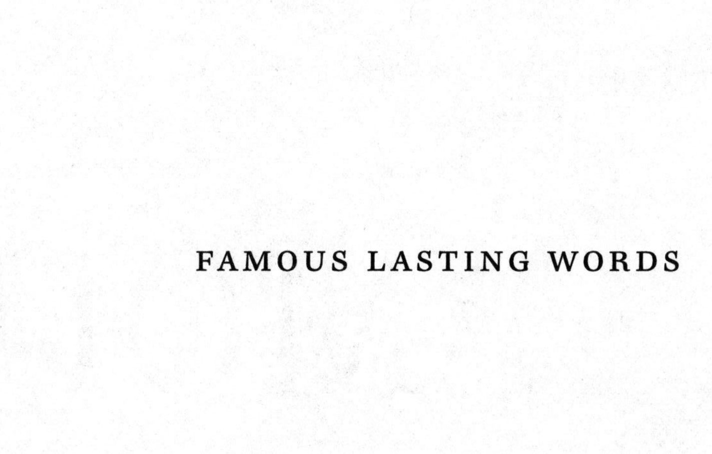

FAMOUS LASTING WORDS

FAMOUS

Great Canadian Quotations

John Robert Colombo's

LASTING WORDS

DOUGLAS & McINTYRE
VANCOUVER/TORONTO

00 01 02 03 04 5 4 3 2 1

Douglas & McIntyre Ltd.
2323 Quebec Street, Suite 201
Vancouver, British Columbia
V5T 4S7

CANADIAN CATALOGUING IN PUBLICATION DATA
Main entry under title:
John Robert Colombo's famous lasting words

Includes index.
ISBN 1-55054-800-X

1. Quotations, Canadian (English)* 2. Canada—Quotations, maxims, etc.
I. Colombo, John Robert, 1936– II. Title: Famous lasting words.
PN6081.J64 2000 C818'.02 C00-910789-4

For
Peter Urs Bender
Voice of Silver
Heart of Gold

Jacket design and photo illustration by Peter Cocking
Original maple leaf photo copyright © Mike Zens/Corbis
Text design by Peter Cocking
Typesetting by Tanya Lloyd / Spotlight Designs
Printed and bound in Canada by Friesens
Printed on acid-free paper ∞

We gratefully acknowledge the financial support of the Canada Council for the Arts, the British Columbia Ministry of Tourism, Small Business and Culture, and the Government of Canada through the Book Publishing Industry Development Program (BPIDP) for our publishing activities.

CONTENTS

PREFACE

John Robert Colombo's Famous Lasting Words is an original collection of Canadian quotations. It consists in the main of remarks made by Canadians about all aspects of life, along with observations made by non-Canadians about life in this country. The quotations have been selected to meet the needs of readers today and researchers tomorrow. This is a brand-new "quote book" that sheds light on life experienced in Canada in the year 2000.

It offers the reader a many-faceted, mosaic-like view of the country and its people. The compilation attempts to offer a perspective, historical and national, on issues of common concern, on human nature, and on the world at large. It is designed to be a work of popular reference, ideal for readers, browsers, and users who have a special interest in Canadian impression, interpretation, expression, and communication. The selection includes not only current remarks but also some of the most famous observations made in the past. There is something here for both the generalist and the specialist; the book is a combination of conventional information and unconventional insights. It offers ammunition for a volley of editorials and a multitude of columns and articles.

This is a commodious compilation. In round numbers, there are 6,000 brand-new quotations. (In point of fact, in all, there are 6,600 quotations, because I added to the new quotations some 600 quotations of the famous and familiar variety, so the total exceeds 6,600.) There are 2,500 contributors. The organization is by subject; there are 1,300 alphabetically arranged subjects (from A to Zoos). Within subjects, the quotations are arranged chronologically (from the earliest to the latest). The span of time covered is one millennium. The earliest quotations are those associated with the Norse colonist Leif Ericsson, traditionally dated A.D. 1000. I will leave it to the reader to discover the most recent quotation; the cutoff date is 1 July 2000. To guide the reader, there are 600 "see also" entries. At the back of the book there appears a useful index of contributors almost 10,000 lines long. Needless to say, each quotation is complete in itself. Each is followed by a source note, which names and identifies the contributor, cites the source of the passage (book, magazine, newspaper, unpublished remark, etc.), and, as required, appends a note of explanation.

John Robert Colombo's Famous Lasting Words is a new publication, but it appears in the wake of the five previous "quote books" that I have compiled over the last quarter-century. These are *Colombo's Canadian*

Quotations (1974), *Colombo's Concise Canadian Quotations* (1978), *Colombo's New Canadian Quotations* (1987), *The Dictionary of Canadian Quotations* (1991), and *Colombo's All-Time Great Canadian Quotations* (1994). So the present book marks the appearance of the sixth volume of Canadian quoted matter, another "small step" in my attempt to document and dramatize the country's past achievements, present possibilities, and future prospects.

John Robert Colombo's Famous Lasting Words has a title that may raise an eyebrow, so here are some comments on it. The name John Robert Colombo appears in the title because the compilation is the product of one person's determined browsing. No two people would compile the same quote book. It is not the work of a committee. Indeed, there are elements in the selection and treatment of quoted matter that embrace both scholarship and showmanship. Only a number of these quotations are truly famous; yet all of them ought to be famous, or they ought to be of lasting note or able to sustain interest. Finally, these quotations are enduring words of power.

The quotations are taken from a great range of sources. The bulk of them originally appeared in books, journals, magazines, and newspapers. The electronic media supplied most of the rest—I heard them on the radio, overheard them on television, or found them on the Internet. A small number derive from oral and manuscript sources and appear here for the first time anywhere.

It has been estimated that there are between two hundred and six hundred familiar Canadian quotations. Pre-eminent among these are statements like "The 20th century belongs to Canada" (Sir Wilfrid Laurier's widely quoted touchstone of national aspiration and achievement); "Fuddle-duddle" (Pierre Elliott Trudeau's expletive); and "The medium is the message" (Marshall McLuhan's formulation, the most widely known Canadian quotation of all time). These touchstones should be familiar to every Canadian. No collection of Canadian quotations is complete without them. It is good to be reminded that they are there.

The familiar and unfamiliar quotations are found throughout the book. Here are some of the new ones that stick like burrs in the mind and that will probably emerge as "keepers": "We serve two million Canadians a day, but we serve them one at a time" (George Cohon on McDonald's treatment of customers); "I wasn't born in Canada, but if I have a choice, I will be next time" (Red Skelton); "A demand for loyalty is usually an admission that confidence does not exist" (Reeves Hagan on leadership); and "The Canadian dollar will disappear in our lifetime" (Peter C. Newman's prediction). Thousands of these quotations appear here and many of them are destined to brighten the pages of future quote books.

This collection is markedly a contemporary collection. More than half the quoted matter reflects the present period rather than past times. The past is covered for its intrinsic interest and for its influence on the present. But the last two decades are represented in depth. Quotations that shed light on the concerns of the 1980s and 1990s are favoured. (The concerns of these decades remain with us in the 2000s, though they are mainly dire ones—recession, cutbacks, unemployment, free trade, global unrest, globalization, separatism, assaults on national sovereignty, etc. So much doom and gloom is the stock in trade of quote-collectors!) Space has been found for such subjects of contemporary concern as Management, Medicare, and Motivation (to glance at just the M's). About three dozen new subjects are included, subjects like Leonard Cohen, Food Banks, Internet, Partition, and Nunavut. What used to be called "the French fact" resounds in all its rhetorical flourishes; here are the last words (it is hoped) on the Meech and Charlottetown accords; here are such gemstones as "money and the ethnic vote" (Jacques Parizeau) and Lucien Bouchard's talismanic words: "magic wand," "*virage*," "humiliation" (guaranteeing him a seat in the coven that includes his predecessor Maurice Duplessis, who was so fond of the words "no encroachments").

The selection of the quotations and the weight given the subjects should be seen in light of the fact that the book is both a "cultivated crop" and a "random harvest." Certain subjects had to be represented because they are of pressing concern. Other subjects just happened to generate bright "quotable quotes." Because the book is national in spirit, I have taken pains to represent all parts of the country, but it is not possible to do justice to every one. Canada is very much a nation of regions and a cluster of centres. Every region or province should have its own quote book. It may be that central Ontario and in particular the Greater Toronto Area are very well represented, but I hope not at the expense of other regions and centres. There are quotations here that will be meaningful to every reader, browser, or user of this book.

I mentioned earlier that this compilation is national in spirit. As well, it is somewhat eclectic in spirit. It charts the mainstream; then it charts more than a few of the tributaries. Now and then it ventures into interesting-looking ponds, brooks, and creeks. If a handful of the quotations are what journalists might describe as "a stretch," they are included because they express my conviction that a tome like this one should be bounteous enough to offer a few surprises—delicious discoveries, odd bits of information, peculiar insights, such as serendipitous references to Canada in the letters of John Stuart Mill, a short story by Graham Greene, or a novel by Margaret Drabble. These are the bounty of broad interests, the booty of wide reading.

Whether mainstream or tributary in interest, quotations may be classified in a number of ways. I have found three: in terms of types, in terms of kinds, in terms of classes. Here is what I have in mind.

Quotations are of three *types*. There are (1) proverbial expressions (traditional generalizations on life of no known provenance). There are (2) aphorisms (concise and clever commentaries on observations or expressions of opinion). And there are (3) quotations proper (statements about particular events and experiences).

Quotations are of three *kinds*. There are (1) historically important quotations (they summarize actions adopted or positions taken). There are (2) socially significant quotations (they embody widespread notions at a given time and place). And there are (3) psychologically relevant quotations (they seem to apply to all mankind).

Quotations are of three *classes*. There are (1) familiar quotations (identifiable, recurring, memorable). There are (2) characteristic quotations (apt or applicable). And there are (3) informational quotations (rich in knowledge or lore).

Quotations of all types, kinds, and classes will be found in the pages of the present collection, as long as they meet my criteria for inclusion. To be included, a quotation has to be *important* or *interesting* (or both). There is no denying the importance of the poem that begins "In Flanders fields the poppies blow." John McCrae's sonnet has importance that is at once national, social, and cultural. There is no denying the continuing interest of the quip "The Americans are our best friends, whether we like it or not." Robert Thompson's remark remains the country's best-loved malapropism. Thus importance or interest warrant inclusion.

I hope this book is a well-mannered contribution to cultural history because it gives expression to the hopes and fears of the Canadian people. It offers access to the aspirations and trepidations—not to say the consternations—of men and women moved to action by sentiment, passion, emotion, or thought. Epic battles once fought are refought in warring words on the printed page. The book has no single narrator; there is no "coral king" (in the words of Morris Shumiatcher found elsewhere). No narrative is the norm. The present book resembles, in pictorial terms, a mosaic. Its structure juxtaposes disparate elements and arranges them in an overall pattern—a confused medley viewed up close, a somewhat ordered composition viewed from afar. It is a mosaic of words, of voices, and of expressions about life in this part of the world. In my mind the book is one way to draw attention to our diversity as well as to our unity, perhaps to our distinctiveness and our individuality as a nation composed of disparate peoples.

This book is as varied and various as the land and the people, as the country that is still revealing its strengths and weaknesses. Yet Canadians hardly know their own country. This is not stop-press news. The concern has found expression for at least the last century. For instance, here are the words of the Toronto editor J. Castell Hopkins. In 1898, he wrote, "Canada only needs to be known in order to be great." He had in mind the relationship between national knowledge (a form of self-knowledge) and self-worth (or self-esteem). He is affirming that we must know ourselves if we are to know our country, and once we know our country, the country and its population are destined for greatness. Hopkins' affirmation is as true today as it was 102 years ago when it was first published. So I will repeat it for the new millennium: "Canada only needs to be known in order to be great."

ACKNOWLEDGEMENTS

In this undertaking I was assisted by more than one hundred men and women, many of whom I will thank by name.

My researcher Alice Neal shared with me much of the burden of securing quotations and checking sources. I am grateful to her as well as to the librarian Philip Singer who handled the challenging research and reference questions. Assisting them were the talented and helpful librarians of three institutions: Metropolitan Toronto Reference Library; Canadiana Library, North York Public Library; John P. Robarts Reference Library, University of Toronto. From time to time I consulted with the helpful librarians at the *The Toronto Star, The Globe and Mail,* and the CBC's Broadcast Centre, Toronto. Thank you, Alice! Thank you, librarians!

The aphorism is an overlooked and undervalued artform and its place has yet to be assured in the canon of Canadian writing. To remedy this situation, I have gone out of my way to include a plethora of aphorisms from published books and unpublished manuscripts. I am indebted to the aphorists who shared their terse, tempered expressions of opinion with me and my readers: Ara Baliozian, Peter Urs Bender, Raymond Canale, L.S. Cattarini, Robert (Bob) Edwards, Frank Feather, Ronald Hambleton, Maurus E. Mallon, Frank Ogden, Robert Priest, Robin Skelton, Betty Jane Wylie. The lot of the aphorist-fancier is a happy one given the astute statements of Robertson Davies, Louis Dudek, Northrop Frye, John Kenneth Galbraith, Stephen Leacock, and Marshall McLuhan. Also members of this illustrious circle are Conrad Black, John Ralston Saul, and Pierre Elliott Trudeau. Numerous amusing passages derive from the "celebrity interviews" conducted by R.E. Knowles, Presbyterian minister, novelist, columnist, interviewer, and "Special Writer" for *The Toronto Star.* From 1920 to 1940, Knowles wheedled and needled the rich and the famous. For the use of these interviews I am grateful to Jean O'Grady, editor of *Famous People Who Have Met Me: The Life and Interviews of R.E. Knowles* (1999). Some quotations from European travel literature were supplied and translated by Karen E. Beeler. Multilingual Helene Issayevitch graciously contributed a number of translations from Quebec sources.

Over the decades, professional colleagues have made signal contributions to my undertaking: Don Bastian, Dick Beddoes, Nelson Doucet, Edith Fowke, Walter L. Gordon, Anthony M. Hawke, Mel Hurtig, William Kilbourn, Carlotta Lemieux, J.G. McClelland, Alberto Manguel, Jack Stoddart,

William Toye, Jan Walter. I remain indebted to them as well as to associates: Renu Barrett, Peter Urs Bender, W. Ritchie Benedict, Kamala Bhatia, Joel Bonn, Paul Bura, Cecelia Carter-Smith, Catherine Colombo, Jonathan Colombo, Theo Colombo, Douglas Cunningham, Ted Davy, Charlotte and Peter Dorn, Craig Ertl, Jane and David Gotlib, William Gough, Cyril Greenland, Bill Harnum, Sylvia Jonas, Eric Koch, Heath Macquarrie, Ted Mann, Desmond Morton, Alan Rayburn, Michael Richardson, Paul Roazen, Anna Sandor, James B. Simpson, E. Russell Smith, Stephen Smith, Nicholas Stethem, Sandy Stewart, Arkadi Tcherkassov, Sheldon Teitelbaum, Marcello Truzzi, Dwight Whalen, Tom Williams, and Hiroko Yasuda.

I am grateful to Scott McIntyre of Douglas & McIntyre for showing the enthusiasm of a friend and the expertise of a publisher, qualities so characteristic of Jack McClelland, his mentor and mine. Especially to be thanked are Douglas & McIntyre's editor Lucy Kenward, marketing director Kelly Mitchell, and managing editor Terri Wershler, and designer Peter Cocking and typesetter Tanya Lloyd. Thanks are due to Naomi Pauls for the preparation of the index. William Toye was extraordinarily generous with his time and attention, insights, and experience. Carlotta Lemieux most observantly scrutinized the manuscript. Thanks to one and all!

My principal debt is to my wife, Ruth, who has so lovingly fostered my multiplicity of endeavours.

A

The shelves of books we haven't written, like those of books we haven't read, stretch out into the darkness of the universal library's farthest space. We are always at the beginning of the beginning of the letter *A*.

Alberto Manguel, bibliophile, referring to books unwritten and books unread, *A History of Reading* (1996).

ABILITY

The common man is capable.

Characteristic remark of **J.J. Tompkins**, adult educator and a leader of the Antigonish Movement, as recalled by activist priest Harvey (Pablo) Steele in *Agent for Change: The Story of Pablo Steele* (1973) as told to Gary MacEoin.

Competence scares nobody, but capability is alarming.

Robin Skelton, poet and aphorist, *A Devious Dictionary* (1991).

ABORIGINAL PEOPLES See also INDIAN PEOPLES, INUIT, LAND CLAIMS, METIS PEOPLE, NATIVE PEOPLES

We advocate recognition of Aboriginal nations within Canada as political entities through which Aboriginal people can express their distinctive identity within the context of their Canadian citizenship.

Renewal: Volume 5: Report of the Royal Commission on Aboriginal Peoples (1996), co-chaired by René Dussault and Georges Erasmus.

Aboriginal peoples are not racial groups; rather they are organic political and cultural entities.

Restructing the Relationship: Volume 2, Part One: Report of the Royal Commission on Aboriginal Peoples (1996), co-chaired by René Dussault and Georges Erasmus.

The term aboriginal obscures the distinctiveness of the First Peoples of Canada—Inuit, Métis, and First Nations.

Looking Forward, Looking Back, Volume 1: Report of the Royal Commission on Aboriginal Peoples (1996), co-chaired by René Dussault and Georges Erasmus.

The Government of Canada today formally expresses to all Aboriginal people in Canada our profound regret for past actions of the federal government which have contributed to these difficult pages in the history of our relationship together.

"Statement of Reconciliation: Learning from the Past," read by Jane Stewart, Minister of Indian Affairs, Ottawa, 7 Jan. 1998, printed in *The Globe and Mail* the following day.

ABORTION See also BIRTH CONTROL

Every child a wanted child, every mother a willing mother.

Henry Morgentaler, physician, credo, *Abortion and Contraception* (1982).

Abortion? Nobody regards the rights of the dead as more important than those of the living, and where a choice has to be made the rights of the living must also take precedence over those of the unborn. If we believe in freedom, we cannot impose on women, against their wills, a servitude that can be prevented. If we don't believe in freedom, why not bring back the inquisition?

George Woodcock, author, contributor to *If I Were Prime Minister* (1987) edited by Mel Hurtig.

I'm not necessarily opposed to abortion, but then I'm not necessarily opposed to killing.

George Jonas, columnist, "Live and Let Die," *The Idler*, No. 25, Sept.–Oct. 1989.

Abortion is a decision between a woman, her doctor, and God.

Attributed to Alberta Premier **Ralph Klein** by Scott Feschuk in "Western Voices," *The Globe and Mail*, 7 April 1995.

Children who are born and loved and nurtured well do not build concentration camps.

Henry Morgentaler, physician, interviewed on CBC-TV's *Life & Times: Dr. Henry Morgentaler*, 16 Nov. 1999.

Access to safe, legal abortion not only protects the women concerned, it also benefits society at large by decreasing the number of unwanted, neglected or abused children who suffer the consequences all their lives, and benefits society in general by reducing violence and crime.

Henry Morgentaler, physician, Letters to the Editor, *The Toronto Star*, 8 May 2000.

ABUSE

Behind every abusing husband is an abusing mother.

Anne Cools, Senator, addressing a conference on abusive relationships, Ottawa, 7 March 1995, quoted by David Vienneau in *The Toronto Star*, 9 March 1995. The remark was much criticized, as it goes against the conventional wisdom that women are the abused, not the abusers.

ACADIAN PEOPLE

We arrived at Accadia the 26th of November, 1682, and there winter'd.

Perhaps the earliest appearance in print of the place name "Acadia" in explorer **Pierre-Esprit Radisson's** "Fourth Voyage" (1684), *Voyages of Peter Esprit Radisson, Being an Account of His Travels and Experiences* (1885) edited by Gideon D. Scull.

Ave, maris stella, / Dei Mater alma, / Atque semper virgo, / Felix coeli porta, / Felix coeli porta. / Amen.

Lyrics in Latin of the first of six verses of "Ave, Maris Stella," the hymn and national anthem of the Acadian People of New Brunswick, as they appear in *Chansons d'Acadie* (1942) introduced by Marius Barbeau. The Latin canticle, adapted by Acadians about 1630, received *de facto* recognition at an Acadian festival held on 21 July 1881.

Since the arrival of the first colonists, this Acadian stuff, a mixture of the imaginary and the real, has been simmering like a soup made from all the vegetables in the kitchen garden.

Antonine Maillet, Acadian scholar and playwright, *Les cordes de bois* (1977).

Acadia is the ghost of what Canada might have been...it is the story of assimilation.

Heather Menzies, journalist, *The Railroad's Not Enough: Canada Now* (1978).

Cajun. Louisianian of Acadian-English descent; a slurring corruption of Acadian in the same manner that "injun" was taken from Indian.

Paul Dickson, British writer, *What Do You Call a Person From...? A Dictionary of Resident Names* (1990).

If I were to take a poll on the province's largely francophone Acadian Peninsula, I would find more dishonest people there than honest people.

Jocelyn Moreau-Bérubé, New Brunswick Provincial Court Judge, speaking impromptu during a sentencing hearing, Feb. 1998. After complaints were received, she apologized for the remark in March 1999 and the next month was removed from the bench by the N.B. Judicial Council which found, according to *The Toronto Star*, 16 April 1999, "The remarks made by Moreau-Bérubé were unwarranted, offensive, and disparaging to the people of the Acadian Peninsula. They went beyond what is acceptable as far as judicial expression is concerned." According to Kevin Cox in *The Globe and Mail*, 30 July 1999, the province's Court of Queen's Bench ruled she should be reinstated because the remarks were "spontaneous and improvised" and, besides, she did not believe them herself.

ACCIDENT

Misfortune often puts us wise to our own carelessness.

Bob Edwards, publisher, *The Eye Opener*, 18 June 1910.

If you break a leg you have a friend.

John Grierson, first Commissioner, National Film Board of Canada, characteristic remark, recalled about 1970, quoted by Gary Evans in *In the National Interest: A Chronicle of the National Film Board of Canada from 1949 to 1989* (1991).

ACCOMMODATION

The threads of a thousand acts of accommodation are the fabric of a nation.

John Whyte, Alberta's Deputy Attorney General, quoted in the findings of the Supreme Court of Canada on the constitutionality of a unilateral declaration of one province's secession, 20 Aug. 1998, as quoted by columnist Graham Fraser in "Supreme Court Decision," *The Globe and Mail*, 22 Aug. 1998.

ACCOUNTING

Watchdogs do a lot of barking and there is another kind of dog called a guard dog. He doesn't do much barking, but he can be quite effective.

J.J. Macdonell, Auditor General, referring to the guardianship role of the accountant, quoted in *Maclean's*, 13 Dec. 1976.

ACHIEVEMENT See also SUCCESS

Bees, ants, and beavers are marvels of nature in their way. But they show no desire for improvement, and make no effort to improve. Man alone aspires.

Goldwin Smith, essayist, *Guesses at the Riddle of Existence and Other Essays on Kindred Subjects* (1897).

You can't win. A Canadian catch-phrase, dating since ca. 1950 and "expressing the impossibility of coming out on top and the futility of kicking against the pricks" (Leechman).

Entry written by English lexicographer **Eric Partridge** in *A Dictionary of Slang and Unconventional English: Supplement* (8th ed., 1974).

To be human is to participate in human ventures that outlive us.

Frank Feather, futurologist, *G-Forces: Reinventing the World—The 35 Global Forces Restructuring Our World* (1989).

Ninety per cent of achievement is deciding where you want to be and flying over the obstacles.

Linda Lundstrom, manufacturer and retailer of women's and children's clothing, speech, Centennial College, Toronto, 11 Nov. 1992, quoted by Donna Jean MacKinnon in *The Toronto Star* the following day.

Canadians know little about their achievements in the past. They don't even teach them in their schools.

Ralph Nader, U.S. consumer advocate, interviewed on CBC-TV's *Newsworld*, 9 Dec. 1992.

Bad things happen when good people sit on their hands. Good things happen when everyone tries to make a difference. These clichés are true.

Bob Rae, former Ontario Premier, *From Protest to Power: Personal Reflections on a Life in Politics* (1996).

ACID RAIN See also POLLUTION

All that water, and much of it sick from acid rain. More than 14,000 Canadian lakes are nearly fishless.

Priit J. Vesilind, writer, "Common Ground, Different Dreams," *National Geographic*, March 1990.

ACQUIRED IMMUNE DEFICIENCY SYNDROME See AIDS

ACTIVISM

That man who fails while attempting to do right is more to be respected than he who succeeds in doing what is wrong.

R.B. Bennett, Prime Minister, quoted by Andrew D. MacLean in *R.B. Bennett: Prime Minister of Canada* (1934).

The best time is always the present time, because it alone offers the opportunity for action, because it is ours, because on God's scale it is apocalyptic, a time when the lines between good and evil are clearly drawn, and each of us must choose his side, a time when there is no longer room for either the coward or the uncommitted.

Georges P. Vanier, Governor General, quoted in an editorial in *The Toronto Star*, 6 Nov. 1981.

When in doubt, do both.

Maxim of the social and political activist **Kay Macpherson**, serving as the title of her memoirs *When in Doubt, Do Both: The Times of My Life* (1995) written by C.M. Donald.

ACTORS & ACTING See also CULTURE, FILM, TELEVISION, THEATRE

How is it that actors and actresses can set at defiance all the laws of morality, can live in scandalous and admitted wickedness, and lose not one iota of popularity.

Hugh Johnston, Montreal Methodist minister, *Shall We or Shall We Not?* (1886).

Two months later, while chopping trees, I received a brief note: "Join Jean Russell Stock Company in Kamloops, B.C.—Kelly." I left my axe sticking in a tree.

Boris Karloff, fledgling actor, quoting a message received in 1909 from a theatrical agent named Kelly in Seattle, Washington, quoted in *The Book of Lists No. 2* (1980). Born William Henry Pratt, Karloff adopted the name Boris Karloff for his first theatre appearance on a makeshift stage in Kamloops, B.C.

"How does it come that it was reserved for a Canuck like you to achieve the greatest Lincoln success in history?

Great souls know no boundary lines. Neither do their admirers."

Raymond Massey, stage and screen actor noted for his impersonations of the American President, interviewed by R.E. Knowles in *The Toronto Star*, 15 Feb. 1939.

Anyone who becomes an actor is a fool, and I was. Canadians have the greatest respect for the guy who goes to work for American General Electric. Canadians always think more highly of us performers when we leave the country—respect our "courage" in going. It's crazy.

Robert Christie, actor, quoted by June Graham in *CBC Times*, 24 Feb. 1962.

When an actor reads a story aloud, he gets to do all the parts! Surely that is every actor's ambition. Also, he is alone. He cannot be upstaged by a smart fellow actor.

John Drainie, actor, on reading 1,800-word stories written by Canadian writers for CBC Radio, Preface, *Stories with John Drainie* (1963).

I look for that area of the character which is a loser, because I know nobody wins for twenty-four hours a day, no matter what.

William Hutt, actor and director, quoted by Urjo Kareda in *The Toronto Star*, 25 May 1974.

The heartbreak of my life is knowing what Kate Reid could have been.

Nathan Cohen, drama critic, referring to the actress Kate Reid, whom he maintained went from being an ingenue to a character actress without becoming a leading lady, quoted by John Hofsess in *The Canadian*, 30 Aug. 1975.

I've always felt that Americans go into acting to discover themselves and the English to hide themselves.

Don Harron, actor and performer, quoted by Frank Rasky in *The Toronto Star*, 6 March 1976.

I wanted to be a Highlander and wear a kilt. I never even got my pants off.

Melvyn Douglas, suave Hollywood actor, who as an undergraduate at Upper Canada College, Toronto, tried to enlist with a Highland regiment in Toronto during World War I, quoted by Jack Miller in *The Toronto Star*, 15 Oct. 1976.

I'd like to look like Ingrid Bergman, act like Kim Stanley, and drink like Richard Burton.

Kate Reid, actress, quoted by Barbara Greenberg in *Chatelaine*, Oct. 1977.

Do what you do best and New York will come to you.

William Hutt, actor and director, advice to fledgling actor Maxim Mazumdar, quoted by Julia Maskoulis in *Maclean's*, 20 Nov. 1978.

To be a star in your own country is very, very tough. To be a star here is to be able to work.

Carole Laure, film actress, quoted by Rick Groen in *The Globe and Mail's Broadcast Week*, 2 Feb. 1980.

To survive in the theatre as I have for thirty years, an actress must be strong as a horse, tough as old boots, clever as a fox or a rat.

Frances Hyland, actress, quoted by Frank Rasky in *The Toronto Star*, 4 Sept. 1980.

An actor has a nine-to-five job looking for work.

Paul Kligman, radio, television, and stage actor, characteristic remark made in May 1981.

Up to this point my height was the only thing I had in common with Alan Ladd.

Michael J. Fox, film star, quoted by Jamie Portman in *The Toronto Star*, 21 Nov. 1989.

I'm not an actor or an actress but an ACTRA.

Craig Russell, performer known for his female impersonations, punning on his sexuality in terms of the name of the performer's association, recalled by Peter Gzowski on CBC Radio's *Morningside*, 1 Nov. 1990.

All actors are defectors. They leave reality, go into fantasy. They leave who they are and become somebody else. And that's part of the business.

Graham Greene, Oneida actor, quoted by Henri Behar in *The Globe and Mail*, 4 April 1992.

My job as an artist is to search for truth. My job as a craftsman is to perform the results of that pursuit, for the director.

Donald Sutherland, actor, interviewed by Kate Fillion in *The Globe and Mail*, 28 Dec. 1993.

My Canadian half is the reserved half, the diplomatic half, the socially sensitive half; it's the side not prone to wacky or crazy behaviour.

Shirley MacLaine, actress, commenting on her Canadian mother and her American father who met in rural Virginia in the 1940s, interviewed by Deirdre Kelly in *The Globe and Mail*, 20 April 1995.

The essence of being a Canadian actor is being mistaken for somebody else.

Richard Monette, actor, quoted by Michael Kesterton, "Social Studies," *The Globe and Mail*, 30 Aug. 1996.

ADULTERY

Adultery is more often a convenience than a passion.

Robin Skelton, man-of-letters, aphorism, May 1990.

ADVENTURE

The real adventure takes place in the sensibility and imagination of the individual. The real trail must be blazed towards a perception of the universal relations that are present in every parcel of creation, not towards the Arctic circle.

John Lyman, Montreal artist, observation, May 1932, quoted by Dennis Reid in *A Concise History of Canadian Painting* (1973).

Canada is not really a place where you are encouraged to have large spiritual adventures.

Robertson Davies, man-of-letters, quoted by Peter C. Newman, "The Master's Voice," *Maclean's*, Sept. 1972.

I don't go where the money is, I go where the adventure is.

Pierre Berton, author and media personality, quoted by John Hofsess in "The Second Last Spike," *Maclean's*, March 1974.

If we can dream it... we can do it.

Maxim of the Arctic adventurer **Jeff MacInnis** from *Polar Passage: The Historic First Sail through the Northwest Passage* (1989) by Jeff MacInnis with Wade Rowland.

The Journey is not the Adventure.... The Destination is not the Adventure.... Life is the Adventure!

Credo of **Alex Tilley** of Tilley Endurables Inc. adventure clothing from its 1991 catalogue, according to Thelma Dickman, *Leisureways*, April 1992.

The modern adventurers are kids ten to sixteen. What they are learning at their computers or while playing Nintendo video games no institution in the world can teach today. If I, as the boss of a company, had to hire a kid, I would much rather the kid had a certificate of competence from Nintendo than a degree from Harvard or Heidelberg.

Frank Ogden, futurologist, interviewed by Gerd Meissner in *Der Spiegel*, No. 38, 1994.

ADVERTISING See also ADVERTISING CAMPAIGNS, BUSINESS

It is unquestionably the struggle for advertising, rather than readers, that kills newspapers and magazines.

Milton Shulman, Toronto-born, London-based journalist, drama critic, and TV producer, *The Ravenous Eye: The Impact of the Fifth Factor* (1973).

Madison Avenue is a very powerful aggression against private consciousness. A demand that you yield your private consciousness to public manipulation.

Marshall McLuhan, communications pioneer, interview, *Maclean's*, 7 March 1977.

Advertising doesn't always mirror how people are acting, but how they're dreaming.

Jerry Goodis, advertising consultant, quoted by Olivia Ward in *The Toronto Star*, 9 March 1980.

No wonder people watch commercials: They're the last bright flickers of optimism in a gloomy world of dissent.

Jim Fleming, Minister of State for Multiculturalism, address, radio and television news directors, Toronto, 20 June 1980, quoted by Geoffrey Stevens in *The Globe and Mail*, 25 June 1980.

Advertising is closely allied with what is called mass culture, which demands passivity of response and acceptance of unexamined clichés. Mass culture is a most misleading phrase for what it describes because it is something imposed on the so-called "masses" and not produced by them. To call it "popular culture" is clearly still more misleading.

Northrop Frye, cultural critic, "Criticism and Environment" (1983), *The Eternal Act of Creation: Essays, 1979–1990* (1993) edited by Robert D. Denham.

Principle 1: The prospect is more important than the product. / Principle 2: Precision in positioning is everything. / Principle 3: Be read, seen and heard. And be persuasive.

"The Three Principles of Breakthrough Advertising" evolved by **Bern Wheeler**, President, Bern Wheeler Communications Ltd., Toronto, 29 Sept. 1987.

Advertising is one of the greatest forms of education and enlightenment that I know of in this society, and it always has been.

Garth Drabinsky, CEO, Cineplex Odeon Corp., defending the showing of commercials in his company's cineplexes, quoted in *The Toronto Star*, 31 Dec. 1988.

Advertising, n. Words and pictures, often set to music, designed to correct the mistaken impression among consumers that their lives possess meaning in the absence of a receipt for a particular product in their sock drawer.

David Olive, business commentator, *White Knights and Poison Pills: A Cynic's Dictionary of Business Jargon* (1990).

Advertising is a very difficult, unkind, nasty, unforgiving business. But it can be fun.

Gary Prouk, creative director, quoted by Brenda Dalglish in *Maclean's*, 22 Oct. 1990.

Just as business sometimes captures dreams, causing the imagination to soar, advertising sometimes connects with its audience to evoke those dreams and stimulate imagination.

John Dalla Costa, advertising executive, *Meditations on Business: Why Business As Usual Won't Work Anymore* (1991).

PR is BS in Swahili, and most other evolved languages.

Maurus E. Mallon, aphorist, remark made in April 1992.

CQ is more valued than IQ.

Sign in the offices of the **Padulo Integrated Agency**, quoted by Sarah Hampson in "The Adman Who Ate Toronto," *Toronto Life*, Dec. 1995. Expanded it means, "Change Quotient is more valued than Intelligence Quotient."

ADVERTISING CAMPAIGNS See also ADVERTISING

Wants of All Sorts / If you want a slovenly girl or a lazy girl, a poor cook, careless about her work, unattractive in her appearance and who wants to be "out" five nights a week—don't advertise for her in "The Evening Mail." That class of domestic is not a regular reader of "The Mail."

Classified advertisement in *The Halifax Herald*, 29 Dec. 1897.

How do you do, I'm Gilbert Templeton....

Advertising campaign created for **Templeton's T-R-C's**, with the gravelly voice of patent medicine-maker Gilbert Templeton, proprietor. The campaign was launched on radio in 1933 and introduced to television in the 1950s. T-R-C's were first manufactured in Toronto in 1907 and the letters stand for "The Rheumatism Capsules."

Offer Good Only in the United States / Slightly Higher in Canada

Notices that appeared on premiums and products imported from the United States, common in the 1940s and 1950s.

Listen to Sinatra on Clairtone—Sinatra does.

Advertising campaign launched by **Clairtone Sound Corporation Limited**, 1966, to promote Clairtone audio equipment. Quoted by Garth Hopkins in *The Rise and Fall of a Business Empire: Clairtone* (1978). Two years later the glamour company went bankrupt.

Caramilk. One of life's sweet mysteries.

Key line of the advertising campaign launched in 1968 for the Caramilk chocolate bar division of William Neilson Co. Ltd. (now Cadbury Chocolate Canada Inc.). It was conceived by Gary Proulx, then of **Doyle Dane Bernbach**, with art direction by André Morkel, and it asked the question, "How do they get the soft flowing caramel into the Caramilk bar?" In 1980, it became the first Canadian commercial to be inducted into the International Advertising Hall of

Fame, according to Randy Scotland in *Marketing*, 24 Sept. 1990.

How clean are your nooks? How fresh are your crannies?

Line of advertising devised by Eric McMillan of **ReadWhite Media Inc.** to promote the Shower-Toilet, a Japanese device introduced to Canada in 1989, quoted by Michelle Lalonde in *The Globe and Mail*, 18 Aug. 1990.

Ten-ounce, USA-treated cotton duck, solid British brass hardware, sewn with Canadian persnicketiness.

Wording on the label of the famous Tilley Hat manufactured by **Tilley Endurables Inc.**, Don Mills, Ont., 1993.

100,000 Weeks / On the Best-Seller List / The Bible

Message on billboards placed by the **Canadian Bible Society**, Toronto, March 1994.

I'm dedicated to ensuring every new batch of Buckley's tastes as bad as the last.

Message in print advertising for Buckley's Mixture, a non prescription cough medicine, produced by **W.K. Buckley Ltd.** in Toronto. Reproduced by Marina Strauss in *The Globe and Mail*, 18 April 1995.

It tastes awful and it's good for you.

Advertising campaign for W.K. Buckley Ltd.'s Buckley's TRC's, devised by Peter Byrne of **Bensimon Byrne Inc.**, as noted by Marina Strauss in *The Globe and Mail*, 15 May 1997. Another version: "It tastes awful, and it works."

I am Canadian . . . I have a prime minister, not a president . . . it's pronounced "zed," not "zee" . . . Canada is the second-largest land mass, the first nation of hockey . . . and the best . . . part . . . of North America!

Nationalistic sentiments expressed with pride tinged with irony in the monologue (also called a rant) about U.S. misconceptions of Canada delivered by roughly dressed youthful actor Jeff Douglas in the surprisingly successful series of "I am Canadian" 60-second commercials for Molson Canadian beer created for Molson Breweries of Canada by the agency **Bensimon Byrne D'Arcy** launched on television on 17 March 2000 then in movie theatres on 27 March and subsequently live at hockey games. Conceived by art director Michael Smith and writer David Swaine and directed by Kevin Donovan.

ADVICE

"Must" is only for the King of France.

Isaac Columbus, French-born cutler and gunsmith at York (Toronto) at the time of the War of 1812, quoted by Henry Scadding in *Toronto of Old* (1873).

Advice is sought to confirm a position already taken.

Sir William Osler, physician and professor, quoted by William Bennett Bean in *Sir William Osler: Aphorisms from His Bedside Teachings and Writings* (1950).

It is one thing to be entertained by the frolics of circus clowns; it is altogether another thing to take their advice seriously.

Tom Davey, publisher, Editorial Comment, *Environmental Science & Engineering Magazine*, Jan. 1966.

AFFECTION

Life is more than a dexterous manipulation of zippers. I need to hold hands too.

Gerald Lampert, novelist, *Chestnut/Flower "Eye of Venus"* (1978).

Hold on to affection's smallish stuff, I thought, for otherwise it is all hell in a bucket.

Resolve of a character in **Leon Rooke**'s novel *Shakespeare's Dog* (1983).

Let's hear it for hugs. A good hug gives you emotional reassurance, physical support, and a spiritual lift.

Betty Jane Wylie, author, obiter dictum, 1990.

AFRICA

But look here—give this message to your Canadian people—that the greatest asset they have is their snow. If we only had it in Africa, there's no telling what we'd be. . . .

Jan Christian Smuts, Prime Minister, Union of South Africa, interviewed in Toronto by R.E. Knowles, *The Toronto Star*, 3 Jan. 1930.

Many a perfectly competent Central African still does not know that he is supposed to be an Upper Voltaic and that the capital of his country is called Ouagadougou. It is, after all, a hell of a thing to admit.

Edgar Z. Friedenberg, social scientist, "Liberty and the Giant Corporation," *The Disposal of Liberty and Other Industrial Wastes* (1975).

When Black Africa learns the arts of self-discipline, of unity and human leadership, it will undoubtedly emerge on the world scene as a great new powerful sector of the globe. Africa has been a slumbering giant. Now it is slowly awakening.

Frank R. Joubin, prospector, *Not for Gold Alone: The Memoirs of a Prospector* (1986) written with D. McCormack Smyth.

I use the term "Africadian," a word I have minted from "Africa" and "Acadia" (the old name for Nova Scotia and New Brunswick), to denote the Black populations of the Maritimes and especially of Nova Scotia.... If Africadians constitute a state, let it be titled Africadia.

George Elliott Clarke, editor, *Fire on the Water: An Anthology of Black Nova Scotian Writing, Volume I: Early and Modern Writers 1785–1935* (1991).

How can those countries who have stolen land from the red Indians, the aborigines, and the Eskimos dare to tell us what to do with our land?

Robert Mugabe, President of Zimbabwe, referring to Canada, referring to the expropriation of white-owned land, quoted by Linda Hossie in *The Globe and Mail*, 20 Aug. 1993.

If the phrase "African American" denotes every person of African descent in the United States, no matter his or her origins, the phrase African Canadian denotes a fragile coalition of identities consisting of Rastafarian "Dubb" poets from Jane and Finch in Toronto, African Baptist "gospelaires" straight out of Preston in Nova Scotia, and even Haitian born Péquistes in Côte-des-Neiges in Montreal.

Austin Clarke, author, quoted by Graham Fraser in "Identities," *The Globe and Mail*, 30 Aug. 1997.

AGE See also AGING, RETIREMENT, YOUTH

I observe how people are treated after they are dead, / and therefore I drink before I die.

Lines from a Tlingit poem, "Song of Growing Older," *Songs of the Great Land* (1989) edited by John Robert Colombo.

To kill all men over forty was commonly thought to be the plan of Canadian-born Sir William Osler (1849–1919).

Robert Hendrickson, U.S. author, *Human Words* (1972). The misunderstanding is based on an address delivered by the famous physician at Johns Hopkins University in 1905 in which he argued that "the usefulness of men above sixty years of age" was greatly exaggerated.

As you get older virtue becomes easier.

Louis Dudek, man-of-letters, *Epigrams* (1975).

Nobody knows anything, really, until he is fifty!

F.H. Underhill, political scientist, quoted by John A.B. McLeish in *A Canadian for All Seasons: The John E. Robbins Story* (1978).

I am old enough to know that nothing I want will ever happen. I might get a faded facsimile.

Elizabeth Smart, middle-aged memoirist, *The Assumption of the Rogues and Rascals* (1978).

If, as you grow older, you feel you are also growing stupider, do not worry. This is normal, and usually occurs around the time when your children, now grown, are discovering the opposite—they now see that you aren't nearly as stupid as they had believed when they were young teenagers.

Margaret Laurence, novelist, "My Final Hour" (1983), *Up and Doing: Canadian Women and Peace* (1989) edited by Janice Williamson and Deborah Gorham.

Life becomes easier as emotions calm down; as desires decrease, so does the frustration about their lack of fulfillment. But the greatest advantage of old age is that one no longer has to worry about the future, because there is so little of it.

Hans Blumenfeld, architect-planner, *Life Begins at 65: The Not Entirely Candid Autobiography of a Drifter* (1987).

Well, my friends are gone and my hair is grey. / I ache in places where I used to play. / And I'm crazy for love but I'm not coming on. / I'm just paying my rent everyday in the Tower of Song.

Leonard Cohen, poet and singer, "Tower of Song," *I'm Your Man* (album, 1988).

To grow older is to realize the universe is copernican, not ptolemaic, and that self and the loved one do not form the epicentre of the solar system.

Line from **Edward Phillips**' novel *Sunday Best* (1990).

Midlife crisis

"'The midlife crisis,' as a phrase and a concept, was first articulated more than forty years ago [in a paper presented at the British Psychoanalytical Institute] by Toronto-born organizational scientist **Elliott Jacques**," noted Judy Steed, "Organizational Man," *The Toronto Star*, 24 Dec. 1995.

Old age is a clinic full of old men's bodies as shapeless as the Cambodian alphabet.

Louis Dudek, poet and aphorist, "Bitter Pills," *Reality Games* (1998).

AGING See also AGE

Just about the time a man gets comfortably fixed in this world it is time for him to move on to the next.

Bob Edwards, publisher, *The Eye Opener*, 29 June 1911, *The Best of Bob Edwards* (1975) edited by Hugh Dempsey.

I think that at the other end of life there is a change and an unfolding and a new kind of splendour to life which should be seized and enjoyed.

Robertson Davies, man-of-letters, interviewed by Tom Harpur in 1975, *Conversations with Robertson Davies* (1989) edited by J. Madison Davis.

When I was young and in my prime, / I used to block kicks all the time; / But now that I am old and grey, / I only block them once a day.

Doggerel penned and recited by sports columnist **Ted Reeve**, known as the Old Groaner, born in 1902, recalled in his obituary by Trent Frayne in *The Globe and Mail*, 29 Aug. 1983.

Life contains awful things. By the time you've reached a certain age, you notice.

Margaret Atwood, author, "Why I Write," *Quill & Quire*, Aug. 1993.

At eighty, I'm in the prime of senility. All I worry about now is whether there will be anyone left to come to my funeral.

Irving Layton, poet, remark made at his eightieth birthday party, Montreal, quoted in *The Porcupine's Quill*, Fall/Winter 1994.

I like to say that the secret of living to an advanced age is being in love. I have fallen in love with my own vast ignorance.

Clifford Scott, Montreal-based psychoanalyst, referring to his own age of ninety-two years, following the production of *Sessions: A Document from the Psychoanalytic Tapes of Dr. Clifford Scott*, realized by Daniel Brooks, Clare Coulter, and Daniel MacIvor, Tarragon Theatre, Toronto, 18 March 1995.

You won't grow old if you persist in staying young.

Ed Mirvish, theatre personality, quoted by Elaine Dembe in "Passionate Longevity," *Rocky McMountain Buyer's Guide*, Summer 1995.

Women are like cheese, and men are like milk. As women grow older, they become sharper. As men turn older, they curdle.

Antanas Sileika, writer, "Nothing Is Funny to Grumpy Old Men," *The Globe and Mail*, 25 Sept. 1995.

I am in my third age.

The first age is youth. The second is middle years. And the third age is, "You look wonderful!"

Adapted from an observation made by Toronto rabbi **W. Gunther Plaut** at the age of eighty-five, quoted by Warren Gerard in *The Toronto Star*, 28 Sept. 1997.

AGRICULTURE See also FARMING, WHEAT

Agriculture must be the main source of wealth and prosperity of Canada, and if it is not maintained in a healthy and prosperous state, every other profession, trade, and business must inevitably languish.

Agricultural Improvement by the Education of Those Who Are Engaged in It as a Profession; Addressed Very Respectfully to the Farmers of Canada (1837).

Similarly—and again this is not a prediction but a projection of work which I have seen going on—agriculture will be extended well north of the Arctic Circle.

Ritchie-Calder, Lord, British scientist and peer, *The Inheritors: The Story of Man and the World He Made* (1961).

For me, picking blackberries is a simple ritual that acknowledges the changing seasons and reconnects us with the Earth.

David Suzuki, environmentalist, "The Things in Life that Really Count," *Earth Time: Essays* (1998).

AIDS See also DISEASE

I've got gay cancer. I'm going to die and so are you.

Gaetan Dugas, Air Canada flight attendant, early AIDS carrier who boasted of infecting at least 2,500 men across North America during the last decade of his life, according to Randy Shilts in *And the Band Played On: Politics, People and the AIDS Epidemic* (1987). Dugas died of complications from the Acquired Immune Deficiency Syndrome in Quebec City in 1984.

It's a great pity that there is paranoia about AIDS. I don't think AIDS is a particularly contagious disease, certainly not in the context of other things to which people may be exposed.

Kim Campbell, M.P.P., opinion expressed during a debate in the B.C. Legislature in 1987, as noted by Mel Hurtig in *At Twilight in the Country: Memoirs of a Canadian Nationalist* (1996).

AIR

...filled themselves with the first draughts of ozone from the great paradise of spruce which stretches almost unbroken from the Canadian line to the Arctic circle.

C.L. Norton and **John Habberton**, travellers and humorists, *Canoeing in Kanuckia or Haps and Mishaps* (1878).

Not all parts of the world have the power to condition air, but Canada has. Especially in the fall and winter and early spring, the northern part of the continent becomes an almost perfectly designed mechanical refrigerator.

Wolfgang Langewiesche, climatologist, "The Seven American Airs," *A Treasury of Science* (4th edition. 1958), edited by Harlow Shapley, Samuel Rapport, and Helen Wright.

A wonderful freshness, air / that billows like bedsheets / on a clothesline and the clouds / hang in a traffic jam: summer / heads home.

Opening lines of the poem "Light from Canada" descriptive of Nova Scotia by the American poet **James Schuyler** in *The Crystal Lithium* (1972).

Air-Conditioning. An efficient and widely used method for spreading disease.

John Ralston Saul, author, *The Doubter's Companion: A Dictionary of Aggressive Common Sense* (1994).

ALASKA See also BORDER, CANADIAN-AMERICAN; UNITED STATES OF AMERICA

If we had followed the advice of Canada we should have had war with the U.S. over the Alaska Boundary—an inconceivable disaster, so much so that the war office has ceased to include defence of the Canadian frontiers among the contingencies it professes to provide against.

Bertrand Russell, British philosopher, letter to Elie Halévy, 10 March 1905, *The Selected Letters of Bertrand Russell: Volume 1: The Private Years, 1884–1914* (1992) edited by Nicholas Griffin. It concerns Whitehall's indifference to Ottawa's protests over Washington's insistence that the Alaska panhandle belonged to the United States and not to Canada—the Alaska Boundary Dispute.

A Canadian "Polish Corridor" separates the State of Alaska from the main body of the continental United States; and this zone of Canadian territory has come to be of first-class strategic importance for the United States now that the North Pole has come to be a military front between the United States and the Soviet Union.

Arnold J. Toynbee, British historian, "The Case for a Bilingual Canada," *Temper of the Times: An Anthology of Assorted Contemporary Literature* (1969) edited by Ralph Greenfield and Ronald Side.

Consider Alaska, which is more than 1,000 kilometres from the continental United States, separated by Canada. This separation does not create any major problems because Canada and the United States agreed upon the necessary rights of passage to keep the two parts together.

Pierre Bourgault, separatist, *Now or Never! Manifesto for an Independent Quebec* (1991) translated by David Homel.

Alaskans in a hurry should remember that Nome wasn't built in a day.

Maurus E. Mallon, aphorist, *Compendulum* (1995).

ALBERTA See also CALGARY, EDMONTON, PRAIRIE PROVINCES, WESTERN PROVINCES

"Alberta" possesses no significance save that it is the third name of the Duchess of Argyll.

Joseph Pope, bureaucrat, letter addressed to Prime Minister Sir Wilfrid Laurier, 21 Feb. 1905. The following day, Laurier replied, "I regret as much as you do the disappearance of the word 'Assiniboia.' I struggled for it all I could, but it appears that 'Alberta' is now a matter of importance which the members of the North West could not give up. It is really too bad." Quoted in *Public Servant: The Memoirs of Sir Joseph Pope* (1960) edited by Maurice Pope.

Oh, the prairie lights are burnin' bright, / The Chinook Wind is a-movin' in, / Tomorrow night I'll be Alberta Bound.

First lines of "Alberta Bound" with words and music by **Gordon Lightfoot**, copyright 1971 by Early Morning Music, Toronto.

The Born Against syndrome.

A reference to the sense of alienation experienced by Western Canadians with respect to the power bloc of Ontario and Quebec, noted by **Ian Pearson** in "Thou Shalt Not Ignore the West," *Saturday Night*, Dec. 1990.

It's okay for Ontario to say it wants something, it's okay for Quebec to say it wants something, but if Albertans say they want something, everybody suddenly throws their hands up and says that's terrible. Baloney.

Don Getty, Alberta Premier, quoted by George Oake in *The Toronto Star*, 7 Feb. 1992.

To approach the badlands is to find a gap in the known and expected world.

Robert Kroetsch, novelist, referring to the desert-like Badlands of Alberta, quoted by Wayne Grady in *The Dinosaur Project: The Story of the Greatest Dinosaur Expedition Ever Mounted* (1993).

The critics say you can't run government like a business. I respond, well, we can't run government like a government any more.

Ralph Klein, Alberta Premier, quoted by Robert Mason Lee, "The West," *The Globe and Mail*, 10 Dec. 1994.

Alberta, with the strongest and one of the wealthiest economies in the country and the lowest per capita debt, is at the bottom of the barrel in social spending, and in education we're 60th of 63 provinces and states. 60th!

Mel Hurtig, Edmonton-based nationalist, address, awards dinner, Edmonton, 17 Sept. 1997.

ALCOHOL See also BEER, DRINKING, FOOD & DRINK, PROHIBITION, WINE

The traders diluted this rotgut with water and Indians tested the mix by spitting out a swallow on a fire. If it flared up, it was okay; if it sputtered out, they demanded a stronger brew. (That, incidentally, is where the term "firewater" came from.)

Peter C. Newman, columnist, referring to the alcohol sold by unscrupulous traders to the Indians in the early 1800s, *Maclean's*, 6 Aug. 1990.

When I was in Upper Canada, I found no means whatever of social amusement for any class, except that which the tavern afforded: taverns consequently abounded everywhere.

Anna Brownell Jameson, traveller and writer, *Winter Studies and Summer Rambles in Canada* (1838).

We who make whiskey say: "Drink Moderately."

Theme of the advertising campaign launched by Seagram's through the **Blackman Agency** in New York in Oct. 1934 in The New York Times, as noted by Michael R. Marrus in *Mr. Sam: The Life and Times of Samuel Bronfman* (1991). Its Calvert division, headed by William Wachtel, introduced its celebrated "Men of Distinction" advertising campaign. The phrase "Men of Distinction," noted Marrus, "slipped into the vocabulary of the age via newspaper columnists, script writers and even a play in New York."

The pubs—they are called beer-parlours—serve only beer, are not allowed to have whiskey or wine or any spirits at all—and are open only for a few hours a day. There are, in this monstrous hotel, two bars, one for Men, one for Women. They do not mix.

Dylan Thomas, poet, letter written from Vancouver to Caitlin Thomas in Wales, 7 April 1950, *The Collected Letters of Dylan Thomas* (1985) edited by Paul Ferris.

Taverns in Canada: They were the places I really liked—but they wouldn't let my wife in.

Brendan Behan, Irish playwright, *The Wit of Brendan Behan* (1968) compiled by Sean McCann.

Alcohol is, and is likely to remain, Canada's most serious non-medical drug use problem.

Gerald LeDain, dean of law, Chairman of the Royal Commission on the Non-Medical Use of Drugs, *Interim Report*, 15 May 1970.

The United States have their "Wounded Knee," but Canada has its "Bended Elbow," Kenora, Ontario. This is unfortunate because Kenora is the most beautiful Town in Canada, in my estimation—and it is dependant upon the Tourist trade.

Eleanor Jacobson, nurse and activist, exposing alcohol abuse among the Native population, *Bended Elbow: Kenora Ontario Talks Back* (1975).

Americans are plagued with organized crime. We have provincial liquor boards.

Dave Broadfoot, comedian, quoted by Ernest Hillen in *Maclean's*, 30 March 1981.

ALLEGIANCE

The society of allegiance admits of a diversity the society of compact does not, and one of the blessings of Canadian life is that there is no Canadian way of life, much less two, but a unity under the Crown, admitting of a thousand diversities.

W.L. Morton, historian, *The Canadian Identity* (1961).

There's a perverse kind of refusal to accept the here and now in Canada. There's an allegiance to the elsewhere.

Srinivas Krishna, film-maker, quoted by Richard Conniff in "Toronto," *National Geographic*, June 1996.

ALLIANCE PARTY See CANADIAN ALLIANCE

AMATEURISM

This is the role of the great amateurs: to see clearly the issues that academic specialists cannot see because they are limited by the blinders of their institutions and their disciplines.

Robert Fulford, journalist, commenting on specialists and professionals as well as the need for gifted amateurs, *The New York Times*, 16 Feb. 1992.

AMBITION

Make no small plans for they have no power to excite the minds and hearts of men.

Edward Johnson, tenor, General Manager of New York's Metropolitan Opera (1935–50), quoted by Arnold Edinborough in *The Festivals of Canada* (1981).

When I get to where I'm supposed to be... that will be where I'd like to be.

Tantoo Cardinal, actress, discussing life and career, quoted by Brian Gorman in *The Toronto Star*, 12 March 1993.

AMERICA See also NORTH AMERICA, UNITED STATES OF AMERICA

O my America! my new-found-land.

Line from English poet **John Donne**'s "Elegie XIX" (written 1590, published 1633), *Complete Poetry and Selected Prose* (1932), edited by John Hayward. These words are a direct literary reference to Newfoundland, which Sir Humphrey Gilbert had claimed for England in 1583.

He might root out barbarism out of America, and fully discover Terra Australis Incognita, find out the North-East, and North-West passages, drain those mighty Maeotian fens.

Robert Burton, author, "Democritus Junior to His Book," *The Anatomy of Melancholy* (1621) edited by Floyd Dell and Paul Jordan-Smith in 1927.

In the beginning, all was America.

John Locke, English philosopher, *Two Treatises on Government* (1690), as quoted by Michael Ignatieff in *The Needs of Strangers* (1985). Locke had in mind, Ignatieff explained, the state of the American tribes before the advent of "the spiral of need" introduced by European contact.

The inhabitants of the United States insist upon referring to themselves as "Americans," whereas an inhabitant of Mexico is termed a "Mexican," and the term "American" is denied to the people of Canada.

Wyndham Lewis, British artist and author, *America, I Presume* (1940).

The New World was the Outer Space of fifteenth- and sixteenth-century Europe. Travellers set off on terrifying journeys into an unknown that was already peopled, in the popular imagination of the day, with all kinds of fantastic monsters. Some of these adventurers returned with wondrous accounts of the lands and savages they had encountered.

Hugh Brody, author, *Maps and Dreams: Indians and the British Columbia Frontier* (1981, 1988).

When in 1988 George Bush spoke of the need for a kinder, gentler America, he might well have pointed to Canada as his example.

Lawrence Martin, journalist, *Pledge of Allegiance: The Americanization of Canada in the Mulroney Years* (1993). Martin instanced Canada's peaceful nature, broad social programs, cultural programs, public broadcasting, racial tolerance, international peacekeeping. George Bush, U.S. President-elect, in his acceptance speech delivered in Washington, D.C., 20 Jan. 1989, had in mind disadvantaged Americans. Authorship of the words "kinder, gentler America" is claimed by speechwriter Peggy Noonan in her books *What I Saw at the Revolution* (1990) and *Simply Speaking* (1991).

One could not talk to Canadians about America, meaning the United States, because they would instantly point out that they lived in America, too.

Jill Ker Conway, Australian-born, American-educated historian and memoirist who taught at the University of Toronto from 1964 to 1975, *True North: A Memoir* (1994).

The inner life of America is not a place—Canada is a place. Maybe the best place in the world. But if you are Canadian and you have a dream, you leave. Why? Because America is not a place. It is a dream.

Clotaire Rapaille, French anthropologist and marketer, quoted by Jack Hitt in "Does the Smell of Coffee Brewing Remind You of Your Mother," *The New York Times Magazine*, 7 May 2000.

AMERICANISM See UNITED STATES OF AMERICA

ANCESTRY See also HERITAGE

Irish by extraction, English by birth, Canadian by adoption, and Scotch by absorption.

Healey Willan, British-born organist and composer, thumbnail description of himself on CBC-TV's *Spectrum*, 3 Dec. 1980.

The Canadians were the first and the model anti-Americans because the habitants and the Loyalists both wanted to remain free of the United States.

J.L. Granatstein, historian, *Yankee Go Home? Canadians and Anti-Americanism* (1996).

We respect our ancestors' achievements by standing on their shoulders and seeing farther, not by crouching in their shadows and seeing less. Let's do something to inspire our own grandchildren. That's what the ancestors did.

Silver Donald Cameron, columnist, "What to Do with Bluenose II?" *The Globe and Mail*, 27 Sept. 1999.

ANGELS See also BELIEF, SPIRITS

Angels are the things you see / between the things you see.

Lines from an unpublished poem read by the poet **Tom Marshall** at the Bohemian Embassy at The Harbourfront, Toronto, 14 March 1975.

When I returned to a disunited Canada in 1976, I contacted the overlighting angel for its view of the country's situation. This led to my exploring my roots, which I had thought non-existent or irrelevant as I considered myself a citizen of the world, and to my giving a series of exploratory workshops on national identity and the part it had to play in our makeup, if any.

Dorothy Maclean, Ontario-born medium and co-founder of the Findhorn community in Scotland, *To Hear the Angels Sing: An Odyssey of Co-Creation with the Devic Kingdom* (1980).

ANGER

This saying is true / And brutally frank— / Temperament is temper / That's too old to spank.

R.R. Cunningham, publisher and columnist, *The North Battleford News-Optimist*, 1940s, quoted by J. George Johnston in *The Weeklies: Biggest Circulation in Town* (1972).

ANIMAL RIGHTS See also ANIMALS, SEAL HUNT

It is not a question of "them or us." There is no "either-or" situation. There is room for kindness to animals and kindness to humans, room on this planet for both to have rights. I have come to believe, very forcibly, that an understanding of the needs of animals can only lead to a greater understanding of the needs of humans.

Brian Davies, founder of the International Fund for Animal Welfare in 1969, *Red Ice: My Fight to Save the Seals* (1989).

It takes up to forty dumb animals to make up a fur coat. But only one to wear it.

Wording on a **Greenpeace** poster in 1984, noted by Oline Luinenberg and Stephen Osborne in *The Little Green Book: Quotations on the Environment* (1990).

Animal rights people tend to identify with those species closest to us. But animal liberationists tend to be part of the broader struggle for bringing the earth out from under the yoke of human oppression.

Vicki Miller, animal rights activist, in conversation with Farley Mowat, author of *Rescue the Earth! Conversations with the Green Crusaders* (1990).

ANIMALS

See also ANIMAL RIGHTS, BEARS, BEAVERS, BIRDS, CATS, DOGS, HORSES & HORSE RACING, MOOSE, WHALES & WHALING, WILDLIFE, WOLVES, ZOOS

It was somewhere about this time that an inhabitant of Kingston is said to have taken to private wolf breeding, in order to obtain a reward of four dollars per head, offered by Government for their capture.

"An Old Canadian Town," signed by **Fidelis**, referring to Kingston, U.C., in the 1820s, *The Canadian Monthly and National Review*, July 1873.

There never was a man as great as the average dog believes his master to be.

Bob Edwards, publisher, *The Eye Opener*, 4 Aug. 1917.

That's the key: English animal stories are about "social relations," American ones are about people killing animals; Canadian ones are about animals being killed, as felt emotionally from inside the fur and the feathers.

Margaret Atwood, author and critic, *Survival: A Thematic Guide to Canadian Literature* (1972).

Man critically altered the natural equilibrium. In North America close to one hundred mammals and birds have become extinct—without replacement—in the last 32,000 years or so.

John A. Livingston, naturalist, *One Cosmic Instant: A Natural History of Human Arrogance* (1973).

Unless we wish all wild animals to become extinct and tame animals to be further exploited (and ourselves thereby lessened), it is up to us to exercise our dominion, not against but for the animal world.

Dorothy Maclean, medium and co-founder of the Findhorn community in Scotland, *To Hear the Angels Sing: An Odyssey of Co-Creation with the Devic Kingdom* (1980).

Animals confound us not because they are deceptively simple but because they are finally inseparable from the complexities of life.

Barry Lopez, naturalist, *Arctic Dreams: Imagination and Desire in a Northern Landscape* (1986).

I am always dumb to kind animals.

Line from **Edward Phillips**' novel *Buried on Sunday* (1986).

I don't believe in predestiny. You make your own fate, yet I was born to study orangutans and their forest. I believe my affinity for forests comes from my Lithuanian heritage. We are a forest people.

Biruté M.F. Galdikas, zoologist, born to Lithuanian parents in Germany, raised in Canada, a student of orangutans at the Tanjung Puting Reserve in Borneo, "My Life with Orangutans," *Omni*, July 1987.

I'm afraid I can't quite talk to the animals—yet. But they can certainly talk to me. And they do!

Timothy Findley, novelist, interviewed by Alan Twigg in *Strong Voices: Conversations with Fifty Canadian Authors* (1988).

It was now clear that neither God nor Darwinian selection produces and extinguishes species. Committees do.

John A. Livingston, naturalist, referring to the reclassification of the Ipswich sparrow as a subspecies, and not a species, following its apparent extinction, "Nature for the Sake of Nature," *Endangered Spaces: The Future for Canada's Wilderness* (1989) edited by Monte Hummel.

ANNE OF GREEN GABLES See also PRINCE EDWARD ISLAND

Elderly couple apply to orphan asylum for a boy. By mistake a girl is sent them.

Entry in "a faded notebook" dated 1895 made by the young school teacher **L.M. Montgomery**. It blossomed into *Anne of Green Gables* (1908), the classic novel of childhood set in rural Prince Edward Island.

People in other countries might not know the name of our prime minister, but they've heard of Anne.

Robert Fulford, journalist, commenting on the increasing and widespread popularity of the fictional creation Anne Shirley (Anne of Green Gables), quoted by Patricia Orwen in *The Toronto Star*, 18 Aug. 1991.

While Islanders may be sick of Anne of Green Gables, she is ever young in the minds of people from other places. It's a burden Islanders have to bear.

Jack McAndrew, broadcaster, referring to the decision of the government of Prince Edward Island to add Anne Shirley's braided and freckle-faced image to the Island's automobile licence plates, quoted by Kevin Cox in *The Globe and Mail*, 7 Sept. 1992.

ANNEXATIONISM See also CONTINENTALISM

If, today, he should choose to say he thinks it necessary to invade Canada, to prevent the British from invading us, how could you stop him? You may say to him, "I see no probability of the British invading us," but he will say to you, "Be silent; I see it, if you don't."

Abraham Lincoln, future U.S. President, criticizing the presidential power to wage war, letter to William H. Herndon, 15 Feb. 1849, *The Collected Works of Abraham Lincoln* (1953) edited by Roy P. Basler.

Secession first he would put down / Wholly and forever, / And afterwards from Britain's Crown, / He Canada would sever. / And we'll go and capture Canada, / For we've nothing else to do.

Lines from the annexationist's version of "Yankee Doodle" sung in the northern New England states following the Fenian raid on St. Alban's, Quebec, Dec. 1864.

ANSWERS

I think there are all questions and there aren't any answers.

Northrop Frye, cultural critic, interviewed by Harry Rasky, producer of *The Great Teacher: Northrop Frye*, CBC-TV, 25 Dec. 1989.

ANTARCTICA

Scientists in Antarctica have a lot in common with hockey players in Canada (both spend a lot of time on the ice).

Paul Rosenthal, author, *Where on Earth: A Geografunny Guide to the Globe* (1992)

It is to icy Antarctica that we look to find answers to the very roots of civilization—answers which may yet be preserved in the frozen depths of the forgotten island continent.

Rand and **Rose Flem-Ath**, researchers, *When the Sky Fell: In Search of Atlantis* (1995).

ANTHEMS See also MUSIC

God save our gracious Queen, / Long live our noble Queen, / God save the Queen! / Send her victorious, / Happy and glorious, / Long to reign over us, / God save the Queen!

The first verse of "God Save the Queen," the national anthem of the United Kingdom and, unofficially, the royal anthem of Canada. As Percy A. Scholes noted in *The Oxford Companion to Music* (9th ed., 1956), "This must be the best-known tune in the world." He added, "If any attribution is necessary in song-books, the word 'traditional' seems to be the only one possible, or, perhaps 'Traditional; earliest known version by John Bull, 1563–1628.'"

In days of yore, from Britain's shore, / Wolfe, the dauntless hero, came, / And planted firm Britannia's flag / On Canada's fair domain. // Here may it wave, our boast and pride, / And, joined in love together, / The Thistle, Shamrock, Rose entwine / The Maple Leaf forever! // The Maple Leaf, our emblem dear, / The Maple Leaf forever; / God save our Queen, and Heaven bless / The Maple Leaf forever.

First verse of **Alexander Muir**'s once-popular national song "The Maple Leaf Forever" (1867).

O Canada! Our home and native land! / True patriot love in all thy sons command! / With glowing hearts we see thee rise, / The True North strong and free! / From far and wide, O

Canada, / We stand on guard for thee. / God keep our land glorious and free! / O Canada, we stand on guard for thee. / O Canada, we stand on guard for thee.

*

O Canada! Terre de nos aïeux, / Ton front est ceint de fleurons glorieux! / Car ton bras sait porter l'épée, / Il sait porter la croix! / Ton histoire est une epopée, / Des plus brillants exploits. / Et ta valeur, de foi trempée, / Protégera nos foyers et nos droits. / Protégera nos foyers et nos droits.

Words of the official English and French texts of "O Canada" as they appear in the National Anthem Act, 1980, where they are identified as the "National Anthem—Hymne national." Calixa Lavallée composed the stirring tune for Sir **Adolph-Basile Routhier**'s words in 1880; **R. Stanley Weir** wrote the verses for the English version in 1908. Of related interest is the Royal Salute, which is a short composition that combines bars of music from both "O Canada" and "God Save the Queen"; it is played but not sung on semi-official occasions.

Suppose we say it was "Rule Doodle" and "Yankee Britannia" and adjourn to breakfast?

Agreement reached by a Briton and an American visiting Canada in **Jules Verne**'s fantastic-adventure novel *Robur the Conquer, or The Clipper of the Clouds* (1886).

If Your Majesty allows me to be frank, I'll say it is our national anthem after midnight.

Camillien Houde, Montreal Mayor, addressing King George V, Montreal, 18 May 1939, explaining the status of the French-Canadian folk song "Alouette," quoted by Tom MacDonnell in *Daylight Upon Magic: The Royal Tour of Canada—1939* (1989).

What red-blooded Canadian boy cannot recall when "In days of yore, from Britain's shore, / Wolfe, the donkless hero, came?"

Norman Ward, humorist, referring to a misreading of the lyrics of "The Maple Leaf Forever" in "The Donkless Hero," *Mice in the Beer* (1960).

This land is your land, this land is my land, / From Bonavista to Vancouver Island, / From the Arctic Islands to the Great Lakes waters; / This land was made for you and me.

Verse from the modern folk song "This Land Is Your Land," composed by the American singer and songwriter Woody Guthrie in 1956; with the composer's blessing, **Martin Bochner** adapted the lyrics for the Toronto-based folk group The Travellers. There are numerous national adaptations.

O Can... O Can... you see by the dawn's early light....

New words proposed for "O Canada," the national anthem, by the song-writing team of **Marian Grudeff** and **Ray Jessel**, *Spring Thaw*, 1967.

We have a first-rate anthem. Musically "O Canada" is a composition of the mid-19th century and not a particularly adventurous piece of writing. Perhaps it sticks to us because it's so traditional. It was written by a francophone and accepted by anglophones, so it's the perfect bridge between the two societies. Besides, I like it because I've heard that it's the only composition that is performed more often than my own "Fanfares for the Stratford Festival"!

Louis Appelbaum, composer, considering the musical and other characteristics of "O Canada," quoted by John Robert Colombo in *The Globe and Mail*, 1 July 1991.

If you don't believe your country / Should come before yourself, / You can better serve your country / By living somewhere else.

Lines from the title song on the album *Believe in Your Country* (1992) written and performed by **Stompin' Tom Connors**.

I'm very passionate about my national anthem. I think people stand there and sing O Canada lifelessly. I always sing it with verve because I think we live in paradise and I'd like everybody else to know it.

Maureen Forrester, opera singer and contributor to the group celebrity recording of the national anthem, quoted in "O Canada," *Maclean's*, 2 March 1992.

There are few similarities between the English and French versions of "O Canada," our national anthem, apart from the tune.

Mitchell Sharp, former Minister of Finance and Minister of External Affairs, *Which Reminds Me...: A Memoir* (1994).

I now want to know when the public education system is going to teach my kids the words to "God Save the Queen." They've never head it sung in school.

Michael Valpy, columnist, "Culture," *The Globe and Mail*, 28 Nov. 1997.

ANTIGONISH MOVEMENT

The primacy of the individual. Social reform must come through education. Education must begin with the economic. Education must be through group action. Effective social reform involves fundamental changes in social and economic institutions. The ultimate objective of the movement is a full and abundant life for everyone in the community.

J.J. Tompkins, educator, "Six Basic Principles of the Antigonish Movement" (1944), quoted by Alexander Fraser Laidlaw in *The Campus and the Community: The Global Impact of the Antigonish Movement* (1961).

ANTI-SEMITISM See also HOLOCAUST, JEWISH; JEWISH PEOPLE

Achat chez nous.

Slogan of the "Buy at Home" movement in Quebec in the 1930s. "It was aimed at destroying the Jewish retail merchants who had sprung up throughout the province, returning small business to the French Canadian domain where it belonged." Noted by Henry Milner and Sheilagh Hodgins Milner in *The Decolonization of Quebec: An Analysis of Left-Wing Nationalism* (1973). The "Buy at Home" movement was promoted by the right-wing l'Ordre Jacques Cartier, founded in 1928.

No Dogs or Jews Allowed

Warning on a sign reportedly seen in the Beaches, Sunnyside, or Centre Island areas of Toronto in the 1930s. According to historian Pierre Berton, writing to Eric Adams, 7 Sept. 1994, "There is no evidence whatsoever—and I looked into this some years ago—that there was ever a sign in Toronto saying 'No dogs or Jews allowed.'" Noted by Adams in Letters to the Editor, *The Toronto Star*, 30 April 1995.

I am not anti-anyone. I am pro-Québécois. I have never reproached the Journal for having devoted an article to a Jew because he was a Jew, but because he was not a francophone. I have great respect for the Jews, but they take up too much space. I want first of all to help our people who need help more!

Pierre Péladeau, Quebec publisher, quoted by Jean Blouin in "Péladeau tout craché," *L'Actualité*, 15 April 1990. The words come from an interoffice memo Péladeau wrote to the fashion editor of the *Journal* concerning space alloted to Jewish—as distinct from Québécois—fashion personalities. Thereafter Péladeau disavowed any prejudice.

Surely the Nazis were an enemy before whom even Jesus could not have turned his other cheek; he would have been shot first.

Allan Gould, editor, Introduction, *What Did They Think of the Jews?* (1991).

All the same, Jews who have been Quebecers for generations understand only too well that when thousands of flag-waving nationalists march through the streets roaring "Le Québec aux Québécois!" they do not have in mind anybody named Ginsburg. Or MacGregor, come to think of it.

Mordecai Richler, novelist and controversialist, *Oh Canada! Oh Quebec! Requiem for a Divided Country* (1992).

At the Auschwitz–Birkenau concentration camp in Poland, which I once visited, horror-stricken, even the Nazis did not eliminate millions of Jews in a painful or bloody manner. They died in the gas chambers, without suffering.

Jean Bienvenue, Judge of the Quebec Superior Court, remarks made from the bench in 1995, contrasting Nazi practices with a woman who punished her husband by slashing his throat with a razor, as noted by Tu Thanh Ha, "Quebec Judge Unfit, Council Decides," *The Globe and Mail*, 5 July 1996. The remarks were examined by a disciplinary proceeding which concluded in a recommendation that Judge Bienvenue be removed from office.

I do not believe in the gas chamber stuff.

Attributed to **Doug Collins**, newspaperman whose controversial columns appeared in the 1990s in the *North Shore News* ("Voice of North and West Vancouver since 1969"), by journalist Paul Brook, "Freedom's Just Another Word," *Saturday Night*, Nov. 1997. In his column "The Story Keeps Changing," 18 Aug. 1993, Collins asked the following question: "What difference does it make whether the figure was six million, one million, or 300,000, as was stated by the Red Cross after the war?"

ANXIETY

Anxiety information today travels at electronic speeds—what Marshall McLuhan once called the speed of angels—and creates instantaneous communication and community. A community of electronic panic: our special gift to the millennium.

John Fekete, philosopher, *Moral Panic: Biopolitics Rising* (2nd ed., 1995).

We live in an age in which even our anxieties have been privatized.

James Laxer, political scientist, *In Search of a New Left: Canadian Politics after the Neoconservative Assault* (1996).

APHORISMS

Aphorisms give you more for your time and money than any other literary form. Only the poem comes near to it, but then most good poems either start off from an aphorism or arrive at one.

Louis Dudek, poet and aphorist, entry for 1985, *Notebooks 1960–1994* (1994).

APOCALYPSE

The Apocalypse will come, of that there is no doubt, on a magnificent summer's day. The kind of day when the girls are more splendid than ever. It has been said that no one will be recognizable afterwards.

I'll be the one with a red flower in his hand.

Thoughts of the main character as well as the conclusion of **Dany Laferrière**'s novel *Eroshima* (1991) translated by David Homel.

The Armageddon we face is the elimination of the idea that there is anything we can do to make this world one in which we feel at home.

Mark Kingwell, philosopher, *Dreams of Millennium: Report from a Culture on the Brink* (1996).

ARAB PEOPLE

The inhabitants of Emmwas (supposedly the biblical Emmaus) and of two other adjacent villages were expelled from their homes in the wake of the battles of the Six Day War.... The villages were bulldozed, and, later, trees were planted on top of the ruins. The once populated hills of Emmwas became "Canada Park," and Yehoshua's student, who exists somewhere in every Israeli Jewish mind, wondered if one day this park, and similar forests, would be set on fire.

Anton Shammas, Israeli Arab writer, referring to Canada Park in Israel and how it appears to an Arab student, "The Morning After," *The New York Review of Books*, 29 Sept. 1988.

The Soviet Jews should not immigrate to Israel and the occupied territories, but to Canada, which is practically empty.

Attributed to **Yasser Arafat**, Chairman, Palestine Liberation Organization, speech, April 1990.

We are awed by the "real" Arab, the Bedouin tribes people who have survived within an environment as hostile as that of our own Arctic, and who, again like our Inuit, yet have evolved a rich and intricate and pridefully independent lifestyle.

Richard Gwyn, correspondent, *The Toronto Star*, 16 Jan. 1991.

We know we can't make peace with the Jews until the Jews can make peace with the Jews, and the Arabs with the Arabs.

Sam Orbaum, Montreal-raised Israeli columnist, "But Seriously," *The Jerusalem Post Magazine*, 14 Oct. 1994.

ARCHAEOLOGY

The actual presence of early man in eastern Asia is therefore now no longer a matter of conjecture.

Davidson Black, archaeologist and discoverer of the remains of Peking Man in China, conclusion reached in 1926, quoted by Harry L. Shapiro in *Peking Man* (1974).

Our discipline is a very peculiar sort of history. We destroy our evidence in the process of learning more. There is an enormous obligation to record what you see, when you know that no one will ever again see it, as you have, at the moment of discovery.

T. Cuyler Young Jr., archaeologist, Royal Ontario Museum, referring in particular to unearthing ancient treasures in Iran, quoted by Patricia Holtz in *The Canadian*, 15 Jan. 1977.

Such things as actually unearthing with the tip of my digging trowel a beautifully made large stone point thousands of years old, or of being a member of a small survey team suddenly discovering an unknown French fort in the bush near Hudson's Bay have fuelled my sense of being in touch with my own country's ancestral past and helping in a small way to discover it.

Peter Such, author, *Vanished Peoples: The Archaic Forest & Beothuk People of Newfoundland* (1978).

ARCHITECTURE

We must not forget that the architect, more than any other, leads in forming the taste of the country. He inspires, directs, and controls the work of the plasterer, the painter, the woodworker, the ironworker, and the stone mason. He interprets the trend of fashion and translates it into concrete form.

John M. Lyle, architect, "Canadian Architecture," 31 Jan. 1927, *Addresses Delivered before The Canadian Club of Toronto: Season of 1926–27* (1927).

I do not know of any finer specimen of architecture anywhere. The Royal York will give an impetus to noble architecture all over this continent.

Eden Smith, architect known for his Arts and Crafts buildings, commenting on Toronto's Royal York Hotel, interviewed by R.E. Knowles in *The Toronto Star*, 24 Jan. 1930.

Age is something we want to keep. I look on St. Lawrence Hall as our Westminster Abbey. When they lose a cherub, they don't replace it. We should be satisfied to retain the appearance of age; we aren't interested in newness.

Eric Arthur, architect and conservationist, commenting on the restoration of St. Lawrence Hall in Toronto as a Centennial project, quoted by Kenneth B. Smith in *St. Lawrence Hall* (1969).

In 1939 the Canadian Pavilion was overlooked by almost everyone writing about the Fair. Its very ordinariness rendered it instantly forgettable. Today the F.W. Williams-designed pavilion emerges from anonymity as a rare example of Fair architecture that actually looked like everyday buildings of the period.

Larry Zim, Mel Lerner, Herbert Rolfe, authors, referring to the Canadian Pavilion at the New York World's Fair, 1939–40, *The World of Tomorrow: The 1939 New York World's Fair* (1988).

It is the dialogue between building and setting that is the essence of architecture.

Arthur Erickson, architect, quoted by Benjamin Forgey in *The Washington Post*, 18 June 1988. Erickson once said, "Context is everything."

I've developed a sense of Indian warriorship to carry my projects through. Warriorship means you nail your foot to the floor and hold on to the work as if your life depended on it.

Douglas Cardinal, Métis architect and designer of the Canadian Museum of Civilization, quoted by David Lancashire in *Smithsonian*, March 1990.

With writing, you have a blank page and there's nothing stopping you from writing the greatest book in the world. Many things stop you from building the greatest building in the world.

Witold Rybczynski, architect and author, interviewed by Stephen Smith in *The Globe and Mail*, 5 Oct. 1991.

I think that's a big problem in Vancouver—we make buildings so boring that our brains refuse to remember them. If Vancouver had to stand on its architectural merit alone, we'd be clobbered in the beauty sweepstakes by such gems as Duluth, Akron or Sudbury.

Douglas Coupland, author, "Exit," *Vancouver*, Oct. 1997.

Maybe there's a Canadian pride in me that comes to the fore.

Frank Gehry, Toronto-born, Timmins-raised, Los Angeles–based, post-modernist architect, interviewed by Michael Enright on CBC Radio's *This Morning*, 25 Feb. 1998. His maxim is said to be "Being accepted isn't everything."

ARCHIVES

It is an endlessly tantalizing thought that in obscure towns in Australia and Canada, even in the remote hills of India, today may rest documents of untold value for English literary history. Perhaps one of the most dramatic scholarly discoveries of the next few years will occur there—it is not at all impossible.

Robin W. Winks, historian, *The Historian as Detective: Essays on Evidence* (1969).

ARCTIC See also ARCTIC OCEAN, THE NORTH

At last they reached what is now the Arctic Circle. "It is as far as we can go," they said to one another. "The way is blocked by a mountain of snow, a sea of ice. Clearly this is the Back Door of this Fourth World, which Sotuknang said was closed to us."

Spider Woman, however, urged them to go on. "You have the magic powers given you. Use them. Melt this mountain of snow, this sea of ice."

Passage from the traditional account of the ancient migrations of the Hopi people of the Southwestern United States, as recorded by **Frank Waters** in *Book of the Hopi* (1963). Spider Woman urged the Indian clans to melt the snow and ice and bring tropical warmth to the region, the northern boundary of their wanderings. Sotuknang, the God of the Universe, intervened, halted the attempt, punished the Spider Clan, and sent the Hopi people back south where they eventually found their promised homeland in Arizona.

Et Ego in Arctis

Latin phrase employed by **Lord Dufferin**, the titled Englishman who later served as Governor General of Canada, in his book of travel, *Letters from High Latitudes* (1860), subtitled "Being Some Account of a Voyage in 1856 in the Schooner Yacht Foam to Iceland, Jan Mayen and Spitzbergen." Dufferin's words recall the traditional inscription *Et in Arcadia Ego* which appears as the legend on a tomb depicted in a 17th century painting by Gueracino. The legend is translated "I too am in Arcadia." The simple-seeming words are traditionally spoken by the allegorical figure of Death. Dufferin's use of the words, twelve years before coming to Canada, could mean "I too am in the Arctic" or "Even in the Arctic is Death." In recent years the traditional inscription has been associated with the legend of the Holy Grail and the so-called Grail Knights in Nova Scotia, Montreal, and the Niagara region.

This gloomy region, where the year is divided into one day and one night, lies entirely outside the stream of history.

W. Winwood Reade, British author, referring to the Arctic regions, Book III, *The Martyrdom of Man* (1872).

There is something unaccountably oppressive in this Arctic universe. The immensity of these regions, their dreariness, their silent immobility that appears like the stillness of the grave, have a strangely depressing effect. They weigh upon the mind, and bear it down like some fearful incubus, like that half-waking, half-dreaming, indistinct consciousness of weight upon the chest felt in the oppression of nightmare.

Janarius MacGahan, Irish-American war correspondent and member of the Pandora Expedition to the Eastern Arctic, *Under the Northern Lights* (1876).

Ah me, none but those who have experienced it could dream one half the mental depression of that Arctic dark; how the soul takes on the hue of the universe; and without and within is nothing but gloom, gloom, and the rule of the Power of Darkness.

Thoughts of Adam Jeffson, sole survivor of a voyage and then a trek to the North Pole, a point of safety in a world catastrophe, related by the Irish novelist **M.P. Shiel** in his fantasy novel *The Purple Cloud* (1901).

On the first of July last year, on Confederation Day, I had a slab made and on that slab I wrote, "This memorial is erected here today to commemorate the taking possession of all the Arctic Archipelago." I was doing a wholesale business, taking possession for Canada of all lands and islands to the eastward of the international line between Alaska and Canada on the 141st meridian as far north as 90 degrees north.

J.-E. Bernier, Arctic explorer, address, "The Arctic Regions of Canada," Empire Club of Canada, Toronto, 20 Dec. 1909.

We have not as yet had the good fortune of developing in southern Canada any religious sect or other group so unpopular that they have been driven north to help dispel the Arctic desert of Canada.

Vilhjalmur Stefansson, Arctic explorer, address, referring to the role of the Mormons in dispelling the myth of the American desert, "Abolishing the Arctic," Empire Club of Canada, Toronto, 25 Oct. 1928.

I'm going to the Arctic where the flowers are fresh and fair, / I'm going to domesticate a friendly polar bear; / I'll marry an intelligent young lady Esquimo, / And serenade the Arctic moon upon my old banjo.

One stanza of the verse "Northward Ho! After Hearing a Lecture on 'The Friendly Arctic' by Stefansson" composed by versifier **Ronald V. Clarke**, *Cape and Bells: An Anthology of Light Verse by Canadian Poets* (1936) edited by John W. Garvin.

It was like the no-man's-land between the trenches in the War—a colossal no-man's-land created in some campaign of demons, pitted and pocked with shell-holes from some infernal artillery.

Lines descriptive of the Arctic in **John Buchan**'s novel *Sick Heart River* (1941).

When I saw the Arctic, the wildness of it, no trees or vegetation, just tundra rolling for miles, it thrilled me beyond belief. It seemed as if I had been there at some other time.

James Houston, founder of the Eskimo co-operative movement, on visiting Quebec's Ungava area in 1948, quoted by John Ayre in *Saturday Night*, May 1974.

I can see cities in northern Canada north of the Arctic circle. There are vast power potentialities in that area. I can see cities developing there as they are developing today in Norway, if only the government would catch the vision of the possibilities.

John G. Diefenbaker, Conservative leader, address on northern development, early formulation of his Northern Vision, House of Commons, 11 Nov. 1957.

For me, my experience of the Arctic was an experiment in space and time—stepping back into history and forward into the future.

Ritchie-Calder, Lord, British scientist and peer, *The Inheritors: The Story of Man and the World He Made* (1961).

Once Bowman had flown over northern Canada during the height of an auroral display; the snow-covered landscape had been as bleak and brilliant as this. And that arctic wilderness, he reminded himself, was more than a hundred degrees warmer than the regions over which they were hurtling now.

Thoughts of astronaut Dave Bowman, First Captain aboard the spaceship *Discovery*, as he travels in the cold of interplanetary space, passing through "the shadow of Jupiter," in **Arthur C. Clarke**'s novelization *2001: A Space Odyssey: A Novel by Arthur C. Clarke Based on the Screenplay by Arthur C. Clarke & Stanley Kubrick* (1968).

When I flew over the Arctic, devas told me that even the empty frozen wastelands were necessary for certain planetary work.

Dorothy Maclean, medium, *To Hear the Angels Sing: An Odyssey of Co-Creation with the Devic Kingdom* (1980).

Arctic history became for me, then, a legacy of desire—the desire of individual men to achieve their goals. But it was also the legacy of a kind of desire that transcends heroics and which was privately known to many—the desire for a safe and honourable passage through the world.

Barry Lopez, naturalist, *Arctic Dreams: Imagination and Desire in a Northern Landscape* (1986).

The region turns in on itself like any nation. It is organized like Australia, around an inland desert sea, with most of its people living on the coastal periphery. It is not vast like the Pacific. It is vast like the steppes of Asia. It has the heft, say, of China, but with the population of Seattle.

Barry Lopez, naturalist, *Arctic Dreams: Imagination and Desire in a Northern Landscape* (1986).

For the Canadian, the High Arctic is a zone of the mind, and a large part of our consciousness. It is our identity; without it we would be in crisis.

Toni Onley, artist and traveller, *Onley's Arctic: Diaries and Paintings of the High Arctic* (1989).

The Arctic, the lands under the constellation Arktos or the Great Bear, has from the times of classical Greek mythology aroused in humans a sense of wonder and mystery.

Fred Roots, science adviser, "The Polar Regions," *Planet under Stress: The Challenge of Global Change* (1990) edited by Constance Mungall and Digby J. McLaren for the Royal Society of Canada.

The best way to defend our sovereignty is within a coalition with the United States.

Marcel Masse, Minister of National Defence,

statement on Arctic sovereignty in a defence policy paper issued in September, quoted by Peter C. Newman in *Maclean's*, 30 Sept. 1991. Newman added: "To have our Arctic sovereignty protected by the old country that has challenged it is the ultimate surrender. We have become squatters on our own land."

I once stood at Baker Lake (N.W.T.), looking at the barren landscape, in 40 m.p.h. winds, thinking, "This is the geographic centre of Canada." Our centre is above the tree line. It boggles the mind.

Robert Munsch, children's author, "My Canada Includes . . . ," *Maclean's*, 3 Jan. 1994.

The wonder of the Arctic is not in its physical vastness, but rather in its smallness, its intimacy.

James Houston, author and artist, *Confessions of an Igloo Dweller* (1995).

Indeed, without technology—and without the almost imponderable ingenuity that permitted human beings to fashion a tech-dependent existence with little more than bits of bone, skin, moss, and ice—no one in their right or wrong mind could possibly live here.

Sheldon Teitelbaum, correspondent, "The Call of the Wired," *Wired*, Nov. 1997.

ARCTIC OCEAN See also ARCTIC

. . . let us be the first to meet the ships of the Seekers when they come out from the Arctic Seas.

Words spoken by a sea captain's wife in an outport of Newfoundland while waiting with other wives for news of the fate of their husbands and other members of the Franklin expedition in **Wilkie Collins**' melodrama *The Frozen Deep*, a theatrical success in London in 1857, according to David Roberts in "Dickens and the Arctic," *Horizon*, Jan. 1980.

It is only here in these Arctic seas that stark, unfathomable stillness obtrudes itself upon you in all its gruesome reality.

Thoughts of the narrator of the story "The Captain of the Pole Star" in **Sir Arthur Conan Doyle**'s collection *The Captain of the Pole-Star and Other Tales* (1890).

The Arctic consists of an ocean surrounded by large land masses; the Antarctic consists of a land mass surrounded by ocean. From this fundamental opposition, quite different characteristics develop.

David Mountfield, historian, *A History of Polar Exploration* (1974).

The underwater Arctic is the most hostile environment in the world. We know this from first-hand experience.

Joseph A. MacInnis, scientist and undersea explorer, address, Empire Club of Canada, Toronto, 26 Feb. 1976.

The reason we are interested in working here is because the Arctic Ocean is a bit of a canary in a mine shaft.

Harold Welch, marine biologist, interviewed by telephone aboard the icebreaker *Des Groseilliers*, frozen in the Beaufort Sea, quoted by CP, *The Globe and Mail*, 24 Nov. 1997.

ARGENTINA

Vive la République du Québec

Jean Péron, former and future President of Argentina, letter written in 1962 to Santiago J. Lucques, a Montreal academic, noted by *The Toronto Star*, 2 Sept. 1974.

Canada and Argentina are the bookends of the Americas.

Attributed to Prime Minister **Jean Chrétien** during a speech delivered in Buenos Aires, 24 Jan. 1995, quoted by Robert Sheppard in *The Globe and Mail* the following day.

But don't cry for Argentina. The Argentinians could still have had it all if only, as a nation, they had not refused to grow up.

Joe Schlesinger, foreign correspondent, alluding to the theme song of the musical *Evita* and to Argentine attitudes, *Time Zones: A Journalist in the World* (1990).

ARMAMENTS See also CANADIAN ARMED FORCES

The fact that Canada does not effectively apply human rights criteria when it sells military equipment also means that Canadian arms industries serve to strengthen the hand of repression in some Third World countries.

For Canada, this constitutes a form of

"branch plant immorality." As Canadians, we are, whether we like it or not, accomplices in the operations of the American military-industrial machine.

Remi J. De Roo, Bishop of Victoria, "Our War Economy and Conversion for Peace," *End the Arms Race: Fund Human Needs: Proceedings of the 1986 Vancouver Centennial Peace and Disarmament Symposium* (1986) edited by Thomas L. Perry and James G. Foulks.

ARMY See CANADIAN ARMED FORCES

ART & ARTISTS See also COMIC ART, CULTURE, ESKIMO ART, MUSEUMS & GALLERIES, NATIVE ART

He was an exile in the city of exiles; a characteristic item in it, though of a variety exceedingly rare. But he would have been equally an exile in any other city. He had no consciousness of being an exile, of being homeless. He was above patriotisms and homes. Why, when he wanted even a book he only borrowed.

Arnold Bennett, English novelist, describing his friend, the self-exiled painter J.W. Morrice, during the years 1903–04 in Paris, *Evening with Exiles* (1910).

Do not take the paintings too seriously, rather let them take you. The old masters were young servants once. The artistic survey of Canada is in its beginning, and is undertaken entirely at the artists' own expense. The great purpose of landscape art is to make us at home in our own country.

Aphorisms associated with the painters of the **Group of Seven**, "The New Canadian Art," *The Daily Intelligencer* (Belleville, Ont.), 27 Sept. 1919.

All art is a kind of exploring. To discover and reveal is the way every artist sets about his business.

Robert Flaherty, prospector and early documentary filmmaker, quoted by Edmund Carpenter in *They Became What They Beheld* (1970).

After my summers in New Mexico where I had heard the Penitente songs and painted the dark crosses as I felt them there, the Canadian crosses seemed very different. The Canadian crosses were singing in the sunlight. Sometimes there were pottery figures around them—always they had a feeling of gaiety.

Georgia O'Keeffe, painter of the American southwest and painter of the roadside crosses of the Gaspé in 1932, *Georgia O'Keeffe* (1976).

I'll tell you what is the highest work of art—it's of the soul—listen to this: A truly beautiful life is the highest work of art in the world.

Boris Volkoff, dance instructor, interviewed by R.E. Knowles in *The Toronto Star*, 29 Dec. 1939.

The Indian caught first at the inner intensity of his subject, worked outward to the surfaces. His spiritual conception he buried deep in the wood he was about to carve. Then—chip! chip! his crude tools released the symbols that were to clothe his thought—no sham, no mannerism. The lean, neat Indian hands carved what the Indian mind comprehended.

Emily Carr, artist, *Growing Pains: The Autobiography of Emily Carr* (1946), foreword by Ira Dilworth.

Artist awake or be forever fallen

Words on a sign displayed in the 1950s in the studio of painter **F.H. Varley**, now at the Kathleen Gormley Art Centre, Unionville, Ont.

Long, long after the Canadian railroads have crumbled to dust and are no more than a garbled legend, or, worse, a file in some antiquary's records, a song or a picture from this epoch will speak for us, whose maker is now neither celebrated nor rich nor valued in any way, because we simply do not recognize the power of survival, the liveliness, of what he is making.

Tyrone Guthrie, British theatre director, "A Long View of the Stratford Festival," *Twice Have the Trumpets Sounded: A Record of the Stratford Shakespearean Festival in Canada 1954* (1954) by Tyrone Guthrie, Robertson Davies, and Grant Macdonald.

Fundamentally, art is a way of seeing rather than of doing or making.

Alan Jarvis, former Director of the National Gallery, quoted in *CBC Times*, 30 June 1957.

There is so much that I want to do. So many things that I want to say and there is so little time in which to do it.

Paul-Émile Borduas, painter, remark made in

Paris in 1957 to a Canadian couple, quoted in his obituary in *The Toronto Star*, 27 Feb. 1960.

The Group of Seven has been succeeded by the Group of Eleven, a 57 percent increase in less than a generation. For the first time Canadian artists have something in the bank: a mural.

Eric Nicol, humorist, *An Uninhibited History of Canada* (1959) illustrated by Peter Whalley.

Any artist who doesn't think he's the best should quit.

Harold Town, artist, interviewed by Sylvia Fraser in *The Star Weekly*, 17 June 1967.

Few but roses ... many but daisies.

Notion of arts subsidy associated with **Peter M. Dwyer**, Director of the Canada Council, 1967. It is related to another of his phrases concerning "the cultivation of democracy rather than the democratization of culture," as noted by David Silcox in *The Toronto Star*, 1 June 1976.

For the arts to criticize sport, or vice versa, is for the Indians to complain the Eskimos are living high on the hog when both are starving.

Mavor Moore, man-of-the-theatre, quoted by Bruce Kidd in *Weekend Magazine*, 17 July 1976.

To look outward, to enlarge experience, that is, and always has been, the first job of the artist. And it is precisely this which is not only ignored but outspokenly denied by so many of today's painters and poets.

Margaret Fairley, commentator, "The Cultural Worker's Responsibility to the People," *The Marxist Quarterly*, Spring, 1968.

People keep asking me if painting is hard work. Painting isn't work. Painting is making decisions. I make decisions, nothing more.

Barker Fairley, painter, quoted by James Purdie in *The Globe and Mail*, 20 Oct. 1969.

The artist is a person who is expert in the training of perception.

Marshall McLuhan, communications pioneer, "Education in the Electronic Age" (1967), *The Best of Times / The Worst of Times: Contemporary Issues in Canadian Education* (1972) edited by Hugh A. Stevenson, Robert M. Stamp, and J. Donald Wilson.

Modern art, whether in painting or poetry or music, began as a probe and not as a package.

*

Electronic Man approaches the condition in which it is possible to deal with the entire environment as a work of art.

Marshall McLuhan, communications pioneer, *Through the Vanishing Point: Space in Poetry and Painting* (1968) with Harley Parker.

What we call art would seem to be specialist artefacts for enhancing human perception.

Marshall McLuhan, communications pioneer, *Counterblast* (1969).

We may join the Balinese in saying, "We have no art, we do everything as well as possible."

Marshall McLuhan, communications pioneer, *Take Today: The Executive as Dropout* (1972) with Barrington Nevitt.

I am an artist who happens to be an Indian. I am an Indian self that is identified with the Great Spirit and not with the art.

Alex Janvier, artist of Chipewyan ancestry, quoted by Jacqueline Fry in "Treaty Numbers 23, 185, 1171," *Artscanada*, Autumn, 1972.

Writing was fifty years behind painting.

Brion Gysin, painter, British-born, Alberta-raised, collaborator of novelist William Burroughs, proponent of the cut-up/fold-in technique of writing, characteristic remark, 1970s.

Every nation which has made a lasting contribution to mankind has been aware of its artists, for long after our monuments of brick and stone, vitrolite, plastic and concrete have vanished, our words, our art, our legends and our myths will remain as a legacy.

Harry J. Boyle, broadcaster and author, quoted by William French in *The Globe and Mail*, 6 Feb. 1973.

Of all the arts of which traces remain that of the Indians of the Northwest Coast is certainly one of the greatest.

Claude Lévi-Strauss, anthropologist, catalogue for Bill Reid's show at the Vancouver Art Gallery, 1974, quoted by Edith Iglauer in *Saturday Night*, Feb. 1982.

Of all sad fates, the Avant-Garde's the worst; / They were going nowhere, and they got there first.

Satirical couplet from "The Meaning of Modernism" (1975), *Technology and Culture: Six Lectures* (1979) by **Louis Dudek**.

We must try a lot harder. Indian art is a form not found anywhere else in the world. We must say to the white man, "I don't care what you think. This is what I can produce, write, or paint."

George Clutesi, Native artist, quoted by James Hickman in *Artscrafts*, Aug. 1975.

The unconscious is really most marvellous. Waiting there ready to be tapped is all knowledge, all feeling, all understanding. The artist has only to respect it and let it out.

Maryon Kantaroff, sculptor, "Breaking Out of the Family Mould," *Women in the Canadian Mosaic* (1976) edited by Gwen Matheson.

My hope is that the objects I paint have the kind of intensity about them that incites the viewer to introspection.

Christopher Pratt, realist painter, quoted by Gary Michael Dault in *The Toronto Star*, 25 Oct. 1976.

No one in this country takes out his chequebook and says, "I believe in you."

Herman Geiger-Torel, Director, Canadian Opera Company, quoted by William Littler in *The Toronto Star*, 30 Aug. 1975.

Art is anything that people do with distinction.

Louis Dudek, man-of-letters, *Epigrams* (1975).

When I make my sculpture or medal, I first hold the clay in my palm: It nests in it comfortably. I always hope that one day it will nest in another palm and give the same joy that it gives me to create it.

Dora de Pédery-Hunt, medallist, catalogue for an exhibition, Toronto, 1973, quoted by John Brehl in *The Toronto Star*, 4 Dec. 1978.

We know intuitively that we will become great only when we translate our force and knowledge into spiritual and artistic terms. Then, and only then, will it matter to mankind whether Canada has existed or not.

Hugh MacLennan, essayist, "If You Drop a Stone . . . ," *The Other Side of Hugh MacLennan* (1978).

No one ever asked Picasso whether he was influenced by Canadian art, and yet look at his masks: Who's to say Picasso hadn't seen any of our work.

Daphne Odjig, quoted by Adele Freedman, "Reservations Are for Artists: The Dreams of Daphne Odjig," *Toronto Life*, June 1979. Odjig was dubbed "Picasso's mother" by Norval Morrisseau. Picasso himself called her a "remarkable Indian artist."

It was the least talented students who became the strongest advocates of the new fads. I have never known one first-class artist who has taken up modernism.

Kenneth Forbes, portrait painter and art instructor, quoted in his obituary in *The Toronto Star*, 28 Feb. 1980.

Mystery is to illustration what surprise is to writing.

Heather Cooper, illustrator, quoted by Daniel Mothersill in *The Review*, 6 Nov. 1981.

I hesitate to draw the inference that there is a connection between limited funds and liveliness of intellect, but. . . .

Northrop Frye, cultural critic, interviewed by Robert Fulford, "From Nationalism to Regionalism: The Maturing of Canadian Culture," *The Anthology Anthology: A Selection from 30 Years of CBC Radio's Anthology* (1984) edited by Robert Weaver.

Art experts are unfailingly opposed to Art for the simple reason that they are interested in Art—but Art is not interested in Art, Art is interested in life.

Stephen Vizinczey, essayist, *Truth and Lies in Literature* (1986).

The spontaneous is the most beautiful thing that can appear in a picture, but nothing in art appears less spontaneously than that.

Jeff Wall, artist, interviewed by Els Barents in *Jeff Wall: Transparencies* (1986).

I'm aware of being a stranger, an outsider, and that's always an advantage for an artist. It means I can see from the inside and the outside. I have that double vision.

John Hirsch, Hungarian-born, Winnipeg-based theatre director, quoted by Frank Rasky in *The Canadian Jewish News*, 10 Sept. 1987.

The making of an artist is more than the training of hands; it's the training of the eye, the ear, the listening heart.

William Gough, author, *The Art of David Blackwood* (1988).

One never hesitates before a masterpiece.

Shirley Thomson, Director, National Gallery of Canada, defending the controversial acquisition of Barnett Newman's painting "Voice of Fire" for $1.8 million, CBC-TV's *The Journal*, 10 April 1990.

In Poland, we have a terrible economic crisis. Canada, for us, is a very rich country. I would have thought that the government would be considerably more supportive of theatre and of cultural events in general. It's a paradox: such a rich country, unable to support its arts in the way it should. That really was a surprise to me.

Tadeusz Rozewicz, Polish playwright comparing arts subsidies in poor Poland and rich Canada, interviewed in Toronto by Stephen Smith in *The Globe and Mail*, 16 May 1991.

The philistine provides the best definition of art. Anything that makes him rage is first class.

Louis Dudek, poet and aphorist, "Epigrams," *Small Perfect Things* (1991).

It's better to get written up in the social columns than in the art critic's reviews.

Charles Pachter, artist and controversialist, quoted by John Allemang in *The Globe and Mail*, 12 Oct. 1991.

I would include religion with the arts, by the way.

Northrop Frye, cultural critic, interviewed by David Cayley in *Northrop Frye in Conversation* (1992).

The artist's duty to himself is a culmination of immense responsibility and immense irresponsibility. I think those two interlock.

David Cronenberg, film director, interview, *Rolling Stone*, 6 Feb. 1992.

There's more chance to do crazy things in Canada, because nobody pays any attention. In Europe, you're under surveillance as an artist all the time.

R. Murray Schafer, innovative composer, interviewed by Robert Everett-Green in *The Globe and Mail*, 23 Sept. 1993.

When I hesitate, I do not paint. When I paint, I do not hesitate.

Jean-Paul Riopelle, artist, aphorism quoted in an advertisement for his Montreal exhibition *Riopelle: Oeuvres Vives, The Globe and Mail*, 30 Oct. 1993.

I'm more interested in the moment when two objects collide and generate a third. The third object is where the interesting work is.

Bruce Mau, designer, interviewed by Mark Wasiuta and Burton Hamfelt, *Manifesto* (1994).

All art is holy. Not that it is all long-faced and miserable; it can be wild and woolly. But if it transforms you, it is art. And it is holy.

Robertson Davies, man-of-letters, interviewed by Val Ross in *The Globe and Mail*, 8 Oct. 1994.

Somewhere in the world there are rock paintings created by the ancestors of each one of us, and there are songs behind the dancing figures, and thoughts behind the songs. It is a past to be reckoned with, replete with action, violence, wars, discord, resolution, and courage, star-legends with episodes following one on the heels of another.

Paulette Jiles, poet and traveller, *Northern Spirit: Travels among the Cree and Ojibway Nations and Their Star Maps* (1995).

For that is what we must do as artists: demonstrate the shared wholeness of the human condition to our audiences....

Excerpt from "A Letter to the Company on the First Day of Rehearsals, February 20, 1995," written by the actor **Nicholas Pennell** who died days later, read to the members of the Stratford Festival and reproduced in the memorial brochure "A Celebration of the Life of Nicholas Pennell," Festival Theatre, Stratford, Ont., 26 Feb. 1995.

I always feel I'm getting near to something that's got more to it than I can get hold of.

Jack Shadbolt, artist, quoted in "Vancouver Arts," *The Globe and Mail*, 2 Nov. 1995.

I have a profound sense of the power of ordinariness, and of ordinary things. By ordinary, I don't mean a Ford is ordinary compared to a Lamborghini. I mean ordinary in the sense that this is a person, place, or thing that has nothing going for it but the fact of its own existence, the fact that it is. I sense that kind of power. My work is not a celebration of the mundane.

Christopher Pratt, artist, quoted by Chistopher Hume, "Images of a Life Devoted to Art," *The Toronto Star*, 12 Nov. 1995.

An artist in Canada can teach, starve, or go commercial.

A.J. Casson, painter and sometime commercial designer, characteristic remark, quoted by David Twiston Davies in *Canada from Afar: The Daily Telegraph Book of Canadian Obituaries* (1996).

Death and solitude justify art, which draws human aliens together in the mortal family, uniting them against the heart of darkness. Humans must comfort each other, defend each other against the terror of being human.

W.O. Mitchell, raconteur, "The Poetry of Life," address, Writers' Union of Canada, Winnipeg, June 1996, *An Evening with W.O. Mitchell: A Collection of the Author's Best Loved Performance Pieces* (1997) edited by Barbara and Armond Mitchell.

If I ever have a conflict between art and nature, I let art win.

Robert Bateman, wildlife artist, quoted by Max Wyman, "Genuine Bateman," *The Hamilton Spectator*, 12 Oct. 1996.

Man is in a state of becoming, and his arts are part of the definition of what he might become.

Louis Dudek, poet and aphorist, "Selection," *Reality Games* (1998).

I want to make paintings full of colour, laughter, compassion and love. I want to make paintings that will make people happy, that will change the course of people's lives. If I can do that, I can paint for a hundred years.

Norval Morrisseau, Native artist, suffering Parkinson's disease, quoted by Christopher Dafoe, "Such a Long Journey," *The Globe and Mail*, 10 April 1999.

Any fool can learn to paint. The trick is to learn how to see.

Doris McCarthy, artist, quoted in "Landscape and Perspective," *Heritage Matters* (Ontario Heritage Foundation), Spring–Summer 1999.

ASIAN COUNTRIES

The more you see of the Orient, the less you understand.

Allen Abel, correspondent, *Scaring Myself Again: Far-flung Adventures of a TV Journalist* (1992).

Cabot set sail from England on May 2nd, 1497, and landed on Cape Breton Island on June 24th, inadvertently discovering Canada, which he firmly believed was Asia.

Peter Ustinov, media personality, *Ustinov Still at Large* (1993).

"Asian values" are the Western values of about 75 to 100 years ago. They will not be the Asian values of 2025.

Gwynne Dyer, commentator and broadcaster, "Global Culture," *The Globe and Mail*, 27 April 1996.

ASTROLOGY

Now, astrology is an attempt to project upon the stars a kind of intuitive knowledge of what may relate to somebody's life.

Robertson Davies, man-of-letters, interviewed by Terence M. Green in 1982, *Conversations with Robertson Davies* (1989) edited by J. Madison Davis.

Astrology does not always make life easier to live, but it can make it much more meaningful. It can help you to take responsibility for yourself and for the various crises that we must face. Learning to deal with crises is essential for living a wholesome life.

Robin Armstrong, professional astrologer, *Robin Armstrong's Astrological Almanac: 1990* (1989).

I was born at 8:20 a.m.... into an extremely religious home and family. At 8:21 a.m. the doctor slapped me, but I didn't cry. Being a Baptist, I knew I deserved it.

Dave Broadfoot, comic, responding to a request

for birth data by astrologer John McKay-Clements in *The Canadian Astrology Collection: Timed Birth Data of Prominent Canadians* (1998). He was born in North Vancouver, 5 Dec. 1925.

Who am I to doubt the efficacy of the stars?

Farley Mowat, author, responding to a request for birth data by astrologer John McKay-Clements in *The Canadian Astrology Collection: Timed Birth Data of Prominent Canadians* (1998).

ASTRONOMY See also SPACE

I should have liked to have been an astronomer—failing that, to have a few astronomers among my acquaintances. Fancy talking the gossip of the hosts of heaven! I wonder if astronomers feel much interest in earthly affairs.

L.M. Montgomery, author, letter, 26 Feb. 1919, *My Dear Mr. M.: Letters to G.B. MacMillan* (1980) edited by Francis W.P. Bolger and Elizabeth R. Epperly.

Astronomy is terrifying. It describes a hell in which we seem to be the only inhabitants.

Louis Dudek, man-of-letters, *Epigrams* (1975).

Does this vast and magnificent universe in which our earth is but a speck make man seem small and insignificant? Not at all. Just think of it. Such a tiny part of us as the human unaided eye can see to a depth of two million light years.

Helen Sawyer Hogg, astronomer, *The Stars Belong to Everyone: How to Enjoy Astronomy* (1976).

In the Beaver Indian language the word for star is sun, as if they understood the secrets of astronomy.

William Carpenter Bompas, Bishop, *Northern Lights on the Bible: Drawn from a Bishop's Experience During Twenty-five Years in the Great North-West* (1983).

Ian Shelton of the University of Toronto station in the Las Campanas Observatory, Chile, reports a possible supernova in the LMC....

Opening words of the telegram sent on 24 Feb. 1987 by **J. Kunkel**, Las Campanas Observatory, Chile, announcing the discovery of Supernova 1987A in the Large Magellanic Cloud, reproduced by Laurence A. Marschall in *The Supernova Story* (1988).

Stargazers, amateur astronomers, astronomy enthusiasts—whatever we call ourselves—are naturalists of the night. We appreciate what so many ignore.

Terence Dickinson, Preface, *NightWatch: An Equinox Guide to Viewing the Universe* (1983, 1989).

But the earliest legends of each and every unique culture show that we were all, from the beginning, gazing in awe at the night skies, imagining ourselves somehow descended from those wondrous lights, looking to them for blessings, fearing their displeasure, hoping somehow, some day, to ascend once more to the brightness of the stars.

Judith Merril, science-fiction personality, video message included on the CD-ROM affixed to the Martian Lander to the Red Planet and released on Earth as *Visions of Mars* (1994).

ATHLETES See also GRETZKY, WAYNE; SPORTS

Wen I wuz a yung fella, athaletics wuz the nicest way of gittin exosted if you wuzn't already married.

Don Harron, comedian, in the person of Charlie Farquharson, *Cum Buy the Farm* (1987).

Some of the most puzzling questions about sports concern the athletes' motivations for engaging in them.

Susan Butt, psychologist, *The Psychology of Sport: The Behaviour, Motivation, Personality and Performance of Athletes* (1987).

If the purpose of sport is personal growth and self-discovery, the athlete loses all in the Faustian pact with steroids.

Bruce Kidd, champion runner and educator, "Today's Tradition Echoes the Past," *University of Toronto Magazine*, Winter 1989.

You know, the regular four-letter stuff. The universal language.

Eric Lindros, hockey player, during a run-in with a Unified Team member at the Winter Olympics, quoted in *Time*, 2 March 1992.

ATLANTIC OCEAN

For Newfoundlanders living by and upon it, the sea is the ultimate reality. They accept it as their master, for they know they will never master it. The sea is there. It is their destiny. It gives them life, and sometimes it gives them death.

Farley Mowat, author, *The New-Founde-Land* (1989).

ATLANTIC PROVINCES See also MARITIME PROVINCES, NEW BRUNSWICK, NEWFOUNDLAND, NOVA SCOTIA, PRINCE EDWARD ISLAND

Probably the greatest asset of the Atlantic Provinces is our geographic position. We are in that sector of the earth where great civilizations grow. We have the cosmic rays of the Riviera and a benign Creator gave us the cool breezes and sometimes the biting winds from the North Atlantic currents and ice fields to temper our climate into what may be the best in the world to build human beings.

M.M. Coady, adult educator, "A New Orientation" (1951), *The Man from Margaree: Writings and Speeches of M.M. Coady, Educator, Reformer, Priest* (1971) edited by Alexander Fraser Laidlaw.

Of these regions, the Atlantic Provinces have a physical layout and enough common history to justify concerted actions and, indeed, to possess formal collaborative instruments. But they remain obstinately independent in most economic domains. What unites them is the poverty of their land.

F. Kenneth Hare, geographer, "Canada: The Land," *Daedalus: Journal of the American Academy of Arts and Sciences*, "In Search of Canada," Fall, 1988.

The Atlantic Provinces are Canada's Puerto Rico: attached to the country but not really part of it, almost without influence on the life of the nation, impinging on the national consciousness mainly as a nagging socio economic problem and a perennial source of troublesome immigrants.

Silver Donald Cameron, columnist, "Nova Scotia," *The Globe and Mail*, 27 March 1998.

ATOMIC BOMB See also ATOMIC ENERGY, NUCLEAR ARMS

We had grown up taking totally for granted that the generations of mankind and of all creatures are like the leaves on a tree; they fall but a new generation arises, and the earth endures forever. August 6th, 1945, made it impossible ever again to take that reassuring belief for granted. That was the day the first atomic bomb was dropped by the Allies on Hiroshima.

Margaret Laurence, novelist, Convocation Address, York University, June 1980, *Dance on the Earth: A Memoir* (1989).

I heard the blast and saw the flash.... Maybe it was the end of the world for all we knew.... The only thing you can say about the bomb is that it ended the war and got us out of there.

John Ford, retired railway superintendent in St. John's, Nfld., recalling the sight of the atomic bomb exploding over Nagasaki, Japan, 9 Aug. 1945, as quoted in *Maclean's*, 7 Aug. 1995. An RAF flight engineer, Ford was captured by the Japanese in Java; at the time of the explosion of the second atomic bomb, he was an inmate at Fukuoka No. 2 prison camp.

ATOMIC ENERGY See also ATOMIC BOMB, ENERGY, NUCLEAR ARMS, NUCLEAR ENERGY

At the moment of discovery, Soddy exclaimed, "Rutherford, this is transmutation." Rutherford is said to have replied, "For Mike's sake, Soddy, don't call it transmutation. They'll have our heads off as alchemists."

David Lees, journalist, "Living in the Nuclear Shadow," *Toronto Life*, Nov. 1989. Physicist Ernest Rutherford and chemist Frederick Soddy, working at McGill University's Macdonald Physics Building, Montreal, 1901, observed the transformation of the element thorium into radium and wondered what to call the fundamental change in composition.

He took to building his instruments at home, because the Institute was already so contaminated with radioactivity that instruments for the detection of weak gamma rays did not work well. Nobody at that time was as worried about radioactivity as people are now.

Otto Hahn, German-born atomic scientist, describing his work on radioactivity at McGill University under Ernest Rutherford, from Fall 1905 to Summer 1906, in *Otto Hahn: A Scientific Autobiography* (1966) edited by Willy Ley.

It's an elephant!

Gilbert A. LaBine, uranium prospector, exclamation when his Geiger counter made loud cackling noises which indicated the presence of uranium near Beaverlodge Lake, N.W.T., 1925. Quoted by D.M. LeBourdais in *Metals and Men: The Story of Canadian Mining* (1957).

The study of atomic energy will never cease to be both fascinating and unpleasant at the same time.

Bruno Pontecorvo, Italian-born atomic scientist who conducted research in Montreal and Chalk River, Ont., remark made to a colleague in Montreal in 1943 before leaving for Poland, quoted by Margaret Mary Gowing in *Britain and Atomic Energy* (1964).

ATWOOD, MARGARET See also

WRITERS & WRITING, CANADIAN

I had always thought of myself rather as the Mary Pickford of Canadian literature. Spreading joy.

Margaret Atwood, author, "Gettings out from Under," address, Empire Club of Canada, 5 April 1973.

It has long been our opinion that "Margaret Atwood" ("Peggy" to her friends), purported author of some twenty odd books, does not really exist.

Margaret Atwood, author, reviewing her own collection of essays *Second Words, The Globe and Mail,* 20 Nov. 1982.

She's our leading tractarian, our eternal Schoolmarm, and—our national troll. Yes, our national imp inhabiting some bleak underground cave.

Scott Symons, novelist and cultural commentator, "Atwood as-Icon," *The Idler,* No. 28, March–April 1990

Wanting to know an author because you like his work is like wanting to know a duck because you like pâté.

Sign on office wall of Margaret Atwood, noted by Jan Wong, "An Audience with 'a Queen,'" *The Globe and Mail,* 7 Sept. 1996.

Notre Dame des lettres.

Robert MacNeil, broadcaster and author, referring to Margaret Atwood, National Arts Club, New York, 4 Feb. 1997, quoted by Elizabeth Renzetti, "New York Fetes Atwood," *The Globe and Mail,* 5 Feb. 1997.

Margaret Atwood, some time in the century, will win the Nobel Prize for literature.

Allan Fotheringham, columnist, making a millennial prediction, *Maclean's,* 1 Jan. 2000.

AUSTRALIA

You have wowser-ism; we have Toronto.

Pierre Elliott Trudeau, Prime Minister, remark made on a visit to Australia in 1970, quoted by David Spurgeon in *The Globe and Mail,* 17 Sept. 1983. A "wowser" is slang for a "killjoy."

The plaque stands as a record of our gratitude to all those who, so rashly and gallantly, risked their lives for freedom, for our freedom.

Pierre Elliott Trudeau, Prime Minister, address delivered at the unveiling of the memorial dedicated to the Canadan Exiles of 1840, 18 May 1970, Sydney, Australia; quoted by Mark Frank in *1837 Rebellion: A Tour of Toronto and Nearby Places* (1993). A similar memorial outside Hobart, Tasmania, was unveiled by Douglas Harkness, former Minister of National Defence, 30 Sept. 1970.

This place is killing me! I die daily! I miss the sea and the sun, and friendship and talk and real people. I want to get back to the technicolor part of the world.

Alma De Groen, Australian playwright and traveller, describing a stay in Canada, presumably in winter, *Going Home* (1976).

If we had the St. Lawrence River running through us, we would be the most powerful nation on earth.

Sir Robert Gordon Menzies, Australian statesman who died in 1978, contrasting Canada's river system with Australia's, recalled in *Bulletin* (Australia), 4 Oct. 1983.

We memorized the provinces of Canada, and recited them starting in the east and traveling westward. I was used to learning very exact details of topography in order to find my way about a countryside with no signs and few landmarks, but when I asked why we listed Canada's provinces from east to west no one understood why I thought directions important.

Jill Ker Conway, academic, recalling geography lessons from her primary schooling in the Australian outback in the 1940s, *The Road from Corrain* (1989).

Both Australians and Canadians tend to feel undernoticed in and by the world. And as they rejoice in international recognition of their prosperity, civility and good and accessible services, they quietly lament the scarcity of internationally distinguished countrymen.

Conrad Black, publisher, "Media," *The Globe and Mail*, 30 Dec. 1996.

AUTHORITY

Those who pay the piper can rarely carry a tune.

Robin Skelton, man-of-letters, aphorism, May 1990.

The headdress gives me my power, my authority.

Ovide Mercredi, Cree lawyer, National Chief of the Assembly of First Nations, referring to the ceremonial headdress, Saskatchewan reserve, Aug. 1991, quoted by André Picard in *The Globe and Mail*, 6 Nov. 1991.

No human being or human institution is fit to be trusted with any temporal authority that is not subject to cancellation by some other authority.

Northrop Frye, cultural critic, *The Double Vision: Language and Meaning in Religion* (1991).

We may not salute the flag, but we still voluntarily stop at the stop sign, even if it says "Arrêt."

Michael Adams, President, Environics Research Group Ltd., speech, Premier's Summit, Victoria, B.C., 19 Jan. 1995, quoted in *The Globe and Mail*, 20 Feb. 1995.

Freedom even precedes authority, because what comes from the Creator's hands is a free human being. And since we must harmonize freedoms, we create society, and thereby authority. Authority follows freedom.

Georges-Henri Lévesque, priest and social scientist, interviewed by Max Nemni and Monique Nemni, *Cité Libre*, Fall 1999.

AUTHORS See also WRITERS & WRITING

Being an author is a bore; it puts you too much in the limelight.

Paul Hiebert, author, address, CAA, Winnipeg, 1957, quoted by Stan Obodiac in *My Experiences at a Canadian Authors' Convention* (1957).

In a book you offer an immense chunk of yourself, and what you demand in return is an immense chunk of the reader. There is a signficant commitment on both sides. That is the reward.... No other form of communication can compare with this.

Boyce Richardson, author, "Not Enough Space for Our Friends," *The Canadian Forum*, March 1993.

Unidentified bodies in the morgue have a higher recognition rating in Canada than writers.

William Thomas, author, "The Bad, Really Bad, Canadian Book Tour," *The Writers Guild of Canada Newsletter*, Spring 1995.

AUTOMOBILE RACING See also SPORTS

It's the greatest race in the world. If you had a chance of winning a race in your life, make sure its the 500.

Jacques Villeneuve, racing-car driver and son of Formula 1 legend Gilles Villeneuve, on winning the Indianapolis 500, 28 May 1995, quoted by Stephen Brunt in *The Globe and Mail* the following day. Scott Goodyear, another Canadian, received a two-lap penalty and complained, "Everyone knows who really won the race."

My father would be proud of me.

Jacques Villeneuve, auto racer, upon winning the Grand Prix at the 1997 Formula One drivers' championship race, Jerez, Spain, 16 Oct. 1997, referring to his father, champion racer Gilles Villeneuve, quoted by Rick Matsumoto in *The Toronto Star* the following day.

AUTOMOBILES See also TRAVEL

When Solomon said there was a time and a place for everything he had not encountered the problem of parking his automobile.

Bob Edwards, publisher, *The Eye Opener*, 1 July 1922, *The Best of Bob Edwards* (1975) edited by Hugh Dempsey.

According to the usual cliché, the family car has become an extension of the home. I think it offers something more: masterhood. Sexually, spiritually, financially, your life may be "going nowhere." But by climbing onto the driver's seat and taking the car for a spin, you elude the numbness of a dead end.

Mark Abley, traveller, *Beyond Forget: Rediscovering the Prairies* (1986).

Hell must surely consist of driving for eternity along the 401, in a car that never needs refilling, with kidneys that never need draining.

Edward Phillips, novelist, referring to the Macdonald-Cartier Freeway (401) which extends from Windsor, Ont., to the Quebec border, *Sunday Best* (1990).

We're not just building cars and trucks, we're building Canada.

G. Yves Landry, executive, Chrysler Canada, referring to the automotive industry, quoted in his obituary, *The Globe and Mail*, 19 March 1998.

I'm only fourteen, please help me.

Cry of a teenage girl pinned beneath a truck in a 63-vehicle accident in which she and six other motorists were killed on Highway 401 east of Windsor, Ont., 8:00 a.m., 3 Sept. 1999, as recorded by Peter Wise, a survivor, who with other survivors tried to rescue her, quoted in *The Toronto Star* and the *National Post* the following day. According to Ashante Infantry in *The Toronto Star*, 26 Sept., 1999, the teenager was identified as **Marceya LaShawn McLamore**, a native of Rochester, N.Y., who was en route with her father and younger brother to Detroit, Michigan. In that account, she cried out, "Help me! Get me out of here! I'm only 14!"

AUTUMN See FALL

AVIATION See also TRAVEL

The demonstration that no possible combination of known substances, known forms of machinery and known forms of force, can be united in a practical machine by which man shall fly long distances through the air, seems to the writer as complete as it is possible for the demonstration of any physical fact to be.

Simon Newcomb, Nova Scotia–born astronomer, dismissing the notion of heavier-than-air flight in an essay, noted by Arthur C. Clarke in "Hazards of Prophecy" (1962), included by Alvin Toffler in *The Futurists* (1972).

Just one other idea I would put into your minds, and I will not expand it. It is possible that we will have a development of flight with engines without any wings—flying without wings. How about flying without engines?

Alexander Graham Bell, inventor, address, "The Substance of My Latest Research," Empire Club of Canada, Toronto, 1 Nov. 1917.

I'm proud of the title "bush pilot." It originated in Canada, it relates to men of dedicated interest in flying to remote regions, and I hope it will never disappear.

C.H. (Punch) Dickins, northern pilot in the 1930s, interviewed by Bill McNeil in *Voice of the Pioneer* (1978).

Oh, I have slipped the surly bonds of earth, / And danced the skies on laughter-silvered wings; / Sunward I've climbed and joined the tumbling mirth / Of sun-split clouds—and done a hundred things / You have not dreamed of—wheeled and soared and swung / High in the sunlit silence. Hov'ring there, / I've chased the shouting wind along and flung / My eager craft through footless halls of air. / Up, up the long delirious, burning blue / I've topped the wind-swept heights with easy grace, / Where never lark, or even eagle, flew; / And, while with silent, lifting mind I've trod / The high untrespassed sanctity of space, / Put out my hand and touched the face of God.

John Gillespie Magee Jr.'s sonnet "In High Flight" (1941) was chosen as the official poem of the Royal Air Force and of the Royal Canadian Air Force. Magee was a young American pilot who enlisted in Canada and flew with the RAF's Spitfire Squadron. He died in action on 11 Dec. 1941. The text of the poem, found among his personal effects, appears in John Robert Colombo and Michael Richardson's *We Stand on Guard* (1985).

Air services, which are good but tend to be overcrowded, are threading the cities together and making accessible the remoter and wilder parts of this colossal continent, potentially, in spite of its severe climate, one of the richest on the globe.

J.B. Priestley, English bookman and broadcaster, impressions of a five-city tour by Trans-Canada Airlines, "Canadian Notes and Impressions," BBC Radio, *The Listener*, 31 May 1956.

The government has carefully examined and re-examined the probable need for the Arrow aircraft and Iroquois engine known as the CF-105.... The conclusion arrived at is that the development of the Arrow aircraft and Iroquois engine should be terminated now.

John G. Diefenbaker, Prime Minister, announcing the contentious decision to scrap the advanced intercepter aircraft designed and built by A.V. Roe, House of Commons, 20 Feb. 1959, as quoted by Palmiro Campagna in *Storms of Controversy: The Secret Avro Arrow Files Revealed* (2nd ed., 1997).

I am a pre-industrial person. I still regard airplanes in the sky as something between an act of faith and an optical illusion.

Arthur Black, broadcaster, "Bikes," *Basic Black: The Wit and Whimsy of Arthur Black* (1981).

For most pilots, flying is the essence of dreams. It is an escape, an adventure, a love song to the sky. It is a chance to defy gravity, to leave the world behind, to break the bonds of every day.

John Melady, popular historian, *Pilots: Canadian Stories from the Cockpit* (1989).

Call it overreaction, but if God had meant us to fly, he would never have invented Air Canada.

Peter C. Newman, columnist, *Maclean's*, 13 Sept. 1999.

AWARDS & HONOURS See also NOBEL PRIZES, ORDER OF CANADA, TITLES

I want to thank you for everything you've done for Canada, but what have you done for England?

Ben Wicks, cartoonist and master of ceremonies, addressing Mordecai Richler, ACTRA Awards, Toronto, quoted by Sid Adilman in *The Toronto Star*, 26 April 1975.

They'd rather give the Governor General's Award to the Ottawa phone book than to me.

Peter C. Newman, author and popular historian, quoted by Marq de Villiers in *The Canadian*, 9 Oct. 1976.

You know you've been around too long when you see your friends being rewarded for the second time.

Allan J. MacEachen, politician, quoted by Geoffrey Stevens in *The Globe and Mail*, 16 Dec. 1978.

The Arts Engage and Inspire Us.

Motto of the **Governor General's Performing Arts Awards**, established in 1992 to pay tribute to the lifetime achievements of outstanding artists in a variety of creative fields chosen from theatre, dance, classical music/opera, popular music, film, and broadcasting.

When Americans win things such as Miss America crowns, Oscars, murder trial verdicts, and literary prizes, they weep and thank people. When Canadians are awarded things, they look behind them to see if it was meant for somebody else.

Margaret Atwood, author, accepting the National Arts Club's Medal of Honour, New York, 4 Feb. 1997, quoted by Elizabeth Renzetti, "New York Fetes Atwood," *The Globe and Mail*, 5 Feb. 1997.

I'm the King of the World.

James Cameron, Kapuskasing-born film director, quoting a line from his movie *Titanic* which received eleven Oscars, Academy Awards Ceremony, Hollywood, California, 23 March 1998, quoted by Peter Howell in *The Toronto Star* the following day.

AWARENESS See also CONSCIOUSNESS

Look back, not in anger, nor forward with fear, but around with awareness.

Attributed to NFB Film Commissioner **John Grierson** by producer Sydney Newman during an interview with Frank Rasky in *The Toronto Star*, 15 April 1974.

It seems awareness functions like a radio. There are millions of stations we can tune into, but only one channel can be played at a time.

Tim Ward, traveller, *What the Buddha Never Taught* (1990).

No matter which way you turn / There's always something you're not facing.

Robert Priest, aphorist, *Time Release Poems* (1997).

B

BALKAN WAR

Where have all the peace groups gone? Now would have been the time to make a positive contribution to the cause of peace and order in the Balkans and the rest of the world. Yet when put to the test, they have been found wanting. Their silence at this most important moment in history will be their epitaph: "Here lies a movement that cried loudly, but which in the end said nothing."

Ian Holloway, lawyer, "Where Have All the Peace Groups Gone?" *National Networks News* (quarterly publication of the Defence Associations), 15 Oct. 1992.

Will a truck driver from Trenton suddenly find himself under fire on a Bosnian hillside?

Nicholas Stethem, defence analyst, "Reversing Assumptions, Redirecting Policy," *National Networks News* (quarterly publication of the Defence Associations), 15 Oct. 1992.

The pressures are understandable. The evils we see on the ten o'clock news should be addressed by dawn and preferably cured by the weekend, even if conflicts, as in the Balkans, have had six hundred years to develop.

Desmond Morton, historian, "Peace-keeping, Peace-making, War-making: Making a Distinction," *National Networks News* (quarterly publication of the Defence Associations), 15 Oct. 1992.

BALLET See DANCE

BANKRUPTCY

We have overcome all our difficulties following the collapse of Atlantic Acceptance Corporation except for an inadequate supply of our raw material—money.

G.F. Edgar, President of Union Acceptance Corporation, following the collapse of the finance corporation Atlantic Acceptance, quoted in *Maclean's*, 4 June 1966.

The old line is that if you owe the bank $10,000, you are in trouble. If you owe the bank $1 million, the bank is in trouble. In this case, it turns out that if you owe the bank $15 billion, the taxpayer is in trouble.

Allan Fotheringham, columnist, referring to the insolvency of the property developers Olympia & York, *Maclean's*, 11 May 1992.

BANKS & BANKERS See also FINANCE, MONEY

What it came down to was that they had the money and I wanted it.

Edwin Alonzo Boyd, bank robber, explaining why he was attracted to banks in the early 1950s, quoted by Brian Vallée in *Edwin Alonzo Boyd: The Story of the Notorious Boyd Gang* (1997).

"Does it exist?" asked Castang dubiously.

"Better than that—highly thought of. As tax havens go it's cool, and by comparison Switzerland is talkative: you won't need to utter at all."

Exchange between the chief of police and police detective Castang as he assumes the identity of "Harold Greenpeace, Attaché de Director, The Bank of Nova Scotia, Paris" in **Nicolas Freeling**'s detective novel *Wolfnight* (1982).

The strange sight of a sod hut in the middle of the prairie open for business under a large Canadian Bank of Commerce sign astonished one visitor to pioneer Saskatchewan.

William Kilbourn, historian, "The Peaceable Kingdom Still," *Daedalus: Journal of the American Academy of Arts and Sciences*, "In Search of Canada," Fall, 1988.

...the worst errors in banking are regularly made in the largest amount by the highest officials.

John Kenneth Galbraith, essayist and economist, *The Culture of Contentment* (1992).

It is no secret that it is the ultimate ambition of all chartered banks to prevent customers from darkening their doors, muddying their floors and harassing their employees—if any—with their grubby little deposit slips and minuscule cheques made out to "cash." Not that serving millions of modestly paid Canadians by providing for their banking needs is not a profitable business, but that serving their needs while keeping them out of the bank can be even more profitable.

Dalton Camp, columnist, "Do Customers Come First?" *The Toronto Star*, 12 Jan. 1997.

We have not put up a red stoplight [for the mergers], nor have we issued a green light. What we have done is put up a flashing yellow light.

Harold MacKay, chairman of the Federal Task Force on the Future of Financial Services, referring to the proposed but abandoned plan to merge the CIBC and the Bank of Montreal, quoted by Shawn McCarthy and Suzanne Craig in *The Globe and Mail*, 16 Sept. 1998.

The only banks that won't be merging are the food banks and the sperm banks.

Peter C. Newman, author, discussing possible bank mergers, interviewed by David Israelson, "Business," *The Toronto Star*, 15 Nov. 1998.

BASEBALL See also SPORTS

We had never heard of Guelph; we did not care anything about rube baseball teams. Baseball was not play to us; it was the hardest kind of work, and of all things, an exhibition game was an abomination. The audience was strange to us. The Indians, the French Canadians; the huge, hulking bearded farmers or traders or trappers, or whatever they were, were new to our baseball experience.

Passage from the title story of **Zane Grey**'s *The Red Headed Outfield and Other Stories* (1912), a baseball yarn set in Guelph, Ont.

Well, you see they have these polar bears up there and lots of fellows trip over them trying to run the bases and they're never much good any more except for hockey or hunting deer.

Casey Stengel, baseball personality, offering reasons for Canadian disinterest in baseball, quoted by Mordecai Richler in *Weekend Magazine*, 7 April 1979.

... as I was sitting on the verandah of my farm home in eastern Iowa, a voice very clearly said to me, "If you build it, he will come."

The voice was that of a ballpark announcer. As he spoke, I instantly envisioned the finished product I knew I was being asked to conceive.

Passage from **W.P. Kinsella**'s short story "Shoeless Joe Jackson Comes to Iowa" (1979) included in *Shoeless Joe Jackson Comes to Iowa* (1980). Kinsella revised and expanded the story to novel length and titled it *Shoeless Joe* (1982). The disembodied voice urges an Iowa farmer to clear a baseball diamond in his wheat field and await the arrival of deceased baseball great Shoeless Joe Jackson, who was wrongly disgraced in the 1919 White Sox scandal.

The seven words in quotation marks are known far and wide; this affirmation of faith over fate is the most widely known quotation of Canadian origin between the 1980s and the 2000s. It reached its widest audience through the movie version of the novel *Field of Dreams*, written and directed by Phil Alden Robinson and released in 1989.

The phrase "field of dreams" is also remembered. The image of the baseball diamond has been re-imagined to apply to the ice rink by columnist Joey Slinger writing in *The Toronto Star*, May 10, 1993: "The field of our dreams is flooded and frozen and has a net at either end."

Baseball is easy. Life is hard.

Ferguson (Fergie) Jenkins, baseball player, referring to the two events that took place within the space of four days, his wife's death and notification that he would be inducted into the Baseball Hall of Fame in Cooperstown, N.Y., the first Canadian to be so honoured. Quoted by Rosie DiManno in *The Toronto Star*, 20 July 1991.

Our Americans are better than their Americans.

Lloyd Robertson, CTV News anchor, CTV News, after the Toronto Blue Jays won their way into the World Series, 14 Oct. 1992, quoted in *The Toronto Star*, 18 Oct. 1992.

No clock says it's over. We might play forever, a hundred innings, a thousand. A timeless and a lovely mythology. The game invites myth, even demands it to fill the dreamy spaces.

W.P. Kinsella, author and baseball fan, quoted by Trent Frayne in "Sports Watch," *Maclean's*, 5 April 1993.

BASKETBALL See also SPORTS

Toronto Raptors? I don't even know what a raptor is and if I did I would bet it never lived in Ontario.

Allan Fotheringham, columnist, *Maclean's*, 27 Oct. 1997.

BASQUE PEOPLE

In fact, north of the 48th parallel they do not constitute a group large enough to safeguard their cultural traits. They have nevertheless contributed the genius of their race to our nation.

Mario Mimeault, historian, "Basques in New France," *Basque Studies Newsletter* (University of Nevada, Reno), April 1994. The author discusses the presence of Basque whalers on the coasts of Labrador and Newfoundland before the arrival of Jacques Cartier and the continued immigration of Basques to New France and Quebec.

BEACHES

The beach is magic, an infinitely complex and beautiful ballet of the shore and the land, a pas de deux between change and resistance. Caught up in the dance are the animals and plants that live there. The beach is not just a strip of sand: it is a community, a wild and living thing.

Silver Donald Cameron, author, *The Living Beach* (1998).

BEARS See also ANIMALS

The artistic and philosophical evocation of the polar bear by Eskimo and pre-Eskimo cultures leads one to believe that their insight derives from a special affinity with the bear. To an extent, the Eskimo and the polar bear are alike, the lines of their successful adapation to the Arctic being parallel.

Barry Lopez, naturalist, *Arctic Dreams: Imagination and Desire in a Northern Landscape* (1986).

There's an old trapper's tale that says the best way to defend yourself against a polar bear attack is to shoot your buddy and run like hell.

Folklore recalled by the Arctic adventurer **Jeff MacInnis** in *Polar Passage: The Historic First Sail through the Northwest Passage* (1989) by Jeff MacInnis with Wade Rowland.

Most of the wastes are actually south of most of the rest of Canada and around the latitude of Antibes, although everyone acts with cheerful stoicism, as if there were polar bears round the next bend in the road: indeed there is a special train called the Polar Bear Express which runs all the way up to Moosonee, the latitude of Ilfracombe or Blankenberghe; they could as well call it the Mastodon Mail or the Giant Sloth Slow for all your chance of seeing its eponym from the observation car. This proves that climate is all in the mind, a thing to remember as Britain braces itself for its first tsunami.

Eric Korn, columnist and antiquarian, *The Times Literary Supplement*, 15 June 1990.

BEAUTY See also FASHION

If all the ladies of Canada are as beautiful as you, Madame, I have indeed made a conquest.

George III, King of England, addressing Joseph-Gaspard de Léry's wife, Charlotte, during an audience shortly after the Conquest of Quebec in 1759. Quoted by C.W. Jefferys in *The Picture Gallery of Canadian History: Volume 1, Discovery to 1763* (1942).

So many pretty girls—never so many in one town before—beauty of girls, & of little children of both sexes so common as to be almost monotonous—but then one has the occasional relief of the other sort—or one can look in the glass.

Mark Twain, humorist, on women in Montreal in 1881, Notebook 19, *Mark Twain's Notebooks & Journals, Volume II (1877–1883)* (1975), edited by Frederick Anderson, et al.

The Grecian Urn was more beautiful before John Keats got hold of it.

George Bowering, poet, "Selected Errata," *The Brick Reader* (1991) edited by Linda Spalding and Michael Ondaatje.

I'm beautiful. It's lasted quite a long time, this beauty of mine, but it won't be lasting much longer because I'm forty now, as I'm writing this, forty now and probably by the time you read it forty-one, and so on and so forth, and we all know it ends up as worms or ashes, but for the time being I'm still beautiful. More or less. Less than I used to be....

Nancy Huston, Prairie-born, Paris-based author, "Dealing with What's Dealt," *Salamagundi*, Spring–Summer, 1995.

BEAVERS See also ANIMALS; EMBLEMS, NATIONAL

All the beavers in the world must be sad that Grey Owl is gone....

Tribute to the naturalist and writer **Grey Owl** that appeared upon his death in 1938 in *The Children's Newspaper*, as noted by English author Peter Underhill in *No Common Task: The Autobiography of a Ghost hunter* (1983).

It's our national mascot, the beaver. If Canada wants to play hardball with the big guys, then the buck-toothed rodent with the bug eyes has got to go.

Arthur Black, broadcaster and humorist, "Our Symbol—The Rat," *That Old Black Magic* (1989).

The beaver devastates the forest, pollutes the water and leaves a bleak, moribund, albeit often fascinating landscape. Yet for a Canadian to criticize the beaver would be close to treasonous.

Anton Kuerti, pianist and essayist, "All that Glitters Is Not Gould," *The Globe and Mail*, 12 Feb. 1994.

BEAVERBROOK, LORD

Winston and I are the only two people to have served in both wartime cabinets.

Max Aitken, Lord Beaverbrook, British publisher and Canadian philanthropist, making an observation about Sir Winston Churchill in later years, as recalled by his Canadian-born daughter Janet Aitken Kidd in *The Beaverbrook Girl: An Autobiography* (1987).

What the proprietorship is aiming at...is power, but power without responsibility—the prerogative of the harlot through the ages.

Stanley Baldwin, British Prime Minister, speaking in 1931 against the two press barons, Lord Rothermere and Lord Beaverbrook, employing "a moment of rhetorical flourish" attributed to Rudyard Kipling by Janet Aitken Kidd in *The Beaverbrook Girl: An Autobiography* (1987).

Beaverbrook is not a bad man: He is only a bad boy.

John Buchan, Governor General Lord Tweedsmuir, quoted by Alan Wood in *The True History of Lord Beaverbrook* (1965).

Here I must say, in my eighty-sixth year, I do not feel greatly different from when I was eighty-five. This is my final word. It is time for me to become an apprentice once more. I have not settled in which direction. But somewhere, sometime soon.

Lord Beaverbrook, guest at the banquet held in his honour in London, England, 25 May 1964, organized by Lord Thomson of Fleet. He died two weeks later.

BEER See also ALCOHOL

Anyway you can't buy draught Bass in Toronto....I went to Canada during the war....Couldn't get any draught Bass, not even in Toronto, and they seemed to reckon that was pretty English....You can't get draught Bass in Toronto. I've tried it.

Tirade delivered by the worker Archie who has no plans to leave England for Canada in **John Osborne**'s play *The Entertainer* (1957).

Canadian beer is labelled five per cent by volume....American beer is generally four per cent by weight. Taking the density of alcohol into account, both Canadian and American beers have the same alcohol content. However, it is true that American beer is more tasteless, since they put much more carbon dioxide in their beer, thereby selling more air.

Marco Polverari, McGill University, "A Canadian Myth," Letters to the Editor, *Maclean's*, 29 June 1992.

BELIEF See also ANGELS, BIBLE, BUDDHISM, CATHOLICISM, CHRISTIANITY, DOUBT, FAITH, GHOSTS, GOD, JUDAISM, NEW AGE, PARAPSYCHOLOGY, PSYCHICAL RESEARCH, RELIGION, SPIRITS, SPIRITUALISM, SPIRITUALITY, SUPERNATURAL, SUPERSTITION

The Europeans have a strong mind to Inherit a Place in the Country of Souls, and yet they never think of their Creator, but when they dispute with the Hurons.

Baron de La Hontan, French traveller, "A Conference or Dialogue between the Author and Adario, a Note Man among the Savages," *New Voyages to North-America...from 1683 to 1694...Done into English* (1703).

Agnosticism is right, if it is a counsel of honesty, but ought not to be heard if it is a counsel of despair.

Goldwin Smith, essayist, *Guesses at the Riddle of Existence and Other Essays on Kindred Subjects* (1897).

Tell the students of the University of Toronto this from me, simple, but perhaps helpful to some, I say to them: Be above mere authority in matters of the mind; they must, in the last analysis, follow their own judgment—their own feeling of truth. I tell those students this—they must profess no belief without conviction. To conform, means often death; to non-conform—in this is often life, often life eternal.

Albert Einstein, mathematician, offering "a

short message," interviewed in Princeton, N.J., by R.E. Knowles, *The Toronto Star,* 27 Jan. 1934. Knowles added: "He said no more. I asked for no more. Surely the students of the University of Toronto need no more."

I believe in "probably," "perhaps"—and also in "Thus says the Lord."

Abraham Feinberg, rabbi, *Storm the Gates of Jericho* (1964).

In an age when no one believes anything, gospels and revelations abound.

Irving Layton, poet and aphorist, *The Whole Bloody Bird (obs, aphs & Pomes)* (1969).

There is enlightenment in questions, but only barbarism in belief.

Louis Dudek, man-of-letters, *Epigrams* (1975).

Feeling is also believing.

Wilson Bryan Key, sociologist, *Media Sexploitation* (1976).

More beliefs are occasioned by inertia than by credulity.

Robin Skelton, poet and aphorist, *A Devious Dictionary* (1991).

I can't imagine that a spoken certainty can exist without an unspoken uncertainty behind it.

Josef Skvorecky, author, quoted by J.M. Coetzee in *The New York Review of Books,* 3 Oct. 1996.

Why is it then that some people cannot be persuaded about the reported factual accuracy of facts and events, any more than they are willing to listen dispassionately to another point of view, in a debate about ideas?

Louise Arbour, former chief prosecutor of the United Nations' war crimes tribunals for Rwanda and the Balkans, newly appointed member of the Supreme Court of Canada, address, International Press Freedom Awards, Toronto, "The Incurable Deficits of Memory," *The Toronto Star,* 20 Nov. 1999.

BERTON, PIERRE See also WRITERS & WRITING, CANADIAN

Berton: "We'd like a piece on the universe."
Callwood: "The universe?"
Berton: "Yes, the universe. Deadline in two weeks."
Callwood: "Fine."

Telephone call from **Pierre Berton**, articles editor of *Maclean's* in the 1950s, to contributing writer **June Callwood**, as recalled in *Maclean's,* 1 Jan. 1996.

I think my nationalism probably emerged on *Maclean's* magazine. I was on it for eleven years, and you couldn't be on *Maclean's* without becoming a nationalist. Its survival depended on the country.

Pierre Berton, journalist, editor, author, media personality, interviewed in *Meet the Media: Eight of Canada's Best-known Journalists Talk with Robert Bullis* (1976).

I once asked Wayne Gretzky if, having been so celebrated so early, he feared a later reaction—the same thing that happened to Berton. Wayne, bless his heart, said, "Is Pierre Berton a Canadian?"

Peter Gzowski, journalist, *The Private Voice: A Journal of Reflections* (1988).

BETHUNE, NORMAN See also CHINESE PEOPLE

The name is BETHune, not BethUNE.

Norman Bethune, physician, surgeon, and revolutionary, recalled by Stanley Ryerson in *Bethune: The Montreal Years* (1978) by Wendell MacLeod, Libbie Park, and Stanley Ryerson.

We must all learn from him the spirit that is so completely free from selfishness. Starting from that point, one can become a person of great use to the people.

Mao Tse-tung, Chairman of the People's Republic of China, appreciating the spirit and the works of Dr. Norman Bethune in *The Little Red Book* as quoted by Robert Payne in Mao Tse-tung (1968).

Born a bourgeois. Died a communist.

Norman Bethune, physician, offering these words for future use as his epitaph in a note written to painter Charles Comfort, 30 Nov. 1939, reproduced in *The Politics of Passion: Norman Bethune's Writing and Art* (1998) edited by Larry Hannant.

Let us remember / That Norman Bethune built the bridge / Canadians walked across / To China / And made it possible / For the Chinese to walk back.

Sylvia DuVernet, poet, *The Muskoka Tree: Poems of Pride for Norman Bethune* (1976).

Canada owes a debt of gratitude to the memory of Dr. Bethune. No single person has done more to cement good relations and understanding between Canada and China. Every Canadian visiting China is welcomed as "a friend from the home country of Pai Ch'iu-en."

Chester Ronning, diplomat and "old China hand," address, dedication of the Bethune Homestead as a National Historic Site, Gravenhurst, Ont., 30 Aug. 1976.

BIBLE See also BELIEF, RELIGION

Moses died before he ever reached Canada.

Student howler collected by educator **Richard Lederer** and included in "The World According to Student Bloopers," *Anguished English* (1987).

Nowhere does the Bible seem to be afraid of the word anthropomorphic.

Northrop Frye, cultural critic, *The Double Vision: Language and Meaning in Religion* (1991).

As I once told my students, there's a verse in John that says "Jesus wept," and that's about all that would be left of the Bible if you demythologized it consistently.

Northrop Frye, cultural critic, interviewed by David Cayley in *Northrop Frye in Conversation* (1992).

BILINGUALISM See also LANGUAGE; LANGUAGE: FRENCH

Unhappily, there is no prospect at present that the English-speaking Canadians will take the other Canadian national language seriously.

Arnold J. Toynbee, historian, "Canada's Identity and Bilingualism," *The Globe and Mail*, 30 March 1961.

For the benefit of those who are not bilingual, I will now continue in English.

John G. Diefenbaker, former Prime Minister, quoted by Thomas Van Dusen in *The Chief* (1968). Van Dusen added, "When he spoke French, he frequently said every English-speaking person from St. John's to Victoria understood."

As a rule of thumb, you say, "If it's federal, it's bilingual."

Keith Spicer, Commissioner of Official Languages, quoted in *The Globe and Mail*, 27 June 1974.

Absolutely no more than five years would be required for all Canadians to become fully and totally bilingual.

Réal Caouette, Créditiste leader, House of Commons, 21 Nov. 1974.

Let's face it. Except for francophones outside of Quebec and anglophones in Montreal, bilingualism is one of the most universally loathed policies ever foisted onto Canada. Francophone Quebecers hate and fear it because they feel—rightly—that it is a threat to their national sovereignty and existence. English Canadians see it as a stupid and expensive failure which seeks only to perpetuate a historic bad joke and which gives unfair job advantages to a tiny French-speaking minority.

Paul Malvern, journalist, *Persuaders: Influence Peddling, Lobbying and Political Corruption in Canada* (1985).

I would end our policy of two official languages, whereby the 15 per cent of Canadians who are presently bilingual are the only ones who can now reasonably aspire to be P.M. someday or to hold top posts in government.

Peter Worthington, journalist, contributor to *If I Were Prime Minister* (1987) edited by Mel Hurtig.

My main goal was to get people to think about languages not as problems but as opportunities. To do that I had to speak to their hearts as well as their minds, to confront their historic fears and prejudices head-on and try to show them new perspectives and new hopes.

Keith Spicer, Commissioner of Official Languages (1970–77), *Language and Society*, Summer 1989.

This country will rise or fall on the bilingual nature of its character. What is Canada without it? There's no country; it's like an adjunct of the United States.

Brian Mulroney, Prime Minister, address, Kitchener, Ont., 13 Feb. 1990.

What does a bilingual sign tell us? In very clear terms, it whispers in our ear: "You are not the only master in your own home."

Yves Beauchemin, novelist, brief presented to the Bélanger Campeau commission on the future of Quebec, reproduced in *The Toronto Star*, 24 Dec. 1990.

We have been told again and again that the most vibrant original culture in Canada is

French Canadian. But at the same time, it's so fragile that the mere sight of a bilingual street sign is sufficient to propel it into the nearest intensive care unit.

Mordecai Richler, novelist, speech, Canadian Club, Winnipeg, 17 Jan. 1992, quoted in *The Toronto Star* the following day.

If the universities were living in the real world they would deny a diploma to anyone who does not speak at least two languages. What a blessing that would be for our children and our country!

Roch Carrier, author, rector of the Collège Militaire Royal, Saint-Jean, Que., quoted by Brigitte Morissette in "Canadian Parents for French," *Language and Society*, Winter 1992.

Bilingualism, n. The late 20th-century requirement that political candidates demonstrate a polished ability to equivocate and prevaricate in both official languages.

David Olive, editor, *Canadian Political Babble* (1993).

There has been a type of rampant institutional bilingualism which has crept into the civil service.

Louise Beaudoin, Quebec Cabinet Minister, announcing a French only language policy for the Quebec civil service to deter immigrants from assuming that English is one of the official languages of Quebec, news conference, 14 Nov. 1996, quoted in "Pas de service en anglais," *The Globe and Mail* the next day.

Canadian language difficulties. Enforced bilingualism had burdened Canada with twice as much writing as most nations. Cereal boxes, cigarettes, the tide tables—everything came in parallel texts, English and French. This grossly fattened all official publications; pamphlets became books, books stout tomes, and the simplest notice turned gabby and verbose. Everything was a translation of something else. Far from reinforcing each other, one version tended to cast doubt on the other, making its meaning tentative and provisional.

Jonathan Raban, English author resident in Seattle, Washington, *Passage to Juneau: A Sea and Its Meanings* (1999).

BIRDS See also ANIMALS, CANADA GOOSE

Every man has his favourite bird; ours is the bat.

Bob Edwards, publisher, *The Eye Opener*, 13 May 1905, *The Best of Bob Edwards* (1975) edited by Hugh Dempsey.

Drip drop drip drop drop drop

Line from of **T.S. Eliot**'s poem *The Waste Land* (1922), Section V, "What the Thunder Said." To the first edition of this poem, Eliot added the following note: "This is *Turdus aonalaschkae pallasii*, the hermi thrush which I have heard in Quebec Country... its 'water-dripping song' is justly celebrated." Eliot changed "Country" to "Province" for the second and all subsequent editions of his influential poem.

It's marvellous that the very folds imprinted on the rock beds by the ages create a trampoline for what is most inviting about life: the soaring, the just-veering-off, and the luxurious drifting of aquatic birds.

André Breton, French surrealist and traveller, describing Bonaventure Island, Gaspé, Que., *Arcanum 17* (1944) translated from the French in 1994 by Zack Rogow.

WRITE BOX 48 / KINGSVILLE / ONT. / CANADA

This request appeared on the tags of some 50,000 birds that were so banded by conservationist **Jack Miner** at his migratory bird sanctuary at Kingsville, Ont., from 1909 to his death in 1944, as noted by James M. Linton and Calvin W. Moore in *The Story of Wild Goose Jack* (1984). As Paul Martin Sr. noted, "Jack Miner wrote Kingsville, Canada, across the skies of North America."

Those are red-wing orioles from Canada.

Observation made by the wagonmaster (actor **James Stewart**) in the Hollywood movie *Bend of the River* (1952), quoted by Pierre Berton in *Hollywood's Canada: The Americanization of Our National Image* (1975). Berton added, "As every amateur [birdwatcher] knows, there isn't any such thing as a red-wing oriole."

One cardinal on a tree branch / outfitted like a lord. // You see how little it takes / to make my day.

Raymond Souster, poet, "Cutting It Short," *Asking for More* (1988).

And on the TV there were still more birds! Such lovely creatures and I thought that we are so lucky to have the animals. What act of goodness did we as humans once commit to deserve such kindness from God?

Thoughts of the narrator of **Douglas Coupland**'s novel *Life after God* (1994).

First you stumble, then you freeze, then you are ours.

Paulette Jiles, poet and traveller, expressing the watch-and-wait attitude of circling ravens, *Northern Spirit: Travels among the Cree and Ojibway Nations and Their Star Maps* (1995).

BIRTH CONTROL

"Now for a social question, Mrs. McClung—do you believe in what is known as 'birth control'?"

"Yes, I believe human intelligence should control the great question of the coming into being of human lives—to give life is surely almost as solemn a thing as to take it. Promiscuity, in this regard, is, in my opinion, neither ethical nor reasonable."

Nellie L. McClung, pioneer author and feminist, interviewed by R.E. Knowles in *The Toronto Star,* 6 Nov. 1935.

I have said, and still think, we must choose between birth control and revolution. We are raising too large a percentage of the dependent class and I do not blame them if they steal and fight before they starve.

A.R. Kaufman, treasurer of the Eugenics Society of Canada, founder of the Parents' Information Bureau, promoter of family planning, letter to the American essayist H.L. Mencken, 10 Aug. 1937, quoted by Angus McLean in *Our Own Master Race: Eugenics in Canada, 1885–1945* (1990).

The first human statement is a scream.

Robin Skelton, poet and aphorist, *A Devious Dictionary* (1991).

BLACK, CONRAD See also NEWS

Lord Black of Wapping would have a faintly erotic air to it.

Allan Fotheringham, columnist, referring to a possible title for publisher Conrad Black and the removal of the offices of his newspaper *The Daily Telegraph* from Fleet Street to Wapping, *Birds of a Feather: The Press and the Politicians* (1989).

From an early age, Mr. Black has not suffered easily the occasions when his conduct has been critically appraised. This indicates that he is human.

David Olive, journalist, "Writ Large," *The Globe and Mail,* 24 Nov. 1990.

I've never begrudged the Left its voice. I just get angry when the Right isn't allowed equal play.

Conrad Black, publisher, remark made to editor John Fraser, "Diary," *Saturday Night,* July–Aug. 1994.

Hollinger is the greatest corporate friend Canadian working print journalists have. We are, as far as I can see, practically the only buyers in Canada of daily newspapers.... In nearly thirty years in this business, we have rarely sold and never closed a daily newspaper.

Conrad Black, CEO of Hollinger Inc. and Hollinger International, upon the acquisition of the Southam Inc. newspapers, annual meeting, Toronto, 29 May 1996, quoted in *The Toronto Star,* 31 May 1996.

The papers are far more supportive of free enterprise than they used to be.

David Radler, executive, Hollinger Inc., which controls 350 papers in six countries with a daily circulation of 6.1 million, quoted by Peter C. Newman, "The Nation's Business," *Maclean's,* 29 Sept. 1997.

Black who enjoys duel citizenship, Canadian and British, who lives in Great Britain and publishes newspapers here, there, and elsewhere....

Misprint in **Dalton Camp**'s column "A Black Day for Our Society," *The Toronto Star,* 23 June 1999, about the opposition of the federal government to the elevation of press baron Conrad Black to the British House of Lords. Black benefits from dual (not duel) Canadian British citizenship.

BLACKS See also SLAVERY

Among all the singular and interesting records to which the institution of American slavery has given rise, we know of none more striking, more characteristic and instructive, than that of Josiah Henson.

Harriet Beecher Stowe, author of *Uncle Tom's Cabin,* referring to former slave Josiah Henson, resident of Chatham, Ont., real-life model of Uncle Tom, preface to *An Autobiography of the Rev. Josiah Henson* ("Uncle Tom") (1881) edited by John Lobb.

An interviewer on the CBC asks me: Isn't it a burden to have to write about being Black? What else would I write about? What would be more important?

Dionne Brand, poet, "Bread Out of Stone," *Language in Her Eye: Views on Writing and Gender by Canadian Women Writing in English* (1990) edited by Libby Scheier, Sarah Sheard, and Eleanor Wachtel.

Sooner or later, we'll have to discuss to what extent one must be black to teach black history. If so, it's racial discrimination in reverse. It would be unconscionable for me to say a Chinese could not teach Shakespeare.

Michael R. Marrus, historian, University of Toronto, discussing "political correctness," quoted by Lynda Hurst in *The Toronto Star*, 2 June 1991.

No one seems to have a problem in identifying us when they want to shoot us.

Zanana Akande, parliamentary assistant to Ontario Premier Bob Rae, referring to police shootings of black youths with respect to the NDP government's targeting of black youths for employment programs, quoted in *The Toronto Star*, 25 June 1992.

We can grab hold of the future by continuing to dream and investing in ourselves.

Cecil Foster, Barbadian-born author and journalist, quoted by Sigcino Moyo in *Now*, 25 Feb. 1993.

BLOC QUÉBÉCOIS See also BOUCHARD, LUCIEN; POLITICAL PARTIES; SEPARATISM

Yes, I have a respect for Canada and even feel an emotional attachment to Canada, as most Quebecers do, even sovereignists. But my first loyalty is Quebec.

Lucien Bouchard, leader of the Bloc Québécois, addressing the editorial board of *The Toronto Star*, 22 Sept. 1993.

First of all, we never have had an Official Opposition that was not a government-in-waiting, that was not perceived by the people as an alternative to the existing government. This gives the present Official Opposition—the Bloc—an aura of unreality difficult to comprehend. It's not only that no one has seen its like before, no one has ever imagined it.

Dalton Camp, columnist, *The Toronto Star*, 23 Jan. 1994.

Think about it: Separatists forever in the House of Commons.

Jacques Parizeau, Quebec Premier, address, Canadian Club of Toronto, 22 Nov. 1994, published in *The Toronto Star* the following day.

BLOOD

We're educated. We know the pros and cons. All we're asking for is an option. Every parent would give their life to save their child, and all we want to do is give our blood.

Kathryn Watcham, mother of four and crusader for directed donations of blood, quoted by André Picard in *The Globe and Mail*, 30 Jan. 1996.

Every single person that has died, and that will die, died for nothing. We simply know now what caused it.

Janet Conners, representative of families with members infected with tainted blood and advocate of extended government compensation for victims and their families, interviewed at the tabling of the commission of inquiry into the tainted-blood situation, headed by Horace Krever, Ottawa, 27 Nov. 1997, quoted by Scott Feschuk and Anne McIlroy in *The Globe and Mail* the following day.

BOOKS See also BOOKS, CANADIAN; BOOKS: DEDICATIONS; BOOKSELLING; CENSORSHIP; CULTURE; LIBRARIES; LITERATURE; READING; WRITERS & WRITING

The book by the popular author flies without wings, as it were.

D.D. Cumming, aphorist, *Skookum Chuck Fables, Bits of History, Through the Microscope by Skookum Chuck* (1915).

It is easier to buy books than to read them and easier to read them than to absorb them.

Sir William Osler, physician and professor, quoted by William Bennett Bean in *Sir William Osler: Aphorisms from His Bedside Teachings and Writings* (1950).

People and books are the most important things in life.

Angus Mowat, Director of Ontario Public Libraries, father of writer Farley Mowat, quoted by Al Purdy in "Angus," *No Other Country* (1977).

One day when I was a struggling bookseller, my seven-year-old daughter, Jane, appeared on a popular local television show. She was asked by the interviewer, "Now, how would you like to tell us all about what your favourite books are?" Without a moment's hesitation Jane answered, with a great big bright smile on her face, "Library books!"

Mel Hurtig, publisher and nationalist, *At Twilight in the Country: Memoirs of a Canadian Nationalist* (1996).

One does not have to be an expert to pick out a great book; it is the not so-great that demand judgement. Important books have their own authority; something masterful is apparent as soon as one begins to read.

Lovat Dickson, man-of-letters, *Wilderness Man: The Strange Story of Grey Owl* (1973).

I propose that we use the term "koob," book spelt backwards, to describe [junk reading]... I've sold a lot of koobs in my day and plan to continue to do so, but I do respect books and I think a distinction must be made.

Jack McClelland, President of McClelland & Stewart, interviewed in 1973, quoted by James King in *Jack: A Life with Writers, The Story of Jack McClelland* (1999).

The proof of civilization rests much more powerfully in the number of bookshops a country has than in the number of writers it can boast. Without customers, bookshops die. Without an audience, writing goes rogue and mutates into something other than literature.

William Hoffer, antiquarian bookseller, "Cheap Sons of Bitches; Memoirs of the Book Trade," *Carry on Bumping* (1989) edited by John Metcalf.

How sad to see / There soon will be, / Despite winged words, / More books than birds.

Lines from **Robert Finch**'s poem "History," *Miracle at the Jetty* (1991).

My books may not be worth reading, but they are written as if they were.

Francis Sparshott, philosopher, entry, *Contemporary Authors Autobiography Series* (1992), Volume 15.

After Gutenberg came out with print, no one went back to the chisel.

Frank Ogden, futurologist, characteristic observation, 19 Feb. 1993.

Books were what you did when it was raining; they were the entertainment, they were the escape, they were the extended family, and I read them all, even when they weren't supposed to be for children.

Margaret Atwood, author, referring to books in summer cottages, "Why I Write," *The Toronto Star*, 5 June 1993.

Within years, a crystal will hold the Library of Congress. Stop worrying about the forests. They have found new friends in technology.

Frank Ogden, futurologist, characteristic observation, March 1993.

A book survives not just for an hour or so; it is there, if you are lucky, for ten or even more years.

Boyce Richardson, author, "Not Enough Space for Our Friends," *The Canadian Forum*, March 1993.

Since I live in Nova Scotia in July and August—one-sixth of the year—I have long mantained that for every six books of Mordecai Richler's on the Canadiana shelf, there should be one of mine.

Calvin Trillin, American essayist, summer resident of Nova Scotia, "Answer Man," *The New York Times Magazine*, 12 July 1998.

I couldn't review your book. I liked it.

Attributed to sometime reviewer **Larry Zolf** by Peter C. Newman, "The Nation's Business," *Maclean's*, 30 Nov. 1998.

BOOKS, CANADIAN

See also BOOKS; LITERATURE, CANADIAN; WRITERS & WRITING, CANADIAN

I published in Canada. I might as well have done so in Kamschatka.

Major John Richardson, author of *Wacousta; or The Prophecy* (1832), a novel more popular in the United States than in the Canadian colonies, quoted by W.R. Riddell in *John Richardson* (1923).

My publishers persuaded me one year to do a tour of the country to stimulate book sales, but it was a depressing experience. I got the impression that Canadians didn't read too many books.

J.B. Priestley, English author, quoted in his obituary by E.C. Farrell in *The Globe and Mail*, 16 Aug. 1984. On one occasion he noted, "Canada is a huge, sad land out of which everything good can come except high spirits."

What delighted me the most—more than, say, the $200,000 that Ghost Fox earned in paperback rights—was the payment I received from my Eskimo friends when it was translated into Eskimo. I got what I asked for: fifteen ivory tusks, my best royalty payment.

James Houston, author and northerner, referring to the translation of the novel into Inuktitut, quoted by Ken Adachi in *The Toronto Star*, 23 March 1980.

Certainly one of the signs of maturity in a country's literature is when all books do not have to aspire to be War and Peace.

Alan Twigg, interviewer, *Strong Voices: Conversations with Fifty Canadian Authors* (1988).

In this country last year, more people caught AIDS than bought a Canadian book.

Scuttlebutt noted by **Susan Musgrave** in *Great Musgrave* (1989) according to Dennis Kucherawy in *The Toronto Star*, 18 Nov. 1989.

BOOKS: DEDICATIONS See also BOOKS

I have been a Bohemian for twenty years, and during that time I have found but one friend whom I could trust as far as I could throw a bull by the tail. To that one—to thee, my Mother, I dedicate this book.

R.K. Kernighan, versifier known as The Khan, who wrote from "The Wigwam," Rockton, Ont., "known from Vancouver to Halifax as Canada's best-gifted poetic genius," *The Khan's Canticles* (1896).

To all the editors who have helped and hindered me over the past thirty years.

Dedication by **Hugh Garner** to *A Hugh Garner Omnibus* (1978).

Riel is dedicated to all historians, who know better than anyone that history is the greatest of all fictions.

Janet Rosenstock, historical novelist, *Riel: Novelization* (1979) written with Dennis Adair.

I would like to acknowledge my mortgage company, which never let me forget that they were behind me, waiting.

Dedication of the novel *Bad Boy* (1989) by **Diana Wieler**.

For all those who stand beside those who stand alone this book is dedicated.

Dedication of **David Adams Richards'** novel *Evening Snow Will Bring Such Peace* (1990).

Books are not dedicated much to places, / Yet places, too, like people, have their faces....

Robert Finch, poet, dedication, *Miracle at the Jetty* (1991).

To those who helped / to see me through / and often see / through me.

Part of the dedication of the art book *Charles Pachter* (1992) written by **Bogomila Welsh-Ovcharov**.

For my grandchildren and their peers—who will need trees as much as books—arrangements have been made to plant a sufficient number of trees to compensate for those used in publishing this volume.

Dedication of **Barbara Smith**'s *Ghost Stories of Alberta* (1993).

The length of the dedication is inversely proportional to the merit of the book.

Joan Givner, author, "Who to Throw the Book At," *The Globe and Mail*, 24 June 1994.

To all the actors and actresses, / stage managers, designers, / and directors / I have ever worked with. / Except two. // Make that three.

One of the dedications of *Also in the Cast: Memoirs of Tony van Bridge* (1995). The last three words appear as an afterthought on the page that follows the dedication.

Dedicated to all Canadian nationalists.

Dedication of *Secret Tales of the Arctic Trails: Stories of Crime and Adventure in Canada's Far North* (1997) edited by **David Skene-Melvin**.

...and for my mortal enemy Philip Morris Inc., which I vow to take down.

Part of the dedication of the book *Culture Jam: The Uncooling of America* (1999) written by **Kalle Lasn**, Estonian-born, Canadian publisher and editor of *Adbusters Magazine*, a Vancouver-based publication that publishes "subverbs" and "uncommercials."

BOOKSELLING See also BOOKS

A home or a people without good books is something more than waste; in short, an empty brain is the devil's workshop.

John Britnell, bookseller and son of the founder and proprietor of the Albert Britnell Book Store, established in Toronto in 1893, closed in 1999, *Books and Booksellers in Ancient and Modern Times with Autobiographical Experiences of the Past Sixty Years* (1923).

In many British cities there are Communist book shops, but not even in London is there a Canadian book shop.

Sir John Wedgewood, British trade official, "Canadian Trade—Handle with Care" (1959), *Empire Club of Canada: Addresses 1958–59* (1959).

No good bookstore should be without the works of William Hazlitt.

Louis Melzack, bookstore owner, later chain-store founder, quoted by Liam Lacey in *The Globe and Mail*, 29 Aug. 1981.

If placed end to end, Harlequin books sold in 1981 could run along both sides of the Nile, both sides of the Amazon, and one side of the Rio Grande. If all the words of all the Harlequin books sold in 1981 were laid end to end, they would stretch 1000 times around the earth, and 93 times to the moon.

Publicity release quoted by **Margaret Ann Jensen** in *Love's Sweet Return: The Harlequin Story* (1984).

BORDER, CANADIAN-AMERICAN

See also ALASKA, CANADA & THE UNITED STATES, FRONTIERS, UNITED STATES OF AMERICA

All the boundaries in the world should be as open, and as happy as the Canadian–United States line. To many diplomats such a boundary is incredible, and yet it exists, one of the longest in the world.

Vachel Lindsay, American poet, *Going-to-the-Stars* (1923).

The boundary between Canada and the United States is a typically human creation; it is physically invisible, geographically illogical, militarily indefensible, and emotionally inescapable.

Hugh L. Keenleyside, diplomat, *Canada and the United States* (1929).

Canada is a land of multiple borderlines.... Canada has the longest coastline in the world, a coastline which represents the frontier for Europe on one side and the Orient on the other.

Marshall McLuhan, communications pioneer, "Canada: The Borderline Case," *The Canadian Imagination: Dimensions of a Literary Culture* (1977) edited by David Staines.

America borders on the magnificent. Canada.

Advertising campaign sponsored by the Canadian Office of Tourism. It was created by writer Cathy Bennett of **Vickers & Benson Limited**, creative director David Peacock, as noted in *Creative Source 5* (1983).

I still yearn, after all these years, to see the border guards as ineffective as possible with as little reason as possible to be effective.

John Kenneth Galbraith, economist and author, commenting on the international border crossing at Windsor–Detroit between the World Wars, "Canadian Customs," *Saturday Night*, Jan. 1987.

And it has come to me that so much of what makes Canada geographically artificial as the nation of the northern half of North America is exactly that: its lack of definition by water.

Rudy Wiebe, novelist, *Playing Dead: A Contemplation Concerning the Arctic* (1989).

Most of us are still huddled tight to the border, looking into the candy store window, scared by the Americans on one side and the bush on the other.

Thoughts of a character in **Mordecai Richler**'s novel *Solomon Gursky Was Here* (1989).

Again and again as I travelled along the border, I imagined its absence. Many Americans do not even imagine its presence.

*

I know Canadians who would happily fold up the boundary line and become part of the United States; I did not meet these people living close to the line.

Marian Botsford Fraser, author, *Walking the Line* (1989).

Borders are interesting because they generate difference and hence newness.

Douglas Coupland, novelist, "Agree/Disagree: 55 Statements about the Culture," *The New Republic*, 2 Aug. 1995.

Borders are ideas erected between age groups, social classes, all sorts of hierarchical entities, so that society may function as predictably and as decently as possible. They are not solid brick walls. Beauty eats them away.

Nancy Huston, Prairie-born, Paris-based author, "Dealing with What's Dealt," *Salamagundi*, Spring–Summer, 1995.

We got guys looking over the Great Wall of China as an excellent model for the Canadian border.

Pat Buchanan, U.S. Republican, ever the presidential hopeful, address, New Hampshire primary, CBC-TV's *The National*, 20 Feb. 1996.

It's tough to see the difference in borders when you're flying around the world at 28,000 kilometres an hour.

Julie Payette, astronaut aboard the space shuttle, quoted by Canadian Press, "Quote Unquote," *The Globe and Mail*, 5 June 1999.

BOREDOM

Civilization is assuredly the state of things which generates ennui and supplies the readiest means of dissipating it.

Kit Coleman, columnist in the 1880s and 1890s, quoted by Ted Ferguson in *Kit Coleman: Queen of Hearts* (1978).

"If you don't know yourself in this country," a Turkish immigrant to Canada told me in 1974, "you die of boredom. Mind you, if you do know yourself you die of boredom anyway."

Jan Morris, Anglo-Welsh traveller and author, *Farewell the Trumpets: An Imperial Retreat* (1978).

It's not that we're boring. We've just got better things to do than talk about the weather. Like survive it.

Josh Freed, columnist, "All Quiet on the Northern Front," *Sign Language and Other Tales of Montreal Life* (1990).

Canada is distinctly not boring, and it is largely its own fault that the world sees it so....Canada really is one of the best of all countries—perhaps the best—and that it is boring only because it says it is.

Jan Morris, Anglo-Welsh traveller, "In Praise of Canada," *The Toronto Star*, 15 June 1992.

The cardinal sin of the nineties is to be boring.

Frank Ogden, futurologist, characteristic observation, 14 Nov. 1992.

BOUCHARD, LUCIEN See also BLOC QUÉBÉCOIS, PARTI QUÉBÉCOIS, POLITICIANS

Mr. Speaker, I entered politics late in life, under trying circumstances, but with the best of intentions. Two reasons prompted me to go into the lion's den. The first is the attraction of the beau risque, the worthy risk of co operating with Mr. Mulroney. The second, Mr. Mulroney himself. In Sept Iles, on a warm day in August 1984, he made the solemn commitment to bring this country together. I knew as well that he had made this commitment by having all provincial premiers sign the 1987 Accord which would enable Quebec to endorse formally the 1982 patriation.... I felt that in reading the [Meech Lake] accord for the first time that Quebec had managed to overcome its humiliation and its just indigation....

Lucien Bouchard, Minister of the Environment, point of order, House of Commons, 22 May 1990. With these words he began his statement announcing his resignation from the Mulroney Cabinet and Government in which he had served for two years as the Prime Minister's "Quebec lieutenant."

I fell in love with an ambassador, married a cabinet minister and now live with a backbencher.... What's coming next?

Audrey Best-Bouchard, wife of maverick politician Lucien Bouchard, founder of the Bloc Québécois, quoted by Lysiane Gagnon in *The Globe and Mail*, 6 June 1992.

Bouchard ... has the habit of being "serially sincere," as one person who knows him well has put it. He believes totally in whatever it is he happens to believe in.

Richard Gwyn, columnist, "Home and Away," *The Toronto Star*, 27 Feb. 1994.

Traitor? Traitor to what? My country is Quebec.

Lucien Bouchard, leader of the Bloc Québécois, interviewed by Peter O'Neil of *The Vancouver Sun*, quoted by Peter C. Newman in "The Nation's Business," *Maclean's*, 13 June 1994.

Que l'on continue. Merci.

Barely legible message scribbled on a piece of paper by Bloc Québécois leader **Lucien Bouchard**, 30 Nov. 1994. It was displayed by the cardiovascular surgeon at Montreal's Saint-Luc Hospital who amputated Bouchard's left leg to stem a near-fatal infection, Dec. 2 press conference, according to Sandro Contenta in *The Toronto Star*, 3 Dec. 1994. It translates "Let us carry on. Thank you." It became a political slogan. Lise Bissonnette called it in "Commentary," *The Globe and Mail*, 3 Dec. 1994, "a beautiful message that could have marked the end of a life, a relay entrusted to all those who share his commitment, close up or from afar."

In his speech, Mr. Bouchard coined Quebec's latest political expression, calling for a virage in the movement—a sharp road turn.

Tu Thanh Ha, journalist, "Analysis," *The Globe and Mail*, 18 April 1995.

We are a people, we are a nation, and as a nation we have a fundamental right to keep and maintain our territory. Canada is not a real country. There are two people, two nations and two territories. And this one is ours.

Lucien Bouchard, Quebec Premier designate, news conference, 27 Jan. 1996, quoted by Rhéal Séguin in *The Globe and Mail*, 29 Jan. 1996.

I accuse Lucien Bouchard of having betrayed the population of Quebec during last October's referendum campaign. By distorting the political history of his province and of his country, by spreading discord among its citizens with his demagogic rhetoric and by preaching contempt for those Canadians who did not share his views, Lucien Bouchard went beyond the limits of honesty and democratic debate.

Pierre Elliott Trudeau, former Prime Minister, "Truth Must Be Restored," *The Montreal Gazette*, 3 Feb. 1996, reprinted in *The Toronto Star*, 6 Feb. 1996.

There is nothing we can say to Lucien Bouchard short of "Good morning, Mr. President" that will please him.

Brian Tobin, Newfoundland Premier, quoted by Robert Lewis, "From the Editor," *Maclean's*, 24 June 1996.

He is a kind of gifted national poet who, in speaking of his own particular desires, speaks of the yearnings of the general community.

Vivian Rakoff, psychiatrist, psychological profile of Lucien Bouchard and the Quebec psyche, "What It Said," *The Globe and Mail*, 25 Aug. 1997.

His role is extraordinary. He will be the last American liberator in the line of Bolívar, the last great anti-colonialist. It is a heady role, and he does it well. I don't think we can afford to wait for him to trip himself up. Within the politics of desire the community of dreamers is forgiving to the dreamer-in-chief. Don't people die for flags and anthems?

Vivian Rakoff, psychiatrist, psychological profile of Lucien Bouchard and the Quebec psyche, "Just What Was Written," *The Globe and Mail*, 26 Aug. 1997. The references are to Quebec Premier Lucien Bouchard and to Simón Bolívar, soldier-statesman who freed six Latin American republics from Spanish rule before his death in 1830.

Extremists on our side are more restrained.

Lucien Bouchard, Quebec Premier, addressing reporters, contrasting separatist and federalist "extremists," *The Globe and Mail*, 22 May 1998.

Perhaps it would be more accurate to state that Lucien Bouchard is seeking optimum "whining conditions."

Peter Ryan, North Vancouver, punning on the Quebec Premier's insistence on "winning conditions" before calling a referendum on sovereignty, Letters to the Editor, *The Globe and Mail*, 20 Dec. 1999.

The boss's latest unilateral declaration of indignation....

Paul Wells, columnist, referring to Quebec Premier Lucien Bouchard's outspoken objection to the name-change of Newfoundland to Newfoundland and Labrador, *National Post*, 7 Dec. 1999.

BOUNDARIES See BORDER, CANADIAN-AMERICAN

BOXING See also SPORTS

A legend, that's what they call me now. It's a nice word to be called. It's better to be a legend than a bum.

Yvon Durelle, light heavyweight champion boxer of the Commonwealth in 1959, quoted by Silver Donald Cameron in *Today*, 14 Nov. 1981.

The big boy upstairs always liked me. He had his hand on my shoulder.

Jimmy McLarnin, professional boxing champion, long retired, quoted by Stephen Brunt in *The Globe and Mail*, 10 June 1991.

BRAIN DRAIN See EMIGRATION

BRAVERY

Inexperience.

Fred Tilston, soldier, holder of the Victoria Cross, the highest award for military bravery awarded by the British Empire, offering a one word explanation of the essential quality of bravery, quoted in his obituary in *The Vancouver Sun*, 26 Sept. 1992.

BRIBERY See CORRUPTION

BRITAIN See BRITISH EMPIRE & COMMONWEALTH, CANADA & THE UNITED KINGDOM, ENGLISH PEOPLE, IRISH PEOPLE, SCOTTISH PEOPLE, UNITED KINGDOM, WELSH PEOPLE

BRITISH COLUMBIA See also VANCOUVER, VANCOUVER ISLAND, VICTORIA, WESTERN PROVINCES

The people of this Colony have, generally speaking, no love for Canada; they have but little sentimentality, and care little about the distinctions between the form of government of Canada and the United States. Therefore no union on account of love need be looked for.

John Sebastian Helmcken, politician, speech, Victoria, 9 March 1870, quoted by R.E. Watters, editor, *British Columbia: A Centennial Anthology* (1958).

Externally, British Columbia appears to be the richest and the loveliest section of the Continent. Over and above her own resources she has a fair chance to secure an immense Asiatic trade, which she urgently desires.

Rudyard Kipling, author and imperialist, describing his visit made in 1907–08, *Letters to the Family: Notes on a Recent Trip to Canada* (1910).

When two men from the ends of the earth meet by a winter fire, their thoughts are certain to drift overseas. We spoke of the racing tides off Vancouver, and the lonely pine-clad ridges running up to the snow-peaks of the Selkirks, to which we had both travelled once upon a time in search of sport.

Passage from **John Buchan**'s story "The Kings of Orion," *The Moon Endureth* (1936).

British Columbia is heaven. It trembles within me and pains with its wonder as when a child I first awakened to the song of the earth at home. Only the hills are bigger, the torrents are bigger.... The Japanese fish, Chinese have vegetable gardens, Hindoos haul wood, and I often feel that only the Chinese of the eleventh and twelfth century ever interpreted the spirit of such a country. We have not yet awakened to its nature.

F.H. Varley, painter and member of the Group of Seven and resident of British Columbia, quoted by Donald Buchanan in "The Paintings and Drawings of F.H. Varley," *Canadian Art*, Spring 1949.

...the huge country round me, the immense separation of prairie, forest, lake and Atlantic beyond, seem like those fabled landscapes by the Styx, an unbridgeable waste of desolation, fit only to be peopled by the dead. These thoughts came in the night, or when I was alone....

Freya Stark, English traveller and author, *Beyond Euphrates: Autobiography, 1928–1933* (1951). She is describing wintering in 1928–29 in the B.C.'s Kootenay Valley.

The lushness and size of everything we saw seemed preposterously exaggerated. Our spirits lifted with the beauty of the place and its lush vegetation, huge waterfalls, deep black fjords and massive dark green pine forests.

Bob Geldof, musician, crossing Canada from

Montreal to Vancouver by bus in 1973, *Is That It?* (1986).

Super, Natural British Columbia

Advertising slogan used by **Tourism British Columbia**, introduced in the late 1980s.

Can you see now why I love B.C. so much? The air's unencumbered here. There are no ghosts. It's just like a new planet.

Ted Hughes, Poet Laureate of England, after a series of visits which ended in 1986, to fellow poet Ehor Boyanowsky, quoted by Frank Moher in the *National Post*, 30 Oct. 1999.

British Columbia is a kingdom all by itself. If you unwrinkled all those sky-seeking mountains as if they were a sheet of crumpled paper, you'd have something even larger, its size nearly a continent: an empire of the loggers. And at the sea's edge, a fisherman's domain.

Al Purdy, poet, "Peter Trower," *The Oberon Poetry Collection* (1992) edited by Michael Macklem.

I wouldn't know there's anything wacky about B.C. politics and B.C. people if I didn't keep reading it in Toronto magazines.

Howard White, author and publisher, quoted by Robert Matas in *The Globe and Mail*, 10 Feb. 1992.

Perhaps as a byproduct, Bennett Columbia, unlike its western neighbours, has never produced a Canadian prime minister and shows no interest, to this moment, in wanting one.

Allan Fotheringham, columnist, referring to previous B.C. Premiers W.A.C. Bennett and his son Bill Bennett, *Maclean's*, 24 Aug. 1992. Other references favoured by "the Foth," a columnist given to epithetical non-descriptions, include BeeCee, the Wet Coast, and the Left Coast.

The difference has something to do with British Columbia being a frontier—as far as you can escape to, and still have medicare.

Peter C. Newman, journalist, "Essay," *Maclean's*, 24 Aug. 1992.

Want a portrait of post-millennial Canadian values? Look at British Columbia today!

Michael Adams, CEO, Environics Research Group Limited, "Personal Fulfilment in the Garden of Eden," Premier's Summit: A Strong and Secure Economy for British Columbians, Victoria, B.C., 19 Jan. 1995.

It was Bruce Hutchison, who achieved international recognition as a brilliant journalist while refusing all his life to leave his province, who invented the label "Lotusland," derived from the Greek mythology of the lotus-eaters.

Allan Fotheringham, columnist, "Column," *Maclean's*, 22 Jan. 1996.

As things look now, British Columbia will be an independent nation inside the first decades of the next century. Talks will fail and new political arrangements will result. One of them will be an independent British Columbia, probably calling itself Cascadia.

Rafe Mair, broadcaster and author, *Canada: Is Anyone Listening?* (1998).

BRITISH EMPIRE & COMMONWEALTH

See also CANADA & THE UNITED KINGDOM, COLONIALISM, EMPIRE, IMPERIALISM, UNITED KINGDOM

Canada you will no doubt find a place of difficulties, or drawbacks—what place on this Earth is not such!

Thomas Carlyle, author, letter of 3 May 1844, *The Letters of Thomas Carlyle to His Brother Alexander with Related Family Letters* (1968) edited by Edwin W. Marrs, Jr. Alexander Carlyle settled in the Brantford district as a farmer.

But, it may be said, are we not part and parcel of a great Empire upon which the sun never sets, which contains three hundred millions of people, whose wealth defies estimate, whose army is perfect in discipline; whose great navy dominates the sea? What have we to fear when this great Empire protects us?

Joseph Howe, Tribune of Nova Scotia, address, Young Men's Christian Assocation, Ottawa, 27 Feb. 1872, *Poems and Essays* (1874).

In losing the United States, Britain lost the smaller half of her American possessions:—the Colony of the Maple Leaf is about as large as Europe.

W.D. Lighthall, editor, *Songs of the Great Dominion* (1889).

I think you perhaps do not realize how great Canada bulks in the imagination of the other great communities within the Empire. I am sure that you cannot realize how all that she does, how every act and word is watched, and keenly watched, throughout the Empire.

Rudyard Kipling, man-of-letters, "Canada's Path to Nationhood," 21 Oct. 1907, *Addresses Delivered before the Canadian Club of Ottawa: 1903–1909 (1910).*

I really consider Canadians, on the average, the brightest people in the empire.

Ramsay MacDonald, Prime Minister of Britain, interviewed in Glasgow, Scotland, by R.E. Knowles in *The Toronto Star,* 20 June 1929.

My own theory about the British attitude is a very simple one. England is an imperialist, capitalist country possessed of enormous vested interests in various parts of the world, and these are loosely held together by a cement of sentimentality.

Norman Bethune, physician and revolutionary, referring to the British attitude to the Spanish Civil War, interviewed in Toronto in June 1937 by William Strange and reprinted in *The Toronto Star,* 13 Sept. 1992.

When I travel about Canada, nothing delights me more than to hear England spoken of affectionately as "the Old Country."

Earl of Athlone, brother of Queen Mary and Governor General of Canada, "Address" (1941), *Empire Club of Canada: Addresses Delivered to the Members During the Year 1940–41* (1941).

The ties that bind the Commonwealth together are family ties—and what a remarkable family it is!

John G. Diefenbaker, Prime Minister, address, 22 June 1957.

Britain never wanted to keep people down, just exploit them, like everybody else.

Graham Spry, enthusiast for public broadcasting, personal communication, 18 Aug. 1976.

Otherwise the Canadian visit was a great refreshment, a genuine honeymoon, and a confirmation that the British Commonwealth works. Even the haired barefoot Canadian young were civilized....

Anthony Burgess, novelist, *You've Had Your Time: Being the Second Part of the Confessions of Anthony Burgess* (1990).

Why can't one of the founding components of the nation assert with pride its own culture? You can't even use the phrase "British North American." You're considered a crackpot, a little old lady, a mental recessive, an anal retentive. But the British North American tradition built the goddam country.

Scott Symons, cultural commentator of British North American ancestry, interviewed in *The Idler,* No. 25, May–June 1990.

Imperial Canada has faded away, leaving behind French Canada, which is arguably a nation but not a state, and the rest of Canada, which is arguably a state but not a nation. Imperial Canada, by contrast, was never a state: it was a state of mind, a state of being, a state of identity.

David Cannadine, historian, address in 1995, Centre of Canadian Studies, University of Edinburgh, *Imperial Canada 1867-1917* (1997) edited by Colin M. Coates.

Whatever the official view of the Commonwealth, it is clearly a rather nebulous but apparently innocuous organization. (Mozambique, with no historic connection, is now a member because South Africa's Nelson Mandela asked for it. How could any country now be excluded?)

Conrad Black, publisher, "Taking Canada Seriously," *International Journal,* Winter 1997-98.

When comedian Martin Short reflected on the humility of growing up saluting Britain's Union Jack, Eugene Levy retorted that he was just "so damn proud to be part of the Commonwealth." Lorne Michaels deadpanned, "Benedict Arnold was one of ours."

Sarah Vowell, columnist, reporting on a panel on Canadian comedy at New York's 92nd Street YMCA, "American Squirm: Canuck Yuks," "Salon Magazine," Internet, 27 Jan. 1999.

In Toronto, I began to have a sense of a new, postmodern Commonwealth, to which Empire could come to atone for some of its sins and (as retired power brokers do) to make a kind of peace....

Pico Iyer, traveller, *The Global Soul: Jet Lag, Shopping Malls and the Search for Home* (2000).

BRITISH PEOPLE

See BRITISH EMPIRE & COMMONWEALTH, ENGLISH PEOPLE, IRISH PEOPLE, SCOTTISH PEOPLE, UNITED KINGDOM, WELSH PEOPLE

BROADCASTING

See also CANADIAN BROADCASTING CORPORATION; COMMUNICATIONS; JOURNALISM; NEWS; RADIO; GZOWSKI, PETER; TELEVISION

One, two, three, four. Is it snowing where you are, Mr. Thiessen? If so telegraph back and let me know.

The first words spoken on the first radio broadcast of the human voice, 23 Dec. 1900. They were uttered by the Canadian-born inventor **Reginald A. Fessenden** at his laboratory on Cobb Island, Potomac River, near Washington, D.C., over a primitive radio device, and were heard by his assistant Thiessen in Arlington, Virginia, eighty kilometres away. Thiessen answered "yes" by telegraph. Fessenden thereupon made the following statement: "This afternoon, here at Cobb Island, intelligible speech by electromagnetic waves has for the first time in the world's history been transmitted." Quoted by Ormond Raby in *Radio's First Voice: The Story of Reginald Fessenden* (1970). This experiment marks the beginning of radio broadcasting.

It is essential that broadcasting be surrounded with such safeguards as will prevent the air becoming what might be described as an atmospheric billboard.

Sir Henry Thornton, pioneer of public broadcasting, address, Advertising Clubs of the World, Philadelphia, Penn., 21 June 1926, quoted by E. Austin Weir in *The Struggle for National Broadcasting in Canada* (1965).

The question before this committee is whether Canada is to establish a chain that is owned and operated and controlled by Canadians, or whether it is to be owned and operated by commercial organizations associated or controlled by American interests. The question is, the State or the United States?

Graham Spry, Chairman of the Canadian Radio League, address, Parliamentary Committee on Broadcasting, 18 April 1932.

Indeed, this is one illustration of the wider issue, is Canada to be a producer, manufacturer, creator and initiator in the many fields of national life or just the distributor of the marble and the mud of other countries?

Graham Spry, enthusiast for public broadcasting, "The Decline and Fall of Canadian Broadcasting," *Queen's Quarterly*, Summer 1961.

To create a national idiom, a national mythology to interpret Canada to Canadians.... We have to sing our own songs and we have to create our own heroes, dream our own dreams or we won't have a country at all.

Pierre Berton, author, Submission to the Special Senate Committee on Mass Media (Davey Commission), 25 March 1970.

Never in human history have so many been subjected to the concepts distributed so far by so few.

Harry J. Boyle, broadcaster and author, "Responsibility in Broadcasting," *Osgoode Hall Law Journal*, Volume 8, Number 1, 1970.

For God's sake. Either we have a country or we don't. Let's decide!

Pierre Juneau, Chairman of the Canadian Radio-Television and Telecommunications Commission, submission to the Senate Committee on Communications, Oct. 1974, during which he defended the CBC's mandate tried to balance the demands of private broadcasters and the needs of public broadcasting.

By following the imperatives and economics of mass programming, we have succeeded in developing a homogenized broadcasting system in which the rich cultural mosaic that makes up the pattern of the country is scarcely represented.

Mavor Moore, man-of-the-theatre, Canada Council's submission on extension of service to northern and remote communities, and satellite distribution of programming and pay television, 3 March 1980.

Offering choices has always been an essential function of public broadcasting. Offering choices has also been central to the public regulation of private broadcasting. What local and regional cultures are to a nation, national cultures are to the international community.

In the meltdown of globalization it is essential to offer programming that reflects the culture of one's own nation, that nourishes the pluralism of cultures and national values.

Bernard Ostry, Chairman, TVO, quoted in *The New York Times*, 31 Dec. 1989.

The big difference between television and radio is the difference between talking to someone in person and talking to them on the telephone.

Jack Webster, broadcaster, *Webster! An Autobiography* (1990).

Canada itself is our niche. The Americans can dump 200 or 300 channels on us, but they are never going to dump Canadian channels on us. All of us involved in this have a major psychological turn around to effect in our thinking.

Keith Spicer, Chairman, CRTC, quoted in *The Ties that Bind*, as noted by Stephen Godfrey in *The Globe and Mail*, 19 Sept. 1992.

The story of our heart is not a multinational product.

Daryl Duke, broadcaster, referring to serious Canadian programming, "Spectator," *The Globe and Mail*, 30 July 1994.

Public broadcasters are always on the defensive. Why doesn't the private sector ever have to justify itself?

Rick Salutin, columnist and novelist, speech, Toronto, Save the CBC Coalition, 18 Nov. 1995, quoted by Greg Quill in *The Toronto Star* the following day.

Maybe the proper question to be asked by these armchair CBC critics is: "Why do we need CTV and Global? We already have access to American networks."

Peter Mansbridge, news anchor of CBC-TV's *The National*, address, University of Regina, 7 March 1996, "Verbatim," *The Globe and Mail*, 8 April 1996.

BROTHERHOOD

We speak of the brotherhood of man as our great security for mutual benevolence and our high inducement to virtuous effort. But is it an absolute certainty that men are brothers? Has science pronounced decisively in favour of the unity of the race? Some men of science certainly have pronounced on the other side.

Goldwin Smith, essayist, "Morality and Theism," *Guesses at the Riddle of Existence and Other Essays on Kindred Subjects* (1897).

I remember during the last war adopting as a kind of motto this phrase: Last century made the world a neighbourhood, this century must make it a brotherhood.

J.S. Woodsworth, M.P., House of Commons, 8 Sept. 1939.

BUDDHISM See also BELIEF, RELIGION

I went to a monastery not to become Buddhist, nor get enlightenment, but to see how the world looks to a Buddhist, and in doing so, loosen the grip my own culture has on my mind.

Tim Ward, traveller, *Arousing the Goddess* (1996).

It's clear he wanted to find a place where Buddhism could have a real home. He liked the elemental quality of life here and the fact that the people were basically good and human and decent and were not caught up in the speed and aggression of modern society.

Moh Hardin, director, Halifax Shambhala Centre, referring to motives of the Tibetan Buddhist teacher Chögyam Trungpa Rinpoche who first visited Halifax in 1977 and nine years later shifted his activities from Boulder, Colorado, to Nova Scotia, quoted by John DeMont in "Media," *Maclean's*, 9 April 1999.

BUDGET

You will have to spend it better and spend less, there's no doubt about it.

Jean Chrétien, Prime Minister, interviewed by *CBC Prime Time*, 15 Dec. 1993, quoted by Edward Greenspon in *The Globe and Mail* the following day.

The budget lends credence to the view that the new gospel of competitiveness is the same old globaloney preached since the invention of steam by chambers of commerce and stockholders the world over.

Dalton Camp, columnist, discussing the Liberal budget of Paul Martin Jr., *The Toronto Star*, 27 Feb. 1994.

Canadians have paid to see the movie *The Deficit.* They don't want to pay to see the sequel.

Paul Martin Jr., Minister of Finance, tabling a new and balanced budget, House of Commons, 24 Feb. 1998.

BULGARIA

The Bulgarian Experience is indestructible. It will only be finished off when all of us have emigrated to Canada. But then Canada itself would be finished.

Sentences from satirist **Stanislav Stratiev**'s meditation "A Bulgarian Tourist Chats to an English Pigeon in Trafalgar Square," *The Bulgarian Experience* (1991).

BUREAUCRACY See also PUBLIC SERVICE

Here you have chiefs in every division, Welfare, Education, Territorial, Administration, and so on, but the biggest chief above all chiefs, I think, is the clock. Yes, a clock, a timepiece, your watch.

Abraham Okpik, Inuit elder, "Life in the South," *Northern Affairs Bulletin*, Sept.–Oct. 1959.

It works in practice, but will it work in theory?

Urban lore popular in Ottawa in the 1970s.

Guidelines for bureaucrats: (1) When in charge, ponder. (2) When in trouble, delegate. (3) When in doubt, mumble.

James H. Boren, Montreal-born business consultant, quoted in *The New York Times*, 8 Nov. 1970.

With this run-away growth of the federal bureaucracy (which really now could be called the "civil self-service" because it grows by feeding upon itself), our society is both witness and victim of an escalating invasion of government into every facet of our lives.

Richard Rohmer, legal counsel, address, Empire Club of Canada, Toronto, 14 March 1974.

Civil servants are supposed to be on tap, not on top.

James Eayrs, historian, *The Toronto Star*, 25 Oct. 1975.

A bureaucrat's job depends on continuous failure which is one thing he can succeed at.

Line from **James Bacque**'s novel *The Queen Comes to Minnicog* (1979).

He is that most despised of human creatures. His activities have brought down upon his shoulders the scorn and outrage of history's multitude. He is homo bureaucratus; the bureaucrat. He is the paper-pusher of the world.

Narration written and spoken by film director **Donald Brittain** in the NFB documentary *Paperland: The Bureaucrat Observed* (1979). The film opens with a bureaucrat (a mandarin) skating to work on Ottawa's Rideau Canal carrying his briefcase.

The corporate system that is at the heart of the modern economy works on the principles of ever-expanding power and ever-diminishing responsibility.

Walter Stewart, journalist, *Too Big to Fail: Olympia & York: The Story Behind the Headlines* (1993).

And though I've been called a bureaucrat, I think bureaucracy is a noble profession, if you believe in the wise and cautious expenditure of public funds.

Shirley Thomson, Director of the Canada Council, quoted by Greg Quill in *The Toronto Star*, 29 Nov. 1997.

BUSINESS See also ADVERTISING, BUSINESS SCHOOLS, CAPITALISM, DEVELOPERS, FREE TRADE, MULTINATIONALISM, TRADE & COMMERCE

The foyer of the T. Eaton Co. seen at night is like Grand Opera.

Christopher Morley, U.S. bookman, referring to bright displays at Eaton's in Toronto, quoted by R.E. Knowles, *The Toronto Star*, 19 Nov. 1937.

I have been working on sizeable projects all my life and somehow I reach a point in the development of a project where I begin to think it is important, and if it is a serious enough project, then I begin to think it is the most important thing in the world.

C.D. Howe, Minister of Trade and Commerce, House of Commons, Summer 1956, quoted by Leslie Roberts in *C.D.: The Life and Times of Clarence Decatur Howe* (1957).

The Canadian political community was not the creation of a people seeking a distinctive national identity. It was the creation rather of certain business, political, religious and cultural interests, seeking the establishment of a monopolistic system of control.

S.D. Clark, sociologist, "Canada and the American Value System" (1964), quoted by Claude T. Bissell in *Great Canadian Writing: A Century of Imagination* (1966).

The only combine that has worked in Canada was fathered by Massey Harris.

Eric Nicol, humorist, *100 Years of What?* (1966) illustrated by Peter Whalley.

Can anyone hope to describe his impressions of Canadians in just a few words? But on the whole, let me say that the Canadian people impressed me very much by their businesslike attitudes, the boldness with which they go about solving their problems and the solutions which they find for those problems.

Alexsei Kosygin, Soviet Premier, interviewed by Bruce West in *The Globe and Mail*, 26 Oct. 1971.

Today, the business of business is becoming the constant invention of new business.

Marshall McLuhan, communications pioneer, *Take Today: The Executive as Dropout* (1972) with Barrington Nevitt.

Being your own boss is freedom to go bankrupt in your own inimitable way.

Peter Dewhurst, business consultant, quoted by Ann Farrell in *The Toronto Star*, 1 April 1975.

Profits aren't an option, they're a necessity. Although they are the last item of an accounting statement, they are just as important, and just as necessary a cost, as any other cost item—wages, taxes, materials, rents.

Ian Sinclair, Chairman, Canadian Pacific, interviewed by Dean Walker in *A Case for the Enterprise System* (1975).

A civilization shaped by market transactions is a civilization responsive to the common appetites, preferences and aspirations of common people.

E.G. Burton, Vice-President of Simpsons Limited, quoted in *The Globe and Mail*, 3 Feb. 1976.

If Canadians can feel that their business machine is working for them, that—more than any number of "O Canada's"—will generate a strong sense of Canada and proud identification with it.

Heather Menzies, journalist, *The Railroad's Not Enough: Canada Now* (1978).

I deal in bread and dreams.

W. Garfield Weston, founder of the Weston food empire, remark quoted in his obituary, *The Globe and Mail*, 23 Oct. 1978.

If there is a hell, there must be a special pit reserved for nice, sweet, charming, intelligent secretaries who have spent their niceness, sweetness, charm and intelligence on covering up for their bosses.

Stephen Vizinczey, novelist, *An Innocent Millionaire* (1983).

In Canada, far more than in the United States, the competitive strategy of working with or through government, or otherwise making use of it, has coloured the evolution of enterprise, the economy, and government itself.

Michael Bliss, historian, *Northern Enterprise: Five Centuries of Canadian Business* (1987).

Our business community is in favour of joining the United States for the simple and obvious reason that it isn't our business community any more, it is theirs.

Eric Kierans and **Walter Stewart**, economist and writer, *Wrong End of the Rainbow: The Collapse of Free Enterprise in Canada* (1988).

We still believe that the customer is king, that service to the community is the essence of private enterprise, that talent has nothing to do with colour of skin.

Thomas J. Bata, world head of the Bata Shoe Company, *Bata: Shoemaker to the World* (1990) written with Sonja Sinclair.

Business unites us. The language of the spreadsheet is universal.

*

Business is not perfect, but it represents one of the few bright lights available to people around the world.

John Dalla Costa, advertising executive, *Meditations on Business: Why Business As Usual Won't Work Anymore* (1991).

The nature of the problem can be seen in the case of Canada, where the majority of manufacturers are owned by foreigners. Canadians have a good standard of living, but they can never have the best. The best jobs (CEO, CFO, head of research, etc.) are back at headquarters, and that is somewhere else. Even if Canadians were to get those jobs, and they don't, they would have to live abroad. There is something at stake!

Lester Thurow, economist, *Head to Head: The Coming Economic Battle among Japan, Europe, and America* (1991).

When someone says, "It is good business," you may be sure it is bad morality.

Robin Skelton, poet and aphorist, A Devious Dictionary (1991).

This is the story of how decent men, remarkable builders, outstanding citizens, screwed up. And what it means to thee and me.

Walter Stewart, journalist, Prologue, referring to the collapse of the development company Olympia & York Investments, Toronto, *Too Big to Fail: Olympia & York: The Story Behind the Headlines* (1993).

We serve two million Canadians a day, but we serve them one at a time.

George Cohon, President, McDonald's Restaurants of Canada Ltd., interviewed in *The Canadian Jewish News*, 4 Nov. 1993.

If everything is predictable, then smart people are useful. But if everything is unpredictable, then adaptive people are essential.

Henry Mintzberg, management consultant, "Regarding Henry," *The Globe and Mail's Report on Business Magazine*, Oct. 1995.

Profitable projects are galactically higher in status than loser (not quite as profitable) projects.

Observation from **Douglas Coupland**'s novel *Microserfs* (1995).

By 1995, every hour of every day, seven days a week, for 365 days of the year, an average of $4.6-million left the country to pay for the foreign investment already in the country, a total outflow exceeding $40-billion. This figure does not include the business service costs directly associated with foreign ownership in Canada. Nor does it include the many billions of dollars in costs associated with purchases of goods from outside Canada due to intercorporate purchasing or transfer pricing.

Mel Hurtig, publisher and nationalist, speech made in 1990, *At Twilight in the Country: Memoirs of a Canadian Nationalist* (1996).

The government should be getting out of the business of being in business.

Characteristic remark of Alberta Premier **Ralph Klein**, as noted on CBC Radio's *This Morning*, 23 March 1998.

BUSINESS SCHOOLS

See also BUSINESS

MBA, n. An academic degree held by bankers who specialize in Third World overlending. The letters stand for Mexico, Brazil and Argentina.

David Olive, business commentator, *White Knights and Poison Pills: A Cynic's Dictionary of Business Jargon* (1990).

Business Schools... acting schools which train experts in abstract management methods to pretend they are capitalists.

John Ralston Saul, author, *The Doubter's Companion: A Dictionary of Aggressive Common Sense* (1994).

It was once suggested to me by Clare Westcott, a longtime aid to Premier Bill Davis of Ontario, that the Harvard Business School has done more to harm democracy than the Communist Party. This is a little unfair to Harvard, but not to the rhetorical excess explicit in mass 1980s business school theory. Mass neoconservative absolutism is guilty of a similar excess.

Hugh Segal, political adviser, *Beyond Greed: A Traditional Conservative Confronts Neoconservative Excess* (1997).

C

CAJUN CULTURE

Quebeckers point with horror at Louisiana as an example of what might have happened to them.... More to the point, French-Canadians might have been more culturally vigorous, rather than less, had they been less exclusive. Quebec, after all, though bigger in population than Louisiana (4.4 million), has made a far less formidable contribution to world culture (all that jazz).

John Grimond, U.K. journalist, commenting on the Cajun culture of Louisiana, "Nice Country, Nice Mess," *The Economist*, 29 June 1991.

CALGARY See also ALBERTA

Calgary...is as quiet as an English country village.... If liquor were sold, Calgary would be the rowdiest place in the Dominion. Prohibition makes it one of the quietiest, most respectable law-abiding places....

W.S. Caine, British parliamentarian and traveller, *A Trip around the World* (1887).

I wanted to see Calgary, anyhow, due to a painful perplexity as to whether Edmonton or Calgary is the finer city. I was so confused for, whenever I talked to an Edmontonian I was told that Edmonton is to Calgary as Paris is to Pittsburgh. Whenever I met a Calgarian I was assured that Calgary is to Edmonton as the New Jerusalem is to Newcastle. I therefore scrutinized both, asked many questions, especially about the climate from November to April and came to the conclusion that I would sooner live in vain than in either of them.

R.E. Knowles, journalist, *The Toronto Star*, 3 Oct. 1928.

With my wife and son I had left England for Canada only a few months before and we were none of us yet accustomed to the great steely neon-lit city which lay on the foothills of the Rockies more than three thousand feet up. The sky seemed higher and larger than our English skies, above the level of the clouds we knew, and the air was cold and fresh like lake water.

Passage from **Graham Greene**'s story "Dear Dr. Falkenheim" (1963), about an English family which settles in "Kosy Nuick," a suburb on the outskirts of Calgary, included in *Collected Stories* (1973).

Shout Calgary, this growing graveyard.

Aritha van Herk, novelist, *Places Far from Ellesmere: A Geografictione: Explorations on Site* (1990).

Can you imagine how much fun it was writing about Calgary in Paris? The word "Calgary," "cowboy boot"—all of these things I had repressed—suddenly became totally, deliciously exotic. I never would have believed it was possible to write a book about that.

Nancy Huston, Alberta-born, Paris-based novelist, quoted by Philip Marchand in *The Toronto Star*, 22 Oct. 1994. In Paris she wrote the same novel twice, once as *Plainsong* in English and once as *Cantique des plaines* in French.

CALIFORNIA See also HOLLYWOOD, UNITED STATES OF AMERICA

Parts of Los Angeles give me the feeling I'm living in a parking lot with neon signs.

Al Waxman, actor, quoted by Laura Berthold Monteros in *The Herald-Examiner*, 26 June 1977.

I'm in Los Angeles. I begin to doubt that I will ever get out.

Murray Campbell, writer, *The Globe and Mail's Destinations*, May 1992.

Los Angeles *is* the apocalyptic landscape, both geologically and socially. There you find a decay of the Western psyche, of that hierarchy of the soul.

Lines from the title song of the album *The Future* (1992) written by **Leonard Cohen**.

Los Angeles is full of Canadians. According to the Los Angeles chapter of the Academy of Canadian Cinema and Television, L.A. is now the third largest Canadian city.

Lesley Ellen Harris, screenwriter, "Made in L.A.," *The Canadian Forum*, Nov. 1993.

It is like Brampton with palm trees.

Carole Pope, singer-songwriter, quoting a friend's description of Los Angeles, noted by Richard Crouse, *Toronto Free Press*, Feb. 1996.

CALLAGHAN, MORLEY See also WRITERS & WRITING, CANADIAN

Strip the language, and make the style, the method, all the psychological ramifications, the ambience of the relationships, all the one thing, so the reader couldn't make separations. Cézanne's apples. The appleness of apples. Yet just apples.

Morley Callaghan, novelist and memorist, *That Summer in Paris: Memories of Tangled Relationships with Hemingway, Fitzgerald and Others* (1963).

The reviewer, at the end of this article, after trying to give an account of these books, is now wondering whether the primary reason for the current underestimation of Morley Callaghan may not be simply a general incapacity—apparently shared by his compatriots—for believing that a writer whose work may be mentioned without absurdity in association with Chekhov's and Turgenev's can possibly be functioning in Toronto.

Edmund Wilson, literary critic, *O Canada* (1965).

And once I met a writer who told me a famous New York editor had asked, "What in the world happened to Morley Callaghan?"

Morley Callaghan, novelist, "The Pleasures of Failure," *Maclean's*, 6 March 1965.

A character of reasonable dimensions, an honest sensible hard-nosed ego-bastard, a talented short-story writer, a good husband, a good Irish Catholic, a good college boxer, and a good expatriate.

Norman Mailer, novelist, on Morley Callaghan, "Punching Papa: A Review of That Summer in Paris," included in *The Long Patrol* (1971) edited by Robert F. Lucid.

I've always flourished.

Morley Callaghan, novelist, quoted by Zena Cherry in *The Globe and Mail*, 17 April 1975.

I've always wanted to go up strange new alleys in my novels. When there are no new alleys, that's the time to stop.

Morley Callaghan, novelist, quoted by Ken Adachi in *The Toronto Star*, 24 Sept. 1977.

CAMPBELL, KIM See also POLITICIANS

Charisma without substance is a dangerous thing.

Kim Campbell, M.P.P., addressing the B.C. Socred leadership convention at Whistler, B.C., which elected William Vander Zalm as its leader and B.C. Premier, July 1986, quoted by Jeff Sallot in *The Globe and Mail*, 18 March 1993. Campbell recalled her "charisma remark" when declaring her candidacy for the Conservative Party leadership in Vancouver, 25 March 1993. According to Hugh Winsor in *The Globe and Mail* the following day, she said: "My great fear was that I might become known as the candidate of substance without charisma."

Who needs a leadership race? I'll just stage a military coup. Don't mess with me. I have tanks.

Kim Campbell, Minister of National Defence, referring to her Conservative leadership intentions, 19 Jan. 1993, quoted by Robert Fife in *Kim Campbell: The Making of a Politician* (1993).

What I think this evening's debate reflects is a strong sense among the candidates that this race is a race within the family, and that at the end of the leadership campaign we will unite as a family to go forward and defeat not just the enemies of the Progressive Conservative party but the enemies of Canadians, and I use that term mildly I suppose.

Kim Campbell, Minister of National Defence and Conservative leadership candidate, leadership forum, Vancouver, 13 May 1993, quoted by Rosemary Speirs in *The Toronto Star*, 15 May 1993. This is the origin of Campbell's so-called "enemies of Canadians" jibe which was directed against citizens who disagreed with the debt and deficit-reduction policies of the Conservative Party. It was disavowed by Jean Charest and other leadership contenders and then by Campbell herself, who explained to reporters, "It was not what I meant to say. As soon as it was out of my mouth, I realized I'd used a stronger word than I meant to use.... I certainly wouldn't mean to offend anybody." Geoffrey York referred to the incident in *The Globe and Mail*, 15 May 1993: "It was an unfortunate echo of another Conservative politician—Prime Minister Brian Mulroney, who last year denounced critics of the Charlottetown constitutional accord as 'enemies of Canada.' Mr. Mulroney was forced to backtrack after using the phrase, which was widely perceived as a symbol of excessive political partisanship."

The more one saw of her the less there was, or so it seemed.

Mordecai Richler, author and journalist, referring to the Conservative leadership contender Kim Campbell, "Hail, Brian, and Farewell," *Saturday Night*, June 1993.

The difference between being the Prime Minister and not being the Prime Minister is that people actually applaud you for barbecuing.

Kim Campbell, Prime Minister, accepting applause for working a grill for two minutes during a photo opportunity at a barbecue, Scarborough, Ont., 23 July 1993, quoted by David Vienneau in *The Toronto Star* the following day.

Our day in the sun will come again I promise you.

Kim Campbell, Prime Minister, conceding electoral defeat, national television, Vancouver, B.C., 25 Oct. 1993, quoted by Ross Howard in *The Globe and Mail* the following day. After a stunning defeat in the general election that day, in which she lost not only her own seat but her Conservative Party lost all but two seats across the country, having been in power for 133 days, she added, "We have a responsibility to bind our wounds, perhaps snurf into a Kleenex, and then return to fight again."

Gee, I'm glad I didn't sell my car.

Kim Campbell, defeated Prime Minister, election night, CBC-TV's *The National*, 25 Oct. 1993. She owned a 1980 Honda Civic.

Ms. Campbell's last words as prime minister were, "Consider yourself hugged." The voters, in need of a hearing aid, must have thought she said "mugged." It's all our fault, I suppose.

Robert Mason Lee, columnist, "The West," *The Globe and Mail*, 27 May 1995.

Being a former prime minister is a bit like having gum on your shoe. It sticks to you... no matter what.

Kim Campbell, former Prime Minister, "The Wit and Wisdom of Kim Campbell," *The Toronto Sun*, 21 April 1996.

CAMPING

In ten years Dorset hasn't changed—it's almost the only place I've ever come back to that hasn't given me an empty feeling from discovering that nothing can be the same again.

E.B. White, writer, letter addressed to Harold Ross in New York from Camp Otter, Dorset, Ont., July 1929, *Letters* (1929) edited by Dorothy Lobrano Guth. White worked as a counselor at Camp Otter, a boy's camp, in the summers of 1920 and 1921 and returned for visits in 1929 and 1930.

CANADA

See also CANADA: ENGLISH; CANADA: FRENCH; CANADA & QUEBEC; CANADA & THE UNITED KINGDOM; CANADA & THE UNITED STATES; CANADA & THE WORLD; CANADIANISM; CANADIANS; CANADIANS & AMERICANS; CHARACTER, NATIONAL; DOMINION; FRENCH CANADIANS; NORTH AMERICA; QUEBEC & CANADA

Ka-Kanata

Iroquoian word, basis of the place-name Canada, said to mean "the land that is clean," according to Native spokesperson Harold Cardinal in *Divided We Stand* (1977) edited by Gary Geddes. This derivation is at odds with the standard etymology of the Iroquoian word *kanatas*, meaning "community" or "group of dwellings."

Even its name is a negative pun. In south German dialect, Keine dah ("nothing there") is pronounced "Kana dah." Portuguese explorers are supposed to have invented the name by saying acada nada ("nothing here"). In fact, Kanata! Kanata! (meaning something like "Yonder are our wigwams!") seem to have been the words spoken by Indians as they greeted Jacques Cartier in Stadacona in 1534.

William Kilbourn, historian, "The Peaceable Kingdom Still," *Daedalus: Journal of the American Academy of Arts and Sciences*, "In Search of Canada," Fall, 1988.

Corsica is of much greater interest than Canada.

Etienne-François, Duc de Choiseul, commentator, letter to Voltaire written following the signing of the Treaty of Paris, 10 Feb. 1763, quoted by Raymond Douville and Jacques Casanova in *Daily Life in Early Canada* (1968) translated by Carola Congreve.

Canada, at this day, is an exact picture of ancient Germany. Although situated in the same parallel with the finest provinces of France and England, that country experiences the most rigorous cold. The reindeer are very numerous, the ground is covered with deep and lasting snow, and the great river of St. Lawrence is regularly frozen, in a season when the waters of the Seine and the Thames are usually free from ice.

Edward Gibbon, historian, comparing in Chapter IX the state of Germany at the time of the Emperor Decius, *The Decline and Fall of the Roman Empire* (1776).

Canada has held, and always will retain, a foremost place in my remembrance. Few Englishmen are prepared to find it what it is. Advancing quietly… nothing of flush or fever in its system, but health and vigour throbbing in its steady pulse: it is full of hope and promise.

Charles Dickens, novelist and traveller, describing a visit to Eastern Canada in 1842, *American Notes for General Circulation* (1905).

Canada is one of the several places where, thanks to the valor and wisdom of our forefathers and to the labour and self-denial of our brethren elsewhere, a certain place has been secured in which a man may sit down and grow strong and wise against whatever chances may befall him.

Rudyard Kipling, author and imperialist, "Canada's Path to Nationhood," 21 Oct. 1907, *Addresses Delivered before the Canadian Club of Ottawa: 1903–1909* (1910).

She is a little too modest.

Rudyard Kipling, author and imperialist, visit of 1907–08, *Letters to the Family: Notes on a Recent Trip to Canada* (1910).

Canada, fifty years ago, was naive, touchy, longing to be praised, young. "What do you think of us?" (said immediately before one had even thought). I always found myself nearly saying, "I think you're a bore."

Enid Bagnol, English author, referring to her honeymoon trip to Canada in 1920, *Autobiography* (1969).

There is really no means of describing the immensity of this great lovely country.

Freya Stark, traveller and writer, letter written after a train journey from Quebec City to a ranch near Creston, B.C., 4 Nov. 1928, *Beyond Euphrates* (1951).

However, I may indulge in a generality and say with conviction that Canada being a young country is full of possibilities that are incalculable. She has neither exhausted her material resources nor those of her mind and character. She has not yet produced in her psychology the self-toxin of fatigue that old civilizations suffer from in the shape of cynicism and spiritual insensitiveness. Her creative youth is still before her, and the faith needed for building up a new world is still fresh and strong.

Rabindranath Tagore, Bengali poet, "Message of Farewell to Canada," Farewell Address to the Fourth Triennial Conference of the National Council of Education of Canada, Vancouver, 14 April 1929; P.C. Mahalanobis, editor, *Visva-Bharati*, Bulletin No. 14, reprinted 1977.

I have been wonderfully received in Canada. Never in my whole life have I been welcomed with so much genuine interest and admiration as throughout this vast country. I am greatly attracted to this country. Immense developments are going forward. There are fortunes to be made in many directions. The tide is flowing strongly.

Winston Churchill, English statesman, letter written from Canada to his wife, Clementine, late 1929, quoted by Alexander Rose, "Winston's Great Canadian Love Affair," *National Post*, 1 May 1999.

Canada's social system stands in sore need of repair.

Reinhold Niebuhr, clergyman, interviewed by R.E. Knowles in *The Toronto Star*, 11 Aug. 1934.

It is clear, to my mind, that the countries which in the future are destined to play a mighty part in world affairs are what we now called the "small" parts—but highly industrialized. And, among these, due chiefly to her infinite plains and prairies, Canada is destined for a foremost place.

André Malraux, French intellectual, interviewed in Toronto by R.E. Knowles in *The Toronto Star*, 2 April 1937.

Canada, the most damned boring country there is….

Louis-Ferdinand Céline, French novelist and fascist, who may or may not have visited Quebec in the 1920s, remark made in the 1930s, quoted by

Frédéric Vitoux in *Céline: A Biography* (1992) translated by Jesse Browner.

I think this about Canada's future—that your country is eligible, in the next twenty-five years—for just about the greatest expansion of any country in the world.

Thomas J. Watson, founder of IBM, interviewed by R.E. Knowles in *The Toronto Star*, 28 Nov. 1938.

I'm thinking hard about the future. This may be the Country. There's so much that is unknown about it—& it is tremendously large & beautiful. And it is enterprising & vital.

Benjamin Britten, English composer, letter written from Toronto, 20 June 1939, quoted by Humphrey Carpenter in *Benjamin Britten: A Biography* (1992). Britten spent about a week in Toronto working on a commission from CBC Radio. As well, he completed the orchestral work *Canadian Carnival*, Opus 19. In a Toronto hotel he and the singer Peter Pears consummated their relationship.

Canada on the whole, it could be said, is busy decanadianizing itself, without being quite ready to abandon the certain advantages of standing apart and politically remaining "Canadian."

Wyndham Lewis, British author and artist, "Nature's Place in Canadian Culture" (1940–44), *Wyndham Lewis in Canada* (1971) edited by George Woodcock.

The most parochial nationette on earth.

Wyndham Lewis, author and artist, resident of the country during World War II, quoted by C.J. Fox in "Through Toronto's Fire and Ice," *The Beaver*, Dec. 1996–Jan. 1997.

Parents unmarried and living abroad, / relatives keen to bag the estate, / schizophrenia not excluded, / will he learn to grow up before it's too late?

Lines from "Canada: Case History: 1945" by **Earle Birney** in *The Collected Poems of Earle Birney* (1975). A quarter-century later Birney was even more pessimistic in "Canada: Case History: 1972": "one moment murderous, the next depressed, / this youth, we fear, has moved from adolescence / into what looks like permanent senescence."

Canada is a broad land—broad in mind and in spirit as well as in physical expanse.

Harry S. Truman, U.S. President, address, joint sitting of the Senate and the House of Commons, 11 June 1947.

She's not interested in all that horse manure about Canada.

Line spoken by the labourer Archie about a letter from a friend who settled in Canada and opened hotels in Toronto and Ottawa in **John Osborne**'s play *The Entertainer* (1957).

Canada is a country where perfectly astounding things are happening to our culture.

Edmund Wilson, American critic, remark made during Summer 1963 while writing *O Canada: An American's Notes on Canadian Culture* (1965), to Richard Hauer Costa who reported the remark in "A Kind of Nationalist," *The Canadian Forum*, Nov. 1980.

Canada is a society rather than a nation. Its coherence depends on a communications system in which the radio and television networks of the Canadian Broadcasting Corporation play a supremely important part. There is no central and controlling myth to focus Canadian diversity and foster its distinctiveness: the Crown, which in theory symbolizes the State, is an absentee landlord.

Kildare Dobbs, essayist, Introduction, *Canada* (1964).

Beneath the warmth of its welcome and the impressive façade of its economic achievement, Canada could not conceal from me the weaknesses of its structure and situation.

Charles de Gaulle, President of France, writing about his third and penultimate trip to Canada in 1960, *Memoirs of Hope: Renewal, 1958–62: Endeavour 1962–* (1970) translated by Terence Kilmartin.

And sometimes I think of myself as a very perplexed man, but now, perhaps because I am in Canada, I think of myself as being quite a happy man and full of hope for the future.

Jorge Luis Borges, Argentine author, interviewed for CBC Radio in Montreal in 1968 by Don Bell, "A Master in Montreal," *National Post*, 24 Aug. 1999.

My generation of Canadians grew up believing that, if we were very good or very smart, or both, we would someday graduate from Canada.

Robert Fulford, columnist and editor, referring to intellectual life in English Canada in the 1950s, "Notebook," *Saturday Night*, Oct. 1970.

No one will ever write a book called Canada's Second Century; there won't be one.

Attributed to **Donald G. Creighton** upon the publication of his book *Canada's First Century: 1867–1967* (1970).

Thousands of miles of wheat, indifference, and self-apology.

Thoughts of a character in **Mordecai Richler**'s novel *St. Urbain's Horseman* (1971).

But Canada as an entity still has value as the DEW Line for the rest of the world, we have the situation of relatively small involvement in the big headaches. The Canadian has freedom of comment, a kind of playful awareness of issues, that is unknown in, say, Paris or London or New York. They take themselves too damn seriously; they have no choice. Here you have a little time to breathe, to think and to feel.

Marshall McLuhan, communications pioneer, quoted by Peter C. Newman in "The Table Talk of Marshall McLuhan," *Maclean's*, June 1971.

Well, you know, states are not immortal... I don't think Canada will last forever. I just want it to last in my time and in my children's time... I don't want to have to answer to my children when they say, "Well, gee, Dad, you were around, you were in politics in the 1970s and you let this country split up... why did you let it happen?"... I don't want that to be.

Pierre Elliott Trudeau, Prime Minister, interview, 19 Oct. 1976.

We are not so much existentialists in our individual lives as in our version of nationhood. Canada invents itself daily. Perhaps the newspaper is our poem, our weather the poem's subject.

Robert Kroetsch, author and poet, "Canada Is a Poem," *Divided We Stand* (1977) edited by Gary Geddes.

Canada is not yet a country that asks for and uses all the possibilities of its people.

Robertson Davies, man-of-letters, quoted by Geraldine Anthony in *Stage Voices: Twelve Canadian Playwrights Talk about Their Lives and Work* (1978).

This country has been like a woman waiting at a window of an old house at a crossroads. She is an ageless wild hard beauty. Men riding by come to her in the night. They use her, but never really possess her. They leave her and ride on, afraid of her fierce domination over them, knowing they can't handle her; she leaves them feeling small, so she is like the old woman who lived in a shoe: she has had so many children she doesn't know what to do because none of them want to claim her and call her "Mother."

Morley Callaghan, novelist, "Canada," *The Toronto Star*, 1 July 1978.

Canada is really a small country in a large overcoat.

Sylvia Fraser, novelist, address, Harvard University, Nov. 1981, quoted in "F.Y.I.," *The Ottawa Citizen*, 9 Aug. 1994.

Canada, noun. A socialist protectorate full of nice people and clean streets, with no crime except teevee.

R.W. Jackson, American writer, *The Diabolical Dictionary of Modern English* (1986).

In older countries the future was inherited, largely predetermined by the past. Here, if we had the will, we could still choose what we would become.

George Galt, journalist and traveller, concluding sentences, *Whistlestop: A Journey across Canada* (1987).

Today, Canada is recognized almost everywhere as a major power, uncomfortable as we may be with that notion, modest as we may be about the reasons for it.

Allan Gotlieb, Canadian Ambassador in Washington, D.C., address, Canadian Club of Ottawa, reported in *The Globe and Mail*, 29 Oct. 1987.

I don't want to go on too much about Canada. I don't want too many people to find out what a jewel it is. We've got unlimited natural resources. No titanium, though. That's what we need—that aircraft metal.

Dan Aykroyd, Ottawa-born movie actor, comedy routine, quoted by Jay Carr in *The Toronto Star*, 19 June 1988.

Canada is the Switzerland of the twentieth century, surrounded by the great powers of the world and preserving its identity by having many identities.

Northrop Frye, cultural critic, "Levels of Cultural Identity" (1989), *The Eternal Act of Creation: Essays, 1979–1990* (1993) edited by Robert D. Denham.

Well, it's still a good place to live, but that's all Canada is now—just a good place to live.

Donald G. Creighton, historian, observation made in 1979, the year of his death, to the cultural journalist Charles Taylor, *Radical Tories* (1992).

I do not remember any other time in history when a nation disintegrated merely through a lack of will to survive, nor do I think ours will.

Northrop Frye, cultural critic, Entry 261, Notebook 1991, *Northrop Frye Newsletter*, Summer 1997.

I want Canada to be a country where people who want to work can find jobs, a country where future generations won't have to debate whether or not there is such a thing as the Canadian identity. Perhaps most of all, I want Canada to be a nation where the vast majority of Canadians can translate their love for their country into real democratic power.

Mel Hurtig, nationalist, *The Betrayal of Canada* (1991).

You don't love Canada; you are part of Canada, and that's that.

Thoughts of the narrator of **Robertson Davies**' novel *Murther & Walking Spirits* (1991).

The great challenge in the next fifty years politically is: Are you going to become the fifty-first state or are you going to remain a nation?

Ralph Nader, consumer advocate, speech, Upper Canada College, Toronto, Feb. 1991, quoted by Bill Taylor in *The Toronto Star*, 12 Dec. 1992.

The idea of Canada as a model for mankind is a grand one—worth defending far more passionately than many of us, or our leaders, do.

Keith Spicer, commissioner, *Citizens' Forum on Canada's Future: Report to the People and Government of Canada*, published as a special feature of *The Toronto Star, The Globe and Mail*, and other newspapers, 29 June 1991.

What's a nice country like Canada doing in a mess like this?

Editorial, "Nice Country, Nice Mess," *The Economist*, 29 June 1991. The "mess" appeared to be the conflict between the new neo-conservative economy and the old reliance on federal spending to maintain traditional differences with the United States.

Canada can't operate this way, because the country never made sense as a profit-making business. Canada was never about just making money; it was about creating a truly new country based on two cultural groups, the French and the English, and enriching it with adventurous peoples from other nations.

Adrienne Clarkson, author and television personality, "Are We Selling Out?" *Homemaker's Magazine*, Oct. 1991.

There is a certain genius in the Canadian political culture which helps to explain the extraordinary resilience it has shown in dealing so constructively and for so long with the stresses and strains of cultural and regional pluralism.

Charles, Prince of Wales, address at Queen's University, Kingston, 28 Oct. 1991, published in *The Globe and Mail* the following day.

Most countries are problems in search of a solution. Canada seems to be a solution in search of a problem.

Thomas d'Aquino, President, Business Council on National Issues, quoted in University of Guelph's "Canada" supplement, *The Globe and Mail*, 4 Dec. 1991.

As for the "political nation" of Cartier and McGee, it is 125 years old, the oldest federation in the world and the only one never to experience a civil war.

Desmond Morton, historian, "One Nation? Two? Any?" *The Toronto Star*, 7 Feb. 1992.

Belgium is well-endowed with ennui, one is seldom thrilled by dispatches from Portugal or Switzerland; but nothing makes your average foreigner turn the page more abruptly than the looming threat of an Ottawa dateline.

Jan Morris, Anglo-Welsh traveller, "In Praise of Canada," *The Toronto Star*, 15 June 1992.

Canada might be described as the Switzerland of the world. To the east is China and Japan; to the west is Europe; to the south is the United States; and to the north is the Arctic, the North Pole, and ultimately the Soviet Union.

David Ketterer, critic, *Canadian Science Fiction and Fantasy* (1992).

Canada is a country that is probably too big for small minds. Canada is a country that is probably too varied for simple minds.

Roch Carrier, novelist, quoted by Ron Graham in *The French Quarter* (1992).

Three oceans, millions of lakes, vast plains, virgin forests, the Rockies, the shores of the St. Lawrence River, and four well-defined seasons: these gifts from the gods form a great nation. Add to them a soul sculpted by three thousand years of Amerindian, Greco-Latin and western culture, and the result is Canada, a shining hour in the history of the world.

Antonine Maillet, folklorist, *Canada: A Portrait: The Official Handbook of Present Conditions and Recent Progress* (54th edition, 1992).

This is not Romania, or Patagonia, or Uganda. It's Canada. You've got what I call a national psychic strike. English Canada has become a crèche, a permanent daycare.

Scott Symons, author, "Deliquescence in Canada," *The Idler*, July–Aug. 1992.

A bad day in Canada is better than a good day in any other country on the globe.

Richard Berryman, columnist, paraphrasing the message on a bumpersticker, *The Hamilton Spectator*, 10 Oct. 1992.

The Forum in Montreal, Vancouver from the sky, Toronto on the ground, Ottawa by the river, Winnipeg over the phone.

Michael J. Fox, movie personality and resident of Los Angeles, interviewed about what he likes best about his native Canada, quoted by Dan Dugas in *The Toronto Star*, 27 Dec. 1992.

A tremendous Canada of light.

Line from the novel *The Adventures of Augie March* (1953) written by former Quebecer **Saul Bellow**, deployed by commentator B.W. Powe as the title of his book of 1993 essays.

Canada today is understood better as being composed of two quite different kinds of societies—an ethnic, European-style nation in Quebec, and a "rest of Canada" that is well on the way to becoming a multi-ethnic World Nation.

Richard Gwyn, columnist, "Home & Away," *The Toronto Star*, 31 Jan. 1993.

It is said that on a world menu, Canada would be the vichyssoise. It's cold, half-French and difficult to stir....

Simon Mills, journalist, *The Sunday Times Magazine*, 3–4 July 1993, quoted by Jim Sheppard in the *Winnipeg Free Press*, 5 July 1993.

Canadians should be natural SF writers, I think, because this country has been shaped, from its inception, by the kind of utopian dreams one encounters only in the most visionary scientific romances.... In short, Canada itself is a continent-spanning megaproject on a truly science-fictional scale. Perhaps Canada is a work of science fiction.

Glenn Grant, anthologist, Introduction, *Northern Stars: The Anthology of Canadian Science Fiction* (1994) edited by David G. Hartwell and Glenn Grant.

Canada is widely thought to be one of the best countries in which to live. In 1994, the United Nations Development Programme measured the quality of life around the world, using a variety of social and economic indicators. Canada placed first.

United Nations Development Programme, *Human Development Report 1994* (1994). "In the three UNDP reports published from 1991 to 1993, Canada was ranked either first or second," in the words of *Gathering Strength: Volume 3: Report of the Royal Commission on Aboriginal Peoples* (1996), co-chaired by René Dessault and Georges Erasmus.

My Canada serves as the conscience for the continent. It has a good welfare system, the best medical services, the safest cities and a new government that promises to create jobs. It can also have a civilized discussion about the status of Quebec—a debate we enjoy watching down here.

John Kenneth Galbraith, Ontario-born economist at Harvard University, "My Canada Includes...," *Maclean's*, 3 Jan. 1994.

Canada. 1. Corresponds primarily to whatever an individual thinks of Canada or Canadians (i.e., associated with the north, cold, haven of safety, etc.) 2. May be indicative of a foreign visa or travel. 3. Might be associated with crossing the border (i.e., going out of bounds or over the line).

Kevin J. Todeschi, scholar, *The Encyclopedia of Symbolism III* (1995).

Unless it is rediscovered, and quickly, this mythic place called Canada may indeed fragment or dissolve into the United States. Or it may continue to exist on maps for decades and even centuries to come, and no one will be able to remember why.

Ron Graham, commentator, *All the King's Horses: Politics among the Ruins* (1995).

Canada has shown the world how to balance freedom with compassion and tradition with innovation, in your efforts to provide health care to all your citizens, to treat your senior citizens with the dignity and respect they deserve, to take on tough issues like the move afoot to outlaw automatic weapons designed for killing and not hunting....

Bill Clinton, U.S. President, address, House of Commons, 23 February 1995, as published in *The Globe and Mail* the following day.

Canada is the largest country in the world that doesn't exist.

Richard Rodriguez, American social commentator of Mexican-Indian background, commenting on the notion that minority groups overtake majority groups, interviewed by Neil Bissoondath on TVO's *Markings*, 3 July 1995.

Canada is in a perpetual crisis and has always been difficult to govern.

Jean Chrétien, Prime Minister, CTV's year-end interview, 26 Dec. 1995, quoted prior to telecast by Edison Stewart in *The Toronto Star*, 19 Dec. 1995.

It's like something terrible is about to happen, this huge heavy ugly gray thing shaped like a tyrannosaurus rex or the country of Canada on the map is hovering over the entire United States of America and is about to fall or break apart and avalanche down on me and cut off my breath....

Thoughts of a character in **Russell Banks**'s novel *Rule of the Bone* (1996).

It has often been said, usually by foreigners, that Canada is a nation in search of a problem. As the year ends, it certainly is a country in search of a major fix. No one really seems to know what to do.

Robert Lewis, editor, "From the Editor," *Maclean's*, 1 Jan. 1996. The magazine's special report was titled "Can Canada Survive?"

Canada, the Country that Dares Not Speak its Name

Title of the lead editorial that dealt with the unwillingness of the federal government to act on behalf of national interests lest it irk Quebec, *The Globe and Mail*, 10 Feb. 1996.

I have not sufficiently visited Canada. You have cleaner air here; you are somehow more civilized. I was handed a copy of your, er *Mail and Globe*? There was an English solidity to it. It has a pleasing un-American feel, the kind of newspaper that hangs on a stick in a men's club.

John Updike, novelist, visiting Toronto, quoted by Val Ross in *The Globe and Mail*, 14 Feb. 1996.

What an enigma Canada is.... Perhaps the very term "Canada" is an anomaly, for it suggests a monolithic identity at dramatic odds with the country's heterogeneity.

Joyce Carol Oates, novelist, "Out of Canada," *The Times Literary Supplement*, 23 Feb. 1996.

Canada is not a country for the cold of heart or the cold of feet.

Attributed to former Prime Minister **Pierre Elliott Trudeau** on a poster exhibited at the Tattered Cover Book Store, Denver, Colorado, June 1996.

Canada is a country that works in practice but not in theory.

Aphorism characteristic of the 1990s that has been used in public addresses by Intergovernmental Affairs Minister **Stéphane Dion**, as noted by columnist Gordon Gibson in *The Globe and Mail*, 9 June 1996. Gibson protested that the reverse is true in that Canada works smoothly in theory but less efficiently in practice.

Then we may say that Canada's hidden destiny is to follow a path that diverges from egotism and violence, and to build a place where people could say, "All the forces and contradictions, the qualities and contrasts of our souls exist here side by side."

B.W. Powe, essayist, *A Canada of Light* (1997).

Canada is above all an idea of what a country could be, a place of imagination. In spite of a recurring desire to find outside inspiration, it is very much its own invention.

John Ralston Saul, commentator, *Reflections of a Siamese Twin: Canada at the End of the Twentieth Century* (1997).

The truth is Canada is cloud-cuckoo-land, an insufferably rich country governed by idiots, its self-made problems offering comic relief to the ills of the world out there, where famine and racial strife and vandals in office are the unhappy rule.

Thoughts of a character in **Mordecai Richler**'s novel *Barney's Version* (1997).

The whole world should invent Canadas. We already have one. We shouldn't lose it.

Stéphane Dion, Minster of Intergovernmental Affairs, address, Quebec Liberal Party meeting, 7 Dec. 1997, quoted by Graham Fraser in *The Globe and Mail* the following day.

Canada has most of the efficiency of America without its inhumanity, and most of the humanity of the British system without its inefficiency.

David Foot, demographer and author, giving reasons why he settled in Canada after being born in Australia and studying at Harvard, interviewed by Michael Posner in *The Globe and Mail*, 7 Feb. 1998.

Canada over the last thirty years has been the best place to live since the dawn of humankind. The best, of all time, anywhere.... They valued social welfare and added that "Halifax is among the best cities in Canada in which to live."

Peter and **Terry March**, philosophers, "Ask a Philosopher," *The Halifax Daily News*, 7 June 1999.

Canada has rarely been the promised land. About the closest we've come is the title of Wayne Johnston's 1998 novel *The Colony of Unrequited Dreams*.

Margaret Atwood, author, "Survival, Then and Now," *Maclean's*, 1 July 1999.

Canada has shown the world how people of different cultures and languages can live in peace, prosperity, and mutual respect.

Bill Clinton, U.S. President, address, conference on federalism, Mont-Tremblant, Que., 8 Oct. 1999, quoted in *The Toronto Star* the following day.

We must not see ourselves as a small country of 30 million people, floundering in a large land mass. We are among the healthiest, best-educated people in the world, with great natural riches. We have two of the world's great languages. We must not see ourselves as people who simply react to trends but as people who can initiate them. We must not see ourselves as people to whom things are done but as people who do things.

Adrienne Clarkson, Governor General, installation address, Ottawa, 7 Oct. 1999, printed in the *National Post* the following day.

CANADA: ENGLISH

See also CANADA, FRENCH & ENGLISH CANADA

A vast collective hesitation.

André Laurendeau, co-chairman of the Royal Commission on Bilingualism and Biculturalism in 1967–70, referring to English Canada, quoted by Gary Geddes in the introduction to *Divided We Stand* (1977).

My observation as regards Canada is that the English-origin people there are—purely as a group—the best people in the country. The English in Canada are not perfect, but they are—in their behaviour and attitudes—the true issue of a race that, beginning with Henry II, brought all people to an even more meaningful equality.

A.E. van Vogt, Prairie-born science-fiction author, *Reflections of A.E. van Vogt* (1975).

What a lot of Frenchification is going on these days!

This includes the tendency to slew certain names around backasswards such as Radio Canada, Air Canada, Hotel Newfoundland, Hill Signal, Brook Corner, Current Swift and so on.

Ray Guy, humorist, "It Takes All Kinds," *That Far Greater Bay* (1976).

There is no English Canadian culture. And that is why today's Canada is an impossible country. On the one hand there is Quebec culture and on the other American culture, of which English Canada represents the backwoods.

Victor-Lévy Beaulieu, Quebec author, *The Toronto Star*, 5 Jan. 1978.

English Canada should build a country—then maybe we would want to be part of it. Be creative—build your own identity. Believe in yourselves and then maybe we'll believe in you, too. The day you believe in Canada as much as I believe in Quebec, ninety per cent of your problems will go away.

Pierre Bourgault, separatist, interviewed following the defeat of the First Referendum, quoted by Hugh Winsor in *The Globe and Mail*, 21 May 1980.

The English Canada is a little like one of those land mines left over from the Second World War, which still turn up from time to time. No trouble if you don't kick it too hard. But like the mine we go off with a considerable bang if detonated. Left alone we tick quietly away, submerged and inoffensive.

Thoughts of a character in **Edward Phillips**' novel *Sunday's Child* (1981).

TROC

Acronym for The Rest of Canada (that is, Canada minus the Province of Quebec), used by political advisers in Ottawa, Fall 1990, according to Eric Kierans on CBC Radio's *Morningside*, 4 Dec. 1990.

In TROC, Canada wasn't an agreement between two entities, it was an arrangement among ten.

Peter Gzowski, journalist and host of CBC Radio's *Morningside*, using the acronym TROC (The Rest of Canada), "Whistling Down the Northern Lights," *The Fourth Morningside Papers* (1991).

My great preoccupation is the difficulty of finding a consensus in English Canada, because English Canada as such does not exist.

Benoît Bouchard, Minister of Industry, Science and Technology, interviewed in Montreal by Graham Fraser in *The Globe and Mail*, 7 March 1991.

Today, English Canada might be more correctly referred to as The Rest of Canada, or TROCANA.

Charles Pachter, artist and essayist, *The Globe and Mail*, 28 March 1991.

Canada outside Quebec

Collective description of the nine provinces and two territories of Canada, abbreviated COQ, pronounced "cock." The phrase alone is cited by columnist Lysiane Gagnon in "Inside Quebec," *The Globe and Mail*, 1 June 1991.

In Quebec, we speak blithely of English Canada, but the people who live there do not identify with this title. We need a handy way of referring to the rest of the country as an entity, even if it lacks for the moment political expression.

Charles Taylor, McGill philosopher, quoted by Alan Freeman in *The Globe and Mail*, 29 June 1991. The expression favoured by Taylor is COQ (Canada outside Quebec).

It's all a rock. In my view the appellation is Canada. I reject the implication that Canada is somehow not viable without Quebec. If Quebec secedes, it's still Canada.

Michael Bliss, historian, quoted by Alan Freeman in *The Globe and Mail*, 29 June 1991.

Can'a.... It seemed to me that it was about right. You take out roughly 25 per cent of the country, it's a little to the right of centre and it's a very awkward-looking thing. And it looks a little Middle Eastern."

Peter Howitt, economist, University of Western Ontario, arguing that Canada Without Quebec should be called "Can'a," according to Alan Freeman in *The Globe and Mail*, 29 June 1991.

Consider the bizarre pool of words left to Canadians outside Quebec. ROC (Rest Of Canada) sounds like a pile of leftovers, and does not reflect the fact that the people it designates are three times as numerous as

Quebec's. "English Canada" is not accurate either, because it obliterates the Quebec English-speaking minority and the French-speaking minorities in other provinces. (This expression does not ignore ethnic minorities because their common language is English.) Some say "Canada Without Quebec" or "Canada Outside Quebec," but these terms are as flawed and illogical as ROC.

Lysiane Gagnon, columnist, "Inside Quebec," *The Globe and Mail*, 3 Aug. 1991.

They call us an "endangered species" and "a vanishing breed." We are the "Urban Anglos," a little pocket of English-speaking Montrealers, struggling for survival against an onslaught of political rhetoric—pawns in the battle for control of Quebec's cultural industries.

Arden Ryshpan, social activist, "The Life of an Urban Anglo," *Actrascope*, Fall 1991.

The rest of Canada, also known as Rocadia, now has to face the prospect of going it alone.

Angeline Fournier-Tombs and **George Tombs**, commentators, offering a new form of TROC (The Rest Of Canada), *The Globe and Mail*, 31 Jan. 1992.

There will be no separation / Let the whole world come and see / My name is Johnny Maple / And I love my fleur-de-lis.

Stompin' Tom Connors, composer and performer, "Johnny Maple" from the album *Believe in Your Country* (1992), quoted by Malcolm McNeil in *The Globe and Mail*, 9 June 1992.

In the rest of Canada, which I prefer to call MOC, Most of Canada, everyone is an immigrant, native peoples excepted. The injunction of our multiculturalism law—that "there is no such thing as an official culture"—gives our own "old stock," the Anglo-Celts, no greater claim to "own" the country than a Somali refugee just off the board.

Richard Gwyn, columnist, "Home & Away," *The Toronto Star*, 31 Jan. 1993.

A key characteristic of English-Canadians (or whomever) is that they are the only people in the country who have only one country. All immigrants are linked to their ancestral homeland. All Quebeckers have *deux pays*, Canada and that part where they feel themselves *maîtres chez nous*. All native people retain, at least in their memory, an image of another country. Only English-Canadians are here alone, emotionally and psychically.

Richard Gwyn, columnist and author, *Nationalism without Walls: The Unbearable Lightness of Being Canadian* (1995).

English-Canadian is now the only hyphen banned from official usage.

Richard Gwyn, columnist and author, *Nationalism without Walls: The Unbearable Lightness of Being Canadian* (1995).

It's time for us to look at the other side of that "default" position and look at ourselves. Once known as English Canadians, now correctly called other Canadians, we have never done this. In the expressive phrase of University of British Columbia political scientist Phil Resnick, we are, "The nation that dares not speak its name."

Richard Gwyn, columnist, "Home and Away," *The Toronto Star*, 21 Jan. 1996.

I've never met an English-speaking Canadian. But I'm sure they are as nice as any other foreigners.

Remark made to an American journalist at the time of the 1995 referendum by Lucien Bouchard's mother, Lac Saint-Jean, Que., noted by John Ralston Saul in *Reflections of a Siamese Twin* (1997).

CANADA: FRENCH

See also CANADA, FRANCE, FRENCH & ENGLISH CANADA, NEW FRANCE, QUEBEC

Canadien, -ne / 1. Settler of French origin in New France as opposed to transient French administrators and missionaries. / 2. Inhabitants of Canada of French origin as opposed to the English.

Léandre Bergeron, lexicographer, *The Québécois Dictionary* (1982).

Gradually there grew up in Auclair's mind the picture of a country vast and free. He fell into a habit of looking to Canada as a possible refuge, an escape from the evils one suffered at home, and of wishing he could go there.

Lines descriptive of a French physician's image of life during the Old Regime in New France while attending an ailing Count de Frontenac at

Versailles, from **Willa Cather**'s historical novel *Shadows on the Rock* (1946).

"I am not the problem," I remember barking to Gérald Godin, the poet in René Lévesque's Parti Québécois Cabinet, "Michael Jackson is the problem."

Peter Gzowski, journalist and host of CBC Radio's *Morningside*, "Whistling Down the Northern Lights," *The Fourth Morningside Papers* (1991).

When duality dies, Canada dies.

Eric Kierans, former cabinet minister, "Blueprints for a Nation," *The Globe and Mail*, 18 Sept. 1993.

There is no lazy judgement to be made about French Canada, that vibrant, prickly, and separatist enclave of French civilization in an Anglo-Saxon world, any more than there is about Dutch South Africa, a society to which it bears in certain fundamentals a striking resemblance.

John Keegan, British historian, *Travels of a Military Historian in North America* (1995).

Whatever may be said—fairly or unfairly—about the rest, French Canada is almost too full of character for comfort.

John Keegan, British historian, *Travels of a Military Historian in North America* (1995), as quoted in *Saturday Night*, July–Aug. 1995.

CANADA & QUEBEC See also CANADA, DISTINCT SOCIETY, PARTITION, QUEBEC, QUEBEC & CANADA

The population of Canada is no more than a million and is divided into two hostile nations. The rigours of the climate limit the expansion of its territory and shut its ports for six months of the year.

Alexis de Tocqueville, French traveller, *Democracy in America* (1835) translated by George Lawrence and edited by J.P. Mayer and Max Lerner in 1966.

If the English and the French inhabitants of Canada cannot live under each other's government, which ought to give way?

John Stuart Mill, political economist, "Radical Party and Canada: Lord Durham" (1838), *Essays on England, Ireland, and the Empire* (1982), edited by John M. Robson, Volume VI of the "Collected Works of John Stuart Mill."

Two solitudes.

The words "two solitudes" were introduced into intellectual discourse to refer to the mutual isolation of the French and English by author and essayist **Hugh MacLennan** in his novel *Two Solitudes* (1945). MacLennan took the phrase from a letter from the German poet Rainer Maria Rilke written 14 May 1904, which appears in *Letters to a Young Poet* (1934), translated by M.D. Herter Norton. Rilke wrote about "the love that consists in this, that two solitudes protect and touch and greet each other."

MacLennan twice discussed the phrase. In an essay in *Century 1867–1967* (1967), he wrote, "Our old division into two solitudes now seems to me to have been a blessing in disguise. It makes uniformity impossible in Canada. What lacked in the past was love and mutual respect. What must come in the future—it is coming now, as a matter of fact—is affection and understanding." In an essay in *Maclean's*, Aug. 1971, he argued that Rilke's phrase is "surely the best practical definition of love ever uttered, whether applied to individuals or to two nations sharing a single state." It is difficult to imagine a time when the phrase will not be applicable to Canadian dualism.

There are not two histories, but one history, as there are not two Canadas, or any great number, but only one. Nor are there two ways of life, but one common response to land and history expressed in many strong variations of the one, it is true, but still one central substance.

W.L. Morton, historian, *The Canadian Identity* (1961).

How come we can't talk to each other any more? / We've got by far too long to end it feeling wrong / And I still share too much with you. // Just one great river always flowing to the sea. / One single river flowing in eternity.

First verse and refrain of "Song for Canada," a patriotic lyric about French-English relations, words by **Peter Gzowski** and music by Ian Tyson, sung by Ian on the Ian & Sylvia album *Early Morning Rain* (1965). The text appeared in *Song to a Seagull: A Book of Canadian Songs and Poems* (1970) edited by Robert Evans.

We are just like two trains on parallel tracks that will never meet.

Adapted from a remark made by Quebec Premier **René Lévesque** about the French and the English in Canada, First Ministers Conference, Ottawa, 13 Dec. 1976, as noted in *The Toronto Star* the following day.

All we want is an independent Quebec within a strong and united Canada.

Yvon Deschamps, comic, quoted by Peter C. Newman in *Maclean's*, 13 Nov. 1978. In French: "Un Québec indépendant dans un Canada uni!"

Rivalry between French and English has done as much for this country as wheat. And I wouldn't want to see all of it ground down, blended, bleached, processed into uniformity, wrapped in plastic, and sold as a substitute for real national development.

Peter Desbarats, journalist, address, Empire Club of Canada, Toronto, 7 Dec. 1978.

The independence we envisage is the only way possible to us because, as I said when I spoke to American businessmen in January 1977, "Canada and Quebec cannot continue to live like two scorpions in the same bottle," to borrow from Churchill's metaphor.

René Lévesque, Quebec Premier, *My Quebec* (1979).

English Canada won't give in until it has a knife at its throat. If we come to the conclusion that Canada is not ready, not willing to negotiate something very serious with Quebec, then let's go straight to a referendum on independence.

Léon Dion, social scientist, Laval University, constitutional adviser to the Bourassa government, testifying before the Bélanger-Campeau Commission on the future of Quebec, 12 Dec. 1990. He favoured a "profoundly renewed federalism," according to Philip Authier in *Montreal Gazette*, 13 Dec. 1990.

My Canada includes Quebec.

Message on fifteen billboards in eleven cities across Canada (in Quebec the message read "Mon Canada comprend le Québec") co-sponsored by Ontario trucking firm owner **Jim Taylor** and the outdoor advertising firm **Mediacom**, as noted by John Godfrey, "Nation's Business," *The Financial Post*, 29 Nov. 1991.

Being an English Quebecker is like living in a hotel. It's comfortable for the moment, but you always know that some day you will have to leave.

Ron Graham, author, *The French Quarter* (1992).

Quebec is *bored* blind by English Canadians. They can't believe how completely we've been selling out, teaspoon by teaspoon over twenty-five years.

Scott Symons, author, "Deliquescence in Canada," *The Idler*, July–Aug. 1992.

Canada is a dream in the making. In most other countries, people have a common origin, the same history, a single religion, one language. Canadians don't have many things in common. That's why we have a lot to share.

Roch Carrier, author, "Canada Is a Grand Dream," *Canadian Living*, September 1992.

CSN

Abbreviation of the French phrase *Canada sans nous* (Canada without Us) used by *Le Devoir* columnist **Daniel Latouche** to refer to English Canada without French Canada, as noted by Pauline Couture in *The Globe and Mail*, 26 Feb. 1993.

If the French never lost the mentality of the conquered, the English never lost the mentality of the conqueror.

Neil Bissoondath, novelist and essayist, *Selling Illusions* (1994).

It is our feeling that we will continue on much as we have... forever pragmatic, forever flexible, forever Canadian.

Michael Adams and **Mary Jane Lennon**, Environics Research Group Limited, "Quebecers—Hedging Their Bets," *The Public Perspective*, Nov.–Dec. 1994.

And so: This book is dedicated to the pure blend that constitutes the fabric of Canada today. May our problems continue to sustain our success.

Henry Mintzberg, management consultant, *The Canadian Condition: Reflections of a "Pure Cotton"* (1995). This is Mintzberg's dedication; he distinguishes between "pure laine," "pure cotton," and "pure furs"—original French-Canadians and Québécois, later arrivals, and Aboriginals.

Things have got to the point where Canadians can never be a constitutionally defined people as long as Quebec is part of Canada.

David J. Bercuson, historian, quoted by John Gray, "Mood Swing," *The Globe and Mail*, 18 April 1995.

Canada without Quebec is no more Canada, and Quebec without Canada is no more Quebec.

Jean Chrétien, Prime Minister, quoted by Edgar M. Bronfman in "Letters," *The New York Times*, 5 Nov. 1995.

Never in my lifetime have I ever felt that there was a contradiction between being a Quebecer and a Canadian.

Jean Charest, address of the federal Conservative leader agreeing to contest the Quebec provincial Liberal leadership, Sherbrooke, 26 March 1998, quoted in *The Toronto Star* the following day.

As long as we're in Canada, we'll go get our booty. And sovereignist premiers have better success than federalist premiers in grabbing money from Ottawa.

Jacques Parizeau, address, Collège de l'outaouais, Hull, Que., 25 Nov. 1998, quoted by Kate Jaimet in the *National Post* the following day.

CANADA & THE UNITED KINGDOM

See also BRITISH EMPIRE & COMMONWEALTH, CANADA, EMPIRE, UNITED KINGDOM

A Nation spoke to a Nation, / A Throne sent word to a Throne: / "Daughter am I in my mother's house, / But mistress in my own. / The gates are mine to open, / As the gates are mine to close. / And I abide by my Mother's House," / Said our Lady of the Snows.

Final verse of **Rudyard Kipling**'s poem "Our Lady of the Snows: Canadian Preferential Tariff, 1897," *The Times* (London), 27 April 1897. It gave dramatic expression to the independent yet subordinate relationship of the Dominion of Canada to Great Britain, the "mother country." Kipling denounced the tariff as an impediment to tourism and immigration as well as a sign of the weakening of the Imperial connection.

I once wrote, for the *Daily Express*, an article on "Why I Stayed on In Canada," instead of coming home, like a sensible chap, to enjoy the delights of the British climate, the lavish elbow-room, the handsome urban development, and the general industrious benevolence, after ten years in two assorted wildernesses.

The most cogent reason could be pared down to five words, "Because I liked the place," and these had to be expanded, in the interests of filling one and a half columns and earning 100 pounds. Dredging about, I came up with what I thought was a fair picture of a country which would really have needed a book to describe its merits, and a good fat appendix to cover the drawbacks.

Nicholas Monsarrat, novelist whose success with *The Cruel Sea* (1951) saw him move from Johannesburg to Ottawa and then to London, *Life Is a Four-Letter Word: Volume II—Breaking Out* (1970).

I don't suppose we found out much about Canada or the Canadians, but we learnt a little about a country of which the English know nothing, which is not surprising when you think how little Canadians seem to know about their land either.

Robert Morley, British actor, referring to a theatrical tour, *The London Observer*, 24 Dec. 1972.

Canadians... were a people more at ease with the non-domestic than the English or Americans, and, toughened by living, in work or leisure, close to natural forces beyond human control, they had learned never to give in.

Jill Ker Conway, Australian-born, American-educated historian and memoirist who taught at the University of Toronto from 1964 to 1975, *True North: A Memoir* (1994).

CANADA & THE UNITED STATES

See also BORDER, CANADIAN-AMERICAN; CANADA; UNITED STATES OF AMERICA

I agree that with Canada in our possession, our people in America will increase so much, that in a century more the number of British subjects on that side of the water would be more numerous than they now are on this; but I have no fears of their becoming either useless or dangerous.

Benjamin Franklin, U.S. patriot and pamphleteer, "Some Account of a Pamphlet, Entitled, The Interest of Great Britain Considered, with Regard to Her Colonies, and the Acquisitions of Canada and Guadaloupe," sometimes called "The Canada

Pamphlet," reproduced in *The Gentleman's Magazine*, May 1760.

In a short time, we have reason to hope, the delegates of Canada will join us in Congress and complete the American union, as far as we wish to have it completed.

Thomas Jefferson, American statesman, letter to John Randolph, Nov. 1775, *The Jeffersonian Cyclopedia: A Comprehensive Collection of the View of Thomas Jefferson* (1900, 1967) edited by John P. Foley.

Our Misfortunes in Canada, are enough to melt an Heart of Stone.

John Adams, U.S. President (1797–1801), letter to Abigail Adams, 26 June 1776, quoted by E.B. White, "A Busy Place" (1976), *Writings from The New Yorker 1927–1976* (1990) edited by Rebecca M. Dale.

Canada acceding to this confederation, and joining in the measures of the United States, shall be admitted into, and entitled to all the advantages of this Union: but no other colony shall be admitted into the same, unless such admission be agreed to by nine States.

Article 11 (the so-called Canadian Article) of the Articles of Confederation, the name of the first constitution of the United States, drafted largely by **John Dickinson** of Pennsylvania, presented to Congress on 12 July 1776, adopted by Congress on 15 Nov. 1777, and accepted as the law of the land from 1781 to 1789, when it was superseded by the U.S. Constitution. Appendix, *The American's Guide: Comprising the Declaration of Independence, the Articles of Confederation, the Constitution of the United States...* (1843).

The annexation of this country to the United States is a tabooed subject but I have always thought if we did not annex you that it would be a good thing for you to annex us.

Mark Twain, humorist, delivering his so-called Second Speech in Montreal, 9 Dec. 1881, quoted by David Ketterer in "Mark Twain's Overlooked 'Second Speech' in Montreal," *Mark Twain Journal*, Fall 1990.

In the late summer of '06, for example, we took ship to Canada, which I had not seen in any particularity for many years, and of which I had been told it was coming out of its spiritual and material subjection to the United States.

Rudyard Kipling, man-of-letters, recalling a tour of the U.S. and Canada in 1906, "The Committee of Ways and Means," *Something of Myself: For My Friends Known and Unknown* (1937).

Why should Canada, when she has made herself what she is, throw the enormous gifts of her inheritance into the hands of others? Whatever the United States may gain, I see nothing for Canada in Reciprocity except a little money which she does not need, and a very long repentance.

Rudyard Kipling, man-of-letters, cabled message, 8 Sept. 1911, quoted by S. Macnaughtan in *My Canadian Memories* (1920).

I see no argument for the union of Canada with the United States. There is excellent feeling between the two countries, but they could no more join at this period of their history than a great oak could combine with a well-rooted pine to make one tree. The roots of each are far too deep. It is impossible.

Sir Arthur Conan Doyle, author and traveller, thoughts on the Grand Trunk Railway in 1914, *Memories and Adventures* (1924).

Canada is more amazing than the United States because the nightmare of false similarity is more general.

Hilaire Belloc, British essayist, letter written in Montreal, 11 March 1923, *Letters from Hilaire Belloc* (1958) edited by Robert Speaight.

It is inconceivable, if history has any meaning whatever, that Canada should unite, politically, with the American Republic.

Hugh L. Keenleyside, diplomat, *Canada and the United States* (1929).

God forbid that I should commit so ghastly an error as doing what I well know to be the one unpardonable sin, of confusing for a single moment the two great commonwealths that occupy the northern continent of America!

G.K. Chesterton, English writer, address, luncheon held to honour Rudyard Kipling sponsored by the Canadian Literary Society and recorded by the BBC, London, England, 1933; "Visiting Canada," *The Chesterton Review*, Nov. 1996.

I cannot see any possible reason to annex Canada. We do not want to have more people in the United States; what we want is to try and improve the mob we have now. And Canada couldn't help us out....

Will Rogers, humorist popular in the 1930s, *The Best of Will Rogers* (1979) compiled by Bryan B. Sterling.

Perhaps I should say "your foreign relations with the United States." But the word "foreign" seems strangely out of place. Canada and the United States have reached the point where we no longer think of each other as "foreign" countries. We think of each other as friends, as peaceful and co-operative neighbours on a spacious and fruitful continent.

Harry S. Truman, U.S. President, address, joint sitting of the Senate and the House of Commons, 11 June 1947.

The more I think over the whole situation, the more I believe... that the U.S. foreign policy at bottom is to bring Canada into as many situations affecting themselves as possible with a view to leading ultimately to the annexation of our two countries....

W.L. Mackenzie King, former Prime Minister, recording in his diary, 30 June 1950, his reactions to Canadian involvement in the Korean War, quoted by C.P. Stacey in *A Very Double Life: The Private World of Mackenzie King* (1976).

Our own history teaches us that co-operation can be closer when differences are recognized.

Louis St. Laurent, Prime Minister, introducing U.S. President Dwight D. Eisenhower to a joint meeting of the Senate and the House of Commons, 14 Nov. 1953.

It is my belief that the greatest threat to Canadian life has nothing to do with Russian bombs and rockets. The frontier to be watched is that easy friendly line to the south, across which your giant neighbour, the United States, sends its products. And the most dangerous of all these importations to you is that large, vague package which may be called "the American Way of Life."

J.B. Priestley, English man-of-letters who made a cross-Canada lecture tour in 1956 (and was known as "Beastly Priestley" for his comments), "Canadians Should Be More Wary," *The Toronto Star*, 26 April 1958, reprinted 17 May 1992.

How indeed could Canada remain separate from America and yet stay alive?

Winston Churchill, British statesman and popular historian, *Book X: "The Great Democracies," A History of the English-speaking Peoples* (1958).

All that we Canadians and Americans, and those who went before us, have built, all that we believe in, is challenged as it has never been challenged before. The new horizons of competition range from the polar areas, and extend to the infinity of outer space. It is for us, all of us to bring to the challenge a response worthy of ourselves and of our two nations.

Dwight D. Eisenhower, U.S. President, joint meeting of the Senate and the House of Commons, 9 July 1958.

We share common values from the past, a common defence line at present, and common aspirations for the future, and indeed the future of all mankind. Geography has made us neighbours. History has made us friends. Economics has made us partners. And necessity has made us allies. Those whom nature hath so joined together, let no man put asunder. What unites us is far greater than what divides us.

John F. Kennedy, U.S. President, addressing a joint sitting of the Senate and the House of Commons, May 17, 1961.

The Americans are our best friends, whether we like it or not.

Robert Thompson, national leader of the Social Credit Party (1961–1967), malapropism quoted by Peter C. Newman in *Home Country* (1973).

Canada, as anti-environment to the U.S.A., is able to perceive many of the ground rules and operation effects of the American environment that are quite imperceptible to the U.S.A.

Marshall McLuhan, communications pioneer, letter to Claude Bissell, 4 March 1965, *Letters of Marshall McLuhan* (1987) edited by Matie Molinaro, Corinne McLuhan, and William Toye.

A large minority of you are deeply sceptical of American methods and oppose the unquestioned extension of American power. Some of us Americans have always wistfully hoped that you Canadians would teach us a lesson or two, though, to be frank, you have usually let us down.

Paul Goodman, U.S. social critic, Massey Lectures, *The Moral Ambiguity of America* (1966).

We of the United States consider ourselves blessed. We have much to give thanks for. But the gift of Providence that we really cherish is that we were given as our neighbours on this great, wonderful continent, the people and the nation of Canada.

Lyndon B. Johnson, U.S. President, address, Expo 67, Montreal, 1967.

Canada has long been another America, an America in the making, but one with a difference. We still have the chance, in this open, half-formed, dimly identified society of ours, to make something new, even marvelous, out of our American heritage.

William Kilbourn, historian, "Some Feelings about the United States," *The New Romans: Candid Canadian Opinions in the U.S.* (1968) edited by Al Purdy.

Living next to you is in some ways like sleeping with an elephant. No matter how friendly and even-tempered the beast, one is affected by every twitch and grunt.

Pierre Elliott Trudeau, Prime Minister, speech, National Press Club, Washington, D.C., March 25, 1969. Lawrence Martin, in *The Presidents and the Prime Ministers* (1982), attributed the authorship of the speech to Trudeau's adviser, Ivan Head.

I would have to say quite candidly that we have had very little success to date in our negotiations with our Canadian friends, which shows, incidentally, that sometimes you have more problems negotiating with your friends than you do with your adversaries.

Richard M. Nixon, U.S. President, press conference, Washington, D.C., 1972, quoted by Walter Stewart in *As They See Us* (1977).

Simply stated, our histories record that for more than a century millions upon millions of Canadians and Americans have known one another, liked one another, and trusted one another.

Canadians are not capable of living in isolation from you any more than we are desirous of doing so. We have benefited from your stimulus; we have profited from your vitality.

Pierre Elliott Trudeau, Prime Minister, address, Joint Session of the U.S. Congress, Washington, D.C., 22 Feb. 1977.

I don't mind saying that right now we're the 13th Federal Reserve District of the United States, plain and simple. [The Federal Reserve, which controls the U.S. money supply and banking, has twelve districts.] And one of the biggest charades that has been pulled in Canada over the last five years is that Canada has an independent monetary policy. We are independent to follow you—with a twenty-four-hour lag.

Carl Beigie, president, C.D. Howe Research Institute, addressing the Canadian Society of New York, quoted in *The Globe and Mail*, 18 Oct. 1980.

Canada is the only country in the world that has all the American opportunities but none of the problems the Americans face.

Valentyn Moroz, Ukrainian dissident historian and Toronto resident, quoted by Victor Malarek in *The Globe and Mail*, 17 April 1981.

Bilateral bliss

This phrase refers to arrangements made between the governments of Canada and the United States to deal with common problems, and was popularized by political commentator **Lawrence Martin** in his study *The Presidents and the Prime Ministers: Washington and Ottawa Face to Face: The Myth of Bilateral Bliss, 1867–1982* (1982).

Canadians are often not really seen by Americans as foreign. We are neighbours, friends, cousins, fellow North Americans; we are Canadians, but we are not foreigners.

Allan Gotlieb, Canadian Ambassador in Washington, D.C., address, Empire Club of Canada, Toronto, 10 Nov. 1983.

I'm not greatly worried about what is called the Americanization of Canada. What people mean when they speak of Americanization has been just as lethal to American culture as it has been to Canadian culture. It's a kind of levelling down which I think every concerned citizen of democracy should fight, whether he is a Canadian or an American.

Northrop Frye, cultural critic, interviewed by Robert Fulford, "From Nationalism to Regionalism: The Maturing of Canadian Culture," *The Anthology Anthology: A Selection from 30 Years of CBC Radio's Anthology* (1984) edited by Robert Weaver.

Good relations, super relations, with the United States will be the cornerstone of our foreign policy.

Brian Mulroney, Prime Minister, interviewed by the editors of *The Wall Street Journal*, 24 Sept. 1984.

He should get up in the morning and say to himself, "Thank God for Canada. What can I do for Canada today?" Canada is the best friend and neighbour that the United States of American can ever conceive of having around the world.

Brian Mulroney, Prime Minister, referring to U.S. President Ronald Reagan, interviewed by Rod McQueen, "Canada Warms Up to U.S. Business," *Fortune*, 4 March 1985.

There is anti-Americanism in Canada, but not enough to get your dogcatcher elected.

Attributed to **Brian Mulroney** at a press conference called to celebrate the re-election of the Conservative Party the previous day, Baie-Comeau, Que., 22 Nov. 1988; alas, while dogcatchers may be elected in the United States, they are appointed in Canada.

Canada may not want to be known as the mouse that roared but, amidst the thunderous trumpeting of the American elephant, we still like to hear ourselves squeak.

John Meisel, CRTC Commissioner, "Broadcast Regulation in Canada: An Audible Squeak," *Friends So Different: Essays on Canada and the United States in the 1980s* (1989) edited by Lansing Lamont and J. Duncan Edmonds.

English Canadian intellectuals see the United States as threatening; Québécois intellectuals see it as a land of liberty. I think there is enormous naïveté in both cases.

Jacques Godbout, Quebec author, interviewed by Sherry Simon in *Other Solitudes: Canadian Multicultural Fictions* (1990) edited by Linda Hutcheon and Marion Richmond.

Sooner of later Canadians are going to become Americans. Too bad.

John Grimond, journalist, "Nice Country, Nice Mess," *The Economist*, 29 June 1991. In a "follow-up report" that appeared in the same U.K. magazine in July 1999, the editors opined, "When all is said and done, Canadians will still be Canadians... Canadian destiny was, and still is, to be a kinder, gentler society. Being American is not a bad thing—but neither is being un-American."

Canada was born out of necessity. People came here because they had to, and that, I think, has given us a rather withdrawn, watchful attitude toward history, which is not typically American at all.

Robertson Davies, novelist, referring to Canadian-American differences, quoted by Philip Marchand in *The Toronto Star*, 1 Oct. 1991.

This forges the Canadian character—an unremitting effort to distinguish itself from the United States. Canada will never be able to escape that influence. Canada and Poland are similar: they're both major errors of location.

John Kenneth Galbraith, economist and author, referring to the concern Canadians have that they will be swallowed up by Americans, interviewed by Diane Francis in *Maclean's*, 2 Dec. 1991.

I began to realize that Canada was one of the United States' best-kept secrets. Later, after visiting my brother and his friends at the University of Toronto's Hart House, I learned that Canada was also the United States' best-kept colony.

Ralph Nader, consumer activist, Introduction, *Canada Firsts* (1992), researched by Nadia Milleron and Duff Conacher.

America needs a strong Canada.

Bill Clinton, U.S. President-Elect, remark made at his campaign headquarters, Little Rock, Arkansas, election night, CTV Network, 3 Nov. 1992.

Our overriding national preoccupation has been about how to limit U.S. power over our national destiny while deriving maximum advantage from our propinquity.

Allan Gotlieb, Ambassador to the United States in the 1980s, quoted by Lawrence Martin in *Pledge of Allegiance* (1993).

The best thing about Canada is that the worst thing that can happen is that we go bust and are bailed out and become part of the United States. Every country in the world would love to have that as their only downside risk.

Andrew Sarlos, entrepreneur, quoted by Diane Frances in *A Matter of Survival* (1993).

The one-way mirror

Phrase attributed to novelist **Margaret Atwood** by Jeffrey Simpson who wrote as follows in *The Globe and Mail*, 3 Sept. 1994: "The novelist Margaret Atwood coined the phrase 'the one-way mirror' to describe Canadian-U.S. relations. We see them, she claimed, but they do not see us."

Ours is the world's most remarkable relationship, the most successful partnership, between any two countries.... We are neighbours by the grace of nature. But we are allies and friends by choice.

Bill Clinton, U.S. President, address, joint meeting of the Senate and the House of Commons, Ottawa, 23 Feb. 1995, as published in *The Toronto Star* the following day.

Long live Canada—Vive le Canada!

Bill Clinton, U.S. President, address, Museum of Civilization, Hull, Que., 24 Feb. 1995, quoted by Dan Lett in the *Winnipeg Free Press* the following day. The U.S. President echoed the "Vive le Québec libre!" cry of Charles de Gaulle in Montreal in 1967.

I must say that's extraordinarily meaningful to us. In a funny way, we owe the White House... to all of you.

Hillary Rodham Clinton, progressive-minded wife of U.S. President Bill Clinton, address, Mount Saint Vincent University, Halifax, N.S., 15 June 1995, quoted by Murray Campbell in *The Globe and Mail* the following day. She was referring to the fact that the British general who during the War of 1812 burned the executive mansion in Washington, D.C., causing the house to be repainted white, and hence known as the White House, lies buried near Halifax.

Canada... our neighbour to the North... all of a sudden transformed into that place from whence... like the North Wind... terror comes....

Words spoken by a film producer (played by Dustin Hoffman) who is evolving a scenario about a "suitcase bomb" from Albania being brought through Canada into the United States in the Hollywood movie *Wag the Dog* (1997) with screenplay by **David Mamet** and **Hilary Henkin**.

"A former Prime Minister of Canada was criticized by some Canadians for having too cozy a relationship with then-Presidents Reagan and Bush. How would you characterize your relationship with President Clinton?"

"Good. And not cozy."

Question from **Richard Scammon**, President of the National Press Club, Washington, D.C., 9 April 1997, following an official visit with U.S. President Bill Clinton. The reference was to Prime Minister Brian Mulroney. Quoted by Graham Fraser, "Chrétien Adjusts Warmth Dial," *The Globe and Mail*, 10 April 1997.

I like to stand up to the Americans. It's popular. But you have to be very careful because they're our friends.

Jean Chrétien, Prime Minister, private talk with Belgian Prime Minister Jean-Luc Dehaene, accidentally recorded at the NATO Summit Conference, Madrid, Spain, 9 July 1997, quoted by Tim Harper in *The Toronto Star* the following day.

We appreciate very profoundly our relations with a strong and united Canada.

Madeleine Albright, U.S. Secretary of State, address in French delivered at the Museum of Civilization, Ottawa, 10 March 1998, quoted by Laura Eggertson in *The Toronto Star* the following day.

We don't dislike Americans. We just fear the United States.

Allan Fotheringham, columnist, "Learning to Love the American Bully Next Door," *Maclean's*, 13 April 1998.

The dissolution of Canada would affect the United States more than any imaginable crisis overseas.

Robert D. Kaplan, correspondent, "Travels into America's Future," *The Atlantic Monthly*, Aug. 1998.

When you go through Canadian customs, officials ask you if you have any guns. When you return to the United States, customs officials ask you if you have any fruit or vegetables.

Marcello Truzzi, Michigan-based sociologist, noting the questions asked by customs officials on both sides of the border, Detroit, Michigan, 11 July 1999.

If I come one more time I have to start paying taxes.

Bill Clinton, U.S. President, speech at the inauguration of the new American Embassy in Ottawa, joking that this is what Prime Minister Jean Chrétien had told him, quoted by James Brooke, "President Goes on Offensive in a Foray into Canada," *The New York Times*, 19 Oct. 1999.

Absorption is the key American experience. The key Canadian experience is feeling strange.

H.S. Bhabra, novelist and broadcaster, who committed suicide in Toronto, 1 June 2000, quoted by Gayle MacDonald and Alexandra Gill, "The Unseen Faces of H.S. Bhabra," *The Globe and Mail*, 3 June 2000.

CANADA & THE WORLD See also

CANADA, THE WORLD

Canada could have enjoyed: / English government, / French culture, / and American know-how. // Instead it ended up with: / English know-how, / French government, / and American culture.

John Robert Colombo's eight-line poem "O Canada" (1965) first published in *The New Romans* (1968) edited by Al Purdy.

Canada is so far away it hardly exists.

Jorge Luis Borges, Argentine author, interviewed by poet and broadcaster Robert Zend in Borges' apartment in Buenos Aires, 4 Oct., 1974. Zend asked him, "What do you think of when you think of Canada?" Borges made the above reply.

The world generally considers Canada an amiable and well-intentioned country, grandiose and inoffensive, but indistinct and somewhat colourless. Most Canadians, after initial reflexive dissent, would find it difficult to demur too fiercely from that judgement.

Conrad Black, publisher, "Out of Uncle Sam's Shadow," *National Post*, 11 Jan. 2000.

CANADA COUNCIL

It's a shocking thing to think that we're going to get a hundred million dollars of unexpected revenue out of two estates.

John Deutsch, Secretary to the Treasury Board, explaining to Cabinet minister Jack Pickersgill in 1956 that the death duties on the estates of industrialists Izaac Walton Killam and Sir James Dunn amounted to windfall profits at a time of a balanced federal budget and could be used to endow an arts council, quoted by Pickersgill during an address delivered at The Canada Council's 25th Anniversary Dinner, Ottawa, 14 June 1982.

That a body be created to be known as the Canada Council for the Encouragement of the Arts, Letters, Humanities and Social Sciences to stimulate and to help voluntary organizations within these fields, to foster Canada's cultural relations abroad, to perform the functions of a national commission for UNESCO, and to devise and administer a system of scholarships....

Key recommendation of the **Royal Commission on National Development in the Arts, Letters and Sciences**, 1949–51 (1951), known as the Massey Commission after its chairman, Vincent Massey.

I think you will agree that, indeed, the world today needs abundant sources of intellectual and moral energies. Canada wants to be one of those sources, and it has already begun to be one of those sources in several international organizations. With that purpose in mind, we must further develop and enrich our own national soul.

Louis St. Laurent, Prime Minister, announcing the government's decision to create the Canada Council, National Conference on High Education, Ottawa, 12 Nov. 1956, quoted by Bernard Ostry in *The Cultural Connection: An Essay on Culture and Government Policy in Canada* (1978).

Whenever the least shred of artistic talent rears its head on the Canadian scene, it seems, some agency of local, provincial or federal Government is there to confer encouragement in the form of a grant or a purchase.

Hilton Kramer, U.S. critic for *The New York Times*, interviewed by *The Globe and Mail*, 8 June 1976.

If you want to promote a country's literature internationally, you can do more by giving to the defence budget than to agencies like the Canada Council. That's why we know more about Russian literature and not half as much as we should about Swiss or Indian writers.

Barbara Amiel, columnist, "Column," *Maclean's*, 1 May 1995.

CANADA DAY See also HOLIDAYS

What does Canada Day conjure up? Canada Post? Canada Manpower? Petro-Canada? Statistics Canada? Air Canada? It's sameness and mediocrity—no ring, no vision, no magic to stir one's blood.

Laura Sabia, feminist and nationalist, remarks, Toronto branch of the Royal Commonwealth Society, 13 Oct. 1982. The national holiday celebrated on July the first was formerly known as Dominion Day.

Canada Day commemorates a lacklustre gathering of first ministers who concluded the political equivalent of a marriage of convenience.

Lysiane Gagnon, columnist, "Inside Quebec," *The Globe and Mail*, 9 July 1994.

Perhaps this compromise or evolutionary solution could be reached by renaming our national day "Dominion Loblaws Day" so that neither food store chain would be excluded.

John Fraser, columnist, "Let's Take Back Our History on Canada Day," *The Toronto Star*, 16 June 1996. Another suggestion was "Dominion Hollinger Day."

My thought for Canada Day is to report the enemy is at the gates, positioned and reinforced by the very institutions and organizations that once were the outriders, arch defenders, and champions of national interest.

Dalton Camp, columnist, "Keeping the Enemy at Bay, on Canada Day," *The Toronto Star*, 30 June 1999.

CANADA GOOSE See also BIRDS; EMBLEMS, NATIONAL

I know of no bird or animal that can equal the Canada Goose for getting well after being wounded. It is said that a cat has nine lives; if that is true, the Canada Goose has at least eighteen, nine on each side of the border.

Attributed to the conservationist **Jack Miner**, Kingsville, Ont., in the 1930s.

Canadian Geese are the thugs of the bird kingdom.

Notice issued by the **Wansworth Council** on Britain's crisis with aggressive fowl, quoted in *Country Life*, 14 April 1994.

CANADIAN ALLIANCE See also MANNING, PRESTON; POLITICAL PARTIES, REFORM PARTY

THINK BIG

Theme of the address delivered by **Preston Manning**, leader of the Reform Party of Canada, leadership convention, Ottawa, 30 Jan. 2000, noted by Paul Wells in the *National Post* the following day. The Reform Party of Canada (RPC) morphed momentarily into the Canadian Reform Alliance Party (CRAP) and thereafter into the Canadian Reform Conservative Alliance (CRCA), known simply as Canadian Alliance, March 2000.

The middle of the road is for yellow lines and dead skunks.

Tom Long, leadership candidate for the Canadian Alliance, quoted by Margaret Wente in "Counterpoint," *The Globe and Mail*, 16 May 2000.

This is a new century, this is a new party, it's a new day for Canada.

Stockwell Day, treasurer of Alberta, elected leader of the newly formed Canadian Alliance, leader of the official Opposition, acceptance speech, Toronto, 8 July 2000, quoted by Tim Harper in *The Toronto Star* the following day.

CANADIAN ARMED FORCES See also DEFENCE, WAR

Gentlemen, I came here only in order to die for the sake of God while serving him in the profession of arms; if I did not think to die here I would leave the country to go and serve against the Turks and not be deprived of that glory.

Raphaël-Lambert Closse, acting Governor of Montreal, where he was killed on 6 Feb. 1662, according to the historian Dollier de Casson, quoted by Marie-Claire Daveluy, "Raphaël-Lambert Closse," *Dictionary of Canadian Biography: Volume I: 1000–1700* (1965).

One well-trained company is worth a brigade of geniuses in the trenches. This must be continually impressed on our recruits by precept and practice.

Passage from *Rapid Training of Recruits* (1916), a handbook for training troops for World War I, quoted by new recruit, Kerry Gillespie, "My Aching Back," *The Toronto Star*, 27 Sept. 1998. The sentiment "is remarkably similar to things I heard during my training eighty years later."

The grain-growing provinces of Manitoba, Saskatchewan and Alberta, which now have a large percentage of Americans, are essentially attractive to the United States and there is just a possibility that they might make the conquest of these provinces the ultimate objective of their campaign.

Scenario of a possible American military invasion of Canada from an untitled document, 12 April 1921, generally referred to as "Defence Scheme No. 1." It was the work of Colonel **J.S. (Buster) Brown**, Director of Military Operations and Intelligence, Ministry of Defence. Such guidelines for the Armed Forces were prepared between 1921 and 1931 when the operation was cancelled.

Elite means small; better equipped means nothing but the further application of spit and glue to what we have now.

Nicholas Stethem, defence analyst, "My War with the Army," *Maclean's*, March 1975.

The Canadian Forces are the best-paid, most rank-inflated military organization in NATO.

Desmond Morton, historian, "Thinking about Canadian Defence in the Nineties," *National Networks News* (quarterly publication of the Defence Associations), 1 Oct. 1990.

Canada is the only country in the world which has a smaller reserve army than their regular army.

Remark made in *Esprit de Corps* magazine as quoted by Michael Kesterton in "Social Studies," *The Globe and Mail*, 12 April 1995.

They have borrowed a title that is essentially Canadian and is time-honoured. The term Militia is unknown in U.S. military terminology, their part-time soldiers are termed National Guard and are state-designated.

In Canada the Militia has been the bulwark of our defences ever since they assisted the British regulars to repel the American invasions of 1812–14.

Strome Galloway, Colonel (Ret'd.), Letters to the Editor, *The Globe and Mail*, 3 May 1995. The letter was occasioned by U.S. commentators calling fundamentalist-minded, ultra-patriotic, paramilitary groups "militia" groups. Galloway continued, "This new U.S. bastard-military must not be linked to our time-honoured defenders."

The day after a Yes win, Quebec should immediately create a department of defence, the embryo of a major state, and offer all Quebecers serving in the Canadian Forces the chance to integrate into the Quebec Forces while keeping their rank, seniority and retirement funds as a means to ensure a better transition.

Jean-Marc Jacob, M.P., Bloc Québécois defence critic, quoted in a communiqué issued by Bloc leader Lucien Bouchard's office, 26 Oct. 1995, immediately prior to the Second Quebec Referendum. It was denounced as treasonous by Jim Hart, Reform Party's defence critic, yet Jacob retained his position as vice-chair of the Commons defence committee, as noted by Diane Francis in "Political Correctness and the Jacob Affair," *Maclean's*, 22 July 1996.

Our inquiry has revealed some of the frightening effects of this demoralization and corruption within the Canadian officer corps.... If this process goes on long enough, it will seriously weaken a new generation's ability to continue our progress. This in itself is a form of "debt" that we are handing down to our children.

Peter Desbarats, commissioner, *Somalia Cover-up* (1997).

As General MacKenzie told us yesterday, you could put the whole Canadian army in Toronto's Maple Leaf Gardens and still have a thousand seats left over.

Attributed to retired **General Lewis MacKenzie** by Peter Desbarats in *Somalia Cover-up* (1997).

Soldiers are not firefighters. They can be, if we want them to be, in addition to everything else. But soldiers are the deliverers of organized violence on behalf of the state, for the achievement of certain objectives.

David J. Bercuson, historian, rejecting the notion that recruits to the Armed Forces should be on short-term contracts, quoted by Allan Thompson, "Shape U-u-u-p!" *The Toronto Star*, 17 Sept. 1998.

Maximum amount that the Canadian government has agreed to spend on a soldier's sex-change operation: $40,000.

Item from "Harper's Index," *Harper's Magazine*, Dec. 1998.

CANADIAN BROADCASTING CORPORATION

See also BROADCASTING, NEWS

The policy which guides operations of the CBC National News Service is based on the primary conception that this service is in the nature of a public trust; to present all significant news of the day's happenings in Canada and abroad, factually, without bias or distortion, without tendentious comment, and in clear and unambiguous style.

Dan McArthur, news editor and drafter of the CBC National News Policy, formulated 1 Jan. 1941 when the Canadian Broadcasting Corporation, established in 1936, introduced its radio network news service.

The CBC is nothing more than an enormous party line.

Jimmy James, broadcaster associated with the Golden Age of Radio Broadcasting in Canada, quoted by Scott Young in *The Globe and Mail*, 3 March 1975.

I see the CBC as a sort of domestic British Empire. Both were created and developed by a rather insular breed, exhibiting alternate flashes of brilliance and idiocy. At this moment there are many critics who would extend the analogy even further, gloomily predicting that the sun is already setting on the CBC also, and that, beset from without and within, its complete disintegration is close at hand.

Max Ferguson, broadcaster, *And Now... Here's Max: A Funny Kind of Autobiography* (1967).

Sex in Canada is taken care of by the Canadian Broadcasting Corporation, which is staffed by people who wish they'd gone to London. Using tax money, they put on playlets about homosexuals who are just as good as you are, and about nymphomaniacs who are even better.

Henry Morgan, New York comic who spent from 1971 to 1975 in Toronto, "Oy, Canada," *Penthouse*, June 1972.

We have erected at the CBC twin towers, a dual system to promote the aspirations and protect the integrity of both language groups. Malevolence has not imprisoned us in two separate worlds, a sense of justice and fair play has.

Barbara Frum, television personality, referring to the dual character of CBC/Radio Canada, address, Destiny Canada Conference, York University, Toronto, 28 June 1977.

Nowhere have we been more successful in satisfying our need to communicate than with CBC radio. No other institution has contributed so much to Canadian cultural and political life, helping us to know and define who we are.

Morris Wolfe, critic, Introduction to the record album, *Fifty Years of Radio: A Celebration of CBC Radio 1936–1986* (1986).

It must be recognized that the basic move to curtail subsidies to the CBC is a move in the right direction. Unfortunately, the government has not gone far enough and, in our view, has missed a sterling opportunity to do something truly constructive.

Walter Block and **Michael Walker**, economists with the Fraser Institute, *Lexicon of Economic Thought* (1989).

Undoubtedly, I did go too far when I said the CBC was "a lousy left-wing, Liberal-NDP pinko network." My critics have repeated this hyperbole ad nauseum. But most of them have ignored the fact that I also said that I believe in the CBC despite my misgivings about its performance in news and current affairs. I also made it clear that none of my criticisms had anything to do with its drama, music, sports and other presentations.

John Crispo, political economist, member of the CBC's Board of Directors, referring to an appearance before the CRTC, "Critiquing the Critics," *The Globe and Mail*, 18 May 1991.

The CBC should be kept out of the newsroom. A government-owned press is the antithesis of a free-press.

Marjorie Nichols, columnist, *Mark My Words: The Memoirs of a Very Political Reporter* (1992) written with Jane O'Hara.

As the railway has linked us through the movement of people and goods, the CBC has linked us through the flow of ideas, music and entertainment from coast to coast. The CBC is the living expression of our commitment to nurturing a distinctive Canadian culture and identity.

George Radwanski and **Julia Luttrell**, social commentators, *The Will of a Nation: Awakening the Canadian Spirit* (1992).

Can a network devoted to news, sports and commercial programming be any longer considered a public broadcaster? The leaders of the CBC run from the dreams that made this country possible. They flee the requirement placed upon them to establish value and be a moral force within the nation. Ultimately, in the guise of a tainted commercialism, they betray the responsibilty to define and protect who we are.

Daryl Duke, broadcaster, "Spectator," *The Globe and Mail*, 30 July 1994.

Our horizons have broadened because we have listened in the United States to the CBC.

Bill Clinton, U.S. President, address, joint meeting of the House of Commons and the Senate of Canada, Ottawa, Senate Debates, 23 Feb. 1995.

There's a lot of talk about deficits these days. And it's very important that we talk about deficits—like the fact that between 7:00 and 10:00 p.m. on our television screens there is a deficit of Canadian programming, and if it weren't for the CBC, there would be hardly any.... This is a cultural deficit that I think should concern us more than anything else.

Tony Manera, former CBC President, speech, Toronto, Save the CBC Coalition, 18 Nov. 1995, quoted by Christopher Harris in *The Globe and Mail* the following day.

Wherever I travel in this country, CBC is always there.

Sylvia Tyson, composer-singer, speech, Toronto, Save the CBC Coalition, 18 Nov. 1995, quoted by Greg Quill in *The Toronto Star* the following day.

Our business is to work for our shareholders and deliver our shareholders, the Canadian public, a channel devoted to their interests. Their Canadian interests. To offer them an insight into their country that no one else does and no one else can.

Peter Mansbridge, news anchor of CBC-TV's *The National*, address, University of Regina, 7 March 1996, "Verbatim," *The Globe and Mail*, 8 April 1996.

Radio to Call Our Own

Slogan of **CBC Radio** to mark its sixtieth anniversary, the year beginning on 2 Nov. 1996, to celebrate the creation of the Canadian Broadcasting Corporation on 2 Nov. 1936.

CANADIANISM See also CANADA

The university must stand sponsor in this country for a healthy Canadianism.

Alfred Fitzpatrick, Principal of Frontier College, *The University in Overalls: A Plea for Part-Time Study* (1920).

Canadianism is made up of over three centuries of successful struggle with a recalcitrant environment, of over a century's original and successful political adaptation and inventiveness, and of a kind of conservatism which history has shown can be converted by adversity into stubborn, indomitable will.

J.B. Brebner, historian, Presidential Address, Canadian Historical Association, 1940.

Canadiana, Canadiana, / Mens sana in corpore sana, / Other names are top banana, / But we'll still take Canadiana.

Verse from "Culturality Squad" written by **Tim Porteous** and **James Domville** from the McGill musical comedy *My Fur Lady* which opened in Montreal on 7 Feb. 1957 and subsequently toured the country.

"The dirty little hypocrite is a Canadian. Look here." He put the letter on the table between us, and speared at it with his forefinger. "He spells the word 'labor' l,a,b,o,u,r. It's the British spelling, still current in Canada. He isn't even American. He's an impostor."

Passage from the novel *The Galton Case* (1959) written by **Ross Macdonald**, pen name of Kenneth Millar, the California detective-story writer who was raised in Canada.

As Canadian as possible—under the circumstances.

E. Heather Scott, radio listener, completed this

now widely quoted statement of social and cultural identity (along the lines of "As American as apple pie") to win a contest in the early 1960s on CBC Radio's *This Country in the Morning*, a precursor of *Morningside*, as noted by radio host Peter Gzowski in *This Country in the Morning* (1974).

It is the allegiance of the solitary to his solitude.

Jean-Charles Falardeau, historian, defining the essential characteristic of Canadians, quoted by V.S. Pritchett, "Across the Vast Land," *Holiday*, April 1964.

Fuddle-duddle.

Pierre Elliott Trudeau, Prime Minister, Centre Block, Parliament Hill, 16 Feb. 1971. Accused earlier of uttering "a four-letter word" in the House of Commons, Trudeau denied the charge as "an absolute untruth." Later, outside the House, asked by CTV's parliamentary reporter Max Keeping if he had told the Tory M.P.s to "fuck off," Trudeau replied, "No, it was fuddle-duddle." That led M.T. McCutcheon, M.P., to quip, "Mr. Trudeau wants to be obscene but not heard." The cheeky euphemism appealed to the younger generation and the words even appeared on T-shirts.

The genius of Canada remains essentially a deflationary genius.

Jan Morris, Anglo-Welsh travel writer, "On the Confederation Special," *Travels* (1976). Over the years, Morris has described and redescribed the Canadian national style, finding something appealing in either the pattern or the cut of the cloth. "After a few days in Ottawa I began to think that perhaps some recondite accommodation kept this city itself in a balance—that some unwritten compact between the prosaic and the fantastic sustained its bland composure," she wrote of Ottawa in "Government Town," *Saturday Night*, Jan. 1987. "It is part of the civic genius—part of the Canadian genius, too—to reduce the heroic to the banal," she noted in "Suddenly Saskatoon," *Saturday Night*, July–Aug. 1990. "Cheer up! You have drawn a second prize, I would say, in the Lottario of Life," she advised Torontonians in "Flat City," *Saturday Night*, June 1984. In the Introduction to *City to City* (1990), she wrote of the country: "I think it deserves better of itself—more recognition of its own virtues, more readiness to blow its own trumpet, a little less becoming diffidence, a bit more vulgar swagger." Morris, a world traveller and perceptive essayist, concluded: "While it may not be the most thrilling of countries, [Canada] has a genuine claim to be considered the best."

A character actor like, say, Peter Sellers, can produce from his hat Englishmen, Americans, Indians, Frenchmen, Arabs, Mexicans, etc., etc. But what would he do if asked to sketch in a Canadian? What would he wear? What mannerisms might he assume? How would he speak? How would he suggest to an international audience Canadian-ness?

Thoughts of a character in **John Metcalf**'s novel *General Ludd* (1980).

It's clear to me that there is a Canadian personality. I can see it. I don't know why you can't.

Joseph Papp, New York theatre director, interviewed by Ray Conlogue in *The Globe and Mail*, 23 May 1981.

Proud to be Canadian

These four words first appeared on a t-shirt designed for a Toronto office picnic by **Sheila Craig Casgrain** in May 1991. They were so popular the t-shirts were produced in quantity and offered to Members of Parliament. A grass-roots movement supported by the Canadian Education Association was formed to make young Canadians more aware of their feelings about Canada.

I'm a very moderate person in most ways. I'm moderate in my obsessions with news, and quite immoderate in my desire to protect my family. Maybe this is the Canadian part of me—the natural moderate.

Bill Cameron, broadcaster and journalist, quoted by Roderick Jamer in *TV Guide*, 22 Aug. 1992.

What we need to do is discover all things that unite us as Canadians.

Neil Bissoondath, novelist and critic of multiculturalism, panelist, CTV's *W5*, 31 Jan. 1994, printed in "Verbatim," *The Globe and Mail*, 7 Feb. 1995.

Still, a Canadian syndrome exists. Its main symptom seems to be a perverse and provincial belief that universal human failings can be identified as Canadian characteristics.

Robert Fulford, columnist, "Canadians Have No Monopoly on Spite," *The Globe and Mail*, 26 Oct. 1994.

One primal definition of Canadianism has to be that we are among the few peoples in the world who, given a chance to become Americans, have chosen not to.

Richard Gwyn, columnist and author, *Nationalism without Walls: The Unbearable Lightness of Being Canadian* (1995).

CANADIAN PACIFIC RAILWAY See RAILWAYS

CANADIANS See also CANADA; CANADIANS & AMERICANS; IDENTITY, NATIONAL

One individual chooses Tuponia and another Hochelaga, as a suitable name for the new nationality. Now I would ask any hon. member of this House how he would feel if he woke up some fine morning and found himself, instead of a Canadian, a Tuponian or a Hochelagander. I think, sir, we may safely leave for the present discussion of the name as well as the origin of the new system proposed.

Thomas D'Arcy McGee, future Father of Confederation, objecting to wrangles over the new name for the new country, Legislative Assembly, Quebec, 9 Feb. 1865, *Parliamentary Debates on the Subject of the British North American Provinces* (1865).

He talked about Canada. All Canadians do. But about himself? No.

Henry Van Dyke, essayist, referring to a street musician in Ottawa, "A Lover of Music," *The Ruling Passion: Tales of Nature and Human Nature* (1901).

Towns, villages, woods, farms, streams, were spread out before the eye as far as the rim of the earth—the country of the hardiest and simplest race in the Western hemisphere, peaceful, contented neighbours of the great republic.

James Creelman, Canadian-born newspaper correspondent, *On the Great Highway: The Wanderings and Adventures of a Special Correspondent* (1901).

The people are 19 parts American, and one part Colonial, therefore are very insulted if called Americans.... They are a despicable race, exceedingly bourgeois, quite uncultured, very rude, very stupid and very narrow and pious. They are naive, childish and hold the simplest views of the problems of life. They care for nothing except money-making and sport, they chew gum instead of smoking or drinking, and their public meetings are monuments of sentimental platitudes. They are horror-struck with me because I don't know the date of the King's birthday, for they take their loyalty like everything else in dead seriousness and have no sense of humour.

Ernest Jones, psychoanalyst, biographer of Freud, Toronto resident before the Great War, letter to Sigmund Freud, 10 Dec. 1908, *The Complete Correspondence of Sigmund Freud and Ernest Jones: 1908–1939* (1993) edited by R. Andrew Paskauskas.

The woman was trying to say that she was not English but Canadian, but she couldn't make herself heard above the din.

Description of a woman at a Hollywood dinner party held during World War II as depicted by **Henry Miller** in "Soirée in Hollywood," *The Air-Conditioned Nightmare* (1945).

Ah yes, the Canadians of the future,—the true Canadians.

Remark uttered by a Monseigneur of the Old Regime in the historical novel *Shadows on the Rock* (1946), set in New France, by **Willa Cather**.

My fellow Canadians....

John G. Diefenbaker, Prime Minister (1957–63), characteristic manner of beginning public speeches.

Canadians are masters of what Bertrand Russell has called the twentieth century's highest achievement: the technique of suspended judgment. Canadians experiment with technology from all over the world, but rarely adopt any technical stratagem broadly.

Marshall McLuhan, communications pioneer, and Bruce R. Powers, communications specialist, authors of *The Global Village: Transformations in World Life and Media in the 21st Century* (1989).

I am awed by the ability of Canadians to live in Canada without falling upon their knees.

Robin Skelton, author and academic who emigrated from England to Canada in 1963, "O Canada!" in *Notes for a Native Land: A New Encounter with Canada* (1969) edited by Andy Wainwright.

These great, cheerful enormous men and their diminutive wives may not be as elegant as the French or hustle as much as the Americans. They may not, as Prince Philip once wisely told them to, have quite made up their minds about us, but they still drink the Queen's health in water and even if they are happiest with a label pinned on their lapel, explaining who they are and what convention they are attending, they are our friends, our allies, and in some ways our creation. We owe them and the late General Wolfe a good deal.

Robert Morley, British actor, reflections on a theatrical tour across Canada, *The London Observer*, 24 Dec. 1972.

How is it that together we feel we are less than the sum of our pieces? By God, we are a nation of gripers. A great land, a diverse and gifted people, a still awkward but potentially dynamic nation, dissipating its strength in acrimony and meanness.

Barbara Frum, television personality, address, Destiny Canada Conference, York University, Toronto, 28 June 1977.

Frankly, it no longer matters who were the first Canadians or who were the second Canadians. There is only one sorrow and one pity we must avoid at all costs—let none of us be the last Canadians.

David Crombie, Toronto Mayor, address, General Meeting of the Progressive Conservative Party, Quebec City, 4 Nov. 1977, quoted by *The Toronto Star* that day.

Canadians are a sort of bridge between Americans and Europeans, with a freshness that doesn't exist in Europe anymore and a sophistication often lacking in the U.S.

Peter Ustinov, British actor who played the lead in Stratford Festival's *King Lear*, interviewed by Lawrence O'Toole in *Maclean's*, 1 Oct. 1979.

In the welter of statistics about selected ethnic origins (singular or multiple) in the last census, one finding was often overlooked. Of the 25,309,330 people living in Canada in 1986, only 69,065 declared themselves to be Canadians.

Charlotte Gray, journalist, "Speaking in Tongues," *Saturday Night*, Dec. 1989.

In today's world, only one person in every 200 is a Canadian.

Margaret Catley-Carlson, President of CIDA, "Aid: A Canadian Vocation," *Daedalus: Journal of the American Academy of Arts and Sciences*, "In Search of Canada," Fall, 1988.

To be respected we Canadians must learn to seem a trifle dangerous.

Remark made by a Canadian-born character in **John Kenneth Galbraith**'s novel *A Tenured Professor* (1990).

Assistant: One of the witnesses is dead. The other has moved to Canada.

Lawyer: Same thing.

Exchange between an assistant and her lawyer boss (played by James Woods) in the movie *True Believer* (1989), as noted by Josh Freed in *Geist 5*, Oct.–Nov. 1991.

I don't think I ever met a Canadian I didn't like, and that's about as bad a thing as I can think of to say about anyone.

Ray Guy, columnist, quoted by Wayne Johnston in *The Globe and Mail*, 29 Jan. 1991.

Being a Canadian these days is like living with a beautiful and talented woman who keeps slashing her wrists.

Michael Ignatieff, commentator, *The Observer*, 10 Feb. 1991.

If you are a Canadian, you have a bond with alienated Americans... in a way, Canadians are expatriate Americans from birth.

David Cronenberg, movie director, quoted by Brian D. Johnson in *Maclean's*, 20 Jan. 1992.

Being Canadian has never been a nationality; it's a condition.

Peter C. Newman, author and columnist, *Maclean's*, 10 Feb. 1992.

Are Canadians boring? British and American bores have accused Canada of being the most boring nation on the planet, a land of plodding and humorless yokels, tediously earnest and "nice" and, when all is said and done, about as entertaining as a four-hour sermon on chastity or fifteen minutes with any book by Peter C. Newman.

Christopher Dafoe, columnist, *Winnipeg Free Press*, 2 May 1992.

We know how to dress for winter / We're not afraid of snow / And we love our country quietly / And hope Quebec won't go / Forgive us we're Canadian / And some might think us bland / But there's nowhere that we'd rather be / Than the vast and frozen land.

Verse from the comic song "Forgive Us We're Canadian" (1993) composed by **Mark Leiren-Young** and **Kevin Crofton** for their show and album *Local Anxiety: Forgive Us We're Canadian* (1994).

The Canadian people are solid people, responsible people, compassionate people, people with a feeling for others. Even as you criticize and question many things in your country, let me tell you there are many things we can learn from your society. So please remain Canadian.

Mikhail Gorbachev, former Soviet President, address in Toronto, 31 March 1993, quoted by Paul Moloney in *The Toronto Star* the following day.

The world-wide perception seems to be that it is the common desire of every Canadian to cease to be a Canadian.

Glenn Grant, anthologist, Introduction to Grant and David G. Hartwell's *North Stars: The Anthology of Canadian Science Fiction* (1994).

Canada's a land of contrasts; we have cold, deep lakes and warm, shallow people.

Maurus E. Mallon, aphorist, *Compendulum* (1995).

If we don't define ourselves, we are going to allow others to define us.

Leonard Cohen, singer/singwriter, audio track, CBC Museum, Broadcast Centre, Toronto, Jan. 1995.

We're proud to be Canadian / We're awfully nice to strangers, our manners be our curse / It's cool in many ways to be Canadian / We won't say that we're better, it's just that we're less worse.

Chorus of the song "Proud to be Canadian," written and performed by the **Arrogant Worms** on their CD *Caterwaul & Doggerel* (EMI, 1995).

I've always enjoyed Canadians. They're different than anyone else in the world—they're so deep.

Peter Townsend, British composer, interviewed at the revival of his rock opera *Tommy*, Toronto, 9 March 1995, quoted by Serena French in *The Globe and Mail* the following day.

It's hard to grab a cup of coffee without someone saying hello. Sometimes it's an imposition, but people in Canada, they're always very friendly.

David Duchovny, actor and star of the TV series *X-Files*, filmed in Vancouver, quoted by Guy Saddy in *TV Guide*, 11 March 1995.

Canada isn't a country at all, it's simply geography. There's no emotion there... there are no Whitmans, no Twains, no Cranes. Half the English Canadians wish they were really English, and the other half wish they were Americans. If you're going to be anything, you have to choose. Even Catholics don't regard Limbo as something permanent.

Thoughts of a character in **Guy Vanderhaeghe**'s novel *The Englishman's Boy* (1996).

I look at Canadians and think, "These are the people my mother always wanted me to hang out with in highschool."

Garrison Keillor, writer and performer, CBC Radio's production of *A Prairie Home Companion*, broadcast from Vancouver, 24 Feb. 1996, as quoted by Peter Goddard in *The Toronto Star* two days later.

The Rose phrased her question in the sort of friendly, cheerful and helpful Canadian manner that brought an accusatory pall over the entire exchange.

Passage from **Robert Stone**'s novel *Damascus Gate* (1998) set in Jerusalem; one of the characters, nicknamed The Rose, comes from Alberta.

CANADIANS & AMERICANS

See also CANADA, CANADA & THE UNITED STATES, CANADIANS

I do not see any difference between Canadians and Americans.

George Bernard Shaw, Anglo-Irish playwright, addressing members of the Canadian Authors' Association on a visit to London, 13 July 1933, quoted by William D. Lighthall in *The Bookman*, Spring 1937.

I wonder if Canadians have ever stopped to think that they are living alongside for three thousand peaceful miles the most idealistic people in the world. Perhaps you do, and it may make you shudder sometimes.

Arthur Crock, Washington Bureau Chief of *The New York Times*, "Address" (1933), *Empire Club of Canada: Addresses Delivered to the Members During the Year 1933–34* (1934).

Canadians are a fine tribe of people. They are hardy—they got to be to live next to us.

Will Rogers, humorist popular in the 1930s, *The Best of Will Rogers* (1979) compiled by Bryan B. Sterling.

My curiosity at being in a new country was mildly appeased by the difference—the almost imperceptible difference—between the Canadian and the inhabitant of the States. The Canadians speak with a stronger American accent. That is the main distinction.

Wyndham Lewis, British artist and author, *America, I Presume* (1940).

While Americans are benevolently ignorant about Canada, most Canadians seem malevolently informed about the United States.

Merrill Denison, author, "4,000 Miles of 'Irritation,'" *Saturday Review of Literature*, 7 June 1952.

An English-speaking Canadian in the United States is in the same fortunate position as a Scotsman in England. He need not feel as if he were a foreigner, because he will not be treated as one. But, if the question did arise, he could be confident of holding his own.

Arnold J. Toynbee, historian, "Canada's Identity and Bilingualism," *The Globe and Mail*, 30 March 1961.

If the national mental illness of the United States is megalomania, that of Canada is paranoid schizophrenia.

Margaret Atwood, poet, Afterword, *The Journals of Susanna Moodie* (1970).

I have certain advantages from having been brought up in two cultures, Canadian and American. They're closely related but, nevertheless, they're different so it's like looking through binoculars as compared with looking through a telescope. You see things in more depth.

Ross Macdonald, detective-story writer who was born in California and raised in Ontario, quoted by Sam Grogg Jr., in "Ross Macdonald: At the Edge," *Journal of Popular Culture*, No. 7, 1973.

You can have a Canadian friend, and he can see in you an American friend, but history will have placed a national qualification on your friendship.

John Keats, American social critic, resident of an island in the Thousand Islands region, *Of Time and an Island* (1974).

Ugly American, Smugly Canadian

Remark on national styles recorded by **Jeanette Harris** in *Canada: The Land and Its People* (1977).

As a friend of mine remarked the other day: "You ask an American how he's feeling and he cries 'Great!' You ask a Canadian and he answers 'Not bad,' or 'Pas mal.'"

Pierre Berton, author and television personality, writing an imaginary letter to Uncle Sam, *Why We Act like Canadians* (1983).

While Americans are reading *The Joy of Sex*, Canadians are reading *Gray's Anatomy*.

Sandy Stewart, writer and broadcaster, quoted by William French in *The Globe and Mail*, 31 Jan. 1985.

If I were Canadian, I suspect I'd be touchy about it.

Remark made by the intelligence agent known as Mr. Smith (played by Alan Bates) in the BBC-TV movie *Pack of Lies* (1986), based on the play by **Hugh Whitmore**, about a curious couple who claim they are Canadians but turn out to be Americans.

In some unarticulated and mostly polite way, Canadians feel more secure with a tidy line between them and the Americans.

Marian Botsford Fraser, author, *Walking the Line* (1989).

There are still some differences between Canada and the U.S. In the States everyone remembers where they were when Kennedy was shot; in Canada we all know where we were when Henderson scored.

Mark Leiren-Young, playwright, referring to the assassination of U.S. President John F. Kennedy and hockey player Paul Henderson's winning goal in the Canada-U.S.S.R. hockey series of 1972, in the revue *We Love You Brian Mulroney and Other Horror Stories* (1992).

I'm a Canadian, and Canadians are educated to watch America very closely—just as women are educated to watch men very closely—because what America does affects us.

Leonard Cohen, poet and songwriter, interviewed by Karen Schoemer in *The New York Times*, 29 Nov. 1992.

Americans have great and noble principles and they go to hell trying to live up to them. Canadians also have great and noble principles, but they go to heaven figuring out ways to get around them.

Attributed to linguist **Noam Chomsky** by Christopher Dafoe in *The Globe and Mail*, 13 March 1993.

"I remember a time when America wasn't Canadian," somebody laments in an old *Saturday Night Live* sketch that posited an invasion of the United States by its deceptively innocuous neighbour from the North. *Spy* magazine (co-founded by the Ottawa-born E. Graydon Carter) once ran a mock-paranoid feature titled "The Canadians Among Us."

Rick Marin, comic, "The Most Entertaining Americans? Canadians," *The New York Times*, 27 June 1993.

Canadians have an even more intense reverence for America than the Americans themselves.

Adapted from an observation made by Canadian-born band leader **Paul Shaffer**, quoted by Rick Marin in "The Most Entertaining Americans? Canadians," *The New York Times*, 27 June 1993.

I came to understand that at the core of every Canadian being is the determination to differentiate himself or herself from the supposedly crass society which presses upon Canada's southern border, and that the need operates as a set of blinkers preventing some kinds of critical scrutiny of Canadian institutions.

Jill Ker Conway, Australian-born, American-educated historian and memoirist who taught at the University of Toronto from 1964 to 1975, *True North: A Memoir* (1994).

Americans are like Canadians on speed.

Josh Freed, columnist and author, inteviewed by Peter Gzowski on CBC Radio's *Morningside*, 15 Nov. 1994.

The best all-around Americans, in my view, are Canadians.

Thoughts of the narrator of the novel *Independence Day* (1995) written by the U.S. author **Richard Ford**.

Britons put up with, Americans fix, while Canadians cope.

Attributed to sociologist **Margaret Mead** by Alexander Craig, "Quebec, Anyone?" *The Canadian Forum*, June 1995.

I think Canada is funny because it's a country right on our border that is the complete opposite of ours and is everything we would like to be. And I know that sounds strange because you see Canadians trying their hardest to become Americans.

Michael Moore, American filmmaker, interviewed by Shirley Knott, "More Moore," *The Toronto Star*, 12 Aug. 1995.

Studies have shown that Canadians want not to be Americans. What they do want is to be rich and independent enough to continue to debate the Canadian identity.

Nicholas Stethem, strategy analyst, address, "Failure of History and Loss of the Future," Royal Ontario Museum, Toronto, 11 Oct. 1996.

The average Canadian discounts automatically his home and native land by about 33.3 percent, especially in the presence of Americans.

Bruce McCall, humorist, adapted from *Thin Ice: Coming of Age in Canada* (1997).

Many Americans merely think of Canada as the "Maple Leaf" state. But, that's okay with me, because I think of Florida as the "sunshine" province.

Tim Cerantola, columnist, "Canada, Eh?" *The Hamilton Spectator*, 28 June 1997.

"Canadians give thanks sooner than Americans," she said, and the quip—was it really extemporaneous?—was snatched at by Canadian listeners, as always grateful for any morsel of attention and praise from our great neighbour, and became a kind of anthem on the events of the week.

Passage from **Hugh Hood**'s futuristic novel *Great Realizations* (1997).

If Canada was ordained to be anything, it was to be snowy and reasonable. I wanted to remove myself from American morality plays. I wanted to live a snowy and reasonable life.

Stephen Strauss, science columnist and former American, "Why I Became a Canadian," *The Globe and Mail*, 1 July 2000.

CANOES

It is strange that all my ailments vanish as soon as I seat myself in a canoe.

Sir George Simpson, Governor, Hudson's Bay Company, quoted by John S. Galbraith in *The Beaver*, Winter 1960. Simpson was governor of more than one-quarter of North America from 1821 for almost forty years.

A Canadian is somebody who knows how to make love in a canoe.

Pierre Berton, author and television personality, quoted by Dick Brown in *The Canadian*, 22 Dec. 1973.

In John Robert Colombo's *Canadian Quotations*, Pierre Berton is quoted saying "a Canadian is someone who knows how to make love in a canoe." Pierre says he didn't say it, or if he did he took it from someone else, but whoever the authority is, if that's the test, I fail. I do know how to gunwale a canoe... portage it, right it without getting out of the water, and sail it home with my hockey sweater tied to a paddle. But make love? You got me.

Peter Gzowski, journalist, *The Private Voice: A Journal of Reflections* (1988).

Few people have any idea what it is, what a toll it takes, to average over thirty miles a day in a canoe, regardless of weather, weariness, or sickness.

Don Starkell, canoeist, *Paddle to the Amazon: The Ultimate 12,000-Mile Canoe Adventure* (1987).

Western art starts with the figure; West Coast Indian art starts with the canoe.

Bill Reid, Haida carver, interviewed by *Equinox*, quoted by Christopher Dafoe in *The Globe and Mail*, 16 Nov. 1991.

A really good paddle should come alive in your hands and put a smile on your face.

Ray Kettlewell, master paddle-maker, characteristic remark, Canoe Expo, Etobicoke, Ont., 8 April 1994.

God first created the canoe and then thought up the ideal country to go with it.

Attributed to paddler **Bill Mason** by Donna Carter in "Peterborough Canoe Museum Makes a Big Splash," *The Globe and Mail*, 16 May 1997.

CANUCK

Canuck is a Canadian and unites *Canadian* and *Chinook*, the name of an Indian tribe that lived on the Columbia River and traded with the Hudson Bay traders.

John D. Jacobson, compiler, offering a somewhat dubious etymology for no-longer-fashionable slang word "Canuck," *Toposaurus: A Humorous Treasury of Toponyms* (1990).

CAPE BRETON ISLAND See also NOVA SCOTIA

Cape Breton is the land of my love, / The land of trees and high mountains. / Cape Breton is the land of my love; / We deem it the most beautiful land on earth.

English translation of the Gaelic chorus of the anthem "Cape Breton Is the Land of My Love" (Oran Do Cheap Breatainn), composed by **Dan Alex MacDonald** of Framboise, Richmond County, C.B.I., *Gaelic Songs in Nova Scotia* (Bulletin No. 198, 1964) edited by Helen Creighton and Calum MacLeod.

I have travelled around the globe. I have seen the Canadian and the American Rockies, the Andes and the Alps and the Highlands of Scotland; but for simple beauty, Cape Breton Island outrivals them all.

Alexander Graham Bell, inventor and summer resident of Cape Breton Island, N.S., quoted by Wes Rataushk in *Silver Highway: A Celebration of the Trans-Canada Highway* (1988).

Whatever the landscape had of meaning appears to have been abandoned, / unless the road is holding it back, in the interior, / where we cannot see, / where deep lakes are reputed to be....

Elizabeth Bishop, New England poet who in 1911–17 lived in Great Village, N.S., "Cape Breton Island," *The Complete Poems 1927–1979* (1983).

A Cape Breton fishing village is a way of life, a confrontation with the elements, not a tourist attraction.

Stephen Brook, English travel writer, *Maple Leaf Rag: Travels across Canada* (1987).

Nineteen years ago I discovered Cape Breton when I was looking for a place I could afford to take my kids in the summer. I took the map of Nova Scotia and drove to the place with the fewest roads. I figured it would be isolated and I was right. It was years before anyone in the community figured out that I was a celebrity.

Philip Glass, minimalist composer, quoted in *Saturday Night*, Dec. 1987.

Home is Cape Breton, and I'm here to stay.

Rita MacNeil, singer and composer and resident of Big Pond, Cape Breton Island, N.S., quoted by Ann Finlayson in *Maclean's*, 7 Nov. 1988.

Oh, how I long to be in her arms again, / Oh, how I long to see those waves come rolling in; / And I will leave her never more, / My bonnie, my Cape Breton Shore.

Refrain of **John Allan Cameron**'s song "My Cape Breton Shore" (1970s) quoted by Martin Melhuish in *Celtic Tides: Traditional Music in a New Age* (1998).

Cape Breton is one of those places around which it is impossible to drive without imagining that you are in an automobile commercial.

Rebecca Mead, writer, "Sex, Drugs, and Fiddling," *The New Yorker*, 20 Dec. 1999.

CAPITALISM See also BUSINESS, FREE ENTERPRISE, LABOUR, UNIONS

The supreme task of the twentieth century will be to find out how to make the many improvements of our scientific age yield happiness to all, instead of profit to a few, and the completion of this task is due now at any time. Ways of improvement must be found.

William Irvine, politician, *The Farmers in Politics* (1902).

Conflicts exist, but only because capitalism exists.... Capital needs competition, yet kills it through monopoly; it needs peace, yet breeds war; it needs outlets for investment, but this develops rival capitalisms; it needs flexibility, yet creates rigidity.

David Lewis and **Frank Scott**, socialists, *Make This Young Canada: A Review of C.C.F. History and Policy* (1943).

Capitalism is a heartless, callous, cynical and hypocritical economic system. It is a lie that honest labour brings economic security. Those who have the most economic security, like Rita Hayworth's parasitical husband Ali Khan, do not labour at all.

Leslie Morris, communist, *The Canadian Tribune*, 9 Jan. 1950, *Selected Writings of Leslie Morris: 1923–1964* (1970).

Economic expansion accompanied by widespread suffering and injustice is not desirable social progress. A society motivated by the drive for private gain and special privilege is basically immoral.

"Winnipeg Manifesto: 1956 Winnipeg Declaration of Principles of the Co-operative Commonwealth Federation," reproduced in *The Decline and Fall of a Good Idea: CCF-NDP Manifestos 1932 to 1969* (1974) introduced by Michael S. Cross.

Capitalism must be replaced by socialism, by national planning of investment, and by the public ownership of the means of production in the interests of the Canadian people as a whole.

"The Waffle Manifesto: For an Independent Socialist Canada" (1969) reprinted in *The Canadian Forum*, Dec. 1989.

These days the typical capitalist is not a banker or some wealthy man sitting in an ivory tower. By and large, the capitalist is the individual Canadian citizen who has any kind of savings.

J.S. Land, President, IAC Limited, interviewed by Dean Walker in *A Case for the Enterprise System* (1975).

Greed is essential to the proper functioning of our economic system. Of course, we don't call it greed in polite company. On the supply side, we call it hustle or ambition or push-and-shove. On the demand side, we call it consumerism or, playfully, "shop till you drop."

William A. Dimma, corporate executive, address at York University, Toronto, quoted by Michael Valpy in *The Globe and Mail*, 29 Nov. 1989.

Capitalism's ability to "deliver the goods" economically has been much exaggerated. As a political system, it fails miserably to address the ordinary needs and demands of its citizens. As a moral system, it utterly fails to enlist people's will to a shared freedom, to justice, to equality, to community, or to love. If the best democratic socialism can offer is "a little more of this and a little more of that," we might as well pack our bags and call it a day.

Bob Rae, NDP leader, address, "A Socialist's Manifesto," *The Globe and Mail*, 1 Oct. 1990.

Self-maximizing owners of international capital have been accorded well-defined transnational rights to rule the world's production and distribution, uncontrolled by a single effective human right or environmental limit to their private profit-seeking for themselves.

John McMurtry, philosopher, University of Guelph, "The Contradictions of Free Market Doctrine—Is There a Solution?" a paper prepared for the Westminster Institute Conference, "Surviving Globalization: Economic, Social, and Environmental Dimensions," London, Ont., May 1995.

The central challenge to 21st century capitalism, and ultimately to the world order itself, is to ensure that the opportunities and rewards of this explosion of enterprise are shared with literally billions of people.

Thomas d'Aquino, President, Business Council on National Issues, 12 Jan. 1995, *National and Global Perspectives*, Winter 1994–95.

Each economic system does tend to be more at home in certain circumstances than in others. Capitalism is happiest in a non-democratic society.

John Ralston Saul, author, *The Doubter's Companion: A Dictionary of Aggressive Common Sense* (1994).

Is the new capitalism fertile ground for the extension of human freedom? Hardly.

James Laxer, political scientist, *In Search of a New Left: Canadian Politics after the Neoconservative Assault* (1996).

I do not wish to receive my policing services from General Motors any more than I wish to buy my cars from the government.

Henry Mintzberg, economist, from an essay in the *Harvard Business Review*, quoted by Ed Finn, "Waiting for the Flood," *The Canadian Forum*, April 1998.

CAPITAL PUNISHMENT See also CRIME

Perhaps it is eligible that incorrigible offenders should sometimes be cut off. Let it be done in a way that is not degrading to human nature.

Joseph Brant, Native leader, quoted by William L. Stone in *Life of Joseph Brant—Thayendanegea; Including the Indian Wars of the American Revolution* (1838).

Some part of us still believes that men should kill.

Robin Skelton, poet and aphorist, *A Devious Dictionary* (1991).

I sometimes think it's not individual human beings but this world we all inhabit that requires the death sentence.

Sentence from **Eric McCormack**'s novel *The Mysterium* (1992).

We all know that capital punishment works not when it fits the crime but when it grotesquely exceeds it. If the punishment for drunk driving were the electric chair, who would risk frying for one last beer?

H.S. Bhabra, novelist, "Progressive Culling," *The Globe and Mail*, 20 Sept. 1994. Bhabra calls "white-collar criminals" "felons in French cuffs."

CAREERS See also WORK

I'm just a kept woman who pays her own way.

Barbara Frum, writer and broadcaster and wife of a dentist turned property developer, quoted by Paul King in *Homemaker's Magazine*, May 1975.

I thought of myself as specifically not having a career but, rather, as having some kind of destiny.

Leonard Cohen, poet and singer, quoted by Sheldon Teitelbaum in *The Los Angeles Times Magazine*, 5 April 1992.

To paraphrase the late Andy Warhol: In the future, everyone will have a good job—for fifteen minutes.

Barbara Moses, career consultant, *Career Intelligence* (1997).

If you choose a career you love, you will never work a day in your life.

Mark Cullen, gardening specialist, quoting "a Chinese proverb," conference, Toronto, 19 Jan. 1999.

Career activism means *becoming an intelligent actor in your own life:* developing a thorough understanding of your current situation, and then taking steps to change it for the better.

Barbara Moses, career consultant, *The Good News about Careers: How You'll Be Working in the Next Decade* (1999).

CARIBBEAN ISLANDS

Some are for keeping Canada, some Guadaloupe. Who will tell me what I shall be hanged for not keeping?

William Pitt the Elder, Prime Minister of Great Britain, address on the future of Britain's military acquisitions, House of Commons in 1759. At the time Canada meant Quebec, and Guadaloupe referred to a chain of islands in the Lesser Antilles in the Caribbean Sea. Since 1816, La Guadeloupe has been a French overseas département. Pitt's remark was quoted by Hilda Neatby in *Quebec: The Revolutionary Age 1760–1791* (1966).

I hope the day will come when we have political union with some of the Caribbean countries. This motion should not be talked out today but should be given some serious study. In time we may reach a common market relationship and achieve a measure of political association.

Lorne Nystrom, Member for Yorkton-Melville, House of Commons, 16 Dec. 1977.

CARTOON ART See COMIC ART

CATHOLICISM See also BELIEF, CHRISTIANITY, RELIGION

You are a grain of mustard seed that shall rise and grow until its branches overshadow the earth. You are few, but your work is the work of God. His smile is on you, and your children shall fill the land.

Sieur de Maisonneuve, French colonist, delivering a sermon-like speech on the founding of the settlement of Ville-Marie, today's Montreal, 18 May 1642, quoted by Francis Parkman in *The Jesuits of North America in the Seventeenth Century* (1867).

I listen to my curé, my curé listens to the bishop, the bishop listens to the pope, the pope listens to our Lord Jesus Christ, who aids with the Holy Spirit to render them infallible on the teaching and government of his Church.

Bishop Ignace Bourget, sermon, 1850s, quoted by Ron Graham in *God's Dominion: A Sceptic's Quest* (1990).

And yet I love their religion. There is something beautiful and almost divine in the faith and obedience of a true son of the Holy Mother. I sometimes fancy that I would fain be a Roman Catholic,—if I could; as also I would often wish to be still a child, if that were possible.

Anthony Trollope, English novelist and traveller, responding to the Catholicism of Quebec, *North America* (1862).

After our parish there is another parish, and another, and another, all alike, and each with its own church steeple, its curé, its buried dead, its old soil worked by fathers and fathers' fathers which one loves more than oneself. There you have it, this country of ours!

Words of old Uncle Jean in **Adjutor Rivard**'s novel *Chez nous* (1914) translated by W.H. Blake in 1924.

A true French Canadian should remain forever a Catholic.

George-Étienne Cartier, Father of Confederation, quoted by John Boyd in *Sir George-Étienne Cartier, Bart.* (1914).

One person who seemed to understand me was Archbishop Neil McNeil. I used to go to him often when I couldn't take it any more. He was a small man, and on one occasion two tears rolled down his cheeks.

"Catherine," he said, "pray for my priests. They are hidebound."

Catherine de Hueck Doherty, Catholic founder of Friendship House in Toronto in the 1930s, turning to the Archbishop of Toronto, *Fragments of My Life* (1979).

The Catholic religion is the only religion—all sects are derivative. Buddhism and similar oriental philosophies and mythologies are not religions in any sense. They have no convenants and no sacraments and no theology. The very notion of "comparative" religion is ridiculous.

Marshall McLuhan, communications pioneer, letter, 5 Sept. 1935, *Letters of Marshall McLuhan* (1987) edited by Matie Molinaro, Corinne McLuhan, and William Toye.

This is the spot. The institute will be here or it will be nowhere.

Étienne Gilson, French theologian, referring to the residence now known as Gilson House, 8 Elmsley Place, on the campus of St. Michael's College, University of Toronto, where in 1929 he helped to establish the world-famous institute which in 1939 was renamed the Pontifical Institute of Mediaeval Studies. Quoted by Margaret McGrath in *Gilson Bibliography* (1982).

Over a glass of brandy he lectured me about the conversion of Canada to Roman Catholicism. I do not think he was being realistic.

G.K. Chesterton, man-of-letters, unpublished recollection of a meeting in Toronto with priest and author Dean Harris, quoted by Michael Coren in "Exile Here at Home," *Canadian Notes & Queries*, Spring 1992.

...I had turned over a Protestant's drab atheism for an old-fashioned popish cure, I had hoped to deduce from my sense of sin the existence of a Supreme Being. On those frosty mornings in rime-laced Quebec the good priest worked on me with the finest tenderness and understanding.

Passage reflecting the thoughts of the oddly named seducer Humbert Humbert in **Vladimir Nabokov**'s novel *Lolita* (1955, 1958).

Without pride or any falsification of the facts, I can assure you that at seven o'clock every evening, while I was reciting the rosary on the radio, all of Montreal was kneeling, praying with the pastor.

Paul-Émile Cardinal Léger, recalling on TV in 1984 his Cardinalship in Montreal which extended from 1953 to 1967, quoted by Michael Higgins in *The Toronto Star*, 14 Dec. 1991.

When a man is accountable only to God the Father who is in Heaven, he can afford to take a few liberties with temporal history. It is dangerous, but not everyone has the imagination to perceive that. We live in a surrealist world.

Jean-Paul Desbiens, teacher, *The Impertinences of Brother Anonymous* (1962) translated from the French by Miriam Chapin.

The French won't take over and neither will the Pope, although he's not the menace he used to be.

Pierre Elliott Trudeau, Prime Minister, remark made at an Ottawa press conference, 25 Nov. 1976, quoted by Hugh Winsor in *The Globe and Mail* the following day.

There will be a cult devoted to Mary (or whatever she comes to be called) as long as there are economic conditions that produce the father-ineffective family. And as long as there is a cult devoted to Her, there will be people who speak with the goddess face to face.

Michael Carroll, psychologist, concluding sentences, *The Cult of the Virgin Mary: Psychological Origins* (1986).

Once a Catholic, often an anti-Catholic.

Michael Coren, biographer, "Friend of the Fairies," *The Idler*, July–Aug. 1992.

Could anyone younger than forty understand, or even care, how powerful and confident the Church was before it began leaking priests, and its teachings on birth control, celibacy, homosexuality, and the role of women began to feel like ancient freight?

Philip Milner, author and academic, *The Yankee Professor's Guide to Life in Nova Scotia* (1993).

I have often said at public occasions that it is good to belong to a Church that can change its mind.

Gregory Baum, theologian, "A Letter from the Pope," *The Canadian Forum*, Dec. 1993.

The Sacrifice of the Mass is the greatest form of theatre possible and the one in which the audience is necessarily participant—in which there is no audience.

Marshall McLuhan, communications pioneer, referring to the Catholic celebration of the Mass, quoted by John Kelly in *Who Was Marshall McLuhan?* (1994) edited by Barrington Nevitt and Maurice McLuhan. Kelly, a Catholic priest and friend of McLuhan, continued, "That statement is loaded with orthodox theology but spoken like an artist. It may well be the greatest statement McLuhan ever made and it is so perfect that I would dishonour his memory by offering comment. I only wish I could have said it. It was unrehearsed, spontaneous, brilliant: one sentence about which libraries could be and have been written. It is quintessential McLuhan, total involvement and ultimate breakthrough."

Kneeling to receive Communion is not a criminal offence.

Ruling of the **Supreme Court of Canada** against arrest of Roman Catholics in Nova Scotia for "disturbing the solemnity of a church service" by refusing to follow a new directive to stand while receiving the sacrament, news summary, 30 Sept. 1985, as noted by James B. Simpson in *Simpson's Contemporary Quotations* (1997).

The greatest criminal organization outside the Mafia.

Mischievous, tongue-in-cheek remark made by broadcaster and former Catholic **Michael Enright**, as noted by Michael Posner, "Son of Morningside," *The Globe and Mail*, 10 May 1997. Enright, subsequently appointed host of CBC Radio's *This Morning*, successor to *Morningside*, was taken to task by Catholic organizations. "The Catholic Church, the largest criminal organization in the world after the Mafia" is how the remark was quoted by Thomas Langan, "Crossroads," *The Globe and Mail*, 29 Sept. 1997.

CATS See also ANIMALS

Or what if it was cats and not humans who invented technology—should cats build scratching-post skyscrapers covered entirely with shag carpeting? Would they have TV shows starring rubber squeak toys?

Thoughts of the narrator of **Douglas Coupland**'s novel *Life after God* (1994).

CBC See CANADIAN BROADCASTING CORPORATION

CCF See NEW DEMOCRATIC PARTY

CELEBRITIES See also FAME, SHOW BUSINESS

The celebrity goes up like a rocket, comes down like a stick.

Louis Dudek, man-of-letters, *Epigrams* (1975).

Stars are vacuums filled by others' fantasies.

Gina Mallet, film and theatre critic, *The Toronto Star*, 23 Dec. 1979.

CELTIC PEOPLE See WELSH PEOPLE

CENSORSHIP See also BOOKS, FREE SPEECH, NEWS, OBSCENITY, PORNOGRAPHY

Yes, gentlemen, come what will, while I live, Nova Scotia shall have the blessing of an open and unshackled press.

Joseph Howe, publisher of *The Novascotian*, impassioned address to the jury, Halifax, May 1835. News of his acquittal for libel marked a turning point in the history of the press in British North America. *The Speeches and Public Letters of The Hon. Joseph Howe* (1858) edited by William Annand.

Stowed away in a Montreal lumber room / The *Discobolus* standeth and turneth his face to the wall; / Dusty, cobweb-covered, maimed, and set at naught, / Beauty crieth in the attic and no man regardeth: / O God! O Montreal!

Lines from English satirist **Samuel Butler**'s poem "A Psalm of Montreal," *The Spectator*, May 18, 1878. Butler wrote it after a visit to the old Montreal Museum of Natural History in 1874, where he saw that the plaster cast of Myron's *Discobolus* had been relegated to the storage room. This act of curatorial prudery inspired him to write the satiric verse. In 1913, the poet Rupert Brooke wrote: "I made my investigations in Montreal. I have to report that the *Discobolus* is very well, and, nowadays, looks the whole world in the face, almost quite unabashed." Would that this were so in the 2000s! The *Discobolus*, part of the permanent collection of the Montreal Museum of Fine Arts, was loaned for display purposes in the 1960s and then disappeared from view. Perhaps it languishes to this day in some Montreal "lumber room."

And in this connection I may perhaps be permitted to say that no book of a questionable character, no pernicious literature of any description has ever been seen or discovered either in my shop or on my shelves, nor has my catalogue ever been disgraced or contaminated with obnoxious or obscene literature of any kind. Nothing has been offered for sale that I could not read aloud in my own family circle.

John Britnell, bookseller and proprietor of the Albert Britnell's Book Shop, founded in Toronto in 1893, *Books and Booksellers in Ancient and Modern Times with Autobiographical Experiences of the Past Sixty Years* (1923).

I can only say that the American Mercury acknowledges no allegiance to King George V, and that it is interested in definitions of treason framed by Canadian politicians only as it is interested in other amusing imbecilities.

H.L. Mencken, writer and editor of the journal *American Mercury*, denounced in 1924 by Canadian M.P.s for its "treasonable" editorial about the decline of British culture, as noted by Edgar Kemler in *The Irreverent Mr. Mencken* (1950).

Doesn't that conjure up a lovely picture! Americans sneaking over the border into Canada to see it and no doubt being conscience-stricken that they are being un-American.

Charlie Chaplin, film personality, noting that his feature film *The King in New York* (1957) was being exhibited in Canada but not in the United States, according to William D. Grant, "That Old Movie Bug," *Canadian Fandom*, Oct. 1957.

It's such an honour being banned in Italy, the mother of sensuality. It's like being asked to straighten your tie in a bordello. It's ironic that the pictures were removed on the complaint of a cardinal. I regard censorship as a cardinal sin.

Harold Town, artist, when two drawings in his "Enigma" series were removed as indecent from the Venice Biennale in 1964. Quoted by Pierre Berton in *The Toronto Star*, 31 Oct. 1992.

We were a propaganda arm of our governments. At the start the censors enforced that, but by the end we were our own censors. We were cheerleaders.

Charles Lynch, war correspondent, referring to censorship during World War II, quoted by Phillip Knightley in *The First Casualty* (1975).

If the government may forbid an English sign, is it so far a step to forbid an English book? And if an English book how about certain French books?

W. Earle McLaughlin, bank president, referring to Quebec's "sign law," address, Quebec City, 18 April 1977, quoted by Douglas H. Fullerton in *The Dangerous Delusion: Quebec's Independence Obsession* (1978).

If you can put a control on the speed of a guy charging down the highway at 110 miles an hour and couple that with seat-belt legislation and say it's good for all mankind in this province, then it seems to me you can consider a seat-belt on your psyche. That's all we're talking about, a check.

Donald Sims, head of the Ontario film censor board, quoted by Sid Adilman in *The Toronto Star*, 7 Oct. 1978.

If literary filth is to have official Government recognition, it should come first to our own Canadian trash.

W.O. Mitchell, novelist, letter to then-premier Ernest Manning when the Alberta Cabinet denounced the schoolroom use of Salinger's novel *The Catcher in the Rye*, from *W.O. Mitchell: Novelist in Hiding* (1980).

I'm against cutting it. I have been reading in the newspapers here what your censor board wants and I think perhaps in Ontario there is too much Victorian moralistic thinking.

Günter Grass, German author of the novel *The Tin Drum*, when the movie version was banned by the Ontario censor board, quoted by Sid Adilman in *The Toronto Star*, 28 April 1980.

Canada is certainly the most over-censored country in the free world, if not in terms of the severity of the practice, then in terms of the variety and profusion of its censorial flora.

Malcolm Dean, journalist, *Censored! Only in Canada: The History of Film Censorship—The Scandal Off the Screen* (1981).

Censorship is practically always wrong, because it invariably fastens on the most serious writers as its chief object of attack, whereas the serious writer is the ally of social concern, not its enemy.

Northrop Frye, cultural critic, address, Empire Club of Canada, Toronto, 19 Jan. 1984.

However rationalized it may be, censorship is always an attack on human intelligence and imagination and is always a sign of weakness, not of strength, in those who enforce it.

Northrop Frye, cultural critic, "Introduction to Canadian Literature," address, Moscow, 10 Oct. 1988, *Northrop Frye Newsletter*, Spring 1989.

It's my belief that it is better to have a world in which we laugh at the evil things that are in the world, than a world where we must carefully consider whether or not anything can offend anyone.

Brad Templeton, computer programmer, quoted by Luisa D'Amato in "UW Computer System Used to Send Racial Jokes," *The Kitchener-Waterloo Record*, 9 Nov. 1988. Templeton, born near Toronto, then on the faculty of the University of Waterloo, Ont., living in Silicon Valley since 1991, introduced the Internet to Canada in 1981 and established the popular website rec.humor.funny, which some members of the community found objectionable.

Censoring pornography is like using an aspirin to cure cancer: it might ease the pain, but does not eliminate the disease, and may well have serious side effects.

Lynn King, Ontario judge, quoted by Susan G. Cole in *Pornography and the Sex Crisis* (1989).

What has been so ridiculous about Canada is that we have *eight* censorship boards for the ten provinces.

Gerald Pratley, film historian, commenting on the profusion of boards, quoted by Jan Uhude in *Vision and Persistence: Twenty Years of the Ontario Film Institute* (1990).

The quantum leap from racism to censorship is neither random nor unexpected, since the issue of censorship is central to the dominant cultures of liberal democracies like Canada.

Marlene Nourbese Philip, activist, "The Disappearing Debate," *Language in Her Eye: Views on Writing and Gender by Canadian Women Writing in English* (1990) edited by Libby Scheier, Sarah Sheard, and Eleanor Wachtel.

If you aim for the Marquis de Sade you hit Margaret Laurence every time.

Comment on censorship attributed to novelist **Marian Engel**, CBC Radio's *Morningside*, 2 April 1991.

Loompanics Unlimited cannot be responsible for any shipment of books seized by any government body. This applies in particular to Canada, where many books are banned, and to prisoners, whose keepers often confiscate books. If you are a prisoner or a Canadian, you are advised to check with your authorities before ordering books. We cannot be responsible for books seized by ANY government....

"Special Notification Regarding Books Seized by Authorities" which prefaces **Loompanics Unlimited**'s 1991 *Main Catalogue: The Best Book Catalogue in the World*. The mail-order company based in Port Townsend, Washington, specializes in "unusual books" on fake I.D., guerrilla warfare, anarchism, libertarianism, etc.

Nothing good can ever come of censorship. Cutting one person's tongue will never give another person a voice, but it turns the silencer into a dictator.

Alberto Manguel, essayist, *The Globe and Mail*, 12 March 1992.

It's an undignified position for Canada to be seen to be handcuffing writers.

David Irving, British historian and Holocaust denier, addressing reporters following a deportation hearing in Vancouver, 30 Oct. 1992, quoted by Deborah Wilson in *The Globe and Mail* the following day.

Somewhere in Canada yesterday, a group requested a court ban on the publication/broadcast of a certain work for certain reasons. The court granted the ban on publication/broadcast and, in addition, imposed a ban on reporting the fact of the ban.

First paragraph of three paragraphs headed "Banned" that appeared on the front page of *The Globe and Mail*, 5 Dec. 1992. It referred to the decision of an Ontario judge to restrict in Ontario exposure to the CBC-TV production *The Boys of St. Vincent* which dealt with abuse by Christian brothers of their charges.

Canada became the first country in the world to pass, unanimously, an all-party resolution condemning the Iranian government for its appalling human rights record and calling for the withdrawal of the fatwa and bounty. That was a remarkable thing.

Salman Rushdie, author who had been living under a fatwa of the Iranian government, statement read to the 1993 PEN Benefit on the first anniversary of his appearance there, 7 Dec. 1992, printed in *The Toronto Star*, 16 Dec. 1993.

Every time I go to Canada I'm immediately on radio and television. I was there last week for a day, and I had three interviews on national CBC. In the United States people with similar views, not just me, are marginalized, excluded, no reviews. You rarely find such books in the libraries; the media are almost totally closed off.

Noam Chomsky, U.S. linguist and media critic, interviewed by David Barsamian for *The Media Monopoly* (1983) edited by Ben Bagdikian, as quoted by Geoff Hendricks in *eye*, 17 Dec. 1992.

Censorship is to art as lynching is to justice. We ought to fight the former as ardently as the latter.

Henry Louis Gates Jr., historian and chair of Afro-American studies at Harvard University, referring to attempts of some militant members of Toronto's black community to ban the revival of the musical *Show Boat*, address, Performing Arts Centre, North York, 28 Oct. 1993, quoted by Kellie Hudson in *The Toronto Star* the next day.

Donham's First Law of Censorship states that "Most citizens are implacably opposed to censorship in any form—except censorship of whatever they personally happen to find offensive."

Parker Barss Donham, political columnist, "An Unshackled Internet: If Joe Howe Were Designing Cyberspace," address at the Symposium on Free Speech and Privacy in the Information Age, University of Waterloo, Waterloo, Ont., 26 Nov. 1994. Donham added, "Since delivering this paper, I have been fiddling with a draft Second Law of Censorship: 'Everything offends someone; everyone is offended by something.'"

Telling one horror story after another, Ms. Strossen notes that Canada's anti-pornography law, which is modelled after the one written by Ms. MacKinnon and Ms. Dworkin, has been used to censor lesbian, gay and feminist works (and even two of Ms. Dworkin's books)....

Abbe Smith, deputy director, Criminal Justice Institute, Harvard Law School, reviewing Nadine Strossen's *Defending Pornography: Free Speech, Sex, and the Fight for Women's Rights* (1995) "Freedom to Be Grossed Out," *The New York Times Book Review*, 29 Jan. 1995. The allusion is to U.S. feminists Catharine MacKinnon and Andrea Dworkin and their influential model law that "defined pornography as a form of sex discrimination; it would authorize lawsuits for damages and injunctive relief." Struck down by the U.S. Supreme Court in 1986, its "pornophobic" principles were allowed to stand unchallenged in Canada. Smith continued, "Canadian Customs officials confiscated a book entitled *Hot, Hotter, Hottest*, thinking it was some kind of sex tract, instead of a cookbook about spicy food."

I have a T-shirt from a librarians' conference that says, "There's something in my library to offend everyone."

Susan Musgrave, author, "If you Want to Write," *In 2 Print*, Sept. 1995.

Champions of the marketplace of ideas should not be buyers in the marketplace of facts.

Louise Arbour, former chief prosecutor of the United Nations' war crimes tribunals for Rwanda and the Balkans, newly appointed member of the Supreme Court of Canada, address, International Press Freedom Awards, Toronto, "The Incurable Deficits of Memory," *The Toronto Star*, 20 Nov. 1999.

Literature is in principle uncompliant with authority. It is subversive. That is why it is feared in authoritarian societies.

Robert Bringhurst, poet and translator of Haida stories, "Since When Has Culture Been about Genetics," *The Globe and Mail*, 22 Nov. 1999.

CENTENNIAL YEAR See also EXPO 67

In that sense, 1967 was the last good year before all Canadians began to be concerned about the future of our country.

Pierre Berton, author and media personality, referring to the high spirits and bonhomie characteristic of the celebration of the Centennial of Confederation and the world's fair *Expo 67, 1967: The Last Good Year* (1997).

CENTRAL CANADA See ONTARIO, QUEBEC

CENTRALIZATION

One of the many curious aspects of Canada's constitution is that it was devised in the 1860s with the aim of creating a strong federal government, yet Canada is today more decentralized than any other Western country with the possible exception of Switzerland.

John Grimond, journalist, "Nice Country, Nice Mess," *The Economist*, 29 June 1991.

There is a great fallacy in the land, expressed by the cliché that "Canada is the most decentralized federation in the world." Canada may be decentralized by government functions, but power in Ottawa, especially, is terribly overconcentrated in the Prime Minister's hands, and in the service of Central Canada.

William Thorsell, newspaper editor, speech, Vancouver Institute, 20 Sept. 1997, printed in *The Globe and Mail*, 27 Sept. 1997.

CEREMONY

Ceremony was invented by a wise man to keep fools at a distance.

Bob Edwards, publisher, *The Eye Opener*, 6 May 1916, *The Best of Bob Edwards* (1975) edited by Hugh Dempsey.

CHAMPLAIN, SAMUEL DE

In our beloved Georgian Bay, which lies on the great water route he took from the French River to Huronia, there is a cairn, placed on a small island, between a tennis court and Champlain's Gas Bar & Marina, which commemorates his passage and quotes from his journal: Samuel de Champlain / by canoe / 1615 / "As for me, I labour always to prepare a way for those willing to follow."

Adrienne Clarkson, Governor General, installation address, Ottawa, 7 Oct. 1999, printed in the *National Post* the following day.

CHANCE

The unusual always attracts attention, and is easily made a source of mystery. Once, many years ago, my hand at bridge consisted of all the spades in the pack, an event to be expected only once in 779,737,580,160 times. But as the same is true of every other hand that can be mentioned, there was really no occasion for great wonder, although, of course, not all hands are equally noticeable and desirable.

Chester E. Kellogg, McGill statistician, "New Evidence (?) for 'Extra-Sensory Perception,'" *The Scientific Monthly*, Oct. 1937.

You turn right instead of left and your life changes forever without your knowing any change has come.

Lines from the novel *For Those Who Hunt the Wounded Down* (1993) by **David Adams Richards**.

CHANGE

We cannot in Canada continue as we are. We must become something greater or something infinitely less.

Stephen Leacock, humorist, "Greater Canada: An Appeal" (1907), *The Social Criticism of Stephen Leacock* (1973) edited by Alan Bowker.

I know that I create my own world, and while I can still suffer in it, not being able to blame anything or anyone else does negate emotional and mental stress and turns me to the area where I can make effective change: myself.

Dorothy Maclean, medium, *To Hear the Angels Sing: An Odyssey of Co-Creation with the Devic Kingdom* (1980).

If you want to know who is going to change this country, go home and look in the mirror.

Maude Barlow, Chairperson, Council of Canadians, address, speech, League of Canadian Poets, Toronto, May 25, 1991.

Those who want change control change, or think they do.

Ken Dryden, former hockey star and author, *The Moved and the Shaken: The Story of One Man's Life* (1993).

Ninety percent of everything you'll interact with ten years from now hasn't been developed yet. You've got to live with uncertainty and be comfortable with it. The ones who succeed in the future are those who learn to walk on quicksand and dance with electrons.

Frank Ogden, futurologist, quoted by Patrick

Cotter in "Keeping Up with Tomorrow," *Chief Information Officer Journal*, March–April 1993.

There are many radical changes that we need to make to save the planet, but we are not likely to make them until we have changed ourselves—our ways of thinking and feeling and living that weigh so heavily on the earth today.

James George, former Canadian Ambassador, *Asking for the Earth: Waking up to the Spiritual/Ecological Crisis* (1995).

Improvement is the enemy of change... you can't change if you're improving... unless you threaten the survival of the organization... then real change... isn't available until you bankrupt how it is... if you don't bankrupt it well, if you don't create a great crisis, you'll improve it to death... it's very brave work, you have to have an enormous amount of courage... you have to go through all kinds of false starts, mess, morass, nastiness... it's ugly. The only thing uglier... is living in a survival mode.

John Snobelen, Ontario Minister of Education, formerly private-sector consultant on organizational change, address to new staff, July 1995, quoted by Gerald Caplan in *The Toronto Star*, 14 Feb. 1997. As part of the Ontario Conservative government's Common Sense Revolution, all existing institutions were deemed to be in the state of "crisis."

Everything interesting happens at the edge of chaos. The idea that you can arrive at a state where things are finished, where no further change is possible or necessary—that's a state of death, and the only thing that can result from it is decay.

Jane Jacobs, essayist, quoted by Noah Richler, "Wealth in Diversity," *National Post*, 18 March 2000.

CHARACTER, NATIONAL See also CANADA; IDENTITY, NATIONAL

Theoretically, some twenty-four million Canadians should be able to live happily and fruitfully in so vast and productive a country. In practice, they are willy-nilly involved in the confusion and tumult and fantasies of a world going through one of those periods of breakdown and change that occur from time to time in our human history.

Malcolm Muggeridge, English commentator, "The Land that Time Forgot," *The Canadian*, 13 Oct. 1979. "The Mug" served as journalist-in-residence at the University of Western Ontario in 1978–79.

I would like Canada to come out, as it were. It has little to be diffident about, much to be proud of, and I believe the world would welcome the more assertive presence upon the international scene of an amiable, slightly eccentric, young giant with a bit of swagger. No other country can quite fill the role: only Canada the Good and the Bold.

Jan Morris, Anglo-Welsh traveller, "In Praise of Canada," *The Toronto Star*, 15 June 1992.

The background of this country is so different from any other country—the geographical background, the ethnic background, the historical background. None of that changes. The Canadian Shield can't be sandpapered away in a day.

Pierre Berton, author and broadcaster, quoted in *Maclean's*, 1 July 1994.

CHAREST, JEAN See also POLITICIANS

I have news for you. I intend to make this country work, because if there's one commitment I made to my children, it's that I'm going to pass on to them the country that I received from my parents. I am going to make this happen.

Jean Charest, Conservative leader, Leadership Debate, CBC-TV, 12 May 1997.

First, let's recall who Jean Charest really is. First, its John Charest; his real name is John, that's what's on his birth certificate, not Jean. It suits him fine to be Jean to us. That is not his real name. John is his real name and we must not forget it.

Suzanne Tremblay, Bloc Québécois M.P., campaign rhetoric, Rimouski, Que., quoted by Rhéal Séguin in *The Globe and Mail*, 26 May 1977. Bloc Québécois leader Gilles Duceppe explained that "it was probably not the best way for her to express her views," noting that everyone who lives in the province, "regardless of origin, is a Quebecker."

Apparently, the name written on the birth certificate is John. It isn't Jean, the way that some had thought it was. Again, I'm sorry. I admit—my mother was of Irish origin. I was baptized in an Irish parish and, no, I won't do it again, because I'll only do it once.

Jean Charest, Conservative leader, campaign rhetoric, Lindsay, Ont., quoted by Rhéal Séguin in *The Globe and Mail*, 26 May 1977.

Charest's speech will be "For a strong Quebec in a united Canada"... and Bouchard's will be "For a sovereign Quebec in partnership with Canada."

Ian MacDonald, political consultant, quoted by Rhéal Séguin in "Face-off," *The Globe and Mail*, 28 March 1998.

Jean Charest would make a good Prime Minister of Canada.

Attributed to Quebec Premier **Lucien Bouchard**, drawing attention to the federalist beliefs of Quebec Liberal leader Jean Charest, election campaign, 2 Nov. 1998.

CHARITY See also DONATIONS, PHILANTHROPY

In a world like ours differences in faith are much less important than agreement in charity. Faith, or the rejection of faith, often revolves around the question, "Why would a good God permit so much evil and suffering?" Charity starts with the question: "Why do we permit so much evil and suffering?" and that is a question on which all men and women of good will can act instead of arguing in circles.

Northrop Frye, cultural philosopher, "The Dedicated Mind," address, Service of Thanksgiving, 5 Oct. 1986, *Vic Report*, Winter, 1986–87.

To give is to give.

Paul Reichmann, developer and philanthropist, alluding to his private philanthropy and that of his various companies, all of which is kept very quiet, quoted by Walter Stewart in *Too Big to Fail: Olympia & York: The Story Behind the Headlines* (1993).

Redressing historic grievances is not a charity according to the Income Tax Act. Charities should not be a mechanism for social justice. That dollar isn't there for the advancement of any political cause, however righteous.

Anne Cools, Senator, on charities, quoted by Adele Freedman in "White Woman's Burden," *Saturday Night*, April 1993.

Mr. Harris: We want Justice not Charity

Wording on the sign displayed by the three surviving **Dionne** quintuplets—**Annette, Cécile,** and **Yvonne**—at a press conference in Toronto to reject the meagre compensation package offered by Ontario Premier Mike Harris because the Dionne Quintuplets were made wards of the state in 1934, noted in *Maclean's*, 9 March 1998.

CHARLOTTETOWN See also PRINCE EDWARD ISLAND

The Cradle of Confederation

Unofficial motto of Charlottetown, capital and sole city of Prince Edward Island, which in 1864 hosted the first of the conferences that led to Confederation and the creation of the Dominion of Canada in 1867.

CHARLOTTETOWN ACCORD See also CONSTITUTION

It's come to the point that we're talking about humiliation on every street corner.

Jean Chrétien, Liberal leader, referring to Robert Bourassa's refrain and Brian Mulroney's reverberation of Quebec's years of "humiliation" since the signing of the Constitution in 1982, quoted by Ingrid Peritz in *The Montreal Gazette*, 28 Dec. 1991.

Canadians today face the choice we have faced repeatedly throughout our history: in 1774, 1791, in 1840, in 1867 and 1980. That choice is simple: Quebec will either be a distinct society within Canada or it will develop as a distinct society outside Canada.

Brian Mulroney, Prime Minister, address, business group, Montreal, 23 Oct. 1991, as quoted by Graham Fraser in *The Globe and Mail*, 26 Oct. 1991. The concept of Quebec as a "distinct society" is associated with the Charlottetown Accord and applies to Quebec whether within or without Confederation.

Canadians in every province, including Quebec, would vote overwhelmingly "yes" to this referendum question: "Are you in favour of a 10-year moratorium on all discussions of constitutional change?"

Michael Bliss, historian, referring to the referendum on the Charlottetown Accord, "Let's Shut Up and Keep the Status Quo," *The Globe and Mail*, 17 Jan. 1992.

NON

Celebrated one-word editorial, signed by publisher and editor **Lise Bissonnette**, *Le Devoir*, 9 July 1992. The three-letter word appeared in two-inch capital letters spread over three columns occupying one-quarter of the newspaper page. Bissonnette was rejecting the constitutional arrangement struck 7 July 1992, a precursor of the Charlottetown Accord. Under the heading "In Reply to Ms. Bissonnette," the editors of *The Globe and Mail* took it upon themselves to respond on 10 July 1992: "NONsense."

All Canadians win. We get to keep Canada—the most magnificent country in the world.

Brian Mulroney, Prime Minister, press conference, announcing tentative agreement of First Ministers and aboriginal and other leaders at the so-called Canada Round of negotiations for constitutional reform, known as the Charlottetown Accord, Ottawa, 22 Aug. 1992, quoted by Edison Stewart in *The Toronto Star* the following day.

The first ministers are like a group of priests who are trying to work out a liturgy that all Catholics and Protestants can live with. And boy, that's hard.

Michael Bliss, historian, expressing surprise the First Ministers found a consensus in the Charlottetown Agreement on Senate reform, Native self-government, and Quebec autonomy, quoted in *The Hamilton Spectator*, 22 Aug. 1992.

This is a very good day for Canada.

Brian Mulroney, Prime Minister, press conference called to announce unanimity among First Ministers, in agreeing to the Charlottetown Accord, Charlottetown, P.E.I., 28 Aug. 1992, quoted by Edison Stewart in *The Toronto Star* the following day.

Charlottetown Accord / Canada is a democracy committed to a parliamentary and federal system of government and to the rule of law.... [Unity and Diversity]

*

The Aboriginal peoples of Canada, being the first peoples to govern this land, have the right to promote their languages, cultures and traditions and to ensure the integrity of their societies, and their governments constitute one of the three orders of government in Canada....

*

Quebec constitutes within Canada a distinct society, which includes a French-speaking majority, a unique culture and a civil law tradition....

*

Canadians are committed to racial and ethnic equality in a society that includes citizens from many lands who have contributed, and continue to contribute, to the building of a strong Canada that reflects its cultural and racial diversity....

*

The Constitution should be amended to recognize that the Aboriginal peoples of Canada have the inherent right of self-government within Canada....

*

Canada is a social and economic union within which, to the extent provided below, persons, goods, services, and capital may move freely across provincial and territorial boundaries.

Key clauses of the Charlottetown Constitutional Accord of the First Ministers and Native and Territorial leaders for Constitutional Reform, 28 Aug. 1992, reproduced in *The Globe and Mail*, 1 Sept. 1992. The national referendum on the adoption of the Accord was held on 26 Oct. 1992 and it was defeated.

Maybe the 20th century never really did belong to us; but if we don't, as a country, vote "Yes" on Oct. 26, we won't belong to the 21st.

Peter C. Newman, columnist, referring to referendum on the Charlottetown Accord, "Business Watch," *Maclean's*, 14 Sept. 1992.

When the United Nations... looks at all other countries and says this is the best place in the world to live, we should take this seriously. And we should recognize that, once, Beirut was one of the best places in the world to live, and it gave in to anger—that so many of the things that we see on the news today used to be whole communities until they gave in to anger. This could happen here. If we lose this, we lose the country.

Joe Clark, Minister of Constitutional Affairs, interview, CBC-TV's *Midday*, quoted by Edison Stewart in *The Toronto Star*, 17 Sept. 1992. This is the origin of Clark's notorious "second Beirut" remark, the dire warning being that if Canadians rejected the Charlottetown Constitutional Accord, the country would descend into the chaos of Beirut, the capital of strife-torn Lebanon. Michael Bliss and other commentators took exception to Clark's "scare tactics."

The Charlatan Accord.

Humorous reference to the Charlottetown Accord made by political satirist **Charlie McKenzie** in *The Globe and Mail*, 24 Sept. 1992.

If we vote No, we rip up those historic gains.

Brian Mulroney, Prime Minister, melodramatically ripping a sheet of foolscap, speech, Sherbrooke, Que., 26 Sept. 1992.

You think you'll have peace if you vote Yes. You'll have peace if you vote No. Because No means we've had enough of the Constitution, we don't want to hear any more about it.... The blackmail will continue if you vote Yes.... They made a mess that deserves a big No.

Pierre Elliott Trudeau, former Prime Minister and critic of the Charlottetown Accord, speech, Maison du Egg Roll, Montreal, 1 Oct. 1992, quoted in *The Toronto Star* two days later.

And the right to self-determination for Quebec, that's still on the Quebec Liberal Party's platform. What does it mean? It means that the blackmail will continue if you vote Yes.

Pierre Elliott Trudeau, former Prime Minister and critic of the Charlottetown Accord, speech, Maison du Egg Roll, Montreal, 1 Oct. 1992, quoted in *The Globe and Mail* the following day.

The current mess shows the consequences of treating people as members of minorities with special rights rather than as people, all of whom should have the same rights.

Editorial, *The Economist*, 17 Oct. 1992.

Do you agree that the Constitution of Canada should be renewed on the basis of the agreement reached on Aug. 28, 1992? YES NO

Wording of the referendum ballot for constitutional reform, the so-called Charlottetown Accord, calling for a Yes or No response, 26 Oct. 1992.

Is it conceivable that any referendum on such a fundamental question enjoying such overwhelming official sponsorship could fail in any other advanced country?

Conrad Black, publisher, referring to the referendum on the Charlottetown Accord then being held, address, Canadian Club of Toronto, 26 Oct. 1992, quoted in *The Globe and Mail* the following day.

The Charlottetown agreement is history.

Brian Mulroney, Prime Minister, conceding the fact that the electorate decisively rejected the Charlottetown Accord, CBC-TV's *The National*, 26 Oct. 1992, quoted by Edison Stewart in *The Toronto Star* the following day.

Accord sinks, Canada stays afloat.

Headline on an article about the state of the country following the referendum on the Charlottetown Accord, written by **Warren Gerard** in *The Toronto Star*, 1 Nov. 1992.

Certain nationalists, taking upon themselves the role of spokespersons for all French-speaking Canadians, gargle out a few gratuitous statements: "Quebec" wants more autonomy and "Quebeckers" feel humiliated by the federal government. Like hell they do. These nationalists are speaking only for themselves; they are not "Quebec."

Pierre Elliott Trudeau, former Prime Minister, on Prime Minister Brian Mulroney's insistence that the patriation of the Constitution "humiliated" the Quebec people, *Memoirs* (1993).

CHARTER OF RIGHTS See CONSTITUTION, RIGHTS

CHEESE See also FOOD & DRINK

The federal government has laid down national standards for everything from income support to milk quality (which is why you cannot buy a decent cheese in Canada, even in Quebec), and money is made available to the provinces, even in their exclusive jurisdictions, so long as they meet these standards.

John Grimond, journalist, "Nice Country, Nice Mess," *The Economist*, 29 June 1991.

CHEMISTRY

Great chemists are to be found in various reference sources, but usually in roles other than as chemists. I cannot find any other learned profession whose professional skills impact so drastically on society in medicine, our judicial system (through forensic science) and on the environment, yet whose members remain unlicensed. Perhaps chemists developed a formula to make their profession invisible.

Tom Davey, "Editorial Comment," *Environmental Science & Engineering*, Sept. 1993.

CHERRY, DON See also HOCKEY

It isn't easy to become Don Cherry. For starters, you need to have a mother named Maude and a father named Delmar.

Don Cherry, sports personality, *Quotations from Chairman Cherry* (1991).

I'm proud to call myself a redneck.

Don Cherry, hockey commentator, noting that others call him "a redneck" because of his opposition to the motion for hyphenated Canadianism, quoted by Leslie Scrivener in *The Toronto Star*, 23 May 1993. Actually, his friends call him "Grapes."

Lower Slobovia attacking Slimea.

Characterization of events in Yugoslavia in 1994 by sports broadcaster **Don Cherry** after CBC-TV News cut into his "Coach's Corner" segment of *Hockey Night in Canada* to report on developments in the Balkans, as noted by Lindsay Scotton in *The Toronto Star*, 22 April 1995.

My rough, tough image and all that, and here I am dressed like Little Lord Fauntleroy!

Don Cherry, sports personality, quoted by Balke Gopnik in "Men," *The Globe and Mail*, 21 May 1998.

CHILD CARE

Child care is one of those items—like a causeway to Prince Edward Island—that is regularly promised just before an election.

Doris Anderson, feminist, *The Unfinished Revolution: The Status of Women in Twelve Countries* (1991). The causeway, called the Confederation Bridge, was opened between New Brunswick and Prince Edward Island in 1997.

I would just as soon hire a nanny to have sex with my husband as I would to raise my children. These are private affairs, and our children deserve their privacy and our attention.

Deborah Maes, Toronto mother, "A World without Mothers," *The Globe and Mail*, 9 July 1998.

CHILDREN See also FAMILY

It is not so much a woman's duty to bring children into the world as it is to see what sort of a world . . . she is bringing them into.

Nellie L. McClung, suffragette, "Women's Place in the Universe" (1915), quoted by Candace Savage in *Our Nell: A Scrapbook Biography of Nellie L. McClung* (1979).

I take my place with the children.

J.S. Woodsworth, M.P., declining to make unanimous the motion to affirm that a state of war exists with Germany through the invocation of the War Measures Act, House of Commons, 8 Sept. 1939. He added, "It is only as we adopt new policies that this world will be at all a livable place for our children who follow us."

Parents receive more training in how to raise pigs than in how to raise children.

Paraphrased from a remark made by **Dr. Brock Chisholm**, April 1945, noted by Allan Irving in *Brock Chisholm: Doctor to the World* (1998).

There, in Montreal, poor Growler was savaged by a dog and died.

E.H. Shepard, illustrator of *Winnie the Pooh* (1926), quoted by Catherine Milner, "Model Pooh Bear Savaged in Montreal," *National Post*, 6 April 1999. In a letter written to a fan in 1971, Shepard mentioned the fate of Growler, the teddy bear that had served as the model for A.A. Milne's Pooh Bear. It was owned by an English girl whose parents took her to Montreal for the duration of World War II; there Growler came to a sad end.

Diaper backwards spells repaid. Think about it.

Marshall McLuhan, communications pioneer, quoted by Richard J. Schoeck in *Who Was Marshall McLuhan?* (1994) edited by Barrington Nevitt and Maurice McLuhan.

Childbearing is coming very close to being another once-noble accomplishment.

Judith Merril, author, obiter dictum, 7 Sept. 1979.

David, we're pregnant.

Caption to a popular cartoon in the "For Better or for Worse" strip drawn by **Lynn Johnston**, depicting a beaming wife and her surprised husband. *David, We're Pregnant* (1975).

No matter how you bring up your children, you turn out badly.

*

Not all children turn out badly; some turn out disastrously.

*

You should treat your children as strangers whom you happen to like—if, that is, you happen to like them.

Richard Needham, newspaper columnist, *The Wit and Wisdom of Richard Needham* (1977).

Every new generation that is born into this world is a fresh barbarian invasion that will seize and grasp and demand and consume everything in sight, until it is civilized into understanding its duty to give and yield and respond and produce.

Morris C. Shumiatcher, advocate, quoted by Richard J. Needham in *The Globe and Mail*, 9 June 1980.

There's no such thing as the Canadian boy next door; they're all hockey players.

Jonathan Welsh, actor, quoted by Sid Adilman in *The Toronto Star*, 29 Dec. 1980.

There is nothing more peaceful than a sleeping child.

D. Murray Dryden, philanthropist, characteristic remark, *For the Love of His Children* (1991). Dryden is the founder of Sleeping Children Around the World, an organization based in Islington, Ont., that donates "bedkits" to the underprivileged children of Third World countries.

The only thing better than having a grandchild, in my prejudiced view, is being one. Especially at Christmas.

Peter Gzowski, essayist and broadcaster, "The Great Great Great Great Grandchild of Sir Casimir, I," *Selected Columns from Canadian Living* (1993).

I don't think things will ever be normal ever again. But yes, I do have to get back to school, back to my normal routine, back to the snow.

Craig Kielburger, 13-year-old activist who spent seven weeks touring five Asian countries with poor records for child labour, returning home to Thornhill, Ont., 30 Jan. 1996, quoted by Bruce DeMara, "Teen Activist Returns Home," *The Toronto Star*, 31 Jan. 1996.

We never outlive the horrors of childhood. The horrors of adulthood that follow are a positive relief.

Louis Dudek, poet and aphorist, *The Caged Tiger* (1997).

And for the first time in human history, children are an authority on a topic of critical importance to society. They are becoming a massive force for the transformation of every institution in society.

Don Tapscott, futurologist, referring to the "Net-Gen" or Net Generation of children who have grown up with digital technology, interviewed by Beppi Crosariol, *The Globe & Mail's Report on Business Magazine*, Nov. 1997.

Once again childhood was lying in wait behind the summer heat, the smell of the breeze, the slightest word. All-powerful childhood.

Thoughts of the narrator of **Louise Dupré**'s *Memoria: A Novel* (1998) translated from the French by Liedewy Hawke.

CHILE

In Chile, the word cana means prison, and the colloquial meaning of the words "in Canada" is "in the cooler."

Beatriz Zeller, Santiago-born, Toronto-based librarian and translator, observation, 1 July 1980.

In spite of all of the problems, I prefer Chile as a society where things happen. In Canada, I feel nothing happens. People go to shopping malls.

Mirna Concha, Chilean-born Canadian retornada or returnee, quoted by Isabel Vincent in *The Globe and Mail*, 16 Sept. 1993.

CHINESE PEOPLE See also BETHUNE, NORMAN

I think you Canadians ought to thank God to have the Chinamen here to do the manual work for you.

Tom Chue Tom, Chinese missionary at New Westminster, B.C., testimony, *Report of the Commissioners Appointed to Inquire into the Subject of Chinese and Japanese Immigration into the Province of British Columbia*, Sessional Paper No. 54, 1902.

One day of happiness in China is better than a hundred days of happiness in Canada.

Chinese saying of the 1920s noted in Denise Chong's memoir "The Concubine's Children" included in *Many-Mouthed Birds: Contemporary Writing by Chinese Canadians* (1991) edited by Bennett Lee and Jim Wong-Chu.

If blood be the price of freedom and national integrity, God knows China has paid in full.

James G. Endicott, missionary and peace activist, "China, the Democratic Front in the Far East" (1941), *Empire Club of Canada: Addresses Delivered to the Members during the Year 1941–42* (1942).

China's rainfall is too little or too much, comes too early or too late, or falls in the wrong places.

Line of narration from the script written and spoken by **Roy Faibish** of the documentary *The 700,000,000*, about life in the People's Republic of China, CBC-TV, 4 Nov. 1964.

Mao, Mao everywhere and not a thought to think.

Joe Schlesinger, foreign correspondent, referring to the pervasive cult of Mao Tse-tung in China in the 1970s, *Time Zones: A Journalist in the World* (1990).

If the Chinese dare to make their alphabet phonetic, Chinese culture will dissolve in ten years.

Marshall McLuhan, communications pioneer, Montreal International Book Fair, quoted by Christie McCormick in *The Montreal Gazette*, 16 May 1975.

To the Chinese, there is virtue in money and the acquisition of it. They were never ashamed of working hard, for it meant that one day they would be able to return from "the golden mountain," as they called Canada, with a lot of money.

Adrienne Clarkson, broadcaster, *Today Magazine*, 7 Nov. 1981.

Our research suggests that the environmental pressures in China may cause the country's fragmentation. This is not the received wisdom: most experts have been distracted by the phenomenal economic expansion in China's coastal areas; they have tended to project these trends onto the rest of the country and to neglect the dangers posed by resource scarcities. The costs of misreading the Chinese situation could be very high.

Thomas F. Homer-Dixon, co-ordinator of the Peace and Conflict Studies Program, University College, University of Toronto, "Environmental Scarcities and Violent Conflict: Evidence from Cases," *International Security*, Summer 1994.

China will probably have the next century pretty well to itself as far as culture, & perhaps even civilization, are concerned.

Northrop Frye, cultural critic, diary entry, 19 Aug. 1942, *Northrop Frye Newsletter*, Fall 1996.

Living in China has made me appreciate my own country, with its tiny, ethnically diverse population of unassuming donut-eaters. I had gone all the way to China to find an idealistic, revolutionary society when I already had it right at home.

Jan Wong, correspondent, *Red China Blues: My Long March from Mao to Now* (1996).

Trying to do business North American style in China, for example, is like trying to eat spaghetti with chopsticks. It's messy and it's not going to be successful.

Colin D. Watson, Spar Aerospace Limited, speech, 18 Nov. 1997, *National and Global Perspectives* (Business Council on National Issues), Spring 1998.

Trade between Canada and China surges on like the Fraser River toward the Pacific Ocean.

Jiang Zemin, President of China, speech, APEC forum, Vancouver, 23 Nov. 1997, broadcast on CBC Radio the following day.

CHOICES

As my grandfather used to say, "You can do anything you want, but you can't do everything you want."

George Torok, training consultant, presentation, Canadian Association of Public Speakers, Toronto, 11 Aug. 1997.

CHRÉTIEN, JEAN

See also LIBERAL PARTY, POLITICIANS

Mr. Chrétien speaks French just like he speaks English.

Lysiane Gagnon, columnist, "Inside Quebec," *The Globe and Mail*, 7 Nov. 1992.

It's true. I speak out of one side of my mouth. I'm not a Tory. I don't speak out of both sides of my mouth.

Jean Chrétien, Liberal leader, remark made early in the election campaign, well before the Conservative TV commercials that distorted his appearance, quoted by Kenneth Whyte in *Saturday Night*, Feb. 1994.

Jean Chrétien's place in Canadian history will depend upon whether he is the last Québécois to be prime minister of Canada.

John Saywell, historian, *Canada: Pathways to the Present* (1994).

I repeat in front of the nation and in front of God, if you want, because my name is Chrétien and I have no problem with that, that I never discussed security with anybody with the RCMP.

Jean Chrétien, Prime Minister, denying the allegation that the Prime Minister's Office instructed the RCMP to use force to deal with student protest in Vancouver, the so-called Peppergate inquiry, House of Commons, 26 Oct. 1999.

This is my life.

Jean Chrétien, Prime Minister, address, national convention, Liberal Party, Ottawa, stating his intention to seek a third term of office, quoted by Anne McIlroy, "P.M. Tries to Rally Liberals," *The Globe and Mail*, 18 March 2000.

CHRISTIANITY See also BELIEF, CATHOLICISM, RELIGION

'Twas in the moon of wintertime / When all the birds had fled, / That Mighty Gitchi Manitou / Sent angel choirs instead. / Before their light the stars grew dim, / And wand'ring hunters heard the hymn: / "Jesus, your King, is born: / In excelsis gloria!"

Jean de Brébeuf, Jesuit missionary, composed the first Canadian Christmas carol, writing it in the Huron tongue at Sainte-Marie-among-the-Hurons (near present-day Midland, Ont.) in 1641. The Huron lyrics were translated into French before the year 1800. The English version is an interpretation made by J.E. Middleton in 1926.

Brother, if you white people murdered the Saviour, make it up yourselves. We had nothing to do with it. If he had come among us, we should have treated him better.

Red Jacket, Seneca chief, addressing Christian missionaries about 1811, quoted by William Canniff in *The Settlement of Upper Canada* (1869).

John, I would like you to be a missionary to the Indians in North America.

Florence Nightingale, English nurse, addressing John Smithurst, English gentleman and fiancé, who in 1839 duly set out as a missionary to the Red River Settlement but eventually settled in Elora, Ont., where he ministered to the English congregation of the Church of St. John the Evangelist which now houses Communion plates which she donated to the congregation.

When he landed in 1848, there were no Christians here, and when he left, in 1872, there were no heathen.

Words on the headstone of **John Geddie**, Presbyterian missionary, raised in Pictou, N.S., who preached on the New Hebrides Islands in the South Pacific. He was sent there to take the place of the missionary John Williams who was murdered and eaten by headhunters. Geddie fared better and died in Geelong, Australia, 14 Dec. 1872, as noted by John S. Moir, "John Geddie," *The Canadian Encyclopedia* (2nd ed., 1988).

The effect produced by the teaching of Jesus and his disciples is, beyond question, the most momentous fact in history.

Goldwin Smith, essayist, "The Miraculous Element in Christianity," *Guesses at the Riddle of Existence and Other Essays on Kindred Subjects* (1897).

The name of the Church, formed by the union of the Presbyterian, Methodist and Congregational Churches in Canada, shall be "The United Church of Canada."

Article, The United Church of Canada Act, 1924, reproduced in *Historical Documents of Canada: Volume V: The Arts of War and Peace, 1914–1945* (1972) edited by C.P. Stacey.

"I guess I'm a mystic, all right," was Aimee's final and painless verdict. "I preach a message specially imparted to me."

Aimee Semple McPherson, Los Angeles-based evangelist, visiting her hometown of Ingersoll, Ont., interviewed by R.E. Knowles, *The Toronto Star*, 9 July 1929. For her showmanship, she was called "the Mae West of the Tabernacles."

"Tell your Canadian people," he began, "to stand fast by the principles that have made Canada one of the most admired nations in the world. If Canada is 'Conservative,' it is the Conservatism of Christianity. If she is slow of progress, her progress is that of certainty. Tell her to hold fast the traditions of the Scriptures."

Charles E. Coughlin, right-wing broadcaster from the Shrine of the Little Flower, Royal Oak, Detroit, interviewed by R.E. Knowles, *The Star Weekly*, 6 Jan. 1934.

"Sex is here to stay," said a young man, somewhat sententiously, tonight at a discussion group. He's right, of course. But so, I hope, is the Church. It is about time, therefore, that there was a much better understanding between the two.

Arnold Edinborough, editor, *Some Camel... Some Needle and Other Thoughts for the Day* (1974).

I also realize that God's revolution is going to go on with or without me. But I don't want to get left behind. So this is my prayer: Lord, start a revolution and start it in me!

Leighton Ford, Canadian-born evangelist and brother-in-law of Billy Graham, *One Way to Change the World* (1970).

You see, I cannot consider myself a totally orthodox Christian because I can't accept the Christian urging toward perfection. I don't think that perfection is possible or even, in psychological terms, desirable for human beings.

Robertson Davies, man-of-letters, "A Talk with Tom Harpur," *The Toronto Star*, 16 Feb. 1974, *The Enthusiasms of Robertson Davies* (1979) edited by Judith Skelton Grant.

In the next eleven days I shall cross your country from one ocean to the other.... I have some questions to ask you and I would also like to hear yours.

Pope John Paul II, Supreme Pontiff of the Roman Catholic Church, address, Quebec City, 9 Sept. 1984.

"The Orange and the Green, with the Snow in Between, 1832–40"

Title of an academic study of the Orange Lodge and Irish Catholicism in Canada, presented by **Harold Senior**, Celtic Arts Festival, St. Michael's College, Toronto, 16 March 1985.

Two thousand years ago, Jesus stood on a rock to preach. If Jesus were to come back today, he'd probably say, "Gee, I have to go on a talk show."

Morton Weinfeld, sociologist at McGill University, quoted by Sandra Contenta in *The Toronto Star*, 8 Nov. 1992.

Over a hundred thousand weeks on the best seller list.

Message on billboards placed by the **Canadian Bible Society**, Toronto, March 1994.

It often seems to me that Christianity is an embarrassment to God.

Thoughts of a character in **Paul William Roberts**' novel *The Palace of Fears* (1994).

Christ's disciples should stop acting like Christians and start behaving as Christians.

Maurus E. Mallon, aphorist, *Compendulum* (1995).

CHRISTMAS See HOLIDAYS

CHURCH See also BELIEF

The average man goes to church six times a year and has attended Sunday school for two afternoons and can sing half a hymn.

Stephen Leacock, humorist, Preface, *Winnowed Wisdom* (1926).

I am a woman and have a woman's perspective, but I don't bring womanhood to the House of Bishops, I bring myself.

Victoria Matthews, Canada's first female Anglican bishop, fifth woman bishop in the Anglican world, anticipating consecration on 12 Feb. 1994, quoted by Jack Kapica in *The Globe and Mail*, 7 Dec. 1993.

Mieux un Archevêque Roy qu'un Cardinal Léger.

Celebrated pun, "Better a royal archbishop than a light-weight cardinal," recalling Quebec Premier Maurice Duplessis's preference for Archbishop Maurice Roy over Cardinal Léger of Montreal, as noted in the latter's obituary, quoted by David Twiston Davies in *Canada from*

Afar: The Daily Telegraph Book of Canadian Obituaries (1996).

CITIES & TOWNS See also PLACES and the following cities: CALGARY, CHARLOTTETOWN, EDMONTON, FREDERICTON, HALIFAX, MONTREAL, NIAGARA FALLS, OTTAWA, QUEBEC CITY, REGINA, SAINT JOHN, ST. JOHN'S, TORONTO, VANCOUVER, VICTORIA, WHITEHORSE, WINNIPEG, YELLOWKNIFE

But we have shown that in every millennium of the past the centres of wealth and power have been found farther north than they were a thousand years before.

Vilhjalmur Stefansson, Arctic explorer, address, "Abolishing the Arctic," Empire Club of Canada, Toronto, 25 Oct. 1928.

We have medicare, legal care, but where is our city care?

John C. Parkin, architect, address, Toronto Teachers' Art Association, 5 Feb. 1963.

The future of a city may be very much like a world's fair—a place to show off new technology—not a place of work or residence whatever.

Marshall McLuhan, communications pioneer, "Address at Vision 65" (1966), *The Essential McLuhan* (1995) edited by Eric McLuhan and Frank Zingrone.

Men may find God in nature, but when they look at cities they are viewing themselves.

John C. Parkin, architect, address, Toronto, 22 Aug. 1969.

City dwellers are the only majority group I know that allow themselves to be over-governed, under-represented and ignored.

David Crombie, Mayor of Toronto, address, Annual Convention, Manitoba Progressive Conservative Party, *The Globe and Mail*, 8 March 1975.

A mathematical phenomenon exists in our suburbs—multiplication by subdivision.

Attributed to Metro Chairman **F.G. Gardiner**, noted in his obituary, *The Globe and Mail*, 23 Aug. 1983.

Suburbs in the sky.

Description of highrise apartment buildings attributed to **Marshall McLuhan** in the 1960s, first heard in May 1995.

Outer Canada

Reference to small-town Canada, as distinct from big-city Canada, as a region for growth, popularized by parliamentarian and author **David Kilgour** in *Inside Outer Canada* (1990).

Canada is one of the most urbanized countries in the world and yet our collective psyche is stuck in the country, as if there is an inherent contradiction between the idea of the north and the enjoyment of city life.

Joe Berridge, urban planner, *The Globe and Mail*, 31 May 1991.

A friend suggested stopovers in small towns. But the myth of the Canadian small town held no charm for me. Mean spirits and dried-out hearts ruled those tree-lined streets and leafy porches. It was time to stop pretending that neighbourliness survived only in hamlets that time has insulated.

Kildare Dobbs, travel writer, *Ribbon of Highway: By Bus along the Trans-Canada* (1992).

Try standing in front of a class and asking what is the capital of Canada. The eyes stare back at you, indifferent, hostile, some of them look the other way. You say it again. "What is the capital of Canada?" While you wait in the silence, absolutely the victim, your own mind doubts itself. What is the capital of Canada? Why Ottawa and not Montreal? Montreal is much nicer, they do a better espresso, you have a friend who lives there. Anyway, who cares what the capital is, they'll probably change it next year.

Thoughts of a school teacher in England in the novel *Written on the Body* (1992) by **Jeanette Winterson**.

If Canada were not a country, however fragmented, but, instead, a house, Vancouver would be the solarium-cum-playroom, an afterthought of affluence; Toronto, the counting room, where money makes for the most glee; Montreal, the salon; and Edmonton, Edmonton, the boiler room.

Mordecai Richler, novelist and controversialist, *Oh Canada! Oh Quebec! Requiem for a Divided Country* (1992).

No city ever became great without a subway.

Allan Lamport, former Mayor of Toronto, speaking on the fortieth anniversary of the city's subway system, which he promoted, quoted in *The Toronto Star*, 30 March 1994.

And yes we still do dream of cities where there is still no past and where the future remains entirely unwritten, of cities where there are grassy canyons and water glazed by the sun into gold, of a billion butterflies floating through a billion coral trees, of water piped in from heaven and where there are limitless gleaming wide white freeways that will lead us off into infinity.

Douglas Coupland, author, *Polaroids from the Dead* (1996).

For a city to be a great international city, it must learn from and respect its heritage, it must build on and favour its economic strengths, it must provide vibrant civic spaces, it must value civility, it must celebrate beauty, it must value great cultural and educational institutes and it must prize architecture of the highest order of excellence. This, I believe, is the destiny of Toronto.

Allan Gotlieb, chairman of the Ontario Heritage Foundation, address, 7 April 1999, forum on Toronto's city plan, "What Makes a Great City?" *The Globe and Mail*, 12 April 1999.

CITIZENSHIP See also OATH OF ALLEGIANCE

As for myself, my course is clear. A British subject I was born—a British subject I will die.

Sir John A. Macdonald, Prime Minister, appealing for the retention of British ties, House of Commons, 7 Feb. 1891. He was born in Scotland a subject of the Crown, and he died in Canada a subject of the Crown. The Canadian Citizenship Act of 1947 created the status of Canadian citizen while retaining the status of British subject. With the Citizenship Act of 1977, Canadian citizens ceased to be British subjects, becoming instead citizens of the Commonwealth.

I took possession of Baffin Island for Canada in the presence of several Eskimo, and after firing nineteen shots I instructed an Eskimo to fire the twentieth, telling him that he was now a Canadian.

Joseph-Elzéar Bernier, mariner, claiming the Arctic archipelago for Canada on 1 July 1909 and doing so in an imaginative ceremony of his own devising, recalling the occasion in an address to the Empire Club of Canada in 1926.

I speak as a citizen of Canada.

W.L. Mackenzie King, Prime Minister, accepting the first citizenship certificate at a special ceremony organized by the Secretary of State, Ottawa, 3 Jan. 1947; the Canadian Citizenship Act came into effect 1 Jan. 1947; until that time Canadians were "British subjects" and not "Canadian citizens"; quoted by J.W. Pickersgill and D.F. Forster in *The Mackenzie King Record: Volume 4, 1947–1948* (1970).

A Canadian is a Canadian is a Canadian.

Attributed to Prime Minister **Pierre Elliott Trudeau** following the victory of the Parti Québécois in the provincial election of 15 Nov. 1976, by Iona Campagnolo, House of Commons, 24 Oct. 1977.

If I were born at the North Pole, I would remember the North Pole. If I were born in Canada, I would be a Canadian. There is no miracle in that. It is a very natural thing.

Marc Chagall, painter, interviewed by Harry Rasky at St. Paul de Vence, France, for the TV documentary *Homage to Chagall—The Colours of Love*, as quoted by Rasky in his memoirs *Nobody Swings on Sunday: The Many Lives and Films of Harry Rasky* (1980).

I would suggest that any country that does not claim the full loyalty of its citizens old or new, any country that counts citizens old or new who treat it as they would a public washroom—that is, as merely a place to run to in an emergency—accepts for itself severe internal weakening. It is perhaps inevitable that for many newcomers Canada is merely a job.

Neil Bissoondath, author, "A Question of Belonging," *The Globe and Mail*, 28 Jan. 1992.

There should be a law that Canadians would not be granted citizenship until they've crossed this country by car or, if they can find one, by train. That kind of odyssey would serve to remind us that even if we've always suffered from constitutional indigestion, our forefathers performed a series of miracles to originally settle this country.

Peter C. Newman, columnist, *Maclean's*, 6 July 1992.

I am a citizen of Canada, and I make this commitment to uphold our laws and freedoms; to respect our people in their diversity; to work for our common well-being, and to safeguard the honour of this ancient northern land.

English draft of the revised Oath of Citizenship released by **Citizenship and Immigration Canada**, as noted by Michael Valpy in *The Globe and Mail*, 26 Jan. 1995. Here is the wording of the old Oath: "I swear that I will be faithful and bear true allegiance to Her Majesty Queen Elizabeth the Second, Queen of Canada, Her Heirs and Successors, and that I will faithfully observe the laws of Canada and fulfill my duties as a Canadian citizen."

Canada's Citizenship Act of 1947 was the first in the world to make no distinction between native-born and newcomers.

Richard Gwyn, columnist and author, *Nationalism without Walls: The Unbearable Lightness of Being Canadian* (1995).

Aboriginal people are both Canadian citizens and citizens of their particular nations. Thus they hold a form of dual citizenship, which permits them to maintain loyalty to their nation and to Canada as a whole.

Restructuring the Relationship: Volume 2, Part One: Report of the Royal Commission on Aboriginal Peoples (1996), co-chaired by René Dussault and Georges Erasmus.

I learned to be a Canadian through a series of eternally virginal public school teachers, who treated me only as bright—and not bright yellow.

Adrienne Clarkson, Governor General, installation address, alluding to her Chinese ancestry, Ottawa, 7 Oct. 1999, printed in the *National Post* the following day.

CIVILIZATION

There is only one first-class civilization in the world today. It is right here, in the United States and the Dominion of Canada.

Unidentified professor addressing a meeting of "the venerable Order of Elks" in Los Angeles, as satirized by **Aldous Huxley** in his travel book *Jesting Pilate: An Intellectual Holiday* (1926).

The Canadians are a great people, with every human good quality; but having had to struggle pretty hard for a livelihood, they have been apt to miss some of the essentials of civilization. In scientific and technical work, they are quite admirable, but in what might be called "the humanities" they are a little backward....

John Buchan, Governor General Lord Tweedsmuir, observation made in Jan. 1937, quoted by Janet Adam Smith in *John Buchan: A Biography* (1965).

I have always had hopes that civilization here in Canada could make some kind of contribution to mankind.

A.R.M. Lower, historian, interviewed by Ramsay Cook in *The Craft of History* (1973) edited by Eleanor Cook.

The measure of a civilization is how much you can take for granted.

Louis Dudek, man-of-letters, *Epigrams* (1975).

North American civilization is one of the ugliest to have emerged in human history.

Arthur Erickson, architect, quoted by Daniel Stoffman in *The Toronto Star*, 11 Oct. 1981.

Dictatorships try to suppress the critical intelligence wherever they can; our own society is profoundly and perversely anti-intellectual; some religious groups think that only blind faith can see clearly. All such attitudes are dangerous to civilized life and abhorrent to the gospel.

Northrop Frye, cultural critic, "The Dedicated Mind," address, Service of Thanksgiving, 5 Oct. 1986, *Vic Report*, Winter, 1986–87.

Civilization begins with man's effort to say something, and ends with the effort to interpret what has been said.

Louis Dudek, poet and aphorist, "Epigrams," *Small Perfect Things* (1991).

Civilization is, at least in part, about pretending that things are better than they are.

Jean Vanier, founder of the L'Arche and Daybreak movement for the intellectually disabled, interviewed by Leslie Scrivener, "Canada's Disciple to the Disabled," *The Toronto Star*, 14 Nov. 1998.

We must not forget that this complexity is whole. To be complex does not mean to be fragmented. This is the paradox and the genius of our Canadian civilization.

Adrienne Clarkson, Governor General, installation address, Ottawa, 7 Oct. 1999, printed in the *National Post* the following day.

CLARK, JOE See also POLITICIANS

Joe Who?

Bold headline on the front page of *The Toronto Star*, 23 Feb. 1976. The news story concerned the election of dark-horse candidate Joe Clark to the leadership of the federal Conservative Party. "Joe Who?" became the nickname of the future Prime Minister. When Clark showed a determination to make changes, he was rechristened (briefly) "Joe Do."

Joe Clark is the cultural incarnation of English Canada, colourless, odourless and tasteless.

Victor-Lévy Beaulieu, author, *The Toronto Star*, 5 Jan. 1978.

A fine, Christian gentleman, a good husband and father, but not made by Almighty God to be Prime Minister of Canada. We certainly wouldn't be content with him as premier of Newfoundland. He's not big enough or strong enough for that. Let's be charitable and say he'd make a good mayor of a small town.

J.R. (Joey) Smallwood, former Premier of Newfoundland, on the stature and prospects of future Prime Minister Joe Clark, quoted by Frank Rasky in *The Toronto Star*, 24 Nov. 1979.

Trudeau was five-foot-ten and looked six-foot-one. Clark was six-foot-one but looked five-foot-ten.

Jack Webster, broadcaster, *Webster! An Autobiography* (1990).

Big man, little chin.

Description of Joe Clark by **Brian Mulroney** that equates stature with chin-size, current in Conservative circles, 19 Feb. 1993. Liberal circles quipped of Mulroney: "Little man, big chin."

My life has always been dull. I'm still waiting for the 15 minutes Andy Warhol promised.

Joe Clark, politician, announcing his retirement, Ottawa, 20 Feb. 1993, quoted by Hugh Winsor in *The Globe and Mail*, 22 Feb. 1993. By then Clark, at 54, had spent 35 years in politics, 20 as an M.P., 7 as Conservative leader, and 9 months as Prime Minister.

Joe Clark has never made an important decision in his political life that was correct. He keeps inflicting mortal wounds on himself without ever coming back to life politically. It is feline to have more than one life but unique to him to have only recurrent deaths.

Conrad Black, publisher, "Out of Uncle Sam's Shadow," *National Post*, 11 Jan. 2000.

Joe Clark will never set the world on fire, except by accident.... Joe Clark has the necessary brains and energy. He lacks heft, or gravitas, a weightiness of character.

Peter C. Newman, columnist, "Joe Clark Has No Gravitas," *National Post*, 19 Feb. 2000.

CLASS, SOCIAL See also ESTABLISHMENT, SOCIETY

One of the advantages of visiting a Dominion, is that one comes to meet on equal terms people into whose life one never could enter in England. In the towns one is absolutely relegated to one's own class: in the country this is widened if you are a sportsman or woman.

Freya Stark, traveller and writer, observation recorded in notebook, entry for 10 Jan. 1929, Creston, B.C., *Beyond Euphrates* (1951).

Let the Old World, where rank's yet vital, / Part those who have and have not title. / Toronto has no social classes— / Only the Masseys and the masses.

B.K. Sandwell, editor, "On the Appointment of Governor-General Vincent Massey, 1952," included in *The Blasted Pine* (1957) edited by F.R. Scott and A.J.M. Smith. It was widely felt that members of the wealthy Massey family, especially Vincent and his actor brother Raymond, "put on airs."

In America, only a corporation may still lawfully segregate facilities by class.

Edgar Z. Friedenberg, social scientist, "Liberty and the Giant Corporation," *The Disposal of Liberty and Other Industrial Wastes* (1975).

There's nothing wrong with overdogs!

E. Graydon Carter, Canadian-born founder of *Spy* and editor of *Vanity Fair*, interviewed by Val Ross, *The Globe and Mail*, 2 June 1993. In Carter's eyes, *Spy* was edited for "underdogs," *Vanity Fair* for "overdogs."

We've just about arrived at the classless society; few today have any class.

Frank Ogden, futurologist, "Point of View Vanishing," syndicated newspaper column, 23 Oct. 1995.

CLAYOQUOT See also PROTEST

Perhaps [the Crown] would ask Christ to pay for his cross, and Joan of Arc to pay for her firewood.

Peter Scott, journalist, reacting to the suggestion that the protesters at Clayoquot Sound, B.C., pay the court costs, *The Victoria Times-Colonist*, 7 Oct. 1993, as quoted by Ronald B. Hatch in "The Clayoquot Show Trials," *Clayoquot & Dissent* (1995).

CLIMATE See WEATHER

CLOTHES See FASHION

COHEN, LEONARD See also WRITERS & WRITING, CANADIAN

He may well be the greatest poet Canada has ever produced in English. He is certainly Canada's first international writer.

Kenneth Rexroth, American poet and critic, "Poetry into the '70s," *The Alternative Society: Essays from the Other World* (1970).

I'm an eccentric, a minor, minor poet and that's all I ever wanted to be. I don't want to be in the mainstream. The mainstream is like the Ganges. I'm a little rivulet, a leaky genital....

Leonard Cohen, poet, quoted by Stephen Williams in *Toronto Life*, Feb. 1978.

He is a singular entity: a kind of rock-and-roll Lord Byron, a cultural scholar in the unlikely medium of pop.

Karen Schoemer, writer, describing Leonard Cohen, "Leonard Cohen, the Lord Byron of Rock-and-Roll," *The New York Times*, 29 Nov. 1992.

I'm not really interested in being the oldest folksinger around.

Leonard Cohen, folksinger and Buddhist monk, quoted by Pico Iyer, "In Person," *The Globe and Mail*, 1 May 1999.

Leonard Cohen's never going to bring my groceries in.

Refrain from the amusing song "Leonard and Me" written and performed by singer **Nancy White**, heard on *The Vinyl Cafe*, CBC Radio, 19 June 1999.

COHEN, NATHAN See also WRITERS & WRITING, CANADIAN

In my profession, idealism is both a sedative and a salvation.

Nathan Cohen, critic, *The Theatre Week*, April 1949, quoted by Wayne E. Edmonstone in *Nathan Cohen: The Making of a Critic* (1977).

Gentlemen! Gentlemen!

Characteristic greeting of **Nathan Cohen**, moderator of *Fighting Words*, popular on CBC Radio and TV from 1952 to 1962. According to Barbara Moon in *Maclean's*, 8 June 1957, he said of his voice: "I know I sound like God."

A Canadian Jew came to interview me for the wireless.

Evelyn Waugh, English novelist, referring to the visit of critic and broadcaster Nathan Cohen for a CBC Radio interview, diary entry, 18 Aug. 1956, *The Diaries of Evelyn Waugh* (1976) edited by Michael Davie.

I am, in fact, the *only* drama critic in Canada. The rest are reviewers.

Nathan Cohen, critic, quoted by Barbara Moon in *Maclean's*, 8 June 1957.

I not only know what I like, but why.

Nathan Cohen, critic, CKFM Radio, 12 Jan. 1966, quoted by Wayne E. Edmonstone in *Nathan Cohen: The Making of a Critic* (1977).

I've got a vision of perfection in the temple of my mind.

Nathan Cohen, critic, quoted by Paul King in "A Remembrance of Nathan Cohen," *Toronto Life*, May 1971.

He was not too big to do little things / Nor too small to do big things / He was totally involved in life

Epitaph on the headstone of **Nathan Cohen** (1902–1971), Faband Labour Zionist Alliance, Mt. Sinai Memorial Park, Toronto, Ont.

COINCIDENCE

Coincidence petrifies men but liberates women.

Urjo Kareda, writer, "The Occult," *Homemaker's Digest*, Jan.–Feb. 1972.

A coincidence is a piece of design that one cannot find a use for.

Northrop Frye, cultural critic, "Cycle and Apocalypse in Finnegans Wake" (1985), *Myth and Metaphor: Selected Essays, 1974–1988* (1990) edited by Robert D. Denham.

COLD

I'll tell you where I feel a coward. When the cold wind blows. I am a coward when it comes to cold. I can't wait to get indoors. I dread every moment when I have to step out and go to an engagement. All I can do is grit my teeth, bear with it, and get out of the cold as quickly as possible. You want to torture me, you want me to confess or anything of the sort, just put me out into the cold, wintry Toronto weather.

Wole Soyinka, Nigerian-born writer, interviewed in Toronto in January by Stuart McLean, *PEN Canada's Newsletter*, March 1996.

COLD WAR See also WAR

Canada is the biggest country in the Free World.

Americanism heard during the so-called Cold War (1945–90) between the United States and the Soviet Union.

Dangerous living had never appealed to me, and adventure always associated itself with unromantic danger in my mind. But that night of September 5, 1945, during the long walk from Somerset Street to Range Road, I came as close to becoming a hero as I ever will.

Igor Gouzenko, Soviet defector, referring to his departure from the Russian Embassy with classified documents, *This Was My Choice: Gouzenko's Story* (1948).

I'm absolutely certain the Cold War began in Ottawa. I've argued that it was the most important thing that ever happened in Canada in terms of geopolitics.

Robert Fulford, journalist, quoted by John Sawatsky in *Gouzenko: The Untold Story* (1984).

Mr. Brown who came to us from Prague....

Circumspect words of the priest who conducted the funeral service of Igor Gouzenko in a church somewhere in Metropolitan Toronto. The Russian defector died on 28 June 1982. He was born in Rogachov, near Moscow, not Prague, Czechoslovakia. It is doubtful that the priest even knew the identity of "Mr. Brown" or "Mr. Peter Brown." Quoted by William Stevenson in *Intrepid's Last Case* (1983).

The Cold War had come to Canada with a vengeance; to a substantial extent, the Cold War had *begun in Canada*.

J.L. Granatstein and **David Stafford**, historians, *Spy Wars: Espionage and Canada from Gouzenko to Glasnost* (1990).

One of the absurdities of the Cold War is that 15 billion years of evolution could have ended in 15 minutes of nuclear war.

Hubert Reeves, cosmologist and commentator, quoted by André Picard in *The Globe and Mail*, 14 May 1993.

Canadians had to make themselves feel at home occupying the territory which separated the world's two nuclear giants, each with their missiles poised to fly over Canadian territory. This made them perpetual mockers of the heroic, insisters that no one become excited by ideas, that the only way to live was to be determinedly pragmatic. These qualities found wonderfully positive expression in Canadian peacekeeping activities, and support of the United Nations, but I thought them also a straitjacket for Canadian intellectual life, and a barrier to firing the imagination of the young women and men I taught.

Jill Ker Conway, academic and memoirist, *True North: A Memoir* (1994).

COLLEGES & UNIVERSITIES See also EDUCATION

Change within a university encounters all the difficulties of moving a cemetery.

Attributed to **Sidney Smith** who resigned the presidency of the University of Toronto in 1959 to join the cabinet of Prime Minister John G. Diefenbaker.

Traditionally, universities were judged by the fame of their faculties. They may soon be judged by the fame of their students.

Edmund Carpenter, anthropologist, "Reclassification," *Human Alternatives: Visions for Us Now* (1971) edited by Richard Kostelanetz.

My grandfather was Principal of Queen's University; my father was Headmaster of Upper Canada College; I, myself, am head of the Department of Religion at McMaster University; my son is a janitor here.

George P. Grant, philosopher, private communication, 1976. He was referring to his grandfather, George M. Grant, Principal of Queen's, and his father, William L. Grant, head of the private high-school.

The British, for example, are not prejudiced against "the British"; the Americans are not prejudiced against "the Americans." But the universities in Canada are profoundly prejudiced against those they call "the Canadians" (of whatever origin)—just as our foreign and domestic capitalists are.

Anthony Wilden, commentator, *The Imaginary Canadian* (1980).

University is a place where knowledge is not found, but sought.

Vincent Bladen, academic, quoted by John Picton in *The Toronto Star*, 15 Feb. 1981.

The university is a community in which the intellect and the imagination have a continuously functional place, and so gives us a sense of what human life could be like if these qualities were always functional in it.

Northrop Frye, cultural critic, "The View from Here" (1983), *Myth and Metaphor: Selected Essays, 1974–1988* (1990) edited by Robert D. Denham.

There is no irony whatever in saying that the memory of one's experience as a student is more real than the experience itself.

Northrop Frye, cultural critic, sermon, Service of Thanksgiving, Toronto, 5 Oct. 1986.

To be educated in private schools in Ontario and then at a university in Newfoundland is not normal. It is not even sensible.

John Fraser, cultural commentator, discussing his own educational background, *Telling Tales* (1986).

You and I who belong to the university share common goals and a common experience. This is not an institution divided between those who read and those who are read to—between teachers and pupils—but between those who, if they merit the title of professor, are life-long students, and yourselves, students of more recent date.

John Polanyi, scientist, "No Genuine Ivory Tower Is Ever Irrelevant," *The Vancouver Sun*, 9 Sept. 1989.

Our universities now take on the structure of supermarkets and make courses of study out of the specious agendas of post-modern complaints.

Frank Zingrone, communications theorist, "Wired Society Leaves Democracy Twitching," *The Toronto Star*, 6 Oct. 1994.

If all we did at Princeton was train a terrifically well-qualified and very smart group of white males, we would be failures. It's as simple as that. At one time that was an acceptable way to meet civic responsibility. But at this time and this place, we have the responsibility to do better than that.

Harold T. Shapiro, Montreal-born President of Princeton University, quoted by Kimberly J. McLarin in "Education Life: Profile," *The New York Times Magazine*, 2 April 1995.

A university is not a continuation of high school; it is a research institution dedicated to the advancement of knowledge, and those who do not contribute to this end ought not to be employed there.

David J. Bercuson, **Robert Bothwell**, and **J.L. Granatstein**, historians, *Petrified Campus: The Crisis in Canada's Universities* (1997).

COLONIALISM See also BRITISH EMPIRE & COMMONWEALTH

We formerly estimated the cost of transporting the people to Canada, and settling them there, at ten times the expense of locating them on the waste lands. Others have since estimated it at thirty times. We know not, nor is it material, which guess is nearest the truth. Neither have we spoken of the benefit of employing our own labour in the improvement of our own country, instead of the improvement of countries which will not always be ours.

John Stuart Mill, political economist, *Newspaper Writings*, "The Condition of Ireland," 2 Dec. 1846, on emigration from Ireland, edited by Ann P. Robson and John M. Robson, Volume XXIV of the "Collected Works of John Stuart Mill."

It is the weakness of you French—planting a drop of your precious blood in outlandish veins, in the wilderness and fancying that that addition makes them French—that by this the wilderness is converted! civilized, a new link in the chain. Never. Great as your desire may be.

William Carlos Williams, American poet and essayist, "The Founding of Quebec," *In the American Grain* (1925).

He had been in Canada the year before, and had fixed upon two areas, one in British Columbia and the other on the Peace River, for a great national experiment.

Passage descriptive of a scheme to generate colonial wealth from **John Buchan**'s novel *The Gap in the Curtain* (1932).

Canadians ask themselves whether they have become free of Britain's colonial influence only to fall under the spell of the United States' economic imperialism.

Walter L. Gordon, statesman, *A Choice for Canada: Independence or Colonial Status* (1966).

Dependence, provincialism, colonialism, whatever term is used is not the best kind of life. An inferior status produces an inferior people.

A.R.M. Lower, historian, quoted by Ian Lumsden in *Close the 49th Parallel, Etc.: The Americanization of Canada* (1970).

It would be a mistake to evoke the image of Canada as a seething colony struggling to break loose. Canada bears rather the signs of a successful lobotomy to which it has voluntarily assented.

Abraham Rotstein, economist, "Canada: The New Nationalism," *Foreign Affairs*, Oct. 1976, included by Grant S. McClellan in *Canada in Transition* (1977).

COLOUR

We live in a world of darkness, but the colour comes from the inner world to the outer world. Can you imagine if these buildings were purple and red and shocking pink?

Norval Morrisseau, Ojibwa artist, discussing his art and its relationship with the world, quoted by Christopher Dafoe, "Such a Long Journey," *The Globe and Mail*, 10 April 1999.

COMEDY See also HUMOUR & HUMORISTS

The world's greatest comedienne.

Description of Toronto-born comedienne Beatrice Lillie, Lady Peel, offered by **Noel Coward**, as noted in *The Toronto Star's Centennial Magazine*, Nov. 1992.

My name. José Jimenez.

Characteristic greeting of **Bill Dana**, B.C.-born humorist and comic, creator of José Jimenez, the character of a semi-literate Mexican, for television, seen for the first time in 1959 on *The Steve Allen Show*, according to Laurence J. Peter in *The Laughter Prescription* (1982). Astronaut Alan Shepard, the first American in space, told takeoff control, "You're on your way, José." Quoted by John Picton in *The Toronto Star*, 14 Nov. 1982.

To Err Is Human, To Farce Divine

Motto of the Royal Canadian Air Farce, and the title of its CD, according to comedian **Dave Broadfoot**, CBC Radio, 21 Aug. 1992.

We weren't troublemakers—in fact, I always thought we were somewhat bland. There was a reviewer once in the States who said we looked like "two accountants desperately trying to find the balance." Yet, in many ways, I think that "safeness" is what led to our longevity.

Frank Shuster, comedian, referring to the long-lasting Wayne and Shuster comedy team, quoted by Bill Brioux in *TV Guide*, 26 June 1993.

Good day, eh?

Salutation popularized by comedian **Dave Thomas** of the McKenzie Brothers in the 1970s, quoted in *The Globe and Mail*, 28 July 1993.

All I did was write about the adolescent, heavy-metal experience as I knew about it growing up in Scarborough, Ontario.

Mike Myers, comedian, commenting on his character Wayne Campbell of the TV series *Wayne's World*, quoted by Colin MacLean in a Jumbo Video promotional pamphlet in 1997. Myers recalled that "my parents were born in Liverpool, England, and we moved to Canada in 1956. I was brought up in an English household."

My Boyfriend's Back and There's Gonna Be Laundry

Title of a routine written and performed by

comic **Sandra Shamas** in the 1980s, included in *Sandra Shamas: A Trilogy of Performances* (1997).

Mojo is libido, essence, right stuff, what the French call a certain I don't know what.

Mike Myers, Toronto-born comic, defining the word mojo which caught on with the movie *Austin Powers: The Spy Who Shagged Me* (1999). It seems to be a cross between life energy and sex appeal.

COMIC ART See also ART & ARTISTS, HUMOUR & HUMORISTS

One mythical cartoon was supposed to have appeared in the *Calgary Eye Opener*. It portrayed a small farmer standing in the middle of his vast wheat field during a blistering hailstorm. The cut-line simply reads, "God damn the CPR!" We checked through the existing microfilm of *The Eye Opener*, but could not discover the cartoon.

Terry Mosher, cartoonist, referring to the tabloid published by Bob Edwards, Preface, *The Hecklers: A History of Canadian Political Cartooning and a Cartoonist's History of Canada* (1979).

Harry, the *Star Weekly* does not go to press without Mr. Frise.

J.E. Atkinson, publisher of *The Toronto Star*, to its editor, Harry Hindmarsh, about 1936, concerning the appearance of "Birdseye Centre" (later "Juniper Junction"), a popular weekly cartoon feature created by Jim Frise, quoted by Greg Clark in his preface to *Birdseye Centre by Frise* (1965).

If you draw without a caption, then it can be funny in any language.

*

Dignity is nonsense.

George Feyer, cartoonist, interviewed on CBC-TV, 1 Dec. 1954.

By profession I am a cartoonist, and my work is displayed through the medium of the Sunday comic section. But in reality I am an illustrator, and my methods are those of an illustrator.

Hal Foster, cartoonist and creator of the strip "Prince Valiant," quoted by Allen Willette in *Top Cartoonists Tell How They Create America's Favourite Comics* (1964). Foster drew Prince Valiant from 1937 to 1980 and placed the text within the frame, not the balloon.

The more serious you are, the less people pay attention to you.

Roland Berthiaume, editorial cartoonist for *Le Jour* who signed his name Berthio, quoted in *Time*, 29 Dec. 1974.

Psychoanalysts are constantly sending in wretched ideas for drawings about psychoanalysts, and for reasons that nobody fully understands, a large proportion of our would-be artist-contributors are Canadians.

Brendan Gill, writer on *The New Yorker*, commenting on unsolicited ideas for cartoons, *Here at The New Yorker* (1975).

The World's not lost while live the comics.

Line from **Earle Birney**'s poem "Lines for Lotos-Eaters" (1975), *The Collected Poems of Earle Birney* (1975).

So enjoy. And remember that enjoying art is part of enjoying life. Remember, too, that the verb "to enjoy" means "to put joy into."

Frank Kelly Freas, Canadian-raised illustrator, dean of science-fiction artists, *Frank Kelly Freas: The Art of Science Fiction* (1977).

Most cartoonists are guys who can't stand authority.

Terry Mosher, cartoonist who signs his work Aislin, comment, documentary movie *The Hecklers*, quoted by John Brehl in *The Toronto Star*, 20 Jan. 1979.

All you need to be a cartoonist is a sheet of paper, a two-dollar pen and a sense of humour. The sense of humour is especially important if, as in my case, it takes thirty years to save up the two dollars.

Jim Unger, cartoonist who introduced the cartoon "Herman" in Ottawa in 1974, *The 1st Treasury of Herman* (1979).

A cartoon never hurt any politician. They manage to do that with their own mouths.

Duncan Macpherson, editorial cartoonist, quoted by Peter Desbarats and Terry Mosher in *The Hecklers: A History of Canadian Political Cartooning and a Cartoonist's History of Canada* (1979).

By creating Adam in His own image and likeness, God made the first caricature. Thus, God is the patron saint of all caricaturists!

Robert LaPalme, cartoonist, *The Art of Political Cartooning in Canada: 1980* (1980).

We are the last magicians. We have the potential, in a day and age when everything is thoroughly logical, to bring people magic. At Nelvana, that's all we are after.

Frank Nissen, director of animation at Nelvana Productions, quoted by Ann Johnston in *Maclean's*, 28 April 1980.

I just came up here to help out. Very cold country, and Toronto was not a very creative city. I was earning a living in those days, that's all.

Ralph Bakshi, cartoonist, creator of "Fritz the Cat," the first x-rated cartoon, who worked on the TV series *Rocket Robin Hood* in Toronto, quoted by Ron Base in *The Toronto Star*, 1 March 1981.

The political cartoon is the greatest vehicle for delivering the message of the day. It really has historical value, and it's one of the finest visual records there are.

Ben Wicks, cartoonist, creator of "The Outcasts," quoted by Bruce Blackadar in *The Toronto Star*, 2 May 1982.

Comics, like TV, reinforced the notion that Canada was a backwater. In fact, comics were a welcome escape from our own culture's seeming dullness. Life in America, we just knew, was more exciting. Superman might visit his Fortress of Solitude in our Arctic from time to time, but never Toronto or Montreal, let alone Halifax where I lived.

John Bell, researcher, "Yes, There Are Canadian Comics," *Canuck Comics* (1986) edited by John Bell.

Comics that were written and drawn and published in Canada in the Forties bought new by me in Painesville, Ohio. Comics that were my joy and a source of early inspiration for the stories I have spent my life writing.

Harlan Ellison, U.S. science-fiction writer, recollecting the adolescent joys of reading Toronto-published comic books issued in 1941–47, "Dreams of Joy Recaptured," *Canuck Comics* (1986) edited by John Bell.

Now that the paper's anniversary has arrived, I can tell you I have very fond memories of *The Toronto Star*. It was a very important part of my life.

Joe Shuster, comic-book artist and co-creator (with writer Jerry Siegel) of "Superman," recalling his early years in Toronto in 1930s as a *Star* paperboy, interviewed in Los Angeles by Henry Mietkiewicz, *The Toronto Star*, 26 April 1992. Clark Kent, Superman's alter ego, originally worked as a reporter for "the Daily Star," later "the Daily Planet."

We all look forward every day to that one page in the paper where the small truths lie, hoping for a laugh, or a little sarcasm, or a punchline that will ease the burden just a bit. I learned that our work is taken seriously, and despite the reduction in numbers and size, the comics matter a great deal.

Lynn Johnston, creator of "For Better or for Worse" comic feature, *It's the Thought that Counts... For Better or For Worse Fifteenth Anniversary Collection* (1994).

COMIC BOOKS & STRIPS See COMIC ART

COMICS, STAND-UP See HUMOUR & HUMORISTS

COMMERCIALS See ADVERTISING

COMMON MARKET

We are seeking a system in which two nations, one whose motherland would be Québec, the other free to rearrange the rest of the country as it pleases, associate in an original application of the contemporary "common market" model, forming a new whole that could, for instance, be known as The Canadian Union.

René Lévesque, separatist, address, 15 Sept. 1967, *Quotations from René Lévesque* (1977) edited by Jean Côté and Marcel Chaput, translated by Robert Guy Scully and Jacqueline Perrault.

It will greatly aid Quebec to achieve the commitment it has made, that is to make of Quebec a French state within the Canadian common market.

Robert Bourassa, Quebec Premier, quoted in *Le Monde Diplomatique, Le Monde*, Jan. 1975. At that time Bourassa's vision was "Cultural Sovereignty within a Canadian Common Market."

COMMON SENSE

It would appear to us that the matters under consideration do not call so much for the exercise of military skill or the application of military experience as the consideration of international law and the exercise of the common-place quality of common sense.

Sir Robert Borden, Prime Minister, letter to Governor General the Duke of Connaught in 1916, *Robert Laird Borden: His Memoirs* (1938). The last seven words are occasionally recalled.

Canada would not be so fine a country if its citizens were not so well endowed with common sense.

Philippe Deane Gigantes, author and Senator, *The Road Ahead* (1990).

We believe in the common sense of the common people.

Preston Manning, leader of the Reform Party, "in innumerable speeches promoting the Reform Party of Canada," as noted by Brian Bergman, "Rough Waters on the Right," *Maclean's*, 24 May 1999.

COMMONWEALTH See BRITISH EMPIRE & COMMONWEALTH

COMMUNICATIONS See also BROADCASTING, MEDIA, TELECOMMUNICATIONS, TELEPHONE

Shortly before mid-day I placed the single earphone to my ear and started listening.... The answer came at 12:30 when I heard, faintly but distinctly, pip-pip-pip. I handed the phone to Kemp: "Can you hear anything?" I asked. "Yes," he said, "the letter S"—he could hear it. I knew then that all my anticipations had been justified.

Guglielmo Marconi, Italian-born inventor of wireless telegraphy, describing the reception of a signal in Morse Code from Poldhu, Cornwall, in his hut on Signal Hill, Nfld., cited by Leslie Bailey in *Scrapbook 1900–1914* (1957).

So much of the practical development of the telephone has been in the United States that I think the fact that the telephone was invented in Canada should be more widely known than it is—at least in the United States.

Alexander Graham Bell, inventor, address, "The Substance of My Latest Research," Empire Club of Canada, Toronto, 1 Nov. 1917.

A people forms itself by acting, by creating—that is, by communicating. It finds itself through the act of communication.

Hector de Saint-Denys-Garneau, poet, *The Journal of Saint-Denys-Garneau* (1962) translated by John Glassco.

Another very useful remark was made to me by a student who said: "Why are your letters to the newspapers so plain and your other writing so difficult and obscure?" This question highlights the difference between exposition and exploration...the actual process of dialogue and discovery is not compatible with packaging of familiar views.

Marshall McLuhan, communications pioneer, "Education in the Electronic Age" (1967), *The Best of Times / The Worst of Times: Contemporary Issues in Canadian Education* (1972) edited by Hugh A. Stevenson, Robert M. Stamp, and J. Donald Wilson.

Communication is what people with nothing to say do to people who won't listen.

Marshall McLuhan, communications pioneer, quoted by Richard J. Schoeck in *Who Was Marshall McLuhan?* (1994) edited by Barrington Nevitt and Maurice McLuhan.

The singing Muse translates herself into a writer: she who had required men to listen now invites them to read.

Eric A. Havelock, classicist and theorist of oral cultural communication, *The Muse Learns to Write: Reflections on Orality and Literacy from Antiquity to the Present* (1963).

Of all areas of public policy, communication policy is most vital. Communications form the central nervous system of a nation. Who controls the system controls the nation. The system must be seen as a whole, and the parts in relation to the whole.

Graham Spry, enthusiast for public broadcasting, quoted in *The Toronto Star*, 13 Feb. 1970.

We need a set of communication symbols as universal as the figures. You can go into a restaurant anywhere in the world and the menu will tell you the price of a meal but you may not know what you are going to eat.

Carl Dair, typographer, statement reproduced in the privately printed volume "Carl Dair in Quotes" (*Wrongfount 6*, 1968).

In either case communication is a one-way street. Wherever we turn, there is that same implacable voice, unctuous, caressing, inhumanly complacent, selling us food, cars, political leaders, culture, contemporary issues, and remedies against the migraine we get from listening to it. It is not just the voice we hear that haunts us, but the voice that goes on echoing in our minds, forming our habits of speech, our processes of thought.

Northrop Frye, cultural theorist, "Communications," *The Listener*, 9 July 1970. Frye had in mind messages emanating from the two "establishments"—political in socialist countries and economic in the United States.

Lack of communication has held Canada together for one hundred years. Once we can speak each other's language, the mystique of being what we are is gone.

Dave Broadfoot, comedian, *Sex & Security: A Frank and Fearless Political Testament by the Honourable Member of Parliament for Kicking Horse Pass* (1974).

If there were an International Need to Communicate Award, Canada would win every year. Our huge land mass, small population, and proximity to the United States have created in us an obsession with keeping in touch with one another.

Morris Wolfe, critic, Introduction to the record album, *Fifty Years of Radio: A Celebration of CBC Radio 1936–1986* (1986).

Teleconferencing and conference calls are poor substitutes for handshakes.

F. Kenneth Hare, geographer, "Canada: The Land," *Daedalus: Journal of the American Academy of Arts and Sciences*, "In Search of Canada," Fall, 1988.

Today, the whole world is becoming a satellite dish, where everything that is knowable is known instantly and collectively. Nothing can be hidden.

Frank Feather, futurologist, *G-Forces: Reinventing the World—The 35 Global Forces Restructuring Our World* (1989).

A sentence that has shock value carries more information than one that does not.

Frank Ogden, futurologist, quoted in an interview in *The Toronto Star*, 2 June 1992.

There was never a Toronto school of Communications. It was simply a bunch of islanders watching the greatest show on earth.

Edmund Carpenter, communications theorist, referring to the group in Toronto in the 1950s concerned with the effects of media on society, "Remembering Explorations," *Canadian Notes & Queries*, Spring 1992.

The only way we can be alive in this country is through advanced technologies of communication. We need the telephone, the telegraph, the radio, the satellite dish, TV and the computer, air travel and trains. The paradox is that these technologies do not solidify individual identity; they do not focus a singular identity for any one person.

B.W. Powe, critic, *A Tremendous Canada of Light* (1993) as reproduced in *The Toronto Star*, 11 July 1993.

While we humans, with our opposable thumbs, have been "doing our thing" throughout our brief history, perhaps dolphins and whales have learned the more subtle inner arts of being-communication that we have been too busy with externals to discover.

James George, former Canadian Ambassador, *Asking for the Earth: Waking up to the Spiritual/Ecological Crisis* (1995).

COMMUNISM See also IDEOLOGIES, MARXISM, SOVIET UNION

Canada? You know, there are many farmers there, and a young bourgeoisie, who, like the Swiss, should have a strongly developed sense of property.

Leon Trotsky, communist leader, remark made to fellow prisoners in Spain, prior to his detention in Amherst, N.S., 3–29 April 1917, quoted by Hans Werner in *Saturday Night*, Aug. 1974.

Jesus Christ was born in a barn.

John Boychuck, a founder of the Communist Party of Canada, referring to the CPC's clandestine formation in a barn outside Guelph, Ont., 27 Nov. 1921. The barn has long been demolished, but its farmhouse still stands at 257 Metcalf St., Guelph. When Boychuck was interviewed by *The Canadian Magazine*, 22 Jan. 1972, he said, "Oh, fifty years ago, I thought I'd see something. Now, maybe, another fifty years."

Scott: Why do you refuse paid advertisements in the *Montreal Star* for the CCF, even when M.J. Coldwell is coming to speak, when you carry ads all the time for the Communist Party?

McConnell: Because they aren't dangerous; the CCF is.

Exchange between **F.R. Scott**, a founder of the CCF, and **J.M. McConnell**, publisher of the *Montreal Star,* in the latter's office in 1944, as recalled by Scott in 1976. The newspaper never referred to the CCF but would carry advertisements for meetings of the Communist Party. This was noted with characteristic irony by F.R. Scott, constitutional law authority, "*The Montreal Star* and the CCF: Another Monopoly at Work" (1944), *A New Endeavour: Selected Political Essays, Letters, and Addresses* (1986) edited by Michiel Horn.

The Communist Party has no right to the word socialist, since what it calls "scientific socialism" is the negation of the most fundamental part of socialism, namely its respect for the individual human being.

F.R. Scott, constitutional law authority, "The Fundamentals of Socialism" (1950), *A New Endeavour: Selected Political Essays, Letters, and Addresses* (1986) edited by Michiel Horn.

You're right. I got a telegram from Joe Stalin this morning ordering me to ask for a park for Ward 4.

Joe Salsberg, Toronto alderman, communist member of the Ontario Legislature in the 1940s and 1950s, facing objections that he took orders from Moscow, quoted in his obituary by Nicolaas van Rijn in *The Toronto Star,* 9 Feb. 1998.

I have no regrets, and I hope that you will not consider it bravado if I tell you that my only hope is that I shall not be found wanting by the many workers who have placed their confidence in me, and whom I have tried to represent.

Tim Buck, leader of the Communist Party of Canada, address to the judge and jury after being found guilty of violating Section 98 of the Criminal Code, *Yours in the Struggle: Reminiscences of Tim Buck* (1977) edited by William Beeching and Phyllis Clarke.

By intelligent individual and group action, the masses can repossess the earth. The democratic formula, of which economic co-operation is a vital part, is adequate. It takes the appeal out of the Marxian call to arms and says instead: "Workers of the world, arise! You need not be proletarians."

M.M. Coady, adult educator and co-founder of the Antigonish Movement, "The Challenge from the Left" (1954), *The Man from Margaree: Writings and Speeches of M.M. Coady, Educator, Reformer, Priest* (1971) edited by Alexander F. Laidlaw.

I believe that our movement fulfills the righteous purposes of God in history and that God uses Communists for the establishment of peace whether they know it or not.

James G. Endicott, President of the Canadian Peace Council in 1960, quoted by Ivan Avakumovic in *The Communist Party in Canada: A History* (1975).

The "Moscow Gold" myth was always a good propaganda point with the powers-that-be, but I would sure enjoy seeing a lot of them having to live on it.

Tom McEwen, newspaperman, *The Forge Glows Red: From Blacksmith to Revolutionary* (1974). Immediately following the collapse of the Soviet Union, the Communist Party of Canada sold its national headquarters building in Toronto.

Marx had it all wrong: as the state grows stronger, communism withers away.

Louis Dudek, man-of-letters, *Epigrams* (1975).

I'm a living example their system can be beaten. I did escape and I'm still alive. I'm a bad example as far as the Soviets are concerned.

Igor Gouzenko, Soviet defector, quoted by John Picton in *The Toronto Star,* 25 Nov. 1979.

Communism is a myth of plentitude at the end of time.

Michael Ignatieff, essayist, *The Needs of Strangers* (1985).

All of us knew, of course, what McCarthy had done to those with left-wing sympathies in the U.S., but were oblivious to the fact that Canada had been the first English-speaking country in the world to declare its Communist Party an unlawful organization and to jail its leaders.

Morris Wolfe, journalist, referring to U.S. Senator Joseph McCarthy, "Hard Labour," *The Canadian Forum*, Dec. 1991.

In those days, if anyone ever asked me, "Are you or are you not a Communist?" I'd always reply, deadpan, "We're not allowed to tell."

Ted Allan, playwright and member of the International Brigade during the Spanish Civil War, interviewed by Len Scher in *The Un-Canadians: True Stories of the Blacklist Era* (1992).

Is Marx right after all, for more reasons than he imagined, that we are faced with a choice between world capitalism and world survival?

John McMurtry, philosopher, University of Guelph, "The Contradictions of Free Market Doctrine—Is There a Solution?" a paper prepared for the Westminster Institute Conference, "Surviving Globalization: Economic, Social, and Environmental Dimensions," London, Ont., May 1995.

COMMUNITY See also PLACES

Look and listen for the welfare of the whole people and have always in view not only the present, but also the coming generations, even those whose faces are yet beneath the surface of the ground—the unborn of the future Nation.

Counsel from the traditional Great Law of Peace of the **Iroquois Confederacy**, reproduced by Craig MacLaine and Michael S. Baxendale in *This Land Is Our Land: The Mohawk Revolt at Oka* (1991).

To really save one man you must transform the community in which he lives.

J.S. Woodsworth, social reformer, quoted by Alan Phillips in *Into the 20th Century: 1900–1910* (1977).

The individual cannot live by bread alone; and the true life of the community must reside in those intangibles which derive their chief value from being enjoyed in common.

Hilda Neatby, educator and Massey Report commissioner, "The Massey Report: A Retrospect," *The Tamarack Review*, Issue One, Autumn, 1956.

A Citizen Who Cared for Her Community

Inscription on the memorial erected in the Toronto park dedicated to the memory of writer **Margaret Fairley** (1885–1968), presented to the city by her friends in 1973.

A nation may be considered as a community of communities. The nation is an organic entity of goals and resources.

Léon Dion, sociologist, expressing a notion of nationhood, *Quebec: The Unfinished Revolution* (1976) translated by Thérèse Romer. Prime Minister Joe Clark was comfortable with the concept that Canada was a "community of communities" for it met the needs of Conservatives and seemed to solve some of the problems that exist for separatists. Pierre Elliott Trudeau ridiculed the notion as "ten premiers and the Prime Minister as a kind of head waiter to take their orders" and the idea as "a loose confederation of shopping centres."

"Canada" is a political entity; the cultural counterpart that we call "Canada" is really a federation not of provinces but of regions and communities.

Northrop Frye, cultural critic, interviewed by Robert Fulford, "From Nationalism to Regionalism: The Maturing of Canadian Culture," *The Anthology Anthology: A Selection from 30 Years of CBC Radio's Anthology* (1984) edited by Robert Weaver.

Yet the human community is losing something essential, and nearly everyone senses it. It is something that won't sit still for quantification, still less for qualification. But losing it is making some of us very, very uneasy.

Brian Fawcett, cultural commentator, *Public Eye: An Investigation into the Disappearance of the World* (1990).

Collectivity, after all, is perhaps the single characteristic of Canadian society that sets us most apart from our giant neighbour to the south.

Peter Gzowski, journalist and host of CBC Radio's *Morningside*, "Whistling Down the Northern Lights," *The Fourth Morningside Papers* (1991).

. . . we all belong to something before we are anything. . . .

Northrop Frye, cultural critic, *The Double Vision: Language and Meaning in Religion* (1991).

It would be difficult to determine on whom the right to unilateral secession should be conferred. With more than 3,000 human groups in the world conscious of a collective identity, the creation of each new state would risk creating within that state minorities who would in turn claim their own independence.

Stéphane Dion, Minister of Intergovernmental Affairs, address, Nordic Association for Canadian Studies, Reykjavik, Iceland, 5 Aug. 1999, quoted by Jack Aubry in the *National Post* the following day.

COMPANIONSHIP

And I just want to hold you closer than I've ever held anyone before / You say you've been twice a wife and you're through with life / Ah, but Honey, what the hell's it for? / After twenty-three years you'd think I could find / A way to let you know somehow / That I want to see your smiling face forty-five years from now.

Lines from **Stan Rogers**' song "Forty-five Years," *Fogarty's Cove* (1973), quoted by Chris Gudgeon in *An Unfinished Conversation: The Life and Music of Stan Rogers* (1993).

COMPASSION

My wish is to live in a society where compassion is not a crime.

John Hofsess, founder, The Right to Die Society, "Fatal Contract," *The Globe and Mail*, 19 Sept. 1992.

I don't think compassion ever goes completely out of favour.

Bob Rae, former Ontario Premier, press conference to announce his plan to resign, quoted by Martin Mittelstaedt, *The Globe and Mail*, 15 Jan. 1996.

COMPENSATION

I was underpaid for the first half of my life; I don't mind being overpaid for the second half.

Pierre Berton, author, quoted by Gary Ross in *The Canadian*, 5 April 1975.

COMPETITION

Competition creates resemblance.

Marshall McLuhan, communications pioneer, observation made in 1966 as quoted by George Leonard in *Who Was Marshall McLuhan?* (1994) edited by Barrington Nevitt and Maurice McLuhan.

A little talent will get you a long way in an uncompetitive society, protected by tariffs and government rewards. A Canadian has been defined as somebody who does not play for keeps. Even his anti-trust laws fail to enforce business competition as ruthlessly as the American ones.

William Kilbourn, historian, Introduction, *Canada: A Guide to the Peaceable Kingdom* (1970).

The competition no longer is the factory next door but one halfway around the world.

Hugh Hamilton, executive, Northern Telecom, quoted by Susan Goldenberg in *Global Pursuit: Canadian Business Strategies for Winning in the Borderless World* (1991).

Canadians dislike excellence, at least if it is Canadian (since the British were beaten by the Americans and the French were beaten by the British, Canada is founded upon a firm tradition of being trounced). Canadians suffer from what Mr. Valaskakis calls "a passion for bronze," the ability to always put in the middling performance apparently appropriate to a middle-sized power.

Editorial feature, "Survey on Canada," *The Economist*, 19 June 1991, reprinted in *The Globe and Mail*, 19 July 1991. The reference is to Greek-born Quebec commentator Kimon Valaskakis.

A society based on competition is therefore primarily a society based on losers.

John Ralston Saul, author, *The Doubter's Companion: A Dictionary of Aggressive Common Sense* (1994).

We don't succeed today because we are American, German, or Japanese—or from Quebec. We succeed when we are able to meet the competition, wherever it may come from. We must therefore stimulate entrepreneurship, the willingness to take risks.

Paul Desmarais, head of the Power Corporation of Canada, address, Sept. 1996, "Industry and Competitiveness," *National and Global Perspectives*, Winter 1996–97.

I find competition bracing. I find it exciting. I find it exhilarating. I find it almost impossible to be any other way.

George Cohon, senior chairman, McDonald's Restaurants of Canada, *To Russia with Fries* (1997) written with David Macfarlane.

COMPROMISE

There's the joke: Why does the Canadian cross the road? To get to the middle. We will solve this issue the Canadian way, by meeting in the middle.

David Crombie, former Toronto Mayor, referring to the Quebec referendum, "Bracing for 1995," *The Toronto Star*, 1 Jan. 1995.

Compromise is an essential and necessary part of the discourse of politics. Just as it abhors a vacuum, a healthy politics rejects absolutes. The revolutionary left and the radical right both start from a very different premise: that they are armed with truth, and that this truth is incompatible with the blurring tendencies of parliamentary life and coalition politics.

Bob Rae, former Ontario Premier, *From Protest to Power: Personal Reflections on a Life in Politics* (1996).

COMPUTER INDUSTRY See also COMPUTERS

In terms of, say, a computer technology we are headed for cottage economics, where the most important industrial activities can be carried on in any individual little shack anywhere on the globe.

Marshall McLuhan, communications pioneer, observation made in 1970, "A McLuhan Sourcebook," *The Essential McLuhan* (1995) edited by Eric McLuhan and Frank Zingrone.

Information Processing

Neologism: "The key phrase, 'information processing,' was coined by **Marshall McLuhan**, who was asked by IBM to explain to them, in succinct language, what computers are all about," according to Peter Bishop in *Fifth Generation Computers* (1986).

I am *danielu@microsoft.com.*

Opening sentence of **Douglas Coupland**'s first-person novel *Microserfs* (1995). The narrator is "a bug checker in Building Seven" of Microsoft.

Thought: one day the word "gigabits" is going to seem as small as the word "dozen."

Observation of the narrator of **Douglas Coupland**'s novel *Microserfs* (1995).

The technology isn't important—the opportunities are.

Jim Carroll and **Rick Broadhead**, computer specialists, *The Canadian Internet Advantage* (1995).

I was always interested in building things.

James Gosling, founder of California-based Sun Microsystems Inc., deviser of the computer language Java, referring to his student years at the University of Calgary, quoted by John Markoff in *The Globe and Mail*, 17 Oct. 1995.

The microchip will take its rightful place among history's four greatest inventions—the others being fire, the wheel, and hotel room service.

Peter C. Newman, journalist, "The Dawn of a New Millennium," *Maclean's*, 30 Dec. 1996.

COMPUTERS See also COMPUTER INDUSTRY, CYBERSPACE, INFORMATION, INTERNET

The plaintive coffins no longer furnish interesting tears. / Wealth and a pleasure filled with joy waste away sadness together with its roots.

Two lines of computer-written "poetry," as programmed by **Jean Baudot** of the computer sciences division of the University of Montreal. Quoted from the first such collection, *La machine à écrire* (1964) by Jacques Vallée in *Forbidden Science* (1992) who calls such lines "some pearls of wisdom that would have enchanted Jean Cocteau."

Computers may replace men, but they will never replace women.

Louis Dudek, man-of-letters, *Epigrams* (1975).

In the past college graduates had to be numerate and literate; in the future they will have to be numerate, literate—and computerate.

John Robert Colombo, editor, remark, general-education committee, Mohawk College, Hamilton, Ont., May 1979.

The issue, then, is not that everyone might be controlled by robots, but that we will all come to think like robots, and not be disturbed by that at all.

Heather Menzies, academic, *Fast Forward and Out of Control: How Technology Is Changing Your Life* (1989).

It is relatively easy to design a system that converts rigid syntax to computations; it is much harder to design a system that tolerates mistakes or accepts a broader range of program descriptions.

A.K. Dewdney, computer specialist, "Algorithms: Cooking Up Programs," *The Turning Omnibus: 61 Excursions in Computer Science* (1989).

And a further note, a found poem from my spell-check: "Stopped at: Ottawa. Replacement: Oneiric."

Eric Korn, columnist, referring to his word processor's spell-check function, *The Times Literary Supplement*, 15 June 1990.

The word processor I am working on goes along fine for a while, but then, when I'm not paying attention, it starts turning out utter nonsense which gets published and makes me look like a moron.

Joey Slinger, humorist, "Getting Even," *If It's a Jungle Out There, Why Do I Have to Mow the Lawn* (1992).

Typewriters reward caution with fidelity; word processors encourage a carefree facility, only to betray it with grotesque calamities.

Francis Sparshott, philosopher, entry, *Contemporary Authors Autobiography Series* (1992), Volume 15.

I predict, quite fearlessly, that there will be at least one VR machine in every home in Canada within a generation. They will become as ubiquitous as TV sets today.

Bob Hunter, columnist, referring to computers that create the Virtual Reality experience, "City," *eye*, 21 Jan. 1993.

A naked woman working at a computer. Which attracts you most?

Opening line of **Candas Jane Dorsey**'s short story "(Learning About) Machine Sex" included in *Northern Stars: The Anthology of Canadian Science Fiction* (1994) edited by David G. Hartwell and Glenn Grant.

Shallit's First Law: Every new medium of expression will be used for sex. / *Shallit's Second Law*: Every new medium of expression will come under attack, usually because of Shallit's First Law.

Jeffrey Shallit, computer scientist, University of Waterloo, Treasurer of Electronic Frontier Canada, quoted by Joe Chidley in "Red Light District," *Maclean's*, 22 May 1995.

With the computer, you recover the autonomy you lost in television. The computer is an electronic book.

Derrick de Kerckhove, communications theorist, speech, "From Marconi to McLuhan," Italian Trade Commission, Toronto, 16 Sept. 1996.

In 1995 the electronic games industry had revenues of $17 billion—greater than the entire American motion picture industry.

Don Tapscott, consultant, *The Digital Economy: Promise and Peril in the Age of Networked Intelligence* (1996).

Computers have reversed the identity-destroying effects of electronic media and offer a new sort of identity. Do you have a personal web site yet?

Frank Zingrone, academic, "Electric Reality," *Canadian Review of American Studies*, Vol. 27, No. 3, 1997.

Inuktitut is polysynthetic, grouping words together like German. The translation of computer, like a big brain, in Greenlandic Inuktitut is: nakuarsuamikqarasaasiaqarpunga. Put that on your computer and watch it explode!

Lois Darroch, author and *Arctic traveller, Time Between: Akuningini* (1998).

CONFEDERATION See also CONSTITUTION, DOMINION

My deliberate opinion is that the question is simply one of Confederation with each other or of ultimate absorption in the United States, and every difficulty placed in the way of the former is an argument in favour of those who desire the latter.

Sir Alexander Tilloch Galt, Father of Confederation, letter to Sir Edward Bulwer-Lytton, London, England, 22 Nov. 1858, quoted by O.D. Skelton in *The Life and Times of Sir Alexander Tilloch Galt* (1920).

We come to Your Majesty, who have given us liberty, to give us unity, that we may preserve and perpetuate our freedom.

Thomas D'Arcy McGee "visualized the fathers of Confederation approaching Queen Victoria and addressing her in the florid oratory of the day," noted by John Conway, "An 'Adapted Organic Tradition,'" *Daedalus: Journal of the American Academy of Arts and Sciences*, "In Search of Canada," Fall, 1988.

True to her high traditions, to Britain's ancient glory / Of patient saint and martyre, alive in deathless story; / Strong, in their liberty and truth, to shed from shore to shore / A light among the nations, till nations are no more.

Lines from "Dominion Day, 1874," a patriotic verse written by **Agnes M. Machar**, included by W.D. Lighthall in *Songs of the Great Dominion* (1889). It ends, "A noble future in her eyes, the Britain of the West."

In geographical area, this Confederation of the British North American Provinces is even now large—it may become one day second only in extent to the vast territories of Russia.

Lord Carnarvon, Henry Howard Molyneux, British Secretary of State for the Colonies, opinion on the passage of the BNA Act, 1867, as he recalled on his visit to Quebec, 1 Sept. 1883.

Confederation, which was supposed to cure everything and make everyone rich, has been but a coalition of miseries and of provinces being bled of their populations.

Arthur Buies, Quebec essayist, *Chroniques canadiennes: humeurs et caprices* (1884).

Confederation has held sway. Whether it will last twenty or thirty years, I do not know; but one day it must dissolve.

Henri Bourassa, Quebec nationalist, address in Montreal, *Le Devoir*, 23 Dec. 1921, quoted by Michael Oliver in *The Passionate Debate* (1991).

In the Hearts and Minds of the / Delegates Who Assembled / In This Room on September 1, 1864 / Was Born the Dominion of Canada // Providence Being Their Guide / They Builded Better Than They Knew.

Inscription on the bronze plaque erected in 1917 (but not unveiled until 1 July 1927), Legislative Chamber, Province House, Charlottetown, P.E.I. Here the basis was established for the confederation of the colonies of British North America. The inscription's last two lines are taken from English and American poetry. "Providence being their guide" comes from *Paradise Lost* (1667), in which John Milton describes the expulsion of Adam and Eve from the Garden of Eden. "They builded better than they knew" comes from "The Problem," *Poems* (1847), in which Ralph Waldo Emerson wrote about the need for belief. The lines remain a powerful pastiche of British thought and American sentiment, and as such are completely Canadian.

Canada had become a nation, and shining prospects lay before her.

Winston Churchill, British statesman and popular historian, referring to Confederation, *Book X: The Great Democracies, A History of the English-speaking Peoples* (1958).

I had no more than glimpsed the underlying realities which make the Canadian Federation a State that is perpetually uneasy, ambivalent and artificial.

Charles de Gaulle, President of France, impressions during 1960, *Memoirs of Hope: Renewal, 1958–62: Endeavour 1962–* (1970) translated by Terence Kilmartin. The French statesman made official visits to Canada in July 1944, Aug. 1945, April 1960, and July 1967.

To confess one's inability to make Canadian Confederation work is, at this stage of history, to admit one's unworthiness to contribute to the universal order.

Pierre Elliott Trudeau, constitutional specialist, "Toward Political Realism," *The Canadian Forum*, May 1964. Trudeau was one of six French-Canadian intellectuals who signed this manifesto which appeared simultaneously in *The Canadian Forum* and *Cité Libre*.

Confederation had been a political union of several provinces, not a cultural compact between two ethnic communities, English and French.

Donald C. Creighton, historian, *Canada's First Century: 1867–1967* (1970). Here the BNA Act, 1867, is defined as a "political act" or "political pact" vs. a "cultural compact."

Once in every generation, we've had to conquer our fate over again.

A.R.M. Lower, historian, interviewed by Ramsay Cook in *The Craft of History* (1973) edited by Eleanor Cook.

Confederation itself was not a French idea or a British idea. It was an idea born of this land.

The need for it arose from a shared experience and common problems. Its fulfillment sprang from shared attitudes and beliefs.

Elizabeth II, Queen of Canada, address, State Dinner, Silver Jubilee, Government House, 16 Oct. 1977, printed in *The Globe and Mail* the following day.

Confederation means sovereignty in association and association in sovereignty.

René Lévesque, Quebec Premier, quoted by Douglas Fullerton in *The Toronto Star*, 22 May 1978.

Will we be highly centralizing? Will we be a loose confederation of shopping centres, as some wag said about Los Angeles? Will we be something in between? I don't know.

Pierre Elliott Trudeau, Prime Minister, address, 23 March 1981, quoted by Robert Sheppard and Michael Valpy in *The National Deal* (1982).

The funniest thing about Canada is that it was founded by a bunch of lawyers scratching away with quill pens. It almost ended the same way, with lawyers using ballpoints.

Charles Lynch, newspaperman, *A Funny Way to Run a Country: Further Memoirs of a Political Voyeur* (1986).

If Confederation was a business arrangement more than a love-match—and we think it was—Quebec has gained far more from it than it has lost.

David J. Bercuson and **Barry Cooper**, historian and political scientist, *Deconfederation: Canada without Quebec* (1991).

Confederation is the best invention after democracy. It is based on the respect of differences. A day will come when countries will join up in a world confederation where individuals are no longer sacrificed to tribal rivalries.

Roch Carrier, author, quoted by Pauline Couture in *The Globe and Mail*, 8 Sept. 1992.

We speak of the Fathers of Confederation, but nobody talks about the fathers of Canada, indicating clearly enough that Confederation was an episode in Canada's evolution, not a brand-new beginning. A few intellectuals may indulge in loose talk about the Canadian founding, but they ought to know better.

Barry Cooper, political scientist, noting the evolutionary nature of the establishment of the country, "An Unfounded Nation," *National Post*, 3 July 1999.

CONQUEST OF 1759

The paths of glory lead but to the grave.

Line from **Thomas Gray**'s "Elegy, Written in a Country Churchyard" (1749), which was recited by General James Wolfe the night before he led the assault on the Plains of Abraham, 15 Sept. 1759.

Gentlemen, I would rather have written those lines than take Quebec.

James Wolfe, General, quoted by Francis Parkman in *Montcalm and Wolfe* (1884) who noted, "None were there to tell him that the hero is greater than the poet."

The Death of Wolfe on the Plains of Abraham = On a path to fame, both he and his war foe fell

Anagram attributed to the puzzle constructor **Sam Weller** in 1881 by O.V. Michaelsen in "Best Anagrams and Antigrams," *Word Ways: The Journal of Recreational Linguistics*, Nov. 1990.

The long siege of Quebec in 1759, or the glorious and desperate defence by the French, is an event almost entirely forgotten by us nowadays—as also, it seems, is the existence of the entire Canadian nation.

Alfred de Vigny, French poet, "Les Français au Canada" (1851), *Oeuvres complètes* (1948) edited by F. Baldensperger.

It is quite remarkable that I have never heard a man of the people blame Louis XV for the disasters that befell the Canadians after the colony was left to its own resources. If anyone accused the monarch, Jean-Baptiste would retort, "Bah! It was La Pompadour who sold the country to the English!" And he would launch into abuse of the lady.

Philippe-Joseph Aubert de Gaspé, memoirist, *A Man of Sentiment: The Memoirs of Philippe-Joseph Aubert de Gaspé 1786–1871* (1988) translated by Jane Brierley from the original French edition of 1866.

CONSCIENCE

When you come down to it, a good many radical opinions are fundamentally nothing but bad conscience.

Thoughts of a character in the novel *Miss Silver's Past* (1974) by **Josef Skvorecky**.

CONSCIOUSNESS See also AWARENESS

Cosmic Consciousness, then, is a higher form of consciousness than that possessed by the ordinary man.

Richard Maurice Bucke, alienist and philosopher, *Cosmic Consciousness: A Study in the Evolution of the Human Mind* (1901). Bucke coined the term "cosmic consciousness" to refer to an ecstatic or mystical state of awareness in a presentation before the American Medico-Psychological Association, Philadelphia, May 18, 1894.

Electricity makes possible—and not in the distant future, either—an amplification of human consciousness on a world scale, without any verbalization at all.

Marshall McLuhan, communications pioneer, "Playboy Interview" (1969) conducted by Eric Norden, *The Essential McLuhan* (1995) edited by Eric McLuhan and Frank Zingrone.

Sometimes we wonder whether humanity is capable of living in any world at all where consciousness is really a function of life.

Northrop Frye, cultural philosopher, "The Dedicated Mind," address, Service of Thanksgiving, 5 Oct. 1986, *Vic Report*, Winter, 1986–87.

I once read a book on problems in perception that contained the phrase, "The word *cat* cannot stretch you." But it can—if you are in an altered state of consciousness.

Audrey Thomas, novelist, contributor to *The Fourth Morningside Papers* (1991) edited by Peter Gzowski.

And the acceptance of psychic discomfort is the acceptance of consciousness.

John Ralston Saul, philosopher, final line, *The Unconscious Civilization* (1995).

Small enzymes of consciousness can have large catalytic effects on a whole culture. Anyone who has made yogurt knows that.

James George, former Canadian Ambassador, *Asking for the Earth: Waking up to the Spiritual/Ecological Crisis* (1995).

CONSERVATION

I have spent a lifetime in conservation affairs and have gradually but inescapably been convinced that up until the present time all we conservationists have been able to achieve is fight a delaying action.

John A. Livingston, naturalist, *One Cosmic Instance: A Natural History of Human Arrogance* (1973).

The Mohawks prophesied that, seven generations after the white people came, the elm trees would die, and then the maples. They predicted that birds would fall from the sky and fish die in the water. Then, they said, "man would grow ashamed of how he had treated his mother and provider, the earth."

Kevin Marron, researcher and author, *Witches, Pagans, and Magic in the New Age* (1989).

The future is R's.

Slogan introduced in Fall 1990 for the Blue Box recycling program sponsored by **Ontario Multi-Material Recycling Incorporated** (OMMRI), established in Toronto in 1986, to introduce the curbside collection system. The three R's are Recycling, Reduction, and Reuse.

If conservationism can make everyone a dollar, conservationism has a future.

Marq de Villiers, commentator, *Water* (1999).

Until you catch the last fish, until you cut the last tree, until you poison the last river, then and only then will you understand that money cannot be eaten.

Cree proverb recalled by a Native elder on CBC Radio's *Cross-Country Checkup*, 7 Nov. 1999.

CONSERVATISM See also CONSERVATIVE PARTY

But the conservatism, the Toryism you find on this side is reflected in that single verse of Tennyson: "That man's the true conservative / That lops the mouldered branch away." The mouldered branch is this played-out idea that when this country reaches a certain stage of development, we shall cling to old conditions and not encourage new production, new manufactures.

R.B. Bennett, Prime Minister, House of Commons, 12 April 1929. Bennett recalled the "mouldered branch" on 2 July 1931 and and 7 June 1934.

All around the Right is risin', people we need organizin', / "Smash the Right" is our song, because know the Right is wrong.

Chorus of "Smash the Right" (1983), a collective song sung by unionist **Arlene Mantle**, reproduced in *The Canadian Wobbly Songbook* (1990) compiled by Jerzy (George) Dymny.

In a world gone mad the word "Conservative" offers hope of common sense and orderly progress. It is a word which carries into the realm of practical politics the Biblical injunction "prove all things; hold fast that which is good."

George Drew, Colonel and Conservative, address, Toronto, 17 April 1940, quoted by Robert M. Hamilton in *Canadian Quotations and Phrases: Literary and Historical* (1952).

The emergence in the West of a renascent intellectual right, rigorous and articulate, has been a long time coming and is a development of great significance.

Conrad Black, publisher and capitalist, Spring Convocation, Faculties of Business and Humanities, McMaster University, printed in *The Globe and Mail*, 7 June 1979.

The inexorable outcome of neo-conservatism thus will be to make Canadians into poorer Americans rather than distinctive North Americans.

Richard Gwyn, columnist and author, *Nationalism without Walls: The Unbearable Lightness of Being Canadian* (1995).

Government's role is not to see how many people we can employ, it is to deliver the services that the public wants government to deliver with the best quality and the best price.

Mike Harris, Ontario Premier, leader of the Common Sense Revolution, quoted by Mary Janigan in "The Harris Revolution," *Maclean's*, 10 June 1996.

It all boils down to the slightly improbable case that the rich are not working because they have too little income, while the poor are not working because they have too much.

John Kenneth Galbraith, economics, finding paradox in the economics of neo-conservatives, address, Toronto, 9 Jan. 1997, quoted by John Ibbitson in *The Toronto Star* the following day. Galbraith went on to call it "the horse-and-sparrow theory of economics... if you feed the horse enough oats, some will pass through to the road for the sparrow."

CONSERVATIVE PARTY See also

CONSERVATISM, POLITICAL PARTIES

"My most important, immediate task, as Conservative leader," Col. Drew observed, "is to convince the people of Ontario that the primary purpose of the Conservative Party is to give them good government."

George A. Drew, Army Colonel and future Ontario Premier, interviewed by R.E. Knowles in *The Toronto Star*, 10 Dec. 1938.

Neo-Conservative. The exact opposite of a conservative. Neo-conservatives are the Bolsheviks of the Right.

John Ralston Saul, author, *The Doubter's Companion: A Dictionary of Aggressive Common Sense* (1994).

Common Sense. For a Change.

Campaign slogan of the **Progressive Conservative Party of Ontario** approaching the election of 15 June 1995, which saw its leader Mike Harris elected Premier of Ontario.

We're the only political party with perfect gender parity.

Jean Charest, leader, Conservative Party, referring to the fact that the party was represented by two members, Elsie Wayne and Jean Charest, in the House of Commons, noted by Susan Delacourt, "Election Notebook," *The Globe and Mail*, 6 May 1997.

I want to assure you I am not a member of any organized political party. I am a federal Progressive Conservative.

Hugh Segal, Conservative spokesperson, addressing a Progressive Conservative Party gathering, quoted by Bruce Wallace in *Maclean's*, 20 April 1998.

People ask, "Mr. Orchard, are you a Conservative?" If the word "conserve" means anything at all, I am a Conservative. I want to conserve our nation, I want to conserve our economy, I want to conserve our environment and I want to conserve the border between ourselves and our powerful neighbour to the south.

David Orchard, Conservative leadership contender, quoted in *The Globe and Mail*, 14 Aug. 1998.

Founded 133 years ago, the Conservative Party today constitutes governments in five provinces representing almost 65 per cent of Canada's GDP.

Brian Mulroney, former Prime Minister, address, Conservative Party gathering, Markham, Ont., 9 June 2000, published in *The Globe and Mail* the following day.

CONSPIRACY THEORIES

A conspiracy need not have anti-social or criminal purposes or motivations. A conspiracy can equally be a more or less clandestine group of men and women dedicated to positive and progressive social ideals, and the conspiracy of the Holy Grail seems always to have been precisely this.

Michael Bradley, author, *The Columbus Conspiracy: An Investigation into the Secret History of Christopher Columbus* (1991).

National governments do *not* want their subjects to have a planetwide orientation.

Stanton T. Friedman, flying-saucer researcher, *Top Secret/Majic* (1996).

I slowly realized that I was being spied on, presumably by Canadian, American, British, French and Russian agencies hostile to the disclosures in the first book.

James Bacque, researcher, *Crimes and Mercies: The Fate of German Civilians under Allied Occupation, 1944–1950* (1997), as quoted by Brian Loring Villa, "Crimes and Rumours of Crimes," *The Globe and Mail*, 18 Oct. 1997. In his first book, *Other Losses: An Inquiry* (1989), Bacque argued that the Allies were responsible for the deaths of German prisoners of war—"the missing million"; in the later book, he argues that the Allies killed off nine million German civilians as well.

The conspiracy is this cigarette-smoking man who has a Canadian accent, we don't know why. And he seems to have killed Kennedy and a few other important people in American history and he has a Canadian accent, and we don't know why.

David Duchovny, actor, referring to the TV series *X-Files* and its cigarette-smoking man, "cancer man," played by Vancouver actor William B. Davis, interviewed by John Allemang, "Television," *The Globe and Mail*, 25 July 1999.

CONSTITUTION See also

CHARLOTTETOWN ACCORD,
CONFEDERATION, RIGHTS & FREEDOMS

"America," says he (in his speech on the Canada Constitution bill), "never dreamed of such absurd doctrine as the Rights of Man."

Tom Paine, revolutionary writer, criticizing the views of the English conservative Edmund Burke as expressed in a speech in the House of Commons, *Rights of Man* (1791).

It shall be lawful for the Queen, by and with the Advice of Her Majesty's Most Honourable Privy Council, to declare by Proclamation that, on and after a Day therein appointed, not being more than Six Months after the passing of this Act, the Provinces of Canada, of Nova Scotia, and New Brunswick shall form and be One Dominion under the name of Canada; and on and after that Day those Three Provinces shall form and be One Dominion under that Name accordingly.

*

It shall be lawful for the Queen, by and with the Advice and Consent of the Senate and House of Commons, to make Laws for the Peace, Order, and good Government of Canada.

Articles from the **British North America Act**, 1867, commonly called the BNA Act, passed in the British Parliament on 29 March 1867; it became effective on 1 July 1867.

A careful consideration of the general position of British North America induced the conviction that the circumstances of the times afforded the opportunity, not merely for the settlement of a question of personal politics, but also for the simultaneous creation of a new nationality.

Lord Monck, Governor General of British North America, Throne Speech, Parliament of Canada, Quebec, 19 Jan. 1865, addressed the notion that the provinces should be united into a confederation. The concept of "a new nationality" (as distinct from the American ideal of "a new nation") originated in 1858 with the Montreal lawyer Alexander Morris, who was later appointed Lieutenant-Governor of Manitoba;

the notion was popularized by Father of Confederation Thomas D'Arcy McGee.

Phineas Finn, when the session began, was still hard at work upon his Canada bill, and in his work found some relief for his broken back.

Passage about the fictional British Cabinet minister and "the Canada Bill" in **Anthony Trollope**'s novel *Phineas Finn: The Irish Member* (1869).

The ink was scarcely dry upon our Constitution when we began to think constitutionally.

George W. Ross, educator, "The Evolution of Canadian Sentiment," address to the Empire Club, Toronto, 12 May 1905, included in *Builders of the Canadian Commonwealth* (1923) edited by George H. Locke.

There's a wind blowing for constitutional change. Yes, that's precisely what it is—wind.

Eugene Forsey, constitutional authority, address, Committee for an Independent Canada, Toronto, 15 Oct. 1977.

The government has resolved to provide Canada with a new Constitution by the end of 1981.

Pierre Elliott Trudeau, Prime Minister, tabling a document called "A Time for Action: Toward the Renewal of the Canadian Federation," House of Commons, 12 June 1978. It called for its signing on or before 1 July 1981 to mark the 50th anniversary of Canada's accession to the Statute of Westminister.

The strength of Canada's new Constitution lies not in the words it contains, but in the foundation upon which it rests, the desire of the people of Canada that their country remain strong and united.

Pierre Elliott Trudeau, Prime Minister, address, Patriation Ceremony, Ottawa, 17 April 1982.

I believe that the challenge of re-Confederation can be just as positive in 1990 as it was in 1867 when the original founders and builders of this country accomplished their great work.

Brian Mulroney, Prime Minister, address, Buckingham, Que., 16 Dec. 1990, quoted in *The Globe and Mail*, 18 Dec. 1990.

We sometimes forget that the attempt to solve the Quebec question has generated five different constitutions.

David J. Bercuson and **Barry Cooper**, historian and political scientist, *Deconfederation: Canada without Quebec* (1991). They instanced arrangements in 1763, 1774, 1791, 1841, 1867, excluding 1982 as "neither fish nor fowl nor good red herring."

Much of the debate is not substantive; it's psychological. What this country needs may be psychoanalysis, not a constitution.

Pierre Fortin, member, Bélanger-Campeau Commission, quoted in University of Guelph's "Canada" supplement, *The Globe and Mail*, 4 Dec. 1991.

On the list of 100 priorities, the Constitution is 101st.

Ross Thatcher, former Saskatchewan Premier, characteristic remark quoted by Jeffrey Simpson in *The Globe and Mail*, 18 Oct. 1991.

Weirdly, a few Quebec nationalists have had the outrageous *chutzpah* to say in recent years that they, of all people, are sick of constitutional talk!

Robert Fulford, columnist, "The Country that Dare not Speak Its Name," *The Globe and Mail*, 17 July 1996.

There is no point throwing more raw meat to constitutional cannibals. The sooner we vaporize the Lévésque-Parizeau-Bouchard fairyland of painless independence, the greater is our public service to all Canadians, Quebec in particular.

Conrad Black, Chairman of Hollinger Inc., address at Annual General Meeting in Toronto, 27 May 1997, quoted by Robert Brehl in *The Toronto Star* the following day.

Our ancestors did not wait for constitutional change to build our country.

Jean Charest, Prime Minister, *My Road to Québec* (1998).

Only in the constitutional arena did he leave a permanent mark: the Charter of Rights and Freedoms, described by many as the most Americanizing act of any government since Confederation (and not regrettable for that), and patriation of the Constitution through a domestic amending formula over the objections of Quebec's National Assembly.

William Thorsell, columnist, referring to the legacy of Trudeau's years in office, "Pierre Trudeau and the Dance of the Acolytes," *The Globe and Mail*, 24 Jan. 1998.

CONSUMERISM

The problem with markets dependent on consumption is that the consumer cannot be relied upon to know what he or she wants.

John Ralston Saul, author, *The Doubter's Companion: A Dictionary of Aggressive Common Sense* (1994).

When something is pitched toward the widest possible audience, a downsizing of ambition will follow. McDonald's doesn't even *try* to make the best hamburgers around, just the most accessible, and the most reliably predictable.

Guy Gavriel Kay, novelist, "Other Voices," *The Toronto Star*, 19 Feb. 1994.

People without the money to purchase the goods they need, about twenty percent of the world's population and increasing, do not have under the rules of the free market the right to live.

John McMurtry, philosopher, University of Guelph, "The Contradictions of Free Market Doctrine—Is There a Solution?" a paper prepared for the Westminster Institute Conference, "Surviving Globalization: Economic, Social, and Environmental Dimensions," London, Ont., May 1995.

Let me believe that in consuming, I am communing.

David Beers, journalist, referring to the lifestyle of Vancouver, "Sustainable Fantasy," "Vancouver Arts," *The Globe and Mail*, 2 Nov. 1995.

The average North American consumes five times more than a Mexican, ten times more than a Chinese person, and thirty times more than a person from India. (Burp!) We are the most voracious consumers in the world, a world that could die because of the way we North Americans live. Give it a rest. November 26th is Buy Nothing Day.

Text of an advertisement for Buy Nothing Day, a campaign inaugurated in 1997 by **Adbusters Media Foundation**, a social marketing operation in Vancouver led by activist Kalle Lasn.

If every human being wanted to live like we do in Toronto, we'd need five more planets. So there is no way our lifestyle can be enjoyed by everybody on Earth, but everybody wants to be like us.

David Suzuki, geneticist and broadcaster, musing on the eve of the new millennium, quoted by Leah Eichler, "Sightings," Reuters News Service, Internet, 21 Dec. 1999.

CONTENTMENT

Contentment consists largely in not wanting something that is out of your reach.

Bob Edwards, publisher, *The Eye Opener*, 11 Feb. 1911, *The Wit and Wisdom of Bob Edwards* (1976) edited by Hugh Dempsey.

CONTINENTALISM See also

ANNEXATIONISM, FREE TRADE

Do not forget that the King of France is the owner of all this continent.

Marquis de La Jonquière, Governor of New France, letter addressed to Edward Cornwallis, Governor of Nova Scotia at Halifax, about 1749, quoted by G.W. Wrong in "The Historical Background," *Canada: Reprinted from the Canadian Number of The Times, May 15, 1939* (1939).

I can't help thinking that it would be a grand thing to see one Government rule from the Equator to the North Pole.

John British, British statesman, letter to Sir Charles Tupper in 1867, reproduced in Tupper's *Recollections of Sixty Years in Canada* (1914).

The annexation of this country to the United States is a tabooed subject but I have always thought if we did not annex you that it would be a good thing for you to annex us. Then there are other ways to bring this thing about. It may be brought about by peaceful means—by invisible agencies.

Mark Twain, humorist, address at the Windsor Hotel, Montreal, 8 Dec. 1881, quoted by David Ketterer in "Mark Twain's Overlooked 'Second Speech' in Montreal," *Mark Twain Journal*, Fall 1990.

We must decide whether the spirit of Canadianism or of Continentalism shall prevail on the northern half of this continent.

Sir Robert Borden, Prime Minister, campaign speech in 1911, quoted by Robert Craig Brown in *Robert Laird Borden: A Biography, Volume I: 1854–1914* (1975).

The momentous move towards uniting the two countries economically is very gratifying to me. For more than a decade my pop urged in his newspapers that Canada become part of the U.S.

William Randolph Hearst, Jr., remark made on 11 Oct. 1987, referring to his namesake father, the influential newspaper publisher, quoted by Mel Hurtig in *The Betrayal of Canada* (1991).

CONVERSATION

Ever notice how little attention is paid to people who talk too much?

Bob Edwards, publisher, *The Eye Opener*, 25 April 1914, *The Wit and Wisdom of Bob Edwards* (1976) edited by Hugh Dempsey.

Confused, I resorted to the basic principle of good interviewing: when in doubt, shut your mouth and really listen.

Silver Donald Cameron, author and interviewer, *Conversations with Canadian Novelists* (1973).

If, as Schopenhauer claims, each farewell is a preparation for death, then every greeting is an affirmation of life.

Maurus E. Mallon, aphorist, 2 May 1993.

CONVICTION

An intellectual conclusion can only become an emotional conviction leading to direct action if the ideas in one's head have been indissolubly linked to the desires of one's heart by some deep personal experience.

James George, former Canadian Ambassador, *Asking for the Earth: Waking up to the Spiritual/Ecological Crisis* (1995).

CO-OPERATION See also CREDIT UNION

We want our men to look into the sun and into the depths of the sea. We want them to explore the hearts of flower and the hearts of fellow men. We want them to live, to love, to play and pray with all their being. We want them to be men, whole men, eager to explore all the avenues of life and to attain perfection in all their faculties.

M.M. Coady, adult educator and co-founder of the Antigonish Movement, widely quoted peroration of *Masters of Their Own Destiny* (1939) included in *The Man from Margaree: Writings and Speeches of M.M. Coady, Educator, Reformer, Priest* (1971) edited by Alexander F. Laidlaw.

Co-ops are the only way to secure the future of mankind.

M.M. Coady, adult educator and co-founder of the Antigonish Movement, quoted by Yousuf Karsh in *Karsh Canadians* (1978).

Co-operation is no longer simply advantageous; in order to survive it is an absolute necessity.

Pierre Elliott Trudeau, Prime Minister, address, Mansion House, London, England, March 1975, reproduced by C. David Crenna in *Pierre Elliott Trudeau: Lifting the Shadow of War* (1987).

At 30 below, there are no self-made men (or women, much less children). A rugged individualist won't last till spring if things go wrong. But if peole have the ability to co-operate, they can survive. Nature gives an annual, compulsory seminar in dependence and responsibility.

Margaret Catley-Carlson, President of CIDA, "Aid: A Canadian Vocation," *Daedalus: Journal of the American Academy of Arts and Sciences*, "In Search of Canada," Fall, 1988.

If competitive individualism is the mark of America, then the co-operation of groups within large institutional structures expresses an essential Canadian value.

William Kilbourn, historian, "The Peaceable Kingdom Still," *Daedalus: Journal of the American Academy of Arts and Sciences*, "In Search of Canada," Fall, 1988.

It would be folly not to acknowledge the hazards along the way toward a better world. But it would be a still greater folly if we were deterred by fear from treading the only path that offers hope, the path to security through global co-operation.

John C. Polanyi, scientist and peace activist, address, Pugwash International Conference, *The Globe and Mail*, 28 July 1989.

COPYRIGHT

Copyright is one of the most boring and complex subjects known to man.

J.G. (Jack) McClelland, publisher, quoted in *Time*, 24 Feb. 1975.

Copyright laws and attempts to protect intellectual property are becoming obsolete. Individual intellectual property rights will become absurd once collective knowledge is shared in a single electronic global brain, accessible to all.

Frank Feather, futurologist, *G-Forces: Reinventing the World—The 35 Global Forces Restructuring Our World* (1989).

In the end, what transpires on the field is usually not what is planned, but something that is totally unpredictable. That is one of the reasons why sports games are so appealing to their spectators. No one can foresee what will happen. This is not the same as a ballet, where, barring an unforeseen accident, what is performed is exactly what is planned. No one bets on the outcome of a performance of *Swan Lake*. Ballet is, therefore, copyrightable, but team sports events, despite the high degree of planning involved in them, are not.

Decision written by Justice **J.J.A. Linden**, FWS Joint Sports Claimants vs. Copyright Board et al., Federal Court of Appeal, 3 June 1991. The Federal Court of Appeal has held that there is no copyright in professional sporting events such as NHL hockey games.

Copyright is a European invention, first legalized in Venice in 1476.

Alberto Manguel, essayist, *The Globe and Mail*, 12 March 1992.

The deceased no longer has a career.

Nicholas Borkovich, Judge, Ontario Court's General Division, 23 Nov. 1995. Judge Borkovich dismissed an application by the estate of the late pianist Glenn Gould for an interim introduction to halt the distribution of *Glenn Gould: Some Portraits of the Artist as a Young Man* (1995) by Jock Carroll.

One of the basic problems in understanding copyright is that we cannot see it.

Lesley Ellen Harris, lawyer and specialist in intellectual property, opening sentence of the *Introduction to Canadian Copyright Law* (1995).

Children's book publishers, to give one example, may now have to pay a fee, if they want to use archival photos of the Royal Canadian Mounted Police in school history books. The fee is payable not to the Canadian Government but to the Disney corporation, which owns the commercial licensing rights.

Patrick Parrinder, critic, reviewing Rosemary J. Coombe's *The Cultural Life of Intellectual Properties* (1999), *The Times Literary Supplement*, 12 March 1999.

In my books the word "copyright" means "copy it right."

Peter Urs Bender, motivational speaker, characteristic remark, 11 May 2000.

CORPORATISM

Corporate welfare bums.

David Lewis, leader, New Democratic Party, speech, New Glasgow, N.S., 3 Aug. 1972, as noted by Walter Stewart in *Divide and Con* (1973). Lewis branded as "corporate welfare bums" those corporations, large and small, which avoided paying their fair share of business taxes as well as those businesses which pressed all levels of government for additional grants, concessions, subsidies, deferrals, remissions, depreciations, and incentives. What sparked research into this matter was business writer Alexander Ross's column in *The Toronto Star*, 17 April 1972.

Until now, "corporate values" was an oxymoron.

John Dalla Costa, advertising executive, *Meditations on Business* (1991).

The acceptance of corporatism causes us to deny and undermine the legitimacy of the individual as citizen in a democracy.

John Ralston Saul, commentator, *The Unconscious Civilization* (1995).

The world's corporations, taken together, cannot feel the pain of a single maimed child.

Silver Donald Cameron, columnist, "The Dignity of Labour," *The Halifax Herald*, 13 Sept. 1998.

We demonize corporations for their unwavering pursuit of growth, power and wealth. Yet, they are simply carrying out genetic orders. That's exactly what corporations were designed—by us—to do. Trying to rehabilitate a corporation, urging it to behave responsibly, is a fool's game. The only way to change the behaviour of a corporation is to record it.

Credo or motto of **Kalle Lasn**, Estonian-born, Vancouver-based consumer activist, publisher and editor of *Adbusters Magazine*, Internet, 5 Dec. 1999.

Despite our openness to trade, Canada is home to far fewer transnational corporations than Denmark, South Korea, Switzerland or Sweden. Canada is home to two of the top 150 global companies. The Netherlands has six and Switzerland five.

Brian Mulroney, former Prime Minister, address, Conservative Party gathering, Markham, Ont., 9 June 2000, published in *The Globe and Mail* the following day.

CORRECTNESS, POLITICAL See POLITICAL CORRECTNESS

CORRUPTION See also CRIME, PATRONAGE

These hands are clean!

Caption to **J.W. Bengough**'s cartoon "Whither Are We Drifting?" *Grip*, 6 Aug. 1873. Prime Minister Sir John A. Macdonald is shown absolving himself of all charges of corruption in connection with the Pacific Scandal. Yet in his left hand he holds a sign that says "Send me another $10,000," and in his right a charter for the "Prorogation and Suppression of the Investigation."

Let's get corruption out of the trade unions... and back into management where it belongs.

Dave Broadfoot, comedian, spoken as the Senator from Kicking Horse Pass, quoted by Ron Evans in *The Toronto Telegram*, 7 April 1964.

There's always corruption. It's bad when it's more than fifteen percent.

Michel Brunet, historian, taking a long view of the prevalence of corruption in government, interviewed by Ramsay Cook in *The Craft of History* (1973) edited by Eleanor Cook.

Bribes may appear to be more efficient than advertising: they reach their target. And the variety and volume of bribes would lead one to think they are efficient. However, the expectation of bribes has, over recent decades, created in Quebec a culture of political exploitation, a culture which nourishes secessionism.

Albert Breton, economist, "Secessionism, a Proposal for Discussion," *Cité Libre*, March 1998.

COSMOPOLITANISM

The trouble is localism. We live too far from the sea. The broad peoples are the people who do commerce on great waters and whose coasts are swept by the ocean.

Sigmund Samuel, philanthropist, interviewed by R.E. Knowles, *The Toronto Star*, 1 Aug. 1929.

COTTAGES

Canadians, like Russians, dream of possessing a dacha and presumably a maple of their own one day.

Robert Morley, British actor, *A Musing Morley* (1974).

The homegrown mythology, which remains close to the city's heart, is about going someplace else, escaping each summer to "cottage country" and the wild north.

Richard Conniff, U.S. journalist, "Toronto," *National Geographic*, June 1996.

COUCHICHING CONFERENCE

The motto of the conference was plain living and high thinking. High living and plain thinking would have been more agreeable. But deliberately the guests of the conference lived in spartan conditions, and Murray Ross, looking like a boy scout, plunged into the cold lake water every morning.

Han Suyin, Chinese-American author, referring to her appearance at the 1959 Couchiching conference and to the President of York University, *My House Has Two Doors* (1980).

COUNTRY

Whatever country you are in, your own is perhaps more cruel.

Marie-Claire Blais, novelist, quoted by Margaret Atwood in *Maclean's*, Sept. 1975.

If you don't believe your country should come before yourself / You can better serve your country by living somewhere else.

Lines from the title song of the 1992 album *Believe in Your Country* written and performed by **Stompin' Tom Connors**.

We are made special by our territory, and not one precious inch of it must be lost or allowed to be taken away, not one stone, not one stick, not one blade of grass, not one earthworm below the surface, not one iota of slime on that earthworm below the surface of "our territory," and so on. To realize how strong our territorial interest is, try travelling abroad without a passport.

E.L. Stone, advocate and author, *Pleasura & Realitas: The Dialectic of Dominating Impulses* (1993).

In many ways, countries are like people. They need to be told, passionately and at regular intervals, how much we love them. How much we care. How important they are to the fabric of our lives.

Lorraine Monk, editor, *Canada: Romancing the Land* (1996) with poems by Miriam Waddington.

It's tough to build a country to match a dream.

Deborah Coyne and **Michael Valpy**, constitutional lawyer and columnist, *To Match a Dream: A Practical Guide to Canada's Constitution* (1998).

COURTESY

It was more of a surprise to discover how different Canadians were—they were so polite!

Thoughts of the narrator of **John Irving**'s novel *A Prayer for Owen Meaney* (1989).

Canadians will say "Thank you" to a bank machine.

Rick Marin, comic, "The Most Entertaining Americans? Canadians," *The New York Times*, 27 June 1993.

COURTS

The Supreme Court is like the Tower of Pisa—it always leans the same way.

Attributed to Quebec Premier **Maurice Duplessis** in the 1950s by Quebec Deputy Minister Bernard Landry, noted by Karen Unland in *The Globe and Mail*, 12 May 1997.

CREATION

The one essential idea is that in its nature Creation is essentially inscrutable; we can never hope to know just how it was accomplished; we cannot expect to know the process or the details, for we have nothing with which to measure it.

George McCready Price, Maritime-born creationist, anticipator of Scientific Creationism, *Q.E.D.* (1917).

A dandelion is as much a proof of a creator as a comet is.

R.E. Knowles, columnist, interviewing an astronomer, *The Toronto Star*, 3 June 1935.

CREATIVITY

I do feel quite convinced that one's creativity is enhanced primarily by the more-or-less single-minded pursuit and development of one's own resources without reference to the trends, tastes, fashions, etc. of the world outside.

Glenn Gould, pianist, letter of 14 Feb. 1974, *Glenn Gould: Selected Letters* (1992) edited by John P.L. Roberts and Ghyslaine Guertin.

To be a creator is to be in touch, sometimes in uncomfortably close touch, with what psychiatrists call the Unconscious—and not always one's personal Unconscious, but the vast, troubled Unconscious of mankind.

Robertson Davies, man-of-letters, "Gleams and Glooms" (1976), *One Half of Robertson Davies: Provocative Pronouncements on a Wide Range of Topics* (1977).

Creativity can be described as the ability to reshape a situation.

Peter Gzowski, radio personality, "Celebrity Class," *The Canadian*, 24 Feb. 1979.

Add a pinch of hope to a state of oppression and you have creativity.

Louis Dudek, man-of-letters, "The Mermaid Inn," *The Globe and Mail*, 23 May 1981.

We are limited only by our lack of creativity. Our buildings should symbolize the exuberance of a free nation that encourages individual effort and creativity.

Douglas Cardinal, architect, "Museum of Man Proposal, 1983: From Earth Creatures to Star Creatures," *The Canadian Forum*, Oct. 1989.

Nothing that man makes is genuinely alive.

Northrop Frye, cultural critic, "Literature as a Critique of Pure Reason," *Myth and Metaphor: Selected Essays, 1974–1988* (1990) edited by Robert D. Denham.

The creative process for me is extremely important. Whenever the ego surrenders to the archetypal images of the unconscious, time meets the timeless. Insofar as those moments are conscious, they are psychological—they belong to the soul. They are in time, illuminating, not rejecting, the timeless.

Marion Woodman, Jungian psychotherapist, interviewed by Anne A. Simpkinson, *Conscious Femininity: Interviews with Marion Woodman* (1993).

CREDIT UNION See also CO-OPERATION

Keep the monkey working.

Alphonse Desjardins, founder of North America's credit union movement (savings and loan society or caisse populaire) in Lévis, Que., 6 Dec. 1900, quoted by George Boyle in *The Poor Man's Prayer: The Story of Credit Union Beginnings* (1951).

Through credit unions, co-operative stores, lobster factories and sawmills, we are laying the foundations for an appreciation of Shakespeare and grand opera.

M.M. Coady, adult educator and co-founder of the Antigonish Movement, *Masters of Their Own Destiny* (1939).

CRIME See also CAPITAL PUNISHMENT, CORRUPTION, JUSTICE & INJUSTICE, LAW, MURDER, PATRONAGE, POLICE, ROYAL CANADIAN MOUNTED POLICE, SEXUAL OFFENCES

The main thing is to shoot first and never miss.

Bat Masterson, gunfighter, sheriff of Dodge City, then sports columnist in New York City, quoted by Carl W. Breihan in *Great Gunfighters of the West* (1977). Masterson was born of American parents in Henryville, Eastern Townships, Canada East, in 1853; he died in New York in 1921. He was played with aplomb by actor Gene Barry on television.

I am telling you, there has never been a greater scoundrel in these United States than Canada Bill.

Line of dialogue spoken by one Westerner to another in the **Karl May**'s *Canada Bill* (1911), a novel of the Wild West, translated by Fred Gardner in 1971.

Have strong suspicions that Crippen London cellar murderer and accomplice are among saloon passengers.

Part of the wireless message sent to London by **Captain H.G. Kendall**, master of the CP liner *Montrose*, three days out of Antwerp en route to Quebec City. On 31 July 1910, Inspector Dew of Scotland Yard was able to board the *Montrose* at Farmer Point, Gulf of St. Lawrence, and arrest the wife-murderer Dr. Crippen. Cited by Leslie Bailey, *Scrapbook 1900–1914* (1957).

I never told him that I was his mother. But he turned out badly, he drank, then took drugs. I managed to pay his passage out to Canada.

Admission made by a spinsterish English housekeeper about Charles Kent, her illegitimate son and a murder suspect, to the investigator Hercule Poirot in **Agatha Christie**'s novel *The Murder of Roger Ackroyd* (1926).

How could you, Mrs. Dick?

Refrain of a popular ditty (with its double-entendre) associated with the 1946 Evelyn Dick murder case in Hamilton, Ont. It served as the title of the 1990 stage play based on the Dick murder trial.

I recognized him as Hal Banks. I went up to him and said, "Mr. Banks?" and he said, "Yes, what do you want?" I said I wanted an interview and he told me to beat it.

Robert Reguly, investigative reporter with *The Toronto Star* who in one day located former Seafarers International Union boss Hal Banks sitting on a yacht in Brooklyn after the FBI and the RCMP had failed to do so, appearing on CBC-TV, 4 Oct. 1964, quoted by Eric Koch in *Inside This Hour Has Seven Days* (1986).

There are crimes which make men afraid; there are crimes which make us afraid of being men.

Bruno M. Cormier, forensic psychiatrist, "On the History of Men and Genocide" (1966), *Breaking the Chains: Bruno M. Cormier and the McGill University Clinic in Forensic Psychiatry* (1998).

I do not believe that every vulture is a maladjusted nightingale.

T. George Street, Chairman of the National Parole Board, address, Empire Club of Canada, Toronto, 1970, quoted by Scott Young and Margaret Hogan in *The Best Talk in Town* (1979).

Sanctioned by the majesty of the law, society expiates its own guilt by the punishment of its criminals.

Guy Richmond, prison physician, *Prison Doctor: One Man's Story that Must Be Told in Canada Today* (1975).

We are creating the kind of society where the criminal is out of jail before his victim is out of hospital.

Richard Needham, newspaper columnist, *The Wit and Wisdom of Richard Needham* (1977).

If we closed every jail and prison tomorrow, data show that it would have zero effect—nothing would get worse, nothing would get better.

J.W. (Hans) Mohr, specialist in criminal justice, quoted by Eileen Morris in *Homemaker's*, Nov. 1980.

The dream of a crook is a man with a dream.

Line from **Stephen Vizinczey**'s novel *An Innocent Millionaire* (1983).

Are there gangsters and Mafia there too?

Jorge Luis Borges, man-of-letters, referring to Canada, interviewed by Raul Galvez in Buenos Aires, Argentina, June 1985, *From the Ashen Land of the Virgins* (1988).

I've never had the slightest problem defending clients whom other people have regarded as "professional" or "organized" criminals. I've defended such clients (among many other things) on drug-related charges of various kinds. I might have had a big problem, though, had I ever been called upon to defend the *idea* of say, trafficking in illicit drugs.

Edward L. Greenspan, lawyer, *Greenspan: The Case for the Defence* (1987) written with George Jonas.

That the violent crime rate of the Canadian metropolis is only 10 to 20 percent of that of the American (murders average 70 a year in Toronto but 700 in Detroit) is more than a matter of strict gun control in Canada and the lack of it in the United States. It is a matter of the two societies differing in their attitudes toward authority.

William Kilbourn, historian, "The Peaceable Kingdom Still," *Daedalus: Journal of the American Academy of Arts and Sciences*, "In Search of Canada," Fall, 1988.

"Mysteries are very popular in Canada. Very fashionable," he said.

Thoughts of a character commenting on the vogue for mystery-style entertainments in *The Edge* (1988), **Dick Francis**'s crime novel set aboard a transcontinental train.

Potentially today's expelled student in Toronto is next month's armed robber in Alberta.

Scott Newark, general counsel for the Canadian Police Association, quoted by Canadian Press, "Study Documents School Violence," *The Globe and Mail*, 24 Aug. 1994.

Think about it: How many victims of violent crime do you know? Now think: How many people do you know who are affected by something like the collapse of a major company. Millions of Canadians suffer when incompetence, misapplication or malfeasance strike a financial institution or professional body. Only a few hundred are victims of violent crime on any given day. It isn't the morons on the street who are a danger to most of us, it's the men in suits.

H.S. Bhabra, novelist, "Progressive Culling," *The Globe and Mail*, 20 Sept., 1994.

In 1995 Toronto had 2 murders per 100,000 people versus 65 for Washington, D.C.

Richard Conniff, U.S. journalist, "Toronto," *National Geographic*, June 1996.

Crimes can never safely be boxed in the historical past; they remain locked in the eternal present, crying out for vengeance.

Michael Ignatieff, author, "Articles of Faith," *Index on Censorship*, Sept.–Oct. 1996, as reprinted in "Readings," *Harper's*, March 1997.

CRITICS & CRITICISM

See also CULTURE

The greatest number of sticks and stones are found under the good apple trees.

Timothy Eaton, founder of the T. Eaton Co., on criticism, quoted by George G. Nasmith in *Timothy Eaton* (1923).

Criticism is to art what history is to action and philosophy to wisdom.

Northrop Frye, cultural critic, *Anatomy of Criticism* (1957).

Critics are the conscience of the public and not its mouthpiece.

Chester Duncan, composer and commentator, quoted by Stan Obodiac in *My Experiences at a Canadian Authors' Convention* (1957).

In our time there has grown up a sharp distinction between the reviewer and the critic. The reviewer is a newspaper hack. The critic is an exalted person, generally a university professor, whose own style may be dull, who may use long hard words, and who generally, but not always, is concerned with the world of long-dead authors.

William Arthur Deacon, literary critic, "The Reviewer" (1959), reprinted by Clara Thomas and John Lennox in *William Arthur Deacon: A Canadian Literary Life* (1982).

Although we may not be in the middle of the cultural gold rush we had hoped for, there is certainly plenty to pan.

Tony Emery, art connoisseur, *Canadian Art*, Jan.–Feb. 1962.

This is to inform you that some crackpot is using your name and has recently written to me over your signature, putting forth views so eccentric in nature and so much at variance with your usual logical style that the letter could not possibly be from you. I felt I owed it to you to bring this to your attention.

John G. Diefenbaker, Prime Minister, standard reply to crackpot letters from cranks, quoted by Thomas Van Dusen in *The Chief* (1968).

I respect the effort that goes into even a bad performance.

Herbert Whittaker, drama critic, quoted in *Time*, 15 Sept. 1975. He served for twenty-six years with *The Globe and Mail* as "Canada's best-loved, if least feared, drama critic."

Sibelius once remarked that nobody had ever seen a statue of a critic. Statues of playwrights, on the other hand, are seen very frequently, and usually in theatres, where they belong.

Robertson Davies, man-of-letters, Preface, *Question Time* (1975).

A barking dog is often more useful than a sleeping lion.

Roy Thomson, newspaper publisher, *After I was Sixty: A Chapter of Autobiography* (1975) by Lord Thomson of Fleet.

A critic at best is a waiter at the great table of literature.

Louis Dudek, man-of-letters, "The Mermaid Inn," *The Globe and Mail*, 23 May 1981.

Let them eat Hansard.

Attributed to former Prime Minister **Joe Clark** in *The Globe and Mail*, 28 Dec. 1981. When his administration was criticized, he made reference to the written record of the House of Commons.

A publication devoid of invective is likely also to be a publication devoid of readers. When, for example, was the last time you saw a line-up to buy the *Canadian Bar Review?*

A. Alan Borovoy, General Counsel, Canadian Civil Liberties Association, *When Freedoms Collide: A Case for Our Civil Liberties* (1988).

He told the story of the Maritime fisherman carrying a pail of lobsters up from the wharf. Another fisherman warns him that the lobsters might escape because there's no lid on the pail. "Oh, no," says the first fisherman. "These are Canadian lobsters, boys. As soon as one makes it to the top, the others will drag him down."

Derek Burney, Ambassador to the United States, address, Empire Club of Canada, Toronto, 30 Nov. 1989.

If you want to sell paintings, it's most useful to appear in the social columns than in the art columns.

Charles Pachter, artist, quoted by Gerald Hannon in *Toronto Life*, Dec. 1989.

The bigger the dog, the happier the flea.

Robin Skelton, poet and aphorist, *A Devious Dictionary* (1991).

I learned a long time ago that you can't argue with people who buy ink by the barrel and paper by the ton.

Brian Mulroney, Prime Minister, referring to press criticism, interviewed by Kevin Doyle and Anthony Wilson-Smith in *Maclean's*, 8 March 1993.

If you turn on a light, you're going to attract bugs.

Proverbial expression frequently used by Alberta Premier **Ernest Manning** and on occasion by his son **Preston Manning**, founder of the Reform Party, notably during a campaign prior to the General Election of 25 Oct. 1993, as quoted by Ian Pearson in *Saturday Night*, Dec. 1990.

Given an apple, Canadians immediately look for the razor.

Mordecai Richler, novelist, press reception for the Giller Prize, Jan. 1994, quoted by Jack Rabinovitch, "Feedback," *The Toronto Star*, 27 Jan. 1996.

CROWN, THE

The idea of adding British America to the Queen's title is laughably pedantic and absurd, and the notion of giving the colonies representatives in the H. of C. cannot be entertained by anyone who has one grain of statesmanship in his head.

John Stuart Mill, political economist, writing to John Robertson, 28 Dec. 1838, *The Early Letters of John Stuart Mill* (1963), edited by John M. Robson, Volume XII of the "Collected Works of John Stuart Mill."

CRUELTY

Why is there cruelty when tenderness exists?

Question asked in **Roch Carrier**'s novel *Heartbreaks along the Road* (1987) translated by Sheila Fischman.

CUBAN PEOPLE

Long live Cuba and the Cuban people! Long live Prime Minister Commander Fidel Castro, long live the friendship of Cuba and Canada!

Pierre Elliott Trudeau, Prime Minister, greeting Fidel Castro, state visit, Havana, Cuba, 28 Jan. 1976. Trudeau's "Viva Cuba, Viva Castro!" convinced some people that he was a socialist who embraced communist dictators. Richard Gwyn noted: "The salutation was quite routine, and actually was added to Trudeau's original text by a departmental Latin affairs expert."

We respect you, we admire you, we want to say you are truly a great people.

Fidel Castro, President of Cuba, addressing External Affairs Minister Lloyd Axworthy, Havana, 22 Jan. 1997, quoted by Linda Diebel in *The Toronto Star* the following day. Castro also called Canada "one of the most able countries in all history."

Something happens to their brains when they hit Cuba. My theory is that it's the ratio of sunlight to oxygen to ocean here.... Unfortunately, they're so sexually deprived, they make you work harder than anyone else on the planet.

Remarks about Canadian tourists made by a Havana woman who sometimes works as a prostitute in **Christina García**'s novel *The Agüero Sisters* (1997).

CULTURAL APPROPRIATION See also CULTURE

Canada Council director Joyce Zemans is mistaken when she says, "We have a new need for authenticity." We do not. We have an old need and a present need and a continuing need for authenticity; an authenticity that is achieved only when a writer or any other artist works at the height of his or her intellectual, imaginative and moral powers. That does not change.

Richard Outram, poet, Letters to the Editor, *The Globe and Mail*, 28 March 1992.

[At] a seminar on Cultural Appropriation which is to be held in Calgary in October... he feigns ignorance of Canada's leading role in the debate on communitarianism and ethnic minorities... and as for the notion that a white man cannot write about or represent in court a black or brown man, or vice versa—well, it leaves him gobsmacked...."Are you telling me that a person can only represent or speak for that category of person which he or she happens to be? Isn't that rather restrictive?"

Passage from **Margaret Drabble**'s satiric novel *The Witch of Exmore* (1996) about an English literary academic who attends a conference in Calgary.

CULTURE See also ACTORS & ACTING; ART & ARTISTS; CRITICS & CRITICISM; CULTURAL APPROPRIATION; CULTURE, NATIONAL; DANCE; FILM; FOLKLORE; GROUP OF SEVEN; LITERATURE; MUSIC; MYTHOLOGY; PAINTING; TELEVISION; THEATRE; WRITERS & WRITING

"Culture," that forbidden word... was sedulously avoided in the report.

Hilda Neatby, educator and Massey Report

commissioner, "The Massey Report: A Retrospect," *The Tamarack Review,* Issue One, Autumn, 1956.

The world's culture is not, praise heaven, one amorphous grey, but a rich and ever-changing colour scheme; and we shall serve ourselves and the world best by heightening our own hues.

Mavor Moore, man-of-the-theatre, "Radio and Television," *The Arts in Canada: A Stock-Taking at Mid-Century* (1958) edited by Malcolm Ross.

Our whole cultural habitat, which we once viewed as a mere container of people, is being transformed by these media and by space satellites into a living organism, itself contained within a new macrocosm or connubium of a supraterrestrial nature.

Marshall McLuhan, communications pioneer, "Playboy Interview" (1969) conducted by Eric Norden, *The Essential McLuhan* (1995) edited by Eric McLuhan and Frank Zingrone.

A man of culture is the man who shares several cultures.

Jean-Louis Gagnon, publisher, "Canada—Unity in Diversity," *Canada: Pictures of a Great Land* (1976) edited by Jürgen F. Boden and Hans Scherz.

If you get on a jet plane, you can't expect a different culture in the place where the plane lands, but you will find different people, and the creative people will be aware of the differences.

Northrop Frye, cultural critic, interviewed by Robert Fulford, "From Nationalism to Regionalism: The Maturing of Canadian Culture," *The Anthology Anthology: A Selection from 30 Years of CBC Radio's Anthology* (1984) edited by Robert Weaver.

Ideally, no student should receive a degree, be it in arts or sciences, without at least a minimal level of cultural literacy (much as some universities are adopting minimum language-proficiency requirements).

Morton Weinfeld, sociologist, McGill University, "How Cultured is Canada?" *The Globe and Mail,* 6 Aug. 1990.

I think the first measure of any citizen-based culture must be, not its rhetoric or myths or leaders or laws, but how few of its own citizens it kills.

John Ralston Saul, commentator, LaFontaine-Baldwin Lecture, Toronto, *The Globe and Mail,* 24 March 2000. He notes that "we have killed in political strife among us less than a hundred citizens—most of them on a single day at Batoche."

CULTURE, NATIONAL See also CULTURE

Culture is not a national god in Canada. (By culture I mean nothing exotic, but only the knowledge and love of the best that has been thought and said, a recognition of the excellent and a resolution to rest satisfied with nothing less, a liberation from the vulgar, the superficial, the provincial.)

E.K. Brown, critic, "The Immediate Present in Canadian Literature" (1933), *Responses and Evaluations: Essays on Canada* (1977) edited by David Staines.

French-Canadian culture consists of little more than Maurice Richard and Lili St. Cyr.

Attributed to journalist and M.P. **Douglas Fisher** at Laval University, Quebec, referring to the hockey star and the stripper, late 1950s, according to Joseph Schull in *The Great Scot: A Biography of Donald Gordon* (1979).

The Canadians of her acquaintance were always mocking their own city, their own university, their own music and galleries.... If she pointed out something that was genuinely good, they resented her intrusion; if she said nothing they resented her silence.

Thoughts of an American academic who teaches at a university in a Canadian border city in **Joyce Carol Oates**' story "Customs," *Crossing the Border: Fifteen Tales* (1976). Oates once taught at the University of Windsor.

Culture is not the icing on the national cake, nor is it the pan in which you bake the cake. It is the cake itself.

Bernard Ostry, Secretary General, National Museums of Canada, quoted by George Gamester in *The Toronto Star,* 7 April 1976.

We are not so much in need of protection as an opportunity to excel.

Mordecai Richler, author, *The Canadian,* 14 Aug. 1976.

In the CBC, they have the best television network in North America—well, let us say, the least bad. In the Stratford Festival, they also have the best drama company in North America.

Clives Barnes, critic of *The New York Times*, *The Vancouver Promise*, 27 Nov. 1976.

Canadian culture pre-dates the Canadian identity. When the possibility of Canada still lay remote in the future, our writers struggled to articulate what they were, what they were to become.

John Moss, critic, *Sex and Violence in the Canadian Novel: The Ancestral Present* (1977).

If we hitch a political development to a cultural one, as in separatism, we get a kind of neo-fascism; if we hitch a cultural development to a political one, we get a pompous, bureaucratic pseudo-culture.

Northrop Frye, cultural critic, address, Empire Club of Canada, Toronto, 19 Jan. 1984.

To paraphrase John Lennon, cultural policy is what happens when the government isn't making other plans.

Roy MacSkimming, cultural consultant, comment made in 1988, quoted by Charlotte Gray in *Saturday Night*, Dec. 1991.

There's an American vulture / That's tryin' to eat our culture / And without you I don't think we can survive.

Lines from the song "Stompin' Tom, We Need Ya," written and performed by country singer **Washboard Hank**, heard on CBC Radio, 19 June 1992.

Finestone: In my view, there isn't any one Canadian identity. Canada has no national culture.

Ormiston: No national culture?

Finestone: Well, where's your national culture?

Ormiston: I think a lot of people would feel uncomfortable with that.

Finestone: Well, I think our national culture is fairness and equality and equal opportunites.

Interview with **Sheila Finestone**, Federal Secretary of State for Multiculturalism and the Status of Women, conducted by interviewer **Susan Ormiston**, conducted on 31 Jan. 1995, with Eric Malling, CTV's *W5*.

"Looney Tunes" was our introduction to American culture.

E. Graydon Carter, editor-in-chief of *Vanity Fair*, referring to the cartoons he saw on television growing up in Ottawa in the 1950s, quoted by Rick Marin in "The Most Entertaining Americans? Canadians," *The New York Times*, 27 June 1993.

I think that Canada can protect its culture in all sorts of ways. It can have cultural support, fairs and communications—and all that sort of thing.

Carla Hills, U.S. trade representative, briefing with reporters in Washington on the eve of a congressional vote on extending the Free Trade pact with Canada to include Mexico, quoted by Linda Diebel in *The Toronto Star*, 25 May 1991.

A totally popular culture would be an immovable culture, admitting no difference or disagreement. To prevent that happening to our polity, we subsidize the existence of an opposition in Parliament. What we do when we subsidize unpopular art, believe it or not, is subsidize democracy.

Ronald Bryden, theatre critic, *The Globe and Mail*, 22 Aug. 1991.

How much longer before we believe in our genius, before we showcase our own.

Robert Lantos, film producer, accepting Air Canada's award for outstanding contribution to the film business, Toronto, 26 Nov. 1991, quoted by CP in *The Toronto Star* the following day.

The one place that Canadian culture doesn't come from is Ottawa.

Greg Curnoe, artist, quoted in University of Guelph's "Canada" supplement, *The Globe and Mail*, 4 Dec. 1991.

We once had a culture here. I mean, a *collective culture*. It was based on hope. It thrived on multiplicity. At its heart lay the belief that we were here to help one another.

Timothy Findley, novelist, "When You Write about This Country," *The Canadian Forum*, Sept. 1992.

We do not have respect for our own culture. We have no equivalent of the British Council, the Swedish Institute, the Goethe Institute or the Italian Cultural Institute. And I don't accept the argument that they've had culture longer than we have. It's not that much longer.

*

People are ignorant of their own ignorance—that's how successful the colonization and cultural imperialism has been from abroad.

Greg Gatenby, literary organizer, Harbourfront's International Festival of Authors, quoted by *eye*, 15 Oct. 1992.

The message in the end of multiculturalism is that there really is no definable, hard, solid, Canadian culture.

Neil Bissoondath, novelist and critic of multiculturalism, panelist, CTV's *W5*, 31 Jan. 1994, printed in *The Globe and Mail*, 7 Feb. 1995.

There is a hard truth to the American position that culture is business; what that means for us in Canada is that business is culture—that without Canadian business, whether book publishers or magazine publishers, there won't be much by way of Canadian culture.

Mel Watkins, economist, "The Business of Culture," *The Canadian Forum*, May 1994.

We're only as good as our past. If we destroy our cultural and institutional memories, we'll just be another Idaho.

Daryl Duke, television producer, quoted by Peter C. Newman in "The Nation's Business," *Maclean's*, 25 July 1994.

I have a social security system, therefore I exist.

Marcel Masse, former federal Minister of Culture, epitomizing the English-Canadian approach to culture and identity, quoted in *The Canadian Forum*, Dec. 1994.

That Canada might wish to create space for its own cultural products, while still giving consumers access to an incredible range of U.S. products, has always struck American entertainment moguls as literally incomprehensible.

Jeffrey Simpson, columnist, "The Americans Encounter the Unimaginable World of Canadian Culture," *The Globe and Mail*, 10 March 1995.

If you can't protect what you own, you don't own anything.

Jack Valenti, President, Motion Picture Association of America, dismissing Canadian cultural exceptions in the Canada-U.S. Free Trade Agreement as foolish, anti-free trade, and symptoms of world-wide "infection," interviewed by Laura Eggertson in *The Toronto Star*, 17 March 1995.

When the government sets about defending culture it's time to defend oneself against the government.

Louis Dudek, poet and aphorist, "Bitter Pills," *Reality Games* (1998).

Canada is one of mankind's greatest achievements. It's comparable in every way to the great civilizations of the past. There's never been a country before based on the ideal of multiculturalism and peace. The problem is that Canada doesn't get any credit for the great things it has produced.

Tyler Cowan, economist and author of *In Praise of Commercial Culture*, interviewed by Christopher Hume, "The Bottom Line on Culture and the Market," *The Toronto Star*, 13 March 1999.

CURIOSITY

Curiosity is almost as good as genius, and anyone who wants it can cultivate it at home.

Louis Dudek, poet and aphorist, "Epigrams," *Small Perfect Things* (1991).

Curiosity, it appears to me, is the great preservative and the supreme emollient.... We have lost all when we cease to be curious about ourselves, for that means that we have indeed abandoned hope. When we succumb to the bodily and mental habits of those who have given up all hope of change or improvement, we have fitted the latch of the tomb. It is not easy to fight this fight, for old age has its seductions.

Robertson Davies, man-of-letters, *The New York Times Book Review*, 12 May 1991.

Our curiosity should be profound, since our knowledge is superficial.

Louis Dudek, poet and aphorist, *The Caged Tiger* (1997).

CURLING See also SPORTS

Everyone who has attempted to play a curling stone, no matter what may be his occupation, generally feels all his cares and anxieties disappear as he concentrates on nothing else but defeating his opponents.

Lord Dufferin, Governor General, address, opening of the Toronto Curling Club, 12 Feb. 1877, quoted in *The Globe* the following day.

The sport at witch Canajuns generally end up nummer 1 in the wirld is yer Curlin. Canajuns has become the teem to beet in yer Sliver Brooms and yer Bryers. The wife and I likes to curl up togethr all winter with our own bumspeels, taking turns neelin down to git our rocks off wile the uther pardner brakes wind in front.

Don Harron, comedian, in the person of Charlie Farquharson, *Cum Buy the Farm* (1987).

Every small town in Saskatchewan has to have two things: a hockey rink and a curling rink.

Amber Holland, technical director, Saskatchewan Curling Association, quoted by Francine Dubé, *National Post*, 26 Feb. 2000.

CYBERSPACE See also COMPUTERS

I coined the word "cyberspace" in 1981 in one of my first science fiction stories and subsequently used it to describe something that people insist on seeing as a sort of literary forerunner of the Internet.

William Gibson, author, "The Net Is a Waste of Time," *The New York Times Magazine*, 14 July 1996. The Vancouver-based author coined the word in his novel *Neuromancer* (1984), according to Michael L. Benedikt in *Cyberspace: First Steps* (1992). Cyberspace is a form of "virtual reality."

"Cyberspace" is what everyone remembers from *Neuromancer*. But to me, as a writer, it was a throwaway concept. I invented cyberspace because I needed something to replace the aliens-and-spacecraft part of science fiction.

William Gibson, author, interviewed by H.J. Kirchhoff, "In Person," *The Globe and Mail*, 2 June 1995.

I tried to come up with a name for it. I literally did sit down at a typewriter one night and go, "Dataspace? Noooo. Infospace? Boring. Cyberspace? Hmmm. It's got sibilance. It sounds interesting." What did it mean? I had no clue. It was like an empty chocolate cup awaiting the whipped cream.

William Gibson, novelist, interviewed by Brian D. Johnson in "Mind Games with William Gibson," *Maclean's*, 5 June 1995.

The world has changed. Some already see cyberspace as their sovereign state.

Frank Ogden, futurologist, "Constructive Destruction Will Let in the Future," "As Prime Minister, I Would . . ." *Canada's Brightest offer Innovative Solutions for a More Prosperous and United Country: Volume Two* (1996) with a foreword by Frank Stronach.

CYBORGS

People find me peculiar. They think it's odd that I spend most of my waking hours wearing eight or nine Internet-connected computers sewn into my clothing and that I wear opaque wrap-around glasses day and night, inside and outdoors. . . . Despite the peculiar glances I draw, I wouldn't live any other way. I have melded technology with my person and achieved a higher state of awareness than would otherwise be possible.

Steve Mann, computer engineer, University of Toronto, pioneer in "wearable computers," "Cyborg Seeks Community," Internet, May–June 1999.

CYCLING See also SPORTS

Cycling. Cross-Canada. The trans-Canada record is 13 days 9 hr. 6 min., by Bill Narasnek of Lively, Ontario, cycling 3,751 miles from Victoria, British Columbia, to Halifax, Nova Scotia, July 5–18, 1991.

Peter Matthews, editor, *The Guinness Book of Records* (1996).

CYNICISM

Cynics are but cowards in disguise.

Mary Pitawanakwat, human-rights activist, accepting the Woman of Courage Award of the National Action Committee on the Status of Women in 1994, quoted by Rudy Platiel, "Larger Lives," *The Globe and Mail*, 23 Dec. 1995.

Cynicism. An effective social mechanism for preventing communication.

John Ralston Saul, author, *The Doubter's Companion: A Dictionary of Aggressive Common Sense* (1994).

D

DAMAGE

Sometimes you have to bite the bullet, eat your socks, and shut your mouth. Let's go out and try to minimize the damage.

Attributed to **Pat Burns**, coach of the Toronto Maple Leafs (1992–96).

DANCE See also CULTURE

Dancing isn't a tournament. The only competition you have is yourself and your expectations.

Karen Kain, ballerina, upon winning the International Ballet Competition with Frank Augustyn in 1973, quoted by Alan Edmonds in *The Canadian*, 16 Feb. 1975.

What matters most, of course, is what happens on the stage. That's what a dance company exists for. Everything else—history, happiness, heartbreak—is extra: the process is the product.

Max Wyman, author, *The Royal Winnipeg Ballet: The First Forty Years* (1978).

All my life, I worked as hard as I could to attain as much as I could and grow as much as possible, without ever thinking about what the end result would be. I have been surprised over the years by the results, which are the ones I could never have really dreamed of. The way it has turned out has gone beyond what I expected, or what anyone else expected.

Veronica Tennant, principal dancer, quoted by Deirdre Kelly in *The Globe and Mail*, 4 Feb. 1989.

There are places inside us that have no limitations.

Robert Desrosiers, dancer, "Robert Desrosiers: A Portrait in the First Person," *The Originals*, Vision TV, 7 Dec. 1991.

DAVIES, ROBERTSON See also WRITERS & WRITING, CANADIAN

A lot of people complain that my novels aren't about Canada. I think they are, because I see Canada as a country torn between a very northern, rather extraordinary, mystical spirit which it fears and its desire to present itself to the world as a Scotch banker. This makes for tension. Tension is the very stuff of art. Plays, novels—the whole lot.

Robertson Davies, man-of-letters, "The Master's Voice: The Table Talk of Robertson Davies," quoted by Peter Newman in *Maclean's*, Sept. 1972.

I was not scholarly, except in ancient phonology, but others were—Robertson Davies, for instance, whose silvery Oxford cadences reminded me that British speech was acceptable in Canada, and that Canada's dominion status conferred a cosmopolitanism not really acceptable south of the Great Lakes.

Anthony Burgess, novelist, *You've Had Your Time: Being the Second Part of the Confessions of Anthony Burgess* (1990).

The theme of the portion of life that is unlived, for whatever reason, has long appealed to me.

Robertson Davies, man-of-letters, quoted by Geraldine Anthony in *Stage Voices: Twelve Canadian Playwrights Talk about Their Lives and Work* (1978).

If I had to choose a character standing for myself, it would be the Ugly Duckling. Oh yes, the Ugly Duckling. You see, no one thought much of him when he was a duck. But when they found out he was a swan, opinion changed. I may not be the world's foremost swan, but I am not a duck.

Robertson Davies, man-of-letters, quoted by Val Ross in *The Globe and Mail*, 28 Sept. 1991.

You wouldn't expect an answer if you wrote to Shakespeare, would you?

Reply of Robertson Davies' secretary to a letter of inquiry about an obscure reference in *The Cornish Trilogy*, as noted by Sara Earley, Calgary, Letters to the Editor, *The Globe and Mail*, 6 Oct. 1999.

He was the greatest comic novelist in the English language since Charles Dickens.

John Irving, novelist, "Obituary," *Maclean's*, 18 Dec. 1995.

DEATH See also DYING WORDS, EUTHANASIA, SUICIDE

His Will be Done. If it be our Fortunes to end our Days here, we are as neer Heaven, as in England....

Thomas James, English sea captain and Arctic explorer, *The Dangerous Voyage of Capt. Thomas James: In His Intended Discovery of the North West Passage into the South Sea* (written in 1633, published in 1740). James comforted his crew during foul weather off Danby's Island (which he named) in James Bay, 29 Nov. 1631.

The world holds a larger share of sorrow than joy, and it ought to be a consolation to know that we will not live forever. To be robbed of death would be the most frightful thing that could happen to us.

Kit Coleman, columnist in the 1880s and 1890s, quoted by Ted Ferguson in *Kit Coleman: Queen of Hearts* (1978).

They know no seasons but the end of time.

A reference to the repose of the dead, last line of **Archibald Lampman**'s poem "In Beechwood Cemetery" (1894), *Poems* (1900) edited by D.C. Scott.

No wild animal dies of old age. Its life has soon or late a tragic end. It is only a question of how long it can hold out against its foes.

Ernest Thompson Seton, naturalist, *Wild Animals I Have Known* (1898).

You know, it is not forbidden to desire death in order to be with God.

Brother André, Montreal religious, quoted by Henri-Paul Bergeron in *Brother André, C.S.C., The Apostle of Saint Joseph* (1938) translated by Réal Boudreau.

It isn't so much that dying is tragic, for death comes to us all, but dying without meaning. Life is never tragic; the tragedy is living without meaning.

J. Roby Kidd, adult educator, observation made in 1973, quoted in the memorial booklet *Roby Kidd: 1915–1982* (1982).

Well, I'm all packed and ready to go. I'm an aged agnostic, unafraid of death and undeluded with thoughts of a life hereafter.

Greg Clark, newspaperman, then 82, quoted by Frank Rasky in *The Toronto Star*, 7 June 1975.

And now there is nothing more to say except the familiar phrase of my old Micmac friends when talking of things past: Kes-pe-ah-dooksit—"Here the story ends."

Thomas H. Raddall, novelist, last sentence of *In My Time: A Memoir* (1976).

I offer this for your consideration. If the human psyche cannot be measured and is not limited by time and space and is not material then perhaps it can survive death.

Allen Spraggett, author and parapsychologist, quoted by Nancy Reynolds in *The Niagara Falls Review*, 24 Aug. 1976.

The dead are not terrifying, nor are they incomprehensible. They can be understood, communicated with, and freed.

Ian Currie, researcher, *You Cannot Die: The Incredible Findings of a Century of Research on Death* (1978, 1993).

Every time I make a horror movie, I'm rehearsing my own death.

David Cronenberg, film director, quoted in *Maclean's*, 16 Feb. 1981.

We have needs of the spirit because we are the only species whose fate is not simply a mute fact of our existence but a problem whose meaning we attempt to understand.

Michael Ignatieff, essayist, *The Needs of Strangers* (1985).

I can face death, but I cannot face watching myself disappear from within. Nowadays, when the world comes knocking at the door of Claude Jutra, there's no one *home*. I don't know who I am anymore.

Claude Jutra, filmmaker, on his Alzheimer's disease, quoted by John Hofsess, "Candle in the Wind," *Homemaker's Magazine*, Nov–Dec. 1991. A few months after the conversation, Jutra committed suicide on 5 Nov. 1986.

For many Canadians, a funeral and its aftermath can be the third most expensive purchase of a lifetime after a house and a car, but that purchase is usually made under the gun on the worst day of their lives, a time funeral directors refer to as "at need."

Bronwyn Drainie, journalist, "Happier Endings," *Toronto Life*, April 1987.

Death is the only mystery we all solve.

Robin Skelton, poet and aphorist, *A Devious Dictionary* (1991).

I was never so amazed in my life as when the Sniffer drew his concealed weapon from its case and struck me to the ground, stone dead.

Celebrated opening sentence of **Robertson Davies**' novel *Murther & Walking Spirits* (1991). The events of the novel are related by the spirit of the newly dead man.

The one indisputable human right is the right to say: *No more!*

John Hofsess, writer, "Love and Death," *Last Rights*, April–May 1993.

Even Lazarus, on the narrative level anyway, would have had to die again.

Northrop Frye, cultural critic, "Notebook 1993," edited by Robert D. Denham, *Northrop Frye Newsletter*, Summer 1993.

In modern middle-class culture, the absence of death in most people's early years creates a psychic vacuum of sorts. For many, thoughts of a nuclear confrontation are one's first true brush with nonexistence, and because they are the first, they can be the most powerful and indelible.

Thoughts of the narrator of **Douglas Coupland**'s novel *Life after God* (1994).

The sun shines as if there is no death.

Nicholas Catanoy, poet, *Notes on a Prison Wall: A Memoir/Poem* (1994).

If I were to die and go to heaven, I would want to go as an eye, one that could travel to the bounds of the universe and see everything that there is to see.

Phyllis Gotlieb, poet, science-fiction writer, comment, 7 Jan. 1994.

I guess the time you learn you're going to die is the time you really understand you are human.

W.O. Mitchell, raconteur, "The Poetry of Life," address, Writers' Union of Canada, Winnipeg, June 1996, *An Evening with W.O. Mitchell: A Collection of the Author's Best Loved Performance Pieces* (1997) edited by Barbara and Armond Mitchell.

Death is part of creation, part of God's plan for us on earth. We hope that it is not the end just as birth is not the beginning, but we know nothing of that. Being human we are, by definition, limited in what we can fathom, yet we are able to accept what is given to us.

Dow Marmur, rabbi, Holy Blossom Temple, Toronto, *Choose Life: Thoughts on Grief and Growth* (1999).

DEBT & DEFICIT

For one generation to run up a debt that future generations will have to pay is morally wrong.

Kim Campbell, Minister of National Defence and Conservative leadership candidate, address, Ottawa leadership convention, 12 June 1992, quoted by Rosemary Speirs in *The Toronto Star* the following day.

There is no example of a nation becoming rich by paying its debts.... There are dozens of examples of nations becoming rich by defaulting or renegotiating.

John Ralston Saul, author, *The Doubter's Companion: A Dictionary of Aggressive Common Sense* (1994).

Deficits are not a sin, but a necessity.

William Vickrey, Victoria-born economist and Nobel laureate, emeritus professor at Columbia University, quoted by Stephen Handelman in *The Toronto Star*, 9 Oct. 1996.

DECENCY

I believe we should die with decency, so that at least decency will survive.

Nicholas Catanoy, poet, *Notes on a Prison Wall: A Memoir/Poem* (1994).

DEDICATIONS See BOOKS: DEDICATIONS

DEEDS

The Lord was asking me for deeds as well as for words. There is a great difference between one thousand conferences and one good deed.

Attributed to **Paul-Émile Cardinal Léger** when he resigned as Archbishop of Montreal to serve in a humanitarian capacity in Africa in 1967, obituary, *The Toronto Star*, 13 Nov. 1991.

DEFEAT See also FAILURE

One of the worst stings of defeat is the sympathy that goes with it.

Bob Edwards, publisher, *The Eye Opener,* 8 June 1912, *The Wit and Wisdom of Bob Edwards* (1976) edited by Hugh Dempsey.

I believe in the dignity of defeat.

Richard Hatfield, New Brunswick Premier, conceding defeat in the provincial election of 1987, quoted in his obituary by Jonathan Ferguson in *The Toronto Star,* 27 April 1991.

DEFENCE See also CANADIAN ARMED FORCES, NORTH ATLANTIC TREATY ORGANIZATION, WAR

World War III could have broken out and ended before we disentangled ourselves and climbed through the babel of the Canadian skies.

J.G. Ballard, author, recalling the confusing, multilingual nature of NATO pilot-training in the early 1950s at Moose Jaw, Sask., *The Kindness of Women* (1991).

Defensively, as well as geographically, we are joined beyond any possibility of separating.

Dwight D. Eisenhower, U.S. President, joint meeting of the Senate and the House of Commons, 14 Nov. 1953.

The economic burden of armaments is now almost overpowering, and where public opinion can bring itself effectively to bear on government, the pressure is nearly always for the greatest possible amount of butter and the fewest possible number of guns.

Lester B. Pearson, diplomat, Nobel Peace Prize Lecture, Oslo, Norway, 11 Dec. 1957. The text is taken from *The Four Faces of Peace and the International Outlook* (1964) edited by Sherleigh G. Pierson.

Shall Canada's role be that of powder-monkey or peacemaker?

James M. Minifie, correspondent, contrasting a continental or an independent defence policy, *Peacemaker or Powder-Monkey: Canada's Role in a Revolutionary World* (1960).

For good or ill, in Canada, defence is not a major issue; after all, other people do it for us.

Nicholas Stethem, defence analyst, "The Canadian Armed Forces in the 1980s," *Jane's Defence Review,* No. 2, 1980.

The best defence is a non-offensive defence.

Project Ploughshares, *What Makes Canada Secure?* (1991), the background document for the Citizens' Inquiry into Peace and Security in Canada.

The only thing that's real about this defence is the cost.

John Polanyi, scientist, interviewed regarding the federal government's decision to spend $4.4 billion for helicopters suitable for anti-submarine warfare, quoted in *The Globe and Mail,* 25 July 1992.

In December 1944, I had to visit a radar research station in Canada, wearing only light clothing, when the air temperature was –30oC (-22oF). I remember walking two miles after dark and seriously wondering if I could ward off hypothermia. On that visit, I had to climb 50 feet up a vertical steel ladder in the middle of a field, without gloves. I still remember my fingers sticking to the metal. There would have been a scandal in [the British] Parliament if service personnel had been required to suffer such conditions.

Fred Hoyle, English scientist and novelist, *Home Is Where the Wind Blows: Chapters from a Cosmologist's Life* (1994).

Canadian defence policy must satisfy four criteria. It must protect our security, preserve our sovereignty, respect sentiment and, above all, observe strict economy.

Desmond Morton, historian, "Canadian Defence Policy: A Civil-military Dialogue of the Deaf," *National Networks News* (quarterly publication of the Defence Associations), July 1994.

Canada cannot be defended by Canadians.

Attributed to the Chief of Defence Staff, General **John de Chastelain** by John Dixon, "Control," *The Globe and Mail,* 7 Feb. 1995. Dixon explained, "Our borders are too long and our strategic situation too difficult for our small and diffuse population to defend the country against a determined aggressor. Our security must always be a function of world security, and we have a particularly large stake in those institutions that make and keep international peace."

DEFICITS See DEBT & DEFICIT

DELINQUENCY

To rise above one's station is rebellion; to fall from it is delinquency.

Northrop Frye, cultural critic, "Repetitions of Jacob's Dream" (1983), *The Eternal Act of Creation: Essays, 1979–1990* (1993) edited by Robert D. Denham.

DEMOCRACY

Democracy is rarely beautiful in its workings, for the many still refuse to be refined, restrained, and artistic.

George M. Wrong, historian, remark made in 1917, quoted by Walter Stewart in *Divide and Con: Canadian Politics at Work* (1973).

Democracy: A mockery that mouths the word and obstructs every effort on the part of an honest people to establish a government for the welfare of the people.

Charles E. Coughlin, "the radio priest," address, 1 Aug. 1938, quoted by George Seldes in *The Great Quotations* (1960).

The basic flaw in the democratic process is not that the average man is incapable of intelligent participation in the affairs of state. It is that he must be rendered incapable of doing so in order to prevent him from using his formal political powers to challenge the existing distributions of wealth and power.

Edgar Z. Friedenberg, social scientist, "Liberty and Rancor," *The Disposal of Liberty and Other Industrial Wastes* (1975).

Democracy is not a system of public participation. It is a system where leaders are chosen.

Jean Drapeau, long-time Montreal Mayor, quoted by Nick Auf der Maur in *The Billion-Dollar Games: Jean Drapeau and the 1976 Olympics* (1976).

To save democracy, turn off the TV sets.

Marshall McLuhan, communications pioneer, quoted by Richard Gwyn in *The Toronto Star*, 25 Oct. 1992.

In Canada, the real political power is once removed. It's inaccessible, unaccountable. You can't have political democracy when your economy is absentee owned.

Ralph Nader, consumer advocate, interviewed by Bill Taylor in *The Toronto Star*, 12 Dec. 1992.

Countries that have soldiers in charge seem, more often than not, to be the ones where democracy is but a flickering candle sitting in an open window with a forecast of rain.

L.W. MacKenzie, Major-General, Canadian Armed Forces, open letter written on the eve of retirement, *The Globe and Mail*, 21 Jan. 1993.

If you tell someone in Toronto that you think freedom and democracy are wonderful, they give you a strange look, as if you are raving about how nice oxygen is.

Jan Wong, correspondent, *Red China Blues: My Long March from Mao to Now* (1996).

The idea of democracy was an American import into Canada, without which we would still be governed by a Family Compact. A healthy society takes good ideas wherever it can find them.

Michael Bliss, columnist, "Opinion," *The Toronto Star*, 21 May 1996.

Let us not forget that the object of democracy is a free people, not free institutions.

Henry Mintzberg, management consultant, "The Myth of 'Society Inc.'" *Report on Business Magazine*, Oct. 1996.

Democracy is not a short-term goal, and not just a flag to be waved by one country: it is the long-term hope of the entire human species.

Louis Dudek, poet and aphorist, "Towards a Democratic Art," *Reality Games* (1998).

We are one of the oldest democracies in the world—152 years without civil war or coup d'état. Look around at our allies. Compare.

John Ralston Saul, commentator, LaFontaine-Baldwin Lecture, Toronto, *The Globe and Mail*, 24 March 2000.

DEMOGRAPHY

Demographics explain about two-thirds of everything.

David K. Foot and **Daniel Stoffman**, demographer and journalist, *Boom, Bust & Echo: How to Profit from the Coming Demographic Shift* (1996).

DENTISTRY See also MEDICINE

My idea as regards the management of a dental practice is that the department of accounts should receive as careful thought and forethought as the carving of an impression for an oral restoration.

J.M. Ritchie, dentist, address, Toronto Forum on Dental Practice Management, 11 March 1935, quoted by Ralph Crawford in the editorial, *Journal of the Canadian Dental Association*, Nov. 1991.

We have just visited your dentist. Have you?

Slogan on the delivery vans of the national dental-supply company **Ashe Temple Ltd.**, founded in Toronto. The slogan has been in use "for many years."

DEPRESSION

Depression is private expression of public despair. But people want to find solutions—they're hoping for happy endings.

Lionel Tiger, biologist, quoted by Olivia Ward in *The Toronto Star*, 6 May 1979.

I experience both depression and its treatment as continuous mass-cultural phenomena, not individual disease and one-to-one therapy. Depression has always been for me, and remains, a self-punishing language, a prolonged sensation of filthiness and worthlessness, of embarrassement at being alive; a sickening deadness I enviously compare to the liveliness other people seem to enjoy.

John Bentley Mays, critic, *In the Jaws of the Black Dogs: A Memoir of Depression* (1995).

Statistically, this is a recession but psychically the result has been depression.

Bruce Powe, media observer, quoted by Trish Crawford in "Bracing for 1995," *The Toronto Star*, 3 Jan. 1995.

DEPRESSION, ECONOMIC

Bennett is my shepherd, I am in want, / He maketh me to lie down on park benches, / He leadeth me beside still factories, / He restoreth my doubt in the Conservative party, / He leadeth me in the paths of destruction, / For my party's sake.

Opening lines of "The Psalm of Bennett," a parody of the 23rd Psalm and a gripe against Prime Minister R.B. Bennett, quoted by **Edgar R.E. Chevrier**, House of Commons, 4 April 1932.

If this book has any viewpoint it is that the Depression brought out more of the best than it did the worst in people; that people, if left alone, tend to work out their own problems for themselves; that expert advice, particularly in economic matters, is most useful when it is completely ignored; that so much was learned from the Depression that it will never happen again.

James H. Gray, historian, *The Winter Years: The Depression in the Prairies* (1966).

Artists stand depressions quite well, depressions look as much like their regular brand of prosperity.

David Milne, painter, quoted in *Time*, 10 Feb. 1975.

Crash, n. An inappropriate term. Use *correction.*

David Olive, business commentator, *White Knights and Poison Pills: A Cynic's Dictionary of Business Jargon* (1990).

A form of economic disaster common throughout history. In 1973 the word was deleted from all Western languages and replaced by the term recession.

John Ralston Saul, author, *The Doubter's Companion: A Dictionary of Aggressive Common Sense* (1994).

DEPTH

Mud sometimes gives the illusion of depth.

Marshall McLuhan, communications pioneer, quoted by Richard J. Schoeck in *Who Was Marshall McLuhan?* (1994) edited by Barrington Nevitt and Maurice McLuhan.

DESIGN See also TYPOGRAPHY

Design, to define it very briefly, is the art of assembling diverse elements into an organized unit.

Carl Dair, typographer, *Design with Type* (1952, 1967).

Signage / Wayfinding

Credit for the first use of the word *signage* to refer to a system or a family of symbols for non-verbal communication in public places goes to Toronto-based graphic designer **Paul Arthur** who in 1962 designed the glyphs used as signs at the Winnipeg airport and then at the Edmonton airport; thereafter he acted as chief designer of signs at Expo 67. Arthur subsequently popularized another term, *wayfinding*, to refer to designing directions.

"Wayfinding refers to ways of getting around a building" is the definition given in Arthur's report prepared with Romedi Passini *1-2-3 Evaluation and Design: Guide to Wayfinding—Helping Visitors Find Their Way around Public Buildings* (March 1987). The information comes from Paul Arthur and Romedi Passini's *Wayfinding: People, Signs, and Architecture* (1992).

If there is a distinction between art and design, it is that art is about failure and design is about success.

Bruce Mau, designer, quoted by Elizabeth Crinion in "Maximal Mau," *Azure*, May–June 1994.

We are happy amateurs, not sad professionals.

Bruce Mau, graphic designer, lecture, recalling a saying current in the field, quoted by Pamel Houng in *The Globe and Mail*, 16 May 1996.

Is there such a thing as a recognizable Canadian design? The short answer is no. The Canadian style is no style.

Christopher Hume, columnist and art critic, "Master of the Utilitarian," *The Toronto Star*, 21 Aug. 1997.

DESIRE See also SEX

Desire seems to have boiled down to shopping.

Douglas Coupland, novelist and aphorist, writing in *The New Republic*, quoted by Bruce Blackadar in *The Toronto Star*, 20 Aug. 1995.

DESPAIR

And night is wrapped in mystery profound. / We cannot lift the mantle of the past: / We seem to wander over hallowed ground: / We scan the trail of Thought, but all is overcast.

Concluding lines of **Charles Sangster**'s poem "The Red Man," *The St. Lawrence and the Saguenay, and Other Poems* (1856).

DESTINY

Canada's destiny lies in the North.

Attributed to the Arctic explorer **Vilhjalmur Stefansson** during a Toronto address, by Norman Phillips in *The Toronto Star*, 3 Nov. 1959.

All we know is that the mystics, seers, mediums, and prophets who have peered deeper into the mystery assure us that the end is worth the long, drawn-out drama of creation, the weary rounds of the wheel of rebirth, the thirst and hunger of the quest—abundantly, supremely, transcendentally worth it all....

Allen Spraggett, broadcaster and writer, concluding paragraph of *The Case for Immortality* (1974).

The knowledge that you can have is inexhaustible, and what is inexhaustible is benevolent. The knowledge that you cannot have is of the riddles of birth and death, of our future destiny and the purposes of God. Here there is no knowledge, but illusions that restrict freedom and limit hope. Accept the mystery behind knowledge: it is not darkness but shadow.

Northrop Frye, cultural critic, annual baccalaureate service, Metropolitan United Church, Toronto, 10 April 1988, quoted by Alexandra Johnston in *Vic Report*, Spring 1991.

DEVELOPERS See also BUSINESS, DEVELOPMENT

They are building Rome in a day, in Toronto.

Pier Georgio Di Cicco, poet, commenting on Italian-born Canadian developers and builders, quoted by Carmin Priolo in *Thornhill Month*, March 1990.

Until the day of reckoning, few asked what this far-from-distinguished Canadian real estate operator, product of what has been called a roller-coaster career, could do for, say, Bloomingdale's.

John Kenneth Galbraith, economist and essayist, *A Short History of Financial Euphoria* (1990). The reference is to the spectacular bankruptcy of Robert Campeau who at one point acquired ownership of Bloomingdale's in New York City.

The Reichmann brothers, with Robert Campeau the Canadian gift to financial excess, are indubitably broke with depressive effect on the banks that were captured by their euphoric mood. Perhaps it is to their credit that, like Donald Trump, they erected monuments that will long commemorate their adventure.

John Kenneth Galbraith, economist and essayist, referring to the Reichmann's Olympia & York Investments' Canary Wharf development on the Isle of Dogs, London, *A Short History of Financial Euphoria* (1990).

For what it's worth, I hope there is some truth to the rumour of Albert Reichmann having complained that One Canada Place was too good for the British: The building is, as Black would have it, an elegant structure, monstrous not by North American standards but chiefly in contrast to the decrepit 18th- and 19th-century tenements in The City which London's investment bankers continue to prefer.

David Olive, columnist, "Owe & Why," *The Globe and Mail's Report on Business Magazine*, Aug. 1992. One Canada Place is the name of the centrepiece of the Canary Wharf development project in London, England; the reference is to Conrad Black. The Reichmann interests temporarily lost control of the mammoth commercial development on London's Isle of Dogs in the crash of 1992–93.

DEVELOPMENT See also DEVELOPERS

In the case of Canada, not merely great regions, but the *whole country* has been picketed out in great rectangles for future development.

Oswald Spengler, German historian, *The Decline of the West* (1918), Volume II. The observation, which applies only to the Prairies, takes the form of a footnote written in 1926 by the authorized English translator Charles Francis Atkinson.

We are surely the only country in the world that is changing from a developed country to an underdeveloped country. Day by day, we become more of a colony, and the disturbing thing to me is that so many Canadians seem willing to embrace the idea of being economically annexed by a country which is about to go through some pretty choppy waters itself.

Allan Blakeney, Saskatchewan Premier, National Press Club, Ottawa, 9 April 1980, quoted in *The Globe and Mail* the following day.

My life has exceeded even my own fantasies.

Mortimer Zuckerman, Montreal-born, McGill-educated, Boston-based property developer and publishing executive, proprietor of *The Atlantic Monthly* and *U.S. News & World Report*, quoted by Marci McDonald in *Maclean's*, 27 Jan. 1986.

DICTATORS

Happy are peoples who have found dictators.

Attributed to l'**Abbé Lionel Groulx**, Quebec priest and patriot, writing in 1934 in his publication *L'Action nationale*, by Mordecai Richler in "A Reporter at Large: Inside/Outside," *The New Yorker*, 23 Sept. 1991.

DIEFENBAKER, JOHN G. See also POLITICIANS

You have got to make him a combination of Churchill, de Gaulle, Moses, God, and maybe the Devil, because he has got a bit of that in him. This combination usually wins votes. Do that.

Maurice Duplessis, Quebec Premier, offering advice to Pierre Sévigny who was then arranging for Duplessis's Union Nationale party to endorse the Conservative leader John G. Diefenbaker in the 1957 federal election, quoted by Peter Stursberg in *Diefenbaker: Leadership Gained, 1956–62* (1975).

Oh, it's not easy for us—the Macmillans, the Kennedys, the Audenaurs, and the de Gaulles....

John G. Diefenbaker, Prime Minister, equating himself with some world leaders of the 1960s, *Time*, 15 June 1962.

As for the critics, well, big-game hunters don't go after gophers!

John G. Diefenbaker, former Prime Minister, remark made during the autographing session at Simpsons in Toronto for the first volume of *One Canada* (1977), as noted by Carolyn Weir in *The Right Honourable John George Diefenbaker* (1979).

DIET See also WEIGHT

It is easiest to fast / just after eating.

Robert Priest, aphorist, *Time Release Poems* (1997).

DIFFICULTIES

You can go through a red light but you can't go through a red truck.

Louis Dudek, man-of-letters, *Epigrams* (1975).

As any prophet can perceive, our present hang-ups are due to the incompatibility of sequential thinking with the simultaneities of electric living.

Barrington Nevitt, communications, consultant, *ABC of Prophecy: Understanding the Environment* (1985).

Old Age and Treachery Will Always Overcome Youth and Skill.

Saying on a card printed for demonstration purposes at the **Mackenzie Heritage Printery Museum**, Queenston, Ont., 1 Oct. 1994.

You never understand the cross until you are nailed to it.

Robert Bendavid, physician and surgeon, aphorism, 16 Sept. 1996.

DIGNITY

One of the great ideals of the feminists' cultural revolution is that all human beings be encouraged to find their own dignity and pursue their own truth.

Naomi Goldenberg, feminist, *Changing the Gods: Feminism and the End of Traditional Religions* (1979).

DINOSAURS

Dinosaurs Are Alive and Well and Living as Birds

Wayne Grady, author, *The Dinosaur Project: The Story of the Greatest Dinosaur Expedition Ever Mounted* (1993).

DIPLOMACY

There should be no secret diplomacy of that kind. In other words, the covenants should be open, as well as the policies on which they are based. But the detailed negotiations leading up to them need not be so.

Lester B. Pearson, diplomat, *Diplomacy in the Nuclear Age* (1959). This seems to be the origin of the concept of "open convenants secretly arrived at" that is associated with Pearson who was awarded the Nobel Prize for Peace in recognition of his work at the United Nations Security Council in containing the Suez Crisis.

It is said that during the New York newspaper strike the quality and quantity of diplomatic reporting around the world diminished perceptibly: without *The New York Times* to tell them what to say, the diplomats fell silent.

James Eayrs, historian, noted in Sept. 1969, *Diplomacy and Its Discontents* (1971).

Wherever I have been *en poste* as diplomat, I have used poetry to get through to the local people and the local intellectuals and literary groups. It has been a marvellous passkey.

R.A.D. Ford, poet and diplomat, remark made after seventeen years in Moscow where he served as the Dean of the Diplomatic Corps, quoted by Burt Heward in the *Ottawa Citizen*, 19 July 1980.

By buying simultaneously into both globalization and peace-building, Canada appears committed both to fanning the flames and to joining in the bucket brigade.

Daryl Copeland, diplomat, writing in *Canadian Foreign Policy*, quoted by Paul Knox in *The Globe and Mail*, 17 Sept. 1997.

DISABILITIES See also FOX, TERRY

It's what's left that counts.

Harold Russell, double amputee, *The Best Years of My Life* (1981) written with Dan Ferullo. Born in the Maritimes, Russell lost both hands during a munitions training session at a U.S. Army Base in 1944. Russell won two Academy Awards for his portrayal of the handless veteran in the movie *The Best Years of Our Lives* (1946). He is the sole actor ever to win two Oscars for the same role.

The designers of cities, transportation systems, and public buildings appear to live in a fantasy world and act as if the population consisted entirely of Olympic athletes with fast reflexes and 20/20 vision. Survival in the cities is increasingly dependent on a high degree of agility and visual acuity.

Cyril Greenland, commissioner, *Vision Canada: The Unmet Needs of Blind Canadians* (1976), a study that found the blind to be "the poorest of the poor."

People ask me if Rick's wheelchair is motorized. I say, yes, one in each shoulder.

Tom Norman, volunteer for the U.S. wing of Rick Hansen's Man in Motion world tour, quoted in *The Globe and Mail*, 4 Jan. 1988.

We can't have women representing themselves or the next thing you'll know we'll have to have the crippleds and coloureds.

John Crosbie, Minister of Fisheries, explaining to Judy Rebick of the National Action Committee on the Status of Women why no women drew up the Charlottetown Agreement, St. John's, Nfld., 8 Oct. 1991, quoted in *The Globe and Mail* two days later. Crosbie later explained, "These were not racist or anti-disabled or sexist remarks. They were common-sense remarks. I was referring to coloured people as opposed to white people. I was referring, yes, to the crippled. I've been making donations to associations with respect to crippled children for many years."

DISARMAMENT

These proposals are not starry-eyed idealism. They are plain, realistic common sense. The romanticists are those who still believe that modern armaments can make a nation safe.

Philip Noel-Baker, British statesman, son of Canadian Quakers, discussing disarmament proposals, *The Arms Race: A Program for World Disarmament* (1958).

The Venus de Milo is the Goddess of Disarmament.

Al Boliska, broadcaster, *The World's Worst Jokes* (1966).

DISASTER

A St. Valentine's Day Massacre is just a word until you have one.

Max Ferguson, broadcaster, *And Now... Here's Max: A Funny Kind of Autobiography* (1967).

Canadian disasters do have a way of not happening, doomsday being postponed forever.

Mordecai Richler, author, *Life*, 9 April 1971.

DISCIPLINE

Discipline as traditionally conceived involves a great deal of antagonism between the educator and the educand.

Attributed to mental-health specialist **William Line** as a characteristic observation, by Dr. Jack Griffin in 1986.

DISCOVERIES See also EXPLORATION

I shall give this country a name and call it *Helluland*.

Words from the Old Icelandic epic narrative *Greenlander's Saga* and attributed to the Viking colonist **Leif Ericsson**, also known as Leif the Lucky. Helluland means "slab-land" in Old Icelandic. He likely landed on Baffin Island in the Eastern Arctic about A.D. 1000 The passage is quoted from *The Vinland Sagas* (1965), translated from the Old Icelandic by Magnus Magnusson and Hermann Palsson. Ericsson made two more landfalls—on the Labrador coast, which he called Markland (or "forest-land"), and at L'Anse aux Meadows at the northeastern tip of Newfoundland, which he called Vinland (or "wine-land").

This land he called Prima vista, that is to say, First seen.

John Cabot, Genoese navigator, words upon landing at the site of Cape Bonavista, Nfld., 24 June 1497, quoted by Richard Hakluyt in *The Principal Navigations, Voyages, Traffiques and Discoveries of the English Nation* (1598). The key words are sometimes given as Terra Primum Vista, Latin for "first-seen land"; they refer to the historic landfall made by Cabot. John Quinpool in *First Things in Acadia* (1936) ranks this "three-word account of the discovery of America" with Julius Caesar's gem of brevity, "Veni, vidi, vici."

In fine I am rather inclined to believe that this is the land God gave to Cain.

Jacques Cartier, French navigator, journal entry made sailing past the bleak northern shore of the Gulf of St. Lawrence, today's Labrador and Quebec, Summer 1534. The words appear in "Première relation," *The Voyages of Jacques Cartier* (1924), translated by H.P. Biggar. Cartier's image of the desolate region is the earliest (and most powerful) image associated with the new land based on personal experience. In the King James version of the Bible, the accursed Cain wandered into the land of Nod that was "east of Eden." Cartier's reference gave rise to the false etymology for the country's name "Cain-ada." The historian Laurier LaPierre asked a good question in *Canada My Canada* (1992): "If Canada is the land of Cain, what, on earth, did Abel inherit?"

The sayd men did moreover certify unto us, that there was the way and beginning of the great river of Hochelaga and ready way to Canada, which river the further it went the narrower it came, even into Canada.

Jacques Cartier, French navigator, journal entry, 26 July 1535, "A Shorte and Briefe Narration" (1535), *The Principal Navigations, Voyages, Traffiques and Discoveries of the English Nation* (1598) edited by Richard Hakluyt. Here is the first recorded use of the word "Canada," from *kanata*, a Huron-Iroquois word for "village." Cartier is describing what he heard from the Indians on the banks of the St. Lawrence River upriver past Hochelaga, the Native settlement on the future site of Montreal.

And because that place and country hath never heretofore been discovered, and therefore had no special name, by which it might be called and known, her Majesty named it very properly Meta Incognita, as a mark and bound utterly hitherto unknown.

Sir Martin Frobisher, explorer, "The Third Voyage of Captain Frobisher, Pretended for the Discovery of Cataya, by Meta Incognita, Anno Do. 1578," *The Three Voyages of Martin Frobisher: In Search of a Passage to Cathay and India by the North-West, A.D. 1576–8*. From the *Original 1578 Text of George Best* (1938) edited by Vilhjalmur Stefansson. The text has been modernized for presentation here. Stefansson explained, "The Queen received Frobisher at Court, with thanks and a gift of £100. To the newly discovered land she gave the name 'Meta Incognita.'"

We are as near to heaven by sea as by land!

Sir Humphrey Gilbert, English mariner, claimed Newfoundland as England's first overseas colony on 5 Aug. 1583. On the return voyage, he was aboard the frigate *Squirrel* when, encountering rough weather and icebergs near the Azores, it sank; Gilbert and all hands were lost. "We are as near to heaven by sea as by land!" he roared to his crew as the frigate went down. His words, it is said, were overheard by the crew aboard his companion ship, the *Golden Hind*. These stirring words remain among the most memorable words in the literature of exploration.

I now mixed up some vermilion in melted grease, and inscribed, in large characters, on the South-East face of the rock on which we had slept last night, this brief memorial—"Alexander Mackenzie, from Canada, by land, the twenty-second of July, one thousand seven hundred and ninety-three."

Sir Alexander Mackenzie, first explorer to cross the American continent north of Mexico, doing so, 22 July 1793, mostly on foot, from Montreal to Dean Channel, Bella Coola River, B.C., where he left this memorial, *Voyages from Montreal on the River St. Lawrence, through the Continent of North America, to the Frozen and Pacific Oceans* (1801).

Chapter I.—The discovery of Canada by the French and its recovery by the British—the original inheritors of the earth.

Peter McArthur, satirist, one of ten chapter headings for an unwritten history called "Canada, Her History, Customs and Resources" mentioned in the section "Canada as She Is Misunderstood" from *To Be Taken with Salt: Being an Essay on Teaching One's Grandmother to Suck Eggs* (1903).

One thousand years ago, Europe and America were brought together by Vikings. Our knowledge of the world has grown faster than our sense to take care of it. Now we must set the right course ahead and open up a new era.

Message on a blue banner flown by the *Gaia*, the Norwegian-built, Viking-style long ship which left the Norwegian port of Bergen on 17 May and docked at L'Anse aux Meadows, Nfld., 2 Aug., thereby recreating Leif Ericsson's expeditionary voyage made almost 1000 years earlier; quoted by E. Kaye Fulton in *Maclean's*, 12 Aug. 1991.

DISCOVERY

The joys of discovery and understanding are so great in themselves that the failure to receive lesser rewards is no great loss in the end.

Bernard Grad, biochemist and parapsychologist, "Experiences and Opinions of an Unconventional Scientist," *Men and Women of Parapsychology: Personal Reflections* (1987) edited by Rosemarie Pilkington.

Only puny secrets need protection. Big discoveries are protected by public incredulity.

Marshall McLuhan, communications pioneer, quoted by Richard J. Schoeck in *Who Was Marshall McLuhan?* (1994) edited by Barrington Nevitt and Maurice McLuhan.

DISCRIMINATION See also PREJUDICE, RACE & RACISM

Let her feel in the sacred dawn of her life that the expectation of the human destiny is upon her as upon other young sister countries of hers, which have just entered into the cycle of their promise. She will have to solve, for the salvation of man, the most difficult of all problems, the race problem, which has become insistent with the close contact of communities that had their isolation for centuries in their geographical and cultural exclusiveness.

Rabindranath Tagore, Bengali poet, "Message of Farewell to Canada," Farewell Address to the Fourth Triennial Conference of the National Council of Education of Canada, Vancouver, 14 April 1929; P.C. Mahalanobis, editor, *Visva-Bharati*, Bulletin No. 14, reprinted 1977.

No country could open its doors wide enough to take in the hundreds of thousands of Jewish people who want to leave Europe; the line must be drawn somewhere.

Frederick Charles Blair, Director of the Immigration Branch of the Department of Mines and Resources, letter to O.D. Skelton, Undersecretary of State for External Affairs, 16 June 1939, as quoted by Irving Abella and Harold E. Troper, "The Line Must Be Drawn Somewhere," *The Canadian Jewish Mosaic* (1981) edited by M. Weinfeld, W. Shaffir, and I. Cotler. The statement "None is too many" is often attributed to Blair, but it was spoken by an unnamed senior official with the Department of Immigration, who gave this reply to journalists in early 1945 when asked how many Jews would be allowed into Canada after World War II.

To treat everyone the same may be to offend the notion of equality. Ignoring differences may mean ignoring legitimate needs.

Rosalie Abella, chairperson, Royal Commission on Equality in Employment, *Equality in Employment* (1984).

Of course racism and discrimination can be found in Canada, just as they can everywhere, but probably to a lesser extent than in practically any other country and certainly than in any other country that receives so many newcomers—an influx nearly 1 per cent of the total population, beginning next year. Immigrants to Canada live in a tolerant country that genuinely welcomes both immigrants and refugees; indeed, it finds it almost impossible to send people away once they have turned up.

Editorial feature, "Survey on Canada," *The Economist*, 19 June 1991, reprinted in *The Globe and Mail*, 19 July 1991.

DISCUSSION

Many a good argument is ruined by some fool who knows what he is talking about.

Marshall McLuhan, communications pioneer, quoted by Richard J. Schoeck in *Who Was Marshall McLuhan?* (1994) edited by Barrington Nevitt and Maurice McLuhan.

DISEASE See also AIDS, ILLNESS

Ask not what disease the person has, but rather what person the disease has.

Attributed to **Sir William Osler** by Oliver Sacks in *An Anthropologist on Mars* (1995).

The keynote of postmodern life is the solitude and sense of precariousness arising from ruptures in intimate relationships.

Edward Shorter, historian of society and medical practice, From *Paralysis to Fatigue: A History of Psychosomatic Illness in the Modern Era* (1992).

In my dreams I could scale the mountains high, / In my dreams I face the samurai. / In my dreams I stroke my lover's hair, / In my dreams I travel everywhere. / In my dreams I kiss and never tell, / In my dreams I'm not a languid shell. / In my dreams I never convalesce, / In my dreams I don't have ALS.

Poem by **Dennis Kaye** from *Laugh, I Thought I'd Die: My Life with ALS* (1994). Kaye suffers the degenerative disease Amyotrophic Lateral Sclerosis (ALS).

Neither diseases nor the diseased exist in isolation. It is the isolation of our specialists, locked up inside their narrow sectors, which makes them believe that a disease is a phenomenon with natural limits.

John Ralston Saul, author, *The Doubter's Companion: A Dictionary of Aggressive Common Sense* (1994).

DISSENT

When speaking favorably of the government and the system in general, you are advertising; but should you dissent from it, then you are promoting subversive propaganda.

André Carpentier, author, *Axel et Nicholas suivi de Mémoires d'Axel* (1973) quoted by Claude Janelle in *Citations québécoises modernes* (1976).

DISTINCT SOCIETY See also CANADA & QUEBEC, MEECH LAKE ACCORD, QUEBEC, TWO NATIONS

What counts is not that the *Canadiens* had formed a society different from other societies, but that they had formed a society which was distinct.

Guy Frégault, historian, "The Colonization of Canada in the Eighteenth Century" (1957), *Society and Conquest* (1977), translated and edited by Dale Miquelon. This is the earliest known use of the words distinct and society with respect to Quebec. The phrase distinct society, as a variant of the discredited special status, took on a life of its own with the ill-fated Meech Lake Accord: "The Constitution of Canada shall be interpreted in a manner consistent with... the recognition that Québec constitutes... a distinct society."

What we need in Canada is not special status for Quebec as much as a new status for all provinces.

Eric Kierans, public figure, *Social Sciences in Canada*, symposium, Calgary, quoted in *The Independencer*, Aug.–Sept. 1977.

No one can deny that Quebec is, culturally and sociologically, a distinct society. So is Newfoundland.

Eugene Forsey, authority on the constitution and critic of the Meech Lake constitutional accord, *A Life on the Fringe* (1990).

... having recognized that Quebec is a distinct society, I say to my friends in Quebec I believe it is the responsibility of all of the citizens of Quebec to place Canada first and recognize that, like all of the other provinces, Quebec is second.... Canada must come first.

Clyde Wells, Newfoundland Premier, after giving qualified assent to the Meech Lake Accord, Ottawa, quoted by Patrick Doyle in *The Toronto Star*, 10 June 1990.

English Canada must clearly understand that Quebec is today and forever a distinct society, capable of ensuring its own development and destiny.

Robert Bourassa, Quebec Premier, responding to the collapse of the Meech Lake Accord, 22 June 1990, quoted in *Maclean's*, 24 Dec. 1990.

I think the Tories got the wrong end of the stick, as usual. Instead of declaring Quebec a "distinct society," they should just declare the rest of Canada an "indistinct society." That would confirm what everybody thinks of us anyway.

Mordecai Richler, commentator, "The People Speak," *The Globe and Mail*, 25 Sept. 1991.

We want to be recognized as a distinct society, too. If the government is willing to recognize the distinct society in Quebec and give it powers to preserve and protect their culture... why can't the same treatment be given to us.

Elijah Harper, Cree and Manitoba M.P.P., quoted by Donald Campbell in the *Winnipeg Free Press*, 25 Sept. 1991.

Distinct society—I could care less! As far as I'm concerned, it's irrelevant.... Quebec is a global society!

Léon Dion, political scientist, testifying before an Ottawa committee, 10 Dec. 1991, quoted by Graham Fraser in *The Globe and Mail* the following day.

Thanks to the miracle of modern cookery, we have "assymetrical federalism." It has meat and potatoes and the same thin gruel it had before—and I call it stew.

Clayton C. Ruby, attorney, referring to the catchphrase assymetrical federalism (euphemism of the year 1992 for distinct society, separate status, Two Canadas, etc.; associated with the so-called Canada Round of the Mulroney administration's constitutional reform package introduced late in 1991), Letters to the Editor, *The Globe and Mail*, 7 Feb. 1992.

Who knows if in fifty years from now, as its thriving Asian population keeps expanding, British Columbia wouldn't become the most "distinct" of all provinces.

Lysiane Gagnon, columnist, "Inside Quebec," *The Globe and Mail*, 8 Aug. 1992.

A society cannot be distinct in relation to another, in fact, without that other one being distinct in relation to the first.

Pierre Elliott Trudeau, former Prime Minister, "Trudeau Speaks Out," *Maclean's*, 28 Sept. 1992.

The irony is that Quebec's difficulties are the same as Canada's. The more it tries to have a loose, functional definition of its political community, the less distinct it gets. The more it relies on a hard-core definition of what constitutes the Quebec nation, the more it paints itself into an ethnic corner from which it prides itself it has escaped.

Stephen Schecter, essayist, *Zen and the Art of Post-Modern Canada* (1993).

Though Quebec nationalism insisted on separation because it claimed to be a "distinct society," it actually emerged as a significant force precisely when Quebec ceased to be the "distinct society" it had so patently and unmistakably been until the 1960s.

Eric Hobsbaum, English historian, *Age of Extremes: The Short Twentieth Century 1914–1991* (1994).

We must recognize that Quebec's language, its culture and institutions make it a distinct society.

Jean Chrétien, Prime Minister, address to Quebec and the nation, CBC-TV, 25 Oct. 1995.

Make "Distinct" Extinct

Slogan of the Toronto group **Canadians Against Distinct Society Status**, advertisement, *The Globe and Mail*, 27 Nov. 1996.

The notion of "distinct society" actually does more to divide Quebeckers than separation itself.

Guy Bertrand, intervenor in the federal appeal to the Supreme Court of Canada to study the legality of a unilateral declaration of Quebec independence, open letter to New Brunswick Premier Frank McKenna, "Commentary," *The Globe and Mail*, 11 Sept. 1997.

Consequently, the Legislature and Government of Quebec have a role to protect and develop the unique character of Quebec society within Canada.

Resolution of nine of the country's Prime Ministers—the conference was boycotted by Quebec Premier Lucien Bouchard—at a meeting in Calgary, 14 Sept. 1997, quoted by Edison Stewart in *The Toronto Star* the following day.

Canadians are not revolutionaries: they are rebels and reformers. And in spite of our growing intimacy with American commerce and culture, Canada remains a distinct society on the northern half of the North American continent.

Michael Adams, pollster, *Sex in the Snow: Canadian Social Values at the End of the Millennium* (1997).

The most distinct societies in all of North America are in Newfoundland and Labrador and Quebec. And what is the Newfoundland and Labrador experience? That you can be different, you can be distinct, you can have a great love and a great passion for your country, but an equal love and passion for your own people and your province and you don't have to choose between the two.

Brian Tobin, Newfoundland Premier, speaking on the occasion of the fiftieth anniversary of Newfoundland entering Confederation, 31 March 1999, St. John's, Nfld., quoted by Graeme Hamilton in the *National Post*, 1 April 1999.

DIVERSITY

Canada's very nature is contained in the fact that it has as many faces as a Buddhist deity. Our identity crisis really seems to lie in an attempt to cling to the illusion that uniformity and unity are the same thing and that they are equally desirable—neither of which, of course, is true.

George Woodcock, author and critic, *The Canadians* (1979).

Our monoculture is another form of suicide; diversity gives us survival.

Rosalie Bertell, scientist and social activist, "Radioactivity: No Immediate Danger?" *Ms.*, Sept.–Oct. 1991.

DIVORCE

In the last couple of decades ... people often went back and forth to the divorce court the way a tongue returns to a sore tooth time and time again, just to see if it still hurts and finds that, in fact, it does.

Merle Shain, essayist, *Courage My Love: A Book to Light an Honest Path* (1988).

One of the ironies of marriage today is that it is about love and we have forgotten the economic union—until there's a divorce.

Alan Mirabelli, representative, Vanier Institute of the Family, quoted by Vivian Smith in "Fifth Column," *The Globe and Mail*, 17 Dec. 1992.

A goodwill divorce is like having all your teeth extracted and having to smile.

Irena F. Karafilly, aphorist, "Thoughts for the Millennium from A to Z," *The Montreal Gazette*, 30 Dec. 1999.

DOGS See also ANIMALS

Man, strong as he was, might capture him, but man with all his magic would never break him. Not if he gave his life in fighting man's bending him to his will.

Lines from **Jack O'Brien**'s popular children's book *Silver Chief: Dog of the North* (1933).

... but what if, say, it was *dogs* and not people who had invented these things. How would *dogs* express their essential dogginess with inventions? Would they build space stations shaped like big bones that orbited the earth?

Thoughts of the narrator of **Douglas Coupland**'s novel *Life after God* (1994).

Forget the Dog / Watch out for the Kids

Sign on the porch of a house in Kitchener, Ont., April 1998.

DOMINION See also CANADA, CONFEDERATION, DOMINION DAY

His dominion shall be from sea to sea.

That the Dominion of Canada should be the title and name of the new country was the recommendation of **Samuel Leonard Tilley** at the pre-Confederation conference in London, England, Dec. 1866. He found the word dominion in the King James version of the Bible: "His dominion shall be from sea to sea" (Zechariah 9:10); "He shall have dominion also from sea to sea" (Psalm 72:8). The favoured title had been Kingdom, but it was deemed monarchical and possibly offensive to American republican sentiment.

Dominion as the title of a country is a distinctively Canadian word. It is the only distinctive word we have contributed to political terminology. Other countries throughout the Commonwealth borrowed it from us.

Eugene Forsey, historian, expressing a preference for Dominion Day rather than Canada Day, Letters to the Editor, *The Globe and Mail*, 16 July 1982.

Postmodern Dominion

Coinage of cultural commentator **Robert Fulford** at a conference on citizenship, Ottawa, Jan. 1992. The words imply that Canada is a notional state rather than a national state. "Fulford was the first, I believe, to use the term to describe Canada's national condition. His bracketing of the hot-button word with the archaic 'Dominion' especially caught my fancy." So noted Richard Gwyn in *Nationalism without Walls* (1995). Fulford's address appeared in *Belonging: The Meaning and Future of Canadian Citizenship* (1993) edited by William Kaplan.

DOMINION DAY See also DOMINION, HOLIDAYS

Dominion Day celebrates one of the greatest feats of modern history: the making of a new nation, and a new kind of nation, by a handful of people of differing origins, differing languages, differing creeds, differing histories, and differing interests, and in the face of obstacles that might well have daunted the boldest and most resolute statesmen. Everything was against them.

Eugene Forsey, constitutional authority, address delivered on 19 June 1956, quoted by Gordon Towers in the House of Commons, 13 March 1979.

Give us back Dominion Day, give us back the word "Dominion."

Michael Valpy, columnist, *The Globe and Mail*, 1 July 1994. Dominion Day—the anniversary of Confederation, 1 July—was renamed Canada Day on 9 July 1982.

The assault on "Dominion" especially was characterized by bad law, bad history, bad logic.... The perpetrators of this performance did almost all their work darkly, at dead of night.... Finally they changed the name of "Dominion Day" by Act of Parliament—put through the House of Commons by something very close to sneak-thievery, when it is pretty certain there was not even a quorum.

Eugene Forsey, constitutional specialist, *A Life on the Fringe: The Memoirs of Eugene Forsey* (1990).

We are the only country in the world, so far as I know, to use the word to describe our own confederation, and unquestionably we are the most significant country to do so. What folly moved a handful of parliamentarians to trash this splendid title in favour of "Canada Day"—only one letter removed from the name of a soft drink—must remain one of the inexplicable lunacies of a democratic system temporarily running to seed.

Robertson Davies, man-of-letters, on the word dominion and Canada Day, Letters to the Editor, *The Globe and Mail*, 10 July 1993.

DONATIONS see also CHARITY

A donation that is seen and managed as an investment is a much more dynamic and productive activity than a simple donation per se.

A.L. Flood, chief, Canadian Imperial Bank of Commerce, address, *New Trends in Corporate Giving*, 25 April 1996, quoted in *National and Global Perspectives*, Autumn 1996.

DOUBT See also BELIEF

Never believe what you cannot doubt.

Robin Skelton, poet and aphorist, *A Devious Dictionary* (1991).

When in doubt, mumble.

Maxim of **James H. Boren**, aphorist, quoted by Stewart MacLeod in *Maclean's*, 30 March 1992.

The only human activity capable of controlling the use of power in a positive way.

John Ralston Saul, author, defining doubt, *The Doubter's Companion: A Dictionary of Aggressive Common Sense* (1994).

DOUKHOBORS

Canada is very slowly drawing together the elements of an enduring nationality, and as a factor in this evolution they will certainly contribute a valuable influence from their sturdy spirituality.

Albert E.S. Smythe, editor, "The Doukhobors," *The Lamp: A Theosophical Monthly*, Volume II, 15 Oct. 1899.

Tommy declared that he would become a Doukhobor to please her, but she said something about the inability of Ethiopians to change their skin.

Line about young lovers in **John Buchan**'s story "A Lucid Interval," *The Moon Endureth* (1912)

DREAMS

I know not if Religion has ever any Share in what they generally call *the Festival of Dreams*, and which the Iroquois, and some others, have more properly called *the turning of the Brain*. This is a Kind of *Bacchanal*, which commonly lasts fifteen Days, and is celebrated about the End of Winter.

Pierre-François-Xavier de Charlevoix, historian, *A Voyage to North-America: Undertaken by Command of the Present King of France* (1766).

And the story is told / Of human veins and pulses, / Of eternal pathways of fire, / Of dreams that survive the night, / Of doors held ajar in storms.

E.J. Pratt, poet, concluding lines of "Newfoundland" (1923), *E.J. Pratt: Complete Poems* (1989) edited by Sandra Djwa and R.G. Moyles.

The Indian lives by dreams, is inspired by them, guided by them—we are mystics if we are anything.

Grey Owl, author and naturalist, interviewed by R.E. Knowles in *The Toronto Star*, 2 March 1936.

Canadians should learn to express their dreams for the future in the terms of the actual future facing their land and their own selves and descendants.

Donald A. Wollheim, U.S. editor, "Whither Canadian Fantasy?" *Uncanny Tales*, Dec. 1942.

Our dreams are all we own.

Words engraved on the hearthstone of the farmhouse known as Owl Pen by versifier **Kenneth McNeill Wells** in *The Owl Pen* (1947).

And who knows some day, maybe, our dreams will all come true.

Words of the theme song of **Mart Kenny** and His Western Gentlemen, formed in 1931.

One night a man had a dream. He dreamed he was walking along the beach with the Lord. Across the sky flashed scenes from his life.

Opening lines of the prose poem "Footprints" written by **Margaret Fishback Powers**, Thanksgiving 1964, Echo Lake Youth Camp, Kingston, reproduced in *Powers' Footprints: The Story Behind the Poem that Inspired Millions* (1993).

No one goes after her dream—whether it's in France or across the street—without changing.

Sheila Kieran, writer, "The Day I Ran Away to Paris," *Chatelaine*, Oct. 1974.

Has there ever in history been another nation of people who collectively fantasized about the great things they could accomplish if only they had the luck to live somewhere else.

Martin Knelman, critic, writing in *Saturday Night*, April 1980.

Everything flies away; only dreams remain.

Chapter heading of **Roch Carrier**'s novel *Heartbreaks along the Road* (1987) translated by Sheila Fischman.

I think I'm just the average person who had the very good fortune to realize his own dreams.

Rick Hansen, wheelchair athlete and fund-raiser for the Man in Motion world-wide tour, receiving the Order of Canada, Ottawa, 29 March 1988, quoted in *The Toronto Star* the following day.

But I think the humorist vision sees things in proportion because it sees them out of proportion. In other words the customary proportions of things are somehow all wrong. Perhaps that's why we have dreams to remind us every night that we've spent the previous day in a world of petrified nonsense.

Northrop Frye, cultural critic, Afterword, *Daymares: Selected Fictions and Dreams* (1991) by Robert Zend.

What is real? What is imaginary? Half of our life is lived in dreams.

Ludwig Zeller, poet and artist, quoted by Beatriz Zeller, editor of *Focus on Ludwig Zeller, Poet and Artist* (1991).

One could dream big dreams in this vast continental landscape, its eastern shore looking across to Europe, and its western shore home to vessels that sailed to the Orient, but it was safest to keep them to oneself, or scale them down and introduce them to others with a deprecating remark.

Jill Ker Conway, Australian-born, American-educated historian and memoirist who taught at the University of Toronto from 1964 to 1975, *True North: A Memoir* (1994).

A border separates our peoples, but there are no boundaries to our common dreams.

Bill Clinton, U.S. President, address, joint sitting of the House of Commons and the Senate of Canada, Ottawa, Senate Debates, 23 Feb. 1995.

I believe that when you have a passion or a dream in your life, nothing can stop you or even slow you down. It becomes the fuel of your life, the sunshine in your day.

Sylvie Frechette, synchronized swimmer, quoted by Peter Urs Bender in *Leadership from Within* (1997) with Eric Hellman.

DRESS See FASHION

DRINKING See also ALCOHOL, BEER, FOOD & DRINK, WINE

The next Sunday night, when we ordered only beer, the waiter told us that he was not permitted to serve beer without food. When he saw how disappointed we looked, he suggested, "Why don't you have a ham sandwich?" So we ordered one. The waiter picked up a sandwich, slightly yellow with age, from a neighbouring table, brought it to us, and said, "Now, what do you want to drink?" A little while later the same "prop" sandwich was transferred to another table.

Otto Hahn, scientist, referring to Quebec's liquor laws as they affected a Sunday dinner with drinks, Windsor Hotel, Montreal, *Otto Hahn: A Scientific Autobiography* (1966) edited by Willy Ley. Hahn, the German-born physicist, worked under Ernest Rutherford at McGill University's Macdonald Physics Building between Fall 1905 and Summer 1906.

A drunkard / likes to be drunk. / An alcoholic / can't stand to be sober.

Alden Nowlan, poet and aphorist, "Scratchings," *I'm a Stranger Here Myself* (1974).

Most Canadians still think drinking is the stuff of comedy.

Line from **Edward Phillips**' novel *Sunday Best* (1990).

There's hardly a village left in Canada, even the traditional Prairie whistle stop, which doesn't have an espresso bar in the shadow of its grain elevator.

James Barber, chef, *Peasant's Choice: More of the Best from The Urban Peasant* (1994).

DRUG TRADE

The extent to which any particular drug is to be deemed to be undesirable will depend upon its relative potential harm, both personal and social.

Gerald LeDain, dean of law, Chairman of the Royal Commission on the Non-Medical Use of Drugs, *Interim Report*, 15 May 1970.

Tobacco is probably our most dangerous drug. It kills more of us than all the others combined and doubled.

Neil Boyd, criminologist, *High Society: Legal and Illegal Drugs in Canada* (1991).

I was offered pot on occasion. I preferred corned beef.

Hugh Segal, Conservative adviser, April 1993, responding to reporters, quoted by David Olive in *Canadian Political Babble* (1993).

DUPLESSIS, MAURICE See also POLITICIANS

We do not want the Quebec legislature to be towed by Ottawa. It must be driven by the people of Quebec.

Translation of the inscription on the base of the statue of Quebec Premier **Maurice Duplessis** on the grounds of the National Assembly, Quebec City. The sentences come from a speech he delivered in the National Assembly in 1944.

The bishops eat from my hand.

Attributed to **Maurice Duplessis**, Premier of Quebec (with one break) from 1936 to 1959. According to Conrad Black in *Duplessis* (1977), this remark is "possibly Duplessis's most famous line of all, frequently uttered in the Assembly and in conversation, but difficult to find in contemporary newspapers. Everyone who knew Duplessis remembers this."

Circonférences

French neologism that means "going around in circles" created by Quebec Premier **Maurice Duplessis** to characterize the dominion-provincial conferences of the 1950s, according to Conrad Black, "Canada," *The Globe and Mail*, 7 Nov. 1995.

On veut notre butin.

Attributed to former Quebec Premier **Maurice Duplessis** by Ingrid Peritz and Tu Thanh Ha, "Column One," *The Globe and Mail*, 17 Nov. 1998. It means "Give us our booty" or "Give us our spoils" or "Give us our plunder."

Co-operation Always, Assimilation Never.

Translation of the inscription on the pediment of statue erected to honour Maurice Duplessis, Trois-Rivières, Que., as noted by Robert McKenzie, "Quebec Honours 'Le Chef,'" *The Toronto Star*, 7 Sept. 1999.

DUTY See also RESPONSIBILITY

My slogan, "Do the duty closest to me."

Jack Miner, conservationist, *Jack Miner on Current Topics* (1929).

DYING WORDS See also DEATH, EPITAPHS

Children, children, look to yourselves, the world is mad....

Norman McLeod, missionary and colonist who in 1851 led Cape Breton Islanders first to Australia and then to Waipu, N.Z., dying words, 14 March 1866, quoted by Flora McPherson in *Watchman against the World* (1993).

Keep the Festival alive!

Louise Manny, folklorist, who in Sept. 1957 founded the Miramichi Folk Festival, dying words and inscription on the memorial raised in her honour in the City Park, Newcastle, N.B., noted in Aug. 1991.

Future generations will weep for us; they'll call us the Dark Ages.

Clarence Meredith Hincks, founder of the Mental Health movement in Canada, dying words, Toronto, 17 Dec. 1964, quoted by Robert Weil, "Take a Look Back, Doctor," *The Medical Post*, 16 July 1996.

I'm afraid to die, but it pains too much to live.

Samuel Bronfman, founder of the Seagram whisky empire, dying words, addressed to his physician, Montreal, 10 July 1971, quoted by Michael R. Marrus in *Mr. Sam: The Life and Times of Samuel Bronfman* (1991).

The game is just about over.

Dick Beddoes, sports commentator, Toronto, 22 Aug. 1991, dying words quoted in his obituary by Milt Dunnell in *The Globe and Mail*, 26 Aug. 1991.

Life is hell, most people are bastards, and everything is bullshit.

George Black, financier, last words to his son Conrad Black before the former's fatal fall from a banister, quoted by Jennifer Wells in *The Globe and Mail's Report on Business Magazine*, Dec. 1993.

Huh-Lo!... Thanks for everything and so long for now.

With these words newspaperman and broadcaster **Clyde Gilmour** opened and closed his weekly program *Gilmour's Albums*, carried by CBC Radio for 40 years and 8 months. His last program, recorded in July 1997 was rebroadcast on *As It Happens* on the day of his death, 7 Nov. 1997.

E

EARTH

With satellite and electronic antennae as probes, the planet ceases in a way to be the human environment and becomes a satellite itself—a probe into space, creating new space and environments for the planet.

Marshall McLuhan, communications pioneer, "Address at Vision 65" (1966), *The Essential McLuhan* (1995) edited by Eric McLuhan and Frank Zingrone.

Earth, planet wandering in space, insignificant sphere on the shore of infinity, unique perhaps with your cargo of sufferings and aspirations, perhaps the sole speck in the universe conscious of your destiny and for that reason tragic,—what will become of you, what will become of us all?

Gabrielle Roy, author, *Man and His World* (1967) edited by Guy Robert.

God gave a piece of this darn world to every race of people, and this land happened to be our land. We Indians own this continent from the tip of South America to the North Pole.

James Gosnell, President, Nisga'a Tribal Council of B.C., address, National Association of Indian Chiefs, Penticton, B.C., April 1982, quoted in *The Toronto Star*, 2 May 1982.

Earth is but a mote of dust adrift in the ocean of space. The fact that Earth harbours creatures who are able to contemplate their place in the cosmic scheme must make our dust speck at least a little special.

Terence Dickinson, Preface, *NightWatch: An Equinox Guide to Viewing the Universe* (1983, 1989).

When you see Earth from space, it is small. It is a planet to explore.

Roberta Bondar, astronaut aboard the *Discovery*, 22–30 Jan. 1992, *Maclean's*, 24 Feb. 1992.

You begin to understand that this earth we live on—once thought insensate, inanimate, dead by scientists, theologians and such—has an emotional, psychological and spiritual life every bit as complex as that of the most complex, sensitive and intelligent of individuals.

Tomson Highway, playwright, "What a Certain Visionary Once Said," "Bank of Montreal: A Portrait of Canada," *Saturday Night*, May 1992.

We usually cherish things that are unique. Why not the Earth?

Roberta Bondar, astronaut, *Touching the Earth* (1994).

The most important thing is to serve the Earth, and to take a biocentric viewpoint, not an anthropocentric viewpoint of things.

Paul Watson, Sea Shepherd, interviewed by Alexander Blair-Ewart in *Mindfire: Dialogues in the Other Future* (1995).

There are no passengers on Spaceship Earth. We are all crew.

Marshall McLuhan, communications pioneer, quoted on the television documentary *Space Suite* (NASA/York University, 1998) shown on TVO, 4 Nov. 1998.

EASTER See HOLIDAYS

EATON'S

Icons belong in museums and churches, not shopping malls.

Sean Silcoff, journalist, on the collapse of the department-store empire established by Timothy Eaton in 1869, "Life after Eaton's," *Canadian Business*, 10 Sept. 1999.

ECOLOGY See also ENVIRONMENTALISM, GREENPEACE, NATURE, WILDERNESS, WILDLIFE

We are now in a struggle to retain the land. I believe that we are not only fighting for the land, but also for the animals living on it, the trees, the barren lands. We are fighting for the wind, the moon, sun and stars to keep on shining down. Only the Inuit can stand up....

Willie Thrasher, Inuit musician, "Willie Thrasher Tells about His Music" (1976), quoted by Penny Petrone in *Northern Voices: Inuit Writing in English* (1988).

Man is an inescapable part of all nature, that its welfare is his welfare, that to survive he cannot continue acting and regarding himself as a spectator looking on from somewhere outside.

Fred Bodsworth, naturalist and novelist, *Canada Writes: The Members' Book of the Writers' Union of Canada* (1977) edited by K.A. Hamilton.

The planet does not need "saving." It has periodically been coming apart—only to be pasted together again—since the proverbial Garden of Eden. Fundamentally, the Earth is in orbit within a self-correcting stable-state environment—the solar system. Our responsibility is to help it self-correct, and I believe we have the ability to do so.

Frank Feather, futurologist, *G-Forces: Reinventing the World—The 35 Global Forces Restructuring Our World* (1989).

The new culture, following the lead of quantum science, will be imbued with a sense of the interconnectedness of everything. It is not the individual that is all-important; it is the whole, the immensity, that is Life. We are the leaves on that tree.

James George, former Canadian Ambassador, *Asking for the Earth: Waking up to the Spiritual/Ecological Crisis* (1995).

What can, and I think must, be discussed and disseminated is a world-view that is both traditional and scientific, one that has either been forgotten or not yet fully discovered, on the basis of which a new culture can be built in time to save our planet from becoming a wasteland because of mindless and conscienceless human behaviour, which we can legitimately call sleep.

James George, former Canadian Ambassador, *Asking for the Earth: Waking up to the Spiritual/Ecological Crisis* (1995).

ECONOMICS See also ECONOMY, CANADIAN; FINANCE; INFLATION; RECESSION; RESOURCES

Forty years of hard work on economics has pretty well removed all the ideas I ever had about it. I think the whole science is a wreck and has got to be built up again.

Stephen Leacock, humorist, Preface, *Hellements of Hickonomics in Hiccoughs of Verse: Done in Our Social Planning Mill* (1936).

In the unplanned society, it's dog eat dog; in the planned society, both of them starve to death.

Richard Needham, columnist, "A Writer's World," *The Globe and Mail*, 28 Jan. 1977.

Economy has broken away from the reins of polity.

Michael Ignatieff, essayist, *The Needs of Strangers* (1985).

The rule will often be here reiterated: Financial genius is before the fall.

John Kenneth Galbraith, economist and essayist, *A Short History of Financial Euphoria* (1990, 1993). Galbraith first iterated "the oldest rule of Wall Street" in an article in the *Atlantic* in 1987.

If economics is sovereign, there is no right and wrong.

Eric Kierans and **Walter Stewart**, economist and writer, *Wrong End of the Rainbow: The Collapse of Free Enterprise in Canada* (1988).

Economics, n. A study of the incomprehensible with a view to rendering it unintelligible, happily with no impact on the subject.

David Olive, business commentator, *White Knights and Poison Pills: A Cynic's Dictionary of Business Jargon* (1990).

A large number of America's economic problems, and those of the West, could be solved by shutting down the Chicago School of Economics.

John Ralston Saul, author, *The Doubter's Companion: A Dictionary of Aggressive Common Sense* (1994).

If economists were doctors, they would today be mired in malpractice suits.

John Ralston Saul, author, *The Unconscious Civilization* (1995).

Economists can talk about globalization and technological change in the abstract all they want, but governments must not. We cannot treat the restructuring we are all living through as if it were some mechanical concept of academic interest only. It is a phenomenon with very real human consequences.

Paul Martin Jr., Minister of Finance, budget speech, House of Commons, 18 Feb. 1997.

Due to the Economy Our Dresses Cost as Much as $6.00 / Goodwill

Message on a billboard for the charity outlet **Goodwill Services**, Toronto, 17 Aug. 1997.

A country that isn't fair to its rich will soon become too broke to be fair to its poor.

Frank Ogden, futurologist, aphorism on business card, 7 March 2000.

ECONOMICS, CANADIAN See also ECONOMICS

Pray excuse my not having sooner answered your letter, as my whole spare time and thoughts were occupied with poor Canada....

John Stuart Mill, political economist, writing to John Hill Burton from India House, 23 Jan. 1838, *The Early Letters of John Stuart Mill* (1963), edited by John M. Robson, Volume XII of the "Collected Works of John Stuart Mill."

Our first job must be to see that our own house is in order.

Walter L. Gordon, statesman, *Troubled Canada: The Need for New Domestic Policies* (1961).

Toronto and Montreal are economic suburbs of each other.

Jacques Parizeau, Parti Québécois Minister of Finance, quoted in *The Toronto Star*, 16 Nov. 1976.

A recession is when your neighbour loses his job. A depression is when you lose your job. Economic recovery is when Pierre Trudeau loses his job.

Brian Mulroney, Conservative leader, fundraising speech, Toronto, quoted by Nora McCabe in *The Globe and Mail*, 7 May 1982.

The more Canada's economy is tied to that of our powerful neighbour, the more Canada operates as a branch plant of the American military-industrial complex in a high-tech nuclear age.

Remi J. De Roo, Bishop of Victoria, "Our War Economy and Conversion for Peace," *End the Arms Race: Fund Human Needs: Proceedings of the 1986 Vancouver Centennial Peace and Disarmament Symposium* (1986) edited by Thomas L. Perry and James G. Foulks.

Attempts to restore economic health by cutting back on the public sector are equivalent to the medieval notion of bleeding to cure the patient.

Harold Chorney, political economist, Concordia University, Montreal, quoted in *The Toronto Star*, 21 March 1993.

This is a $700 billion gross domestic product economy. If you believe you can kick start that with a $2 billion investment in sewers, then you believe you can start a 747 with a flashlight battery.

Preston Manning, leader of the Reform Party of Canada, referring to the Liberal job plan, leadership debate, CBC-TV, 4 Oct. 1993, quoted by Rosemary Speirs and David Vienneau in *The Toronto Star* the following day.

I even managed to establish a Canadian tradition—unintentionally. My staff had been told—probably by a shoe manufacturer—that it was tradition for a minister of finance when presenting his first budget to wear a new pair of shoes. I fell for it. So did the press, which gave enormous publicity to my new shoes. About five years ago an investivative journalist, searching for the origins of the tradition that most of my successors followed, could not find that any of my predecessors as minister of finance had worn new shoes at budget time. Was it traditional? Perhaps not in 1965. It is now, after more than a quarter of a century.

Mitchell Sharp, former Minister of Finance and Minister of External Affairs, *Which Reminds Me...: A Memoir* (1994).

Such abstract concepts as knowledge, design and service look unfamiliar to those who have traditionally seen Canada as a land of rocks, trees and cyclical performance.

Deirdre McMurdy, columnist, "The Bottom Line," *Maclean's*, 7 Feb. 1994.

Remember that this is not inevitable. I call it the TINA Syndrome—"There Is No Alternative." To say that is intellectual terrorism, and I deeply object to it. I hope you do too.

Maude Barlow, chair, Council of Canadians, address, referring to cuts to culture and the arts in the interests of debt and deficit reduction, Toronto Theatre Alliance, 11 Dec. 1995, quoted by H.J. Kirchhoff in *The Globe and Mail* the following day.

The more money you have, the more intolerable you find life in Canada.

Charles Gordon, columnist, citing a paradox of the Canadian rich, *The Edmonton Journal*, 28 March 1999, as quoted by Mel Hurtig in *Pay the Rent or Feed the Kids* (1999).

EDITORS See also PUBLISHING

The only writers permitted use of the word "we" around here are editorial writers and people with tapeworms.

H. Napier Moore, editor of *Maclean's*, offering guidelines in the 1930s to new recruit Lotta Dempsey who recalled it in her memoirs, *No Life for a Lady* (1976).

Book editors are different from newspaper editors. Book editors make a writer, newspaper editors ruin one.

Peter Worthington, newspaperman, quoted by Beverley Slopen in *The Toronto Star*, 7 Oct. 1984.

The ideal anthologist's coat of arms should show a pair of eyeglasses, couchant, to symbolize the act of reading; a pencil, rampant, representing the passion for scribbling on margins; and the motto *de gustibus non disputandum*—there's no accounting for taste.

Alberto Manguel, anthologist, "Sweet Are the Uses of Anthology," *The New York Times Book Review*, 23 Aug. 1987. In a professional vein, he added, "An anthologist is a reader with a purpose."

No editors of ours have ever retired because of interference from my associates or me.

Conrad Black, capitalist, "Letter of the Day" Conrad Black's Response to the CBC," *The Hamilton Spectator*, 26 Oct. 1996.

EDMONTON See also ALBERTA

Edmonton, the most northerly city in Canada, is described as "a city with no past, some present, and an illimitable future."

Robert Donald, newspaperman, *The Imperial Press Conference in Canada* (1921).

My beloved Edmonton.

Attributed to **Pierre Elliott Trudeau**, Ottawa, 25 May 1983.

I don't want Edmonton to grow too big. If it grows too big it might lose some of its friendliness. People might not participate as much. And you might not be able to see the sky, and Edmonton is not Edmonton if you can't see the sky.

Joe Shoctor, benefactor and booster, quoted by Kenneth Bagnell in "Northern Light," *The Imperial Oil Review*, Winter, 1989.

Edmonton: here the world rests outside the glass of cold, winter speculations.

Aritha van Herk, novelist, *Places Far from Ellesmere: A Geografictione: Explorations on Site* (1990).

The biggest difference between L.A. and Edmonton was that instead of people looking at me, I was looking at them.

Wayne Gretzky, hockey player, referring to the effect of his transfer from Edmonton to Los Angeles (or "Hockeywood"), *Gretzky: An Autobiography* (1990) with Rick Reilly.

Edmonton is a lot like Moscow... without the charm.

Alan Hustak, Montreal journalist, one-time resident of Calgary, characteristic remark, Oct. 1991.

The capital of Alberta is a city you come from, not a place to visit, unless you happen to have relatives there or an interest in an oil well nearby.

Mordecai Richler, novelist and controversialist, *Oh Canada! Oh Quebec! Requiem for a Divided Country* (1992).

Edmonton isn't exactly the end of the world. But you can see it from there.

Ralph Klein, former mayor of Calgary and premier-elect of Alberta, quoted by Miro Cernetig in "Edmonton," *The Globe and Mail*, 10 Dec. 1992.

Seven thousand eight hundred miles from the Land of Khem lies the city of Edmonton.

Jonathan Cott, U.S. author, *Isis and Osiris: Exploring the Goddess Myth* (1994). Land of Khem is an ancient reference to Egypt. Cott is tracing the global dissemination of the myth of Isis and Osiris in modern times.

I must say it's really great to be in this part of Canada where we've never been before. I thought it was going to be a lot colder than this.

Mick Jagger, member of The Rolling Stones rock band, referring to their concert in Edmonton,

4 Oct. 1994, quoted by Gwen Dambrofsky in the *Winnipeg Free Press*, 6 Oct. 1994.

I very much like the *size* of Edmonton... not too big... not too small. But, most of all, I have always loved the strong sense of community we have had, the civility, the compassion, the thousands of good, altruistic, socially concerned people I have met here over the years.

Mel Hurtig, nationalist, address, awards dinner, Edmonton, 17 Sept. 1997.

EDUCATION

See also COLLEGES & UNIVERSITIES; EDUCATION, CANADIAN; HUMANITIES; LEARNING; SCHOOLS; SCIENCE & SCIENTISTS; TEACHERS & TEACHING; TECHNOLOGY

What is a student but a lover courting a fickle mistress who ever eludes his grasp?

Sir William Osler, physician and professor, quoted by William Bennett Bean in *Sir William Osler: Aphorisms from His Bedside Teachings and Writings* (1950).

Whoever ceases to be a student has never been a student.

George Iles, aphorist, *Canadian Stories: Together with... Jottings from a Note-Book* (1918).

Higher education—ah yes, that is what teaches you to cinch the argument by calling your opponent a fascist.

Richard Needham, newspaper columnist, *The Wit and Wisdom of Richard Needham* (1977).

That which cannot be graded is rarely taught.

Robin Skelton, poet and aphorist, *A Devious Dictionary* (1991).

Learning a living.

This phrase, a variant of "earning a living," was used by communications pioneer **Marshall McLuhan** in 1957, according to Philippe Dean Gigantes in *The Road Apart* (1990).

How do I know that you won't indoctrinate us?

Protest of a first-year student in her introductory philosophy course, Concordia College, University of Alberta, noted by Gary Colwell in *You Won't Believe This, but..." Responding to Student Complaints and Excuses* (1996).

The trouble with a cheap specialized education is that you never stop paying for it.

Marshall McLuhan, communications pioneer, quoted by Richard J. Schoeck in *Who Was Marshall McLuhan?* (1994) edited by Barrington Nevitt and Maurice McLuhan.

If you don't have an education, you really have to use your brains.

Attributed to a philosophical-minded New York cab driver in 1967 by adult educator J. Roby Kidd, as recalled by John O'Leary of Frontier College in Dec. 1997.

Education on all levels has to move from packaging to probing, from the mere conveying of data to the experimental discovering of new dimensions of experience. The search will have to be for patterns of experience and discovery of principles of organization which have universal application, not for facts.

Marshall McLuhan, communications pioneer, "Electronics and the Psychic Drop-Out" (1970), *This Book Is About Schools* (1970) edited by Satu Repo.

There are no courses in remedial metaphor.

Northrop Frye, cultural critic, reacting to the speech of an educator who is described as being fluent without being articulate and cannot break out of "an armour of ready-made phrases," *The Stubborn Structure* (1970).

Again, I have always tended to distrust conceptions of teaching which regarded it as a personal encounter between teacher and taught. It seems to me that the authority of the subject being taught is supreme over both teacher and student.

Northrop Frye, cultural critic, "The Critic and the Writer," address, Learned Societies, McGill University, Montreal, May 1972, *Northrop Frye Newsletter*, Winter 1991–92.

The purpose of education is to instill a decent apprehension of one's ignorance.

Eric Nicol, humorist, *Letters to My Son* (1974).

Schooling you get in the schoolroom. Education you get in the poolroom.

Ed Mirvish, self-educated merchandiser, quoted by George Gamester in *The Toronto Star*, 23 June 1977.

Is it a sin to be rude to people who are in need of a rude awakening?

Ara Baliozian, writer and teacher, *Portrait of a Genius and Other Essays* (1980).

Let me first say that the educated person, in my lexicon, is one who has a tolerance for ambiguity and a capacity to countenance a multitude of viewpoints.

Stanley R. Barrett, sociologist, *Is God a Racist? The Right Wing in Canada* (1987).

Humanity, alone of all organisms, has elected to transform its environment instead of simply adapting to it, and so only human beings have a lifelong commitment to experiment, trial and error, uncertainty, and all the other burdens of continuing knowledge.

Northrop Frye, cultural critic, "Some Reflections on Life and Habit" (1988), *Myth and Metaphor: Selected Essays, 1974–1988*. Charlottesville, N.C.: University of Virginia, 1990. Edited by Robert D. Denham.

In education the appetite does indeed grow with eating. I have never known anyone to abandon study because they knew too much.

John C. Polanyi, scientist, "No Genuine Ivory Tower Is Ever Irrelevant," *The Vancouver Sun*, 9 Sept. 1989.

When teachers disagree the student learns.

Robin Skelton, poet and aphorist, *A Devious Dictionary* (1991).

If schools were factories, we would have closed them ten years ago because they're not producing a saleable product.

Frank Ogden, futurologist, characteristic remark, April 1991.

A good modern education is essential, to nurture the body, starve the mind, and shrivel the soul.

Maurus E. Mallon, aphorist, observation, 29 July 1992.

The first school had a hearth and was called home.

Andrew Nikiforuk, education writer, *School's Out: The Catastrophe in Public Education and What We Can Do About It* (1993).

If you think training won't get you a job, try ignorance.

Arthur Kroeger, former deputy minister of employment and immigration, quoted in *The Globe and Mail*, 26 Jan. 1994.

I Touch the Future—I Teach

Message on a bumpersticker reported by advertising guru Jerry Goodis, Toronto, Jan. 1995.

In Singapore schooling isn't even compulsory, yet everyone wants to go to school. Why?

Frank Ogden, futurologist, "Constructive Destruction Will Let in the Future," *"As Prime Minister, I Would . . ." Canada's Brightest offer Innovative Solutions for a More Prosperous and United Country: Volume Two* (1996) with a foreword by Frank Stronach.

If the public was informed about what's going on in our schools, they'd burn down the Ministry of Education and shoot everybody in it.

Harry Jiles, founder of two private schools, The Toronto French School in 1962 and the Giles School in 1989, quoted by Jerry Amernic in the *National Post*, 19 Feb. 2000.

EDUCATION, CANADIAN

See also EDUCATION

Its school system, founded on the Massachusetts plan, is one of the best and most comprehensive in the world.

Walt Whitman, American poet, visitor to Ontario and Quebec in Summer 1880, "Notes for a Lecture," 14 Aug. 1880, Hamilton, Ont., *Walt Whitman's Diary in Canada* (1904) edited by W.S. Kennedy. On his visit to London, Ont., Whitman encountered the pious belief that Ontario's system of public primary and secondary schools was "one of the best" if not "the best" in the world. The myth persists: "There is no better public system in the world than in Ontario. . . . If there is a better public system in the world than Ontario's, show me where it is. We'll try to duplicate what is better than ours," wrote Terry Gray, school superintendent, "Full Marks for the School System," *The Globe and Mail*, 8 Sept. 1992.

Whenever and Wherever / People Shall Have Occasion / To Congregate, / Then and There / Shall Be / The Time, Place and Means / Of / Their Education.

Words of the educator **Alfred Fitzpatrick** engraved on the plaque outside Frontier College, which he founded in Toronto in 1899. The plaque reproduces, within its crest, the following unattributed motto: "I Would Not Have the Labourer Sacrified to the Result...Let There Be Worse Cotton and Better Men."

My father who owned the wagon-shop / And grew rich shoeing horses / Sent me to the University of Montreal / I learned nothing and returned home....

Lines from **Edgar Lee Masters**' poem "Percy Bysshe Shelley," *Spoon River Anthology* (1915).

But, oh, another thing: I forgot, in my message to your people, to say this: Let Canada be on guard never to change her system of education—never to tamper with it—it is the best I know in the world.

Charles E. Coughlin, right-wing broadcaster, Shrine of the Little Flower, Royal Oak, Detroit, interviewed by R.E. Knowles, *The Star Weekly*, 6 Jan. 1934.

What I really learned was the meaning of boredom, and I learned that so well that I have never been bored since then.

Judith N. Shklar, Harvard-based political scientist, born in Russia, describing her attendance at a leading private school in Montreal during the Second World War, "A Life of Learning" (1989), *Liberalism without Illusions: Essays on Liberal Theory and the Political Vision of Judith N. Shklar* (1996) edited by Bernard Yack.

How can you teach Milton to a class in heat?

Attributed to cultural critic **Northrop Frye** with respect to teaching English to returned servicemen in the late 1940s and early 1950s, by Edmund Carpenter, "Remembering Explorations," *Canadian Notes & Queries*, Spring 1992.

In brief, Canada educates its young people to be cautious Americans and venturesome Europeans. Is this the golden mean?

Charles E. Phillips, educator, "Education," *The Culture of Contemporary Canada* (1957) edited by Julian Park.

I just got involved more or less gradually. But when I realized that Canada must be the only country in the world where high school kids aren't taught their own literature, then I had to tell them and their teachers about it. I had to tell them what they're missing.

James (Jim) Foley, teacher, organizer of the first Canada Day to celebrate Canadian writing, Port Colborne High School, 1971, quoted by Al Purdy in *Weekend Magazine*, 15 June 1974.

If they had their way, do you think taxi-drivers would be happier with a degree in literature?

Paul Sauvé, Quebec Minister of Youth, quoted by Gérard Pelletier in *Years of Impatience: 1950–1960* (1984).

We no longer have a broad education, only an inflated one.

Robin Skelton, poet and aphorist, *A Devious Dictionary* (1991).

I am really elated to be here. I spent the happiest decade of my life here.

Allan Bloom, academic identified with the University of Chicago, author of *The Closing of the American Mind*, professor of philosophy at the University of Toronto in 1970–79, returning to the same university to deliver a guest lecture, Jan. 1988, quoted in his obituary in *The Toronto Star*, 9 Oct. 1992.

The only way to get a decent high-school education in Canada these days is to go to university.

Charlie McKenzie, concierge, Rhinoceros Party of Canada, quoted by Stewart MacLeod in *Maclean's*, 30 March 1992.

I can remember when I was teaching Sanskrit at the University of Toronto, my greatest fear was that the next day no students would show up. "Why should we?" they would say. "We aren't learning anything worthwhile." I needed them to reappear to validate what I was doing.

Jeffrey Moussaieff Masson, professor-analyst-memoirist, *My Father's Guru: A Journey through Spirituality and Disillusion* (1993).

I was at the Ritz after a long lunch, and I was going to buy some cigars. Bernard Landry was checking his coat—we'd never met—and he said to me, "I hate you, you're a racist." I wasn't really on top of it after this long lunch, and I said, "You're nothing but a provincial bumpkin." And he said: "I have a university degree!"

Mordecai Richler, referring to meeting Quebec's Deputy Premier in Montreal's Ritz Hotel, interviewed by Elizabeth Renzetti, "Literary Lion," *The Globe and Mail,* 27 Sept. 1997.

EFFICIENCY

There is nothing so efficient / as the last match.

Robert Priest, aphorist, *Time Release Poems* (1997).

EFFORT

The only true memorial is the continuation of effort.

William E. Blatz, physician, specialist in child development, quoted by Zena Cherry in *The Globe and Mail,* 2 June 1966.

Be bold / or be bowled over

Robert Priest, aphorist, *Time Release Poems* (1997).

EGYPT

O, the East is but the West, with the sun a little hotter; / And the pine becomes a palm, by the dark Egyptian water; / And the Nile's like many a stream we know, that fills its brimming cup,— / We'll think it is the Ottawa, as we track the batteaux up! / Pull, pull, pull! as we track the batteaux up! / It's easy shooting homeward, when we're at the top!

First verse and refrain of **W.W. Smith**'s song "The Canadians on the Nile" to be sung by the Canadian boatman who rowed to Khartoum to save General "Chinese" Gordon, included by William Douw Lighthall in *Songs of the Great Dominion* (1889).

O mystic Nile! Thy secret yields / Before us; thy most ancient dreams / Are mixed with far Canadian fields / And murmur of Canadian streams.

Verse written by **Charles G.D. Roberts** quoted by Albert E.S. Smythe in *The Lamp: A Theosophical Monthly,* Volume I, Aug. 1895.

EH?

Anglosaxophones may boast their famous four-letter words, but Canada's great little two-letter word "eh?" tops them all when it comes to ubiquity. Neither provincial boundaries nor the Property and Civil Rights section of the B.N.A. Act has been able to stop the relentless spread of "eh?" into every corner of the country.

Mark M. Orkin, linguist, *French Canajan, Hé?* (1975). Orkin went on to note, "Broadly speaking, hé may be used in every life-situation where Canajan 'eh?' is called for. For all practical purposes the two words are interchangeable."

"Not bad, eh?" could well be our national motto. Instead, of course, it is *A Mari usque ad mare*—from sea unto sea.

Peter Gzowski, journalist, *The Private Voice: A Journal of Reflections* (1988).

Eh? could come from the American *huh?,* the British *what?* or *aye?,* or the French *hein.* I think it is a sort of combination of all, as is most of our language.

Marg Meikle, radio personality known as The Answer Lady, *Dear Answer Lady: A Compendium of Astonishing Facts and Arcane Origins for the Passionately Curious and Easily Distracted* (1992).

ELECTIONS See also POLITICS, VOTES

Elections are not won by prayers alone.

Joseph-Israël Tarte, Minister of Public Works, Laurier's "Quebec lieutenant," Liberal election victory of 1896.

Those who are opposed to me are lefties, pinkos, and hamburgers. Anybody without a university education is a hamburger.

Attributed to **Tom Campbell**, Mayor of Vancouver (1967–72), dubbed "Tom Terrific" for his flair for publicity.

I'm glad I won a majority. Now I can go back to being arrogant and telling everyone to fuddle-duddle off.

Attributed to Prime Minister **Pierre Elliott Trudeau** at a celebration party at 24 Sussex Drive, upon re-election in 1974, quoted by Richard Gwyn in *The Toronto Star,* 3 Oct. 1974.

The People's Choice—The candidate the people have been told they have chosen.

Dick Beddoes, sports columnist, *The Globe and Mail,* 8 Oct. 1976.

Every election is a contest between heritage and impulse, as the verities of the past compete with the risks of the future.

Peter C. Newman, columnist, *Maclean's*, 5 Dec. 1988.

One problem with Canadian elections is that they're often all over by the time the program hits the Manitoba border.

Knowlton Nash, news anchor and broadcaster, *Prime Time at Ten: Behind-the-Camera Battles of Canadian TV Journalism* (1987).

Okay, we've won. What do we do now?

Brian Mulroney, Prime Minister, addressing Conservative staffers on his second landslide victory in the general election, 17 Sept. 1988.

Elections are to democracy what weddings are to marriage. In democracy as in marriage, you have to work at it or lose it.

Joe Schlesinger, foreign correspondent, *Time Zones: A Journalist in the World* (1990).

I think the results stank.

Rita Johnston, B.C. Premier and Social Credit leader, on the NDP electoral landslide with the loss of her own seat and the end of sixteen years of Socred government, 17 Oct. 1991, quoted by Robert Matas and Deborah Wilson in *The Globe and Mail* the following day.

This election wrote an epitaph for Canada as a two-party state. In fact, we've come dangerously close to becoming a one-party state. Trust Canadians to invent a new system of government: an elected dictatorship.

Peter C. Newman, columnist, discussing the Liberal landslide in the General Election of 25 Oct. 1993, "The Nation's Business," *Maclean's*, 1 Nov. 1993.

ELECTRICAL POWER See also ENERGY

I had hoped to live to forge a band of iron around the Hydro to prevent its destruction by politicians.

Sir Adam Beck, founder, Ontario Hydro-Electric Power Commission (now Ontario Hydro), deathbed remark made in 1925, quoted in an advertisement for the Power Workers' Union, *The Toronto Star*, 29 Feb. 1996.

Electricity has made angels of us all—not angels in the Sunday school sense of being good or having wings, but spirits freed from flesh, capable of instant transportation anywhere.

Edmund Carpenter, anthropologist, *Oh, What a Blow that Phantom Gave Me!* (1973).

Toronto's SkyDome stadium uses enough electricity to light Prince Edward Island.

Canadian Press news item, "Social Studies," *The Globe and Mail*, 13 July 1990.

I try to decipher the code of the electroscape...

B.W. Powe, cultural commentator, coining the word electroscape for the topography created by the electronic media, *Outage: A Journey into Electric City* (1995).

ELITISM

A society should not be damned as elitist because it recognizes and rewards excellence, creating an elite. We are too ready to suppose the opposite. And yet at the Olympics we do not consider that the games are staged for the benefit of the athletes. It does not, moreover, need to be explained to us that among the athletes only a very few will win. Nor that later those same few will lose. We are all aware that it is the community as a whole that wins, both that day and in the future.

Unless of course we bar the way to excellence in the interest of equity, in which case we all lose.

John C. Polanyi, scientist and Nobel laureate, quoted in the *Winnipeg Free Press*, 22 Sept. 1991.

ELOQUENCE

Long speeches are not appreciated by those who starve.

Adario, Iroquois chief of the 17th century, quoted by Robert Prévost in *Petit dictionnaire des citations québécoises* (1988).

EMBLEMS, NATIONAL See also BEAVERS, CANADA GOOSE, FLAGS, MAPLE LEAF, SYMBOLS

We are the only country in the world with both a national animal and a national bird that are edible. Do the British eat lions, or have you ever seen an American or a German eat an eagle? Russians eat bears, and so do we, but they don't taste as good as beaver.

Charles Lynch, newspaperman, *A Funny Way to Run a Country: Further Memoirs of a Political Voyeur* (1986).

They also took the Iroquois emblem as their national coat of arms with one important difference. The arrows in the talons of the eagle are pointing up on theirs—"flying." Ours are turned downward in peace. That is why the Americans have always been at war with other nations and will be till they learn to bury their arms like the Great Law teaches.

Johnny Cree, Kanesatake faithkeeper, quoted by Craig MacLaine and Michael S. Baxendale in *This Land Is Our Land: The Mohawk Revolt at Oka* (1991).

What could be more Canadian? Is it possible that there's a single citizen in this country that wouldn't recognize—*instantly*—a hockey stick?

Arthur Black, broadcaster and humorist, referring to the giant hockey stick at Duncan, B.C., as the quintessential national symbol, *Black in the Saddle Again* (1996).

EMIGRATION See also IMMIGRATION

Canada is a headless nation with its brains scattered all over the world.

Attributed to political scientist **Harold Adams Innis** by correspondent Marvin Fremes, Letters to the Editor, *The Globe and Mail*, 11 Dec. 1996.

You could make an enormously wonderful university out of the Canadian faculty at Harvard, Cornell, Stanford and Berkeley... There's more Canadian content in the U.S. scientific establishment than on the television screen in my hotel room here in Kingston.

Richard Taylor, Canadian-born, U.S.-based Nobel laureate in Physics, address to the Royal Society of Canada in 1991, quoted by Lawrence Martin in *Pledge of Allegiance* (1993).

A nation that sends an important segment of its young people abroad, for lack of options at home, risks losing them forever. It has chosen provincialism as a way of life, and thereby called into question its reason for existence.

John C. Polanyi, scientist and Nobel laureate, "Call for Excellence," *Maclean's*, 9 Nov. 1992.

Canada is trying to make it into the 21st century with two-thirds of its brains removed.

Peter Stangeby, professor, University of Toronto's Institute for Aerospace Studies, referring to the brain drain, Letters to the Editor, *The Toronto Star*, 20 Jan. 1999.

EMOTIONS See also FEELINGS

We're a country of rich natural resources. Our problem is that the greatest natural resource of human emotion for Canada remains virtually untapped. Whoever touches it now and uses it positively will deserve to be called a hero. Let's hope it happens soon.

Harry J. Boyle, broadcaster and author, "In Praise of Praising Heroes," *Maclean's*, 17 Dec. 1979.

EMPIRE See also BRITISH EMPIRE & COMMONWEALTH, CANADA & THE UNITED KINGDOM, IMPERIALISM

What has been done before, we shall be proud to do again; and never be guilty of the baseness of basking in the sunshine of the empire, and forsaking it in the storm.

William Kirby, writer and antiquarian, *Counter Manifesto to the Annexationists of Montreal* (1849), written under the pseudonym Britannicus.

In the scrolls of the future it is already written that the centre of the Empire must shift—and where, if not to Canada?

Line from **Sara Jeannette Duncan**'s novel *The Imperialist* (1904).

Canada is not an ex-empire. This is an enormous strength when competing for international contracts.

John Ralston Saul, President, Canada PEN International, quoted in University of Guelph's "Canada" supplement, *The Globe and Mail*, 4 Dec. 1991.

EMPLOYMENT See also LABOUR, WORK

The youth of today face a bleak future, energy shortages, a national crisis of unity and the prospect of the worst unemployment since the dirty thirties.... The first step in making Canada work as a nation is putting the nation back to work.

Ed Broadbent, NDP leader, address, United Steelworkers, Winnipeg, 6 May 1977, quoted in *The Toronto Star*, 6 May 1977.

Any system that cannot provide employment for its workforce, with self-respect and human dignity, is not efficient. That is the first goal, and all else flows from it.

Eric Kierans and **Walter Stewart**, economist and writer, *Wrong End of the Rainbow: The Collapse of Free Enterprise in Canada* (1988).

When Brian Mulroney said, "Jobs, jobs, jobs," I thought he meant in Canada!

Dave Broadfoot, comedian, quoted by Dennis Kucherawy in *eye*, 16 Jan. 1992.

Many economists calculate that nearly 70 per cent of the manufacturing jobs lost since the Free Trade Agreement was signed will not reappear. Ask St. Catharines.

Peter C. Newman, columnist, *Maclean's*, 9 March 1992.

The most enlightened retraining policy a government can deliver is to give the unemployed, or anyone else, the generic skills to enable them to be self-employed.

Diane Francis, columnist, *Maclean's*, 11 Jan. 1993.

Jobs are going the way of child labour, slavery, and indentured service.

Frank Ogden, futurologist, quoted in "Towards 2000: A Progress Report," *The Globe and Mail*, 4 March 1993.

We will only have true employment equality between men and women when we have as many incompetent females in positions of authority as we have incompetent males.

Sheelagh Whittaker, President, EDS Canada, "It Matters Who Makes It," NFB Symposium, Sept. 1993.

Jobs cannot be created. Economies are created and they in turn create jobs.

John Ralston Saul, author, *The Doubter's Companion: A Dictionary of Aggressive Common Sense* (1994).

Canada could create more jobs if that became the country's economic priority and policy adjustments were made. Those are political decisions a nation makes. They are not completely dictated by global markets.

Paul Krugman, economist, Sloan School of Management, Cambridge, Mass., interviewed by Jonathan Ferguson, "Loosen Up, He Says," *The Toronto Star*, 23 March 1997.

ENDEAVOUR

If you ask me the difference between Canada and England it is that in England, if you want to do something new, people say that it hasn't been done before, so better not risk it, while in Canada they have never done anything before and are willing to try.

Robin Skelton, author and academic who emigrated from England to Canada in 1963, quoted in *The Guardian Weekly*, 24 Oct. 1970.

ENEMIES

I believe that one day, very soon, people will set aside their differences and come together as one. Maybe not because we love one another, but because we need each other to survive. Then, together, we will fight our common enemies.

Maria Campbell, Native spokesperson, *Halfbreed* (1973).

All my known enemies are pseudo-intellectuals, artistic charlatans and specious socialists with cunning eyes, avaricious inclinations, flaccid bodies, theatrical garments and ignoble records of service to Queen and country.

McKenzie Porter, columnist, sentence from a column in *The Toronto Sun* in the 1975, quoted by Peter Worthington, "Irrepressible Ken Porter," *The Toronto Sun*, 11 April 1999.

ENERGY See also ATOMIC ENERGY, ELECTRICAL POWER, OIL INDUSTRY

Concerning one aspect of the sun's influence on the earth there is not much doubt. Except for radioactivity and certain other forms of atomic energy, all sources of power come directly or indirectly from the sun, and it is the energy from the sun which maintains life on the earth.

Peter M. Millman, astronomer, *This Universe of Space* (1961).

Very clearly, there is not now, never has been, and never will be, a permanent energy shortage in the world.

Frank Feather, futurologist, *G-Forces: Reinventing the World—The 35 Global Forces Restructuring Our World* (1989).

If I was able to sell power to Hydro, and the bank would lend me the money. I'd be a wind farmer. That's the future.

George Wright, farmer who uses solar and wind-generated power and partner in Metcalfe Wind Electric, Metcalfe, Ont., quoted by Kelly Egan in *The Montreal Gazette*, 22 May 1997.

ENGINEERING

This is a world where countries like Mexico and the Philippines are producing four times as many engineers as we are.

C.E. Ritchie, Chairman and CEO, Bank of Nova Scotia, "Do Canadians Really Want to Compete?" address, The Canadian Club, 29 April 1991.

ENGLISH CANADA See CANADA: ENGLISH

ENGLISH PEOPLE See also BRITISH EMPIRE & COMMONWEALTH, UNITED KINGDOM

Everything else is partial, compared to London; when a Canadian settles down in London it is just about the same as drawing your chair up to the fire, at the old homestead.

Matthew Halton, foreign correspondent and broadcaster, interviewed on his return from London, England, by R.E. Knowles, *The Toronto Star*, 13 Aug. 1938.

One with the nameless are they all; there never was a Brown / Who rose above the rank and file to gain the world's renown; / One with a common host they are, by dale and copse and fen— / But England's made and moulded by the lives of common men.

One verse of **Audrey Alexandra Brown**'s poem "The Browns," *A Dryad in Nanaimo* (1934).

It may seem strange to begin a history of Canada in an English city, a bustling maritime centre of narrow streets in a pocket of the hills where the Avon joins the Severn. But that is where the story rightly begins: in the city of Bristol....

Opening sentences of **Thomas B. Costain**'s narrative history called *The White and the Gold: The French Regime in Canada* (1954). Bristol was John Cabot's seaport.

The British obsession with class made me an enigma. I seemed unclassifiable: I had an "impenetrable" accent; I was Indian; I had grandparents who worked in a factory; I was a Christian with a Hindu father. And to top it all off, I was Canadian—this, I was informed, was "really the last straw."

Akaash Maharaj, scholarship student who was elected president of the Oxford Student Union, "Dreams of Oxford Tainted by Racism," *The Toronto Star*, 23 Oct. 1994, written with Peter Cheney.

ENTERPRISE

Nothing binds a people together like entering in a spirit of common enterprise and friendly co-operation on a project that is completely useless.

Line from **James Bacque**'s novel *The Queen Comes to Minnicog* (1979).

In Canada, you've got to come to them with a flourishing flower. Americans, you can go to them with the seeds and they'll help you make them grow. A certain type rises to the top in this country—talentless. In the U.S. talent rises. Here, the morons reach the top and the talented are kept in their places.

Jim Unger, cartoonist, Ottawa resident, quoted by Roy MacGregor in *Maclean's*, 16 April 1979.

It is no longer enough for an enterprise to be better and more efficient than the enterprise across the street. Industries—and countries themselves—have to be as good as the most efficient competitor on the other side of the globe. This new reality has brought about one of the greatest attitudinal turnarounds of this century.

Diane Francis, columnist, *Maclean's*, 20 Dec. 1993.

ENTERTAINMENT

An entertainer gives you those good old songs that you want to hear. An artist wants to give you what you *don't know* you want. Something you might know you want the next time, but you never knew you wanted before.

David Cronenberg, film director, interview, *Rolling Stone*, 6 Feb. 1992.

The second you make someone feel something then you have entertainment value.

Kiefer Sutherland, actor, quoted by Paul McKie in the *Winnipeg Free Press*, 13 March 1992.

ENTREPRENEURSHIP

The future does not have to be dim, but we will only succeed if we reward entrepreneurs, not special interest groups, lobbies or politicians who buy our votes.

Diane Francis, columnist, "A Mission Statement to Revive Canada," *Maclean's*, 30 Aug. 1993.

Become an outlaw. Grab the latest technology and run with it. When they do catch you, you'll be in charge.

Frank Ogden, futurologist, quoted by Rod McQueen in *The Financial Post*, 4 June 1994.

I don't have an entrepreneurial bone in my body. For me, personally, I just get fascinated building things that are good.

James Gosling, Calgary-educated computer programmer who developed the Java computer application program in 1995, interviewed by Tyler Hamilton, "Java Inventor Brews Cool Stuff," *The Globe and Mail*, 19 Nov. 1998. The slogan of Java is "Write once, run anywhere."

ENVIRONMENT See also ENVIRONMENTALISM, RESOURCES

I suggest that, as the human population grows and environmental damage progresses, policymakers will have less and less capacity to intervene to keep this damage from producing serious social disruption, including conflict.

Thomas F. Homer-Dixon, political scientist, "On the Threshold: Environmental Changes as Causes of Acute Conflict," *International Security*, Fall, 1991.

Environmental scarcity has insidious and cumulative social impacts, such as population movement, economic decline, and the weakening of states. These can contribute to diffuse and persistent sub-national violence. The rate and extent of such conflicts will increase as scarcities worsen.

Thomas F. Homer-Dixon, co-ordinator of the Peace and Conflict Studies Program, University College, University of Toronto, "Environmental Scarcities and Violent Conflict: Evidence from Cases," *International Security*, Summer 1994. By "environmental scarcity," Homer-Dixon refers to the degradation and depletion of environmental resources, population growth, and unequal resource distribution.

Multiply our individual choices that affect our environment five billion times and we can begin to see that every time we just do what all the others are doing we are contributing to the stress of the planet in ways that are cumulatively dangerous.

James George, former Canadian Ambassador, *Asking for the Earth: Waking up to the Spiritual/Ecological Crisis* (1995).

ENVIRONMENTALISM See also ECOLOGY, ENVIRONMENT, PROTEST

Bottle caps and metal cans do not disintegrate for at least a hundred years on the tundra. Fifty to one hundred years of plant growth can be snuffed out by a beer can.

Ann H. Zwinger, environmental advocate, *Land above the Trees* (1972) by Ann H. Zwinger and Beatrice E. Willard.

I do not feel like a freak. I feel normal. And sometimes I wonder if the rest of the world is normal, especially that part of it that goes round plundering the natural world.

Paul Watson, ecologist and environmental activist, *Sea Shepherd: My Fight for Whales and Seals* (1982) as told to Warren Rogers.

For decades I have been preaching that we must discard the concept of "waste" to be "disposed of" as obsolete, and replace it by the notion of by-products to be reused and recycled.

Hans Blumenfeld, architect-planner, *Life Begins at 65: The Not Entirely Candid Autobiography of a Drifter* (1987).

Well, slowly but surely consumers are beginning to comprehend the extent of the power that they hold in their hands; they are becoming aware that they can use the every-day process of consumption to demonstrate support for the environment. They're beginning to realize that they play a very important part in market forces.

Dave Nichol, President, Loblaw International Merchants, Summit on the Environment, Toronto, 11 Sept. 1989.

My specific thought about garbage sprang from the realization that Canadian society has travelled in my lifetime from returnable glass bottles for milk to throwaway plastic bags. This is not progress. Moreover, in the same lifetime, Canadian cities have abandoned horse-drawn carts doing door-to-door milk routes. This probably isn't progress either.

Michael Valpy, columnist, *The Globe and Mail*, 29 Dec. 1989.

And if it made sense to preserve those fragile islands at the edge, then it makes sense to preserve the gentle planet on which they float, somewhere between ocean wave and brilliant sky. Earth is calling us home.

Elizabeth E. May, social activist, *Paradise Won: The Struggle for South Moresby* (1991).

In British Columbia, environmentalists are often compared to watermelons: green on the outside, pink on the inside. Not so in Ontario. Lacking B.C.'s benign climate a curious political mutation seems to have occurred. Ontario cabinet ministers have reversed the order, being pink on the outside and very, very green on the inside.

Tom Davey, publisher, editorial, *Environmental Science & Engineering*, June 1992.

Today, if you were to randomly throw a stick in any environmental conference, the odds are very good that your missile would connect with a lawyer.

Tom Davey, publisher, editorial comment, *Environmental Science & Engineering*, March 1996.

I think it would be wonderful if things collapsed for a few days. Chaos would happen… but it would be an amazing opportunity for people to really start thinking about things—and a global collapse would really make people think.

David Suzuki, geneticist and broadcaster, musing on the eve of the new millennium, quoted by Leah Eichler, "Sightings," Reuters, Internet, 21 Dec. 1999.

EPITAPHS See also DYING WORDS, MEMORIALS, WAR DEAD

Wm. Pierce, Died Feb. 31, 1860. / Aged 73 Years.

Epitaph on a gravestone, Old St. Mary's Cemetery, Picton, Ont., as reported by Margaret McBurney and Mary Byers in *Homesteads: Early Buildings and Families from Kingston to Toronto* (1979). "Ever since it was reported in Ripley's 'Believe It or Not,' visitors have come considerable distances to see the tablet of a man who achieved fame by dying on a day that never dawned."

Callaghan moved to Dale Avenue in 1951. Neighbours often saw and talked to him as he crossed this bridge with his wife and dog, Nikki, then with his dog, then alone until he died in 1990.

Well-worded inscription on the plaque that honours author Morley Callaghan, erected by the **Toronto Historical Board** in 1992. It marks the footbridge near the house on Dale Avenue in the Rosedale district of Toronto now occupied by his son Barry Callaghan.

He Died Learning

Self-selected, pre-need epitaph of broadcaster **Lister Sinclair**, quoted by Christopher Harris in *The Globe and Mail*, 21 Jan. 1995.

Here Lies a Man Who Tried to Do the Right Thing

Joe Salsberg, former Communist Member of the Ontario Legislature, proposing the wording of his epitaph, noted in his obituary by Nicolaas van Rijn in *The Toronto Star*, 9 Feb. 1998.

EQUALITY

As long as a flag waves over a person disenfranchised on account of sex, that flag is not big enough for me—so long as a church refuses absolute equality to woman with men, so long as it closes its pulpits to the natural teachers and preachers of our race, just so long is that church too small for me.

Flora MacDonald Denison, early feminist and poetry fancier, inscription in a copy of *Whitman's Poetical Works*, quoted by Mary Savigny in *Bon Echo: The Denison Years* (1997).

As far as I am concerned, as long as I am president, promotions are not going to be made because the person is French Canadian. He has to be something else as well…. Promotion on the CNR is made on merit. I don't care if he is black, white, red or even a Scotsman. Scotsmen sometimes get promoted, too.

Donald Gordon, President of the CNR, quoted in *The Globe and Mail*, 21 Nov. 1962. Gordon, a man of Scots background, appearing before the Commons Railways Committee, responded to questions about discrimination against French Canadians raised by Gilles Grégoire. When Lionel Chevrier expressed disbelief there was not one suitable person in Quebec to fill a senior position, Gordon replied: "What you are really asking for is discrimination."

When the citizen is not equal to all the other citizens in the state, we're in the presence of a dictatorship which sets the citizens in a hierarchy based on their beliefs.

Pierre Elliott Trudeau, former Prime Minister and critic of the Charlottetown Accord, speech, Maison du Egg Roll, Montreal, 1 Oct. 1992, quoted in *The Globe and Mail* the following day.

Everyone has an equal right to inequality.

John Ralston Saul, author, *The Doubter's Companion: A Dictionary of Aggressive Common Sense* (1994).

Indeed, the potential for internal division among the "disadvantaged" is just as great as the potential for separation from the "dominant white male." Group thinking has a nearly unlimited potential for subdividing into narrower and narrower concentrations of some essential bioquality.

John Fekete, philosopher, *Moral Panic: Biopolitics Rising* (2nd ed., 1995).

EROTICISM See also PORNOGRAPHY

How would the world look, how would it feel if as much time, money and creativity as are spent on eroticizing power, hierarchy, violence, male dominance and female submission were spent on a truly transformative project like eroticizing equality? The world of eroticized equality is so far away from so much of our experience that we can barely imagine it, let alone start creating it.

Susan G. Cole, feminist, *Pornography and the Sex Crisis* (1989).

The environment is saturated with utopian eroticism of the sort found in Calvin Klein underwear advertisements, while the social machine we work and live with is drenched with sedative, amnesiac grease.

John Bentley Mays, critic, *In the Jaws of the Black Dogs: A Memoir of Depression* (1995).

ERROR

I'd never have made a scientist. Being wrong actually bothers me.

Maurus E. Mallon, writer and aphorist, Jan. 1992.

ESKIMO See ESKIMO ART, INUIT

ESKIMO ART See also ART & ARTISTS, INUIT

...a distrust of extreme facility; a work of art, I thought, should be carved in marble, not in soapstone.

John Buchan, Governor General Lord Tweedsmuir, learning to appreciate soapstone carvings, *Memory Hold-the-Door* (1941).

What excited me most, however, was visiting the headquarters of the Hudson Bay Company to look at their collection of Eskimo carvings. These astonishing works, small and carved out of soapstone, had a depth of form and purity of line that made me swear that if I were a Canadian I would buy them all, corner the lot, against the time, only a few years hence, when the Eskimo, under our influence, will have lost his miraculous touch.

J.B. Priestley, English bookman and broadcaster, impressions of a five-city tour, "Canadian Notes and Impressions," BBC Radio, *The Listener*, 31 May 1956.

We could do that.

Osuitok, Inuit hunter and carver, Cape Dorset, N.W.T., Winter 1957, addressing Indian and Northern Affairs officer James Houston, who recorded the remark in *Confessions of an Igloo Dweller* (1995). Osuitok marvelled at the printing of cigarette packs; Houston, an artist himself, then explained the offset printing process. Houston subsequently studied silkscreen printing in Japan and then introduced printmaking to the Eastern Arctic as a complement to its soapstone carving.

Inuit stonework is simply a cheap Henry Moore that everybody can have, and then feel warm inside in their feelings towards native peoples.

Edmund Carpenter, anthropologist, quoted by Blake Gopnik and Graham Fraser in *The Globe and Mail*, 3 Sept. 1999.

ESPIONAGE

Imagine this little Canadian country boy fooling the entire Canadian government, not to mention Reader's Digest, Quentin Reynolds and Random House! The only way we can get out of this is to laugh it off.

Bennett Cerf, New York publisher and TV personality, addressing R. DeWitt Wallace, publisher of *Reader's Digest*, whose magazine ran an article on the Canadian impostor George DuPré which drew world-wide attention to his supposed espionage feats. Biographer Quentin Reynolds ghosted DuPré's memoirs and Cerf's Random House published the book. "We're going to announce that this book isn't non-fiction, but fiction, and we're going to change the name of it immediately from *The Man Who Wouldn't Talk* to *The Man Who Talked Too Much*," Cerf explained in *At Random: The Reminiscences of Bennett Cerf* (1977). "The interesting thing is that the book sold about five times as well after the exposure as it did before."

But two years later...the revelations of a young Russian cypher-clerk in Ottawa had created a new demand for men of Smiley's experience.

Passage from **John le Carré**'s novel *Call for the Dead* (1961) that refers to how Igor Gouzenko's defection in Ottawa in 1945 affected the British security service and the espionage career of the novel's agent George Smiley.

It was Dwyer's last direct service to SIS that, by a brilliant piece of analysis of the known movements of the two men, he conclusively eliminated Peierls. Thereafter, the finger pointed unwaveringly at Fuchs.

Kim Philby, English spy, referring to the Secret Intelligence Service activities in the postwar period of Peter M. Dwyer, who in later years headed the Canada Council, *My Silent War* (1968).

Only eight hours after leaving London, Bond was driving a Hertz U-drive Plymouth saloon along the broad Route 17 from Montreal to Ottawa and trying to remember to keep on the right side of the road.

Sentence from the title story included in *For Your Eyes Only* (1960) written by **Ian Fleming**. In the story James Bond visits "the Headquarters of the Royal Canadian Mounted Police" in Ottawa.

Someone once said that a journalist is really no longer any good to his employer once he gets to understand something about how his society really works. That's true of intelligence officers too.

Ian Adams, journalist and novelist, quoted by Stephen Overbury in *Content*, March–April 1980.

Young Canadian Richard Hannay (Robert Donat) visits London and befriends Miss Smith (Lucie Mannheim), a spy, who is murdered in his flat under mysterious circumstances. As she lies dying, she is able to reveal to Richard enough information to send him on a cross-country mission to prove his innocence.

Synopsis of Alfred Hitchcock movie *The Thirty-Nine Steps* (1935), based on the popular novel by **John Buchan**, which turns the South African adventurer Hannay into a Canadian, *Video One Preview*, 18 Feb. 1991.

"No, you don't know me. I've been away in Canada," I said.

Evasive comment made by British espionage agent Bernard Samsom in **Len Deighton**'s novel *Faith* (1994).

Canada must realize that our political allies have become our economic competitors. Canada must provide for itself an increased capability to contribute at least to defensive efforts against foreign economic espionage, if not an offensive capability.

Peter A. Hammerschmidt, research officer, Canadian Institute of Strategic Studies, *Stategic Datalink*, Nov. 1997.

ESTABLISHMENT See also CLASS, SOCIAL; SOCIETY

In other words, *the status quo* as *quid pro quo*.

Charlie McKenzie, concierge, Rhinoceros Party, writing in *The Globe and Mail*, 24 Sept. 1992.

ETERNITY

As our personal future narrows, we become more aware of another dimension of time entirely, and may even catch glimpses of the powers and forces of a far greater creative design.

Northrop Frye, cultural critic, observation made in 1978, quoted by Albert C. Hamilton in *Vic Report*, Spring 1991.

ETHICS See GOOD & EVIL

ETHNICITY See also MULTICULTURALISM

The result of this [prevalence of national societies] is that, in a great measure, the population of Canada is composed of foreign nationalities, and any one not connected with either has been almost an outcast—at least deprived of certain advantages—and natives of the soil are often more anxious to be considered English, Irish or Scotch than Canadians.

William Canniff, historian, "Canadianism: Some of the Reasons Why a New Canadian Political Party Should Be Established," Letters to the Editor, *The London Times*, 11 Dec. 1873.

Canadians are the third-largest ethnic group in America.

June Callwood, author, *Portrait of Canada* (1981).

...an idea that for the moment lacks a name—call it "ethnic possession"—has been gathering strength. Increasingly, racial groups are laying claim not only to objects produced by their ancestors (and now in museums) but also to the culture and history surrounding those objects.

Robert Fulford, journalist, "Into the Heat of the Matter," *Rotunda*, Summer 1991.

In a world darkened by ethnic conflicts that literally tear nations apart, Canada has stood for all of us as a model of how people of different cultures can live and work together in peace, prosperity and understanding.

Bill Clinton, U.S. President, address, joint meeting of the House of Commons and the Senate of Canada, Ottawa, Senate Debates, 23 Feb. 1995.

Ethnic isn't a dirty word and anyway it's an adjective, not a noun.

Ben Viccari, commentator on CFMT, Toronto, 2 Feb. 1997.

EUROPE

Having watched the disintegration of Mitteleuropa as a boy, I shall be spending the next few years witnessing the pangs of its rebirth. History, I hope, will do better this time. It has to. It certainly could not do any worse.

Joe Schlesinger, Czech-born CBC-TV foreign correspondent, *Time Zones: A Journalist in the World* (1990).

What is white? What is English? What indeed is Europe? I remember, a few years ago, coining this term of which I'm very proud: "Euroeccentricity." This broad critique that Canadians of non-European origin make about Eurocentrism is very incomplete and inadequate, given the variety of European experience, Irish vs. English, for example, or Ukrainian vs. Polish.

Myrna Kostash, author, interviewed by Mark Abley in "The Culture of Nationalism," *The Canadian Forum*, Sept. 1994.

The first minute I get off that plane, whether it is the airport in Madrid, in Paris, in Frankfurt, in Rome, or in Amsterdam, this smell always hits me like a ton of bricks, a smell in the air unlike anything I've ever smelled over here on this side of the Atlantic.... That is my first impression: one of blood, the smell of human blood.

Tomson Highway, playwright, Native spokesperson, referring to the odour of the European continent, "Arts Cut," *The Toronto Star*, 22 Oct. 1995.

EUTHANASIA See also DEATH, SUICIDE

I want to ask you gentlemen, if I cannot give consent to my own death, then whose body is this? Who owns my life?

Sue Rodriguez, victim of ALS (amyotrophic lateral sclerosis, Lou Gehrig's disease, a progressive and terminal illness), made a videotaped presentation to a House of Commons justice subcommittee, Nov. 1992, in which she urged amendments to the section of the Criminal Code that makes it a crime for one person to assist another's suicide; quoted by Deborah Wilson in *The Globe and Mail*, 5 Dec. 1992. Subsequently the Supreme Court of Canada denied Rodriguez's request for a physician-assisted death.

I refuse to be intimidated by the traditional stigmata associated with suicide. I intend to take charge of my own life *and* my death. I will demonstrate to thousands of other Canadians that *a good death* is possible and that there is an alternative to endless suffering.

Position statement evolved by **John Hofsess**, Executive Director, Right to Die Society of Canada, "The $100,000 Question," *Last Rights*, Dec.–Jan. 1993.

I still feel I did what was right. I don't think you people are being human.

Robert Latimer, Saskatchewan farmer found guilty of second-degree murder in the death of his severely disabled 12-year-old daughter, quoted in "The Year," *The Toronto Star*, 31 Dec. 1994.

I'm a religious person. A loving father gave Tracy to a loving Father. When I think about that peace then I'm all right.

Laura Latimer, wife of Robert Latimer and mother of disabled 12-year-old Tracy Latimer who was killed on 24 Oct. 1993, testifying in a court in Battleford, Sask., 3 Nov. 1997, quoted by David Roberts in *The Globe and Mail* the following day.

EVIL See also GOOD & EVIL

I knew the wickedness that is in the heart of man.

Lord Beaverbrook, newspaper publisher, concluding line of his memoirs in the *Atlantic Advocate*, as noted by Anne Chisholm and Michael Davie in *Beaverbrook: A Life* (1992).

It is the old story: Mephistopheles did not lack intelligence, but goodness.

Archibald Lang Fleming, consecrated first Bishop of the Arctic in Winnipeg in 1933, *Archibald the Arctic* (1957).

I have expressed this elsewhere by suggesting that love or charity begins by asking the question, "Why do we permit so much evil and suffering?"

Northrop Frye, cultural critic, *The Double Vision: Language and Meaning in Religion* (1991).

The minute you say evil, I think Christianity.

David Cronenberg, film director, interview, *Rolling Stone*, 6 Feb. 1992.

EVOLUTION

No Adam, no fall; no fall, no atonement; no atonement, no saviour. Accepting Evolution, how can we believe in a fall?

Dictum associated with Seventh Day Adventist and pioneer, New Brunswick–born creationist George McCready Price in *Back to the Bible: or, The New Protestantism* (3rd, 1920). Although associated with it, Price attributed the authorship of the dictum to English socialist **Robert Blatchford**, as noted by Ronald L. Numbers in *The Creationists* (1992).

No polly-wog evolution theories for me. We're not children of a gorilla, we're children of God.

Aimee Semple McPherson, evangelist, expressing anti-evolutionary principles, interviewed by R.E. Knowles, *The Toronto Star*, 9 July 1929.

EXCELLENCE

In the arts, centres of excellence are absolutely imperative. It's tough if you live in Saskatchewan, but you don't have the same right to an opera house that Toronto has.

Greg Gatenby, artistic director, Harbourfront Reading Series, panel on Culture in the Greater Toronto Area, *The Toronto Star*, 8 July 1995.

Women try to be perfect. We tend to focus on that rather than on doing our best. Focus on excellence rather than perfection.

Roz Usheroff, entrepreneur, quoted by Sheena Jarvis, "Striving for Perfection," *City Woman*, March 1996.

As for relevance, we will never find a better guarantee of that than is inherent in excellence. For whenever we make a discovery that changes people's thinking, we shall, to the same extent, change their doing. The only truly irrelevant science, as we all know, is mediocre science.

John C. Polanyi, scientist, address, Nobel Laureate Gala Dinner, 28 Aug. 1997, "Ideas," *The Toronto Star*, 1 Oct. 1997.

EXECUTIVES See also MANAGEMENT

The corporate executive is not a capitalist but a technocrat in drag.

John Ralston Saul, author, *The Doubter's Companion: A Dictionary of Aggressive Common Sense* (1994).

Although it never appears in their job descriptions, clairvoyance is a much-sought-after attribute in CEOs. Knowing what will happen, or at least guessing right, is part of what is expected from business leaders.

John Dalla Costa, advertising executive, *Meditations on Business: Why Business As Usual Won't Work Anymore* (1991).

I never met a group of managers or executives who felt overpaid or underworked.

Peter Urs Bender, motivational speaker, characteristic remark, 11 May 2000.

EXERCISE

If they had Nautilus on the Concorde, I would work out all the time.

Attributed to the Canadian-born supermodel **Linda Evangelista**, Internet, 15 Aug. 1995.

EXISTENTIALISM

We come from the unknown at birth, and we rejoin it at death with all our questions about it unanswered. Sometimes we wonder whether humanity is capable of living in any world at all where consciousness is really a function of life.

Northrop Frye, cultural critic, sermon, Service of Thanksgiving, 5 Oct. 1986.

EXPECTATIONS

You never get what you expect, only what you inspect with respect.

Roger E. Keeley, Canadian Professional Sales Association, motto, quoted by Peter Urs Bender in *Leadership from Within* (1997) with Eric Hellman.

EXPERIENCE

I know what I have experienced and I know what it has meant to me.

Words inscribed on the monument raised to the memory of explorer **Vilhjalmur Stefansson** at his birthplace, Arnes, Man., quoted in *The Point and Beyond: Arnes and District 1876–1990* (1992) compiled by the committee.

You can't judge a man until you've walked a mile in his moccasins.

Proverbial expression, said to be of Native origin, possibly Algonkian, common in the 1970s.

What seems to reason and experience to be perpetually coming apart at the seams may seem to the imagination something on the point of being put together again.

Northrop Frye, cultural critic, Preface, *The Bush Garden* (1971).

When you're writing out of the total embrace of the experience of the emotion of the moment, what comes out of there is really authentic.

Leonard Cohen, poet and performer, interviewed by Alan Twigg in *Strong Voices: Conversations with Fifty Canadian Authors* (1988).

Given a choice between the vividness of my memory and scientific doubt, I'll take my own experience: I was there; science was not.

Sylvia Fraser, novelist and journalist, *The Book of Strange: A Journey* (1992).

Experience can happen in an armchair.... I have tried to keep open to the pores of experience....

Jack Shadbolt, artist, quoted by Christopher Dafoe in *The Globe and Mail*, 10 July 1992.

Perhaps it is time to go in quest of the Grail (or Snark) of unmediated experience.

Tom Henighan, author, *The Presumption of Culture* (1996).

EXPLANATIONS

He was one of those men who when looking for a scapegoat always managed to find it tethered in someone else's backyard.

Attributed to corporate lawyer and "orator-general" **Leonard Brockington** by Sir Edwin Leather in 1980.

EXPLORATION See also DISCOVERIES, PIONEERS

He spoke also of yet another island of the many he found in that ocean. It is called Vinland because vines producing excellent wine grew wild there.... Beyond that island, he said, no habitable land is found in that ocean, but every place beyond it is full of impenetrable ice and intense darkness.

Adam of Bremen, annalist who died about 1076, paraphrasing the observations of the Danish voyager and king Svein Ulfson, in his *Historia* (first published in 1579), noted by Francis J. Tschan in his translation of *History of the Archbishops of Hamburg-Bremen* (1959) and quoted by Tryggvi J. Oleson in *Early Voyages and Northern Approaches: 1000–1632* (1963).

In the seaport of Saint Malo, 'twas a smiling morn in May, / When the Commodore Jacques Cartier to the westward sail'd away.

Opening lines of **Thomas D'Arcy McGee**'s ballad "Jacques Cartier," *The Poems of Thomas D'Arcy McGee* (1869) edited by Mrs. J. Sadlier.

And so because that I will not be tedious in this history of these Canadians, ye that note that these people universally are afflicted with continual cold, because of the absence of the sun.

André Thevet, Franciscan friar and chronicler, *The New Found World, or Antarctike, Wherein Is Contained Wonderful and Strange Things, as Well as Human Creatures, as Beasts, Fishes,*

Fowles, and Serpents, Trees, Plants, Mines of Gold and Silver (1568) translated into English by Thomas Hacket. This is the first printed reference to Canada in the English language. (The original was published in French ten years earlier.)

I would rather be hanged at home than starve abroad.

Said to be the complaint of a rebellious sailor aboard Henry Hudson's Arctic-exploration vessel *Discovery,* but not found in the account kept by survivor Abacuk Pricket of the subsequent mutiny, 22 June 1611, which saw Hudson and his son and seven other crew members forced into a shallop and cut adrift in the open sea of Hudson Bay, while the rest of the ship's company sailed for England.

I cannot find words to describe our situation at times. We had to pass where no human being should venture. Yet in those places there is a regular footpath impressed, or rather indented, by frequent travelling upon the very rocks.

Simon Fraser, explorer, entry for 26 June 1808, "Journal of a Voyage from the Rocky Mountains to the Pacific Ocean Performed in the Year 1808," *The Letters and Journals of Simon Fraser* (1960) edited by W. Kaye Lamb. The trail across the Rocky Mountains was set by Natives "in the most difficult and dangerous part of the Fraser Canyon, which centres upon Hell's Gate and the Black Canyon," according to W. Kaye Lamb, editor of *The Letters and Journals of Simon Fraser: 1806–1808* (1960).

Not a cape was turned, not a river entered, but a Jesuit led the way.

George Hubert Howe Bancroft, historian, remark made in 1834, quoted by Reuben Gold Thwaites in his Introduction to *The Jesuit Relations and Allied Documents* (1954) edited by Edna Kenton. Thwaites added, "Bancroft was inexact... in his oft-quoted phrase."

When an explorer climbs a hill or rounds a headland he is always struck with surprise at what he finds on the other side. What he sees is never quite what he expected.

Robert A. (Bob) Bartlett, sea captain, *The Log of Bob Bartlett: The Truth Story of Forty Years of Seafaring and Exploration* (1928).

We had many great explorers in the Arctic.... When they got there they didn't know where they were! And, of course, like Christopher Columbus, when they got back they had no idea where they had been or what they had discovered. The people that lived there didn't know they were being discovered because they had no idea that they were lost!

Stuart M. Hodgson, N.W.T. Commissioner, address, Empire Club of Canada, Toronto, 13 March 1975.

Radisson, Radisson, / Canada's courageous pioneer; / Raddison, Raddison, / Lord of the Wilderness, / The man who knew no fear.

Lyrics of the theme song of CBC-TV's *Radisson,* celebrating the French explorer Pierre-Esprit Radisson, its answer to the American TV series *Davy Crockett,* launched in Feb. 1957 and cancelled before it ran its thirty-nine weeks. Quoted by Alexander Ross in *The Booming Fifties: 1950–960* (1977).

I am an explorer. I adventure into the present. I make startling discoveries.

Marshall McLuhan, communications pioneer, interviewed by Linda Sandler in *Miss Chatelaine,* 3 Sept. 1974.

What is a Philistine? Oh, some of them are very nice people. They are the salt of the earth, but not its pepper. A Philistine is someone who is content to live in a wholly unexplored world.

Thoughts of a character in **Robertson Davies**' novel *The Lyre of Orpheus* (1989).

EXPO 67 See also CENTENNIAL YEAR

The Quebec Tercentenary was the greatest work of art ever conceived, prepared and carried out in Canada. It was the flower of the national life brought to perfection by the skill of many minds, exactly at the propitious moment.

Sir Arthur G. Doughty, Dominion Archivist, *The King's Book of Quebec* (1911). The Tercentenary of Quebec, which marked the city's three hundredth anniversary, was proclaimed in Quebec City on 20 July 1908. The attendant festivities were not equalled until Expo 67 in Montreal.

I think its significance is that it has taken the world's best and condensed it to one area so that we can look at it in a day and say, "That's how man can live."

Allan Fleming, designer, referring to Expo 67, quoted by Dusty Vineberg in *The Montreal Star*, 23 Sept. 1967.

This was big league stuff. Expo made us all realize that, hey, we weren't that bad.

Frank Shuster, comedian, on performing with his partner Johnny Wayne at Expo 67, quoted by Bill Brioux in *TV Guide*, 24 May 1997.

EXTERNAL AFFAIRS See FOREIGN AFFAIRS, INTERNATIONALISM

EXTRATERRESTRIAL LIFE See also UNIDENTIFIED FLYING OBJECTS

Long-distance radio listening attracts amateurs, too. Bob Stevens bought for one dollar a 60-foot early warning radar up in the Northwest Territories; he hung in there, living in the shack next to it as long as he could, finally leaving town emaciated and frozen nearly solid.

Paul Horowitz, physicist, Harvard University, referring to Robert Stevens' shoestring SETI (Search for Extra-Terrestrial Intelligence), Hay River, N.W.T., "Extraterrestrial Intelligence: The Search Programs," *Carl Sagan's Universe* (1997) edited by Yervant Terzian and Elizabeth Bilson.

F

FAILURE See also DEFEAT

Failure is due, far oftener, to lack of principle than to lack of ability.

C.L. Burton, merchandiser, interviewed by R.E. Knowles in *The Toronto Star*, 2 Feb. 1937.

It is easier to fail than to succeed because when you fail no one ever expects anything from you.

Larry Solway, broadcaster and writer, characteristic remark first recorded in 1970.

It's lovely to be a failure in Canada because it doesn't feel like a failure.

John Hirsch, theatre director, quoted by Philip Marchand in *Saturday Night*, June 1975.

Success dehumanizes people, but failure makes them fall back on something in themselves.

Brian Moore, novelist, quoted by Martin Knelman in *The Canadian*, 21 May 1977.

Loss is given us, and we take it.

Line from **Fraser Sutherland**'s poem "Forms of Loss," *Whitefaces* (1986).

...the eloquence of failure may be the only eloquence remaining in our time....

Robert Kroetsch, poet and author, "Author's Note," *Complete Field Notes: The Long Poems of Robert Kroetsch* (1989).

I think the real explanation of...failure is often disarmingly simple: The people running the business just aren't having fun any more.

George Cohon, senior chairman of McDonald's Restaurants of Canada, *To Russia with Fries* (1997) written with David Macfarlane.

FAIRIES See SPIRITS

FAITH See also BELIEF

Faith is a belief in something you know isn't so.

Bob Edwards, publisher, *The Eye Opener*, 29 June 1918, *The Wit and Wisdom of Bob Edwards* (1976) edited by Hugh Dempsey.

We lose faith in mankind whenever our faith does not take us beyond mankind.

Albert W.J. Harper, Ottawa aphorist, *Thoughts and Afterthoughts* (1984).

All faith is founded on good faith, and where there is good faith on both sides there is also the presence of God.

Northrop Frye, cultural critic, *The Double Vision: Language and Meaning in Religion* (1991).

If only we had faith in our own contradictions—public/private, French/English—we'd be a great nation.

Scott McIntyre, publisher, interviewed by Val Ross in *The Globe and Mail*, 18 Jan. 1992.

I can't say that I left Asia with a new faith. In fact I lost most of what I'd started with...I really had next to nothing left in the way of doctrinal faith to guide me.

Tim Ward, writer and traveller, conclusion upon completing two years of travel in the East, *The Great Dragon's Fleas* (1993).

Some say, "Cast your bread upon the water, and it will return to you one hundred fold." A Canadian says, "What am I going to do with a hundred loaves of wet bread?"

Dave Broadfoot, comedian, quoted in *The Canadian 1993 Household Almanac* (1992).

Faith is the hypostasis of what is hoped for, the elenchus of the unseen. The only thing truly unseen, the world across death, may, according to my principle, be what enables us to see what is visible.

Northrop Frye, cultural critic, "Notebook 1993," edited by Robert D. Denham, *Northrop Frye Newsletter*, Summer 1993.

Raspberries are best not washed. After all, one must have faith in something.

James Barber, chef, *Peasant's Choice: More of the Best from The Urban Peasant* (1994).

FALL See also SEASONS

Along the line of smoky hills / The crimson forest stands, / And all the day the blue-jay calls / Throughout the autumn lands.

First verse of **W.W. Campbell**'s celebrated poem "Indian Summer," *Lake Lyrics and Other Poems* (1889).

Another potent remembrance of this and subsequent tours is the turn of the leaf in Canada, so flaming and complete in its chromatic scale from lemon to scarlet as to appear almost unreal.

Lillie Langtry, British actress, who toured North America five times between 1882 and 1915, *The Days I Knew* (1925).

I am an autumn junkie. It is the perfect season for depraved Calvinists who require every intoxicant to be tinged with melancholy, who aren't happy unless every binge carries a whiff of mortality.

Joey Slinger, humorist, "Going for Gold," *If It's a Jungle Out There, Why Do I Have to Mow the Lawn* (1992).

Fall is the season that's the most romantic, the most melancholic, and the most conducive to being a writer. And you have Fall here for, like, nine months.

k.d. lang, singer and composer, referring to the weather in Vancouver, quoted in "Vancouver Arts," *The Globe and Mail*, 2 Nov. 1995.

FAME See also CELEBRITIES, REPUTATION

"I'm world-famous," Dr. Parks said, "all over Canada."

Line from **Mordecai Richler**'s satiric novel *The Incomparable Atuk* (1963). Famous is Andy Warhol's prediction: "In the future everyone will be famous for fifteen minutes." Less famous is the Canadian variant: "In the future everyone will be famous for fifteen minutes, thirty in Newfoundland."

Fame is mainly the privilege of being pestered by strangers.

Louis Dudek, man-of-letters, *Epigrams* (1975).

I know what it is to scale the Heights / And fall just short of fame. / But not one in ten thousand knows my name.

Lines from **Stan Rogers**' stirring song "MacDonnell on the Heights" (1982), From *Fresh Water* (1982), as quoted by Chris Gudgeon in *An Unfinished Conversation: The Life and Music of Stan Rogers* (1993). Colonel John MacDonnell (or Macdonell) fought under Sir Isaac Brock, sharing Brock's fate (but not his fame) at the Battle of Queenston Heights in the Niagara Peninsula, a decisive engagement in the War of 1812.

I didn't regard myself as a celebrity, but being well known made life a hell of a lot more pleasant. I always got a seat in a busy restaurant.

Jack Webster, broadcaster, *Webster! An Autobiography* (1990).

If all else fails, immortality can always be assured by spectacular failure.

John Kenneth Galbraith, economist and essayist, quoted by David Olive in *White Knights and Poison Pills: A Cynic's Dictionary of Business Jargon* (1990).

It could be our national motto. Canada: Where even famous people think they should behave themselves.

Stephen Strauss, science columnist, "Mind and Matter," *The Globe and Mail*, 4 Sept. 1993.

Fame is based on what people say about you, reputation on what they think of you.

Louis Dudek, poet and aphorist, distinction made in 1985, *Notebooks 1960–1994* (1994).

Saintliness is the only way in which a man can become famous without credentials.

Nicholas Catanoy, poet, *Notes on a Prison Wall: A Memoir/Poem* (1994).

Postfame.

Neologism devised to refer to the aftermath of acclaim, first used by **Doug Coupland** in his novel *Polaroids from the Dead* (1996).

I was lonely being the only star on King Street.

Ed Mirvish, showman, referring to the performing artists honoured with "stars" in the Canadian Walk of Fame on Toronto's King Street in front of the Royal Alexandra Theatre which he owns, quoted by Greg Quill in *The Toronto Star*, 14 June 1998.

FAMILY See also CHILDREN, FATHERS, MOTHERS, PARENTHOOD

You may tell your people how impressed I have been, for years, by the strength and beauty of Canadian home life. There are more families together—that's my point—in Canada than anywhere else.

Henry Ford, U.S. industrialist, interviewed by R.E. Knowles, *The Star Weekly*, 30 Dec. 1933.

There is only one certainty, human in its complexity and seeming paradox: in our search for intimacy, emotional safety, and nurture, for that "haven in a heartless world," we have never found a design more fraught with the potential for disappointment—and richer in possibilities—than the family.

Sheila Kieran, author, *The Family Matters: Two Centuries of Family Law and Life in Ontario* (1986).

Living in a real family taught you how to fight back. The other kind of family... just taught you how to duck.

Thoughts of a character in **Diana Wieler**'s novel *Bad Boy* (1989).

Nobody brings out your shortcomings more quickly than a member of your own family.

Line from **Edward Phillips**' novel *Sunday Best* (1990).

All families are creative accidents.

Robin Skelton, poet and aphorist, *A Devious Dictionary* (1991).

One of the great mysteries of the universe is that there are parents who seem to do almost everything right and their children grow up with insecurities, complexes, anxieties, and self-doubt.

Nathaniel Branden, author of books on self-esteem, quoted by Pat Young in *Vitality Magazine: Toronto's Monthly Wellness Journal*, Sept. 1991.

When you're seeking to form a new family, it's easier for most people to choose someone from a similar family than to write a letter, "Dear Mom, I just met the most wonderful Inuit."

Lionel Tiger, Canadian-born anthropologist at Rutgers University, quoted by John Tierney, "New York's Parallel Lives," *The New York Times Magazine*, 19 Oct. 1997.

FARMING See also AGRICULTURE

I have seen an epitaph that was inscribed on the tomb of a poor man who had been a sufferer by such a transaction. It was as follows:

Shed not a tear for Simon Wruggle, / For life to him was a constant struggle; / He preferred the tomb and death's dark fate / To farming mortgaged real estate.

Robert Read, Senator, recalling an inscription, Senate of Canada, 28 April 1880.

Up! be stirring, be alive, / Get upon a farm and thrive! / He's a king upon a throne / Who has acres of his own!

Refrain of **Alexander McLachlan**'s "Acres of Your Own," *Songs of the Great Dominion* (1889) edited by W.D. Lighthall.

I like both the work and the play here, the time out of doors and the time for coming home. I like the summer and the winter, the monotony and the change. Besides, I like a flannel shirt, and liberty.

Moira O'Neill, Irish poet who in her youth ranched in 1885 with her husband near High River, Alta., "A Lady's Life on a Ranch," *Blackwood's Magazine*, Jan. 1898, quoted by T.B. Higginson in "Moira O'Neill in Alberta," *Alberta Historical Review*, Spring 1957.

On the death of Sir Charles we inquired for this young gentleman and found that he had been farming in Canada. From the accounts which have reached us he is an excellent fellow in every way.

Speech of Dr. Mortimer about the young heir Sir Henry Baskerville in **Sir Arthur Conan Doyle**'s novel *The Hound of the Baskervilles* (1902).

City people envy the farmer—but not to such an extent that they take advantage of the continuous opportunities to become one.

Bob Edwards, publisher, *The Eye Opener*, 12 Aug. 1912.

I do not know that it is such a paradox to claim that, from the social point of view, a Quebec farmer is worth a New York multi-millionaire.

Edouard Montpetit, Quebec nationalist, "The Excellence of the French-Canadian Farmer," *The Quebec Tradition: An Anthology of French-Canadian Prose and Verse* (1946) edited by Séraphin Marion and translated by Watson Kirkconnell.

A homesteader is the only man who can start with nothing, lose money all his life, and die rich.

George Stepherd, pioneer on the *Prairies, West of Yesterday* (1965).

The farmer must plan and work by guess and by God, the least rewarding combination conceivable.

James M. Minifie, correspondent, *Homesteader: A Prairie Boyhood Recalled* (1972).

For all Westerners, even city people, the farm is the touchstone, our fertility symbol, the core of our mythology. He is the grass roots, the salt of the earth, the moral fibre of the nation: he is The People.

Heather Robertson, memoirist, *Grass Roots* (1973).

Haying, raking, swathing, mowing, driving trucks and tractors and teams, quietening horses, taking cattle back and forth to the reserve, dehorning, vaccinating, branding, anything that was to be done. I worked outside with him, just as a man would, anything that was to be done.

Irene Murdoch, farmer, quoted by Florence Bird in *Anne Francis: An Autobiography* (1974). In Oct. 1973, the Supreme Court ruled that Mrs. Murdoch was not entitled to any portion of her husband Alex Murdoch's 480-acre ranch property in Alberta. This happened when she sought a divorce. She made the above reply to the Alberta judge who asked her the nature of her contribution to the family farm during twenty-eight years of marrage.

One of the reasons for growing a garden is to develop an attunement with nature, with all life.

Dorothy Maclean, medium, one of the original founders of the Findhorn Community in Northern Scotland, quoted in *The Findhorn Garden* (1975) by The Findhorn Community, with a Foreword by William Irwin Thompson.

Farmers are professional complainers. They complain about the weather, they complain when there is too much sun, when there is too much rain.

Pierre Elliott Trudeau, Prime Minister, addressing a rural audience, Rimouski, Que., 4 April 1979, as noted by Liane Heller in *The Toronto Star*, 17 Jan. 1983.

The Ice Age brought Canada's good soil for potatoes to grow in the State of Idaho. The Free Trade Agreement brought the good potatoes from Idaho to Canada.

Steve Rubin, Montreal commentator, remark, 14 Oct. 1991.

While it's true that Canada occupies the second-largest area of any nation on earth, the area of Canada's Class One agricultural land is actually smaller than the province of New Brunswick.

Tom Davey, editor and publisher, "What Garbage Crisis?" *The Toronto Sun*, 27 Aug. 1994.

One of the achievements of the century has been the general escape from what Marx, with some exaggeration, called the idiocy of rural life.

John Kenneth Galbraith, economist, address, London School of Economics, "World Tour," *The Globe and Mail*, 6 July 1999.

When all the small farmers are gone there will be no one left, except for those few Amerindian people living in the traditional manner, who understands how nature works in an intimate, personal, daily way over a small piece of ground. This is wisdom gleaned slowly over generations, for the most part never expressed coherently nor in writing, and thus, not saved in any way accessible to the rest of us.

Sharon Butala, author, "Fields of Broken Dreams," *The Globe and Mail*, 4 March 2000.

FASCISM

We will not march on Ottawa. When we go we will go as M.P.'s in Pullman cars.

Adrien Arcand, Quebec fascist, referring to the On to Ottawa Trek, remark made on 23 Feb. 1938, quoted by Lita-Rose Betcherman in *The Swastika and the Maple Leaf: Fascist Movements in Canada in the Thirties* (1975). One of Arcand's followers is racist Ernst Zundel.

It has become fashionable for priests to become activists these days. I guess I was a pioneer.

Charles E. Coughlin, so-called Radio Priest, silenced in 1940 for making fascist and anti-Semitic statements on international radio from the pulpit of the Shrine of the Little Flower, Royal Oak, Michigan, interviewed by George Gamester in *The Toronto Star*, 8 May 1976.

The Hitler We Loved and Why

Title of a book signed **Christof Friedrich** but said to be written by racist Ernst Zundel, according to *The Toronto Sun*, 19 April 1978, as noted by

Stanley R. Barrett in *Is God a Racist?* (1987). Barrett wrote about Zundel's denial of authorship in *The Globe and Mail*, 22 Feb. 1985: "I suppose the attributed author's name, Christof Friedrich, Zundel's two middle names, might have been a mere coincidence."

...traditional but outdated electoral procedures and new developments in the party structures both within and outside Parliament are opening the way to a quasi-totalitarianism which, for the lack of a better name, I would call five-year fascism.

George Woodcock, social commentator, referring to current Canadian electoral practices and procedures, the maximum period between elections being five years, "Five-Year Fascism," The *Canadian Forum*, Dec. 1990.

FASHION See also BEAUTY

If we cannot fit you, you may as well start a factory on your own.

Business slogan of **W. Tawse & Son's Popular Boot and Shoe Store**, 25 Wyndham St., Guelph, Ont., advertisement in *Guelph Directory for 1875/6/7* (1875).

About one-half the children born in this country die before they are five years of age, and no doubt this terrible mortality is largely due to this instrument of torture known as the *modern corset*.

B.G. Jefferis, medical crank, *Search Lights on Health, Light on Dark Corners; A Complete Sexual Science and a Guide to Purity and Physical Manhood* (1894).

A woman is always suspicious of another woman who dresses better than herself.

Bob Edwards, publisher, *The Eye Opener*, Summer Annual, 1923, *The Wit and Wisdom of Bob Edwards* (1976) edited by Hugh Dempsey.

Both the Canadians and Americans dress their children like Eskimos in winter; both chew gum; both affect the attire of the lumberjack and seek to astonish by the violence of their sports jerseys or their formal freakishness.

Wyndham Lewis, British artist and author, *America, I Presume* (1940).

As I watched her remove her wedding ring, I thought: Now she's naked—except for her clothes. Women are members of the largest secret army in the world. Each woman covers up her uniform with clothes.

Raymond Canale, Italian-born, Toronto-based playwright, observations made in 1975.

Just because I'm interested in Yves Saint Laurent doesn't mean I'm not interested in Nietzsche.

Adrienne Clarkson, stylish broadcaster, quoted by Knowlton Nash in *Prime Time at Ten* (1987).

I was always obsessed with fashion—with the magazines, the models and the poses. Now, Arab princes want to marry me.

Linda Evangelista, Italian-born fashion model raised in St. Catharines, Ont., quoted by Tom Fennell in *Maclean's*, 9 Dec. 1991.

"Not-Yet-Famous Tilley Hat"

Slogan and description of the distinctive sports cap designed and manufactured by Alex Tilley of **Tilley Endurables Inc.**, noted by Thelma Dickman in "Canada's Glad Hatter," *Leisureways*, April 1992.

You have a choice: to look your best or to look fashionable.

Lise Watier, cosmetics manufacturer, quoted by Trisee Loxley in *The Globe and Mail*, 22 Oct. 1992.

In Espérance the girls stand out like parakeets. The matrons of stodgy Ontario next door may dress themselves like sofas at a funeral, but here in Espérance the hot-blooded Québécois make a carnival every day, in radiant cottons and gold bracelets that smile at you across the street.

Description from **John le Carré**'s espionage novel *The Night Manager* (1993). A small part of the action takes place in the fictional northern Quebec community of "Espérance."

Shoes are such a personal artifact. They tell you about the owner's social standing, habits, culture, and religion. That's what makes them special.

Sonja Bata, founder, The Bata Shoe Museum, Toronto, brochure called *The Bata Shoe Museum*, May 1995.

Fashion is what each of us does about Naked.

Gale Garnett, commentator, "Fashion & Design," *The Globe and Mail*, 28 Nov. 1996.

I don't think people want bulky clothes—even in Canada.

Bill Blass, U.S. fashion designer, interviewed by Tim Blanks, CBC-TV's *Fashion File*, 10 Jan. 1999.

FATHERS See also FAMILY

Every man who amounts to a damn has several fathers... the fathers you choose for yourself are the significant ones... no man knows his father.

Thoughts of a character in **Robertson Davies**' novel *The Manticore* (1972).

FEAR

Fear alone stands in the way of developing a land larger than the United States.

Vilhjalmur Stefansson, Arctic explorer, address in Toronto in 1923, quoted in *The Globe and Mail*, 18 Nov. 1959.

As a very eminent psychiatrist once said to me: "We attract what we fear." What we fear is the portion of life that remains unlived. Our task, if we seek spiritual wholeness, is to be sure that what has been rejected is not, therefore, forgotten, and its possibility wiped out.

Robertson Davies, man-of-letters, "Gleams and Glooms" (1976), *One Half of Robertson Davies: Provocative Pronouncements on a Wide Range of Topics* (1977).

On Fear: Fear is a state of mind in *itself*, irrespective of what one is afraid *of*.

Northrop Frye, cultural critic, interviewed by Allan Gould, "Chatelaine's Celebrity I.D.," *Chatelaine*, Nov. 1982.

Everyone is frightened of something, and some people are frightened of everything. This is really the beginning.

Thoughts of the narrator of **Paul William Roberts**' novel *The Palace of Fears* (1994).

Sometimes the shadow is bigger / than the cat

Robert Priest, aphorist, *Time Release Poems* (1997).

The only thing I fear is my own mouth.

Mel Lastman, Mayor of North York, candidate for Mayor of Greater Toronto, quoted by John Barber, "Toronto," *The Globe and Mail*, 4 Nov. 1997.

FEDERALISM See also FEDERAL-PROVINCIAL RELATIONS

I hold strongly the view that Canadian federalism can be assisted by the study of Canadian history.

Sir Campbell Stuart, Montreal-born chief of propaganda in London during World War II, *Opportunity Knocks Once* (1952).

Canada provides us with an irony. No student of federalism can avoid studying the Canadian experience, for it is one of the oldest and most articulated in the world. But few Canadians are students of federalism. In spite of the fact that Canadians live in one of the world's most unique federal experiments, most of us have only the faintest notion of the nature, origins, and workings of our system.

John Paul Harney, political scientist, "New Forms of Federalism" (1977), *Canada's Third Option* (1978) edited by S.D. Berkowitz and Robert K. Logan.

It will endeavour to make a virtue of its tolerance of decentralization: Canada will be the first post-modern nation-state with a weak centre acting as a kind of holding company for a few activities, chief among them the business of handing out equalization payments. The richer provinces will complain, but at least they will be left to get on with most of their own affairs virtually unimpeded by the centre.

Editorial feature, "Survey on Canada," *The Economist*, 19 June 1991, reprinted in *The Globe and Mail*, 19 July 1991.

FEDERAL-PROVINCIAL RELATIONS See also FEDERALISM

The stated distribution of federal money to the provinces is an anomaly which we could not reconcile with the public spirit and dignity of the States, nor recognize as a proper function of the Government.

Charles Dudley Warner, American travel writer, *Studies in the South and West* (1889).

While the ship of state now sails on larger ventures and into foreign waters she still retains the watertight compartments which are an essential part of her original structure.

Celebrated judgement of **Lord Atkin**, Judicial Committee of the Privy Council, in the Labour

Conventions case of 1936–37, concerning interpretation and implementation within Canada of international treaties concluded by the federal government, as noted by P. Macklem et al., editors, *Canadian Constitutional Law* (2nd, 1997).

To unify ourselves in the strict sense of the word would be to work for the King of Prussia—I mean for the President of the United States. We will live decentralized or risk dying paralysed around Ottawa.

André Laurendeau, editor, "Is There a Crisis of Nationalism?" (1952–53), *French-Canadian Nationalism: An Anthology* (1969) edited by Ramsay Cook.

Paradoxically, rigidity at the centre has always seemed a greater danger to unity in Canada than independence on the verges.

George Woodcock, author, *The Canadians* (1979).

The genius of Canadian federalism ... lies in your consistent ability to overcome differences through reason and compromise.

Pierre Elliott Trudeau, Prime Minister, address, Patriation Ceremony, Ottawa, 17 April 1982.

Le beau risque

Phrase ("The fine risk") associated with federalism and with the return to power of Quebec Premier **Robert Bourassa** in 1985, quoted by Pierre Elliott Trudeau in *Maclean's*, 28 Sept. 1992.

The average Albertan pays an annual tax of $900 to enable a province like Newfoundland, which receives 60 percent of its budget from the general slush fund, to remain semi-solvent and attached to the confederation.

Charles F. Doran, School of Advanced International Studies, Johns Hopkins University, "Will Canada Unravel?" *Foreign Affairs*, Sept.–Oct. 1996.

While espousing partnerships, Ottawa will largely do what it thinks best; while proclaiming solidarity, provinces will act in their own individual self-interest.

Jeffrey Simpson, columnist, "Show of Solidarity," *The Globe and Mail*, 10 Dec. 1997.

Our founding principles are diversity and unity: Canada is a federation, not just a nation, and that says it all.

Bob Rae, former Premier of Ontario, "An Unfounded Nation," *National Post*, 3 July 1999.

FEELINGS See also EMOTIONS

Feeling is the power that drives art.

David Milne, painter, quoted by Anne McDougall in *Anne Savage: The Story of a Canadian Painter* (1977).

I think ... no, I do not think, I feel ....

Laurier LaPierre, historian and broadcaster, characteristic remark, address, Committee for an Independent Canada, Toronto, 15 Oct. 1977. He has been dubbed "Sir Wilfrid Laurier LaPierre."

You get bitter / and then you get better

Robert Priest, aphorist, *Time Release Poems* (1997).

FEMINISM See also MONTREAL MASSACRE, WOMEN

The country is yours, ladies; politics is simply public affairs. Yours & mine & everyone's. The government has enfranchised you, but it cannot emancipate you; that is done by your own processes of thought.

Nellie L. McClung, suffragette, remarks made in 1917, quoted by Linda Rasmussen, et al., in *A Harvest Yet to Reap: A History of Prairie Women* (1976).

For millions of years women have catered to the male ego, only to produce a breed of male with utter delusions of grandeur. Women have a moral duty to save the world from the terrible mess men have made of it.

Kim Campbell, student at the University of British Columbia, campus newspaper *The Ubyssey*, Nov. 1965, quoted by Tim Harper in *The Toronto Star*, 27 March 1993.

Feminism is the only way to alleviate the kind of horror and pain that exists now in the relationship between men and women.

Maryon Kantaroff, sculptor, quoted by Mary McAlpine in *The Vancouver Sun*, 22 Nov. 1974.

Most leading feminists are deservedly cast-off wives, pseudo-intellectual frumps and incurable lesbians, a vociferous motley of shrews, viragos, prudes and charlatans.

Attributed to newspaperman **McKenzie Porter** in a column in *The Toronto Sun* in 1975 by Peter

Worthington, "Irrepressible Ken Porter," *The Toronto Sun,* 11 April 1999.

When Nora slammed the door in Ibsen's nineteenth-century play, *A Doll's House,* the sound was a slam that (slowly, slowly) was heard around the world.

Betty Jane Wylie and **Lynne MacFarlane**, authors, *Everywoman's Money Book* (1989).

I think that's what feminism is. The coming together of all the colours of sisters and cousins.

Anne Cameron, writer, "The Operative Principle Is Trust," *Language in Her Eye: Views on Writing and Gender by Canadian Women Writing in English* (1990) edited by Libby Scheier, Sarah Sheard, and Eleanor Wachtel.

We have been there. We have all been there.

Doris Anderson, feminist, *The Unfinished Revolution: The Status of Women in Twelve Countries* (1991). This is the refrain the author adds to her case histories of social and economic difficulties faced by women in Western countries today.

Am I the only one who doesn't know whether to wear red lipstick to a feminist gathering?

Sandra Shamas, comedian and star of the show "My Boyfriend's Back and There's Gonna Be Laundry," quoted by Martin Knelman in "The Wickedest Witch of the North," *Toronto Life,* Dec. 1991.

I'm not a feminist, I do exactly what I want.

Sara Botsford, actress, quoted by John Haslett Cuff in *The Globe and Mail,* 23 May 1992.

We, their sisters and brothers, remember, and work for a better world. In memory, and in grief, for all the women who have been murdered by men. For women of all countries, all classes, all ages, all colours.

Controversial inscription for the proposed Women's Monument Project to be erected in Vancouver. Designed by the artist **Beth Alber**, the "marker of change" consists of fourteen pink granite benches, one for each of the young Montreal women slain at the École Polytechnique on 6 Dec. 1989. As noted by Henry Gale in *The Globe and Mail,* 23 Nov. 1994, the inscription's words "murdered by men" were immediately judged provocative. Noting the increase in modern society of violence against women, Alber argued, "But there is a human face behind the fist, and most of the time it's a man's."

Biofeminists began to speak, not just *for* women, but *instead of* and over the voices of the women who spoke for themselves.

John Fekete, philosopher, *Moral Panic: Biopolitics Rising* (2nd ed., 1995).

What feminists do in the legal system is to expose its previously unseen maleness and attempt to deconstruct it, in order to make room for the viewpoints, the concerns, and the experience of women.

Mary Eberts, lawyer and feminist, quoted by Nicolaas van Rijn in *The Toronto Star,* 8 Oct. 1996.

I think social feminism, genuine social & intellectual equality between men & women, a centrally important issue. Feminist *literary* criticism is mostly heifer-shit.

Northrop Frye, cultural critic, Entry 400, Notebook 1993.1, *Northrop Frye Newsletter,* Summer 1997.

I am delighted to hear that Canada seems to be edging back toward the cosmopolitan pleasure principle after its recent years in the ice grip of MacKinnonite censorship. (Point of information for Americans: Catharine MacKinnon's totalitarian anti-porn measures, which were twice struck down by the courts as unconstitutional in the United States, were foolishly adopted in Canada and led to tremendous trouble for gay bookstores, whose shipments were seized at the border. Ironically, the writings of MacKinnon's fanatical anti-porn cohort, Andrea Dworkin, were also seized.)

Camille Paglia, American cultural critic and columnist, "Ask Camille," Internet magazine "Salon," 10 June 1997.

FENCES

The important question in terms of function is, what is the fence intended to keep out? Or in? The best fence, in rural traditions, horse-high, bull-strong and sheep-tight—in imperial measure, that converts to about six feet high for horses, five feet for cattle and at least four feet for sheep. The size of the rails determines the size of the escape gaps between them, but on average, sheep need a five-rail fence, horses and cattle three or four. A five-foot-high four-rail fence is standard.

Charles Long, writer, "Getting the Hang of It," *Harrowsmith*, May–June 1987.

FICTION See LITERATURE, STORIES

FILM See also ACTORS & ACTING; FILM, CANADIAN; HOLLYWOOD; NATIONAL FILM BOARD

The world's first full-length feature, running for more than an hour, was premiered on December 24, 1906, at the Athenaeum Hall in Melbourne, Victoria. Made for $2,250, Charles Tait's *The Story of the Kelly Gang* was an epic drama about the Australian bushranger Ned Kelly. But nobody knows the name of the star. He was an unidentified Canadian from a theatrical touring company who walked off the set shortly before the film was completed. The movie was finished with a stand-in playing the remaining scenes in long-shot.

"Movie Firsts," *The People's Almanac Presents The Twentieth Century* (1995) by **David Wallechinsky**.

Beside this film the unusual photoplay, the so-called "dramatic" work of the screen, becomes as thin and blank as the celluloid on which it is printed.

Unsigned review of *Nanook of the North* (1922), the world's first documentary film, *The New York Times*, 19 June 1922.

You're only as good as your last picture.

Marie Dressler, star of stage and screen, born in Cobourg, Ont., originator of the observation according to Leslie Halliwell in *The Filmgoer's Book of Quotations* (1978).

Brother against brother, bride against bride—family skeleton shakes its bones as young wife comes to stay, and the curious thing we call the family becomes the flaming crucible of love and jealousy, of tragedy and triumph, behind the life-worn walls of Jalna, homestead of the Whiteoaks.

RKO press release for the movie *Jalna* (1935), based on Mazo de la Roche's novel, as quoted by Ronald Hambleton in *Mazo de la Roche of Jalna* (1966).

Good-bye, Mr. Massey.

"Visual errors are legion in movies, but mistakes on the sound track are much rarer—usually they can be corrected. One of the few examples occurred in *Abe Lincoln in Illinois* (1940). There is a scene at a railroad depot where Lincoln, played by Raymond Massey, is setting out for Washington for his inauguration as president. The crowds wave and cheer and call out 'Good-bye, Mr. Lincoln!' All except one absent-minded extra who hollers, 'Good-bye, Mr. Massey.'" Noted by David Wallechinsky in "Movie Oddities," *The People's Almanac Presents The Twentieth Century* (1995).

I always think of Canada in terms of fresh air. In my 20s, I was a stage actor on the road, and played in Toronto, Hamilton, Ont., Montreal, and lots of tiny places you probably never heard of. I couldn't always afford the best hotels, and in winter there was no shortage of fresh air, nicely refrigerated.

Cecil B. DeMille, Hollywood director, recalling his youth as a touring actor, quoted by his daughter Cecilia DeMille Harper as told to Bob Willett, *Liberty*, Dec. 1956. Cecilia noted: "Father has a deep liking for Canadians. My adopted sister, Katherine, was born in Vancouver, B.C., daughter of an ex-high school principal there, Edwin Lester. And Father's public relations chief is ex-Torontonian Art Arthur, brother of Hye Bossin, editor of *Canadian Film Weekly*."

The movie, physiologically, is the union of the eye and the foot.

Marshall McLuhan, communications pioneer, observation made in 1964, "A McLuhan Sourcebook," *The Essential McLuhan* (1995) edited by Eric McLuhan and Frank Zingrone.

My heart grew lighter as we travelled west: cities looked cleaner. Our route was Winnipeg, Tacoma, Seattle, Vancouver, Portland. In Winnipeg and Vancouver, audiences were essentially English and in spite of my pro-American leanings it was pleasant to play before them.

Charles Chaplin, vaudeville actor, recalling his trip across Canada in 1913 to join the Keystone Film Company of Mack Sennett in Hollywood and become the "little tramp," *My Autobiography* (1964).

Spontaneous behaviour and dialogue is purer than re-expression if you can record it well.

Allan King, documentary filmmaker, quoted by Bernadette Andrews in *The Toronto Telegram*, 5 April 1969.

I think they're going to give you an Oscar for finishing a film.

Ted Kotcheff, film director, referring to financing difficulties and ever-present awards, quoted in *The Toronto Star*, 30 March 1976.

The body is the wellspring of horror.

David Cronenberg, director of horror movies, quoted by Lawrence O'Toole in *Maclean's*, 16 July 1979.

I'm photogenic. I want to use it to seduce millions.

Carole Laure, film actress, quoted in *Canada Today/D'Aujourd'hui*, Nov. 1979.

I knew my films were good because the audience told me.

Ivan Reitman, Czech-born, Hamilton-raised film producer and director, quoted by Ron Base in *The Toronto Star*, 8 June 1981.

We used to talk, we talked all the time, and I told him about my idea. I wanted to build a multi-mini-cinema that could run foreign films. My idea was to build about twelve screens having a small enough number of seats that you could keep a picture running a long time until people found out about it. You know, with foreign pictures it takes a long time before people decide they want to see them.

Nat Taylor, film exhibitor, exponent on the multiplex or cineplex theatre, original investor in what became Cineplex Odeon, infusing his youthful fellow partner Garth Drabinsky with the notion that revitalized film exhibition, quoted by Jaimie Hubbard in *Public Screening: The Battle for Cineplex Odeon* (1990).

Can you believe that Warren Beatty is half-Canadian—the top half.

Attributed to film personality **Shirley MacLaine**, Warren Beatty's sister, by Rick Groen in *The Globe and Mail*, 30 Dec. 1990.

What's IMAX? It sounds like a makeup—Eye Max, beautiful eyes.

Paul McCartney, former Beatle, visiting Toronto on 25 Oct. 1991 to promote his concert film *Get Back*, unaware that the Rolling Stones' *At the Max* was the same day premiering in the giant-screen IMAX format; quoted by Peter Howell in *The Toronto Star* the following day.

I've never met a movie I didn't like. Even a bad picture, you know, is interesting.

Attributed to **Elwy Yost**, host for two decades of TVO's "Saturday Night at the Movies," by Eric Kohanik in *The Hamilton Spectator*, 20 Nov. 1993.

It now seems bizarre that Shakespeare's plays survived their first 400 years on earth in much better shape than D.W. Griffith's films survived their first four decades.

Robert Fulford, columnist, "The Ideology of the Book," *Queen's Quarterly*, Winter 1994. Fulford had in mind loss of almost all the silent cinema produced between 1910 and 1930: "Today no more than ten per cent of these silent films exist."

If you walk from Edmonton to Guatemala, you will learn more than even in five years of film school.

Werner Herzog, German film director, speaking in Edmonton, quoted by Geoff Pevere in *The Globe and Mail*, 12 March 1996.

Ultimately everyone wants his own adjective... I want to be "Cronenbergesque."

David Cronenberg, film director, once known as the Baron of Blood, interview, CBC-TV, 25 April 1999.

FILM, CANADIAN See also FILM

I have another ambition, and that is, to go home, back to Canada, and make some big pictures there. I am still—always will be—a Canadian, never having given my allegiance to any other country. I have wanted to see Canada as a motion picture centre for years, and one day I am going to have my desire fulfilled, in spite of a decided obstacle, which is in my way.

Allan Dwan, Canadian-born Hollywood director, *Maclean's*, 1 Feb. 1920, reprinted as "Canada Has a 'Movie' Future," *Maclean's*, 1 Jan. 1996.

Hmmnn, not bad... not bad.

Joseph Goebbels, Nazi propaganda minister, watching footage from a World War II propaganda film produced by the National Film Board, from the narration of the film *Has Anybody Here Seen Canada?* (1979) directed by John Kramer.

Rather a good bit of luck. Saw a rather good film. *Nanook of the North.* All about Eskimos. Of course, it's old, but—

Lines spoken by the actor **Denholm Elliott** to Ralph Richardson, playing his father, in the British film *The Holly and the Ivy* (1953).

I didn't care much for the script, but the scenery in Canada was beautiful.

Marilyn Monroe, movie star, recalling being on location in Banff, Alta., for the filming of *River of No Return* (1954), a Western set in the 1880s, directed by Otto Preminger.

Goin' Down the Road is a classic. It was the first Canadian movie I saw that made me think, "Hey, we can make movies in Canada—they don't have to come from Britain or the States."

Roger Abbott, comic with the Royal Canadian Air Farce, on the 1970 Canadian film directed by Don Shebib, quoted by Bill Brioux in *TV Guide*, 13 July 1996.

I loved Duddy Kravitz. I was Duddy Kravitz and I recognized Duddy in myself as you have to recognize him in you. He's in everybody.

Richard Dreyfuss, American actor who played the lead in *The Apprenticeship of Duddy Kravitz* (1974) directed by Ted Kotcheff based on Mordecai Richler's novel, quoted by James McLarty in *Motion*, July–Aug. 1974.

Scripts don't just flutter down with the snowflakes in Montreal.

Geneviève Bujold, actress, explaining why she moved from Montreal to Malibu, quoted by George Gamester in *The Toronto Star*, 27 Feb. 1975.

The Canadian way to make a film is to gather a dozen well-known Canadians and bring in George C. Scott as the star. Why?

Tony van Bridge, actor, quoted by Herbert Whittaker in *The Globe and Mail*, 24 May 1975.

I just wanna thank my mother, the man, and the mountain.

F.R. (Budge) Crawley, film director, accepting an Oscar for the documentary *The Man Who Skied Down Everest* (1976), quoted by Robert Hughes in *Time*, 12 April 1976, who called it "the most richly bogus solemnity of the evening."

Earlier this year I spent three months in Los Angeles as part of my efforts to become a screenwriter in Canada.

Lesley Ellen Harris, screenwriter, "Made in L.A.," *The Canadian Forum*, Nov. 1993.

Canadians make movies about people who are smaller than life.

Quip heard at the Banff Television Festival, noted by Kate Barris in *The WGC News* (*The Writers Guild of Canada Newsletter*), Autumn 1994, who added, "It hurts, but it's true."

The last big American film outta here described our crews as "Mexicans in sweaters"—we thought that was very funny.

Mark Desroches, B.C. Film Commissioner, referring to a U.S. film crew attracted to shooting locales on the West Coast, quoted by Stefan Schwartz and Richard Holmes in "Art Forms," *The Globe and Mail*, 28 Sept. 1994.

Film is an art made with lenses.

Robert LePage, stage and film director, interviewed by Shelagh Rogers, CBC Radio's *Morningside*, 27 Nov. 1995.

FINANCE

See also BANKS & BANKERS; ECONOMICS; FINANCE, PERSONAL; INTEREST; INVESTMENT; MONEY; STOCK MARKET; TAXES

Once a nation loses control over its currency and its credit, it does not matter much who in that nation makes laws. Once in control, money lenders will ruin any country.

W.L. Mackenzie King, Prime Minister, speech, quoted by Adrien Lambert in the House of Commons, 1 Dec. 1978.

Life is less amusing since I became Minister of Finance.

John C. Crosbie, Minister of Finance, following the electoral victory of Joe Clark, quoted by Wayne Cheveldayoff in *The Globe and Mail*, 24 Oct. 1979.

The Minister of Finance has just announced that Canada had a better third quarter than Bulgaria.

Dave Broadfoot, comedian, quoted by Sid Adilman in *The Toronto Star*, 4 Jan. 1992.

Finance Ministers are normally the only rational members of any cabinet.

Paul Martin Jr., Minister of Finance, address, Association of Canadian Investment Dealers, London, England, 11 April 1994, quoted by Paul Koring in *The Globe and Mail* the following day.

Thus transfer payments bail out provincial governments from about half the harm that their policies cause.

David R. Henderson, Canadian-born research fellow with the Hoover Institution, "If Quebec Separates, Almost Everybody Wins," *The Wall Street Journal*, 19 Jan. 1996.

Everyone with humanity and compassion would be opposed to the policies of the Department of Finance.

Attributed to Finance Minister **Paul Martin Jr.** by investigative journalist Linda McQuaig, interviewed by Michael Enright, CBC Radio, 23 March 1999.

If there is a single issue that could lead to the breakup of Canada, it's the exchange rate.

Robert Mundell, Ontario-born economist, Nobel laureate, quoted by Peter Shawn Taylor, "Nobel Prize a Triumph for a Low-Key Economic Maverick," *National Post*, 14 Oct. 1999.

FINANCE, PERSONAL See also FINANCE

There is the possibility, even the likelihood, of self-approving and extravagantly error-prone behaviour on the part of those closely associated with money.

John Kenneth Galbraith, economist and essayist, *A Short History of Financial Euphoria* (1990, 1993).

Do you sincerely want to be rich?

Rhetorical question asked of future sales representatives by **Bernie Cornfeld**, founder of Investors Overseas Services Ltd., a mutual-fund holding company chartered in New Brunswick in 1969, which went spectacularly bankrupt in 1970; quoted in Cornfeld's obituary, *The Toronto Star*, 1 March 1995.

Ninety per cent of financial planning is spending less than you make.

David Chilton, financial planner, *The Wealthy Barber: Common Sense to Financial Planning* (1989).

FINLAND

I was also very drawn to the country itself, resembling, as it did in climate and landscape, the severe beauties of Canada. The Finns share with Canadians the mystique of living in the presence of the North, in the way other peoples live with mountains or the sea, something always present even when they sleep.

Robert MacNeil, broadcaster and memoirist, referring to a visit in 1962, *The Right Place at the Right Time* (1982).

FIREARMS See also WEAPONRY

For the next hour we're going to look at the full question of gun ownership and gun control, and we are going to put forward the following proposition: That all guns... should be totally banned. Now, in doing this, we're stretching some CBC journalistic policies here. This morning we make no claims to impartiality or objectivity. We are saying flat out: Get rid of guns.

Michael Enright, host, introducing a panel discussion on the subject of firearms in private hands, CBC Radio's *This Morning*, 29 April 1999. Enright's statement and the panel's position were criticized. The CBC's ombudsman, according to a CP news story, 17 Nov. 1999, ruled that the host and panel members should have remained impartial and objective.

Can this be the Canada of old, carved out of wilderness by independent men and women of uncommon valour?

Charlton Heston, movie actor and President of the National Rifle Association of America, address, B.C. Wildlife Federation, Prince George, B.C., 13 April 2000, printed in the *National Post* the following day. He warned that registration of handguns and long guns would lead to confiscation.

FIRST MINISTERS' CONFERENCES

It is interesting to note how quickly political personalities can change, thus casting doubt on the significance of agreements reached by the First Ministers—the Prime Minister and ten premiers (Executive Federalism). A striking illustration of how the key players in the 1982 Constitution have largely disappeared... all within a decade.

Marjorie Bowker, retired judge and critic of federal agreements, noting the short political lives of most so-called key players in constitutional agreements, *Canada's Constitutional Crisis: Making Sense of It All* (1991).

FIRST NATIONS See ABORIGINAL PEOPLE, INUIT, MÉTIS PEOPLE, NATIVE PEOPLES

FISH & FISHING See also SPORTS

I'se the b'y that builds the boat, / And I'se the b'y that sails her! / I'se the b'y that catches the fish / And takes 'em home to Lizer.

Fifth of five verses of "I'se the B'y that Builds the Boat," traditional Newfoundland dance ditty, included by Edith Fowke in *The Penguin Book of Canadian Folk Songs* (1973). George Woodcock in *The Canadians* (1979) wrote that it "combines authentic detail with a kind of wild surrealist fantasy."

For the supreme test that proves fishing to be a real sport is that no true fisherman is dependent upon his luck for his happiness.

Helen E. Williams, essayist, *Spinning Wheels and Homespun* (1923).

I hope the Canada business comes off. It would be an interesting change. I believe there's incredible fishing in Canada, if you care about that.

George Orwell, author, letter to George Woodcock who was planning to return to Canada, 23 March 1948, *The Collected Essays, Journalism and Letters of George Orwell: Volume IV: In Front of Your Nose: 1945–1950* (1968) edited by Sonia Orwell and Ian Angus.

You can look it up if you like: according to *Colombo's Canadian Quotations* no Canadian of any significance has ever uttered a public word on caviar.

Jurgen Gothe, writer and broadcaster, "Caviar," *enRoute*, Oct. 1977.

Although the industry has many problems, a shortage of fish is not one of them.

Sentence from the **Task Force on Atlantic Fisheries**, 1982, quoted by John Speers in "Atlantic Fishery Bound for the Rocks?" *The Toronto Star*, 8 July 1989.

The idea of a youngster, a pole cut from the alders, a can of worms and a lazy summer's day has become as outdated as martinis, cars that owners can fix and voting for the candidate.

Roy MacGregor, columnist, *Ottawa Citizen*, 27 May 1987. The column discusses the "re-invention" of sports that require computerized fishing reels with "built-in memory chips" and language in which "fish are no longer found at different depths, but display certain suspension characteristics."

But it's never the actual fishing that stays with you, only the quality of your surroundings: its smells and sounds—its feel—so that suddenly, years later, you can catch the odour of wet pine needles, or hear the happy giggle of fast water running over stones, and be transported back, immediately and totally.

Hume Cronyn, actor, recalling vacations at La Roche, Que., *A Terrible Liar: Memoirs* (1991).

We are the world's largest exporter of fish products, but if you want a state-of-the-art vessel, or if you want to master the techniques of aquaculture, you take a trip to Norway. Today, that is no longer good enough.

C.E. Ritchie, Chairman and CEO, Bank of Nova Scotia, "Do Canadians Really Want to Compete?" address, The Canadian Club, 29 April 1991.

It is difficult to get international publicity on overfishing—you don't see any famous actresses running over to kiss and cuddle a codfish.

John C. Crosbie, Minister of Fisheries, encouraging Japanese officials to end overfishing in the Northwest Atlantic, quoted by Canadian Press, 15 Dec. 1992.

Feel sorry for the scientist who says fish are cold-blooded; if you've ever seen the joyous leap of a trout on a May morning, you'll know that it's the poor *scientist* who's cold-blooded.

Maurus E. Mallon, aphorist, 18 Feb. 1993.

Then afterward I saw this documentary about how codfish have been gill-netted into extinction in Newfoundland in Canada, so I went out to Burger King to get a Whaler fishwich-type breaded deep-fried filet sandwich while there was still time.

Narration from **Douglas Coupland**'s novel *Microserfs* (1995).

That lost, lonely, unattractive, unwanted turbot clinging by its fingernails to the edge of the Grand Banks is safe.

Brian Tobin, Minister of Fisheries, reaching an

agreement in the Canada-Spain fisheries dispute, news conference, Ottawa, 15 April 1995, quoted by Shawn McCarthy in *The Toronto Star* the following day.

The fish don't carry flags. They swim and they don't carry passports.

Jean Chrétien, Prime Minister, referring to the border-crossing salmon at the time of the West Coast salmon-fishing dispute, CBC Radio's *National News*, 21 July 1997.

The fishery is the DNA of Newfoundland life.

Rex Murphy, broadcaster, convocation address, Memorial University, St. John's, Nfld., published in *The Globe and Mail*, 13 Nov. 1997.

Farm salmon are bred to be fat, dumb and happy. In the wild, you want a fish that is lean, mean and able to evade predators.

Fred Whoriskey, researcher, Atlantic Salmon Federation, contrasting farm and fresh salmon, quoted by Kelly Toughill, "Wild Salmon Decimated by Farm Fish," *The Toronto Star*, 25 June 1999.

FITNESS See also HEALTH

These men are about evenly matched. That's because the average thirty-year-old Canadian is in about the same shape as the average sixty-year-old Swede. Run. Walk. Cycle. Let's get Canada moving again. This message is from the Canadian movement for personal fitness, PARTICIPaction.

Wording of the fitness commercial shown on national television a total of six times, Fall 1973. Conceived by **Keith McKerracher**, President of the Institute of Canadian Advertising, it was sponsored by the Fitness and Amateur Sports' National Advisory Council. No advertising agency was involved and no research was conducted, yet it struck a responsive chord in the hearts of Canadians.

FLAGS See also EMBLEMS, NATIONAL

The Canadian service flag has a maple leaf in it—a live leaf, and when it begins to turn crimson, it is very pretty.

William Faulkner, future novelist, writing from Toronto to his mother, 9 July 1918, *Thinking of Home: William Faulkner's Letters to His Mother and Father 1918–1925* (1922) edited by James G. Watson.

Now I ask you, how are you going to be able to see that white flag in winter?

John G. Diefenbaker, former Prime Minister, criticizing the design of the Maple Leaf flag in the House of Commons, as noted in *Time*, 26 June 1964. Diefenbaker later complained that schoolchildren would confuse the proposed Maple Leaf design with the flag of Peru.

This is the flag of the future, but it does not dishonour the past.

Lester B. Pearson, Prime Minister, address, intro ducing the new Maple Leaf flag to replace the old Union Jack of Great Britain, House of Commons, 15 Dec. 1964.

Quebec's flag (barely forty years old) includes a white cross to symbolize Christianity and four *fleurs-de-lis* "to evoke the kingdom of France"; Quebec's emblem is the lily that was the symbol of France until the revolution.

John Grimond, journalist, "Nice Country, Nice Mess," *The Economist*, 29 June 1991.

I think there should be four flags, one for every season: a very small maple leaf for spring, sort of yellowish green, a big green leaf for summer, a red one for fall, and just a white outline of a leaf for winter. Family rituals could be built around changing the flag.

Leonard Cohen, poet and songwriter, quoted by Brian D. Johnson in "Life of a Lady's Man," *Maclean's*, 7 Dec. 1992.

I can also report, having just spent some time in cottage country north of Toronto, that the Canadian flag looks natural and noble in green and watery settings, whereas it seems kitschy and faintly embarrassing in an urban context—just the opposite of the Stars and Stripes.

Bronwyn Drainie, columnist, "Spectator," *The Globe and Mail*, 18 Sept. 1993.

Unlike the Americans, we do not salute our flag; as a matter of fact, we got along for a century without one.

Mitchell Sharp, former Minister of Finance and Minister of External Affairs, *Which Reminds Me...: A Memoir* (1994).

There were too many flags on display.

Suzanne Tremblay, Bloc Québécois M.P., griping about the Maple Leaf flags at the Canadian athletes' quarters at Nagano, Japan, at the conclusion of the Winter Olympic Games, 22 Feb. 1998. In response, the Reform Party organized a bout of flag-waving in the House of Commons, as noted by Tim Harper in *The Toronto Star,* 18 March 1998.

FLORIDA See also UNITED STATES OF AMERICA

It is likely that Florida will be annexed by Quebec before they will reclaim Labrador.

Steve Rubin, Montreal commentator, 14 Oct. 1991.

...thirty miles up a two-lane highway from the employment opportunities of Key West, meaning forty-five minutes if there's no road construction and I don't get caught behind some sun-dazed Canadian tourists. I hate the drive....

Barbara Ehrenreich, American travel writer, "Nickel-and-Dimed," *Harper's Magazine,* Jan. 1999.

FLOWERS See also GARDENS

There is not a flower that buds, however small, that is not for some wise purpose.

George Copway, Ojibwa chief, *The Traditional History and characteristic Sketches of the Ojibway Nation* (1850).

Be not such a Canadian thistle!

Exclamation about a difficult person found in **Herman Melville**'s novel *The Confidence-Man: His Masquerade* (1857).

In the tropics it is the plants that live intensely, thrusting up and flowering overnight, while the work of man proceeds so slowly as to be at times quite imperceptible.

Colin McPhee, Montreal-born composer, long-time resident of Bali, *A House in Bali* (1946).

She would rather that you brought her a daisy than that you sent her a dozen roses.

Richard Needham, newspaper columnist, referring to an agreeable woman, *The Wit and Wisdom of Richard Needham* (1977).

Although man is a miracle, to many the flower is a more compelling expression of perfection.

Dorothy Maclean, medium, *To Hear the Angels Sing: An Odyssey of Co-Creation with the Devic* Kingdom (1980).

This seems to me to be a rather dead country. I can't feel you have nearly enough flowers. I find Canada rather depressing, that people here all grow the same old flowers in their gardens.

John Fowles, novelist, interviewed in Toronto, quoted by Philip Marchand, "Artsnews & Reviews," *The Toronto Star,* 7 May 1998.

FOLKLORE See also MYTHOLOGY

The Canadian Pacific Railway Company...is a true empire-builder. It has a romantic sense of nation building. They have taken these foreign groups, have fostered their folk-lore, their songs, their dances, their customs, and are winning these people for Canada—they are weaving them into our own life.

Charles W. Gordon, imperialist and novelist who wrote as Ralph Connor, discussing the CPR's role in fostering local lore and national cultures during the 1920s, interviewed by R.E. Knowles in *The Toronto Star,* 30 April 1929.

We don't know what we don't have.

Carole Carpenter, folklorist, York University, about the loss of lore over time, 1986.

When a reader, in Yellowknife, Northwest Territories, wrote offering to be my listening post for urban legends up there, I thought, "Sure, ha ha; urban and suburban folklore can't possibly get that far into the wilds." A week later, he sent me notes on a couple of good ones he had just heard in Yellowknife. When I got a similar call from White Horse [sic] up in the Yukon, I listened.

Jan Howard Brunvand, folklorist, collector of urban legends, *Curses! Broiled Again! The Hottest Urban Legends Going* (1989).

I feel, if I collect from the folk, I should return to the folk.

Edith Fowke, folklorist, sharing the songs of the people with the people through publication, interviewed by Val Ross in *The Globe and Mail,* 5 May 1994.

There's no pretense that these are anonymous folk tales; they're only anonymous if some ass didn't write down the names of the storytellers.

Robert Bringhurst, author, referring to translations of Haida traditional tales, quoted by

Christopher Dafoe in "In Person," *The Globe and Mail*, 24 June 1995.

FOOD & DRINK See also ALCOHOL, BEER, CHEESE, WINE, VEGETARIANISM

An honest brew makes its own friends.

Attributed to **John Molson**, founder of Molson Breweries in Montreal in 1786, recalled in advertisements in 1999.

Our inns are bad: that is to say, many of them clean and comfortable enough, and the landlords almost uniformly civil and obliging, but the proverb of "God sending meat and the devil cooks" never was so fully illustrated as in this country; for, with the superabaundance of the raw material, the manufactured article of a good dinner is hardly to be found in a public-house in the province.

William (Tiger) Dunlop, colonist, referring specifically to waystations in early Ontario, *Statistical Sketches of Upper Canada for the Use of Emigrants* (1832).

October 17—Travelled 15 miles, made supper of toasted rawhide.sealskin boots. Palatable. Feel encouraged.

One of the final entries in the diary for 1906 kept by **Isaac O. Stringer**, Bishop of the Yukon, later Archbishop of Rupertsland, while stranded in a snowstorm on Edmonton Trail between Fort McPherson and Dawson City, Yukon Territory, as quoted by Frank A. Peake in *The Bishop Who Ate His Boots: A Biography of Isaac O. Stringer* (1966). If Charles Chaplin based the boot-eating scene in his movie *The Gold Rush* (1926) on Stringer's experience, the actor-director was influenced by the oral tradition, as the first printed reference to the episode appeared in Stringer's biography in 1966.

Canada's a wealthy country, / As all have said; / For here the rich man and the poor / Can have white bread.

One of six stanzas of a settler's song, loosely translated, recorded in Ukrainian in Kamsack, Sask., quoted by Robert B. Klymasz in *An Introduction to the Ukrainian-Canadian Immigrant Folksong Cycle* (1970).

It's hard to be hungry and be a Christian.

Line from the novel *Such Is My Beloved* (1934) by **Morley Callaghan**.

Finally, all the meals served by this air line seem to have been designed by and for a schoolgirl of twelve, being composed almost exclusively of sweet stuff, jelly, whipped cream, chocolate, with no flavours enjoyed by the elderly male.

J.B. Priestley, English writer on a tour of Canada, referring to food served on TCA flights, "I Heard the Monotonous, Mournful Voices of Canadian Women," *Liberty*, Aug. 1956.

25 Wonderful Things You Can Do with Snow

Fictitious title of a cookbook compiled by radio personality **Kate Aitken**, according to Max Ferguson on CBC Radio's *Rawhide* in the 1950s.

Outside the bar a sign read / ARCTIC CLUB BAR / Admission to Members only / Membership Tickets available / on request from Barman.

Sign reportedly seen in the Arctic in the 1960s by artist Dorothy McCarthy in *The Good Wine: An Artist Comes of Age* (1991).

He would slip me one of those strong white peppermints that say (still, I think) CANADA on them.

Recollection of **Elizabeth Bishop** who as a child in the 1910s grew up in Great Village, N.S., where her grandfather fed her peppermints in church, recalled in a letter to Anne Stevenson written in 1964, quoted in *Becoming a Poet* (1989) by Elizabeth Bishop with Marianne Moore and Robert Lowell.

If you're interested in cooking, you're also just naturally interested in art, in love, and in culture.

Jehane Benoît, cooking authority, *The Canadian Magazine*, 28 Dec. 1974.

I am beginning to realize the part that food plays in Canadian life—surely greater than in any other country I know. Even in Vancouver, I noticed the extravagant number of food advertisements on the television screens. The Canadian is first and foremost an eating man and putting on weight is his besetting sin, even as a child, in fact especially then.

Description from French author and traveller **Michel Tournier**'s novel *Gemini* (1975).

The ingredients for a successful party? Good company, good food, good wine... and goodbye!

Raymond Canale, Italian-born playwright and Toronto-based aphorist, observation made in 1975.

While going through the newspapers one day, I spotted an ad announcing that one of our favourite Gaijin-type supermarkets was holding what they chose to call a "Canadian Food Festival."

Now I don't recall seeing any ad in any paper ever that aroused my curiosity like that one did. What, I was asking myself, *do* Canadians eat? And I couldn't for the life of me come up with anything.

Think about it—you non-Canadians, anyway—and I bet you'll be hard-pressed for an answer to that one as I was.

Don Maloney, American businessman, columnist for *The Japan Times*, referring to a display in a foreign-style supermarket in Tokyo, "What Do Canadian Eat?" *Japan: It's Not All Raw Fish* (1975).

If you eat better, you love more.

Eugene Whelan, Minister of Agriculture, characteristic remark, address, Calgary, quoted in *The Toronto Star*, 19 Nov. 1976.

Good things grow in Ontario.

Advertising campaign, **Ontario's Agriculture and Food** department, launched with a full-page advertisement in *The Globe and Mail*, 9 Nov. 1977. "Say it over a few times," noted Bill Newman, Ontario's Minister for Agriculture and Food. "It grows on you."

Pepsi maewest... Name given by Quebec Anglophones to the Québécois (pejorative).

Léandre Bergeron, lexicographer, referring to the traditional preference of the French Canadian worker for a bottle of Pepsi-Cola and a Mae West (a chocolate-coated little cake), *The Québécois Dictionary* (1982).

Nobody born after 1910 can make good gravy.

Tim Burke, columnist, *The Montreal Gazette*, 12 Jan. 1983.

Abundance also seemed to breed a vague indifference to food, manifested in a tendency to eat and run, rather than to dine and savour.

Harvey A. Levenstein, historian, *Revolution at the Table: The Transformation of the American Diet* (1988).

Poutine is a fast food of choice of Québécois: a plate of french fries sprinkled liberally with cheese curds and covered with gravy just hot enough not to melt the cheese. Add spaghetti sauce and you have poutine italienne and various ingredients for local variations—shrimps in Matane, pieces of pork fat in pig-raising country north of Quebec City.

Unsigned article, *The Globe and Mail*, 28 Oct. 1989.

With over 70,000 new chemicals added to our environment since the 1940s, how could anyone say that our food supply is the best it's ever been?

Zoltan P. Rona, physician, specialist in holistic medicine, *The Joy of Health: A Doctor's Guide to Nutrition and Alternative Medicine* (1991).

Indeed, it's my opinion there's more mutual understanding fostered over kitchen tables than across all the boardroom tables of the nation!

John Robert Colombo, author, Foreword, *Ethnic Eating: The Canadian Scene Cookbook* (1991).

Chips and vinegard or *poutine*, butter tarts or *tourtière*, dim sum or bagels or chapati or baklava are *à votre choix*. Where else in the world is all this diversity so taken for granted?

Charles Pachter, artist and essayist, *The Globe and Mail*, 28 March 1991.

We do not need to be swallowed up by our obsession with food. We need to be free of it. There are limits to health and, beyond those limits, real things to do in a real world.

Scott Mowbray, food writer, *Food Fight: Truth, Myth and the Food-Health Connection* (1992).

Beware the enterprise not launched with champagne. Remember the Titanic; no bottle was broken over its bow.

Opening sentences of **Tony Aspler**'s mystery novel *Blood is Thicker than Beaujolais* (1993).

I like to write romances almost as much as I like to live them, and most of my cookbooks are blatant attempts to seduce, to encourage people to experiment and wander up the sideroads of their imaginations.

James Barber, chef, *The Urban Peasant: Quick & Simple* (1993).

I discovered the butter tart and, much to my amazement, also discovered that it was unique to us. There's no other country in the world that has this patisserie. As the croissant is to France and as the doughnut is to America, the butter tart is to English Canada.

Charles Pachter, artist, "A Romance with Canada," 23 June 1994, *The Empire Club of Canada: Addresses 1994–95* (1995).

There are only four basic recipes: bake, boil, fry, and screw up.

James Barber, chef, in conversation with Bronwyn Drainie on CBC-TV's *Morningside*, 7 Nov. 1994.

The only thing as good as your Crispy Crunch is someone else's.

Slogan on a campaign launched in 1995 for Crispy Crunch chocolate bar, first manufactured by William Neilson Ltd. of Toronto in 1936, now produced by **Cadbury Chocolate Canada**, in *The Globe and Mail*, 29 Feb. 1996. When the bar was introduced in the United States in 1991, the wrapper's slogan read: "Canada's Favorite Bar."

You can often buy one thousand litres of municipal drinking water usually for much less than the cost of one litre of bottled water.

Tom Davey, editor and publisher, "Canada's Water Quality Record," *Environmental Science & Engineering*, March 1995.

Canada has a little white wine, but it's kind of hard to drink.

Paul Bocuse, French chef, dining at Mont Tremblant, Que., tasting a 1993 Inniskillin Chardonnay from southern Ontario, as quoted by Ray Conlogue in *The Globe and Mail*, 11 March 1995.

The bread you buy is yours to eat. The bread you make is yours to experience. One is forgettable, the other memorable.

John Howard, Vice-President of J.M. Schneider Ltd., speaking to shareholders on the popularity of bread-making machines and meatless food products, noted in *The Toronto Star*, 31 March 1995.

Doughnut outlets represent 20 percent of the Canadian fast-food market, as opposed to only 2 percent of the U.S. one.

Charles Trueheart, correspondent, "Hard Times for Canadian Doughnut," *International Herald Tribune*, 26 Sept. 1995.

Waking up in Ottawa is not something I expect to do more than two or three times in this lifetime and two of those times have already happened. This is not solely because Ottawa coffee is possibly the worst in Canada and Canadian coffee on the whole the bitterest and weakest you will ever encounter, though these truths have some bearing.

Germaine Greer, Australian-born author, describing a book-promotion and lecture tour, "Letter from New York," *The Times Literary Supplement*, 7 Aug. 1999.

The Europeans are saying, "If you want to find out if GMOS are dangerous, just watch Canada. They're doing the experimenting for us." And I think that you don't put people in an experiment unless they have been told and asked for our permission. We haven't been told or asked. We're guinea pigs.

David Suzuki, geneticist and broadcaster, commenting on genetically modified organisms, quoted by Leah Eichler, "Sightings," Reuters News Service, Internet, 21 Dec. 1999.

FOOD BANKS See also HUNGER, POVERTY

The only real way to eradicate food banks—and the poverty they represent—is to generate the political will to make poverty unacceptable.

Carolyn Jack, commentator, "Food Banks and the Politics of Hunger," *The Canadian Forum*, Dec. 1991.

Somehow under the business genius of Brian Mulroney and Michael Wilson, Canada has become a nation of food banks.

Mel Hurtig, publisher, address in Winnipeg, quoted by Paul Samyn in the *Winnipeg Free Press*, 28 Jan. 1993.

Across the country, the more than 2,000 food banks now exceed the number of any fast-food chains, including McDonald's.

Richard Gwyn, columnist and author, *Nationalism without Walls: The Unbearable Lightness of Being Canadian* (1995).

FOOLS

An illiterate fool can be a useful fool, he can wash floors, but a fool with a doctorate is deadly. No amount of learning can cure stupidity, and higher education positively fortifies it.

Speech from **Stephen Vizinczey**'s novel *An Innocent Millionaire* (1983).

The wise man will learn from the fool, but the fool will learn from nobody.

Peter Urs Bender, speaker, characteristic remark, 17 Feb. 2000.

FOOTBALL See also SPORTS

Tell me, Stuke—what's wrong with the B.C. Lions?

Chiang Kai-shek, Chinese nationalist leader in Taiwan, first question asked of Annis Stukus, football writer for *The Vancouver Sun* in the 1950s, according to Stuart Keate in *Maclean's*, 8 Sept. 1980.

The Canadian Football League is contemplating an opening-day ceremony in which the prime minister will throw out the first drunk.

Eric Nicol and **Dave More**, humorists, *The U.S. or Us: What's the Difference, Eh?* (1986).

Glory is almost totally absent from modern warfare. The contemporary warrior is quite likely to be blown to smithereens by an enemy located fifty miles away. Only on the football field can the young men of today have an even chance of winning glory and living to tell the tale.

Christopher Dafoe, columnist, referring to professional football's annual Grey Cup game, *Winnipeg Free Press*, 23 Nov. 1991.

I've been to seven Super Bowls, to the World Series, and to dozens of sporting events all around the world, and never, and I do mean never, have I seen anything like Grey Cup weekend in Winnipeg.

Peter King, reporter for *Sports Illustrated*, writing about the Grey Cup game held in Winnipeg on 24 Nov. 1991, quoted by John Douglas in the *Winnipeg Free Press*, 26 Nov. 1991.

Canadian is better . . . our balls are bigger.

National television advertising slogans for the **Canadian Football League**, Spring 1996.

I write all the time that if the Canadian Football League is allowed to die, it will signify the end of Canada. And I haven't been to a CFL game in years. I think I'm finally growing up.

Allan Fotheringham, columnist, *Maclean's*, 27 Oct. 1997.

FORCE

One's appreciation of a club depends entirely upon the end from which one contemplates it.

W.L. Morton, historian, "Cleo in Canada: The Interpretation of Canadian History," *The University of Toronto Quarterly*, April 1946.

FOREIGN AFFAIRS See also FOREIGN AID, INTERNATIONALISM, TRADE & COMMERCE

Our external relations are enveloped in what might be called a highly luminous but cloudy halo. The plain man who makes no pretence at the investigation of legal or constitutional subtleties must be in despair when he attempts to understand them.

Sir Clifford Sifton, politician, "Some Canadian Constitutional Problems," *Canadian Historical Review*, March 1922.

Canadian foreign policy should be soundly based upon two main principles. One is the defence of Canadian territory from invasion. The other is the creation of a new world order, a real League that will supersede our petty national sovereignties.

F.R. Scott, constitutional law authority, "What Kind of Peace Do We Want?" (1939), *A New Endeavour: Selected Political Essays, Letters, and Addresses* (1986) edited by Michiel Horn.

. . . from the bosom of the British mother onto the bony lap of the American uncle.

Reference to Canada shifting its attention from Britain in the Mackenzie King years to the United States in the Mulroney years, noted by **Norman Hillmer**, "From Bosom to Bony Lap," *Acadiensis*, Autumn, 1981.

Foreign affairs are already conducted by the provinces in parallel with the federal government; in Paris, *La Maison du Québec* has more representatives than the Canadian embassy.

Editorial feature, "Survey on Canada," *The Economist*, 19 June 1991, reprinted in *The Globe and Mail*, 19 July 1991.

The Canadian external policy is a subject often discussed in intellectual circles. I hear that it is inconsistent, low profile, uncommitted, ambivalent—in a word, bleak. Again I say, Thank God! Our external policy has made

Canada a friend of all. Everybody knows that a Canadian passport opens most doors. Even the separatist Quebeckers want it!

Roch Carrier, author, referring to separatist-minded friends in the 1960s, "Canada Is a Grand Dream," *Canadian Living*, September 1992.

The boundaries on the map and in the mind seem to be in flux. Few things are sure any more, and there can be little doubt that Canadian good sense will continue to be needed in the world arena. The umpire will always be indispensable on the international playing field.

Norman Hillmer and **J.L. Granatstein**, historians, concluding lines, *Empire to Umpire: Canada and the World to the 1990s* (1994).

Canada is not a "middle power" but a mini-superpower.

Attributed to U.S. foreign-affairs adviser **Henry Kissinger** by Alan Sullivan, moderator, seminar, Canadian Institute of Strategic Studies, Toronto, 6 Nov. 1997.

Herein lies the irony: by buying simultaneously into both globalization and peace-keeping, Canada appears committed both to fanning the flames and to joining in the bucket brigade.

Daryl Copeland, diplomat, "Foreign Policy, Foreign Service and the 21st Century: The Challenge of Globalization," *Canadian Foreign Policy*, Winter 1997.

FOREIGN AID See also FOREIGN AFFAIRS

While aid to Africa increased more than ten-fold between 1970 and 1988, Africans are poorer. After $100 billion in investments, Africa's economy shrunk by 20%—the GNP of that entire continent compares to that of Belgium, which has a land mass 1% the size of Africa.

Patricia Adams, Executive Director, Probe International, mailer, Jan. 1995.

Aid spending has been reduced almost 50 percent since 1989, and there has been barely a peep in response.

Daryl Copeland, diplomat, "Foreign Policy, Foreign Service and the 21st Century: The Challenge of Globalization," *Canadian Foreign Policy*, Winter 1997.

FOREIGN INVESTMENT

We can now be bought by foreigners with our own money.

Peter Desbarats, journalist, *Canada Lost/Canada Found* (1981).

If we fail to invest in our own future we will be exporters of yesterday's product and importers of tomorrow's technology.

Attributed to Ontario Premier **David Peterson** in *The Globe and Mail*, 1 Jan. 1990.

FORESTRY See also TREES

Nothing can exceed the sensation of loneliness which is experienced in the interminable forests where, for hundreds of miles, no object is recognisable beyond the tops of the trees.

Patrick Matthew, writer and traveller, *Emigration Fields* (1839).

...some partial relief from one of the most burdensome of our monopolies, that which taxes us from a million to a million and a half a year for the privilege of buying bad timber from Canada instead of good from the Baltic, has been declared to be in immediate contemplation.

John Stuart Mill, political economist, "State of Politics in 1836" (1836), *Essays on England, Ireland, and the Empire* (1982), edited by John M. Robson, Volume VI of the "Collected Works of John Stuart Mill."

Forests aren't just for employment; they're also for enjoyment.

Attributed to **Adam H. Zimmerman**, President, Northwood Mills Ltd., formed in 1961 by Noranda in British Columbia.

Next to trees, people are our most important resource.

Attributed to **Wesley Black**, British Columbia Cabinet Minister, 1963.

One tree will make a million matches. One match will destroy a million trees.

Jack Miner, conservationist, *Wild Goose Jack* (1969).

To know what we once had and what we've lost, we would need to ask a tree.

Elizabeth E. May, ecologist, *At the Cutting Edge: The Crisis in Canada's Forests* (1989). One chapter of this book is titled "What Was Once a Land of Trees. . . ."

What a piece of work is a man! In action how like an angel! And the only piece of man's handiwork that can be seen by the angels as they guard or at least regard the earth from geostationary orbit at 37 thousand kilometres is the great wound wrought in the temperate rain forests of Vancouver Island by MacMillan Bloedel and other logging companies. Or so at least British Columbians glumly boast.

Eric Korn, columnist, referring to clear-cutting of forests, sole manmade mark on earth visible from the TIROS satellite, "Remainders," *The Times Literary Supplement*, 13 April 1990.

About sixty per cent of Canada's Pacific forest has by now been destroyed, mostly in the past forty years. In the United States, less than ten per cent survives.

Catherine Caufield, U.S. reporter, "A Reporter at Large: The Ancient Forest," *The New Yorker*, 14 May 1990.

Think of it. Canada probably cuts down more trees than any country in the world, but we import chainsaws. We have the world's biggest pulp and paper industry, but much of the most sophisticated machinery comes from Finland.

C.E. Ritchie, Chairman and CEO, Bank of Nova Scotia, "Do Canadians Really Want to Compete?" address, The Canadian Club, 29 April 1991.

Canada is the Brazil of the North. Brazil is losing one acre of forest every nine seconds. We're losing one acre every twelve seconds.

Colleen McCrory, ecologist and foe of logging interests, resident of New Denver, B.C., recipient of the Goldman Environmental Foundation prize, quoted by Peter Kuitenbrouwer in the *Winnipeg Free Press*, 30 April 1992.

It has always been the land—which really means its forests—that has anchored our sense of who we are and what we want to become. The shape and growth of our landscape has been the most potent influence on formation of the Canadian character. Let's not flatten it.

Peter C. Newman, columnist, "Business Watch," *Maclean's*, 16 Aug. 1993.

I look at our northern Saskatchewan forests and see trees in danger of clear-cutting. Yet the cousin of a friend of mine from Hong Kong looked at those same trees and saw chopsticks.

Pat Lorjé, Saskatchewan M.L.A., speech, Federal NDP Renewal Conference, Ottawa, 27 Aug. 1994, *The Globe and Mail*, 20 Sept. 1994.

The northern boreal world was unique and unlike any other on earth, still undisturbed, with deep linkages to other sub-arctic cultures and its unbroken chain of story-lives going back into the pre-Colombian past.

Paulette Jiles, poet and traveller, *Northern Spirit: Travels among the Cree and Ojibway Nations and Their Star Maps* (1995).

The sad truth is that there really is no such thing as reforestation; once a forest is gone, all the planting in the world will not bring it back. But it is possible to raise a crop of trees that are conveniently spaced, tall, straight, and highly marketable—a tree farm, not a forest.

Susanna Haley, observer in British Columbia, Letters to the Editor, *Harper's*, Sept. 1997.

FOX, TERRY

Somewhere the hurting must stop....I'm not a dreamer...but I believe in miracles. I have to.

Terry Fox, amputee, resident of New Westminster, B.C., letter addressed to the head office of the Canadian Cancer Society, 15 Oct. 1979. He requested the society's aid in sponsoring his "run across Canada to raise money for the fight against cancer." Fox's Marathon of Hope raised millions for cancer research. The one-legged runner jogged from St. John's, Nfld., to Thunder Bay, Ont., two-thirds of the way across Canada.

How many people do something they really believe in? I just wish people woud realize that anything's possible if you try. Dreams are made if people try.

Terry Fox, marathon runner, speaking from his hospital room in Thunder Bay, Ont., quoted in *The Globe and Mail*, 4 Sept. 1980. He died of cancer in New Westminster, B.C., 28 June 1981. Annual charity runs are held in his memory.

He united Canadians as they have never been united before.

Inscription on the Terry Fox Memorial, outside Thunder Bay, Ont., unveiled 26 June 1982.

Inspiring all to never lose, / It'll take a long, long time for someone to fill your shoes. / It'll take somebody who is a lot like you, / Who never gave up on a dream.

Lines from the song "Never Give Up on a Dream" written and performed by **Rod Stewart**, rock 'n' roll singer and performer, benefit, Boston, Mass., 5 Aug. 1989.

FRANCE See also CANADA: FRENCH; LA FRANCOPHONIE; NEW FRANCE; QUEBEC; QUEBEC & FRANCE; ST. PIERRE & MIQUELON

Are the streets being paved with gold over there? I fully expect to awake one morning in Versailles to see the walls of the fortress rising above the horizon.

Complaint attributed to **Louis XV**, King of France (1715–74), concerning the cost of building and maintaining the Fortress of Louisbourg, addressed to Sébastien de Vauban, the military architect who pressed for further funds. Its reconstruction, undertaken by Parks Canada in 1961, has proven to be even more costly. The vision is worthy of the surrealist painter Magritte.

There was a time when we too might have created a great French nation in the wilds of America and might have shared the destinies of the New World with the English. There was a time when France possessed in North America a territory almost as vast as the whole of Europe.

Alexis de Tocqueville, French traveller, *Democracy in America* (1835) translated by George Lawrence and edited by J.P. Mayer and Max Lerner in 1966.

Three million French Catholics—for with us French and Catholic are synonymous—three million French Catholics, descended from 60,000 poor peasants, separated from France a hundred and fifty years ago, must say in a loud enough voice what the French race has done and what it could do if it wished to.

Henri Bourassa, publisher and nationalist, *Le Canada à Lourdes* (1914) quoted by Joseph Levitt in *Henri Bourassa on Imperialism and Bi-culturalism, 1900–1918* (1970).

We have found at Ottawa, at Quebec, at Montreal, renewed and moving proofs of the fraternal understanding which unites France and Canada. This friendship and understanding has been dedicated anew by the blood of Canadian soldiers and the blood of French soldiers which has been poured out in the common struggle.

Charles de Gaulle, leader of the Free French, address, Ottawa, 12 July 1944, quoted by Gordon Barthos, "The President Forgot the General's Debt," *The Toronto Star*, 25 July 1997.

Officially separated for two centuries, with differences that go back even further, the Frenchman and the Canadian have neither the same past nor the same future. Therefore, they do not share a same present, a same continuity, a same life, a same mode of being.

Etienne Gilson, theologian, quoted by Gratien Gélinas in "A National and Popular Theatre" (1949) reproduced by Renate Usmianti in *Gratien Gélinas* (1977).

You are Quebec! You are the French Canadians! No passage of time has been able to remove from the mind and the heart of France the memory and the loss of her children that she left there almost two hundred years ago.

Charles de Gaulle, French President, welcoming Quebec Premier Jean Lesage to Paris, Oct. 1961, quoted by William Johnson, "Decades of Meddling in Canadian Affairs," *Cité Libre*, Number 2, April–May 1998.

Scratch a French Canadian and you will find a "Gaulois."

Jean Lesage, Quebec Premier, addressing a group of French parliamentarians in Paris, Oct. 1961, quoted by Dale C. Thomson in *Vive le Québec libre* (1988) who explained that a Gaulois was "an inhabitant of historic pre-French Gaul, known for his rugged ways and bawdy humour."

One day or another Quebec will be free.

Charles de Gaulle, French President, prediction made in a private meeting to French Cabinet Minister Alain Peyrefitte, 24 April 1963, as noted by Peyrefitte in the third volume of *C'était de Gaulle: La France redevient la France* (2000).

We must above all establish a special cooperation with French Canada and we must not allow what we do for it and with it to be drowned in a business concerning the two Canadas as a whole. Besides, French Canada must necessarily become a state and it is with this in mind that we must act.

Charles de Gaulle, French President, notation on a letter sent to Prime Minister Lester B. Pearson, 4 Sept. 1963, quoted by William Johnson, "Decades of Meddling in Canadian Affairs," *Cité Libre*, Number 2, April–May 1998.

When Mr. Malraux speaks of autonomy, what he means is independence. I don't know whether it will happen in ten, twenty or thirty years, but French Canada must become independent and, consequently, must shake off, violently or otherwise, the state of dependence in which it finds itself.

Charles de Gaulle, French President, Cabinet meeting, Paris, 23 Oct. 1963, quoted by William Johnson, "Decades of Meddling in Canadian Affairs," *Cité Libre*, Number 2, April–May 1998.

It is out of the question that I should deliver a message to Canada to celebrate its "Centenary." We can have good relations with Canada as a whole, as it is now. We must have excellent relations with French Canada. But we have no reason to congratulate either the Canadians or ourselves for the creation of a "state" established on our past defeat and on the integration of a part of the French people in a British entity. Moreoever, this entity has become quite precarious.

Charles de Gaulle, French President, notation made in 1966 on a letter of invitation to visit Expo 67, quoted by William Johnson, "Decades of Meddling in Canadian Affairs," *Cité Libre*, Number 2, April–May 1998.

I intend to strike a mighty blow. It's going to cause a fuss. But it has to be done. It's the last occasion to repair the cowardice of France.

Charles de Gaulle, French President, addressing his son-in-law prior to his visit to Quebec in 1967; quoted by Anne and Pierre Rouanet in *Les trois derniers chagrins du Général de Gaulle* (1980), as translated by William Johnson in *The Globe and Mail*, 31 July 1980.

I will tell you a secret that you must not repeat. This evening here, and all along my route, I found myself in an atmosphere just like that of the liberation.... Vive Montréal! Vive le Québec! Vive le Québec libre! Vive le Canada français et vive la France!

Charles de Gaulle, French President, address from the balcony of Montreal's City Hall, 24 July 1967. He deliberately incurred the wrath of federalists and curried favour with the separatists by employing their slogan "Québec libre." Montreal Mayor Jean Drapeau and Prime Minister Lester B. Pearson publicly disavowed de Gaulle's démarche. He cancelled a visit to Ottawa and promptly returned to Paris. The most stylish response to the French President's speech was made by Pauline Vanier, widow of the Governor General; she had the following terse comminiqué conveyed to de Gaulle: "1940."

Vive de Gaulle!

René Lévesque, Quebec leader, following the French President's "Vive le Québec libre" speech, *La Presse*, 31 July 1967, Quotations from René Lévesque (1977) edited by Jean Côté and Marcel Chaput, translated by Robert Guy Scully and Jacqueline Perrault. Almost ten years later he told Agence France-Presse, 22 Nov. 1976: "General de Gaulle's 'Vive le Québec libre' did more for Québec's publicity than ten million dollars spent by an ad agency could ever have done."

W *pour* Waterloo... O *pour* Ontario... U *pour* Utrecht... L *pour* Laval... D *pour* Dien Bien Phu... V *pour* Vichy....

Line from **Francine du Plessix Gray**'s novel *Lovers and Tyrants* (1967) in which the narrator is explaining how her editor, an Englishman who detests the French, dictates cables from France to England, letter by letter, for the sake of the Paris operators—wickedly using the first letters of French historical disasters.

Ambassador, I can assure you that as long as I sit here, there will not be any murderous little sentences shot by my ministers against Canada.

François Mitterrand, French President, addressing Canadian Ambassador Michel Dupuy in 1981, repudiating his predecessor Charles de Gaulle's "Québec libre" speech of 1967, quoted by Marci McDonald in his obituary, "Riddle of the Sphinx," *Maclean's*, 22 Jan. 1996.

If France didn't have us she'd be enclosed in her little hexagon in Europe with no access to the science or culture of North America.

Jacques Godbout, Quebec author, contributor to *Mapping Literature: The Art and Politics of Translation* (1988) edited by David Homel and Sherry Simon.

France will accompany Quebec along its way, respecting scrupulously your orientations and your decisions. You are the ones, quite obviously, who hold in your hands your destiny.

Alain Juppé, French Prime Minister, speech, Quebec City, 11 June 1996, quoted by William Johnson, "Decades of Meddling in Canadian Affairs," *Cité Libre*, Number 2, April–May 1998.

Whatever path Quebec chooses, France will accompany it. Quebec can count on the friendship and the solidarity of France.

Jacques Chirac, French President, statement made following a meeting with Quebec Premier Lucien Bouchard, Paris, 29 Sept. 1997, quoted by Sandra Contenta in *The Toronto Star* the following day.

Be assured that France will accompany Quebec on the path it chooses.... I would be tempted to say to you that to accompany Quebec on the path it will choose does not mean to precede it.

Lionel Jospin, Prime Minister of France, statement made to reporters following a meeting with Quebec Premier Lucien Bouchard, Paris, 30 Sept. 1997, quoted by Rhéal Séguin in *The Globe and Mail*, 1 Oct. 1997.

It is regrettable that, since the beginning of the 1960s, French governments have often acted as our enemy. That must change. We Canadians, whenever France has called, have always responded: "*Vive la France!*" But we would like to hear occasionally, "*Vive le Canada!*"

William Johnson, columnist, "Decades of Meddling in Canadian Affairs," *Cité Libre*, Number 2, April–May 1998.

FRANCOPHONIE, LA See also FRANCE

Who speaks for France?

Pierre Elliott Trudeau, Prime Minister, responding to French President Valéry Giscard d'Estaing who asked who would represent Canada at the Francophonie meeting to be held in Dakar in a month's time, 24 Nov. 1980, quoted by Bill Fox in *The Toronto Star* the following day.

I think it's very important for non-francophones to know the value of la Francophonie.... If I can persuade them to acquire a second language like French, it will enrich them and it will reinforce the specificity of Canada.

Boutros Boutros-Ghali, secretary-general of l'Agencie de la Francophonie, interviewed in Paris prior to a visit to the French-language summit, Moncton, N.B., quoted by Alan Freeman, "English Language No Threat to French, Boutros-Ghali Says," *The Globe and Mail*, 8 Sept. 1998.

FREDERICTON See also NEW BRUNSWICK

My city, Fredericton, a jewel in a dream.

Line from **Sir Charles G.D. Roberts**' poem "Two Rivers" (1937), *Collected Poems* (1985) edited by Desmond Pacey.

Life to a man in Fredericton without the elms above him is unthinkable.

Bruce Hutchison, newspaperman, *The Unknown Country: Canada and Her People* (1942).

FREEDOM

There is more real freedom in Canada than in the United States and people may express their opinion with far less restraint. In the States they are afraid of the majority of their own party.

Johann Georg Kohl, German traveller, *Travels in Canada and through the States of New York and Pennsylvania* (1861) translated from the German by Mrs. Percy Sinnett.

I am still, I am glad to say, enough of an Englishman that it gives me a glow of pride to think that twice in the same hundred years men have escaped from the American Republic to Canada to find freedom.

G.K. Chesterton, English writer, address, luncheon held to honour Rudyard Kipling sponsored by the Canadian Literary Society and recorded by the BBC, London, England, 1933; "Visiting Canada," *The Chesterton Review*, Nov. 1996. Chesterton referred to the arrival of the Loyalists and then of "the poor black people who ran or swam across the river or whatever." History would add the Vietnam war resisters of the 1970s.

I'd sooner be in jail—sooner be there than free but fettered!

Tim Buck, leader of the Communist Party of Canada, interviewed upon his release from the

Kingston Penitentiary, interviewed by R.E. Knowles in *The Toronto Star*, 26 Nov. 1934.

Sooner or later, men prefer to be free.

F.R. Scott, poet and professor of law, "The Democratic Manifesto" (1941), *Brick: A Journal of Reviews*, No. 30, Summer 1987.

There are ghettos and châteaux in every country. It isn't "*Vive le Québec libre*" but "*Vive l'univers libre.*"

Robert Charlebois, chansonnier, quoted by Robert McKenzie in *The Toronto Star*, 10 April 1969.

Only the tiniest fraction of mankind want freedom. All the rest want someone to tell them they are free.

Irving Layton, poet and aphorist, *The Whole Bloody Bird (obs, aphs & Pomes)* (1969).

We dedicate this monument as a record of our gratitude to all those who so rashly and so gallantly risked their lives for freedom.

Pierre Elliott Trudeau, Prime Minister, address, Carabita Park, Sydney Harbour, Australia, 18 May 1970, as noted in *The Globe and Mail* the following day. Australia's penal colonies accepted the Rebels of 1837: 58 from Lower Canada, 24 from Upper Canada.

Freedom for Hungary! Freedom for all!

Geza Matrai, Hungarian-born Canadian activist and protester, who had to be physically restrained from further assaulting Soviet Premier Alexei Kosygin as he strolled with Prime Minister Trudeau across Parliament Hill, Ottawa, 19 Oct. 1971.

When freedom is lost, everyone watches everybody.

Bruno M. Cormier, psychiatrist and penologist, *The Watcher and the Watched* (1975).

Hesitation is the beginning of freedom.

Louis Dudek, man-of-letters, *Epigrams* (1975).

The questioning mind requires the freedom to pursue the truth wherever it leads; indeed, it is unable to operate in the absence of such freedom. This includes not only the freedom to say, without fear, what is true but also to determine where the truth is most likely to be found.

John C. Polanyi, scientist, "The Scientist as Citizen: Freedom and Responsibility in Science," *Queen's Quarterly*, Spring 1992.

What has "freedom," at any recorded period in history, ever meant for more than one per cent of the total population? What did it really mean even for them?

Northrop Frye, cultural critic, "Notebook 1993," edited by Robert D. Denham, *Northrop Frye Newsletter*, Summer 1993.

Freedom cannot exist for those with no means to act freely.

John McMurtry, philosopher, University of Guelph, "The Contradictions of Free Market Doctrine—Is There a Solution?" a paper prepared for the Westminster Institute Conference, "Surviving Globalization: Economic, Social, and Environmental Dimensions," London, Ont., May 1995.

An occupied space which must be reoccupied every day.

John Ralston Saul, author, *The Doubter's Companion: A Dictionary of Aggressive Common Sense* (1994).

FREE ENTERPRISE See also CAPITALISM

I know of no country that has retained liberal democracy and fundamental western values that does not have a mixed free-enterprise or modified capitalist system.

John Crispo, political economist, address, Empire Club of Canada, 25 Jan. 1979.

Free market proponents really mean "freedom from government intervention" *that is not necessary or profitable to private business.*

*

The historically developed "mixed" society in which the free market is complemented by a public sector guaranteeing what the free market cannot, is now being rapidly dismantled in Canada and across the world by proponents of a "true free market."

John McMurtry, philosopher, University of Guelph, "The Contradictions of Free Market Doctrine—Is There a Solution?" a paper prepared for the Westminster Institute Conference, "Surviving Globalization: Economic, Social, and Environmental Dimensions," London, Ont., May 1995.

FREE SPEECH See also CENSORSHIP

...what is important about free speech in a democracy is not only that everyone has a right to express an opinion, however ill-considered, but that fools should have full liberty to speak so that they can be recognized to be fools.

Northrop Frye, cultural critic, Entry 774, Notebook 1997.1, *Northrop Frye Newsletter,* Summer 1997.

We strongly support free speech and we believe that *all* authors and publishers must support the following fundamental freedoms: freedom of thought, belief, opinion and expression, including freedom of the press and other media of communication. These fundamental freedoms are embodied in the Canadian Charter of Rights.

Statement made by **Avie Bennett**, Chairman of McClelland and Stewart Inc., rejecting a demand that a book be withdrawn from publication, *Newsletter of the Canadian Centre of International PEN,* Dec. 1990.

FREE TRADE See also CONTINENTALISM, FREE TRADE AGREEMENTS, NORTH AMERICAN FREE TRADE AGREEMENT, TRADE & COMMERCE

It is in vain to suppose that a free trade system will be beneficial to a new and struggling colony, which has nothing to export but raw materials; it is rather calculated to enrich an old commonwealth, whose people by their skill and labour make such raw materials valuable, and then return them for consumption. The result of the system alluded to has been that the suppliers of the raw material at last become hewers of wood and drawers of water to the manufacturers.

Abraham Gesner, scientist, critic of reciprocity, *The Industrial Resources of Nova Scotia* (1849).

I say to discuss free-trade or protection as abstract principles in a country of four millions, lying alongside of forty millions of people, with a boundary line, as the Hon. Finance Minister has said, three thousand miles in length, is simply nonsense. I say what Canada wants is a national policy—a policy that shall be in the interest of Canada, apart from the principles of free-trade, apart from the principles of protection.

Sir Charles Tupper, Father of Confederation, House of Commons, 25 Feb. 1876.

It is proposed to form a union for commercial purposes.... It is said that a large proportion of the merchants of Canada are in favour of this step, as they believe it would materially add to the business of the country by removing the restrictions that now exist on trade between Canada and the States.

Walt Whitman, American poet and Canadian visitor, "Summer Days in Canada," 22 June 1880, *Walt Whitman's Canada* (1992) edited by Cyril Greenland and John Robert Colombo.

Continental Union should take place. Not only are the countries coterminus and interlocked, but their population, the bulk of it at least, is identical, while in their products they are complements of each other; Canada supplying timber, minerals, and water-power, the United States manufacturing on a large scale.

Goldwin Smith, essayist, *Commonwealth or Empire* (1902).

No Truck Nor Trade with the Yankees!

Slogan of the **Conservative Party** devised by one of its ministers, Sir George E. Foster, for the election of 1911, which was fought over the issue of reciprocity, a form of free trade. The slogan was effective; the electorate rejected the free-trade agreement reached by Prime Minister Sir Wilfrid Laurier and U.S. President William Howard Taft. Instead of free trade with the United States, Canada continued the policy of Imperial preference.

I do not understand how nine million people can enter into such arrangements as are proposed with ninety million strangers on an open frontier of four thousand miles, and at the same time preserve their own national integrity.... Whatever the United States may gain, I see nothing for Canada in Reciprocity except a little money which she does not need, and a long repentance.

Rudyard Kipling, author and imperialist, cable sent in support of the anti-reciprocity movement, 8 Sept. 1911, quoted by S. Macnaughtan in *My Canadian Memories* (1920).

If there was ever a right time for the Empire, it is now.

Lord Beaverbrook, publisher and imperialist, promoting Empire Free Trade, 24 Oct. 1929, quoted by Janet Aitken Kidd in *The Beaverbrook Girl: An Autobiography* (1987).

Something more than commercial agreements, however, is required to explain why Canada and the United States exchange more than two billion dollars worth of goods a year. Ambassador Atherton has aptly given the reason as not "free trade," but "the trade of free men."

Harry S. Truman, U.S. President, address, joint sitting of the Senate and the House of Commons, 11 June 1947.

How often I've been told, / To throw away a nation / For a pocketful of gold. / On the pocket-books of Wall Street / The old nation is a state / And of the northern mysteries / What memories remain?

Verse from the song "Pocketful of Gold" (1972) composed by **Stan Rogers**, quoted by Chris Gudgeon in *An Unfinished Conversation: The Life and Music of Stan Rogers* (1993).

Again, if we are really serious about competitiveness, we should be prepared to establish an *internal* Free Trade Agreement among the provinces and the federal government. Why not negotiate a formal agreement that encompasses services, procurement and the full range of interprovincial barriers?

C.E. Ritchie, Chairman and CEO, Bank of Nova Scotia, "Do Canadians Really Want to Compete?" address, The Canadian Club, 29 April 1991.

The choice for rich countries is simple: accept the products or the people from poor countries. That is why opposing free trade is like opposing gravity.

Diane Francis, columnist, *Maclean's*, 27 April 1992.

FREE TRADE AGREEMENTS

See also FREE TRADE, NORTH AMERICAN FREE TRADE AGREEMENT

Sooner or later, commercial imperatives will bring about free movement of all goods back and forth across our long border; and when that occurs, or even before it does, it will become unmistakably clear that countries with economies so inextricably intertwined must also have free movement of the other vital factors of production—capital, services, and labour.

George W. Ball, U.S. Undersecretary of State, *The Discipline of Power* (1968).

In fact, the key to our own future security may lie in both Mexico and Canada becoming stronger countries than they are today....

Ronald Reagan, announcing his candidacy for the U.S. Presidency, New York City, 13 Nov. 1979, marking the first use of the phrase "A North American Accord," quoted by Geoffrey Stevens in *The Globe and Mail*, 25 Nov. 1980.

Bilateral free trade with the United States is simplistic and naive. It would only serve to further diminish our ability to compete internationally.

Michael Wilson, Minister of Finance, quoted in *Maclean's*, 13 June 1983.

Canadians rejected free trade with the United States in 1911. They will do so again in 1983.

Brian Mulroney, Conservative leader, quoted in *Maclean's*, 13 June 1983.

Our politicial sovereignty, our system of social programs, our commitment to fight regional disparities, our unique cultural identity, our special linguistic characters—these are the essence of Canada. They are not at issue in these negotiations.

Brian Mulroney, Prime Minister, address on free trade issues, University of Chicago, Chicago, 4 Dec. 1985.

Canadians kid themselves if they think that any free trade arrangement will stop American directors from deciding that, if there is a plant to be closed, it should be in Brampton rather than Buffalo.

Eric Kierans and **Walter Stewart**, economist and writer, *Wrong End of the Rainbow: The Collapse of Free Enterprise in Canada* (1988).

The free trade agreement should really be called... the sale-of-Canada agreement. Canada's not open for business, Canada is up for sale.

Mel Hurtig, nationalist and publisher, quoted by Joseph Hall in *The Toronto Star*, 21 April 1990.

For example, the prospect of the European single market was the direct cause of the free trade agreement between the U.S.A. and Canada.... It flies in the face of everything that Canada has ever felt important. Even now, Canadians are not enthusiastic; they simply had no choice but to throw in their economic lot with their dominating neighbour. After Canada, there is now an even bigger question: Does Mexico in its turn have any choice?

Peter F. Drucker, U.S. management consultant, *Managing for the Future: The 1990s and Beyond* (1991).

We are setting out to create—in the jargon of the economists—the level playing field. We're bringing it down to the American level.

J.L. Granatstein, historian, quoted by Dennis Kucherawy in *eye*, 16 Jan. 1992.

Free trade is desirable depending on where you sit—and whether you have a job.

Robert MacNeil, broadcaster and author, interviewed by Peter Gzowski on CBC Radio's *Morningside*, 27 Feb. 1992.

This is a good day for Americans, a good day for North Americans.

George Bush, U.S. President, responding to the completion by Canadian, American, and Mexican negotiators of the first draft of the North American Free Trade Agreement, CBC Radio, 12 Aug. 1992.

From Yukon to Yucatan!

Rallying cry of proponents of the North American Free Trade Agreement (NAFTA), which links the economies of Canada, United States, and Mexico, as noted by Peter C. Newman in "Business Watch," *Maclean's*, 17 Aug. 1992.

The important ethical question here is: Who do you stand with and why? The men in suits who say free trade has been good or the unemployed people who say it has cost them their livelihood?

Timothy Findley, novelist, "When You Write about This Country," *The Canadian Forum*, Sept. 1992.

Far from being a catastrophe, the free trade initiative with the United States has had the overall effect of making Canadians less parochial and more globally minded.

Thomas d'Aquino, President and CEO, Business Council on National Issues, "Right of Reply," *The Canadian Forum*, Dec. 1992.

Thanks to free trade, the greatest bout of genius ever to spring from the forehead of Brian Mulroney, most of Ontario's manufacturing base has moved to Memphis, Mobile and Miami.

Allan Fotheringham, columnist, *Maclean's*, 7 Dec. 1992.

FTA + NAFTA + GST = UIC

Formula of nationalist **Mel Hurtig**, address, Toronto, National Party of Canada, 12 Jan. 1993. The abbreviations stand for Free Trade Agreement, North American Free Trade Agreement, Goods and Services Tax, and Unemployment Insurance Commission.

We don't *hafta* have Nafta.

Slogan of the **Canadian Union of Public Employees** in *The Canadian Forum*, April 1993.

Only donkeys don't change their minds.

Brian Mulroney, Prime Minister, explaining how he could oppose Free Trade in 1983 and promote it in 1988, quoted in *The Toronto Star*, 25 Feb. 1993.

There is a Tooth Fairy and there is an Easter Bunny.

Ross Perot, U.S. presidential hopeful and critic of free trade agreements, responding to U.S. Vice-President Al Gore's bright vision of employment opportunities in Canada following implementation of NAFTA, CNN's *The Larry King Show*, 9 Nov. 1993.

Every day we see the enormous benefits that this partnership gives us—in jobs, prosperity and the great creative energy that trade brings. We have only seen the beginning.

Bill Clinton, U.S. President, address, House of Commons, 23 Feb. 1995, as published in *The Toronto Star* the following day.

Globalized free trade has brought us, we might say, to the age of disposable humanity.

John McMurtry, philosopher, University of Guelph, "The Contradictions of Free Market Doctrine—Is There a Solution?" a paper prepared for the Westminster Institute Conference, "Surviving Globalization: Economic, Social, and Environmental Dimensions," London, Ont., May 1995.

You Canadians are pygmies. If all of Canada were an American state, it would rank fifth or sixth in GDP terms. Yet you think trade decisions will be made in Ottawa. They will be made in Washington.

Lester Thurow, U.S. economist, NAFTA critic, address, Municipal Finance Officers Association, Muskoka, Ont., June 1995, quoted by Donald Coxe in *The Globe and Mail*, 10 July 1995.

As co-founders of the North American Free Trade Agreement (NAFTA), we should urge the United States government to join us in advising Britain that if it wished to do so and if our joint efforts to reduce trade barriers between Europe and North America did not proceed quickly enough, it would be welcome in NAFTA.

Conrad Black, publisher, "Taking Canada Seriously," *International Journal*, Winter 1997–98.

It's a great irony that Canadians became so excited about Brian Mulroney's Free Trade Agreement with the United States, but only yawned when he signed the North American Free Trade Agreement, an act which is proving to have much more profound consequences.

Peter C. Newman, columnist, "The Nation's Business," *Maclean's*, 27 July 1998.

FRENCH & ENGLISH CANADA See also CANADA: ENGLISH; CANADA: FRENCH; FRENCH CANADIANS; QUEBEC

We live in a country of mixed population, let us not forget it. We are the minority in this country, let us not forget it either. Let us live in peace with the Protestants, the English, and the Freemasons.

Lines from **Jules-Paul Tardivel**'s futuristic novel *Pour la patrie* (1895).

No country is enriched by the co-existence of two cultures if one half of the population cannot appropriate the cultural product of the other half.

Proposition discussed by panelists on CBC Radio's weekly discussion program *Fighting Words*, 12 Nov. 1957, hosted by Nathan Cohen. As noted by Morris Wolfe in *Fifty Years of Radio* (1986), the panelists were broadcaster René Lévesque, teacher Raymond Gagnier, writer Solange Chaput-Rolland, and *Cité Libre* magazine editor Pierre Elliott Trudeau.

We are then, French and English Canadians alike, the heirs to Lord Durham. If Canada is ever to become a place where French and English Canadians can live in full harmony, recognizing the validity of each other's culture, then Lord Durham will have to become a genuinely historical figure.

Ramsay Cook, historian, Introduction, *The Heirs of Lord Durham: Manifesto of a Vanishing People* (1978).

We see political exchange all the time, but we (in French-speaking Canada) don't know much about English artists, except the big ones. English Canada doesn't even know who the big ones are in French Canada.

Edith Butler, Acadian chansonnière, quoted in the *Winnipeg Free Press*, 30 June 1990.

French Canada aspires to nationhood while English Canada fears the loss of it. Within this entire history, only Newfoundland has a cautionary tale to tell—to everyone.

John Fraser, editor, convocation address, Memorial University, St. John's, Nfld., 31 Oct. 1992, reproduced in *The Globe and Mail*, 19 Nov. 1992.

Quebec must be the only place in the world where a well-paid middle-aged white male can have the cachet that comes with being a minority.

Jan Wong, columnist, "Why Should I? This Is My Home," *The Globe and Mail*, 26 Nov. 1999.

FRENCH CANADIANS See also CANADA, FRENCH & ENGLISH CANADA, QUEBEC, LES QUÉBÉCOIS

When the French are in a scrape, they cry out on behalf of the human species. Yet, when the French are on top, there are none more bloody or more inhumane.

James Wolfe, General, quoted by Sam Allison in *French Power: The Francization of Canada* (1978).

. . . The Hindoos are a more ignorant and more passive people than the French Canadians.

John Stuart Mill, political economist, "Penal Code for India" (1838), *Writings on India (1828–71)*, edited by John M. Robson, et al., Volume XXX of the "Collected Works of John Stuart Mill."

Nos institutions, notre langue et nos droits.

Motto of *Le Canadien,* the nationalist newspaper founded in Montreal by Étienne Parent in 1831; the words, which translate "Our institutions, our language and our rights," are said to be those of **Ludger Duvernay**.

They are thrifty;—but they do not thrive. They do not advance, and push ahead, and become a bigger people from year to year as settlers in a new country should do. They do not even hold their own in comparison with those around them.

Anthony Trollope, English novelist and traveller, *North America* (1862).

Most French-Canadian country-women become stout and wrinkled in middle life, owing to the excessive heat of the houses in winter, badly cooked food, and hard work; but those who have to go up and down these steep hills become especially clumsy.

W. George Beers, writer, "The Canadian Mecca," *The Century Magazine,* May 1882. The hills are those around Ste-Anne-de-Beaupré, Que.

We are French Canadians, but our country is not confined to the territory overshadowed by the Citadel of Quebec; our country is Canada, it is the whole of what is covered by the British flag on the American continent, the fertile lands bordered by the bay of Fundy, the Valley of the St. Lawrence, the region of the Great Lakes, the prairies of the West, the Rocky Mountains, the lands washed by the famous ocean whose breezes are said to be as sweet as the breezes of the Mediterranean.

Sir Wilfrid Laurier, Leader of the Opposition, address at the dedication of Cartier-Brébeuf Memorial Park, Quebec City, 25 June 1889.

Perhaps nothing will surprise the visitor more than the persistence of the French type in Canada, and naturally its aggressiveness.

Charles Dudley Warner, American travel writer, *Studies in the South and West* (1889).

First of all, it may be observed that the name, French-Canadian, is somewhat of a misnomer; at any rate, the people of the French race in Canada rarely if ever use it when speaking of themselves. They do not, as a rule, recognize the compound word; they simply call themselves Canadian.

Byron Nicholson, commentator, *The French-Canadians* (1902).

Strangers have surrounded us whom it is our pleasure to call foreigners; they have taken into their hands most of the rule, they have gathered to themselves much of the wealth; but in this land of Quebec nothing has changed. Nor shall anything change, for we are the pledge of it.... These people are a race which knows not how to perish.... In this land of Quebec naught shall die and naught change....

Profound peroration of French journalist and traveller **Louis Hémon**'s novel *Maria Chapdelaine* (1916) that celebrates the traditional life of the farming folk of the Lac Saint-Jean region of Quebec.

It is very strange. The Canadian French have this power through an intense, rather sullen organization. They love to call themselves a Conquered People—and you know what that means in the way of expansion and tenacity! They treat their hierarchy as a sort of Cadre, like the officers of an Army.

Hilaire Belloc, British essayist, letter written in Montreal, 11 March 1923, *Letters from Hilaire Belloc* (1958) edited by Robert Speaight.

The good point about the French in Quebec is that they have dwelt immemorially on the same soil amidst the same conditions and traditions. That is what makes a civilization!

H.P. Lovecraft, writer of supernatural tales, letter, 31 Oct. 1930, quoted by L. Sprague de Camp in *Lovecraft: A Biography* (1975). Lovecraft visited Quebec City in 1930, 1932, and 1933.

He is a Canuck—a Frenchman from Quebec—and I expect his mind works different from yours and mine.

Comment of an Anglo-Saxon about the character of a French-Canadian businessman in **John Buchan**'s novel *Sick Heart River* (1941).

The tragedy of French-Canada is that you can't make up your minds whether you want to be free-choosing individuals or French-Canadians choosing only what you think your entire race will approve.

Comment made by Huntley McQueen to Anathase Tallard in **Hugh MacLennan**'s novel *Two Solitudes* (1945).

"Ah yes, the Canadians of the future,—the true Canadians."

Exclamation of a character concerning native-born children in New France in **Willa Cather**'s historical novel *Shadows on the Rock* (1946).

If the future of mankind in a unified world is going to be on the whole a happy one, then I would prophesy that there is a future in the Old World for the Chinese, and in the island of North America for the *Canadiens*. Whatever the future of mankind in North America, I feel pretty confident that these French-speaking Canadians, at any rate, will be there at the end of the story.

Arnold J. Toynbee, historian, *Civilization on Trial* (1948).

We want French Canadians to stop thinking of themselves as second-class citizens and realize that all Canadians are second-class.

Dave Broadfoot, comedian, quoted by Constance Mungall in *The Toronto Star Weekly*, 8 May 1965.

A *Tabernac* of French Canadians.

Group term or term of venery for Quebecers, as noted by James Lipton in *An Exaltation of Larks: The Ultimate Edition* (1968, 1993).

For the time being, the French Canadian still exists. He is difficult to spot or to define, more so than the American or the Frenchman. But one need only wander through the Beauce or Charlevoix Counties and even in certain areas of our cities to recognize this singular being. And to have recognized in oneself that irrefutable *élan*....

Fernand Dumont, writer, *La vigile du Québec* (1971).

Groulx is also credited with the policy of *La revênche des berceaux*—the Revenge of the Cradles, which meant it was the duty of French-Canadian women to breed as many children as their bodies could produce in order to gain for Quebec a political majority in Canada.

Hugh MacLennan, novelist and essayist, referring to nationalist Canon Lionel Groulx, *The Toronto Star*, 18 May 1980.

I had thought the French-Canadian thing was a joke. I thought they might say "merci" or something every now and again, but that would be the extent of it. It is very unsettling to arrive in North America and not understand anything. I said "s'il vous plaît" a few times....

Bob Geldof, musician, flying into Montreal from Dublin in 1973, *Is that It?* (1986).

In spite of their more or less vigorous denials, I often have the impression that there is a fatigue that comes from being Canadian—an almost impossible undertaking and a heavy responsibility given the proximity of the United States. This is a complex question, and I haven't really succeeded in figuring out what they feel about it. What I'm struck by is the fact that they hardly seem to notice the problem and live in this twilight zone without regrets and apparently without worries.

André Laurendeau, Quebec nationalist, diary entry for 1964, "A Québécois Journal," translated by Pat Smart, *The Canadian Forum*, Nov. 1990.

FRENCH LANGUAGE See LANGUAGE: FRENCH

FRIENDSHIP

You do not know who is your friend or your enemy until the ice breaks.

Identified as an Inuit proverb in *The Canadian 1993 Household Almanac* (1992).

The difference between a friend and an acquaintance is that a friend helps where an acquaintance merely advises.

Bob Edwards, publisher, *The Eye Opener*, 20 Aug. 1921, *The Best of Bob Edwards* (1975) edited by Hugh Dempsey.

Nobody can be a friend of mine if I can't call him a son of a bitch.

Sam Bronfman, distiller, quoted by Peter C. Newman in *Bronfman Dynasty: The Rothschilds of the New World* (1978).

A friend is one who knows enough about you to become your worst enemy.

Louis Dudek, poet and aphorist, Oct. 1991.

i will not say good-bye / there are no good-byes / between friends / just long, long silences / until the next hello

Verse of the poem "Lesson" in **Gianna Patriarca**'s *Daughters for Sale* (1997).

Peace is friendship / Friendship is love / When you put them together / It's one big hug

Verse composed by **Lina-Marie Leone** and engraved in stone, Prospect Cemetery, Toronto, Sept. 1998.

FRONTIERS See also BORDER, CANADIAN-AMERICAN

The American frontier was a transient experience; the Canadian frontier is perpetual.

W.L. Morton, historian, *The Canadian Identity* (1961).

Welcome to the northeast's last frontier: to the United States government it's known as the St. Regis Indian Reservation, to the Canadian the St. Regis Indian Reserve. To the Mohawks, the land straddling New York State, Ontario, and Quebec is Akwesasne, "Land Where the Partridge Drums."

Rick Hornung, journalist, *One Nation: Under the Gun* (1991).

FRYE, NORTHROP See also GARRISON MENTALITY; WRITERS & WRITING, CANADIAN

Really, it is most exciting to me to know that at last we have the critic we have been waiting for. But it goes further than that. I think you will also prove to be the religious teacher we have been waiting for.

Edith Sitwell, English poet, letter of 29 April 1948 acknowledging receipt of Northrop Frye's *Fearful Symmetry, Selected Letters of Edith Sitwell* (1997) edited by Richard Greene.

I'm not a very conventional scholar. I'm not a scholarly authority in any one thing. I'm more like the hero in Carlyle's *Sartor Resartus*: The Professor of Things in General.

Northrop Frye, cultural critic, quoted by Gillian Cosgrove in *The Toronto Star*, 7 Aug. 1980.

My critical theory... that literature is born out of other literature.

Northrop Frye, cultural critic, interviewed by Susan Gabori, "Beginnings," *The Toronto Star*, 3 Jan. 1981.

General Attitude Toward Life: That of a liberal bourgeois intellectual, which I consider the flower of humanity.

Northrop Frye, cultural critic, interviewed by Allan Gould, "Chatelaine's Celebrity I.D.," *Chatelaine*, Nov. 1982.

Literature seems to me to revolve around what I call the primary concerns of humanity, those that have to do with freedom, love, and staying alive, along with the ironies of their frustration, as distinct from the secondary or ideological concerns of politics and religion, for which the direct verbal expression is expository rather than literary.

Northrop Frye, cultural critic, "Auguries of Experience" (1987), *The Eternal Act of Creation: Essays, 1979–1990* (1993) edited by Robert D. Denham.

There is a misapprehension widely afoot to the effect that Northrop Frye is primarily a literary and social critic.

Maggie Helwig, writer, arguing his status as a "mage" or "prophet," "The Prospero Figure: Northrop Frye's Magic Criticism," *The Canadian Forum*, Oct. 1987.

Our most extraordinary literary imagination does not work with poetry, prose fiction, or drama. It belongs to an essayist, the one who wrote *Anatomy of Criticism: Four Essays*.

Eleanor Cook, scholar, referring to mythopoeic criticism, "'A Seeing and Unseeing in the Eye': Canadian Literature and the Sense of Place," *Daedalus: Journal of the American Academy of Arts and Sciences*, "In Search of Canada," Fall, 1988.

The knowledge that you can have is inexhaustible, and what is inexhaustible is benevolent. The knowledge that you cannot have is of the riddles of birth and death, of our future destiny and the purposes of God. Here there is no knowledge, but illusions that restrict freedom and limit hope. Accept the mystery behind knowledge: It is not darkness but shadow.

Northrop Frye, cultural critic, Commissioning at the Baccalaureate Service, Victoria University, Toronto, 10 April 1988, reprinted by Jean O'Grady and Alvin Lee in *The Bible and Religion* (1998).

Literature is a human apocalypse, man's revelation to man, and criticism is not a body of adjudications, but the awareness of that revelation, the last judgement of mankind.

Northrop Frye, cultural critic, quoted by A.C. Hamilton in *Northrop Frye: Anatomy of His Criticism* (1990). Of the significance of this aphorism, Hamilton wrote: "In fumbling for an answer, I came to realize that anything Frye says forms part of all he says. This one gnomic sentence encapsulates his entire vision of literature and the function of literary criticism. I realized that if it alone of all his writings had survived, like an anthropologist shaping Neanderthal man from one bone sliver, I could reconstruct the *Anatomy*."

Indeed, a good nickname for him (he was always drawing these circles with crosses over them on the blackboard) might be Monsieur Mandala.

James Reaney, poet, writing of Northrop Frye and his mythopoeic imagination, "He Educated Our Imagination," *The Toronto Star*, 24 Jan. 1991.

People don't realize that I'm building temples to—well, "the gods" will do. There's an outer court for casual tourists, an inner court for those who want to stay for communion (incidentally, the rewards of doing so are very considerable). But I've left a space where neither they nor I belong.

Northrop Frye, cultural critic, Notebook, edited by Robert D. Denham, *Northrop Frye Newsletter*, Summer 1993.

It doesn't matter how often I'm mentioned by other critics: I form part of the subtext of every critic worth reading.

Northrop Frye, cultural critic, Notebook, edited by Robert D. Denham, *Northrop Frye Newsletter*, Summer 1993.

We all know the doggerel poem about critics: "Seeing an elephant, he exclaimed with a laugh, / What a wondrous thing is this giraffe." Perhaps one of his greatest gifts to writers was his lifelong work to ensure that if you created an elephant, it would never again be mistaken for a giraffe.

Margaret Atwood, author, memorial tribute, quoted in *Vic Report*, Spring 1991.

As a Vic freshman I had been a devout atheist, but after two years in the air force I reconsidered, and during my sophomore year I became an agnostic. By the time I graduated I believed in God. He was Northrop Frye.

Don Harron, humorist and former student, memorial tribute, *Vic Report*, Spring 1991.

Only Ulysses can bend the bow of Ulysses.

Robertson Davies, man-of-letters, offering a response to the rhetorical question of who will "replace" Northrop Frye who died on 22 Jan. 1991, heard on CBC Radio's *The National* the following day.

FUN

Fun is a much under-estimated activity. In North America we tend to think of it as something trivial, as something that isn't part of the real world. You do your work, which is serious, and then when you want to do nothing, or nothing of any import—when you want to goof off—you have fun.

George Cohon, senior chairman of McDonald's Restaurants of Canada, *To Russia with Fries* (1997) written with David Macfarlane.

FUR TRADE

On no account let your ladies wear furs. You have no idea what wretches the North-Western Indians are; and, above all, their women.

John Stuart Mill, political economist, presenting a rhetorical argument against an importation, "The New Corn Law" (1824–45), *Essays on Economics and Society* (1967), edited by John M. Robson, Volume IV of the "Collected Works of John Stuart Mill."

Some errors in earlier volumes have been discovered and corrected.... The most amusing is the fact that the references to the Fur trade in the *Principles* turned out to be nothing of the sort, but a misprint for Free Trade—a disappointment to Canadians.

Jean O'Grady, indexer, referring to *Mill's Principles of Political Economy*, Introduction, *Indexes to the Collected Works of John Stuart Mill* (1991) edited by Jean O'Grady with John M. Robson.

In 1739 the first French-Canadian fur traders, who trapped beaver from the Athabaska to the Mississippi, arrived. Some settled here. Isolated Taos became an outfitting post for these new mountain men, a place to winter and stock up on mules, saddles, and wilderness supplies.

Alexandra Mayes Birnbaum, travel writer,

Birnbaum's 1994: Santa Fe & Taos (1994). The traders wintered at Taos, New Mexico.

FUTURE See also MCLUHAN, MARSHALL; OGDEN, FRANK; PREDICTION & PROPHECY; TIME

The Archaic Period represents, indeed, as one of its most peculiar characteristics, the abundance of native gold; but the true *Golden Age of Man* lies before him, not behind.

Sir Daniel Wilson, historian, coiner of the word "prehistoric," *Prehistoric Annals of Scotland* (2nd ed., 1863).

All the future lies before us / Glorious in that sunset land.

Frederick G. Scott, Anglican Canon and versifier, epigraph quoted by W.D. Lighthall in *Songs of the Great Dominion* (1889).

I have not the least fear of the future. I regard it as certain as sunrise.

Sir William Van Horne, General Manager of the CPR, quoted by Walter Vaughan in *Sir William Van Horne* (1926).

Canada, as I have said, has no past, it has only a future.

Donald A. Wollheim, U.S. science-fiction editor, "Whither Canadian Fantasy?" *Uncanny Tales*, Dec. 1942.

Let her double her fourteen million population, along with the continued discovery of new oil and mineral wealth, and her potency will rival that of the United States.

Merrill Denison, author, "4,000 Miles of 'Irritation,'" referring to Canada's future, *Saturday Review of Literature*, 7 June 1952.

To strive, even dimly, to foresee the wonders of Canada's next generation is to summon the utmost powers of the imagination.

Dwight D. Eisenhower, U.S. President, joint meeting of the Senate and the House of Commons, 14 Nov. 1953.

The future is here now. The teacher of the future is always the present and it is very difficult to look at the present. Everything that is going to happen in ten or twenty years is happening now, right under our noses.

Marshall McLuhan, communications pioneer, "Education in the Electronic Age" (1967), *The Best of Times / The Worst of Times: Contemporary Issues in Canadian Education* (1972) edited by Hugh A. Stevenson, Robert M. Stamp, and J. Donald Wilson.

The future is on hold.

Judith Merril, science-fiction personality, commenting on the climate of opinion at the time, remark, 7 Sept. 1979.

To sacrifice the present, which exists, to a future which does not exist, and certainly will never exist in any presently recognizable form, is as perverse a notion as any in history.

Northrop Frye, cultural critic, "Some Reflections on Life and Habit" (1988), *Myth and Metaphor: Selected Essays, 1974–1988* (1990) edited by Robert D. Denham.

At the end of the day, the people of this great country will decide upon the future they want.

Charles, Prince of Wales, address at Queen's University, Kingston, 28 Oct. 1991, reproduced in *The Globe and Mail* the following day.

Travelling to the future is like travelling to any distant place. You really never get to know exactly what it's like until you arrive.

Frank Ogden, futurologist, "The Most Visionary Developments of the Century to Come," *Leaders*, Jan.–March 1992.

Give me back the Berlin Wall / Give me Stalin and St. Paul/ I've seen the future, brother: it is murder

Lines from the title song of the record album *The Future* (1992), the text of which is included in **Leonard Cohen**'s *Stranger Music: Selected Poems and Songs* (1993).

The future has become one of those topics, like education, on which everyone pontificates. Today, in a sense, we are all futurists.

Robert Fulford, columnist, "The Ideology of the Book," *Queen's Quarterly*, Winter 1994.

Human numbers and the acceleration of human activities made possible by advances in science and technology have reached the point at which we are now the architects of our own future. We literally have responsibility for our own evolution.

Maurice Strong, Chairman of the Earth Council, Preface, *Asking for the Earth* (1995) by James George.

Beyond argument, the Canada of tomorrow is going to have to be decisively different from the Canada of yesterday.

Richard Gwyn, columnist and author, *Nationalism without Walls: The Unbearable Lightness of Being Canadian* (1995).

Nothing is comfortably contemporary: postmodern is by now neo-quaint. We have entered the Prefuture Era.

Sam Orbaum, Montreal-raised Israeli columnist, "But Seriously," *The Jerusalem Post Magazine*, 20 Jan. 1995.

One of Canada's great strengths in the past has been that you always come to the future *second*, you let someone else make the mistakes.

Peter Druker, management consultant, address, Toronto, quoted by Douglas Bell in "Paradigms Lost Paradigms Found," *The Globe and Mail's Report on Business Magazine*, July 1995.

Only by claiming our own future—and that of our immediate families and communities—will the human spirit prevail.

Peter C. Newman, journalist, "The Dawn of a New Millennium," *Maclean's*, 30 Dec. 1996.

The future is a wonderful country: You can do anything there.

Hamilton Southam, benefactor, observation shared with his granddaughter Sophia, Ottawa, 15 March 2000.

G

GAELIC PEOPLE

Listen to me, as when ye heard our father / Sing long ago the song of our shores— / Listen to me, and then in chorus gather / All your deep voices, as ye pull your oars: / Fair these broad meads—these hoary woods are grand; / But we are exiles from our fathers' land.

Verse from the "Canadian Boat-Song (from the Gaelic)" which expresses a Highland Scot's lament at his exile in the New World. It appeared anonymously in *Blackwood's*, Sept. 1829, but authorship has been ascribed to a Scots versifier, **David Macbeth Moir**, who never visited North America but who corresponded with the Scots-Canadian colonist and novelist John Galt.

This dearest of Isles / Is so fertile and fair, / That no other island / May with it compare; / Here Gaelic was spoken / In ages gone by, / And here it will live / Till the ocean runs dry.

Second of six verses of the Gaelic song "The Isle of Heather" with lyrics attributed to **Murdo Macleod** and to **Donald Macrae** and translated by Henry Whyte. Apparently "the most famous Gaelic song" was written on a train between Sudbury and the Lakehead. *Lewis Gaelic Songs and Melodies* (1982) and *The Minstrelsy of the Scottish Highlands* (n.d.) edited by Alfred Moffatt.

GALLERIES See MUSEUMS & GALLERIES

GAMES & GAMBLING See also LOTTERIES

Never lose more today than you can win back tomorrow.

Llewelyn Davies, Montreal-born racing enthusiast, quoted by Jim Coleman in *A Hoofprint on My Heart* (1971).

Trivial Pursuit will forever stand as the Canadian standard for The-Stupidest-Move-I-Ever-Made. It will do this for no other reason than the main chance was blown by too many journalists who knew the game's inventors but refused to back them, and who can be counted on to dine out on their misfortune for as long as it takes to make up through freelance articles what they lost through God's idea of a cruel joke.

Roy MacGregor, columnist, *Ottawa Citizen*, 22 May 1987.

"What about a board game," I said to my friend, "called Bureaucracy? The winner would be the first one to discover the rules of the game."

John Galt, journalist and traveller, *Whistlestop: A Journey across Canada* (1987).

P.S. My favourite Trivial Pursuit question is this: *Who invented Trivial Pursuit?* The answer, of course, is two Canadians, but nobody, not even masters of the game, can remember their names.

Barry Callaghan, essayist, "Canadian Wry," (1985), *Canadian Content* (1992) edited by Sarah Norton and Nell Waldman. John Haney and Scott Abbott invented *Trivial Pursuit* in a Toronto pub in 1981 and successfully launched the game a year and a half later.

From the moment a government encourages its citizenry to finance the state by gambling—which means by idle dreaming—instead of through creativity, work and productivity, that state is in an unacknowledged crisis.

John Ralston Saul, author, *The Doubter's Companion: A Dictionary of Aggressive Common Sense* (1994).

GARBAGE

When and why does one man's garbage become another's historical artifact? The Parks Canada rule is that anything that is older than forty years takes on an aura of ancient truth-telling.

Stephen Strauss, science columnist, *The Globe and Mail*, 28 March 1992.

New York spends more on garbage collection—though to very little effect—than the whole world spends on the United Nations.

Hugh Keenleyside, diplomat, quoted by Donn Downey in his obituary, *The Globe and Mail*, 30 Sept. 1992.

GARDENS See also FLOWERS

Garden folk are invariably kindly folk.

Jack Miner, conservationist, *Jack Miner and the Birds and Some Things I Know about Nature* (1923).

Even during the worst of the drought, gardens in our part of the country were always adequate, and vegetables were at their best about haying time. There would have been no advantage in skimping them to see the produce saved, for there was no sale for it thereabouts, and anyhow it would have been shocking to take money for vegetables from neighbours.

Heather Gilead, Alberta farm memoirist, *The Maple Leaf for Quite a While* (1967).

Canadians are a bit like spectators in their solemn land, always partly aware of trespassing on the Eden of Gitchi Manitou.

Elizabeth Kilbourn, commentator, The Centennial Art Show, July 1968.

For Everyone a Garden

Moshe Safdie, architect, *For Everyone a Garden* (1974) edited by Judith Wolin. The book jacket shows an apartment at Montreal's Habitat with its own compact garden.

My theory is: If a lawn is dangerous for children and dogs, it probably isn't good for plants.

Marjorie Harris, columnist, *The Globe and Mail*, 29 Feb. 1992.

My garden is not a hobby. It is a fascination, an amazement. It is, occasionally, an obsession.

Marjorie Harris, writer and gardener, *The Healing Garden* (1996).

GARRISON MENTALITY See also FRYE, NORTHROP

It must realize its latent nationalism, a nationalism neither racial like the French nor dominant—a "garrison" nationality—like that of Ontario, but environmental and, because of the diversity of its people, composite.

W.L. Morton, historian, "Cleo in Canada: The Interpretation of Canadian History," *The University of Toronto Quarterly*, April 1946. The subject is Western Canada; this is an early use of the notion of the "garrison mentality" popularized two decades later by Northrop Frye.

Small and isolated communities surrounded with a physical or psychological "frontier," separated from one another and from their American and British cultural sources... are bound to develop what we may provisionally call a garrison mentality.

Northrop Frye, cultural critic, "Conclusion," *Literary History of Canada* (1965). Frye noted with a sense of dismay or disappointment how inarticulate was the society of Upper Canada and Southern Ontario.

At present I am concerned rather with a more creative side of the garrison mentality, one that has had positive effects on our intellectual life.

Northrop Frye, cultural critic, Preface, *The Bush Garden: Essays on the Canadian Imagination* (1971).

I've spoken of the garrison mentality in Canadian life and I got that idea from watching academics digging holes in palisades around themselves.

Northrop Frye, cultural critic, interviewed by Adele Freedman in *The Globe and Mail*, 3 Oct. 1981.

What corresponded to the frontier in American life was never a border in Canada. It was a circumference: a frontier surrounded and enclosed all the tiny communities wherever they were.

Northrop Frye, cultural critic, "Criticism and Environment" (1983), *The Eternal Act of Creation: Essays, 1979–1990* (1993) edited by Robert D. Denham.

Canadians are now, however, one of the most highly urbanized people in the world, and the garrison mentality, which was social but not creative, has been replaced by the condominium mentality, which is neither social nor creative and which forces the cultural energies of the country into forming a kind of counterenvironment.

Northrop Frye, cultural critic, "Levels of Cultural Identity" (1989), *The Eternal Act of Creation: Essays, 1979–1990* (1993) edited by Robert D. Denham.

GAYS & GAY RIGHTS See also HOMOSEXUALITY

This side is trying to distance itself from the raunchy gay sex of the seventies and eighties.

Now, joked one gay man, S&M means Scarborough and Mississauga.

Alanna Mitchell, journalist, referring to changes in lifestyles in two staid Toronto communities, "Gay in the Nineties," *The Globe and Mail*, 29 June 1991.

We're here, we're queer and we're not going away.

Chant of gay activists at Queen's Park, Toronto, following defeat of a spousal-rights benefits bill, quoted in *The Hamilton Spectator*, 11 June 1994.

Biopolitics and moral panic dovetail, then, as natural allies, aggressive and virulent.

John Fekete, philosopher, *Moral Panic: Biopolitics Rising* (2nd ed., 1995).

GENERATION X

Generation X.

The designation Generation X—for the generation of North Americans born in the mid-1960s who are in no hurry "to find themselves" because they give equal value to life experience and education—was popularized by Vancouver-based fiction writer **Douglas Coupland** in his satiric novel *Generation X: Tales for an Accelerated Culture* (1991). It is not certain whether he originated the phrase which is sometimes abbreviated to Gen X; he certainly adopted it and became identified with it. *Shampoo Planet* (1992), his second work, surveyed the adolescent world of "global teens" who are most at home in shopping malls. Apparently, the descriptions "Generation X" and "Xers" have some history in Britain to refer to post–Baby Boom Punkers.

GENIUS

I wish I lived in a town where the streets and squares were named after great men instead of developers, mayors and trees. Why can't we have cities which honour genius at every corner? How could people aspire to anything but money when there is nothing in their surroundings to remind them of the immortals who created things which do not lose their value with inffation.

Stephen Vizinczey, novelist, Foreword, *In Praise of Older Women* (1965, 1990).

One may recognize genius partly by its impertinence.

Robin Skelton, poet and aphorist, *A Devious Dictionary* (1991).

Genius is to the mind what the opposable thumb is to the body.

Maurus E. Mallon, aphorist, *Compendulum* (1995).

GEOGRAPHY See also LAND

We are fortunate both in our neighbours and in our lack of neighbours. It may be that this fortunate position is not due to any special virtue on our part, that it is an accident of geography and of history, but one has only to be in any European country a day to realize how relatively fortunate a position it is, and what folly it would be to throw it away. It is equally true, I should add, that if some countries have too much history, we have too much geography.

W.L. Mackenzie King, Prime Minister, speech, House of Commons, 18 June 1936. The last twelve words have been widely quoted.

In a right Rebellious Geography, East and West do not so much meet as radiate from a common centre. The Yang-Tse-Kiang is a tributary of the St. Lawrence and both flow from Parnassus through the Land of Sweet Living.

Barker Fairley, painter and professor, Introduction to *J.E.H. MacDonald / Catalogue* (1937).

Canada is so big as to seem invisible.

Brian Moore, novelist, *Canada* (1963, 1968).

Canada will always be so infinitely bigger physically than the small nation who live in it—even if its population is doubled—that this monstrous, empty, habitat must continue to dominate it psychologically and also culturally.

Wyndham Lewis, British artist, "Nature's Place in Canadian Culture" (1940–44), *Wyndham Lewis in Canada* (1971) edited by George Woodcock.

There is a thousand miles of forest, / A thousand miles of plain, / A thousand miles of mountains, / And then the sea again.

Ditty quoted by **Frederick W. Gershaw**, Senator, address, Senate of Canada, 12 March 1959, who added, "Someone has said that, on travelling from the Atlantic to the Pacific."

We're a long, thin country shaped like a railway....

Pierre Berton, author and media personality, address, Empire Club of Canada, Toronto, 7 Nov. 1985.

As I sit in my Toronto home, I am 2,740 miles south of the northern tip of Ellesmere Island, Canada's northernmost land for all practical purposes. If I swivel my chair and look directly south, there, a bit over the horizon but the same distance away, is Bogotá, the capital of Colombia. The District of Columbia, in contrast, is a mere hour's travel by jet.

F. Kenneth Hare, geographer, "Canada: The Land," *Daedalus: Journal of the American Academy of Arts and Sciences*, "In Search of Canada," Fall, 1988.

Know something? Canada, which we tend to think of as a thin ribbon of city lights stretched out along the forty-ninth parallel, is as high as it is wide. It's as far from Eureka, on Ellesmere Island, to Point Pelee in Ontario (which in fact is south of parts of California) as from Carbonear to Skidegate. The north is enormous.

Peter Gzowski, journalist and host of CBC Radio's *Morningside*, "Whistling Down the Northern Lights," *The Fourth Morningside Papers* (1991).

Southernmost Canada is south of northernmost Pennsylvania and within 138 miles of the United States' Mason-Dixon Line. One goes north from Windsor, Ontario, to enter Detroit, Michigan.

George J. Demko, geographer, *Why in the World: Adventures in Geography* (1992).

Space, land and winter—these are the overwhelming realities of Canada.

Wade Davis, ethnobotanist and essayist, *Shadows in the Sun* (1992).

Whether one is crossing Canada on a train or just looking at it on a map, the country is just too big for sparkle. The mind instinctively shies away from a subject that extends across so much territory.

Jan Morris, Anglo-Welsh traveller, "In Praise of Canada," *The Toronto Star*, 15 June 1992.

It's the second-largest land mass in the world, next to the Soviet Union. They have a lock on the world's largest supply of party ice . . . and just think of what they can do with Zamboni technology.

Michael Moore, documentary film-maker, quoted by Yardena Arar in *The Globe and Mail*, 4 July 1992.

So stand up and be proud and sing out very loud / We stand out from the crowd cuz Canada's really big.

Chorus of the song "Canada's Really Big" written and performed by the **Arrogant Worms** on their CD *Caterwaul & Doggerel* (1995).

GEOLOGY

He divided the Precambrian into two eras: the Archean, in which no life yet existed, and the Algonkian, in which life had arisen and gradually developed.

Charles D. Walcott, American geologist and coiner of the term Algonkian for a division of a geographical era, after 1879, as noted by Herbert Wendt in *Before the Deluge* (1968) translated from the German by Richard and Clara Winston.

The history of the last million years has been more completely recorded in the deposits in the neighbourhood of Toronto than anywhere else in Canada or perhaps the world.

Adapted from an observation made by geologist **Arthur P. Coleman**, with respect to Toronto's Scarborough Bluffs, author of *Ice Ages: Recent and Ancient* (1926) and *The Last Million Years* (1939).

This is perhaps the oldest country in the world. Till yesterday it seemed destined to eternal solitude.

Stephen Leacock, humorist, *Canada: The Foundations of Its Future* (1941).

A graduate, *magna cum lava*, / Of Ottawa's College of Mines, / He died while at work in Ungava / By failing to read the French signs.

Lines from **Nathan Fast**'s verse "The Status of Canadian Geology" (1957), *The Blasted Pine* (2nd ed., 1967) edited by F.R. Scott and A.J.M. Smith.

No mortal mother made me / to feel the warm blood flow; / the years have not betrayed me / to hunger and to know. // A wiser mother made me; / from searings and from shock; / the cooling years have stayed me. / I am the rock.

"The Rock" inspired by the topography around Georgian Bay from **Barker Fairley**'s *Poems of 1922 or Not Long After* (1972).

The continents are floating about the globe like froth in a pot.

J. Tuzo Wilson, geologist and proponent of the theory of continental drift, quoted by Hanoch Bordan in *The Toronto Star,* 4 March 1978.

Chunks of granite in the Northwest Territories are among the world's oldest rocks: more than 4 billion years.

George J. Demko, geographer, *Why in the World: Adventures in Geography* (1992).

GERMANY

Canada, at this day, is an exact picture of ancient Germany. Although situated in the same parallel with the finest provinces of France and England, that country experiences the most rigorous cold. The reindeer are very numerous, the ground is covered with deep and lasting snow, and the great river of St. Lawrence is regularly frozen, in a season when the waters of the Seine and the Thames are usually free from ice.

Edward Gibbon, historian, Chapter IX, *Decline and Fall of the Roman Empire* (1776–88).

GHOSTS See also BELIEF

There's no literature on earth I relish as I do a good ghost story.

L.M. Montgomery, novelist and diarist, April 1930, *The Selected Journals of L.M. Montgomery: Volume IV: 1929–1935* (1998) edited by Mary Rubio and Elizabeth Waterston. Montgomery is referring to fictional ghosts: "A volume of Marion Crawford's ghost stories cheered me up tonight. Ghost stories always do."

And this brings us to the Great Amherst mystery of 1879... it is a mystery, and one which becomes more, and not less, interesting the more that we examine it.

Sacheverell Sitwell, English author, referring to the poltergeist reported in the house of Esther Cox, Amherst, N.S., 1879, *Poltergeists* (1940).

No ghosts in Canada? The country which too vigorously asserts its normality and rationalism is like a man who declares that he is without imagination; suddenly the ghosts he has denied may overcome him, and then his imaginative flights make poets stare. Unfortunately, he also needs the help of the psychiatrist, and there are no psychiatrists who minister to whole nations.

Robertson Davies, man-of-letters, article in *Holiday,* April 1964, *The Well-Tempered Critic: One Man's View of Theatre and Letters in Canada* (1981) edited by Judith Skelton Grant.

Ghost, ghost, you are more alive still / than half the people in this room.

Lines from **Elizabeth Brewster**'s poem "At the Poet's Birthplace," *In Search of Eros* (1974).

There is nothing supernatural about ghosts. They are part of the world in which we live, and they follow laws which we are beginning to understand more fully as more and more research into parapsychology continues to be done.

Robin Skelton and **Jean Kozocari**, *A Gathering of Ghosts: Hauntings and Exorcisms from the Personal Casebook of Robin Skelton and Jean Kozocari* (1989).

I believe in them the way Shakespeare believed in them. They're a way of exemplifying something which you know to be true but which is very hard to give substance to.... It doesn't really mean that people are floating around in nighties looking for somebody to scare.

Robertson Davies, man-of-letters, quoted by Mel Gussow in "A Moralist Possessed by Humour," *The New York Times Book Review,* 5 Feb. 1995.

GIFTS & GIVING See also PHILANTHROPY

You took my hand. That was the only time you took something and I got it back.

Raymond Canale, Italian-born, Toronto-based aphorist, 1975.

Some people do you favours hoping you'll reciprocate in triplicate.

Maurus E. Mallon, aphorist, *Compendulum* (1995).

GLAMOUR

Glamour defies death and assuages our anxiety about loss. Youth is therefore inherently glamorous. Vitality is glamorous. And intense living—surviving in high style at the brink—is the most glamorous scenario of all.

Douglas Kirkland, photojournalist, *Light Years: Three Decades of Photography among the Stars* (1987) edited by Judith Thurman.

GLOBALIZATION See also GLOBAL VILLAGE

The multinational firm.

The concept of business multinationality was

conceived and given currency in 1961 by **Howe Martyn**, Professor of Political Economy, the American University, Washington, D.C. In a letter written in 1973, Martyn, a Canadian citizen, noted: "I coined the term for a course, finding subsequently, however, a similar earlier use. I prefer my original term 'multinational firm' because it avoids the suggestion of an American monopoly of this development conveyed by 'corporation' which is the American term for what others call limited company or *société anonyme*." By the 1990s, the term was largely superseded by global corporation.

But now Canada has become a kind of global Switzerland, surrounded by the United States on the south, the European common market on the east, the Soviet Union on the north, China and Japan on the west.

Northrop Frye, cultural critic, "Conclusion to a Literary History of Canada" (1965), *The Bush Garden: Essays on the Canadian Imagination* (1971).

Think Globally, Act Locally

Maxim of the futurist movement in the 1970s, popularized if not coined by futurologist **Frank Feather**. By the 1990s, the four words were reduced to the one-word neologism glocal.

In the world of tomorrow, the old concepts of right and left do not mean anything. Protectionism is not left-wing or right-wing, it is simply passé. Globalization is not right-wing or left-wing. It is simply a fact of life.

Jean Chrétien, Liberal leader, address, Liberal Party's policy convention, Aylmer, Que., 22–24 Nov. 1991, quoted in an editorial in *The Globe and Mail*, 26 Nov. 1991.

Globalization and competitiveness are thus far more than trendy buzz words. They refer to a fundamental shift in the character of the economic relationships between individuals and between societies.

Peter J. Nicholson, bank executive, *Finding Common Ground* (1992) introduced by Jean Chrétien.

If globalization means that your society will be threatened by the lowest common denominator, I want nothing to do with it.

Mel Hurtig, nationalist, quoted by Steven Wild in the *Winnipeg Free Press*, 29 March 1992.

Does local turbulence—the Slovenians, the Croats, the Kurds, the Estonians, the Québécois, the Mohawks—impede the growth of the world supermarket? Of course not: Global order feeds on local chaos; that's what these events are all about.

Frank Zingrone, academic, "Culture and What Surrounds It," *Journal/Newsletter of Computers, Evolution and Society*, Winter 1992.

It's hard to be globally minded when you're sleeping under a bridge.

Murray Dobbin, commentator and critic of globalization, "Right of Reply," *The Canadian Forum*, Dec. 1992.

1. The Global Economy is inevitable. 2. The Global Economy will produce more goods at lower prices. 3. To resist the Global Economy is to deny the Third World its opportunity. 4. The Global Economy is the future.

John Ralston Saul, author, *The Doubter's Companion: A Dictionary of Aggressive Common Sense* (1994). These are the "four banners" that identify arguments on behalf of the Global Economy, according to Saul, who defines the Global Economy in this way: "The modern form of ideology is economic determinism."

The Age of Networked Intelligence is creating a borderless world where nation states become less important. Money, communications, business transactions, and information are becoming bits that lack awareness and respect for national boundaries.

Don Tapscott, consultant, *The Digital Economy: Promise and Peril in the Age of Networked Intelligence* (1996).

We are moving from globalization to planetization.

Derrick de Kerckhove, communications theorist, speech, "From Marconi to McLuhan," Italian Trade Commission, Toronto, 16 Sept. 1996.

What is a borderless world? It is a world emptied of every value and principle except one—accumulation.

Eric Kierans, economist, quoted by Linda McQuaig in *The Cult of Impotence* (1998).

This study began in the Himalayas. I had been inside the Dalai Lama's monastery, listening to the monks' chanting. As I went outside, I was startled to hear a radio blaring another, more mundane mantra. We all know the words: "We must compete in the new global marketplace."

John McMurtry, philosopher, opening words of his study *Unequal Freedoms: The Global Market as an Ethical System* (1998).

GLOBAL VILLAGE See also GLOBALIZATION; MCLUHAN, MARSHALL

The new electronic independence recreates the world in the image of a global village.

Marshall McLuhan, communications pioneer, *The Gutenberg Galaxy* (1962). The notion that the world's parochial cultures and countries are being transformed into one, planet-wide community characterized by interconnected needs and uniform services was pioneered and popularized by McLuhan in the 1960s. McLuhan built on this idea from Wyndham Lewis's *America and Cosmic Man* (1948): "The earth has become one big village, with telephones laid on from one end to the other, and air transport, both speedy and safe...."

If the world is becoming a global village, it will also take on the feature of real village life, including cliques, lifelong feuds and impassable social barriers.

Northrop Frye, cultural critic, "Communications," *The Listener*, 9 July 1970.

We can see everybody else in the world now and they can all see us. Essentially, it's turning us all back into villages. Which is just as well—because our cities are dying.

Gwynne Dyer, media personality, interviewed by Scott Steele, "Eve of Destruction?" *Maclean's*, 5 Sept. 1995.

GLORY

A nation without glory is like a man without courage.

Garnet Wolseley, Army general, *The Story of a Soldier's Life* (1903).

There'll be enough glory for all of us if we can get it right.

Remark made by **Frederick G. Banting** to Charles H. Best with respect to credit for the discovery of insulin, identified with the television series, CBC-TV's *Glory Enough for All*, 16–17 Oct. 1988.

GOD See also BELIEF

But there is one thing which we struggle to keep out of our mind: the true condition of our soul in the sight of God.

Louis Riel, Métis leader and mystic, diary entry, 11 Aug. 1885, *The Diaries of Louis Riel* (1976) edited by Thomas Flanagan.

The Christian God's substance is not above history; is the substance of history itself.

Leslie Dewart, philosopher, *The Future of Belief: Theism in a World Come of Age* (1966).

"God is going to change," I thought. "We women are going to bring an end to God."

Naomi Goldenberg, feminist, *Changing the Gods: Feminism and the End of Traditional Religions* (1979).

I have a sense of human consciousness saying that God is too mighty to speak through small things. Human consciousness thus seeks to limit God to certain categories, although the atom has proved mighty. Everything, all detail, is important. Every cell and every speck of dust are important and speak in a divine voice. The human task is the ordering and manifesting of a new world; we show you how it is done in our small world, and let our divinity speak to you.

Dorothy Maclean, medium, quoting the "Landscape Angel" (1971), *To Hear the Angels Sing: An Odyssey of Co-Creation with the Devic Kingdom* (1980).

I'm not a pessimist because I don't believe the coming holocaust will be, by any means, the end. Man is not the boss. He will not wipe out the world on which he lives. It is God who will end the world when He knows its purpose has been fulfilled. That purpose is a happy one: the population of heaven with souls who want to share existence with Him for all eternity.

William Kurelek, artist, *Someone with Me: The Autobiography of William Kurelek* (1980).

One cannot live a day without being concerned about food, but one may live all one's life without being concerned about God.

Northrop Frye, cultural critic, distinguishing between primary and secondary concerns and calling into question Paul Tillich's notion that religious concern is "ultimate," "Framework and

Assumption" (1985), *Myth and Metaphor: Selected Essays, 1974–1988* (1990) edited by Robert D. Denham.

For even gods are mortal. After millennia, our own gods are showing signs of weariness. Christianity, with its pastoral symbolism, is beginning to feel uncomfortable in the concrete and plastic jungles we have built around us.

W.A. Kenyon, archaeologist, *Mounds of Sacred Earth: Burial Mounds of Ontario* (1986).

The *Bible* says that God made man in His image, but even 2,400 years ago Herodotus knew better. It is the other way around, man makes his gods in his image.

Michael Bradley, writer, *Chosen People from the Caucasus: Jewish Origins, Delusions, Deceptions and Historical Role in the Slave Trade, Genocide and Cultural Colonization* (1992).

A human being is a microcosm of the macrocosm. That we are in fact "made in God's image" is probably one of the few remnants of true information that has been handed down to us correctly by tradition.

James George, former Canadian Ambassador, *Asking for the Earth: Waking up to the Spiritual/Ecological Crisis* (1995).

We have components of godliness—the DNA of the divine plan of the universe resides in every one of us.

Duke Redbird, Native spokesperson, interviewed by Ron LeBlanc in "Duke Redbird," *The Core* (Toronto tabloid), Feb. 1995.

Ultimately, human experience is determined by what is happening in the brain. And the experience of God can be generated by a process that has nothing to do with whether God exists or not.

Michael Persinger, psychologist, referring to the "helmet" he devised that exposes the brain with low-intensity electromagnetic waves, quoted by Mark Nichols, "The God Machine," *Maclean's*, 22 Jan. 1996.

I believe that God is more than Jesus. God is huge, mysterious, wholly beyond our comprehension and beyond our total understanding. Jesus therefore does not represent or embody all of God, but embodies as much of God as can be in a person. But to me that does not diminish the divine that Jesus embodies.

Bill Phipps, Moderator of the United Church of Canada, interviewed by *Maclean's*, 15 Dec. 1997.

It is not within the power of any government to issue the orders to God.

Lucien Bouchard, Quebec Premier, referring to the effects of the ice storm that devastated Eastern Ontario, Montreal, and Quebec's South Shore, press conference, Montreal, CBC-TV, 14 Jan. 1998.

GOLD See also KLONDIKE, YUKON TERRITORY

In due time the gold of Klondyke will find its way to the great cities of the world. But the old dilemma will keep continually reproducing itself.

George Bernard Shaw, Anglo-Irish playwright, *The Perfect Wagnerite: A Commentary on the Nieblung's Ring* (1898). Shaw equated the greed for gold in Wagner's opera *Das Rheingold* (1869) with the greed of the Klondike Gold Rush of 1897 in the Yukon Territory.

GOLF See also SPORTS

Give me the five iron... no, on second thought, give me that other club, no, no give me that one I bought up in Toronto. Ah yes, that Canadian Club.

Comedy routine attributed to comedian **W.C. Fields**, with reference to Canadian Club rye whiskey, from a vaudeville routine of the 1930s.

In some parts of Africa, native tribes practise the strange custom of beating the ground with sticks and uttering wild, blood-curdling yells. Anthropologists call this a primitive form of self-expression. We call it golf.

Al Boliska, broadcaster, *Fore-Play: Every Golf Joke Ever Told* (1971).

Every swing is a challenge.

George Knudsen, champion golfer, quoted by Jim Gray in *The Toronto Star*'s *The City*, 3 Sept. 1978.

If T.S. Eliot had been a Canadian golfer, he wouldn't have called April the cruellest month. He would have reserved his bitter epitaphs for the long wasteland of winter when drives are shovelled rather than sliced, and where eager duffers lapse into a state of wintry inactivity.

Paul McLaughlin, journalist, *TV Guide*, 15 Jan. 1982.

I punished my golf clubs by leaving them in the garage all winter. The garage is cold and the roof leaks. It is full of spiders. The golf clubs needed to be punished because they lacked distance and accuracy, the two qualities every decent golf club ought to possess. One of these days I will take them out of the garage and see whether they have mended their ways.

Joey Slinger, humorist, "Getting Even," *If It's a Jungle Out There, Why Do I Have to Mow the Lawn* (1992).

GOOD & EVIL See also MORALITY, RIGHT & WRONG

The good which we do to others yields us a deeper and more lasting satisfaction than the good which we do to ourselves.

Goldwin Smith, essayist, "Morality and Theism," *Guesses at the Riddle of Existence and Other Essays on Kindred Subjects* (1897).

The idea of good and evil is a myth created by the politicians, the priests and all those who have an interest to keep us at their mercy.

Brock Chisholm, first Director-General of the World Health Organization, address, Fall 1945, quoted by Allan Irving in *Brock Chisholm: Doctor to the World* (1998).

I have expressed this elsewhere by suggesting that love or charity begins by asking the question, "Why do *we* permit so much evil and suffering?"

Northrop Frye, cultural critic, *The Double Vision: Language and Meaning in Religion* (1991).

I sometimes characterize Canadians as a sullen people addicted to doing good.

Adrienne Clarkson, Governor General, interviewed by Brian Stewart, Rideau Hall, Ottawa, CBC-TV, 14 Oct. 1999.

GOODS & SERVICES TAX See also TAXES

Of all the things that are wrong with the GST, surely a tax on reading stands out as the most regressive and offensive cultural and educational measure ever introduced by a government.

Allan MacEachen, Senator, address, Senate of Canada, 5 Nov. 1990.

BTT / VAT

BTT or Business Transfer Tax: name proposed in June 1986 for the future GST. (Other meanings: God Save the Taxpayer, Government Screwing Taxpayers, Goddam Stupid Tax.) VAT or Value-Added Tax: name proposed in 1994 for a rejigged GST. (Other meanings: Very Awful Tax, Vote Away this Tax). *Q.* How does a Canadian pupil recite the alphabet? *A.* A-B-C-D-E-F-G-S-T. . . .

GOULD, GLENN See also MUSIC

Except for a few octagenarians, I'm really the first person who has, short of having a nervous collapse or something, given up the stage.

Glenn Gould, pianist, who performed his last public concert on Easter Sunday 1964, "Notes to Glenn Gould: Concert Dropout" (1968), quoted by Geoffrey Payzant in *Glenn Gould: Music and Mind* (1978).

At the same time, I think that if I were required to spend the rest of my life on a desert island, and to listen or play the music of any one composer during all that time, that composer would almost certainly be Bach.

Glenn Gould, pianist, letter of 22 May 1967, *Glenn Gould: Selected Letters* (1992) edited by John P.L. Roberts and Ghyslaine Guertin.

It's not that Mozart died too soon; he died too late.

Attributed to pianist **Glenn Gould** by William Aide in *Starting from Porcupine* (1996).

Gould is a wonderful figure, a sort of self-displaced person.

Don DeLillo, novelist, observation made in a letter to commentator B.W. Powe, 7 June 1992.

There are more books in the Metro Toronto library about Gould (15) than about Paderewski, Rachmaninoff, or Casals, some of the most colourful great artists of our century.

Anton Kuerti, pianist and essayist, "All that Glitters Is Not Gould," *The Globe and Mail*, 12 Feb. 1994.

GOVERNANCE See also GOVERNMENT

We have among us no splendid villains above the control of our laws. Daring wickedness is here never suffered to triumph over helpless innocence.

Joseph Brant, Mohawk leader, quoted by William L. Stone in *Life of Joseph Brant—Thayendanegea; Including the Indian Wars of the American Revolution* (1838).

The question is not whether we need global government but what form it should take. The great weakness of the present system is that it is state-centric. The geo-centric vision of planetary government, where the greatest amount of power would instead be vested in its transnational global authority, is no longer a utopian dream—it is an absolute necessity.

Frank Feather, futurologist, *G-Forces: Reinventing the World—The 35 Global Forces Restructuring Our World* (1989).

It may not be fashionable to talk about love and solidarity as political and economic duties. These are, we are told, private things best left to private moments. But they are public values as well. There is a will to solidarity, to community, and to love. It can break barriers of class, of upbringing, of colour, of language. It reminds us that we have duties as well as rights: responsibilities to the earth itself, duties to take care of ourselves, to take care of others.

Bob Rae, NDP leader, election campaign address delivered in 1990 before being elected Ontario Premier, *The Globe and Mail*, 1 Oct. 1990.

The thought of a world government is frightening on one level, but represents the only way mankind can solve its two biggest problems: poverty and pollution.

Diane Francis, columnist, *Maclean's*, 27 April 1992.

GOVERNMENT See also GOVERNANCE, OPPOSITION, PARLIAMENT, POLITICS, SENATE

Most of any government's troubles come from trying to uphold the blunders it makes.

Bob Edwards, publisher, *The Eye Opener*, 19 April 1919.

I once heard Sir Wilfrid Laurier say in reply to an editor of a newspaper which was criticizing certain of his colleagues: "You good people want me to have a Cabinet of angels, but you do not send me angels to make a Cabinet out of."

W.L. Mackenzie King, Prime Minister, "Appreciations" (1919), *The Message of the Carillon and Other Addresses* (1927).

I do not mean to say that private gain is never extreme, that all missionaries are angels. But I do say that they represent the only basis on which it has yet proved possible to develop the assets of a country. We must get rid of the incubus of government activity. It is a blight which is spreading all over the world.

Stephen Leacock, humorist, address, The Canadian Club of New York, 10 March 1923, quoted by Hugh A. Anderson in *The Kinship of Two Countries: A History of The Canadian Club of New York* (1964).

Canada has made no contribution to political theory or to the science of government. The oldest dominion, it has followed British developments, practices, and customs. We walk by the still waters and along the quiet paths of traditions, and our historical origins lie across creative politics.

W.P.M. Kennedy, historian, "The Government of the Canadian Federation," *Handbook of Canada: Issued by the Local Committee on the Occasion of the Meeting of the British Association for the Advancement of Science at Toronto, August, 1924* (1924).

Not life, liberty, and the pursuit of happiness, but peace, order, and good government are what the national government of Canada guarantees. Under these, it is assumed, life, liberty, and happiness may be achieved, but by each according to his taste. For the society of allegiance admits of a diversity the society of compact does not, and one of the blessings of Canadian life is that there is no Canadian way of life, much less two, but a unity under the Crown admitting of a thousand diversities.

W.L. Morton, historian, *The Canadian Identity* (1961). Morton distinguished the aims of the Declaration of Independence, 1776, from the objectives of the British North America Act, 1867.

Government, it seems, is a kind of inert mass upon which impression may be made only by constant and unremitting pressure, by the reiteration if ideas, by unrelenting advocacy, by constant repetition, as in the Chinese water torture.

James Eayrs, historian, noted in Jan. 1967, *Diplomacy and Its Discontents* (1971).

The true test of a government is found in its ability to provide its people with a sense of worth, of accomplishment, of fulfillment.

Pierre Elliott Trudeau, Prime Minister, address in Peking, China, Oct. 1973, quoted by James Eayrs in *The Canadian,* 22 May 1976.

Legislation cannot alter the human body by a single centimeter—except to destroy it. It cannot improve the human brain—except to inhibit it. It cannot affect human compassion—except to institutionalize it.

Morris C. Shumiatcher, advocate, CMA Journal, 3 Sept. 1977.

When I think of the way we run our economy and our governments, I'm reminded of those startling photographs that sometimes emerge from a Canadian spring—interlocking skeletons of two stags who have locked horns, gotten stuck, and died when unable to eat and survive the winter. I sometimes wonder how different we really are from those Canadian deer.

Bob Rae, leader of the Ontario NDP, future Ontario Premier, speech, *The Toronto Star,* 10 Oct. 1982.

When governments talk morality they intend repression.

Robin Skelton, poet and aphorist, *A Devious Dictionary* (1991).

This is a difficult country to govern.

Brian Mulroney, Prime Minister, observation made to reporters, Manicouagan, Que., 21 Aug. 1986, quoted in *The Toronto Star,* 25 Feb. 1993.

The state is not a vestigial remnant of a past age, as neoconservatives would have us believe; rather, it is a vital institution that can act as our "equalizer," and we should regard it as such.

James Laxer, economist, *False God: How the Globalization Myth Has Impoverished Canada* (1993).

For years governments have been promising more than they can deliver, and delivering more than they can afford.

Paul Martin Jr., Minister of Finance, budget speech, House of Commons, 22 Feb. 1994, quoted by Alan Freeman in *The Globe and Mail* the following day.

If you're a mayor and you have a problem, what do you do? You blame the provincial government. And when you're the provincial government and you have a problem, what do you do? You blame the federal government. And for us, we cannot blame the Queen any more, so we blame the Americans once in a while.

Jean Chrétien, Prime Minister, referring to criticism of the federal budget, in conversation with Peter Gzowski on CBC Radio's *Morningside,* 1 March 1995, quoted by Susan Delacourt in *The Globe and Mail* the following day.

We never went far enough to satisfy child-care advocates, arts organizations, columnists, and others who demand the full moon or nothing at all. Now they have their starless sky.

Bob Rae, former Ontario Premier, referring to the demands of identity groups on his NDP government and its defeat by the Conservatives in the next election, *From Protest to Power: Personal Reflections on a Life in Politics* (1996).

Attacks on government are attacks on the fabric of society. We have individual needs, to be sure, but a society that allows them to undermine collective needs will soon destroy itself. We all value private goods, but they are worthless without public goods—such as policing and economic policies—to protect them.

Henry Mintzberg, management consultant, "The Myth of 'Society Inc.'" *Report on Business Magazine,* Oct. 1996.

We did not elect the provincial premiers to undo national programs; we elected the federal government to apply strong national standards, and provincial governments to deliver services.

Maude Barlow, chair of the Council of Canadians, interviewed by Graham Fraser, *The Globe and Mail,* 9 Dec. 1998.

Canada is divided by great mountains, great prairies, Great Lakes, and eleven governments that really grate.

Hugh Arscott, aphorist, *Hugh's Views* (Volume I), 1998.

GOVERNOR GENERAL See also MONARCHY, PARLIAMENT

I also append my valuable signature to a great deal without knowing in the least why, and run out to the most notorious gossips to pick up the last bits of news, political or social, with which to regale his Excellency, who duly rings for me for that purpose when he has read his letters.

Laurence Oliphant, British-born aide to Governor General Lord Elgin, appointed Superintendent-General of Indian Affairs, Ottawa, letter to his mother in England, summer 1854, quoted by Ann Taylor in *Laurence Oliphant: 1829–1888* (1982). Oliphant was unstable and subsequently joined the Brotherhood of the New Life established by cult leader Thomas Lake Harris.

Man, according to Aristotle, is a political animal, but there is an exception in the case of a Governor General. His views on public policy can only be the views of his Ministers. If he touches on the subject he must confine himself to what may be called Governor-Generalities.

John Buchan, Lord Tweedsmuir, Governor General (1935–40), *Canadian Occasions: Addresses* (1940).

Nothing touched me quite as much as this comment in a Canadian newspaper: "He made the Crown Canadian." It was too generous a tribute; but that was what I had tried to do.

Vincent Massey, first native-born Governor General (1952–59), *What's Past Is Prologue* (1963).

Call me Madame.

Adrienne Clarkson, Governor General, establishing the style of address, prior to her installation as the 26th Governor General of Canada, Ottawa, 7 Oct. 1999.

There's only one Governor General.

John Ralston Saul, author and commentator on public affairs, press conference convened to announce the forthcoming appointment of his wife, Adrienne Clarkson, Ottawa, 8 Sept. 1999, quoted in *The Toronto Star* the following day.

I am very honoured to be the first woman of neither founding nation to be Governor General of Canada—it has deep meaning for me.

Adrienne Clarkson, referring to her Chinese background, press conference, Ottawa, 8 Sept. 1999, quoted in *The Toronto Star* the following day.

I am Adrienne Clarkson *and you're not.*

Caricature of the imperturbable image of TV personality Adrienne Clarkson, host of CBC-TV's *Adrienne Clarkson Presents,* launched June 1990, subsequently popularized by the comedy team of CBC Radio's *Double Exposure,* as noted by Peter C. Newman in "The Nation's Business," *Maclean's,* 25 July 1994. The jibe recalls the droll signoff employed by historian and TV personality Laurier LaPierre for his Montreal-based TV show in the mid-1970s: "I am Laurier LaPierre . . . and you are you."

GRAFFITI

My Canada Does Not Include Politicians.

Bumper sticker noted in "Social Studies, *The Globe and Mail,* 10 May 1993.

Canadians are such polite people they write graffiti in full sentences.

Garrison Keillor, author and performer, CBC Radio's *Encore,* concert, rebroadcast on 5 Aug. 1996.

GRASS

Please Walk on the Grass

Wording on signs in Toronto's public parks introduced by **Thomas (Tommy) W. Thompson**, first Parks Commissioner, Metropolitan Toronto (1955–81); inscription, memorial, Mount Pleasant Cemetery, noted by Mike Filey in *Mount Pleasant Cemetery: An Illustrated Guide* (1999).

GREAT BRITAIN See UNITED KINGDOM

GREAT LAKES

For in their interflowing aggregate, those grand fresh-water seas of ours,—Erie, and Ontario, and Huron, and Superior, and Michigan,—possess an ocean-like expansiveness, with many of the ocean's noblest traits; with many of its rimmed varieties of races and of climes.

Evocation of the Great Lakes by the character Don Sebastian in **Herman Melville**'s novel *Moby Dick; or, The Whale* (1851).

Lake Ontario was a vast plain, upon which disported skaters, walkers, riders, drivers, and that most fairy-like of "white-wings," the ice-boat. Did you ever fly across the silvery ice on runners, with sails bending before the wind? It is an experience.

Sir Henry Irving, English actor in Toronto, *Henry Irving's Impressions of America: Narrated in a Series of Sketches, Chronicles, and Conversations* (1884) by Joseph Hatton.

There is a quiet horror about the Great Lakes which grows as one revisits them.

Rudyard Kipling, man-of-letters, *Letters to the Family: Notes on a Recent Trip to Canada* (1908).

The legend lives on from the Chippewa on down / Of the big lake they call Gitche Gumee. / Superior, it is said, never gives up her dead / When the gales of November come early.

Refrain of **Gordon Lightfoot**'s song "The Wreck of the Edmund Fitzgerald" (1975). The *Laker* sank in Lake Superior, 10 Nov. 1975.

The lake was an inside ocean: birds screeched into its blue, shells stuck up like toenails in its strand. It might even have harboured a swimming dragon.

Description or evocation of Lake Ontario in **Cynthia Ozick**'s novel *The Cannibal Galaxy* (1983).

GREATNESS

It is as a nation among nations that you stand today, it is as a great nation among great nations that you will be judged.

Rudyard Kipling, man-of-letters, "Canada's Path to Nationhood," 21 Oct. 1907, *Addresses Delivered before the Canadian Club of Ottawa: 1903–1909* (1910).

Every human life is insignificant until you make yourself great.

Athol Murray, priest and founder of Notre Dame College, Wilcox, Sask., message to students, quoted by Jack Gorman in *Père Murray and The Hounds* (1977).

It takes centuries before the mountain peaks emerge. Most contemporaries are about the same size.

Northrop Frye, cultural critic, quoted by Gillian Cosgrove in *The Toronto Star*, 7 Aug. 1980.

One must start early to become a great man.

Line from **Stephen Vizinczey**'s novel *An Innocent Millionaire* (1983).

GREEK PEOPLE

A great city falls into ruin, but a ruin lasts forever.

George Galt, writer and traveller, referring to the once-great Greek city of Delos, *Trailing Pythagoras* (1982).

Toronto has been written in the history of modern Greece.

Andreas Papandreou, Prime Minister of Greece, who spent five years of his exile as an economist at York University, address, Toronto, 30 March 1983, quoted by Lorne Slotnick in *The Globe and Mail* the following day.

How strange . . . a Greek shoemaker in Toronto!

Jorge Luis Borges, man-of-letters, expressing surprise upon learning the size of the Greek population of Toronto, interviewed by Raul Galvez in Buenos Aires, Argentina, June 1985, From the *Ashen Land of the Virgins* (1988).

GREENPEACE See also ECOLOGY

Don't Make A Wave

Message on banners to protest the U.S. testing of a one-megaton nuclear bomb at Amchitka, Aleutian Islands, Alaska, 2 Oct. 1969. The Don't Make A Wave Committee became the **Greenpeace Foundation**. Quoted by Michael Brown and John May, journalists, *The Greenpeace Story* (1989).

I often say, out on the lecture circuit, that if Greenpeace had started in any country other than Canada, the head office would still be in that country. Can you imagine the Germans or Brits or Americans or Spaniards giving up the title copyright? Not on your life?

Bob Hunter, columnist, one of the founders of Greenpeace (now Greenpeace International) in Vancouver, *eye*, 18 Feb. 1993.

We have an environmental movement that is run by people who want to fight—not to win.

Patrick Moore, ecologist, a founder of the environmental advocacy group Greenpeace, "The Great Green Con-trick," *The Mail* (England), 7 May 2000.

GRETZKY, WAYNE See also ATHLETES, HOCKEY

I skate to where the puck is going to be, not where it's been.

Wayne Gretzky, hockey star, *Let's Do It!* (1985).

Boys who wanted to be Charlie Conacher grew up to produce sons who wanted to be Bobby Orr. Those sons are producing kids who want to be Wayne Gretzky.

Dick Beddoes, sports personality, *Greatest Hockey Stories* (1990).

I played because I loved it. I played because I idolized the great players of the game, the Bobby Orrs, the Gordie Howes, and the Bobby Hulls. I had a passion for it. I didn't do it for any other reason but a passion.

Wayne Gretzky, hockey personality, press conference in New York City, announcing his retirement from professional hockey, 16 April 1999, printed in the *National Post* the next day.

No one else better captures what my country is, the country of my heart, where the boys are on the ice until dark, until the women call them home, and they come in, high colour on their cheeks, smelling sweaty but sweet, so male, so different from us, and so wondrous.

Christie Blatchford, sports columnist, "The Boy Inside the Man," *National Post*, 17 April 1999.

The best description, ever, of Gretzky was from Russia's national hockey coach who exclaimed in wonderment at first encountering this magician on skates: "He appears from nowhere, he passes to nowhere, and there is a goal!"

Allan Fotheringham, columnist, "Needed: Gentlemen in Sports," *Maclean's*, 10 May 1999.

He is the champion we all could have been. Hardworking, hard playing, skilled, knowing what he is and what he isn't, what he can and cannot do, respectful, and largely content, he is the face that Canadians would most like to present to the world.

Ken Dryden, hockey personality, on hockey superstar Wayne Gretzky, "The Ordinary Superstar," *National Post*, 11 May 1999.

I probably miss the game more than the game misses me.

Wayne Gretzky, hockey superstar, press conference, induction into the Hockey Hall of Fame, Toronto, 22 Nov. 1999, quoted by Cam Cole in *The Globe and Mail* the following day.

GROUP OF SEVEN See also ART & ARTISTS, CULTURE, PAINTING

He lived humbly but passionately with the wild. It made him brother to all untamed things of nature. It drew him apart and revealed itself wonderfully to him. It sent him out from the woods only to show these revelations through his art. And it took him to itself at last.

Inscription on the cairn erected to the memory of Tom Thomson, identified as "artist, woodsman, and guide," who drowned in Canoe Lake, Algonquin Park, Ont., 8 July 1917. The inscription was the work of fellow artist **J.E.H. MacDonald**, and the memorial was erected on the shore of Canoe Lake on 27 Sept. 1917.

The Group of Seven were really pre-Canadian in the sense that they were imaginative explorers. Their literary counterparts would not be our established writers so much as people like David Thompson and Samuel Hearne.

Northrop Frye, cultural critic, interviewed by Robert Fulford, "From Nationalism to Regionalism: The Maturing of Canadian Culture," *The Anthology Anthology: A Selection from 30 Years of CBC Radio's Anthology* (1984) edited by Robert Weaver.

Sadly, most Canadians are able to name more members of the Seven Dwarfs than of the Group of Seven.

E. Kaye Fulton, arts reporter, article on the Group of Seven, *Maclean's*, 30 Oct. 1995.

I sought out the Thomson Gallery, which majors in the works of Canada's revered landscape painters, the Group of Seven. I was the only visitor and, as I admired their placid, mystical scenes, now imprisoned on the ninth floor of a shopping centre, I felt I had stumbled on some safe-deposit box for the Canadian spirit.

Nigel Tisdall, English travel writer, describing a visit to the Thomson Gallery in Toronto, "Into the Great Green Yonder," *The Daily Telegraph*, 26 Sept. 1998.

GROWTH

I'm looking forward to continued growth in the last third of my life and I would like to be at the crest of the mountain in the 21st century and if not live in the promised land at least have a glimpse of it before I go off to the happy hunting ground.

Duke Redbird, Native spokesperson, interviewed by Ron LeBlanc in "Duke Redbird," *The Core* (Toronto tabloid), Feb. 1995.

GST See GOODS & SERVICES TAX

GUILT

I wish that you suffer enough guilt to grow a conscience, but not so much as to sour your life.

June Callwood, social activist, graduation speech, McMaster University's social science faculty, "Quotables," *The Hamilton Spectator*, 4 June 1994.

GULF CRISIS See also WAR

Deficits have got nothing to do with the defence of freedom.

Brian Mulroney, Prime Minister, explaining that the expense of sending and maintaining Canadian troops in the Persian Gulf are supportable, 12 Nov. 1990, quoted by Susan Delacourt in *The Globe and Mail*, 15 Nov. 1990. He later noted that social programs would be reduced to compensate for the expense.

We have just had the first North-South war—in the gulf.

Ivan Head, president, International Development Research Centre, referring to the Third World in terms of "the North-South" division, quoted by Gerald Utting in *The Toronto Star*, 20 July 1991.

I must confess that I do not ever want to find myself in the position I was in in Zurich at the meeting of the International Institute for Strategic Studies in September following the Gulf War. I was sitting in a Gasthaus drinking with a group of senior RAF and other Allied officers. I was thoroughly enjoying the party until I heard the top joke of the evening. Shouted question: "How many awards for valour did Canada give out in the Gulf War?"

Answer?—general laughter!

Nicholas Stethem, defence analyst, "Myth, Policy and Power: The Defence Investment," *National Network News* (quarterly publication of the Defence Associations), July 1994.

GZOWSKI, PETER See also BROADCASTING, RADIO

I've climbed a lot of hill.

Peter Gzowski, writer and radio personality, characteristic remark, quoted by Edna Hampton in *The Globe and Mail*, 12 Feb. 1972.

When I grow up I want to be Paul Hiebert... on my way to becoming Paul Hiebert, I'd like to be W.O. Mitchell... I don't think I'll ever be Paul Hiebert or W.O. Mitchell. I started too late.

Peter Gzowski, writer and radio personality, referring to his favourite Prairie writers, *Peter Gzowski's Book About This Country in the Morning* (1974).

Morningside continued to be, as I once described it, a kind of village bulletin-board to the nation....

Peter Gzowski, journalist and host of CBC Radio's *Morningside*, "Whistling Down the Northern Lights," *The Fourth Morningside Papers* (1991).

This is the only program in the world that will tell you what to do if you are charged by a muskox.

Peter Gzowski, host, interviewing a guest who spoke about muskoxen and how to survive a muskox charge, CBC Radio's *Morningside*, 31 Oct. 1996.

And from the Temple Garden Spa in Moose Jaw, Saskatchewan, Canada—this is not goodbye, it's *au revoir*. As in see you again, we'll meet again. See you soon, I hope. I'm Peter Gzowski.

Peter Gzowski, host of CBC Radio's *Morningside*, final words on the last broadcast of the long-running, three-hour-long, five-day-a-week program, Moose Jaw, Sask., 30 May 1997, quoted in "Au Revoir, Peter Gzowski," *The Globe and Mail* the following day.

H

HAITI

That's my dream. My body in Miami, my spirit in Montreal, my heart in Port au Prince.

Dany Laferrière, novelist, commenting on his love of Florida, his residence in Montreal, and his childhood in Haiti, quoted by Val Ross in *The Globe and Mail*, 8 June 1991.

Haiti has had independence for a long time and is looking for democracy. Quebec has had democracy for a long time and is looking for independence.

Bernard Landry, Parti Québécois member, addressing a group of ethnic leaders, quoted by David Johnston in *The Montreal Gazette*, 7 Oct. 1991.

When it was not popular anywhere in the world to worry about poor, beleaguered, abandoned Haiti, Canada was truly a friend of Haiti.

Bill Clinton, U.S. President, address, joint meeting of the House of Commons and the Senate of Canada, Ottawa, Senate Debates, 23 Feb. 1995.

HALIFAX See also NOVA SCOTIA

It would be easy to fall into the local rhythm of a place like Halifax. No one pretended that this was the centre of things. You were accepted easily, it seemed whoever you were.

George Galt, journalist and traveller, *Whistle-stop: A Journey across Canada* (1987).

Haligonian. This North American demonym has a long history... in print as early as 1840...

Paul Dickson, British writer, *What Do You Call a Person From... ? A Dictionary of Resident Names* (1990).

My goal was Halifax in Nova Scotia, a city on the extreme end of the Trans-Canadian Highway. In many ways it was like the end of the continent, a sort of Ultima Thule, a land on the far reaches of the earth.

David Hatcher Childress, adventurer, referring to Halifax and the Trans-Canada Highway (which ends east of St. John's, Nfld.), *Lost Cities of North & Central America* (1992).

Seven Richest Nations to Meet in Poorest Corner of Canada.

Headline in *The Washington Post*, concerning the meeting of the G7 nations in Halifax, N.S., June 1995, according to Allan Fotheringham, "Column," *Maclean's*, 26 June 1995. "And then one of the U.S. networks says Halifax is basically on a par with Akron, Ohio, with 'a small and shabby downtown' where restaurants serve food 'usually found at hockey games.'"

HAPPINESS

Whether this is, as Leibnitz thought, the best, or, as Schopenhauer thought, the worst, of all possible worlds, neither of them could really tell. Neither of them had any means of verifying his hypothesis by comparison or in any other way. Practically it is a very different world for different men.

Goldwin Smith, essayist, "Morality and Theism," *Guesses at the Riddle of Existence and Other Essays on Kindred Subjects* (1897).

Life has not been—never can be—what I once hoped it would be in my girlhood dreams. But I think, taking one thing with another, that I am as happy as the majority of people in this odd world and happier than a great many of them.

L.M. Montgomery, author, diary, 5 Jan. 1917, *The Selected Journals of L.M. Montgomery: Volume II: 1910–1921* (1987) edited by Mary Rubio and Elizabeth Waterston.

Some discontents are ignoble... but there is a certain discontent which I believe does ennoble because it impels us to try to improve our surroundings—to measure our happiness by what we can *put into* our environment, not by what we can *get out*.

L.M. Montgomery, author, letter, *My Dear Mr. M.: Letters to G.B. MacMillan* (1980) edited by Francis W.P. Bolger and Elizabeth R. Epperly.

Tomorrow is the happiest day in a man's life.

Bob Edwards, publisher, *The Eye Opener*, 23 Aug. 1919, *The Wit and Wisdom of Bob Edwards* (1976) edited by Hugh Dempsey.

It's easy to be happy. All you have to do is to be foolish.

Bob Edwards, publisher, *The Eye Opener*, Summer Annual, 1922.

Happiness always prefers a cabin to a castle.

Arthur Heming, naturalist and novelist, *The Drama of the Forests* (1947).

Sir Charles Forte: You know, Roy... it's happiness that really counts.

Lord Thomson of Fleet: Ah yes, but happiness cannot buy money.

Exchange between the British catering magnate **Sir Charles Forte** and the Canadian-born British press lord **Roy Thomson**, quoted by George Gamester in *The Toronto Star,* 15 April 1975.

We envy the happiness of other people mainly because we believe in it.

Irving Layton, poet and aphorist, *The Whole Bloody Bird (obs, aphs & Pomes)* (1969).

Happiness is a moral question, not a question of wealth and property. On the mountain, we have more unhappy people than there are in the slums.

Jean Drapeau, long-time Montreal Mayor, quoted by Carl Dow in *The Canadian,* 19 Sept. 1970.

Happiness was invented by adults to mend broken hearts.

André Langevin, author, *L'élan d'Amérique* (1972).

I know people were happier in the old days. But I know for sure they were not happy every day.... Nobody can be happy every day.

Peter Pitseolak, Inuit artist, *People from Our Side* (1975) edited by Dorothy Eber.

Happiness I've said is a by-product. It is not a primary product of life. It is a thing which you suddenly realize you have because you're so delighted to be doing something which perhaps has nothing whatever to do with happiness.

Robertson Davies, man-of-letters, interviewed by Bronwyn Drainie in 1979, *Conversations with Robertson Davies* (1989) edited by J. Madison Davis.

Your way of seeing things changes as you get older. Now if I were given a choice between being happy and being famous, I'd take happiness every time.

Alice Munro, author, quoted by Martin Knelman in *Saturday Night,* Nov. 1979.

Two people can only be happy together if they're equally happy apart.

Richard Needham, columnist, "A Writer's World," *The Globe and Mail,* 16 May 1980.

The only way to become relatively happy is to be utterly unconcerned with pain and death. But this is impossible to achieve.

Louis Dudek, poet and aphorist, dated 1992, *Notebooks 1960–1994* (1994).

As soon as one is unhappy one becomes moral.

Nicholas Catanoy, poet, *Notes on a Prison Wall: A Memoir/Poem* (1994).

If human life and happiness are the standard, not all cultural traditions are equal.

Nathaniel Branden, Ontario-born participant in the human potential movement, *The Six Pillars of Self-Esteem* (1994).

I was happy once, but I'm all right now.

Jann Arden, singer, interviewed on CFCF Radio's *Montreal AM,* 26 Sept. 1997.

The taste of happiness is like *crème de menthe* on Sunday.

Louis Dudek, poet and aphorist, "Bitter Pills," *Reality Games* (1998).

HATE

Luck and love are blind; science and hate see in the dark.

Maurus E. Mallon, aphorist, June 1993.

At the core of our being, no matter how polished and successful our exterior, is the worm of self-hatred, self-loathing.

Neil McKenty, author, *The Inside Story: Journey of a Former Jesuit Priest and Talk Show Host towards Self-discovery* (1997).

HEALING See also HEALTH, MEDICINE

For many years, accounts of cures among primitive peoples by medicine men, shamans and the like aroused little attention among psychiatrists. The development of modern psychotherapy has drawn attention to the mystery of the mechanism of psychological healing and shown how many of its details still puzzle us.

Henri Ellenberger, historian of psychiatry, *The Discovery of the Unconscious* (1970).

Some call it healing; some call it regeneration. No matter what it is called, it is the same process—people taking control of their individual lives.

Gordon Peters, Ontario Native chief, Toronto, 18 Nov. 1993, quoted in *Renewal: Volume 5: Report of the Royal Commission on Aboriginal Peoples* (1996), co-chaired by René Dussault and Georges Erasmus.

When we are most vulnerable to external threats which we have feared all our lives, then, in a paradoxical way, we have made ourselves most available for healing.

Neil McKenty, author, *The Inside Story: Journey of a Former Jesuit Priest and Talk Show Host towards Self-discovery* (1997).

HEALTH See also FITNESS, HEALING, HEALTH CARE, MEDICINE

I cannot express the emotion that swept over me when I held your letter... it was the finest present I ever got in my long life—now in its seventy-fifth year.

Charles Bliss, inventor of the Blissymbols in Australia, writing to teacher Shirley McNaughton and occupational therapist Margrit Beesley in the early 1970s, when he learned from them that the Ontario Crippled Children's Centre in Toronto was making use of his colourful symbols in their work with handicapped children. Subsequently the Blissymbolics Communication Institute was established in Toronto in 1975. Quoted by Elizabeth S. Helfman in *Blissymbolics: Speaking without Speech* (1981).

If I felt any better, I'd be arrested.

Conn Smythe, hockey personality, contemplating his eightieth birthday, quoted by Bob Pennington in *The Toronto Star*, 30 Jan. 1975.

If it's supposed to be good for some of the teeth of some of the children some of the time, why put it in the water of all the people all of the time?

Gordon Sinclair, broadcaster, characteristic comment on compulsory fluoridation of municipal drinking water, a practice recommended by the dental profession, 13 Dec. 1979.

I've always been interested in why some people seem to get along with a minimum of disease and others are, in the true meaning of the word, patients all their lives, sufferers.

Robertson Davies, man-of-letters, quoted by Mel Gussow in "A Moralist Possessed by Humour," *The New York Times Book Review*, 5 Feb. 1995.

1 in 4 Canadians / Suffer from / Mental Illness / Please Help / 979 6909

Wording on a sign on the lawn of the **Clarke Institute of Psychiatry**, Toronto, Aug. 1995. (There is lack of agreement between subject and predicate.) When questioned, the Clarke's executive director wrote on 13 Oct. 1995: "This statement is based on the finding that psychiatric illness was found in one-quarter of the adult patients in a study of general medical practice as reported by Barrett, J.E. et al. in *The Prevalence of Psychiatric Disorders in a Primary Care Practice, Archives of General Psychiatry*, December 1988; 45 (12): 1100–1106." No relationship between the number of "adult patients" and the general population of "Canadians" is established.

We're now starting to realize that there are two aspects to health: getting better and feeling better. Conventional medicine is good at the first, complementary medicine often better at the second. There is treating disease and there is the doctor-patient relationship. Both are important.

Robert Buckman, physician, quoted by Lynda Hurst, "Natural Medicine Breaks Through," *The Toronto Star*, 17 Jan. 1998.

HEALTH CARE See also HEALTH, MEDICARE, MEDICINE

The challenge for the future may be to find ways to discover and express our collective values with respect to the definition of health itself. What sort of outcomes as opposed to services do we as a community think worth buying? And through what institutional channels, present or projected, do we give effect to those views?

Robert G. Evans, economist and health care specialist, "'We'll Take Care of It for You': Health Care in the Canadian Community," *Daedalus: Journal of the American Academy of Arts and Sciences*, "In Search of Canada," Fall, 1988.

Our problem is that we're the second-wealthiest country in the world, but, unfortunately, we're living right next door to the wealthiest country in the world. If we were halfway between Albania and Romania, we wouldn't have any problem.

Charles Wright, Vancouver General Hospital, commenting on the "brain drain" of medical specialists to the United States, quoted by Graham Fraser, Susan Delacourt, and Richard Mackie in *The Globe and Mail*, 9 June 1992.

All countries have a stake in the Canadian system being maintained, even in its attenuated state.

Ralph Nader, U.S. consumer advocate, statement, committee of the House of Commons examining the government's decision to extend patent protection for foreign-owned pharmaceutical distributors, Ottawa, 2 Dec. 1992, quoted by Drew Fagan in *The Globe and Mail* the following day.

Judging from the media coverage, Americans seem quite hung up on how health care is rationed in Canada. It's true, Canada does ration health care according to the severity of illness, compared to the U.S. which rations according to the patient's bank balance.

Lisa Priest, journalist, "Caught in the Middle of a U.S. Debate," *The Toronto Star*, 15 Feb. 1994.

Canada is a sparsely populated nation with a shortage of gunshot wounds, crack addicts and huge tort judgments. What can we really learn from a medical system devoted to hockey injuries and sinus infections caused by trying to pronounce French vowels?

P.J. O'Rourke, humorist, writing in *The Wall Street Journal*, as quoted by Linda Priest in *The Toronto Star*, 15 Feb. 1994.

If you ask the average Canadian how we differ from Americans, he or she would most often first say "health care." Odd way to define citizenship perhaps, but maybe not.

Joe Berridge, urban planner, "Is Toronto Different from U.S. Cities? Was It Planned that Way?" *The Globe and Mail*, 10 April 1995.

The only thing more expensive than good health care is no health care.

Emmett Hall, retired judge and proponent of public health insurance, quoted in his obituary by Don Downey in *The Globe and Mail*, 14 Nov. 1995.

The Americans admire your health system, not knowing anything about it, because it must be better than ours.

Michael Korda, American author and publisher, interviewed by Vicki Gabereau on CBC Radio's *Gabereau*, 29 May 1996.

Even in the midst of societies in torment, I had met passionate individuals dedicated to alleviating the suffering of others.

Tim Ward, traveller, *The Great Dragon's Fleas* (1993).

At the end of the Trudeau era, Canada was the only country in the world besides North Korea to have outlawed private medicine, and current political wisdom blames successor governments for the health care disaster created twenty years ago.

Conrad Black, publisher, "Taking Canada Seriously," *International Journal*, Winter 1997–98.

I would exchange my Canadian citizenship for an American one if I did not have to worry about medical insurance.

Attributed to novelist **W.P. Kinsella** by Evelyn Lau in "Me and W.P.," *Vancouver Life*, Oct. 1997.

We're all ten minutes away from being a patient.

Michael Decter, investor, Lawrence & Company, which favours the "med-tech" field, quoted by Diane Francis, "High-tech Saviour of Health Care," *The Financial Post*, 22 Feb. 2000.

HEART

Scan not its outer, but its inner part / 'Twas not the head composed it, but the heart.

Concluding lines of **Sir Charles G.D. Roberts**' poem "Epistle to W. Bliss Carman" (1878), *Selected Poetry and Critical Prose* (1974) edited by W.J. Keith.

It was one thing to speak from the heart. And quite another to speak from the heartburn.

Line from **Morley Torgov**'s novel *A Good Place to Come From* (1974).

A man's heart melts; a woman's breaks.

Raymond Canale, Italian-born playwright and Toronto-based aphorist, observation made in 1975.

Don't tell the physiologists, but every heart worthy of the adjective "human" has hidden chambers, hundreds of them.

Maurus E. Mallon, aphorist, 22 October 1992.

Ymwrandawed dyn a'l galon

These words in Welsh (meaning "A man must pay heed to his innermost heart") appear on the bookplate of **Robertson Davies**, noted by Val Ross in *The Globe and Mail*, 8 Oct. 1994.

It doesn't interest me what you do for a living. / I want to know what you ache for, and if you dare to dream of meeting your heart's longing.

Opening lines of the poem "The Invitation" (1994), *The Invitation* (1999), composed by **Oriah Mountain Dreamer**, born at New Liskeard, Ont., whose name was the gift of a Cherokee medicine man.

HEAVEN & HELL

I believe in heaven and hell—on earth.

Abraham Feinberg, rabbi, *Storm the Gates of Jericho* (1964).

Hell is a place like this world only a little warmer.

Louis Dudek, man-of-letters, *Epigrams* (1975).

I sometimes think a Canadian's idea of heaven is an eternal panel discussion.

Marc Lalonde, Minister of Finance, quoted in *The Toronto Star*, 4 Oct. 1982.

If there is a heaven it's no doubt already filled—with horses, chickens, lambs, and other poor creatures. People will simply not get in.

Louis Dudek, poet and aphorist, dated 1985, *Notebooks 1960–1994* (1994).

Man alone is responsible for hell, and much as he would like to pursue his cruelties beyond the grave, he is blocked from doing so.

Northrop Frye, cultural critic, *The Double Vision: Language and Meaning in Religion* (1991).

I once met in the Yukon an elderly Sekani man who was completely confounded by a missionary's notion of heaven. He couldn't believe anyone could be expected to give up smoking, drinking, swearing, carousing and all the things that made life worth living in order to go to a place where they didn't allow animals. "No caribou?" he would say in complete astonishment. He couldn't conceive of a world without wild things.

Wade Davis, ethnobotanist and essayist, *Shadows in the Sun* (1992).

The abolition of hell has created major problems in the maintaining of a general ethical standard.

John Ralston Saul, author, *The Doubter's Companion: A Dictionary of Aggressive Common Sense* (1994).

HERITAGE See also ANCESTRY, PAST, TRADITION

Je suis un chien qui ronge lo / En le rongeant je prends mon repos / Un temps viendra qui n'est pas venu / Que je morderay qui maura mordu.

Quebec City's famous "Golden Dog" inscription which consists of four lines of old French embellished with the gilded figure of a dog gnawing on a bone. Carved in stone and placed over the lintel of a private residence on Rue Baude, the inscription was later affixed to the portal of the Quebec City post office, where it may be seen to this day. The lines, which recall a tale of vengeance that dates back to 1737, inspired William Kirby's historical novel *The Golden Dog* (1877, 1896). They may be translated: "I am a dog that gnaws his bone / I crouch and gnaw it all alone / The time will come which is not yet / When I'll bite him by whom I'm bit."

Why should the inhabitant of an historic spot sometimes know less about it than the stranger who comes to gain information?

Janet Carnochan, archivist, address, "A Plea for Historical Societies," Beaver Dams and Thorold Historical Society, 24 June 1895, published in *The Welland Tribune*, 5 July 1985.

Irish by extraction, English by birth, Canadian by adoption, and Scotch by absorption.

Amusing self-definition of composer **Healey Willan**, recalled by Godfrey Ridout, "Healey Willan," *Canadian Music Journal*, Spring 1959.

I am intensely proud of my Newfoundland heritage, my Ontario heritage, my Nova Scotian heritage, my Quebec heritage; proud also of the Prairies and British Columbia, of which, by virtue of being a Canadian, I can claim some share. I am proud of our British heritage and our French heritage. But I am prouder still of the Canadian heritage which subsumes and transcends them all and without which all would perish miserably.

Eugene Forsey, historian, convocation address, "Speak for Canada!" *Queen's Alumni Review*, Jan.–Feb. 1980.

Abandon my country? / Forsake my heritage? / I do not see the need. / My birthright began / This country's history.

Lines from Native writer **Rita Joe**'s poem "Legacy," *Song of Eskasoni: More Poems of Rita Joe* (1988) edited by Lee Maracle.

Trouble is, there's no Canadian heritage any more, absolutely none. We're a nonentity, a generic country, we're nothing, and it's sad. And there's a few guys left like me that will come on and say, "I want Jesus Christ in the prayer, I want to observe Victoria Day," and somehow or other when you talk like that, you're a bigot, and it's amazing to me.

Don Cherry, hockey commentator, quoted by Bill Brioux in *TV Guide*, 16 April 1994.

We make a great mistake by associating the inheritance of physical characteristics with far more complex traits of human personality and behaviour.

David Suzuki, scientist and broadcaster, "Ancestors—The Genetic Source," *Far and Wide: Essays from Canada—Reflections in Non-fiction* (1996) edited by Sean Armstrong.

HEROES See also LEADERSHIP

The Great Master of Breath calls me to go. I have patiently waited his summons. I am ready—farewell.

Traditional farewell to his people of **Hiawatha**, semi-legendary leader under semi-mythological Dekhanawideh of the Six Nations Confederacy, "Six Nation Indian Traditions," *The Lamp: A Theosophical Monthly*, Volume 11, 15 Dec. 1896.

Yes, we do well to keep green the memory of our heroes of the past, to raise monumental piles, to emulate their brave deeds.

Janet Carnochan, archivist, address, "A Plea for Historical Societies," Beaver Dams and Thorold Historical Society, 24 June 1895, published in *The Welland Tribune*, 5 July 1985.

The so-called hero is only playing the role of Santa Claus for grown-ups. That's just the grown-up's way of getting an emotional outlet.

Attributed to the polar explorer **Vilhjalmur Stefansson** during a Toronto interview by R.E. Knowles in *The Toronto Star*, 5 Nov. 1929.

I had never heard of Ulysses, but before I was ten years old I knew that I was descended from classical heroes.

Alden Nowlan, poet and essayist, referring to Nova Scotians who built and sailed three-masted schooners "even round the Horn," "Alden Nowlan's Canada," *Maclean's*, June 1971.

Canada hasn't had any heroes since Johnny Canuck.

Leo Bachle, pen name of cartoonist Lex Barker, quoted in *The Toronto Star*, 1 Aug. 1974. Bachle was only fifteen years old when he created "Johnny Canuck" and drew the comic book for Toronto's Bell Features during World War II.

Superman never made any money / Savin' the world from Solomon Grundy, / And sometimes I despair the world will never see / Another man like him....

Lines from "Superman's Song" from the album *The Ghosts that Haunt Me* (1991) composed and performed by **Brad Roberts** and the Winnipeg group **Crash Test Dummies**.

Traitors have saved nations. Heroes have ruined them.

Nicholas Catanoy, poet, *Notes on a Prison Wall: A Memoir/Poem* (1994).

U.S. people are good at inventing heroes that weren't, like Paul Bunyan and Abner Doubleday. We cancel heroes that really were. A charming habit, but one which our vulnerable country cannot afford.

Axel Harvey, historian of astrology, arguing for recognition of Canadian astrologers with good predictive reputations, "Postscript: The Rootless Science," included by John McKay-Clements in *The Canadian Astrology Collection: Timed Birth Data of Prominent Canadians* (1998).

We need real heroes to coax out the potential heroes who reside in our secret selves. We need real heroes to give us the courage to follow our dreams, break free from the herd, blow away convention and aspire to great things.

Michael Valpy, columnist, on the fall of hockey builder R. Alan Eagleson, "Culture," *The Globe and Mail*, 8 Jan. 1998.

It is often said that Canadians love to lionize their stars and love even more to tear them down. There is some perverse sense of the democratic in Canadians that makes us chop off any head that rises above the others.

Ken Dryden, hockey personality, "The Ordinary Superstar," the *National Post*, 11 May 1999.

HIGH-TECH INDUSTRY See

COMPUTERS, INDUSTRY

HISTORY & HISTORIANS See also

HISTORY, CANADIAN

If we cannot engrave on bronze the exploits of our forefathers, we can at least inscribe them in the pages of history.

P.-J.-O. Chauveau, French-Canadian historian, quoted by H. Beaumont Small as the conclusion to his *Chronicles of Canada; or A Concise History of the Leading Events in the Old Provinces of the New Dominion* (1868).

Historians sometimes tell the truth, not always the whole truth, certainly never anything but the truth, and nothing is to be despised which gives a peep at the life as it really was.

Robina Lizars and **Kathleen Macfarlane**, local historians, *Humours of '37: Grave, Gay and Grim: Rebellion Times in the Canadas* (1897).

It is conceded to the antiquarian that he performs certain useful functions that the historian does not undertake, and perhaps does not wish to undertake. He keeps alive an interest in local history. He marks historic sites and attempts to preserve historic buildings. He collects historical material, which may often be trivial but which is sometimes not without a positive value.

Edgar Andrew Collard, antiquary, "All Our Yesterdays," *The Montreal Gazette*, 13 Aug. 1994. This column first appeared on the editorial page on 14 Aug. 1944, inaugurating a series of 2,600 weekly articles on popular history.

After all, history is life itself.

George M. Wrong, historian, advising W. Stewart Wallace to choose History over English, quoted by Wallace (who became a notable librarian and antiquarian) in "The Life and Work of George M. Wrong," *Canadian Historical Review*, Sept. 1948.

Men have need of history because, without it, the past would be likely to crush them.

Guy Frégault, historian, *La guerre de la conquête* (1955).

Historians are concerned with disasters of the past, and insurance men with disasters of the future.

John Roberts, Secretary of State, quoted in *The Globe and Mail*, 26 Nov. 1977.

Perhaps no truly objective history of anything is ever popular.

Elwy Yost, TV host and movie enthusiast, *Magic Moments from the Movies* (1979).

History is a burden, yet it offers the gift of possibility.

George Galt, writer and traveller, *Trailing Pythagoras* (1982).

The powerful write history; the powerless suffer it. History hurts.

Joe Schlesinger, foreign correspondent, *Time Zones: A Journalist in the World* (1990).

History is the social memory of human experience....

Northrop Frye, cultural critic, *The Double Vision: Language and Meaning in Religion* (1991).

History is about the *drama* of human life; it is about people, individual, self-conscious, free.

Modris Eksteins, historian, "The Lydians and Us," *The Idler*, July–Aug. 1992.

History doesn't repeat itself: history repeats myth.

Northrop Frye, cultural critic, "Notebook 1993," edited by Robert D. Denham, *Northrop Frye Newsletter*, Summer 1993.

After half a century of exploring the past, I can truly say that such researchs will bring anyone very close to the wonder and mystery of life; for history constantly reminds us that those who lived in the past were once as real as we are. Before long we shall be the shadows that they seem to us now.

We are all, the living and the dead, bound together by the same ultimate mystery—the mystery that gives life its depth, its wonder, and perhaps even its hope. To have touched the past, even in fragments, is to have touched something immense in its intangible meaning.

Edgar Andrew Collard, antiquary, "All His Yesterdays," *The Montreal Gazette*, 13 Aug. 1994.

It is in our nature to travel into our past, hoping thereby to illuminate the darkness that bedevils the present. And it is in the nature of things that we can seldom manage, in that fine old phrase, to part the veils of time.

Farley Mowat, author, Foreword, *Aftermath: Travels in a Post-War World* (1995).

The history of the world keeps changing to fit the current needs of the world, so I make no apology for presenting a history that fits my own needs.

Paul William Roberts, author and traveller, *In Search of the Birth of Jesus: The Real Journey of the Magi* (1995).

If you're going to keep stirring up history, you must remember to open the lid slowly, to let the steam out of the pot.

Line from **Anne Michaels**' novel *Fugitive Pieces* (1996).

History is memory, inspiration, and commonality—and a nation without memory is every bit as adrift as an amnesiac wandering the street. History matters, and we forget this truth at our peril.

J.L. Granatstein, historian, *Who Killed Canadian History?* (1998).

HISTORY, CANADIAN See also HISTORY & HISTORIANS

The history of the country can be traced no further than from the arrival of the Europeans; for everything that happened before that period is more like fiction or a dream than like anything that really happened.

Peter Kalm, Swedish traveller, *Travels into North America* (1770–71) translated from the Swedish by J.R. Forster.

Canada will some day do justice to my memory.

Said to be the dying words of **Lord Durham**, author of the famous *Report* (1839) on conditions in the Canadas, as noted by John Buchan in "Lord Durham" (1938), *Canadian Occasions: Addresses* (1940).

These unmemoried heights are inhuman—or rather, irrelevant to humanity. No recorded Hannibal has struggled across them; their shadow lies on no remembered literature. They acknowledge claims neither of the soul nor of the body of man.

Rupert Brooke, English poet and traveller, responding to the sight of the Rocky Mountains, *Letters from America* (1916).

In the annals of the world there is no more illuminating and inspiring history than the history of Canada.

W.L. Mackenzie King, Prime Minister, quoted by Charles H. Mackintosh in *Chronicles of Canada's Diamond Jubilee: Commemorating Sixty Years of Confederation* (1929).

Thus there emerged the three decisive fields of Canadian historical interpretation: the French survival, the dominance of Ontario, and the subordination of the West...

W.L. Morton, historian, "Cleo in Canada: The Interpretation of Canadian History," *The University of Toronto Quarterly*, April 1946.

Dull as our history unquestionably is, I happen to be proud of it—precisely because it is dull. After all, what does exciting history mean? Only that a country has *failed* to live up to the ideals of a normal human society.

Michael Bliss, historian, "Argument," *Maclean's*, 21 Aug. 1965.

History is a party to which Canada has not been invited.

Robert Fulford, columnist and author, recalling his feelings growing up in the 1940s, CBC-TV's *The Great Culture Hunt*, 31 March 1976.

There are two possible reasons for a Canadian knowing little or nothing about this country's history and geography: (1) that he wasn't born and brought up here and (b) that he was.

Richard Needham, newspaper columnist, *The Wit and Wisdom of Richard Needham* (1977).

French Canadians can never forget their history, and English Canadians can never remember theirs.

John Roberts, Secretary of State, quoted in *The Globe and Mail*, 26 Nov. 1977.

Exploring and taming Canada's resources has been a Heroic epic and it is only the poor quality of our history teachers that has failed to bring that truth home.

Peter C. Newman, columnist, *Maclean's*, 6 July 1992.

In the 1960s, curriculum experts in ministries of education from coast to coast decided that "social studies" were more important than history, and stopped teaching history—of Canada or anything else—to the next generation.

David J. Bercuson, historian, *Maple Leaf Against the Axis: Canada's Second World War* (1995).

Very few of us in this country share the same past, but all of us can share the same future. Especially if we refuse to permit the past to poison that future.

Roméo LeBlanc, Governor General, address on being sworn in as Canada's 25th Governor General, Ottawa, 8 Feb. 1995, quoted in *The Globe and Mail* the following day.

Where's Laurier in the history books of French Canada.... So I'm not being hopeful.

Pierre Elliott Trudeau, former Prime Minister, discussing the role of the Quebec intelligentsia's separatist revision of history, interviewed by Peter Gzowski on CBC Radio's *Morningside*, 22 Oct. 1996.

Canada is not one of the world's youngest nations, but given the way we treat our past, the nation might have been formed in 1967 rather than 1867. Can there be any other country that scants its past as Canadians do?

J.L. Granatstein, historian, "Canada Needs Its Historical Memory Back," the *National Post*, 19 April 1999.

HOCKEY See also CHERRY, DON; GRETZKY, WAYNE; HOCKEY VIOLENCE; SPORTS

Hurly on the long pond on the ice....

Earliest known printed reference to the game of hurly, an antecedent of the game of hockey, made by **T.C. Haliburton** in *The Attaché; or, Sam Slick in England* (1844), describing the game played in the early 1800s on the ice of Long Pond, near Windsor, N.S. The site of this early game borders on the present-day campus of King's-Edgehill School, according to Roy Mayer in *Inventing Canada: 100 Years of Innovation* (1997).

Superstar

According to sports personality Dick Beddoes, the term "superstar" is of hockey origin and was coined by **Frank Patrick** when he ran hockey teams on the West Coast in the 1900s. (It now refers to a stellar performer in any field who is paid top dollars.) In *Greatest Hockey Stories* (1990), Beddoes traced the term back to 31 Oct. 1909, when Frederick (Cyclone) Taylor left the Ottawa Senators for the Renfrew Creamery Kings, signing an "unheard-of contract of $5,250 for one season.... On that date the golden era of hockey was ushered in."

He shoots! He scores!

Foster Hewitt, sports broadcaster, describing for radio listeners the hockey match between the Toronto Maple Leafs and the Boston Bruins, Toronto's Mutual Street Arena, 4 April 1933. It was a long game. After five hours of play, at 1:45 a.m., Ken Doraty, the smallest player on either team, whipped the puck into the Boston net. An exhausted Hewitt murmured (rather than roared): "He shoots! He scores!" This is the birth of the most famous phrase in Canadian hockey history. Hewitt covered Maple Leaf and National Hockey League games on radio and then television from 1923 to within a few years of his death in 1985. The equivalent in French is "Il lance et compte."

And the man called Richard had something of the passionate glittering fatal alien quality of snakes.

William Faulkner, novelist, Madison Square Garden, describing the gaze of hockey personality Maurice (Rocket) Richard, as noted by Andy O'Brien in *Rocket Richard* and Jean-Marie Pellerin in *Maurice Richard: L'idole d'un peuple*.

Hockey is the Canadian metaphor, the rink is this country's vast stretches of water and wilderness, its extremes of climate, the player a symbol of our struggle to civilize such a land. Some people call it our national religion. Well, what better?

Bruce Kidd and **John Macfarlane**, runner and writer, *The Death of Hockey* (1972).

Hockey has been the source of community pride and national unity; if the CPR held the country together during the early years of Confederation, certainly *Hockey Night in Canada* has done so in recent years.

Bruce Kidd, runner and academic, quoted in *Canadian Dimension*, July 1969.

The game is bigger now, but it will never be bigger than a small boy's dreams.

Attributed to hockey star **Bobby Hull** by sportsman Dick Beddoes in the 1970s.

Hockey. Origins. The game probably originated in 1860 at Kingston, Ontario, Canada, but Montreal and Halifax also lay claims as the originators.

Norris and **Ross McWhirter**, editors, *Guinness Book of World Records* (10th ed., 1971).

No, I had never seen either Bobby Orr or Bobby Hull in the flesh until they were shooting at me.

Ken Dryden, goaltender, quoted by Andy O'Brien in *Les Canadiens: The Story of the Montreal Canadiens* (1971).

A cleared pass from the far side. Liapkin rolled one to Savard. Savard clears a pass to Stapleton. He cleared to the open wing to Cournoyer. Here's a shot! Henderson made a wild stab for it and fell. Here's another shot, right in front—they score! Henderson scores for Canada! And the fans and the team are going wild! Henderson, right in front of the Soviet goal with 34 seconds left in the game!

Foster Hewitt, hockey broadcaster, covering the last half-minute of the final Team Canada–Soviet summit series Moscow, 28 Sept. 1972, as quoted in *The Toronto Star's Centennial Magazine: The Hundred*, Nov. 1992.

When I scored that final goal, I finally realized what democracy was all about.

Paul Henderson, hockey star, quoted by Dick Beddoes in *Hockey Night in Minsk* (1972). Beddoes attributed these words to Henderson after he scored the all-important goal the evening of 28 Sept. 1972, when Team Canada battled the Soviet team in Moscow's Luzhniki Stadium. With thirty-four seconds left in the game, left-winger Paul Henderson scored the winning goal. Throughout all eight games in the series, Canadian fans chanted, "Da, da, Canada! / Nyet, nyet, Soviet!"

Hockey is the Canadian specific.

Al Purdy, poet, expressing the Canadian fascination with hockey aptly and succinctly, quoted by Dick Beddoes and John Roberts in *Summit 74* (1974).

The difference between a hockey player and a football player or a baseball player is this: Hockey guys play if they can breathe.

Conn Smythe, hockey personality, quoted by Trent Frayne in "Conn Smythe: The Big Wind from Lake Ontario" in *The Madmen of Hockey* (1974).

Clausewitz said of the Prussian army that every private soldier carried a field-marshall's baton in his knapsack. Every player with the Canadiens carries the Plains of Abraham on his back, and bears the inescapable duty to redress that ancient wrong, not just in the finals or the semis, but every time he takes to the ice to play against anyone.

Dennis Braithwaite, columnist, *The Toronto Star*, 9 May 1978.

Over the last half century, it has been accepted in professional hockey circles that most fans, as a rule, have two favourite teams—their home team and the Montreal Canadiens.

Herbert Warren Wind, essayist, *The New Yorker*, 19 March 1979.

Seasons vanish forever, but not Gordie Howe. If he's too old to play hockey, then we're all too old for childhood dreams. If Gordie Howe is too old, then it's too late for Halloween. If Gordie Howe is old, Canada is old. It isn't true. It's not. Is it?

Dick Beddoes, sports columnist, on the retirement at age fifty-one of hockey star Gordie Howe, *The Globe and Mail*, 31 Oct. 1979.

Once I started a speech at a noisy NHL awards banquet in Montreal with the words, "Gentlemen, and Frenchmen," which I correctly figured would get their attention.

Conn Smythe, hockey personality, *If You Can't Beat 'Em in the Alley* (1981) written with Scott Young.

How would you like a job where, every time you make a mistake, a big red light goes on and 18,000 people boo?

Jacques Plante, hockey star who donned a protective face mask in 1959, the first professional goalie to do so. The above remark was attributed to him the year before his death in Switzerland, 26 Feb. 1986.

Hockey is Canada's game. Nothing else is; nothing else will be.

Ken Dryden and **Roy MacGregor**, sportsman and journalist, *Home Game* (1989).

Okay. Drop the blessed puck. Maybe the Maple Leafs will win another Stanley Cup before the year 2018. Perhaps, too, the New York Rangers, who haven't won one since 1940. Doesn't matter who wins. If the game is good, we all win.

Dick Beddoes, sports personality, *Greatest Hockey Stories* (1990).

Hockey is in some ways a sport, in some ways a business, but mostly it is a tribe with its own cruelties and allegiances.

Alan Eagleson, hockey personality, *Power Play: The Memoirs of Hockey Czar Alan Eagleson* (1991) written with Scott Young.

Somewhere in our souls is a spiritual Canada. Most probably, its bedrock is of snow and ice, winter and the land. And if we were to penetrate it a little deeper, chances are we would find a game.

Ken Dryden and **Roy MacGregor**, hockey star and writer, *Hockey and Life in Canada* (1992).

You can never lose unless you try.

Sentiment attributed to hockey superstar, Big Bobby Clobber, a character created by comic **Dave Broadfoot**, "Bobby Clobber, Public Relater," *The Great Big Book of Canadian Humour* (1992) edited by Allan Gould.

The field of our dreams is flooded and frozen and has a net at either end.

Joey Slinger, columnist, writing about hockey in terms of the baseball metaphor created by W.P. Kinsella, *The Toronto Star*, 20 May 1993.

I'll tell you what Canadians do better than anyone else in the world—that's produce hockey games. *Hockey Night in Canada* does a hockey game better than ABC, NBC or CBS ever could.

Dan Matheson, sports anchor, quoted by Bill Brioux in *TV Guide*, 26 June 1993.

We like your style of fire on ice. We like your appreciation for the game and we like the way you produce players who establish new standards for the game.

Anatoly Tarasov, Soviet coach and Russian hockey personality, referring to the Canadian game, quoted in his obituary by James Christie in *The Globe and Mail*, 24 June 1995.

To an outsider, hockey often seems to be the one place where Canadians unleash anarchic impulses, which might explain why they love it to such uncharacteristic excess.

Richard Conniff, American journalist, "Toronto," *National Geographic*, June 1996.

They say the game has changed. But it's still four corners, three zones, two legs, and a puck.

Ron MacLean, hockey player, advertisement for National Hockey League, CBC-TV, 26 Aug. 1996.

Hockey should be finished before the snow is off the ground.

W.P. Kinsella, author, quoted by Anthony Jenkins in "Person, Place, Thing," *The Globe and Mail*, 7 June 1997.

Rock 'em, Sock 'em hockey!

Hyperbole associated with hockey broadcaster **Don Cherry** who released action-packed videos devoted to the game throughout the 1990s.

We played because we had nothing better to do. That's why hockey will live in this country. We didn't dream of becoming NHL stars. You thought about just getting to the next stage of the game. Our heroes were the guys who were ahead of us at the local rink. It was always just about the next step.

Wendel Clark, hockey player from Kelvington, Sask., quoted by Sarah Hampson, "The Puck Stops Here," *The Globe and Mail*, 10 Feb. 2000.

The Stanley Cup doesn't live here any more—by here I mean Canada, our home and native land.

Allan Makin, columnist, *The Globe and Mail*, 10 May 2000.

HOCKEY VIOLENCE See also HOCKEY

If the good Lord didn't want red-blooded Canadian boys to spend Saturday mornings shattering each others' bicuspids, why did He give us elbows?

Jim Cormier, old-time hockey enthusiast, "Ice Follies," *enRoute*, Nov. 1933.

If you can't lick 'em in the alley, you can't beat 'em on the ice.

Conn Smythe, hockey personality, characteristic remarks used to justify both manly qualities and hockey violence, first recorded in an interview conducted by Trent Frayne in 1952. Smythe backtracked somewhat for Bob Pennington of *The Toronto Star*, 1 Oct. 1973: "I did not mean that you scare the other guy but that you show him there is no fear in you."

It remains a game of pain.

Trent Frayne, sports writer, *The Mad Men of Hockey* (1974).

Hockey is the only team sport in the world that actually *encourages* fighting. I have no idea why we let it go on.

Wayne Gretzky, hockey player, *Gretzky: An Autobiography* (1990) with Rick Reilly.

Canadians are less likely to shoot someone. However, we are more likely to club someone over the head with a hockey stick.

Tim Cerantola, columnist, "Canada, Eh?" *The Hamilton Spectator*, 28 June 1997.

HOLIDAYS See also CANADA DAY, DOMINION DAY

My Canada Includes Florida

Message on a bumpersticker seen in Toronto, 12 Dec. 1994.

Three "national" holidays—for Quebec, Canada, and the United States—take place within ten days of each other at this time of year. It is possible they are lined up like this to encourage reflection on the true nature of our countries, and on the things we have in common.

Reed Scowen, columnist, *The Montreal Gazette*, 8 July 1995. Scowen had in mind Quebec's Saint-Jean-Baptiste Day (24 June), Canada's Dominion Day (1 July), and the United States Independence Day (4 July).

New Year's Day

We are on the threshold of the New Year. Oh, I wonder what it will bring me! I only ask release from worry—I would be content with that.

L.M. Montgomery, author, journal entry, 1 Jan. 1906, Cavendish, P.E.I., *The Selected Journals of L.M. Montgomery: Volume 1: 1889–1910* (1985) edited by Mary Rubio and Elizabeth Waterston.

Cheer up! Happy New Year! All the good people don't die young. Lots of them live to a ripe old age and die poor.

Bob Edwards, publisher, *The Eye Opener*, 1 Jan. 1910.

Ten, nine, eight, seven, six, five, four, three, two, one.... Happy New Year!... And now, "When the Saints Come Marching In."

Guy Lombardo, leader of The Royal Canadians dance band, greeting the New Year. First on radio and then on television, first from the ballroom of the Taft Hotel and then at that of the Waldorf-Astoria, from the 1930s to his death in 1977, Lombardo and his Royal Canadians ushered in the New Year by broadcasting "the sweetest music this side of heaven."

And I said to the man who stood at the gate of the year: / "Give me a light, that I may tread safely into the unknown!" / And he replied: / "Go out into the darkness and put your hand into the Hand of God. / That shall be to you better than light and safer than a known way." // So, I went forth, and finding the Hand of God, trod gladly into the night / And He led me toward the hills and the breaking of day in the lone East. // So, heart, be still! / What need our little life, / Our human life, to know, / If God hath comprehension? / In all the dizzy strife / Of things both high and low / God hideth His intention.

M. Louise Haskins, Maritime-based poetess, "The Gate of the Year," *Poetry Please! 100 Popular Poems from the BBC Radio 4 Programme* (1985) with a foreword by Charles Causley. "The Gate of the Year" was recited by King George VI in his New Year's broadcast, Christmas 1939.

Easter

Life can begin again! That is the central message of Easter, on which all the rest is commentary.... This is why Easter always belongs to all people, not just to those who call themselves Christians.

Tom Harpur, journalist, *Harpur's Heaven and Hell* (1983).

24th of May

The twenty-fourth of May / Is the Queen's Birthday; / If you don't give us a holiday, / We'll all run away.

Traditional ball-bouncing rhyme known to generations of Canadian children and quoted in this form in **Sara Jeannette Duncan**'s novel *The Imperialist* (1904) set in Brantford, Ont. The idea of setting aside a day each year to celebrate the British Empire and then Queen Victoria's birthday, 24 May occurred to Mrs. Clementina Fessenden, a schoolteacher in Hamilton, Ont. Her notion was taken up by George W. Ross, Ontario Minister of Education, and within a few years "the Queen's Birthday" was the focus of Imperial celebrations throughout the British Empire. The rhyme has outlasted the Empire, and so has the statutory holiday which is still observed on the Monday closest to the 24th of May.

I remember being struck by the extraordinary proliferation of Union Jacks and portraits of royalty in shops and public places; a generation later, I still find it amazing (as, I now know, did Leacock over a century ago) that any country in the late twentieth century should celebrate Queen Victoria's birthday with a national holiday.

W.J. Keith, academic, commenting on imperial sentiment in Ontario in the 1950s and in the 1990s, *Literary Images of Ontario* (1992).

Any nation that continues to celebrate Queen Victoria's birthday eighty-five years after the sour-duck breathed her last must hold in its psychic cupboard of toys any number of archaic baubles that can't help but render ineffective any emergent sense of a distinctly Canadian national identity.

Stephen Brook, English travel writer, *The Maple Leaf Rag: Travels across Canada* (1987).

St-Jean-Baptiste Day

I, myself, no longer celebrate the holiday of Saint Jean on the 24th. It is too depressing.

Hélène Jutras, commentator, *Québec Is Killing Me* (1995) translated by Jutras and Michael Gnarowski.

Canada Day

What is the difference between Dominion Day and Independence Day, between the First of July and the Glorious Fourth?.... not much—only forty-eight hours.

James Eayrs, political scientist, "Canadianism: Back and Forth on the Nation Swing," *The Toronto Star*, 3 July 1975.

Thanksgiving

Forgiveness and celebration are at the heart of community. These are the two faces of love. Celebration is a communal experience of joy, a song of thanksgiving.

Jean Vanier, founder of L'Arche, *Community and Growth: Our Pilgrimage Together* (1979).

Remembrance Day

Instead of fading away, as every good soldier should, you continue transformed: the arm of the state becomes its appendix.

Nicholas Stethem, defence analyst, "My War with the Army," *Maclean's*, March 1975.

But when daylight comes she's up and away / Ready to start another full day / Such is the life of a Red Cross Nurse / When the curse of war descends on earth / But men never learn from years before / That nobody ever wins a war

Lines from a verse written by **Ella Mae Bongard**, Canadian nurse who served during the Great War, *Nobody Ever Wins a War: The World War One Diaries of Ella Mae Bongard* (1998)

Christmas

If we do not wrap up a little love with our Christmas gift what is the use?

Bob Edwards, publisher, *The Eye Opener*, 20 Dec. 1913, *The Wit and Wisdom of Bob Edwards* (1976) edited by Hugh Dempsey.

To make a child believe, against the evidence of his own senses, such stories as that of Santa Claus bringing his bag of toys down the chimney, is to subject his capacity to think and make him easy meat for demagogues and mob orators.

Brock Chisholm, first Director-General of the World Health Organization, address, April 1945, the first assault on the sacrosant figure of Santa Claus, quoted by Allan Irving in *Brock Chisholm: Doctor to the World* (1998).

There is something seriously screwed up about an economy that can grow a Christmas tree on land best suited to raising bumper crops of townhouses and condominiums, nurture it, cut it down and put it on a truck and sell it to a guy like me, who lives smack in the middle of several *thousand square miles* of Christmas trees.

Arthur Black, broadcaster, "paper," *Basic Black: The Wit and Whimsy of Arthur Black* (1981).

To this day Canadians are the only people who believe that Santa lives in Canada.

Steven Freygood, writer, *Headless George and Other Tales Told in Canada* (1983).

With my own kids grown to sophistication—and to sleeping in—I need someone around me who believes in Santa Claus, and who thinks that anyone still in bed at Christmas dawn has wasted half the day.

Peter Gzowski, essayist and broadcaster, "The Great Great Great Great Grandchild of Sir Casimir, I," *Selected Columns from Canadian Living* (1993).

To me, Christmas has always been a very loving, fairy tale kind of time. My memories, of course, are always drawn back to the early days and all the beautiful things that I remember. But then, isn't that what we all do when it comes to Christmas? We take the good that we remember.

Rita MacNeil, singer-songwriter, quoted by Lee Ann Nicholson, *TV Guide*, 11 Dec. 1993.

Goodbye for now, may all your dreams come true and here's a fine Merry Christmas to you.

Greetings sent by **Santa Claus** (expedited by volunteers from Canada Post) to youngsters, who since the 1970s have been able to post personal letters to Santa Claus, c/o North Pole, Canada HOH OHO.

HOLLYWOOD See also CALIFORNIA, FILM, SHOW BUSINESS

Sam: Tell me, Edgar, are we buying all this stock in M-G-M just so you can get laid?

Edgar: Oh, no, Pop, it doesn't cost $40 million to get laid.

Conversation between **Sam Bronfman** and his son and successor **Edgar** when Seagram's bought what they thought was a controlling interest in the Metro-Goldwyn-Mayer studio in Hollywood in 1967, quoted by Peter C. Newman in *Bronfman Dynasty: The Rothschilds of the New World* (1978).

Imagine you, Gladys Smith, of Toronto, Canada, with the Queen of Siam in your bathtub.

Mary Pickford, silent film star born Gladys Smith, on entertaining the King and Queen of Siam at Pickfair, the mansion in Beverly Hills which she shared with her husband Douglas Fairbanks Sr. in the 1920s, quoted by Robert Windeler in *Sweetheart: The Story of Mary Pickford* (1973).

In some ways I didn't grow up in Grand Falls, I grew up in Hollywood. Ever since I can remember I went to movies, as often as I could. And so I began to dream of going to that other "hometown" of my imagination.

Gordon Pinsent, actor and writer, native of Newfoundland, sometime resident of Los Angeles and Toronto, quoted by John Hofsess in "Pinsent's Progress," *Maclean's*, Aug. 1974.

In film, compromise is a way of life. The only time when I didn't have stomach trouble was when I was in jail.

Edward Dmytryk, director, born in Grand Forks, B.C., of such movies as *Farewell My Lovely* (1944) and *The Caine Mutiny Court Martial* (1954), who was one of the so-called Unfriendly Ten, in his memoirs, *It's a Hell of a Life but Not a Bad Living* (1978).

If there's anything Hollywood can do on cue, it's make a grown man cry.

William Thorsell, columnist, "Television's Bright Lights," *The Globe and Mail*, 30 March 1996.

HOLOCAUST, JEWISH See also ANTI-SEMITISM, JEWISH PEOPLE

It took six million victims for the world, awakened and stunned, to rule that when men kill men because they are men, such an abomination will no longer be called the persecution of Christians by Romans, of Christians by other Christians, but it will be a crime against humanity, regardless of who are the guilty and who are the victims.

Bruno M. Cormier, psychiatrist, "On the History

of Men and Genocide" (1966), *Breaking the Chains: Bruno M. Cormier and the McGill University Clinic in Forensic Psychiatry* (1998).

The authentic Jew of today is forbidden to hand Hitler yet another, posthumous victory.

Emil Fackenheim, rabbi and philosopher, "The 614th Commandment" (1978), *The Jewish Thought of Emil Fackenheim: A Reader* (1987) edited by Michael L. Morgan. There are 613 commandments in the Talmud and 613 bones in the human body. Fackenheim's "614th commandment" is the most widely known and notable Canadian quotation of specific Jewish interest.

Even if you no longer can discover the uniqueness of the Torah in, say, celebrating the Sabbath, which is one of the Commandments we read today, you will still discover the uniqueness of your heritage because of anti-Semitism. This is the typical experience of the assimilated Jew: he has often lost observance, but is kept Jewish by the hostility of his environment.

Dow Marmur, rabbi, Holy Blossom Temple, "Anti-Semitism as Revelation," *Walking toward Elijah: Sermons on the Jewish Festivals* (1988) edited by David Azen.

As long as I draw breath, I will see to it that nobody profits from the ashes of the Holocaust.

Edgar Bronfman, Canadian-born chairman of the Seagram Company Ltd., head of the World Jewish Congress, and leader of the World Jewish Restitution Organization, Toronto address, quoted by Sandra Contenta in *The Toronto Star*, 23 March 1997.

Q. Did you lose any members of your family in the Holocaust?

A. I consider the entire Jewish people my family and I lost six million.

Edgar Bronfman, head of the World Jewish Congress, Toronto address, answering a frequently asked question, quoted by Sandra Contenta in *The Toronto Star*, 23 March 1997.

Luckily, you can't stage a Holocaust while CNN is watching.

Peter C. Newman, columnist, referring to international press reaction to the Serb atrocities against the Ethnic Albanians in Kosovo, Yugoslavia, "The Nation's Business," *Maclean's*, 9 April 1999.

HOME See also HOUSING, IGLOOS

Let others far from foreign grandeurs roam, / Dearer to me the loveliness of home.

Lines from **William Kirby**'s poem "The U.E.—A Tale of Upper Canada" (1864), *Canadian Idylls* (2nd ed., 1894).

We had our troubles, ne'er a doubt, / In those wild woods alone; / But then, sir, I was bound to have / A homestead of my own.

First verse of "Fire in the Woods; or, The Old Settler's Story" by **Alexander McLachlan** included by W.D. Lighthall in *Canadian Poems and Lays: Selections of Native Verse, Reflecting the Seasons, Legends, and Life of the Dominion* (1893).

Home is the place where many a man shows up at a disadvantage.

Bob Edwards, publisher, *The Eye Opener*, 4 May 1912, *The Wit and Wisdom of Bob Edwards* (1976) edited by Hugh Dempsey.

We have to talk in terms of a million human beings at a time, and in terms of how they want to live. We cannot continue to design homes as if there were still a landed aristocracy.

Moshe Safdie, architect and designer of Montreal's Habitat, quoted by Robert Fulford in *This Was Expo* (1968).

Eskasoni is my home, a place of peace and harmony / Where bannock and tea are served / To anyone who is kind enough to visit.

Lines from **Rita Joe**'s poem "The Art of Communication," *Song of Eskasoni: More Poems of Rita Joe* (1988) edited by Lee Maracle.

May you prosper / here among those you love / and there / amid the vast village / of stars and fostering suns.

Lines from **Don Gutteridge**'s poem "Say Uncle," *Love in the Wintertime* (1990).

Homesick sometimes means sick of home.

Maurus E. Mallon, aphorist, *Compendulum* (1995).

HOMOSEXUALITY See also GAYS & GAY RIGHTS

I may have to go on calling myself a lesbian into great old age, not because it is any longer true but because it takes such a long time to make the simple point that I have the right to be.

Jane Rule, writer, "Hindsight," *A Hot-Eyed Moderate* (1986).

That would be something. Svend Robinson as Minister of Defence.

Brian Mulroney, Prime Minister, slighting the NDP's defence critic who earlier became the first Member of Parliament to acknowledge his homosexuality, quoted in *The Globe and Mail,* 21 Nov. 1988.

How can we expect the church to deal with homosexuality, when it hasn't even dealt with sexuality.

Nancy Radclyffe, pastor, Metropolitan Community Church, Toronto, a congregation that includes gay and lesbian worshippers, quoted by Salem Alaton in *The Globe and Mail,* 22 Feb. 1992.

I'm a lesbian, but my music isn't lesbian music. They have to realize that's the way I feel and respect it.

k.d. lang, country-and-twang singer, after publicly announcing her sexual orientation, quoted by John Lyons in the *Winnipeg Free Press,* 19 Aug. 1992.

There is a difference between being attracted to a person of the same sex and acting on those feelings. It is not sinful to have homosexual tendencies, but sexual acts between people of the same sex are morally wrong because they do not respect the law of God in creating us male and female.

Guidance to Roman Catholic congregants from the pastoral letter issued by **Aloysius Ambrozic**, Archbishop of Toronto, its intent being to bring pressure to bear on the Ontario Legislature which was examining a bill that would grant same-sex couples the legal rights now extended to common-law heterosexual couples, quoted by Nicolas van Rijn in *The Toronto Star,* 29 May 1994.

HONESTY

Definition of a hypocrite: one who is too kind to be wholly honest and too honest to be wholly kind.

Alden Nowlan, poet and aphorist, "Scratchings," *Between Tears and Laughter* (1971).

Honesty is the best fallacy.

Ronald Hambleton, writer and aphorist, 1991.

HONOUR

A man should preserve his integrity, though he must sell his soul to do it.

Eric Nicol, humorist, *Letters to My Son* (1974).

HOPE

There is a mental therapy in hope, in the expression of a positive faith that a tunnel, however dark the passage-way, has an exit into some measure of sunlight. To believe otherwise means inertia, frustration, and continuous darkness.

E.J. Pratt, poet, address, April 1953, Queen's University, Kingston, Ont., quoted by David G. Pitt in *E.J. Pratt: The Master Years, 1927–1964* (1986).

Hope springs eternal: unfortunately it usually springs prematurely.

Northrop Frye, cultural critic, *The Double Vision: Language and Meaning in Religion* (1991).

I felt at home here. Perhaps I had found a country which has the right size of population so that it is an extended village. You don't get lost in it, except geographically... I was also attracted by the fact that ours is a country whose history lies in the future; a place where one can have hope.

John C. Polanyi, scientist, explaining why he settled in Canada, interviewed by Knowlton Nash in *Visions of Canada: Searching for Our Future* (1991).

HORSES & HORSE RACING See also ANIMALS, SPORTS

You trust in God. I trust my horse.

François Vielle, scout known as Crazy Vielle, addressing two Jesuit missionaries stranded on the plains near Fort Whoop-Up, quoted by Paul F. Sharp in *Whoop-Up Country: The Canadian-American West, 1865–1885* (1973).

Give the horse the ride he likes.

Attributed to Cuban-born Canadian jockey **Avelino Gomez**, as noted by Sylvia Fraser in *The Star Weekly,* 1 Oct. 1966.

All my life I have heard of men who became wealthy as a result of betting on horses but, strangely enough, I never met one of those elusive Midases. The only person I have known who could actually produce evidence that they won money consistently through horse-betting were bookmakers.

Jim Coleman, racing columnist, *A Hoofprint on My Heart* (1971).

Every man who has acquired a bit of money should have a hobby and a worry—and he can have both, if he owns a racehorse.

James Speers, promoter of horse racing on the Prairies in the 1930s and 1940s, quoted by S.F. Wise and Douglas Fisher in *Canada's Sporting Heroes* (1974).

I myself never surrendered. But they got my horse, and *it* surrendered.

Line spoken by actor **Chief Dan George** to fellow actor Clint Eastwood in the movie *The Outlaw Josey Wales* (1976).

I don't feel the least bit sorry for Northern Dancer because he's young, rich, and handsome, and his entire sex life lies before him.

Attributed to sportswriter **Scott Young** on the retirement of the champion thoroughbred Northern Dancer in 1970, by broadcaster Andy Barrie, CBC Radio, 24 Oct. 1995.

HOUSE OF COMMONS See also PARLIAMENT

They do one of two things—they grow, or they swell.

John G. Diefenbaker, former Prime Minister, referring to newly elected Parliamentarians, quoted by Scott Young in *The Globe and Mail*, 7 Nov. 1974.

O Lord, help my words to be gracious and tender today, for tomorrow I may have to eat them.

Lines said to be inscribed on the opening page of Prime Minister **Pierre Elliott Trudeau**'s briefing book for answers to questions expected to be raised by Opposition members in the House of Commons, according to *The Globe and Mail*, 21 March 1977.

I was elected as the member for the Lac-Saint-Jean riding... to represent the interests of Quebec within the national government.

Lucien Bouchard, Environment Minister, defining his conception of his responsibilities as a Member of Parliament, quoted in an editorial, *The Toronto Star*, 14 April 1990.

Grant us wisdom, knowledge and understanding to preserve the blessings of the country for the benefit of all and to make good laws and wise decisions.

Closing of the English text of the prayer recited each day by members of the House of Commons, unanimously adopted on 18 Feb. 1994. It was reproduced by Allan Thompson in *The Toronto Star* the following day.

HOUSING See also HOME

Working people who, in old age, own homes are unpoor. But working people, in old age, who don't own homes, are poor.

David B. Greenspan, advocate, "The Politics of Affordable Housing," address, Urban Land Institute, N.Y., 26 Oct. 1980.

The only way to live comfortably in an apartment building is to pretend you are the sole tenant.

Line from **Edward Phillips**' novel *Sunday Best* (1990).

Who lives next to subways? In a disproportionately high number of cases the answer seems to be—people in public housing.

Edward Relph, geographer, *The Toronto Guide: The City/Metro/The Region* (Annual Conference, Association of American Geographers, Toronto, April 1990).

The Canadian domestic archetype was once the log cabin. Now it is the sprawling bungalow.

Witold Rybczynski, architect and essayist, "If the House Fits," *Saturday Night*, April 1997.

HUDSON'S BAY COMPANY

The Hudson's Bay Company is simply a mercenary Corporation; there is not an officer in it with a soul above a beaver skin.

David Douglas, botanist, who visited the West in 1827, after whom the Douglas Fir was named, quoted by Hubert H. Bancroft in *History of the Northwest Coast* (1890).

The Hudson's Bay Company once controlled a Hollywood film studio. It made 37 feature films. During World War One, they owned and operated the third-largest fleet in the world. They lost 110 ships while sending supplies to France and Russia. Also, the only corporate directorship Sir Winston Churchill accepted when he retired from politics was with the Hudson's Bay Company because, eight generations before, his ancestor the Duke of Marlborough had been a governor of the company.

Peter C. Newman, author, quoted by Ben Knight in *Coles Booktalk*, Christmas 1991.

On a lighter note, Thomas Courchene has come up with one of the better lines of the year. Hearing of the rumoured move of Hudson's Bay Company warehouses over the border to New York State, Courchene suggests a new book: *The History of Canada in Three Centuries—From Buffalo to Buffalo.*

Mel Hurtig, nationalist, referring to the political scientist Thomas Courchene, *The Betrayal of Canada* (1991).

HUMANISM

Yet who really knows whether we need freedom more than we need solidarity, or fraternity more than equality? Modern secular humanism is empty if it supposes that the human good is without internal contradiction. These contradictions cannot be resolved in principle, only in practice.

Michael Ignatieff, essayist, *The Needs of Strangers* (1985).

Practical humanism is the voyage towards equilibrium without the expectation of actually arriving there.

John Ralston Saul, author, *The Unconscious Civilization* (1995).

I believe Humanism to be a philosophy of life, or a lifestance, which is meaningful, positive and relevant to our present-day knowledge of ourselves and the world, and a framework of values to live by.

Henry Morgentaler, physician, Honorary President of the Humanist Association of Canada, "Humanism Today," *Humanist in Canada*, Winter 1995–96.

HUMANITIES See also EDUCATION, SCHOLARSHIP

We cannot live in one element or the other, only in both.

Donald Hebb, psychologist, referring to the twin elements of science and imagination, "A World of Thought," *Essay on Mind* (1980).

The basis of my own approach, as a teacher of the humanities, has always been that we participate in society by means of our imagination or the quality of our social vision, and that training the imagination and clarifying the social vision are the only ways of developing citizens capable of taking part in a society as compicated as ours.

Northrop Frye, cultural critic, "The View from Here" (1983), *Myth and Metaphor: Selected Essays, 1974–1988* (1990) edited by Robert D. Denham.

HUMANITY See also LIFE

I often ask myself what advantages our "good society" possesses over that of the "savages," and find, the more I see of their customs, that we have no right to look down upon them.

Franz Boas, anthropologist, working in 1883, Kekerton, an island south of Pangnirtung, N.W.T., quoted by John Goddard in "N.Y.T. and Y.T.," *The Penguin Guide to Canada* (1989) edited by Alan Tucker.

The hardest place to look is inside yourself, but that is where you will find the beast, blocking your path to other men. Conquer it, and you can truly join the world.

Line from the soundtrack of *Labyrinth*, the NFB-produced film, directed by Roman Kroitor, exhibited at the NFB Pavilion at Expo 67, quoted by Robert Fulford in *This Was Expo* (1968).

Humanity's leading characteristic in my opinion is ignorance, second is his laziness, and third may be his vanity. These are strong human traits and they are very dangerous in the decisions that people make. They become very dangerous when applied to international things.

Cyrus Eaton, Pugwash-born, Cleveland-based industrialist, interviewed for CBC-TV's *Cyrus Eaton: The Prophet of Pugwash*, 9 Nov. 1977.

To strive for perfection is to kill love because perfection does not recognize humanity.

Marion Woodman, analyst and author, *Addition to Perfection: The Still Unravished Bride* (1982).

After all is said, / a simple hello / how are you / I love you / would have done.

Lines from **Don Gutteridge**'s poem "Said and Done," *Love in the Wintertime* (1990).

In fact, humanity literally has the capacity to exterminate itself, thus joining the many other species that have become extinct.

Allen Tough, futurologist, *Crucial Questions about the Future* (1991).

Changing human to humane takes one letter and most of a lifetime.

Maurus E. Mallon, aphorist, 18 Feb. 1993.

So what exactly is it that *humans* do that is specifically human?

Thoughts of the narrator of **Douglas Coupland**'s novel *Life after God* (1994).

HUMAN NATURE

We despair of changing the habits of men; still we would alter institutions, the habits of millions of men.

George Iles, aphorist, *Canadian Stories: Together with... Jottings from a Note-Book* (1918).

People who don't have faith in human nature are forever cleaning up the mess made by people who do.

Richard Needham, newspaper columnist, *The Wit and Wisdom of Richard Needham* (1977).

HUMAN RIGHTS See RIGHTS, HUMAN

HUMILITY

It was as if humility had an arse.

Line from **Daniel Richler**'s novel *Kicking Tomorrow* (1991).

Such awe-inspired humility is usually derived from nature—the macro-mysteries of outer space and the micro-mysteries of genetics, the redwoods of California, the Rockies of British Columbia, the Great Barrier Reef of Australia, each has the potential to move our spirit.

John Dalla Costa, advertising executive, *Meditations on Business: Why Business As Usual Won't Work Anymore* (1991).

HUMOUR & HUMORISTS See also COMIC ART; HUMOUR, CANADIAN; JOKES; LAUGHTER; LEACOCK, STEPHEN; MALAPROPISMS; NEWFIE JOKES; WIT

In its larger aspect, humour is blended with pathos, until the two are one and represent, as they have in every age, the mingled heritage of tears and laughter that is our common lot on earth.

Stephen Leacock, humorist, address, The Canadian Club of New York, 10 March 1923, quoted by Hugh A. Anderson in *The Kinship of Two Countries: A History of The Canadian Club of New York* (1964).

The key to happiness and freedom is a sense of humour and a sense of humour is nothing more or less than the ability to laugh at oneself.

Jim Unger, cartoonist who began to draw the cartoon "Herman" in Ottawa in 1974, Introduction, *The 1st Treasury of Herman* (1979).

Actually, *levity* is the soul of wit.

Maurus E. Mallon, aphorist, 20 Nov. 1992.

Dad always said it was easy writing 500 funny words a day. All he had to do was roll a blank sheet of paper into the typewriter and stare at it until beads of blood appeared on his forehead.

Stephen Lautens, son of newspaper columnist and humorist Gary Lautens, "A Short Note about Dad," *The Best of Gary Lautens* (1995).

The enemies of laughter, by the way, deserve to be treated with the same abhorrence as the enemies of truth.

Peter C. Newman, columnist, "The Nation's Business," *Maclean's*, 31 May 1999.

HUMOUR, CANADIAN See also HUMOUR & HUMORISTS; LEACOCK, STEPHEN

Canadians, it seems to me, are terrified by the idea of not being something. A man whom I shall not name once pounded the table in front of me saying, Goddamnmit it, I do have a sense of humour.

Larry Zolf, broadcaster, interviewed in *Meet the Media: Eight of Canada's Best-known Journalists Talk with Robert Bullis* (1976).

I think Canadians have always been good laughers. I used to run into that all the time. An interviewer in the middle of an interview on television would look at me and say, "Dave, do Canadians have a sense of humour?" I'd say, "No, that's why I'm in the clothing business."

Dave Broadfoot, comic, quoted by John Lyons in the *Winnipeg Free Press*, 19 Aug. 1992.

The British novelist Kingsley Amis put a fictitious tome titled *Canadian Wit and Humour* on his list of the World's Shortest Books. "Worthwhile Canadian Initiative" was the winner of *The New Republic* magazine's Most Boring Headline contest.

Rick Marin, comic, "The Most Entertaining Americans? Canadians," *The New York Times*, 27 June 1993.

Canadian humour expressed people's delight in mocking authority or deflating large ideas. This was an attitude necessary to preserve the regional and local, but there was an astringent quality to it I didn't enjoy.

Jill Ker Conway, Australian-born, American-educated historian and memoirist who taught at the University of Toronto from 1964 to 1975, *True North: A Memoir* (1994).

HUNGARIAN PEOPLE

The thing about Canada is that I have never felt like a foreigner here. From the first moment I was absolutely at home. I could not have gone to England and become an Englishwoman because I was still in a way Hungarian. But I can be a Canadian without having to give up my feelings for the country I came from.

Dora de Pédery-Hunt, medallist, born in Hungary, resident in Canada, quoted by John Brehl in *The Toronto Star*, 4 Dec. 1978.

I am a Hungarian patriot still and will die as such. But I am happy that I am out. I am happy that I am out because I am not a masochist.

George Faludy, Hungarian-born poet, Canadian citizen and Toronto resident from the 1960s to the 1980s, interviewed by Alan Twigg in *Strong Voices: Conversations with Fifty Canadian Authors* (1988).

HUNGER See also FOOD BANKS, POVERTY, THIRD WORLD

Headlines pass; breadlines continue.

Robin Skelton, poet and aphorist, *A Devious Dictionary* (1991).

HUNTING See also ANIMALS, SEAL HUNT

In the Arctic a man's life is a perpetual hunt. It is his very existence.

Jan Welzel, traveller, *The Quest for Polar Treasurers* (1933) translated from the Czech by M. and R. Weatherall.

Bing Crosby: You should take it easy, go up to Canada, and shoot a buck.

Al Jolson: I'd rather go to Las Vegas and shoot two bucks.

Inane dialogue from the radio program *The Chesterfield Show* heard in the United States and Canada in 1949.

HYDRO-ELECTRIC See ELECTRICAL POWER, JAMES BAY PROJECT

HYPNOTISM

There is danger of a real sort in hypnotism, but not where the reader has been taught to expect it. The highly emotional orator and mob leader is, from the psychologist's viewpoint, a much more effective hypnotist than any laboratory product. It is he who leads humanity by the nose into its bloody wars.

George H. Estabrooks, Canadian-born psychologist, *Hypnotism* (1943).

I can hypnotize a man—*without his knowledge or consent*—into committing treason against the United States.

George Estabrooks, Canadian-born psychologist and specialist in hypnosis, boast made in the early 1940s, quoted by W.H. Bowart in *Operation Mind Control* (1978).

I

ICE

You mind the last Ice Age? (And I don't meen the winter of '87 in Sinjons, Nofunland.) I'm tockin bout a cuppla millenema ago wen sumboddy tern down the wirld's thermalstat and everybuddy that had been in heet cum all of a suddin over friggid. Canda wuz at that time enjoin a topical climacks, and our first sittizens wuz them prehysterical Land Rovers like yer bucktooth Tyger and yer hairy Mastoidon....

Don Harron, comedian, in the person of Charlie Farquharson, *Cum Buy the Farm* (1987).

I looked out at the icebergs. They were so beautiful they also made you afraid.

Barry Lopez, naturalist, describing the appearance of icebergs in Davis Strait, N.W.T., *Arctic Dreams: Imagination and Desire in a Northern Landscape* (1986).

Icebergs smaller than houses the Newfoundlanders contemptuously refer to as "bergy bits."

Marq de Villiers, commentator, *Water* (1999).

ICELANDIC PEOPLE

Where the settlers' dreams were buried / in the mounds at Sandy Bar. / Infant hopes of sturdy manhood / came to naught at Sandy Bar.

Lines from the verse "Sandy Bar" (1920) written in Icelandic by **Guttormur J. Guttormsson**, the bard of Riverton, Man., who became Poet Laureate of Iceland. He died in 1966 and was buried at Sandy Bar cemetery. The poem appears in English in Heather Alda Ireland's *Aurora: English Translations from Iceland Poems* (1933).

You are caught in the act of trying to convince others of the existence of a reality they know nothing of. It is not unlike insanity: you have an idea of yourself and your reason for being, your background and purpose, your priorities and beliefs, but people around you do not share any of these. They look at you, nod their heads and at best are patient. This is no way to live. How does it feel to be in a world where all your deepest instincts are privatized?

Kristjana Gunnars, editor of Icelandic background, Introduction, *Unexpected Fictions: New Icelandic Canadian Writing* (1989).

Everyone knows me as being Icelandic, but the truth is that 50 per cent of my life was spent being brought up Protestant, Orange, Irish. My grandfather was an Orangeman, a Mason, who marched in the Orange parade every year, and I learned to walk along with King Billy on his white horse. That was a big part of my life, although it hasn't surfaced in my writing.

W.D. Valgardson, author of Icelandic and Irish ancestry, interviewed by Judith Miller in *Other Solitudes: Canadian Multicultural Fictions* (1990) edited by Linda Hutcheon and Marion Richmond.

In a 1994–95 Gallup poll of 18 nations, Canadians ranked second only to Icelanders as the world's happiest people.

Jeremy Daniel, writer, *Family Circle,* 16 Sept. 1996, reprinted in *Reader's Digest,* July 1997.

I don't want to be identified as an Icelander. I'm a Canadian, but I'm proud of my background.

George Johnson, Lieutenant-Governor of Manitoba, the first Queen's representative of Icelandic descent, quoted by John Lyons in the *Winnipeg Free Press,* 4 Dec. 1990.

ICE STORM

Ice storms are a major hazard in all parts of Canada except the North.

"Ice Storm '98," *The 1999 Canadian Global Almanac* (1998).

It's like the *Titanic*. You are living in it. You can't believe it's happening. It was a beautiful disaster.

Gary Gallon, writer, describing the experience of living through Ice Storm '98 which immobilized Montreal, Quebec's Eastern Townships, and Eastern Ontario, 10–15 Jan., "Damage," *The Globe and Mail,* 12 Jan. 1998.

Some people even said they were sad when the lights went on, but they were grateful to have at least been warm and fed. There are many stories to be told—there are tales of frustration and anger and love....

Carolyn Smart, poet, "Ice Storm Diary," Writers in Electronic Residence, *Maclean's,* 9 Nov. 1998.

IDEALS See also IDEAS

Canada is too young to fall a victim to the malady of disillusionment and scepticism, and she must believe in her great ideals in the face of contradiction—for she has the great gift of youth, she has the direct consciousness of the stir of growth within, which should make her trust her own self which is the only sure way of trusting the world.

Rabindranath Tagore, Bengali poet, "Message of Farewell to Canada," Farewell Address to the Fourth Triennial Conference of the National Council of Education of Canada, Vancouver, 14 April 1929; P.C. Mahalanobis, editor, *Visva-Bharati*, Bulletin No. 14, reprinted 1977.

Idealist: a cynic in the making.

Irving Layton, poet and aphorist, *The Whole Bloody Bird (obs, aphs & Pomes)* (1969).

IDEAS See also IDEOLOGIES, IMAGINATION, INTELLIGENCE

Only now are we rounding up facts and ideas instead of cattle and horses. The younger ones have never been brought into captivity before, and even some of the older have developed a good deal of resistance. Others are simply hidden in a remote corner. None must be left to be buried in the winter's snow.

John E. Robbins, editor, expressing his "sense of adventure" in editing *The Encyclopedia Canadiana*, completed in 1958, quoted by John A.B. McLeish in *A Canadian for All Seasons: The John E. Robbins Story* (1978).

When an idea seizes the masses, it becomes a material force.

Leslie Morris, communist, *The Canadian Tribune*, 20 Jan. 1960, *Selected Writings of Leslie Morris: 1923–1964* (1970).

For ultimately only ideas prevail; ultimately men cannot be moved except they be persuaded; ultimately freedom alone unites mankind.

W.L. Morton, historian, *The Canadian Identity* (1961).

As a rule, the most dangerous ideas are not the ones which divide people, but those on which they agree.

Stephen Vizinczey, essayist, *The Rules of Chaos* (1969).

An idea in the mind of an individual scientist could make a $100 billion defence system obsolete overnight. The mind of a single citizen somewhere in the world holds within it the potential of generating an idea that could lead us to the cure for cancer, the way to feed the starving millions, or the achievement of world peace.

Laurence J. Peter, educator, *Peter's People* (1979).

I give him credit for being closed-minded in an open-minded way.

Howard Eisenberg, psychologist and parapsychologist, commenting on the McGill psychologist D.O. Hebb who would dismiss evidence rather than discount theory, address, University of Toronto, 16 March 1989.

Material things look smaller at a distance, mental things look bigger.

Louis Dudek, poet and aphorist, "Epigrams," *Small Perfect Things* (1991).

Somebody said that *Paradise Lost* was a monument to dead ideas, and my comment on that was that there were no dead ideas, there were only tired readers.

Northrop Frye, cultural critic, interviewed by David Cayley in *Northrop Frye in Conversation* (1992).

Ideas are harder to change than leaders. That may be because they matter more.

Desmond Morton, historian, "A Time to Think about Leadership," *The Toronto Star*, 6 June 1993.

I used to worry that ideas were finite, but they're infinite, they really are. They just come and come and come and....

Douglas Coupland, author, interviewed by Philip Marchand, *The Toronto Star*, 7 Oct. 1995.

You're a product of your past and you wonder about your future.

Tom Daly, film producer, remark made to Colin Low in 1954, quoted by D.B. Jones in *The Best Butler in the Business: Tom Daly of the National Film Board of Canada* (1996).

I grew up believing that loving the life of books and argument, of imagination and the adventure of ideas, is loving part of life itself.

Bob Rae, former Ontario Premier, *From Protest*

to Power: Personal Reflections on a Life in Politics (1996).

IDENTITY See also IDENTITY, NATIONAL

Identity cannot be preserved either by cutting oneself off from others or by dissolving oneself in others, but only by the flexibility of a larger group where there are great variations of character, and sharp differences of opinion and emphasis, yet all contained within the sense of a common heritage and a common destiny.

Northrop Frye, cultural critic, Foreword, *The Prospect of Change: Proposals for Canada's Future* (1965) edited by Abraham Rotstein.

We all belong to something before we are anything....

Northrop Frye, cultural critic, *The Double Vision: Language and Meaning in Religion* (1991).

Who Do You Think You Are? is the title of one of Alice Munro's short story collections, and no Canadian needs to ask for a translation, because we have all had this indignant and scornful question addressed to us at some point in our lives, when others might have thought we were getting too big for our boots.

Margaret Atwood, author, Foreword, *Charles Pachter* (1992) by Bogomila Welsh-Ovcharov.

All the ills of mankind spring from belonging to a race, a nation, a city, a group of some kind. The ideal would be to belong to none, and to care for all—but who is capable of that?

Louis Dudek, poet and aphorist, 1987, *Notebooks 1960–1994* (1994).

Truth is related to identity. What you believe to be true depends, in some measure, on who you believe yourself to be. And who you believe yourself to be is mostly defined in terms of who you are not.

Michael Ignatieff, author, "Articles of Faith," *Index on Censorship*, Sept.–Oct. 1996, reprinted in "Readings," *Harper's*, March 1997.

IDENTITY, NATIONAL See also CANADIANS; CHARACTER, NATIONAL; IDENTITY, NATIONALISM

They felt, I suspect, that they were duller than they ought to be. They were wondering if they were not too cautious, and yet had steeled themselves against being incautious.

J.B. Priestley, English writer on a tour of Canada, referring to the suggestion that Canadian businessmen were "smug and complacent," in "I Heard the Monotonous, Mournful Voices of Canadian Women," *Liberty*, Aug. 1956.

The average Canadian doesn't know who the hell he is. In one part of the country he thinks he's a Frenchman who is being exploited by English Protestants. Ontario feels vaguely American, vaguely British, and vaguely. British Columbia wants to be an American state. Victoria thinks it's the nicest part of London, and Vancouver, on the Pacific, is making love to Japan. Canada in general is united in thinking that Newfoundland is really Brooklyn.

Henry Morgan, New York comic who lived in Toronto from 1971 to 1975, "Oy, Canada," *Penthouse*, June 1972.

One disadvantage of living in Canada is that one is continually called upon to make statements about the Canadian identity, and Canadian identity is an eminently exhaustible subject.

Attributed to cultural critic **Northrop Frye** by John Meisel in *The Toronto Star*, 15 Oct. 1977.

Everyone belongs somewhere. Yet much of the conflict in the history, and the pre-history, of mankind has been about who belongs where.

Ramsay Cook, historian, Introduction, *Canada, Quebec, and the Uses of Nationalism* (1986).

A nation's identity is (not "is in") its culture, and culture is a structure with several levels.

Northrop Frye, cultural critic, "Levels of Cultural Identity" (1989), *The Eternal Act of Creation: Essays, 1979–1990* (1993) edited by Robert D. Denham. Frye discerned three levels of culture: a level of lifestyle, a level of ideology and historical process, a level of creativity and of education in the arts and sciences."

In Canada, the time has come to address a centrally important question. If what we have in common is our diversity, do we really have anything in common at all?

Reginald W. Bibby, sociologist, *Mosaic Madness: The Poverty and Potential of Life in Canada* (1990).

Canadians ... are not in any way objectionable because no one in the world even knows what a *real* Canadian behaves like. Even in Canada. Canadians think other Canadians are just polite Americans. (Quebec is the exception, of course, but I still have family there, so I'd best leave that alone.)

Sam Orbaum, Montreal-raised Israeli columnist, "Friday Feuilleton," *The Jerusalem Post*, 28 Jan. 1991.

Canada is the existence of not being. Not English, not American. It is the mathematics of not being. Subtle flavour. We're more like celery as a flavour, know what I mean?

Mike Myers, Toronto-born comic, quoted by Chris Heath in "Mike Myers," *Rolling Stone*, 10 June 1999.

Ethnicity does not replace Canadian identity; it *is* Canadian identity.

Harold Troper, sociologist, "Multiculturalism," *Encyclopedia of Canada's Peoples* (1999) edited by Paul Robert Magocsi.

The search for Canada is a personal journey. The search for a national identity is a journey without an end. It began a long, long time ago. It will continue into the far distant future.

Lorraine Monk, editor, *Canada: These Things We Hold Dear: An Album of Photographic Memories* (1999).

So Canada enters the millennium with no real rationale as a country. Except for Australia and New Zealand, whose isolation from any kindred nationality gives them a sort of identity, Canada is the only substantial country in the world with no cultural, linguistic, or tribal homogeneity nor any distinct revolutionary, ideological, or geopolitical tradition to give it an organizing principle.

Conrad Black, publisher, "Out of Uncle Sam's Shadow," the *National Post*, 11 Jan. 2000.

IDEOLOGIES See also COMMUNISM, IDEAS, LIBERALISM & LIBERAL PARTY, MARXISM

Canada should have more philosophic strategy and less political tactics. We are held back by the myopic view, the overriding regionalism, parochialism, provincialism that have dogged our path. There are "isms" today—let's make them "wasms." Let us work for, believe in and take pride in "Canada."

Sidney Smith, president, University of Toronto, address, Canadian Club of London, Ont., 1956, quoted by Russell R. Merifield in *Speaking of Canada: The Centennial History of The Canadian Clubs* (1993).

The only ism for Canadians is Canadianism.

Brian Moore, novelist, *Canada* (1963, 1968).

As a rule, when Mr. Theory makes an error, Mr. Practice pays for it.

Peter Humeniuk, Winnipeg-based aphorist, *My Quotations and Comments* (1975).

While English Canadians are just beginning to express a nationalism long felt by their historians, French Canadian historians are starting to reject a nationalism long felt by their people. Having had their fill of traditional nationalism, younger historians are beginning to search their past for other things: politics, economics, classes, even revolutions.

Susan Mann, historian, *Action Française: French Canadian Nationalism in the Twenties* (1975).

Whoever wishes to escape the totalitarianism of the new ideology (striving to draw status from science itself) will have to start listening to society's humblest and most under-privileged ranks: the pioneer farmers of the Lower Saint-Lawrence and the Gaspé Peninsula, clinging to their wood-lots and their rocky soil, the people of the forgotten slums of Montréal, Québec, and other cities.

Léon Dion, political scientist, *Quebec: The Unfinished Revolution* (1976) translated from the French by Thérèse Romer.

If noxious or foolish doctrines can never be refuted, perhaps they can be laughed to death.

Irving Layton, poet, Foreword, *The Covenant* (1977).

Between the Left and the Right there's nowhere to go but down.

Midge Decter, Canadian-born American social commentator, quoted by her former husband Norman Podhoretz in *Breaking Ranks: A Political Memoir* (1979).

What would astonish a primitive tribesman about the state of our spirits is that we believe we can establish the meaningfulness of our private existence in the absence of any collective cosmology or teleology.

Michael Ignatieff, essayist, *The Needs of Strangers* (1985).

This whole anti-P.C.-ism thing is a put-up job—the right doesn't have a Communist Party to attack any more.

Chandler Davis, mathematician, political activist, commenting on "politically correct" thinking, quoted by Lynda Hurst in *The Toronto Star*, 2 June 1991.

Right and left have lost their meaning not because they are too ideological, but because they are not ideologies at all. They are theologies, useful only for denouncing heretics.

Editorial, "Today Is Tomorrow to Yesterday's Man," *The Globe and Mail*, 26 Nov. 1991.

We have no need of a new Jerusalem. Instead, we simply need to practise what we preach: reducing, for as many of our fellow citizens as possible, the often appalling gap between what we promise and what we deliver, the gap between fine words about justice and fairness and the grim reality of life for our fellow human beings.

Michael Ignatieff, commentator, address, Queen's University, Kingston, 22 Oct. 1991, *Queen's Quarterly*, Winter 1991.

I'm White, I'm Straight, I'm Sorry

Title of an "ode to the politically correct" from the revue *We Love You Brian Mulroney and Other Horror Stories* (1992) written by **Mark Leiren-Young** and **Kevin Crofton**.

You can't eat ideology, but ideology can eat you.

John Tory, political organizer, address, Public Affairs Association, Toronto, quoted in *eye*, 30 April 1992.

When I was a boy in High River I used to lie in the fields and study the heavens. And I noticed a very peculiar thing about birds. They have two wings, a left wing and a right wing. And if they had only one wing, they would fly around in circles.

Joe Clark, future Prime Minister, warning listeners against ideological extremism, as quoted by David Olive in *Canadian Political Babble* (1993).

It is the duty of intellectuals to be rude to the movements.

John Fekete, philosopher, quoting Feri Fehér, *Moral Panic: Biopolitics Rising* (2nd ed., 1995).

Ideologies are often adopted as poses by people who wish to avoid engaging in discourses they find tiresome.

Douglas Coupland, novelist, "Agree/Disagree: 55 Statements about the Culture," *The New Republic*, 2 Aug. 1995.

If I adhere to any creed today, it's a belief in human dignity and strength. Anything I do believe in today has to stand up to reason—and be explainable to my five-year-old son.

Jan Wong, correspondent and former ideologue, *Red China Blues: My Long March from Mao to Now* (1996).

IGLOOS See also HOMES

Most experts believe that igloos were first conceived somewhere in the vastness of the Canadian Arctic where man was faced with a treeless expanse and was forced to invent and dwell with his family in that small monument to human genius in the face of adversity, the household dome of snow.

James Houston, author and artist, *Confessions of an Igloo Dweller* (1995).

"Igloo" is a more generic term than southerners realize. In the Inuit language, any shelter can be referred to as an iglu, including a modern house. At Nunuvat Arctic College in Iqaluit, for instance, Igloo Building is offered as a credit course in the Language and Culture program.

Communications Division, **Statistics Canada**, *Canada Year Book 1999* (1998).

IGNORANCE

A little learning is a dangerous thing, but a lot of ignorance is just as bad.

Bob Edwards, publisher, *The Eye Opener*, 20 Aug. 1921, *The Best of Bob Edwards* (1975) edited by Hugh Dempsey.

When we overcome our anger and disappointment at ignorance, we may learn to appreciate it. We have so much of it that we should make the best of it. When we are able to love our ignorance from which all new good will come, life may become easier.

W.C.M. Scott, psychiatrist, "On Positive Affects" (1981), *Psychoanalysis and the Zest for Living: Reflections and Psychoanalyatic Writings in Memory of W.C.M. Scott* (1998) edited by Michel Grignon.

Our most stubborn assumptions are precisely those that remain unconscious: the biases that we bring to bear when we are judging each other's culture but which we ourselves are not aware of.

Mavor Moore, former Chairman, Canada Council, *Cultures and Writers: A Cultural Dialogue of Ethnic Writers* (1983) edited by Yvonne Grabowski.

Canada is so huge that Canadians don't know one another. Canada is covered by ignorance about itself. Canadians don't know their country. We don't travel it. We don't know our history, we don't read our literature. Having two languages cuts the reality of the country into parts that sometimes are impermeable.

Roch Carrier, author, "Canada Is a Grand Dream," *Canadian Living*, September 1992.

What is the true value of knowledge? That it makes our ignorance more precise.

Thoughts of a character in **Anne Michaels**' novel *Fugitive Pieces* (1996).

ILLNESS See also DISEASE

A creative illness succeeds a period of intense preoccupation with an idea and search for a certain truth.... The subject emerges from his ordeal with a permanent transformation in his personality and the conviction that he has discovered a great truth or a new spiritual world.

Henri F. Ellenberger, Montreal psychiatrist and theorist, *The Discovery of the Unconscious* (1970). According to psychiatrist Anthony Storr, Ellenberger introduced the term "creative illness" to characterize "a creative solution to the subject's problems, albeit a creative solution which does not stand up to critical examination."

If the national mental illness of the United States is megalomania, that of Canada is paranoid schizophrenia.

Margaret Atwood, author, quoted by Carole McKenzie in *Quotable Women* (1992).

Men get the killing diseases. Women get the crippling diseases.

Ruth Wilson, physician, Queen's University, quoted by Vivian Smith in *The Globe and Mail*, 24 April 1993.

IMAGINATION See also IDEAS

Imagination is but a free thinking. The imaginative are blessed with a facility in the association of facts. High latent force develops when such a man is faced with a perplexing problem, and wide spark gaps are bridged.

Sir Frederick Banting, scientist, quoted by Lloyd Stevenson in *Sir Frederick Banting* (1945).

For in the secret places of his imagination every Canadian sawing firewood at his summer cottage is a lumberjack, every suburbanite on skis a *coureur de bois*, every Sunday canoer a *voyageur*.

Kildare Dobbs, essayist, Introduction, *Canada* (1964).

The function of the historical imagination in reading is to change "potentially" into "actually" whenever possible.

Northrop Frye, cultural critic, "Harold Innis: The Strategy of Culture" (1982), *The Eternal Act of Creation: Essays, 1979–1990* (1993) edited by Robert D. Denham.

I believe that the roots of the imagination are physical roots, real roots.

Anne Hébert, poet and author, quoted by Donald Smith in *Voices of Deliverance: Interviews with Quebec and Acadian Writers* (1986) translated by Larry Shouldice.

If there has been a single principal theme in our century's aesthetics, it is that the life of imagination and the life of action are one and the same.

Modris Eksteins, historian, *Rites of Spring: The Great War and the Birth of the Modern Age* (1989).

Once we accept an imaginative literalism, everything else falls into place: without that, creeds and dogmas quickly turn malignant.

Northrop Frye, cultural critic, *The Double Vision: Language and Meaning in Religion* (1991).

Can our imagination chase / Intelligence's why? / Or does intelligence outface / Imagination's eye?

Robert Finch, poet, "Vexed Question," *Miracle at the Jetty* (1991).

What you dream never quite materializes. This strange, empty land with its mountains, silver, mysterious, vast presences, exists only in your mind. Once you touch the mountain, it becomes a paltry handful of pebbles and dirt. But wait—look at it. You hold the mountains in your hand!

Mark Frutkin, novelist, *Invading Tibet* (1991).

What exactly is it like in the Canada of the imagination, adrift in this Ark of Ice, on the cold-fusion fluid of tomorrow?

Lesley Choyce, editor, Introduction, *Ark of Ice: Canadian Futurefiction* (1992).

Our brains are our broomsticks, sleighs, wings, burning bushes, magic carpets, ointments, Aladdin's lamps....

Thoughts of a character in the novel *Instruments of Desire* (1997) by **Nancy Huston**.

IMMIGRATION See also REFUGEES

I think a stalwart peasant in a sheep-skin coat, born on the soil, whose forefathers have been farmers for ten generations, with a stout wife and a half-dozen children, is good quality.

Sir Clifford Sifton, Minister of the Interior from 1896 to 1905, encouraged the immigration to western Canada of Ukrainian and Doukhobor farmers and labourers, as noted in "The Immigrants Canada Wants," *Maclean's*, 1 April 1922.

The result of all this is a perfectly marvellous "expansion"—everywhere new railroads are being built, new houses erected, new mines opened, new factories started, new industrial enterprises set going—parallel with the new acres being brought under cultivation.

Beatrice and **Sidney Webb**, British socialists, describing how British investment of labour and capital is developing Canada, following a visit for the Poor-Law Commission of 1911, "Minority Report," quoted by Helen MacMurchy in *Third Report on Infant Mortality* (1912).

...that subject which engaged her attention, and not merely her attention...that project for emigrating young people of both sexes born of respectable parents and setting them up with a fair prospect of doing well in Canada.

Passage from **Virginia Woolf**'s novel *Mrs. Dalloway* (1925) in which is described the pet project of Mrs. Dalloway's friend Lady Bruton who hopes in this manner to deal with "the superfluous youth of our ever-increasing population."

In consequence, it was quite common to find the second generation, grandchildren of the pioneers, innocent of the English language, unconformed to Canadian customs, unabsorbed in Canadian life and untouched by the Canadian spirit. The mass spirit is to be commended—but these foreigners should be distributed in smaller groups.

Charles W. Gordon, imperialist and novelist who wrote as Ralph Connor, interviewed by R.E. Knowles in *The Toronto Star*, 30 April 1929.

If you put pants on a penguin, it could be admitted to this country.

David A. Croll, Senator, ridiculing the immigration policies of the 1950s, quoted by R. Douglas Francis, Richard Jones, and Donald B. Smith in *Destinies: Canadian History since Confederation* (1988).

I can only marvel at the way you accept strangers. You don't know what you're getting in for, but you accept strangers.

Richard Rodriguez, Mexican-American critic of affirmative action and multiculturalism, interviewed in Toronto by Philip Marchand in *The Toronto Star*, 4 March 1993.

If we were to stop the tap of immigration tomorrow and not let one person in, the last Canadian would die in 175 years.

Sergio Marchi, Minister of Immigration, interviewed by Geoffrey York in *The Globe and Mail*, 27 June 1994.

Pier 21 represents a lot of things to a lot of people. We shouldn't regard it as just a landmark. It is really a symbol for the age that has passed. A time when people came to Canada by ship with hope for a better life. And many of them came here with nothing but their dreams.

John LeBlanc, retired federal immigration officer, address, 1 July 1994, on the 125th anniversary of Canada's first Immigration Act, ceremony to mark the unveiling of the plaque at Pier 21 on the Halifax waterfront, which saw the disembarking of generations of immigrants who crossed the Atlantic by ship. Quoted in *Canadian Scene*, 19 Aug. 1994. Pier 21 closed its gates on 31 March 1971 after nearly two million immigrants had passed through them.

In Japan we were able to buy, in effect, a visa to Canada, which had, as is now common knowledge, a less than generous immigration policy.

Judith N. Shklar, Harvard-based political scientist, born in Russia, educated in Montreal, discussing her family's exodus from Europe immediately before the Second World War, "A Life of Learning" (1989), *Liberalism without Illusions: Essays on Liberal Theory and the Political Vision of Judith N. Shklar* (1996) edited by Bernard Yack.

We have virtually no monuments to the multicultural nature of Canada, to salute those who came here seeking a fresh and better future—which, when you think about it, includes just about all Canadians. We're a nation of boat people.

Peter C. Newman, columnist, "Pier 21," *Maclean's*, 22 July 1996.

Every immigrant who landed at Pier 21 has two stories: the story they came from and the story they started when they landed in Canada.... There was one thought attached to every single immigrant who set foot here: gratitude.

Rosalie Abella, Justice of the Court of Appeal for Ontario, address to mark the dedication of Pier 21 in Halifax, which from 1928 to 1971 served as a point of entry for half a million immigrants, many of them refugees, of whom Justice Abella was one, 30 June 1999, "Welcome to Pier 21," *The Globe and Mail*, 2 July 1999.

I believe that my parents, like so many other immigrants, dreamed their children into being as Canadians.

Adrienne Clarkson, Governor General, installation address, alluding to her Chinese ancestry, Ottawa, 7 Oct. 1999, printed in the *National Post* the following day.

IMMORTALITY

The world is not only what we can see. It is enormous, and also has room for people when they die and no more walk about down here on earth.

Nalungiaq, Eskimo shaman, expounding the traditional Netsilik belief system, quoted by Knud Rasmussen in *The Netsilik Eskimos: Social Life and Spiritual Culture: Report of the Fifth Thule Expedition, 1921–24* (1931).

If only we could accept our immortality, how differently we should live.

Joe Fisher, journalist, *Cotopaxi Visions: Travels in Ecuador* (1992).

IMPERIALISM See also BRITISH EMPIRE & COMMONWEALTH, EMPIRE

Hundreds of years ago, the hairy Britons crept wonderingly down to the shore and watched the wind fill the sails of the mighty Roman galleons as they set out for Imperial Rome. I love Canada more than any other country, but we are still the hairy Britons and London is Imperial Rome. You will have to come to London.

Lord Beaverbrook, Canadian-born British press baron, interviewed in 1918 by the correspondent Beverley Baxter for his memoirs *Strange Street* (1935).

The American empire is a central reality for Canadians. It is an empire characterized by militarism abroad and racism at home. Canadian resources and diplomacy have been enlisted in support of that empire.

"The Waffle Manifesto: For an Independent Socialist Canada" (1969) reprinted in *The Canadian Forum*, Dec. 1989.

All permission fees received by the author are being utilized in the struggle against American cultural and economic imperialism in Canada and throughout the Third World.

Note accompanying the reprinting of author **Dave Godfrey**'s story "The Hard-Headed Collector" in *The Canadian Century: English-Canadian Writing Since Confederation* (1973), an anthology edited by A.J.M. Smith for Gage Educational Publishing Limited, a well-established Toronto publishing house that had been acquired by American interests.

INDEPENDENCE

You fought to remain colonists instead of struggling to become independent, then do remain slaves!

Marquis de Lafayette, French general who fought with the Americans in the Revolutionary War, upon learning of French-Canadian resistance to the American Revolution of 1776, quoted by Louis Landry in *Encyclopédie du Québec* (1973).

For to pursue independence seriously is to make visible the necessity of socialism in Canada.

"The Waffle Manifesto: For an Independent Socialist Canada" (1969) reprinted in *The Canadian Forum*, Dec. 1989.

The Independence movement is linked to a universal phenomenon: Québec is at the tail end of the great colonial liberation era which followed the Second World War. If we don't hurry, we're about to miss the boat. Like it or not, we are a colony within Canada.

René Lévesque, separatist, quoted in *La Presse*, 9 Jan. 1969, *Quotations from René Lévesque* (1977) edited by Jean Côté and Marcel Chaput, translated by Robert Guy Scully and Jacqueline Perrault.

The road to independence must be paved with sound financing.

Jacques Parizeau, Quebec Minister of Finance, quoted by Peter C. Newman in "Column," *Maclean's*, 13 June 1977.

The independence we envisage is the only way possible to us because, as I said when I spoke to American businessmen in January 1977, "Canada and Quebec cannot continue to live like two scorpions in the same bottle," to borrow from Churchill's metaphor.

René Lévesque, Quebec Premier, *My Québec* (1979) translated by Gaynor Fitzpatrick.

Freedom is not magic. Proclaiming your independence does not necessarily make you independent or free. To me, they were rejecting the most challenging opportunity: to be partners in a big country in North America, a country that would be the future of the world.

Roch Carrier, author, referring to separatist-minded friends in the 1960s, "Canada Is a Grand Dream," *Canadian Living*, September 1992.

If every racial and ethnic group that occupies a specific piece of land... became a separate nation, we might have 800 countries in the world, we may have a difficult time having a functioning economy or functioning global polity.

Bill Clinton, U.S. President, address, conference on federalism, Mont-Tremblant, Que., 8 Oct. 1999, quoted in *The Toronto Star* the following day. Quebec Premier Lucien Bouchard told reporters, "Of course he had Quebec in his mind. It was obvious. Who would say the contrary?"

INDIA

The evidence of Hindu and Buddhist influences all over America from Alaska to the Andes is overwhelming.

Marius Barbeau, folklorist, referring to pre-Columbian occulation of the continent, letter of 18 Dec. 1961, reproduced by scholar Chaman Lal in *Hindu America: Revealing the Forgotten Story of the Imprints of Hindu and Buddhist Cultures on the Ancient Americas* (6th edition, 1966).

Though in the intervening long summers and winters I have wandered over many lands in many climes and lived among diverse races—black, brown, yellow, and white—I remain as convinced as I was twenty years ago that there is no country in the world as beautiful as Canada, and there are no people in the world nicer than the Canadians.

Khushwant Singh, Indian novelist and for six months information officer with the Indian High Commission in Ottawa, address, Expo 67, Montreal, "Orient Pearl in the World Oyster," *Man and His World: The Noranda Lectures* (1968).

The only place in the world where you'll find more Goans is in Goa, for example.

Sue Zesiger, writer, commenting on the number of immigrants in Toronto from the territory of Goa on the west coast of India, "Best Cities," *Fortune*, 11 Nov. 1996.

There is a saying in Indian: Patience is the sandal which the wise man wears because he cannot pave the road with leather.

Tim Ward, traveller and writer, *Arousing the Goddess* (1996).

INDIAN PEOPLES See also ABORIGINAL PEOPLES, LAND CLAIMS, MÉTIS PEOPLE, NATIVE PEOPLES

Our sons shall wed your daughters, and henceforth we shall be one people.

Samuel de Champlain, explorer and colonist, "Brief Narrative" (1599), *Voyages to New France: 1599–1603* (1971) translated by Michael Macklem.

Marvel you not at the thin population of America, nor at the rudeness and ignorance of the people; for you must account your inhabitants of America as a young people, younger a thousand years at the least than the rest of the world....

Speech of "the Governor of Bensalem," the capital of the New Atlantis in the Pacific Ocean, in **Sir Francis Bacon**'s speculative work *The New Atlantis* (1627).

A remarkable sameness characterized the countenances of the whole nation—a dull, phlegmatic want of expression with very little variation.

James Cook, English sea captain, description of the Nootka at Nootka Sound, Vancouver Island, 31 March 1778, *Seventy North to Fifty South: The Story of Captain Cook's Last Voyage* (1969) edited by Paul W. Drake.

What has become of the spirit, the wisdom, and the justice of your nations? Is it possible that you should barter away your ancient glory, and break through the most solemn treaties, for a few blankets or a little rum or powder.

Joseph Brant, Mohawk leader, address to leaders of the Six Nations, quoted by William L. Stone in *Life of Joseph Brant—Thayendanegea; Including the Indian Wars of the American Revolution* (1838).

Should you ask me, whence these stories? / Whence these legends and traditions, / With the odours of the forest, / With the dew and damp of meadows, / With the curling smoke of wigwams, / With the rushing of great rivers, / With their frequent repetitions, / And their wild reverberations, / As of thunder in the mountains? / I should answer, I should tell you, / "From the forests and the prairies, / From the great lakes of the Northland."

Familiar opening lines **H.W. Longfellow**'s narrative poem *The Song of Hiawatha* (1855) set largely in the region north of Lake Superior.

The Dominion has done very well by its Indians, of whom it has a hundred thousand. It has tried to civilize them by means of schools, missions, and farm instructors....

Charles Dudley Warner, American travel writer, *Studies in the South and West* (1889).

His mind ran over possibilities, deserts, angry Americans, Japanese, Chinese—perhaps Red Indians! (Were there still Red Indians?)

Thoughts of the character Bert Smallways on Goat Island in the Niagara River in **H.G. Wells**' imaginative novel about a German air invasion of America, *The War in the Air and Particularly How Mr. Bert Smallways Fared While It Lasted* (1908).

Forget that I was Pauline Johnson, but remember always that I was Takahionwake, the Mohawk that humbly aspired to be the saga singer of her people, the bard of the noblest folk the world has ever seen, the sad historian of her own heroic race.

E. Pauline Johnson, poet, referring to her Indian name, meaning "double wampum," quoted by Ernest Thompson Seton in his introduction to Johnson's *The Shagganappi* (1913).

I want to get rid of the Indian problem. I do not think as a matter of fact, that the country ought to continuously protect a class of people who are able to stand alone.... Our objective is to continue until there is not a single Indian in Canada that has not been absorbed into the body politic and there is no Indian question, and no Indian Department, that is the whole object of this Bill.

Duncan Campbell Scott, Deputy Superintendent General of Indian Affairs, testifying before the Special Committee of the House of Commons examining the Indian Act amendments of 1920, noted by John Leslie in *The Historical Development of the Indian Act* (1978).

One memorial stone reads: / "We, near whose bones you stand, were Iroquois. / The wide land which is now yours, was ours / Friendly hands have given us back enough for a tomb."

Carl Sandburg, U.S. poet, Iroquois epitaph, "Section 85," *The People, Yes* (1936) included in *Complete Poems* (1950).

The Indian, on this continent, has suffered wrongs, and endured indignities, through the centuries, such as almost no other race has ever been called on to endure.

Grey Owl, author and naturalist, interviewed by R.E. Knowles in *The Toronto Star,* 2 March 1936.

I am a chief, but my quiver has no arrows and my bow is slack. My warriors have been lost among the white man's cities. They have melted away into the crowds as once they did amid the forests. But this time they will not return. Yes, my quiver is empty, my bow is slack.

Chief Dan George, elected chief and Native elder, address, March 1967, Playhouse Theatre, Vancouver, *Abundant Rivers* (1972), Indian Heritage Series, Volume 3.

Why, I'm proud to be part Indian and part white because... / Man, I've got the best of two worlds.

Lines from **Brant Joseph Maracle**'s poem "The Best of Two Worlds," *The Fever and Frustration of the Indian Heart* (1972).

From great-grandparents to great-grandchildren we are only knots in a string.

Naskapi expression quoted by Fraser Symington in *The First Canadians* (1978).

These are still the men of tomorrow. / The proud races, / The men of peace, / The quiet ones.

Lines from Micmac poet **Rita Joe**'s poem "Men of Peace," *Poems of Rita Joe* (1978).

I lost my talk / The talk you took away. // Let me find my talk / So I can teach you about me.

Lines from Micmac poet **Rita Joe**'s poem "I Lost My Talk," *Song of Eskasoni: More Poems of Rita Joe* (1988).

Like the Celtic tradition, there is a rich mythology in Cree, but one which is specific to our landscape. We inherited about 10,000 years of a tradition, a literary tradition that happens to be oral.

Tomson Highway, Cree playwright, interviewed by Ann Wilson in *Other Solitudes: Canadian Multicultural Fictions* (1990) edited by Linda Hutcheon and Marion Richmond.

Inside a *gwam,* you could be anywhere, Finland or Quebec, 1992 B.C. or 1992 A.D.; but you are at home. It is outside time, magical.

Arauco, a Canadian-born Micmac, discussing the gwam or wigwam in which members of his band live near Kittila in Finland, quoted by Carl Honoré in *The Globe and Mail,* 18 April 1992.

I don't know why they're so scared. I don't know what one poor little Indian can do.

Elijah Harper, Cree, opponent of the Meech Lake Accord, following announcement that he would run as a Liberal candidate in the northern Manitoba riding of Churchill, St. John's, Nfld., *The Toronto Star,* 26 March 1993.

I didn't hear my first Haida song until I was sixteen and I didn't see my first Haida dance until I was twenty-two. My children have a head start. We're reconnecting with that belief of what it is to be Haida.

Robert Davidson, artist and Haida elder, quoted by Christopher Dafoe in *The Globe and Mail,* 3 July 1993.

We've made enough mistakes for them. It's time for them to make their own mistakes.

Jean Chrétien, Prime Minister and former Minister of Indian Affairs, quoted by Edward Greenspon in *The Globe and Mail,* 22 Nov. 1996. The remark, said to be characteristic, was quoted upon the tabling of the Royal Commission on Aboriginal Peoples.

INDIGNATION

Moral indignation is a technique used to endow the idiot with dignity.

Marshall McLuhan, communications pioneer, quoted by Philip Marchand in "Obsolete," *Forward through the Rearview Mirror* (1996) edited by Paul Benedetti and Nancy DeHart.

INDIVIDUALISM

The basic assumptions of possessive individualism—that man is free and human by virtue of his sole proprietorship of his own person, and that human society is essentially a series of market relations—were deeply embedded in the seventeenth-century foundations.

C.B. Macpherson, political scientist, *The Political Theory of Possessive Individualism* (1962).

INDUSTRY See also LABOUR, MANUFACTURING

A central objective of Canadian socialists must be to further the democratization process in industry. The Canadian trade union movement throughout its history has waged a democratic battle against the so-called rights or prerogatives of ownership and management.

"The Waffle Manifesto: For an Independent Socialist Canada" (1969) reprinted in *The Canadian Forum*, Dec. 1989.

The Japanese have their high-tech and the Americans have their car industry. We can become the best in the world perhaps in food sciences, water technology, clean air technology—and the good part is that these are all things we're already good at.

Patrick Carson, environmental affairs specialist for Loblaws and co-author of the booklet *Green Is Gold*, quoted by Ben Knight in *Coles' Booktalk*, Spring 1991.

INFLATION See also ECONOMICS

One of the greatest allies Stalin has in the world today is inflation.... We cannot beat Stalin with a fifty-six-cent dollar.

John G. Diefenbaker, Member of Parliament, House of Commons, 20 April 1951.

INFORMATION See also COMPUTERS

In the age of information, it is information itself that becomes environmental. The satellites and antennae projected from our planet, for example, have transformed the planet from being an environment into a probe.

Marshall McLuhan, communications pioneer, *Through the Vanishing Point: Space in Poetry and Painting* (1968) with Harley Parker.

Faced with information overload, we have no alternative but pattern-recognition.

Marshall McLuhan, communications pioneer, *Counterblast* (1969).

To paraphrase Marshall McLuhan, the medium is also the money. Much of the new wealth today is being generated by people trading in information.

E.G. Burton, President of Simpsons Limited, quoted in *Carleton Journalism Review*, Winter 1977.

If you wish to acquire anybody's relevant knowledge quickly, start with their ignorance.

Barrington Nevitt, communications consultant, *The Communication Ecology: Re-presentation versus Replica* (1982).

Energy is no longer the most important or profitable concern in the world. Information is.

Allan Fotheringham, columnist, observing that International Thomson Organization sold off its North Sea oil interests in favour of expanding its newspaper chain, *Birds of a Feather: The Press and the Politicians* (1989).

Those who do not learn will become the peasants of the Information Age. Societies that do not give all their people future-related education will be left behind.

Frank Feather, futurologist, *G-Forces: Reinventing the World—The 35 Global Forces Restructuring Our World* (1989).

Paper remains the best, the fastest and the most democratic interactive medium around. It is the best "random-access memory" available.

Derrick de Kerckhove, communications theorist, "The Future," *The Globe and Mail*, 5 March 1994.

Voodoo priests believe they receive information from a hierarchy of gods. We get ours through a hierarchy of technology.

Frank Ogden, futurologist, quoted by Laura Jeffrey in *The Globe and Mail*, 13 April 1994.

With a computer, Western European technology is able to reduce all technological information to zero and one. The Chinese achieved this thousands of years ago with the I Ching. They were able to reduce all human phenomena down to yin and yang.

Duke Redbird, Native spokesperson, interviewed by Ron LeBlanc in "Duke Redbird," *The Core* (Toronto tabloid), Feb. 1995.

INFORMATION HIGHWAY See COMPUTERS, INTERNET

INNOCENCE

Oh dear! What a pain! / What a primitive way to meet and chat! / We in Canada are blessed / With innocent freedom!

Boast of the wealthy Canadian merchant named Slook from the libretto *La Cambiale di Matrimonio* (The Promissory Note of Marriage), premiered in 1810, the earliest operatic farce written and composed by the Italian composer **Gioacchino Rossini**, "one of the greatest storytellers in music who ever lived," according to Greg Gatenby who translated part of it for *The Wild Is Always There: Canada through the Eyes of Foreign Writers* (1993).

It crosses Farb's mind that days—unlike babies—are never born innocent....

Thoughts of the lawyer named Isadore Farb in **Morley Torgov**'s novel *St. Farb's Day* (1990).

INNOVATION

I think the opportunity for progress is a metre wide. But we've only gone a centimetre.

David Mitchell, founder of the Ernest Manning Awards which reward innovators, quoted by Cathryn Motherwell in *The Globe and Mail,* 18 Nov. 1991.

We constantly test new products. We're consumer-driven so what will happen ten years from today will depend on what consumers want to happen ten years from today.

George Cohon, President, McDonald's Restaurants of Canada Ltd., interviewed in *The Canadian Jewish News,* 4 Nov. 1993.

INSECTS

When a cockroach is in love or mounts another cockroach, he feels as if all the stars are looking down at him, he feels at one with the cosmos. Cockroaches or human beings, it's the grandest emotion.

Irving Layton, poet, observation made in 1972, *Taking Sides: The Collected Social and Political Writings* (1977) edited by Howard Aster.

INSPIRATION

I have long considered the creative impulse to be a visit—a thing of grace, not commanded or owned so much as awaited, prepared for. A thing, also of mystery.

Loreena McKennitt, Celtic composer and singer, album note, *The Visit* (1991).

INSTITUTIONS

The prestige of Canadian institutions is inversely proportionate to their profitability.

Kildare Dobbs, author, "The Almost Invisible, Almost Unknown, All-Canadian Honour," *Smiles and Chukkas & Other Vanities* (1995).

Someone once told me, "Create an institution and you have a Canadian asking to be a member of it."

Ferry de Kerckhove, foreign-affairs officer, presentation, seminar, Canadian Institute of Strategic Studies, Toronto, 6 Nov. 1997.

INTEGRITY

Nobody wholly trusts a man of integrity.

Robin Skelton, poet and aphorist, *A Devious Dictionary* (1991).

INTELLIGENCE See also IDEAS, SECURITY & INTELLIGENCE, THOUGHTS, WISDOM

There are many enemies to intellectual life, but they may be all classed under the one head as *the world.*

William Dawson LeSueur, philosopher, "The Intellectual Life" (1875), *A Critical Spirit: The Thought of William Dawson LeSueur* (1977) edited by A.B. McKillop.

But a new country has to *import* its Shakespeares and Newtons, as it imports the choicer wines. As to Einstein, the present-day Newton, the United States has got hold of him, I am afraid. Then Canada should hold out for a Leibnitz.

Wyndham Lewis, author and artist, "On Canada" (1940–44), *Wyndham Lewis in Canada* (1971) edited by George Woodcock.

Joueurs de piano

French for "piano players," the term used by Quebec Premier **Maurice Duplessis** in the 1950s for intellectuals not to his liking, as noted by Jean Provencher in *René Lévesque: Portrait of a Québécois* (1975) translated by David Ellis.

Intelligent life may turn out to be a short-term evolutionary dead end. It has already had a cataclysmic effect on the rest of the biosphere.

Brian Fawcett, cultural commentator, *Public Eye: An Investigation into the Disappearance of the World* (1990).

Most people, upon hearing the word *intelligence,* would think of the CIA before they would Einstein. This is not a minor matter of linguistic evolution. Intelligence, after all, was one of the central conceptions of the rational revolution.

John Ralston Saul, author, *Voltaire's Bastards: The Dictatorship of Reason in the West* (1992).

On our planet, it's the human being whose intelligence has outstripped that of any other living species. Elsewhere in the universe, the situation might be different.

Hubert Reeves, astrophysicist, *Malicorne: Earthly Reflections of an Astrophysicist* (1993) translated from the French edition of 1900 by Donald Winkler.

I'm also intelligent. Less so than Simone Weil. My intelligence, too, is already going downhill—though differently from my beauty—and it, too, will end up as worms or ashes. But still. For the time being I'm quite intelligent.

Nancy Huston, Prairie-born, Paris-based author, "Dealing with What's Dealt," *Salamagundi,* Spring–Summer, 1995.

In place of thought, we have opinion; in place of argument, we have journalism; in place of polemic, we have personality profiles; in place of reputation, we have celebrity.

Michael Ignatieff, essayist, "The Decline and Fall of the Public Intellectual," *Queen's Quarterly,* Fall 1997.

INTEREST See also FINANCE

Interviewer: Name the world's greatest invention.

Bronfman: Interest.

Response of **Sam Bronfman**, distiller and philanthropist, quoted by Robert Kaiser in *The Toronto Star,* 14 Aug. 1975.

INTERNATIONALISM See also FOREIGN AFFAIRS

"The new internationalism is upon us." No country stands to gain or lose more than Canada.

Harold Adams Innis, social scientist, alluding to the theme of C. Foreman's *The New Internationalism* (1934), "Economic Nationalism," *Papers and Proceedings of the Sixth Annual Meeting of the Canadian Political Science Association, 1934* (1934).

I believe that the greatest contribution that Canada can make to Great Britain is to maintain the most friendly possible relations with the United States.

J.S. Woodsworth, M.P., declining to make unanimous the motion that a state of war exists with Germany through the invocation of the War Measures Act, House of Commons, 8 Sept. 1939.

Lester B. Pearson: Canadians have the United States to the south and the Soviet Union to the North. We feel pressure from both directions.

L.M. Kaganovitch: As far as we are concerned, friendly pressure.

Lester B. Pearson: The strongest pressure I know is friendly pressure.

Adapted from an exchange that took place at a friendly dinner in Moscow in 1956 hosted by future Prime Minister **Lester B. Pearson** and the Soviet representative **L.M. Kaganovitch**, as quoted by Mitchell Sharp in *Which Reminds Me...: A Memoir* (1994).

Why so much for countries in Asia and so little for the rights of Quebec?

Maurice Duplessis, Quebec Premier, objecting to the assistance that Canada committed to the Colombo Plan, *Le Temps,* 17 May 1956. Quoted by Herbert F. Quinn in *The Union Nationale: A Study in Quebec Nationalism* (1963). This became the party slogan in the 1956 provincial election campaign, as Léon Dion noted in *Quebec: The Unfinished Revolution* (1976) translated by Thérèse Romer: "Duplessis gives to his province, while the Liberals give to foreigners."

The greatness of any country or group is to be found in what it gives to the world. It seems to me that it is in that direction that Canada will be great, not by its power but by its giving, by its radiance, by its example.

Elizabeth II, Queen of Canada, address, Expo 67, Montreal, April 1967, quoted in *Weekend Magazine,* 30 April 1997.

When Canada stamps its foot, the world does not shake. But when Canada, beginning to shake off its diffidence, its inwardness, speaks loud and clear, the world echoes back, whether in its recognition of Canadian artistry or its appreciation of Canadian goodheartedness in an ever-troubled world.

Stephen Brook, English travel writer, *Maple Leaf Rag: Travels across Canada* (1987).

We live between the two superpowers, but we do not see them as morally equivalent in any way.

Brian Mulroney, Prime Minister, addressing a joint sitting of U.S. Congress, 27 April 1988, quoted in *The Toronto Star* the following day.

There are so many great things we can do as masters in our own house, but very little we can do as frightened tenants who have nothing left with which to pay the rent.

Mel Hurtig, nationalist, *The Betrayal of Canada* (1991).

How hypocritical do we appear to the nations of the South as we offer them a hand while standing on their bootstraps?

Ivan L. Head, Director, International Development Research Centre, rhetorical question, *On a Hinge of History: The Mutual Vulnerability of North and South* (1991).

On the whole, we have had the luxury of needing to do little thinking about the world. And if we play a less vigorous role in world affairs today than fifty years ago, it is not without broad public acquiescence.

John Cruickshank, journalist, reviewing Arthur Andrew's *The Rise and Fall of a Middle Power* (1993), *The Globe and Mail*, 26 Feb. 1994.

INTERNET See also COMPUTERS

The next medium, whatever it is—it may be the extension of consciousness—will include television as its content, not as its environment, and will transform television into an art form.

Marshall McLuhan, communications pioneer, observation made in 1970, "A McLuhan Sourcebook," *The Essential McLuhan* (1995) edited by Eric McLuhan and Frank Zingrone. Here is an anticipation of the 500-channel universe and the Internet.

It is apparent that Canada is in danger of having inadequate Internet networking capacities compared to the U.S. The current state of the planned upgrade makes one wonder if Canada is building a dirt road while our neighbours to the south build an information highway.

Jim Carroll and **Rick Broadhead**, computer specialists, *Canadian Internet Handbook: 1994 Edition* (1994).

I consider it to be the third most significant development in human communication after the invention of the printing press and the telephone. It is quickly becoming the network by which we will begin to access the whole of human knowledge.

Jim Carroll, computer consultant, defining the Internet as an "information appliance," *The Toronto Star*, 2 Nov. 1994.

The Internet promises to achieve what no charter of rights can: putting printing presses in the hands of many.

Parker Barss Donham, political columnist, address, Symposium on Free Speech and Privacy in the Information Age, University of Waterloo, Waterloo, Ont., 26 Nov. 1994.

Mindful of Pierre Berton's book *The Last Spike*, which describes the role of the Canadian Pacific Railway in nation building, one student of Canadian history labelled Canada's information highway "The Next Spike."

David Johnston, Deborah Johnston, and Sunny Handa, specialists, *Getting Canada Online: Understanding the Information Highway* (1995).

If we do it right, and do the right thing, the Age of Networked Intelligence can be an age of unprecedented wealth, fairness, true democracy, and social justice.

Don Tapscott, author, *The Digital Economy: Promise and Peril in the Age of Networked Intelligence* (1996).

The Internet will one day plug together every computer chip in the world.

Jim Carroll and **Rick Broadhead**, Internet specialists, *1996 Canadian Internet Handbook* (1996).

I imagine that the World Wide Web and its modest wonders are no more than the test pattern for whatever the 21st century will regard as its equivalent medium. Not that I can even remotely imagine what that medium might actually be.

William Gibson, author, "The Net Is a Waste of Time," *The New York Times Magazine*, 14 July 1996.

The Internet is destined to become the world's most important communications medium, gobbling up traditional analogue media as quickly as they can be switched over to digital technology. Private commercial and financial communications have already gone digital and migrated on-line more or less en masse; public services are quickly following.

Wade Rowland, science and technology writer, *Spirit of the Web: The Age of Information from Telegraph to Internet* (1997).

INTERPRETATION

Some things increase the gain of exploration / By constantly eluding explanation.

Lines from **Robert Finch**'s poem "Cautionary Treizaine," *Miracle at the Jetty* (1991).

INTERVIEWS See also NEWS

Many a great man's reputation for wit is due to his having been interviewed by a bright reporter.

Bob Edwards, publisher, *The Eye Opener*, 22 Feb. 1919.

You may say that I said that I have nothing to say.

Arthur Meighen, sometime Prime Minister, refusing to explain why he was inactive in a federal election campaign, interviewed by R.E. Knowles in *The Toronto Star*, 23 July 1930.

What does it feel like to be a genius?

R.E. Knowles, interviewer, questioning the violinist Jascha Heifetz, *The Toronto Star*, 18 Oct. 1933. Heifetz's response was somewhat equivocal: "I see what you mean."

"Mr. Kreisler, what is art?" I asked. "Mr. journalist, what is love?" was the apt reply.

R.E. Knowles, interviewer, questioning the violinist Fritz Kreisler, *The Toronto Star*, 14 Nov. 1933.

I don't see any point in making anything but controversial statements. There is no other way of getting any attention at all. I mean you cannot get people thinking until you say something that really shocks them; dislocates them.

Marshall McLuhan, communications pioneer, "Education in the Electronic Age" (1967), *The Best of Times / The Worst of Times: Contemporary Issues in Canadian Education* (1972) edited by Hugh A. Stevenson, Robert M. Stamp, and J. Donald Wilson.

I'm not responsible for the answers. I'm only responsible for the questions.

Barbara Frum, broadcaster and interviewer, quoted by Clyde Gilmour in *The Toronto Star*, 12 Dec. 1981.

Most television interviewing is done to show off the interviewer, not his subject.

Robert MacNeil, broadcaster and memoirist, *The Right Place at the Right Time* (1982).

The most rewarding compliment I can receive about my work is to be told I have asked exactly the question the listener would have asked if he were in my place.

Peter Gzowski, host of CBC Radio's *Morningside*, in *The Private Voice: A Journal of Reflections* (1988).

Anything said off the cuff has usually been written on it first.

Robin Skelton, poet and aphorist, *A Devious Dictionary* (1991).

A bad interview is like a bad blind date. You've invited him to your house so as the evening progress you can't flee, however much you might want to. If only it were his place—you could sneak off into the night, leaving no forwarding address.

Pamela Wallin, TV interviewer, *Since You Asked* (1998).

INTIMACY

Sexual services do not survive and thrive unless they fulfill specific needs. When we discover that our piece of plastic currency can be used to buy an orgasm (the so-called ultimate sexual climax), we suddenly realize that there is a great need for intimacy. We are forced to recognize the problems in maintaining close relationships.

Jack Pollock, artist and memoirist, observations made in 1983, *Dear M: Letters from a Gentleman of Excess* (1989).

Facetime.

Neologism devised to refer to a one-on-one relationship first used by Doug Coupland in his novel *Polaroids from the Dead* (1996).

INTOLERANCE

Zero tolerance. Quite apart from whatever particular moral targets it is aimed at, this is in and of itself an ugly slogan of intolerance. But let nobody be fooled. You cannot get to tolerance by getting more and more deeply immersed in intolerance. Illiberalism will never expand the horizons of freedom and diversity.

John Fekete, philosopher, *Moral Panic: Biopolitics Rising* (2nd ed., 1995).

INTUITION

Nine-tenths of a woman's intuition is suspicion.

Bob Edwards, publisher, *The Eye Opener*, 22 Feb. 1919.

INUIT See also ABORIGINAL PEOPLES, ESKIMO ART, NATIVE PEOPLES, NUNAVUT

Eskimaux Indians

First use in English of these words to refer to the Eskimo (today's Inuit) was made by fur trader **Arthur Dobbs** in *An Account of the Countries Adjoining to Hudson's Bay* (1744).

Never in my life have I seen such a joyous and carefree people, full of mirth though starving, full of humour though freezing in their poor, tattered clothing....

Knud Rasmussen, Danish Arctic explorer, describing life in a small fishing settlement on King William's Island, N.W.T., in 1925–26, quoted by Tryggvi J. Oleson in *Early Voyages and Northern Approaches: 1000–1632* (1963).

Yes, the Canadian was certainly the most isolated people on earth, except for the Eskimo.

Wyndham Lewis, British artist, "Hill 100: outline for an Unwritten Novel" (1942), *Wyndham Lewis in Canada* (1971) edited by George Woodcock.

On the assumption that the future of mankind is to be very catastrophic, I should have prophesied, even as lately as a few years ago, that whatever future we might be going to have would lie with the Tibetans and Eskimos, because each of these peoples occupied, till quite lately, an unusually sheltered position. "Sheltered" means, of course, sheltered from the dangers arising from human folly and wickedness, not sheltered from the rigors of the physical environment.

Arnold J. Toynbee, historian, *Civilization on Trial* (1948).

Eskimo . . . what period?

Michael Langham, artistic director, Stratford Festival, when informed by actor-director David Gardner that the Canadian Players troupe would produce Shakespeare's play *King Lear* in an Eskimo setting. The production was premiered with William Hutt wearing snow-goggles, Crest Theatre, Toronto, 23 Oct. 1960.

There are only very few Eskimos, but millions of whites, just like mosquitoes. It is something very special and wonderful to be an Eskimo—they are like the snow geese. If an Eskimo forgets his language and Eskimo ways, he will be nothing but just another mosquito.

Abraham Okpik, Inuit elder, "What does It Mean to Be an Eskimo?" *North*, March–April 1963.

There are two men fighting. They are both Inuit. One is the first and the other the last Eskimo. I don't know who will be the one to die first.

Inuit lore quoted by Stephen Guion Williams in *In the Middle: The Inuit Today* (1983).

Canadians like to talk about us eating frozen meat and living in the cold. It gives Canada something that other countries don't have. Everybody likes the Inuit.

Nellie Cournoyea, Inuit spokesperson, "The Independent Inuit," *Maclean's*, 14 July 1986.

When I began the book, a current spelling for white man was *kabloona*, big eyebrows. This has since progressed from *kabluna, kadluna, kalunait, qadlunaq* to *qallunaaq*. I have used the latter because it is the latest.

Lois Darroch, author and Arctic traveller, referring to Inuktitut, *Time Between: Akuningini* (1998).

The Inuit in the high Arctic, for example, teach us that there are other possibilities, other ways of being, other ways of living on the planet. This idea is one that can only fill you with hope.

Wade Davis, anthropologist, "What's Next?" *Saturday Night*, Dec. 1999–Jan. 2000.

INVENTION

Almost all great discoveries and inventions have been made by men who united theoretical and practical knowledge.

John Langton, pioneer settler and writer, "The Importance of Scientific Studies to Practical Men," *Supplement to the Canadian Journal*, March, 1854.

The telephone was conceived in Brantford in 1874, and born in Boston in 1975.

Alexander Graham Bell, inventor, address, "The Substance of My Latest Research," Empire Club of Canada, Toronto, 1 Nov. 1917.

If there is a characteristic that unites us it is a deep reluctance to believe that the wheel either has been or can be invented.

I.M. Owen, columnist, *Saturday Night*, March 1978.

Innovation is always the mother of necessities, old and new.

Barrington Nevitt, communications, consultant, *ABC of Prophecy: Understanding the Environment* (1985).

INVESTMENT See also FINANCE

But it need scarcely be pointed out that human personality is more dependent on the right to own a home than on the right to own a piece of paper on which are printed the magic words "Ten Shares of CPR Preferred Stock."

F.R. Scott, constitutional law authority, "Gare aux mots!" (1945), *A New Endeavour: Selected Political Essays, Letters, and Addresses* (1986) edited by Michiel Horn.

In our kitchen life we knew stock only as the base for soup. It has taken on added seasoning since we broadened our base of understanding. Stock is not soup, but you still have to watch the pot!

Betty Jane Wylie and **Lynne MacFarlane**, writer and financial consultant, *Everywoman's Money Book* (1989).

A broker is someone who invests your money until it's his.

*

Wealth beyond your wildest dreams is possible if you learn the golden secret: Invest ten percent of all you make for long-time growth. If you follow that one simple guideline, someday you'll be a very rich man."

David Chilton, investment adviser, *The Wealthy Barber: The Common Sense Guide to Successful Financial Planning* (1989).

When the Indians sold Manhattan to the Dutch for beads worth twenty-four dollars, it seemed like the natives got taken. But if they had invested that money at 8 percent interest, today their tribe would be worth trillions of dollars.

Lines spoken by the barber Roy Miller in investment adviser **David Chilton**'s *The Wealthy Barber: The Common Sense Guide to Successful Financial Planning* (1989).

Speculation, n. A reckless, irresponsible and avaricious gamble that does not pay off, as opposed to an "investment," which does.

David Olive, business commentator, *White Knights and Poison Pills: A Cynic's Dictionary of Business Jargon* (1990).

I Went to a Broker, and Now I'm Broke

Title of Chapter Ten, devoted to brokers, in **Walter Stewart**'s *The Golden Fleece: Why the Stock Market Costs You Money* (1992).

IRAQ

But nobody spoke of the human rights of this Canadian citizen of U.S. nationality. After he came to Iraq, they killed him.

Saddam Hussein, President of Iraq, referring on television to the murder in Brussels of Canadian-born arms engineer Gerald Bull, 22 March 1990, quoted by Dale Grand in *Wilderness of Mirrors: The Life of Gerald Bull* (1991).

[The U.S. has] no opinion on Arab-Arab conflicts, like your border disagreement with Kuwait.

April Glaspie, Vancouver-born U.S. Ambassador to Iraq, appointed in 1988, meeting with the Iraqi President Saddam Hussein on 25 July 1990 in Baghdad, one week before Iraq's invasion of Kuwait, recalled during Glaspie's appearance before the U.S. Senate Foreign Relations Committee, March 1991, as quoted by Robert D. Kaplan in *The Arabists: The Romance of an American Elite* (1993).

If Iraq was the cradle of civilization, the bough must have broken, the baby falling into a brutally battered childhood, because it had certainly grown into one hell of a disturbed adult.

Paul William Roberts, author, observation prompted by the sign in the Baghdad airport in 1990 that read "Welcome to Iraq: The Cradle of Civilization," *comment*, 1995.

IRISH PEOPLE See also BRITISH EMPIRE & COMMONWEALTH, UNITED KINGDOM

Deep in Canadian woods we met / From one bright island flown, / Great is the land we tread, but yet / Our hearts are with our own.

Verse from an unnamed traditional Irish song (which resembles the "Scottish Boat-song") sung in Limerick in the 1950s, as recalled by a character in Frank McCourt's *Angela's Ashes: A Memoir* (1996).

I've a certain affection for Canada. Only thing I know is the Fenians tried to invade at some time and they finally caught up with Thomas D'Arcy McGee on the steps of your Parliament.

Brendan Behan, Irish playwright, quoted by Jack Gale in *The Toronto Star*, 2 Nov. 1960. Behan was in Toronto as a mystery guest on CBC-TV's *Front Page Challenge*.

Ireland is the Israel that failed.

Irving Layton, poet and aphorist, *The Whole Bloody Bird (obs, aphs & Pomes)* (1969).

Celticity (if this is a word) is not dreamy twilight, as some think. It's something madder.

Gerald Owen, reviewer, "Briefly Noted," *The Idler*, March 1992.

The animosities here are not as lethal as in Ireland, where people speak the same language. The friction appears to be worse when people speak the same language. In Canada the two linguistic groups are living in somewhat separate worlds and that cushions the anger.

Conor Cruise O'Brien, Irish writer, interviewed by Michael Coren in "Irish Ires," *Saturday Night*, Dec. 1994.

ISLAM

The Sufi Message of Love, Harmony and Beauty, which is yet in its infancy in Canada, is charged with greatest energy; motivating the Sufi brothers and sisters in a strong movement of wisdom, inspiring all more and more toward the materialization of its great Ideals.... The day might come when Lake O'Hara shall be known in Canada as the sacred Sufi hill.

Hidayat Inayat Khan, son of mystic and musician Inayat Khan, leader of the International Sufi Movement, who in 1982 led the first in a series of annual retreats at Lake O'Hara, Rocky Mountains, *Sufi Teachings: Lectures from Lake O'Hara* (1996), as noted in "The Man from Kaf Mountain," *B.C. Bookworld*, Summer 1996.

Sufism is a process. By this I mean to suggest the kind of process involved in aging cheese, or fermenting wine. Sufism is the processing of human beings.

Murat Yagan, Istanbul-raised, Vancouver-based carpenter and teacher of the Ahmusta Kebzeh tradition of Islam, quoted in "The Man from Kaf Mountain," *B.C. Bookworld*, Summer 1996.

ISRAEL See also JEWISH PEOPLE

Teach your children Hebrew, and Jewish culture and traditions, and send them to Israel.

David Ben-Gurion, President of the State of Israel, address, Beth Tzedec Synagogue, Toronto, quoted in *The Globe and Mail*, 21 March 1967.

If two men are in love with one woman, one is out of luck, but if two peoples are in love with the same land, they can divide it. Once Jews understand this, they can hope for relief from their current agony.

Reuben Slonin, rabbi and author, "Palestinians, Israelis in the Holy Land," *The Toronto Star*, 22 Jan. 1988.

Mordecai Richler is as forcefully committed to Israel splitting into two states as he is to Canada remaining one.

Sam Orbaum, Montreal-raised Israeli journalist, "Make 'em Mad, Mordecai Richler!" *The Jerusalem Post Magazine*, 6 Nov. 1992.

What's going on in Israel is tragic; what's happening in Canada is a farce.

Mordecai Richler, novelist, comparing racial tensions among Arabs and Jews in Israel with separatist pretensions in Quebec, quoted by Sam Orbaum in "Make 'em Mad, Mordecai Richler!" *The Jerusalem Post Magazine*, 6 Nov. 1992.

We now speak less of survival and more of continuity. The difference between the two terms is substantive. For, whereas our quest for survival forced us to be primarily reactive to threats from outside, the stress on continuity prompts us to be proactive, to formulate Judaism positively in the light of the opportunities within the challenges without.

Dow Marmur, rabbi, Holy Blossom Temple, Toronto, Introduction, *On Being a Jew: A Reform Perspective* (1994).

The tourists finally find democracy at its best when they tour a kibbutz, the world's purest form of communism.

Sam Orbaum, Montreal-raised Israeli columnist, "But Seriously," *The Jerusalem Post Magazine*, 14 Oct. 1994.

ITALIAN PEOPLE

Such is Toronto. A brisk city of getting on for half a mill inhabitants, the largest British city in Canada (in spite of the cheery Italian faces that pop up at you out of excavations in the street), liberally endowed with millionaires, not lacking its due nature of destitution, slavery and slums.

Rupert Brooke, poet and traveller, *Letters from America* (1916).

Avero una casetta picolina in Canada, con gelsomini e fiori di lillà.

Lyrics of the popular song "La Casetta in Canada" (A Cottage in Canada) sung in Italy in the 1950s, according to Mark Quinn in *The Toronto Star*, 14 Oct. 1997. It translates: "I have a little cottage in Canada with jasmine and lilacs."

Do you know that there are more Italians living in Toronto, Ontario, than in Venice, Italy, and the Vatican City, combined? It's true!

Bruce Lovatt, journalist, *Bet You Didn't Know* (1981).

I love the Italians. I love the way they just get a thrill out of being alive. The Italians are people who know we are all born to die, so they live every moment of every day.

Barbara Frum, TV personality, quoted by Clyde Gilmour in *The Toronto Star*, 12 Dec. 1981.

What Milan made me understand is that Toronto is one of the world's great cities. It's just too bad it's in Canada.

Bruce Cockburn, composer-singer, after returning from a trip to Italy, quoted by Peter Goddar in *The Toronto Star*, 13 Aug. 1982.

Favourite Cities: When I was a student in Italy, the first places I saw were Pisa and Siena. Siena has remained in my mind with great vividness as a place full of colour and warmth and life.

Northrop Frye, cultural critic, interviewed by Allan Gould, "Chatelaine's Celebrity I.D.," *Chatelaine*, Nov. 1982.

On behalf of the government and people of Canada, I offer a full and unqualified apology for the wrongs done to our fellow Canadians of Italian origin during World War II.

Brian Mulroney, Prime Minister, address, National Congress of Italian Canadians, Concord, Ont., 4 Nov. 1990.

In a recent meeting in Toronto with then-prime minister of Italy Giulio Andreotti, Prime Minister Brian Mulroney joked that the first generation of Italian Canadians had built downtown Toronto and the second generation owned it.

Nino Ricci, novelist, "A Canadian Love Affair," *The Toronto Star*, 4 June 1992.

JAMAICA

Canada can give us, the Third World, the results of experience. I honestly do believe that Jamaica and Canada can make a real contribution to the international dialogue.

Michael Manley, Prime Minister of Jamaica, speech delivered during an official visit to Canada, quoted by Robert Turnbull in *The Globe and Mail*, 25 Oct. 1976.

JAMES BAY PROJECT See also WATER

We the representatives of the Cree bands that will be affected by the James Bay hydro project, or any other project, oppose these projects because we believe only the beavers have the right to build dams in our territory....

Opening resolution of the **Cree of Northern Quebec** to the Minister of Indian Affairs following the Quebec government's decision on 30 April 1971 to proceed with the James Bay Project, as quoted by André Picard in "Background," *The Globe and Mail*, 24 May 1995.

Quebec is a vast hydroelectric plant in the bud, and every day millions of potential kilowatt-hours flow downhill and out to sea. What a waste!

Robert Bourassa, Quebec Premier, referring to the James Bay Project, a gargantuan hydro-electric power project planned for Northern Quebec, quoted by Ron Graham in *The French Quarter* (1992).

Flooding Quebec to Light New York

Heading for **Sam Howe Verhovek**'s cover story, "Power Struggle," *The New York Times Magazine*, 12 Jan. 1992.

Who would consider the total elimination of the Hudson River? Yet great rivers have been destroyed where my people live.

Matthew Coon Come, chief of the Grand Council of the Cree, appearing before an environment-assessment panel at the United Nations, expressing fear for his people should Phase Two of the James Bay Project be completed, quoted by Sam Howe Verhovek, "Power Struggle," *The New York Times Magazine*, 12 Jan. 1992.

Whatever else has been done, it is beautiful. A monument we have created, like the Agora in Athens, or the pyramids in Egypt, or what is left from the Aztecs. It would take half of New York to rival it. Like all the other monuments, it was achieved at great cost. People paid, maybe even a way of life.

Stephen Schecter, essayist, referring to work on Phase Two of the James Bay Project, *Zen and the Art of Post-Modern Canada* (1993).

JAPANESE PEOPLE

Canada is estimated to be moving away from Europe at the rate of a few yards a year. This is excellent except that it brings us nearer Japan.

Stephen Leacock, humorist, "The Empty Continent," *Canada: The Foundations of Its Future* (1941).

The sound policy and the best policy for the Japanese Canadians themselves is to distribute their numbers as widely as possible throughout the country where they will not create feelings of racial hostility.

W.L. Mackenzie King, Prime Minister, writing in his diary in 1944, quoted by David Olive in *Canadian Political Babble* (1993). King is said to have written in his diary in 1945: "It is fortunate that the use of the [atomic] bomb should have been upon the Japanese rather than upon the white races of Europe."

As final resting place, / Canada is chosen. / On citizenship paper, / Signing / Hand trembles.

Takeo Ujo Nakano, Japanese-born Canadian poet, traditional five-line tanka, read before Emperor Hirohito and Empress Nagako, Tokyo, Japan, 1964, *Within the Barbed Wire Fence: A Japanese Man's Account of His Internment in Canada* (1980) written with Leatrice Nakano.

Like the Japanese, the Canadian suffers from a space problem. But while the first is cramped into a tiny, scattered archipelago, the second is reeling with vertigo in the midst of his vast plains.

Description from French author and traveller **Michel Tournier**'s novel *Gemini* (1975).

Love letter from Canada / It might be very happy only if you were here with me / Love letter from Canada / Trees have turned their colour / Walking on the street I moved to tears / The beautiful sunset in Canada reminds me of your voice / Please send me your kisses and stop my breath by your kisses / Love letter from Canada / I am a lonely traveler without you.

Lyrics from "Love Letter from Canada" as translated from the Japanese by **Hiroko Yasuda**. The ballad was so popular it made the Japanese hit parade in 1978. It was recorded by the composer-singer Masaki Hirao, according to *The Toronto Star*, 30 May 1978.

Japan and Asia should be considered the Near West, not the Far East.

Attributed to former Prime Minister **Pierre Elliott Trudeau** by executive Mamoru Iwamoto in *Destinations*, 3 Dec. 1990.

Nearly half a century ago, in the crisis of wartime, the government of Canada wrongfully incarcerated, seized the property of, and disenfranchised thousands of citizens of Japanese ancestry. We cannot change the past. But we must, as a nation, have the courage to face up to these historical facts.

Brian Mulroney, Prime Minister, offering the apologies of the government and people of Canada to Japanese Canadians for the injustices visited upon them during World War II; the apology, accompanied by a comprehensive redress, was delivered in the House of Commons, 22 Sept. 1988.

We have shown our contrition, we feel very rigorously contrite.... I expressed my apologies for the unbearable sufferings and the pains that were caused by the Japanese state against the Canadian people who experienced such sufferings in the Asian Pacific at the hands of the Japanese state.

Toshiki Kaifu, Prime Minister of Japan, official apology for war crimes, Tokyo, *The Toronto Star*, 29 May 1991.

The apology Canada's Hong Kong veterans got this week from Japanese Prime Minister Toshiko Kaifu is only half the apology they deserve. The other half should come from Prime Minister Brian Mulroney for the actions of the Canadian government in the early 1950s which, in what can only be described as reprehensible behaviour, actually signed away the rights of these same veterans to seek financial compensation from the Japanese government for the inhuman treatment they received during the forty-four months they spent in Japan's prisoner of war and slave labour camps.

Fred Cleverley, columnist, *Winnipeg Free Press*, 30 May 1991.

Build a few *ryokan* in North America and psychiatrists would be out of business.

Gabrielle Bauer, travel writer, Tokyo, *My Everest: A Canadian Woman in Japan* (1995). A *ryokan* is a Japanese-style inn that caters to creature comforts.

The Japanese have a higher per capita income than Americans or Canadians, but the average Japanese puts only 40 percent as much carbon dioxide into the atmosphere as the average American or Canadian.

Maurice Strong, Chairman of the Earth Council, quoted by James George in *Asking for the Earth* (1995).

It is the nearest approximation to a science-fictional planet we can actually live in, with deeply strange yet tantalizingly permeable relationships forcing us to constant decipherment on pain of anomie.

Darko Suvin, scholar, *Lessons of Japan: Assayings of Some Intercultural Stances* (1996).

In 1955, Canada and Japan had the same size economy. Today, Japan's economy is four times the size of Canada's, a result achieved by following an independent national policy and refusing to allow the sale to foreign companies of key industries. Even in its current downturn, Japan's unemployment rate is roughly half that of Canada's.

David Orchard, commentator, "The Siren Song of the U.S. Dollar," *Cité Libre*, Winter 2000.

JEALOUSY

I am only jealous when I'm not in love.

Raymond Canale, Italian-born playwright and Toronto-based aphorist, observation made in 1975.

JEWISH PEOPLE See also ANTI-SEMITISM; HOLOCAUST, JEWISH; ISRAEL; JUDAISM

For a while he dallied in Odessa, where, at last, he secured a false passport and, under a false name, took off with his family for America—sailed all the way to Canada! There they had a hard time at first, but, some years later, letters reporting that they were "making a living" began coming from him. These were followed by handsome pictures in which everyone looked like lords and barons.... But precisely how one "made a living," and precisely what life in America was like, could in no way be discovered from them.

Sholom Aleichem, Yiddish humorist, describing his beloved uncle Nissel Rabinowitsch and his family and how they left the Pale of Settlement and settled in 1882 on the Prairies, the future Province of Manitoba, *The Great Fair: Scenes from My Childhood* (1955). A later edition is titled *From the Fair: The Autobiography of Sholom Aleichem* (1985) translated by Curt Leviant.

I do not look back fondly to my college days at McGill University, either. That may have something to do with the then prevailing entrance rules: 750 points for Jews and 600 for everyone else. Nor was it an intellectually exciting institution....

Judith N. Shklar, Harvard-based political scientist, born in Russia, educated at McGill University in Montreal during and after the Second World War, "A Life of Learning" (1989), *Liberalism without Illusions: Essays on Liberal Theory and the Political Vision of Judith N. Shklar* (1996) edited by Bernard Yack.

Canada Needs More Jews

Title of an article written by communications pioneer **Marshall McLuhan** in 1944 but never published. McLuhan argued, according to biographer Philip Marchand in *Marshall McLuhan: The Medium and the Messenger* (1989), that Canada would benefit from Jewish energy, imagination, reverence for art, love of learning, and sense of community.

Who wants a Jew? This is our life, to hammer on doors.

Thoughts of a character in **Adele Wiseman**'s novel *The Sacrifice* (1956).

Jews have been the scapegoats not only for a single group, at a specific point in time, but have been the scapegoats for a whole civilization. No other form of prejudice has been so deeply entrenched in our civilization to a point where we can say it has succeeded in transforming the persecutors and the victims.

Bruno M. Cormier, psychiatrist, "On the History of Men and Genocide" (1966), *Breaking the Chains: Bruno M. Cormier and the McGill University Clinic in Forensic Psychiatry* (1998).

The Jew is neither a race nor a religion but a complaint.

Irving Layton, poet and aphorist, *The Whole Bloody Bird (obs, aphs & Pomes)* (1969).

To live in Canada, to write in French, is for me the pursuit of an undertaking that did not come to an end with my ancestors, the Jews of Babylon.

Naim Kattan, author and arts administrator, born in Baghdad, "Écrire en français," *Boundary 2: A Canadian Issue*, Fall, 1974.

This unprecedented crisis in post-modern Jewish identity is the result of two enormous facts. Of these one is the state of Israel. The other, however, has an enormity forcing us to view it quite by itself: *every Jew alive today would either be dead or be unborn but for a geographical accident.*

Emil Fackenheim, philosopher, "Post-Holocaust Anti-Jewishness, Jewish Identity, and the Centrality of Israel" (1987), *The Jewish Thought of Emil Fackenheim: A Reader* (1987) edited by Michael L. Morgan.

If there are common characteristics of this somewhat unique group, the Jews, I can think of three which I value: a respect for learning, stemming from a tradition of "the people of the Book"; a desire for social justice, handed down from the prophets; and cosmopolitanism, resulting from 2000 years of diaspora. In Israel the first two are weakening and the third is fiercely rejected; I am inclined to say that the Israelis, by becoming a nation, have ceased to be Jews.

Hans Blumenfeld, architect-planner, *Life Begins at 65: The Not Entirely Candid Autobiography of a Drifter* (1987).

Paradoxically, we Jews only began to achieve our religious objectives when we stopped praying and started doing.

Dow Marmur, rabbi, Holy Blossom Temple, Toronto, "Walking toward Elijah," *Walking toward*

Elijah: Sermons on the Jewish Festivals (1988) edited by David Azen.

Your view of the Jew is the measure of you.

Maurus E. Mallon, writer, aphorism, 18 March 1992.

The Plains of Abraham isn't a reference to the Israeli air force.

Attributed to **Irving Abella**, historian, President of the Canadian Jewish Congress, quoted by Warren Gerard in *The Toronto Star*, 24 May 1992.

To be Jewish means, to almost every Jew, to see oneself as a link in a long chain.

Dow Marmur, rabbi, Holy Blossom Temple, Toronto, "The God of My Parents—the God of My Children," *On Being a Jew: A Reform Perspective* (1994).

Today, we Jews in North America worry more about assimilation than about anti-Semitism. Absorption not anti-Semitism seems to be our greatest threat in North America.

Irving Abella, President, Canadian Jewish Congress, New Year's message, *The Canadian Jewish News*, 1 Sept. 1994.

The difference between the Jews and the WASPS is that Jews say mean things they don't mean, and WASPS say nice things they don't mean.

A. Alan Borovoy, lawyer, characteristic observation, 31 Dec. 1996.

JOHNSON, DANIEL See also POLITICIANS

He would go to a meeting of Toronto bond dealers and tell them, "Quebec won't separate if we can live in Canada as a group." Then, on his return to Quebec he would boldly declare: "Unless Quebec can live in Canada as a group, we'll separate!" Journalists would subtract one statement from the other, come up with zero, and Johnson would promptly attack the press for misrepresenting his position.

Peter C. Newman, columnist, referring to Daniel Johnson, Union Nationale leader and Premier of Quebec, "The Nation's Business," *Maclean's*, 19 Sept. 1994.

JOKES See also HUMOUR & HUMORISTS, NEWFIE JOKES

The joke is a form of hidden grievance.

Marshall McLuhan, communications pioneer, address, Multicultural Conference, Mohawk College, Hamilton, Ont. 19 May 1977. He elaborated: "Humour is always based on an abrasive interplay of cultures."

Ah, jokes. My own theory is we're the funniest nation on earth, and a lot of comedy on American television, from "SCTV" to "The Kids in the Hall" to "Saturday Night Live," supports it.

Peter Gzowski, broadcaster and writer, "Gzowski's Canada," *Canadian Living*, Sept. 1996.

Our Merchandise is All Indian Made, Canadian Made, or Imported.

Advertising slogan, **The Canoe**, a Native craft shop in Duncan, B.C., July 1975.

JOUAL See also LANGUAGE: FRENCH

Joual... 1. Horse. 2. Derogatory term used since 1960 in certain intellectual circles in Quebec, referring to the Québécois language.

Léandre Bergeron, lexicographer, defining "joual," the Quebec term for slang, *The Québécois Dictionary* (1982).

Quebec at the height of the British Empire was called the Joual in the Crown.

Maurus E. Mallon, writer and aphorist, Jan. 1992.

Before, professors taught in *joual*, and it was practical because no one could rival our excellence. We spoke *joual* and we were the best at it in the world.

Pierre Elliott Trudeau, former Prime Minister, address, Royal Society of Canada, quoted by André Picard in *The Globe and Mail*, 14 April 1994.

JOURNALISM See also BROADCASTING, JOURNALISTS, NEWS

Civilization itself rests upon the mind and conscience of the whole people, and for this mind and conscience, the press is the best vehicle of expression the world has yet evolved.

Joseph E. Atkinson, first publisher of *The Toronto Star* from 1899 to 1948, quoted in that newspaper on 1 Jan. 1992.

Newspapers are the daily cardiograms of humanity's heartbeat.

Fred Edge, reporter, *Don't Tell Me About It... Write It!* (1963).

Perhaps the hardest thing to learn, in refining my editorial judgment, was a sensitivity to cliché. Journalism is cliché, after all. The more popular the journalism, the more blatant and unabashed is the resort to hackneyed situations and hackneyed responses, formula stories where you have merely to fill in the blanks to produce the professional effect.

Robert MacNeil, broadcaster and memoirist, *The Right Place at the Right Time* (1982).

Today, there are more people involved in preparing the news than in making the events.

Barrington Nevitt, communications consultant, *The Communication Ecology: Re-presentation versus Replica* (1982).

There is no doubt that journalism is hasty, incomplete, sometimes inaccurate, occasionally misleading, and frequently flawed. It's an imperfect necessity. I also believe that journalism is the hinge of democracy: It is the only way we're going to find out about the events and issues that dominate our lives.

Knowlton Nash, broadcaster and correspondent, *Prime Time at Ten: Behind-the-Camera Battles of Canadian TV Journalism* (1987).

Of course, the bottom line is the scorecard; without it you have nothing, you're dead.

David Franklin Radler, president of Hollinger Inc. and publisher of its chains of dailies and weeklies, quoted by Peter C. Newman in *Maclean's*, 3 Feb. 1992.

I was often irritated by the naysaying of Canadian journalism, a characteristic which resonated with some deep need in the Canadian psyche.

Jill Ker Conway, Australian-born, American-educated historian and memoirist who taught at the University of Toronto from 1964 to 1975, *True North: A Memoir* (1994).

So to the fun stuff. The rationalization for *Frank's* existence. Here it is: The only true limit on power is information. That's what Frank tries to give anyone willing to buy it.

Geoff Heinricks, national affairs editor of *Frank* magazine, address, Royal Ontario Museum, Toronto, 27 Jan. 1995.

A sense of morality, a passion for freedom, and a large and fearless capacity for righteous anger are at the heart of journalism. Otherwise, it's nothing but selling ads.

Peter Desbarats, commissioner, *Somalia Cover-up* (1997).

So, we arrive at a Monty Python situation: *The Los Angeles Times* covers Canada from Manhattan, *The New York Times* covers Canada from Denver, and *The Boston Globe* covers Canada from a farm in northern Vermont.

James Brooke, Canada bureau chief of *The New York Times*, once resident in Toronto, subsequently resident in Evergreen, Colorado, "Why *The New York Times*'s Canada Bureau Isn't in Canada," *The Globe and Mail*, 4 Oct. 1999. He added, "In Canada, as best I can make out, there are three resident American correspondents: Associated Press, *Business Week* and *The Washington Post*."

JOURNALISTS See also JOURNALISM, NEWS

I learned that the good journalist must be ready, at all times, to write about anything he is called upon to write. Similarly, the good editor must be ready to take an interest in anything that turns up; it may all be grist to his mill. "*Nihil putavit a se alienum*" would be the inscription I would be satisfied to have put upon my tombstone, when I have finished with this world.

R.S. Lambert, founding editor of the BBC magazine *The Listener* and subsequently CBC Radio's Superintendent of School Broadcasting, discussing his first journalistic assignment for *The Economist* (to write about "Economic Conditions in Roumania"), *Ariel and All His Quality: An Impression of the BBC from Within* (1940).

My own all-time favourite from this school, which I may well have written myself, appeared over an article by Sidney Katz, quite a nice piece of reporting on its own, but labelled, I'm afraid, "Canada's a nation of dental cripples."

Peter Gzowski, journalist, on writing article heads for *Maclean's* in the 1950s, *The Private Voice: A Journal of Reflections* (1988).

To work, gentlemen, we have a government to overthrow.

Val Sears, newspaperman, Ottawa reporter for *The Toronto Star*, exhorting other members of the Press Gallery, when the 1962 election got underway and anti-Diefenbaker feeling was high across the country. Quoted by John G. Diefenbaker in *One Canada: Memoirs of the Right Honourable John G. Diefenbaker: The Tumultuous Years, 1962–1967* (1977).

STAR MAN FINDS HAL BANKS

Banner headline on *The Toronto Star*, 1 Oct. 1964. It took the *Star*'s investigative reporter, Robert Reguly, merely two days to locate Hal C. Banks on the Brooklyn waterfront. Banks was a gangster as well as Canadian Director of the Seafarers' International Union of North America. He had jumped bail in Canada and his name was on the "most wanted" lists of the RCMP and FBI, which seemed unwilling to pursue him.

Look at everybody who crosses this lobby. In every one of them there is a story.

Jack Scott, columnist with *The Vancouver Sun*, recalling advice of his father, also a newspaperman, sitting in the lobby of the Hotel Vancouver, quoted by Allan Fotheringham in *Birds of a Feather: The Press and the Politicians* (1989).

I think the role of a political journalist is not to have definite partisan loyalties. My interpretation of journalistic objectivity is to be against everybody who's in power.

Peter C. Newman, author, quoted by Robert Chodos in "Peter Newman Stands on Guard for Thee," *Toronto Life*, Aug. 1974.

Avoiding errors rather than assembling data is always a reporter's major problem. Errors have an extraordinary life expectancy. They pass from originator through plagiarist to rewrite man and on through the chain until they reach the wire services, by which time they have become an article of faith which no newspaperman dare contradict.

James M. Minifie, correspondent, *Expatriate* (1976).

Communist countries never expel correspondents for telling lies.

Ross H. Munro, China correspondent for *The Globe and Mail*, explaining the context of his expulsion, Nov. 1977.

I've always figured my job was simple: to tell people what I know—within the laws of good taste and libel. Readers should know what the insiders know, and that's what I have tried to do here.

Stevie Cameron, parliamentary correspondent, *Ottawa Inside Out* (1990).

Media scrums (a horde of reporters and photographers crowding in on a "hot" politican) seem to best represent the curious mating rite which brings opposites instantly together.

Robert J. Fleming, administrative consultant, *Canadian Legislatures 1992: Issues, Structures and Costs* (1992).

The hungry journalist, just like the hungry boxer, is always the best.

Joe Fisher, journalist, *Cotopaxi Visions: Travels in Ecuador* (1992).

I used to believe that there were three qualities essential to a journalist's craft: curiosity, compassion, and serendipity, the ability to find what you are not seeking. If the first two could be cultivated, I would say, the third would certainly follow.

Allen Abel, correspondent, *Scaring Myself Again: Far-flung Adventures of a TV Journalist* (1992). When Abel moved from print to television journalism, he wrote: "But the international television crew, burning money like jet fuel in a jumbo, needs to add a fourth ingredient: local help."

As a journalist I know it's often the detail that doesn't fit that points to a deeper, underlying truth.

Sylvia Fraser, novelist and journalist, *The Book of Strange: A Journey* (1992).

If there's one thing journalism teaches you, it's how to write fast. You may not write well, but you write fast.

Robert MacNeil, journalist, broadcaster, memoirist, novelist, quoted by Martin Townsend in *Quill & Quire*, Jan. 1992.

What can be said about any profession in which Barbara Amiel is widely considered to be a success?

John Hofsess, journalist, referring to newspaper and magazine columnist Barbara Amiel, Editorial, *Last Rights*, Feb.–March 1992.

It's fine to be an *indépendantiste* newsperson; it is even better to be an independent one.

Keith Spicer, CRTC Chairman, speaking in Chicoutimi, Que., about separatist-minded Quebec journalists, quoted in *The Toronto Star*, 8 May 1992.

If you're a feminist, you'll be *ipso facto* a better reporter than someone who pretends to be neutral.

Michelle Landsberg, columnist, addressing a conference in Ottawa for women in the media, 14 Dec. 1992, quoted by Tim Harper in *The Toronto Star* the following day.

The so-called profession of journalism is heavily cluttered with abrasive youngsters who substitute what they call commitment for insight, and, to a lesser extent, with aged hacks toiling through a miasma of mounting decrepitude.

Conrad Black, publisher, quoted by Nicholas Coleridge in *Paper Tigers* (1993).

I was merely, to borrow and blend a Jesuitical maxim, somewhat economical with the truth.

Michael Coren, columnist and broadcaster, on the scanty research and the semi-scandalous sensationalism of his column for *Frank* magazine, *Aesthete: The Frank Diaries of Michael Coren* (1993).

A columnist has to be someone who climbs out of bed in the morning and flies into a rage.

Attributed to sometime columnist **Ralph Allen** by full-time columnist Joey Slinger during an interview by Peter Gzowski on CBC Radio's *Morningside*, Fall 1992.

Most journalists these days have been to university, and one of the things university trains us to do is to complete a writing task approximately 37 seconds before it is due.

Parker Barss Donham, political columnist, address, Symposium on Free Speech and Privacy in the Information Age, University of Waterloo, Waterloo, Ont., 26 Nov. 1994.

I can't think of a better way to make a living. I was paid to go out there and watch the world.

Joe Schlesinger, CBC-TV foreign correspondent, retiring in 1994 after twenty-one years in the field, quoted by Bill Brioux in "Joe Schlesinger Retires," *TV Guide*, 25 June 1994.

Get it first, but first get it right.

Dick Beddoes, newspaperman and sports personality, referring to scoops, quoted by Ken McKee, "TV, Radio Sports," *The Toronto Star*, 7 Oct. 1994.

Look it up—you'll remember it longer; screw it up and you'll remember it forever.

Dean Tudor, journalist and professor, Ryerson Polytechnic University, Toronto, characteristic remark, 12 Nov. 1996.

The late Barbara Frum defined our job most clearly once in a conversation over brunch: "Just tell me something I don't already know about something that matters to me—or should." The phrase "or should" is crucial, because our readers are seeking direction to important things they're not yet aware of, among other things.

William Thorsell, Editor-in-Chief of *The Globe and Mail*, address, Sing Tao School of Journalism, University of British Columbia, Vancouver, 18 Sept. 1998, printed in *The Globe and Mail*, 3 Oct. 1998.

The Forces of Darkness

Words used by CBC-TV's investigative journalist **Terry Milewski** in an e-mail sent to University of British Columbia student protester Craig Jones concerning the obfuscatory tactics of the Prime Minister's Office. The e-mail came to light in Oct. 1998 during the RCMP's Public Complaints Commission inquiry into the Force's use of pepper spray (a scandal dubbed "Spraygate" or "SprayPEC") to quell student demonstrators at the APEC Summit, Nov. 1997. The phrase "the Forces of Darkness," which recalls the language of the movie *Star Wars*, led the PMO's communications director Peter Donolo to file a complaint against the CBC and Milewski, alleging bias in reporting. The CBC publicly exonerated Milewski of the charge but then privately reprimanded him. Then he wrote "Who's Next" for *The Globe and Mail*, 10 Nov. 1998, and was reprimanded again. "I am not allowed to comment, and I am not allowed to comment on why I cannot comment," he complained to *The Globe and Mail* the following day.

My own conception is that a good reporter can only at times be a gentleman, but in general, cannot, and cannot ever perceive himself as a gentleman.

William Johnson, former journalist, president of Alliance Quebec, interviewed by Graham Fraser, "Canada," *The Toronto Star*, 6 Feb. 2000.

JOY

As many griefs as you can bear / as many joys as you desire

Lines from **Harry Howith**'s poem "Fragments of the Dance," *Fragments of the Dance* (1969).

If you cannot feel pain at some of the harsh circumstances of life, it is very likely that you have ceased to feel joy at some of the satisfactions and delights of life. When that happens, one lives at all times under a mental and spiritual cloud; it is always wet weather in the soul.

Robertson Davies, man-of-letters, "The Deadliest of the Sins" (1962), *One Half of Robertson Davies: Provocative Pronouncements on a Wide Range of Topics* (1977).

The question is, can our haste to succumb to joy, regardless of all other longings, reveal anything beyond the measure of our forlornness and despair.

Stephen Vizinczey, novelist and essayist, "Postscript: On the Acts of Writing and Reading" (1977), *In Praise of Older Women* (1965).

JUDAISM See also BELIEF, JEWISH PEOPLE, RELIGION

Judaism strongly affirms the afterlife, but it refuses to speculate and to fret about what it is going to be like. Such knowledge is beyond human reach.

Dow Marmur, rabbi, Holy Blossom Temple, Toronto, *Choose Life: Thoughts on Grief and Growth* (1999).

JUDGEMENT

I learned... not to trust value judgments too much, even when they come from the pit of the stomach, which is where the sixteenth-century alchemist Helmont located the soul.

Northrop Frye, cultural critic, "The World as Music and Idea in Wagner's *Parsifal*" (1982), *Myth and Metaphor: Selected Essays, 1974–1988* (1990) edited by Robert D. Denham.

To discriminate, in every area, this is what we need to learn in our undiscriminating society.

Louis Dudek, poet and aphorist, "Radical Notes 1944," *The Nashwaak Review*, No. 2, 1995.

Non-judgemental is another spelling of amoral.

Maurus E. Mallon, aphorist, 30 June 1995.

JUSTICE & INJUSTICE See also CRIME, LAW, PRISONS

Justice must be the same on the banks of the Saskatchewan or of the Qu'Appelle, as on those of the Red River or the Assiniboine.

Edward Blake, leader of the Liberal Party, address, delivered on the eve of the execution of Louis Riel, which took place in Regina on 16 Nov. 1885.

The Supreme Court of Canada is like the Tower of Pisa, always leaning in one direction.

Attributed to Quebec Premier **Maurice Duplessis** in the 1950s by André Picard, "Québécois Voices," *The Globe and Mail*, 23 May 1996.

Someone once asked President Kennedy: "What will you do to correct the injustices that the Negroes have been suffering in the United States since the Civil War?" He replied: "We will be just in our time." It is not a question of correcting the past; the past cannot be corrected. We must rather ensure that justice will prevail today, tomorrow, and the day after tomorrow. That is what I am proposing.

Pierre Elliott Trudeau, leader of the Liberal Party, address, Quebec City, 15 June 1968.

The universe may not be just or, as seems more likely to me, it may be just in ways that we cannot yet understand.

Ian Stevenson, psychiatrist and psychical researcher, "Some Questions Related to Cases of the Reincarnation Type," *Journal of the American Society for Psychical Research*, Oct. 1974.

Never pray for justice, because you might get some.

Thoughts of the narrator of **Margaret Atwood**'s novel *Cat's Eye* (1988).

The scales of Justice know the grocer's thumb.

Robin Skelton, poet and aphorist, *A Devious Dictionary* (1991).

The justice system serves all but the just.

Maurus E. Mallon, aphorist, 26 March 1993.

There's a sort of cynical saying going around the courts that if you plead guilty, you get mercy. If you get found guilty by a judge, you get justice.

David Humphrey, Ontario Justice, referring to plea bargaining, quoted by Tracey Tyler in *The Toronto Star*, 12 June 1993.

A judge cannot try to steer a middle course between partiality and impartiality.

Antonio Lamer, Chief Justice of the Supreme Court of Canada, address, National Judicial Institute, 2 May 1994, "Verbatim," *The Globe and Mail*, 6 May 1994.

I have a vested interest in injustice.

A. Alan Borovoy, lawyer, head, Canadian Civil Liberties Association, characteristic remark, 31 Dec. 1996.

No matter what we do, justice alone will never bring peace to our planet.

Louise Arbour, chief prosecutor of the United Nations' war crimes tribunals for Rwanda and the Balkans, quoted by Sylvie Halpern in "Madame Justice for All," *enRoute*, June 1998.

One of the aims and purposes of the criminal sanction, and of international criminal justice, is to eradicate the malign untruths, to deny all moral equivalency while asserting the universality of the rule of law.

Louise Arbour, former chief prosecutor of the United Nations' war crimes tribunals for Rwanda and the Balkans, newly appointed member of the Supreme Court of Canada, address, International Press Freedom Awards, Toronto, "The Incurable Deficits of Memory," *The Toronto Star*, 20 Nov. 1999.

KILLING

Human beings are the only creatures that kill from a distance.

Robin Skelton, poet and aphorist, *A Devious Dictionary* (1991).

KINDNESS

There is very little anyone can do for anyone else... in the end it's a matter of waiting things out in an improvised shelter and thinking as kindly of yourself as possible.

Thoughts of a character in the title story of **Carol Shields**' fiction collection *The Orange Fish* (1989).

In this world you have to take your bits and ends of kindness where you can find them....

Remark attributed to Grace Marks in **Margaret Atwood**'s novel *Alias Grace* (1996).

KING, W.L. MACKENZIE See also POLITICIANS

The motto of the Prime Minister's Office should be "Industry Without Humanity."

Quip attributed to the "orator-general" **Leonard W. Brockington** with reference to the title of Prime Minister Mackenzie King's book *Industry and Humanity* (1918), as recalled by James A. Gibson in correspondence, 31 Oct. 1994.

"Not necessarily conscription, but conscription if necesary."

W.L. Mackenzie King, Prime Minister, House of Commons, 7 July 1942. Ever the artful dodger, King employed the seven words, which appear in quotation marks in Hansard, the official record of the proceedings of the House of Commons, and repeated them like a mantra to cool the Conscription Crisis of World War II. His formulation is elastic to the point of being plastic. It is now believed that the phraseology originated in an unsigned editorial titled "Mr. King on Conscription," *The Toronto Star*, 11 June 1942. The anonymous editorial writer argued as follows: "But the government says enough are coming forward; that enough may continue to come forward, and that conscription for overseas duty, which it is willing to impose if necessary, may never be necessary at all." According to writer David MacDonald, the wording of this passage was drawn to King's attention by his adviser J.S. (Jack) Pickersgill, and King eagerly adapted it to his own purposes.

I never saw a touch of greatness in him.

Norman A. Robertson, civil servant, on learning of the death of former Prime Minister W.L. Mackenzie King in 1950, as reported by Douglas LePan, quoted by J.L. Granatstein in *A Man of Influence: Norman A. Robertson and Canadian Statecraft 1929–68* (1981).

He skilfully avoided what was wrong / Without saying what was right, / And never let his on the one hand / Know what his on the other hand was doing.

Lines from **F.R. Scott**'s satiric poem "W.L.M.K." (1957), *Selected Poems* (1966).

His verbal currency was invariably tendered in the highest denominations; but in practical politics he always dealt in very small change.... He made both big words and small deeds serve his turn. There was at once more in him than met the eye, and a great deal less than filled the ear.

Donald C. Creighton, historian, *Canada's First Century: 1867–1967* (1970).

I remember the election of 1935 when the Rt. Hon. W.L. Mackenzie King, then member for Prince Albert, ran on a platform of "King or Chaos." We got both.

John G. Diefenbaker, former Prime Minister, speech, House of Commons, 10 March 1971.

But another way of putting it would be that he delivered us from the bosom of the British mother onto the bony lap of the American uncle, and he preserved a semblance of national unity by deflecting the issue, and leaving it for today's generation to face.

Charles Lynch, columnist, "Mackenzie King's Carpet Hid Canada's Problems," *Ottawa Citizen*, 18 Dec. 1996.

Mackenzie King was an uncommon man, but studying him can teach us something about our common humanity.

Paul Roazen, historian, *Canada's King: An Essay in Political Psychology* (1998).

KISSES See also LOVE

Kissing, fondling and caressing between lovers—this should never be tolerated under any circumstances, unless there is an engagement to justify it, and then only in a sensible and limited way. The girl who allows a young man the privileges of kissing her or putting his arms around her waist before engagement will at once fall in the estimation of the man she has thus gratified and desired to please.

B.G. Jefferis, medical crank, *Search Lights on Health, Light on Dark Corners; A Complete Sexual Science and a Guide to Purity and Physical Manhood* (1894).

Nobody wants to kiss but once.

John Robert Colombo, anthologist, on rereading rather than simply reading a book once, quoted by Doris Giller in *The Toronto Star*, 19 Oct. 1991.

And sometimes when the night is slow / The wretched and the meek / Gather up our hearts and go / A thousand kisses deep.

Lines from **Leonard Cohen**'s song "A Thousand Kisses Deep" premiered on videotape at the Leonard Cohen Event, Montreal, 13 May 2000, quoted by Stephanie Nolen, "He's Their Man," *The Globe and Mail*, 15 May 2000.

KLONDIKE See also GOLD, YUKON TERRITORY

Oh, my Heart, my Life, my Soul, / I will meet thee when the ice-worms nest again.

Lines from versifier **Robert W. Service**'s song included in his novel *The Trail of '98: A Northland Romance* (1910). It signals his adieu to the North and his eventual retirement to the south of France.

It was in the Klondike I found myself. There nobody talks. Everybody does things. You get your true perspective. I got mine.

Jack London, American adventurer, Yukon resident, and novelist, "Jack London by Himself," *The Star Rover* (1915).

She Made the Frozen North—Red Hot! / When it's forty below and there's nothing but snow, that's where the West begins....

Promotional copy for the Paramount movie *Klondike Annie* (1936) starring Mae West. Noted by Fergus Cashin in *Mae West: A Biography* (1981).

I was right there where it happened in the Dominion Saloon in Dawson City, and I always relate this story because I actually saw it. It is not just a poem, but a record of a real happening.

Michael (Mike) Mahoney, Ottawa resident and former Yukon prospector, claiming he witnessed the incident that inspired Robert Service to write the ballad "The Shooting of Dan McGrew," interviewed at Niagara Falls, as quoted by the reporter of the *Niagara Falls Evening Review*, 17 Feb. 1937.

All the things I am and have, I owe to the North. That far-off cold and silent land has made better men of all who have ever come out of it.

Robert W. Service, versifier, interviewed in Vancouver in 1949, quoted by James Mackay in *Vagabond of Verse: Robert Service—A Biography* (1995).

Gold lured hardy fortune-hunters to Australia, and to the bleak recesses of Canada, where they discovered a more practical if less respectable El Dorado than had dazzled the Elizabethan adventurers.

Winston Churchill, British statesman and popular historian, *Book X: "The Great Democracies," A History of the English-speaking Peoples* (1958).

"I like Robert Service, too," Marilyn said. "Gosh, those days in the Klondike! I get chills just reading about the frozen North."

Marilyn Monroe, movie star, referring to the Bard of the Yukon who celebrated the Klondike Gold Rush in his verse, quoted by Robert F. Slatzer in *The Life and Curious Death of Marilyn Monroe* (1974).

KNOWLEDGE

That we are made and intended to pursue knowledge is as certain as that we are made and intended for the improvement of our estate and we cannot tell how far or to what revelations the pursuit may lead us.

Goldwin Smith, essayist, *Guesses at the Riddle of Existence and Other Essays on Kindred Subjects* (1897).

Nothing is too small to know, and nothing is too big to accept.

Sir William Van Horne, General Manager of the CPR, quoted by Walter Vaughan in *Sir William Van Horne* (1926).

The knowledge industries and the educational industries are the biggest in the world so far. I mean they make General Motors look very small indeed.

Marshall McLuhan, communications pioneer, "Education in the Electronic Age" (1967), *The Best of Times / The Worst of Times: Contemporary Issues in Canadian Education* (1972) edited by Hugh A. Stevenson, Robert M. Stamp, and J. Donald Wilson.

Knowledge that tries to do without experience becomes paranoid; experience that tries to do without knowledge becomes schizophrenic.

Northrop Frye, cultural critic, "Some Reflections on Life and Habit" (1988), *Myth and Metaphor: Selected Essays, 1974–1988* (1990) edited by Robert D. Denham.

The vast unknown is there, in all the fields of knowledge. We should always point to that, and invite students to go to the frontier, to begin the adventure.

Louis Dudek, poet and aphorist, entry of 1989, *Notebooks 1960–1994* (1994).

Know what thou art not, and it follows as night the day thou wilt then truly know thyself.

W.O. Mitchell, writer, quoting the advice of "an old woman," "Bank of Montreal: A Portrait of Canada," *Saturday Night*, May 1992.

Knowledge is doubling every eighteen months (most of it now coming from outside North America). It is impossible to know everything about anything. Your best hope is to learn how to access information. Your biggest mistake may be your unwillingness to pay for information.

Frank Ogden, futurologist, *The Last Book You'll Ever Read and Other Lessons from the Future* (1993).

We no longer cast spells against the unknown; we cast spacecraft into the void.

Rand and **Rose Flem-Ath**, researchers, *When the Sky Fell: In Search of Atlantis* (1995).

What is more contemptible than a civilization that scorns knowledge of itself?

John Ralston Saul, author, *The Unconscious Civilization* (1995).

You will find much less pleasure in demonstrating your knowledge than in finding yet more fascinating proof of your ignorance. If you are wise enough to understand how little you know, you will always realize how much delight remains in learning more.

William Thorsell, editor and columnist, convocation address, June 1995, printed as "Knowledge," *The Globe and Mail*, 10 June 1995.

All minds are passive to impressions 90% of the time, and probably people are more affected by oracles than they admit.

Northrop Frye, cultural critic, diary entry, 3 July 1942, *Northrop Frye Newsletter*, Fall 1996.

That which "everybody knows" is usually false.

Ron Haggart, writer and broadcaster, characteristic remark, June 1999.

KOREAN WAR See also WAR

Personal investigations reveal undeniable evidence large scale continuing American germ warfare on Chinese mainland urge you protest shameful violation United Nations agreements.

Text of the telegram sent by missionary and peace activist **James G. Endicott** to Lester B. Pearson, Minister of External Affairs, April 1952. Endicott's germ-warfare charges in Korea were defiantly denied by the United States authorities but in time they were proven to be only too true, as noted by Stephen Endicott in *James G. Endicott: Rebel Out of China* (1980).

Each uniquely mounted nameplate / On this Korean Veterans' Wall / Tells the story of a Person / Who rallied to their country's call.

First of four verses composed for the plaque to be attached to the Korea Veterans Wall of Remembrance, Meadowvale Cemetery, Brampton, Ont. The verses were composed by **J.E. (Jack) La Chance**, veteran of the 1st and 2nd Battalion (1950–52), in honour of the 26,971 Canadians who fought (including the 516 who fell) in the Korean War, whose names are inscribed on the Wall erected by the Korea Veterans Association of Canada. *City of North York Management Committee Report No. 3*, 30 Jan. 1996.

KUWAIT See GULF CRISIS

L

LABOUR See also CAPITALISM, EMPLOYMENT, INDUSTRY, UNEMPLOYMENT, UNIONS, WORK

Central to the creation of an independent socialist Canada is the strength and tradition of the Canadian working class and the trade union movement.

"The Waffle Manifesto: For an Independent Socialist Canada" (1969) reprinted in *The Canadian Forum*, Dec. 1989.

Whatever ill will the public may think of politicians, it appears that they think even worse of labour unions.

Kim Campbell, Socred member, B.C. Legislature, April 1987, quoted by Tim Harper in *The Toronto Star*, 27 March 1993.

Fishermen and miners and factory workers risk their bodies and their lives; the shareholders only risk money. Money can be replaced; fingers and fathers can't.

Silver Donald Cameron, columnist, "The Dignity of Labour," *The Halifax Herald*, 13 Sept. 1998.

Instead of the conservative motto, "A fair day's wage for a fair day's work," we must inscribe on our hammer the revolutionary watchword, "Abolition of the wage system."

Preamble of the **Industrial Workers of the World**, reproduced in *The Canadian Wobbly Songbook* (1990) compiled by Jerzy (George) Dymny.

LABRADOR See also NEWFOUNDLAND

This country shall be named after its natural resources: It shall be called *Markland*.

Words attributed to the Norse explorer **Leif the Lucky** around A.D. 1000 in *The Vinland Sagas: The Norse Discovery of America* (1965) translated from the Old Icelandic by Magnus Magnusson and Hermann Palsson. The word *Markland* means "forest-land"; its local is likely Labrador.

I shall never find in the wilds of Labrador any greater wildness than in some recess of Concord, i.e., more than I import into it.

Henry David Thoreau, American essayist, entry, 30 Aug. 1865, *Journal: Volume 1, 1837–1844* (1981) edited by John C. Broderick.

The shadow of Newfoundland lies flat and still. / Labrador's yellow, where the moony Eskimo has oiled it.

Elizabeth Bishop, New England poet who in her youth in 1911–17 summered in Great Village, N.S., "The Map," *The Complete Poems 1927–1979* (1983).

There is a cold air coming off Labrador, but not so bad as Syria. The sea is grey, exactly the colour of the seagulls with the white under their wings. They are still following us—lovely creatures. I have the joy of the *Odyssey:* it made me forget even the roll of the waves, such is the triumph of beautiful words.

Freya Stark, traveller and writer, letter written in the Gulf of St. Lawrence aboard the S.S. *Athenia*, 26 Oct. 1928, *Beyond Euphrates* (1951).

Dear land of mountains, woods and snow, / Labrador our Labrador. / God's noble gifts to us bestow, / Labrador our Labrador, / Thy proud resources waiting still, their splendid task will soon fulfil, / Obedient to thy Maker's will, / Labrador our Labrador.

First of three verses of "Ode to Labrador," the unofficial anthem of Labrador. The words were written by **Dr. H.L. Paddon**, North West River, to be sung to the traditional Christmas tune "O Tannenbaum." Words and music appear in *Songs of Labrador* (1993) edited by Tim Borlase.

Labrador's moment in history has arrived. Finally, after four centuries, it begins to look as if the land no longer belongs to Cain.

Pierre Berton, author and media personality, *The Mysterious North* (1956). The reference is to Jacques Cartier's description in 1534 of Labrador's south shore as "the land that God gave to Cain."

... and in Northwest River I met a dear old lady who told me her life's ambition was to see a cow.

Sandra Gwyn, writer, "Labrador on the Brink of the Future," *Saturday Night*, Dec. 1978.

Great Whale River, Eskimo Point / Indian House Lake, Caribou Pass / but still no name for the whole / I was willing to name the parts / but not the whole.

Lines from **Kenneth White**'s poem "Labrador or the Waking Dream," *The Blue Road* (1983).

In fact, Quebec has as much a claim to Labrador as it does to upstate New York, and a much better claim to southern Ontario, which was genuinely a French possession prior to 1763. So far as Canada is concerned, there is nothing to discuss regarding Labrador.

David J. Bercuson and **Barry Cooper**, historian and political scientist, referring to Quebec's rejection of the decision of the Judicial Committee of the Privy Council of 1927 that established the present-day boundaries of Labrador, *Deconfederation: Canada without Quebec* (1991).

To be a part of this great land, / Should be the pride of any man, / To know that we were born on these great shores, / So listen while I tell, / And it makes my old heart swell, / I'm proud to be a son of Labrador.

First verse of the song "Sons of Labrador" with words and music by **Sid Dicker**, *Nain, Songs of Labrador* (1993) edited by Tim Borlase.

In Russia, one of the definitions of what is the North is "where grain does not grow." Here the grain definitely does not grow. Caribou grow here—altogether 600,000 of them on the whole of the Labrador peninsula. Very tasty.

Arkadi Tcherkassov, Russian geographer, "A Homesick Russian's Thoughts about the Ukraine—in the Heart of Labrador!" *Grainews*, June 1994.

LACROSSE See also SPORTS

Lacrosse has undergone some changes since the white man rescued it from savagery. It still requires the speed and endurance of the Indian, the courage of the Spartan, the fortitude of the Stoic, the patience and self-denial of a Job. To all must be added the strategic ability and tactical skill of a Wellington.

Description of the game of Lacrosse, *The Montreal Herald* in 1892, quoted by Henry Roxborough in *One Hundred—Not Out* (1966).

LAKES See GREAT LAKES, WATER

LAND See also GEOGRAPHY

The soil of the earth from one end to the other is the property of people who inhabit it. By birthright, the Onkwehonwe, the original beings, are the owners of the soil which they own and occupy and none other may hold it. The same law has been held from the oldest times.

Article of the "Great Law of Peace" of the **Iroquois Confederacy**, reproduced by Craig MacLaine and Michael S. Baxendale in *This Land Is Our Land: The Mohawk Revolt at Oka* (1991).

...far away at the portals of the setting sun, lies the Great Lone Land.

Sir William Francis Butler, traveller, *The Great Lone Land: A Narrative of Travel and Adventure in the North-West of America* (1872).

Money to us is of no value, and to most of us unknown; and as no consideration whatever can induce us to sell our lands, on which we get sustenance for our women and children, we hope we may be allowed to point out a mode by which your settlers may be removed, and peace thereby obtained.

Joseph Brant, Mohawk leader, address to Commissioners of the United States, quoted by William L. Stone in *Life of Joseph Brant—Thayendanegea; Including the Indian Wars of the American Revolution* (1838).

It has been said that he that would describe Canada must use for his pen a mountain crag and for ink the waters of the Arctic Sea. It is, I suppose, a way of saying that only a fool would attempt to, that a wise man, given the choice, would prefer to spend his time chasing shooting stars with a butterfly net.

Kenneth McNeill Wells, essayist, *Colourful Canada* (1959).

Look as he would, the land had no face.

Thoughts of a character in **Rudy Wiebe**'s novel *First and Vital Candle* (1966).

They came to the land in ignorance, perhaps expecting miracles which would not occur, but at least with caring, seeing it as a gift and not an affliction.

Lines about city folk who return to the land in **Margaret Laurence**'s novel *The Diviners* (1974).

There are some parts of Canada still owned by Canadians, but they are too scattered to make a country.

Louis Dudek, man-of-letters, *Epigrams* (1975).

This land-and-water-scape is pre-Cambrian; in other words its age is unknown. Before man, before any animals, or any vegetation, it was. It goes back to frost and fire, to the primeval volcano and the ur-glacier. Its granite is the product of upheavings and downsinkings, and all the convulsive writhings of cosmic chaos.

Kathleen Coburn, scholar, *In Pursuit of Coleridge* (1977).

We must treat this land of ours with respect and with deference. To me, the land is as animate and as living, as complex as any human being. Our future lies as much in partnership with this land as it does in our partnerships with each other.

Tomson Highway, playwright, *Canada: A Portrait: The Official Handbook of Present Conditions and Recent Progress* (54th edition, 1992).

A certain ancient aboriginal visionary of this country once said: "We have not inherited this land, we have merely borrowed it from our children."

Tomson Highway, playwright, "What a Certain Visionary Once Said," "Bank of Montreal: A Portrait of Canada," *Saturday Night*, May 1992.

Aboriginal peoples have not lost their spiritual relationship with the land because they never had one. Indigenous societies are not characterized by their respect for the environment, but by their primitive technology and a subsistence economy.

Frances Widdowson and **Albert Howard**, researchers, "Impolite Society," *The Globe and Mail*, 2 May 1998.

LAND CLAIMS

See also INDIAN PEOPLES, NATIVE PEOPLES, OKA STANDOFF

O Canada, your home's on native land. . . .

Attributed to Native activist **Elijah Harper**, noting that Native land claims include Parliament Hill, seat of the Government of Canada, Aug. 1991.

At present some 370 specific and 30 comprehensive land claims are outstanding, and another 100, relating to disputes that precede Canada's confederation in 1867, could be added. Some of them are large: more than three-quarters of British Columbia is claimed by natives.

John Grimond, journalist, "Nice Country, Nice Mess," *The Economist*, 29 June 1991.

Why should the First Nations be the only landless people in the world? Why do we always have to be placed in the position of having to beg to the rest of Canada for land that once belonged to our ancestors?

Ovide Mercredi, Cree lawyer, National Chief of the Assembly of First Nations, quoted by André Picard in *The Globe and Mail*, 6 Nov. 1991.

When a robber robs a bank, is the money his?

Matthew Coon Come, Quebec Cree leader, referring to unsettled land claims, quoted by John Gray in *The Globe and Mail*, 15 Oct. 1994.

LAND MINES

It is this generation's pledge to the future and a bridge to the millennium.

Lloyd Axworthy, Foreign Minister, on signing in Ottawa on 3 Dec. 1997 the treaty banning the production, export, and use of anti-personnel land mines, quoted in *The Globe and Mail*, 8 Dec. 1997.

LANGUAGE

See also BILINGUALISM; LANGUAGE: ENGLISH; LANGUAGE: FRENCH; SPEECH & SPEECHES

Pas d'admission. / No admission. / Keep out.

Public notice in Joliette, Que. "Street names and notices in Joliette are in French, but sometimes the English equivalents are added. One inhibitory notice warning people away from the high-power cables was in French, English, and American," according to Robert Donald in *The Imperial Press Conference in Canada* (1921).

Language was the first outering of the central nervous system. In language we put all of ourselves outside.

Marshall McLuhan, communications pioneer, *Counterblast* (1969).

Language is at once the most vulgar of all media and the greatest work of art that ever can be devised by man.

Marshall McLuhan, communications pioneer, observation, "A McLuhan Sourcebook," *The Essential McLuhan* (1995) edited by Eric McLuhan and Frank Zingrone.

In our language lingers something of those who went before us, and to know something about our language can make our lives a little richer.

R.E. McConnell, editor, *Our Own Voice: Canadian English and How It Came to Be* (1978).

Each language is a unique description of the world, shaping and shaped by culture and environment, imposing categories on inchoate experience; its death is the phonic and gnostic equivalent of extinction of a species.

Ronald Wright, author, *Time Among the Maya: Travels in Belize, Guatemala, and Mexico* (1989).

It's a city where Greek stops to ask directions of Ukrainian, and they stumble along in shaky French—each slowly realizing the other can't be a native Québécois, because if he were, he'd have switched to English.

Robyn Sarah, writer, referring to Montreal, "Paradigm Found," *The Globe and Mail*, 20 July 1996.

It's difficult to overemphasize the importance of language as the vehicle of identity—it provides a zone of safety for values and it structures the world it describes. It is, in short, a kind of primary oxygen.

Vivian Rakoff, psychiatrist, psychological profile of Lucien Bouchard and the Quebec psyche, "What It Said," *The Globe and Mail*, 25 Aug. 1997.

LANGUAGE: ENGLISH See also LANGUAGE

It seems highly expedient, and decidedly for the advantage of the Canadians themselves, that the English language should be universally prevalent in Canada.

Hugh Gray, traveller, *Letters from Canada, Written during a Residence There in the Years 1806, 1807, and 1808* (1809).

In Canada two-thirds of the white population are Anglophones and the rest are Francophones.

Early reference to terms for English-speakers and French-speakers, found in **Deniker**'s *Races of Man* (1900).

In Ontario which is as violently Orange as Belfast (though not at all of our European savour) they pass laws compelling all children to learn in English: their English.

Hilaire Belloc, British essayist, letter written in Montreal, 11 March 1923, *Letters from Hilaire Belloc* (1958) edited by Robert Speaight.

My aunt was bitten by an ant in Ontario while she was singing Schubert's *Ave Maria*.

Sentence devised by playwright and language-reformer **George Bernard Shaw** to illustrate his pet phonetic alphabet, noted by Michael Kesterton, "Social Studies," *The Globe and Mail*, 2 Nov. 1995.

And yet the stubborn fact remains that Canadian English is *not* the same as General American, and one may seriously question whether it ever will be.

Mark M. Orkin, linguist, *Speaking Canadian English: An Informal Account of the English Language in Canada* (1970).

The reason you can't make right turns on red lights in Quebec is because the word "right" is an English word.

Steve Rubin, Montreal aphorist, 14 Oct. 1991.

Tell them they all sound like Randolph Scott. They do not say "house" or "mouse," they say "hoose" or "moose." I love it.

Mel Brooks, American comedian, on Canadian pronunciation, quoted by J.A. Davidson, "Talking 'Funny': The Canadian Language," *The Beaver*, June–July 1993.

This Sign is Illegal.

Wording on a placard carried by a protester at the celebration to mark the anniversary of the passage of Bill 101 in Quebec City, as seen on CBC-TV's *The National*, 26 Aug. 1997.

LANGUAGE: FRENCH See also BILINGUALISM, JOUAL, LANGUAGE

People laugh at what appears uncommon and ridiculous. In Canada nobody ever hears the French language spoken by anyone but Frenchmen, for strangers seldom come here and the Indians are naturally too proud to learn French and compel the French to learn their own language.

Peter Kalm, Swedish traveller, *Travels into North America* (1770–71) translated from the Swedish by J.R. Forster.

I can speak French, but I cannot understand it. But I am charmed by the fluency of the language as it flows from their lips.

Mark Twain, humorist, delivering his so-called Second Speech in Montreal, 9 Dec. 1881, quoted by David Ketterer in "Mark Twain's Overlooked 'Second Speech' in Montreal," *Mark Twain Journal*, Fall 1990.

La langue, gardienne de la foi.

Henri Bourassa, nationalist and publisher, address, Notre Dame, Montreal, 1910. "The language, guardian of the faith." Quoted by Michael Oliver in *The Passionate Debate* (1991).

Ever since the close of the Eighteenth Century patriotic French-Canadians have been voicing fears that the French language would be obliterated from their country, soon or late, by the growth of English, but so far it has not happened.

H.L. Mencken, lexicographer, *The American Language: Supplement 1* (1945, 8th printing 1961).

We speak a language that was English. When Richard Coeur de Lion first heard Turkish he said: "He spik lak a fole Britain." From which orthography one judges that Richard himself probably spoke like a French-Canadian.

Ezra Pound, poet, *How to Read* (1931).

The French language has survived in North America for one reason only: because Canada has survived.

Donald C. Creighton, historian, "Towards the Discovery of Canada" (1956), *Towards the Discovery of Canada: Selected Essays* (1972).

As long as this state does not exist, we will have to forget about good French and assume the inferiority of the people to whom we belong by speaking the same language they speak: *le joual.*

Gerald Godin, poet and future politician, referring to the future state of Quebec, "Le joual politique," *Parti Pris*, March 1965.

I think of Quebec first because this province is the only one in which I feel completely at home, the only one which allows me to live freely in French twenty-four hours a day.

Solange Chaput Rolland, writer, *My Country, Canada or Quebec?* (1966).

Canady French

Name of the variety of French spoken in the Quebec of North America in **Vladimir Nabokov**'s other-dimensional novel *Ada* (1969).

We are an uncultured stammering people / yet we are not deaf to the uniqueness of a tongue / speak with the accent of Milton and Byron and Shelley and Keats / *speak white* / and forgive us if we reply / only in the harsh songs of our ancestors / and the deep pain of Nelligan.

Lines from **Michèle Lalonde**'s poem of protest "Speak White" which was distributed by the McGill français marchers, Feb. 1969, translated by John Robert Colombo for *How Do I Love Thee: Sixty Poets of Canada (and Québec) Select and Introduce Their Favourite Poems from Their Own Work* (1970).

I can speak French very easily. There's not an English-speaking person in Canada who doesn't understand me perfectly when I speak French.

John G. Diefenbaker, former Prime Minister, quoted in *The Globe and Mail*, 22 May 1975.

We want to make it necessary to speak French to live in Quebec.

Fernand Lalonde, Solicitor-General of Quebec, quoted by Richard Cleroux in *The Globe and Mail*, 27 Aug. 1975.

French is and has always been the language of the people of Quebec.

Camille Laurin, Quebec Cabinet Minister, introducing Quebec's "language law," Bill 101, National Assembly, Quebec City, May 1977; it was passed on 28 Sept. 1977.

The Quebec accent is ridiculous and grotesque.

Attributed to the French novelist **Françoise Sagan** in an interview in Feb. 1989, as quoted by Stephen Godfrey in *The Globe and Mail*, 3 March 1989.

The citizens of Quebec are so interested in speaking French that they may leave the Canadian federation just to do it. People in France are arguing about whether there should be a hyphen in "weekend" and people in Quebec are arguing about whether it's okay to arrest someone for putting an English word like "weekend" on a sign, hyphen or no hyphen. It's only a matter of time before anybody who wants to speak real French will have to go to Quebec.

Calvin Trillin, columnist and essayist, 4 July 1990.

Skin is superficial; language is not. Those who doubt this should spend a few days in a totally French environment where they can't understand what is being said and what is going on. Feeling like a foreigner in one's own country is a strange, unsettling experience.

Lysiane Gagnon, columnist, "Inside Quebec," *The Globe and Mail*, 25 Sept. 1993.

Our language celebrates our love, our beliefs, and our dreams for this land and for this country. In order that the profound sense of belonging to a distinct people is now and for all time the very bastion of our identity, we proclaim our will to live in a French-language society.

Text of the Preamble to the Declaration of Sovereignty Bill, written by a committee consisting of singer **Gilles Vigneault**, playwright **Marie Laberge**, sociologist **Fernand Dumont**, and constitutional-law specialists **Andrée Lajoie** and **Henri Brun**. The document was read at a special ceremony held at the Grand Theatre, Quebec City, 6 Sept. 1995. The text was tabled in Quebec's National Assembly, 7 Sept. 1995, and published in *The Toronto Star* that day.

We talk funny. In our word, you take the *autoroute* or the *Métro* downtown to present the *deputy* who's giving the main *conférence* at the *colloque*. And after that you're the *animator* at a *concertation* table on the *global* situation in the professional *corporations*. On your way home after the table, you'll stop at the *dépanneur* to grab a *baguette* and a *tourtière*, with maybe a little *poutine* for your kid in *secondary five*, who is cramming to get into a good *CEGEP*.

Joan Fraser, editor, *The Gazette*, Conference on Canada & Quebec: Perspectives and Strategies, Vancouver, 2 March 1996.

My saying a few words in English isn't going to shrink the borders of Quebec.

Charles Aznavour, French singer, persisting in introducing some of his songs in English after shouts of "En français!" at a concert at the Molson Centre, Montreal, quoted by Ray Conlogue, "Arts Review," *The Globe and Mail*, 9 Nov. 1996.

Parisians may say they find the Québécois accent *charmant*. In fact, to them, it sounds like the way peasants talk. It's *très très mal vu*. It's the classic hick accent: almost like the Belgians, and there are two jokes a day on the television about the Belgians.

Louis-Bernard Robitaille, Quebec-born correspondent in Paris, interviewed by Taras Grescoe, "The French Paradox," *The Globe and Mail*, 9 Jan. 1999.

LATIN AMERICA

Strictly speaking, a linguistic definition would mean that Quebec, too, ought to be considered a part of Latin America, as it lies within America and is inhabited by a people who speak a Romance language.

Martin W. Lewis and **Kären E. Wigen**, geographer and historian, *The Myth of Continents: A Critique of Metageography* (1997).

LAUGHTER See also HUMOUR & HUMORISTS

The man who can laugh when he isn't amused is always popular.

Bob Edwards, publisher, *The Eye Opener*, 4 June 1910, *The Wit and Wisdom of Bob Edwards* (1976) edited by Hugh Dempsey.

More than anything else I like to hear people laugh. Farce, for me, is just heightened reality. It's reality carried to almost its ridiculous extremes. Turn a farce over and you've got a tragedy, practically.

William Hutt, actor, quoted by Kevin Prokosh in the *Winnipeg Free Press*, 17 Feb. 1992.

Talk can always follow laughter, but laughter can't always follow talk.

Charlie McKenzie, concierge, Rhinoceros Party of Canada, quoted by Stewart MacLeod in *Maclean's*, 30 March 1992.

LAW See also CRIME; JUSTICE & INJUSTICE; LAW & ORDER; LAWYERS; RIGHTS, CIVIL

To the Iroquois, peace *was* the law. They used the same word for both. Peace (the Law) was righteousness in action, the practice of justice between individuals and nations.

Paul A.W. Wallace, historian, *The White Roots of*

Peace (1946). Wallace noted that among the Iroquois the Great Peace and the Great Law were synonymous; "noble" was the radical meaning of the word translated as either "peace" or "law."

The constant goal of any future system of laws which we must adopt must always be, in the last analysis, the preservation of the cultural and spiritual values of our two great civilizations.

F.R. Scott, constitutional law authority, "Canadian Federalism and the Provinces: Some Lessons from the War" (1943), *A New Endeavour: Selected Political Essays, Letters, and Addresses* (1986) edited by Michiel Horn.

The purpose of law is turning passion to reason.

F.R. Scott, professor of law and poet, remark made in June 1960.

Law is the transposition of philosophy to the practical plain.

Guy Favreau, Minister of Justice, quoted by Richard Gwyn in *The Shape of Scandal: A Study of a Government in Crisis* (1965).

The Common Law has grown like a great coral reef. A coral reef is made up of the minutest of living bodies that live and that die, whose spiny skeletons, billions of them, go to make up the body of a great shoal. There is no master plan. There is no "coral king" that directs the birth and death of these tiny organisms whose lives are destined, in the aggregate, to become a thing very different from what they seemed originally to be.

Morris C. Shumiatcher, advocate, *CMA Journal*, 3 Sept. 1977.

People are driven to the law by intense pain or intense hate and are quite immune to practical considerations.

Line from **Stephen Vizinczey**'s novel *An Innocent Millionaire* (1983).

Justice is blind, but the jury system is its guide dog.

John Weingust, lawyer, "Letters to the Editor," *The Globe and Mail*, 25 Sept. 1991.

We have created in law what we abhor in medicine: a two-tiered legal system. Alternative dispute resolution for the rich. Contingency fees for the poor. And they call this justice.

Clayton Ruby, lawyer and columnist, "Talking Point," *The Toronto Star*, 27 March 1996.

LAW & ORDER See also LAW

Law and order are contradictory terms. Mussolinis and Hitlers had order. I prefer law.

George Jonas, essayist, aphorism, Sept. 1975.

Those who enforce the law must at all times be distinguishable from those who infringe it.

John C. Polanyi, scientist, "Beating a Bully but Losing a War," *The Globe and Mail*, 9 April 1991.

When law replaces custom the community dies.

Robin Skelton, poet and aphorist, *A Devious Dictionary* (1991).

What *is* it about the prospect of safe streets that so scares liberals?

Maurus E. Mallon, aphorist, *Compendulum* (1995).

LAWYERS See also LAW

The lawyer is ever more excited by two of the most powerful drives of human nature, pride and love of money.

Lines from **Antoine Gérin-Lajoie**'s two-part novel *Jean Rivard* (1862–64).

And you may place it in the hands of your solicitor, or any other part of his anatomy your ingenuity may devise or his complacency permit.

Leonard W. Brockington, orator and business executive, letter sent in the 1940s in response to receipt of a letter of insult, quoted by Al Boliska in *Wipeouts!* (1969).

To state a lie firmly, categorically and with great authority, undeterred by the fact that all concerned know it to be a lie, is one of the principal activities defined by the term *practising law*.

Line from **Stephen Vizinczey**'s novel *An Innocent Millionaire* (1983).

The defence of unpopular causes is the greatest of challenges that a lawyer will meet in his career at the Bar.

Morris C. Shumaitcher, advocate, "The Abuse of

Power by a Political Minority," Law Society of Upper Canada, Toronto, Special Lecture Series, Fall 1979.

I haven't the slightest moral conflict defending people accused of homicide, sexual assault, business fraud, environmental offences, or even crimes against humanity. I don't "draw the line" at anything. If I defended *crimes*, maybe I would—but I don't defend crimes. I only defend innocent people. Until they are found guilty there are no other kinds of people for me to defend, and what differences does it make what an innocent person is accused of?

Edward L. Greenspan, lawyer, *Greenspan: The Case for the Defence* (1987) written with George Jonas.

Lawyer, n. A specialist who renders legal that which the company has already done.

David Olive, business commentator, *White Knights and Poison Pills: A Cynic's Dictionary of Business Jargon* (1990).

People say the judge is master of the law. That's not true. The law is master of the judge.

Henry Steinberg, Quebec Superior Court Judge, quoted by Bill Taylor in *The Toronto Star*, 6 March 1993.

LEACOCK, STEPHEN See also HUMOUR & HUMORISTS; HUMOUR, CANADIAN; WRITERS & WRITING, CANADIAN

Lord Ronald said nothing; he flung himself from the room, flung himself upon his horse and rode madly off in all directions.

Line from **Stephen Leacock**'s sketch "Gertrude the Governess: or, Simple Seventeen," *Nonsense Novels* (1911). It is said that "riding madly off in all directions" entered the language when U.S. President Theodore Roosevelt made use of it in a political address, giving credit to Leacock for these words which so vividly convey the idea of a state of confusion.

To Stephen Leacock / Who certainly *ought* to like most of the stuff in this book as he wrote it himself first. / Gratefully / Bob Benchley

Robert Benchley, American humorist, inscription on the fly-leaf of his first book, presented to Leacock in 1922, as quoted by Stephen Franklin in the *Jackdaw Leacock* (1970).

His lectures were crowded. Adam Smith, John Stuart Mill, and Malthus would come to life. He, before Winston Churchill, saved the British Empire every Monday, Wednesday, and Friday, at three o'clock, in Room 20.

John T. Culliton, fellow professor at McGill University in Montreal in the 1930s, quoted by Barbara Nimmo in *Last Leaves* (1945).

I shall not altogether die.

Stephen Leacock, humorist, "Three Score and Ten," *My Remarkable Uncle and Other Sketches* (1942).

Sadder still, Stephen Leacock, formerly a hero of mine and of many others, has long bitten the dust. Even his very best story, "Soaked in Seaweed"... is as dead as a doornail or the Marx Brothers films. Poor Leacock's Canadian upbringing laid him low in the end.

Kingsley Amis, English man-of-letters reviewing an anthology of humour, "The Sound of Dying Laughter" (1990), *The Amis Collection: Selected Non-Fiction 1954–1990* (1990).

LEADERSHIP See also HEROES

The chiefs of the League of Five Nations shall be mentors of the people for all time. The thickness of their skin shall be seven spans, which is to say that they shall be proof against anger, offensive action and criticism.

Article of the "Great Law of Peace" of the **Iroquois Confederacy**, reproduced by Craig MacLaine and Michael S. Baxendale in *This Land Is Our Land: The Mohawk Revolt at Oka* (1991).

Our wise men are called Fathers; they truly sustain that character.

Joseph Brant, Mohawk leader, referring to elders, quoted by William L. Stone in *Life of Joseph Brant—Thayendanegea; Including the Indian Wars of the American Revolution* (1838).

If the leader strides forward too fast, he may be hidden from his followers by the curvature of the earth.

George Iles, aphorist, *Canadian Stories: Together with... Jottings from a Note-Book* (1918).

On Political Leaders in History: Most of the people who rank as great leaders—say, Lenin—seem to me to be utter creeps.

Northrop Frye, cultural critic, interviewed by

Allan Gould, "Chatelaine's Celebrity I.D.," *Chatelaine*, Nov. 1982.

Ordinarily we associate authority with leadership, but Canada is the sort of environment in which we can see most clearly that leadership is a conception that modern society is trying to outgrow.

Northrop Frye, cultural critic, "The View from Here" (1983), *Myth and Metaphor: Selected Essays, 1974–1988* (1990) edited by Robert D. Denham.

The capacity of Canadians to do great things in and for the world endures undiminished. It needs only political leadership, and a belief in ourselves, to break the spell.

Eric Kierans and **Walter Stewart**, economist and writer, *Wrong End of the Rainbow: The Collapse of Free Enterprise in Canada* (1988).

Maybe I'm not a true leader because my legs are too short.

Louis Laberge, President of the Quebec Federation of Labour, known as P'tit Louis, diminutive in stature but not in standing, quoted in *The Globe and Mail*, 4 Dec. 1989.

What this country needs is not more leadership, it is more partnership, more participation by the people in the decisions that affect their lives, and a major reform in our institutions, like Parliament and the political parties, that will provide for such participation.

George Woodcock, author and social commentator, "Five-Year Fascism," *The Canadian Forum*, Dec. 1990.

I come from a history of "I don't know, what do you think?"

Audrey McLaughlin, NDP leader, referring to her style of consensual leadership, quoted by Graham Fraser in *The Globe and Mail*, 1 Dec. 1990.

When journalists noticed that Canadians saw little difference between Liberals and Conservatives, they discovered a leadership crisis.

David J. Bercuson and **Barry Cooper**, historian and political scientist, *Deconfederation: Canada without Quebec* (1991).

The essence of leadership is making people feel good.

Said to be the dictum of Prime Minister **Jean Chrétien**, according to David Olive in *Canadian Political Babble* (1993).

A leader who read and thought and spoke in more than sound bites would disturb us because he would sound undecided. He would be forcing us to listen and respond to the authentic noises of a human brain functioning in a position of responsibility.

John Ralston Saul, author, *The Doubter's Companion: A Dictionary of Aggressive Common Sense* (1994).

Leadership starts with leading ourselves, not directing others. Leaders see possibilities, not problems.

Peter Urs Bender, communicator, "Finding the Leader within You," *CGA Magazine*, Oct. 1996.

Leadership + Presentation Skills = Success

Peter Urs Bender, motivational speaker, offering a formula that relates "power presentations" and "leadership" motivation, *Leadership from Within* (1997) with Eric Hellman.

Leadership is the art of getting people to do what they don't want to do and have them enjoy the experience.

Lewis MacKenzie, retired Major-General, quoted by Peter Urs Bender in *Leadership from Within* (1997) with Eric Hellman.

Management is maintaining the status quo; leadership is setting a new direction.

George Torok, motivational speaker, characteristic remark, 26 March 2000.

Anyone can manage when things go right. It takes a leader to take charge when things go wrong.

George Torok, motivational speaker, characteristic remark, 11 May 2000.

LEARNING See also EDUCATION

A little learning is a boring thing.

Line from **Edward Phillips**' novel *Sunday Best* (1990).

When you listen, it's amazing what you can learn. When you act on what you've learned, it's amazing what you can change.

Audrey McLaughlin, NDP leader, *A Woman's*

Place: My Life in Politics (1992) written by Rick Archbold.

There is no dirtier word in the 1990s than the word "elite." Yet there is also nothing more fundamental to the progress of humanity than the existence of elites—the elites of learning.

William Thorsell, newspaper editor, convocation address, June 1995, printed as "Knowledge," *The Globe and Mail*, 10 June 1995.

LEBANESE PEOPLE

I am a Canadian and proud of it. I am an Islander and proud of it. I am a Canadian and an Islander of Lebanese extraction and I am proud of that as well.

Joe Ghiz, Premier of Prince Edward Island, election campaign in 1986, quoted in his obituary in *The Toronto Star*, 10 Nov. 1996.

LEGENDS See also MYTHOLOGY, STORIES

Legends are but the true stories of impossible people.

Augustus Bridle, critic, *Sons of Canada: Short Studies of Characteristic Canadians* (1916).

The Glorious Kingdom of Saguenay had no more existence than Olympus of the Gods. But, like Olympus, Saguenay was thought to exist, and the men who had this thought found it a powerful driving force to action. Very often, in the lives of men, not the truth, but what they feel to be the truth, is important, and must be sought out with care and precision. For what men have believed to be facts has always been the dynamic fact of history.

Joseph E. King, historian, referring to the motive force of the legend of a pre-Columbian society on the banks of the Saguenay River, "The Glorious Kingdom of Saguenay," *Canadian Historical Review*, 31 (1950).

Our legends come from living in a land that contains so much power.

David Adams Richards, novelist, "Northern New Brunswick: A Personal Perspective," "Bank of Montreal: A Portrait of Canada," *Saturday Night*, May 1992.

LEISURE See also PLAY

Having nothing to do is great for about an hour or two.

Louis Dudek, poet and aphorist, "Bitter Pills," *Reality Games* (1998).

LÉVESQUE, RENÉ See also PARTI QUÉBÉCOIS, POLITICIANS

I am first a Québécois, and second—with rather growing doubt—a Canadian.

René Lévesque, Quebec minister, address in Toronto in 1963, quoted by Peter Desbarats in *René: A Canadian in Search of a Country* (1977).

I go to bed, I sleep, I wake with the feeling of urgency.

René Lévesque, Quebec Premier, *My Québec* (1979) translated by Gaynor Fitzpatrick.

They were the two poles of Quebec politics. Lévesque is what we are; Trudeau is what we would like to be.

Claude Charron, former Quebec Cabinet Minister, perhaps explaining why the Québécois voted simultaneously for the separatist Lévesque provincially and the federalist Trudeau federally, quoted by Donald Brittain in the NFB/CBC-TV production *The Champions*, CBC-TV, 14–16 Sept. 1986.

I like to think that he appealed to the emotions of the Quebec people, while I was trying to appeal to their reason.

Pierre Elliott Trudeau, former Prime Minister, on René Lévesque, *Memoirs* (1993).

René Lévesque / 24 Aug. 1922–1 Nov. 1987 / New Carlisle / Montreal / La première page de la vraie belle histoire du Québec vient de se terminer / Dorénavant, il fait partie de la courte liste des libérateurs de peuple.

Inscription on the headstone of René Lévesque, Quebec's first separatist premier, Sillery, Quebec. The inscription is based on a tribute composed by his friend and chansonnier **Félix Leclerc**, 2 Nov. 1987: "The first page of the true beautiful history of Quebec comes to an end. Now it departs from the short list of the liberators of the people."

He was the one who led the Québécois to realize they had the inalienable right to decide their own destiny.

Lucien Bouchard, federal Conservative cabinet minister, wording of a telegram sent to the Parti Québécois national council, meeting in his federal riding of Lac-St-Jean, quoted by Rhéal Séguin, "Face-off," *The Globe and Mail,* 28 March 1998. Séguin noted, "This effectively signalled Mr. Bouchard's resignation as a federalist."

LIBERALISM & LIBERAL PARTY See also IDEOLOGIES, POLITICAL PARTIES

The task of liberalism down through the ages has been to resist the predators, to see that the law is not used to despoil society, to see that every man gets what he earns, and, equally important, to see that every man earns what he gets.

E.C. Drury, socialist, former Ontario Premier, *Farmer Premier* (1968).

I wish neither to take nor to give orders.

A.R.M. Lower, historian, defining "the quintessence of liberalism" in 1948, quoted by Carl Berger in *The Writing of Canadian History: Aspects of English-Canadian Historical Writing: 1900–1970* (1976).

The Liberal Party is like the Tower of Pisa—it always appears to be falling, but it never does.

Reginald Whitaker, historian, reviewing a book on the Liberal Party, *The Globe and Mail,* 28 March 1981.

Bourgeois liberals don't mind if you're mental, as long as you're not *judge*mental.

Maurus E. Mallon, aphorist, *Compendulum* (1995).

LIBERTY See also RIGHTS, CIVIL

Liberty, to a rational creature, as much exceeds property as the light of the sun does that of the most twinkling star.

Joseph Brant, Mohawk leader, quoted by William L. Stone in *Life of Joseph Brant—Thayendanegea; Including the Indian Wars of the American Revolution* (1838).

I write also to prove that I can say what I think, that it isn't liberty that is lacking, but the courage to use the liberty that we have.

Jean-Paul Desbiens, teacher, *The Impertinences of Brother Anonymous* (1962) translated from the French by Miriam Chapin.

Liberty has its costs, but perhaps it is necessary to have lived under tyranny to appreciate that it is still a bargain at any price.

George Jonas, columnist, "Freedom Means Never Having to Say You're Hired" (1978), *Politically Incorrect* (1991).

I would renounce, therefore, the attempt to create heaven on earth, and focus instead on reducing the hell.

A. Alan Borovoy, General Counsel, Canadian Civil Liberties Association, personal maxim, *When Freedoms Collide: A Case for Our Civil Liberties* (1988).

The Americans revere a Statue of Liberty. Our most cherished national symbol is a police force.

Michael Bliss, historian and columnist, *The Toronto Star,* 17 Dec. 1993.

We need justice, we need liberty, and we need as much solidarity as can be reconciled with justice and liberty. But we also need, as much as anything else, language adequate to the times we live in.

Michael Ignatieff, essayist, *The Needs of Strangers* (1985).

The three M.P.s (one Conservative, one Liberal, one NDP—if it matters) deserve our admiration for their strength of principle and wisdom. The principle is that you do not let yourself be shamed by those who are shameless. Your hosts are very likely to think it ill-mannered that you mention their crimes. The wisdom is that, far from damaging those whom you wish to protect... you afford them the only protection that it is in your power to give, namely public attention.

John C. Polanyi, scientist, concerning the expulsion from China of three Members of Parliament who protested civil-rights violations, Letters to the Editor, *The Globe and Mail,* 16 Jan. 1992.

LIBRARIES See also BOOKS, LITERATURE

If the Dear Children who may read Books of this small Library should feel grateful & wish to make any return the most acceptable return they can make will be to abstain wholly from the use of all Intoxicating Liquors and Tobacco. 1839. Jesse Ketchum

Wording on the tablet affixed to the Sunday school library endowed by farmer philanthropist and abolitionist **Jesse Ketchum**, Eglinton Methodist (later United) Church, Toronto, as quoted by Patricia W. Hart in *Pioneering in North York: A History of the Borough* (1968).

Don't you know what a library is for? It's to prevent us making damn fools of ourselves.

George Locke, Chief Librarian of Toronto from 1908 to 1937, addressing a library attendant, quoted by Donald Jones in *The Toronto Star*, 3 April 1982.

There can be no effective education without books... and there can be no adequate source of books for everybody without libraries. Good libraries, dynamic librarians, not stagnant ones.

Angus Mowat, librarian, Introduction, *The Public Library Handbook* (1950).

If the library is, as Borges maintains, a model of the universe, let's try to transform it into a human universe... such as the library of the University of Toronto.

Umberto Eco, Italian scholar and author, frequent visitor to the University of Toronto's Robarts Library, referring to Argentine poet Jorge Luis Borges, address, Milan, 1983, quoted by Greg Gatenby in *The Wild Is Always There: Canada through the Eyes of Foreign Writers* (1993).

If there is a group of people who, besides being absolutely indispensable to the scholar, are more courteous, helpful, and self-effacing than librarians, they must live in some world where I can only hope to go when I die.

O.F.G. Sitwell, geographer, *Four Centuries of Special Geography* (1993).

But a Library—well, a Library goes on as far as thought can reach.

Thoughts of the narrator of **Robertson Davies**' novel *The Cunning Man* (1994).

A public library is the most civilized and democratic of public institutions. It is sacrosanct. A library is the very heart of a community's intellectual life. Here books and other media enshrine the wisdom of the ages, the news of the day, the saga of humanity. Every conceivable topic of interest can be explored in a library, every life enriched through a library's infinite sources of information. To the discouraged a library is a beacon of hope, to the poor and lonely an oasis. To everyone it is a friend.

Dwight Whalen, researcher and writer, protesting early closing of the Niagara Falls Public Library as an economy measure in the face of windfall revenue from the newly opened Niagara Casino, *The Niagara Falls Review*, 23 June 1997.

There Is Something in My Library to Offend Everyone

Wording on a t-shirt worn at a librarians' convention, as noted by Susan Musgrave, "The End of the Road," *PEN Canada Newsletter*, Fall 1997.

LIES

How easy it is for a false statement to take wings; how difficult it is to have it corrected when once told incorrectly! How impossible to make people, who have told the same story time after time, acknowledge that there could be any error in it!

Janet Carnochan, author, "Some Mistakes in History," *Ontario Historical Society: Papers and Records, Volume XIII, III* 1915.

Parents should not tell their children falsehoods merely for convenience, for in so doing the children's faith in their parents is destroyed when they learn the truth.

Brock Chisholm, first Director-General of the World Health Organization, address, Rotary Club, Toronto, Feb. 1945, quoted by Allan Irving in *Brock Chisholm: Doctor to the World* (1998).

Whatever a government says is the exact opposite of the truth. Try it. It doesn't work every time, but it works a lot more often than it should.

Silver Donald Cameron, journalist, *Weekend Magazine*, 14 Feb. 1976.

In a dictatorship, the people are afraid to tell the truth to the leaders. In a democracy, the leaders are afraid to tell the truth to the people.

Richard Needham, newspaper columnist, *The Wit and Wisdom of Richard Needham* (1977).

When you are young, you are shocked by the hypocrisy of others; when you are old, you are amused by your own.

Richard Needham, newspaper columnist, *The Wit and Wisdom of Richard Needham* (1977).

The charm of falsehood is not that it distorts reality, but that it creates reality afresh.

Thoughts of a character in **Carol Shields**' novel *Swann* (1987).

It gets easier to fool other people as you get older, but a lot harder to fool yourself.

Line from **Edward Phillips**' novel *Sunday Best* (1990).

The Nazis taught us one thing: that lies that are left unchallenged become truths.

Irving Abella, historian, address, League for Human Rights of B'nai Brith Canada, Toronto, 10 Dec. 1991, quoted by Bob Brent in *The Toronto Star* the next day.

Reichmann Empire on Secure Footing

Title of a column written on the eve of the collapse of the Reichmann's Olympia & York Developments Ltd. by editor and columnist **Diane Francis** in *The Financial Post*, 26 March 1992, as noted by Walter Stewart in *Too Big to Fail: Olympia & York: The Story Behind the Headlines* (1993) who added, "Reclusive, media-shy Paul Reichmann was playing the *Financial Post* like a zither."

I was vividly reminded of Ontario Premier Bob Rae's proclamation of cabinet integrity when Ontario Northern Affairs Minister Shelley Martel proclaimed that she really had *told the truth when she said she had lied.* She later *proved* she had lied through polygraph tests. This must be the first time in recorded history a polygraph has been commissioned by someone to prove she was lying and as unlikely as a rat clinging to a sinking ship.... The fact that a minister of the Crown resorted to a lie detector test to actually prove she lied will surely enter the record books one day.

Tom Davey, editor, editorial, *Environmental Science & Engineering*, June 1992.

LIEUTENANT-GOVERNOR

It is interesting that American and Englishmen pronounce that word differently: the English and Canadian *left-tenant*, the American *loo-tenant*, closer to the French word, meaning place-taker, he who occupies the place of a superior.

Robert MacNeil, broadcaster and memoirist, *Wordstruck: A Memoir* (1989).

LIFE See also HUMANITY, MANKIND

I assure you there cannot well be a more unpoetical and unromantic existence than ours.

Anne Langton, English spinster who settled near Sturgeon Lake, Upper Canada (Ontario), *A Gentlewoman in Upper Canada* (1950).

A little while and I will be gone from among you, whither I cannot tell. From nowhere we came, into nowhere we go. What is life? It is a flash of a firefly in the night. It is a breath of a buffalo in the winter time. It is as the little shadow that runs across the grass and loses itself in the sunset.

Attributed to **Crowfoot**, as the Blackfoot chief lay dying in his teepee overlooking the Bow River, 25 April 1890, by the historian John Peter Turner in *The North-West Mounted Police: 1873–1893* (1950). Hugh Dempsey excluded the speech from his biography of Crowfoot. Historian Robert S. Carlisle, "Crowfoot's Dying Speech," *Alberta History*, Summer 1990, established a prior source: Sir H. Rider Haggard's once-popular novel *King Solomon's Mines* (1885). In the novel, the African chieftain Umbopa speaks these words: "What is life?... It is the glow-worm that shines in the night-time and is black in the morning; it is the white breath of the oxen in winter, it is the little shadow that runs across the grass and loses itself in sunset." Did Turner Canadianize the African references and ascribe the fictitious Umbopa's words to the real-life Crowfoot? Haggard visited the Northwest; Ayesha Peak, west of Alberta's Bow Lake, was named after the immortal Ayesha in his novel *She* (1887).

Each morning founds a dynasty of fate; each evening ends the empire of a day.

Albert E.S. Smythe, editor, "Rays," *The Lamp: A Theosophical Monthly, Volume 1*, Oct. 1894.

What is the life of a man? Our little being is lost in immensity. This thought and that of the impenetrable mystery of existence are likely, rather than cosmic emotion, worship of humanity, or any of the other substitutes for theism, to take possession of the human mind if the belief in a God is withdrawn.

Goldwin Smith, essayist, "Morality and Theism," *Guesses at the Riddle of Existence and Other Essays on Kindred Subjects* (1897).

Life is certainly one darned worriment after another.

L.M. Montgomery, author, journal entry, 13 April 1919, *The Selected Journals of L.M. Montgomery: Volume II: 1910–1921* (1987) edited by Mary Rubio and Elizabeth Waterston.

What was life anyway? A dumb shifting of forces. Grass grew and was trodden down; and it knew not why.

Thoughts of a character in **Frederick Philip Grove**'s novel *Settlers of the Marsh* (1925).

Any depiction of life as it is, is depressing reading.

Stephen Leacock, author, "Why He Selected 'My Remarkable Uncle,'" included by Whit Burnett in *This Is My Best: Over 150 Self-Chosen and Complete Masterpieces, Together with Their Reasons for Their Selections* (1942).

We are a belayed boat and life is out there on the open seas. Let's cut the cables. After that single moment of cutting loose, our position will be beautiful, honest, active; all our newly discovered possibilities will lead to their own reality.

Bruno M. Cormier, writer and future psychiatrist, "Rupture" (1945), quoted by Ray Ellenwood in *Egregore: A History of the Montréal Automatis Movement* (1992).

Modern science has made to almost every one of you the present of a few years.

Sir William Osler, physician and professor, quoted by William Bennett Bean in *Sir William Osler: Aphorisms from His Bedside Teachings and Writings* (1950).

The stage presents things that are make-believe; presumably life presents things that are real and sometimes not well rehearsed.

Erving Goffman, sociologist born in Manville, Alta., who found in the theatrical performance the metaphor for human behaviour in social situations, *The Presentation of Self in Everyday Life* (1959).

You can sing about life or you can try to understand it. You can't do both.

Irving Layton, poet and aphorist, *The Whole Bloody Bird (obs, aphs & Pomes)* (1969).

Perfect from the start / That small cell / Contains / Already / The wrinkles and death / Of an old man

Lines from **Cécile Cloutier**'s poem "Birth" translated by Fred Cogswell in *One Hundred Poems of Modern Quebec* (1970).

I once coined a phrase. And it is that the essence of great living is to have something to wake up to, something to go to, and something to come home to.

Sammy Koffman, proprietor of the Belle Clair Hotel in Ottawa (1953–66), quoted by Earl McRae in *The Toronto Star*, 2 April 1977.

Nothing is as strange as life and the most unlikely people have the most surprising secrets.

R.A. Wells, author, *The Manipulators* (1977).

The first twenty years of your life are ruined by your parents; the next twenty years are ruined by your children; doctors, lawyers, and tax collectors look after the rest.

Richard Needham, newspaper columnist, *The Wit and Wisdom of Richard Needham* (1977).

In all we do we can recognize that we belong to a great universe of life. We can apply our relatedness to everything, and we, and everything, become more alive.

Dorothy Maclean, medium, *To Hear the Angels Sing: An Odyssey of Co-Creation with the Devic Kingdom* (1980).

There is no real / world, my friends. / Why not, then, / let the stars / shine in our bones?

Poem titled "envoi (to begin with)" from **Robert Kroetsch**'s *Advice to My Friends: A Continuing Poem* (1985).

Expect the unexpected because your life is bound to be full of surprises.

Bernard Grad, biochemist and parapsychologist, "Experiences and Opinions of an Unconventional Scientist," *Men and Women of Parapsychology: Personal Reflections* (1987) edited by Rosemarie Pilkington.

I have come to that place in life where / there is nothing below. There are no / lower numbers.

Lines from **Kristjana Gunnars**' journal-like poem in *Zero Hour* (1991).

Life for the young is a situation comedy, for the middle-aged a soap-opera, for the old a documentary.

Louis Dudek, poet and aphorist, "Epigrams," *Small Perfect Things* (1991).

Mischance can wreck a life; so can a missed chance.

Maurus E. Mallon, aphorist, 27 August 1992.

But if the two possibilities, of nothingness and of something that makes sense, weren't equally present, the mind couldn't grow. If I *knew* that there was nothing, my motivation for going on by myself would drop to zero. If there is something, and I *knew* what that something was, the next life would be essentially the same as this one. So the mystery in death guarantees the liveliness of life.

Northrop Frye, cultural critic, "Notebook 1993," edited by Robert D. Denham, *Northrop Frye Newsletter*, Summer 1993.

Yet that life you live is still more fascinating than any novel you'll ever read or any film you'll ever see, even if that fact is being withheld from you. Your life is still your own. It won't be repeated and it can't be passed on.

R. Murray Schafer, composer and theorist, "Dub," *The Canadian Forum*, Nov. 1994.

Let me tell you a secret: there is no such thing as an uninteresting life.

Remark of an older person in **Rohinton Mistry**'s novel *A Fine Balance* (1995).

Stars, stones, canoes, lamps, coins. All these things must be spoken of as Beings, as alive things.

Paulette Jiles, poet and traveller, *Northern Spirit: Travels among the Cree and Ojibway Nations and Their Star Maps* (1995).

The examined life makes a virtue of uncertainty. It celebrates doubt.

John Ralston Saul, author, *The Unconscious Civilization* (1995).

We do not deny that tragedy and loss exist; we accept the tragic dimension of life which cannot be avoided, but we must aim towards the *fullness of life*.

Henry Morgentaler, physician, Honorary President of the Humanist Association of Canada, "Humanism Today," *Humanist in Canada*, Winter 1995–96.

To grow up in those parts of this country called "English Canada" is to grow up with a peculiar certainty of the in-betweenness of things.

Geoff Pevere and **Greig Dymond**, commentators, *Mondo Canuck: A Canadian Pop Culture Odyssey* (1996).

Humans must comfort one another, defend one another, against the terror of being human.

W.O. Mitchell, writer and humorist, first Margaret Laurence Memorial Lecture, annual meeting, Writers' Union of Canada, Winnipeg, 1 May 1996, quoted by Philip Marchand in *The Toronto Star*, 3 June 1996.

Life isn't fair. Did you already find that out? It would be nice if it were. But I do not think it was supposed to be.

Peter Urs Bender, motivational speaker, *Leadership from Within* (1997) with Eric Hellman.

For no life can be other, viewed from the standpoint of the afterlife, than a scene within an eternal present.

Louis Dudek, poet and aphorist, "Biography," *Reality Games* (1998).

LIGHT

. . . and my eyes followed the spin of the fields newly laid out for sowing, the oak woods with hard bronze survivor leaves, and a world of great size beyond, or fair clouds and then of abstraction, a tremendous Canada of light.

Thoughts of a character in **Saul Bellow**'s novel *The Adventures of Augie March* (1965).

We think no shadows when we are the sun.

Line from a poem by **Robin Skelton** in *Timelight* (1975).

LISTENING

Since attentive listeners are, in fact, rare in our society, a person—*any* person—who offers rapt attention to somebody talking starts off with a tremendous advantage right there. It's hardly an arcane skill.

Philip Marchand, writer and exponent of the "new journalism," Introduction to *Just Looking, Thank You: An Amused Observer's View of Canadian Lifestyles* (1976).

LITERACY

It is well known that these western nations have no knowledge of letters. This it is which all who have written of them say that the savages most wondered at, to see that by a piece of paper I make known my will from one end of the world to the other; and they thought that there was enchantment in the paper.

Marc Lescarbot, French lawyer and sometime colonist at Port-Royal, *Histoire de la Nouvelle-France* (1609), translated by W.L. Grant as *The History of New France* (1907).

In our day the electronic media of film, radio and television have brought about a revival of the oral culture that we had before writing, and many of the social characteristics of a pre-literate society are reappearing in ours.

Northrop Frye, cultural theorist, "Communications," *The Listener*, 9 July 1970.

A recent investigation reveals that five million Canadian adults are "functionally illiterate." But why, one wonders, do so many of these seek, and achieve, election?

Robertson Davies, man-of-letters, "The Canadian Imagination," *The Globe and Mail*, 17 Dec. 1977.

Anybody who can do so much as read has an obligation to those who cannot.

John C. Polanyi, scientist, "No Genuine Ivory Tower Is Ever Irrelevant," *The Vancouver Sun*, Sept. 1989.

This is a nation not of illiterates but of ex-literates—supposedly educated people who haven't read a book since they escaped from school. Many of them are university graduates but they learned no love of the printed word.

Crawford Kilian, novelist, quoted by Larry Smith in *The St. Catharines Standard*, 17 Oct. 1990.

The twenty-four per cent of Canadians who are illiterate must be bright enough to get by. It's the ones who can read that worry me.

Louis Dudek, poet and aphorist, "Epigrams," *Small Perfect Things* (1991).

According to the Organization for Economic Cooperation and Development's data, 10 per cent of Canadian university graduates are functionally illiterate in a population where 47 per cent of the entire population are similarly handicapped, able to read only the simplest of texts or unable to read at all.

David Bercuson, Robert Bothwell, and J.L. Granatstein, historians, *Petrified Campus: The Crisis in Canada's Universities* (1997)

Over the world, let us be clear: there is no literate population that is poor; no illiterate population that is other than poor.

John Kenneth Galbraith, economist, *The Socially Concerned Today* (1998).

LITERATURE

See also BOOKS; CULTURE; LIBRARIES; LITERATURE, CANADIAN; MAGAZINES; POETS & POETRY; SCIENCE FICTION; STORIES; THEATRE; WRITERS & WRITING, CANADIAN

It is, of course, quite impossible to have any real understanding of English literature without a thorough knowledge of French, German, Italian, and Spanish literature, to say nothing of Latin and Greek.

Paul Lafleur, head of the English Department, McGill University in the 1930s, remark recalled by his student, Eugene Forsey, in *A Life on the Fringe* (1990).

It is only after long practice and much interest in the work that one can set down plain truth, without over-embellishment or wandering from the point.... When this is done even the truth itself sounds a little better than true, which is the basis of what is called literature.

Stephen Leacock, author, "Why He Selected 'My Remarkable Uncle,'" included by Whit Burnett in *This Is My Best: Over 150 Self-Chosen and Complete Masterpieces, Together with Their Reasons for Their Selections* (1942).

Literature is a human apocalypse, man's revelation to man, and criticism is not a body of adjudication, but the awareness of the revelation, the last judgement of mankind.

Northrop Frye, cultural critic, *Anatomy of Criticism* (1957).

Find a classic that wasn't first regarded as light entertainment.

Marshall McLuhan, communications pioneer, quoted by Quentin Fiore in *Media & Methods*, Dec. 1968.

Nothing but literature, in a culture as verbal as ours, can train the imagination to fight for the sanity and the dignity of mankind.

Northrop Frye, cultural critic, "The Bush Garden," *The Bush Garden: Essays on the Canadian Imagination* (1971).

Great literature is any old stuff you can read without disgust.

Louis Dudek, man-of-letters, *Epigrams* (1975).

The word *classic* as applied to a work of literature means primarily a work that refuses to go away, that remains confronting us until we do something about it, which means also doing something about ourselves.

Northrop Frye, cultural critic, "The Double Mirror" (1981), *Myth and Metaphor: Selected Essays, 1974–1988* (1990) edited by Robert D. Denham.

What I have to say is in my novels. The rest is gossip.

Mordecai Richler, novelist, interviewed by Marlene Kadar in *Other Solitudes: Canadian Multicultural Fictions* (1990) edited by Linda Hutcheon and Marion Richmond.

We write each other's lives—by means of fictions. Sustaining fictions. Uplifting fictions. Lies. This way, we lead one another toward survival.

Sentiments of a character in **Timothy Findley**'s novel *Headhunter* (1993).

Do not read for longer than thirty minutes. The mind cannot absorb what the ass cannot endure.

Greg Gatenby, artistic director of Harbourfront's International Authors' Festival, instructions to recitalists, quoted by Liam Lacey in *The Globe and Mail*, 1 Jan. 1994.

The way I put it is, someone who reads Tolstoy and doesn't recognize the presence of a towering genius is deficient in taste, period.

Philip Marchand, book columnist, "What I Really Think," *Saturday Night*, Oct. 1997.

LITERATURE, CANADIAN See also LITERATURE

You have English, French, and American literature. One result of this is that your Canadian literature is reconstructed, and another result is that by and by you may not have any Canadians at all.

Mark Twain, humorist, delivering his so-called Second Speech in Montreal, 9 Dec. 1881, quoted by David Ketterer in "Mark Twain's Overlooked 'Second Speech' in Montreal," *Mark Twain Journal*, Fall 1990.

The moment we begin to give a nation the unity and simplicity of an animal, we begin to think wildly.... Thus people will say that Spain has entered a final senility; they might as well say that Spain is losing her teeth. Or people will say that Canada should soon produce a literature; which is like saying that Canada must soon grow a moustache.

G.K. Chesterton, British man-of-letters, *What's Wrong with the World* (1910).

By a strange trick of fate the writers of travels who are now remembered make no pretension to literary skill. The narratives which have become classic are the unpolished, but intensely fascinating, accounts of the traders connected with the Hudson Bay Company and its formidable rival, the Northwest Association. Their tales of adventure will be read as long as men delight in pictures of life untrammelled by the conventions of society.

Ray Palmer Baker, historian, *A History of English-Canadian Literature to the Confederation: Its Relation to the Literature of Great Britain and the United States* (1920).

Of course no one believes there is a Canadian literature! I know nothing of Canada, never having been there!

George Bernard Shaw, Anglo-Irish playwright, addressing members of the Canadian Authors' Association visiting London, 13 July 1933, quoted by William D. Lighthall in *The Bookman*, Spring 1977.

I know from Canadian friends how much Canada has to depend for "literary" reading matter on the very dowdiest stuff that comes from this country.

Sylvia Townsend Warner, English novelist, letter written from Dorchester, England, to William Lawson in Toronto, 1 Aug. 1938, quoted by Dorothy Livesay in *Right Hand Left Hand* (1977).

Canada has had writers, and has them now, and they have not been trivial in their achievement. What Canada needs is serious, demanding readers. Before a nation demands masterworks it must be certain that it really wants them. Strong demand brings rich supply.

Robertson Davies, man-of-letters, essay, 1967, *Robertson Davies: The Well-Tempered Critic: One Man's View of Theatre and Letters in Canada* (1981) edited by Judith Skelton Grant.

And the rest of it... Canada? Tell me, what has Canada produced? Nothing. But the south is interesting. What a pity they lost the Civil War—don't you think it is a pity, eh?

Jorge Luis Borges, Argentine writer, discussing North American literature during the course of an interview with the travel writer Paul Theroux in *The Old Patagonian Express* (1979).

The oldest Canadian literary form was the ledger.

Eric Nicol, humorist, *Canada Cancelled for Lack of Interest* (1977) illustrated by Peter Whalley.

Canadian literature is without strong individual characters on the whole, being much more forceful in its presentation of settings. Man appears rather generalized: what has character is the wilderness, the city, the snow, the sea.

Jay Macpherson, poet and scholar, "This Swan Neck of the Woods," *The Spirit of Solitude: Conventions and Continuities in Late Romance* (1982).

If there is such a thing as Canadian literature, actually distinct from the literature of Europe, John Sky of the Q'unaqighawai and Walter McGregor of the Qaiahllanas are two of its earliest and greatest classical authors.

Robert Bringhurst, poet and anthropologist, "That Also Is You," *Native Writers and Canadian Writing: Canadian Literature Special Issue* (1990) edited by W.H. New. Bringhurst is referring to two 19th-century oral poets of the Haida people; another candidate is the Eskimo singer Orpingalik.

Canadian economic and political development today is that of a fully matured Western democracy, but its culture is that of an emergent nation.

Northrop Frye, cultural critic, "Criticism and Environment" (1983), *The Eternal Act of Creation: Essays, 1979–1990* (1993) edited by Robert D. Denham.

I believe Leacock, Stephen Leacock the humorist, was Canadian, wasn't he?... And there is a poet, Pratt... who has a poem... a salute to Canada, yes. He has an "Ode to the Railroad"... a railway poet... doesn't augur well... but, why not? Everything can be a theme for poetry. Kipling wrote to "Our Lady of the Snows, Canada." Our lady of the snows, yes. And with the enormous territory they have....

Jorge Luis Borges, Argentine man-of-letters, interviewed by Raul Galvez in Buenos Aires, Argentina, June 1985, *From the Sahen Land of the Virgins* (1988).

I was told by V.S. Naipaul to go neither to England, which he thought was a decaying civilization, nor to the United States, which would swallow me up. He suggested Canada as a good place. I think it was a very good suggestion.

Neil Bissoondath, Trinidad-born, Toronto-based novelist, interviewed by Andrew Garrod in *Speaking for Myself: Canadian Writers in Interview* (1986).

Canada has the greatest unread literature in the world. What it lacks in greatness it makes up for in unreadability.

Louis Dudek, poet and aphorist, "Epigrams," *Small Perfect Things* (1991).

It is important to note one other thing, in regard to the "classics." No one who has read them at all widely can read, say, Laurence or Atwood or Davies, and not recognize that they are, when all is said, minor writers. I do not mean that they are bad—or mediocre, or negligible—writers. But they are minor—that is, the notes they sound are often true but the range of these notes is limited, and sometimes sharply limited.

Philip Marchand, book columnist, "What I Really Think," *Saturday Night*, Oct. 1997.

When I started out as a scribbler, something like fifty years ago, you could fit all of Canada's quality writers into a Volkswagen and still have room to pick up a hitchhiker. These happy days we could just about fill a bus.

Mordecai Richler, novelist, quoted in the *National Post*, 11 Dec. 1999.

LOBBYISTS

A lobbyist is a legislative consultant like an undertaker is a mortician and a chimney sweep is a flumologist.

E.H. Van Slyke, lobbyist for the Canadian Federation of Independent Business, quoted by Elaine Carey in *The Toronto Star*, 3 Aug. 1978.

If you think talk is cheap, you haven't dealt with a lobbyist lately.

Sean Moore, editor of *The Lobby Monitor*, "Forum File," *The Canadian Forum*, July–Aug. 1994. In 1994, the Department of Industry reported that there were 2,759 registered lobbyists in Ottawa. "Per diem fees usually run between $1,000 and $2,000 and retainers range from $3,000 to $10,000 a month."

LONELINESS

A man becomes lonely because he has never consented to be alone.

André Laurendeau, editor, "You Must Drink Your Own Prose to the Dregs" (1963), *André Laurendeau: Witness for Quebec* (1973) translated by Philip Stratford.

The European habitually goes out to be social and comes home to be alone. The American and Canadian do exactly the reverse.

Marshall McLuhan, communications pioneer, and Bruce R. Powers, communications specialist, authors of *The Global Village: Transformations in World Life and Media in the 21st Century* (1989).

You think we are lonely when we are out on the land. I tell you it's the people in the cities who are lonely.

Roger Kuptana, Inuit of the Arctic, quoted in *Canada's Northwest Territories: 1992 Explorers' Guide* (1991).

A LAKE / A LANE / A LIVE / A LONE

Memorable inscription dedicated to poet bp Nichol, based on the lines of one of his concrete poems, embedded in concrete by artist **David B. Smith**, 30 April 1994, opposite Coach House Press, bp Nichol Lane, Toronto.

All that land and all that sky do make poets. Prairie certainly teaches early that to be human means to be conscious of self—and separation from the rest of the living whole. "Human" therefore equals "lonely."

W.O. Mitchell, raconteur, "The Poetry of Life," address, Writers' Union of Canada, Winnipeg, June 1996, *An Evening with W.O. Mitchell: A Collection of the Author's Best Loved Performance Pieces* (1997) edited by Barbara and Armond Mitchell.

LOONIE See also MONEY

Loonie

First use of the name loonie (subsequently spelled looney) for the one-dollar coin, which features the profile of Queen Elizabeth II on the obverse side and a loon in water on the reverse side, has been claimed by **Charles Cook** of Toronto, Letters to the Editor, *The Globe and Mail*, 9 Jan. 1987. The claim was upheld in Letters to the Books Editor, *The Globe and Mail*, 8 Aug. 1998.

Toonie

Name proposed for the two-dollar Canadian coin, modelled on that of the one-dollar Loonie, when it was introduced, Metropolitan Toronto Zoo, 21 Sept. 1995. Twoonie (or toonie) was the private choice of David Dingwall, Minister of Public Works, who officiated at the launch. A joke making the rounds some weeks prior to Quebec's referendum on sovereignty, 30 Oct. 1995, suggested the new coin should depict Quebec Premier Jacques Parizeau on one side, Bloc Québécois leader Lucien Bouchard on the other, and it should be known as the double loonie.

As a lover of loons, I propose that our $2 coin should display two loons on the reverse side. This should ensure that I would realize my true objective: to have it become known as a *doubloon*.

Kerr Gibson, correspondent, offering the first known instance in print of the pun on the loonie and the old Spanish coin called the doubloon, Letters to the Editor, *The Toronto Star*, 18 Feb. 1993. Sixty million such $2 coins were minted and circulated on 19 Feb. 1996.

The word *toonie* has too much of the nursery about it, but commends itself on grounds of accuracy (two loonies), synergy (loonie toons, suggesting Warner Bros. cartoons) and alliteration (a two-tone toonie).

Warren Clements, columnist, "Sterling Names for the $2 Coin," *The Globe and Mail*, 24 Feb. 1996.

Nanuk is the Inuit word for polar bear. It plays on the representation on the coin's face without making light of it, the language honours Canada's aboriginal heritage, and it has a nice ring to it: the Nanuk of the North.

The Nanuk. That's our choice.

Editorial, "Two Cents on the Twoonie," *The Globe and Mail*, 30 March 1996.

LOTTERIES See also GAMES & GAMBLING

Consider: You are twice as likely to be struck by lightning and twenty times as likely to be a homicide victim, as you are to win a major lottery prize.

Manuel Escott, writer, *The Toronto Star*, 29 July 1979.

Quebecers make the fewest long-distance phone calls, give the least to charity, do less volunteer work and buy more lottery tickets than other provinces.

Brian Dunn, writer, "Why Quebec Advertising Is Different: Advertising Supplement," *Advertising Age*, 22 Nov. 1993.

An American wins the lottery and buys a new Cadillac. The Canadian buys an airline ticket in search of a good time—somewhere else.

Michael Adams, President, Environics Research Group Ltd., speech in Victoria, B.C., "Just What Was Said," *The Globe and Mail*, 20 Feb. 1995.

LOVE See also KISSES, MARRIAGE, MEN & WOMEN, ROMANCE, SEX

These people are too closely absorbed in gaining a livelihood to find leisure for flights of fancy; the struggle for existence is too implacable and inexorable to allow time for indulgence of the imagination. Even Love, the universal theme, is here scarcely mentioned; the fire which in warmer climes glows with such fervent heat here waxes dim, and is scarcely taken into account at all.

Janarius A. MacGahan, Anglo-Irish correspondent, referring to the traditional tales of the Eskimos, *Under the Northern Lights* (1876).

But, O me! how many women since the days of Echo and Narcissus, have pined themselves into air for the love of men who were in love only with themselves!

Anna Brownell Jameson, traveller and writer, *Winter Studies and Summer Rambles in Canada* (1838).

It is very hard—nay, it is impossible to explain why we love some people and have no love for others. I know many people who, I feel sure, are good and admirable. Yet I find no pleasure in their society and in some cases dislike them. Again, there are people who are far from being perfect whom I do love and in whose society I find delight and satisfaction.

L.M. Montgomery, author, diary entry, 5 Feb. 1911, *The Selected Journals of L.M. Montgomery: Volume II: 1910–1921* (1987) edited by Mary Rubio and Elizabeth Waterston.

When a man is in love for the first time he thinks he invented it.

Bob Edwards, publisher, *The Eye Opener*, 24 Nov. 1917, *The Wit and Wisdom of Bob Edwards* (1976) edited by Hugh Dempsey.

Love—why, I'll tell you what love is: it's you at seventy-five and her at seventy-one, each of you listening for the other's step in the next room, each afraid that a sudden silence, a sudden cry, could mean a lifetime's talk is over."

Passage from **Brian Moore**'s novel *The Luck of Ginger Coffey* (1960).

Your body's a small word with many meanings. / Love. If. Yes. But. Death.

Lines from **Alden Nowlan**'s poem "Canadian Love Song," *The Things Which Are* (1962).

Every time you make love, it should be as if it were for the last time.

Bertrand Vac, poet and aphorist, *Mes pensées "profondes"* (1967).

Soft is a feminine privilege / without any angles but love.

Lines from **Sandra Kolber**'s poem "Fleshings," *All There Is of Love* (1969).

Mirrors / are the perfect lovers.

Lines from **Margaret Atwood**'s poem "Tricks with Mirrors," *You Are Happy* (1974).

All honest people have difficulty with the word "love."

John Hofsess, columnist, *Maclean's*, Dec. 1974.

Love: Hours written into life's minutes.

Raymond Canale, Italian-born playwright and Toronto-based aphorist, observation made in 1975.

A husband suspects one other man; a wife, all other women.

Richard Needham, newspaper columnist, *The Wit and Wisdom of Richard Needham* (1977).

Love is not kind or honest and does not contribute to happiness in any reliable way.

Alice Munro, author, quoted by Anne Lamott in "Almost 86'ed" (1985), reprinted in *San Francisco Stories: Great Writers on the City* (1990) edited by John Miller.

Why are we, like velcro, always so reluctant to let go?

Thought of a character in **Edward Phillips**' novel *Buried on Sunday* (1986).

Although much of our life is rooted in the anxiety of time, in other words the fear of death, the continuity of knowledge and wisdom that has brought us here together is rooted in love, a love that is not only as strong as death, but able to cast out its fear.

Northrop Frye, cultural critic, sermon, Metropolitan United Church, Toronto, celebrating the Sesquicentennial of the University of Victoria, 5 Oct. 1986, quoted in *Vic Report*, Spring 1991.

Love was like a childhood for him. It opened him up, he was silly and relaxed.

Thoughts of a character in **Michael Ondaatje**'s novel *In the Skin of a Lion* (1988).

Old lovers go the way of old photographs, bleaching out gradually as in a slow bath of acid: first the moles and pimples, then the shadings, then the faces themselves, until nothing remains but the general outlines.

Thoughts of the narrator of **Margaret Atwood**'s novel *Cat's Eye* (1988).

The lover is not an ideal, nor a fantasy, but only the full humanness of us.

Robert Augustus Masters, writer, *The Way of the Lover: The Awakening and Embodiment of the Full Human* (1989).

From infancy to old age we are loved less and less, but we also become more capable of love.

Louis Dudek, poet and aphorist, "Epigrams," *Small Perfect Things* (1991).

Your palm warm / Upon my body / Shadows now of two— / Me and you.

Lines from **Flavia Cosma**'s poem "It Was," *47 Poems* (1992) translated by Don D. Wilson.

Whatever happens between us now / I think about for hours, / Until it changes me.

Lines from **Don Coles**' poem "K in Love," *Someone Has Stayed in Stockholm: New and Selected Poems* (1994).

Let us give to each other the love we are capable of instead of reserving it for some illusory Deity which does not exist, or a mythical Jesus, or other such idol. We have to find meaning in this life, and possibly transcendence in working for a good cause with other people.

Henry Morgentaler, physician, Honorary President of the Humanist Association of Canada, "Humanism Today," *Humanist in Canada*, Winter 1995/96.

Thirty years later I still do not know why I loved her with a husband's love rather than the blind passion women like her seem to require—only that I did.

Thoughts of a character in **Guy Vanderhaeghe**'s novel *The Englishman's Boy* (1996).

LOYALTY

We may be loyal to Great Britain, but our heart and our thoughts belong to France.

Henri Bourassa, publisher, writing in 1912, quoted by Robert Prévost in *Petit dictionnaire des citations québécoises* (1988).

A demand for loyalty is usually an admission that confidence does not exist.

Reeves Haggan, CBC General Supervisor of Public Affairs in the 1960s, subsequently government adviser, quoted by Eric Koch in *Inside This Hour Has Seven Days* (1986).

You can teach expertise—but you can't teach loyalty.

Attributed to Prime Minister **Brian Mulroney** who was said to favour friends over politicial allies, quoted by Graham Fraser in *The Globe and Mail*, 18 May 1991.

LUCK

Luck is an opportunity seized.

Roy Thomson, Lord Thomson of Fleet, quoted by Peter C. Newman, "The Table Talk of Roy Thomson," *Maclean's*, Dec. 1971.

You know, it's a hell of a lot better to be lucky than smart.

John W. Bassett II, publisher and capitalist, quoted by Charles Taylor in *The Globe and Mail*, 21 Feb. 1974.

Capricious "Dame Fortune," and her sister "Serendipity," both among the most popular of prospector's patronesses, again had their day.

Frank R. Joubin, prospector, *Not for Gold Alone: The Memoirs of a Prospector* (1986) written with D. McCormack Smyth.

I believe in good omens. I don't believe in the bad ones.

Silken Laumann, Olympic rower, quoted by Stephen Brunt in *The Globe and Mail*, 29 July 1992.

M

McLUHAN, MARSHALL See also COMMUNICATIONS, MEDIA

The medium is the message.

This is the most widely quoted aphorism of Canadian origin of all time. It is recognized from Toronto to Timbuktu. **Marshall McLuhan**, pioneer in communications theory and media studies, first uttered the now-famous formulation on the evening of 30 July 1959 at a reception in the Vancouver home of educator Alan Thomas, following a symposium at the University of British Columbia on the subject of music and the mass media. McLuhan first published the aphorism in his book *Understanding Media* (1964) and thereafter punned (or "funned") with it: "The medium is the mess-age," "The medium is the massage," etc. McLuhan had in mind that the content of communiqué is influenced by its form.

The new electronic independence recreates the world in the image of a global village.

This is the first known appearance in print of the words "a global village." The sentence appears in **Marshall McLuhan**'s *The Gutenberg Galaxy* (1962).

The media.

Marshall McLuhan should be credited with the first use of the words the media to embrace all forms of communication, according to cultural commentator Thomas Wolfe, interviewed on CBC-TV's *Marshall McLuhan: The Man with the Message*, 18 Oct. 1984. McLuhan used it in *Counterblast* (1954), where he wrote, "The media are not toys; they should not be in the hands of Mother Goose and Peter Pan executives. They can be entrusted only to new artists, because they are art forms."

Extensions of man.

Phrase used by **Marshall McLuhan** to refer to the arts and the sciences, particularly the technologies, which was originated by Edward Hall who may have found it in Buckminster Fuller, according to Edmund Carpenter, "Remembering Explorations," *Canadian Notes & Queries*, Spring 1992.

McLuhan put a telescope to his ear; / What a lovely smell, he said, we have here.

Satirical couplet from **A.J.M. Smith**'s "The Taste of Space," *Poems* (1967). McLuhan's response was "Synaesthesia!"

I could never stand up to McLuhan—he always had aces to my kings.

Norman Mailer, author, appearing on CBC-TV in the 1960s on a panel moderated by Robert Fulford with McLuhan and Malcolm Muggeridge. Quoted by Philip Marchand in *The Toronto Star*, 7 May 1995. Mailer feared McLuhan, but McLuhan quaked before Muggeridge.

You mean my whole fallacy is wrong?

Rhetorical question asked by **Marshall McLuhan** playing himself in the movie *Annie Hall* (1976). In the scene he steps into the foyer of a Manhattan movie theatre to comment on a statement of actor-director Woody Allen. Noted by Matie Molinaro in *Who Was Marshall McLuhan?* (1994) edited by Barrington Nevitt and Maurice McLuhan.

By and large he has simply acted as a rallying-point for assumptions and prejudices which were already beginning to take shape long before his work became generally known.

John Gross, English cultural journalist, *The Rise and Fall of the Man of Letters: A Study of the Idiosyncratic and the Humane in Modern Literature* (1969).

I am not, by temperament or conviction, a revolutionary; I would prefer a stable, changeless environment of modest services and human scale.

Marshall McLuhan, communications pioneer, "Playboy Interview" (1969) conducted by Eric Norden, *The Essential McLuhan* (1995) edited by Eric McLuhan and Frank Zingrone.

Some people read between the lines. I read between the pages.

Statement made by **Marshall McLuhan** to reading specialist Joel Bonn after taking his speed-reading course in the 1970s. McLuhan maintained that with a new book he always turned to page 69, read it, then consulted the table of contents; if the book was of interest to him, he read only left-hand pages, using his finger as a guide in the standard speed-reading manner.

Ashley, are you sure it's not too soon to go around parties saying, "What ever happened to Marshall McLuhan?"

Caption to a cartoon in *The New Yorker*, 26 Sept. 1970, quoted by Philip Marchand in *Marshall McLuhan: The Medium and the Messenger* (1989).

Man's reach should exceed his grasp, or what's a metaphor?

Parody of the well-known lines "Ah, but a man's reach should exceed his grasp, / Or what's a heaven for?" from Robert Browning's poem "Andrea del Sarto," dear to the heart of **Marshall McLuhan**, as recalled by Northrop Frye in "The Double Mirror" (1981), *Myth and Metaphor: Selected Essays, 1974–1988* (1990), edited by Robert D. Denham.

Writers commonly speak of Marshall's original ideas. He had none. Be grateful. They would have been right off the wall. His genius lay in perceiving, not creating.

Edmund Carpenter, anthropologist, "Remembering Explorations," *Canadian Notes & Queries*, Spring 1992.

He might mention small matters, but when he did, his unflinching directness transformed that subject, no matter how humble. Once we saw a turd in the centre of the broad steps forming the grand entrance to the Royal Ontario Museum. "Human," he said. The bizarre scene this (correct) judgement required would have escaped all conventional minds.

Edmund Carpenter, anthropologist, "Remembering Explorations," *Canadian Notes & Queries*, Spring 1992.

"Global village," properly noted, appears in a Wyndham Lewis book. Marshall liberated the phrase. It will probably (and properly) enter *Bartlett's Familiar Quotations* under the heading *McLuhan*. A more accurate phrase, as Marshall later realized, was global theatre. But this proved unappealing to journalists who considered themselves neutral reporters, not theatrical producers.

Edmund Carpenter, anthropologist, referring to Marshall McLuhan's adoption of the popular phrase, "Remembering Explorations," *Canadian Notes & Queries*, Spring 1992.

"The medium is the message" came from Ashley Montague's lecture, "The Method is the Message," which Marshall and I attended. Marshall improved the wording and extended the concept. "The medium is the massage" came from Sam Zacks. Marshall had been asked to explain his earlier phrase, to which Sam, who favoured steam baths and massages, replied: "You mean, like a massage?" At which point, message became massage, mass-age, mess-age.

Edmund Carpenter, anthropologist, referring to Marshall McLuhan's adoption of the popular phrase, "Remembering Explorations," *Canadian Notes & Queries*, Spring 1992.

McLuhan created the persona of the scholar who was also the cultural commentator, who reconciles in his own mind, in his own person, the terrible division we have between high culture and popular culture.

Camille Paglia, social critic, "Sontag, Fabio, Warhol, & Oldenburg," included by Paul Benedetti and Nancy DeHart in *Forward through the Rearview Mirror* (1996).

Patron Saint: Marshall McLuhan

Credit line on the masthead of early issues of the magazine *Wired*, founded in San Francisco in 1993.

I would have liked to have been Marshall McLuhan—it seemed a ton o'fun—but he had the job pretty much cornered.

Margaret Atwood, author, "Survival, Then and Now," *Maclean's*, 1 July 1999.

He died in 1980 at the age of 69 after a series of strokes, more than a decade before the creation of the Internet. Dear God—if only he were alive today! What heaven the present moment would have been for him! How he would have loved the Web! What a shimmering Oz he would have turned his global village into!

Tom Wolfe, writing about Marshall McLuhan, *Forbes*, Nov. 1999.

He had a breathtaking sweep of vision and a charming aptitude for the startling example. His irreverent, aphoristic wit was perfectly attuned to the brash spirit of my generation, with its absurdist "happenings" and its taste for zinging one-liners—in the satiric style of Lenny Bruce or the gnomic manner of Zen sages and Hindu gurus.

Camille Paglia, social critic and professor, Second Annual Marshall McLuhan Lecture, Fordham University, New York City, 17 Feb. 2000, "The Saturday Essay," *The Globe and Mail*, 26 Feb. 2000.

MADNESS

After all, it is a matter of physical strength: One only becomes mad when one is too tired to ignore the emptiness that surrounds us all.

Robert Elie, poet, *La fin des songes* (1950) quoted by Claude Janelle in *Citations québécoises modernes* (1976).

For example, in Ojibwa traditional culture—which taught that persons could be possessed by spirits and that the possessed ones would have an uncontrollable desire for human flesh—madness took the form of the Windigo Psychosis. Believing what they were "taught," the victims would kill humans, often their own families, and devour their flesh. Similarly, in that pressure cooker that was Eskimo life, the madness took a special northern form known as Arctic Hysteria, in which the victim would rip off his or her clothes and, insensible to danger, race out onto the ice floes.

Elliott Leyton, anthropologist, *Hunting Humans: The Rise of the Modern Multiple Murderer* (1986, 1987).

MAFIA See CRIME

MAGAZINES See also READING, WRITERS & WRITING

I pick up a recent copy of *Maclean's* magazine and what do I read? That modesty has more sex appeal than nudity!

Attributed to newspaper publisher **Grattan O'Leary**, appearing before the Davey Commission on corporate concentration in the media in 1970.

Canadians really do want to know more about Canada. Magazines have constituencies, linked not just by geography, but by public interest.... Be dangerous and stay close to home.

E. Graydon Carter, Canadian-born founder of *Spy* and editor of *Vanity Fair*, interviewed by Val Ross, *The Globe and Mail*, 2 June 1993.

After years of conditioning, many Canadians appear to have succumbed to what might be described as a form of national self-hatred complicated by cross-border hero-worship. This widespread malady can be encountered in full flower at the magazine stand in any Canadian store or airport. Try to find the Canadian magazines. Even hard-bitten Americans have expressed amazement at this tendency to ignore the home product.

Christopher Dafoe, columnist, *Winnipeg Free Press*, 2 April 1994.

MAGIC & MAGICIANS

Previous to this incident I had seen and used various restraints such as insane restraint muffs, belts, bedstraps, etc., but this was the first time I saw a strait-jacket and it left so vivid an impression on my mind that I hardly slept that night, and in such moments as I slept I saw nothing but strait-jackets, maniacs, and padded cells!

Harry Houdini, magician and escape artist, "Handcuff Secrets Exposed" (1908), quoted by Ruth Brandon in *The Life and Many Deaths of Harry Houdini* (1993). During a vaudeville tour of the Maritimes in 1895 or 1896, Houdini was introduced to the strait-jacket in "a large insane asylum" in Saint John, N.B. He devised ways and means of escaping from this form of restraint and soon the release became a feature of his stage act.

Make way for magic! Make way for objective mystery! Make way for love! Make way for what is needed!

Lines from the artistic manifesto *Refus global* (Global Refusal), which was released and distributed in Montreal on 9 Aug. 1948. The manifesto in favour of artistic and imaginative freedom was largely written by the painter **Paul-Émile Borduas**.

MAGICIAN—HAVE RABBIT, WILL TRAVEL

Sign on the motocycle of the young **Doug Henning**, prior to his success on Broadway with *The Magic Show*, quoted in *Time*, 22 July 1974.

My illusions are really a metaphor for all the magic in the world.

Doug Henning, magician, quoted in *The New York Times*, 21 Dec. 1975.

I'm sure that long ago all beings were able to communicate without travelling. Communicate through their brains, through their souls, through their visions. People were able to do magic.

Alanis Obomsawin, Abenaki spokesperson raised on the Odanak Reserve, Que., *Free Spirits: Annals of the Insurgent Imagination* (1982).

The new magic is the belief that science can solve any problem. Meanwhile, ancient magic provides fresh clues for modern scientific discoveries.

Barrington Nevitt, communications, consultant, *ABC of Prophecy: Understanding the Environment* (1985).

Put the words "magic" and "computer" in the same sentence and you are likely to throw a rational person into a state of cognitive dissonance. How could magic, the essence of a shadowy world we chain off with links of logic, invade the computer, the primary expression of our rationality? The dissonance lies in the word "magic" as a symbol of the supernatural. In reality magic is a piece of the natural world, and magicians are logical folk.

A.K. Dewdney, computer specialist, *The Armchair Universe: An Exploration of Computer Worlds* (1988).

I have created as many miracles as there are f's in phenomena.

Stewart James, inventor of innumerable magical effects, "James's Miracle," *Stewart James in Print: The First Fifty Years* (1989), created by Stewart James, edited by P. Howard Lyons and Allan Slaight.

Magic is born in the mind of the practitioner. It takes its strength from our will to see it succeed.

Tamara James, witch, *Lady Tamara's White Witch Book of Spells* (n.d.), quoted by Kevin Marron in *Witches, Pagans, and Magic in the New Age* (1989).

I am somewhat relieved to be able to say that in all my encounters with witches and magicians I did not ever feel that I had come under a spell or suffered a curse. I did, however, learn to respect magic, not as a supernatural force, but as a way of dealing with the world that exerts considerable influence on many people today.

Kevin Marron, author, *Witches, Pagans, & Magic in the New Age* (1989).

You are striving to perform two contradictory feats at once. You are attempting to fool an audience and to entertain them at the same time.

Henry Gordon, magician and writer, *Henry Gordon's World of Magic* (1989).

You will hear the lesser media chortling over the discovery that "I once said that I am a liar, a cheat and a fake." I have said that more than once. In fact I use that expression every time I step on stage, whether as a conjuror or as a lecturer. It's my way of telling my audience, straight up front, that I'm an actor who plays the part of a magician. Yes, I use deception to accomplish my impersonation.

James Randi, Toronto-born conjuror and skeptic of claims of the paranormal known as "the Amazing Randi," *James Randi: Psychic Investigator* (1991).

MALAPROPISMS See also HUMOUR & HUMORISTS

Lake Champlain... the very same waters that Champlain trod.

Malapropism attributed to **P.B. Rynard**, Member of Parliament and cottager on Lake Couchiching, address, opening of the Stephen Leacock Memorial Home, Orillia, Ont., 5 July 1958. "Rynard gave the day a Leacock touch it lacked, though he did so in all innocence," explained James A. (Pete) McGarvey in *The Old Brewery Bay: A Leacockian Tale* (1994).

From one Pacific to the other!

Attributed to Créditiste leader **Réal Caouette** in the 1960s by Jacques Hébert, "*Cité Libre*'s Eternal Youth," *Cité Libre*, March 1998.

All the problems of Saskatchewan are soluble.

Attributed to Saskatchewan Premier **Allan Blakeney** in 1978 by David Olive in *Canadian Political Babble* (1993).

Quebec has been disadvantaged in the auto industry since Confederation.

Attributed to Quebec industry minister **Rodrique Tremblay** in 1979 by David Olive in *Canadian Political Babble* (1993). Confederation occurred in 1867; the regulatory Auto Pact dates from 1965.

Every voyage may start with a single step, but that first step is a whopper, particularly when you are one citizen, out of 27 million, trying to influence the attitudes of people you don't know, on issues you don't fully understand. Yet the challenge is to take an initiative, not be an expert, and most of us have had to step into something new before.

Joe Clark, former Prime Minister, succeeding in sewing together a patchwork of malapropisms, *A Nation Too Good to Lose: Renewing the Purpose of Canada* (1994).

MANAGEMENT See also EXECUTIVES

Don't surprise me.

A.M. Rosenthal, Canadian-born managing editor of *The New York Times*, "cardinal rule of management," quoted by Joseph C. Goulden in *Fit to Print: A.M. Rosenthal and His Times* (1988).

Each of us is a personnel manager of a department of one.

Peter G. Hanson, physician and stress specialist, *Stress for Success: Thriving on Stress at Work* (1989).

Management, n. The art of misdirection.

David Olive, business commentator, *White Knights and Poison Pills: A Cynic's Dictionary of Business Jargon* (1990).

What are we to make of these managers, who have had almost absolute control of Western business for some 30 years, the last 22 of which have been marred by general crisis?

John Ralston Saul, author, *The Unconscious Civilization* (1995).

If we are to manage government properly, then we must learn to govern management.

Henry Mintzberg, management consultant, "The Myth of 'Society Inc.'" *The Globe and Mail*, Oct. 1996.

Management is a curious phenomenon. It is generously paid, enormously influential, and significantly devoid of common sense.

Henry Mintzberg, Professor of Management, McGill University, "Musings on Management," *Harvard Business Review*, July–Aug. 1996.

The most rewarding part of management is working with people. The worst part of management is working with people.

George Torok, motivational speaker, characteristic remark, 11 May 2000.

MANITOBA See also PRAIRIE PROVINCES, WESTERN PROVINCES, WINNIPEG

It is a very moderate calculation to say that, if these regions were occupied by an industrious population, they might afford ample means of subsistence for thirty millions of British subjects.

Lord Selkirk, colonist, calculating the farming potential of the Red River Settlement in present-day Manitoba, *Statement Respecting The Earl of Selkirk's Settlement upon the Red River in North America* (1817).

For how was it possible, we reasoned, with the feeble incredulity of effete Eastern minds, that the same country should be at once a fertile garden and a howling wilderness: that it should be the happy hunting ground of the Indians, and the home of a large and industrious population: that the climate should be temperate and agreeable, while the mercury was frozen in the bulb, and the wind blowing at the rate of fifty miles an hour? These things puzzled us.

Henry Van Dyke, American essayist and travel writer, commenting on descriptions of Manitoba prior to a visit, "The Red River of the North," *Harper's New Monthly Magazine*, May 1880.

Magnificent landscape / Green forests of fir beech chestnut cut with ripe fields of wheat oats buckwheat hemp / Everything breathing abundance / And it's absolutely deserted

Lines from French poet and traveller **Blaise Cendrars**' poem "The North" (1924), *Blaise Cendrars: Complete Poems* (1992) translated by Ron Padgett.

The mace of the Provincial Parliament of Manitoba was fashioned out of the hub of a Red River cart wheel.

Heather Gilbert, observer, quoted by Albro Martin in *James J. Hill and the Opening of the Northwest* (1976).

I love Manitoba, but there are moments when I would gladly give it back to the buffalo. Every Manitoban has felt that way on occasion.

Christopher Dafoe, columnist, "Part of the Oral Tradition," *The Beaver*, Feb.–March 1993.

For it's forty below in the winter / And it's twenty below in the fall. / It just rises to zero in summer, / And we don't have a springtime at all.

Four-line refrain of "Forty Below," sung to the tune of "Red River Valley"; the lyrics, once believed traditional, were written by the journalist **Christopher Dafoe**, as he recalled in "Part of the Oral Tradition," *The Beaver*, Feb.–March 1993. The lyrics first appeared in print in "Coffee Break by Wink," *Winnipeg Free Press*, 30 May 1959.

A glance at the map tells it all. Manitoba is right in the middle, the keystone province, which is probably why many of us think of Manitoba when we hear the term "Central Canada." How central can you get?

Christopher Dafoe, columnist, *Winnipeg Free Press*, 6 Nov. 1993.

MANKIND See also LIFE, MEN, MEN & WOMEN, WOMEN

In such condition, there is no place for Industry; because the fruit thereof is uncertain: and consequently no Culture of the Earth, no Navigation, nor use of the commodities that may be imported by Sea; no commodious Building; no Instruments of moving, and removing such things as require much force; no Knowledge of the face of the Earth; no account of Time; no arts; no Letters; no Society; and which is worst of all, continuall feare, and danger of violent death; And the life of man, solitary, poore, nasty, brutish, and short.

Thomas Hobbes, English philosopher, *Leviathan* (1657). This celebrated passage, about the social state of primitive man who lived in a state of perpetual "warre," appears in Chapter XIII of Hobbes' classic work of political philosophy. It was inspired by the condition of "the savage people in many places of America."

Do not think, young sir, that I compliment or congratulate you on having a kind heart. On the contrary, happy is he—a thousand times happy—who possesses a heart of brass, since he is constrained to live among men.

Philippe-Joseph Aubert de Gaspé, memoirist, *A Man of Sentiment: The Memoirs of Philippe-Joseph Aubert de Gaspé 1786–1871* (1988) translated by Jane Brierley from the original French edition of 1866.

Man is now able to fly through the air like a bird; he's able to swim beneath the sea like a fish, to burrow beneath the ground like a mole. Now if only he could walk the Earth like a man, that would be paradise.

T.C. (Tommy) Douglas, Premier of Saskatchewan (1944–61), leader of the first socialist government in North America, founder of Medicare, statesman, political orator, seen and heard on the CBC-TV documentary *Tommy Douglas: The Fight of a Lifetime*, telecast 1 Feb. 2000, directed by Julia Bennett.

We are so small between the stars / So large against the sky

Line from **Leonard Cohen**'s song "Stories of the Streets" from the album *Songs of Leonard Cohen* (1967).

Since I no longer expect anything from mankind except madness, meanness, and mendacity; egotism, cowardice, and self-delusion, I have stopped being a misanthrope.

Irving Layton, poet and aphorist, *The Whole Bloody Bird (obs, aphs & Pomes)* (1969).

The human race is like toothpaste. One half of one percent is active ingredient, and the rest is filler.

Crad Kilodney, fiction writer, *Putrid Scum* (1991).

On my 70th birthday in May of this year I was asked how I felt about mankind's prospects. This is my reply.

We are behaving like yeasts in a brewer's vat, multiplying mindlessly while greedily consuming the substance of a finite world. If we continue to imitate the yeasts we will perish as they perish, having exhausted our resources and poisoned ourselves in the lethal brew of our own wastes.

Unlike the yeasts, we have a choice. What will it be?

Farley Mowat, author, "Writer's Reflection," Letters to the Editor, *The Globe and Mail*, 20 July 1991.

No matter what his weaknesses are, no matter how many Hitlers he produces, man contains the possibility of freedom because he is creative. And his creativity, I believe, will eventually allow him to make a better world than that made by his predecessors up to now.

Irving Layton, poet, interviewed by Ekbert Faas and Maria Trombacco, *Raging like a Fire: A Cele-*

bration of Irving Layton (1993) edited by Henry Beissel and Joy Bennett.

The only tribe that I belong to, or want to belong to, is the human species and the tribe of all beings and creatures.

Robert Bringhurst, poet, quoted by Philip Marchand, "Simplicity Motivates Poet's Work of a Lifetime," *The Toronto Star*, 15 April 1995.

MANNERS

"Nice," I came to realize quite early, is a pejorative word in Canada, and I could hardly offer a Canadian town a more irritating insult than to say how nice it was. In my own vocabulary nice means essentially good; but then "good," too, if applied to the Canadian national character, apparently does not give pleasure to the indigenes.

Jan Morris, Anglo-Welsh traveller, "In Praise of Canada," *The Toronto Star*, 15 June 1992.

If niceness were an Olympic sport, Canadians would be perennial champions, like Kenyans in the marathon.

Robert Fulford, columnist, "The Country that Dare not Speak Its Name," *The Globe and Mail*, 17 July 1996.

MANNING, PRESTON See also CANADIAN ALLIANCE, POLITICIANS, REFORM PARTY

The only thing I suggest to people in the rest of Canada to reflect on is, I'm the most popular in the province that knows me best. Chrétien is the least popular in the province that knows him the best. People ought to think about what that means both ways.

Preston Manning, Reform leader, referring to Prime Minister Jean Chrétien, interviewed by Dale Eisler in *Maclean's*, 16 June 1997.

Presto!

Nickname based on the one-word spell of the stage magician, created for Reform Party founder and leader Preston Manning by **Christopher Young**, columnist with the *Ottawa Citizen*, as noted by Peter C. Newman in the *National Post*, 15 Jan. 2000.

MANUFACTURING See also INDUSTRY

It was the approval, and the confidence, of the Canadian public that more than anything else made me confident I was on the right track.

Henry Ford, U.S. industrialist, interviewed in Detroit, Mich., by R.E. Knowles, *The Star Weekly*, 30 Dec. 1933. Ford noted that "the first factory I established, outside of here, was in Canada."

You could make it cheaper offshore, I'm told. / Perhaps. But I believe it's the patriot thing to do, to make our clothes here. / Honour. / Patriotism. / Rare words nowadays.

Wording on the plaque in the office of Alex Tilley of **Tilley's Endurables Inc.**, quoted by Susan Goldenberg in *Global Pursuit: Canadian Business Strategies for Winning in the Borderless World* (1991).

Some people are interested in administration, some in power, some in money, but the thing that's motivated me is the desire to feel good about what I manufacture.

Garry H. Weston, Toronto-born son of W. Garfield Weston, Chairman and Managing Director, Associated British Foods, quoted by Anthony Gardner in "The Frugal Billionaire," *The Toronto Star*, 3 May 1992.

MAPLE LEAF See also EMBLEMS, NATIONAL

In days of yore, from Europe's shore, / Wolfe and Montcalm came to fight, / And started first our Great Debate / That bores without respite. // Here may it rage, our fame, our fate, / And join in acrimony / The East, the West, the North and South: / The Maple Leaf forever.

New words for Alexander Muir's one-time patriotic favourite "The Maple Leaf Forever" (1867) contributed by columnist **John Fraser**, "Let's Take Back Our History on Canada Day," *The Toronto Star*, 16 June 1996.

All hail the broad-leaved Maple! / With its fair and changeful dress— / A type of our young country / In its pride and loveliness; / Whether in Spring or Summer, / Or in the dreary Fall, / 'Mid Nature's forest children, / She's fairest of them all.

First of seven verses of "The Maple," composed by **H.F. Darnell**, cleric and versifier, included in *The Fourth Book of Reading Lessons* (1869) in "Canadian Series of School Books."

MAPLE SYRUP

I was regaled here with the juice of the maple; this is the season of its flowing. It is extremely delicious, has a most pleasing coolness, and is exceedingly wholesome; the manner of extracting it is very simple. When the sap begins to ascend, they pierce the trunk of the tree, and by means of a bit of wood, which is inserted in it, and along which it flows, as through a pipe, the liquor is conveyed into a vessel placed under it. In order to produce an abundant flow, there must be much snow on the ground, with frosty nights, a serene sky, and the wind not too cool....

Pierre-François-Xavier de Charlevoix, historian, *Histoire et description générale de la Nouvelle France* (1744).

In the old days, it seems, French Canadians feasted on kiwi fruit, baked beans, pâté and fried eggs. And, of course, maple syrup, which came in a glass flask shaped like the Eiffel Tower, neatly summing up the appeal of Montreal.

Nigel Tisdall, English travel writer, describing a platter served in Montreal called *festin l'ancienne*, "Into the Great Green Yonder," *The Daily Telegraph*, 26 Sept. 1998.

MAPS

I still wish, though, that some cartographer would draw Canada south-side-up so the people, not the ice, could be on top!

James C. Reaney, poet, "Swimming in the Past," *Saturday Night*, March 1988.

Toronto is a big city with a small country called Canada on its outskirts. Look at the map of the world on the wall behind their editors' desks. It shows a big dot on the shore of Lake Ontario labelled "Us. Right smack in the middle of everything." The rest of the map is coloured green and marked "Cottage Country."

Joey Slinger, columnist, referring to parochial-minded newspaper editors, "No Place to Call Home," *The Globe and Mail*, 5 March 1994.

MARITIME PROVINCES See also

ATLANTIC PROVINCES, NEW BRUNSWICK, NOVA SCOTIA, PRINCE EDWARD ISLAND

In the 1930s you had to go by ship. There weren't any transatlantic flights then. I suddenly realized when I was in the middle of the Gulf of St. Lawrence that I was surrounded by five Canadian provinces, all of them invisible.

Northrop Frye, cultural critic, on a transatlantic voyage across the Gulf of St. Lawrence, returning from Oxford University in 1939, interviewed by David Cayley in *Northrop Frye in Conversation* (1992).

Certainly in the Maritimes there has been no loss of identity. We're very sure of that. In Prince Edward Island, if anybody ever said he was alienated, I would say: "You are not alienated. I can tell you exactly who you are; you are the illegitimate son of your Aunt Mary."

J.H. Maloney, former P.E.I. Minister of Development, testifying at a CRTC hearing, quoted by Peter C. Newman in *Maclean's*, 21 Nov. 1988.

If I were Ambassador from the Maritimes to Upper and Outer Canada, here is what I would say to the befuddled heathens of Ottawa and the lesser capitals: You will never understand the Maritimes without understanding Buddhist economics.

Silver Donald Cameron, columnist, "Atlantic Canada," *The Globe and Mail*, 29 Sept. 1997.

MARKETS & MARKETING

Meet a need, go against a trend, keep it simple. Messy sells better than neat.

Axioms of entrepreneur **Ed Mirvish**, founder of Honest Ed's, the world's first discount department store, established in Toronto in 1948, as noted by Ethel A. Starbird in *National Geographic*, Aug. 1975.

The new market is both centralized (through info-globalized producers) and decentralized (through info-localized) customers. Marketing must be "glocalized."

Frank Feather, futurologist, *The Future Consumer* (1994). The originator of the phrase "Think Globally, Act Locally" is attributed to Frank Feather. A catchphrase among futurologists or futurists in the 1960s, by the 1990s it had become a mantra of transnational corporations. SONY founder Aiko Moritz introduced a transistorized version in the four words with his single word: glocal.

Marketing is simply the expression of who you are. You can market positively or negatively, but you cannot not market—just like you cannot not communicate.

Peter Urs Bender and **George Torok**, professional speakers, *Secrets of Power Marketing* (1999).

MARRIAGE See also LOVE, MEN & WOMEN

If a smart and pretty widow, under thirty-five, with a snug jointure or disposable fortune, with three or four ready made sons and daughters (the riches of the Canadian colonist) be inclined to migrate hither, I pledge myself to provide a mate for her.

T.W. Magath, editor, *Authentic Letters from Upper Canada* (1833).

Marriage purifies the complexion, removes blotches from the skin, invigorates the body.

B.G. Jefferis, medical crank, *Search Lights on Health, Light on Dark Corners; A Complete Sexual Science and a Guide to Purity and Physical Manhood* (1894).

Soon after marriage a girl's brain ceases to be a dream factory.

Bob Edwards, publisher, *Eye Opener*, 5 Oct. 1912, *The Wit and Wisdom of Bob Edwards* (1976) edited by Hugh Dempsey.

I believe it would be a good thing to make marriage harder instead of easier, for there is too great a tendency on the part of people to rush into marriage without realizing either its hardships or its binding nature.

Agnes Macphail, pioneer feminist, address, House of Commons, 26 Feb. 1925.

Always let a man think how fine and tolerant he is to put up with you. That's the formula for marital success.

Thoughts of a doctor's wife in **Sinclair Ross**'s novel *As for Me and My House* (1941).

Wedlock, that's what it is. A thick rope pulled tight in order to suffocate each another.

Lines from **Anne Hébert**'s novel *Kamouraska* (1970) quoted by Claude Janelle in *Citations québécoises modernes* (1976).

Some part of each of us is a dark forest and no one can follow us there, so every marriage has a little pocket of unmet needs.

Merle Shain, essayist, *Some Men Are More Perfect than Others* (1973).

Marriage is love with the nerve removed.

Raymond Canale, Italian-born, Toronto-based aphorist, 1975.

Four things that might, just might, help to make a successful marriage—silences, secrets, solitudes, separations.

Richard Needham, newspaper columnist, *The Wit and Wisdom of Richard Needham* (1977).

Love is an arrow, marriage a boomerang.

Ara Baliozian, writer and teacher, *Portrait of a Genius and Other Essays* (1980).

The trouble with marriage is that most people marry someone they don't even know.

Louis Dudek, man-of-letters, "The Mermaid Inn," *The Globe and Mail*, 23 May 1981.

We never found ourselves with the same day off in the same place at the same time. How could we get married? Besides, Teresa is a confirmed bachelor.

Zubin Mehta, symphony conductor, referring to his relationship with opera diva Teresa Stratas, *Zubin* (1978). Stratas's response? "I couldn't see myself going through life as Mrs. Conductor. What Zubin needs is someone to take care of him, and that's not me." Noted by Harry Rasky in his book *Stratas: An Affectionate Tribute* (1988).

Marriage *should* be the cemetery of love: I don't mean a place where love is dead, I mean a place where it doesn't have to be an issue; a place where one's love is affirmed automatically by the situation, and one can be something other than a lover.

Leonard Cohen, poet, interviewed by Eve Rockett in *Homemaker's Magazine*, May 1979.

But post-industrial marriages—at least among well-educated Westerners—are what I call supra-sexual partnerships: intellectual intercourse is "hot" and of primary importance; sexual intercourse also then becomes hot (in a "cool" sense, becoming recreational super-sex) and reinforces the couple's co-creativity.

Frank Feather, futurologist, *G-Forces: Reinventing the World—The 35 Global Forces Restructuring Our World* (1989).

Love in the marital bed is classicism, outside it's romanticism.

Louis Dudek, poet and aphorist, "Epigrams," *Small Perfect Things* (1991).

Even Dante found it easier / to write about / the ineffable shape of God / than about his marriage.

Lines from **Peter Dale Scott**'s poem *Listening to the Candle: A Poem on Impulse* (1992).

I think any man that can make his wife laugh at breakfast is a marvellous husband.

Amelia Hall, actress, quoted by Judith Skelton Grant in *Robertson Davies: Man of Myth* (1994).

As my father said to me on my wedding day, "You're dead for eternity but married forever."

Vicki Gabereau, host, CBC Radio's *Vicki Gabereau Show*, 1 Nov. 1996.

People who are afraid of loneliness shouldn't get married.

Richard Needham, columnist, quoted by Michael Kesterton in *The Globe and Mail*, 20 July 1996.

We've been married a short enough time to still be enjoying it and long enough to be respectable.

Adrienne Clarkson, television personality, referring to her marriage to long-time partner John Ralston Saul, press conference called to announce her future appointment as the 26th Governor General of Canada, Ottawa, 8 Sept. 1999, quoted by Susan Bourette in *The Globe and Mail* the following day.

MARVELS

Lest it be thought that I have no appreciation for the marvellous, I will assert here that I regard Lewis Carroll, puppy dogs and selected sunsets as a few of the "miracles" of my own life. I am not immune to such beauty.

James Randi, Toronto-born conjurer and critic of claims of the paranormal known as "the Amazing Randi," *The Mask of Nostradamus: The Prophecies of the World's Most Famous Seer* (1993).

MARXISM See also COMMUNISM, IDEOLOGIES

Marxism doesn't work. At the end of the Second World War, all Europe was laid waste, so both systems started from the same point. You just have to compare the results in the East and West since then to see which is better.

Sir Edwin Leather, Canadian-born former Governor of Bermuda and author of espionage novels, quoted by William French in *The Globe and Mail*, 8 Dec. 1977.

I've said elsewhere, at least half seriously, that the only true Marxists functioning today teach in the Chicago School of Economics and manage our large corporations. I could add that these same people are the true descendants of Benito Mussolini.

John Ralston Saul, author, *The Unconscious Civilization* (1995).

MASS MEDIA See MEDIA

MATHEMATICS

They told me A equalled B, but I knew it wasn't so. A doesn't equal B and it never has.

Gregory Clark, humorist, giving his reason for failing freshman mathematics two years in a row at the University of Toronto in 1912, speech, accepting its honorary doctorate, quoted in *Weekend Magazine*, 7 June 1975.

I am convinced that everyone uses mathematical thinking at almost every moment of conscious existence.... The trick is to bring the intuitive analytic abilities to the level of conscious awareness so that they can be utilized in a formal way.

A.K. Dewdney, computer columnist, "The Tower of Hanoi and the Chinese Rings," *The Armchair Universe: An Exploration of Computer Worlds* (1988).

I opened an issue of *The Canadian Journal of Geometry* at random and was surprised by how many symbolic systems mathematicians had pressed into service: Greek and Russian letters, of course, but the British pound sterling sign? Capital letters in a florid script that looked as if it came from a wedding invitation?

Thoughts of Arno Strine, the narrator of **Nicholson Baker**'s novel *The Fermata* (1994).

To mathematize is a natural habit of the human mind. Mathematics, as a science, is the systematic exploitation of human delight in totally abstract thought.

A. John Coleman, mathematician, Letters to the Editor, *The Globe and Mail*, 18 Sept. 1996.

MATURITY

We grow old slipping back from the verge of maturity.

Mavor Moore, man-of-the-theatre, *Maclean's*, 8 June 1981.

Perhaps one of the surest signs of middle age is to realize you are far less interested in tailoring yourself to other people's expectations than in trying to live up to those you have set for yourself.

Thoughts of a character in **Edward Phillips**' novel *Sunday Best* (1990).

Nature first created the child. It has been trying slowly to create the adult.

Louis Dudek, poet and aphorist, "Epigrams," *Small Perfect Things* (1991).

Maturity is acceptance of the inevitability of the defeat of your dreams. And that is the reason I am not mature.

Barry Callaghan, author, interviewed by Joyce Davidson, CBC-TV's *Authors*, 15 April 1999.

MEANING

Meaning is not "content" but an active relationship.

Marshall McLuhan, communications pioneer, observation made in 1971, "A McLuhan Sourcebook," *The Essential McLuhan* (1995) edited by Eric McLuhan and Frank Zingrone.

Address a lilac-bloom or a rose, it will tell you what I mean.

Christopher Chapman, photographer, quoted by Gerald Milne Moses in "Reflected Images," *Indigenous People* (1993) published by the Royal Canadian Academy of Arts.

When the politics of meaning are constrained, the range of all of our hopes and desires become diminished with them.

Frank Davey, academic, *Post-National Arguments: The Poetics of the Anglophone-Canadian Novel Since 1967* (1993).

MEDIA See also COMMUNICATIONS; MCLUHAN, MARSHALL; NEWS

New media are new environments. That is why the media are the message.

Marshall McLuhan, communications pioneer, "Address at Vision 65" (1966), *The Essential McLuhan* (1995) edited by Eric McLuhan and Frank Zingrone.

There is a conspiracy to turn us off, us people, to make of us well-programmed, responsive robots. It is a conspiracy that works particularly well because the conspirators do not know there is a conspiracy and believe their actions to be good.

Patrick Watson, broadcaster, *Conspirators in Silence* (1969).

The message of the media is that everything becomes cliché.

Louis Dudek, man-of-letters, *Epigrams* (1975).

Today's high school graduate probably has spent more than twice as much time watching TV and movies as attending classes.

T.H.B. Symons, commissioner, *The Symons Report: An Abridged Version of Volumes 1 and 2 of "To Know Ourselves; the Report of the Commission on Canadian Studies"* (1978).

Media fallout

Term coined by communications pioneer **Marshall McLuhan** to refer to "the panic caused by the impact of sense impressions that our minds have not been adequately prepared to receive," in the words of Northrop Frye, "The Dialectic of Belief and Vision" (1985), *Myth and Metaphor: Selected Essays, 1974–1988* (1990) edited by Robert D. Denham.

We look to the media to fill us in, but we don't count on it. After all, their job is to report the news, not to get at the truth.

Duncan Cameron, academic, "Mulroney's New Deal," *The Canadian Forum*, Sept. 1992.

In the final analysis, media is about business, not truth.

John Haslett Cuff, arts critic, referring to a libel action launched by Baton Broadcasting Inc. against *The Globe and Mail*, quoted by Scott Anderson in "Media," *eye*, 6 May 1993.

The media are now, in administrative techniques, an industry like the others; more profitable than most, perhaps more strategic than any.

Conrad Black, publisher and capitalist, "The Rights of the Press," *Contemporary Issues in*

Political Philosophy (1976) edited by W.R. Shea and J. King Farlow.

In our media we are twice colonized. Once by the United States, once by Toronto. It is no wonder that as the century ends we feel like exiles in our own cities, our own provinces, our own country.

Daryl Duke, TV personality, "Exiles in Our Own Country," *Canadian Perspectives* (The Council of Canadians), Spring 1999.

MEDICARE See also HEALTH CARE, MEDICINE, SOCIAL PROGRAMS

To Our Patients / This Office Will Be Closed after / July 1st, 1962 / We Do Not Intend to Carry on Practice / Under / The Saskatchewan Medical Care / Insurance Act

Wording on signs that appeared in May 1962 in "every doctor's office in Saskatchewan," when Medicare was first introduced, reproduced by Heather Robertson in *Grass Roots* (1973).

I think it's wrong that people should be punished financially for being stricken by illness when they're old or broke (or both). If there is a benchmark of the difference between the American way of doing things and the Canadian way, in fact—and how our political processes have come to reflect that difference—it is, surely, that in the 1980s no major American political party is far enough to what we call the left to stand for a national program of medicare, while in Canada no party would dare stand far enough to the right to oppose it. Our political centre of gravity is different.

Peter Gzowski, host of CBC Radio's *Morningside*, in *The Private Voice: A Journal of Reflections* (1988).

There may be some loss of superstars to the United States, but that is hard to document—individual anecdotes do not make a trend. In any case, there is always some leakage of stars in any field from countries with small populations to populous neighbours (the Gretzky effect).

Robert G. Evans, et al., "Controlling Health Expenditures—The Canadian Reality," *The New England Journal of Medicine*, 2 March 1989.

User fees are not about making the rich pay. They are about making the sick pay. And poor people tend to be in worse health than rich people.

Robert G. Evans, economist, quoted in *The Atkinson Letter*, "Can Medicare Be 'Saved'?" *The Toronto Star*, 1 Dec. 1996.

We also became one of only three or four countries in the entire world (the others being Communist dictatorships) to abolish private medicine.

Conrad Black, publisher, commenting on changes since the 1960s led by the Trudeau administrations, "Out of Uncle Sam's Shadow," *National Post*, 11 Jan. 2000.

MEDICINE See also DENTISTRY, HEALING, HEALTH, HEALTH CARE, MEDICARE, PSYCHIATRY, SCIENCE & SCIENTISTS

Dr. Williams' Pink Pills for Pale People

Wording on the label of a patent medicine produced and promoted by manufacturer **Senator George Fulford** of Brockville, Ont., based on a formula devised by Hamilton-based William Jackson (better known for Roman Meal) in the 1870s, according to *Maclean's* (Business Magazine), Nov. 1905. As June Callwood explained in *Naughty Nineties: 1890–1900* (1977), the Pink Pills were overtaken by Dodd's Kidney Pills in 1964. Fulford's catchy slogan made it into *The Oxford Dictionary of Quotations*. The original label explained, "These Pills Make Weak People Strong.... Recommended by the Liberal Minded Doctor and Trained Nurse."

I See and Am Silent

Motto of the first school of nursing in Canada, **Dr. T. Mack's General and Marine Hospital**, St. Catharines, Ont., 1874, and quoted by the publications of the Mack Training School for Nurses, 1874–1949.

It is too easy to forget that the end we serve is not our careers—to rise in our profession and receive accolades from our peers—but humanity. If we are no better than pedlars seeking profit, albeit in honours not dollars, then we should leave medicine. I'll return to my one-time role of hardware merchant, at which I was very successful, and you to whatever clerk's roles you wish.

Joseph Workman, psychiatrist, address, Toronto Medical Students, 1883, reproduced in Christine I.M. Johnston in *Joseph Workman: The Father of Canadian Psychiatry* (2000).

To us as a profession belongs the chief glory of the century. The gradual growth of a deep sense of the brotherhood of man, such an abiding sense as pervades our own profession in its relation to the suffering, which recognizes the one blood of all the nations, may perhaps do it. In some development of socialism, something that will widen patriotism beyond the bounds of nationalism, may rest the desire of the race in this matter; but the evil is rooted and grounded in the abyss of human passion, and war with all its horrors is likely long to burden the earth.

Sir William Osler, physician and teacher of medicine, address to the American Medical Association, 1896, quoted by Michael Bliss in *William Osler: A Life in Medicine* (1999).

It was at Oxford during Osler's tenure that I carried out my first post-mortem examination. I screwed my courage to the sticking place and had made a beginning when I was startled by the voice of Sir William. "That is splendid," he said. "It is always best to do a difficult job the wrong way first. Then you never forget."

Wilder Penfield, surgeon-in-training, recalling the words of his illustrious teacher Sir William Osler, quoted in *Canada Today/D'Aujourd'hui*, Dec. 1979.

(1) Look after the poor widows—the rich can look after themselves. (2) When you see an eighty-year-old man lying dead in bed, don't search under the bed for a gun. (3) Don't cause any trouble for the government and especially not for the medical profession. If a doctor does something wrong take him in the back room and give him hell, but don't let the public or the press learn about it.

Smirle Lawson, Chief Coroner of Toronto, instructions given to junior coroner Morton Shulman in 1952, who quotes them in his memoir *Coroner* (1975).

In every medical school in the world, doctors are taught to answer one question: "What kind of a disease does this person have?" In the real world, the trick is to figure out the opposite question: "What kind of a person does this disease have?"

Peter G. Hanson, physician and author of *Stress for Success*, characteristic observation, Nov. 1991.

With holistic medicine you can put all your aches in one basket.

Maurus E. Mallon, aphorist, 2 May 1993.

If *The Toronto Star* were my doctor, I'd be dead.

Dalton Camp, Tory strategist and weekly political columnist for *The Toronto Star*, who on 15 May 1993 became Canada's oldest heart-transplant patient, quoted by Michael Smith in "Heart Transplant: Who's First in Line?" *The Toronto Star*, 27 June 1993. Camp, in his mid-seventies, objected to the suggestion, attributed to an unidentified surgeon, that the operation was "the ultimate in Tory patronage." On 30 June, the *Star* ran an apology but thereafter refused to print Camp's next column which criticized Smith's article and the suggestion that Camp had received preferential treatment. If Camp's new lease on life resulted in columns notably more Red Toryish than earlier ones, it was hazarded that his new heart had been donated by a West Indian woman on welfare.

In my opinion, drinking water professionals have done as much, if not more, to wipe out many lethal diseases than the medical profession. The record is quite incredible. Cholera and typhoid outbreaks were common killers in Canadian cities—not in the Dark Ages—but within living memory. Sanitary sewerage, too, played a major role in curbing diseases.

Tom Davey, editor and publisher, "Canada's Water Quality Record," *Environmental Science & Engineering*, March 1995.

Medicine is all right until you have something wrong with you, then it's usually quite useless.

Louis Dudek, poet and aphorist, *The Caged Tiger* (1997).

Trust your body first, your doctor second.

Rudolf Flak, oncologist, maxim, quoted by Kate Fillion in "Lives Lived," *The Globe and Mail*, 24 April 1998.

MEDITATION

Transcendental meditation, the prolonged effort to think of nothing, is a technique perfectly suitable for Canadians. They've been doing it now for almost a century.

Louis Dudek, man-of-letters, *Epigrams* (1975).

MEECH LAKE ACCORD See also DISTINCT SOCIETY, QUEBEC

Quebec constitutes, within Canada, a distinct society.

Key provision of the Meech Lake constitutional accord, adopted for future provincial ratification at an all-ministers' conference, Ottawa, 3 June 1987. The Accord, by granting constitutional recognition of the distinctive character of the Province of Quebec, sought to provide for "two distinct societies (*deux nations*)" in Canada. The Accord failed to be ratified in Manitoba and Newfoundland. As Manitoba Premier Gary Filmon explained, "We have an aboriginal past and a multicultural future... not just the French-English duality that is seen as the fundamental characteristic." Newfoundland Premier Clyde Wells stated, "I am not rejecting Quebec. I am rejecting a Canada with a Class A province, a Class B province and eight Class C provinces."

The real monster is not in Loch Ness, it's in Meech Lake.

Sam Burger, controversialist, quoted by Tim Burke in *The Montreal Gazette*, 8 Dec. 1987.

It was with some hesitancy that I finally accepted the accord.... I finally concluded that we had to pull ourselves out of the ghetto and prostration where Pierre Trudeau's arrogant deception had confined us. I said to myself that we had to take that opportunity to turn the page on the bitterness of the recent past and, with Brian Mulroney, begin to write a glorious chapter highlighted by acts of faith, tolerant gestures, and open dialogues.

Lucien Bouchard, Member of Parliament, House of Commons, 22 May 1990. Speaking on a point of privilege, Bouchard announced his change of party affiliation.

Clyde Wells, Premier of Newfoundland and Labrador*

The most famous asterisk in Canadian constitutional history appears here. Premier Wells, like nine other provincial premiers and Prime Minister Mulroney, added his signature to the final communiqué attached to the Meech Lake constitutional accord at the First Ministers' Conference, Ottawa, 9 June 1990, but Wells' signature is the only one followed by an asterisk. It directs the reader to the following addendum: "*The Premier of Newfoundland endorses now the undertaking in Part I of this document and further undertakes to endorse this agreement if the Constitutional Amendment, 1987 (the Meech Lake Accord), is given legislative or public approval following the consultation provided for in Part I." The text is taken from *The Toronto Star*, 11 June 1990. Subsequently, the the Manitoba legislature failed to ratify it and Newfoundland's adjourned before considering it.

Right here, I told them when it would be. I told them a month ago when we were going to meet. It's like an election campaign; you count backward. I said, "That's the day we're going to roll the dice."

Brian Mulroney, Prime Minister, indiscretion shared with interviewers, 24 Sussex Drive, Ottawa, 11 June 1990. He boasted to reporters how one month earlier he and his advisers had determine the federal strategy to deal with the Meech Lake constitutional accord and to set a First Ministers' meeting the first week of June. Mulroney assumed, mistakenly, that the outcome was "in the bag." The pressure tactic backfired, in part because of the boast made above, as noted by Susan Delacourt and Graham Fraser in *The Globe and Mail*, 12 June 1990.

No, Mr. Speaker.

These three words had an immense impact on the state of the nation; they changed the face of the country in the 1990s. They were spoken in Manitoba's Legislative Assembly by **Elijah Harper**, Ojibwa-Cree member, who thereby withheld the unanimity required for the Legislature to table and then ratify the Meech Lake constitutional accord by its deadline. Harper said "No, Mr. Speaker" a total of nine times between 12 and 22 June 1990.

I certainly hope we are bringing an end to Canada as we know it because Canada as we know it is not something we want to continue.

Georges Erasmus, National Chief, Assembly of First Nations, on the opposition of leaders to the Meech Lake Accord, quoted by Darcy Henton in *The Toronto Star*, 20 June 1990.

It would simply not be possible in the United States for eleven politicians to be sitting around a table negotiating the breakup of their country without millions of Americans publicly demonstrating their refusal to accept this outrage.

Peter Jennings, Toronto-born ABC-TV news anchor, referring to the Meech Lake Accord, *Maclean's*, 25 June 1990.

Meech Lake... has entered even linguistics: Two years ago in Winnipeg I overheard an Indian chief say, "No thank you very Meech, but no."

Arkadi Tcherkassov, Russian commentator, "Our Man in Moscow," *Grainews*, July 1992.

I think the Quebec people now believe the myth that somehow the rejection of Meech Lake was a slap in the face by English Canada to French Canada.

Pierre Elliott Trudeau, former Prime Minister, referring to the myth that the Accord was promoted by separatists but rejected by federalists, press conference, 6 Nov. 1995, quoted by Hugh Winsor in *The Globe and Mail* the following day.

MEETINGS

A committee meeting is where bureaucrats are born, ideas are killed, and the status quo preserved.

James H. Boren, neologist, *Fuzzify! Borenwords and Stategies for Bureaucratic Success* (1982).

If I were King of the World, there would be fewer meetings, and every meeting would be shorter.

George Torok, motivational speaker, characteristic remark, 25 March 2000.

There are three types of meetings—boring, complete waste of time, and postponed.

George Torok, motivational speaker, characteristic remark, 11 May 2000.

MEMORIALS See also EPITAPHS, WAR DEAD

In his memorial figure in Kinsmen Park, Hugh Cairns, the city's one Victoria Cross holder, is dressed for a game of football, and this is the only place I know in the British Empire that has acclimatized Lutyens' solemn design for a cenotaph by putting a clock in it.

Jan Morris, Anglo-Welsh traveller, writing about Saskatoon, Sask., "Suddenly Saskatoon," *Saturday Night*, July–Aug. 1990.

In Memory of / the 229 Men, Women and Children / Aboard Swissair Flight 111 / Who Perished off These Shores / September 2, 1998 / They Have Been Joined to the Sea and the Sky

Words engraved on the stone that marks the memorial to the victims of Swissair Flight 111 at Peggy's Cove, N.S., unveiled one year following the disaster. Quoted in *The Globe and Mail*, 2 Sept. 1999.

MEMORY

Who will remember our dead? Who will remember us?

Shawnawdithit, last of the Beothuk people, before her death in Newfoundland in 1829, quoted by Rudy Wiebe in *Playing Dead* (1989).

Memory is cultivated and praised, but who will teach us to forget?

George Iles, aphorist, *Canadian Stories: Together with... Jottings from a Note-Book* (1918).

No one dies until the last person dies who remembers his name.

Murray McLauchlan, singer-composer, vigil to mark the death of the Beatle John Lennon, Toronto, 10 Dec. 1980, quoted by Paul McGrath in *The Globe and Mail*, 11 Dec. 1980.

Forgetting the right things is better than remembering the wrong things.

James H. Boren, neologist, *Fuzzify! Borenwords and Stategies for Bureaucratic Success* (1982).

Society, like the individual, becomes senile in proportion as it loses its continuous memory.

Northrop Frye, cultural critic, "Literary and Mechanical Models" (1989), *The Eternal Act of Creation: Essays, 1979–1990* (1993) edited by Robert D. Denham.

The skin is like an elephant. It doesn't forget.

Gary Sibbald, dermatologist, Women's College Hospital, Toronto, quoted by Sean Fine in *The Globe and Mail*, 31 May 1991.

Memo writers never remember.

Robin Skelton, poet and aphorist, *A Devious Dictionary* (1991).

Layer after layer of autumn leaves / are swept away / Something forgets us perfectly

Lines from **Leonard Cohen**'s poem "For E.J.P.," *Stranger Music: Selected Poems and Songs* (1993).

I call false memory syndrome *invented* because no impartial committee of psychiatrists has ever approved it for inclusion in the *Diagnostic and Statistical Manual of Mental Diseases-III-R*, or any other professional manual, though that is what its scientific-sounding nomenclature implies. This "syndrome" exists because, on a particular day, a lobby group decided that it did.

Sylvia Fraser, novelist and journalist, "Freud's Final Seduction," *Saturday Night*, March 1994.

People begin as dreams and end as memories.

Robert Priest, aphorist, *Time Release Poems* (1997).

Memory is a fiction that I can write.

Thoughts of the lead character in **Terence M. Green**'s novel *A Witness to Life* (1999).

We are not commanded to believe, but we are commanded to remember. Without memory there can be neither continuity nor identity.

Dow Marmur, rabbi, Holy Blossom Temple, Toronto, *Choose Life: Thoughts on Grief and Growth* (1999).

MEN See also MANKIND, MEN & WOMEN

Men will never disappoint us if we observe two rules: (1) to find out what they are; (2) to expect them to be just that.

George Iles, aphorist, *Canadian Stories: Together with... Jottings from a Note-Book* (1918).

Male bonding.

The concept of male bonding—the behaviour whereby men form groups—was given its present currency by the Montreal-born anthropologist **Lionel Tiger** in his book *Men in Groups* (1969). Interviewed by Bill Taylor in The Toronto Star, 17 Feb. 1992, Tiger explained: "It was a robust notion, sure. It never occurred to me that it would become a part of the language."

Men don't remain babies all their lives; around forty, most of them become boys.

Richard Needham, newspaper columnist, *The Wit and Wisdom of Richard Needham* (1977).

Young men exaggerate; old men pretend.

Robin Skelton, poet and aphorist, *A Devious Dictionary* (1991).

A man is an insane woman.

Title of a poem in **Ann Diamond**'s collection *Terrorist Letters* (1992).

MEN & WOMEN See also LIFE, LOVE, MANKIND, MARRIAGE, MEN, SEX, WOMEN

I have always noticed that if there was a cheer for the Governor-General, and that cheer was followed by another for Lady Lansdowne, the last cheer seemed to me to be the heartier, but there was never any heart-burning on my part on that account.

Lord Lansdowne, Governor General, remark made at Bowood, his estate in Wiltshire, England, Summer 1888, after serving as Governor-General, quoted by John Cowan in *Canada's Governors-General 1867–1952* (1952).

But this is courtship all the world over—the man all tongue; the woman all ears.

Line from **Emily G. Murphy**'s autobiographical novel *Janey Canuck in the West* (1910).

I have no desire to be equal to man. I prefer to maintain my superiority.

L.M. Montgomery, author, quoted by her son Chester Montgomery in Hilda M. Ridley's biography *The Story of L.M. Montgomery* (1973).

A man wants a wife who can bake bread like her mother. A woman wants a husband who can make dough like her father.

Bob Edwards, publisher, *The Eye Opener*, 7 Sept. 1912, *The Wit and Wisdom of Bob Edwards* (1976) edited by Hugh Dempsey.

If a man understands one woman he should let it go at that.

Bob Edwards, publisher, *The Eye Opener*, 23 Aug. 1919, *The Wit and Wisdom of Bob Edwards* (1976) edited by Hugh Dempsey.

Sitting in the restaurant the other day we heard a lady complain all men she'd met are underage, overage or average.

R.R. Cunningham, publisher and columnist, remark made in 1940s, quoted by J. George Johnston in *The Weeklies: Biggest Circulation in Town* (1972).

Men search for happiness; women for fulfilment.

Raymond Canale, Italian-born, Toronto-based aphorist, 1975.

When he sees an attractive member of the opposite sex, a man takes a second look. A woman can pack everything into the first look.

Eric Nicol, humorist, *Canada Cancelled for Lack of Interest* (1977) illustrated by Peter Whalley.

Men offer love in the hope of getting sex; women offer sex in the hope of getting love; both are cheated.

Richard Needham, newspaper columnist, *The Wit and Wisdom of Richard Needham* (1977).

I think virginity should be renewable in the same way a man can get divorced and become a bachelor again.

Sylvia Fraser, author, quoted by John Burgess in *The Toronto Star*, 16 March 1980.

In my observations as a lay person, the words "male" and "female" have become obsolete. Feminine and masculine characteristics often seem to be totally interchangeable. I prefer the word *androgynous*. I find that most people whom I consider to be close to complete human beings are, in fact, a mélange: a melding of both the sensitive and the strong.

Jack Pollock, artist and memoirist, observations made in 1983, *Dear M: Letters from a Gentleman of Excess* (1989).

The more educated a man the less likely he is to believe that women can think and wear earrings at the same time.

Aileen Burford Mason, medical researcher, characteristic comment, Aug. 1990.

Men who like women rarely fall in love.

Robin Skelton, poet and aphorist, *A Devious Dictionary* (1991).

Who knows what evil lurks in the hearts of men? An older woman knows. But how much older do you have to get before you acquire that kind of wisdom?

Thoughts of a character in **Margaret Atwood**'s novel *The Robber Bride* (1993).

Men and women occupy different worlds. We walk down the same streets but it is as the lion and the zebra share the savannah. One runs for its supper, the other for its life.

Craig McInnes, journalist, "The Beast Within," *The Globe and Mail*, 16 Jan. 1993.

Men and women are looking for a friend to sleep with.

Wendy Dennis, author, characteristic remark, CJRT Radio, Toronto, 22 Sept. 1994. After interviewing men for a book about sex today, Dennis concluded that a man wants a "sex buddy" rather than a "sex bunny."

People are human beings first and men and women afterwards. Their bodily functions are different; their environments are different, though the difference in this century has been greatly decreased.

Northrop Frye, cultural critic, diary entry, 24 Aug. 1942, *Northrop Frye Newsletter*, Fall 1996.

Women love, men lust—clearly the real story is much *more* complicated, and far more interesting. The truth is that women are capable of all kinds of emotions and behaviour and so are men.

Kate Fillion, journalist, *Lip Service: The Truth about Women's Darker Side in Love, Sex, and Friendship* (1996).

The way to a man's heart is through his stomach, but the way to a woman's usually involves a jeweller.

Susan Kastner, columnist, "World of Women Whirls Us Away," *The Toronto Star*, 15 Sept. 1996.

If a man can't fix it, he can't face it.

Shirley Bobier, social work co-ordinator, characteristic remark, Aug. 1999.

Men blame circumstances. Women blame themselves.

*

For a woman, no man is a solution; at best, only a compromise.

Susan Ioannou, writer and editor, aphorisms, 7 March 2000.

MENNONITES

What is the mysterious connection between the doctrine of non-resistance and worldly prosperity? Why do they always go together?

Henry Van Dyke, American essayist and travel writer, thoughts occasioned by visiting Mennonite settlements in southern Manitoba, "The Red River of the North," *Harper's New Monthly Magazine*, May 1880.

I visited a friend who has lived there most of her life, and who writes about the Mennonite people, their customs, their cooking, and, more than anything, their life-view, which is to us amazingly untouched by this century, amazingly simple and related to one another. Naturally, outsiders tend to regard their way of life as archaic, but sometimes one wonders if their view won't endure longer than ours.

Margaret Laurence, novelist, discussing writer Edna Staebler and the Mennonites of Waterloo County, "Down East," *Heart of a Stranger* (1976).

MENOPAUSE

I have been the guest on so many hour-long call-in shows in all parts of North America that I am no longer surprised to pick up the telephone and hear a hesitant voice ask, "Is this the menopause lady?"

Janine O'Leary Cobb, women's health specialist who launched the newsletter *A Friend Indeed* in March 1984, *Understanding Menopause: Answers and Advice for Women in the Prime of Life* (1993).

Menopause is not an equal-opportunity employer. Men get it too, but they get to enjoy it. They buy red sports cars and leave their wives for someone young and skinny enough to fit into the front seat.

Dorothy Lipovenko, reporter, "Biological Bugaboo," *The Globe and Mail*, 13 Jan. 1995.

MENTAL HEALTH See HEALTH, PSYCHIATRY

MERCHANDISING

It will not be in my day, but I hope you will live to see the Store closed all day Saturday. The week's work will be done between Monday morning and Friday evening. Saturday will be a day for play. Sunday will be a day for rest and worship, and people will return to work on Monday morning refreshed in body and in spirit.

Timothy Eaton, founder of the T. Eaton Co. who died in 1907, addressing his son Sir John Craig Eaton about early closing on Saturdays, from an advertisement designed by Sir John, 31 Dec. 1918. *Golden Jubilee, 1869–1919: A Book to Commemorate the Fiftieth Anniversary* (1919).

We know how to subsidize, but we don't know how to merchandise. In Canada, we haven't learned how to acquaint the public with what we do.

Harry Boyle, broadcaster, interviewed on TVO's *The Government We Deserve*, 5 Dec. 1976.

If you're going to give anything away… charge a nickel.

Ed Mirvish, merchandiser, advice to film exhibitor Reg Hartt, quoted by Adam Czerechowicz in *The Toronto Star*, 1 Nov. 1979.

Dave Nichol has launched more failed new products than anyone I know. On the other hand, he has launched more new products than anyone in the history of the world.

Galen Weston, Chairman and President of George Weston Ltd., announcing the retirement of Dave Nichol who as president of Loblaws merchandising department launched both No Name and President's Choice products, quoted by John Deverell in *The Toronto Star*, 5 July 1994.

MÉTIS PEOPLE See also ABORIGINAL PEOPLES; INDIAN PEOPLES; NATIVE PEOPLES; RIEL, LOUIS

I am French / I am English / And I am Métis / But more than this / Above all this / I am Canadian and proud to be free.

Lines from **Duke Redbird**'s monologue "I Am a Canadian" performed before Queen Elizabeth II, Silver Jubilee Celebrations, Ottawa, 17 Oct. 1977. The text appears in *Loveshine and Red Wine* (1981).

We defy definitions of race. Our blood can be of many origins. We defy those who want to talk of percentages of this parentage or that. We defy definitions that are based on colour. We come in many hues. We defy cultural definitions for we speak many tongues and live as part of many cultures. We defy those who try to delimit our citizenship for there are no simple criteria.

Definition of "Métisness" according to the **Métis National Council** in a conference report of 1991, as quoted by Sheila Jones in "Identity," *The Globe and Mail*, 3 Aug. 1996.

METRIC COMMISSION

The reason there are ten provinces is because Canada was destined to go metric.

Steve Rubin, Montreal aphorist, 14 Oct. 1991.

I like living in a country where adults still announce, "I'll never understand the metric system as long as I live," and be proud of it.

Rick Green, comedian and host of TVO's *Prisoners of Gravity*, "My Canada Includes . . . ," *Maclean's*, 3 Jan. 1994.

MEXICO & MEXICANS See also NORTH AMERICA

Canada and Mexico, as the saying goes, have one common problem between them. This problem, of course, is their relationship with the United States.

Saying recorded by historian **J.C.M. Ogelsby** in *Gringos from the Far North: Essays in the History of Canadian-Latin American Relations, 1866–1968* (1976).

Mexicans are not Spaniards. A Mexican is a Spanish-speaking person with Maya blood and hereditary memory of the highly developed pre-Colombian Maya culture.

Sheila Gostick, political satirist, *The Toronto Star*, 17 Aug. 1992.

Canadians, I believe, see Mexico as Sicilian, dark, closed, Catholic, threatening.

Richard Rodriguez, American commentator of Mexican ancestry, interviewed by Richard Gwyn in "Opinions," *The Toronto Star*, 7 Feb. 1993.

MIGRATION

Emparons-nous du sol

"Let us seize the sun for ourselves." Slogan devised by **Abbé François Labelle**, the so-called King of the North who urged the settlement of the Laurentians, and adopted by the Congress of Colonization of 1898 to redirect the flow of French immigrants from the New England states to the Quebec North. Quoted by Joseph Levitt in *Henri Bourassa and the Golden Calf: The Social Program of the Nationalists of Quebec* (1969).

MILITARY POWER

This is a very militaristic country we live in, a country with a long military history, a country where violence is as Canadian as apple pie, a country where the game we talk is not the game as it really exists.

J.L. Granatstein, historian, quoted by Dennis Kucherawy in *eye*, 16 Jan. 1992.

MILLENNIUM

The next millennium was not getting off to a promising start.

Thoughts of the narrator of **Paul William Roberts**' novel *The Palace of Fears* (1994).

Around the world, and in our own imagination, a new Global Culture is being born. Its main values, astonishingly, are Democracy, Peace, and Equality.

Gwynne Dyer, journalist and broadcaster, CBC Radio's *Millennium*, 24 March 1996.

As the millennium turns, I think we're on the verge of a great global mind shift—a transformation of human affairs comparable in scale to the Renaissance and the Enlightenment.

Kalle Lasn, non-consumer advocate and co-founder of Adbusters Media Foundation in Vancouver in 1995, "People, Get Ready," *The Globe and Mail*, 31 Dec. 1999.

MIND

I conclude that there is no good evidence... that the brain alone can carry out the work that the mind does.... I believe that one should not pretend to draw a final scientific conclusion, in man's study of man, until the nature of the energy responsible for mind-action is discovered, as in my own opinion, it will be.

Wilder Penfield, neurosurgeon, *The Mystery of the Mind* (1975).

The mind is an observer from outer space.

Louis Dudek, man-of-letters, *Epigrams* (1975).

Matter thinks in humans.

E.L. Stone, advocate and author, *Pleasura & Realitas: The Dialectic of Dominating Impulses* (1993).

We're trapped in a prison of the mind and we think constantly of escape.

Louis Dudek, poet and aphorist, "Bitter Pills," *Reality Games* (1998).

MINING

A mine is a hole in the ground with a liar sitting on top of it.

Attributed to humorist **Mark Twain** with respect to Ontario mining promotion, dating from his years in Buffalo, N.Y., 1870s.

In the town of Springhill, Nova Scotia, / Down in the dark of the Cumberland Mine, / There's blood on the coal and the miners lie, / In roads that never saw sun nor sky, / Roads that never saw sun nor sky.

Verse of **Ewan MacColl** and **Peggy Seeger**'s ballad "The Springhill Mining Disaster" (1958) that commemorates the collapse of the deepest mine in North America, Springhill Mine, N.S., 23 Oct. 1958, killing seventy-four miners.

Give me a glass of water and I'll sing you a song.

Maurice Ruddick, miner known as the Singing Miner, made the above boast when he was rescued after more than eight days underground, Springhill Mining Disaster of 1958, quoted by Dale Brazao and John Spears in *The Toronto Star,* 13 May 1992.

There may come a day when some of Canada's biggest mines will be among the igloos.

R.A.J. Phillips and **G.F. Parsons**, writers, *This Is the Arctic* (1964).

I would say that ninety per cent of our natural wealth still awaits discovery.

Stephen B. Roman, founder of Denison Mines, the world's largest producer of uranium, quoted by Lawrence F. Jones and George Lonn in *Historical Highlights of Canadian Mining* (1973).

Although mineral production is an industry, mineral search—prospecting—is a romantic adventure.

Frank R. Joubin, prospector, *Not for Gold Alone: The Memoirs of a Prospector* (1986) written with D. McCormack Smyth.

We don't have the glitz. We don't have the press.... We just generate wealth. We quietly, in a boring, dull way produce most of the things human beings need.

Peter Munk, mining magnate, address, Council of the Americas, New York, 15 Sept. 1995, quoted by Brian Milner in "World Watch," *The Globe and Mail,* 18 Sept. 1995.

MINORITIES

In an age of mass audiences it is the minorities who stand firm, and their loyalties are international.

Robert Weaver, magazine editor and radio producer, "Books," *Mass Media in Canada* (1962) edited by John A. Irving.

At the same time, if the prophetic voice so frequently comes from the outsider, it follows that society's most effective defence against prophecy is toleration. The realization of this, in our society, has helped to create an almost obsessive preoccupation with the subcultures or countercultures of various minorities, blacks, Chicanos, homosexuals, terrorists, drug addicts, occultists, yogis, criminals like the holy and blessed Genet—wherever it may still be possible to make out a case for social hostility or discrimination.

Northrop Frye, cultural critic, "The Responsibilities of the Critic" (1976), *Myth and Metaphor: Selected Essays, 1974–1988.* Charlottesville, N.C.: University of Virginia, 1990, edited by Robert D. Denham.

Visible minorities are, in fact, the invisible members of our society. Canada will be the ultimate loser if we do not take advantage of the skills and abilities which visible minority Canadians have to offer.

Commissioners, *Report of the Special Committee on the Participation of Visible Minorities in Canadian Society,* March 1984.

For the purpose of this report, visible minorities have been defined as non-whites who are not participating fully in Canadian society. The approximate non-white population of Canada is 1,864,000 or 7 per cent of the population.... Ten visible minority groups were established: Black, Indo-Pakistani, Chinese, Korean, Japanese, South East Asian, Philipino, Other Pacific Islanders, West Asian and Arab, and Latin American.

Commissioners, *Report of the Special Committee on the Participation of Visible Minorities in Canadian Society,* March 1984. The commissioners added an eleventh or "mixed" group as well as a twelfth group for "total aboriginals."

I recall a class in which I was discussing the Canadian concept of a "visible minority," which means a minority capable of being recognized easily, such as blacks or Native Americans. A student raised her hand and asked whether Jews were a visible minority. I responded: "No, we are an audible minority."

Alan M. Dershowitz, lawyer and law professor, Harvard University, Princeton, N.Y., *Chutzpah* (1991).

Canada is a country of minorities; the anglophones are a minority put upon by the Americans; the francophones are put upon by the anglophones; the aboriginal people are put upon by the anglophones and francophones; and other cultural minorities feel left out.

John Ralston Saul, President, Canada PEN International, quoted in University of Guelph's "Canada" supplement, *The Globe and Mail*, 4 Dec. 1991.

MIRACLES

Shall I say that miracles are wrought here? If I denied that such were the case, the ex-votive offerings in yonder pyramids would belie my words.

Louis-Joseph Bruchési, Archbishop of Montreal, blessing the addition to the chapel of St. Joseph's Oratory, Mount Royal, Montreal, Nov. 1910, quoted by George H. Ham in *The Miracle Man of Montreal* (3rd ed., 1922).

Suppose some holy nun in Toronto should cure a broken leg—I wouldn't believe it simply because I heard it, but because it could certainly be.

G.K. Chesterton, man-of-letters, referring to his belief in miracles, interviewed in Toronto by R.E. Knowles in *The Toronto Star*, 3 Oct. 1930.

A miracle is not explained by being analyzed—and life is indeed a miracle.

Louis Dudek, poet and aphorist, 1988, *Notebooks 1960–1994* (1994).

MISSIONARIES

The missionary should constantly have before him a picture of himself with a suitcase in his hand.

William Charles White, missionary in China, on leaving China, quoted by Lewis C. Walmsley in *Bishop in Hanoi* (1974).

The task of our missions is not to make a Hindu a better Hindu. It is to make him a Christian, because that is Right.

Paul Smith, son of the founder and pastor of the People's Church, an evangelical tabernacle in Toronto, quoted by Marq de Villiers in *Weekend Magazine*, 8 Feb. 1975.

MISTAKES

You've got to make yards out of everything—even your mistakes.

Philip A. Gagliardi, B.C. Highways Minister, quoted by Ray Gardner in *Maclean's*, 24 Oct. 1959.

I've certainly made mistakes, but life doesn't give you all the cards at the same time. You have to take them as they're dealt. I've had both peaks and valleys and, hopefully, I'm on my way to the summit again.

Corey Hart, Montreal-born popular singer, quoted by Stephen Ostick in the *Winnipeg Free Press*, 26 May 1992.

MODERATION

Moderation is clear firmness. It is the opposite of intemperance and confrontation.

George P. Grant, philosopher, *The Toronto Star*, 7 July 1977.

For while moderation may be necessary physiologically, it may be a calamity for the psyche and the imagination.

Douglas LePan, poet and essayist, *Bright Glass of Memory: A Set of Four Memoirs* (1979).

Well, as my friend Professor Donald Creighton once remarked, the man who asks me to jump out of a third storey window can, I suppose, be described as "moderate" by comparison with one who wants me to jump from the seventh storey; but in either case I shall be dead.

Eugene Forsey, political commentator, "'French' and 'English'" *Essays on the Canadian Constitution* (19882).

MONARCHY See also GOVERNOR GENERAL, ROYAL TOURS

Red Crow

Title of Red Crow or Mekastro granted by the Kainai Chiefs of the Blood Indians of Alberta to the **Prince of Wales**; it was accorded in 1919 to Edward Albert, Prince of Wales (subsequently Edward VIII and Duke of Windsor); in 1977 to Charles, Prince of Wales.

I'm on display so much, sometimes for hours, that I dodge into a washroom whenever I see one.

Prince of Wales, later Edward VIII, still later Duke of Windsor, remark made to an unnamed professor, overheard by R.G. Everson and published in the poem "The Day I Spent with Edward, Prince of Wales," *Indian Summer* (1976).

Canada was quick to teach me that mere civility—the polite but distant bow, the right word to the right person, a mild interest in a carefully selected assortment of local projects and good works—was no longer an adequate Royal export. As Lloyd George had shrewdly surmised, the Dominions wanted, if not a vaudeville show, then a first-class carnival in which the Prince of Wales should play a gay, many-sided, and natural role.

Prince of Wales, later Edward VIII, still later Duke of Windsor, *A King's Story: The Memoirs of H.R.H. the Duke of Windsor* (1951).

Virtually any female I meet is liable to be sized up as a future spouse. So I shall be very careful as to whose nose I rub.

Charles, Prince of Wales, Frobisher Bay, *Time*, 5 May 1975. The Inuit Tapirisat of Canada denounced the Prince for this remark because it showed "no respect for Inuit integrity." In the Eastern Arctic in 1977, Charles was dubbed Attanniou Ikeneega ("The Son of the Big Boss"); in the West he was named Mekastro ("Red Crow") by the Kainai Chiefs of the Blood Indians, resuscitating the name accorded in 1919 to Edward Albert, Prince of Wales (subsequently Edward VIII and Duke of Windsor).

God Save Everyone from the Queen

Sign carried by **Zoltan Szoboszloi**, self-styled iconoclast and anti-monarchist of Hungarian background, demonstrating at the Queen's Silver Jubilee Dinner, Parliament Hill, Ottawa, 16 Oct. 1977, quoted by Helen Bullock in *The Toronto Star* the following day.

When it comes to national unity, the Crown could be the golden clasp which holds this country together—a focal point above political parties, a symbol beyond elected personalities, a lifebuoy in a sea of despair.

Strome Galloway, monarchist, Letters to the Editor, *The Globe and Mail*, 2 Nov. 1977.

Better we have the Queen as Head of State than, say, Keith Davey.

René Lévesque, Quebec Premier, referring to Liberal Senator Keith Davey, First Ministers' Conference, 9 Aug. 1978.

I would go as far as to say that, in the unconscious minds of most Canadians, Canada no longer has a head of state. There is only a governor-general representing an anachronism—a shadow symbolizing a memory at the pinnacle of the nation.

William Thorsell, "Let Us Compare Mythologies" (1990), *Canadian Content* (1992) edited by Sarah Norton and Nell Waldman.

The Queen has no personal power; but the Crown is the foundation of Canadian political, legal and social practice, and the guarantor of our rights and freedoms. The Queen offers a reasonable alternative to anarchy, republicanism, communism or fascism.

Heather Robertson, columnist, "The Queen, Like Her or Lump Her," *The Canadian Forum*, May 1991.

A constitutional monarchy, then, is a wonderful form of government. The pity is that we don't have one any more.

William Christian, political scientist, "Holiday Musings, *The Globe and Mail*, 20 May 1991.

Canada is no longer a British progeny in the eyes or hearts of most of us. The only person more embarrassed than a typical Canadian at the spectre of Charles as King of Canada would be Charles the King himself.

William Thorsell, columnist, *The Globe and Mail*, 25 May 1991.

Every time I come to Canada, and I've been here many times since 1970, a little more Canada seeps into my bloodstream. And from there, straight into the heart.

Charles, Prince of Wales, address, Winnipeg, 25 April 1996, quoted by David Roberts in *The Globe and Mail* the following day.

It's time for Canada to ditch that inbred family of promiscuous mediocrities, still pretending to reign over us.

Peter C. Newman, columnist, discussing Royal reaction to the funeral of Diana, Princess of Wales, "The Nation's Business," *Maclean's*, 15 Sept. 1997.

MONEY

See also FINANCE, LOONIE, STOCK MARKET, WEALTH

A millionaire might offer more for a life belt as a souvenir than a drowning man could pay for it to save his life.

Stephen Leacock, humorist, *The Unsolved Riddle of Social Justice* (1922).

Of course money talks as much as ever, but what it says nowadays makes less cents. Then again let's put it this way—there are bigger things than money. Bills for instance.

R.R. Cunningham, publisher and columnist, 1940s, quoted by J. George Johnston in *The Weeklies: Biggest Circulation in Town* (1972).

What's a million?

Catch-phrase identified with **C.D. Howe**, who served as "Minister of Everything" in the Cabinets of Mackenzie King and St. Laurent. Howe never uttered these words. Howe may have been a pragmatist as well as a parliamentarian, but he was also a disciplinarian when it came to expenditures. He defended a review of budget estimates in the House of Commons on 19 Nov. 1945, with these words: "I daresay my honourable friend could cut a million dollars from this amount; but a million dollars from the war appropriation bill would not be a very important matter." The bill in question called for the expenditure of $1,365 million. The following day, John G. Diefenbaker, then a Conservative backbencher, rose in the House of Commons and deliberately misquoted Howe. Diefenbaker claimed that Howe had said, "We may save a million dollars, but what of that?" Howe was outraged, but the pattern was set. Thereafter the "Minister of Everything" was known as C.D. ("What's a million?") Howe.

Making money is the least important thing in the world, unless you're making it to advance a good cause.

W. Garfield Weston, founder of George Weston Ltd. and financier, characteristic remark made in the 1950s.

In the economic sphere cash becomes credit: Money becomes the poor man's credit card.

Marshall McLuhan, communications pioneer, *Take Today: The Executive as Dropout* (1972) with Barrington Nevitt.

There are doubtless things money won't buy, but one can't think of them at a moment's notice.

Richard Needham, newspaper columnist, *The Wit and Wisdom of Richard Needham* (1977).

Things that are current create currency.

Marshall McLuhan, communications pioneer, quoted by Richard J. Schoeck in *Who Was Marshall McLuhan?* (1994) edited by Barrington Nevitt and Maurice McLuhan.

There's nothing more nervous than a million dollars. It doesn't speak French, it doesn't speak English, and it moves pretty fast.

Jean Chrétien, Prime Minister, quoted by Adam Mayers and Patrick McKeough in *Surviving Canada's Separation Anxiety: Taking Control of Your Financial Future* (1996).

Not everyone wants to be a millionaire. Most people are content just to live like one.

Brian K. Costello, investment adviser, *Taking Care of Your Money: Multi-Dimensional Investing that Works* (1997).

Nothing sets such stern limits on the liberty of the citizen as a total absence of money.

John Kenneth Galbraith, economist and essayist, *The Socially Concerned Today* (1998).

The Canadian dollar will disappear in our lifetime.

Peter C. Newman, columnist, "The Nation's Business," *Maclean's*, 27 July 1998.

MONSTERS See OGOPOGO, SASQUATCH

MONTREAL See also QUEBEC

Montreal has 40,000 inhabitants, and is the seat of the Provincial Government. It looks like an old English town.

George Moore, English author, *Journal of a Voyage across the Atlantic with Notes on Canada and the United States and Return to Great Britain in 1844* (1845).

Montreal is rotten to the core and if all Canada be like it the sooner we have done with it the better.

Lord Elgin, Governor General of British North America (1847–54), letter to Earl Grey, 1849, *The Elgin-Grey Papers* (1937) edited by A.G. Doughty.

This is the first time I was ever in a city where you couldn't throw a brick without breaking a church window.

Mark Twain, American humorist, address, Windsor Hotel, Montreal, 7 Dec. 1881, quoted by

Stephen Leacock in *Queen's Quarterly*, Summer 1935.

The most astonishing thing was the city itself, consisting as it does of two sectors, one English-Canadian and one French-Canadian. The border between these two areas was invisible, but it went right through the city. If you took the electric streetcar in the English sector the conductor would say, "Tickets, please." But after a certain undistinguished cross street had been passed, the same conductor would call out, "Les billets, Messieurs, s'il vous plaît."

Otto Hahn, German-born atomic scientist, describing his work at the Macdonald Physics Building, McGill University, Montreal, under Ernest Rutherford, from Fall 1905 to Summer 1906, in *Otto Hahn: A Scientific Autobiography* (1966) edited by Willy Ley.

Go to Atlantic City for a week, or up to Montreal.

Advice of the narrator to Nick Carraway in **F. Scott Fitzgerald**'s novel *The Great Gatsby* (1925).

The place you really have in mind is Montreal. It is a grand town, with good hotels and magnificent saloons.

H.L. Mencken, author, letter of 24 June 1931 to Philip Goodman, *The New Mencken Letters* (1977) edited by Carl Bode. Mencken spent his honeymoon in Quebec City in 1930 but preferred Montreal.

Montreal is a very fine city, with beautiful buildings, banks and such-like, far more ornamental than any of their kind I have seen in England.

Freya Stark, traveller and writer, letter written after a stopover in Montreal en route to Creston, B.C., 4 Nov. 1928, *Beyond Euphrates* (1951).

I also went to Canada. Montreal is four-fifth imitation American, and one-fifth imitation English—but the beer and ale were splendidly real.

Thomas Wolfe, American novelist, letter to Henry T. Volkening, 9 Aug. 1929, *The Letters of Thomas Wolfe* (1956) edited by Elizabeth Nowell.

Suddenly I was back in Paris, listening to my occult friend Urbanski who had gone one winter's night to a bordel in Montreal and when he emerged it was Spring. I have been to Montreal myself but somehow the image of it which I retain is not mine but Urbanski's.

Passage from **Henry Miller**'s autobiographical work *The Colossus of Marousi* (1941).

Montreal is a world-city now with most of the symptoms of one, but in those days it was as a visiting Frenchman described it, an English garrison encysted in an overgrown French village.

Thoughts of a character reminiscing about the Montreal of the 1920s in **Hugh MacLennan**'s novel *The Watch that Ends the Night* (1957).

We finally went to Montreal. It was not a city one could easily like. Montreal was politically held together by an equilibrium of ethnic and religious resentments and distrust. And in retrospect, it is not surprising that this political edifice eventually collapsed with extraordinary speed.

Judith N. Shklar, Harvard-based political scientist, born in Russia, educated at McGill University in Montreal during and after the Second World War, "A Life of Learning" (1989), *Liberalism without Illusions: Essays on Liberal Theory and the Political Vision of Judith N. Shklar* (1996) edited by Bernard Yack.

This is a city of hatreds. I can smell them.

Brendan Behan, Irish playwright, addressing writer Tony Aspler during a drive north along St. Lawrence Boulevard, Montreal, Sept. 1960, as quoted by Aspler in *Travels with My Corkscrew: Memoirs of a Wine Lover* (1997).

Montreal is the only place where a good French accent isn't a social asset.

Brendan Behan, Irish playwright, *The Wit of Brendan Behan* (1968) compiled by Sean McCann.

If the Chanukah candles were being extinguished, other candles no less colourful and bright were being lit.

Irving Layton, poet, quoted in *The Montreal Star*, 21 April 1969. Layton, a confirmed Montrealer, feeling that Quebec nationalism was inimical to its Jewish population, moved to Toronto but later returned to the city of his birth.

Montreal is en route to becoming *The City* of the world. Twenty years from now, no matter what happens, it will have achieved this position, and it will be referred to in all parts of the world as *The City*.

Jean Drapeau, long-time Montreal Mayor, quoted in *Sports Illustrated*, 27 Sept. 1970.

In Montreal shortly before I left Canada I had the same feeling—like the frightening stillness and oppressiveness just before a thunderstorm. The storm that is shaking the world settles now here, now there, and Montreal seems fated to be another Belfast or Beirut.

Malcolm Muggeridge, English commentator, "The Land that Time Forgot," *The Canadian*, 13 Oct. 1979.

I love Montreal but it is so slight, so young, so much younger than the bearded West Coast.

George Bowering, poet and essayist, "Montreal," *Craft Slices* (1985).

Paris, London, and Rome are said to be cosmopolitan capitals; Montreal is a "multicultural city." The word "cosmopolitan" refers to an indigenous culture that is open to the world; "multicultural" connotes a mixture in which no culture or identity predominates.

Alice Parizeau, Polish-born Quebec writer, contributor to *Mapping Literature: The Art and Politics of Translation* (1988) edited by David Homel and Sherry Simon.

It is above all an inconsolable city—it weeps still for that clash of distant powers which, two centuries ago, first tossed it from empire to empire, culture to culture. It has not, after all Got Away.

Jan Morris, Anglo-Welsh travel writer, "The Battle for Montreal," *Saturday Night*, July 1988.

One of the anomalies of Montreal is that it is not very beautiful. It ought to be, but it isn't. It lacks the grand touch, the unmistakable artefact—few are the people in the world who, invited to imagine the look of Montreal, could envisage anything specific at all. It lacks chic, too, whatever its publicists say.... So it is by cameos, not by panoramas, that I shall remember my visit.

Jan Morris, Anglo-Welsh travel writer, "The Battle for Montreal," *Saturday Night*, July 1988.

The once cosmopolitan city of Montreal is in danger of becoming a linguistic Beirut. Sensibilities have become dulled to the point where the presence or absence of an apostrophe or an *accent aigu* is a political statement, and spray paint has replaced civilized discourse.

Witold Rybczynski, architect and essayist, interviewed by *Liberté* in 1989, quoted by Mordecai Richler in "A Reporter at Large: Inside/Outside," *The New Yorker*, 23 Sept. 1991.

Actually, Canada *has* been held hostage for at least twenty years by a quarrel endemic to a Montreal suburb. But that suburb is Outremont, not Westmount; Outremont, where the following political figures were either raised or are still resident: Pierre Elliott Trudeau, Robert Bourassa, Jacques Parizeau, Claude Ryan, Camille Laurin.

Mordecai Richler, novelist and essayist, *Oh Canada! Oh Quebec! Requiem for a Divided Country* (1992).

The grace of Montreal is to survive its successive leaders. That may be its secret, a lovely pragmatic endurance that makes the city tolerant toward the empty dreams of its paladin mayors, obsessed with impressing the whole planet.

Lise Bissonnette, columnist, writing in *Le Devoir* about Montreal's 350th birthday celebrations, quoted in *The Hamilton Spectator*, 30 May 1992.

But I love Montreal. It's a wonderful city to be in. You walk the streets and there's a gait.... They can amble, or they can cavort, but there's a gait that relates to something in the centre of their pelvis.

Scott Symons, author, "Deliquescence in Canada," *The Idler*, July–Aug. 1992.

In Montreal, you have to spend the first few seconds or moments of every encounter determining, first of all, which language you are going to speak. This runs quite deep. A great deal of energy is spent trying to establish situations in which you do not murder each other.

Leonard Cohen, poet and singer, interviewed by Winfried Siemerling, "Loneliness and History," *Take This Waltz: A Celebration of Leonard Cohen* (1994) edited by Michael Fournier and Ken Norris.

McGill generally behaves as if it could as easily be in Paris, London, New York, San Francisco or Beijing. That's wrong. It ought to behave as if it is here in Montreal.

Bernard J. Shapiro, Montreal-born Principal of McGill University, quoted by Kimberly J. McLarin in "Education Life: Profile," *The New York Times Magazine*, 2 April 1995.

English Montrealers are just about the only unfashionable minority in all of Canada.... We are the only minority English-speaking group north of the Rio Grande.

Joan Fraser, editor, *The Gazette*, Conference on Canada & Quebec: Perspectives and Strategies, Vancouver, 2 March 1996.

In Montreal, and only in Montreal, is to be found the paradigm of the Canada we have come so close to losing; the two founding peoples, the successive waves of immigrants, co-existing peacefully in a bilingual, multicultural society, celebrating difference. Elsewhere, it has been an idea; here, in Montreal, a reality. Only in Quebec, out of everywhere in Canada, has this vision flourished as a lived reality—and in Quebec, only in Montreal.

Robyn Sarah, writer, "Paradigm Found," *The Globe and Mail*, 20 July 1996.

This is a time for all of us, wherever we live in Canada, to say, "We are all Montrealers."

Jean Chrétien, Prime Minister, announcing subsidies to Montreal-area businesses, quoted in an editorial in *The Toronto Star*, 25 Oct. 1996.

MONTREAL MASSACRE See also FEMINISM, WOMEN

Women to one side. You're all a bunch of feminists!... Women to one side. You are all feminists, I hate feminists.

Marc Lépine, disgruntled student and mass murderer, École Polytechnique, Université de Montréal, Montreal, 4:30 p.m., 6 Dec. 1989. He shot and killed fourteen women students of engineering and wounded twelve others before taking his own life.

If those 14 students had lived to pursue their careers, they would have represented one-half of one per cent of all women engineers in Canada. That may not sound like much, but when 14 people can make a dent in the statistics, there is a problem. The sad reality is that fewer than 3 per cent of all engineers are women.

Leigh Dayton, columnist, *The Globe and Mail*, 13 Jan. 1990.

Who's going to break the silence? / Who's going to fight the fight? / Stand up and be counted / And give us back the night.

Cynthia Kerr, composer, refrain of "Give Us Back the Night," quoted by Kerr in "Have Your Say," *The Toronto Star*, 8 Sept. 1991. The song is associated with the Montreal Massacre and was recorded in Jan. 1991. One of the voices of the chorus was that of Nina De Villiers, a high-school student from Hamilton, Ont., who one evening in Aug. 1991 was raped and murdered.

In memory, and in grief, for all the women murdered by men, / For women of all countries, all classes, all ages, all colours, / We, their sisters and brothers, remember and work for a better world.

Controversial wording proposed for the inscription to appear in seven languages on the monument to commemorate the fourteen women students murdered in the Montreal Massacre, 6 Dec. 1989, to be erected in Vancouver, quoted by Christopher Dafoe in *The Globe and Mail*, 29 July 1993.

MOON

They can have the moon. The moon is dead. We killed it by standing on its face—by planting a windblown flag where there is no wind and by saying *this moon is mine*. Talk about the death of the imagination. Talk about *appropriation*.

Timothy Findley, novelist, "When You Write about This Country," *The Canadian Forum*, Sept. 1992.

One that touched me most was one of the most dramatic I've ever been involved with, and that was the moon landing. That was a story of great hope and optimism.

Lloyd Robertson, veteran CTV newsanchor, when asked which news stories over the years affected him the most, quoted by Paul Welsby in *TV Guide*, 27 Aug. 1994.

MOOSE See also ANIMALS

Beaver are boring. Moose are magnificent.

David Lewis Stein, journalist, discussing the moose photographs of naturalist Michael Runtz, *The Toronto Star,* 5 Oct. 1991.

MORALITY See also GOOD & EVIL, RIGHT & WRONG

Some people are too good to be interesting.

Bob Edwards, publisher, *The Eye Opener,* 25 Oct. 1911, *The Best of Bob Edwards* (1975) edited by Hugh Dempsey.

Sometimes it seems as if we simply traded the threat of nuclear oblivion for the reality of moral oblivion.

Brian Fawcett, novelist and columnist, *The Globe and Mail,* 26 April 1991.

Like the other animals, we find and pick up what we can use, and appropriate territories. But unlike the other animals, we also trade and produce for trade. Because we possess these two radically different ways of dealing with our needs, we also have two radically different systems of morals and values—both systems valid and necessary.

Jane Jacobs, commentator, Preface, *Systems of Survival: A Dialogue on the Moral Foundations of Commerce and Politics* (1992).

Non-judgmental is an alternate spelling of amoral.

Maurus E. Mallon, aphorist, 22 Oct. 1992.

Immorality is doing wrong of our own volition. Amorality is doing it because a structure or an organization expects us to do it.

John Ralston Saul, author, *The Doubter's Companion: A Dictionary of Aggressive Common Sense* (1994).

To remain life-size in a time of moral diminishment. This is the challenge for all of us today.

Mary Jo Leddy, activist theologian, abbess of Romero House, a centre for refugees, Toronto, quoted by Susan Kastner in *The Toronto Star,* 31 May 1997.

MORTALITY

You begin to feel that instead of the world being created for you, you are only an accidental atom, an insect, upon it, and that it is a wonder you have not perished long ago.

Janarius A. MacGahan, Irish-American war correspondent and member of the Pandora Expedition to the Eastern Arctic, commenting on living conditions, *Under the Northern Lights* (1876).

Every year nearly Ten Thousand Children in Ontario, under the age of five years, go to their graves. We would think ten thousand emigrants a great addition to our population. It is a question if ten thousand emigrants from anywhere would equal in value to us these ten thousand little Canadians of Ontario, whose lives are sacrificed to our carelessness, ignorance, stupidity and eager haste to snatch at less valuable things.

Helen MacMurchy, physician and author, *Infant Mortality: Special Report* (1910).

MOTHERS See also FAMILY

It's my belief that between mothers and daughters there is a kind of blood-hyphen that is, finally, indissoluble.

Thoughts of a character in **Carol Shields**' novel *Swann* (1987).

Tell a pregnant woman that her unborn child hears her voice or senses her love, and she's bound to agree. For mothers intuitively know what scientists have only recently discovered: that the unborn child is a deeply sensitive individual who forms a powerful relationship with his or her parents—and the outside world—while still in the womb.

Thomas Verny, psychiatrist, founder of the Pre- and Perinatal Psychology Association of North America, and **Pamela Weintraub**, journalist, *Nurturing the Unborn Child: A Nine-Month Program for Soothing, Stimulating, and Communicating with Your Baby* (1991).

MOTIVATION

Then Ajax leapt, or was propelled from behind, into the fray.

Attributed to humorist **Stephen Leacock** and called his "famous line" by F.R. Scott, *Brick: A Journal of Reviews,* No. 30, Summer 1987.

Two areas of study allow special insight into the signficance of *competence motivation.* These are the play activities of children and the leisure activities of adults.

Susan Butt, psychologist, *The Psychology of*

Sport: The Behaviour, Motivation, Personality and Performance of Athletes (1987).

There are only two types of motivation: fear and desire. Your greatest fear or desire always wins.

George Torok, motivational speaker, characteristic remark, 25 March 2000.

Mountain climbers will scale a mountain because "it is there." Why don't teenagers clean the messes in their rooms for the same reason?

George Torok, motivational speaker, characteristic remark, 11 May 2000.

MOTTOS

Je me souviens.

Motto of the **Province of Quebec**, French for "I remember." Recalled are the glories of the Ancien Régime—the language, laws, and religion of Quebec before the Conquest of 1759. The motto was selected to be inscribed beneath the coat of arms of the National Assembly in Quebec City, 9 Feb. 1883. The architect Eugène Taché took the words from a three-line poem, which runs: "*Je me souviens / Que né sous le lys, / Je crois sous la rose.*" The poem is of unknown origin; the words mean: "I remember / That while under the fleur de lys [of France], / I grow under the rose [of England]." The three lines imply co-existence; the three words suggest separate existence. In 1978, "Je me souviens" replaced "La Belle Province" as the inscription on Quebec's automobile licence plates.

Je me souviens runs the motto on every car number plate in Quebec. That comes from a poem which goes, "I remember that I was born under the *fleur-de-lis* and grew up under the rose." Everyone knows how to interpet it: "Born French but screwed by the English ever since." Quebeckers carry their chip not on their shoulders but on their cars.

John Grimond, journalist, "Nice Country, Nice Mess," *The Economist*, 29 June 1991.

A mari usque ad mare.

Motto of the **Dominion of Canada**. The official translations are "From Sea to Sea" and "D'un océan à l'autre." Samuel Leonard Tilley found it in the King James Version of the Bible (Zechariah 9:10): "His dominion shall be from sea to sea" and recommended it at the pre-Confederation Conference, London, England, Dec. 1866. The notion that Canada extends from sea to sea is repeated in the national anthem "O Canada"; in the 1908 English version by R. Stanley Weir, the second and third verses refer to the land extending "from East to Western Sea." Since the late 1950s and the Northern Vision of Prime Minister John G. Diefenbaker, it has been fashionable to speak of Canada as a country extending "from sea to sea to sea"—from the Atlantic to the Pacific to the Arctic.

The little envelopes of granulated sugar have the arms of the Canadian provinces on them, Newfoundland, Ontario, British Columbia, and so on, along with the motto: "Explore a part of Canada and you'll discover a part of yourself."

Description from French author and traveller **Michel Tournier**'s novel *Gemini* (1975).

Early Frost Warning in Effect, Needs Some Assembly, Divided We Stand, Batteries Not Included, In Cod We Trust (*E Pluribus* UIC), 27 Million Served.

Suggested replacements, "The Great Canadian Search for a New National Motto," *Geist*, Dec.–Jan. 1994.

MOUNTAINS See also ROCKY MOUNTAINS

Poets of all ages have done much to create a vision of immutability by extolling the "immortal mountains" and "changeless hills," but this is all imaginary. There is immortality in nature. As with civilization, there is constant modification, alteration and even revolution.

Earl C. Denman, adventurer and first Canadian mountaineer to attempt to scale Mount Everest, *Alone to Everest* (1954).

And our mountains are neither higher / nor more beautiful than the mountains / praised and loved by other nations.

Lines from **Al Purdy**'s poem "Home Thoughts," *The Collected Poems of Al Purdy* (1986) edited by Russell Brown.

I want you to imagine you are driving north, across the Lions Gate Bridge, and the sky is steely gray and the sugar-dusted mountains loom blackly in the distance. Imagine what lies behind those mountains—realize that there are only more mountains—mountains until the North Pole, mountains until the end of the world, mountains taller than a thousand me's, mountains taller than a thousand you's.

Douglas Coupland, author, "Coupland's Vancouver," *Vancouver*, Oct. 1997.

MOVIES See FILM

MOWAT, FARLEY See also WRITERS & WRITING, CANADIAN

He's always fought for endangered species—wolves, whales and now *Canadians*.

Gale Garnett, actress and host, introducing Farley Mowat, recipient of the Council of Canadian's first Take Back the Nation Award, Toronto, 21 Nov. 1991.

A good reporter goes where the story takes him. Mowat takes the story where he wants it to go. To him, facts are not sacred.

Peter Worthington, columnist, "Why All the Fuss about Farley," *The Toronto Sun*, 14 May 1996.

The first great non-fiction narrative of Western literature, *The Histories*, took some such liberties and is still widely read 2,500 years later. My guess is, that's longer than Farley Mowat's books will endure, but who knows—if he had been roaring around Persia in his kilt in the 5th century B.C. when Herodotus penned *The Histories*, perhaps we'd still be reading *People of the Camel* today.

George Galt, columnist, "Spectator," *The Globe and Mail*, 18 May 1996. Galt refers to criticism that Mowat's "subjective non-fiction," as in *People of the Deer* (1952), plays fast and loose with the facts.

MULRONEY, BRIAN See also POLITICIANS

In Quebec—and it is very obvious—there are wounds to be healed, worries to be calmed, enthusiasms to be rekindled, and bonds of trust to be established. The men and women of the province have undergone a collective trauma.

Brian Mulroney, Conservative leader, nomination meeting in his riding, Sept-Iles, Que., 6 April 1984. With this speech he moved to "bring Quebec into the Constitution ... with honour and enthusiasm." Written with his one-time friend Lucien Bouchard, it planted the seeds of Quebec's dissatisfaction, supposedly stemming from Prime Minister Trudeau's 1982 patriation of the Constitution. Trudeau would later dismiss the idea of Quebec's discontent as "humiliation at every streetcorner."

As for us, we have only been in power for two months, but I can tell you this: Give us twenty years, and it is coming, and you will not recognize this country. Moreover, the whole area of federal-provincial relations will also be completely changed.

Brian Mulroney, Prime Minister, maiden speech as Prime Minister, uttering prophetic words, House of Commons, 7 Nov. 1984.

He's a genius, a master of mindless phrase, mindfully wrought. And he can do it in two languages, too, with ease.

Barry Callaghan, essayist, "Canadian Wry," (1985), *Canadian Content* (1992) edited by Sarah Norton and Nell Waldman.

You know, we're very lucky to have Muldoon as prime minister, because he got into office not by America-bashing but by saying kind words about us.

Clairborne Pell, member of the U.S. Senate's foreign relations committee, referring in spirit if not in fact to Prime Minister Brian Mulroney in 1986, quoted by Lawrence Martin in *Pledge of Allegiance* (1993).

She thinks him an empty windbag.

Bernard Ingham, press secretary to British Prime Minister Margaret Thatcher, giving an off-the-record answer to the question posed by reporters, "What does Mrs. Thatcher think of Prime Minister Brian Mulroney," Commonwealth Conference in Vancouver in 1987, according to Allan Fotheringham in *Birds of a Feather: The Press and the Politicians* (1989).

Brian Mulroney? Deep down, he's on our side.

Pierre Bourgault, separatist, *Now or Never! Manifesto for an Independent Quebec* (1991) translated by David Homel.

Mulroney claimed that all his life he's wanted to be prime minister in the worst possible way. And he's succeeded beyond his wildest dreams.

Mark Breslin, comic, *Son of a Meech: The Best Brian Mulroney Jokes* (1991).

People wielding great power must be held responsible for how they wield it. There is fury in the land against the prime minister. Although I respect him much more than many, I have to say that, in my view, our consensual editing understates the discontent with him.

Keith Spicer, commissioner, *Citizens' Forum on Canada's Future: Report to the People and Government of Canada*, published as a special feature of *The Toronto Star, The Globe and Mail* and other newspapers, 29 June 1991.

There may be a belief among North American politicians that Irish ancestry is a sure-fire vote-getter, which may explain the sudden appearance of our very own Brian Mulroney this week in the fabled land of saints and scholars, described by at least one observer as an example of the snake returning to Ireland.

Christopher Dafoe, columnist, *Winnipeg Free Press*, 14 July–Aug. 1991.

I may have many critics but my only enemies are the enemies of Canada.

Brian Mulroney, Prime Minister, keynote address, Conservative National Convention, Toronto, 7 Aug. 1991, quoted by Rosemary Spiers in *The Toronto Star* the next day.

Lyin' Brian, Go to Hell, / Canada's Not Yours to Sell.

Couplet yelled by demonstrators outside the Conservative Convention, Toronto, 10 Aug. 1991, quoted by Geoffrey Stevens in *The Toronto Star*, 18 Aug. 1991. Credit for the sobriquet "Lyin' Brian" goes to journalist Claire Hoy, as noted Stevie Cameron in *Ottawa Inside Out* (1990).

We expected that he would behave like a statesman, and not like a petty parish-pump politician—which he does too often.

Léon Dion, political scientist, testifying before an Ottawa committee, 10 Dec. 1991, quoted by Graham Fraser in *The Globe and Mail* the following day.

Prime Minister Brian Mulroney has figured out the platform upon which he can win the next election in these troubled times: jobs for the rich.

Clayton Ruby, advocate, quoted in "Flashback," *The Globe and Mail*, 28 Dec. 1991.

Alas, only one eventuality had not been foreseen: that one day the government of Canada might fall into the hands of a wimp.

Pierre Elliott Trudeau, former Prime Minister, remark made "just a few years" after his retirement, quoted by Ron Graham in *The French Quarter* (1992).

More Canadians think Elvis Presley is alive than think Brian Mulroney can run this country.

Alan Gregg, pollster, quoted by Bill Casselman on CBC Radio's *The Radio Show*, 23 May 1992.

Brian Mulroney is the best prime minister the United States has ever had—his view of the world is an American view.

Nelson Riis, NDP House Leader, quoted by Anthony Wilson-Smith in *Maclean's*, 1 June 1992.

Unlike some who have written him off, I would never underestimate a French-speaking Irish-Canadian.

Richard M. Nixon, former U.S. President, questioned about Prime Minister Brian Mulroney on a visit to Toronto to address the 61st anniversary Hollinger dinner, 23 June 1992, quoted in *The Toronto Star* the following day.

Mother Teresa not being available, I volunteered.

Brian Mulroney, Prime Minister, explaining why he led the Yes campaign in the referendum on the Charlottetown Accord, "Quotes of the Year," *The Toronto Star*, 27 Dec. 1992.

Charming and charismatic, but he lacked any real political experience.... As leader of the Progressive Conservatives, I thought he put too much stress on the adjective as opposed to the noun.

Margaret Thatcher, former British Prime Minister, *The Downing Street Years* (1993).

Brian understands.

Ronald Reagan, U.S. President, characteristic comment with referring to Prime Minister Brian Mulroney, quoted by Lawrence Martin in *Pledge of Allegiance* (1993).

When the history of the Mulroney government is written, the title can be, "Prime Minister of Canada, on loan from Washington." I have never seen a head of state so contemptuous of preserving the sovereignty of a nation.

Ralph Nader, U.S. consumer advocate, interviewed by Joe Chidley in *Maclean's*, 11 Jan. 1993.

Mulroney is the only Canadian prime minister we have a city named after—Moose Jaw.

Michael Magee, comic, creator of the character Fred C. Cobbs, quoted by Sid Adilman in "Eye on Entertainment," *The Toronto Star*, 11 Feb. 1993.

You can be, these days, a popular prime minister or you can be an effective one. You can't be both.

Brian Mulroney, Prime Minister, referring to himself and to British Prime Minister John Major, press conference at No. 10 Downing Street, London, England, 11 May 1993, quoted by Paul Koring in *The Globe and Mail* the following day.

In the end, history may not be kind to Brian Mulroney, and if not, it may not be due to his policies. History may conclude, as have some of his contemporaries, that the poor boy from Baie Comeau was not guided by principle, but driven by an ambition and vanity so great that he ultimately could not be trusted.

John Saywell, historian, *Canada: Pathways to the Present* (1994).

We can't say that Brian Mulroney didn't warn us. "Ya dance with the lady what brung ya," he told Canadians, long before his first government was elected. It was a succinct summation of the one principle by which he governed. Interpret it as simple loyalty to one's friends or confirmation that to the victor go the spoils; the result is the same.

Stevie Cameron, investigative journalist, *On the Take: Crime, Corruption and Greed in the Mulroney Years* (1994).

The legacy of the Mulroney years is that Canadians have lost their faith in government, and they've lost their trust in politicians. Politicians everywhere are paying for what those bozos did.

Stevie Cameron, political journalist, "The Mulroney Years," 17 Nov. 1994, *The Empire Club of Canada: Addresses 1994–95* (1995).

I know full well that if you let a lie go around the world, you spend the rest of your life chasing it.

Brian Mulroney, former Prime Minister, explaining why he launched a lawsuit for libel against the federal government and the RCMP, which were investigating the possibility of kickbacks in the Airbus affair, quoted by Sandro Contenta in *The Toronto Star*, 20 April 1996.

MULTICULTURALISM

It has been alleged that we desire to create antagonism between native-born Canadians and Canadians by adoption. The contrary is the fact. Our earnest desire is to do away with all invidious distinctions of nationality, creed, locality or class, and to unite the people of the Dominion, as Canadians, through affection for and pride in Canada, their home.

W.A. Foster, founder of the Canada First movement, *Canada First* (1890).

It is indeed a mosaic of vast dimensions and great breadth.

Victoria Hayward, American traveller, *Romantic Canada* (1922). This is the first known use of the word "mosaic" to refer to Canada's social and cultural diversity. Sociologist John Porter examined the structure of Canadian society horizontally (to study ethnicity) and vertically (to study class) and published his findings in *The Vertical Mosaic* (1965). The ethnic composition of Canada is routinely contrasted with that of the United States, the former a "mosaic," the latter a "melting pot" (coined by the British writer Israel Zangwill).

I wish to emphasize the view of the government that a policy of multiculturalism within a bilingual framework is basically the conscious support of individual freedom of choice. We are free to be ourselves. But this cannot be left to chance. It must be fostered and pursued actively.

*

For although there are two official languages, there is no official culture, nor does any ethnic group take precedence over any other. No citizen or group of citizens is other than Canadian, and all should be treated fairly.

Pierre Elliott Trudeau, Prime Minister, announcing the implementation of a policy of multiculturalism within the framework of bilingualism, House of Commons, 8 Oct. 1971.

The ethnic mosaic has made for a more colourful and interesting Canadian way of life. Those who make up this mosaic share the goal of retaining the clarity of that mosaic, for in the clarity of their culture distinctiveness lies its beauty.

Edward R. Schreyer, Governor General, address, installation, Ottawa, 22 Jan. 1979; House of Commons, 26 Jan. 1979.

I liken Canada to a garden. A mosaic is a static thing with each element separated and divided from the others. Canada is not that kind of country. Neither is it a "melting pot" in which the individuality of each element is destroyed in order to produce a new and totally different element. It is rather a garden into which have been transplanted the hardiest and brightest of flowers from many lands, each retaining in its new environment the best of the qualities for which it was loved and prized in its native land.

John G. Diefenbaker, late Prime Minister, quoted by Dean Wood in "Multiculturalism: Appreciating Our Diversity," *Accord*, Nov.–Dec. 1980.

Canada has a federal minister of multiculturalism, whose job it is to watch the cultural mosaic in case the pieces become unstuck.

Eric Nicol and **Dave More**, humorists, *The U.S. or Us: What's the Difference, Eh?* (1986).

Canada is not so much a multicultural country as it is a country with a few multicultural cities.

Pat Carney, journalist and politician, "The Golden Dragon," *Saturday Night*, Nov. 1989.

I'm dead set against official multiculturalism.... if people want to keep their distinctive cultures after migrating to Canada, by all means encourage them to do so at their own expense.

Jack Webster, broadcaster, *Webster! An Autobiography* (1990).

A Canadian is a hyphen... we're diplomats by birth.

Joy Kogawa, novelist, interviewed by Magdalene Redekop in *Other Solitudes: Canadian Multicultural Fictions* (1990) edited by Linda Hutcheon and Marion Richmond.

I think that multiculturalism is something like those ethnic fast food areas you find in shopping centres of the third generation across Canada. Life, thought, literature would become a bit like these super-cafeterias.

Jacques Godbout, Quebec author, interviewed by Sherry Simon in *Other Solitudes: Canadian Multicultural Fictions* (1990) edited by Linda Hutcheon and Marion Richmond.

I know what multiculturalism means. It means the Scots own the banks and the Portuguese get to clean them.

Herb Denton, one-time correspondent for *The Washington Post*, quoted by Suanne Kelman in *The Globe and Mail*, 30 Oct. 1990.

We acknowledge that our "melting pot" is at least a double-boiler.

Jack McLeod, political scientist, *The Globe and Mail*, 27 Dec. 1991.

Multiculturalism indeed may decay into multinationalism, and Canada will lose all sense of being a collective community.

Richard Gwyn, columnist, "Home & Away," *The Toronto Star*, 7 March 1993.

No other nation has a policy of official multiculturalism.

Richard Gwyn, columnist and author, *Nationalism without Walls: The Unbearable Lightness of Being Canadian* (1995).

We are becoming a society where multiculture means no public culture.

Michael Valpy, columnist, *The Globe and Mail*, 3 May 1995.

Multiculturalism is the masochist celebration of Canadian nothingness.

Gad Horowitz, political scientist, quoted by Gina Mallet in "Multiculuralism: Has Diversity Gone Too Far?" *The Globe and Mail*, 15 March 1997.

I consider myself Egyptian by birth, Bulgarian by origin, French by culture, and Canadian by choice.

Hélène Issayevitch, Toronto-based interpreter and translator, characteristic remark, 13 June 1999.

MULTINATIONALISM See also BUSINESS

It has always been a recognized theory that the worker would rather work for a multinational than be out of a job.

Pierre Elliott Trudeau, Prime Minister, interviewed by James Reston, *The New York Times*, 3 Oct. 1982.

American corporate capitalism is the dominant factor shaping Canadian society. In Canada, American economic control operates through the formidable medium of the multinational corporation. The Canadian corporate elite has opted for a junior partnership with these American enterprises. Canada has been reduced to a resource base and consumer market within the American empire.

"The Waffle Manifesto: For an Independent Socialist Canada" (1969) reprinted in *The Canadian Forum*, Dec. 1989.

These two dynamics—adversarialism and the lack of social responsibility—make the planet the playground for multinational activity.

Austin G. Thorne, labour official, *Finding Common Ground* (1992) edited by Jean Chrétien.

MURDER See also CRIME

I suppose you know that it is practically certain that Jack the Ripper was on our rolls as Dr. Neill Cream....

Stephen Leacock, humorist, letter dated 15 May 1935, addressed to Charles Martin, Dean of Medicine at McGill University, quoted by Don Bell in *The Toronto Star*, 17 Feb. 1979. According to the executioner at London's Newgate Prison, 15 Nov. 1892, as the trap fell, Cream's last words were, "I am Jack—." *Time*, 20 Jan. 1975. Rumours persist that Dr. Thomas Neill Cream, the Glasgow-born, McGill-trained sadistic physician, was the original Jack the Ripper.

She cut off his arms! / She cut off his legs! / She cut off his head! / How could you, Mrs. Dick? / How could you, Mrs. Dick?

Schoolyard ditty (and pun) popular in 1946, when Mrs. Evelyn Dick of Hamilton, Ont., was charged with the murder of her infant son, whose body was found encased in cement, and the murder and dismemberment of her husband, whose torso was found, recalled in 1991 with the premiere of the stage play *How Could You, Mrs. Dick?* by Douglas Rodgers. Noted by Vit Wagner in *The Toronto Star*, 1 Nov. 1991.

If you're a Canadian and you come to our state, don't murder anybody.

George W. Bush II, Texas Governor, giving gratuitous advice to the delegation from Canada that pleaded in vain for a reprieve from the death sentence on Canadian-born convicted murderer George W. Faulder, quoted on CBC Radio News, 9 Dec. 1998.

May God have mercy on this broken society and all the hurting people in it.

Dale Lang, church minister, speaking at the funeral held for his 17-year-old son, Jason, who was murdered by a teenage gunman at their high school, civic auditorium, Taber, Alta., 19 April 1999, quoted by Ric Dolphin in the *National Post* the following day.

MUSEUMS & GALLERIES See also ART & ARTISTS

A good museum is not a dead repository of curios but a living expression of past and present cultures.

T.A. Heinrich, Director, Royal Ontario Museum from 1955 to 1962, remark made in 1958, quoted in his obituary in *The Toronto Star*, 28 Jan. 1981.

A newsman inquired why he hadn't left his art collection to Canada. "Nobody asked me," Hirshhorn replied crisply. "I love Canada and it's been good to me. But some of the people are asleep up there."

Comment made by **Joseph Hirshhorn** in Washington on 17 May 1966 when the speculator and investor who made his fortune in gold and uranium dealing on Toronto's Bay Street signed an agreement with the U.S. Government to donate his fabulous collection of art to an institution that he would build in Washington that would bear his name, quoted by Barry Hyams in *Hirshhorn: Medici from Brooklyn* (1977).

I paid no attention to these scraps at the time, merely wondering if they were Indian relics.

J.E. Dodd, relic-hunter, who claimed he stumbled upon a cache of Viking weapons (iron sword, axe, shield-handle) on 24 May 1930 but may have "salted" them near Beardmore, Ont., as quoted by O.C. Elliott in "The Case of the Beardmore Relics," *Canadian Historical Review*, Sept. 1941.

Certainly the time is not far distant when the collections of the Northwest Coast will move from anthropological museums to take their place in the art museums among the arts of Egypt, Persia, and the Middle Ages. For this art is not unequal to those great ones and unlike them has displayed, during the century and a half of its known development, a prodigious diversity and had an apparently inexhaustible power of renewal.

Claude Lévi-Strauss, anthropologist, "The Art of the Northwest Coast at the American Museum of Natural History," *Gazette des Beaux Arts*, Sept. 1943.

I would shudder to think of a day arriving when an institution like ours, the National Gallery of Canada, is in any way forced by federal legislation, or indeed public opinion, to spend some fixed sum of money on Canadian art, for this simple reason: This year might be a very lean year. We might find comparatively few works of art, paintings, drawings, sculpture, or whatever, by Canadians that we regard as worthy of a place in the National collection.

Alan Jarvis, director, National Gallery, address, "A World without Frontiers," Empire Club of Canada, Toronto, 6 Dec. 1956.

Where are the museums for forgotten sounds?

R. Murray Schafer, composer and theorist, *The Tuning of the World* (1977).

A collector is the sort of person who owns works by six members of the Group of Seven and lives in torment until he can fill the gap with a purchase of the seventh.

Douglas Duncan, collector, quoted by Lester B. Pearson, remarks on the opening of the Duncan exhibition, National Gallery, Ottawa, 4 March 1971, reproduced in *Douglas Duncan: A Memorial Portrait* (1974) edited by Alan Jarvis.

The function of a public gallery is to preserve the past up to yesterday. Tomorrow is where the artist belongs.

Harold Town, artist, *The Canadian*, 8 Jan. 1977.

All you have to do is sit in the foyer of the new National Gallery. The greatest picture in this gallery is the view across the river to the Parliament buildings. There it is. You have Parliament Hill, you have that octagonal neo-Gothic library.

Scott Symons, author, "Deliquescence in Canada," *The Idler*, July–Aug. 1992.

Security guards are the only modern component of modern art museums.

Douglas Coupland, novelist and aphorist, quoted in *The New Republic*, quoted by Bruce Blackadar, "Magazines," *The Toronto Star*, 20 Aug. 1995.

We don't want to *teach*—but in appealing to people's sense of wonder, that's when learning occurs. A museum is a place of secrets, of magic and wonder.

Robert James, executive director, Glenbow Centre, quoted by Val Ross in "International Museums Day '96," *The Globe and Mail*, 11 May 1996.

MUSIC See also ANTHEMS; GOULD, GLENN; MUSIC: CONTEMPORARY; MUSIC: POPULAR; OPERA; RECORD INDUSTRY; SONGS; SOUND

The whole point of music is to have a party.

Murray McLauchlan, singer-composer, quoted in *Grapevine*, 23 Dec. 1961.

Among the Dene, it is said the child is born with a drum in its hand.

Northwest Territories, Department of Education, Culture and Development, Dene Kede—*Education: A Dene Perspective* (1993), quoted in *Gathering Strength: Volume 3: Report of the Royal Commission on Aboriginal Peoples* (1996), co-chaired by René Dessault and Georges Erasmus.

Those Canadians who made up the British half were too stubborn to enjoy music, and those who belonged to the French half were too stupid.

Louis Moreau Gottschalk, French-educated virtuoso pianist who performed in Toronto and Montreal, *Notes of a Pianist* (1881) translated by Robert E. Peterson and edited by Jeanne Behrend in 1964.

I have married an Englishman, and have made my home in England, but I still remain at heart a French-Canadian.

Madame Albani, born Marie Louise Emma Cécile Lajeunesse at Chambly, Que., took her professional name from the city of Albany, N.Y., where she studied opera, *Forty Years of Song* (1911).

Music is sound.

Motto of **Healey Willan**, composer and organist, quoted by F.R.C. Clarke in *Healey Willan: Life and Music* (1983).

If you're going to spend all that money, John, for God's sake, do the thing properly.

Audrey Mildmay, Canadian-born opera singer and wife of English opera impressario John Christie, concerning plans to launch the first season of the Glyndebourne opera festival, England, May 1934, quoted by Kenneth Bagnell in *The Globe and Mail*, 12 July 1997.

Being a composer in Winnipeg is almost a contradiction in terms, or like that old school problem in physics: Is the sound still there if no one hears it?

Chester Duncan, composer, commentator, and resident of Winnipeg, Man., *Wanna Fight, Kid?* (1975).

I'm extremely grateful for everything Canada has done for me. I am, however, getting a bit tired of knocking on doors after hammering away on the piano for thirty years for six to eight hours a day.

Sheila Henig, musical prodigy and professional pianist, letter written to a friend, quoted by Harry Henig and Madeline Thompson in *Elusive Summit: The Biography of Sheila Henig* (1981). She commited suicide on 14 May 1979.

The only time I ever felt unfaithful to my wife was listening to Mozart—I felt such love.

George P. Grant, philosopher and music-lover, CBC-TV, 13 Feb. 1980, quoted by William Christian in *George Grant: A Biography* (1993).

I went through the agonies trying to be a serious musician. In Canada, in 1938, I twigged to the fact I'm a comedienne.

Anna Russell, singer and comedienne who presents *Wagner's Ring, I'm Not Making This Up, You Know: The Autobiography of the Queen of Musical Parody* (1985).

Being human is an accomplishment like playing an instrument. It takes practice. The keys must be mastered. The old scores must be committed to memory. It is a skill we can forget. A little noise can make us forget the notes.

Michael Ignatieff, essayist, *The Needs of Strangers* (1985).

Visitors to Westminster Abbey can't help noticing, as they enter that hallowed hall, a simple inscription carved into the marble at their feet. It reads, "Remember Winston Churchill." May all who visit this hall and see the plaque we are unveiling today remember Ernest MacMillan.

William Littler, music critic, address, unveiling of the plaque in honour of teacher and conductor Sir Ernest MacMillan (known as Lord Largo for his partiality to classical compositions with slow and stately tempos), Toronto's Massey Hall, quoted in *The Toronto Star*, 26 Aug. 1989.

When non-Jews hear my music, they think it's modern and Canadian. When Jews hear it, they recognize something of their heritage.

Srul Irving Glick, composer of classical compositions much influenced by the Jewish spirit, quoted by Paula Citron in *The Toronto Star*, 24 Nov. 1991.

What can Canada put forth to make the world take notice (apart from surtitles in opera houses, which were invented in Canada)?

Bernard Levin, British columnist, "Bravo!" *The Toronto Star*, 18 March 1995.

Sibelius is a Canadian composer. Without him I could never have written music.

Harry Freedman, composer, referring to Finnish composer Jean Sibelius, interviewed by Adrienne Clarkson, quoted by John Ralston Saul in *Reflections of a Siamese Twin* (1997).

There are a handful of eminent musical dynasties, but can there be four other brothers who achieved comparable distinction in the world of music in Europe and North America?

Eric Koch, author and biographer, Preface, *The Brothers Hambourg* (1997), a study of Mark, Jan, Boris, and Clement Hambourg who from 1910 to 1973 enriched the musical life of Toronto, Canada, and the world.

MUSIC: CONTEMPORARY

See also MUSIC

The universe is your orchestra.

R. Murray Schafer, composer and theorist, *The*

New Soundscape: A Handbook for the Modern Music Teacher (1969).

Technology is never neutral and recording technology has, since its invention, discriminated in favour of the human voice and against the sounds of nature.

R. Murray Schafer, composer and theorist, "Dub," *The Canadian Forum*, Nov. 1994.

I invite you to join the 20th century before we leave it.

Harry Somers, composer, characteristic remark to student audiences of new music, recalled the day following his death by friend and composer Alexa Louie, CBC Radio's *As It Happens*, 10 March 1999.

MUSIC: POPULAR See also MUSIC

Way Down East Music

Phrase associated with the group **Don Messer and His Islanders** on CBC-TV's *Don Messer's Jubilee* in the 1950s and 1960s. Country & Western Music was known, in Atlantic Canada at any rate, as Country & Eastern Music.

There's one girl in Kingston, Ontario, who's written me thousands of letters and I don't see anything wrong with that. Why, at Christmas I got 40,000 Christmas cards from around Toronto alone. I can't read every one of the letters I get, but that's not to say that I don't really thank the people who send them. 'Cause I do.

Elvis Presley, rock 'n' roll performer, press conference, Maple Leaf Gardens, Toronto, reported in *The Toronto Telegram*, 1 April 1957. "He reported that he gets more fan mail from Toronto and Winnipeg than any other cities in North America," noted the reporter for *The Globe and Mail* the same day.

The word "Beatlemania" was created by Ottawa journalist Sandy Gardiner in 1963, writing about the Beatles while on a visit to Britain. Capitol Records retitled the Beatles album *With the Beatles* as *Beatlemania* when it was released here.

Robert Davis, writer, "What Do You Know about Canada, Eh?" *The Toronto Star*, 1 July 1994.

Radio was inseparable from the rise of jazz culture as TV has been inseparable from the rise of rock culture.

Marshall McLuhan, communications pioneer, observation made in 1972, "A McLuhan Sourcebook," *The Essential McLuhan* (1995) edited by Eric McLuhan and Frank Zingrone.

Too many jazz pianists limit themselves to a personal style, a trademark, so to speak. They confine themselves to one type of playing. I believe in using the entire piano as a single instrument capable of expressing every possible musical idea. I have no one style. I play as I feel.

Oscar Peterson, jazz pianist, quoted in *The Toronto Star*, 14 Feb. 1972.

I can't stand to see moonlight go to waste… perhaps it's the merchant in me.

Leonard Cohen, poet, concert, Théâtre du Nouveau Monde, Montreal, 20 Feb. 1975.

I would not exist today as a singer if Félix Leclerc had not come from Canada to France and opened the way.

George Brassens, French chansonnier, paying tribute to Quebec's Félix Leclerc, CBC Radio's *Morningside*, 24 June 1977.

Nobody likes my music but my fans.

Guy Lombardo, leader of The Royal Canadians dance band, quoted by Beverly Fink Cline in *The Lombardo Story* (1979).

Rise again, rise again—though your heart it be broken / And life about to end / No matter what you've lost, be it a home, a love, a friend / Like the *Mary Ellen Carter*, rise again.

Lines from **Stan Rogers**' song "The Mary Ellen Carter" (1979), *Between the Breaks* (1979), quoted by Chris Gudgeon in *An Unfinished Conversation: The Life and Music of Stan Rogers* (1993). "The Mary Ellen Carter" was Rogers' signature song; it celebrates the spirit of seamen who resolve to "raise again" a sturdy, twenty-year-old vessel which sank; its owners refused to raise it for insurance reasons. The refrain runs, "Rise again, rise again, that her name not be lost / To the knowledge of men."

What kind of music do we play?… Folk, sort of. Eclectic. Canadian. Songs with a sense of place…. Songs with roots. Funny things. Orphaned songs. Songs that picked us to sing them. Songs that we like and that we think you'll like as well.

Bob Bossin, composer and singer and founder of The Stringband, liner notes for the album *The Stringband* (1979).

It is simply that his voice runs warm at some times and hot at others but always sounds lonely. Neil Young sounds like the wind on the Prairies. There is, unfortunately, no other way to describe it.

Douglas Fetherling, author, "Neil Young: 'That's My Sound, Man,'" *Some Day Soon: Essays on Canadian Songwriters* (1991).

Leonard Cohen, as usual, is making a comeback.

Douglas Fetherling, author, "Leonard Cohen: The Sound of Mercy," *Some Day Soon: Essays on Canadian Songwriters* (1991).

I was the Bryan Adams of 1944.

Mart Kenney, bandleader, reminiscing about the popularity of Mart Kenney and the Country Gentlemen during the Second World War, quoted by Mark Miller in *The Globe and Mail*, 12 Nov. 1992.

I'll be brief with modern music: rap is crap, and rock's a crock.

Maurus E. Mallon, aphorist, 22 June 1992.

He is the Picasso, I am the Matisse. I love Matisse, but I am in awe of Picasso.

Leonard Cohen, singer-songwriter, comparing and contrasting himself with Bob Dylan, quoted by Peter Howell in *The Toronto Star*, 19 Nov. 1992.

We take the music seriously, not ourselves, and I think that's why audiences respond so well.

Holly Cole, Nova Scotia–raised jazz singer, quoted by C. Lee Cranford in *TV Guide*, 2 Jan. 1993.

The music industry has disenfranchised people from a variety of musical expressions. When people come across music that is different, they are drawn to it.

Loreena McKennitt, Manitoba-born, singer-composer of "eclectic Celtic" music, quoted in *Time*, 12 Dec. 1994.

As a musician, I have to thank you especially for Oscar Peterson, a man I consider to be the greatest jazz pianist of our time.

Bill Clinton, U.S. President, address, joint meeting of the House of Commons and the Senate of Canada, Ottawa, Senate Debates, 23 Feb. 1995.

I studied thousands of years of knowledge and I discovered I carried a lot in my soul. Being a rock star is like being a king or a queen and I swear some of us are reincarnated from kings or queens. I was a high priestess.

Alannah Myles, singer-songwriter, interviewed by Christopher Dafoe in *The Globe and Mail*, 23 Sept. 1995.

She makes me cream my jeans / When she comes my way.

Lines from **Carole Pope**'s song "High School Confidential," quoted by Elizabeth Renzetti in *The Globe and Mail*, 12 Dec. 1995.

Always respect the instrument and make it sound like it loves you, because it does. Satisfy yourself. If you do something to get an audience reaction, then that's dishonest and usually bad music.

Oscar Peterson, jazz pianist, interviewed by Bruce W. Culp in "The Importance of Being Oscar," *The Globe and Mail*, 5 Oct. 1996.

He had to *learn* to play the blues.

Miles Davis, American Black blues musician, dismissing the musical artistry of Montreal-born Canadian Black blues pianist Oscar Peterson, quoted by Graham Fraser in "Identities," *The Globe and Mail*, 30 Aug. 1997.

I've always known that I was half-Canadian. It's nothing really new to me.

Eric Clapton, British rock performer, speaking at a press conference in Toronto to launch his new record album *Pilgrim*, with its single "My Father's Eyes," quoted by Alan Niester in *The Globe and Mail*, 30 March 1998. He was born to an English mother in England; his father, Edward Walter Fryer, was a Canadian soldier stationed in England during World War II, who returned to Toronto where he died in 1985.

Muzak goes in one ear and out some other opening.

Anton Kuerti, pianist, quoted by David Barber in *Better than It Sounds: A Dictionary of Humorous Musical Quotations* (1998).

I came into the folk scene because it was easy and I did it as a hobby in art school to make some money—there was never any ambition or desire to be a performing animal.

Joni Mitchell, folksinger-songwriter, who is still surprised by her long-lasting success in the music industry, quoted in the *Winnipeg Free Press*, 19 Sept. 1998.

Céline Dion has become an American or universal performer. In her soul she is neither a Quebecer nor a Canadian. Her songs reflect nothing of what Quebecers experience.

Suzanne Tremblay, Bloc M.P., comments made in Feb. 1999 before a House of Commons Heritage Committee, quoted by Francine Dubé, "Bloc M.P. Questions Dion's 'Soul,'" *National Post*, 6 April 1999.

I want to do what people expect from me. And that is not Ashley MacIsaac not on drugs, that is Ashley MacIsaac on drugs.

Ashley MacIsaac, folk fiddler turned rock fiddler, interviewed by Rebecca Mead, "Sex, Drugs, and Fiddling," *The New Yorker*, 20 Dec. 1999.

Blame Canada! Blame Canada! / It seems that everything's gone wrong since Canada came along. / Blame Canada! Blame Canada! / They're not even a real country anyway. / Blame Canada! Blame Canada! / With all their hockey hullabaloo / And that bitch Anne Murray too. / Blame Canada! Blame Canada! / Canada's dead and gone, / There'll be no more Céline Dion. / We must blame them and cause a fuss / Before somebody thinks of blaming us!

Lines from the song "Blame Canada" composed by **Trey Parker** and **Marc Shaimin** for the movie *South Park: Bigger, Larger & Uncut* (1999). The song was nominated for an Academy Award in March 2000, as noted by Jonathon Gatehouse in the *National Post*, 28 March 2000. One columnist suggested that the song might be adopted as the anthem of the Parti Québécois or, failing that, the Bloc Québécois.

MYSTERIES

But what could the disappearance of one Ambrose, in Texas, have to do with the disappearance of another Ambrose, in Canada? There was in these questions an appearance of childishness that attracted my respectful attention.

Charles Fort, collector of anomalies, referring to the disappearances of writer Ambrose Bierce and Toronto theatre-owner Ambrose Small, *Wild Talents* (1932). He concluded, "Somebody's collecting Ambroses."

The knowledge that you can have is inexhaustible, and what is inexhaustible is benevolent. The knowledge that you cannot have is of the riddles of birth and death, of our future destiny and the purposes of God. Here there is no knowledge, but illusions that restrict freedom and limit hope. Accept the mystery behind knowledge: It is not darkness but shadow.

Northrop Frye, cultural critic, ordained minister of the United Church of Canada, address, annual baccalaureate service, Metropolitan United Church, Toronto, 10 April 1988, as quoted by Alexandra Johnston in *Vic Report*, Spring 1991.

The fantastic is the real that most people want to ignore.

Robertson Davies, novelist, interviewed by Harry Rasky on *The Magic Season of Robertson Davies*, CBC-TV, 27 Dec. 1990. Davies went on to discuss those aspects of reality that are "inexplicable but inescapable."

Consider the crop circles worldwide. Are crop circle formations, and the Canadian ones in particular, reflective of not only the country's unique *agriculture* but of its unique *culture* as well?

Michael Strainic, specialist in UGMS (Unidentified Ground Markings), "Once Upon a Time in the Wheat," *MUFO UFO Journal*, Dec. 1991.

Why the inhabitants of Easter Island put up all those immense statues is a profound & inscrutable mystery. Almost as profound and inscrutable as why anybody would carve a gigantic head of Theodore Roosevelt on a mountain in South Dakota.

Northrop Frye, cultural critic, "Notebook 1993," edited by Robert D. Denham, *Northrop Frye Newsletter*, Summer 1993.

It is much more interesting to stand at the door of a mystery than to imagine you have already entered.

Louis Dudek, poet and aphorist, entry for 1979, *Notebooks 1960–1994* (1994).

I'm fascinated by those who assume that man with his five senses and his remarkable ability to think and investigate will somehow put salt on the tail of all the secrets of the universe.

Robertson Davies, man-of-letters, quoted by Mel Gussow in "A Moralist Possessed by Humour," *The New York Times Book Review*, 5 Feb. 1995.

MYSTICISM

The great sea has set me in motion, / Set me adrift, / Moving me as the weed moves in a river. // The arch of sky and mightiness of storms / Have moved the spirit within me, / Till I am carried away / Trembling with joy.

Uvavnuk, Eskimo shaman and singer, quoted by Knud Rasmussen in *Across Arctic America: Narrative of the Fifth Thule Expedition* (1927).

May the blessing of our Masters rest on us all, illuminating our minds, and filling our hearts with love.

Annie Besant, world president of the Theosophical Society, offering benediction, Toronto, 3 Nov. 1926, quoted in *The Canadian Theosophist*, 15 Nov. 1926.

Mysticism is just tomorrow's science dreamed today.

Marshall McLuhan, communications pioneer, "Playboy Interview" (1969) conducted by Eric Norden, *The Essential McLuhan* (1995) edited by Eric McLuhan and Frank Zingrone.

MYTHOLOGY See also FOLKLORE, LEGENDS

In the folds of the hills, under Coyote's eye....

Opening sentence of **Sheila Watson**'s novel *The Double Hook* (1959).

In Canada the mythical was simply the "prehistoric" (this word, we are told, is a Canadian coinage), and the writer had to attach himself to his literary tradition deliberately and voluntarily.

Northrop Frye, cultural critic, "Conclusion to a Literary History of Canada" (1965), *The Bush Garden: Essays on the Canadian Imagination* (1971).

The myths are my reality.

Statement of Morag Gunn in **Margaret Laurence**'s novel *The Diviners* (1974).

Samuel Butler remarked that a chicken was merely an egg's device for producing more eggs; similarly, a poet often seems to be merely a myth's device for reproducing itself again in a later period.

Northrop Frye, cultural critic, *Creation and Recreation* (1980).

I don't think Canada has really found its dearest and deepest myth—which is going to be the myth of the northland.

Robertson Davies, man-of-letters, interviewed by Kaarina Kailo in *Other Solitudes: Canadian Multicultural Fictions* (1990) edited by Linda Hutcheon and Marion Richmond.

Critics may ignore the language of myth and metaphor; but no poet can possibly be a poet of any significance who does not learn to speak it constantly and consistently.

Northrop Frye, literary critic, "Notebook 1993," edited by Robert D. Denham, *Northrop Frye Newsletter*, Summer 1993.

N

NAFTA See NORTH AMERICAN FREE TRADE AGREEMENT

NAMES See also PLACES

The Indian guides of the early explorers called out *kanata* every time they passed a village on the St. Lawrence, and the explorers mistook the word for the name of the country.

H.L Mencken, lexicographer, referring to the Indian word for the French *ville, The American Language: Supplement II* (1948).

They used to call us "pea-soupers"; we called them "craw-fish."

René Lévesque, Quebec Premier, referring to slurs for French Canadians and English Canadians during his youth in New Carlisle, Que., *My Québec* (1979).

Now the most minimal and therefore most powerful word, spoken or written, about any human being is *name*, and anyone who can hide that goes beyond secret into engima, that is, into intentional and impenetrable obscurity.

Rudy Wiebe, novelist, *Playing Dead: A Contemplation Concerning the Arctic* (1989).

All are called Canadians, Ontarians, Torontonians. Right there, you have Indian names. There is an additional psychic magic that happens there, just as a result of that name. So I think that white culture in Canada is very much changing and transforming as a result of living with native culture; likewise Cree culture, native culture.

Tomson Highway, Cree playwright, interviewed by Ann Wilson in *Other Solitudes: Canadian Multicultural Fictions* (1990) edited by Linda Hutcheon and Marion Richmond.

That's why I prefer the name we call ourselves. Annishnawbe translates as meaning, basically, the good beings or the people.

Drew Hayden Taylor, Annishnawbe playwright, rejecting such names as Adirondack, Ojibway, etc., "An Aboriginal Name Claim," *The Globe and Mail*, 1 June 1993.

Most white people, at some time in their lives, would like to think they have an Indian name existing somewhere in the universe, a sort of authentic title of the self, our inside nature-self with a label.

Paulette Jiles, poet and traveller, *Northern Spirit: Travels among the Cree and Ojibway Nations and Their Star Maps* (1995).

It is instructive to compare the explorers' Arctic namings with the Inuit nomenclature for the same landscapes, which usually interested the Victorians not at all; though in retrospect it is the indigenous names for the inhabited parts of the northern ice which seem substantive, and the European ones a ghostly overlay.

Francis Spufford, historian, "Traces in the Snow," *The Times Literary Supplement*, 18 July 1995.

NATION See also NATIONALISM

A nation is an association of reasonable beings united in a peaceful sharing of the things they cherish, therefore to determine the quality of a nation, you must consider what those things are.

Epigraph from the writings of **St. Augustine** appended to the opening of the Massey Commission, formally known as the *Report of the Royal Commission on National Development in the Arts, Letters and Sciences* (1951).

Deux nations

Slogan referring to the two-nation concept of the Dominion as composed of Quebec and the rest of Canada, popularized in the 1960s by Montreal financier and Conservative thinker **Marcel Faribault**. As Dalton Camp noted in *Points of Departure* (1979): "Among the hardships imposed upon the French in Canada is that they must accept responsibility for the English translation of the meaning of their words. If only Faribault had said *deux peuples!*" Another Conservative, Prime Minister Diefenbaker, extolled the opposite of *deux nations*: "One Canada."

Canada seems to have moved from a pre-national to a post-national phase of existence without ever having been a nation.

Northrop Frye, cultural critic, address, Options Conference, University of Toronto, 15 Oct. 1977, quoted by Daniel Stoffman in *The Toronto Star*, 17 Oct. 1977.

A nation is an idea, not an entity.

Robin Skelton, poet and aphorist, *A Devious Dictionary* (1991).

Wherever I went, I found a struggle going on between those who still believe that a nation should be a home to all—and that race, colour, religion, and creed should be no bar to belonging—and those who want their nation to be home only to their own. It's the battle between the civic and the ethnic nation. I know which side I'm on. I also know which side, right now, is winning.

Michael Ignatieff, essayist and broadcaster, *Blood and Belonging: Journeys into the New Nationalism* (1994).

A state-nation rather than a nation-state. A nationless-state. A post-sovereignty state. A postmodern one. Benedict Anderson's evocative term "imagined community" fits us better than any of these.... The quality that makes us truly one of a kind is that we are an *invented* community.

Richard Gwyn, columnist and author, *Nationalism without Walls: The Unbearable Lightness of Being Canadian* (1995).

No nation carries divine assurance of immortality. Perhaps Canada—lacking visionary federal leadership and a strong federalist presence in Quebec—cannot avoid decline and eventual disintegration. Not much can be done to build a country without a dream to match, without will and vision, without determination and courage.

Deborah Coyne and **Michael Valpy**, constitutional lawyer and journalist, *To Match a Dream: A Practical Guide to Canada's Constitution* (1998).

NATIONAL ANTHEM See ANTHEMS

NATIONAL FILM BOARD See also FILM

The Film Board has been important in saying to countries of very different kinds, all over the world, that *the film is an instrument of great importance in establishing the patterns of national imagination.*

John Grierson, former Film Commissioner, quoted in 1970 by James Beveridge in *John Grierson: Film Master* (1978). In 1939, Grierson wrote the NFB's mandate: "The National Film Board will be the eyes of Canada. It will, through a national use of cinema, see Canada and see it whole... its people and its purpose."

NATIONALISM See also IDENTITY, NATIONAL; NATION; NATIONALITY; PATRIOTISM

He is a poor being who is not proud of his country.

Janet Carnochan, archivist, address, "A Plea for Historical Societies," Beaver Dams and Thorold Historical Society, 24 June 1985, published in *The Welland Tribune*, 5 July 1895.

In this country, where nationalism is only just beginning to flower again, everything is *national*: maple butter, poets, industries, conservatories, beer and historians.

The word horrified me; I detested it just as I detested the rhapsodies on our race.

André Laurendeau, statesman, describing in 1935 Quebec of the 1920s, quoted by Michael Oliver in *The Passionate Debate* (1991).

A strong and dominant national feeling is not a luxury in Canada, it is a necessity. Without it this country cannot exist. A divided Canada can be of little help to any country, and least of all to itself.

W.L. Mackenzie King, Prime Minister, quoted in *Bulletin 69*, Information Division, Department of External Affairs, as quoted by Allan S. Evans and Lawrence A. Diachun in *Canada: Towards Tomorrow (1976).*

Nationalism: a snarl wrapped up in a flag.

Irving Layton, poet and aphorist, *The Whole Bloody Bird (obs, aphs & Pomes)* (1969).

If I can talk in my own name, my position is this. I have no objections *on nationalistic grounds* to any amount of decentralisation; but I do have objections *on democratic grounds.* For I feel that the people of Quebec (a majority of whom happen to be French speaking) will never learn the art of self government if all their problems are solved (albeit happily) from the outside by a government not wholly responsible to them.

Pierre Elliott Trudeau, letter, 19 Oct. 1956, quoted by Michael Oliver in *The Passionate Debate* (1991).

You can't stand up for Canada with a banana for a backbone.

John G. Diefenbaker, former Prime Minister, referring to the Pearson administration, quoted by James Johnston in *The Party's Over* (1971).

A nationalist is a separatist who's gained twenty-five pounds.

Tim Burke, columnist, *The Montreal Gazette*, 12 Jan. 1983.

Canadian nationalism is kitsch, the construction of a world out of sentiment. It rejects reality, for the greater part of the Canadian identity that is simply human will always outweigh the smaller part that is distinctly Canadian. It is inherently collectivist, for it must as well exaggerate those trivial characteristics that identify the group, rather than recognize the far greater differences between individuals within the group.

Andrew Coyne, journalist, *Saturday Night*, July 1989.

Nationalism is the only way that mediocrity can blow its own horn.

Louis Dudek, poet and aphorist, "Epigrams," *Small Perfect Things* (1991).

It seems unlikely that Canada's future is going to be as a country with a strong national purpose. The glue that holds the place together is no more adhesive than maple syrup, and there is little prospect of replacing it with something stickier.

John Grimond, journalist, "Nice Country, Nice Mess," *The Economist*, 29 June 1991.

Canada is the only country in the world where being a nationalist automatically disqualifies someone—in media eyes—as a serious person.

Michael Valpy, columnist, *The Globe and Mail*, 17 Sept. 1993.

Nationalism is a form of speech that shouts, not merely so that it will be heard but so that it will believe itself.

Michael Ignatieff, essayist and broadcaster, *Blood and Belonging: Journeys into the New Nationalism* (1994).

What I mean by "Canadian nationalism" is a passionate attachment to a cumulative achievement or experience, that hasn't got anything to do with denigrating or fearing or hating other cultures. Just knowing that something precious would be lost to the human gene-pool if Canada fell apart, keeps me loyal.

Myrna Kostash, author, interviewed by Mark Abley in "The Culture of Nationalism," *The Canadian Forum*, Sept. 1994.

If Canada's nationalism stands silent and deep in the land, the particular nationalisms of the aboriginal peoples, though much battered, are rooted in the bedrock beneath us.

Nicholas Stethem, defence analyst, "Strategic Notebook," *Sitrep: Newsmagazine of the Royal Canadian Military Institute*, Oct. 1995.

NATIONALITY See also NATIONALISM

Being a Canadian nationalist is the closest one can become to being a world citizen today. The passport is honoured everywhere in the world. The attitude to world affairs is a really international one.

Judith Merril, author, obiter dictum, 7 Sept. 1979.

I have never had a compelling reason to change my citizenship, but then I don't believe that the colour of your passport should matter. I believe that a reporter should be stateless. It is not a matter of loyalty, but integrity.

Morley Safer, Toronto-born news broadcaster, first with the CBC and then with CBS in New York City, quoted by Laura Goldstein in *The Globe and Mail*, 17 Nov. 1979.

On my passport, issued in "Hull, Quebec," I have whited out the U in Hull and substituted an E.

Ann Diamond, columnist, "Last Word," *The Suburban*, 22 Dec. 1993.

NATIVE ART See also ART & ARTISTS, ESKIMO ART, NATIVE PEOPLES, TOTEM POLES

Every man his own Leonardo.

William (Bill) Reid, master Haida craftsman, epitomizing the Haida esthetic, "The Art—An Appreciation," *Arts of the Raven: Masterworks of the Northwest Coast Indian* (1967) edited by Wilson Duff.

I don't think an art form reaches a peak, I think a carver reaches a peak.

Robert Davidson, Haida carver at Masset, B.C., quoted by Peter L. MacNair in *artscanada*, Dec. 1973.

Does one have to be a Canadian Indian to appreciate the subtle and serene stare of the Gitksan moon mask? Does one have to be Italian to appreciate the mysterious smile of the Mona Lisa? Of course not! True art is timeless and transcends nationality. What we need is to educate the public in our history and in our aesthetics.

Tom Hill, Native curator, *The Arts in Canada: Today and Tomorrow: Based on Papers Prepared for the 45th Couchiching Conference of the Canadian Institute on Public Affairs* (1976) edited by Dean Walker.

When I paint a picture just for Norval, it's no good... the Spirit knows a much better set of colours than I do.

Norval Morrisseau, Ojibwa artist, quoted by Gary Michael Dault in *The Toronto Star*, 29 Aug. 1977.

NATIVE PEOPLES See also ABORIGINAL PEOPLES, INDIAN PEOPLES, INUIT, LAND CLAIMS, MÉTIS PEOPLES, NATIVE ART

[The Native Americans] are incapable of civilization. They have no motive force, for they are without affection and passion. They are not drawn to one another by love, and are thus unfruitful. They hardly speak at all, never caress one another, care about nothing, and are lazy.

Immanuel Kant, German philosopher, quoted by Henry Steel Commager in *The Empire of Reason* (1977). The source is Kant's lectures on Philosophical Anthropology at Königsberg (1772). Kant apparently added that the Americans were "incapable of governing themselves and destined for extermination."

English and French besides some Cannibals.

Inscription placed across much of present-day Ontario and Quebec on a map of the world titled "Chart of the World Shewing the Religion, Population and Civilization of Each Country" (1815), prepared for evangelical purposes by an English cartographer **James Wyld**. Reproduced by Peter Barber and Christopher Board in *Tales from the Map Room: Fact and Fiction about Maps and Their Makers* (1993).

Our job is to try to fit ourselves into the new scheme of life which the Great Spirit has decreed for North America. And we will do that, keeping always before us the old Blackfoot proverb: *Mokokit-ki-ackamimat*—Be Wise and persevere.

Sylvester Clarke, Chief Buffalo Child Long Lance, Native spokesperson, *Long Lance* (1929).

We are going to have to teach the white man the Indian way of life. If we don't, he is going to kill us all.

Duke Redbird, Native artist and spokesperson, quoted by Marty Dunn in *Red on White* (1971).

They came to a wigwam. It was a long wigwam with a door at each end. The man inside the wigwam said, "I have lived here since the world began."

Rita Joe, Micmac poet (who coincidentally shares the name of the principal character in George Ryga's play *The Ecstasy of Rita Joe*), *Poems of Rita Joe* (1978).

In the four-hundred-plus years between the original European probe of Newfoundland and the final conquest of the Northwest Territories, a holocaust befell the Indians of Canada.

Robert Hunter and **Robert Calihoo**, environmental writer and Native activist, *Occupied Canada: A Young White Man Discovers His Unsuspected Past* (1991).

I'm a dreamer. But what's the alternative?

Ovide Mercredi, Cree lawyer and Native activist, National Chief of the Assembly of First Nations, quoted by André Picard in *The Globe and Mail*, 6 Nov. 1991.

On this continent, indigenous and indigent are synonymous.

Maurus E. Mallon, aphorist, 2 Aug. 1993.

There was a time before the road.

First line of the life story of **Justa Monk**, leader of the Portage Reserve in central British Columbia, as set down in *Justa: A First Nations Leader* (1994) as told to **Bridget Moran**.

The largest obstacle to an independent Quebec is probably the rights of aboriginal peoples. In the event Quebec tries to secede, we also have the right to self-determination, to control of our resources and our lands.

Matthew Coon Come, Grand Chief of the Quebec Crees, Conference of the American Council of Quebec Studies, Washington, D.C., 18 Nov., quoted in *The Globe and Mail*, 24 Nov. 1994.

There is a term used in Ontario, most often in Toronto, that is an offshoot of Annishnawbe, the word Ojibway people use to describe themselves. The term has been modified to accommodate the growing aboriginal middle-class that has appeared in Toronto and other major cities. They are sometimes referred to as "Anishsnobs."

Drew Hayden Taylor, columnist and Native, "Talking Point," *The Globe and Mail*, 14 Sept. 1995.

The Government of Canada today formally expresses to all Aboriginal people in Canada our profound regret for past actions of the federal government which have contributed to these difficult pages in the history of our relationship together.

Sentence from "Statement of Reconciliation: Learning from the Past" signed on behalf of the Government of Canada by Jane Stewart, Minister of Indian Affairs and Northern Development, and Ralph Goodale, Federal Interlocutor for Métis and Non-status Indians, printed in *The Toronto Star*, 28 March 1998.

Today, the Nisga'a canoe returns. It carries a cargo of hope.

Joseph Gosnell Sr., hereditary chief of the Nisga'a people, initialing the first land-settlement treaty his people concluded with the federal government since 1887, New Aiyansh, Nass Valley, B.C., 4 Aug. 1998, quoted by CP in *The Globe and Mail*, 5 Aug. 1998. The specific reference is to Nisga'a ancestors who paddled their canoes to Victoria in search of a settlement to the land claims but returned empty-handed in 1887.

NATO See NORTH ATLANTIC TREATY ORGANIZATION

NATURAL RESOURCES See NATURE

NATURE See also ECOLOGY, PARKS, POLLUTION, RESOURCES, WILDERNESS, WILDLIFE

I really do not know where I shall halt. I feel like Milton's Adam and Eve—"The world was all before them where to choose their place of rest."

John Muir, botanist, conservationist, and future founder of the Sierra Club, who spent two youthful years (1864–66) exploring the region south of Georgian Bay, living on a farm at Meaford, County Grey, Canada West, today's Ont., letter, 1 March 1864, *The Life and Letters of John Muir* (1924) edited by William Frederic Badé.

The Canadian consciousness must always, to a peculiar degree, be implicated with nature, seeing that Canada is first and foremost an agricultural nation, and, still more important, is everywhere on the frontiers of the wilderness.

Wyndham Lewis, British artist, "Nature's Place in Canadian Culture" (1940–44), *Wyndham Lewis in Canada* (1971) edited by George Woodcock.

I was convinced then, and still am, that there is a capricious element in nature. Nature is not entirely predictable. If it were, there would be little romance in geology and prospecting. The manner in which rock formations form often suggests that random, or capricious, forces were at work in their creation. A less elegant synonym for capricious is probably teaser and the latter is probably one of the most used adjectives in the lexicon of many bush prospectors in pursuit of their mother lode.

Frank R. Joubin, prospector, *Not for Gold Alone: The Memoirs of a Prospector* (1986) written with D. McCormack Smyth.

Within the next 24 hours, as we go about our daily lives, 54 species of animals and plants will disappear forever—at least 20,000 species a year are lost as the rain forests of the world are destroyed.

Anita Gordon and **David Suzuki**, science broadcasters, *It's a Matter of Survival* (1990).

Vinyl is as natural as lichen.

Christopher Dewdney, poet, interviewed by Philip Marchand, *The Toronto Star*, 15 May 1993.

Nature is prodigal with details but parsimonious with principles.

Jane Jacobs, essayist, *The Nature of Economies* (2000).

NATURE, HUMAN

A theory of human needs is a particular kind of language of the human good. To define human nature in terms of needs is to define what we are in terms of what we lack, to insist on the distinctive emptiness and incompleteness of humans as a species.

Michael Ignatieff, essayist, *The Needs of Strangers* (1985).

My sense is that nature unites artist and scientist—and indeed all curious humans.

Adapted from "A Personal Statement" made by space artist **Jon Lomberg** in "Artist of the Cosmos" on the Internet homepage of the Planetary Society, 12 October 1996.

NAVY See CANADIAN ARMED FORCES

NDP See NEW DEMOCRATIC PARTY

NEEDS

Need makes us short-sighted. Necessity, blind.

Ara Baliozian, writer and teacher, *Portrait of a Genius and Other Essays* (1980).

To create needs is to create discontent, and to invite disillusionment. It is to play with lives and hopes.

Michael Ignatieff, essayist, *The Needs of Strangers* (1985).

NEGOTIATION

Whoever starts to negotiate on his knees is very likely to end up flat on his face.

Lucien Bouchard, Liberal Cabinet Minister, letter of resignation from the federal cabinet of Brian Mulroney over Jean Charest's revisions to the Meech Lake Accord, May 1990, quoted in the *National Post*, 1 Dec. 1998.

Canadians prefer to negotiate. Whether they are any good at it is another matter. They want to deliberate for days, if not weeks or years. They're also hopeless, helpless, shameless nitpickers.

James Blanchard, former U.S. Ambassador to Canada, *Behind the Embassy Door: Canada, Clinton and Quebec* (1998).

I am more interested in proposition than in opposition.

Jack Layton, once-radical and politically correct Toronto city councillor, based on a remark quoted by Jack Lakey in "The Mellowing of Jack Layton," *The Toronto Star*, 4 Jan. 1999.

NETHERLANDS, THE

Ottawa is the key to my and my family's close relationship with Canada.

Princess Margriet of the Netherlands, daughter of the Dutch Queen Juliana, born in Ottawa during World War II, opening Ottawa's Canadian Tulip Festival, CBC Radio's *National News*, 17 May 1995.

There used to be a saying, "I'd rather have a Dutch whore than a Canadian nurse." You see in Amsterdam or Rotterdam or wherever you were, when you went on leave the nurses or the Red Cross girls, or any others who were in the war for fun, why, they wanted all the things they got at home.

Unnamed veteran of the European campaign in World War II, quoted by Barry Broadfoot in *Six War Years 1939–1945: Memories of Canadians at Home and Abroad* (1974).

NEUTRALISM & NEUTRALITY

Canada's best protection would lie in neutrality, and its neutrality could be of a different and far more positive kind than the passive neutrality of the European countries that keep out of military alliances merely to save themselves from the perils of war. Canada's neutrality could be an active one, aimed not at keeping out of international problems but at resolving them peacefully and rationally.

George Woodcock, author, contributor to *If I Were Prime Minister* (1987) edited by Mel Hurtig.

Those who insist that defence is useless in the thermonuclear age will be joined by those who regard it as needless in the wake of Capitalism's triumph.

Desmond Morton, historian, "Thinking about Canadian Defence in the Nineties," *National Networks News* (quarterly publication of the Defence Associations), 1 Oct. 1990.

Canadian territory should not be made available to any other country for the purpose of attacking or threatening a third country.

Project Ploughshares for the Citizens' Inquiry into Peace and Security, quoting a statement by

Canadian church leaders, *What Makes Canada Secure: Background Document for the Citizens' Inquiry into Peace and Security in Canada* (1991).

NEW AGE See also BELIEF

I think a very decisive, radical change is imminent, because in the psychological history of mankind there has been something which you can call a new revelation about every 2,000 years.

Robertson Davies, man-of-letters, quoted by Tom Harpur in *The Toronto Star*, 2 Oct. 1981.

After the almost unimaginable horrors we have seen in this century, we have reached a manic-depressive psychosis in which we swing wildly from a despairing conviction that the human race is near its own extermination to euphoria about a coming age of Aquarius when everything will be for some reason wonderful.

Northrop Frye, cultural critic, "The View from Here" (1983), *Myth and Metaphor: Selected Essays, 1974–1988* (1990) edited by Robert D. Denham.

New Age Section Moved to Science Fiction

Sign (in Day-Glo orange ink) spotted in an Ontario bookstore, as noted by Michael Shermer in *Why People Believe Weird Things: Pseudoscience, Superstition, and Other Confusions of Our Time* (1997).

NEW BRUNSWICK See also ATLANTIC PROVINCES, FREDERICTON, MARITIME PROVINCES, SAINT JOHN

They say that everything in New Brunswick that is worth owning belongs to either God, the Government or the Irvings.

Alden Nowlan, poet and writer, "What about the Irvings?" in *Canadian Newspapers: The Inside Story* (1980) edited by Walter Stewart.

I don't think politics and business mix. New Brunswick is too small for politics.

K.C. Irving, industrialist, quoted by Peter C. Newman in *Debrett's Illustrated Guide to the Canadian Establishment* (1983).

As for [N.B. Premier Frank] McKenna, his contribution, whatever else, was a public relations triumph. Speaking to the nation—something New Brunswick premiers rarely get to do—from the theatre of the national press club, McKenna could say, "We should spike our guns with flowers." This should become a keeper for Colombo's book on Canadian quotations, even though, at any other moment, it would have been a clanger.

Dalton Camp, political columnist, writing about McKenna's contribution to the revision of the Meech Lake Accord, *The Toronto Star*, 25 March 1990.

Once you've been Premier of New Brunswick why would you want to be Prime Minister of Canada?

Frank McKenna, New Brunswick Premier, interview, Fredericton, 8 Oct. 1997, following the announcement that he would retire as Premier, quoted by Kevin Cox in *The Globe and Mail* the following day.

NEW DEMOCRATIC PARTY See also POLITICAL PARTIES, SOCIALISM

God, sir, is a New Democrat!

Stanley Knowles, CCF-NDP stalwart, veteran parliamentarian, characteristic remark recalled by Peter Warren, letter, *Maclean's*, 7 July 1997.

The New Democratic Party must be seen as the parliamentary wing of a movement dedicated to fundamental social change. It must be radicalized from within and it must be radicalized from without.

"The Waffle Manifesto: For an Independent Socialist Canada" (1969) reprinted in *The Canadian Forum*, Dec. 1989.

The New Democratic Party can, should and must become the green party of Canada, that is, a party thoroughly committed to a radical environmental policy and using all reasonable means at its disposal to advance it.

Lynn McDonald, former M.P., "Can the NDP Become the Green Party of Canada?" *The Canadian Forum, Dec.* 1989.

I take particular pleasure in exceeding other people's expectations.

Audrey McLaughlin, NDP leader, *A Woman's Place: My Life in Politics* (1992).

More people believe Elvis is alive than support the NDP.

Attributed to **Svend Robinson**, NDP Member of

Parliament, as noted in "Parliament Hill," *The Hamilton Spectator,* 26 Dec. 1995.

As New Democrats, we never made government, but we always made a difference. The very things that have made Canada special in the eyes of the world are the very things that are under attack today.

Alexa McDonough, NDP leader, Winnipeg speech, quoted by Scott Feschuk, "McDonough Lurking in Wings," *The Globe and Mail,* 31 March 1997.

NEWFIE JOKES See also HUMOUR & HUMORISTS, JOKES

The last refuge of the bore is the Newfie joke.

Tim Burke, columnist, *The Montreal Gazette,* 12 Jan. 1983.

It seemed that our turn to be ridiculed had come round. Before us there were the Irish, the Jews, the Blacks, the Poles and others. The hurtful part was that many of the people who heard and repeated the damned things knew nothing else of Newfoundland or Newfoundlanders. At their height, I got snickers at the mere mention of Newfoundland in places as far apart as Barbados and Vancouver.

Ray Guy, humorist, "Peace, Good Wife; We May Entertain Angels Unaware," *Ray Guy's Best* (1987).

In this sense *we are all Newfoundlanders.* So never laugh at a Newfie joke unless you want to laugh at yourself.

John Fraser, columnist, referring to the experience of Newfoundlanders in renouncing their national sovereignty in place of provincial status, "The Last Laugh," *Saturday Night,* March 1992.

NEWFOUNDLAND See also ATLANTIC PROVINCES, LABRADOR, ST. JOHN'S

Now we have two tasks on our hands. On alternate days we must gather grapes and cut vines, and then fell trees, to make a cargo for my ship.

Words attributed to Old Norse explorer **Leif Ericsson** (c. A.D. 1000), *The Vinland Sagas: The Norse Discovery of America* (1965) translated from the Old Icelandic by Magnus Magnusson and Hermann Palsson. Leif the Lucky referred to the region as vinland, or "wine-land," and the locale is most likely Newfoundland.

In this colony an unbroken tradition points to Cape Bonavista, Newfoundland, as the first land seen.

D.W. Prowse, historian, referring to the tradition that John Cabot made his historic landfall on 24 June 1497 at Cape Bonavista, Nfld., not in the Maritimes. "'Bonavista! Oh! good sight'" is the natural exclamation the old Italian might make, as after his long and dangerous voyage he first caught sight of land, bright and green with the springing grass of June. There is no other cape with the same name on the eastern shore of North America."

Terra Nova, of the Codfish, is a cold place. The inhabitants are idolaters, some worship the sun, others the moon, and many other kinds of idols. It is a fair place, but savage.

Pietro Andrea Mattioli, inscription on a map of Terra Nova, today's Newfoundland, 1546, quoted in "What Newfoundland Means to Me," *National Post,* 27 March 1999.

What Seas abounding with fish? What shores so replenished with fresh and sweet waters? The wants of other Kingdomes are not felt here.

Sir Richard Whitbourne, colonist, *A Discourse and Discovery of New-found-land* (1622), as quoted by Gillian T. Cell, "Sir Richard Whitbourne," *Dictionary of Canadian Biography: Volume I: 1000–1700* (1965).

No athenaeum, or rink, or library; no townhall or museum; no greenhouses, conservatories, or parks. Nothing, absolutely nothing to be seen but the bare, cold, unappealing necessities of life.

John Mullaly, traveller, reacting to the capital city of St. John's, *A Trip to Newfoundland* (1855).

Then hurrah for our own native isle, Newfoundland! / Not a stranger shall hold one inch of its strand! / Her face turns to Britain, her back to the Gulf. / Come near at your peril, Canadian Wolf!

One verse from "An Anti-Confederation Song" (1869) popular among Newfoundlanders who were opposed to entering Confederation in 1869. *Old-Time Poetry and Songs of Newfoundland* (1940) edited by Gerald S. Doyle.

That foggy little island, although always somewhat of a rough diamond, is a valuable jewel, and is the first that was set in the imperial crown.

Earl of Dunraven, Irish politician and noted sportsman who hunted in Newfoundland in 1879, *Canadian Nights: Being Sketches and Reminiscences of Life and Sport in the Rockies, the Prairies and the Canadian Woods* (1914).

Manuel's talk was slow and gentle—all about... legends of saints, and tales of queer dances or nights away in the cold Newfoundland baiting-ports.

Line of description from **Rudyard Kipling**'s novel *Captains Courageous: A Story of the Grand Banks* (1897), a novel rich in Great Island fishing lore.

If you have ever lived in a Newfoundland Outport, be proud of it—and grateful. If you were born in one, be prouder still.

Arthur Scammell, folksong composer, "Outport Heritage," *Atlantic Guardian*, Vol. 1, No. 5, 1945.

If such a decision is made, it must be made by the 50,000 poor families and not by the 5,000 who are confident of getting along in any case.

Joseph R. (Joey) Smallwood, advocate of union with Canada, addressing the Newfoundland Legislature in 1946 on behalf of Confederation with Canada, quoted by Richard Gwyn, *The Toronto Star*, 19 Dec. 1991.

The acquisition of Newfoundland will take its place, in strategic importance, with the acquisition by the United States of Alaska and Louisiana.

John G. Diefenbaker, Member of Parliament, House of Commons, 8 Feb. 1949.

Floreat terra nova

Latin inscription (May the New Land Flourish) on the reverse side of the silver dollar, designed by **Thomas Shingles** and minted in 1949, to commemorate Newfoundland's entrance into Confederation, 1 April 1949.

Our time spent together will ebb like the tide, / Distance may part us but never divide; / We want you to know we are proud that you came— / Some things have changed but the folks are the same.

Last verse of "A Newfoundland Come Home Song" written by versifier **A.R. Scammell** for *Come Home Year* (1966) and included in *Scammell's My Newfoundland* (1966).

Welcome to Newfoundland / Britain's Oldest Colony / Canada's Youngest Province

Highway sign, near Port-aux-Basques, Nfld., 1960s.

You might think it's goofy, / But the man in the moon is a Newfie, / And he's sailing on to glory, / Away in the golden dory; / He's sailing on to glory / Away in the golden dory.

Lines from composer **Stompin' Tom Connors**' song "The Moon-Man Newfie" (1971).

At midnight on March 31, 1949, that old dream of the Fathers of Confederation finally came true. The oldest settlement in North America became the newest Canadian province and we then understood the meaning of the words "A mari usque ad mare."

Pierre Elliott Trudeau, Prime Minister, address on the 25th anniversary of Newfoundland's joining Confederation, House of Commons, 1 April 1974.

When New York was a swamp, we were growing daisies in Newfoundland.

Joseph R. (Joey) Smallwood, former Premier of Newfoundland, characteristic remark, quoted by Dick Beddoes in *The Globe and Mail*, 10 Dec. 1975.

This is not a land for welfare and soft living and the comforts of a complex society. It is a land that demands a spirit in which North Americans no longer believe, though their ancestors believed in it with passion—the spirit of heroes—a land whose black rocks confront the Arctic ice, and whose naked hills stare up to the implacable stars.

Harold Horwood, author, *Beyond the Road: Portraits and Visions of Newfoundlanders* (1976) by Stephen Taylor and Harold Horwood.

Newfoundland is the only province of Canada to have freely decided to enter Canada through a referendum.

Brian Peckford, Newfoundland Premier, addressing the First Ministers' Conference, Ottawa, 15 Sept. 1980, quoted by Bren Walsh in *More than a Majority: The Story of Newfoundland's Confederation with Canada* (1985). Walsh added, "That's a supposition concerning which this book, if it does nothing else, certainly raises reasonable doubts." It was Walsh's thesis that the results of the referendum on Confederation were rigged, the majority of Newfoundlanders having voted against Confederation.

Newfoundland, for example, was (I think) three hours, 35 minutes, and some seconds behind GMT before standardization, and elected to round off to three hours, 30 minutes—owing, I suppose, to the native perversity of its inhabitants, who delighted in being out of sync with the rest of Canada.

Cecil Adams, U.S. journalist, *The Straight Dope: A Compendium of Human Knowledge* (1984).

It was an unparalleled pleasure to live amongst the outport children of Burgeo—soft-spoken, calm, imbued with an innate and entirely natural politeness, uninhibited in their affections. But it was agony to watch what happened to them as they reached adolescence and began to suffer from the disintegration of the human fabric in the coves by the sounding sea.

Farley Mowat, naturalist and sometime resident of the outport community of Burgeo, Nfld., *The New-Founde-Land* (1989).

If you took the word "fight" out of the political vocabulary of Newfoundland politicians, they'd have nothing else to say.

Ed Roberts, government official, with special reference to Nfld. Premier Clyde Wells, quoted by Jeffrey Simpson in *The Globe and Mail*, 24 Sept. 1991.

I hadn't been on the island ten minutes before I knew this was going to be an exceedingly important place for me.

E. Annie Proulx, Vermont novelist with Canadian ancestors who set her novel *The Shipping News* (1992) on the Great Island, quoted in *Quill & Quire*, Jan. 1994. She went on to say: "My ideal temperature is about 22 degrees—Fahrenheit."

One of the problems of Newfoundland is also one of its advantages. We're midway between Frankfurt and Calgary. I don't know if people realize that or not.

Clyde Wells, Nfld. Premier, quoted by Alan Freeman in *The Globe and Mail*, 30 Nov. 1992.

This whole shouting and bawling about foreign overfishing—sure, they are out there and sure, they take a lot of fish and sure, they misbehave—but just about any Newfoundlander ever born would kill the last living creature if he thought he could get a six-pack of beer for it.

Christopher Pratt, Newfoundland-born painter, quoted by Joseph Hall in *The Toronto Star*, 13 Feb. 1994.

Upon this beautiful, bleak land, a nation as distinct as Quebec but guarded by sea rather than by language, has taken root. Again like Quebec, it has gone beyond mere endurance, or *la survivance*, to discover its own distinctive voice, in the theatre, in films, in music, in satire, in painting.

Richard Gwyn, columnist and summertime resident of Clay Cove, Bonavista Bay, "Opinion," *The Toronto Star*, 13 Feb. 1994.

Lewis Carroll might have imagined Newfoundland; few Canadians have been able to do so.

Dalton Camp, columnist, "Amid Poverty and Corruption, a Great People," *The Toronto Star*, 13 Feb. 1994.

Weather, rock and water; shore, sea and sky: these are the elements which framed our being here. The nod of their triple intersection . . . is the outport: the outport is the house of our being.

Rex Murphy, broadcaster, convocation address, Memorial University, St. John's, Nfld., published in *The Globe and Mail*, 13 Nov. 1997.

Someone once asked how you can tell which ones are Newfoundlanders when you visit heaven. The answer is, you can always tell the Newfoundlanders because they're the ones who want to go home.

John C. Crosbie, politician, "What Newfoundland Means to Me," *National Post*, 27 March 1999.

NEW FRANCE

See also CANADA: FRENCH; FRANCE; QUEBEC

Our world has just discovered another world (and who will guarantee us that it is the last of its brothers, since the daemons, the sibyls, and we ourselves have up to now been ignorant of this one?) no less great, full, and well-limbed than itself, yet so new and so infantile that it is still being taught its ABC; not fifty years ago it knew neither letters, nor weights and measures, nor clothes, nor wheat, nor vines.

Michel de Montaigne, French essayist, writing in the 1580s, *The Complete Works of Montaigne: Essays, Travel Journal, Letters* (1957) translated by Donald M. Frame.

The King regards his Canadian subjects ... as his own children.

Attributed to **Louis XIV**, the Sun King, King of France and of New France, Versailles, France, 1663.

However starved New France may have been for settlers, it never lacked administrators.

Alan Gowans, architect, *Church Architecture in New France* (1955).

The Quebec of 1995, which stands behind the Acadians and the francophones in Canada, is all that remains in North America of the New France of yesteryear.

Jacques Parizeau, Quebec Premier, addressing members of the French National Assembly, Paris, 24 Jan. 1994, quoted by Robert McKenzie in *The Toronto Star* the following day.

NEWS See also BLACK, CONRAD; BROADCASTING; CANADIAN BROADCASTING CORPORATION; CENSORSHIP; COMMUNICATIONS; GZOWSKI, PETER; INTERVIEWS; JOURNALISM; JOURNALISTS; MEDIA; NEWSPAPERS; PRESS; RADIO; TELEVISION

Something you want to remember around here, son, there are three things of importance, in this order: *The Toronto Star*, the Liberal Party, and Jesus Christ.

Jim Kingsbury, managing editor of *The Toronto Star* in the 1940s, addressing Tom Cossitt, then a junior reporter, quoted by Michael Enright in *Maclean's*, 20 Oct. 1975.

The business of getting the *news* is mostly the art of getting to *people*.

Fred Edge, reporter, *Don't Tell Me About It ... Write It!* (1963).

The newspapers have to have bad news, otherwise there would be only ads, or good news. Without bad news we could not discern the ground rules of the environment.

Marshall McLuhan, communications pioneer, "Address at Vision 65" (1966), *The Essential McLuhan* (1995) edited by Eric McLuhan and Frank Zingrone.

Show me a man who is completely objective and I'll arrange to have his tombstone made.

Norman DePoe, broadcaster, quoted in *Maclean's*, May 1968.

News, far more than art, is artifact.

Marshall McLuhan, communications pioneer, observation made in 1969, "A McLuhan Sourcebook," *The Essential McLuhan* (1995) edited by Eric McLuhan and Frank Zingrone.

Viewed from Central Asia, it doesn't look very significant.

Pierre Elliott Trudeau, Prime Minister, responding to a Canadian Press reporter who asked for his reaction to Paul Hellyer's resignation from the Liberal Party during Trudeau's visit to Central Asia, quoted by Claude Balloune in *The Last Post*, Oct. 1972.

Honesty and integrity matter most. And I have a deep respect for the truth. And I'm prepared to ask dangerous questions to get it—even if I risk making a fool of myself I'm prepared to lose in order that the audience wins. You have to take chances.

Barbara Frum, co-host of CBC Radio's *As It Happens*, quoted by James Quig in *Weekend Magazine*, 31 May 1975.

An explosion has to kill a lot of people in Tokyo to make the front page of the *Toronto Star*. It only has to kill one person in Toronto.

Pierre Berton, author, *Meet the Media: Eight of Canada's Best-known Journalists Talk with Robert Bullis* (1976).

An editor I once worked for gave me the best advice a journalist ever got. "People want to read about people, places, and things. In that order."

Roger Burford Mason, writer, recalling the advice of Hertfordshire editor Eric Scott, "Bookshelf," *Thornhill Month*, Aug. 1991.

In Canada, the press is addicted to creating news by the elevation and destruction of reputations. It is easier to manufacture news than to report it.

Conrad Black, newspaper proprietor and columnist, "Why Does the Press Savage Success?" *The Globe and Mail's Report on Business Magazine*, March 1986.

If they discovered life in other planets and galaxies, think how much more bad news we could get.

*

The news has been very bad every day now for about a million years.

Louis Dudek, poet and aphorist, "Epigrams," *Small Perfect Things* (1991).

The classic definition of news can be summarized, I think, as "what went wrong yesterday."

William Thorsell, publisher, article, *The Globe and Mail*, 12 Dec. 1991.

Anything that will alarm the public is news.

Louis Dudek, poet and aphorist, sarcastic definition, "Radical Notes 1944," *The Nashwaak Review*, No. 2, 1995.

News is what someone wants suppressed.

Neil Reynolds, newspaper publisher and editor, offering a tongue-in-cheek definition of news on a journalism panel conducted by Peter Gzowski, CBC-TV's *Morningside*, 15 May 1995.

From the National Newsroom of CBC Radio this is the CBC National News.

Program identification, somewhat redundant, heard on CBC Radio, 25 Oct. 1995.

We have lots of faith in print. Given what they want, people will keep on reading.

David Radler, executive, Hollinger Inc., quoted by Peter C. Newman, "The Nation's Business," *Maclean's*, 29 Sept. 1997.

NEWSPAPERS See also NEWS

A newspaper, to attract and hold public support, must have politics, conviction, loyalty and principles. In short, it must have a personality.

John W. Dafoe, editor of the *Winnipeg Free Press* (1901–44), on being asked in the 1930s why he was so dedicated to the Liberal Party, quoted by Allan Levine in the *Winnipeg Free Press*, 17 Oct. 1991.

To be a successful newspaper proprietor you need prejudice and breadth of vision. It's a rare combination.

Lord Beaverbrook, publisher, remark made in 1956, quoted by Anne Chisholm and Michael Davie in *Beaverbrook: A Life* (1992).

For enough money, I'd work in hell.

Attributed to financier **Roy Thomson** by Adrian Havill in *The Last Mogul* (1992). The British biographer Havill added, "Although the metaphor is wrong, he could have been speaking of the cold northern Ontario winters."

Subscription Rates. Since many subscribers may live in the "bush," subscriptions may be paid in either cash or kind.

Notice carried in the first issue of *Drum*, 6 Jan. 1966, the first newspaper published inside the Arctic Circle, at Inuvik, N.W.T.

People don't actually read newspapers—they get into them every morning like a hot bath.

Marshall McLuhan, communications pioneer, "Playboy Interview" (1969), *The Essential McLuhan* (1995) edited by Eric McLuhan and Frank Zingrone.

Wherever the capitalist system exists, the newspapers will be owned by capitalists.

Alden Nowlan, poet and writer, "What about the Irvings?" in *Canadian Newspapers: The Inside Story* (1980) edited by Walter Stewart.

For most people who work here, I suspect, there are two *Globes*. One is the Platonic Ideal, which exists as a public trust and which calls us to our highest standards of excellence. The other *Globe* is the messy, flawed, aggravating, typo-ridden paper we publish every day, usually good enough and sometimes superb, but always imperfect.

Margaret Wente, editor and columnist, writing to mark the paper's 150th anniversary, *The Globe and Mail*, 5 March 1994.

Publishing it on newsprint rather than on stone tablets is a concession to convenience, although its prose still causes less robust readers to risk a hernia, and an eternity of torment should they ignore its injunctions.

Joey Slinger, columnist with The Toronto Star, commenting on *The Globe and Mail*, "No Place to Call Home," *The Globe and Mail*, 5 March 1994.

We are not in the business of selling you newspapers; we are in the business of buying your time.

William Thorsell, editor-in-chief, "Papermaking," *The Globe and Mail*, 6 Feb. 1995.

Editors who work for us have the right to voice their opinions after they stop working for us.

Attributed to **David Radler**, executive, Hollinger Inc., by Peter Gzowski on CBC Radio's *Morningside*, 17 Oct. 1996.

The fabricated and orchestrated concern is that we are so extremely conservative in our views, so overbearing in our methods, and so commercially avaricious, that we will cause our newspapers to come precipitately down market as they assault the readers with extreme opinions.

Conrad Black, capitalist, "Letter of the Day" Conrad Black's Response to the CBC," *The Hamilton Spectator*, 26 Oct. 1996. He was referring to a CBC-TV program about his commercial empire and legal action directed against his press concentration.

We own only slightly over 40 per cent of this country's daily newspaper circulation, which hardly constitutes a monopoly.

Conrad Black, publisher, chairman and CEO of both Hollinger Inc. and Southam Inc., shareholders' address, 26 May 1998, published in "Verbatim," *The Globe and Mail*, 28 May 1998.

NEW YEAR'S DAY See HOLIDAYS

NEW ZEALAND

While we share many advantages, we also have some common problems. We have the Maoris, and you have the French Canadians.

Sir Keith Holyoake, Prime Minister of New Zealand, welcoming Prime Minister Pierre Elliott Trudeau in 1970, as recalled by Charles Lynch in *A Funny Way to Run a Country* (1986).

What I remembered was the nineteenth-century anglophone society of the Canadian west coast that I found surviving in Victoria when I got there thirty years ago. I could not help thinking, as I looked at New Zealand with that memory in mind, how narrowly Canadians had escaped a continuing colonialism. "There," I thought, "but for the grace of Quebec, go we!"

George Woodcock, travel writer, "From Rotorua to Tasman Bay" (1979), *Letter from the Khyber Pass and Other Travel Writing* (1993) edited by Jim Christy.

NIAGARA FALLS

My Fall was stopped by a terrible Squash, that sounded louder to my ears than the Cataract of *Niagara;* after which I was quite in the Dark for another Minute....

Jonathan Swift, Anglo-Irish author, making an early reference to Niagara Falls, in "A Voyage to Brobdingnag," *Travels into Several Remote Nations of the World* (1726), popularly known as *Gulliver's Travels.*

Nature will be Nature still, while palaces shall decay and fall in ruins. Yes, Niagara will be Niagara a thousand years hence! The rainbow, a wreath over her brow, shall continue as long as the sun, and the flowering of the river—while the work of art, however, impregnable, shall in atoms fall!

George Copway, Native spokesperson, *Recollections of a Forest Life, or the Life and Travels of Kah-se-ga-gah-bowh* (1847).

She ordered him to sit down. He obeyed; then, looking at the weir: "It's like Niagara." He began to talk of distant countries and long journeys.

Passage about the French lovers on the Seine above Nogent in **Gustave Flaubert**'s novel *Sentimental Education* (1869) translated by Anthony Goldsmith in 1941.

Niagara Falls must be the second major disappointment of American married life.

Oscar Wilde, Anglo-Irish wit, visitor to Niagara Falls, "honeymoon capital of the world," Feb. 1882, quoted by Kevin O'Brien in *Oscar Wilde in Canada* (1982).

The master banalities of art: the Mona Lisa, La Dame aux Camelias and Celeste Aïda. The master banalities of nature: Niagara Falls, the Gulf Stream and the blood-sweating hippopotamus.

H.L. Mencken, American man-of-letters, "The Smart Set," *The American Mercury*, 1916.

The idea is to be nailed in a packing case, thrown over Niagara Falls, and eventually make an escape!

Harry Houdini, magician and escape artist, quoted by Walter B. Gibson in *Houdini's Escapes and Magic* (1932), as cited by Ruth Brandon in *The Life and Many Deaths of Harry Houdini* (1993). Houdini was describing the role he wrote for himself in the early silent feature film *The Man from Beyond* (1920).

The roar of Niagara is the Delphian voice of the great spaces of North America.

Sir Osbert Sitwell, English traveller and writer, *The Four Continents: Being More Discursions on Travel, Art and Life* (1954).

A wave pushed me way out in the air when I got to the edge. I felt like I was flying.

Roger Woodward, seven-year-old boy who survived a plunge over Niagara Falls, "How I Rode over Niagara," *The Toronto Star*, 11 July 1960.

Niagara Falls, said Gertrude Stein, is beautiful for thirty seconds.

Lewis Thomas, essayist, attributing a sentiment about the cataract to the remarkable American literary stylist, *Et Cetera, Et Cetera: Notes of a Word-Watcher* (1990).

O Canada's Niagara Falls, you at once feed not only the curious mind and eyes of humanity but also the aspiring heart of humanity.

Prayer of **Sri Chinmoy Kumar Ghose**, Indian-born, New York–based guru and peace activist, recited at the dedication ceremony of Niagara Falls as a Sri Chinmoy International Peace Falls, Niagara Falls, Ont., 15 April 1992.

Maybe they should send divorcees here.

Nicholas Shakespeare, English novelist, upon visiting Niagara Falls and learning that it was the Honeymoon Capital of the World, quoted by Philip Marchand in *The Toronto Star*, 2 Nov. 1996.

Ladies and Gentlemen, *this* is Niagara Falls!

Highpoint of the recorded commentary of a male voice heard aboard the *Maid of the Mist* at the foot of Niagara Falls, noted by Jody Alesandro in "Coming to Terms with Niagara," *The New York Times*, 29 Sept. 1996.

NOBEL PRIZES See also AWARDS & HONOURS

Gosh, I am thunderstruck and overwhelmed. I am aware that in the work which I have done and which was in the minds of the Nobel committee, I was the spokesman for Canada and not operating in any personal capacity. Therefore the award is a tribute to the efforts Canada has made since World War II to bring about peace and better international relations. I am proud beyond words to be the only one chosen to receive it. My feeling of gratitude for an honour of this kind is very much increased when I think of the great men who have previously received it.

Lester B. Pearson, President of the U.N. General Assembly, learning from the reporter that he was the recipient of the 1957 Nobel Peace Prize, quoted by Bruce MacDonald in *The Toronto Star*, 12 Oct. 1957.

There is a responsibility. The fact that this prize, for no good reason I think, tends to open doors to you gives you an obligation to go through those doors and talk to the person who's been hiding behind.

John C. Polanyi, recipient of the 1986 Nobel Prize for Chemistry, quoted by Lydia Dotto in *Alumni Magazine* (University of Toronto), Winter 1986.

When, on *Morningside*, I told Robertson Davies that a few days earlier in an interview with me Anthony Burgess had suggested he, Davies, be given the Nobel Prize for Literature, he said, "Goodness gracious, I'm sure I don't deserve it."

Peter Gzowski, journalist, *The Private Voice: A Journal of Reflections* (1988).

There's a little bit of a tendency to feel that we cannot do first-rate things in Canada because we're too small. This award says the science done here is as good as the science done anywhere, and you can do science in B.C. as well as anywhere in the world.

Michael Smith, biochemist at the University of British Columbia, co-recipient of the 1993 Nobel Prize for Chemistry, quoted by Robert Matas in *The Globe and Mail*, 14 Oct. 1993.

How on earth could they pick me?

Bertram Neville Brockhouse, retired scientist, response to learning he was co-recipient of the

1994 Nobel Prize for Physics for work in nuclear physics on the behaviour of atoms conducted at the National Research Laboratory at Chalk River some forty years earlier, 12 Oct. 1994, as noted in an editorial in *The Toronto Star* the following day.

The only Australians or Canadians who are well known in the world are a few entertainers. The two countries together have fewer Nobel Prize winners than many American university campuses, and a smaller population and lower standard of living than the combination of California and Illinois.

Conrad Black, publisher, "Media," *The Globe and Mail*, 30 Dec. 1996.

My entire culture in math and theoretical physics has its origins in my time in Toronto.

Walter Kohn, Professor at University of California at Santa Barbara, 1998 Nobel laureate in Chemistry, who arrived in Canada from Germany in 1940 and spent time in an alien detention centre, graduated with his Bachelor's from the University of Toronto in 1945, his Master's the following year, quoted in the *University College Alumni Magazine*, Winter 1999.

NOISE See also SOUND

Noise is any sound signal which interferes. Noise is the destroyer of things we want to hear.

R. Murray Schafer, composer and theorist, *Ear Cleaning: Notes for an Experimental Music Course* (1967).

Noise is the fifth element in which we live.

Robertson Davies, man-of-letters, commencement address, Toronto French School, 18 June 1982, *TFS's Bi-Line* (1982).

Lawn care has also become a persistent source of noise pollution which has grown dramatically in recent years. By itself, one gas-powered lawn mower is bearable, but the cumulative effect of several mowers can drench an entire subdivision with industrial strength noise for several hours. If a new factory were to emit such protracted noise near a residental area, it is certain that indignant demonstrations would erupt at municipal offices.

Tom Davey, editor and publisher, "Urban Life Gets Louder," *The Toronto Sun*, 27 Nov. 1994.

NORAD See DEFENCE

NORTH, THE See also ARCTIC, NORTHERN LIGHTS, NORTH POLE, NORTHWEST PASSAGE, NORTHWEST TERRITORIES, NUNAVUT, WILDERNESS, YUKON TERRITORY

And that true North, whereof we lately heard.

The words "true North," so rich in resonance, first appeared in **Alfred Lord Tennyson**'s poem "O Loyal to the Royal in Thyself," *Idylls of the King* (1873). England's poet laureate composed the line after reading an editorial in *The Times*, 30 Oct. 1872, which advised Canada to seek its independence from Britain. Tennyson felt this advice to be gratuitous, patronizing, and unpatriotic. R. Stanley Weir introduced the words into the English version of "O Canada" (1908): "With glowing hearts we see thee rise, / The True North, strong and free."

All lands between the two lines up to the North Pole should belong and do belong to the country whose territory abuts up there.

Pascal Poirier, Senator, 20 Feb. 1907. Poirier was presenting what is now known as the "sector theory" with respect to possession and sovereignty. The Senate resolution went unpassed, as noted by R.A.J. Phillips in *Canada's North* (1967).

Canada is not just a narrow fertile fringe along the top of the U.S. border. All of the country can be made fertile, right up to the northern sea coast.

Vilhjalmur Stefansson, Arctic explorer, interviewed by *The Toronto Star*, 18 Nov. 1929.

The North is the only place where Nature still can claim to rule, the only place as yet but little vexed by man. All over the globe there spread his noisy failures; the North alone is silent and in peace. Give man time and he will spoil that too; but the time had not, thank Heaven, as yet arrived.

Stephen Leacock, humorist, "Reflections on the North" (1936), *Northern Treasury: Selections from The Beaver* (1956) edited by Clifford Wilson.

I could see a Canada that answered not only the description on the main doorway of the House of Commons, "Canada from Sea to Sea," but "Canada from Sea to Seas." Today, these ideas are regarded as the fundamental policy for the development of the North.

John G. Diefenbaker, Conservative leader, address, Massey Hall, Toronto, 25 April 1957. This address, Diefenbaker once explained, was the genesis of his Northern Vision, yet the concept did not catch on until he spoke on the same subject in Winnipeg in Feb. 1958. He also maintained that it was the origin of the New Frontier policy of U.S. President John F. Kennedy who apparently borrowed it in 1960 (without attribution) and used it to great advantage.

Like the aurora glowing greenly in the August night, the north continues to elude us. It remains as it was in Leif Ericsson's time, a secret land of mystery, enigma, and legend.

Pierre Berton, author, *The Mysterious North* (1959).

Our North is not only the last frontier, but a permanent frontier.

Marie-Josée Drouin, commentator, *Canada Has a Future* (1978), a report prepared for the Hudson Institute of Canada by Drouin and B. Bruce-Biggs.

The North is fine if you are white, not bad if you are an Eskimo, but downright discouraging if you are an Indian.

Gordon Gibson, entrepreneur, *Bull of the Woods: The Gordon Gibson Story* (1980) written with Carol Renison.

It is difficult to go far north without becoming a philosopher.

Glenn Gould, pianist, quoted by Tim Page in *The Glenn Gould Reader* (1984).

I know it fairly well, but not the North. It's so cold up there. Trees and bears... that have their coats.... And the interminable snow, yes. But Alaska must be worse.

Jorge Luis Borges, man-of-letters, referring to Canada and the North in particular, interviewed by Raul Galvez in Buenos Aires, Argentina, June 1985, *From the Ashen Land of the Virgins* (1988).

The north focuses our anxieties. Turning to face the north, we enter our own unconscious. Always, in retrospect, the journey north has the quality of dream.

Margaret Atwood, essayist, "True North" (1987), *Canadian Content* (1992) edited by Sarah Norton and Nell Waldman.

Beyond Saskatoon, the vast wilderness of northern Canada extended to the planet's edge, touched only by the aurora borealis and the condensation trails of military jets surfing on the upper limits of the atmosphere. Here the great radars of the Norad chain and the Russian defence system bayed at each other like lions staked to the ice.

J.G. Ballard, author, recalling his NATO pilot-training at Moose Jaw in the 1950s, *The Kindness of Women* (1991).

You have not seen Canada until you have seen the North.

Pierre Elliott Trudeau, Prime Minister, quoted in *Canada's Northwest Territories: 1992 Explorers' Guide* (1991).

The Yukon and Northwest Territories remain our last frontier. We need ways to allow the people living there to be heard more in Ottawa and at the constitutional table. We need to make a concerted effort to learn much more about the unique challenges, opportunities and culture of the North. And we need to bring the idea of North more vividly into the imagination of Canadians as a unifying factor.

Keith Spicer, commissioner, *Citizens' Forum on Canada's Future: Report to the People and Government of Canada*, published as a special feature of *The Toronto Star, The Globe and Mail*, and other newspapers, 29 June 1991.

"North" is a word like *vision*, or *apocalypse*, or *maya*.

John Flood, publisher, catalogue, Penumbra Press, Fall 1991 Frontlist & Recent Backlist.

We belong to the North. Our elites try to pretend that we are in New York or Paris or Milan, but our literature, music, painting and actions are all determined by the fact that we live in the North.

John Ralston Saul, President, Canada PEN International, quoted in University of Guelph's "Canada" supplement, *The Globe and Mail*, 4 Dec. 1991.

This depth is what makes Canada so enticing—the idea that at the border you can start walking north and disappear into a land that rolls on to some impossibly distant shore. Perhaps only the Sahara and parts of the Amazon also evoke this feeling—the sense that a journey, once initiated, need never end.

Wade Davis, ethnobotanist and essayist, *Shadows in the Sun* (1992).

The North is not on the compass. It is right here.

Pierre Morency, author, quoted by Adrienne Clarkson, Governor General, installation address, Ottawa, 7 Oct. 1999, printed in the *National Post* the following day.

One Land, Many Voices

Words engraved on the silver band that encircles the head of the ornamental mace designed for use by the **Legislative Assembly of the Northwest Territories**. The words appear in the Territories' ten official languages: Chipewyan, Cree, Dogrib, Gwich'in, North Slavey, South Slavey, Inuvialuktun, Inuinnaqtun, English, French. The mace was unveiled 14 Jan. 2000, reproduced in the *National Post* the next day. The mace represents the authority of the Assembly's Speaker.

NORTH AMERICA See also AMERICA, CANADA, MEXICO & MEXICANS, UNITED STATES OF AMERICA

"By the way, Grey Owl," I digressed, "what is your theory as to how the red Indian ever came on this continent in the first place?"

"Impossible to say—some contend that this continent is the cradle of the whole human race. Difficult to dogmatize—but," he added with a sad smile (the only kind known to the Indian), "the fact remains that we are here."

Interview with **Grey Owl**, naturalist and author, conducted by interviewer R.E. Knowles in *The Toronto Star*, 2 March 1936.

America is a country that has passed from barbary to decadence without even having known civilization.

Leonard W. Brockington, orator and business executive, quoted by Wyndham Lewis, "Hill 100: Outline for an Unwritten Novel" (1940–44), published by George Woodcock in *Wyndham Lewis in Canada* (1971).

Our peoples are North Americans. We are the children of our geography, products of the same hopes, faith and dreams....

John G. Diefenbaker, Prime Minister, introducing U.S. President Dwight D. Eisenhower before a joint sitting of the Senate and the House of Commons, 9 July 1958.

Canada exists in America by the operation of geography, the needs of imperial strategy, the development of an historical tradition, and the conscious will of the Canadian people. It is not, more than other states, an historical accident or an artificial creation.

W.L. Morton, historian, *The Canadian Identity* (1961).

The North Americans, consisting of Canadians, the U.S. citizens, and Mexicans, are evolutionarily cross-breeding into a single hybrid family of world humans.

R. Buckminster Fuller, visionary engineer, *Critical Path* (1981) written with Kiyoshi Kuromiya.

There is no such thing as a North American identity. If you're not Canadian, or American, you simply lack identity.

John Hofsess, journalist, *Inner Views: Ten Canadian Film-makers* (1975).

European observers sometimes classify me as a hybrid curiosity, neither fully American nor satisfactorily European, stuffed with references to the philosophers, the historians, and poets I had consumed higgledly-piggledly, in my Midwestern air.

Saul Bellow, Quebec-born, Chicago-based author, Foreword, *The Closing of the American Mind* (1987) by Allan Bloom.

Our greatest destiny could be to do all we can to ensure that North American liberal, democratic, English-speaking capitalism continues to be the foremost political influence in the world.

Conrad Black, publisher, address, Canadian Club of Toronto, 26 Oct. 1992, quoted by Bob Papoe in *The Toronto Star* the next day.

I am a North American bi-national. Most of the time, I happily pick and choose between my two selves, Canadian and American, depending on which nationally it is least embarrassing to admit at any particular moment.

Adam Gopnik, Montreal-born, New York–based essayist, quoted by Charles Oberdorf in "The Talk of The New Yorker," *Saturday Night*, Feb. 1994.

Mexico is passion, Canada is ignorance, and the United States is aggression. There are three ways to ignore who we are.

Chogyam Trungpa Rinpoche, Buddhist leader, resident of Halifax, N.S., drawing a map of North America, as recalled by a follower, noted by David Swick in *Thunder and Ocean: Shambhala and Buddhism in Nova Scotia* (1996).

We are North Americans by birth, on either side of the line. The rest is just survey stakes and politics.

Charlton Heston, movie actor and President of the National Rifle Association of America, address, B.C. Wildlife Federation, Prince George, B.C., 13 April 2000, printed in the *National Post* the following day.

NORTH AMERICAN FREE TRADE AGREEMENT See also FREE TRADE, FREE TRADE AGREEMENTS

The role of Canada's negotiators in the NAFTA talks is to ensure that Canada's interests do not get lost in the shuffle.

John Crispo, political economist, referring to the North American Free Trade Agreement, *The Toronto Star*, 4 June 1991.

NAFTA has come into the world with blood on its hands. And the indications are that more blood will be shed before the tragic story is over.

James Laxer, columnist, referring to the peasant uprising in Mexico's southern state of Chiapas, *The Toronto Star*, 23 Jan. 1994.

The success of NAFTA, which is generating new jobs and creating new markets from Monterrey to Medicine Hat, is the proof. As the Prime Minister has said so well, we in NAFTA are on our way to becoming the four amigos. That phrase will go down in history; I wish I had thought of it.

Bill Clinton, U.S. President, address, joint meeting of the House of Commons and the Senate of Canada, Ottawa, Senate Debates, 23 Feb. 1995. Prime Minister Jean Chrétien first used the phrase "the four amigos" to refer to the four "friends"—Canada, United States, Mexico, and Chile.

There are thousands of pages of rules to protect corporate and business rights, over 20,000 pages of them in the most recent General Agreement on Tariffs and Trade (GATT), but no rules to protect human rights or the quality of the environment.

John McMurtry, philosopher, University of Guelph, "The Contradictions of Free Market Doctrine—Is There a Solution?" a paper prepared for the Westminster Institute Conference, "Surviving Globalization: Economic, Social, and Environmental Dimensions," London, Ont., May 1995.

NORTH ATLANTIC TREATY ORGANIZATION See also DEFENCE

When I ask you to support a North Atlantic Treaty, I am simply asking you to pay an insurance premium which will be far, far less costly than the losses we would face if a new conflagration devastated the world.

Louis St. Laurent, Prime Minister, CBC Radio, 11 Nov. 1948. On Remembrance Day, St. Laurent announced that Canada would join the North Atlantic Treaty Organization (NATO) on 28 March 1949. Quoted by J.W. Pickersgill in *My Years with Louis St. Laurent: A Political Memoir* (1975).

I bear solemn witness to the fact that NATO heads of state and of government meet only to go through the tedious motions of reading speeches, drafted by others, with the principal objective of not rocking the boat.

Pierre Elliott Trudeau, former Prime Minister, NATO address, urging the West to adopt the principle of renouncing the initial use of nuclear weapons once conventional forces are built up, quoted in *The New York Times*, 14 Nov. 1984.

The most valuable military contribution NATO can now make to security is to join the Soviet Union in reducing military forces and eliminating offensive capabilities and strategies.

Project Ploughshares for the Citizens' Inquiry into Peace and Security, *What Makes Canada Secure: Background Document for the Citizens' Inquiry into Peace and Security in Canada* (1991).

NORTH POLE See also THE NORTH

By the north pole, I do challenge thee. / I will not fight with a pole, like a northern man: I'll slash; I'll do it by the sword. I bepray you, let me borrow my arms again.

Punning reference to the North Pole in **William Shakespeare**'s play *Love's Labour's Lost* (c. 1594).

Q. Where can a man look south in all directions?

A. When he is standing at the North Pole.

Well-known conundrum first published by **Henry van Etten** in *Mathematical Recreations* (1624) as noted by David Wells in *The Penguin Book of Curious and Interesting Puzzles* (1992).

Occult teaching corroborates the popular tradition which asserts the existence of a fountain of life in the bowels of the earth and in the North Pole. It is the blood of the earth, the electro-magnetic current which circulates through all the arteries, and which is said to be found stored in the "navel" of the earth.

H.P. Blavatsky, theosophist, *The Secret Doctrine* (1885), II, Notes.

The pole at last!!!! The prize of 3 centuries. My dream and goal for 23 years. *Mine* at last! I cannot bring myself to realize it. It all seems so simple and commonplace.

Robert Peary, Arctic explorer, who trekked to the North Pole from Cape Columbia on Ellesmere Island with an African American black, Matt Henson, and two Eskimo guides, diary entry, 6 April 1909, *The North Pole* (1910).

What a cheerless spot to have aroused the ambitions of man for so many ages! Endless fields of purple snows, no life, no land, no spot to relieve the monotony of frost. We were the only pulsating creatures in a dead world of ice.

Dr. Frederick Cook, Arctic explorer, who with two Eskimo guides, may have attained the North Pole via Axel Heiberg Island on 21 April 1909, *My Attainment of the Pole* (1909).

That extraordinarily overrated abstraction, the Pole.

Wyndham Lewis, British artist, "Leviathan and the Canadian Ahab" (1946), *Canada: A Guide to the Peaceable Kingdom* (1970) edited by William Kilbourn.

All compasses point to Canada!

Dictum of versifier **J.S. (Joe) Wallace** who proposed it for the Centennial of Confederation, as noted by John Robert Colombo in "Canada's Banned Poet," *The Canadian Forum*, July 1960.

As the quest for the North Pole lost its grip on the popular imagination, Tibet would replace it as the next mysterious, but far more complex, closed land.

Peter Bishop, historian, *The Myth of Shangri-La: Tibet, Travel Writing and the Western Creation of Sacred Landscape* (1989).

NORTHERN LIGHTS See also THE NORTH

Superstition maintains that if the Aurora Borealis is seen in either Britain or America it is a portent of war. This happened in 1939 when the Northern Lights, as the display is also called, were seen as far south as London; and in America, just prior to the attack on Pearl Harbor, they were seen on three successive nights as far south as Cleveland, Ohio.

Peter Haining, English author and anthologist, *Superstitions* (1979).

NORTHWEST PASSAGE See also THE NORTH

I am mad north-north-west; when the wind is southerly, I know a hawk from a handsaw.

Speech of the Dane in **William Shakespeare**'s *Hamlet, Prince of Denmark* (c. 1601), a likely reference to the North-West Passage.

They forged the last link with their lives.

Inscription on the statue of Arctic explorer Sir John Franklin, who sought the Northwest Passage, in his native town, Spilsby, Lincolnshire, England, erected in 1855; it was unveiled following his disappearance and presumed death in the Eastern Arctic in 1847; the wording was suggested by his friend and biographer **Sir John Richardson**, as noted by Frances Joyce Woodward in *Portrait of Jane: A Life of Lady Franklin* (1951).

The quest for the North-West Passage is so extraordinary a phenomenon of the human spirit that, it seems, only the sense of glory can account for it: Man was for the last time in history "face to face with something commensurate to his capacity for wonder."

George Malcolm Thomson, British historian, concluding passage (with the quoted words of Sir Herbert Read), *The North-West Passage* (1975).

Ah, for just one time, I would take the Northwest Passage / To find the hand of Franklin reaching for the Beaufort Sea / Tracing one warm line through a land so wild and savage / And make a Northwest Passage to the sea.

Chorus of **Stan Rogers**' song "Northwest Passage" (1980), quoted by Chris Gudgeon in *An Unfinished Conversation: The Life and Music of Stan Rogers* (1993).

Every age but ours has had its El Dorado, its Happy Isles, or its North-West Passage to lure the adventurous into the unknown. A lifetime ago men could still dream of what might lie at the poles—but now the North Pole is the crossroads of the world.

Arthur C. Clarke, scientist and science-fiction author, *The Snows of Olympus: A Garden on Mars* (1994).

NORTHWEST TERRITORIES See also THE NORTH, NUNAVUT, YELLOWKNIFE

Now we have done better than Bjarni where this country is concerned—we at least have set foot on it. I shall give this country a name and call it *Helluland*.

Words attributed to the Norse explorer **Leif Ericsson** in *The Vinland Sagas: The Norse Discovery of America* (1965) translated from the Old Icelandic by Magnus Magnusson and Hermann Palsson. The word Helluland means "slab-land," and the tentative identification is Baffin Island, N.W.T.

The tidal current...had borne all the ships whose names are like jewels flashing in the night of time, from the *Golden Hind* returning with her round flanks full of treasure, to be visited by the Queen's Highness and thus pass out of the gigantic tale, to the *Erebus* and *Terror*, bound on other conquests—and that never returned. It had known the ships and the men.

Passage from **Joseph Conrad**'s novel *Heart of Darkness* (1902).

It was the borderline between the prosaic world, where things went by rule and rote and where all fitted to the human scale, and the world as God first made it out of chaos, which had no care for humanity.

Lines descriptive of the Northwest Territories from **John Buchan**'s novel *Sick Heart River* (1941).

Few have seen the cliffs of Baffin or the eskers of the tundra but we all live cheek by jowl with the wilderness; and all of us, I think, feel the empty and awesome presence of the North.

Pierre Berton, author and TV personality, writing an imaginary letter to Uncle Sam, *Why We Act like Canadians* (1983).

Within reach, yet beyond belief.

Advertising slogan of the **Northwest Territories**, *Canada's Northwest Territories: 1992 Explorers' Guide* (1991).

A Land Beyond Words

Inscription on a cairn on the highest point of Dogrib Rock, Northwest Territories, composed by **Rudy Wiebe** and others, as noted in his book *A Discovery of Strangers* (1994). He added: "En route, tracing as canoe will allow, Franklin's route of October 1821: Starvation Lake to Fort Enterprise 19 vii 1988 A University of Alberta-Canada Council Research Project." The novelist was a member of six-person trek: The Land, Air and Water Expedition of 1988, Edmonton, Alberta, to Obstruction Rapids, N.W.T.

It's simple to say. It's easy to spell. Bob is the same in everyone's language.

Steve Tomkins, bartender, principal sponsor of the movement to give the commonplace name Bob to the non-Nunavut part of the Northwest Territories, quoted by Lydia Hurst in *The Toronto Star*, 29 Dec. 1996.

Canada's Northwest Territories boasts a land mass a third the size of the United States, yet you could squeeze its population (of which aboriginals make up half) into a large stadium. Its climate is almost as inhospitable as that awaiting the first human colonists on Mars.

Sheldon Teitelbaum, correspondent, "The Call of the Wired," *Wired*, Nov. 1997.

Baffin Island lies four and a half hours northeast of Yellowknife by air. This makes it closer to Danish Greenland, a few hundred kilometres directly northeast, than to the nearest Canadian metropolis, Montreal, roughly 2,000 air kilometres to the south—in other words, as far away from Montreal as Miami Beach.

Sheldon Teitelbaum, correspondent, "The Call of the Wired," *Wired*, Nov. 1997.

NOVA SCOTIA See also ATLANTIC PROVINCES, CAPE BRETON ISLAND, HALIFAX, MARITIME PROVINCES

Neptune, if e'er thou hast thy favour cast / On

those whose lives upon thy waves are passed, / Good Neptune, grant us what we most desire, / Safe berth in friendly port, so thine Empire / May thereupon be known in countless regions / And soon be visited by all the nations.

Final stanza composed by **Marc Lescarbot**, French lawyer, poetaster, and sometime colonist at Port-Royal, from his celebratory verse "August 1606: Farewell to the Frenchmen Returning from New France to Gallic France" (1607) translated by F.R. Scott in *The Poetry of French Canada in Translation* (1970) edited by John Glassco.

May the building that shall rise from this foundation perpetuate the Loyalty and Liberality of the Province of Nova Scotia.

Sir George Prevost, Governor, dedicating the cornerstone of Province House, Halifax, N.S., 12 Aug. 1811, quoted by Elizabeth Pacey and Alvin Comiter in *Historic Halifax* (1988).

The name, Nova Scotia, has no meaning to the masses and is otherwise not a name we would have chosen. Acadia is a land of poetry and song.

Sir Adams George Archibald, Father of Confederation, address, Nova Scotia Historical Society, 1878, quoted by John Quinpool in *First Things in Acadia: The Birthplace of a Continent* (1936).

If God came here on Earth with us and asked if he could rest, / I'd take him to my Nova Scotia home, the place that I love best.

Lines from **Hank Snow**'s song "My Nova Scotia Home" (1950s), quoted in his obituary by Adrian Humphreys, *National Post*, 21 Dec. 1999.

It must be Nova Scotia; only there / does one see gabled wooden houses / painted that awful shade of brown. / The other houses, the bits that show, are white.

Lines from the poem "Poem" written by the American poet **Elizabeth Bishop** who in her youth in 1911–17 lived in Great Village, N.S., *The Complete Poems 1927–1979* (1983).

Greatest Tides. The greatest tides in the world occur in the Bay of Fundy, which separates Nova Scotia from Maine and the Canadian province of New Brunswick. Burncoat Head in the Minas Basin, Nova Scotia, has the greatest mean spring range with 47.5 feet, and an extreme range of 53.5 feet.

Norris and **Ross McWhirter**, editors, *Guinness Book of World Records* (10th ed., 1971).

We're proud of being what we are and where we are. Nova Scotia is the most magnificent anchorage on the Atlantic coast of North America. That's what her history and her future are all about.

Gerald A. Regan, Premier of Nova Scotia, quoted by Charles McCarry in *National Geographic Magazine*, March 1975.

I feel most real in Nova Scotia. That's where I feel like me to me.

Anne Murray, singer, quoted by David Livingstone in *Anne Murray: The Story So Far* (1981).

In Nova Scotia, Castang, they wait for Eskimo Nell, who comes once a year when the fleet's in.

Remark made to the police detective Castang in **Nicolas Freeling**'s crime novel *Wolfnight* (1982). Castang had assumed the identity of "Harold Greenpeace, Attaché de Director, The Bank of Nova Scotia, Paris."

Nova Scotia lies one time zone closer to England than most of North America....

Robert MacNeil, broadcaster and memoirist, *Wordstruck: A Memoir* (1989).

When you're a dynamo, the energy comes from an inner calmness. It was my Canadian past. My mother is Canadian, born in Nova Scotia. I spent a lot of time in Canada when I was young. I think my mystical leanings probably come from Nova Scotia.

Shirley MacLaine, entertainer and exponent of New Age thought, "People," *Maclean's*, 15 Aug. 1994.

No Nova Scotian lives more than fifty miles from the sea, and the great majority hug the coast.

David Swick, journalist, *Thunder and Ocean: Shambhala and Buddhism in Nova Scotia* (1996).

Nova Scotia is one of those noble places buffeted by man's indomitable yet hopeless desire for rapport with the sea.

Sam Orbaum, Montreal-raised Israeli columnist, "Travel," *The Jerusalem Post*, 28 June 1996.

Nova Scotia is connected with Tibet.... Personally, I regard this particular location, province, as a sacred place.

Chogyam Trungpa Rinpoche, Buddhist leader, remark adapted from his address in Halifax in 1984, as noted by David Swick in *Thunder and Ocean: Shambhala and Buddhism in Nova Scotia* (1996). In 1979, eight years before his death, Trungpa moved the world headquarters of his Tibetan Buddhist community from Denver, Colorado, to Halifax, N.S.

Our history is actually the story of a little buried nation—a nation almost at the level of independence before Canada was born; a people welded together by centuries of shared experience; a strikingly civilized community; a society which will endure and evolve on this rocky, salt-washed terrain even if Canada itself should dissolve.

Silver Donald Cameron, columnist, *The Halifax Herald*, 19 April 1998.

Since I live in Nova Scotia in July and August—one-sixth of the year—I have long maintained that one-sixth of my books should be counted as Canadian content.

Calvin Trillin, American essayist and summer resident, *The New York Times Magazine*, 12 July 1998.

NUCLEAR ARMS See also ATOMIC BOMB, ATOMIC ENERGY, NUCLEAR ENERGY

I never heard a convincing explanation of what that strong team of British nuclear scientists at Chalk River at the end of 1944 was supposed to be doing.... The obvious explanation of the presence of the strong British nuclear group in Montreal was that they were there as a listening post, to pick up whatever they could from the signs and portents, which was just what I had done myself.

Fred Hoyle, English scientist and novelist, recalling a visit in 1944 to the nuclear facilities at Chalk River, Ont., and Montreal, with respect to the Manhattan Project, *Home Is Where the Wind Blows: Chapters from a Cosmologist's Life* (1994).

We shall not, so long as we are pursuing the ways of disarmament, allow the extension of the nuclear family into Canada.... We do not intend to allow the spread of nuclear arms beyond the nations which now have them.

John G. Diefenbaker, Prime Minister, election speech, Brockville, Ont., 1962, as he recalled in the House of Commons, 25 Jan. 1963.

The fact that being eighteen years old and at the beginning of your life, you ponder the grave threat hanging over humanity, says a lot about you.

Konstantin Chernenko, Soviet President, open letter addressed to Laurie Piraux, a Calgary student whose social studies assignment required her to express her fears about the nuclear arms race in an unsolicited letter addressed to the Soviet President, who to everyone's surprise answered it on 23 Jan. 1985, quoted in *The Toronto Star* the following day.

If you were to fix radiation limits at levels that were really protective of human health, you couldn't get anybody to make bombs.

Rosalie Bertell, Grey Nun of the Sacred Heart and peace activist, interviewed in Toronto, 12 March 1986, quoted by Robert Del Tredici in *At Work in the Fields of the Bomb* (1987).

Can you tell me why there are fifty thousand nuclear weapons in the world? Do these weapons make any military sense?

Richard Handler, writer, *Canadian Institute for International Peace and Security Magazine*, Spring, 1987, quoted by Peter Gzowski in *The New Morningside Papers* (1987).

I believe that our land should be declared a nuclear-weapons-free zone, with absolutely no testing of nuclear arms by both sides, monitored by neutral countries, and that there should be a freeze on the production and testing of nuclear weapons.

Margaret Laurence, novelist, "My Final Hour" (1983), *Up and Doing: Canadian Women and Peace* (1989) edited by Janice Williamson and Deborah Gorham.

Remember your duty to humanity.

Joseph Rotblatt, British scientist, campaigner for the reduction of nuclear arms, and co-founder of the International Pugwash Conference in 1957, acceptance speech, Nobel Prize, Oslo, Norway, 10 Dec. 1995, quoted in *The Toronto Star* the following day. The first Pugwash Conference was hosted by Cyrus Eaton at his summer home at Pugwash, N.S., in July 1957.

NUCLEAR ENERGY See also ATOMIC ENERGY, NUCLEAR ARMS, NUCLEAR WINTER

Arriving in Montreal, Mr. Ehrenburg complimented this province as being the locale of two great cultures, English and French; then, to give an acid zest to his compliment he added—"two great cultures working in harmony together to produce—an atomic bomb." The irony, we feel, would have come with better grace if it came from the representative of a culture which had already discovered the atomic secrets but in the interests of morality had decided to abandon them.

A.M. Klein, poet, referring to Russian writer and Soviet apologist Ilya Ehrenburg who toured Canada, "In Defence of the Atom" (1964), *Beyond Sambation: Selected Essays and Editorials, 1928–1955* (1982) edited by M.W. Steinberg and Usher Caplan.

So the bad news about Darlington is that we are who we are. No society in human history ever willingly gave up power in either a literal or a metaphoric sense, so the prognosis is not good; in the meantime, if we don't like nuclear power, we had better start turning off some lights.

David Lees, journalist, "Living in the Nuclear Shadow," *Toronto Life*, Nov. 1989. The reference is to Ontario's Darlington Nuclear Generating Station, one of the world's largest, most expensive, and least productive.

Claiming nuclear production of energy is "clean" is like dieting but stuffing yourself with food between meals.

Rosalie Bertell, Grey Nun of the Sacred Heart and peace activist, "Radioactivity: No Immediate Danger?" *Ms.*, Sept.–Oct. 1991.

When you get right down to it, using a nuclear reactor to generate electricity is just another way to boil water for steam to spin the turbines. If someone tells you the nuclear core that contains the controlled fission process is called a calandria and it's Greek to you, you're right. It's the Greek word for kettle.

Advertisement for **Atomic Energy of Canada Limited** (AECL), *The Directory of Sources*, Summer 1992.

I'll give you my own theory: that the nuclear unit was operated over all those early years as some sort of special nuclear cult. I'm told this is not that unusual in utilities elsewhere in the world.

Bill Farlinger, Chairman of Ontario Hydro, admitting to poor management of the nuclear power-generating facility division, 13 Aug. 1997, quoted by William Walker in *The Toronto Star* the following day.

NUCLEAR WINTER See also NUCLEAR ENERGY

A single night below freezing is enough to destroy the Asian rice crop. A 2 to 30C average local temperature drop is sufficient to destroy all wheat production in Canada, and 3 to 40 all grain production.

Carl Sagan and **Richard Turco**, scientists, *A Path Where No Man Thought* (1990).

NUDITY

The stripper puts on her audience by taking off her clothes.

Marshall McLuhan, communications pioneer, *Take Today: The Executive as Dropout* (1972) with Barrington Nevitt.

Mr. Diefenbaker, once faced with an audience of angry, disrobing women, said: "You can't scare me. I was brought up on a farm." It was thought that he lost conservative female votes by this quip.

Nicholas Monsarrat, author, *Life Is a Four-Letter Word: Volume II-Breaking Out* (1970). It is said Diefenbaker faced a group of Doukhobor women who protested policies by disrobing in public. When Mackenzie King was asked what he would do in such circumstances in the 1940s, he said, "I would call for the leader of the Opposition."

Few Canadian nudes are energetic, pathetic or ecstatic.

Jerrold Morris, art dealer and critic, rendering a judgement on the inner life of nude figures in art, *The Nude in Canadian Painting* (1972).

Canadians now seem to be leading the way in pagan fantasy. More power to them!

Camille Paglia, American cultural critic and columnist, referring to a recent decision by the Toronto authorities to permit women to go topless in public, "Ask Camille," Internet magazine "Salon," 10 June 1997.

It is acceptable to publicly display graphic photographs of willing models, but not acceptable to sunbathe topless. We know why, of course. Photographs of half-naked women are considered artistic; half-naked people on the beach are vulgar. Such are the strange values of our prim society.

Catherine Ford, writer, "To Top It Off...," *enRoute*, June 1998.

NUNAVUT See also THE NORTH, NORTHWEST TERRITORIES, YUKON TERRITORY

Our collective agreement is far more than a simple exercise in cartography. It is, at its core, an important act of nation-building.

Brian Mulroney, Prime Minister, signing the agreement to transfer title of much of the Eastern Arctic to its Inuit inhabitants and to create the Territory of Nunavut by the year 1999, Iqualuit, 25 May 1993, quoted in *The Toronto Star* the following day.

At a time when people are attempting to dismantle Canada, the people of Nunavut are trying to complete it.

The Nunavut Implementation Commission, quoted in *The Canadian Global Almanac 1996* (1995).

The whole Nunavut saga is a magnificent symbol of Canada's flexible democracy at its best. The result is a government build around the Inuit people, so that it is truly their land now.

J.L. Granatstein and **Norman Hillmer**, historians, "Canada's Century," *Maclean's*, 1 July 1999.

NURTURING

So I've been reticent to celebrate female nurturing in case I wind up adding to this disavowal of women's experience. For me, nurturing has been a furtive and guilty pleasure, delicious, dangerous and doubly intoxicating because the needs of a child, a friend or a lover so often seem in competition with the time required to write a book and the labour involved is never commensurate with the recognition you get for it.

Susan Swan, novelist, *The Globe and Mail*, 8 June 1991

NUTRITION

No substance known to medicine has so many healing properties.

Evan Shute, physician and proponent of Vitamin E therapy, quoted by Bill Trent in *Weekend Magazine*, 27 May 1972.

OAS See ORGANIZATION OF AMERICAN STATES

OATH OF ALLEGIANCE See also CITIZENSHIP

I swear/affirm that I will be faithful and bear true allegiance to Her Majesty Queen Elizabeth the Second, Queen of Canada, her heirs and successors, according to law and that I will faithfully observe the laws of Canada and fulfill my duties as a Canadian citizen.

Wording of the **Oath of Allegiance** published in *The Globe and Mail,* 27 Jan. 1996, when suggestions were that the Minister of Citizenship would drop references to the Queen.

OBSCENITY

For the purposes of this Act, any publication a dominant characteristic of which is the undue exploitation of sex, or of sex and any one or more of the following subjects, namely, crime, horror, cruelty and violence, shall be deemed to be obscene.

Definition of obscenity from the Criminal Code, R.S., C.C-34, s.1959; 1993, c.46, s.1.

OBSOLESCENCE

You know, there's an old saying in the business world: If it works, it's obsolete. And it's only when a thing has become obsolete that everybody is sufficiently familiar with it to make it work.

Marshall McLuhan, communications pioneer, CBC-TV, 1970, quoted by Paul Benedetti and Nancy DeHart in *Forward through the Rearview Mirror* (1996).

OCEANS

At the top look down, look down, and see / My broad enchanted land, / Where South is love and Death lies North, / And Oceans on either hand.

Last verse of the poem "Nocturne" composed by radio actor **J. Frank Willis** and read each week on the CBC Radio musical program *Atlantic Nocturne* (later *Nocturne*), which premiered in 1951, quoted by Morris Wolfe in *Fifty Years of Radio* (1986).

Canada has the longest ocean coastline of any country in the world.

Jon Lien, specialist in the behaviour of whales, "Eau Canada! A New Marine-Parks System," *Endangered Spaces: The Future for Canada's Wilderness* (1989) edited by Monte Hummel.

The ocean's bottom is more interesting than the moon's behind.

Attributed to Newfoundland biologist **Frederick Aldrich** by Maura Hanrahan in "Natural Resources," *The Globe and Mail,* 30 Aug. 1994.

OCTOBER CRISIS See also TERRORISM, WAR MEASURES ACT

The Front de Libération du Québec is not a messiah, nor a modern-day Robin Hood. It is a group of Quebec workers who have decided to use every means to make sure that the people of Quebec take control of their destiny.

Preamble to "The FLQ Manifesto" read under duress on the late-evening TV news programs, in French on Société Radio-Canada and in English on the Canadian Broadcasting Corporation, 8 Oct. 1970. Three days earlier, the **Front de Libération du Quebec** (FLQ) had kidnapped British trade commissioner James Cross.

Trudeau: Yes, well there are a lot of bleeding hearts around who just don't like to see people with helmets and guns. All I can say is, go on and bleed, but it is more important to keep law and order in the society than to be worried about weak-kneed people who don't like the looks of—

Ralfe: At any cost? How far would you go with that? How far would you extend that?

Trudeau: Well, just watch me.... Yes, I think the society must take every means at its disposal to defend itself against the emergence of a parallel power which defies the elected power in this country and I think that goes at any distance.

Pierre Elliott Trudeau, Prime Minister, interviewed by CBC-TV reporter Tim Ralfe, Parliament Hill, Ottawa, 13 Oct. 1970. It was the second week of the October Crisis and Trudeau answered the interviewer's question about the measures the government would take to deal with the emergency. Reproduced in *The Toronto Star* the following day. The War Measures Act was invoked on 16 Oct. 1970.

This is the hour of the last chance for democratic change. Quebec no longer has a government. The bit of country over which we had any control has been swept away by the first hard blow.

René Lévesque, Quebec opposition leader, address protesting the implementation of the War Measures Act, Paul Sauvé Arena, Montreal, 19 Oct. 1970, quoted in *The Toronto Star* the following day and by John Saywell in *The Rise of the Parti Québécois 1967–76* (1977).

In the face of the arrogance of the federal government and its lackey Bourassa, in the face of their obvious bad faith, the FLQ has therefore decided to act.

Pierre Laporte, minister of unemployment and assimilation, has been executed at 6:18 tonight by the Dieppe cell (Royal 22nd). You will find the body in the trunk of the green Chevrolet (9J-2420) at the St. Hubert base, entry no. 2.

We shall overcome.

FLQ

Handwritten communiqué found outside Place des Arts, 17 Oct. 1970, published in *The Globe and Mail* two days later; reproduced by John Saywell in *October 70: A Documentary Narrative* (1971).

What the October Crisis taught me was that it is absolutely essential to have, at the helm of state, a very firm hand, one that sets a course and never alters.

Pierre Elliott Trudeau, Prime Minister during the October Crisis of 1970, *Memoirs* (1993).

One could retort quite curtly that the Canadian prime minister who suspended civil liberties in 1970, opening the way to imprisonment without cause for a mere crime of opinion, 500 citizens including some poets, without any charges being laid, and with no recourse, and who condoned 3,000 searches without warrant, is in no position to give lessons in democracy.

Lucien Bouchard, open letter, referring to former Prime Minister Pierre Elliott Trudeau, published in *The Montreal Gazette*, 10 Feb. 1996, and in *The Toronto Star*, 13 Feb. 1996.

OGDEN, FRANK See also FUTURE

The world's greatest information collector.

Description of futurologist Frank Ogden by scientist and author **Arthur C. Clarke**, quoted by Patrick Cotter in "Keeping Up with Tomorrow," *Chief Information Officer Journal*, March–April 1993.

Although I am a futurist today, if I don't change tomorrow I will be a historian.

Frank Ogden, futurologist, observation, 1 Feb. 1993.

My idea of long-range planning is lunch.

Frank Ogden, futurologist, *Ogdenisms: The Frank Ogden Quote Book* (1994).

I try to keep one foot in the Silicon Valley, the other in the jungle.

Frank Ogden, futurologist, quoted by John Shoesmith in *Computing Canada*, 14 March 1995.

In times of panic, chaos or rapid change, the bizarre rapidly becomes acceptable.

Frank Ogden, futurologist, *Dr. Tomorrow's Future World* (1999).

OGOPOGO

I'm looking for the Ogopogo, / The bunny-hugging Ogopogo. / His mother was a mutton, his father was a whale. / I'm going to put a little bit of salt on his tail. / I'm looking for the Ogopogo.

Local version of the English music-hall number, written by Ralph Butler, adapted by **H.F. Beattie** of the Okanagan Valley on 23 Aug. 1926. "Bunny-hugging" refers to a 1920s dance and "his mother was a mutton" alludes to an eye-witness's description of Ogopogo as having a sheep's head. Noted by Mary Moon in *Ogopogo: The Okanagan Mystery* (1977).

OIL INDUSTRY See also ENERGY

Oil is a non-renewable resource. To turn a popular phrase upside down: When you use it, you lose it.

Arden R. Haynes, Chairman, Imperial Oil, address, Empire Club of Canada, 26 Jan. 1989.

In northern Alberta lies the world's largest single reserve of crude oil, a mammoth patch of energy the size of England, roughly 1.7 trillion barrels of it.

Diane Forrest, journalist, "Unearthing Alberta's Buried Treasure," *Imperial Oil Review*, Summer 1991.

After all, oil is a commodity we consume on our way to buy more while driving on a petroleum-based surface.

John Ralston Saul, author, *The Doubter's Companion: A Dictionary of Aggressive Common Sense* (1994).

I find it illogical that there is not one single economist at the University of Alberta who specializes in the petroleum industry. Equally incredible is that most of the information the government employs to formulate public petroleum policy comes from the industry itself.

Mel Hurtig, nationalist, address, awards dinner, Edmonton, 17 Sept. 1997.

OKA STANDOFF See also LAND CLAIMS, PROTEST

A band of terrorists.

Brian Mulroney, Prime Minister, referring to the members of the Warrior Society of the Mohawks who took part in the Oka Standoff, news conference, Ottawa, 28 Aug. 1990, quoted in *The Toronto Star* the following day.

Canada has now lived through a crisis of a kind and magnitude it has perhaps never seen before. Its armed forces were set to move in against native people. An awful rift almost opened up in Canadian society. The long-term consequences no one could have been sure about. But one thing is certain. Canada has moved further down the road towards social unrest and racial hatred.

Phil Fontaine, leader, Assembly of Manitoba Chiefs, on the Oka Standoff, quoted in the *Winnipeg Free Press*, 31 Aug. 1990.

Are you ready to die?

Ronald "Lasagna" Cross, Mohawk Warrior of mixed Mohawk and Italian ancestry, resident of New York City, confronting and taunting an imperturbable soldier, Private Patrick Cloutier of the Canadian Armed Forces, outside the treatment centre, Kanesatake, Que., 1 Sept. 1990; the words of the nationally televised encounter were quoted by Rick Hornung in *One Nation: Under the Gun* (1991) who added, "Eventually, Lasagna walked away, but for the media and the Canadian public, that confrontation remained the quintessential scene of the treatment-centre standoff."

The tragedy at Oka and the collapse of the Meech Lake Accord have forced Canadians to think about what kind of a nation they live in and what kind of a society they want theirs to be.

David Maybury-Lewis, anthropologist, *Millennium: Tribal Wisdom and the Modern World* (1992).

OLYMPIC GAMES See also SPORTS

I was just like any kid of twenty. I was simply bewildered by it all. I didn't like running. Oh, I was so glad to get out of it all.

Percy Williams, champion runner, recalling his feelings when he won the 100-metre race at the 1928 Amsterdam Olympics, 30 July 1928, and two days later won the 200-metre event, thereby qualifying as "the world's fastest human." Quoted by Ray Gardner in "How Percy Williams Swept the Olympics" in *Maclean's Canada: Portrait of a Country* (1960) edited by Leslie F. Hannon.

The Montreal Olympics can no more have a deficit than a man can have a baby.

Jean Drapeau, Mayor of Montreal, announcing the "self-financing" 1976 Olympic budget of $310 million at a press conference in Montreal, 29 Jan. Thereafter, Aislin published his celebrated cartoon in *The Montreal Gazette* which showed the pregnant Mayor on the phone yelling, "'Ello, Morgentaler?" Aislin is the pen-name of cartoonist Terry Mosher; Dr. Henry Morgentaler is known for his advocacy of abortion on demand.

Today, in the midst of impressive, moving Olympic pageantry featuring heads of state, politicians and official rhetoric about amateurism, competition, team spirit and national pride, let's remember what these Games are really about—mankind in a contest with space, time, gravity and each other.

Jack Ludwig, novelist, on the opening of the 22nd Olympiad in Montreal, *The Canadian*, 17 July 1976.

A chinook could cause great havoc here.

Gordon Taylor, competition organizer, checking the weather forecast for the first day of the snow-sculpting contest of the 1988 Calgary Olympics, quoted by Brian Brennan in *The Calgary Herald*, 2 March 1988.

Montreal is still paying forty million a year for two weeks of the Olympics.

Louis Dudek, aphorist, "Epigrams," *Small Perfect Things* (1991).

To be a Canadian at the Olympics is to know the art of losing gracefully.

Jim Proudfoot, sports columnist, *The Toronto Star*, 30 July 1992.

This is the most Olympic thing someone can do. It's more than anything the honour of it all.... I've been world champion four times but I've never really felt this Canadian before.

Kurt Browning, figure-skating champion, carrying the Canadian flag at the opening ceremonies of the 1994 Winter Olympics in Lillehammer, Norway. Quoted by Jim Morris in the *Winnipeg Free Press*, 12 Feb. 1994.

I wanted to perform and sell magic moments to people.

Jean-Luc Brassard, champion skier, referring to his childhood dream of joining a circus, recalled after he won a gold medal in freestyle skiing (moguls) at the 1994 Winter Olympics in Lillehammer, Norway, quoted by Randy Starkman in *The Toronto Star*, 17 Feb. 1994.

I didn't do anything.

Myriam Bédard, champion biathlete, first Canadian woman to win two gold medals at a single Winter Olympics, after claiming her second gold at the 1994 Winter Olympics at Lillehammer, Norway, quoted in *Maclean's*, 7 March 1994.

I'm Jamaican, man. I'm Jamaican first. You've got to understand that. That's where I was born. That's home. You can never take that away from me. I'm a Jamaican-born Canadian sprinter.

Donovan Bailey, sprinter, 100-metre gold medalist and world record breaker at the 1996 Atlanta Summer Olympic Games, 27 July 1996, quoted by Chris Young in *The Toronto Star* the following day.

Everybody wants to win all the time and it is tough when you do not win. It is the worst feeling in the world. And that is the way we feel right now. There are no words to describe it.

Wayne Gretzky, hockey personality, speaking to the press following Team Canada's 2-1 shootout loss to the Czech Republic, 1998 Winter Olympics, Nagano, Japan, 20 Feb. 1998, quoted by Alan Adams in *The Toronto Star* the following day.

ONTARIO See also OTTAWA, TORONTO

I leave you to imagine whether we suffered in the midst of this abundance in the earthly paradise of Canada; I call it so, because there is assuredly no more beautiful region in all Canada.

Early reference to the region of North America now known as Ontario by the French Sulpician missionary **René de Galinée** who explored the Great Lakes area in 1669–70 and raised a cross at the site of Port Dover, Ont.; so described by him in *Voyage de MM Dollier & Galinée* (1878) translated by James H. Coyne in 1903.

I've had enough of this inert / Ontario, this eunuch sea / And pastured fenced nonentity....

Lines from **Earle Birney**'s poem "Eagle Island" (1938), *The Collected Poems of Earle Birney* (1975).

Give us a place to stand / And a place to grow / And call this land / Ontario.

Chorus of the song "Ontar-i-ar-i-ar-io" which was loudly sung throughout the documentary film *A Place to Stand* directed by Christopher Chapman for the Ontario Pavilion at Expo 67 in Montreal. Words by **Richard Morris**, tune by Dolores Claman.

Ontario must be more than a place to stand; it must be a place in which to stand tall, to be proud of one's own heritage, to be secure in one's own culture.

William G. Davis, Premier of Ontario, address on multiculturalism, referring to the film *A Place to Stand* produced for Expo 67's Ontario, 4 May 1977, quoted in *Annual Report of the Ontario Advisory Council on Multiculturalism 1977–1978* (1978).

Quebec will be as French as Ontario is English.

Attributed to Quebec Cabinet Minister **Camille Laurin** and "principal architect of Quebec's language law"; Bill 101 was passed by the Quebec National Assembly on 26 Aug. 1977.

Southern Ontario, formerly one of the most brutally inarticulate communities in human history, now finds itself in possession of James Reaney, Alice Munro, Robertson Davies, Margaret Laurence, Al Purdy and a dozen other people. The community as a whole has not grasped the real importance of this fact.

Northrop Frye, cultural critic, address, Options Conference, University of Toronto, 15 Oct. 1977, quoted by Daniel Stoffman in *The Toronto Star*, 17 Oct. 1977.

Ontario is the hardest province to grasp. Partly because of its size and the diversities of its dimensions. And because it represents the standard against which the other regions measure their differences. And because for many, Ontario *is* Canada.

Heather Menzies, journalist, *The Railroad's Not Enough: Canada Now* (1978).

Ontario, is there any place you'd rather be?

Advertising campaign created for the Ontario Ministry of Tourism. It was written by Claus Mohr of the **McLauchlan, Mohr** agency and introduced in the 1960s. Quoted by David Parry in *The Canadian*, 10 Jan. 1976.

Yours to Discover

Advertising campaign created for the Province of Ontario by Dianne Axmith of **Camp Associates**, Toronto, launched in May 1980.

When knowledge is absent, theory abounds. Why would anyone study Ontario? Happy times have no historian.

Desmond Morton, historian, Foreword, *The Happy Warrior: Political Memoirs of Donald C. MacDonald* (1988).

For most of the time, I never thought of myself as an Ontarian. It seemed like a soupy concept, an oddly awkward word. In my mind, I was always a Canadian.

Christina McCall, author, "Ontario on My Mind," "Bank of Montreal: A Portrait of Canada," *Saturday Night*, May 1992.

Ontario has for decades been the part of Canada that dared not speak its name. The country was based on the premise that everyone else could speak ill of us in Ontario and at the same time this inherently wealthy place would continue to bankroll Canada.

Bob Rae, Ontario Premier, addressing a conference of educators, Toronto, 8 Nov. 1993, quoted by Martin Mittelstaedt in *The Globe and Mail* the following day.

Ontario has been, and in some measure still is, a compound of aggressiveness, conservatism, and the conviction that its values should be the model for the rest of Canada.

James Struthers, commentator, description of the province in the Series Introduction to *The Limits of Affluence: Welfare in Ontario, 1920–70* (1994).

I like the idea of southwestern Ontario being a separate little principality. After all, it's as large as many European countries, and larger than some. It could be called "Sowesto."

James Reaney, poet and playwright, interviewed by Philip Marchand in *The Toronto Star*, 26 Oct. 1997.

Whether you see Ontario as primarily a province of Canada or as one of 60 states in the continental grid, it's heartland country. Ontario expects to be at the centre of North American political evolution, not on the fringes, not on any cutting edge.

Michael Bliss, historian, "Heartland Dynasties," *National Post*, 4 June 1999.

OPERA See also MUSIC

If you can feel in a vast audience that even one person knows, understands and appreciates the study you have put upon a role to make it true to life, you are rewarded for your pains.

Kathleen Howard, opera singer, born at Niagara Falls, Ont., *Confessions of an Opera Singer* (1918).

With this production of *Elektra* the Canadian Opera Company introduces the projection of "surtitles" on the proscenium arch above the stage. The English surtitles were prepared by Sonya Friedman.

Note from the program for the COC's production of Richard Strauss's *Elektra*, O'Keefe Centre, Toronto, 21 Jan. 1983. Surtitles were introduced to the world of opera by the Canadian Opera Company. They are now internationally employed for the simultaneous translation of foreign-language theatrical and musical productions of all sorts.

Opera is about sex, love, and death. I'm just trying to be accurate.

Robert Carsen, opera conductor, referring specifically to nudity on stage, quoted by Philip Anson, "Opera's Man of the Hour," *The Globe and Mail*, 8 Nov. 1999.

OPINION See also OPINION POLLS

A man has reached the age of discretion when he is willing to admit that other men may have opinions different from his without being fools.

Bob Edwards, publisher, *The Eye Opener,* 19 Oct. 1912, *The Wit and Wisdom of Bob Edwards* (1976) edited by Hugh Dempsey.

To me, he who never changes his mind is as despicable as he who never changes his shirt.

Attributed to Prime Minister **Sir Wilfrid Laurier** when in the House of Commons in Oct. 1917 a Liberal crossed the floor to join Borden's Union Government, only to be dismissed as a "turncoat," much to Sir Wilfrid's dismay.

The public doesn't know what it wants, or thinks it wants, until it gets it.

Harry J. Boyle, broadcaster and author, "Responsibility in Broadcasting," *Osgoode Hall Law Journal,* Volume 8, Number 1, 1970.

People do not possess opinions; they are possessed by them.

Robin Skelton, poet and aphorist, *A Devious Dictionary* (1991).

I'm not smart enough to have an opinion, but if I were, I'm sure I'd have yours.

Crad Kilodney, author and aphorist, characteristic remark, July 1993.

OPINION POLLS See also OPINION, PREDICTION & PROPHECY

Disasters, malfunctions, misfortunes cannot individually be brought to the attention of the policy-maker in advance of their occurrence. Trends, tendencies and dispositions may be.

James Eayrs, political economist, *Fate and Will in Foreign Policy* (1967).

Public opinion does not exist. It is created at the moment you begin questioning.

Normand Bourdon, commentator, "Que penser des sondages d'opinion?" *Perspectives,* 4 Aug. 1973.

I used to have a rule that if a question had more than seventeen words it was bad.

Donald Monk, President, Canadian Facts Ltd., market-research firm, quoted by Claire Hoy in *Margin of Error: Pollsters and the Manipulation of Canadian Politics* (1989).

Tory leader Joe Clark often picked up on the "Government by Goldfarb" theme to indicate the Liberals paid more attention to polls than to doing what they thought was right. But then the Tories were no different, and the wonder is that "Decision by Decima" hasn't become the slogan of current critics of the Conservative government.

Claire Hoy, journalist and author, referring to Liberal and Conservative pollsters, *Margin of Error: Pollsters and the Manipulation of Canadian Politics* (1989).

I can envision a new game-show program, with a winning award of $100,000, to the single Canadian who can prove not to have been interviewed by anyone by July 1.

Allan Fotheringham, columnist, *Maclean's,* 31 Dec. 1991.

We answer more public opinion polls but vote less.

Thelma McCormack, sociologist, "The Problem with Polls," *The Canadian Forum,* July–Aug. 1992.

What people have come to share is less and less based on exchange of immediately personal stories, and more and more on mythic participation in a common fate captured in numbers. This is the legacy of polling and numbers research.

John Fekete, philosopher, *Moral Panic: Biopolitics Rising* (2nd ed., 1995).

The only poll that's important is the one that's held on election day.

Gary Filmon, Manitoba Premier, interviewed on CBC-TV's *National News,* 20 April 1995.

OPPORTUNITY

Every crisis is an opportunity.

Harry Browne, investment adviser, *You Can Profit from a Monetary Crisis* (1974).

Canadians have such a head start, just being here. They could have been born in Bulgaria, or some corrupt society. Instead, they were born with everything—education, opportunity, expectations.

Peter Munk, entrepreneur, quoted by Joan Sutton in *The Toronto Star,* 19 Jan. 1980.

People say we're opportunistic, and I hope so. I think that's a compliment.

Samuel Belzberg, corporate head and corporate raider, accepting the 1985 Businessman of the Year Award from the Vancouver Chamber of Commerce, quoted in *The Globe and Mail's Report on Business Magazine*, Sept. 1990.

You miss one hundred percent of shots you don't take.

Attributed to hockey personality **Wayne Gretzky** in June 1996.

Not very long ago, many Canadians feared that for the first time in Canadian history, their children would not have the same opportunities or the same standard of living they had known. Today, we can see that Canada's children, the first of what might be called "the global generation," will experience a wholly new richness of choice and opportunity.

Matthew W. Barrett, CEO, Bank of Montreal, address, 7 May 1997, *National and Global Perspectives*, Summer 1997.

OPPOSITION See also GOVERNMENT

A well organized and vocal minority will always prevail over a disorganized and irresolute majority.

Chris Axworthy, M.P., quoted in *Last Rights*, Feb.–March 1992.

Opposition creates the illusion that there is good policy and bad policy, and that political life is simply a matter of choosing the good over the bad, in a relatively painless way. Rhetorical dragons are slain with rhetorical swords, and even drowned in a flood of eloquent wounds.

Bob Rae, former Ontario Premier, *From Protest to Power: Personal Reflections on a Life in Politics* (1996).

You might be alone at first, but you won't be alone at the end of the day if your arguments are valuable and you know how to express them.

Stéphane Dion, Minister of Intergovernmental Affairs, quoted by Daniel LeBlanc, "In Ottawa," *The Globe and Mail*, 4 Dec. 1999.

OPTIMISM

Cynicism is merely the art of seeing things as they are, instead of as they ought to be.

Bob Edwards, publisher, *The Eye Opener*, 14 March 1914, *The Wit and Wisdom of Bob Edwards* (1976) edited by Hugh Dempsey.

I'm somewhat optimistic. I see little hope for mankind.

Louis Dudek, poet and aphorist, entry in 1960s, *Notebooks 1960–1994* (1994).

Optimism is the best working hypothesis.

Attributed by **John Peters Humphrey**, principle author of the original draft of the UN Declaration of Human Rights, quoted at the time of his death, 14 March 1995.

ORDER & DISORDER

As a matter of fact there is only one perfect order: that of cemeteries. The dead never demand anything and they enjoy their equality in silence.

Jean-Louis Gagnon, commentator, *La mort d'un nègre suivi de la fin des haricots* (1961) quoted by Claude Janelle in *Citations québécoises modernes* (1976).

Our Canada is the most orderly land in the world (with the exception of Disneyland).

Gordon Gibson, columnist, "Commentary," *The Globe and Mail*, 18 Feb. 1997.

ORDER OF CANADA See also AWARDS & HONOURS

It seems to me very characteristic of Canada that its highest Order should have for its motto: "Looking for a better country." The quotation is from the New Testament, where the better country really is the City of God, but the feeling it expresses has more mundane contexts.

Northrop Frye, cultural critic, "Conclusion to a Literary History of Canada" (1965), *The Bush Garden: Essays on the Canadian Imagination* (1971). The Order of Canada was established 1 July 1967; its Latin motto is taken from the Epistle to the Hebrews, 11:16: *Desiderantes meliorem patriam.*

Ceremonial and insignia, properly understood and properly applied, are surely the hallmarks of a really human and civilized community, society and country. They are brakes on egotism, accolades of merits, dykes against disorder.

Conrad Swan, York Herald of Arms-in-Ordinary

to Her Majesty Queen Elizabeth II, first Canadian to be appointed to this office established in Britain in 1484, address, Empire Club of Canada, Toronto, 3 April 1975.

ORGANIZATION OF AMERICAN STATES

Why any Canadian with anything better than a cabbage perched on the top of his neck wants us to join the Organization of American States is beyond me. It would be the perfect way to lose friends and influence people the wrong way.

Eugene Forsey, constitutional authority, discussion membership in the OAS, speech, 10 Feb. 1976, reprinted by Warren Clements in *The Globe and Mail*, 6 June 1979.

ORIGINALITY

We Canadians never recognize originality because we have no real use for it. We *fire* the man who thinks up something new.

Brian Moore, novelist, resident of Canada from 1948 to 1960, quoted by William French in *The Globe and Mail*, 14 June 1975.

The trouble with recognizing originality is that it doesn't look familiar.

Dennis Burton, artist, diary entry, quoted in *The Globe and Mail*, 29 June 1978.

OTTAWA See also ONTARIO, PARLIAMENT

Ottawa is a sub-arctic lumber-village converted by royal mandate into a political cockpit.

Goldwin Smith, essayist, quoted by Edwin C. Guillet in *Pioneer Inns and Taverns* (1956).

The ghosts of the old chiefs must surely chuckle when they note that the name by which Canada has called her capital and the centre of her political life, Ottawa, is an Indian name which signifies "buying and selling."

Rupert Brooke, English poet and traveller, *Letters from America* (1916).

Ottawa remains in its soul a small town—not quite like the old, small settled communities of the East, but more a lumbering settlement in the Ottawa Valley. That spirit still pervades the place.

Charles Ritchie, diplomat and diarist, entry for 18 Jan. 1950, *Diplomatic Passport: More Undiplomatic Diaries, 1947–1962* (1981).

Start from the North Pole; strike a bead for Lake Ontario; and the first spot where the glacier ceases and vegetation begins—that's Ottawa!

Wilfrid Eggleston, newspaperman, quoting an unidentified American, *The Queen's Choice: A Story of Canada's Capital* (1961).

The sun rises over the Chateau Laurier and sets beyond the Supreme Court Building.

Don Braid, commentator, quoted by David J. Bercuson and Barry Cooper in *Deconfederation: Canada without Quebec* (1991).

I dislike Ottawa as a city. I wish the capital were somewhere else, preferably Montreal.

Richard Hatfield, New Brunswick Premier, remark made in Aug. 1983, quoted by Jonathan Ferguson in *The Toronto Star*, 27 April 1991.

"What's the difference between yogurt and Ottawa?" Answer: "More culture in yogurt"—wit from a time capsule.

B.W. Powe, commentator, *The Solitary Outlaw* (1987).

When I went up to Ottawa, / I met a man who sang tra-la. / "What did you do with the country today?" / "I gave it away to the U.S.A."

Lines from a poem in **Dennis Lee**'s *The Difficulty of Living on Other Planets* (1987).

No wonder the Canadian political system shows such a strong tendency toward sycophancy the higher one rises. The only way to get applause in this town is to pay for it.

Roy MacGregor, columnist, *Ottawa Citizen*, 3 June 1988.

And a further note, a found poem from my spell-check: "Stopped at: Ottawa. Replacement: Oneiric."

Eric Korn, columnist and antiquarian book dealer, referring to the "Ottawa-avoidance" of his computer's spell-checker, *The Times Literary Supplement*, 15 June 1990.

Ottawa is the second coldest national capital, next to Ulaanbaatar, Mongolia.

David Phillips, climatologist, *The Day Niagara Falls Ran Dry!: Canadian Weather Facts and Trivia* (1993).

How far is it to Ottawa? / Three score miles and ten. / Can I get there by CPR? / Yes, but not back again.

Verse titled "Is Anybody There?" written by **Jim Parr**, as cited by J.G. Keogh in Letters to the Editor, *The Globe and Mail*, 1 Dec. 1993.

Men in Ottawa have nothing hard in their pants except cellular phones.

Attributed to NDP leader **Audrey McLaughlin** by Peter C. Newman in "The Nation's Business," *Maclean's*, 19 June 1995.

Though I love New York, I disapprove of it. Dreary as Ottawa was, it was in the end a better place than New York. Canadians believe that happiness is living in a just society; they will not sing that Yankee song that capitalism is happiness, capitalism is freedom. Canadians have a lively sense of decency and human dignity. Though no Canadian can afford freshly squeezed orange juice, every Canadian can have juice made up from concentrate. The lack of luxury is meant to coincide with the absence of misery. It doesn't work altogether, but the idea is worth defending.

Germaine Greer, Australian-born feminist and author, describing cities on a book-promotion and lecture tour, "Letter from New York," *The Times Literary Supplement*, 7 Aug. 1999.

OWNERSHIP, FOREIGN

No other country in the world would sell off so much ownership and control of its natural resources to foreigners. Mr. Mulroney and Mr. Epp would probably sell Parliament Hill if they got the right price.

Mel Hurtig, nationalist, referring to Prime Minister Brian Mulroney and Energy Minister Jake Epp's decision to allow U.S. investors to increase their holdings in Canadian gas and oil companies, quoted by Jim Morris in the *Winnipeg Free Press*, 26 March 1992.

We have long deserved to be in the *Guinness Book of Records* for having the highest level of foreign ownership of any of the industrialized countries in the world.

Mel Watkins, economist, "The Business of Culture," *The Canadian Forum*, May 1994.

P

PACIFIC RIM

Canadians should recognize the Pacific Region not as the Far East but as the New West.

Pierre Elliott Trudeau, Prime Minister, remark made in 1970, quoted by William Dalton in *The Globe and Mail*, 12 May 1990.

The Pacific is our future.... For Canada, our trade with the Pacific is bigger than our trade with the European continent by fifty percent. The Pacific is getting more and more important for all of Canada.

Jean Chrétien, Prime Minister, press conference, Canberra, Australia, 15 Nov. 1995, quoted by David Vienneau in *The Toronto Star* the following day.

PACIFISM See PEACE

PAIN & SUFFERING

Shared pain is lessened, and shared joy is increased. What more do you need to know?

Lines from **Jeanne Robinson** and **Spider Robinson**'s novel *Stardance* (1979).

Pain is, *can*, be useful. But only if you use it. You have to be *willing* to suffer. You have to accept it. This principle of accepting pain can work, even at the dentist, during childbirth, bursitis, sinusitis, even the death of people you love.

Elizabeth Smart, novelist and diarist, "How to Mend a Broken Heart" (Feb. 1982), *Autobiographies* (1987) edited by Christina Burridge.

Suffering is real. But it's caused by wanting something that's not real. We want a stable sense of self, but the world doesn't support it.

Tim Ward, traveller, *What the Buddha Never Taught* (1990).

God comes through the wound.

Marion Woodman, analyst, quoted by Neil McKenty in *The Inside Story* (1997).

The truth, if it is to be believed, must be authored by those who have suffered its consequences.

Michael Ignatieff, author, "Articles of Faith," *Index on Censorship*, Sept.–Oct. 1996, as reprinted in "Readings," *Harper's*, March 1997.

Pain is a condition of life, not a reason for death.

Eric Neufeld, Crown prosecutor in the Robert Latimer case of Battleford, Sask., which involved euthanasia, quoted by Scott Feschuk and David Roberts in *The Globe and Mail*, 7 Nov. 1997.

PAINTING See also ART & ARTISTS, CULTURE, GROUP OF SEVEN

If you can't paint it with the back of a broom, it is not worth doing. Work from the shoulder, not the fingertips.

Maxims of the painter and teacher **Carl Schaefer**, as recalled by the wildlife artist Robert Bateman, address, Empire Club of Canada, Toronto, 13 Nov. 1986.

Whatever I think of, I dismember.

Jack Shadbolt, painter, known for image recreation, quoted by Stephen Godfrey in *The Globe and Mail*, 2 June 1988.

PARAPSYCHOLOGY See also BELIEF, PSYCHICAL RESEARCH

Personally, I do not accept ESP for a moment, because it does not make sense. My external criteria, both of physics and of physiology, say that ESP is not a fact despite the behavioural evidence that has been reported.

D.O. Hebb, psychologist, referring to the statistical studies of Extrasensory Perception carried out by J.B. Rhine, "The Role of Neurological Ideas in Psychology," *Journal of Personality*, No. 20, 1951.

The world is wide and there is much in it, and the mind is deep. Psychical research for all that anyone can say to the contrary may be as necessary in terms of insight as any other study, and may, in the end be more harmless and edifying.

A.R.G. Owen, scientist and parapsychologist, and **Victor Sims**, newspaperman, *Science and the Spook: Eight Strange Cases of Haunting* (1971).

The main purpose of this book is to suggest that many anomalous experiences may be amenable to examination in terms of normal psychological processes, without recourse to such variables as "special powers," visitors from outer space, voodoo spells, or toxic substances in the water supply.

Graham Reed, psychologist, Foreword, *The Psychology of Anomalous Experience: A Cognitive Approach* (2nd ed., 1988).

For example, there have been experiments in ESP and telepathy which may have established the fact that some human beings possess such powers. They certainly established the fact that the majority of people either do not possess them at all or possess them in an erratic, unreliable, and very largely useless form.

Northrop Frye, cultural critic, "Literary and Mechanical Models" (1989), *The Eternal Act of Creation: Essays, 1979–1990* (1993) edited by Robert D. Denham.

PARENTHOOD See also FAMILY

A woman never stops to consider how very uninteresting her children would be if they were some other woman's.

Bob Edwards, publisher, *The Eye Opener,* 9 Aug. 1919.

If you don't talk back to your parents they'll never learn anything.

Don Harron, comic, quoted by Martha Harron in *A Parent Contradiction* (1988).

Fathering a boy is just the start of being a father to a boy.

Maurus E. Mallon, aphorist, *Compendulum* (1995).

PARIZEAU, JACQUES See also PARTI QUÉBÉCOIS, POLITICIANS

We had already torn the sheet in half. The only solution appeared to be to rip it all the way. When I boarded the train at Windsor station, I was a federalist. When I descended in Banff, I was a separatist.

Jacques Parizeau, Parti Québécois leader, characteristic remark, quoted by Barry Came in "The Private Parizeau," *Maclean's,* 12 Sept. 1994. The enlightenment occurred on the train in 1967 (some accounts say 1968). Planning to deliver a lecture on federalism, Parizeau ended up delivering one on separatism. At the time he was an economic adviser to Premier Daniel Johnson, as noted by Robert McKenzie in *The Toronto Star,* 13 Sept. 1994.

Just what is Parizeau smoking? He's like the adolescent who hates his parents and wants to move out of his house to get his freedom but not unless his parents pay the rent, give him his allowance, assume half his debts and buy him a car. Give me a break.

Diane Francis, columnist, "The Insiders," *The Financial Post,* 16 Dec. 1991.

We are going to settle this in 1995. We are going to give ourselves a country.

Jacques Parizeau, leader of the Parti Québécois, prior to the provincial election, 12 Sept. 1994, as quoted by Clyde H. Farnsworth in *The New York Times,* 11 Sept. 1994.

Like lobsters thrown in boiling water.

Remark attributed to Quebec Premier **Jacques Parizeau** at a private meeting of the ambassadors of fifteen European Union countries, German Embassy, Ottawa, 13 June 1995. The remark compared the fate of Quebecers following a Yes vote in the forthcoming referendum to that of lobsters. The resulting controversy—*l'affaire des homards*—gave rise to jokes about the "tempest in the lobster pot" and "How would you like your Péquiste today, grilled, steamed, or thermidor?" Chantal Hébert broke the story in *La Presse,* 11 July 1995. She wrote, "After a Yes, Quebecers will be like lobsters, Parizeau told a group of European ambassadors to Ottawa." Paul Wells of *The Montreal Gazette* on 12 July 1995 explained that "a lobster pot is not a cooking vessel but a wood trap with a one-way gate: an animal that crawls in, on the seabed, cannot get out. If Parizeau did say that, the denials would amount to merely a statement that Parizeau had never mentioned boiling water." On July 11, Quebec's Deputy Premier Bernard Landry denied that the remark had been made. Parizeau himself was unavailable for comment, as were all fifteen ambassadors. It seems likely that Parizeau compared Quebecers after a Yes vote in the referendum to lobsters being caught but not being boiled.

It's true we are beaten, it's true. But by what, basically? By money and the ethnic vote.

Jacques Parizeau, Quebec Premier, nationally televised concession speech, Palais de Congrès, Montreal, concerning the defeat of the second Quebec Referendum, 30 Oct. 1995. Quoted by Robert McKenzie in *The Toronto Star* the following day.

By Jove!

Characteristic exclamation of one-time Quebec Premier **Jacques Parizeau**, said to date back to student days at the London School of Economics, as noted by William Walker in *The Toronto Star*, 1 Nov. 1995.

Quebec is standing tall. The people of Quebec, by its majority vote yesterday, has just affirmed to the world that it exists. This affirmation, serene and democratic, cannot be erased by anything or anyone.

Jacques Parizeau, Quebec Premier, "The Speech Jacques Parizeau Never Got to Give," *The Globe and Mail*, 23 Feb. 1996. In an act of hubris that went awry, flushed with confidence that the sovereignists would win the forthcoming referendum, Premier Parizeau prepared and videotaped a victory speech a week or two prior to the second Quebec Referendum on 30 Oct. 1995, which the sovereignists narrowly lost. Parizeau resigned as Premier and the speech was broadcast on 12 Feb. 1996 and then published, a bric-à-brac about what might have been.

He'll be around longer than Lucien Bouchard.

Terry Mosher, cartoonist known as Aislin, quoted by Anthony Jenkins in "Person, Place, Thing," *The Globe and Mail*, 3 Jan. 1998.

PARKS See also NATURE, ROCKY MOUNTAINS

Fifty Switzerlands in One

Description of the Rocky Mountains in the pamphlet *Fifty Switzerlands in One: Banff the Beautiful, Canada's National Park* (1923) written by **N.K. Luxton**.

In fact there is one spot in North America where drainage is split among three oceans, and from this spot—at The Snow Dome in the icefields where Banff and Jasper National Parks come together—your cup of tea could be spilled to flow eventually into the Arctic Ocean, the Atlantic Ocean, and the Pacific Ocean.

David M. Baird, writer, *Banff National Park: How Nature Carved its Splendour* (1968).

Why, in Canada, can the federal government designate twenty per cent of the land mass for future parks, but not have the same political will to designate twenty per cent of the total land mass of Canada for Indian people? Why the double standard?

Ovide Mercredi, Cree lawyer, National Chief of the Assembly of First Nations, quoted by André Picard in *The Globe and Mail*, 6 Nov. 1991.

If I were the king of the world I would turn Canada, the whole country, into an international park. An international ecological mega-garden. That would be the best possible future for Canada.

Tomson Highway, playwright, "What's Next?" *Saturday Night*, Dec. 1999–Jan. 2000.

PARLIAMENT See also GOVERNMENT, HOUSE OF COMMONS, OTTAWA, PARLIAMENT HILL, POLITICS, SENATE

Some hon. Members: Hear, hear!
Some hon. Members: Oh, oh!

Yeah and nay and their euphemisms employed by the reporters for Hansard, the official record of proceedings of the Senate and the House of Commons, for approval and disapproval respectively.

Farmers will give their Members of Parliament wide scope, as long as they remember the price of oats.

Attributed in so many words to CCF leader **T.C. (Tommy) Douglas** in the 1950s by Warren Caragata in *Maclean's*, 28 Feb. 1994.

I greet you as your Queen. Together we constitute the Parliament of Canada.

Elizabeth II, Queen of Canada, first reigning monarch to open the Canadian Parliament, Ottawa, 1957. Speech from the Throne, 1 Feb. 1958, joint meeting of Senate and the House of Commons.

The perfect parliament / would include / delegates from / the living, / the unborn / and the dead.

Alden Nowlan, poet and aphorist, "Scratchings," *I'm a Stranger Here Myself* (1974).

When you come to Parliament on your first day, you wonder how you ever got here. After that, you wonder how the other 263 Members got here.

Attributed to Prime Minister **John G. Diefenbaker** by Robert Shelley in *The Great Canadian Joke Book* (1976).

PARLIAMENT HILL See also PARLIAMENT

Goddess, Maiden, Mother, Crone.... In you, through you, I banish all forces of evil that fetter and chain and bind those who serve us in this place, elected and non-elected.

Robin Skelton, poet and witch, performing the Ritual of Healing and Blessing at the foot of Parliament Hill, Ottawa, 21 June 1990, as quoted by John Robert Colombo in *Mysteries of Ontario* (1999). Skelton, an author as well as a practitioner of Wicca, was incensed that the Mulroney administration would impose the Goods and Services Tax on books. Three years later, almost to the day, there was a new Prime Minister.

PARTIES, POLITICAL See POLITICAL PARTIES

PARTI QUÉBÉCOIS See also BOUCHARD, LUCIEN; LÉVESQUE, RENÉ; PARIZEAU, JACQUES; QUEBEC, SEPARATISM

English-speaking Canadians will have to face the fact that if Canada is to continue to exist, there must be true partnership, and that partnership must be worked out as between equals.

André Laurendeau and **A. Davidson Dutton**, commissioners, *Preliminary Report of the Royal Commission on Bilingualism and Biculturalism* (1965). This appearance of the notion of "between equals" may have inspired René Lévesque to adopt "Equal to Equal" as the slogan of the Parti Québécois for the Referendum of 1980, although Lévesque said it was his own idea.

I never thought I could be as proud to be a Quebecker as I am tonight.... We're not a minor people. We're maybe something like a great people.

René Lévesque, founding leader of the Parti Québécois, speaking as Quebec's Premier-designate, victory speech, Montreal, 15 Nov. 1976. The next day the cartoonist Aislin drew for *The Montreal Gazette* the image of a surprised Lévesque saying, "O.K., everybody, take a Valium!" The "proud-to-be-a-Quebecker" reference was recalled by Prime Minister Trudeau following the outcome of the Quebec referendum on sovereignty-association, 20 May 1980.

Politically, this is probably the most beautiful and perhaps the greatest night in the history of Québec.

René Lévesque, Quebec premier-elect, *La Presse*, 16 Nov. 1976, *Quotations from René Lévesque* (1977) edited by Jean Côté and Marcel Chaput, translated by Robert Guy Scully and Jacqueline Perrault.

The Parti Québécois wants to create its own country out of the pocketbooks of the rest of us.

Howard Galganov, civil rights activist, interviewed by Michael Enright on CBC Radio's *As It Happens*, 13 Sept. 1996.

Basically, this party is not a party. It is organized hope.

Jacques Parizeau, retiring as Quebec Premier and leader of the Parti Québécois, final speech as leader, news conference, 27 Jan. 1996, quoted by Rhéal Séguin in *The Globe and Mail*, 29 Jan. 1996.

Their platform has two plans only: referendum and separation.

Jean Charest, federal Conservative leader, agreeing to contest the Quebec provincial Liberal leadership, address, Sherbrooke, 26 March 1998, quoted in *The Toronto Star* the following day.

PARTITION See also CANADA & QUEBEC, REFERENDA, SECESSION, SEPARATISM, SOVEREIGNTY, SOVEREIGNTY-ASSOCIATION

In the first place, English Canada should accept separation only if Quebec leaves Confederation as it entered it, with exactly the same boundaries that it had in 1867—minus, of course, the territory of Labrador, which was awarded to Newfoundland by the Privy Council's decision of 1927.

Donald G. Creighton, historian, "Beyond the Referendum" (1977), *The Passionate Observer: Selected Writings* (1980). This is an early expression of the "partition" theory of the 1990s, relished in English Canada, rejected in French Canada.

Who Gets Ungava?

Rhetorical question asked in the booklet *Who Gets Ungava?* (1991) issued by lawyer **David Varty** about the title and fate of territories transferred by the federal government to the Quebec government in 1898 and 1912 in the event of Quebec's secession.

When Quebec leaves Canada it surrenders all territory it gained while it was part of Canada.

David Jay Bercuson and **Barry Cooper**, historian and political scientist, referring in particular to Rupert's Land, *Deconfederation: Canada without Quebec* (1991).

To those who will say that a majority of a people has the right to secede, others will reply that nothing permits one to reserve for oneself the title of a people or a nation; and if Canada is divisible then Quebec is too, and that if a minority within Canada has the right to remove itself from Canada, then a minority in Quebec has the right to remove itself from a secession that it doesn't want.

Stéphane Dion, newly appointed Minister of Intergovernmental Affairs, address for *Cité Libre* magazine in Montreal, Jan. 1994, quoted by Jeffrey Simpson in *The Globe and Mail*, 27 Jan. 1996.

If Quebeckers have a right to the integrity of their territory, then certainly the Crees' right to the integrity of our territory cannot be denied.

Matthew Coon Come, Grand Chief of the Crees, address delivered to Crees meeting in Quebec, printed in *The Globe and Mail*, 26 Sept. 1995.

Canada is divisible because it is not a real country. There are two peoples, two nations and two territories and this one is ours. It will never, never be partitioned.

Lucien Bouchard, Quebec Premier designate, news conference in Montreal, 27 Jan. 1996, quoted by Robert McKenzie in *The Toronto Star* the following day.

I am very well aware that Canada is a very real country for the people in this room and right across Canada.

Lucien Bouchard, Quebec Premier, address to anglophone Quebeckers, Centaur Theatre, 11 March 1996, quoted by Sandra Contenta in *The Toronto Star* the following day.

Before sovereignty, it is not possible. And after sovereignty, it will be too late. We call that aggression. *Tough luck*. There is no reason for which the territory of Quebec can be hacked to bits.

Jacques Parizeau, former Quebec Premier, address, CEGEP Edouard Montpetit, Longueuil, Que., 21 May 1997, quoted by Eric Siblin in *The Montreal Gazette* the following day.

PARTNERSHIP

I believe that it's only through teamwork and partnership that positive change can be effectively managed.

Susan Thompson, Winnipeg's first woman mayor, quoted by Radha Krishnan Thampi in the *Winnipeg Free Press*, 4 Nov. 1992.

PAST See also HERITAGE, TIME, TRADITION

We share a past but not a history, a situation which seems to put the future very much in doubt.

Daniel Francis, commentator, *National Dreams: Myth, Memory and Canadian History* (1971).

We always talk about ourselves as a country with a great future, but we never talk about ourselves as a country with a sort of living past.

Robertson Davies, man-of-letters, interviewed by Silver Donald Cameron in 1971, *Conversations with Robertson Davies* (1989) edited by J. Madison Davis.

At one and the same time never has so much money been put into the organized study of the past and never has the past had less meaning in our lives.

George Grant, philosopher, "Research in the Humanities" (1979), *Technology and Justice* (1986).

A nation that repudiates or distorts its past runs a grave danger of forefeiting its future.

Donald G. Creighton, historian, *The Passionate Observer: Selected Writings* (1980).

Every experience is a recognition of having had it an instant earlier. It follows that the past is the sole source of knowledge, even though it extends up to the present moment.

Northrop Frye, cultural critic, *The Double Vision: Language and Meaning in Religion* (1991).

A people who have no collective past can have no collective future.

Richard Gwyn, columnist and author, *Nationalism without Walls: The Unbearable Lightness of Being Canadian* (1995).

Conservatives falsify the past, socialists falsify the future, and liberals falsify the present, so someone once said. It may even be true—in most countries. Canada is different. Ours is a nation where everyone—liberal, socialist, and conservative—seems to be engaged in an unthinking conspiracy to eliminate Canada's past.

J.L. Granatstein, historian, *Who Killed Canadian History?* (1998).

PATIENCE

The things that come to the man who waits are seldom the things he waited for.

Bob Edwards, publisher, *The Eye Opener*, 27 Jan. 1912.

I can't wait / to be patient.

Robert Priest, aphorist, *Time Release Poems* (1997).

PATRIOTISM See also NATIONALISM

I love France that gave us life; I love England that gave us freedom; but Canada, my country, my native land, holds first place in my heart.

Sir Wilfrid Laurier, address in Paris, France, 2 Aug. 1897, quoted by Robert Prévost in *Petit dictionnaire des citations québécoises* (1988).

We are swayed by no patriotic sentiments that might unite our diverse provincial interests in the common cause of our country. Our politics are a game of grab.

Sara Jeannette Duncan, novelist and essayist, article in *The Week*, 30 Sept. 1886, *Sara Jeannette Duncan: Selected Journalism* (1978) edited by Thomas E. Tausky.

Patriotism is a natural, almost familial virtue, easy-going when it is satisfied, but embittered when frustrated; it then tends toward politics and becomes nationalism.

Jacques Ferron, physician and author, *Historiettes* (1969).

Sometimes it seems that people of nations / outside my own country's boundaries are dancing / and shouting in the streets for joy / at their great good fortune in being citizens / of whatever it is they are citizens of

Lines from **Al Purdy**'s poem "Home Thoughts," *The Collected Poems of Al Purdy* (1986) edited by Russell Brown.

Cause if you don't believe your country / Should come before yourself, / You can better serve your country / By living somewhere else.

Lines from **Stompin' Tom Connors**' title song on the 1992 album *Believe in Your Country*, quoted by Malcolm McNeil in *The Globe and Mail*, 9 June 1992.

Atlantic to Pacific / Canada is Terrific

Words on the bumpersticker issued to promote the **Army, Air Force, and Navy Veterans of Canada,** noted in Toronto, Dec. 1992.

The thing that makes me proudest of being a Canadian is that I don't have to be proud of being a Canadian.

Brian Fawcett, writer, responding to a question about patriotism directed to him as a panelist, Vancouver International Writers' Festival, as noted by Stan Persky in *The Globe and Mail*, 11 Dec. 1993.

If I have learned anything in a lifetime of studying Canada, it is that our low-key, diffident style masks an intense love for the country and its institutions.

Michael Bliss, historian, "Massive Backlash," *The Toronto Star*, 22 Sept. 1995.

PATRONAGE See also CRIME, CORRUPTION

Let's face it, there's no whore like an old whore. If I'd been in Bryce's position I'd have been right in there with my nose in the public trough like the rest of them.... I hope this is all off the record. I'm taking the high road now.

Brian Mulroney, Conservative leader, campaign indiscretion committed during casual conversation aboard a flight between Montreal and Baie-Comeau, Que., referring to the ambassadorship accepted by Liberal Bryce Mackasey, 14 July 1984, quoted by Neil Macdonald in the *Ottawa Citizen* two days later.

What this party wants is two feet right in the trough.

Attributed to the late Conservative Senator **Allister H.G. Grosart** by L. Ian MacDonald in *The Montreal Gazette*, 24 July 1985.

PEACE See also PEACEKEEPING & PEACEMAKING

I, Dekanahwideh, and the Confederated Chiefs, now uproot the tallest pine tree, and into the cavity thereby made we cast all weapons of war. Into the depth of the earth, deep down into the underwater currents of water flowing to unknown regions, we cast all weapons of strife. We bury them from sight and we plant again the tree. Thus shall the Great Peace be established.

Words attributed to the half-mythical Iroquois statesman **Dekanahwideh** who, with the assistance of the half-legendary Ojibwa chief Hiawatha, founded the Great League of the Iroquois (the Five later Six Nations Confederacy) perhaps in the early 1450s near the present-day site of Kingston, Ont. The words come from Paul A.W. Wallace's *The White Roots of Peace* (1946), as do Dekanahwideh's final words to his people: "If the Great Peace should fail, call on my name in the bushes, and I will return."

I suggest that the common people of the country gain nothing by slaughtering the common people of any other country.

J.S. Woodsworth, M.P., declining to make unanimous the motion that a state of war exists with Germany through the invocation of the War Measures Act, House of Commons, 8 Sept. 1939.

I want to make the world of the "here and now" a more attractive place in which to live.

Cyrus Eaton, Canadian-born American industrialist and founder of the Pugwash Conferences, July 1957, quoted by Frank R. Joubin in *Not for Gold Alone: The Memoirs of a Prospector* (1986) written with D. McCormack Smyth.

The grim fact, however, is that we prepare for war like precocious giants and for peace like retarded pygmies.

Lester B. Pearson, President of the United Nations General Assembly, future Prime Minister, acceptance speech, Nobel Prize for Peace, Oslo, Norway, 11 Dec. 1957; *The Four Faces of Peace and the International Outlook* (1964) edited by Sherleigh G. Pierson.

True peace is a condition of harmony whereby all people are treated as responsible agents, as subjects of their own destiny, sharing common goals and promoting values recognized as meaningful by the majority.

Rémi J. De Roo, Bishop of Victoria, Moderator's Welcome, *The True North Strong & Free? Proceedings of a Public Inquiry into Canadian Defence Policy and Nuclear Arms* (1987), introduced by Mel Hurtig.

In the Mandarin language, the printed characters for peace may be translated as "rice in the mouth" and "a roof over your head"... there is a third meaning to the Chinese character—two hearts beating together in understanding, friendship, harmony, and love.

Lois Wilson, Christian activist, *Turning the World Upside Down: A Memoir* (1989).

Isaiah may imagine a state in which the lion lies down with the lamb, but we live in a state in which the lion could not exist without eating lambs, or something dietetically equivalent.

Northrop Frye, cultural critic, *The Double Vision: Language and Meaning in Religion* (1991).

The obvious fact that people of comfortable circumstance live peacefully together and those afflicted by poverty do not goes largely unnoticed.

John Kenneth Galbraith, essayist and economist, *The Culture of Contentment* (1992).

Better a rude peace than a civil war.

Maurus E. Mallon, aphorist, 18 Feb. 1993.

In the wrong hands even doves are dangerous.

Robert Priest, aphorist, *Time Release Poems* (1997).

Indeed, shoot an arrow of peace into the air and get a quiver of suspicions and paranoias in return.

Marq de Villiers, commentator, *Water* (1999).

PEACEKEEPING & PEACEMAKING

See also PEACE, UNITED NATIONS

The Rush-Bagot agreement in 1817... originally was intended to limit and to regulate the naval vessels of both countries on the great lakes. It has become one of the world's most effective disarmament agreements and is the basis for our much-hailed unfortified frontier.... The Rush-Bagot agreement was stated in less than 150 words.

Harry S. Truman, U.S. President, address, joint sitting of the Senate and the House of Commons, 11 June 1947.

The whole world knows what happens when a beautiful woman is shipwrecked on a desert island with an Englishman, a Frenchman, and an American. The only activity credible for a Canadian in their company would be standing on guard as a one-man peace-keeping force.

Passage from **John Metcalf**'s satiric novel *General Ludd* (1980).

Any Canadian disarmament proposal is a proposal to disarm someone else.

E.L.M. Burns, General, Canadian Forces, referring to such negotiations in the early 1960s, quoted by Richard and Sandra Gwyn in "The Politics of Peace," *Saturday Night*, May 1984.

Peacekeeping comes naturally to Canadians, as history has shown. The image of a Canadian soldier wearing his blue beret, standing watch at some lonely outpost in a strife-torn foreign land with binoculars at the ready, is very much an element of the modern Canadian mosaic, and a proud part of our national heritage.

Paul D. Manson, General and Chief of the Defence Staff, Department of National Defence, address, Empire Club of Canada, 17 Nov. 1988.

If I could have one wish, it would be to dump the entire population of Canada in Sarajevo for about six hours. Perhaps then they'd realize Canada is the best damn country in the world.

Lewis W. MacKenzie, Major-General, Canadian Armed Forces, speaking in Toronto, 31 Sept. 1992, quoted in *The Toronto Star* on 4 Oct. 1992.

If you are a commander of a U.N. mission, don't get in trouble after 5:00 p.m. or on the weekend. There is no one in the U.N. to answer the phone!

Lewis W. MacKenzie, Major-General, retired, UN Chief of Staff for peacekeeping in Sarajevo, Yugoslavia; press conference, Ottawa, 28 Jan 1993, quoted by Jeff Sallott in *The Globe and Mail* the next day. In his memoirs, *Peacekeeper: The Road to Sarajevo* (1993), MacKenzie explained: "Yes, I said that. My friends and former bosses in the UN were hurt and replied that, indeed, they had talked to me many times after 5:00 p.m. They were absolutely right, but they missed my point: They talked to me from home, a reception or, in some cases, from bed, but that isn't the same as being able to report to a command headquarters on a twenty-four-hour basis." He noted in a letter written after his retirement and printed in *The Globe and Mail*, 21 Jan. 1993, "Countries that have soldiers in charge seem, more often than not, to be the ones where democracy is but a flickering candle sitting in an open window with a forecast of rain."

The American bandleader John Philip Sousa would have been driven crazy by this country. How do you write a march for peacekeepers?

Joe Clark, former Prime Minister, Inter-American Press Association, Toronto, 19 Oct. 1994, quoted by Susan Delacourt in *The Globe and Mail* the following day.

There is no lack of demand for an armed force which can put a new roof on a hospital in the afternoon, deliver aid in the evening, and fight a pitched battle at dawn.

Nicholas Stethem, defence analyst, "Strategic Notebook," *Sitrep: Newsmagazine of the Royal Canadian Military Institute*, Nov. 1995.

In general, we have made too much of our role as peacekeepers. With rare exceptions, where there is peace there is no need for peacekeepers and where there is war they are of no use.

Conrad Black, publisher, "Taking Canada Seriously," *International Journal*, Winter 1997–98.

The UN is not a sovereign country. It's us. It's all of us. If the UN did not intervene, then by extension it is all of us. We all have a responsibility for the genocide in Rwanda.

Roméo Dallaire, Major-General, former commander of the Canadian peacekeeping contingent under UN command in Rwanda, Central Africa, appearing before a tribunal in Arusha, Tanzania, 25 Feb. 1998, quoted by Scott Straus in *The Globe and Mail* the following day.

I know God exists, because I shook the hand of the devil.

Roméo Dallaire, Major-General, quoted by Allan Thompson, "Haunted by Rwanda, Dallaire Leaves Army," *The Toronto Star*, 12 April 2000. The retiring General was referring to the requirement that he negotiate with Hutu leaders whose death squads had massacred rival Tutsis and were planning further massacres, a warning that took the form of the urgent message dated 11 Jan. 1994 sent to UN's defence chief General Maurice Baril but which went unheeded.

PENSIONS See also SOCIAL PROGRAMS

When governments indulge in policies that hurt large enterprises, they end up hurting pensioners!

Paul H. Leman, President, Alcan Aluminum Limited, interviewed by Dean Walker in *A Case for the Enterprise System* (1975).

Today's Generation X can say goodbye now to ever getting back a part of its Canada Pension Plan contributions.

Richard Gwyn, columnist, "Home & Away," *The Toronto Star*, 4 April 1993.

PEOPLE

Early to bed and early to rise...and you'll miss a lot of interesting people.

Flora MacDonald Denison, suffragette, characteristic remark made about 1915 to her son Merrill Denison, as recalled in Oct. 1972.

People really do think of themselves as specialized machines nowadays. "That's just my speed" is a most revealing remark.

Marshall McLuhan, communications pioneer, letter to Ezra Pound, 16 Aug. 1948, *Letters of Marshall McLuhan* (1987) edited by Matie Molinaro, Corinne McLuhan, and William Toye.

To me, everybody is the main character in his own life story. Anyone who goes out of his way to be eccentric or to be overwhelmingly noticeable is attempting, whether he knows it or not, to be the main character in somebody else's life.

Jack Hodgins, novelist, interviewed by Alan Twigg in *Strong Voices: Conversations with Fifty Canadian Authors* (1988).

I'm still searching for an answer to the question: "What are people for?"

Concluding line of *Webster! An Autobiography* (1990) by broadcaster **Jack Webster** (who credits novelist Kurt Vonnegut with the inspiration).

It's my life's theme—either we're all ordinary, or none of us are.

Carol Shields, novelist, quoted by Val Ross in *The Globe and Mail*, 19 April 1995. Shields' novel *The Stone Diaries* won the 1993 Governor General's Award, the 1994 U.S. National Book Critics Circle Award, and the 1995 Pulitzer Prize for Fiction.

PERFECTION

I don't think that perfection is possible or even, in psychological terms, desirable for human beings.

Robertson Davies, man-of-letters, interviewed by Tom Harpur in 1974, *Conversations with Robertson Davies* (1989) edited by J. Madison Davis.

To strive for perfection is to kill love because perfection does not recognize humanity.

Marion Woodman, analyst and author, *Addition to Perfection: The Still Unravished Bride* (1982).

I see a harsh world softened by a second look.

Christopher Chapman, photographer, quoted by Gerald Milne Moses in "Reflected Images," *Indigenous People* (1993) published by the Royal Canadian Academy of Arts.

PESSIMISM

Pessimism is a form of intellectual laziness.

Jean Drapeau, long-time Montreal Mayor, aphorism directed against critics of the Montreal Olympics, July 1975.

"Behind every silver lining there's a cloud," I tell myself when things threaten to get bright.

Glenn Gould, pianist, quoted by Tim Page in *The Glenn Gould Reader* (1984).

Pessimists are those who are always waiting for the rain. As for me, I'm already wet.

Leonard Cohen, poet and singer, quoted by Christof Graff in "Cohen in Nazi-Land," *Take This Waltz: A Celebration of Leonard Cohen* (1994) edited by Michael Fournier and Ken Norris.

PHILANTHROPY See also CHARITY, GIFTS & GIVING

Greater love hath no man than this: to present gifts after checking their tax deductibility.

John G. Diefenbaker, former Prime Minister, quoted by Bruce Garvey in *The Toronto Star*, 18 Sept. 1975.

No one can foreclose on good deeds.

Louis Mayzel, developer and philanthropist, quoted by William Koene in *Loyal She Remains: A Pictorial History of Ontario* (1984).

Giving money requires even more prescience, more imagination, more executive skill, than making it.

Francis Winspear, investor and philanthropist, quoted by Brian Laghi, "Lives Lived," *The Globe and Mail*, 10 Feb. 1997.

The funding environment has so changed that not every charity, because it's a good idea, can survive. You'll be giving less and less to more and more until finally you'll be doing nothing about everything.

Anne Golden, President of the United Way, quoted by Margaret Philp in *The Globe and Mail*, 16 March 1998.

To paraphrase a Hasidic saying: Take care of your own soul and of another person's body.

Dow Marmur, rabbi, Holy Blossom Temple, Toronto, *Choose Life: Thoughts on Grief and Growth* (1999).

PHILOSOPHY

It takes as long to become a man as it does to become a philosopher.

D.D. Cumming, aphorist, *Skookum Chuck Fables, Bits of History, Through the Microscope by Skookum Chuck* (1915).

I have often thought of giving up philosophy to become a novelist about Toronto (1900–1939).

George P. Grant, philosopher, remark made to anthologist John Robert Colombo in June 1975.

Philosophy books, alas, don't usually have painted illustrations. But the words of which they are made are, in a sense, illustrations of the thought. So the reader of a philosophy book is like someone who finds an illustrated book with the text erased. His task of reading is like trying to supply again the missing text, working from the pictures.

Graeme Nicholson, philosopher, *Seeing and Reading* (1984).

Personally, I have always found questions more interesting than answers, and probes more exciting than products. All of my work has been experimental in the sense of studying effects rather than causes, and perceptions rather than concepts.

Marshall McLuhan, communications pioneer, letter to John C. Polanyi, 4 Jan. 1974, *Letters of Marshall McLuhan* (1987) edited by Matie Molinaro, Corinne McLuhan, and William Toye.

The fact is, I do find philosophy interesting. That is because, on a good day, I find everything interesting, because everything is strange. Philosophy is no less interesting than other things. Taking the line of least resistance has sufficed to lead me through a career of inexhaustible fascination.

Francis Sparshott, philosopher, entry, *Contemporary Authors Autobiography Series* (1992), Volume 15.

George Parkin Grant / 1918–1988 / Out of the Shadows and Imaginings into the Truth

Inscription on the tombstone of the philosopher **George P. Grant**, Cemetery, Terrence Bay, N.S., noted by William Christian in *George Grant: A Biography* (1993).

PHOTOGRAPHY

Photographs are what happen when you and the subject meet, and you use a camera to describe the meeting.

Freeman Patterson, photographer, *Photography for the Joy of It* (1977).

Photography, from the moment of its invention, has been one of the most moving and powerful instruments of communication ever devised. It is not only a silent language, but also a visual language, an alphabet that the entire world can read.

Lorraine Monk, editor, Preface, *Photographs that Changed the World* (1989).

I've always been extremely sensitive to people's moods. It seems that I am blessed with being able to win their faith immediately.

Yousuf Karsh, portrait photographer, quoted by Ben Knight in *Coles' Booktalk*, Christmas 1992.

Every picture I've made is an experiment in the gray area between the theatrical and the real.

Jeff Wall, photo-artist, quoted by Vick Goldberg, "Photos that Lie—and Tell the Truth," *The New York Times*, 16 March 1997.

Photography revolutionized the world of communication. It has democratized societies. Everyone acquired ancestors.

Lorraine Monk, editor, *Canada: These Things We Hold Dear: An Album of Photographic Memories* (1999).

PIONEERS See also EXPLORATION

Now the class of people to whom this country is so admirably adapted are formed of the unlettered and industrious labourers and artisans. They feel no regret that the land they labour on has not been celebrated by the pen of the historian or the lay of the poet.

Catharine Parr Traill, pioneer settler and author, *The Backwoods of Canada: Being Letters from the Wife of an Emigrant Officer* (1836).

And if you could tough it, you was tough. And if you couldn't tough it, well, you passed away.

Lorne Saunders, Northern Ontario pioneer, quoted by Cathy Wismer in *Faces of the Old North* (1974).

From Doon and Shannon / From Clyde and Dee / They spend their poverty / Over the rich acres / They sowed their children / Broadcast upon the untested soil.

Inscription on the monument to the Scots pioneer settlers of the area, City Park, Newcastle, N.B., noted in Aug. 1991.

PLACES

See also CALGARY; CHARLOTTETOWN; CITIES & TOWNS; COMMUNITY; EDMONTON; FREDERICTON; HALIFAX; MONTREAL; NAMES; NIAGARA FALLS; OTTAWA; PLACES: COMMUNITIES; QUEBEC CITY; REGINA; SAINT JOHN; ST. JOHN'S; TORONTO; VANCOUVER; VICTORIA; WHITEHORSE; WINNIPEG; YELLOWKNIFE

Each corner of Canada stabs my soul for I am in love with the whole.

John Fisher, broadcaster, *John Fisher Reports: An Anthology of Radio Scripts* (1949).

My dear friend, there are other places in the world besides New York, and it should not surprise you to know that there are people who like to live in those places.

Kurt Weill, German-American composer, advice to Andrew Allan about 1955, when the Toronto-based radio producer was considering moving to New York City, quoted by Allan in *Andrew Allan: A Self-Portrait* (1974).

It's not really the places themselves that matter but what happens in them. I don't know what's going to happen here yet. Ask me later.

Speech of a character in **Paul Geddes**' futuristic, Ottawa-based thriller *The Ottawa Allegation* (1973).

The general place-name pattern of Canada offers an occasional poetic grotesquerie such as Medicine Hat and Moose Jaw. (Both of these are apparently translations of Indian names, but the reasons for their appellation are uncertain.) On the whole, however, the name-pattern is conservative and even monotonous as compared with that of the United States.

George R. Stewart, American philologist, *Names on the Globe* (1975).

Where is here?

Northrop Frye, cultural critic, asking a conundrum-like question, "Haunted by Lack of Ghosts," *The Canadian Imagination* (1977) edited by David Staines.

Why am I here? So I won't have to be / Elsewhere.

Lines from **David McFadden**'s poem "Pictograms by Starlight," *My Body Was Eaten by Dogs: Selected Poems* (1981) edited by George Bowering.

There is something abnormal about everywhere.

Mavis Gallant, Paris-based author, quoted by Wayne Grady in *Today*, 5 Dec. 1981.

It's difficult to love a city authors have ignored.

Jon Whyte, poet, "The Place Where Nothing Happens, *Calgary Magazine*, May 1983.

Ahead lies an open, wild landscape, pointed off on the maps with arresting and anomalous names: Brother John Glacier and Cape White Handkerchief. Navy Board Inlet, Teddy Bear Island, and the Zebra Cliffs. Dexterity Fiord, Saint Patrick Canyon, Starvation Cove. Eskimos hunt the ringed seal, still, in the broad bays of the Sons of the Clergy and Royal Astronomical Society islands.

Barry Lopez, naturalist, *Arctic Dreams: Imagination and Desire in a Northern Landscape* (1986).

The Toronto skyline is more beautiful to me than the familiar silhouette of Prague Castle. There is beauty everywhere on earth, but there is greater beauty in those places where one feels that sense of age which comes from no longer having to put off one's dreams until some improbable future....

Thoughts of Daniel Smiricky, Czech immigrant in Canada, in **Josef Skvorecky**'s novel *The Engineer of Human Souls* (1989).

Banff (adj.) Pertaining to, or descriptive of, that kind of facial expression which is impossible to achieve except when having a passport photograph taken. Manitoba (n.) A re-courtship ritual. The tentative and reluctant touching of spouses' toes in bed after a row. Vancouver (n.) One of those huge trucks with whirling brushes on the bottom used to clean streets.

Douglas Adams and **John Lloyd**, British satirists, *The Deeper Meaning of Liff* (1990). Liff, a neologism created by the authors, refers to "a common object or experience for which no word yet exists."

You may clasp the magic of this place merely by calling the names off a map. To travel Newfoundland is like wandering through an incantation. Bareneed, Gaultois, St. Bride's and Angel's Cove; Trepassey, Twillingate, L'Anse aux Meadows and Harbour Grace; Brigus and Burgeo; Blow Me Down and Bonavista; Isle aux Morts, Random Island and Little Heart's Ease; Comfort Cove and Cappahayden; Come by Chance and Carbonear: the place names of Newfoundland are the poetry of a scrupulous people, and the naming of the outports was a rebellion of delight against a grim tapestry of austerities we have, for the most part, forgotten.

Rex Murphy, broadcaster, convocation address, Memorial University, St. John's, Nfld., published in *The Globe and Mail*, 13 Nov. 1997.

PLACES: COMMUNITIES See also PLACES

Antigonish, N.S.

"How do you get from Vancouver to Antigonish?" is a riddle Antigonishers like to ask those from away. Answer: You head east on the Trans-Canada and turn left at the first stoplight.

Philip Milner, author and academic, *The Yankee Professor's Guide to Life in Nova Scotia* (1993).

Athabasca, Alta.

Though the distance from Calgary to Athabasca was little more than three hundred miles, the journey took a traveller to the borders of another world.

Description of the landscape of northern Alberta from English horror writer **Clive Barker**'s novel *Cabal* (1985).

Baddeck, N.S.

There was an inspiration in the air that one looks for rather in the mountains than on the sea-coast; it seemed like some new and gentle compound of sea-air and land-air, which was the perfection of breathing material.... There is a harmony of beauty about the Bras d'Or at Baddeck which is lacking in many scenes of more pretension.

Charles Dudley Warner, American traveller, *Baddeck, and That Sort of Thing* (1895). Warner's description of the Bras d'Or Lakes, Baddeck, Cape Breton Island, N.S., led Alexander Graham Bell to visit and then build his summer home.

Barren Lands, N.W.T.

Every day he was learning something in Barren Lands. In such places a man must learn or he will die.

Violet Clifton, biographer, referring to the experiences of her husband the world traveller Talbot Clifton in the *Barren Lands, The Book of Talbot* (1933).

Belle Isle, Que.

Gull against in the wind, in the windy straits / Of Belle Isle, or running on the Horn, / White feathers in the snow, the Gulf claims, / An old man driven by the Trades / To a sleepy corner.

Lines from **T.S. Eliot**'s poem *Gerontion* (1920) with a reference to the Strait of Belle Isle.

Belleville, Ont.

And this is a country where the young leave quickly / unwilling to know what their fathers know / or think the words their mothers do not say.

Lines from **Al Purdy**'s poem "The Country North of Belleville," *The Cariboo Horses* (1965).

Bracebridge, Ont.

Halfway to the North Pole

Wording on a sign in Bracebridge, Ont., midway between the Equator and the North Pole, according to the *Canadian Automobile Association's Tourbook: Ontario* (1994).

Bradford, Ont.

Bradford is a multi-dimensional doorway, a vortex to a parallel universe. My belief is that the vortex just recently opened, likely in the past thirty years.

Joyce Halfin, conference organizer, referring to

the so-called Bradford Triangle (the area that lies within the north-of-Toronto communities of Bradford, Uxbridge, and Aurora), quoted by Mark Bourrie in *The Toronto Star,* 13 March 1994.

Brantford, Ont.

I just remember Brantford as being this peaceful place, with acres of trees and farmland and beautiful scenery. It was actually very inspiring for me; it's probably why I later went into art.

Phil Hartman, Brantford-born comedian and actor, quoted by Andrew Ryan in *TV Guide,* 27 June 1998.

Brigus, Nfld.

I am a lonely American in this dismal little British colony.

Rockwell Kent, U.S. painter and illustrator who lived in Brigus, Conception Bay, Nfld., during World War II until he was deported as an alleged German spy, *It's Me, O Lord* (1955).

Buctouche, N.B.

This was my first home. It was my home all through my growing-up years. I now live in Bermuda, but my heart is still here, here in New Brunswick, here in Buctouche.

K.C. Irving, businessman, accepting an award from the Buctouche Rotary Club in 1988, quoted in his obituary, *The Vancouver Sun,* 14 Dec. 1992.

Cambridge, Ont.

Everybody comes from somewhere. Me, I come from Galt.

Peter Gzowski, essayist and broadcaster, a native of Galt, now part of Cambridge, Ont., "The Centre of the Universe," *Selected Columns from Canadian Living* (1993).

Cape Tennyson, N.W.T.

Captain Inglefield has called an Arctic promontory Cape Tennyson after me which makes me as proud as Lucifer. So don't let your major-domo look down upon me!

Alfred Lord Tennyson, England's poet-laureate, postscript to a letter to his brother Frederick Tennyson, 9 Dec. 1852, quoted by Francis Spufford, "Traces in the Snow," *The Times Literary Supplement,* 18 July 1995. Cape Tennyson is on the southeastern tip of Ellesmere Island, N.W.T.

Carillon, Que.

Since the Frenchmen have been here / They have called it Sault-Marie; / But that is a name for priests, / And not for you and me.

Lines from **Robert Louis Stevenson**'s narrative poem *Ticonderoga: A Legend of the West Highlands* (1887), reprinted in 1923 with the editorial note that explains "Sault-Marie" is a misnomer for Carillon, Que.

Chalk River, Ont.

Never before had such a talented group of scientists been brought together in Canada with a single purpose.

C.J. Mackenzie, atomic scientist, referring to the contingent of Canadian, British, French, and other foreign scientists brought together at the Montreal Lab (Université de Montréal) and at Chalk River in the early 1940s, *Early Years of Nuclear Energy Research in Canada* (AECL, May, 1980).

Churchill, Man.

As new lands are opened up and the wilderness becomes populated with new millions, Canada may well be the site of the greatest city in the world. New York already shows signs of decay and it may be replaced by a new world centre of commerce now a tiny port named after a man who will become a legendary hero—Churchill.

Cecil Williams, theosophist and lecturer, "Canada's Glorious Future," *The Canadian Theosophist,* Sept.–Oct. 1955.

Climax, Sask.

Climax—Home of Rape

Wording on the road sign recalled "some years ago" (prior to renaming rapeseed canola) by antiquarian bookseller Tom Williams, communication, 1998.

Cobalt, Ont.

For we'll sing a little song of Cobalt, / If you don't live there it's your fault. / Oh, you Cobalt, where the big gin rickies flow, / Where all the silver comes from, / And you live a life and then some, / Oh, you Cobalt, you're the best old town I know.

Chorus of the traditional lyric "The Cobalt Song" (1910) reproduced by J.B. Macdougall in *Two Thousand Miles of Gold* (1946).

Cobourg, Ont.

As a child, I seldom lived more than a few months in any one place. Sometimes the months stretched into a year, but not often. I am told we paused long enough in Cobourg, Canada, for me to get born and be duly christened Leila von Koerber.

Marie Dressler, stage and screen star, born in Cobourg, Ont., in 1869, *My Own Story* (1934) as told to Mildred Harrington.

Collingwood, Ont.

I've just come back from Collingwood. They don't believe in Canada anymore!

John Turner, Liberal leader, addressing former minister Lloyd Axworthy about the views of business people he met while vacationing at Collingwood on Georgian Bay, quoted by Lawrence Martin in *Pledge of Allegiance* (1993).

Consort, Alta.

She's done more to put us on the map than anybody and we are extremely pleased with her. She's still personable and very approachable and her preferred lifestyle is insignificant to me.

Marlene Arp, Mayor of Consort, Alta., a village southeast of Edmonton, birthplace of k.d. Lang, referring to the "torch and twang" singer's sexual orientation, quoted by Ted Clarke in *The Toronto Sun*, 1 June 1992.

Crabtree Mills, Que.

O country doubly split! One way / Tugged eastward; one to the U.S.A.; / One way tugged deep toward silver Rome; / One way scotched stubborn here at home; / What panacea for your ills? (Le Sacré Coeur de Crabtree Mills.)

Verse written by **Theodore Spencer** included by F.R. Scott and A.J.M. Smith in *The Blasted Pine: An Anthology of Satire, Invective and Disrespectful Verse Chiefly by Canadian Writers* (1957, 1967).

Creston, B.C.

There were more churches and chapels than shops in Creston, I believe....

Freya Stark, English traveller and author, *Beyond Euphrates: Autobiography, 1928–1933* (1951). She wintered in B.C.'s Kootenay Valley in 1928–29.

Dawson, Y.T.

Dawson City... is, in my view, the single most interesting community in Canada. But then I am biased, for it was here that I was raised, in the days when the river was a broad highway linking it to the outside world, when the familiar sound of the steamboat whistle echoed over the rounded hills, when the chut-chug of the paddle-wheel was as soothing as a lullaby and when no ghosts yet haunted the river of my childhood.

Pierre Berton, author, "River of Ghosts" (1994), reprinted in *Worth Repeating: A Literary Resurrection: 1948–1994* (1998).

Dildo, Nfld.

A few more meanings are: (1) a West Indian tree; (2) a chorus or refrain of old songs; (3) a long, narrow arm of water; (4) a small town in the Basque area of Spain.

Gerald Smith, chairman, Dildo Area Community Economic Task Force, referring to the name of the Newfoundland community Dildo (population 1,100), as quoted by Lew Gloin, "Words," *The Toronto Star*, 11 March 1995.

Edberg, Alta.

Edberg: *Deadberg* (the other schools chanted at the ball tournaments). The road to there is paved with old intentions, farma boy in pick-ups, telephone wires, the dart of gophers.

Aritha van Herk, novelist, *Places Far from Ellesmere: A Geografictione: Explorations on Site* (1990).

Ellesmere Island, N.W.T.

Explorers say that harebells rise / from the cracks of Ellesmereland / and cod swim fat beneath the ice / that grinds its meagre sands

Lines from **Earle Birney**'s poem "Ellesmereland I" (1952), *The Collected Poems of Earle Birney* (1975).

And now in Ellesmereland there sits / a town of twenty men / They guard the floes that reach to the Pole / a hundred leagues and ten

Lines from **Earle Birney**'s poem "Ellesmereland II" (1965), *The Collected Poems of Earle Birney* (1975).

Here you are closer to Russia than to yourself.

Aritha van Herk, novelist, *Places Far from Ellesmere: A Geografictione: Explorations on Site* (1990).

Ellesmere Island, which is nearly as large in area as England and Scotland combined, is so hostile, the nearest tree is 2,100 miles to the south.

George J. Demko, geographer, *Why in the World: Adventures in Geography* (1992).

Flin Flon, Man.

This must be the hole old Flin Flon came out of.

Tom Creighton, prospector, referring to Josiah Flintabbety Flonatin, hero of J.E. Preston-Muddock's dime novel *The Sunless City* (1905), a copy of which he found here in 1913.

Fort Chimo, Que.

Ungava means, in Eskimo, "the farthest place." But civilization has reached even the "farthest place," in the form of an agglomeration known as Fort Chimo.

Kenneth White, poet, *The Blue Road* (1983).

Fort Selkirk, Y.T.

On the globe I owned as a child, Fort Selkirk appeared in the same bold type as Boston and Dublin. The North seemed crowded with metropolises, until I learned that mapmakers merely dislike empty splashes of colour.

John Hildebrand, sports writer, *Reading the River: A Voyage Down the Yukon* (1988).

Fort Whoop-up, Alta.

We're just a-whooping it up!

Joe Wye, whisky and fur trader, making light of his activities at the "fur fort," between 1869 and 1871, as noted in *The Alberta Historical Review*, April 1953.

Gander, Nfld.

Here were the last cup of coffee and the last bun in the Western Hemisphere.

Christopher Isherwood, author, describing a flight from New York to Gander, thence from Gander to London, in 1947, "Coming to London" (1957), included by Paul Fussell in *The Norton Book of Travel* (1987).

What's good for Goose Bay is sauce for Gander.

A modern maxim supplied by humorist **Allan Gould**, quoted by Warren Clements in *The Globe and Mail*, 28 Sept. 1991.

Goderich, Ont.

This surely must be the prettiest town in all of Canada.

Remark attributed to **Queen Elizabeth II** on a visit to the picturesque town of Goderich, Ont., quoted by David Scott in "Ontario," *The Penguin Guide to Canada* (1989, 1991) edited by Alan Tucker.

Golden, B.C.

Aptly named.... The sky is blue, the snow is white, the train is red. We are trapped in a Technicolor photo out of the *National Geographic* magazine.

Description from French author and traveller **Michel Tournier**'s novel *Gemini* (1975).

Grand Pré, N.S.

Nought but tradition remains of the beautiful village of Grand Pré.

Line from **Henry Wadsworth Longfellow**'s narrative poem *Evangeline: A Tale of Acadie* (1847).

Great Slave Lake, N.W.T.

At the northern end of the sweeping Mackenzie Highway you come to eleven thousand square miles of cold, cold pond called the Great Slave Lake....

Tom Lodge, traveller, *Beyond the Great Slave Lake* (1957).

Guysborough, N.S.

Now there's no train to Guysborough / Or so the man said / So it might be a good place to be.

Lines from **Stan Rogers**' song "Guysborough Train" (1972), quoted by Chris Gudgeon in *An Unfinished Conversation: The Life and Music of Stan Rogers* (1993). The song refers to the Nova Scotia government's rescinded promise to build a rail line to the town of Guysborough at the foot of Chedabucto Bay.

Hamilton, Ont.

Hamilton has an imaginary, Bergmany quality. It is isolated and in darkness and is very much unto itself. But there is also the fanciful romanticism of the city, for it has an exotic strain. You either become like it, and carry a lunch bucket, or you become its antithesis, a fairy princess, like Sylvia Fraser.

John Reeves, photographer, native of Hamilton, observation made about the city and another native, the novelist Sylvia Fraser, obiter dictum, 28 Sept. 1979.

I can go about my business with relative anonymity in Hamilton.

Glenn Gould, pianist, hiring musicians for the Hamilton Philharmonic, quoted in "Memories" by Robert J. Silverman in *Glenn Gould by Himself and His Friends* (1983) edited by John McGreevy.

High River, Alta.

The more I see of Ottawa, the better I love High River.

Dan Riley, Senator, quoted by Grant MacEwan, "The Cowboy Senator," *Fifty Mighty Men* (1958).

Hudson Bay, Sask.

Hudson Bay, the Moose Capital of the World

Al Mazur, publisher of *The Hudson Bay Post-Review*, published in the northeastern frontier of Saskatchewan, quoted by Andrew King in *Pen, Paper and Printing Ink* (1970).

Ile d'Orléans, Que.

The Isle of Orleans reposes like an emerald in the water at the point where the fate of a continent was decided.

W. George Beers, writer, "The Canadian Mecca," *The Century Magazine*, May 1882.

Ingersoll, Ont.

"How does it feel to be back in the little bay, after the big stormy ocean?" I asked Mrs. McPherson—Aimee. "Thrilling," wherewith Aimee thrilled eyes, voice, lovely frame from tip to toe all uniting to thrill.

Aimee Semple McPherson, evangelist, native of Ingersoll, Ont., builder of the Angelus Temple, Echo Park, Los Angeles, interviewed in Ingersoll by R.E. Knowles in *The Toronto Star*, 9 July 1929.

Jasper, Alta.

An adaptation of an ancient story occurs to me. A New York man reached heaven, and as he passed the gate, Peter said, "I'm sure you will like it." A Pittsburgh man followed, and Peter said, "It will be a very great change for you." Finally, there came a man from Jasper Park. "I'm afraid," said Peter, "that you will be disappointed."

Sir Arthur Conan Doyle, signing the guestbook at Jasper Park Lodge, when the main lodge opened in 1923, quoted by Ken Becker, "Jasper Quietly Manages International Traffic," *The Financial Post*, 23 Aug. 1999.

Kenora, Ont.

Nobody in Canada can know the true situation here unless he or she lives here and has to live with this situation day in and day out.

Eleanor M. Jacobson, nurse and activist, *Bended Elbow: Kenora Ontario Talks Back* (1975). Anastasia M. Shkilynyk wrote, "This book is a highly partisan and harshly negative account of Indians in Kenora, but it expresses feelings and perceptions that are widely shared among white residents of the town."

Kingsmere, Gatineau Park, Que.

It is good to have some familiar, well-loved place to spend time in, until one gets used to eternity.

Percy J. Philip, correspondent for *The New York Times*, who would commune at Kingsmere, "I Talked with Mackenzie King's Ghost," *Fate*, Oct. 1955.

Kingston, Ont.

But the trains never stop in Kingston prison, mama, / They just keep right on passing by. / No, the trains never stop in Kingston prison, mama, / Nothing stops in Kingston, but time.

Chorus of **Roy Payne**'s song "Trains Never Stop in Kingston," reproduced by Bob Davis in *Singin' About Us* (1976).

You get this wonderful old Ontario town, beleaguered by the crud, all the plastic, neon-light, shopping-plaza crud that's been installed since, say, 1960.

Scott Symons, author, "Deliquescence in Canada," *The Idler*, July–Aug. 1992.

It's always difficult to explain to visitors the perennial fascination of life in this small city, once a colonial outpost for two empires, quiet key to the heart of the continent.

Mary Alice Downie and **M.-A. Thompson**, editors, Introduction, *Written in Stone: A Kingston Reader* (1993).

Lake of the Woods, Ont.

Timing is important at Lake of the Woods, unless you are impervious to the bites of black flies. We hit things with the fall colours at their best and with the black flies disappearing before the onset of winter.

Fred Hoyle, English scientist and novelist, recalling a motor trip made in Sept.–Oct. 1976, *Home Is Where the Wind Blows: Chapters from a Cosmologist's Life* (1994).

Lethbridge, Alta.

Chief Mountain, which you can see from here, was once overturned. The fossils that belong near Chief Mountain's summit are found at its base.

Immanuel Velikovsky, theorist, address, convocation dinner, after receiving an honorary degree of Doctor of Arts and Science, University of Lethbridge, Alta., 11 May 1974, *Recollections of a Fallen Sky: Velikovsky and Cultural Amnesia* (1978) edited by E.R. Milton.

Liverpool, N.S.

Liverpool proved to be six hours' journey from Yarmouth, and turned out to be the very prettiest little town I ever visited.

Zane Grey, novelist and frequent visitor to Nova Scotia, *Tales of Swordfish and Tuna* (1927).

London, Ont.

In the course of the morning we passed through the pretty little town of London with avenues of shady trees whose abundant foliage was still, in July, bright and fresh as in the early summer. Yet the sun has great power here, for London, Ontario, is six hundred miles nearer the Equator than London, England, being further south than Nice and Florence.

Vaughan Cornish, traveller, *The Travels of Ellen Cornish: Being the Memoir of a Pilgrim of Science* (1913).

Louisbourg, N.S.

The gloomiest spectacle the sight of man can dwell upon is the desolate, but once populous, abode of humanity. Egypt itself is cheerful compared with Louisbourg!

Frederic S. Cozzens, writer, *Acadia; or, A Month with the Blue Noses* (1859).

Manitoulin Island, Ont.

Manitoulin is a sort of "middle earth," neither north nor south, and for the early natives it was a palace of dreams and legends.

David E. Scott, travel writer, "Ontario," *The Penguin Guide to Canada* (1989, 1991) edited by Alan Tucker.

Marathon, Ont.

Strictly speaking, the idea of suburbia is meaningless within the context of Marathon.... And the result, despite the conscientious stratification of the town, is a curiously compromised emotional unilaterality.

Glenn Gould, pianist, visitor to the small town of Marathon, Ont., "The Search for Petula Clark" (1967), *The Glenn Gould Reader* (1984) edited by Tim Page.

Medicine Hat, Alta.

This is the granary of the whole world, the cornucopia out of which cereals flow to Latin America, China, Russia, the Indies, Africa, to all of starving mankind.

Description from French author and traveller **Michel Tournier**'s novel *Gemini* (1975).

I have fallen in love with American names, / The sharp names that never get fat, / The snakeskin-titles of mining claims, / The plumed war-bonnet of Medicine Hat, / Tucson and Deadwood and Lost Mule Flat.

Lines from **Stephen Vincent Benét**'s poem "American Names," *Ballads and Poems: 1915–1950* (1931).

Midland, Ont.

No longer is it: "See Naples and Die." The more satisfying and healthful saying is: "See Midland, and Live." Be amongst the thousands of "happy fugitives from the bondage of routine" to visit Midland—the land of exhilarating winter and sunny summer skies.

George R. Osborne, historian, *Midland and Her Pioneers* (1975).

Moose Factory, Ont.

An "exploding stove" was any catastrophe, natural or human, from a flood in Medicine Hat, Wyoming, to an angry policeman in Moose Factory, Ontario.

Remark of a movie producer in **Nathanael West**'s novel *The Day of the Locust* (1939). The proper location of Medicine Hat is Alberta.

Moose Jaw, Sask.

All citizens of the British Empire seem all to be citizens of that sacred Indian city called Moose Jaw.

Vachel Lindsay, poet, remark made in 1927, quoted by John Robert Colombo in *Canadian Literary Landmarks* (1984).

Moose Javian. Geographer Alan Rayburn notes that this does not conform to any established pattern, "although it may be related to Shavian, the literature of George Bernard Shaw."

Paul Dickson, British writer, *What Do You Call a Person From... ? A Dictionary of Resident Names* (1990).

Nelson, B.C.

Nelson is a pleasant little town with a high street and two trams, and a few stone houses among the wood. It clambers steeply uphill, with the lake—there as narrow as a river—below it and steep hills on all sides shutting it in. It is the only two of any size (and I suppose is smaller than Ventimiglia), between us and Vancouver, six hundred miles away.

Freya Stark, traveller and writer, letter written about visiting Nelson, B.C., while a winter resident at Creston, B.C., 30 Nov. 1928, *Beyond Euphrates* (1951).

New Liskeard, Ont.

It was a paradox common enough in Canada. A place could nurture its history or its future, seldom both. For New Liskeard the future appeared to be shrinking.

John Galt, journalist and traveller, *Whistlestop: A Journey across Canada* (1987).

Niagara-on-the-Lake, Ont.

Niagara is as near Heaven as any town whatever, and nearer than some others.

William Kirby, 19th-century archivist and resident of Niagara-on-the-Lake, Ont., quoted by Beverly Gray in *The Globe and Mail*, 23 Dec. 1978.

Some whimsical part of me christened this unique Ontario town "Brigadoon." For some time I remained convinced that, in the winter, it just disappeared in the mists of time. In fact there is something strange about the place.

Tony van Bridge, actor with the Shaw Festival, *Also in the Cast: The Memoirs of Tony van Bridge* (1995).

North Bay, Ont.

North Bay is home for me because I was here when I was eight until I was eleven.... When I think about my childhood, about when I was a kid, I think about here.

Michael J. Fox, movie star, on his return to North Bay to visit the home where the Fox family lived from 1968 to 1971 when his father was stationed at the Canadian Forces Base North Bay; *The Globe and Mail*, 17 July 1991. Fox was born in Edmonton and spent his teenage years in Burnaby, B.C.

North York, Ont.

North York City / The heart of the golden horseshoe

Advertising slogan for the City of North York, part of the Greater Toronto Area, created by **Padulo Integrated** and introduced on 18 April 1994.

Norval, Ont.

I love Norval as I have never loved any place save Cavendish. It is as if I had known it all my life—as if I had dreamed young dreams under those pine and walked with my first love down that long perfumed hill.

L.M. Montgomery, author, resident of the manse in Norval, Ont., in the 1930s, quoted by Patricia Mestern, "Lucy Maude's Other Province," *The Globe and Mail*, 29 Aug. 1998.

Okanagan Valley, B.C.

An animal in Okanagan Lake, other than a sturgeon, that is more than three metres in length, and the mates or offspring of that animal.

Reference to Ogopogo, lake monster reportedly seen in the waters of Okanagan Lake, B.C., protected by B.C.'s environmental legislation, Regulation 168–90, as noted by **Terry Glavin** in *The Edmonton Journal*, 23 Aug. 1992.

Orillia, Ont.

Orillia is probably the best Canadian town in which to bring up a family; but if you want rivers, trout-streams, lakes—heaven in general—you've got to turn to Algoma.

J.W. Curran, publisher of *The Sault Star*, interviewed by R.E. Knowles in *The Toronto Star*, 27 Nov. 1933.

Oshawa, Ont.

We are in Oshawa, suffering from Oshawa.

E.B. White, writer, letter addressed to Katharine S. White from Hotel Genosha, Oshawa, Ont., 4 July 1930, en route to Camp Otter, near Dorset, complaining about the sounds of construction, *Letters* (1929) edited by Dorothy Lobrano Guth.

Paris, Ont.

If you feel inclined to live to be a nonagenarian, then go and exist in Paris. Ontario's Paris,

I mean, of course, one of the most picturesque towns on this western hemisphere, hill-girt, sunny slopes on every hand, and the (sometimes) placid Grand river meandering fondly lingering amid the scenic and arboreal charm.

R.E. Knowles, columnist, *The Toronto Star*, 26 May 1992.

Peggy's Cove, N.S.

The tiny harbour on the rocky, sea-girt Nova Scotian coast with its tumble-down shanties and its derelict fishing boats rusting to dust beside the crumblng wharves while dead seagulls wash in and out on the oily tide is the most richly picturesque spot in the country.

Joey Slinger, humorist, "Moving with the Times," *If It's a Jungle Out There, Why Do I Have to Mow the Lawn* (1992).

Peterborough, Ont.

Inevitably, every place is influenced by its past and Peterborough, because of its past, has not had a well-developed inner life.

Robertson Davies, man-of-letters, interviewed by Ralph Hancock in 1963, *Conversations with Robertson Davies* (1989) edited by J. Madison Davis.

Do you know the area north of Peterborough? When I was reporting there, incest was just the beginning of what really went on.

Robertson Davies, journalist, quoted by Elina MacNiven in *The Toronto Star's Broadcast Week*, 23 Feb. 1980.

Toronto's great good fortune in being located so close to such really productive municipalities as Peterborough....

Michael Bliss, historian, "Better and Purer: The Peterborough Methodist Mafia and the Renaissance of Toronto," *Toronto Remembered: A Celebration of the City* (1984) edited by William Kilbourn.

Pointe-au-Pic, Que.

It is heady as champagne, but without the "morning after."

William Howard Taft, U.S. President and long-time summer resident of Murray Bay, Pointe-au-Pic, Que., quoted in *Charlevoix: Tourist Guide* (1994–95).

Porcupine, Ont.

The greatest pianist ever produced by the Porcupine. I've often thought of self-promotion in these terms, but who down south would ever know that the Porcupine is a geographical area, and not the animal that never quite makes it across highways?

William Aide, pianist, *Starting from Porcupine* (1996).

Prince George, B.C.

I couldn't help thinking of the "Big Shot" when we went to Prince George, B.C. The northern town has a mascot they call Mister P.G. (pronounced peegee). The towering, forty-foot statue of a lumberjack with a hard hat greets you as you come into town. It used to be made of B.C. timber; now it's plastic.

Michel Gratton, journalist, *Still the Boss: A Candid Look at Brian Mulroney* (1990).

Pugwash, N.S.

There are two things to do here—swim and think.

Attributed to **Cyrus Eaton**, millionaire and humanitarian, native of Pugwash, N.S., a village on the Northumberland Strait, quoted by John Demont, "Toasting the Prize," *Maclean's*, 23 Oct. 1995.

I can just see people all over the world scurrying for their atlases to see where Pugwash is.

Vivian Godfree, inhabitant of Pugwash, N.S., following the announcement that the Swedish Academy had awarded the 1995 Nobel Prize for Peace to the British nuclear physicist Joseph Rotblat as chairperson of the Pugwash Conferences on Science and World Affairs, established in Pugwash in July 1957, quoted by John Demont, "Toasting the Prize," *Maclean's*, 23 Oct. 1995.

Queen Charlotte Islands, B.C.

Current maps show Haida Gwaii, the Queen Charlotte Islands, as the western-most extremity of Canada, but to some of us who live on that coast now, they are also the region's spiritual capital: Nothing like Rome, and not much like Jerusalem, but something like a rainy, untouristed Cyclades, Eleusis, Delphi, Thebes.

Robert Bringhurst, poet and anthropologist, "That Also Is You," *Native Writers and Canadian Identity* (1990) edited by W.H. New.

Red River Valley, Man.

We realized at once what we had heard before, that it was in fact a lake without any water in it.

Henry Van Dyke, American essayist and travel writer, "The Red River of the North," *Harper's New Monthly Magazine*, May 1880.

Sable Island, N.S.

Yet I venture to state that in the whole of this great Dominion there is no spot more beloved by those who live upon it, no spot more desolate.

Helen Creighton, folklorist, "Sable Island," *Maclean's*, 1 Dec. 1931.

Ste-Agathe-des-Monts, Que.

Sand—glorious sunsets—no paths, planks of wood—fields of large white daisies with millions of fireflies—flat patches of water reflecting the sky.

Mrs. Patrick Campbell, touring British actress, relaxing for ten weeks at Ste-Agathe-des-Monts, Que., 1910, quoted by Alan Dent in *Mrs. Patrick Campbell* (1961).

St. Andrews-By-The-Sea, N.B.

Awaiting development! If there is any town on earth that would be the apple of any developer's eyes, it is St. Andrews, New Brunswick—St. Andrews By The Sea, to use the vulgar sobriquet wished upon it by earlier entrepreneurs.

Jan Morris, Anglo-Welsh traveller, "New Brunswick," *Saturday Night*, May 1990.

St. Catharines, Ont.

I have heard said that St. Catherine [*sic*] is picturesque! I seek in vain to discover the beauties of a country that I have heard spoken of so highly. As well seek the beauty of a woman falling into the water and whom somebody has just drawn out....

Louis Moreau Gottschalk, French-educated virtuoso pianist, *Notes of a Pianist* (1881) translated from the French by Robert E. Peterson in 1964. He visited St. Catharines, Ont., 13 May 1864.

St. Mary's, Ont.

But none the less, St. Mary's is St. Mary's still.

Arthur Meighen, Prime Minister and native of St. Mary's, Ont., "Response to a Welcome Home," 16 Aug. 1920, *Unrevised and Unrepented: Debating Speeches and Others* (1949).

Saskatoon, Sask.

In Saskatoon, Saskatchewan, / Shakespeare's voice seemed in the air, / And something in the prairie live....

Lines of **Vachel Lindsay**'s poem "Two Poems Geographical: II Saskatoon, Saskatchewan (The Shakespearean Christmas Tree)," *Going-to-the-Stars* (1926).

You don't know a rhyme for Saskatoon, do you?

Question addressed by cowboy actor Roy Rogers to his wife and sidekick Dale Evans in the movie *Along the Navajo Trail* (1946).

And there's an advantage in living in Saskatoon in that it isolates you from all those extracurricular things like literary feuding, literary social life, all those things that sometimes attach themselves to writing and sometimes deflect from writing.

Guy Vanderhaeghe, novelist, interviewed by Alan Twigg in *Strong Voices: Conversations with Fifty Canadian Authors* (1988).

Saskatoon, the very name of which is likely to evoke a snigger, is in fact a model city and ought to be an examplar for civic planners everywhere.

Jan Morris, Anglo-Welsh traveller, "In Praise of Canada," *The Toronto Star*, 15 June 1992.

Sault Ste. Marie, Ont.

I do not believe there is, in all Canada, a town quite so quick to welcome, so slow to release, the stranger within her gates; nor any whose citizens so cordially unite to show kindness, to provide interesting days and nights, for those fortunate enough to be their grateful guests.

R.E. Knowles, columnist, during an interview with local newspaper publisher J.W. Curran, *The Toronto Star*, 27 Nov. 1933.

I want to rename this the City of Smiles.

Roberta Bondar, astronaut, native of Sault Ste. Marie on her triumphal return, quoted in *Maclean's*, 2 March 1992.

SCARBOROUGH, ONT.

We offer murder, deceit and infidelity. (Sounds just like Scarborough, doesn't it?)

Line from an advertisement for the new season of the Shaw Festival, *The Globe and Mail*, 30 Aug. 1993. The reference elicited criticism from Scarborough's mayor, as noted by Stan Josey in *The Toronto Star* the following day. The campaign was produced by the advertising agency of **Geoffrey B. Roche and Partners.**

The combination "ough" can be pronounced in nine different ways. The following sentence contains them all: "A rough-coated, dough-faced, thoughtful ploughman strode through the streets of Scarborough; after falling into a slough, he coughed and hiccoughed.

Linguistic lore from the Internet, 25 July 1997.

Sherbrooke, Que.

Oh, the year was 1778, / (How I wish I was in Sherbrooke now!) / A letter of marque came from the King / To the scummiest vessel I've ever seen.

Verse from **Stan Rogers**' song "Barrett's Privateers," quoted by Chris Gudgeon in *An Unfinished Conversation: The Life and Music of Stan Rogers* (1993).

Sioux Lookout, Ont.

I look back on those days in Sioux Lookout as if to a lost paradise.

Thoughts of the narrator of **Robertson Davies**' novel *The Cunning Man* (1994).

Smithers, B.C.

...with Smithereens (as the locals are known)....

Val Ross, journalist, referring to Smithers, B.C., *The Globe and Mail*, 15 May 1993.

South Moresby, B.C.

These shining islands may be the signposts that point the way to a renewed harmonious relationship with this, the only world we're ever going to have.

Elizabeth E. May, social activist, *Paradise Won: The Struggle for South Moresby* (1991).

Springhill, N.S.

The Springhill story—tragic, courageous, dramatic: a reporter's dream story, a miner's nightmare. It is a story we would rather not have to tell—and it's a story that the town, Springhill, Nova Scotia, would like to forget.

Kingsley Brown, CBC Radio reporter, concluding coverage of the Springhill Mining Disaster of 1958, CBC Radio, quoted in *CBC Times*, 15 Nov. 1958.

Stratford, Ont.

I was driving into Stratford. Such a pretty place, and suddenly all I could see were these big Kentucky Fried Chicken and McDonald's hamburger signs—and I asked myself, "Why do Canadians put up with it?"

Eli Wallach, actor, visiting Stratford, Ont., quoted by Jack Miller in *The Toronto Star*, 18 Oct. 1975.

Sudbury, Ont.

Once described as "Canada's Pittsburgh without the orchestra," Sudbury now has its own symphony....

Peter C. Newman, columnist, *Maclean's*, 1 April 1991.

Ingram: I'm sure you will enjoy your trip to Sudbury.

Hawking: It sounds like hell on Earth.

Exchange between science journalist **Jay Ingram** and cosmologist **Stephen Hawking** who was lecturing at the University of Toronto, prior to travelling to Sudbury, Ont., where in his wheelchair he would descend two miles in an elevator to see the Sudbury Neutrino Observatory, quoted by Jay Ingram, "A Little Touch of Hawking in the Night," *The Toronto Star*, 3 May 1998.

Swastika, Ont.

We'll call it the Swastika mine, after that charm on your necklace.

Bill Dusty, prospector for the Tavistock Mining Partnership, to a "young lady" wearing a necklace with a charm who asked him what the new mine was to be called. "The Swastika Mining Company Limited was formed, capitalization $750,000 in one dollar shares, and some shares were sold locally at five cents each in 1908," explained S.A. Pain in *Three Miles of Gold: The Story of Kirkland Lake* (1960).

Unity Mitford, the daughter of Lord Redesdale, who had a crush on Hitler, was conceived at a place called Swastika in Ontario. It was here that the Redesdales owned a goldfield, where they would go panning on their summer holidays.

Paul Sieveking, columnist for *Fortean Times*, "Names," *The Sunday Telegraph*, 1 Dec. 1996.

Thousand Islands, Ont.

The Lake itself, the passages of the thousand islands and of the successive rapids, were a great delight.

Edward Carpenter, English poet, referring to a trip made in Summer 1884 to London, Ont., *My Days and Dreams: Being Autobiographical Notes* (1921).

Any suggestion of fatigue of labour of poverty is missing from this gracious setting for multimillionaires

Line from the poem "The Thousand Islands" from the suite *Kodak* (Documentary) (1924) composed by the French traveller and writer **Blaise Cendrars** and included in *Blaise Cendrars: Complete Poems* (1992) translated by Ron Padgett.

Thunder Bay, Ont.

Nanibozhu lies sleeping still, but there is a sleeping giant that is stirring in his sleep. He moves, he wakes, he stretches himself, he will arise.

Bernard McEvoy, traveller, evocation of the sight of the Sleeping Giant at Thunder Bay, Ont., *From the Great Lakes to the Wide West: Impressions of a Tour between Toronto and the Pacific* (1902).

Two towns stand on the shores of the lake less than a mile apart. What Lloyds is to shipping, or the College of Surgeons to medicine, they are to the Wheat. Its honour and integrity are in their hands; and they hate each other with the pure, poisonous, passionate hatred which makes towns grow.

Rudyard Kipling, man-of-letters, *Letters to the Family: Notes on a Recent Trip to Canada* (1908). Kipling was referring to Fort William and Port Arthur, two towns on Lake Superior, now collectively known as Thunder Bay.

When one reaches Port Arthur one feels that one is at last in touch with ancient Canada, the Canada of Parkman....

Sir Arthur Conan Doyle, author and traveller, travelling across Canada by train from West to East, *Our Second American Adventure* (1923).

Five thousand years before the Egyptians erected the pyramids at Gizeh, Paleo-Indians hunted, fished and manufactured stone tools and weapons in Thunder Bay....

Joseph M. Mauro, historian, *Thunder Bay: The Golden Gateway of the Great Northwest, A History* (1981).

Timmins, Ont.

Timmins gave me a lot of freedom to think broadly.

Myron Scholes, Nobel laureate, economist at Stanford University, California, referring to his place of birth, Timmins, Ont., quoted by AP-CP-Reuter, *The Toronto Star*, 16 Oct. 1997.

In Timmins you play hockey every day.

Frank Gehry, Toronto-born, Timmins-raised, Los Angeles–based architect, interviewed by Michael Enright on CBC Radio's *This Morning*, 25 Feb. 1998.

Trenton, Ont.

Canada? Well, now, what d'you know about that? I was looking for Trenton, New Jersey. My compass must have gone haywire.

Line spoken by the young American pilot (played by actor Tyrone Power) who lands his Harvard trainer at Trenton, Ont., accidentally "on purpose," to join the British Commonwealth Air Training Plan in the Hollywood movie *A Yank in the R.A.F.* (1941). **Darryl F. Zanuck** wrote the script, signing it Melville Crossman, according to Ted Barris in *Behind the Glory* (1992).

Valcourt, Que.

Never forget that our company saw the light of day in a small garage in Valcourt, and it was the people of our village and the surrounding areas who always helped me make it what it is today. Always be humane in your relations with your employees.

Joseph-Armand Bombardier, inventor of the snowmobile, addressing his heirs on his deathbed in 1964, quoted by Alexander Ross in "The Corporate Reality," *Weekend Magazine*, 29 Nov. 1975. His words were actually his "moral testament," drawn up with the help of writer Charles Leblanc eleven days before his death on 18 Feb. 1964, as noted by Alexander Ross in *The Risk Takers* (1975).

Val Marie, Sask.

Prairie Dog Capital of Canada / Home of Bryan Trottier

Wording on signs outside Val Marie, Sask., noted by Mark Abley in *Beyond Forget: Rediscovering the Prairies* (1986).

Vulcan, Alta.

Vulcan wasn't known as a tourist haven before, but people from all over the world come here now.

Royal Elmer, merchant in Vulcan, Alta., who sells *Star Trek* memorabilia, quoted by Ken Ramstead in *TV Guide*, 5 March 1994. Vulcan was named for the ancient Roman god of fire, not TV's Mr. Spock.

Washago, Ont.

Oh, she's divine; she must be mine: she's Bridget from Washago.

Line from **LaRena Clark**'s folksong "Bridget from Washago," *A Family Heritage: The Story and Songs of LaRena Clark* (1994) by Edith Fowke with Jay Rahn.

Windsor, Ont.

Is there anybody here from Windsor?

Paul Martin Sr., Member of Parliament, Cabinet Minister, Senator, and Ambassador, between 1935 and 1979, question asked whenever he delivered a speech as a way of alluding to his constituency, in and around Windsor, Ont.

Windsor's identity is so enmeshed with Detroit's that most postcards of Windsor are of the Detroit skyline. Moreover, Detroiters go to lunch in Windsor as if they were going to a delicatessen down the street.

Isabel Wilkerson, correspondent, *The New York Times*, 21 Sept. 1987.

Yellowknife, N.W.T.

Where Yesterday Rubs Shoulders with Tomorrow.

Unofficial motto of the city of Yellowknife, noted by Peter Lesniak in "Travel," *The Globe and Mail*, 11 April 1987.

Yukon River, Y.T.

Our own odyssey is over, but the river's has only begun.

Pierre Berton, author, after rafting the Yukon River, *Drifting Home* (1973).

Zionville, N.B.

No place has ever been home to me like Canada was.

William Kotzwinkle, U.S. novelist, who with his wife, novelist Elizabeth Gundy, lived during the 1970s and 1980s on a farm at Zionville, N.B., quoted by Philip Marchand in *The Toronto Star*, 1 Nov. 1996.

PLAINS OF ABRAHAM See also QUEBEC, CONQUEST OF

Here Died / Wolfe / September 13th / 1759

Terse inscription on the Wolfe Monument, Avenue Wolfe-Montcalm, off the Grande-Allée, Quebec City. It marks the site where the Commander of the British expedition that took Quebec died. The original monument was defaced or destroyed on a number of occasions by patriotes and separatists. The first memorial was a stone which the Army rolled here to indicate the spot where Wolfe died in 1759. The second memorial was erected in 1832. The third memorial was erected by the British Army stationed in Canada in 1849. The fourth monument, which reproduced the column of the third one, with the same decorative helmet, two inscriptions, etc., was erected by the National Battlefields Commission in 1913. It was destroyed on 29 March 1963. The fifth memorial was erected by the **National Battlefields Commission** in July 1965. One of the casualties of time has been the word "Victorious." The original inscription appeared as follows: "Here Died / Wolfe / Victorious / September 13th / 1759."

My prenticeship I past, where my leader breath'd his last, / When the bloody die was cast on the heights of Abraham; / And I servèd out my trade when the gallant game was play'd, / And the Moro low was laid at the sound of the drum.

Lines with a reference to the Battle of the Plains of Abraham (1759) from **Robert Burns**' poem "The Jolly Beggars: A Cantata," "Posthumous Pieces," *The Complete Poetical Works of Burns* (1897).

I saw the Plains of Abraham, and the spot where the lamented Wolfe stood when he made the memorable remark that he would rather be the author of Gray's "Elegy" than take Quebec. But why did he say so rash a thing? It was because he supposed there was going to be international copyright. Otherwise there would be no money in it. I was also shown the spot where Sir William Phipps stood when he said he would rather take a walk than take two Quebecs. And he took the walk.

Mark Twain, American wit and writer, referring to monuments in Quebec City, address, Windsor Hotel, Montreal, 8 Dec. 1881, reproduced in *The New York Times,* 10 Dec. 1881.

Some men love honour, / Other men love groats, / Here Wolfe reaped laurels, / Lord Dalhousie, oats.

Ditty composed to recall the fact that Lord Dalhousie, Governor in Chief of Canada from 1819 to 1828, had sown and raised a crop of oats on the Plains of Abraham where Generals Wolfe and Montcalm fell in battle, quoted by Robina and Kathleen Macfarlane Lizars in *The Days of the Canada Company* (1896).

The death of Wolfe on the Plains of Abraham = On a path to fame, both he and his war foe fell

Anagram attributed to the puzzle-constructor **Sam Weller** in 1881 by O.V. Michaelsen in "Best Anagrams and Antigrams," *Word Ways: The Journal of Recreational Linguistics,* Nov. 1990.

Where, but only here will you be able to see French-speaking soldiers, disguised in English uniforms, performing a borrowed ceremony for the benefit of American cameras.

Narration about the "friendly invasion" of Quebec by three million American tourists each year from the NFB documentary film *Québec-U.S.A. ou l'Invasion pacifique* (1962) directed by Claude Jutra and Michel Brault, quoted by Gary Evans in *In the National Interest: A Chronicle of the National Film Board of Canada from 1949 to 1989* (1991).

I had often wondered how the American War of Independence would have gone if the English general James Wolfe hadn't died there in battle with French forces under Montcalm. Maybe George Washington wouldn't have been able to beat him. Maybe, with Wolfe in command of the British forces, there would have been no rupture. Maybe he would have sided with Washington. Who knows?

Fred Hoyle, English scientist and novelist, recalling a motor trip made in Sept.–Oct. 1976, *Home Is Where the Wind Blows: Chapters from a Cosmologist's Life* (1994).

Never in the history of colonial wars has the victor treated the vanquished so generously.

Henry Steele Commager, U.S. historian, referring to the victory of the English over the French at the Battle of the Plains of Abraham in 1759, quoted by Allan Fotheringham in *Maclean's,* 16 March 1998.

Québec was not defeated on the Plains of Abraham, France was.

Louis Dudek, poet and aphorist, "In a Nutshell," *Reality Games* (1998).

PLANNING

When schemes are laid in advance, it is surprising how often the circumstances fit in with them.

Sir William Osler, physician and professor, quoted by William Bennett Bean in *Sir William Osler: Aphorisms from His Bedside Teachings and Writings* (1950).

Strategic planning, n. Planning undertaken with care and deliberation, as opposed to normal planning.

David Olive, business commentator, *White Knights and Poison Pills: A Cynic's Dictionary of Business Jargon* (1990).

Today, the old ground rules pushed to extremes have begun to reverse their previous effects. Therefore, *plan very carefully and prepare to do the opposite.*

Barrington Nevitt, communications consultant, *The Communication Ecology: Re-presentation versus Replica* (1982).

My idea of long-range planning is lunch.

Frank Ogden, futurologist, *Ogdenisms* (1994).

If you fail to plan, you plan to fail.

Alex Baumann, champion swimmer, favourite saying, quoted by Peter Urs Bender in *Leadership from Within* (1997) with Eric Hellman.

PLAY See also LEISURE

Play is that for the sake of which work is done, the climactic Sabbath vision of mankind.

Northrop Frye, cultural critic, "Conclusion to a Literary History of Canada" (1965), *The Bush Garden: Essays on the Canadian Imagination* (1971).

Pastimes replay past times.

Barrington Nevitt, communications consultant, *The Communication Ecology: Re-presentation versus Replica* (1982).

PLAYWRIGHTS See LITERATURE, THEATRE, WRITERS & WRITING

PLEASURES

Somehow the people who do as they please seem to get along just about as well as those who are always trying to please others.

Bob Edwards, publisher, *The Eye Opener*, Summer Annual, 1923.

In order that her creatures shall not be indifferent to her demands, nature has made the act of sexual intercourse a supreme physical pleasure of life.

Alfred Henry Tyrer, Anglican minister and birth-control enthusiast, *Sex, Marriage and Birth Control: A Guide-book to Sex Health and a Satisfactory Sex Life in Marriage* (10th ed., 1936).

There is no pleasure greater than giving it.

Robin Skelton, poet and aphorist, *A Devious Dictionary* (1991).

POETS & POETRY See also CULTURE, LITERATURE, WRITERS & WRITING

I loved to hear the recital of his adventures in the polar seas. He described his fishing, and his combats, with a natural poetry; his recital took the form of an epic poem, and I seemed to be listening to a Canadian Homer singing the *Iliad* of the North.

Description of Ned Land, the Quebec-born whaler and "prince of harpooners," in **Jules Verne**'s novel *20,000 Leagues Under the Sea* (1869).

Darkness built its wigwam walls close around the camp.

Line of **Isabella Valancy Crawford**'s verse, inscribed on the plaque on a boulder, Isabella Valancy Crawford Park, Toronto, June 1992, near where she lived her last years and died 12 Feb. 1887.

Poet by the Gift of God

Inscription on the memorial raised to **Isabella Valancy Crawford**, Little Lake Cemetery, Peterborough, Ont. *Peterborough: Land of Shining Waters, An Anthology* (1967) edited by Ronald Borg.

No country on the face of the globe has produced, proportionately, so many volumes of verse as Canada.

John A. Cooper, editor, *Canadian under Victoria* (1901).

So far as I am aware, there has been no single piece of verse that has spoken with so sure an accent as to become current among the Canadian people.

Duncan Campbell Scott, poet, "A Decade of Canadian Poetry" (1901), *Twentieth Century Essays on Confederation Literature* (1976) edited by Lorraine McMullen.

Then entered in that hall of sin, / Into that house of hell / A lusty maid no whit afraid, / Her name was Eskimo Nell.

Lines from the traditional bawdy ballad "Eskimo Nell" (which tells of a northern prostitute's encounter with Dead-Eye Dick and Mexico Pete) included by Alan Bold in *The Bawdy Beautiful: The Sphere Book of Improper Verse* (1979). Bold claims that "Eskimo Nell" is "one of the great modern ballads" and claims it is "the work of a master." It appeared sometime following the publication of Robert Service's *Songs of a Sourdough* (1907).

It is a fact that three out of every six people of any pretension to culture affect verse-writing, and, even in our own young country, "their name is legion."

Mrs. C.M. Whyte-Edgar, editor, Preface, *A Wealth of Canadian Song* (1910).

Today I wrote a poem, canned six jars of tomatoes and re-read *Trilby*.

L.M. Montgomery, author and diarist, line from a journal entry in 1922, quoted by Mary Rubio and Elizabeth Waterston in *The Selected Journals of L.M. Montgomery: Volume III: 1921–29* (1992).

A Canadian poet. Apparently they have poets out there. And...why not? A remarkably growing country.

Lines from **P.G. Wodehouse**'s novel *Leave It to Psmith* (1923).

Emma Goldman: You're the man who makes poetry pay.

Robert Service: I make rhyming remunerative.

Exchange between the anarchist and the poet on the Riviera in the 1930s, quoted by James Mackay in *Vagabond of Verse: Robert Service—A Biography* (1995).

Simply expressed, I write poetry only to reveal my civilization, my sensitivities, my craftsmanship.

A.M. Klein, poet, offering his credo to A.J.M. Smith for *The Book of Canadian Poetry* (1943), quoted by Usher Caplan in *Like One that Dreamed: A Portrait of A.M. Klein* (1982).

The Canadian poets are still suffering traditional taunts from abroad, and still live in the unsympathetic environment of a burgeoning mercantile civilization out of which their American brethren rose to a maturity of expression but a few generations ago.

Kimon Friar, American poet, *The New Republic*, 28 Sept. 1953.

And your meter / should make the reader / Cry. / That's modern.

Lines from **Dennis Lee**'s poem "Free Verse," *First Flowering: A Selection of Prose and Poetry by the Youth of Canada* (1956) edited by Anthony Frisch.

Despite the temporary set-back in Canadian verse when the CNR repainted the walls of its washrooms, poetry in the country continues to thrive. Poetry is not only being written, by Reaney, Macpherson, Dudek and Klein, but it is being read, by Klein, Dudek, Macpherson and Reaney.

Eric Nicol, humorist, *An Uninhibited History of Canada* (1959) illustrated by Peter Whalley.

Poetry is a verdict, not an occupation.

Line from **Leonard Cohen**'s novel *The Favourite Game* (1971).

I have much sympathy for the student who informed in the examinations last May that Pratt had written a poem called "Beowulf and His Brothers."

Northrop Frye, cultural critic, "Conclusion to a Literary History of Canada" (1965), *The Bush Garden: Essays on the Canadian Imagination* (1971). E.J. Pratt was the author of the narrative poem *Brébeuf and His Brethren* (1940).

A poet is someone who is startled out of his trance by his dreams.

Irving Layton, poet and aphorist, *The Whole Bloody Bird (obs, aphs & Pomes)* (1969).

The point of my pencil contains a world.

Louis Dudek, man-of-letters, *Epigrams* (1975).

We're living in too materialistic a society. I'd rather have a few more poets and fewer plumbers.

Pierre Elliott Trudeau, Prime Minister, addressing young Liberals at the University of Toronto, 23 March 1977, quoted in *The Toronto Star* the following day.

Poetry is the shortest possible way of saying the sort of things I want to say.

Earle Birney, poet, quoted by Bruce Ward in *The Toronto Star*, 21 May 1978.

I move in a mythical world all the time, but then myth and reality aren't separate things—it's a way of seeing for me. The mundane is magical, but so is the astronaut going to the moon.

Gwendolyn MacEwen, poet, quoted by Ken Adachi in *The Toronto Star*, 19 Nov. 1978.

Toss / a dart at the map of Canada, / where it lands is / where you'll find me.

Lines from **David McFadden**'s poem "On the Road Again," *My Body Was Eaten by Dogs* (1981) edited by George Bowering.

How beautifully useless, / how deliciously defiant / a poem is!

Lines from **Raymond Souster**'s poem "Cutting It Short," *Asking for More* (1988).

Nothing makes a poem yours and so prepares you to absorb it seriously as committing it to memory. Then you can live with the lines intimately, saying those you wish to dwell on to yourself again and again.

Robert MacNeil, broadcaster and memoirist, *Wordstruck: A Memoir* (1989).

The best poetry is written in fear. I don't know about the best fiction; maybe the best fiction is the best poetry. But the best poetry is written in fear.

George Bowering, poet and esthetician, "Selected Errata," *The Brick Reader* (1991) edited by Linda Spalding and Michael Ondaatje.

Every genuine poet has several other poets hidden somewhere inside him.

Louis Dudek, poet and aphorist, "Epigrams," *Small Perfect Things* (1991).

One idea is to appoint a company Poet Laureate. Supported by the company, this person would have the financial freedom to pursue his or her art. This person would also be the artistic shaman of the company. The company poet would be called upon to write poems that celebrate the accomplishments of a company, or mourn its losses or failures.

John Dalla Costa, advertising executive, *Meditations on Business: Why Business As Usual Won't Work Anymore* (1991).

For as long as man is still capable of emotion, be it love or hate or fear or great joy or sorrow, poems will cry out to be written, and somewhere and somehow poets will spring up to write them down.

Raymond Souster, poet, "Getting On with It," *Contemporary Authors Autobiography Series* (1991), Volume 14.

It has to be one of the most cutthroat businesses north of Wall St., or west of Bay St.

Leonard Cohen, poet, referring to "the fabled envy of poets," quoted by Philip Marchand in *The Toronto Star*, 25 Oct. 1991.

Although I have no statistics at hand it has always been my belief, as a publisher, that more poetry is written in Canada, on a per capita basis, than anywhere else.

Jack McClelland, former publisher, "Irving Layton: Who Doesn't Look like a Poet," *Raging Like a Fire: A Celebration of Irving Layton* (1993) edited by Henry Beissel and Joy Bennett.

If I were named czar tomorrow, the first thing I'd do is fire all the English teachers. They do enormous damage. They take apart poems as if they were crossword puzzles or riddles. They destroy people's innate love of poetry.

Greg Gatenby, poet, founder of the Harbourfront Reading Series, quoted by Rod Currie in *The St. Catharines Standard*, 11 Sept. 1993.

We produce far too many poets of the ordinary, for whose work the market remains limited; what we lack in Canadian mass media are poets of the extraordinary.

Robert Fulford, columnist, referring to the national taste for documentaries, *The Globe and Mail*, 2 Nov. 1993.

I can learn a lot about poetry by listening to birds, for example, or by listening to trees. They speak ancient languages. And if I can't exactly transcribe them word for word, at least I can make some kind of counterpart in my own language.

Robert Bringhurst, poet, quoted by Christopher Dafoe in "In Person," *The Globe and Mail*, 24 June 1995.

On occasion, I imagine Canada a nation of 30 million poets. What disturbs me is how few of them will ever consider purchasing a book of poetry.

Michael Holmes, editor, Introduction, *The Last Word* (1996).

A poem is a preliminary answer to the final question.

Louis Dudek, poet and aphorist, *The Caged Tiger* (1997).

Ancient Chinese wisdom says it best: Poetry is like being alive twice.

James Clarke, poet, "The Essay," *The Globe and Mail*, 16 July 1998.

He came after Homer and before Gertrude Stein, a difficult interval for a poet.

Tongue-in-cheek line from the poem "Red Meat" about the ancient Greek poet Stesichoros that appears in **Anne Carson**'s *Autobiography of Red: A Novel in Verse* (1998).

POLICE See also CRIME, ROYAL CANADIAN MOUNTED POLICE

The American style was to stand aside and let the civilians work out matters for themselves, even at the risk of inefficiency, chaos and bloodshed. The Canadian style was to interfere at every step of the way in the interests of order, harmony, and the protections of life and property.

Jack London, author and adventurer, commenting on the role of the Mounted Police in patrolling the Yukon in the 1890s, quoted by Pierre Berton in *Klondike* (1972).

You ask me if the Warriors are representative of the Mohawk people. Well, I ask you: "Are the Sûrété du Québec representative of Quebec people?

Michèle Rouleau, President, Quebec National Women's Association, referring to the Mohawk Warrior Society, quoted by André Picard in *The Globe and Mail*, 31 July 1990.

POLISH PEOPLE

The Poles? I t'ough' all the Poles was in Canada—ha, ha!

Sentiment expressed by Johnny the Trapper (played with exuberance by **Laurence Olivier**) when the simple French Canadian falls into the hands of menacing Nazi spies who are en route from Hudson Bay to the United States in the movie *The 49th Parallel* (1942).

"To have Canada" is a Polish expression that refers to the achievement of financial success. Emigrés from China describe Canada as "The Golden Mountain."

David Olive in "Notre pays," *The Globe and Mail's Report on Business Magazine*, Aug. 1991.

You have a beautiful country, an excellent country. Make sure it stays the way it is.

Lech Walesa, President of Poland, press conference, Parliament Hill, Ottawa, on the day of the Quebec election that saw the victory of the Parti Québécois, 12 Sept. 1995, quoted by Jeff Sallot in *The Globe and Mail* the following day.

POLITENESS

An American acquaintance told me that the main difference between Canadians and Americans was that Canadians tended to be more polite. Canadians, he said, even say "thank you" when completing their business at automatic cash dispensers!

Charles, Prince of Wales, address at Queen's University, Kingston, 28 Oct. 1991, reproduced in *The Globe and Mail* the following day.

POLITICAL CORRECTNESS

It's not the same as letting native people tell their own stories. Only the people who know the metaphors, the symbols, and the subtleties of the culture can tell the stories.

Lenore Keeshig-Tobias, Ojibwa storyteller, protesting the usurpation of Native themes by non-Natives, addressing a press conference called to launch a TV movie about Native education, quoted by Deirdre Kelly in *The Globe and Mail*, 16 Sept. 1989.

When in doubt, define the opposition as "ideological."

Paul Webster, journalist, "Seeing Canada through a U.S. Prism," *The Toronto Star*, 17 Aug. 1992.

I can't pinpoint exactly where it went off the rails, but there must decidedly have been a moment in time when somebody figured out there was more to be gained by being indignant than by being right.

Eve Drobot, writer, "Come, Let Me Offend You," *Newsweek*, 28 Sept. 1992.

The only culture in Canada it's now socially acceptable to criticize is Anglo Canadian culture. The only ethnic stereotypes it's now politically correct to mock are WASPs, whites, and, as the absolute lowest of the low, white males. Everyone else is a victim.

Richard Gwyn, columnist, "Home & Away," *The Toronto Star*, 28 Feb. 1993.

I spent the first half of my life fighting the Right Wing and I fear that I may be spending my second half fighting the Left Wing.

A. Alan Borovoy, General Counsel, Canadian Civil Liberties Association, referring to incursions made in the interest of "political correctness," Toronto reception, 1 Jan. 1994.

In fact, political correctness is itself a misnomer because what is now going on at the levels of institutional reform is not political but moral administration, not correct or even sane, but deluded and panicked, and especially not laughable but sinister. The only aspect of correctness that characterizes this transformation is correctness in the sense of being correct—the old rightist sense of corporate decorum, and the old leftist sense of orthodoxy.

John Fekete, philosopher, *Moral Panic: Biopolitics Rising* (2nd ed., 1995).

In accordance with our employment equity goals for this occupation, applicants are particularly encouraged from aboriginal peoples, francophones, persons with disabilities and racial minorities.

Sentence from an advertisement for the position of an "Adoption Disclosure Counsellor" placed by the **Ministry of Community and Social Services, Government of Ontario** ("Dedicated to Employment Equity"), "MarketPlace," *The Globe and Mail*, 10 June 1995.

Canadians have financed an increasingly destructive agenda whose outcome is not unity, equality, or fairness but division.

Martin Loney, political scientist, last line of his study *The Pursuit of Division: Race, Gender, and Preferential Hiring in Canada* (1998).

POLITICAL PARTIES

See also BLOC QUÉBÉCOIS, CANADIAN ALLIANCE, CONSERVATIVE PARTY, LIBERALISM & LIBERAL PARTY, NEW DEMOCRATIC PARTY, PARTI QUÉBÉCOIS, POLITICS, REFORM PARTY, SOCIAL CREDIT

Liberal times are good times.... Tory times are hard times.

Liberal Party slogan described by Peter C. Newman in *Maclean's*, 22 July 1991: "The motto dates back to the time when R.B. Bennett, a hard-rock Tory from Calgary, was Canada's prime minister for the worst (1930–1935) of the Depression years."

Without a strong national capitalist class behind them, Canadian governments, Liberal and Conservative, have functioned in the interests of international and particularly American capitalism, and have lacked the will to pursue even a modest strategy of economic independence.

"The Waffle Manifesto: For an Independent Socialist Canada" (1969) reprinted in *The Canadian Forum*, Dec. 1989.

I promise to do absolutely nothing if I'm elected—just like the other parties.

Robert Charlebois, chansonnier, member of the Rhinoceros Party in 1968, quoted by Grattan Gray in *Maclean's*, Sept. 1974.

To switch from the Liberals to the Tories is to switch from blue cheese to green cheese.

Ed Broadbent, NDP leader, remark made in May 1979, quoted by Clive Cocking in *Following the Leaders: A Media Watcher's Diary of Campaign '79* (1980).

We're going to turn this party around 360 degrees.

Malapropism attributed to **John Turner** while leader of the Liberal Party of Canada in the mid-1980s, quoted by Hugh Winsor in "The Power Game," *The Globe and Mail*, 30 June 1999.

We will not accept donations from corporations and we will not accept donations from trade unions or from special interest groups. The present system of financing political parties corrupts the very basis of our democracy.

Mel Hurtig, nationalist, referring to the National Party of Canada, *A New and Better Canada: Principles and Policies of a New Canadian Political Party* (1992).

Historically, the Tories have tended to be the most restrained in their approach, pledging that they will do everything for voters from birth to death, while the more activist Liberals extended that promise to the slightly longer time span covered from womb to tomb. The Socialists, of course, don't believe in any limits and make similar promises from erection to resurrection.

Peter C. Newman, columnist, commenting on social welfare policies, "Business Watch," *Maclean's*, 15 Feb. 1993.

Last year seven-tenths of one percent of adult Canadians made a donation to a political party.

Mel Hurtig, leader of the National Party of Canada, quoted by Murray Dobbin in "The Patriot's Party," *The Canadian Forum*, Oct. 1993.

I will establish a group of 7,000 experts who will practise Transcendental Meditation and Yogic Flying. This group will radiate positivity and harmony throughout the nation and create a unified national consciousness.

Dr. Neil Paterson, leader of the Natural Law Party, campaign promise, advertisement, *The Globe and Mail*, 15 Oct. 1993.

In my continuing education as a Canadian I have learned an important fact of political life in this country, namely that the personal convictions and strengths and weaknesses of the party leaders have more influence on the course of events than the principles of the parties they lead, principles that in any event are not well defined.

Mitchell Sharp, former Minister of Finance and

Minister of External Affairs, *Which Reminds Me...: A Memoir* (1994).

The only difference between the Tories and the Liberals, it might be said, is that the Tories did not do what they said they would, while the Liberals are busy doing what they said they would not.

Andrew Coyne, columnist, "A Decade of Macdonaldism," *The Globe and Mail*, 9 Sept. 1995.

POLITICIANS

See also BOUCHARD, LUCIEN; CAMPBELL, KIM; CHAREST, JEAN; CHRÉTIEN, JEAN; CLARK, JOE; DIEFENBAKER, JOHN G.; DUPLESSIS, MAURICE; JOHNSON, DANIEL; KING, W. L. MACKENZIE; LÉVESQUE, RENÉ; MANNING, PRESTON; MULRONEY, BRIAN; PARIZEAU, JACQUES; POLITICS; PREMIERS; PRIME MINISTERS; TRUDEAU, PIERRE ELLIOTT; VANDER ZALM, WILLIAM

Like men standing on the edge of a cliff, Canadian statesmen are always wanting to jump off.

Charles Wentworth Dilke, British politician, remark made in 1867, quoted by Martin Woollacott in "Nationalism Hastens Canada's Great Divide," *Guardian Weekly*, 5 Nov. 1995.

Well, Mr. Speaker, I have caught some queer fish in my time, but I am afraid that my hon. friend—as during the previous Session, when he sat over in that corner—is too loose a fish for me ever to catch.

Sir John A. Macdonald, Prime Minister, introducing the words "loose fish" for maverick members, House of Commons, 29 Feb. 1876.

Another trouble is that if men start to vote, they will vote too much. Politics unsettles men, and unsettled men mean unsettled bills—broken furniture, broken vows and—divorce.

Speech made by suffragette **Nellie L. McClung** in the manner of Manitoba Premier Sir Rodmond Roblin at "the Women's Parliament," Winnipeg, 28 Jan. 1914, quoted by McClung in *The Stream Runs Fast: My Own Story* (1945).

Heckler: Hey, Tommy, why don't you stand up on a soap box?

Douglas: It doesn't matter because everything I say goes over your head anyway.

T.C. (Tommy) Douglas, politician, characteristic response to a heckler, Saskatchewan speech in 1940s, quoted by Jim Carr in the *Winnipeg Free Press*, 9 April 1995.

A politician is a man who is always interested in wordy causes.

Al Boliska, broadcaster, *The Mahareshi Says....* (1968).

I may be bland, but bland works.

William G. Davis, Ontario Premier (1971–84), noted by Rosemary Speirs in *Out of the Blue: The Fall of the Tory Dynasty in Ontario* (1986).

Flora MacDonald is the finest woman to have walked the streets of Kingston since Confederation.

Cutting remark attributed by Larry Zolf in Jan. 1975 to former Prime Minister **John G. Diefenbaker** about Flora MacDonald, Conservative Cabinet Minister for Kingston and the Islands, friend of Dalton Camp who promoted her bid for Conservative leadership.

I expect to be disagreed with. That's better than being a politician who decides to say nothing serious.

John Sewell, Mayor of Toronto, quoted by Dick Beddoes in *The Globe and Mail*, 22 Oct. 1979.

Let clever politicians, those arsonists disguised as firemen, those sorcerer's apprentices, come and tell us here in Ottawa, before the people, before past, present and future generations, whether or not they repudiate signatures that were freely given, at that time of grace in the national life of this country, at sunrise on June 3, 1987.

Lucien Bouchard, Minister of the Environment, point of order, House of Commons, 22 May 1990. With these words he began his statement announcing his resignation from the Mulroney Cabinet and Government in which he had served for two years as the Prime Minister's "Quebec lieutenant."

Sometimes Canadians complain that our politicians are weak. Thank God they are! I congratulate them for being so. Canadians are wise to select them that way. Too many countries suffer with strong politicians.

Roch Carrier, author, "Canada Is a Grand Dream," *Canadian Living*, Sept. 1992.

Politicians, someone has said, can be divided into those who want to be someone and those who want to do something.

Desmond Morton, historian, "A Time to Think about Leadership," *The Toronto Star*, 6 June 1993.

In entertainment you try to fake sincerity, in politics you fake righteous indignation.

Louis Dudek, poet and aphorist, *The Caged Tiger* (1997).

It's 90 per cent of the politicians who give the other 10 per cent a bad name.

John Crosbie, politician, speech, Niagara Falls Chamber of Commerce, 26 Feb. 1997, quoted in *The Niagara Falls Review* the following day.

POLITICS See also ELECTIONS, GOVERNMENT, PARLIAMENT, POLITICAL PARTIES, POLITICIANS, SENATE

Don't go into politics; it will break your heart.

Sam Jacobs, M.P., advice tendered lawyer Harry M. Budyk, Q.C., in 1937, quoted by Bernard Figler in *Sam Jacobs: Member of Parliament* (Samuel William Jacobs, K.C., M.P., 1871–1938) (1970).

The constitutionality of anything new, even the noblest, has always been questioned, always will be.

William Aberhart, Social Credit Premier of Alberta, interviewed by R.E. Knowles in *The Toronto Star*, 2 Dec. 1938.

What is politics anyway? In the Maritimes, politics is a disease; in Quebec, a religion; in Ontario, a business; on the Prairies, a cause. And in British Columbia, an entertainment.

Attributed to CCF politician **Angus MacInnis** in the 1950s.

In politics, one has to swallow a snake every morning.

Attributed to Senator **Thérèse Forget Casgrain** by Claire Kirkland-Casgrain in the 1950s.

Politics is not the art of the possible. It consists in choosing between the disastrous and the unpalatable.

John Kenneth Galbraith, economist and essayist, letter sent in 1960 to U.S. President John F. Kennedy, quoted by Charlotte Gray in *Saturday Night*, Nov. 1993.

Castration: initiation to political life.

Jacques Languirand, playwright, *Le dictionnaire insolite* (1962).

Don't quote me as saying that we will or we should increase our external aid. That would be my opinion if I had an opinion, but as a member of my government I don't have an opinion.

Paul Martin Sr., veteran politician, press conference, quoted in "Playboy after Hours," *Playboy*, Nov. 1965.

Politics offers yesterday's answers to today's questions.

Marshall McLuhan, communications pioneer, observation made in 1967, quoted by Robert Fleming in *Who Was Marshall McLuhan?* (1994) edited by Barrington Nevitt and Maurice McLuhan.

The vocabulary of politics is very small: there just aren't enough concepts to go around. Consequently, political discourse is crammed with metaphor and analogy. These mislead more often than they instruct.

James Eayrs, historian, "The Bucharest Line" (1966), *Minutes of the Sixties* (1968).

Ever since I got into politics, I've tried to think how the ideas that are important to me will sound to the guys I went to school with when I was a kid in Oshawa.

Ed Broadbent, NDP leader, interviewed by Christina Newman in *The Globe and Mail*, 10 June 1975.

Politics is intrigue from one end to the other.

Réal Caouette, Créditiste leader, House of Commons, quoted by Jacques Grenier in *The Canadian Magazine*, 9 Aug. 1975.

Now that I'm out of politics, I don't have to lie any more.

Dalton Camp, politician turned columnist, *The Globe and Mail*, 4 Dec. 1976.

Everywhere I look in Canada, I get the impression of immense energies trying to find their proper regional outlets, continually blocked and thwarted by unreal political abstractions.

Northrop Frye, cultural critic, address, Options Conference, University of Toronto, 15 Oct. 1977, quoted in *The Globe and Mail*, 17 Oct. 1977.

Nothing changes; it is only perceptions that count. Politics, Canadian politics, at any rate, is altogether the art of the plausible.

George Bain, columnist, quoted in *Policy Options Politiques*, June–July 1980.

Politics is the art of getting elected or re-elected regardless of the cost to the country.

W. Earle McLaughlin, President, Royal Bank, quoted by Roderick McQueen in *Maclean's*, 13 Oct. 1980.

Politics must redress the natural injustice of history.

*

The deepest motivational springs of political involvement are to be located in this human capacity to feel needs for others.

Michael Ignatieff, essayist, *The Needs of Strangers* (1985).

Political reform should be at the top of our national agenda, right next to the economy. Yet, somehow, the Conservatives, Liberals, and New Democrats seem to have almost totally forgotten the issue.

Mel Hurtig, nationalist, *A New and Better Canada: Principles and Policies of a New Canadian Political Party* (1992).

Men on white horses armed with simple solutions are the answer when people decide they've had enough of "politics as usual."

Bob Rae, former Ontario Premier, *From Protest to Power: Personal Reflections on a Life in Politics* (1996).

Perception is a word you hear a lot in politics. My word is conviction.

Stéphane Dion, Minister responsible for National Unity, quoted by E. Kaye Fulton, "Playing Hardball," *Maclean's*, 13 Jan. 1997.

Politics is all about power. Poverty means having no power.

Mel Hurtig, publisher and author, *Pay the Rent or Feed the Kids: The Tragedy and Disgrace of Poverty in Canada* (1999).

POLLS See OPINION POLLS

POLLUTION See also NATURE

Love has to become a stronger power than the poisons of self-interest and powerlessness or else we will all perish.

Anastasia M. Shkilnyk, sociologist, *A Poison Stronger than Love: The Destruction of an Ojibwa Community* (1985).

Think of your own behaviour for a minute. You probably turned on a light when you woke this morning, you used hot water, you had something for breakfast that was either hot or cooked, and you undoubtedly used a forest product and probably took part of your journey there by car. If you did, you supported the forest industry as well as the mining and petroleum industries, you contributed to global warming and proportionately polluted your world far more than any pulp mill.

Adam Zimmerman, Chairman of Noranda Forest Inc., address, Canadian Club, Toronto, quoted in *The Globe and Mail*, 22 Nov. 1989.

The mayor of Elliot Lake, Ontario, Roger Taylor said he had no objection to a permanent dump for radioactive wastes being located near his town, because it was not a dump. "It's a containment initiative."

"Doublespeak," *The People's Almanac Presents The Twentieth Century* (1995) by David Wallechinsky. The semantic distinction was made in 1988.

She came to this conclusion after studying the erosion of life and culture caused by mercury pollution of the water source, from 1963 on, at the Grassy Narrows Reserve, Ont. And where does Canada sit in all this? As one forthright newspaper reporter delicately put it, "Our record stinks on air pollution."

Anita Gordon and **David Suzuki**, science broadcasters, *It's a Matter of Survival* (1990).

Car owners commit sins of emission.

Maurus E. Mallon, aphorist, 18 Feb. 1993.

I am wondering when God is going to punish us for Lake Ontario.

Robertson Davies, man-of-letters, interviewed by Val Ross in *The Globe and Mail*, 8 Oct. 1994.

Chlorofluorocarbons released from an air conditioner in Newfoundland help cause skin cancer in New Zealand.

Carl Sagan, astronomer and author, *Billions and*

Billions: Thoughts on Life and Death at the Brink of the Millennium (1997).

Pollution will be recognized as a serious problem when it interferes with TV reception.

Hugh Arscott, aphorist, *Hugh's Views* (Volume I), 1998.

POPULARITY

Wear unpopularity as a badge of honour.

Brian Mulroney, Prime Minister, alluding to his own unpopularity and to that of U.S. President Clinton, press conference, Washington, D.C., 2 June 1993, quoted by Norma Greenaway in *The Montreal Gazette* the following day.

The quest for popularity is probably a disqualification for greatness.

Brian Mulroney, Prime Minister, guest on CNN's *Larry King Live*, 2 June 1993, quoted by Linda Diebel in *The Toronto Star* later that day.

POPULATION

Indians are having babies because it's the only thing Quebec will pay us to do.

Matthew Coon Come, leader, Grand Council of the Crees, quoted by André Picard in *The Globe and Mail*, 31 July 1991.

I suggest that, as the human population grows and environmental damage progresses, policymakers will have less and less capacity to intervene to keep this damage from producing serious social disruption, including conflict.

Thomas F. Homer-Dixon, co-ordinator of the Peace and Conflict Studies Program, University College, University of Toronto, "On the Threshold: Environmental Changes as Causes of Acute Conflict," *International Security*, Fall 1991.

By the year 2000, more people will live in the cities of Calcutta and Greater Bombay than in all of Canada.

George J. Demko, geographer, *Why in the World: Adventures in Geography* (1992).

Assuming a fertility rate of 1.7 and net migration (immigration minus emigration) of 0, Canada's population would stop growing in 2022 and then begin a long, lingering decline that would continue until the last Canadian, unable to find a mate anywhere from Victoria to St. John's, died of loneliness in 2786.

David K. Foot and **Daniel Stoffman**, demographer and journalist, *Boom, Bust & Echo: How to Profit from the Coming Demographic Shift* (1996).

PORNOGRAPHY See also CENSORSHIP, EROTICISM, SEX

If you want to create pornography you just separate some aspect of sex and life from everything else. That is pornography. It is fragmentation. Sentimentality the same. Take a rich emotion, break it up into bits and you have sentimentality. Sex is fragmentation.

Marshall McLuhan, communications pioneer, "Education in the Electronic Age" (1967), *The Best of Times / The Worst of Times: Contemporary Issues in Canadian Education* (1972) edited by Hugh A. Stevenson, Robert M. Stamp, and J. Donald Wilson.

Pornography is in the groin of the beholder.

Michael Magee, as the comic Fred C. Dobbs, *The Platinum Age of B.S.* (1982).

Pornography is a practice of sexual subordination. Its producers present sexual subordination for their own sexual pleasure, and its consumers get sexual pleasure from the presentation of sexual subordination.

Susan G. Cole, feminist, *Pornography and the Sex Crisis* (1989).

It is absurd that it is illegal to depict a woman sucking a penis but perfectly legitimate to depict her sucking a gun.

Susan G. Cole, feminist, *Pornography and the Sex Crisis* (1989). Cole refers to her own statement which first appeared in "Confronting Pornography: Bound, Gagged and Silenced," *Broadside*, July–Aug. 1983, adding, "Although the statement is often quoted by anti-censorship activists, I no longer hold the view that there is nothing problematic with pornographs presenting women in scenarios of fellatio."

Far from helping us to achieve equality or reduce inequality, the prohibition of pornography infantalizes us.

Thelma McCormack, sociologist and feminist, quoted by Margaret Wente, "Women," *The Globe and Mail*, 15 Oct. 1994.

There is something truly obscene about poking through the works of Alice Munro and Margaret Laurence and Timothy Findley looking for material that might be defined as child pornography.

Marian Botsford Fraser, Chair, PEN Canada, "Notes from the Chair," PEN Canada Bulletin, Dec. 1994.

How can I call myself a feminist if I like porn?

Josey Vogels, columnist, "Dirty Books: A Love/Hate Relationship," *My Messy Bedroom: A Playful Romp through the Pleasures of Sex* (1995).

POST OFFICE

I'm not sure of the answer, but wouldn't it be revolutionary if in the next round of contract talks we heard that CUPW was threatening a strike because they were dissatisfied with the *slow pace* of technological change?

Stephen Strauss, science columnist, referring to the Canadian Union of Postal Workers, *The Globe and Mail*, 28 Sept. 1991.

Moving at a mail's pace.

Pun created by **Barry O'Keefe**, Darmouth, N.S., quoted by Warren Clements in *The Globe and Mail*, 21 Nov. 1992.

There were two interesting items on the newswire this week. First, the United States Postal Service is issuing a 32-cent stamp with Bugs Bunny on it. Second, Canada Post has issued a limited-edition set of Lester B. Pearson commemorative envelopes. Pretty much sums up the difference between our two countries, doesn't it?

Lindor Reynolds, columnist, quoted in the *Winnipeg Free Press*, 28 May 1997.

POVERTY See also FOOD BANKS, HUNGER, STREET PEOPLE, THIRD WORLD

When your barn is well filled, all snug and secure, / Be thankful to God and remember the poor.

Lines written on a barn in 1863 and moved to the grounds of the Rockwood Academy, Rockwood, Ont., as described by Eric Arthur, "Barns," *The Canadian Encyclopedia* (2nd ed., 1988).

Dimes and dollars, dollars and dimes! / An empty pocket is the worst of crimes! / If a man's down give him a thrust, / Trample the beggar into the dust!

Stanza from the traditional verse "A Popular Creed," *The Ontario Workman* (1873), reproduced by N. Brian Davis in *The Poetry of the Canadian People, 1720–1920* (1976).

For the present economic crisis, as we have seen, reveals a deepening moral disorder in the values and priorities of our society. We believe that the cries of the poor and the powerless are the voice of Christ, the Lord of History, in our midst.

Remi J. De Roo, Bishop of Victoria, "Ethical Reflections on the Economic Crisis," an essay released in Ottawa on 5 Jan. 1983 by the Canadian Conference of Catholic Bishops' Episcopal Commission for Social Affairs.

The worst kind of poverty is poverty of the spirit. You can improve your housing and other things, but if you don't improve your spirituality, then you're bankrupt.

Vern Harper, Cree elder and healer, discussing the use of Native ways of dealing with psychiatric disorders, quoted by Helen Armstrong in *Now*, 24 Aug. 1989.

Ours is the first generation to realize that human misery will henceforth be the result of human indifference, and nothing else.

Ivan L. Head, Director, International Development Research Centre, rhetorical question, *On a Hinge of History: The Mutual Vulnerability of North and South* (1991).

Radicals believe that if poverty were equally distributed it would disappear and all would be equally well off.

Louis Dudek, poet and aphorist, entry for 1991, *Notebooks 1960–1994* (1994).

I've seen more beggars during a ten-minute walk in downtown Toronto than I saw throughout my whole three months in Egypt.

Paul William Roberts, travel writer, *River in the Desert: Modern Travels in Ancient Egypt* (1993).

There's been no particular link between children hungry at school and the unemployment rates and welfare rates that are there.... If you go back thirty or forty years ago when it seemed to be that mom was in the kitchen with a hot breakfast cooking as everybody woke up in the morning, that's not the normal situation today.

Mike Harris, Ontario Premier, press conference on the subject of school breakfast programs, Toronto, 6 Nov. 1996, quoted by Thomas Walkom, "Opinion," *The Toronto Star* the following day. Walkom epitomized the attitude in these words: "Children aren't hungry because their parents don't work [but] because their parents—and particularly their mothers—do work."

There are now more than forty thousand poor children in Edmonton. Our collective motto should be "One is too many."

Mel Hurtig, nationalist, address, awards dinner, Edmonton, 17 Sept. 1997.

So, it's not the war against poverty we're to be engaged in, it's the war against the poor.

Mel Hurtig, publisher and author, *Pay the Rent or Feed the Kids: The Tragedy and Disgrace of Poverty in Canada* (1999).

POWER

To many people and to a great number of politicians, the symbols of power are more attractive than the reality of power.

Maurice Lamontaigne, Cabinet Minister, "The Influence of the Politician," *Canadian Public Administration*, Fall, 1968.

Power contracts with a failure to use it.

Bora Laskin, Chief Justice of the Supreme Court of Canada and one of its frequent dissenters, quoted by Richard Gwyn in *The Toronto Star*, 30 Oct. 1975.

One of the signs of the powerful is that they deny they have power.

Peter C. Newman, author, quoted by Marq de Villiers in *The Canadian*, 9 Oct. 1976.

An iron law of history: the qualities needed to obtain power are the exact opposite of those needed to use it wisely.

Richard Needham, newspaper columnist, *The Wit and Wisdom of Richard Needham* (1977).

It is strange, and disturbing, that "power" is always regarded as suspect, if not downright bad ("All power corrupts"), while "freedom" is extolled as the highest ideal. Yet Hobbes expressed a self-evident truth stating that "Freedom and power are identical." Despite the fact that the rational meaning of both terms is identical, we use them with opposite emotional connotations. I think this is very dangerous because it by-passes the question that should be asked: "Freedom from whom and what?"

Hans Blumenfeld, architect-planner, *Life Begins at 65: The Not Entirely Candid Autobiography of a Drifter* (1987).

The single purpose of power is to serve the public weal.

John Ralston Saul, author, *The Doubter's Companion: A Dictionary of Aggressive Common Sense* (1994).

I have always seen the pursuit of power as a responsibility. Power is not immoral. It is a fact of political and public life.

Bob Rae, former Ontario Premier, *From Protest to Power: Personal Reflections on a Life in Politics* (1996).

PRAIRIE PROVINCES

See also ALBERTA, MANITOBA, SASKATCHEWAN, WESTERN PROVINCES

We looked out and beheld a sea of green sprinkled with yellow, red, lilac, and white, extending all round to the horizon. None of us had ever seen a prairie before, and, behold, the half had not been told us! As you cannot know what the ocean is without seeing it, neither can your imagination picture the prairie. The vast fertile beautiful expanse suggests inexhaustible natural wealth. Our uppermost thought must be expressed in the words, "Thank God, the great North-west is a reality."

George M. Grant, nationalist, *Ocean to Ocean: Sandford Fleming's Expedition through Canada in 1872* (1879).

There is a large wheat field, 980 miles long and two hundred and 30 miles broad.

Winston Churchill, British politician, explaining to his mother what he saw in the Winnipeg area on the lecture circuit, Jan. 1901, quoted by Alexander Rose, "Winston's Great Canadian Love Affair," *National Post*, 1 May 1999.

Go softly by that riverside / Or when you would depart / You'll find its every winding / Tied and knotted round your heart.

Lines from **Rudyard Kipling**'s verse apparently inspired by the sight of the Saskatchewan River, quoted by Marjorie Wilkins Campbell, "The Prairie Provinces," *The Face of Canada* (1959).

On the prairie one can see the colour of the air.

Emily G. Murphy, author and homesteader in the Swan River district of Manitoba in 1904, *Janey Canuck in the West* (1910).

Nowhere is there any sign of yesterday—not a cairn, not a monument. Life has passed here, but has left no footstep behind. But stay, the one thing which the old life still leaves is just this one thing—footsteps.

Sir Arthur Conan Doyle, author and traveller, concerning a trip on the Grand Trunk Railway in 1914, *Memories and Adventures* (1924).

Country people have time to tidy up their minds, classify their emotions, and, generally, speaking, get their souls in shape.

Nellie L. McClung, suffragette, "The Spirit of the Times" (1920), quoted by Candace Savage in *Our Nell: A Scrapbook Biography of Nellie L. McClung* (1979).

The Canadians were a hospitable and tolerant desert people, living on the edge of a wilderness of snow and permafrost. Winnipeg, Regina, and Saskatoon were cities of the northern desert, Samarkands of ice. At the end of every street there were white horizons of emptiness. My mind leapt, expanding to fill the void....

J.G. Ballard, author, recalling the sight of the Prairies in the 1950s, *The Kindness of Women* (1991).

Between the Province of Ontario and the Rocky Mountains lay a thousand miles of territory, uninhabited save by a few settlers in Manitoba, a roaming-place for Indians, trappers and wild animals. It was a temptation, so it was argued, to the land-hunger of the United States.

Winston Churchill, British statesman and popular historian, *Book X: "The Great Democracies," A History of the English-speaking Peoples* (1958).

To be born on the Prairies is to be marked forever. Something stays with you and never leaves, no matter where you go.

Frances Highland, actress, quoted by John Gray in *The Canadian*, 27 March 1976.

No one who has stood alone in the middle of a field in Manitoba, Saskatchewan or Alberta can ever doubt that the earth is flat, slowly spinning around its navel, the Prairies.

Alberto Manguel, author, "Prairie Zen," *The Globe and Mail's Destinations*, April 1988.

Here in Canada, really, we are the newest of the New World. My own generation was newest of all. We were the first whites to be born and stained in childhood by the prairie west. It is difficult to be much newer than that and, therefore, historically lonelier.

W.O. Mitchell, author, native of Weyburn, Sask., "Prairie Summer," *Imperial Oil Review*, Summer 1993.

The best soil in Manitoba is found in Saskatchewan.

Dave Phillips, climatologist, CBC Radio's *Radio Noon*, 26 Nov. 1996.

PRAYER

They shall make and address and offer thanks to the Earth...to the Great Creator who dwells in the heavens above who gives all the things useful to men, and who is the source and the ruler of health and life.

Article of the "Great Law of Peace" of the **Iroquois Confederacy**, reproduced by Craig MacLaine and Michael S. Baxendale in *This Land Is Our Land: The Mohawk Revolt at Oka* (1991).

From plague, pestilence and famine, / From battle, murder, sudden death / And all forms of cowlike contentment, / Good Lord, deliver us!

Prayer recalled in the pages of the autobiographical work *In Times like These* (1915) written by **Nellie L. McClung**.

Prayer is not simply words but a state of being that causes something to flow from you. Negative emotional states may also involve the flow of unhealthy, destructive forces.

Bernard Grad, biologist at McGill University who conducted research on the effect of prayers on plant life, quoted by Allen Spraggett in *The Unexplained* (1967). Dr. Grad noted, "Prayer can stimulate cell growth in plants and animals," according to William V. Rauscher and Spraggett in *The Spiritual Frontier* (1975).

O Lord, grant me the simplicity of childhood, the enthusiasm of youth, the wisdom of maturity, and the gentleness of old age.

Prayer attributed to **Marian Wilmhurst** frequently quoted by the prominent Quebec physician Gustave Gingras, *Feet Was I to the Lame* (1977) translated by Joan Chapman.

O God, grant me mediocrity and comfort; protect me from the radiance of Thy light.

Thoughts of a character who sarcastically calls these lines the "national prayer" in **Robertson Davies**' novel *The Lyre of Orpheus* (1988).

I thought I was praying to God, but perhaps / it was only to silence (a silence / that always listens)

Lines from **W.J. Keith**'s poem "Prayer, God, Silence," *Echoes in Silence* (1992).

Prayers are for losers.

Nicholas Catanoy, poet, *Notes on a Prison Wall: A Memoir/Poem* (1994).

PREDICTION & PROPHECY See also FUTURE, OPINION POLLS

The shrewd trader has already rid himself of all holdings that have about them a speculative flavour.

Floyd Chalmers, financial editor, anticipating by days the Stock Market Crash, *The Financial Past*, 24 Oct. 1929.

There is no such thing as a forward-looking person. That is a metaphor from car-driving, and it applies to space but not to time. In time we all face the past, and are dragged backwards into the future. Nobody knows the future; it isn't there to be known. The past is what we know, and it is all that we know. Those who are concerned with prediction and forecasting, like statisticians, can deal with the future only as the analogy of the past.

Marshall McLuhan, communications pioneer, "Education in the Electronic Age" (1967), *The Best of Times / The Worst of Times: Contemporary Issues in Canadian Education* (1972) edited by Hugh A. Stevenson, Robert M. Stamp, and J. Donald Wilson.

Of more signficance than prediction is the vision of alternate modes of life, of changed behaviour patterns that the future might demand or permit.

David Hartwell, science-fiction editor, *Age of Wonders: Exploring the World of Science Fiction* (1984).

We should always bear in mind that most questions that can be posed about the future can more forcefully and meaningfully be posed about the present.

Max Dublin, sociologist, *FutureHype: The Tyranny of Prophecy* (1989).

PREJUDICE See also DISCRIMINATION, RACE & RACISM

Would it not be sensible to stop imposing our local prejudices and faiths on children and to give them instead all sides of every question?

Brock Chisholm, first Director-General of the World Health Organization, address, Fall 1945, quoted by Allan Irving in *Brock Chisholm: Doctor to the World* (1998).

The oldest paradox of prejudice is that it renders its victims simultaneously invisible and overexposed.

Bharati Mukherjee, author born in India who lived in Canada and now lives in the United States, "An Invisible Woman," *Toronto Remembered: A Celebration of the City* (1984) edited by William Kilbourn.

Wherever zero tolerance reigns, zero sense is never far behind.

Margaret Wente, columnist, *The Globe and Mail*, 4 March 2000.

PREMIERS See also POLITICIANS

I am that other Prime Minister who is Québécois.

Pierre Elliott Trudeau, Prime Minister, address, National Assembly, Paris, 10 Nov. 1982, quoted by Jeffrey Simpson in *The Globe and Mail* the next day. The National Assembly had awarded Quebec Premier René Lévesque the Legion of Honour in 1977, and Trudeau was noting that constitutional custom allows the Premier of Quebec the title of Prime Minister, *premier ministre*.

... most of them provincial in more than status....

Mordecai Richler, journalist and author, "A Reporter at Large: Inside/Outside," *The New Yorker*, 23 Sept. 1991.

No provincial premier deserves more than 250 pages in the history books.

Michael Bliss, historian, reviewing the lengthy biography of a provincial premier, *The Globe and Mail's Report on Business Magazine*, May 1992.

Don't compare me to the Almighty; compare me to the alternative.

Bob Rae, Ontario Premier, deflecting criticism by pointing to the vacuum of Opposition leadership, quoted by Judy Steed in *The Toronto Star*, 21 Nov. 1993.

PRESENT See also TIME

The present cannot be revealed to people until it has become yesterday.

Marshall McLuhan, communications pioneer, *War and Peace in the Global Village* (1968), as quoted by Philip Marchand in *Marshall McLuhan: The Medium and the Messenger* (1989).

My interest lies in the present because I'm going to be spending the rest of my life there.

Byron Barwick, astrologer, "Astrologer," monograph, Oct. 1991.

I resist the degradation of the past in the name of the present, and in the name of the unfulfilled hopes of the past. I resist the degradation of the present, in the name of the future, and in the name also of the complex density of our being.

John Fekete, philosopher, *Moral Panic: Biopolitics Rising* (2nd ed., 1995).

PRESS See also NEWS

The newspaper industry in London has long attracted proprietors of immense ego.

Conrad Black, press proprietor, "Hello, Sweetheart, Give Me a Peerage," *Saturday Night*, Dec. 1992.

The press no longer reports government. The press only reports political scandal.

Marjorie Nichols, columnist, *Mark My Words: The Memoirs of a Very Political Reporter* (1992) written with Jane O'Hara.

We can formulate the law-like principle of this unfreedom of the press in a general way: *Nothing which contradicts the value or the necessity of the free market system or its aim of money profit for private corporations will be re-produced in the mass media.* Test this hypothesis against fact. Follow the mass media in all their pervasive circuits of dissemination to see if this principle of their censorship is anywhere disproved.

John McMurtry, philosopher, University of Guelph, "The Contradictions of Free Market Doctrine—Is There a Solution?" a paper prepared for the Westminster Institute Conference, "Surviving Globalization: Economic, Social, and Environmental Dimensions," London, Ont., May 1995.

PRIDE

You've got to keep moving. What you're most proud of today is quite likely to be scrapped five years hence.

Edgar G. Burton, merchandiser, interviewed by R.E. Knowles in *The Toronto Star*, 22 Jan. 1937.

What the masses want are monuments.

Jean Drapeau, Mayor of Montreal, remark made in the 1970s, quoted by Brian McKenna in "Jean Drapeau," *The Canadian Encyclopaedia* (1988).

I'm in a lot of pain right now, but the doctor says I should be okay. Pain lasts for a period of time, but pride lasts a lifetime.

Elvis Stojko, figure skater who overcame painful infirmities to win the 1994 silver medal at the Olympics at Nagano, Japan, press conference, 16 Feb. 1998, quoted by Allan Maki in *The Globe and Mail* later the same day.

PRIME MINISTERS See also CAMPBELL, KIM; CHRÉTIEN, JEAN; CLARK, JOE; DIEFENBAKER, JOHN G.; KING, W.L. MACKENZIE; MULRONEY, BRIAN; POLITICIANS; TRUDEAU, PIERRE ELLIOTT

About Mr. Bennett I need hardly say anything to Canadians. Mr. King: a consummate politician. Mr. Woodsworth: a fine old gentleman.

Harold Laski, British economist who lectured at McGill in the 1920s, commenting on three Prime Ministers, London School of Economics in the mid-1930s, recorded by Mitchell Sharp in *Which Reminds Me...: A Memoir* (1994).

Everybody says Canada is a hard country to govern, but nobody mentions that for some people it is also a hard country to live in.

Line from a speech in **Robertson Davies**' stage play *Fortune, My Foe* (1949).

The Canadian kid who wants to grow up to be Prime Minister isn't thinking big, he is setting a limit to his ambitions rather early.

Mordecai Richler, novelist and columnist, quoted in *Time*, May 31, 1971.

Politicians and prime ministers cannot do without the press, and we cannot do without them; the public might be able to do very well without both.

Charles Lynch, columnist and author, *The Lynch Mob: Stringing Up Our Prime Ministers* (1988).

Whatever the efforts of the opposition, a prime minister with an absolute majority in Canada has not been effectively challenged since the party rebellion that dislodged Sir John A. in 1873. Unless he commits some flagrantly criminal act, he remains immune and as absolute in his actions as he is in his majority.

George Woodcock, author and social commentator, "Five-Year Fascism," *The Canadian Forum*, Dec. 1990.

The art of politics is learning to walk with your back to the wall, your elbows high, with a smile on your face.

Attributed to Prime Minister **John Chrétien** by William Thorsell in *The Globe and Mail*, 21 Sept. 1996.

Prime Ministers are not chosen to seek popularity. They are chosen to provide leadership. There are times when Canadians must not be told what they want to hear, but what they have to know.

Brian Mulroney, former Prime Minister, address, Canadian Club of Toronto, 14 April 1997, quoted by William Walker in *The Toronto Star* the following day.

It's the toughest job in the land.

Jean Chrétien, Prime Minister, leadership debate, CBC-TV, 12 May 1997.

PRINCE EDWARD ISLAND See also ANNE OF GREEN GABLES, ATLANTIC PROVINCES, CHARLOTTETOWN, MARITIME PROVINCES

When I tell you that the technical specifications for the building were based on a lifespan of 1,000 years, you will realize the Centre is just beginning. Long may it flourish.

Frank MacKinnon, political scientist, address, fifteenth anniversary in 1979 of the founding of the Charlottetown Festival, quoted by Arnold Edinborough in *The Festivals of Canada* (1981).

This is Prince Edward Island. / I came back to my birthplace to announce my death. / I said I would ride full gallop into the sea / and not look back. People were furious....

Lines from **Mark Strand**'s poem "My Death," *Selected Poems* (1981). The P.E.I.-born poet was appointed the Poet Laureate of the United States by the Library of Congress in Washington, D.C.

The Premier of Prince Edward Island represents fewer people than the mayor of Sarnia, Ontario.

Remark based on an observation made by broadcaster and essayist **Peter Gzowski** in "Secrets of the Premier's Salad," *Selected Columns from Canadian Living* (1993).

Take this Island now. / A cradle it is: / Small enough to rock / Before the fireplace / On a homey evening— / All red and green and gentle.

Lines from an untitled poem by **Milton Acorn** first published by Chris Gudgeon in *Out of This World: The Natural History of Milton Acorn* (1996).

If all 5.5 billion people on Earth were gathered together in Prince Edward Island and given 60-centimetre squares to stand on, they would occupy only 36 per cent of the island and it would be 1,000 years before they would have to move on to a larger province.

Michael Kesterton, journalist, *Social Studies: The Best of "The Globe and Mail's" Daily Miscellany of Information* (1996).

PRINTING

Inspired typography... could give the world a means of visual communication that hurdles the barriers of race, religion, language, politics and economics and give the human race a common basis of communication and from this understanding and tolerance.

Words of typographer and designer **Carl Dair** displayed on a finely printed sign, Mackenzie Heritage Printery Museum, Queenston, Ont., observed on 1 Oct. 1994.

After Gutenberg came out with print, no one went back to the chisel.

Frank Ogden, futurologist, explaining why he releases computer books rather than publishes books, 17 Nov. 1992.

PRISONS See also JUSTICE & INJUSTICE

I came out a better man than when I went in. I learned much that will aid me in all future activity.

Tim Buck, leader of the Communist Party of Canada, interviewed upon his release from the Kingston Penitentiary by R.E. Knowles in *The Toronto Star*, 26 Nov. 1934.

I was so delighted to be getting away from Fort Henry that I raised no objection. "I understand," I remarked, "I am the first piece of reverse Lend-Lease."

Ernest (Putzi) Hanfstaengle, one-time intimate of Adolf Hitler and memoirist who recalled detention as an "enemy alien" in 1940–42 at Red Rock and then Kingston, Ont., *Hitler: The Missing Years* (1957). He was conditionally released on 30 June 1942 to assist the U.S. war effort.

Bill: You'll just have to take the consequences I'm afraid. It's Canada or jail.

Archie: You know, I've always thought I should go to jail.

Exchange between two characters in London, England, who have no love for Canada in **John Osborne**'s play *The Entertainer* (1957).

Man can come near enough to his utopias. In the meantime, I believe that as long as prisons exist, independent voices must be heard, not outside the walls but inside.

Bruno M. Cormier, psychiatrist, *The Watcher and the Watched* (1975).

Whereas liberty engenders democratic thinking, captivity produces paranoid thinking.

Bruno M. Cormier, forensic psychiatrist, *The Watcher and the Watched* (1975).

I went by bus and plane, to Kabul, via Mazar-i-Sharif. Two incidents in Kabul stay in my mind: a visit to the Kabul Insane Asylum, where I failed to gain the release of a Canadian who had been put there by mistake (he said he didn't mind staying there as long as he had a supply of chocolate bars; it was better than going back to Canada)....

Paul Theroux, American traveller and writer, *The Great Railway Bazaar: By Train through Asia* (1975).

Every fourteen-year-old who has been in prison could be my son.

Dave Barrett, B.C. Premier and former social worker, quoted by Christina Newman in *The Globe and Mail*, 1 March 1975.

You can't kill an idea by putting its author in jail.

John Ross Taylor, fascist, member of the Western Guard, jailed in 1981–82 for promoting racism, quoted by Stanley R. Barrett in *Is God a Racist?* (1987).

Nearly 700 Canadians are currently imprisoned abroad. The laws and customs of the various countries in the world can be shockingly different from those of Canada. Ignorance of laws is no defence from .whatever penalties may be attached to them.

Bon Voyage, But... Tips for Canadians Travelling Abroad, booklet issued by **External Affairs and International Trade Canada**, 1995.

PRIVACY

There's no place for the state in the bedrooms of the nation.

Pierre Elliott Trudeau, Minister of Justice, celebrated bon-mot, Ottawa interview, 22 Dec. 1967. With reference to changes in the Criminal Code, he said, "The state has no place in the nation's bedrooms." Like many a famous aphorism, it is seldom recalled in its original words and it may not be the work of a single person. Trudeau's aphorism is an adapation of lines that originally appeared in an editorial published in *The Globe and Mail*, 12 Dec. 1967: "Obviously, the state's responsiblity should be to legislate rules for a well-ordered society. It has no right or duty to creep into the bedrooms of the nation." The unsigned editorial was written by journalist Martin O'Malley, so he contributed to the formulation of one of the most celebrated of modern Canadian aphorisms, one that brought the name "Trudeau" to the lips of the electorate.

If two consenting adults decide, in the privacy of their bedroom, that a master-slave role-play will nourish their souls and get them off, what's the big deal?

Wendy Dennis, author, *Hot and Bothered: Men and Women, Sex and Love in the '90s* (1992).

I can find out anything I want about anybody I want.

Frank Ogden, futurologist, quoted by Rod McQueen in *The Financial Post*, 4 June 1994.

PROBLEMS

Problems are gateways.

Robin Skelton, poet and aphorist, *A Devious Dictionary* (1991).

What many Canadians do not seem to realize is that in most countries of this world people would say about Canada: "Boy, I wish we had their problems and not ours!"

Arkadi Tcherkassov, Russian commentator, "Our Man in Moscow," *Grainews*, July 1992.

PRODUCTIVITY

The United States and Canada produce wheat for export because they happen to have a "surplus"; they have a surplus because there is a demand abroad for wheat at a profitable price. The same is true of the coffee "surpluses" in Colombia and Brazil.

Lauchlin Currie, Canadian-born economic adviser to Colombia, *Accelerating Development: The Necessity and the Means* (1966).

The knee-jerk response that Canada must become more like the U.S. to become more productive is based on the simplistic assumption that workers need to be disciplined by fear, while corporations and their senior executives need to be stimulated by greed. But social equality and democracy at the workplace boost rather than depress productivity.

Bob White, President, Canadian Labour Congress, "Counterpoint," *Financial Post*, 29 Dec. 1998.

PROFESSIONALISM

That old idea of "trust me" is passé. Professionals now have to earn the public's respect.

Colin McKinnon, head of the communications committee of the Law Society of Upper Canada, referring to a province-wide survey of attitudes towards lawyers, quoted in *The Hamilton Spectator*, 2 May 1992.

We have a saying in our studio: We are happy amateurs, not sad professionals.

Bruce Mau, designer, address, Design Exchange, quoted by Pamela Young in *The Globe and Mail*, 16 May 1996.

PROFITS

Prophets went out with the Old Testament.

William James, CEO, Denison Mines Ltd., addressing the annual meeting at which a stockholder raised a question about future profitability, Toronto, 31 May 1991, quoted by Allan Robinson in *The Globe and Mail* the following day.

Unlike our febrile adversaries in the CBC and the dreary procession of tired and authoritarian leftists trotted through that program, we see no contradiction between quality and profitability.

Conrad Black, capitalist, "Letter of the Day: Conrad Black's Response to the CBC," *The Hamilton Spectator*, 26 Oct. 1996.

PROGRESS

Progress moves not only westward but northward too.

J.-E. Bernier, Arctic explorer, address, "The Arctic Regions of Canada," Empire Club of Canada, Toronto, 20 Dec. 1909.

No one in history ever went forward by taking steps backward.

Jean Drapeau, long-time Montreal Mayor, quoted by Bill Carroll in *Weekend Magazine*, 3 July 1976.

There is no reason to feel complacent about Stalin's Russia, however: many Canadians defend the destruction of their country by such phrases as "you can't stop progress," unaware that "progress" in such contexts is an idol on the same level as the legendary Hindu Juggernaut or the Old Testament Moloch.

Northrop Frye, cultural critic, *The Double Vision: Language and Meaning in Religion* (1991).

The irritating thought nags at us that progress might be a circle rather than a straight line.

Eb Zeidler, architect, quoted by David Olive in *The Globe and Mail's Report on Business Magazine*, Aug. 1992.

When one hears of progress one should ask for whom.

Robin Skelton, poet and aphorist, *A Devious Dictionary* (1991).

PROGRESSIVE CONSERVATIVE PARTY See CONSERVATIVE PARTY

PROHIBITION See also ALCOHOL

I don't even know what street Canada is on.

Al Capone, Chicago bootlegger, denying any Canadian "interests," quoted in 1931 by Roy Greenaway in *The News Game* (1966).

I was called "King Canada," because that's how I wanted to be known in the United States. I gave myself that name, because here in town if the law comes looking for King Canada, well, nobody's going to know who that is. The people in town know me as Blaise Diesbourg but they don't know King Canada.

Blaise Diesbourg, alias the rumrunner King Canada, quoted by C.H. Gervais in *The Rumrunners: A Prohibition Scrapbook* (1980). Apparently the bootlegger was so named by Al Capone.

There are big companies today that had their beginnings in running illegal liquor into the country. What about Sam Bronfman who ran it from Canada across Lake Erie, which we called the Jewish lake?

Meyer Lansky, U.S. gangster and former bootlegger, recalling in the 1970s his inglorious past and that of others, quoted by Michael R. Marrus in *Mr. Sam: The Life and Times of Samuel Bronfman* (1991). Marrus concluded that Lansky had not "a shred of evidence for this contention, and it is highly doubtful if any exists."

PROPAGANDA

Most of what the C.D. Howe Institute and all of what the Fraser Institute produce is propaganda and should be treated as such.

Timothy Findley, novelist, "When You Write about This Country," *The Canadian Forum*, Sept. 1992.

Propaganda gives us the cure because politics fails to give us the prevention.

L.S. Cattarini, aphorist, 30 Sept. 1992.

The idea of scaremongering doesn't bother me at all. This is irrelevant. It's false. All I was doing in there was telling the truth. This is a rough business.

Brian Mulroney, Prime Minister, discussing tactics of the Yes side during the referendum campaign, interviewed on 21 Oct. 1992 by the editors of *The Globe and Mail* and published 23 Oct. 1992.

PROPERTY

Property appreciates. Man? Man simply depreciates.

Speech of the lawyer in **Morley Torgov**'s novel *St. Farb's Day* (1990).

It should be horse tall, bull strong, and skunk tight.

Norman Kopperud, lawyer and "fence-viewer" defining an ideal fence, interpreting the Line Fences Act of Ontario, which dates back to the 1790s, quoted by Trish Crawford in *The Toronto Star*, 3 July 1994.

A society obsessed by property sucks essential capital out of growth areas and sinks it into the passive domain of land, bricks and mortar.

John Ralston Saul, author, *The Doubter's Companion: A Dictionary of Aggressive Common Sense* (1994).

PROSPERITY

What is prosperity? The fact that a bank manager, a railway president, or an industrialist states at an annual meeting that his business has had a prosperous year is no indication as to conditions throughout the country. Prosperity reflects itself in the general conditions of the masses and when they are prosperous, only then can we say we are in a state of prosperity.

A.A. Heaps, socialist member of Parliament, House of Commons, 20 Feb. 1928.

Despite the tough times, compared with just about any other land on earth, Canada still is blessed with the mandate of heaven.

Peter C. Newman, columnist, "From Hope to Defiance," *Maclean's*, 3 Jan. 1994.

PROSTITUTION See also SEX

Women have found out that their bodies might serve in lieu of goods and would be still better received than beaver, so that it is now the most usual and most continual commerce, and that which is most in fashion.

Etienne de Carheil, Jesuit missionary, referring to the position of some women in Montreal, letter to Jean Bouchard, Chevalier de Champigny, Indendant of New France, 30 Aug. 1702, quoted by Francis Parman in *The Old Régime* (1874).

My first trip to Canadian borders, / My first trip to Canadian shores, / Met a gal named Rosie O'Grady, / Better known as the Winnipeg whore.

First verse of the four-verse bawdy folk song "The Winnipeg Whore," according to Edward Cray, compiler of *The Erotic Muse* (1968), "The Winnipeg whore may be Canadian by birth, but she has become a naturalized citizen of the English-speaking world."

Usually it's the Conservatives who say we're villains and the Liberals who say we're victims. The NDP are the best for saying we're working women.

Valerie Scott, leader of the Canadian Organization for the Rights of Prostitutes (CORP), quoted by Tom Speirs in *The Toronto Star,* 10 Jan. 1988.

I am going to ask something unusual of you. Would you please stand up?

Lew Bewley, B.C. judge, addressing a prostitute in court, quoted by Allan Fotheringham, "Allan Fotheringham," *Maclean's,* 2 Nov. 1998.

PROTECTION & PROTECTIONISM

Every man for himself, as the elephant said as he danced among the chickens.

Characteristic remark concerning protectionism attributed to socialist leader **T.C. (Tommy) Douglas** by William Neville in the *Winnipeg Free Press,* quoted by Mel Hurtig in an address, 25 Oct. 1993.

We speak for the dead to protect the living.

Motto of the **Office of the Chief Coroner of the Province of Ontario**, adopted by H.B. (Beatty) Cotnam, Ontario's chief coroner (1962–82), recalled in his obituary notice by Alan Barnes, *The Toronto Star,* 11 July 1995.

The point system for determining Canadian content goes by the acronym MAPL—music, artist, production, lyrics—and assigns one point for each category where a Canadian is predominantly involved. At least two points are required for a record to be treated as Canadian.

Anthony DePalma, journalist, "Rules to Protect a Culture Make for Confusion," *The New York Times,* 14 July 1999. DePalma concluded, "It isn't so simple to be Canadian."

PROTEST See also CLAYOQUOT, ENVIRONMENTALISM, OKA STANDOFF, REBELLIONS

I don't do protests.

Mike Harris, Ontario Premier, informing reporters at Toronto's Metro Conference Centre, where he spoke on the future of education in the province, 19 Nov. 1997, why he was evading protesters, quoted by Jane Armstrong in *The Toronto Star* the following day.

For me, I put pepper on my plate.

Jean Chrétien, Prime Minister, press conference, Ottawa, 15 Sept. 1998, recalled by Rosemary Spiers, "National Affairs," *The Toronto Star,* 15 Sept. 1998. He made this gaffe while assuring reporters that he had nothing to do with the action of the RCMP in pepper-spraying students protesters who wished to demonstrate against the visit to Vancouver of Indonesia's former dictator Suharto and fifteen other Pacific Rim leaders for the APEC (Asian-Pacific Economic Co-operation) summit meeting, Nov. 1997.

PROTOCOL

Protocol will be necessary as long as two people want to walk through a doorway at the same time.

Arthur Beauchesne, Clerk of the House of Commons (1925–49), quoted by Reg Stackhouse in *The Globe and Mail,* 6 Jan. 1977.

PROVINCES See also ALBERTA, BRITISH COLUMBIA, MANITOBA, NEW BRUNSWICK, NEWFOUNDLAND, NOVA SCOTIA, ONTARIO, PRINCE EDWARD ISLAND, QUEBEC, SASKATCHEWAN

Under Lord Dorchester Canada was divided into Lower Canada (named after Professor A.R.M. Lower) and Upper Canada (after Sir Charles Upper).

Eric Nicol, humorist, *An Uninhibited History of Canada* (1959) illustrated by Peter Whalley.

Provincial autonomy means national inactivity.

F.R. Scott, constitutional specialist, adapted from Bora Laskin's paper "Reflections on the Canadian Constitution after the First Century" (1967), *Canadian Federalism: Myth or Reality* (1968) edited by J. Peter Meekison.

Canada is a collection of ten strong provinces with governments loosely connected by fear.

Dave Broadfoot, comedian, quoted by Ernest Hillen in *Maclean's*, 30 March 1981.

One can probably be happy in a province. Many people are. But one cannot meet the challenges of the new age sitting comfortably on a provincialist couch.

Daniel Latouche, social scientist and columnist, "To Be or Not to Be a Province," *The Globe and Mail*, 17 Feb. 1995.

PSYCHIATRY See also MEDICINE

The easiest thing to do is lock the insane in cells and feed them and forget them. The hardest is to find that spark of humanity that dwells in each of us.

Joseph Workman, psychiatrist, address, Toronto Medical Students, 1883, reproduced in Christine I.M. Johnston in *Joseph Workman: The Father of Canadian Psychiatry* (2000).

Every psychoanalyst has a responsibility to share his knowledge with persons other than neurotics at least once a week.

Brock Chisholm, first Director-General of the World Health Organization, speech, New York Psychoanalytic Society, Nov. 1946, Ottawa, quoted by Allan Irving in *Brock Chisholm: Doctor to the World* (1998).

I am a psychiatrist and psychiatry is the science of change. Change can often be painful, very painful.

Camille Laurin, separatist Quebec Cabinet Minister and psychiatrist, interviewed by Richard Cleroux in *The Globe and Mail*, 1 Oct. 1977.

If there is one central intellectual reality at the end of the twentieth century, it is that the biological approach to psychiatry—treating mental illness as a genetically influenced disorder of brain chemistry—has been a smashing success.

Edward Shorter, historian of medicine, *A History of Psychiatry: From the Era of the Asylum to the Age of Prozac* (1997).

PSYCHICAL RESEARCH See also BELIEF, PARAPSYCHOLOGY

If ESP exists it must revolutionize physical and biological science. The existing evidence does not yet require us to take such a step.

D.O. Hebb, psychologist, *Essay on Mind* (1980).

It is a fact that no paranormal, psychic or supernatural claim has ever been substantiated by proper testing.

James Randi, conjuror and sceptic of claims of the paranormal, *James Randi: Psychic Investigator* (1991).

People see me and they don't seem to forget!

Jocelyn (JoJo) Savard, psychic, gaudily gowned founder of the Psychic Alliance, a telephone psychic service, familiar figure from "infomercials" on late-night television, quoted by Marci McDonald, "Telling Fortunes," *Maclean's*, 4 Sept. 1996.

PSYCHOLOGY

My argument is that it is only with the rubble of bad theories that we shall be able to build better ones, and that without theory of some kind, somewhere, psychological observation and description would at best be chaotic and meaningless.

D.O. Hebb, psychologist, "The Role of Neurological Ideas in Psychology," *Journal of Personality*, No. 20, 1951.

The mystic's monopoly on morality has been broken. Man the rational being has found his spokesman and defender, and has been released from his moral underground. That is the imperishable achievement of Ayn Rand.

Nathaniel Branden, psychologist born in Brampton, Ont., who espoused the cause of Objectivism, *Who Is Ayn Rand? An Analysis of the Novels of Ayn Rand* (1962).

Psychology was as colourless and odourless as a Canadian.

Line describing an academic who studies

psychology without much caring for it in **Nina Fitzpatrick**'s novel *The Loves of Faustina* (1995).

PUBLIC INTEREST

Nobody behaves in the public interest unless it is in their own self-interest to do so.

John Crispo, political economist, address, Empire Club of Canada, 25 Jan. 1979.

Unlike the United States, Canada has yet to develop truly effective public interest groups; we live with the mirage that politicians somehow represent us rather than themselves, their party, and the corporate elite.

David H. Flaherty, historian, "Who Rules Canada?" *Daedalus: Journal of the American Academy of Arts and Sciences*, "In Search of Canada," Fall 1988.

PUBLICITY

Self-seeking, self-indulgence, self-display— / From these arise the evils of the day.

Couplet from an untitled verse by 19th-century poet **James DeMille** and quoted by A.R. Bevan in *The Dalhousie Review*, Autumn, 1955.

I always think that in any movie the promotion budget should be as big as the cost of the movie.

Pierre Berton, author, quoted by P.M. Evanchuck in *Motion*, Sept.–Oct. 1973.

PUBLIC RELATIONS

A negative form of imagination. In Mussolini's phrase, "invention is more useful than truth."

John Ralston Saul, author, *The Doubter's Companion: A Dictionary of Aggressive Common Sense* (1994).

Whitewash comes in many colours.

Robert Priest, aphorist, *Time Release Poems* (1997).

PUBLIC SERVICE See also BUREAUCRACY

The position of the public servant is one inch to the left of the party in power.

Attributed to Film Commissioner **John Grierson** by Ralph Foster in James Beveridge's *John Grierson: Film Master* (1978).

You know that, by definition, civil servants are not people who are in a hurry.

Gilles Delaunière, writer, quoted by Robert Prévost in *Petit dictionnaire des citations québécoises* (1988).

First we stopped being servants—now we've stopped being civil.

Remark overheard at an Ottawa picket organized by the **Public Service Alliance of Canada**, quoted by Leslie Papp in *The Toronto Star*, 1 Oct. 1991.

PUBLISHING See also BOOKS, EDITORS

The growth of literature in every country depends a good deal on the enterprise and liberality of its publishers.

Joseph Howe, patriot, *Novascotian*, 30 Dec. 1841.

Book Publishing, Questionable Methods of

Entry in the index to an article that appeared in *The Bystander*, June 1890, published by **Goldwin Smith**.

My own publisher once said to me: "The more real the religious note in a story, the bigger its sale and the longer its vogue."

R.E. Knowles, interviewer and novelist, explaining to Nellie McClung why she should write a "religious" novel, *The Toronto Star*, 12 March 1937.

If a nation has the literature it deserves, it also has the publishers it merits.

Solange Chaput-Rolland, author, *My Country, Canada or Quebec?* (1966).

We also serve who only punctuate.

Thoughts of a character on copy-editing in **Brian Moore**'s novel *I Am Mary Dunne* (1966).

I don't think I have the qualifications to be a really great publisher. I'll probably have to settle ultimately for being the best in Canada.

J.G. (Jack) McClelland, publisher, McClelland and Stewart Ltd., quoted in *Time*, 5 Jan. 1968, as noted in *Jack McClelland: The Publisher of Canadian Literature* (University of Guadalajara, 1996).

I was the punk from Montreal and you were the Prime Minister of Canada . . . You were the real Prime Minister of Canada. You still are. And even though it's all gone down the tubes, the country that you govern will never fall apart.

Leonard Cohen, poet, tribute, *Jack McClelland:*

The Publisher of Canadian Literature (University of Guadalajara, 1996).

If Canadians spoke Swahili and dealt in razbuckniks, Canada would have a healthy and vigorous Canadian-owned book publishing industry. But, because we have the misfortune of speaking English and dealing in dollars, our publishing industry is fighting for its survival.

Peter Martin, publisher, "Brief to the [Ontario] Royal Commission on Book Publishing, March, 1971," *Independence: The Canadian Challenge* (1972) edited by Abraham Rotstein and Gary Lax.

Since nearly all major Toronto publishers are subsidiaries of American firms, they operate largely as extensions of the U.S. editorial-industrial complex, importing books from south of the border, rather than initiating their own.

Richard Kostelanetz, U.S. critic and poet, *The End of Intelligent Writing* (1973).

Authors express themselves in words, publishers in figures.

Hugh Garner, author, characteristic remark, May 1976.

Xerox gives power to the people. It makes everyone a publisher.

Marshall McLuhan, communications pioneer, Montreal International Book Fair, quoted by Christie McCormick in *The Montreal Gazette*, 16 May 1975.

No matter how complex it is, if you look at it in the right way, it becomes even more complex.

Malcolm Lester, publisher, commenting on the Florence Agreement, a treaty to allow the tariff-free movement of books and other commodities across international borders, quoted by Phil Surguy in *Books in Canada*, Jan. 1978.

Any publisher who believes he knows anything about publishing is in for a rude and immediate shock.

J.G. (Jack) McClelland, publisher, addressing the Applebaum-Hébert Cultural Policy Review, attributed by William French in *The Globe and Mail*, 2 Jan. 1982.

The Canadian book business is ten percent books and ninety per cent business.

Attributed to book publisher **John Gray** by Marsh Jeanneret in *God and Mammon: Universities as Publishers* (1989).

Beyond doubt, book publishing can be the most exhilarating of all possible careers. It is surely the least monotonous, and offers never-ending opportunities to indulge both one's cultural and one's commercial interests. It is the profession of professions....

Marsh Jeanneret, former publisher, University of Toronto Press, *God and Mammon: Universities as Publishers* (1989).

Procrustes was an editor.

Robin Skelton, poet and aphorist, *A Devious Dictionary* (1991).

Publishing is like a second marriage—a triumph of hope over experience.

J.G. (Jack) McClelland, former book publisher, quoted by Beverley Slopen in *The Toronto Star*, 25 Jan. 1992.

PUGWASH CONFERENCES

When in 1955 Albert Einstein and Bertrand Russell suggested that some of the world's most distinguished scientists be invited to an informal conference to discuss international tensions, most responded. The first such conference was held in July 1957, at Pugwash, Nova Scotia. Subsequent "Pugwash" conferences have been held in Quebec, Vienna, and Moscow. Though no formal action has resulted, a definite rapport has developed between scientists of the East and West which undoubtedly is a moderating influence in the Cold War climate of today.

Norman Z. Alcock, scientist and peace advocate, *The Bridge of Reason* (1961).

QUALITY

Quality control, n. A concept of rumoured American origin, mass-marketed by the Swiss, and perfected in Japan.

David Olive, business commentator, *White Knights and Poison Pills: A Cynic's Dictionary of Business Jargon* (1990).

As you move toward perfection, it constantly recedes. Quality is not a destination, rather it is a never-ending climb toward an unattainable peak.

Isadore Sharp, founder, Four Seasons Hotels and Resorts, characteristic remark, quoted in Dec. 1992.

QUEBEC

See also CANADA: FRENCH; CANADA & QUEBEC; DISTINCT SOCIETY; FRANCE; FRENCH & ENGLISH CANADA; FRENCH CANADIANS; MONTREAL; PARTI QUÉBÉCOIS; PARTITION; PLAINS OF ABRAHAM; QUEBEC, CONQUEST OF; QUEBEC & FRANCE; QUEBEC CITY; LES QUÉBÉCOIS; QUIET REVOLUTION; REFERENDA; SECESSION; SEPARATISM; SOVEREIGNTY; SOVEREIGNTY-ASSOCIATION; UNGAVA

Along the shores of the said Quebec are diamonds in the slate rocks which are better than those of Alençon.

Samuel de Champlain, French explorer and colonist, "Of Savages" (1603), *The Works of Samuel de Champlain (1922–36)*, translated by H.P. Biggar. Champlain hoped to find precious minerals and metals like those found in the vicinity of Alençon in Normandy. The "diamonds" he found in Quebec proved to be quartz.

I have no reply to make to your general other than from the mouths of my cannon and muskets. He must learn that it is not in this fashion that one summons a man such as I. Let him do the best he can on his side as I will do on mine.

Comte de Frontenac, defender of Quebec, addressing Major Thomas Savage, envoy of Admiral Phips, commander of the English forces, who was demanding the surrender of Quebec, 15 Oct. 1690. Phips was forced to withdraw. The reply appears in W.J. Eccles' *Canada under Louis XIV: 1663–1701* (1964).

Those who are protestants among the *French*, will probably chuse to remain under the *English* government; many will chuse to remove, if they can be allowed to sell their lands, improvements, and effects: the rest in that thin-settled country, will in less than half a century, from the crowds of *English* settling round and among them, be blended and incorporated with our people both in language and manners.

Benjamin Franklin, U.S. patriot and pamphleteer, "Some Account of a Pamphlet, Entitled, The Interest of Great Britain Considered, with Regard to Her Colonies, and the Acquisitions of Canada and Guadaloupe," sometimes called "The Canada Pamphlet," reproduced in *The Gentleman's Magazine*, May 1760.

In all places where the French were few and weakly established, they disappeared. The rest crowded into a narrow area and passed under other laws. The four hundred thousand French inhabitants of Lower Canada now constitute the remnants of an ancient people lost in the flood of a new nation.

*

The French of Canada, who loyally preserve the tradition of their ancient mores, are already finding it difficult to live on their land, and this small nation which has only just come to birth will soon be a prey to all the afflictions of old nations. The most enlightened, patriotic, and humane men in Canada make extraordinary efforts to render people dissatisfied with the simple happiness that still contents them.

Alexis de Tocqueville, French traveller, *Democracy in America* (1835) translated by George Lawrence and edited by J.P. Mayer and Max Lerner in 1966.

Montreal, and even Quebec are, I think, becoming less and less French every day; but in the villages and on the small farms the French remain, keeping up their language, their habits, and their religion.

Anthony Trollope, English novelist and traveller, *North America* (1862).

The French privilege in regard to laws, language, and religion make an insoluble core in the heart of the confederacy, and form a compact mass which can be wielded for political purposes. This element, dominant in the province of Quebec, is aggressive.

Charles Dudley Warner, American travel writer, *Studies in the South and West* (1889).

Keep out of Quebec, I prithee—that is, unless you are one who wants to see Objects of Interest. It is the cloaca of creation.

H.L. Mencken, author, letter of 24 June 1931 to Philip Goodman, *The New Mencken Letters* (1977) edited by Carl Bode. Mencken visited Quebec on his honeymoon in 1930.

Quebec is and doubtless will remain a "homeland" to all French Canadians, except perhaps the Acadians, but this is an historic fact rather than a constitutional rule. All Canada is the homeland for all Canadians. Canada is thus two cultures, but not two states, a federal system and not a dyarchy.

F.R. Scott, constitutional specialist, writing in 1957, quoted by Deborah Coyne and Michael Valpy in *To Match a Dream: A Practical Guide to Canada's Constitution* (1998).

In Lower Canada the French were deeply rooted, a compact, alien community, led by priests and seigneurs, uninterested and untouched by the democratic ideas of liberal or revolutionary Europe, and holding stubbornly like the Boers in South Africa to their own traditions and language.

Winston Churchill, British statesman and popular historian, *Book X: "The Great Democracies," A History of the English-speaking Peoples* (1958).

There are, perhaps, within Quebec, many countries.

Jacques Ferron, physician and author, *Historiettes* (1969).

In a tranquil country we have received the passion of the world.

Anne Hébert, poet, *Mystère de la parole: Poèmes* (1970).

I was convinced then, and remain so now, that Quebec is one of the rare cultures in which you find snobbism based on ignorance. It's amazing but true....

Alice Parizeau, Polish-born Quebec writer, contributor to *Mapping Literature: The Art and Politics of Translation* (1988) edited by David Homel and Sherry Simon.

Quebec is not a province like the others, as all children learn before playing Atari or Nintendo.

Jacques Parizeau, P.Q. leader, addressing a joint meeting of the Empire Club and the Canadian Club, Toronto, 11 Dec. 1990, quoted by Robert Sheppard in *The Globe and Mail* the following day.

We live in a little society on the margins of the American empire. Let's not pretend this is going to become a great society. It never will be.

Denys Arcand, film director, quoted by Michel Coulombe in *Denys Arcand: The True Nature of the Film-maker* (1993).

Quebec, based on the bedrock of Roman Catholicism and Francophone ethnicity, could yet turn out to be North America's most cohesive and crime-free nation-state. (It may be a smaller Quebec, though, since aboriginal peoples may lop off northern parts of the province.)

Robert D. Kaplan, author, "The Coming Anarchy," *The Atlantic Monthly*, Feb. 1994.

Where the French-Canadian nation finds its freedom, there too will be its homeland.

Daniel Johnson, Premier of Quebec (1966–69), quoted by Peter C. Newman in "The Nation's Business," *Maclean's*, 19 Sept. 1994.

Quebec is the political equivalent of the square root of minus one. Nobody knows what it really adds up to but, without it, where would Canada and *francophonie* be?

James Morgan, correspondent, *Financial Times*, 5 Nov. 1995.

Quebec is different but it is not holy. The danger is that too long a dismissal of the first claim results in the vindication of the second.

Clark Blaise, novelist, quoted by Bruce Blackadar, "Magazines," *The Toronto Star*, 21 Jan. 1996.

Quebec is just a big New Brunswick.

Attribed to one-time New Brunswick Premier

Frank McKenna by Chantal Hébert interviewed by Peter Gzowski on "Some of the Best Minds of Our Time," CBC Radio, 1 May 1998.

I was offered a good position by McGill. I went there to visit and loved it, but I was disturbed by the tension between French- and English-speaking Canadians. Having come out of Europe, and having small children, it was specifically that factor that persuaded me not to accept that position. Or I would have. This prize would be a Canadian prize now.

Walter Kohn, Austrian-born Jewish refugee in an internment camp at Trois-Rivières, graduate and postgraduate of the University of Toronto, emeritus professor of physics at the University of California at Santa Barbara, awarded the 1998 Nobel Prize for Chemistry, interviewed by Kate Jaimet, "How Canada Lost Its Nobel Prize," *Ottawa Citizen*, 16 Oct. 1998.

QUEBEC, CONQUEST OF See also PLAINS OF ABRAHAM, QUEBEC

You know that these two nations have been at war over a few acres of snow near Canada, and that they are spending on this fine struggle more than Canada itself is worth.

Lines from French writer **Voltaire**'s novel *Candide, ou l'Optimisme* (1759) in Robert A. Adams' translation *Candide, or Optimism* (1966). The satiric novel appeared the year of the British conquest of New France. The sting of Voltaire's phrase "a few acres of snow" is felt to this day.

Now, God be praised, I will die in peace!

General James Wolfe, dying words uttered upon being informed that Quebec had been taken, Plains of Abraham, 13 Sept. 1759. Quoted by Francis Parkman in *Montcalm and Wolfe* (1884).

I am happy that I shall not live to see the surrender of Quebec.

Marquis de Montcalm, dying words spoken to his aides, 14 Sept. 1759, the day following the unsuccessful defence of Quebec, Battle of the Plains of Abraham. Quoted by Francis Parkman in *Montcalm and Wolfe* (1884).

Perhaps the loss of such a man was greater to the nation than the conquering of all Canada was advantageous....

Oliver Goldsmith, English poet, *An History of England, in a Series of Letters from a Nobleman to His Son* (1764), quoted by Arthur Friedman in Volume IV of the *Collected Works of Oliver Goldsmith* (1966).

They are a people with no history, and no literature.

Lord Durham, English commissioner, *Report on the Affairs of British North America* (1839). This appraisal of Quebec's past and their culture sat ill with the lawyer François-Xavier Garneau, who researched an influential three-volume *Histoire du Canada* (1845–48), vowing, "I shall write the history which you do not even know exists. You will see that our ancestors yielded only when outnumbered. There are defeats which are as glorious as victories."

At first Wolfe complained that he would rather write Gray's Elegy, but on being told that it had been written already (by Gray) he agreed to take Quebec.

Walter Carruthers Sellar and **Robert Julian Yeatman**, English satirists, "Britain Muffles Through," *1066 and All That* (1930).

QUEBEC & CANADA See also CANADA & QUEBEC

I expected to find a contest between a government and a people: I found two nations warring in the bosom of a single state: I found a struggle, not of principles, but of races; and I perceived that it would be idle to attempt any amelioration of laws or institutions until we could first succeed in terminating the deadly animosity that now separates the inhabitants of Lower Canada into the hostile divisions of French and English.

Lord Durham, English commissioner, *Report on the Affairs of British North America* (1839). The words "two nations warring in the bosom of a single state" have passed into the history of French-English relations.

As a people we are on our way to becoming a nauseating bunch of blackmailers.

Pierre Elliott Trudeau, constitutional specialist, sentence from the first article contributed to *Cité Libre* in 1950, referring to Quebec politicians and how they regard Ottawa, as quoted by Lucien Bouchard, open letter, *The Toronto Star*, 13 Feb. 1996.

French Canadians do not feel French; English-speaking Canadians do not feel British;

and neither community feels American—not, at least, if "American" is equated with "United States."

Arnold J. Toynbee, historian, "The Case for a Bilingual Canada," *Temper of the Times: An Anthology of Assorted Contemporary Literature* (1969) edited by Ralph Greenfield and Ronald Side.

He had two sons. One is dead and the other works for the English in Alberta.

Line from the movie *Les années des rêves* (1984) directed by Jean-Claude Labrecque.

Canada without Quebec is not a country.

Attributed to Prime Minister **Brian Mulroney**, giving expression to his government's frustration following the opposition of some provincial governments to the "distinct society" provision of the Meech Lake Accord, Feb. 1990.

What some people call "the rest of Canada" should understand is that Quebecers will never negotiate on their knees, and Quebecers should understand that "the rest of Canada" cannot be expected to negotiate "with a knife at its throat"—as a prominent Quebecer recently recommended.

Brian Mulroney, Prime Minister, address, joint meeting of the Empire Club and the Canadian Club, Toronto, 12 Feb. 1991.

We are living through a farce, but the problem is we are on stage, not in the audience, so our laughter is understandably limited.

Mordecai Richler, novelist and journalist, referring to Quebec's intrusive language laws, "In the Eye of the Storm," *Maclean's*, 13 April 1992.

Quebecers have Canada in their skin, but they have Quebec in their bones.

Jean-François Lisée, commentator, *L'Actualité*, June 1992, quoted by Norman Webster in *The Toronto Star*, 22 June 1992.

I think Quebec will become more French because the anglophones are going to leave and English Canada will become more and more English. Both will be more provincial.

Mordecai Richler, novelist and Quebec resident, quoted by Chris Guly, *Today's Seniors*, Aug. 1992.

Poor things, they have not yet realized that the nationalists' thirst will never be satisfied, and that each new ransom paid to stave off the threat of schism will simply encourage the master blackmailers to renew the threat and double the ransom.

Pierre Elliott Trudeau, former Prime Minister, referring to Quebec's "traditional demands" as a form of "blackmail," "Trudeau Speaks Out," *Maclean's*, 28 Sept. 1992.

Without francophone Canada's panache, vitality and zest for life, Canada would be dishwater dull.

Mordecai Richler, author and host of the BBC-TV special *Oh, Canada! Oh, Quebec!*, telecast in the United Kingdom on 29 Sept. 1992, as noted by David Israelson in *The Toronto Star* the following day.

Canada and Quebec work much better in practice than in theory.

Josh Freed, columnist, interviewed by Simon Durivage, quoted by Pauline Couture in "Québécois Voices," *The Globe and Mail*, 29 Oct. 1992.

If Quebec had been an American state, it would have gone the way of Louisiana. So it is with many thanks to English Canada that this culture has survived.

Mordecai Richler, novelist, quoted by Sam Orbaum in "Make 'em Mad, Mordecai Richler!" *The Jerusalem Post Magazine*, 6 Nov. 1992.

Our objective is still the same—Quebec first in the Canadian federation.

Gil Rémillard, Quebec Minister of Intergovernmental Affairs, National Assembly, 9 March 1993, quoted by Rhéal Séguin in *The Globe and Mail* the following day.

I want to tell you, I know very well who I am ... a proud Québécois and a proud Canadian. And I have said it's possible to have a happy Quebec in a United Canada.

Jean Chrétien, Liberal leader, referring to Bloc Québécois leader Lucien Bouchard's criticism of Chrétien, French-language leaders' debate, Radio-Canada, 3 Oct. 1993, published in *The Globe and Mail*, 5 Oct. 1993.

All these people say, "My Canada Includes Quebec." People in Serbia would say that, too: "My Yugoslavia Includes Dubrovnik."

Of course it does. You're in the dominating culture, you just appropriate everything.

Myrna Kostash, author, interviewed by Mark Abley in "The Culture of Nationalism," *The Canadian Forum*, Sept. 1994.

I can imagine being a Quebecker without being a Canadian, I cannot imagine being a Canadian without being a Quebecker.

Daniel Johnson, Premier of Quebec, campaign speech, quoted by Pierre Bourgault in *The Globe and Mail*, 9 Sept. 1994. Johnson was under pressure from Parti Québécois leader Jacques Parizeau for saying, the previous fall, "I am a Canadian first and foremost." Johnson disavowed the earlier remark by explaining, "It was a slip of the tongue."

We are never totally susceptible to the things that surround us nor totally independent of them. Thus Québec which has made me has also made me dissatisfied with what it has to offer.

Hélène Jutras, commentator, *Québec Is Killing Me* (1995) translated by Jutras and Michael Gnarowski.

The people of Quebec have been free enough to utterly transform their society in little more than three decades, all within the framework of the Confederation. When the people of Quebec have pushed on the door, it has opened. This is tyranny?

David Cameron, political scientist, "Why Thomas Jefferson Would Have Wept," *The Toronto Star*, 21 Jan. 1995.

I am proud to be a Quebecker and a Canadian, and I will do everything I can do to help show how these two loyalties can complement each other so well.

Stéphane Dion, newly appointed Minister of Intergovernmental Affairs, statement released upon appointment, quoted by Jeffrey Simpson in *The Globe and Mail*, 27 Jan. 1996.

Mainly, what we are hearing is a new recognition of the existence, here in the northern part of the American continent, of two profoundly different nations who shortly must decide upon their destiny. No fruitful dialogue can begin without that recognition.

Lucien Bouchard, Quebec Premier, swearing-in speech, 29 Jan. 1996, quoted by Rhéal Séguin in *The Globe and Mail* the following day.

There is not even a "national" Prime Minister in Canada. There is a "federal" Prime Minister, a "federal" Parliament. The word "national" only applies officially to the Quebec National Assembly.

Bernard Landry, Quebec Deputy Prime Minister, referring to Quebec's participation in the so-called Team Canada international trade junkets organized by the Prime Minister and the provincial premiers, 28 Nov. 1996, quoted by Rhéal Séguin in *The Globe and Mail* the following day.

I once described, here in Toronto, the Quebec question as being for Canadians like a visit to the dentist. Well, the visit to the dentist will last a little while longer.... I believe that sooner or later, Quebec will become a country. That country will be as French as Ontario is English.

Jacques Parizeau, former Quebec Premier, address, Upper Canada College, Toronto, 18 Feb. 1997, "Attacked," *The Globe and Mail*, 20 Feb. 1997.

Francophone Canada is at the core of how anglophone Canada sees itself and the country.

John Ralston Saul, author, *Reflections of a Siamese Twin: Canada at the End of the Twentieth Century* (1997).

Canada is my country, but Quebec is my homeland.

Léon Dion, political scientist and influential Quebec government adviser, quoted in his obituary by Tu Thanh Ha in *The Globe and Mail*, 21 Aug. 1997.

One statistic alone tells us everything we need to know. Québec in the last twenty years lost over four hundred thousand people. This betrays a deep malaise. Four hundred thousand people is more than the population of Laval, the second-largest city in Québec.

Jean Charest, Prime Minister, referring to the exodus of anglophones and others from Quebec, *My Road to Québec* (1998).

A fleur-de-lys can't grow if it's choked by a rose bush.

Clermont Dominique, delegate from the Eastern

Townships, Parti Québécois national council, Trois-Rivières, Que., quoted by Sean Gordon, "Protection for Anglos," *National Post*, 26 April 1999.

QUEBEC & FRANCE See also FRANCE, QUEBEC

There can be no question of my addressing a message to Canada to celebrate its centennial. We can have good relations. We must have excellent relations with French Canada. But we are not obliged to offer congratulations for the creation of a state based on our past defeat and on the integration of part of the French people into a British system.

Charles de Gaulle, President of France, handwritten note, responding to a cable from the Quebec Embassy in Ottawa dated 9 Dec. 1966, concerning his Centennial visit, quoted by Alain Peyrefitte, as noted by Robert McKenzie in "Even Now, the de Gaulle of It All!" *The Toronto Star*, 19 July 1997. In all, de Gaulle visited Canada three times: 1944, 1960, and 1967.

I received very interesting offers from universities there. But then I was shocked to learn more about Quebec nationalism. In many ways it is very provincial.

Julia Kristeva, Bulgarian-born French literary critic, interviewed by Ray Conlogue, "Deconstructing Julia," *The Globe and Mail*, 14 Oct. 1999.

QUEBEC CITY See also QUEBEC

This will, some time hence, be a vast empire, the seat of power and learning. Nature has refused them nothing, and there will grow a people out of our little spot, England, that will fill this vast place.

James Wolfe, General, referring to the French at Quebec before the Conquest, extract from one of his last letters to his mother, quoted by Showell Styles in *Wolfe Commands You* (1959).

Every perception of my mind became absorbed into the one sense of seeing, when, upon rounding Point Levi, we cast anchor before Quebec. What a scene!—Can the world produce such another? Edinburgh had been the beau idéal to me of all that was beautiful in Nature—a vision of the northern Highlands had haunted my dreams across the Atlantic; but all these past recollections faded before the present of Quebec.

Susanna Moodie, pioneer writer, *Roughing It in the Bush; or, Forest Life in Canada* (1852).

It was not until the summer of 1864 that I visited Quebec. Travelling, in the first instance, by steamer, on the beautiful St. Lawrence, and by the Thousand Islands, the romantic, old-fashioned aspect of the ancient capital of Lower Canada pleased me hugely.

George Augustus Sala, English correspondent travelling throughout North America, visiting Quebec City in mid-1864, *The Life and Adventures of George Augustus Sala* (1895).

It is said no foe could ever get into Quebeck, and I guess they couldn't. And I don't see what they'd *want* to get in there for.

Charles F. Browne, American writer and speaker known as Artemus Ward, *Artemus Ward: His Travels* (1865).

The population is ugly and apathetic. Despised by the English, they retaliate with hatred and jealousy.

Louis Moreau Gottschalk, French-educated virtuoso pianist, travel diary translated from the French by Robert E. Peterson, published in 1881, and included in *Notes of a Pianist* (1964) edited by Jeanne Behrend. He visited Quebec City on 6 July 1862.

The commerce of Quebec, much reduced, consists of timber, the forests being immense. The garrison consists of two thousand men. The churches, as I have said, are very numerous and exercise a very great authority. Thus they prohibit the theatre but permit travelling circuses, puppet shows, and magic lanterns. I leave you to judge the intellectual level under such a rule.

Louis Moreau Gottschalk, French-educated virtuoso pianist, travel diary translated from the French by Robert E. Peterson, published in 1881, and included in *Notes of a Pianist* (1964) edited by Jeanne Behrend. He visited Quebec City on 6 July 1862.

... they saw the broad pool stretch out in front of them, the falls of Montmorenci, the high palisades of Cape Levi, the cluster of vessels, and upon the right that wonderful rock with its diadem of towers and its township huddled round its base, the centre and stronghold of French power in America.

Lines describing the view from the Quebec Citadel from **Sir Arthur Conan Doyle**'s historical novel *The Refugees: A Tale of Two Continents* (1893) set in the days of New France.

With the help of God, Champlain's work born under the lilies grew under the roses.

Inscription on the medal issued to commemorate the Tercentenary of the **City of Quebec** in 1908, quoted in "Collected Wisdom," *The Globe and Mail*, 17 March 1994.

Many a time I have looked up at the buildings on top of the bluff at Quebec, and thought what a wonderful location it would be for the story of a mythical kingdom.

Allan Dwan, Canadian-born Hollywood director, *Maclean's*, 1 Feb. 1920, reprinted as "Canada Has a 'Movie' Future," *Maclean's*, 1 Jan. 1996.

Quebec was more interesting: it is entirely French-Canadian, and the people speak little or no English, and no French, either, so far as I am concerned. But this place too I found disappointing—it is like Dr. Johnson's dog walking on hind legs: "the wonder is not that he walks well, but that he walks at all." People are interested in Quebec only because it is a French town in America, and that means little to me.

Thomas Wolfe, American novelist, finding Quebec City more interesting than Montreal, letter to Henry T. Volkening, 9 Aug. 1929, *The Letters of Thomas Wolfe* (1956) edited by Elizabeth Nowell.

This place surpasses all my expectations—a veritable dream of archaic city walls, cassellated cliffs, silver spires, various, zigzag precipitous streets, & the leisurely civilization of an older world!

H.P. Lovecraft, American writer of horror fiction, message on a postcard postmarked Quebec City, 1 Sept. 1930, addressed to fellow-writer Robert E. Howard. Described in the catalogue of Science Fiction & Fantasy Literature issued by Barry R. Levin, Spring 1997.

You have been reading travel booklets. Quebec, in fact, is a dreadful hole. The big hotel is bad, and the little ones are mere boarding houses. Once one has looked at the river, which takes from 3 to 4 minutes, there is absolutely nothing to do. Every street runs uphill at an angle of 45 degrees. There are no decent saloons or restaurants, and the wine-list at the hotel is that of a Liverpool-Boston Cunarder.

H.L. Mencken, author, letter of 24 June 1931 to Philip Goodman, *The New Mencken Letters* (1977) edited by Carl Bode. Despite the fact that earlier, in 1930, Mencken had honeymooned in Quebec City, he preferred Montreal.

From the heights of the Dufferin Terrace at Quebec one can discern, only a few miles away, that blue line which marks the end of human habitation; beyond it rock and forest still wait to be conquered. This is the domain of the pioneer. The immense North Country comes down so close that one can almost touch it with the hand.

André Siegfried, sociologist, *Canada* (1937).

Only *nature*, at Quebec, is American—superlatively so. The harbour *is* unbelievably spacious. It is a great gateway, yes, to the "great open spaces" beyond. In that respect Quebec is a truer and more native portal to the American Scene than is the structural phantasmagoria of the city of New York.

Wyndham Lewis, British artist and author, *America, I Presume* (1940).

The stupendous Quebec countryside. At the point of Diamond Cape before the immense breach of the Saint Lawrence, air, light, and water interpenetrate in infinite proportions. For the first time on this continent a real impression of beauty and true magnitude.

Albert Camus, French writer, visitor in May 1946, *American Journals* (1987) translated by Hugh Levick.

It seems that I would have something to say about Quebec and its history of men who came to struggle in the wilderness, driven by a force that was greater than they were. But to what end?

Albert Camus, French writer, visitor in May 1946, *American Journals* (1987) translated by Hugh Levick.

"Everything is fine in Paris alone," goes the saying. It would be just as true to claim that everything is fine only in Quebec City. For Quebec, just as much as Paris, has the grace, elegance, whims and unpredictability of a changing woman. Despite her three centuries and a half she has an air of youthfulness and an exhilarating joie de vivre.

Gérard Filion, editor, "La Vieille Province," *The Face of Canada* (1959).

This is not quite Europe, but certainly not America any more. This moment is not yesterday, but neither is it really today.

Ringuet, author Philippe Panneton, describing the sensation of staring beyond the Citadel of Quebec above the St. Lawrence River, "The Capital," *Canada—This Land, These People: A Reader's Digest Collection* (1968).

Here was the first diocese of North America. It is from here that the seed first sown began its immense growth.

Pope John Paul II, Pontiff, address, Laval University, Quebec City, 9 Sept. 1985, quoted in *The Pope in Canada* (1984) introduced by J.M. Hayes.

I want to live in a place where I feel comfortable, where I feel I can establish roots and where I might be able to settle down after I'm finished with hockey.

Eric Lindros, Ontario-born hockey player, offering one of a number of the reasons why he declined the NHL draft to the Quebec Nordiques, *Fire on Ice* (1991) by Lindros and Randy Starkman.

Quebec City is the capital of a nation. You feel it as soon as you approach. When Quebec talks about being *une nation,* it's real. To say that it's a distinct society is the palest possible understatement. What indeed are we fussing about? This people has been *une nation, un pays, un peuple, depuis trois siècles et quelques,* and Quebec City is the capital, and that is their national legislature, and in Toronto we are still going bald contemplating it.

Scott Symons, author, "Deliquescence in Canada," *The Idler,* July–Aug. 1992.

Welcome to Quebec... one of the smallest nations of the Americas... home of a people that speaks French.

Attributed to Quebec Premier **Lucien Bouchard**, extending greetings to an international gathering of representatives of twenty-eight countries in North, Central, and South America, to promote Quebec separatism, Parliamentary Conference of the Americas, 19 Sept. 1997, as noted by Rhéal Séguin in *The Globe and Mail* and by Robert McKenzie in *The Toronto Star* the following day.

Québec, National Capital

Sign seen on Highway 20 approaching **Quebec City**, noted by correspondent Marie-France Legault of Quebec City, Letters to the Editor, *Cité Libre,* Winter 2000.

QUÉBÉCOIS, LES See also FRENCH CANADIANS, QUEBEC

I don't feel married to Vancouver.

Jean-Paul Desbiens, teacher, *For Pity's Sake* (1965) translated from the French by Frédéric Coté.

We Québécois submit to colonialism. We are a captive people. To change our situation, we must first recognize it.

Léandre Bergeron, lexicographer, *Petit manuel d'histoire du Québec* (1971).

The typical Québécois is a good, two-legged animal, not vicious, credulous, occasionally pious, big-hearted and narrow-minded; he is not known for his initiative and is incompetent but is beautifully submissive, with an ass molded to receive the English boot, and he also has a great contempt for words.

André Brochu, novelist, *Adéodat I* (1973).

A Québécois is anyone who lives in Quebec, who votes in Quebec eventually, who pays his taxes, if he can afford them or can't find a way to evade them.

René Lévesque, Quebec Premier, address, Canadian Jewish Congress, Montreal, 13 May 1977, quoted in *The Globe and Mail* the following day.

We are not a small people. Perhaps we come close to being a great people.

René Lévesque, Quebec leader, quoted in *La Presse,* 15 Nov. 1976, Quotations from René Lévesque (1977) edited by Jean Côté and Marcel Chaput, translated by Robert Guy Scully and Jacqueline Perrault.

A Quebecker is a person who stays here and that's all.

Bernard Landry, Quebec Minister of Economic Development, address, Canadian Club of Montreal, quoted in *The Globe and Mail,* 24 April 1979.

If I follow the reasoning on both sides to its logical conclusion, in two generations there won't be a single Anglophone left in Quebec, but everybody will be speaking English.

Reed Scowen, member of the Quebec National Assembly, farewell speech, Summer 1987, quoted by Mordecai Richler in "A Reporter at Large: Inside/Outside," *The New Yorker*, 23 Sept. 1991.

In the mid-twentieth century, the Quebecers have finally realized that they are perfectly capable of living in step with the rest of North America without giving up the originality of their own culture.

Gérard Pelletier, former Cabinet Minister, "Quebec: Different but in Step with North America," *Daedalus: Journal of the American Academy of Arts and Sciences*, "In Search of Canada," Fall 1988.

We Quebecers are uncertain of our identity and haunted by the fear of a tragic destiny.

Léon Dion, political scientist, "The Mystery of Quebec," *Daedalus: Journal of the American Academy of Arts and Sciences*, "In Search of Canada," Fall 1988.

Quebec is the only jurisdiction in North America where French-speakers can feel completely free, respected and secure.... Quebeckers want to be themselves. This they can accomplish mostly within even today's Canada, and fully within a renewed Canada.

Keith Spicer, commissioner, *Citizens' Forum on Canada's Future: Report to the People and Government of Canada*, published as a special feature of *The Toronto Star*, *The Globe and Mail*, and other newspapers, 29 June 1991.

English-speaking Quebeckers made a subtle distinction: They designate French Canadians of old stock as "Québécois," reserving "Quebecker" for official, legal, non-cultural meanings.

*

So when the need arises, people now resort to heavy and unpleasant expressions such as "Québécois de vieille souche," which means deeply rooted Quebeckers. Not only is this derogatory to newer citizens, it is also historically inaccurate, since it denies a history common to all French-speaking communities throughout Canada.

Lysiane Gagnon, columnist, "Inside Quebec," *The Globe and Mail*, 3 Aug. 1991.

Look at it this way. Many of the *québécois pure laine or vieille souche* are, in fact, the progeny of *les filles du roi*, or hookers, imported to New France by Jean Baptiste Talon, to satisfy the appetites of his mostly functionally illiterate soldiers.

Mordecai Richler, author and commentator, *Oh Canada! Oh Quebec! Requiem for a Divided Country* (1992).

Forget the whales, never mind the cutesy-poo seal pups. If there is a truly endangered species in Canada, it is the non-francophone population of Quebec.

Mordecai Richler, novelist and journalist, "In the Eye of the Storm," *Maclean's*, 13 April 1992.

In fact, most French-speaking Quebecois are "nationalists" to some significant degree—some are federalist nationalists, some are separatist nationalists.

Brian Mulroney, Prime Minister, address, Conservative Party gathering, Ottawa, 28 May 1993, quoted by Susan Delacourt in *The Globe and Mail* the following day.

If they were offered the universe they would demand heaven, and if they got heaven they would claim the angels were in a federalistic conspiracy to centralize power.

Sheila Copps, Deputy Prime Minister, House of Commons, 31 Nov. 1993, quoted by CP and published in *The Hamilton Spectator* the following day.

We are socialists in our souls, but capitalists in our pocketbooks.

Yvon Deschamps, comic, speaking at the St. Jean Baptiste Day celebrations, Montreal, 1994, quoted by André Picard in "Québécois Voices," *The Globe and Mail*, 7 July 1994.

Angryphones

A reference to Quebec's minority of English speakers (anglophones) who grew increasingly angry (hence "angryphones") with the exclusionist policies and practices of two Quebec Premiers, Jacques Parizeau and Lucien Bouchard, following the Second Referendum of 1995.

A Quebecker is whoever wants to be one.

Jacques Parizeau, former Quebec Premier, article in *Le Devoir*, 30 Oct. 1996, translated by Patrick Van de Wille and printed in *The Globe and Mail* the following day.

The feeling of being a Quebecker is one that grows little by little.

Jacques Parizeau, former Quebec Premier, "Quebec," translated by Patrick Van de Wille, *The Globe and Mail*, 19 Dec. 1996.

Our Quebec who are offended / Recognized be thy name / Thy referendum be granted / Thy sovereignty be done / On this earth which is ours / Give us this day our hope hereafter / Forgive us for having been Canadians / As we shall forgive those who will remain so / But deliver us from Canada / Amen our country.

"Prayer of a True Québécois" adapted by **Nadia Khouri** and **Marc Angenot** from the original which appeared in *La Tempête*, No. 4, 1996. The adaptation appeared in *Cité Libre*, June–July 1998. The adaptors explain, "In French there is a play on words. Amen is a homonym of Amène (Bring)."

Are we a people... Québécois? Canadien? Canadien-français?... There is no one in this room who wants to choose. That's the difference! We want to be Québécois. We want to be Canadians. We want these identities, and we have no reason to choose!

Stéphane Dion, Minster of Intergovernmental Affairs, address, Quebec Liberal Party meeting, 7 Dec. 1997, quoted by Graham Fraser in *The Globe and Mail* the following day.

How can you expect the federal government to represent the Québécois people when it pretends that a Québécois people does not exist.

Lucien Bouchard, Quebec Premier, quoted in *Le Figaro* mid-March, as noted by André Picard, "Québécois Voices," *The Globe and Mail*, 25 March 1999.

I am a Québécois and proud of it.

Céline Dion, popular singer, giving her reason for refusing a 1990 music award offered by a Quebec music industry association for an English-language album by the year's best "anglophone artist," recalled by Francine Dubé, "Bloc M.P. Questions Dion's 'Soul,'" *National Post*, 6 April 1999.

QUEBEC REFERENDUM See REFERENDA

QUESTIONS See also QUIZ

In their approach to problems, Orientals tend to ask, "What is the question?" while Westerners tend to ask, "What is the answer?"

Marshall McLuhan, communications pioneer, *City as Classroom: Understanding Language and Media* (1977) with Kathryn Hutchon and Eric McLuhan.

We come from the unknown at birth, and rejoin it at death with all our questions about it unanswered.

Northrop Frye, cultural critic, "The Dedicated Mind," address, Service of Thanksgiving, 5 Oct. 1986, *Vic Report*, Winter, 1986–87.

Answers: A mechanism for avoiding questions.... Answers are the abstract face of solutions.

John Ralston Saul, author, *The Doubter's Companion: A Dictionary of Aggressive Common Sense* (1994).

QUIET REVOLUTION See also QUEBEC

Pas comme les autres.

French phrase common in Quebec with the meaning that Quebec is "not like the others," the others being provinces, characteristic of the Quiet Revolution led by Premier Jean Lesage (1960–66).

The "quiet revolution" was, in fact, the tumultuous outbreak of economic grievances and social discontents which for twenty-five years had been held in check by the petrified incubus of Union Nationale. The deaths of Duplessis and Sauvé and the disintegration of their party had suddenly liberated the long-pent-up energies of mid-twentieth-century Quebec.

Donald G. Creighton, historian, *Canada's First Century: 1867–1967* (1970).

For all intents and purposes, the Quiet Revolution consisted of three or four ministers, twenty civil servants and consultants—and fifty chansonniers.

Jacques Parizeau, separatist, quoted by Graham Fraser in *Parti Québécois: René Lévesque and the Parti Québécois in Power* (1984).

Maybe the difference between the French and the English Canadian quiet revolutions was that ours did not become exclusive or smug.

Jack McLeod, political scientist, commenting on Quebec's Quiet Revolution and English Canada's parallel cultural renaissance, *The Globe and Mail*, 27 Dec. 1991.

QUIZ See also QUESTIONS

It was the world's first quiz show. Within two years, there were over two hundred of them being aired in North America alone, and a great many more elsewhere.

Roy Ward Dickson, quizmaster, *Take a Chance! Confessions of a Quizmaster* (1977). Dickson claimed he invented the "quiz show" with his program *Professor Dick and His Question Box*, first heard on CKCL (later CKEY) Toronto, 15 May 1935.

QUOTATIONS

An aphorism should be like a burr: sting, stick, and leave a little soreness afterwards.

Irving Layton, poet and aphorist, *The Whole Bloody Bird (obs, aphs & Pomes)* (1969).

Proverbs seem to appear very early in the history of a culture, aphorisms in the middle period, epigrams in the late sophisticated state.

Louis Dudek, poet and aphorist, "The Art of the Epigram," *The Antigonish Review*, Autumn, 1976.

I know it is supposed to be dreadful to fake references, but when people insist on quotations that do not already exist, what is an author to do?

Robertson Davies, novelist, writing to his Norwegian publisher Sigmund Hoftun, 13 Aug. 1979, to admit that the title of his novel *Fifth Business* is not taken from a work on theatre by Tho. Overskou (as the text states) but from his own imagination, *For Your Eyes Alone: The Letters of Robertson Davies, 1976–1895* (1999).

Feel free to misquote me.

Charlie McKenzie, concierge of the Rhinoceros Party of Canada, maxim, quoted by Stewart MacLeod in *Maclean's*, 30 March 1992.

Many an epigram is made by inverting a platitude.

Louis Dudek, poet and aphorist, "Bitter Pills," *Reality Games* (1998).

He spent some time looking at an old copy of *Colombo's Canadian Quotations* (note—the book transpires in 2016), reading what people had said about family life. Colombo contended that the most famous Canadian quotation of all was McLuhan's, "The medium is the message." That was likely true, but one that was uttered more frequently, even if it wasn't uniquely Canadian, was "my children hate me."

Passage from **Robert J. Sawyer**'s future-set novel *Factoring Humanity* (1998).

R

RACE & RACISM See also PREJUDICE

Then let us stand united all / And show our father's might, / That won the home we call our own, / For white man's land we fight. / To Oriental grasp and greed / We'll surrender, no never. / Our watchword be "God save the King" / White Canada for ever.

One verse of the song "White Canada for Ever" which was sung to the tune of "The Maple Leaf Forever" in British Columbia in the early 20th century; quoted by Robert Chodos in *The Caribbean Connection* (1977).

This is my first visit to Canada. And I might say that Canada is almost a sacred word to me. All of the negroes knew it, in slavery days, as the Better Land. I have often heard my father say that, to him and to his kin, Canada was always an enchanted name.

Paul Robeson, American singer, interviewed in Toronto by R.E. Knowles, *The Toronto Star*, 21 Nov. 1929.

Whatever the opinion of the Prime Minister or of the government here, we in British Columbia are firmly convinced that once a Jap always a Jap.

A.W. Neill, B.C. Member of Parliament, speech made in Feb. 1941, quoted by David Suzuki in *Metamorphosis: Stages in a Life* (1987).

Just think, three or four kids, that's all we were, and we had the country up in arms.

John Beattie, leader of the Canadian Nazi Party, boast made in 1966, quoted by Stanley R. Barrett in *Is God a Racist? The Right Wing in Canada* (1987).

God is a racist. At least, that is the claim of the Western Guard, a white-supremacist, neo-Fascist organization that reached its zenith in the mid-1970s in Toronto. The slogan "God Is a Racist" appears at different places in the Western Guard's literature...

Stanley R. Barrett, sociologist, *Is God a Racist? The Right Wing in Canada* (1987).

Strange as it may seem, in one respect racists and anti-racists sustain each other. They constitute a bizarre social relationship, the one providing the other with a platform and confirming beliefs in an insidious conspiracy, the other constituting the proof positive that racism is on the increase and that an all-out attack must be launched.

Stanley R. Barrett, sociologist, *Is God a Racist? The Right Wing in Canada* (1987).

Data have shown that, across ages, methods, samples, and time periods, Caucasoid populations fall between those of Mongoloids and Negroids with measures made of intelligence, maturation, personality, sexuality, and social organization. Many of the differences are not counterintuitive, despite repeated suggestions that such beliefs reflect only prejudice and faulty stereotyping.

J. Philippe Rushton, psychologist, "Race Differences in Behaviour: A Review and Evolutionary Analysis," *Personality and Individual Differences*, Vol. 9, No. 6, Issue 9, 1988.

As a child, I was a direct victim of the effects of the braggadocio of geneticists early in this century. Of course, I only realized this long after I myself had become a geneticist. After Pearl Harbor, my family was stripped of all rights of Canadian citizenship for sharing genes that had come from the country of the enemy near the turn of the century.

David Suzuki, scientist and author, *Inventing the Future* (1989).

The national mythology of Canada is to treat the Asian immigrant as a guest worker or as a visitor, no matter how long he or she has lived in Canada, whereas the national mythology of the United States is to include the newcomer.

Bharati Mukherjee, Indian-born author and social commentator, quoted by Philip Marchand in *The Toronto Star*, 14 Oct. 1989.

Canadians, even when they are racist, realize that it's not a nice thing to be.

Neil Bissoondath, Trinidad-born novelist of East Indian origin, interviewed by Aruna Srivastava in *Other Solitudes: Canadian Multicultural Fictions* (1990) edited by Linda Hutcheon and Marion Richmond.

It cost me $40,000 in lost work—but I got a million dollars' worth of publicity for my cause. It was well worth it.

Ernst Zundel, Holocaust denier, remark made in 1985 after being tried and subsequently retried and found guilty of disseminating hate literature, quoted by advocate and author Alan M. Dershowitz in *Chutzpah* (1991).

The word "racism," with its current negative connotations, can be expected to become a complimentary word meaning "what distinguishes one tribe or ethnic group from another."

Frank Ogden, futurologist, "The Most Visionary Developments of the Century to Come," *Leaders*, Jan.–March 1992.

Racists are like cockroaches: When you turn the lights on them, they scatter.

Ian Kagedan, spokesperson, League for Human Rights of B'nai Brith Canada, quoted by André Picard in *The Globe and Mail*, 1 Aug. 1992.

One can only be racist if one has power. Racism without power doesn't mean a damn thing. If you go into the ghetto you will find many blacks and whites who don't like each other. It's not a matter of power or racism. The fact is they just don't like each other. It's as simple as that. But don't call it racism.

Arnold Auguste, publisher of the black weekly paper *Share*, quoted by Paul Palango, "City," *eye*, 6 May 1993.

The more educated you become, the more likely you are to be racist.

Esther Delisle, historian and author of *The Traitor and the Jew* (1993), quoted by Charles Foran in *Saturday Night*, Oct. 1993.

Tolerant is a slightly negative word. It's like saying, "You smell, but I can hold my breath."

David See-Chai Lam, B.C. Lieutenant-Governor, quoted by Brenda Dalglish in *Maclean's*, 7 Feb. 1994.

How can we have a Black Pride Month and not a White Pride Month?

George Burdi, white supremacist, question asked while still a student in a Toronto high school, quoted by Stephan Talty, "Neo-Nazi Mogul," *The New York Times Magazine*, 25 Feb. 1996.

Is this person (mark or specify more than one, if applicable): White; Chinese; South Asian (e.g., East Indian, Pakistani, Punjabi, Sri Lankan); Black (e.g., African, Haitian, Jamaican, Somali); Arab/West Asian (e.g., Armenian, Egyptian, Iranian, Lebanese, Moroccan); Filipino; South East Asian (e.g., Cambodian, Indonesian, Laotian, Vietnamese); Latin-American; Japanese; Korean; Other (specify).

Note: This information is collected to support programs which promote equal opportunity for everyone to share in the social, cultural and economic life of Canada.

Question 19 from the 1996 Census Form, reproduced in "Verbatim," *The Globe and Mail*, 26 April 1996. Reform M.P. Mike Scott suggested that Canadians identify themselves as Martians to "send a signal to the federal government that Canadians have had enough of this garbage." The ten-part division was subsequently defended by Ivan P. Fellegi, Chief, **Statistics Canada**.

Canada is as blatantly racist as the United States. We know it exists. People who don't appear to be Canadian—people of colour—don't get the same treatment. They associate you with your parents' birthplace or your birthplace.... It's an issue.

Donovan Bailey, Canadian sprinter born in Jamaica, quoted by Michael Farber in "Blast from the North," *Sports Illustrated*, 22 July 1996. Advance distribution of the issue resulted in headlines critical of Bailey who, interviewed on 16 July 1996, retracted the remark. Bailey claimed that Farber had misquoted him; Farber rejected the claim. Bailey maintained that what he had said was, "Canada is not as blatantly racist as the U.S., but it exists. That is what I said." Noted by Randy Starkman in "Olympic Row Erupts over Racism Quote," *The Toronto Star*, 17 July 1996.

Sadly, our history with respect to the treatment of Aboriginal people is not something in which we can take pride. Attitudes of racial and cultural superiority led to a suppression of Aboriginal culture and values.

"Statement of Reconciliation: Learning from the Past," read by Jane Stewart, Minister of Indian Affairs, Ottawa, 7 Jan. 1998, printed in *The Globe and Mail* the following day.

RADIO See also BROADCASTING; GZOWSKI, PETER; NEWS

For the first time in the history of Canada the word spoken on Parliament Hill and the sound of the chimes and bells were carried instantaneously in all parts of this vast Dominion. Never before was a national programme enjoyed by the citizens of any land over so vast an area.

W.L. Mackenzie King, Prime Minister, address, Canadian National Exhibition, Toronto, Aug. 1927, referring to the first national Dominion Day broadcast, 1 July 1927, quoted by Morris Wolfe in *Fifty Years of Radio* (1986).

As you know, I have no radio and have never listened to radio if I could possibly avoid it. I am really keen to have the programs given to the Canadian people made as bad as possible, in order that radio may pass out. For that reason alone I am in favour of government control.

Brooke Claxon, Ottawa bureaucrat, letter addressed to Graham Spry in 1930, quoted by Warner Troyer in *The Sound and the Fury: An Anecdotal History of Canadian Broadcasting* (1980).

The amount of fodder that is the antithesis of intellectual that comes over our radios is appalling while the selection of material for broadcasting remains in commercial hands.

Arthur Meighen, former Prime Minister, Vancouver address, 1931, quoted by Frank W. Peers in *The Politics of Canadian Broadcasting, 1920–1951* (1969).

If the radio is not a healing and reconciling force in our national life it will have failed in its high purpose.

Leonard W. Brockington, orator and business executive, address, "Canada Is on the Air," 4 Nov. 1936, delivered by the Chairman of the newly formed CBC.

I'd sooner be on this board of ours than on any university board in Canada. Our enterprise is the University of the People. Our fees are the lowest in the whole educational world. And, as for matriculation, every man, woman and child in Canada has "passed the Entrance."

Nellie McClung, pioneer writer and broadcasting commissioner, interviewed by R.E. Knowles in *The Toronto Star*, 12 March 1937.

Ladies and gentlemen, for a change, most of the news tonight is good.

Lorne Greene, CBC Radio's chief announcer, referring to news coverage during World War II, mentioned by Greene in his memoirs, *Signing On: The Birth of Radio in Canada* (1982), quoted by *Morris Wolfe in Fifty Years of Radio* (1986).

God never spoke to me. The BBC did.

Robert MacNeil, broadcaster and memoirist, recalling the authority of BBC announcers heard on CBC Radio during World War II, *Wordstruck: A Memoir* (1989).

In Canada, as elsewhere, the voice of the BBC was the voice of sanity, civilization, and truth. If the King himself had read the newscasts they could not have had greater authority: the announcers were better readers.

Robert MacNeil, broadcaster and memoirist, recalling the authority of BBC announcers heard on the CBC during World War II, *Wordstruck: A Memoir* (1989).

1. To be successful. 2. To provide information. 3. To entertain. 4. To serve the public interest.

Radio broadcasting policy of **Jack Kent Cooke**, owner of CKEY in Toronto, formulated in 1947, as quoted by Adrian Havill in *The Last Mogul* (1992).

Radio scenery costs nothing and shifts easily.

Robert McDougall, scriptwriter, commenting in 1948 on CBC Radio's Stage series of dramas, quoted by Bronwyn Drainie in *Living the Part: John Drainie and the Dilemma of Canadian Stardom* (1988).

I live right inside radio when I listen.

Marshall McLuhan, communications pioneer, observation made in 1964, "A McLuhan Sourcebook," *The Essential McLuhan* (1995) edited by Eric McLuhan and Frank Zingrone.

Canada has never had a national newspaper and its national magazine industry has often been feeble; but CBC radio, operating with great initiative and independence, has become in a sense our national journalism.

Robert Fulford, columnist and author, *An Introduction to the Arts in Canada* (1977).

Broadcasting on the radio is exactly like a phone call. You talk to one person. I can't imagine any other way to do it.

Clyde Gilmour, host of CBC Radio's long-running *Gilmour's Albums*, quoted by Bruce Kirkland in *The Toronto Star*, 16 May 1978.

Never say anything in a studio you wouldn't say before your very narrow-minded grandmother.

De B. Holly, broadcaster, offering advice, quoted by John Picton in *The Globe and Mail*, 24 Feb. 1979.

The glory of radio is that the audience has to think, has to use its imagination to create the scene with the actor.

John Colicos, actor, quoted by Helen Bulloch in *The Toronto Star*, 2 June 1982.

The thing about radio is, you can talk and talk and talk into that microphone... but you have no real proof that anyone, anywhere is listening.

Arthur Black, broadcaster, *Back to Black: Comic Sketches* (1987).

Listening to the radio was like being told stories; we listened with the intensity of the people who listened for thousands of years in all cultures to the shaman, the bard, the storyteller, the minstrel, who embodied their history, philosophy, literature, drama, and the meaning of life.

*

To be sure, television quickly became the dominant medium, but for historical and cultural reasons, radio meant more to Canada. It was the glue of modern Canadian feeling. Radio has held the nation together, while television is the medium of dissolution, of cultural absorption by the United States. In spite of laws requiring Canadian content, American programs dominate Canadian screens. Canadians watch American but listen Canadian.

Robert MacNeil, broadcaster and memoirist, *Wordstruck: A Memoir* (1989).

I tried to be ubiquitous, querulous, critical and nosey. Those are the qualities I still believe any good hotliner must possess.

Jack Webster, broadcaster, *Webster! An Autobiography* (1990). "Terror in the Name of Talk" is a phrase associated with Webster's Vancouver-based phone-in shows in the 1970s.

Stewart MacPherson (who died on April 16, 1995, aged 86) had one of the most familiar voices on the wireless in Britain when he decided to return to the comparative obscurity of North American radio in 1949.

David Twiston Davies, Canadian-born obituary-writer, *Canada from Afar: The Daily Telegraph Book of Canadian Obituaries* (1996). A Winnipeg-born broadcaster, MacPherson was "a giant of the BBC" and private radio from 1937 to 1949; for family reasons he returned to North America, finally settling in Winnipeg.

Let's get right down to business.

Peter Warren, broadcaster, characteristic opening line, quoted by David Roberts, "The End of the Bombastic Era," *The Globe and Mail*, 20 Oct. 1998. It was recalled when Warren retired as host of CJOB Winnipeg's *Action Line*, North America's longest-running open-line show (1971–98).

I find there really is this whole radio culture out there—people who can't live without the CBC.

Doug Coupland, novelist, interviewed by John Burns in *Quill & Quire*, May 1996.

CBC Radio One / News. And More. CBC Radio Two / Classics. And Beyond.

New **Canadian Broadcasting Corporation** designations for its AM and FM networks, introduced to English-language listeners, 1 Aug. 1997.

It seemed to me that Canada was rather like a big old radio, with the railway tracks running across like a waveband. Twiddle the knob and you can pick up the sounds of the many different cultures that have built this nation, such as the pockets of Irish, Scots and French life that I had rattled through. And, in between, there is just the silence of the lakes and forests, and the brave hoot of the lone train thundering through.

Nigel Tisdall, English travel writer, listening in Vancouver to a radio broadcast that originated in Halifax, after a trip on Via Rail's Transcontinental Train 001, "Into the Great Green Yonder," *The Daily Telegraph*, 26 Sept. 1998.

RAILWAYS See also TRAVEL

Stand fast, Craigellachie!

A cablegram carried these words from **George Stephen**, President of the Canadian Pacific

Railway Company, who was visiting bankers in London to raise needed capital, to his cousin, Donald Smith, Lord Strathcona, who was in Montreal, Nov. 1884. They signalled that Smith was not to lose faith and funds would be found in the nick of time. They were, and the railway construction continued. Lord Strathcona had the honour of driving in the "last spike" at Craigellachie, Eagle Pass, B.C. A plaque marks the spot with this inscription: "Here on November 7, 1885, a plain iron spike welded East to West." Craigellachie is the name of a rocky prominence in northern Scotland; in Gaelic, the word means "the rock of alarm."

Late events have shown us that we are made one people by that road, that that iron link has bound us together in such a way that we stand superior to most of the shafts of ill-fortune....

Sir John A. Macdonald, Prime Minister, address, June 1885, referring to the Canadian Pacific Railway, quoted by Pierre Berton in *The Last Spike: The Great Railway, 1881–1885* (1971).

The CPR is two streaks of rust across the wilderness. It will never pay for the axle grease to turn its wheels.

Reference to the Canadian Pacific Railway attributed to **Edward Blake**, leader of the Liberal Party from 1880 to 1887.

See This World Before the Next by the World's Greatest Travel System, Canadian Pacific.... Canadian Pacific Spans the World.

Advertising slogan of **Canadian Pacific Railway**, noted by E.J. Hart in "See This World Before the Next: Tourism and the CPR," *The CPR West: The Iron Road and the Making of a Nation* (1984) edited by Hugh Dempsey. "Canadian Pacific Spans the World" was the slogan used at the CP Pavilion at a 1911 exposition, London, England.

A Grecian temple and a Canadian Pacific railway have a common factor. They are alike the product of national intelligence.

W.S. Milner, commentator, "The Higher National Life," *Canada and Its Provinces: Volume XIII* (1914).

I'm free to say that, whether or not the C.P. is the greatest in the world, there certainly is no greater.

Sir Donald Mann, railroad builder, referring to the Canadian Pacific, interviewed by R.E. Knowles in *The Toronto Star*, 31 July 1930.

My first American train—the Canadian Pacific—was the most comfortable I have ever travelled in. American luxury is still extreme, although there is no railway that is not bankrupt and the Royal York, the hotel we stayed at in Toronto, and one of the best in America, was bankrupt too.

Wyndham Lewis, British artist and author, *America, I Presume* (1940).

Let me say quite clearly that the promotion policy of the Canadian National Railways has always been based upon promotion by merit. Any man who by reason of experience, knowledge, judgment, education or for any other reason is considered by management to be the best person for a job will receive the promotion—and we do not care whether he is black, white, red, or French.

Donald Gordon, CNR President, appearing before a Parliamentary Commitee, 19 Nov. 1961, quoted by Joseph Schull in *The Great Scot: A Biography of Donald Gordon* (1979). Gordon was burned in effigy for implying that there were no French Canadians with financial backgrounds to warrant consideration as directors.

For there was a time in this fair land when the railroad did not run, / When the wild majestic mountains stood alone against the sun, / Long before the white man and long before the wheel, / When the green dark forest was too silent to be real, / When the green dark forest was too silent to be real. / And many are the dead men, / Too silent / To be real.

Concluding verse of singer-composer **Gordon Lightfoot**'s song "Canadian Railroad Trilogy" (1967) from the album *Sunday Concert* (1967).

The Crow's Nest rates constitute the Magna Carta of the Western farmer.

John G. Diefenbaker, former Prime Minister, referring to protective tariff for farmers, speech, 15 Dec. 1973, *The Wit and Wisdom of John Diefenbaker* (1982) edited by John A. Munro.

I know where my troubles come from! / Oh yes I do, so I'm a-tellin' you / God damn the CPR!

Lines from **Geoffrey Ursell**'s song "God Damn the CPR!" reproduced by Bob Davis in *Singin' About Us* (1976).

Canadian writers get as excited about trains as French writers do about sex. I'm not immune myself.

Silver Donald Cameron, journalist, *Weekend Magazine*, 28 Aug. 1976.

Our national railway is the basic economic institution of our history, the thread that stitched the provinces together and made Canada possible. It is the elemental symbol of Canadian unity.

George Radwanski and **Julia Luttrell**, social commentators, *The Will of a Nation: Awakening the Canadian Spirit* (1992).

There is some truth in the famous quip, by a Quebec opponent of Confederation in the 1860s, that Canada was "a railway in search of a country."

James Laxer, economist, *False God: How the Globalization Myth Has Impoverished Canada* (1993). The quip, which seems to date from the 1960s, has been attributed to humorist Eric Nicol.

Every small town or railway whistle-stop with a bank branch felt it had a future.

Peter C. Newman, author, *The Canadian Revolution: 1985–1995, From Deference to Defiance* (1995).

On long-distance trains, first class is known as "Silver and Blue." Most people assume this is a reference to the Fifties styling of the carriages, which have lots of chunky steel fittings mixed with pale-blue upholstery, but it of course refers to the passengers, who all sport silver hair and blue denim. Riding the rails has become a popular pursuit for retired North Americans, who gather up their credit cards, rail passes and pastel wardrobes to hit the tracks like seasoned hobos.

Nigel Tisdall, English travel writer, describing a journey across Canada by rail, "Into the Great Green Yonder," *The Daily Telegraph*, 26 Sept. 1998.

RANCHING

Hang on to the cow's tail and she'll pull you through.

Attributed to rancher and meat-packing executive **Pat Burns**, advice to hard-pressed cattlemen of southern Alberta during the 1930s.

There are seven or eight neighbouring ranches visible from our window, and nearly every one belongs to a different nationality—Swede, French, German, English—they are all mixed, and Nature is such a big enemy that all the rest become insignificant.

Freya Stark, traveller and writer, letter written on a ranch near Creston, B.C., 4 Nov. 1928, *Beyond Euphrates* (1951).

RCMP

See ROYAL CANADIAN MOUNTED POLICE

READING

See also BOOKS, MAGAZINES

To resist TV, one must acquire the antidote of related media like print.

Marshall McLuhan, communications pioneer, quoted in *Canadian Cultural Mosaic Magazine*, Volume v, 1985.

Bed was made for two things, and neither of them is reading!

Joel Bonn, speed-reading specialist, characteristic remark, 13 Nov. 1981.

Most people are marked for life by the books they once read in school because they read almost nothing else after that.

Louis Dudek, poet and aphorist, "Epigrams," *Small Perfect Things* (1991).

I'm a firm believer that if we don't get kids reading, we'll have a generation of Ninja Turtles, for God's sake.

Bruno Gerussi, actor, identified with the promotion of *The Canadian Encyclopedia*, quoted by John Lyons in the *Winnipeg Free Press*, 19 Sept. 1991.

On the Tube / Take a Night Off / Believe it or not, there are no live sports events on television this evening. Read a book or take a walk.

Headline and entire article, entertainment section, *The Montreal Gazette*, 26 Sept. 1991.

I'm the sort of person who keeps a paperback in the glove compartment of my car. If I slide off the highway one winter's night, I want my last few hours to be spent reading *The Idiot* while slowly freezing to death, rather than wandering off the Trans-Canada looking for a shovel.

Michael Ondaatje, author, characteristic remark, 6 July 1992.

All reading begins in the revolt against narcissism: when a book stops reflecting your own prejudices, whether for or against what you think you "see in it," & begins to say something close to what it does say, the core of the reality in the objective aspect of it takes shape & you start wrestling with an angel.

Northrop Frye, cultural critic, "Notebook 1993," edited by Robert D. Denham, *Northrop Frye Newsletter*, Summer 1993.

Given the pace of miniaturization, it's not inconceivable that ten years from now someone will be lying in bed reading the new Michael Ondaatje novel on a viewer that weighs no more than the 1994 paperback version of *The English Patient*.

Robert Fulford, columnist, "The Ideology of the Book," *Queen's Quarterly*, Winter 1994.

In the epigram I found something short enough for Canadians to read.

Louis Dudek, poet and aphorist, letter, 13 Sept. 1995.

Sometimes it is the book / that opens you.

Robert Priest, aphorist, *Time Release Poems* (1997).

REALITY

If art is a dream, reality is a nightmare.

Louis Dudek, man-of-letters, *Epigrams* (1975).

In the world of reality that we can reach only through dramatic illusion, the past is the source of faith and the future the source of hope. In the world of illusion that we take for reality, the past is only the no longer and the future only the not yet: one vanishes into nothingness and the other, after proving itself to be much the same, vanishes after it.

Northrop Frye, cultural critic, "Shakespeare's The Tempest" (1979), *The Eternal Act of Creation: Essays, 1979–1990* (1993) edited by Robert D. Denham.

Man: the animal that produces a reality it can't stand to look at.

Stephen Strauss, science columnist, referring specifically to man's need to visualize, *The Globe and Mail*, 6 June 1992.

REASON

The irrationality of people is the poetry of the human race.

Irving Layton, poet and aphorist, The *Whole Bloody Bird (obs, aphs & Pomes)* (1969).

Those who believe without reason cannot be convinced by reason.

James Randi, conjuror and sceptic of claims of the paranormal, *James Randi: Psychic Investigator* (1991).

The reasonable person proceeds by compromise, halfway measures, illogical agreements, and similar signs of mature human intelligence. Rationalism is a militant use of language designed to demonstrate the exclusive truth of what it works on and with.

Northrop Frye, cultural critic, *The Double Vision: Language and Meaning in Religion* (1991).

Personally, I won an election advocating the idea that reason was more important than passion. It worked for one election, but the second time around, we ended up with a minority government. I believe that a certain mixture of emotion and reason is needed; but reason must always prevail.

Pierre Elliott Trudeau, former Prime Minister, interviewed by Max and Monique Nemni, "A Conversation," *Cité Libre*, March 1998.

We live in a world shaped by deductive reason. But that's simply the physical world. Our mental landscape, our spiritual lives, yearn for the inexplicable—we want something magical, miraculous, ridiculous.

Daniel David Moses, Native playwright, quoted by Jon Kaplan in *Now*, 23 May 1991.

REBELLIONS See also PROTEST; RIEL, LOUIS; WAR

They are styled rebels and traitors. The words are totally inapplicable to them... being a conquered people, they cherish the feelings of a conquered people, and have made an attempt to shake off their conquerors; is this treason?

John Stuart Mill, political economist, referring to the Rebels (or Revolutionaries) of 1839, "Radical Party and Canada: Lord Durham" (1838), *Essays on England, Ireland, and the Empire* (1982), edited by John M. Robson, Volume VI of the "Collected Works of John Stuart Mill."

Un Canadien errant, / Banni de ses foyers, / Parcourait en pleurant / Des pays étrangers.

First verse of patriot **Antoine Gérin-Lajoie**'s song "Un Canadien Errant" (1838), a moving lament for the exiles of the Rebellion of 1837. John Boyd's English translation appeared in *Canadian Poetry in English* (1954): "Weeping sorely as he journeyed / Over many a foreign strand, / A Canadian exile wandered, / Banished from his native land."

A new state of things now exists in Canada, and the past has ceased to be of importance, save for the guidance of the future.

John Stuart Mill, political economist, "Radical Party and Canada: Lord Durham" (1838), *Essays on England, Ireland, and the Empire* (1982), edited by John M. Robson, Volume VI of the "Collected Works of John Stuart Mill."

In 1837 rebellion shook this land. / In 1837 I took rebellion's hand. / The passion of rebellion's time again I hope to see. / That working folk again must rise and make this country free. / Yes, that working folk again will rise to make this country free.

Last verse and chorus of **Len Wallace**'s song "Rebellion's Time" (1989), reproduced in *The Canadian Wobbly Songbook* (1990) compiled by Jerzy (George) Dymny.

We are going to take up arms for the Glory of God, the honour of religion and for the salvation of our souls.

Gabriel Dumont, Métis leader, rallying cry, 5 March 1885, quoted by Ogden Tanner in *The Canadians: The Old West* (1977).

And now, ladies and gentlemen, from the faraway plains of Canada, we bring you the one, the only, the incomparable Gabriel Dumont! Gabriel Dumont! The man who, with a handful of followers, defeated a vastly superior Canadian army twice before himself giving way in the face of overwhelming odds. The man who rode eight hundred miles through dust, flood, and fire, to elude nearly two thousand Canadian army and police scouts who were sent out to capture him, and who finally reached the blessed sanctuary of the United States of America! Ladies and gentlemen, I give you Gabriel Dumont, the halfbreed General!

Spiel of the circus barker who introduced Gabriel Dumont, Métis leader, to audiences attending **Buffalo Bill's Wild West Show**, which Dumont joined in 1886. Quoted by Sandra Lynn McKee in *Gabriel Dumont: Indian Fighter* (1973).

RECESSION See also ECONOMICS

When I got to Toronto, there was an economic recession, and yet workers everywhere were going out on strike. When I got to Ottawa, public servants were actually storming Parliament Hill. Do you see my point? All the meanings had gone, all sense of direction.... It wasn't an economic thing, it was a psychic depression. And, certainly in English Canada, a psychic depression of large proportions, a catastrophe.

Scott Symons, author, "Deliquescence in Canada," *The Idler*, July–Aug. 1992.

The insane pursuit of the holy grail of balanced budgets will drive the economy into recession.

William Vickrey, economist and Nobel laureate, born in Victoria, B.C., emeritus professor from Columbia University, quoted by Stephen Handelman in *The Toronto Star*, 9 Oct. 1996.

RECONCILIATION

Nations, properly speaking, cannot be reconciled to other nations, only individuals to individuals. Nonetheless, individuals can be helped to heal and to reconcile by public rituals of atonement.

Michael Ignatieff, author, "Articles of Faith," *Index on Censorship*, Sept.–Oct. 1996, as reprinted in "Readings," *Harper's*, March 1997.

RECORD INDUSTRY See also MUSIC

The only excuse for recording a work is to do it differently.

Glenn Gould, pianist, quoted by Tim Page in *The Glenn Gould Reader* (1984).

There's always hope—except for the record business.

Buffy Sainte-Marie, composer and performer, quoted in *The Toronto Star*, 30 Dec. 1987.

I don't want to sell five million records and be rich, and then that's it. I'm afraid of that. I want a career. I want to sing all my life.

Céline Dion, singer, quoted by Charles P. Alexander in *Time*, 28 Feb. 1994.

Equating the pale fire of a recording with the explosion of a production would be like mistaking a passport photograph for a human being.

R. Murray Schafer, composer and theorist, "Dub," *The Canadian Forum*, Nov. 1994.

A record has to be good in four instances. You have to be able to listen to it in the morning, first thing in the morning. You have to be able to cook and eat to it. You have to be able to drive to it, biking or driving. And you have to be able to f—k to it. If you can do all those things, then it's a good record

k.d. lang, composer and singer, quoted by Peter Howell in *The Toronto Star*, 10 October 1995.

REFERENDA

See also PARTITION, QUEBEC, SECESSION, SEPARATISM, SOVEREIGNTY, SOVEREIGNTY-ASSOCIATION

Are you in favour of the passing of an act forbidding the importation, manufacture or sale of spirits, wine, ale, beer, cider and all other alcoholic liquors for use as beverages?

Question asked on the ballot of the federal referendum on Prohibition held in 1898. The results: 51.3% voted yes, 48.7% voted no. Thereupon Prime Minister Sir Wilfrid Laurier decided that Prohibition was a provincial responsibility.

Are you in favour of releasing the government from any obligation arising out of any past commitments restricting the methods of raising men for military service?

Question asked on the ballot of the referendum on conscription held in 1942. The results: 64% voted yes, 36% voted no. Prime Minister Mackenzie King, noting that Quebec rejected it (70.2% voting no), stalled the authorization of conscription for overseas service until 1944.

The old concept of the plebiscite, for example, may take on new relevance; TV could conduct daily plebiscites by presenting facts to 200,000,000 people and providing a computerized feedback of the popular will.

Marshall McLuhan, communications pioneer, "Playboy Interview" (1969) conducted by Eric Norden, *The Essential McLuhan* (1995) edited by Eric McLuhan and Frank Zingrone.

Canadians in every province, including Quebec, would vote overwhelming "yes" to this referendum question: "Are you in favour of a 10-year moratorium on all discussions of constitutional change?"

Michael Bliss, historian, "Let's Shut Up and Keep the Status Quo," *The Globe and Mail*, 17 Jan. 1992.

Before any referendum, Ottawa will have to stop playing the tart, showing too much leg by the roadside, hoping to hitchhike to a new Canadian Jerusalem.

Mordecai Richler, Quebec novelist, speech, Canadian Club of Winnipeg, 17 Jan. 1992, quoted by David Roberts in *The Globe and Mail* the following day.

If the world held a referendum on Canada, the world would vote yes. It is time we said yes as well.

Joe Clark, Minister of Constitutional Affairs, address, Canadian Real Estate Association, Ottawa, 31 March 1992, quoted in *The Toronto Star* the following day.

I don't think you can have a referendum every few years just because you did not like the results of the last one.

Margaret Thatcher, former Prime Minister of Britain, alluding to the forthcoming Quebec referendum, address in Toronto, 5 Feb. 1995, quoted by Robert Sheppard in "The Provinces," *The Globe and Mail*, 7 Feb. 1995.

The *René*rendum, the Referen*dumb*, the *Nev-er*endum

Popular references to the two Quebec referenda of 20 May 1980 and 30 Oct. 1995.

That's why the government of Canada must immediately stage a referendum across the country with the simple question: "Do you want to keep your Canadian citizenship? Yes or No."... I call it the "refer-end-it."

Diane Francis, columnist, "Column," *Maclean's*, 16 Sept. 1996.

In the October 1995 referendum on Quebec separation, a handful of Francophone voters in Quebec decided the fate of Canada. A mere 53,000 voters, out of a constituency of 7.5 million, defeated the sovereignist proposal.

Charles F. Doran, School of Advanced International Studies, The Johns Hopkins University, "Will Canada Unravel?" *Foreign Affairs*, Sept.–Oct. 1996. Doran noted that 94 percent of registered voters in Quebec cast their ballots, that 63 percent of Francophones voted for separation, up from slightly over 50 percent in the 1980 referendum.

I doubt that Quebec will have another referendum before at least 2005. When it does, the separatists will lose again, whether or not

Lucien Bouchard has retired to California. Michael Bliss, historian, "Coming Soon," *The Globe and Mail*, 22 Aug. 1997.

A referendum is a card you always keep up your sleeve.

Attributed to former Quebec Premier **Robert Bourassa** by columnist Jean Lapine, "The Provinces," *The Globe and Mail*, 17 Nov. 1998.

Don't count on me for a losing referendum. I am not a maniac for referendums.

Lucien Bouchard, Quebec Premier, leaders' debate, CBC-TV, 17 Nov. 1998, as quoted by Robert McKenzie in *The Toronto Star* the following day.

We must stop wasting our energy on referendum after referendum. Together, Quebeckers and other Canadians, we must devote our efforts to the economic, social, cultural and environmental issues on which our quality of life depends.

Stéphane Dion, Minister of Intergovernmental Affairs, address, Nordic Association for Canadian Studies, Reykjavik, Iceland, 5 Aug. 1999, printed in *The Globe and Mail* the following day.

We are not committed to a lost referendum.

Lucien Bouchard, Quebec Premier, speaking at a meeting of the Parti Québécois caucus, Shawinigan, Que., 20 Aug. 1999, quoted by Campbell Clark in the *National Post* the following day.

There never will be another referendum on separation in Quebec.

Allan Fotheringham, columnist, making a millennial prediction, *Maclean's*, 1 Jan. 2000.

Referendum I

If Quebec were to vote very massively for a separation . . . I would silently go away, perhaps to fight another day in some other field.

Pierre Elliott Trudeau, Prime Minister, interviewed by Bruce Phillips, taped 20 Dec. 1977, telecast on the CTV Network on 1 Jan. 1978, reproduced in *The Globe and Mail*, 2 Jan. 1978.

Non, merci!

Wording on advertising sponsored by federalist groups in the 1980 referendum campaign on sovereignty-association in Quebec.

Quebecers will vote yes because they prefer equality to subordination, dignity to defeat, liberty to bondage, advance to retreat, pride to humiliation, the status of majority to the status of minority, expansion to the exhausting conflicts which drain its profits, prosperity to federal pittances, a place among free nations to the ghetto it has been locked in for a century by a federal regime.

Camille Laurin, Quebec Cabinet Minister, speech, referring to the forthcoming referendum on sovereignty-association, Quebec National Assembly, 13 March 1980, quoted by Patrick Doyle in *The Toronto Star* the following day.

On these terms, do you give the government of Quebec the mandate to negotiate the proposed agreement between Quebec and Canada?

Basic question asked on the ballot of the referendum on sovereignty-association held on 20 May 1980. (The actual question was over 100 words long in English, longer in French.) The results: 59% voted no, 41% voted yes.

If I understand you properly, you are saying, "Until next time."

René Lévesque, Quebec Premier and Parti Québécois leader, expressing dismay with the results of the Quebec referendum on sovereignty-association, speech, Paul Sauvé Arena, Montreal, CBC-TV, 20 May 1980. Crestfallen, Lévesque employed the French "goodbye"—*à la prochaine fois.*

I never thought I could be as proud to be a Quebecker and a Canadian as I am tonight.

Pierre Elliott Trudeau, Prime Minister, addressing the nation following the pro-federalist outcome of the Quebec referendum on sovereignty-association, Ottawa, CBC-TV, 20 May 1980. He echoed the words that René Lévesque had spoken following the victory of the Parti Québécois in the provincial election of 15 Nov. 1976.

Referendum II

Since the last referendum Québec has been acting like a sovereign state while remaining part of Canada. The solution now is to pretend it's a sovereign state while making sure it remains a part of Canada.

Louis Dudek, poet and aphorist, entry for 1991, *Notebooks 1960–1994* (1994).

If the separatists win this time, we should make it the best two out of three.

Pierre Elliott Trudeau, former Prime Minister, press conference, using hockey parlance, Fall 1993, quoted by Richard Gwyn, "Home and Away," *The Toronto Star*, 22 May 1994.

There never will be a referendum on independence in 1995. Even dumb columnists know that.

Allan Fotheringham, columnist, dumb or wise, *Maclean's*, 3 Oct. 1994.

But next year's referendum has been lost already—by the separatists. Only malignant stupidity by the rest of us could alter this result.

Richard Gwyn, columnist, "The First Borderless State," lecture, Brock University, St. Catharines, 23 Nov. 1994, as printed in *The Toronto Star*, 26 Nov. 1994.

It's now a question of tactics and strategy. Give me a half-dozen Ontarians who put their feet to the Quebec flag, and I've got it.

Jacques Parizeau, leader of the Parti Québécois, interviewed by *The Los Angeles Times*, 11 Dec. 1994, as published by the *Winnipeg Free Press* the following day. Parizeau was referring to the widely reported incident that occurred in Brockville, Ont., in 1989, when a group of anti-French demonstrators trampled on the Quebec flag to protest a bill banning English-language signs.

The question must be decisive, unambiguous, and neutral. Squeezed into a ball, the question is: Quebec: * In. * Out. If it were printed on the tax return every year it would save trees and everyone a lot of bother.

Robert Mason Lee, columnist, "The West," *The Globe and Mail*, 25 Feb. 1995.

Noui au Canada

Title of an article in *L'Actualité*, March 1995, referring to mixed attitudes in Quebec to the Referendum, playing on the French words for no and yes, *non* and *oui*, as quoted by Barbara Wickens in *Maclean's*, 6 March 1995.

Voting *oui-oui* is a *no-no*.

Graffiti for the No side in the referendum, *Magog*, Que., Sept. 1995.

The National Assembly is authorized, within the scope of the Act, to proclaim the sovereignty of Quebec.

First clause in Bill 1, tabled in Quebec's National Assembly, 7 Sept. 1995. The full text of the proposed measure appeared in *The Toronto Star* the following day.

In the end, I suspect, the referendum will be won or lost on the quality of the words.

Daniel Latouche, columnist, "On Quebec," *The Globe and Mail*, 16 Sept. 1995.

If you're going into the voting booth to vote Yes, leave your passport behind.

Jean Charest, Member of Parliament, warning Quebeckers about the consequences of the Yes vote in the forthcoming referendum on Quebec's sovereignty, Montreal rally, 24 Sept. 1995.

You can't break up a country on a judicial recount.

Daniel Johnson, Quebec Liberal leader, dismissing the notion of legitimizing Quebec's secession from Canada on the basis of "50 plus 1" in the Quebec Referendum, quoted by Lysiane Gagnon, "Inside Quebec," *The Globe and Mail*, 26 Sept. 1995.

None can predict the future, but it is possible that Oct. 30 will be our last collective rendezvous. Then, from being a "province like the others," we will perhaps become individuals like the others.

Jacques Parizeau, Quebec Premier, announcement of the date of the referendum on Quebec's Future, 1 Oct. 1995, quoted by Robert McKenzie in *The Toronto Star* the following day.

There is nothing you will do without our consent. I repeat: There is nothing you will do without our consent.

Matthew Coon Come, Grand Chief of the Quebec Crees, announcing a pre-referendum vote for his Cree people, 12 Oct. 1995, quoted by John Gray in *The Globe and Mail* the following day.

What would this jeopardize? Ninety per cent of our exports would be threatened; close to one million jobs.

Paul Martin, Minister of Finance, warning about the economic and work-related implications of Quebec's secession, news conference, Montreal, 17 Oct. 1995, quoted by David Vienneau in *The Toronto Star* the following day. Martin was accused of scare-mongering by Quebec Premier Jacques Parizeau who, later that day, campaigning in Hull, Que., replied, "There are only 3.2 million jobs in Quebec. Past that point they'll have to import unemployment."

A Yes, that has something magic about it, with a magic wand, it transforms the whole situation. It produces within us solidarity and unity.

Lucien Bouchard, leader of the Bloc Québécois, campaign speech, Montreal, comparing the Yes vote to a "magic wand," 15 Oct. 1995, quoted by Jeffrey Simpson in *The Globe and Mail*, 18 Oct. 1995. Prime Minister Chrétien responded by referred to "Lucien in Wonderland."

A, B, C, D, E, F, G, H, I, J, K, L, M, NO, PQ, R, S, T, U, V, W, X, Y, Z

Accidental No message embedded in the English alphabet, as noted by **Andrea Lemphers**, Shallow Bay, Yukon, Letters to the Editor, *The Globe and Mail*, 21 Oct. 1995.

Do you agree that Quebec should become sovereign, after having made a formal offer to Canada for a new Economic and Political Partnership, within the scope of the Bill respecting the future of Quebec and of the agreement signed on June 12, 1995?

Official translation from the French of the question on the ballot for the Referendum on the Future of Quebec, held 30 Oct. 1995, as published by André Picard, "Diary," *The Globe and Mail*, 24 Oct. 1995.

Love is not enough. Just don't love us—recognize us.

Louise Beaudoin, Quebec Minister of Intergovernmental Affairs, interviewed in English, CBC-TV, the night of the Quebec referendum, 30 Oct. 1995.

The history books will return that we have signalled the end of Canada as we know it.... Canada now exists only on paper.

Mario Dumont, leader of the Action Démocratique, reacting to the anticipated outcome of the referendum, CBC-TV, 30 Oct. 1995, quoted by André Picard in *The Globe and Mail* the following day.

NO. 6

Summary of the results the second referendum on the status of Quebec, held 30 Oct. 1995. The results were a near tie: 50.6% voted No, 49.4% voted Yes. The outcome was decided by 0.6% of all the votes cast (with 95% of the electorate voting).

Let's keep the faith. Let's keep hoping because the next time will be the right time and the next time could come more quickly than we believe.

Lucien Bouchard, leader of the Bloc Québécois, concession speech, Palais des Congrès, Montreal, reacting to the outcome of the referendum, CBC-TV, 30 Oct. 1995, quoted by Robert McKenzie in *The Toronto Star* the following day.

It is true that we were beaten by the power of money and the ethnic vote. That only means that the next time instead of getting 60 per cent of the [francophone] votes we will get 63 or 64 per cent.... Three-fifths of us voted Yes. That wasn't enough but soon we will have enough. We will get our country....

Jacques Parizeau, Quebec Premier, concession speech, Palais de Congrès, Montreal, 30 Oct. 1995, quoted by Rhéal Séguin in *The Globe and Mail* the following day.

It's the Jews, Italians, Greeks who vote along ethnic lines. They're the ones who are the racists, not the sovereigntists.

Pierre Bourgault, separatist, quoted on CBC Radio's *National News*, 30 Nov. 1995.

In a democracy, the people are always right. Tonight there is only one winner, and that is the people. Tonight we have every reason to feel proud of Canadian democracy.

Jean Chrétien, Prime Minister, address CBC-TV

on the outcome of the Quebec Referendum, 30 Oct. 1995, quoted by Sandra Contenta in *The Toronto Star* the following day.

Once our partner has drained the last dregs of its incapacity to recognize our reality as a people, another referendum opening will occur, under winning conditions for Quebec. That will be the time of the next referendum.

Lucien Bouchard, leader, Bloc Québécois, news conference, agreeing to seek the leadership of the Parti Québécois and with it the Premiership of Quebec, press conference, Montreal, 21 Nov. 1995, quoted by Edison Stewart in *The Toronto Star* the following day. Bouchard introduced the face-saving formula of requiring "winning conditions" (*conditions gagnantes*) before agreeing to call for the third referendum on Quebec sovereignty. Such winning conditions for the Yes vote, or losing conditions for the No vote, would presumably be based on the results of polls.

There is going to be another referendum.

Richard Gwyn, columnist, "Home and Away," *The Toronto Star*, 8 Dec. 1995.

An old Canadian friend writes that on Monday, Canada dodged a suicide bullet. That is the good news, I suppose. The bad news is that Quebec is busy reloading the gun.

Charles Krauthammer, correspondent, "Sane, Reliable Canada Attempts Suicide—and Will Do So Again," *The International Herald Tribune*, 4 Nov. 1995.

Canada cannot—will not—remain the same after Oct. 30. There will be a leadership contest for the Parti Québécois, which Mr. Bouchard will win. There will be a provincial election, which his party will win. And then there will be another referendum.

Jeffrey Simpson, columnist, "The Man Who Turned All of Canada on Its Collective Head in 1995," *The Globe and Mail*, 28 Dec. 1995.

REFORM

If the Canadas are pacified, and their prosperity secured, I am content.

Lord Durham, author of the *Durham Report*, letter written from London, England, 22 Jan. 1840, addressed to Major John Richardson who quoted the remark in *Eight Years in Canada* (1847).

We have to get over the naive idea that monopolistic exploiters and dictators are going to reform because good men preaching justice and charity tell them to do so. Experience has shown that bad men generally will reform only when they have to.

M.M. Coady, adult educator, quoted by Harvey (Pablo) Steele in *Agent for Change: The Story of Pablo Steele* (1973) as told to Gary MacEoin.

How do we so easily forget that reconciliation and reform are at the heart of the country's creation and survival?

John Ralston Saul, author, *Reflections of a Siamese Twin: Canada at the End of the Twentieth Century* (1997).

REFORM PARTY See also CANADIAN ALLIANCE; MANNING, PRESTON; POLITICAL PARTIES

Quebec wants out of Confederation; we want in.

Slogan of **Preston Manning**, founder and leader of the Reform Party of Canada, quoted in "Nice Country, Nice Mess," *The Economist*, 29 June 1991.

In the unlikely event of a merger between the Reform Party and the Progressive Conservatives—a suggested name for the new party—Reform-a-Tory.

G.M. Yeomans, Mississauga reader, Letters to the Editor, *The Globe and Mail*, 5 April 1996.

REFUGEES See also IMMIGRATION

It is estimated that Jews, with a population of only 275,000 in Canada, participated in the sponsorship of 3,000 Indochinese refugees (comparable to the number sponsored by the members of the Roman Catholic and United Church together). Of this number, over half were sponsored through the efforts of the *organized* Jewish community.

Howard Adelman, philosopher, spokesman for Operation Lifeline, *Canada and the Indochinese Refugees* (1982). This ad hoc committee encouraged families, social and religious organizations, and the federal government to aid in the settlement of the Boat People in 1979–80.

I figure if Canada were to take, maybe, four million, I could get re-elected.

Brian Mulroney, Prime Minister, touring a Vietnamese refugee camp in Hong Kong where he addressed the camp director, making light of the number of refugees and his electoral standing, quoted by Edison Stewart in *The Toronto Star,* 31 May 1991.

We Canadians had a terrible record. Little Dominican Republic, which fits into most of Toronto, took as many Jews in as all of Canada.

W. Gunther Plaut, rabbi, referring to Canada's record with respect to displaced Jews before and during World War II, quoted by Warren Gerard in *The Toronto Star,* 28 Sept. 1997.

Canada, of course, is a nation of refugees. Except for the aboriginals, we are nearly all boat people.

Peter C. Newman, columnist, "The Nation's Business," *Maclean's,* 9 April 1999.

REGINA See also SASKATCHEWAN

The pleasures of Regina are not immediately obvious. Its centre fails to cohere, its buildings are a graceless jumble, and its topography could hardly be flatter. Allowances, however, must be made.

Mark Abley, traveller, *Beyond Forget: Rediscovering the Prairies* (1986).

REGIONALISM

But although nations may dissolve, *regions* do not. If at some future time all Americans were politically one, from Coronation Gulf to Magellanes, people who live north of the 49th parallel and the Great Lakes would still be referred to as "Canadians."

Wyndham Lewis, British artist, "Nature's Place in Canadian Culture" (1940–44), *Wyndham Lewis in Canada* (1971) edited by George Woodcock.

My consciousness of regionalism is breaking down still further to my basic consciousness which is ... 38 Weston St. And only after that: street, block, neighbourhood, city, township, county, province, dominion, world, solar system, cosmos, all of which become larger and more complicated.

Greg Curnoe, artist, referring to his house in London, Ont., quoted by Dennis Reid in *Greg Curnoe: Canada X Biennial, Sao Paulo* (1969).

The problem of regional disparities is rooted in the profit orientation of capitalism. The social costs of stagnant areas are irrelevant to the corporations.

"The Waffle Manifesto: For an Independent Socialist Canada" (1969) reprinted in *The Canadian Forum,* Dec. 1989.

I think the country we know as Canada will, in the foreseeable future, be a federation of regions culturally, rather than a single nation.

Northrop Frye, cultural critic, interviewed by Robert Fulford, "From Nationalism to Regionalism: The Maturing of Canadian Culture," *The Anthology Anthology: A Selection from 30 Years of CBC Radio's Anthology* (1984) edited by Robert Weaver.

The West hates the East, Maritimers hate everybody else. Toronto hates Quebec. Everybody loves to hate Quebec. And everybody hates Toronto, but in Toronto, they just don't understand why everybody hates them.

Anna Woodrow, sociologist, explaining the view of stand-up comics, quoted by Jane L. Thompson, "It's No Joke," *National Post,* 1 May 1999.

Canada became the first country in the history of the world to entrench regional economic equality as an official *raison d'être* of the country, in 1981, attempting, in effect, to move resources to people instead of the other way round.

Conrad Black, publisher, commenting on changes since the 1960s led by the Trudeau administrations, "Out of Uncle Sam's Shadow," *National Post,* 11 Jan. 2000.

REINCARNATION

Everyone asks for proofs of reincarnation. Can anyone provide any proofs against? The onus of proof is on the disbelivers, since the majority of people accept it.

Albert E.S. Smythe, editor, "Sparks," *The Lamp: A Theosophical Monthly,* Volume 1, Sept. 1894.

RELATIONSHIPS

Beware of the man who abases himself before you. He will never forgive you for it.

Irving Layton, poet and aphorist, *The Whole Bloody Bird (obs, aphs & Pomes)* (1969).

Every relationship we have with another person is rather less, or rather more, than we would like it to be.

Richard Needham, newspaper columnist, *The Wit and Wisdom of Richard Needham* (1977).

The mystery of what a couple *is*, exactly, is almost the only true mystery left to us, and we when have come to the end of it there will be no more need for literature—or for love, for that matter.

Mavis Gallant, author, quoted by Julian Barnes in *A History of the World in 10 1/2 Chapters* (1989).

RELAXATION See also STRESS

Relaxation is a natural state, but not a normal one. We have to make it ours again. Give yourself permission to relax. When you breathe as if you are relaxed, you become relaxed.

Eli Bay, creator of Relaxation Response, characteristic advice, 16 May 2000.

RELIGION See also BELIEF, BIBLE, BUDDHISM, CATHOLICISM, CHRISTIANITY, JUDAISM

How many men do you know who let their religions interfere with their business?

Bob Edwards, publisher, *The Eye Opener*, 6 Dec. 1913, *The Best of Bob Edwards* (1975) edited by Hugh Dempsey.

I believe it is the right, and the duty, of the clergy to have a hand in all that affects the moral, even the temporal, welfare of the people.

Charles E. Coughlin, the "radio priest," interviewed by R.E. Knowles in *The Toronto Star Weekly*, 6 Jan. 1934.

We must affirm freedom of religion for everyone, including those who have no religion at all.

Paul-Émile Léger, Cardinal, quoted by Peter Gzowski in *Great Canadians: A Century of Achievement* (1965).

Religion is the debasement of drama into dogma.

Irving Layton, poet and aphorist, *The Whole Bloody Bird (obs, aphs & Pomes)* (1969).

There are some people who are so heavenly minded they are no earthly good.

Philip A. Gagliardi, B.C. Highways Minister, quoted by Kenneth Bagnell in *The Globe Magazine*, 25 July 1970.

Geography even more than religion has made us puritans, although ours is a puritanism tempered by orgy.

William Kilbourn, historian, Introduction, *Canada: A Guide to the Peaceable Kingdom* (1970).

My name is Harvey Pablo Steele. I'm a Roman Catholic priest, and I'm deeply ashamed of my church. In the name of the Father, the Son and the Holy Ghost....

Harvey Steele, socially conscious priest known in Latin America as "Padre Pablo," opening words of the first sermon he delivered upon returning to Scarboro Missions, Toronto, in 1976, quoted in his obituary by Mark Gollom, *National Post*, 19 April 1999.

Religion, one would think, should be / The bond that all unites. / But take a look around and see / The schisms it incites.

Opening lines of **Ernest Buckler**'s verse "I Am Not, Nor Have Ever Been, a Christian Scientist," *Whirligig* (1977).

People of different religions can get along pretty well, providing they aren't religious.

Richard Needham, newspaper columnist, *The Wit and Wisdom of Richard Needham* (1977).

Optimism, not religion, is the opiate of the masses.

Lionel Tiger, biologist, quoted by Rita Christopher in *Maclean's*, 28 May 1979.

Religion in My Life: It has a great deal of importance. Words like "infinite" and "eternal" are not fuzzy to me; they are words that prevent the human spirit from getting claustrophobia.

Northrop Frye, cultural critic, interviewed by Allan Gould, "Chatelaine's Celebrity I.D.," *Chatelaine*, Nov. 1982.

Where is there a religion of simple kindness?

Robin Skelton, poet and aphorist, *A Devious Dictionary* (1991).

Our view of religion is about to change—due to technology. The oft-repeated phrase "only God can make a tree" is no longer true. With the mastery of genetic manipulation humans will start designing their successors. With this will come increased diversity.

Frank Ogden, futurologist, characteristic observation, March 1993.

You are the first generation raised without religion.

Thoughts about Generation X of the narrator of **Douglas Coupland**'s novel *Life after God* (1994).

If human beings were born with a conscience, God would be out of a job.

Irena F. Karafilly, aphorist, "Thoughts for the Millennium from A to Z," *The Montreal Gazette*, 30 Dec. 1999.

Everyone thinks he or she is right. I have never heard anyone ever say, "I think I'm in the wrong religion."

Peter Urs Bender, motivational speaker, characteristic remark, 11 May 2000.

REMEMBRANCE DAY See HOLIDAYS

REPUTATION See also FAME

Character is what you are. Reputation is what you try to make people think you are.

Bob Edwards, publisher, *The Eye Opener*, 27 Jan. 1912, *The Wit and Wisdom of Bob Edwards* (1976) edited by Hugh Dempsey.

A good reputation is better than fame.

Louis Dudek, man-of-letters, *Epigrams* (1975).

It's great to be acclaimed in your own country.

Oscar Peterson, jazz pianist, quoted by Dave Broadfoot in an interview with Sid Adilman in *The Toronto Star*, 4 Jan. 1992.

RESEARCH & DEVELOPMENT See also SCIENCE & SCIENTISTS

...the simple statement that it would be nice to see more industrial research in Canada is apt to be regarded as critical of industry, as ultra-nationalistic, as anti-American, and as showing ignorance of economics.

*

It is important to support people, not projects. If a man is good enough to be supported, surely he is good enough to decide what to work on.

E.W. Steacie, President, National Research Council, address, Ottawa Board of Trade, 6 April 1961, *Science in Canada: Selections from the Speeches of E.W.R. Steacie* (1965).

Neither the prestige of your subject and the power of your instruments / Nor the extent of your learnedness and the precision of your planning / Can substitute for the originality of your approach and the keenness of your observation.

Precept inscribed over the institute devoted to the study of stress at the **University of Montreal**, founded by Hans Selye and mentioned in *In Vivo: The Case for Supramolecular Biology* (1967).

The future of research, in the humanities and social sciences at least, requires that universities at large embrace the principle that the responsibilities for scholarly research and for disseminating its results are inseparable.

Marsh Jeanneret, former publisher, University of Toronto Press, *God and Mammon: Universities as Publishers* (1989).

Toshiba invests more each year in research than all of Canada.

Geraldine Kenney-Wallace, scientist and President of McMaster University, referring to the Japanese electronics conglomerate, quoted by Diane Brady in *Maclean's*, 9 Nov. 1992.

You can stay in Canada and do original research.... If you adequately fund young scientists they'll return the investment well.

Michael Smith, scientist at the University of British Columbia and recipient of the 1993 Nobel Prize in Chemistry, quoted in *The Toronto Star*, 16 Dec. 1993.

The real payoffs you never understand. You should just give good people money and tell them to do good things.

James Gosling, Calgary-educated computer programmer who developed the Java computer application program in 1995, interviewed by Tyler Hamilton, "Java Inventor Brews Cool Stuff," *The Globe and Mail*, 19 Nov. 1998.

RESISTANCE

Right to the End!

Said to be the maxim of **Dollard des Ormeaux**, also known as Adam Dollard, hero of the battle at Long Sault, New France, May 1660, according to Jean-Paul Desbiens in *For Pity's Sake* (1965) translated from the French by Frédéric Coté.

RESOURCES See also ECONOMICS, ENVIRONMENT, NATURE

Rich by nature, poor by policy.

Goldwin Smith, essayist, commenting on the social and economic condition of the Dominion of Canada, *Handbook of Commercial Union* (1888). He noted in *Canada and the Canadian Question* (1891), "'Rich by nature, poor by policy,' might be written over Canada's door. Rich she would be if she were allowed to embrace her destiny and be part of her own continent; poor, comparatively at least, she is in striving to remain a part of Europe."

The most frustrating thing about this great country of ours is the difference between its actual and its potential performance. No other country in the world has as much going for it, and yet we are far from exploiting all our advantages. In every sense, socially, economically, and politically, we are well below our capacity.

John Crispo, political scientist, *Mandate for Canada* (1979).

Now that natural resources are no longer the most valuable currency, Canada must shift its attention to developing its human resources. People with knowledge who live in a culture where they are free to take the risks involved in investigating and inventing are the greatest resources a nation has. To support their scientific research and technological innovation is to invest in our future in Canada.

Geraldine A. Kenney-Wallace and **J. Fraser Mustard**, scientists, "From Paradox to Paradigm: The Evolution of Science and Technology in Canada," *Daedalus: Journal of the American Academy of Arts and Sciences,* "In Search of Canada," Fall 1988.

Technology enables us to harvest previously unattainable "resources" in quantities far in excess of their regenerative capacity, and we pay no attention because, through the span of human history, we have considered those resources infinite and have believed that the human mind would always provide solutions to our problems.

Anita Gordon and **David Suzuki**, science broadcasters, *It's a Matter of Survival* (1990).

Natural resources are no longer important. Nobody in the 21st century—with the exception of a few countries with lots of oil and no people—is going to be rich based on natural resources.

Lester Thurow, management analyst, addressing the Liberal Party's policy convention, Aylmer, Que., 23 Nov. 1991, quoted by David Crane in *The Toronto Star* the following day.

RESPECT

Kneel to nobody; bow to everyone.

Robin Skelton, poet and aphorist, *A Devious Dictionary* (1991).

RESPONSIBILITY See also DUTY

I would hope that I would leave my children the legacy my father left me—to appreciate that one must meet one's responsibilities and must make decisions one is required to make and be prepared to live with them and face the consequences of those decisions.

John W. Bassett, publisher, interviewed in 1978, quoted by Maggie Siggins in *Bassett* (1979).

There's nothing like responsibility to kill a career.

James H. Boren, neologist, *Fuzzify! Borenwords and Stategies for Bureaucratic Success* (1982).

But as an artist, that's where the paradox is, your responsibility to be irresponsible. As soon as you talk about social or political responsibility, you've amputated the best limbs you've got as an artist.

David Cronenberg, film director, interview, *Rolling Stone,* 6 Feb. 1992.

Nobody is responsible in a corporatist society. That's because the real citizens are corporations. Individuals only work for them and follow orders.

John Ralston Saul, author, *The Doubter's Companion: A Dictionary of Aggressive Common Sense* (1994).

RETIREMENT See also AGE

There is an old French saying: "The cemeteries are full of irreplaceable people."

René Lévesque, Quebec Premier, on his impending retirement, quoted by Anthony Wilson-Smith in *Maclean's,* 8 July 1985.

So, don't let retirement scare the daylights out of you. Get an RRDSP—a Registered

Retirement Daylight Savings Plan—now, and make your last years sunny and bright.

Comedy routine "RRDSP" created by CBC Radio's *Double Exposure* comedy team, *The Great Big Book of Canadian Humour* (1992) edited by Allan Gould.

That's no beach you are reaching, it's back to the new grind. After all, somebody has to support your 35-year-old kids.

Frank Ogden, futurologist, speech on retirement, Vancouver, Feb. 1993.

REVELATION

Those who have the habit of revelation lose the habit of thought.

Robin Skelton, poet and aphorist, *A Devious Dictionary* (1991).

REVOLUTION

Revolution without direction bears a close resemblance to war.

Marshall McLuhan, communications pioneer, "Education in the Electronic Age" (1967), *The Best of Times / The Worst of Times: Contemporary Issues in Canadian Education* (1972) edited by Hugh A. Stevenson, Robert M. Stamp, and J. Donald Wilson.

The bourgeoisie has been the only revolutionary class in history. That thought crucifies me.

Irving Layton, poet and aphorist, *The Whole Bloody Bird (obs, aphs & Pomes)* (1969).

A revolution is a good thing as long as it doesn't succeed.

Louis Dudek, man-of-letters, *Epigrams* (1975).

Schreyer: And what have you been up to lately?

Macpherson: Revolution!

Question asked by Governor General **Edward Schreyer** and answered by **Kay Macpherson**, induction ceremony, Order of Canada, Ottawa, 1982, noted in her obituary by Donn Downey in *The Globe and Mail*, 19 Aug. 1999. The citation read: "She has long served humanitarian and social concerns, particularly women's rights."

They sentenced me to twenty years of boredom / For trying to change the system from within. / I'm coming now, I'm coming to reward them. / First we take Manhattan, then we take Berlin.

Verse from **Leonard Cohen**'s song "First We Take Manhattan" from the album *I'm Your Man* (1988).

I fear that we will not exist as a nation, as a people, as an entity in another few years because of external pressure and internal betrayal. We must literally and figuratively take up arms in our own bloody defence to stop this.

Farley Mowat, author and nationalist, addressing the Council of Canadians, Toronto, 21 Nov. 1991, quoted by John Douglas in the *Winnipeg Free Press*, 23 Nov. 1991.

We invented a bizarre mixture of socio-democratic capitalism, which might be called middle-class communism.

John Ralston Saul, President, Canada PEN International, quoted in University of Guelph's "Canada" supplement, *The Globe and Mail*, 4 Dec. 1991.

The role of a true revolutionary is to patiently explain.

Attributed to former Prime Minister **Pierre Elliott Trudeau** by Minister of Indian Affairs Ronald Irwin, according to Geoffrey York in *The Globe and Mail*, 31 Jan. 1994.

RICHLER, MORDECAI See also WRITERS & WRITING, CANADIAN

Notes toward an unwritten portrait of Mordecai Richler: Walks with the loose, shambling gait of a much larger man. Has the mildly surprised air of a lifelong thin man who woke up one morning to find himself in a fat man's body... a guy who looks like an unmade bed with reading glasses....

Jack Todd, columnist, *The Montreal Gazette*, 21 Sept. 1991.

Whenever I have described Quebec's sign laws, whether at dinner parties in New York or London, the other guests have accused me of inventing the details. Mind you, they have also warned me never to put it in a novel. Nobody would believe anything so patently absurd.

Mordecai Richler, novelist and journalist, 28 Sept. 1991.

Foreigner is not the right expression. I think the right expression is he doesn't belong... he is not part of the family.

Michel Bélanger, co-chairperson, Bélanger-Campeau Commission on Quebec's Future, referring to Mordecai Richler and his criticisms of the province's pretensions, quoted by Ingrid Peritz in *The Montreal Gazette*, 28 Dec. 1991.

Next you'll say Mordecai Richler is Mordecai *Richelieu.*

Line of dialogue that ridicules the habit of turning everybody into a French Canadian in the Quebec feature film *La Florida* (1994).

With bracing immodesty, he confirmed that a famous anecdote is true: Many years ago, matriarch Saidye Bronfman said to him, "You've come a long way for a boy from St. Urbain Street." To which he replied, "You've come a long way for a bootlegger's wife."

Elizabeth Renzetti, reporter, referring to Mordecai Richler, "Literary Lion," *The Globe and Mail*, 27 Sept. 1997.

RIEL, LOUIS See also REBELLIONS

I say humbly, through the grace of God I believe I am the prophet of the New World.

Louis Riel, Métis leader, addressing the jury with messianic fervour, Regina, 31 July 1885; *The Queen vs. Louis Riel, Accused and Convicted of the Crime of High Treason* (1886).

He died at dawn in the land of snows; / A priest at the left, a priest at the right; / The doomed man praying for his pitiless foes, / And each priest holding a low dim light, / To pray for the soul of the dying. / But Windsor Castle was far away; / And Windsor Castle was never so gay / With her gorgeous banners flying!

First of two verses of **Joaquin Miller**'s poem "The Rebel," *Joaquin Miller's Poems* (1909).

Today his image casts a sinister shadow, or its saintly light, on all our ways. There he sits, astride the conscience of Canada and will not be unseated nor let go the reins. Or that was how I began to see him. I was observing a man in the very act and parcel of becoming a Canadian legend, a sort of John Brown of the North whose soul was destined to go marching on.

John Coulter, Anglo-Irish playwright, discussing the genesis of his play *Riel*, first broadcast in 1951, *CBC Times*, 6 May 1951.

There was a brief revolt in Manitoba, where wild Indian half-breeds thought that their freedom was endangered, but order was soon restored.

Sir Winston Churchill, statesman and historian, referring to one of the two so-called Riel rebellions, Book XI "Migration of the Peoples," *History of the English-Speaking Peoples* (1956–58).

Things were good when the Conservative Party had only Louis Riel to divide it.

Attributed to Conservative leader **John G. Diefenbaker** when faced by opposition to his leadership led by Dalton Camp, notably between 1963 and 1967. About Camp, a backroom adviser, Diefenbaker was dismissive: "The papers say Dalton Camp is revolting. I cannot disagree." Also: "Better the 'spirit of Camp David' than the 'dispirit of Dalton Camp.'"

It is not Riel we admire, for in many ways he was a man impossible to admire.... It is Riel the symbol who catches our imaginations and what he symbolizes is our inner condition, our consciousness of deprivation and alienation from meaningful existence, our sense of rebellion without hope.

George Woodcock, biographer, referring to Métis leader Louis Riel, *Gabriel Dumont* (1975).

And above all, we should be reminded that Louis Riel was the first Manitoban. He belongs to all of us, warts and all.

Eric Wells, writer, *The Globe and Mail*, 12 March 1992.

No attempt at reconciliation with Aboriginal people can be complete with reference to the sad events culminating in the death of Métis leader Louis Riel. These events cannot be undone; however, we can and will continue to look for ways of affirming the contributions of Métis people in Canada and of reflecting Louis Riel's proper place in Canada's history.

"Statement of Reconciliation: Learning from the Past," signed on behalf of the Government of Canada by Jane Stewart, Minister of Indian Affairs and Northern Development, and Ralph Goodale, Federal Interlocutor for Métis and non-status Indians. It was read by Jane Stewart, Minister of Indian Affairs, Ottawa, 7 Jan. 1998, and printed in *The Globe and Mail* the following day.

Riel might be a hero and a leader to the Métis, but he has no credentials as a hero to all Canadians, and no school should teach his life that way.

J.L. Granatstein, historian, *Who Killed Canadian History?* (1998).

RIGHT & WRONG See also GOOD & EVIL, MORALITY

When logic has brought us to the brink of madness, illogic tries to push us over. We have based our reasoning on ability to deter the enemy, but pride and patriotism prevent us at critical junctures from conceding that our opponents can also deter. Right, we seem to believe, can deter wrong, but wrong cannot deter right.

John C. Polanyi, scientist and peace activist, *International Journal*, Vol. XVII, Winter 1961.

RIGHTS See also CHARTER OF RIGHTS; CONSTITUTION; GAYS AND GAY RIGHTS; RIGHTS, CIVIL; RIGHTS, HUMAN; RIGHTS & FREEDOMS; WOMEN'S RIGHTS

There is no democracy of values, there is only democracy of rights.

Louis Dudek, man-of-letters, *Epigrams* (1975).

For me to live a full human life, my neighbours must be just as free as I am. Their freedom is my freedom, their equality is my equality, their dignity is my dignity. Freedom is indivisible, human rights are universal.

R. Gordon L. Fairweather, Chairman, Human Rights Commission, quoted by Andrew Brewin, House of Commons, 8 Dec. 1978.

If one man's freedom ends where another's begins, we could also say that minority rights end when they trample on the majority.

Pierre Bourgault, separatist, *Now or Never! Manifesto for an Independent Quebec* (1991) translated by David Homel.

It's not of secondary importance, the question of whether we are going to live in a society where personal, individual rights have more importance than collective rights.

Pierre Elliott Trudeau, former Prime Minister and critic of the Charlottetown Accord, speech, Maison du Egg Roll, Montreal, 1 Oct. 1991, quoted in *The Toronto Star* two days later.

Rights arise from fights.

Richard Lubbock, essayist, "My Right to Hurt Animals," *The Idler*, July–Aug. 1992.

Journalists, academics, students, business people and politicians are all ready to man the barricades to protect the "collective rights" of Quebecers against any interference from the Canadian Constitution or the Charter of Rights and Freedoms.

Pierre Elliott Trudeau, former Prime Minister, "Trudeau Speaks Out," *Maclean's*, 28 Sept. 1992.

Canada is the only country in the world in which the majority is the moral guarantor of the minority.

Laurier LaPierre, historian and broadcaster, discussion, CTV, 2 July 1993.

Equal rights for special people now!

Gordon Bowness, columnist, "Bent Dissent," *Pride Guide* (Toronto), 23 June 1995.

RIGHTS, CIVIL See also RIGHTS

We have had more Americanization of Canada from the Charter of Rights and Freedoms than from the Free Trade Agreement.

Adapted from a remark made by Winnipeg Mayor **William Norrie**, with respect to the increase in pornography; quoted by Radha Krishnan Thampi in the *Winnipeg Free Press*, 4 Oct. 1990.

I have no hesitation in stating that, as a basic principle in a liberal democracy, individual rights come first. They are the foundation upon which must rest the recognition of collective rights. The collective rights, to me, are acceptable and necessary to the extent that they are the extension of genuine individual rights.

Claude Ryan, Quebec Minister responsible for the administration of the French Language Charter, outlining the Quebec Liberal government's agenda, Quebec City, 11 Dec. 1992, quoted by Rhéal Séguin in *The Globe and Mail* the following day.

Judges can now restrict your freedom—*even if you've done nothing unlawful*—simply because there are so-called "reasonable grounds" to believe you'll commit certain crimes in the future. I call this punishment by clairvoyance.

A. Alan Borovoy, General Counsel, Canadian Civil Liberties Association, statement, June 1997.

RIGHTS, HUMAN See also RIGHTS

There is a fundamental connection between Human Rights and Peace. We will have Peace on Earth when everyone's Rights are respected.

John Peters Humphrey, author of the first draft the International Bill of Rights which the United Nations adopted as the Universal Declaration of Human Rights, 10 Dec. 1948, quoted in the travelling exhibition titled *Citizen of the World: John Humphreys and the Universal Declaration of Human Rights,* March 1999.

If human rights and harmonious relations between cultures are forms of the beautiful, then the State is a work of art that is never finished.

F.R. Scott, poet and professor of law, written shortly before his death in Montreal, 31 Jan. 1985, *Brick: A Journal of Reviews,* No. 30, Summer 1987.

A state that is exempt from the observation of any human rights has none. A state that is exempt from its laws is exempt from its legitimacy.

George Jonas, columnist, "Human Rights Exemption?" (1986), *Politically Incorrect* (1991).

All of us are human beings first. We are not francophones, anglophones, rich, poor, weak and strong. First we are human beings with rights.... In my belief, rights are rights are rights. There is no such thing as inside rights and outside rights. No such thing as rights for the tall and rights for the short. No such thing as rights for the front and rights for the back, or rights for the East and rights for the West. Rights are rights and will always be rights. There are no partial rights.... Rights are links in a chain of fundamental values that bind all individuals in the society; they must be inalienable, just and fair.

Clifford Lincoln, Quebec Environment Minister, resigning from the Bourassa government which used the notwithstanding clause in the Constitution to introduce Bill 178, legislation that prevented the use of English signs on the exterior of commercial establishments, National Assembly, Quebec City, 20 Dec. 1988, quoted by Benôit Aubin, "Three Ministers Resign over Quebec Bill," *The Globe and Mail* the following day.

So I think it is a critical moment and this is a critical country—in a way, the country that is able to form the bridge between the European initiative and a North American or an American initiative. That's why I am here to ask for help.

Salman Rushdie, author, on day 1,393 of the fatwa directed against him by Iranian authorities, address, House of Commons' Sub-Committee on Development and Human Rights of the Standing Committee on External Affairs and International Trade, Ottawa, 8 Dec. 1992.

In the same way as the Nordic countries in Europe have a long track record in human rights, Canada is, so to speak, the Scandinavia of North America.

Salman Rushdie, author under death threat, guest of Canadian PEN, observation made in Ottawa, Dec. 1992, quoted by Carol Goar in *The Toronto Star,* 12 Dec. 1992.

We can never abolish death, illness, conflict and sorrow. Our lives are short, and we all end in the grave. But we *can* abolish poverty, ignorance, sexism, racism and the other social evils. They are our own creations. Are we even trying to do that any more?

Silver Donald Cameron, columnist, marking the 50th anniversary of the declaration of the UN's Universal Declaration of Human Rights, *The Halifax Herald,* 31 May 1998.

Our new rights reflect a different spirit. Instead of allowing and encouraging people to be good, our courts now seem most interested in indulging them when they are bad. Instead of fostering a common sense of individual responsibility and opportunity, we encourage a sense of collective claims upon the efforts of the less politicized. Everyone is equal, but "historically disadvantaged groups" are more equal.

Linc Byfield, publisher of *Report Newsmagazine* (formerly *Alberta Report, B.C. Report,* and *Western Report*), "'Narrow-mindedness' Goes National," *The Globe and Mail,* 5 Oct. 1999.

RIGHTS & FREEDOMS See also CONSTITUTION, RIGHTS

I am a Canadian, a free Canadian, free to speak without fear, free to worship God in my own way, free to stand for what I think right, free to oppose what I believe wrong, free to choose those who shall govern my country. This heritage of freedom I pledge to uphold for myself and all mankind.

Preamble to the Canadian Bill of Rights, House of Commons, 1 July 1960. The Preamble, not part of the Bill, was the work of Prime Minister **John G. Diefenbaker**. The text appears in the third volume of his memoirs.

Everyone has the following fundamental freedoms: (a) freedom of conscience and religion; (b) freedom of thought, belief, opinion and expression, including freedom of the press and other media of communication; (c) freedom of peaceful assembly; and (d) freedom of association.

Key clause from the **Canadian Charter of Rights and Freedoms**, part of the Constitution Act, 1982, proclaimed by Queen Elizabeth II, Parliament Hill, Ottawa, 17 April 1982.

RIVERS

The Canadian River rises in New Mexico, flows through Texas and Oklahoma to Arkansas, but does not come near Canada.

Robert L. Ripley, cartoonist and columnist, *Ripley's Mammoth Believe It or Not!* (1955).

"If a river could flow on the moon," I thought as I flew over the Black Canyon, "it would probably look like this."

Hugh MacLennan, novelist and essayist, "The Fraser," *Seven Rivers of Canada* (1961).

I wanted to try to *think* like a river even though a river doesn't think. Because every river on this earth, some of them against incredible obstacles, ultimately finds its way through the labyrinth to the universal sea.

Hugh MacLennan, novelist and essayist, *Seven Rivers of Canada* (1961).

Just one great river always flowing to the sea. / Just one river to the sea. / One single river flowing in eternity. / Just one river in eternity. / Two nations in the land that lies along each shore. / But just one river rolling free.

Refrain of "Song for Canada" (1965) with words by **Peter Gzowski** and music by Ian Tyson from the album *Ian and Sylvia* (1970). The song begins, "How come we can't talk to each other any more? / Why can't you see I'm changing too?"

ROCKY MOUNTAINS See also MOUNTAINS, PARKS

Behold the Shining Mountains.

Anthony Henday, traveller and trader, the first European to describe the view of the Rocky Mountains, near present-day Innisfail, Alta., Oct. 17, 1754. According to James G. MacGregor in *Behold the Shining Mountains: Being an Account of the Travels of Anthony Henday, 1754–55* (1954), the Native people of the foothills region called the Rockies "Mountains of Bright Stones."

In the sea of sterile mountains.

Edward Blake, statesman, address to constitutents, South Bruce, Ont., *The Victoria Colonist*, 2 May 1875. George M. Grant had included the phrase (shorn of the word "sterile") in *Ocean to Ocean* (1873). The phrase has also been attributed to one James Morton: "an inhospitable country, a sea of sterile mountains."

If you look for a long while from here, you are seized with a fancy that all the earth is rolling towards the west, and there is nothing beyond the Rockies; they end the world and meet the sky.

Moira O'Neill, Irish poet who ranched in 1885 with her husband near High River, Alta., "A Lady's Life on a Ranch," *Blackwood's Magazine*, Jan. 1898, quoted by T.B. Higginson in "Moira O'Neill in Alberta," *Alberta Historical Review*, Spring 1957.

The Rockies have no majesty; they do not elevate the mind to contemplation of Almighty God any more than they warm the heart of seeming sentinels to watch over the habitations of one's fellow men.

Aleister Crowley, occultist and traveller, *The Confessions of Aleister Crowley: An Autohagiography* (1970) edited by John Symonds and Kenneth Grant. Crowley crossed the country in 1906 and recalled his impressions in 1923.

The sterile mountains which form the whole eastern border of British Columbia may well prove to be the treasure-chest of Canada, though the lid has been difficult to open. Whenever it has been opened a peep of something wonderful has been obtained.

Sir Arthur Conan Doyle, author and traveller, *Our Second American Adventure* (1923).

If it is possible to make reservations in Heaven, I am going to have an upper berth somewhere in the O'Hara ranges of Paradise.

J.E.H. MacDonald, painter, letter, 4 Sept. 1928, concerning the Lake O'Hara region of the Rocky Mountains, quoted by Paul Duval in *The Tangled Garden* (1978).

I said that he fell straight to the ice where they found him, / And none but the sun and incurious clouds have lingered / Around the marks of that day on the ledge of the Finger, / That day, the last of my youth, on the last of our mountains.

Concluding lines of **Earle Birney**'s narrative poem "David" (1940), *The Collected Poems of Earle Birney* (1975).

... we could see across the rolling beige ranchland to the snowy peaks of the Rockies; they changed colour every hour of the day—sometimes they were a hard glittering white, sometimes a pale rose and even at moments a deep blue like storm clouds.

Narration from **Graham Greene**'s story "Dear Dr. Falkenheim" (1963), *Collected Stories* (1982), about an English family which settles in "Kosy Nuick," a suburb on the outskirts of Calgary.

Well, if you really want your Rocky Mountains, keep them!

René Lévesque, Quebec Premier, addressing federalist politician Yves Michaud in 1967, quoted by David Olive in *Canadian Political Babble* (1993).

nobody / belongs anywhere, // even the / Rocky Mountains // are still / moving

Lines from **George Bowering**'s poem "Nobody," *Rocky Mountain Foot* (1969).

Now there is stillness—such a stillness as I have never before heard in my life.

Oliver Sacks, neurologist and author, describing a plateau amid the Rocky Mountains, "Canada: Pause (1960)," *Antaeus*, Spring 1989.

Higher and higher—all life dying away, everything becoming a uniform gray, till mosses and lichens are the Lords of Creation once more.

Oliver Sacks, neurologist and author, describing the vegetation of the Rocky Mountains, "Canada: Pause (1960)," *Antaeus*, Spring 1989.

Jasper is really beautiful. I don't think there's any place more beautiful than the area between Edmonton and Calgary.

Kirk Douglas, actor, quoted by Sid Adilman in *The Toronto Star*, 15 Nov. 1983.

The Rockies exceeded all my brochure-fuelled expectations. Their peaks and folds and crystal waters are just bewitching—it is rather like when you glimpse someone attractive in a crowd and you just cannot keep your eyes off her.

Nigel Tisdall, English travel writer, describing a railway journey through the Rocky Mountains, "Into the Great Green Yonder," *The Daily Telegraph*, 26 Sept. 1998.

ROMAN CATHOLIC CHURCH See RELIGION

ROMANCE See also LOVE

Romantic love is for grown-ups; it is not for children. It is not for children in the literal sense, and also in the psychological sense: not for those who, regardless of age, still experience themselves as children.

Nathaniel Branden, psychologist, *The Psychology of Romantic Love* (1980).

I am somewhere in the mist. / You find me, you take me home. / What happens then? / We decide. / I go, you stay. Unsaid....

Lines from **Fraser Sutherland**'s poem "Insofar as Weather," *Whitefaces* (1986).

I did not intend to enter the story. It happened by accident, believe me. You were wearing sunglasses.

Journal entry in **Robert Kroetsch**'s *Excerpts from the Real World: A Prose Poem in Ten Parts* (1986).

Never mind Mr. Right, I don't even have time for a Mr. Wrong!

Pamela Wallin, television anchor, referring to her busy schedule, quoted by Joyce Singer in *Today's Seniors*, Aug. 1994.

Increasingly, romantic fiction is for women who move their hips when they read.

Paul Grescoe, author, *The Merchants of Venus: Inside Harlequin and the Empire of Romance* (1996).

ROYAL CANADIAN MOUNTED POLICE See also CRIME, POLICE

Maintiens le droit

The official motto of the Mounties: the North-West Mounted Police (1873–1904), Royal North-West Mounted Police (1904–1920), **Royal Canadian Mounted Police** (from 1920). The authorized English version of the French phrase is "Uphold the Right." Its use was proposed in 1873. The Force's oath of office requires recruits to attend to their duties "without fear, favour or affection"—another vivid phrase. Their uniform is the "Scarlet and Stetson." Their unofficial designation is "The Horsemen," and their unofficial motto, which dates from 1877, is "They always get their man."

A letter came to a citizen the other day with the address: Mr. ____, Winnipeg, Manitoba, Indian Territory, where the Mounted Police are.

Item from the *Manitoba Daily Free Press,* 22 Feb. 1879, quoted by Michael Dawson in *The Mountie: From Dime Novel to Disney* (1998).

In the little Crimson Manual it's written plain and clear / Those who would wear the scarlet coat can say good-bye to fear.

Couplet from **Robert Service**'s verse "Clancy of the Mounted Police" (1909), *Ballads of a Cheechako* (1909).

Oh, Rose-Marie, I love you! / I'm always dreaming of you. / No matter what I do, / I can't forget you. Lines from love ballad

"Rose-Marie," hit song of the Broadway operetta *Rose-Marie* (1924), words by **Otto Harbach** and **Oscar Hammerstein II** with music by Rudolf Friml. Jeanette MacDonald and Nelson Eddy starred in the 1936 Hollywood movie *Rose Marie* (without the hyphen). To this day a soft assignment within RCMP ranks is known as "a Rose-Marie posting."

I'm a Mountie Who Never Got His Man.

Title of the amusing song sung by **Bert Lahr** as a bumbling Mountie in the Hollywood remake *Rose Marie* (1954), with Anne Blyth and Howard Keel.

On, King! On, you huskies! / I arrest you in the name of the Crown.

Familiar words from the radio serial *Sergeant Preston of the Yukon* created by **George W. Trendle** and heard on the ABC Radio Network (1947–55). The voice of Sergeant Bill Preston was that of American actor Don Sherwood. His dog was called Yukon King.

Now in the U.S. there's the old F.B.I. / To catch out those nasty red Russians that spy. / But up here in Canada it's plain to see / We're safe in the hands of the RCMP. // The RCMP, the RCMP. / We're safe in the hands of the RCMP.

First verse of eight verses with chorus of "The RCMP" by **The Brothers-in-Law**, a quartet composed of Windsor policemen, on the satiric album *Oh! Oh! Canada* (1965), reproduced by Bob Davis in *Singin' about Us* (1976).

For the last couple of years I've been guarding the flowerbeds in front of the Parliament Buildings in Ottawa.... It's exciting work in its own way. You never hear the bee that has your name on it.

Observation made by Acting Sergeant Maynard Bullock of the RCMP in **James Powell**'s story "The Stollmeyer Sonnets," *Best Detective Stories of the Year* (1976) edited by Anthony Boucher.

Men, we don't have to take this crap from a corporal. From now on it's Sergeant Renfrew.

Richard Simmons, RCMP Commissioner, adding three stripes to Corporal Renfrew's Mountie uniform, transforming him into Sergeant Renfrew, during a performance by comic Dave Broadfoot, RCMP headquarters, Ottawa, quoted by Jim Lotz in *The Mounties: The History of the Royal Canadian Mounted Police* (1984).

I'm a lumberjack / And I'm O.K. / I sleep all night / And I work all day.

Chorus of "Lumberjack Song" from *Monty Python's Flying Circus: Just the Words, Volume One* (1989) to be sung "by the men of the Royal Canadian Mounted Police" written and conceived by **Graham Chapman, John Cleese, Terry Gilliam, Eric Idle, Terry Jones**, and **Michael Palin**.

It's the only country that uses the police force as a symbol for that country. We take that very seriously, and very humbly.

Richard Bergman, Assistant Commissioner of the RCMP, referring to the Mountie's image, quoted by Randy Turner in the *Winnipeg Free Press,* 14 Nov. 1993.

Interestingly, even our police officers (the picturesque Royal Canadian Mounted Police) don't appear dangerous—they look more like museum pieces than dangerous storm troopers.

Mayo Moran, professor of law, "Talking about Hate Speech: A Rhetorical Analysis of American and Canadian Approaches to the Regulation of Hate Speech," *Wisconsin Law Review*, Number 6, 1994.

The "Mountie" novel gives to the world British North America's own unique and most enduring image: a stalwart, red-coated, fur-hatted policeman on snowshoes, accompanied by his trusty husky, pursuing mad trappers across the trackless wastes of the Barren Lands, or, exchanging his ear-flapped winter headgear for a Boy Scout Stetson, riding alone into a camp of hostile Indians.

David Skene-Melvin, anthologist, discussing adventure novels featuring members of the Mounted Police, *Secret Tales of the Arctic Trails: Stories of Crime and Adventure in Canada's Far North* (1997).

My great-grandfather was a Royal Canadian Mounted Policeman, so it's personally very satisfying for me to play the part.

Brendan Fraser, actor, on why he took the role of the Jay Ward Mountie character "Dudley Do-Right" in the 1999 movie of the same name. Quoted by Iain Blair in the *Winnipeg Free Press*, 12 Aug. 1999.

I never joke about culture.

Characteristic remark made by RCMP Constable Benton Fraser, the straight-shooting officer stationed in Chicago, played by actor **Paul Gross** in the TV series *Due South*, as quoted by Jim McKee in "What Is a 'Canadian' Program, Anyway," *Canadian Screenwriter*, Fall 1998.

The Mounted Policeman is the second most recognized image in the world after Coca-Cola.

Philip Murray, RCMP Commissioner, embellishing somewhat the global recognition factor of the Force, NFB's documentary *The Mountie: Canada's Mightiest Myth*, CBC-TV, 22 Oct. 1998.

ROYAL COMMISSIONS

Some day there will be an investigation of the high cost of investigations.

Bob Edwards, publisher, *The Eye Opener*, 2 Dec. 1916, *The Wit and Wisdom of Bob Edwards* (1976) edited by Hugh Dempsey.

The politics of Billy King / Make honest blood to boil. / His omissions were staggering, / His commissions are royal.

Anonymous verse titled "Royal Commissions" (1950s); another such verse, said to be a newspaperman's lament, runs like this: "William Lyon Mackenzie King / Never said a god-damned thing!"

A commission headed by me... cannot be anything but interesting.

Laurier LaPierre, historian and communicator, newly appointed head of a commission on early education in Ontario, press conference, Toronto, quoted by Elaine Carey in *The Toronto Star*, 19 Dec. 1977.

ROYAL TOURS See also MONARCHY

Keep yer fork, Duke, the pie's acomin'.

Punchline of the well-known story about Prince Philip, Duke of Edinburgh, who, while dining in a rural area, was advised by an over-friendly waitress removing the main-course plates to keep his fork for future use. Intrigued with the story, Peter Gzowski conducted an on-air search on CBC Radio's *Morningside* in 1986 to determine the origin of the story. The incident did not involve Prince Philip; it might have happened to the Governor General, the Duke of Connaught, at a Board of Trade dinner in a small community in B.C.'s Peace River district, between 1911 and 1916.

The Queen, I think I told you, is wearing powder blue... and now as she moves away and juts her bow out into the sun... we can make out a great deal of her green boot topping.

Unidentified CBC Radio announcer, momentarily confusing Queen Elizabeth, wife of King George VI, with the Royal Yacht *Britannia*, which was then leaving Halifax harbour on the last day of the Royal Tour, 15 June 1939.

And now, sir, to come to your Royal Highness's more immediate father.

Joseph Clark, Edmonton Mayor, introducing Edward, Duke of Windsor, by way of referring to his ancestors, including his father, George V, at a civic banquet in Edmonton, quoted by Lotta Dempsey in *No Life for a Lady* (1976), who added:

"I'm told that the Prince loved it. After that he refused to refer to King George in any other way than as 'my more immediate father.'"

I can see Her Majesty across the room, looking rather tired as she smiles at all the dignitaries here, probably thinking how good a stiff belt of scotch would taste at this moment.

W.E.S. Briggs, broadcaster, describing Queen Elizabeth II on the Royal Tour of 1957, quoted by Max Ferguson, "Unforgettable Captain Briggs," *The Reader's Digest*, Nov. 1982.

RULES & REGULATIONS

This—the greatest rule for all life and all living—the knowing when to stop. That's the greatest of all the fine arts.

Elizabeth Arden, Ontario-born cosmetics manufacturer, interviewed by R.E. Knowles in *The Toronto Star*, 16 April 1936.

The half-educated may follow rules or dodge around rules; it is only the thoroughly educated who can take liberties with rules.

Northrop Frye, cultural critic, "Some Reflections on Life and Habit" (1988), *Myth and Metaphor: Selected Essays, 1974–1988*. Charlottesville, N.C.: University of Virginia, 1990. Edited by Robert D. Denham.

Canadians love regulation. What rice is to the Japanese, what wine is to the French, regulation is to the Canadians.

Robert Fulford, columnist, *The Globe and Mail*, 22 Dec. 1993.

RUNNING See also SPORTS

There is a certain feeling, moments before the race, when the starter says, "On your mark.... "I find it nearly erotic. It's the adrenalin, sure, but there's more. It's an unbearable mix of fear and excitement, of lightning in your heart, and you can feel it flash to the nerve-ends. It's a feeling of—ignition. It is what a champion feels.

Angella Issajenko, champion runner, *Running Risks: Angella Issajenko* (1990) as told to Martin O'Malley and Karen O'Reilly.

Sport Canada bureaucrats of course—nudge, nudge—never suspected that Ben Johnson might be using the steroids that his competitors were using. Right up to the Dubin inquiry. American world-record holders have since been caught. There has never been a U.S. inquiry. Francis points out the world indoor records taken from Ben were handed retroactively to the drug-crazy East Germans. We have not, at the moment, found a single Sport Canada executive who has been banned for life.

Allan Fotheringham, columnist, *Maclean's*, 21 Jan. 1991.

Ben Johnson made three major mistakes in his young life: He took steroids, he got caught and then he foolishly demanded an inquiry to clear his name. The Canadian Government obliged him....

Vyv Simson and **Andrew Jennings**, sports commentators, *The Lord of the Rings: Power, Money and Drugs in the Modern Olympics* (1992). This is a reference to the sprinter Ben Johnson and to the Dubin Inquiry.

It's over. But I'm forever the fastest man in the world. My 9.79 from Seoul never can be broken. That's why I'm Big Ben forever. The people know that and that's why they love me.

Ben Johnson, sprinter, after being banned from competition for life, quoted by Randy Starkman in *The Toronto Star*, 10 March 1993.

An urban sport whose principal long-term effect is to cripple middle- and upper-middle-class professionals. Enthusiasts include orthopaedic surgeons and running-shoe manufacturers.

John Ralston Saul, author, referring to jogging, *The Doubter's Companion: A Dictionary of Aggressive Common Sense* (1994).

Running. Al Howie (Great Britain) ran across Canada, from St. John's, Newfoundland, to Victoria, British Columbia, a distance of 4,533.2 miles in 72 days 10 hr. 23 min., from June 21 to September 1, 1991.

Peter Matthews, editor, *The Guinness Book of Records* (1996).

Track and field is dumb. A champion runner, who is honoured and worshipped for the rest of his life, is maybe a second faster than the guy who finished last, who goes home humiliated.

Sam Orbaum, Montreal-raised Israeli columnist, "But Seriously," *The Jerusalem Post Magazine*, 26 July 1996.

RUSSIA See SOVIET UNION

RUSSIAN PEOPLE See also SOVIET UNION

When visiting and reading about your country, for me it was always the ideal which I wanted Russia to imitate.

Alexander of Russia, The Grand Duke, "Out of My Life," *Empire Club of Canada: Addresses Delivered to the Members During the Year 1929* (1930).

I am afraid the end has come for us Romanovs.

Grand Duchess Olga Alexandrovna, the last of the Romanovs, interviewed on the eve of her death by Ian Vorres in *The Globe Magazine*, 26 Nov. 1960. The Grand Duchess Olga was the youngest sister of Nicholas II, the last Czar of Russia who was executed by the Bolsheviks at Ekaterinburg in 1917. Olga was the aunt of Anastasia. Olga immigrated to Canada in 1948 with her husband, White Army Colonel Nikolai Koulikovsky, who died in 1957. Olga died in Toronto on 24 Nov. 1960. Their untitled son, Tihon Koulikovsky, lived for many years in Mississauga, Ont. Earlier she had confessed to Vorres, 18 July 1959: "I always laugh, for if I ever start crying I will never stop."

I immediately felt at home in Canada. The vast open spaces reminded me of Russia and gave me a feeling of comfort.

Grand Duchess Olga Alexandrovna, the last of the Romanovs, who died in Toronto, quoted in *Chatelaine*, April 1960.

This planetary consciousness is growing stronger and stronger in all men, but there is a part of the human race which shares the cold and the snow, the ice and the permafrost, and life in the Far North. It is we, the people of Canada, and you, the people of the Soviet Union, who share to the largest extent this Arctic Experience.

Pierre Elliott Trudeau, Prime Minister, address in Leningrad, Russia, 27 May 1971.

I myself can witness, as a geographer, there is no other pair of countries in the world which would be so similar in terms of physical geography, climate, even geology and history of development. Your Great West equals our Great East, Siberia. Your Inuit are like our Northern People. Your voyageurs resemble our Siberian Cossacks. So, it is always fascinating to know how our neighbours are doing, under similar physical conditions.

Arkadi Tcherkassov, geographer, "Our Man in Moscow," *Grainews*, July 1992.

The prairie, with all that sky and all that horizon, does produce creative people. Look at Dostoevsky, Pushkin, Tolstoy—not much difference, I suppose, between the steppes of Russia and the steppes of Saskatchewan.

W.O. Mitchell, author, "Prairie Summer," *Imperial Oil Review*, Summer 1993.

I am for le *Québec libre!* I am for the liberty of *les québécois!*

Vladimir Zhirinovsky, Russian reactionary, interviewed in French by Radio-Canada's correspondent Paule Robitaille in Moscow during the Russian election campaign, Dec. 1993.

In that historical perspective, Quebec may be compared to Ukraine; the stagnating Acadia/Maritimes to Belarus; Ontario to the European part of the present Russia; the Canadian Prairies and the North to Siberia; and British Columbia to the Russian Far East. Thus, both countries throughout their histories had a moving frontier in a process of constant expansion (westward in Canada, eastward in Russia).

Arkadi Tcherkassov, geographer, Russian Association for Canadian Studies, "Historical, Human and Political Geography of Canada and Russia: Some Parallels," 8 July 1993, Moscow, *Canada Viewed from East and West: Second Biennial Conference* (1994). Tcherkassov went on to parallel the role of Quebec's voyageurs with those of Ukraine's Cossacks, and also with Canada as the "Unamerican America" and Russia as the "Uneuropean Europe" or "Unwestern Europe."

Well, they've never seen anything quite like it. We serve 30,000 or 40,000 or 50,000 people a day sometimes. The story I like to tell is that someone from a Russian newspaper said to someone on opening day, "Why are you lined up?" He said, "This is my way of seeing the West without going to the West."

George Cohon, President, McDonald's Restaurants of Canada Ltd., interviewed in *The Canadian Jewish News*, 4 Nov. 1993. Cohon, who oversaw the expansion of the McDonald's fast-food chain into Russia, recalled the response of Russians to the opening of the first McDonald's in Moscow, 31 Jan. 1990. By 1993 there were 14,000 McDonald's restaurants in 70 countries; three were in Moscow. The busiest of all the restaurants was the one in Pushkin Square.

Big countries have unusually big problems. Maybe Canada is the only exception to this rule.

Georgy Arbatov, President, Russian Association for Canadian Studies and Director of the Institute of the U.S.A. and Canada, welcoming address, 7 July 1993, Moscow, *Canada Viewed from East and West: Second Biennial Conference* (1994).

And Canada? What did I know about Canada? I have to be honest. I knew precisely three things: Canada had great hockey teams, it grew a lot of great wheat because the bread we ate every winter was thanks to Canadian wheat, and Canada was where Glenn Gould lived and worked. That was the extent of my knowledge of Canada.

Mikhail Baryshnikov, ballet star, recalling his knowledge of the country prior to his defection from the Kirov Ballet which was performing in Toronto in June 1974, quoted by John Fraser, "Baryshnikov's Defining Moment," *National Post*, 6 June 1999.

S

SAINT JOHN See also NEW BRUNSWICK

As Canadian cities go, Saint John is old; but when compared with European cities it's only a coastal settlement. The real Saint John is only just beginning to be built, and that's true of most Canadian cities.

Alden Nowlan, poet and essayist, "Alden Nowlan's Canada," *Maclean's*, June 1971.

I appear respectable again, riding the waves of sloth towards some climax as dramatic as the twenty-foot tidal drop at Saint John, in the Bay of Fundy. For forty-five minutes, in that New Brunswick harbour, between the ebb and flow of the tide, a ship can traverse the gorge between river and harbour. Forty-five minutes and no more. Just about the time taken by a bout of activity between spells of *accidie*.

Alan Pryce-Jones, English writer, "Viewpoint," *The Times Literary Supplement*, 27 Oct. 1972.

ST. JOHN'S See also NEWFOUNDLAND

In one respect the chief town of Newfoundland has, I believe, no rival: We may therefore call it the fishiest of modern capitals.

G.D. Warburton, Irish adventurer, *Hochelaga, or England in the New World* (1846).

St. John's, Newfoundland, has one of the toughest climates in Canada. Of all major Canadian cities, St. John's is the foggiest, snowiest, wettest, windiest and cloudiest. Furthermore, it has more days with freezing rain and wet weather than any other large city.

David Phillips, climatologist, *The Day Niagara Falls Ran Dry!: Canadian Weather Facts and Trivia* (1993).

ST. LAWRENCE RIVER See also ST. LAWRENCE SEAWAY

When Mrs. Brooke upon her Return to England from Quebec told Mr. Johnson that the Prospect up the River Saint Lawrence was the finest in the World—but Madame says he, the Prospect down the River St. Lawrence is I have a Notion the finest you ever saw.

Dr. Samuel Johnson's sarcastic reply to the novelist Frances Brooke, who spent some years with her chaplain husband at the English garrison at Quebec, noted in Dec. 1777 by Dr. Johnson's friend Mrs. Thrale, *Thraliana: The Diary of Mrs. Hester Lynch Thrale* (1942).

My dear, it's not a river: it's a part of Hell, got loose.... It's like some ghastly dream of Dante's.... God guard you—and me in this place. I don't like these foreign lands—Not wholesome. Pray for me.

Rupert Brooke, poet and traveller, on the St. Lawrence River, letter to Cathleen Nesbitt, 3 July 1913, *Quebec City, The Letters of Rupert Brooke* (1968) edited by Geoffrey Keynes.

The St. Lawrence seemed broader than the Rhine, the Elb and the Danube combined, and it had the additional advantage, unlike European rivers, that it had never been the scene of bloody wars. Bigness in our eyes was synonymous with innocence, or rather naïveté—which struck us as a very attractive feature; we had had enough of non-naïve Europe for a while.

Eric Koch, author and onetime internee, recalling the view from an internee camp outside Quebec City in 1940, *Deemed Suspect: A Wartime Blunder* (1980).

The dream of the commercial empire of the St. Lawrence runs like an obsession through the whole of Canadian history; and men followed each other through life, planning and toiling to achieve it. The river was not only a great actuality; it was the central truth of a religion. Men lived by it, as once consoled and inspired by its promises, its whispered suggestions, and its shouted commands; and it was a force in history, not merely because of its accomplishments, but because of its shining, ever-receding possibilities.

Donald Creighton, historian, *The Empire of the St. Lawrence* (1956).

Every nation has a back door and a front door, and, with Canada, the front door is the back door.

G.K. Chesterton, English writer, referring to the St. Lawrence River which empties into the Atlantic Ocean, address at a luncheon held in honour of Rudyard Kipling sponsored by the

Canadian Literary Society and recorded by the BBC, London, England, 1933; "Visiting Canada," *The Chesterton Review*, Nov. 1996.

The *Odyssey* continued to sing itself inside me up the St. Lawrence's smooth cold stretches—where the wind tastes of ice from Labrador; where the sunsets look immense and remote in their green sky, and the sparse New Brunswick fields, in tiny clusters round the pointed wooden spires, seemed smaller and more touching than anything made by man that I had ever seen.

Freya Stark, English traveller and author, *Beyond Euphrates: Autobiography, 1928–1933* (1951). She is describing a trip up the St. Lawrence on the *Athenia* in Oct. 1928. At the time she was reading Butcher and Lang's translation of the *Odyssey*.

In the past thirty years I have organized fifty-one expeditions. This is the fifty-first, and I think it should have been one of the very first ones because of the importance of this waterway. The Great Lakes system is the biggest freshwater system in the world. The St. Lawrence has been the way of penetration of the North American continent for all the Europeans. It is loaded with history.

Jacques Cousteau, sea explorer, quoted in *Maclean's*, 27 Oct. 1980.

ST. LAWRENCE SEAWAY See also ST. LAWRENCE RIVER

The St. Lawrence project stirs the imagination of men long accustomed to majestic distances and epic undertakings. The proposal for taking electric power from the river and bringing ocean shipping 2,400 miles inland, to tap the fertile heart of our continent, is economically sound and strategically important.

Harry S. Truman, U.S. President, address, joint sitting of the Senate and the House of Commons, Ottawa, 11 June 1947.

ST. PIERRE & MIQUELON See also FRANCE

Little did Champlain imagine . . . that a few more years would see the *fleur-de-lis* lowered forever from the city he founded; and France, once the mistress of the whole American continent north of Mexico, reduced to a few fishing-islands, equal to a square of fifteen miles!

W. George Beers, writer, referring to 17th-century colonist Samuel de Champlain, "The Canadian Mecca," *The Century Magazine*, May 1882.

Maybe they can land the Concorde on St. Pierre and let it roll to a stop on Miquelon.

Marie White, deputy mayor, St. John's, Nfld., learning that the tiny French islands of St. Pierre & Miquelon, located twenty miles off the south coast of Newfoundland, would be celebrating New Year's Day thirty minutes ahead of Newfoundland, quoted by Jonathan Gatehouse in the *National Post*, 27 January 1999.

SAINTS

But who was this saint so revered long ago by the Canadian *voyageur* and habitant, and whose intercession, all the world over, now seems to be supplanting that of all other saints? It might be enough to know that, in 1876, the Pope declared Ste. Anne to be patroness of the Province of Quebec, though it is not stated how this affects the claim of St. Joseph, who has long been the patron of all Canada. But who was Ste. Anne?

W. George Beers, writer, "The Canadian Mecca," *The Century Magazine*, May 1882.

What is a saint? A saint is someone who has achieved a remote human possibility. It is impossible to say what that possibility is. I think it has something to do with the energy of love.

Lines from **Leonard Cohen**'s novel *Beautiful Losers* (1966).

SALESMANSHIP

Goods Satisfactory or Money Refunded.

Famous guarantee from Eaton's Catalogue, once a byword in households across the country. The **T. Eaton Co.** was founded by Timothy Eaton in Toronto in 1869. The company's popular mail-order catalogue was issued annually from 1884 to 1976. The terms of sale were established early on, but the wording that appears above was not used in print in the catalogue until 1913. C.L. Burton of The Robert Simpson Co. Ltd., Eaton's principal competitor, exceeded Eaton's promise in 1928 by ensuring not just goods but also a psychological state: "Satisfaction Guaranteed."

People always laugh at the fool things you try to do until they discover you are making money out of them.

Bob Edwards, publisher, *The Eye Opener*, 31 May

1919, *The Best of Bob Edwards* (1975) edited by Hugh Dempsey.

The secret of a successful sales pitch is a smash opening, a crash finish—and keep them close together.

Tom Kelley, proprietor of Doc Kelley's Medicine Show, quoted by Thomas P. Kelley, Jr., in *The Fabulous Kelley: Canada's King of the Medicine Men* (1974).

Economies are more important than inventories.

Pat Burns, meat packer, quoted by Grant MacEwan in *Pat Burns: Cattle King* (1979).

Give me $50,000 and that's ten deals with a $5,000 deposit each.

Attributed to entrepreneur and sportsman **Nelson Skalbania** in *The Toronto Star*, 1 Nov. 1981.

It's like you never get a second chance to create a first impression.

William Vander Zalm, B.C. Premier, remark made in 1986, quoted by Stephen Osborne and Mary Schendlinger in *Quotations from Chairman Zalm* (1988).

Writer: I want to include you in an article about the five best salesmen of the world.

Cooke: Sir, I am not one of five anything.

Attributed to financier **Jack Kent Cooke** and based on a reply noted by Adrian Havill in *The Last Mogul* (1992).

We say our goal is one hundred percent customer satisfaction. Anyone can say that, but we do a better job delivering on it.

George Cohon, President, McDonald's Restaurants of Canada Ltd., interviewed in *The Canadian Jewish News*, 4 Nov. 1993.

Buy your weaknesses and sell your strengths.

Barbara Mowat, publisher, *Home Business Report*, quoted in an advertisement sponsored by IBM, *Maclean's*, 16 June 1997.

It's almost a religion for Canadians to wait in line. Canadian salespeople and ticket-takers often look as though they're doing the customer a favour by engaging in grubby commerce, while Canadian customers just quietly, patiently, eternally wait.

James Blanchard, former U.S. Ambassador to Canada, *Behind the Embassy Door: Canada, Clinton and Quebec* (1998).

People buy your ideas because they like you.

Peter Urs Bender, motivational speaker, characteristic remark, 11 May 2000.

SANITY & INSANITY

Their ordinary vent for them is a certaine high hill in the North of America, whose people I can easily beleeve to be wholly descended of them, partly in regard to their colour, partly also in regard to the continuall use of Tobacco which the Lunars enjoy exceeding much.

Passage from **Francis Godwin**'s fantasy *Man in the Moone: Or a Discourse of a Voyage Thither by Domingo Gonsales* (1638). It describes how the inhabitants of the Moon exile the insane and morally deficient among them to a "certaine high hill" in the Arctic.

SASKATCHEWAN See also PRAIRIE PROVINCES, REGINA, WESTERN PROVINCES

Her Valley of the Saskatchewan alone, it has been scientifically computed, will support eight hundred millions.

W.D. Lighthall, editor, referring to valley of the Saskatchewan River and a turn-of-the-century prophecy that failed to come true, *Songs of the Great Dominion* (1889).

Let us take possession of Canada! Let our cry be "Canada for the British!"

Attributed to colonist **Isaac Barr** who led two thousand settlers to the Barr Colony, now Lloyminster, Sask., in 1903.

By the banks of the Seine, / With girls so beautiful, / It gives one pain to remain / Quite dutiful. / And yet I've sworn / By the stars above, / Throughout my life to reserve my love / For a girl by the Saskatchewan, / For a girl by the Saskatchewan.... / But hear me say, / It's a very long, long way / From the banks of the Seine, for a girl to go and stay / By the banks of the Saskatchewan.

Verse and chorus of the love duet of the popular song "By the Saskatchewan," written by **C.M.S. McLellan** (lyrics) and Ivan Caryll (music) for the Broadway musical comedy *The Pink Lady* (1911).

Saskatchewan, the land of snow, / Where winds are always on the blow, / Where people sit with frozen toes, / And why we stay here no one knows. // Saskatchewan, Saskatchewan, / There's no place like Saskatchewan. / We sit and gaze across the plain, / And wonder why it never rains, / And Gabriel blows his trumpet sound; / He says: "The rain, she's gone around."

First verse and chorus of **William W. Smith**'s popular song "Saskatchewan" (sung to the tune of the hymn "Beulah Land").

Yes, I believe that hope is still the dominant sentiment out there, after all the tragedy. And where hope is, there you have power. And I believe that southern Saskatchewan's best days are before her yet.

Nellie L. McClung, pioneer writer, referring to the prairie drought and Depression, quoted by R.E. Knowles in *The Toronto Star*, 18 Nov. 1937.

I gazed at the immenseness of the Saskatchewan plain. "Where does it end? This is the wrong planet."

J.G. Ballard, author, recalling the sight of the prairies north of Moose Jaw, Sask., in the 1950s, *The Kindness of Women* (1991).

Open sarsaparilla?... Open Saskatchewan?

Words of an Arab guard struggling to recall the magic words "Open Sesame!" in the Bugs Bunny–Daffy Duck cartoon *Ali Baba Bunny* (1957).

I'm the only political leader in Canada with a Canadian Wheat Board quota book in his pocket.

Grant Devine, Premier of Saskatchewan, remark made 26 April 1982, quoted in *The Globe and Mail* the following day.

As soon as he got back to the gallery, he had Walter look up Saskatchewan in an atlas. Its austere oblong shape turned his heart to ice. Walter said that it was one of the right-angled territories that so frequently contain oil. Oil seemed to Speck to improve the oblong. He saw a Chirico chessboard sliding off toward a horizon where the lights of derricks twinkled and blinked.

Passage describing a fictitious Parisian art dealer named Speck and his assistant Walter in **Mavis Gallant**'s story "Speck's Idea," *Overheard in a Balloon: Stories of Paris* (1985).

In Saskatchewan, politics is a serious matter. You might find someone there who doesn't care about sex or religion, but you'll never find someone neutral about politics. We have more card-carrying ideologues of all political stripes than mosquitoes in a marsh.

Pat Lorjé, Saskatchewan M.L.A., speech, Federal NDP Renewal Conference, Ottawa, 27 Aug. 1994, *The Globe and Mail*, 20 Sept. 1994.

Scratch a Saskatchewan writer and you find a farm.

Anne Szumagalski, poet, quoted by Sharon Butala in "In My Nature," *Quill & Quire*, Aug. 1995.

In Saskatchewan, the weather fills up the interstices of our lives—blizzards, tornadoes, stupendous heat or bitter cold, drought, fire, flood—and distance, measured as the time it takes to get from one place to another, rarely short, and the sky, so vast some settlers fresh from constricted Europe were driven insane.

Sharon Butala, author, "In My Nature," *Quill & Quire*, Aug. 1995.

Where to go, though? We're told by the UN that Canada is the best country in the world to live in. A Canadian economist, using the UN's criteria, has decided that Saskatchewan is the best province. So now the search is on for the best community in Saskatchewan. One reporter put her money on Climax just because of the name.

Teresa Harley, correspondent, "Cold Enough for You?" *The Guardian Weekly*, 24 Dec. 1995.

Vagina, Saskatchewan

Alan Thicke, comic, *How Men Have Babies: The Pregnant Father's Survival Guide* (1999). Thicke explains: "A play on words that will make Canadians laugh out loud. For the rest of you, just read on."

SASQUATCH

The Wendigo and the Sasquatch have powerful, ghostly qualities—but what we lack is a sighting of these apparitions from inside the particular kind of fear experienced by the people who bred them.

Alberto Manguel, anthologist, referring to fictional descriptions of these traditional Native creatures, *The Oxford Book of Canadian Ghost Stories* (1990).

I know I won't be able to convince the world by argument, because it doesn't want to be convinced. I just have to keep on going—and I will do—until one of these creatures is found, dead or alive.

René Dahinden, naturalist, quoted by Don Hunter in *Sasquatch / Bigfoot: The Search for North America's Incredible Creature* (rev. ed., 1993).

Call Bigfoot. Call him Sasquatch, call him Sir, call him anything you like. With our new satellite mobile phone service it's possible.

Advertising supplement for **Bell Mobility** in *The Globe and Mail*, 25 Jan. 1996.

SAUDI ARABIA

If Canadian unity has anything to learn from this group here, it is that it is alive and well and living in Saudi Arabia.

Pierre Elliott Trudeau, Prime Minister, impromptu response to a spontaneous greeting by Canadian workers, anglophone and francophone, living in the foreign compound, Riyadh, Saudi Arabia, 16 Nov. 1980, quoted by Norman Webster in *The Globe and Mail* the following day.

SCENERY

My idea is that the Canadian Chambers of Commerce and the Government ought to make more or less of an inducement to the motion picture producers to use Canadian scenery. If they would make it agreeable to us, we could bring in a great deal of money. The motion picture industry put Southern California on the map, and it would build up locations in Canada the same way.

Allan Dwan, Canadian-born Hollywood director, *Maclean's*, 1 Feb. 1920, reprinted as "Canada Has a 'Movie' Future," *Maclean's*, 1 Jan. 1996.

SCEPTICISM

All sceptics are credulous.

Robin Skelton, poet and aphorist, *A Devious Dictionary* (1991).

SCHOLARSHIP See also HUMANITIES

The document is the model of all real teaching, because it is infinitely patient: It repeats the same words however often one consults it.

Northrop Frye, cultural critic, "Communications," *The Listener*, 9 July 1970.

In scholarship as in life, knowing the right question is always the hardest problem.

Paul Roazen, historian, *Freud and His Followers* (1975).

When the end stage of all academic inquiry ceases to be communication, scholarship will exit only for its own sake, and scholars themselves will be short-changed, along with the community that supplies the funds that make their work possible.

Marsh Jeanneret, former publisher, University of Toronto Press, *God and Mammon: Universities as Publishers* (1989).

The complicated pocket watch of literature has been replaced by a rude drawing of a watch with no moving parts.

William Hoffer, antiquarian bookseller, "Cheap Sons of Bitches; Memoirs of the Book Trade," *Carry on Bumping* (1989) edited by John Metcalf.

For those of us who like to believe that a close reading of the masters of the language can help teach clarity and grace, a strong dose of literary criticism is a depressing refutation.

Beverley Slopen, columnist, referring to the jargon-ridden prose of academic critics of the works of literary stylists, "Book World," *The Toronto Star*, 23 July 1994.

Pedantry is the last refuge of the truly ignorant.

Paul William Roberts, author and traveller, *In Search of the Birth of Jesus: The Real Journey of the Magi* (1995).

The jewel in the crown of the university is the scholarly culture. From time to time that jewel must be examined, held up to harsh lights and polished so that the encrustrations of age are removed.

Peter C. Emberley, scholar, *Zero Tolerance: Hot Button Politics in Canada's University* (1996).

SCHOOLS See also COLLEGES & UNIVERSITIES, EDUCATION

We should try to get our money's worth out of the schools. It's ridiculous having them standing idle twelve months of the year.

Richard Needham, newspaper columnist, *The Wit and Wisdom of Richard Needham* (1977).

We must rid our schools of dangerous, mind-altering drugs, like L.S.D., T.L.C., and P.R.

Maurus E. Mallon, aphorist, Aug. 1992.

I have said many times, and I'm saying it again to you, that a boy who can go through a first-rate boarding-school and emerge in one piece is ready for most of what the world is likely to bring him.

Thoughts of the narrator of **Robertson Davies**' novel *The Cunning Man* (1994).

SCIENCE & SCIENTISTS See also EDUCATION, MEDICINE, RESEARCH & DEVELOPMENT, TECHNOLOGY

There ought to be no doubt whatever that the popular forms of geology and paleontology should be included as sciences of satanic origin.

George McCready Price, Maritime-born creationist, U.S. Baptist college president, and a founder of the Creation Science movement, *The Phantom of Organic Evolution* (1924).

The physiologist believes as someone has said that the advance of our science is limited not by nature's unwillingness to reveal but by man's inability to comprehend.

Charles H. Best, medical researcher, "Recent Advances in Our Knowledge of the Bodily Functions," 10 Feb. 1930, *Addresses Delivered before the Canadian Club of Toronto: Season of 1929–30* (1930).

The science of today is the research of yesterday, and the research of today is the science of tomorrow.

Sir Frederick Banting, scientist, "Science and the Soviet Union" (1935), quoted by Lloyd Stevenson in *Sir Frederick Banting* (1945).

Are there many scientists in Canada? I have never been there, except a little stay in Halifax.

Albert Einstein, mathematician, interviewed at his home in Princeton, N.J., by R.E. Knowles, *The Toronto Star*, 27 Jan. 1934. When pressed, Einstein admitted knowing about Sir Frederick Banting.

Let us be our own authority. We know far more than any of our ancestors. Scientists of this generation have no obligation to admit superiority of knowledge or of wisdom in any body of traditional belief or authority.

G. Brock Chisholm, psychiatrist, White Memorial Lecture, Washington, D.C., Oct. 1945, published as *The Psychiatry of Enduring Peace and Social Progress* (1945).

The apple that debased Adam exalted Newton.

Line from **Lister Sinclair**'s radio drama *Return to Colonus* broadcast on CBC Radio's *Stage 45*, 12 Nov. 1944.

If an electron or a photon is too small to be perceived, a continent is too large.

Donald Hebb, psychologist, "A World of Thought," *Essay on Mind* (1980).

It is the method of scientific research that has made Western civilization a world civilization. It is at the heart and core of our lives, and as such at the heart and core of our education.

George P. Grant, philosopher, "The Battle Between Teaching and Research," *The Globe and Mail*, 28 April 1980.

Humanists may not know the Second Law of Thermodyanmics, but there are also scientists who think the Enlightenment began with Edison.

Louis Dudek, man-of-letters, "The Mermaid Inn," *The Globe and Mail*, 23 May 1981.

Science is the most powerful force shaping our lives today. If we as a people are to deal with that in any kind of enlightened wise way, we had better become more conversant with science—each and every one of us.

David Suzuki, scientist and spokesperson, address, Empire Club of Canada, Toronto, 6 Dec. 1984.

For Science organizes knowledge through concepts that reinforce existing disciplines, whereas Art organizes existing ignorance through percepts that discover new disciplines.

Barrington Nevitt, communications consultant, *ABC of Prophecy: Understanding the Environment* (1985).

So long as society is committed to the proposition that differences between nations can be solved by the extermination of populations, any branch of science can be put to use in killing, and will be.

John C. Polanyi, scientist, "No Genuine Ivory Tower Is Ever Irrelevant," *The Vancouver Sun*, 9 Sept. 1989.

Science, as it advances more deeply into the unknown, resembles more and more the magic from which it emerged.

Louis Dudek, poet and aphorist, "Epigrams," *Small Perfect Things* (1991).

You can do science anywhere. Obviously, it's a tremendous challenge to do it in space.

Roberta Bondar, astronaut aboard the space shuttle *Discovery*, 22–30 Jan. 1992, quoted in *Maclean's*, 24 Feb. 1992.

Everyone says that you must have literacy and numeracy, and what I am saying equally is that you must have sciencey.

William Fyfe, geologist, quoted by Stephen Strauss in *The Globe and Mail*, 10 Jan. 1992.

The Renaissance represented a modest transformation compared with that which science and technology have brought about in recent decades. We scientists, being in the centre of the cultural stream that is presently reshaping the global landscape, have an obligation to offer our services, not as messiahs but as interpreters between the language of science and that of society.

John C. Polanyi, scientist, "The Scientist as Citizen: Freedom and Responsibility in Science," *Queen's Quarterly*, Spring 1992.

The realities that matter are in fact very simple; there's no discovery of note that in retrospect doesn't seem rather obvious. Looking at it from the other end, what lies ahead is totally obscure.

John C. Polanyi, chemist, interviewed by Michael Smith in *The Toronto Star*, 8 Aug. 1993.

The scientist, calculator in hand, is sketching a picture of the world much as the painter does, pencil in hand.

John C. Polanyi, chemist, address at the inauguration of the John C. Polanyi Chair in Chemistry, Toronto, 3 Nov. 1994, published in *The Globe and Mail* the following day.

Scientists make much of their vaunted skepticism, but woe betide anyone who is skeptical of *them*.

Maurus E. Mallon, aphorist, *Compendulum* (1995).

Marvels are meanings out of control. You can expel a topic from science by making it a marvel. Conversely, if you are forced to look a marvel in the face, the thing to do is to bring it into the laboratory. There it will languish and die until the laboratory itself is cast out of science. Then it will become a marvel again, but it has been somehow rendered less potent because it has been declined a laboratory niche.

Ian Hacking, philosopher, *Rewriting the Soul* (1995).

Everyone knows of Alexander the Great, Julius Caesar, Napoleon, Wellington, Patton and Montgomery... but who knows about the water engineers and scientists whose work saved more lives than the generals sacrificed? Who knows about Dr. Albert Edward Berry, a legendary Ontario engineer and scientist whose work in providing drinking water and wastewater projects almost certainly saved thousands of lives?

Tom Davey, editor and publisher, "Canada's Water Quality Record," *Environmental Science & Engineering*, March 1995.

It seems to me that many people here believe science is for sale.

Nancy Olivieri, medical researcher, University of Toronto, referring to the controversy surrounding the suppression of negative research results by a sponsoring pharmaceutical company, quoted by Krista Foss and Nicola Luksic, "Lobbying for Donor Drug Firms," *The Globe and Mail*, 16 Sept. 1999.

SCIENCE FICTION See also LITERATURE

Canadians may appreciate the modern American science-fiction story but it is not exactly that which speaks for the Canadian. The situations are different. Canada, as I have said, has no past, it has only a future.

Donald A. Wollheim, U.S. editor, "Whither Canadian Fantasy?" *Uncanny Tales*, Dec. 1942.

"Realistic" fiction is about things that have happened. "Fantasy" is about things (we are fairly sure) don't happen. "Science fiction" is about things that could happen.

Judith Merril, author, Prologue, *Survival Ship and Other Stories* (1973).

In this chapter, I will argue for an understanding of SF as the *literature of cognitive estrangement.*

Darko Suvin, academic, *Metamorphosis of Science Fiction: On the Poetics and History of a Literary Genre* (1979).

American SF is about problem-solving; Canadian SF spends a good chunk of the novel trying to find the problem. Even then the problem may not be susceptible to resolution.

Lorna Toolis, librarian, Merril Collection of Science Fiction, Speculation, and Fantasy, quoted by Shlomo Schwartzberg in *Now*, 26 March 1992.

Since then he had spent most of his time under hypnosis, being pumped full of the most various kinds of information and living a monastic life in an obscure corner of Canada. (At least, he thought it was Canada, but it might equally well have been Greenland or Siberia.) Now he was here on the Moon, a minor pawn in a game of interplanetary chess.

Thoughts of the agent Sadler in **Arthur C. Clarke**'s future-set novel *Earthlight* (1993).

Canadian science fiction . . . can therefore be defined as a genre which translates the fable of survival so central to the Canadian psyche into a fable of lonely transcendence.

John Clute, critic, "Fables of Transcendence: The Challenge of Canadian Science Fiction," *Out of This World: Canadian Science Fiction & Fantasy Literature* (1995) compiled by Andrea Paradis.

SCOTTISH PEOPLE See also BRITISH EMPIRE & COMMONWEALTH, UNITED KINGDOM

I think the Highlander's life is the best. I mean the clan spirit, their mysticism; you know what I mean.

W.L. Mackenzie King, Prime Minister, interviewed by R.E. Knowles in *The Toronto Star*, 24 Nov. 1928.

I have been told—I need hardly say by a fellow countryman—that you occupy in the States very much the position that a Scotsman does in England.

John Buchan, Governor General Lord Tweedsmuir, address, "Medicine" (1936), *Canadian Occasions: Addresses* (1940).

Edinburgh's idea of stop-press news is a picture of some mouldy old ruin with a description of what it was like two centuries ago!

Roy Thomson, press lord, quoted by Russell Braddon in *Roy Thomson of Fleet Street* (1965). Thomson's company acquired *The Scotsman* newspaper in 1953 and the broadcast licence for Scottish Television Limited in 1957.

SEA

The wholesome Sea is at her gates, / Her gates both East and West. . . .

Lines from **J.A. Ritchie**'s verse "There Is a Land" (1920) inscribed in stone over the main entrance, Centre Block, Parliament Hill, Ottawa.

Again I say, if I had it all to do over again, I should be a sailor just the same. There is nothing so satisfying as the sea.

Robert A. (Bob) Bartlett, sea captain, *The Log of Bob Bartlett: The Truth Story of Forty Years of Seafaring and Exploration* (1928).

SEAL HUNT See also ANIMALS RIGHTS

Nobody could fail to be moved at the thought of such beautiful, innocent creatures being killed and skinned. If we could stir up a controversy about baby harp seals, we knew we could hope to influence public opinion in favour of our actions on behalf of all sea mammals. The more cries of outrage we provoked from pro-sealers, the more we knew we were on the right track.

Paul Watson, ecologist, planning to halt the hunt for the harp seal in Newfoundland, Nov. 1975, *Sea Shepherd: My Fight for Whales and Seals* (1982) as told to Warren Rogers.

At the present rate of killings, the last of the seals will be finished by 1985.

Brigitte Bardot, French movie star, statement made in Paris prior to leaving for Blanc Sablon, Quebec-Labrador border, as part of the protest group representing the International Fund for Animal Welfare in 1977, quoted by Willi Frischauer in *Bardot: An Intimate Biography* (1978).

Until her arrival, the seal hunt story was all about blood and death. But now it was blood and death and sex. No more potent combination could be put together.

Bob Hunter, social activist, referring to the arrival at Blanc Sablon of social activist Brigitte Bardot, *Warriors of the Rainbow* (1979).

SEASONS See also FALL, SPRING, SUMMER, WEATHER, WINTER

Winter for reading and study; summer for loafing and dreaming and getting near to nature; spring and autumn for joyous and active production.

Archibald Lampman, poet, "At The Mermaid Inn" (1892), *Archibald Lampman: Selected Prose* (1975) edited by Barrie Davies.

Canadians love Canada, but not for fifty-two weeks of the year.

Jean Chrétien, future Prime Minister, quoted by Richard Gwyn in *The 49th Paradox* (1985).

It is a curious characteristic of Canadians that they all own, or want to own cottages, usually referred to as "summer" cottages, overlooking the fact that the most beautiful times of the year in the Canadian countryside are autumn and winter, and even spring if you leave out the weeks of break-up.

Charles Lynch, newspaperman, *A Funny Way to Run a Country: Further Memoirs of a Political Voyeur* (1986).

For nine months of the year, Canadians are God's frozen people.

Charlie McKenzie, concierge, Rhinoceros Party, writing in *The Globe and Mail*, 24 Sept. 1992.

You can really tell winter from summer here. In winter, icicles dangle from your nose; in summer, you can bake potatoes on your car's upholstery.

Rick Green, comedian and host of TVO's *Prisoners of Gravity*, "My Canada Includes...," *Maclean's*, 3 Jan. 1994.

SECESSION See also QUEBEC, SEPARATISM, SOVEREIGNTY

The idea of seceding from one of the wealthiest and freest democracies in the world makes about as much sense as it would for you to agree to your genial dentist's proposal that he pull all your teeth out so you won't have to worry about cavities.

David Cameron, political scientist, "Why Thomas Jefferson Would Have Wept," *The Toronto Star*, 21 Jan. 1995.

The likelihood, to be arbitrary, is about two to one that the secession of Quebec will not occur.

Conrad Black, capitalist, "Après-Referendum Scenarios," *The Globe and Mail*, 21 Feb. 1995.

A clear majority vote in Quebec on a clear question in favour of secession would confer democratic legitimacy on the secession initiative which all of the other participants in Confederation would have to recognize.

*

Quebec could not, despite a clear referendum result, purport to invoke a right of self-determination to dictate the terms of a proposed secession to the other parties to the federation.

Excerpts from the summary of the findings of the Supreme Court of Canada on the constitutionality of a unilateral declaration of one province's secession, 20 Aug. 1998, as reproduced in *The Globe and Mail* the following day.

The federalist side wins, but the sovereigntists don't lose.

Jean-Marc Léger, Quebec pollster, commenting on the findings of the Supreme Court of Canada on the legality of unilateral separatism, quoted by Edward Greenspon in *The Globe and Mail*, 21 Aug. 1998.

We have shown that we are the only country in the world which can allow ourselves, calmly, to discuss the problem of secession democratically, which could result in the destruction of Canada. No country in the world has undergone this exercise.

Guy Bertrand, Quebec City lawyer who challenged the validity of the Quebec referendum in 1995, following the findings of the Supreme Court of Canada on the legality of unilateral separatism, quoted by Graham Fraser in *The Globe and Mail*, 21 Aug. 1998.

SECURITY & INTELLIGENCE See also INTELLIGENCE

It is increasingly recognized that real security is not military strength, but the ability of our society to satisfy human needs on a sustainable basis. Those needs include the prevention of war. But they also include adequate food, health care, shelter, a healthy environment, and respect for human rights.

Project Ploughshares for the Citizens' Inquiry into Peace and Security, *What Makes Canada Secure: Background Document for the Citizens' Inquiry into Peace and Security in Canada* (1991).

CSIS has files on nearly 50,000 Canadians and many thousands of organizations. The vast majority of these people and groups are engaged in lawful political dissent. This would be the equivalent of the FBI maintaining active files on one in every 50 Americans.

Trent Sands, U.S. researcher, referring to the Canadian Security and Intelligence Service, *Reborn in Canada: Personal Privacy through a New Identity* (2nd ed., 1991).

Wonders never CSIS.

Pun created by **K.C. Angus**, Kemptville, Ont., quoted by Warren Clements in *The Globe and Mail*, 21 Nov. 1992.

When a prime minister is in the House of Commons talking to the people of Canada, it is as good as having a Bible here. I repeat in front of the nation and in front of God, if you want, because my name is Chrétien ... that I never discussed security with anybody in the RCMP.

Jean Chrétien, Prime Minister, concerning the suggestion that the Prime Minister's Office instructed the RCMP to use force to deal with student protesters at the University of British Columbia, the so-called Peppergate inquiry, House of Commons, 26 Oct. 1999.

SELF-ESTEEM

Occasionally a man is clever enough to know how important he isn't.

Bob Edwards, publisher, *The Eye Opener*, 20 April 1918, *The Wit and Wisdom of Bob Edwards* (1976) edited by Hugh Dempsey.

It takes a rare, dispassionate intelligence to see the self from outside, a rare, compassionate intelligence to see others from inside.

Jane Rule, author, "Notes on Autobiography," *A Hot-Eyed Moderate* (1986).

Genuine self-esteem is what we feel about ourselves when everything is not all right.

Nathaniel Branden, psychologist, *The Six Pillars of Self-Esteem* (1994).

SENATE See also GOVERNMENT, PARLIAMENT, POLITICS

In the Upper House, the controlling and regulating, but not initiating branch, we have the sober second thought in legislation.

Sir John A. Macdonald, parliamentarian, 6 April 1865, characterizing the role of the Upper House of Parliament, quoted by Sir Joseph Pope in *Confederation* (1895). Elsewhere, Pope quotes Macdonald as saying, less elegantly, "The Senate is the saucer into which we pour legislation to cool."

The most vital function the Senate can perform is to stand between the people—the taxpayers—and the encroachments of the all-powerful bureaucracy.

Grattan O'Leary, Senator, *Recollections of People, Press and Politics* (1977).

We don't need a Triple E Senate, we've already got one. It's Entrenched, it's Elitist, and it's Expensive. This is no time to reform the Senate, but to abolish it. That would show the way to establishing Triple A government. Govrnment that's Affordable, Accessible, and Accountable.

Gordon Campbell, Vancouver Mayor, quoted by Peter C. Newman in "Business Watch," *Maclean's*, 24 Aug. 1992. The notion that the Senate should be Triple E (Elected, Equal, and Effective), popularized by Calgary-area grain farmer Bert Brown in the early 1980s, was adopted by the Reform Party.

This country has done marvellously for 125 years without a functioning Senate.

Joe Ghiz, P.E.I. Premier, suggesting the best way to reform the Senate might be to abolish it, quoted by Canadian Press, Dec. 1992.

What keeps Senators going is protocol, alcohol, and geritol.

Old saw attributed to politician **Ernest Manning** by Allan Fotheringham in *Maclean's*, 22 Dec. 1997.

SEPARATISM See also PARTI QUÉBÉCOIS; QUEBEC; PARTITION; REFERENDA; SECESSION; SOVEREIGNTY; SOVEREIGNTY-ASSOCIATION

Quebec is more and more becoming racially

conscious—largely due, I think, to the system of higher education there.

C.G. (Chubby) Power, Cabinet minister, interviewed by R.E. Knowles in *The Toronto Star*, 3 March 1937. Power expressed the belief that "a Liberalism of a new and better kind" would prevail, especially against "a student section, who are known as 'separationists.'"

Look, they can't even fire me in my own language.

Marcel Chaput, scientist and separatist, press conference, waving a letter of dismissal (written in English) from the Defence Research Board for taking unofficial leave to deliver a speech in favour of Quebec's independence at a conference on "The Canadian Experiment—Success or Failure," vowing never to speak English again, Ottawa, 4 Dec. 1961.

All good Quebeckers are separatists at least one hour a day. The rest of the time, they accept their Canadianness with a shrug.

Attributed to bilingualism and biculturalism commissioner **André Laurendeau** in the 1960s by Daniel Poliquin in *The Toronto Star*, 27 Dec. 1990.

What does Quebec want? More!

Attributed to Quebec Liberal Cabinet Minister **René Lévesque** in the early 1960s. As founding leader of the Parti Québécois, Lévesque would answer more directly: "Out!" The rhetorical "What does Quebec want?" was heard across English Canada in the late 1950s and early 1960s, according to a 1970 NFB documentary, quoted by Gary Evans in *In the National Interest: A Chronicle of the National Film Board of Canada from 1949 to 1989* (1991).

As long as one goddamn French Canadian remains on the soil of Quebec, there isn't a chance of integrating us into the hybrid, bicultural monstrosity that you dream about.

René Lévesque, separatist leader, press conference, resolving to form the Parti Québécois in 1968, according to Dan Turner in *The Canadian*, 15 Jan. 1977.

The more I travel, the more separatism seems a small problem. Famine and wars, these are the things that change the world. Not separatism in Quebec.

Monique Leyrac, chansonnière, quoted by Penny Williams in *Maclean's*, April 1967.

It is the destiny of man to unite rather than divide, and as a Canadian I have little sympathy with separatism, which seems to me a mean and squalid philosophy. But I can hardly ignore the fact that separatism is the strongest political force yet thrown up by the age of television.

Northrop Frye, cultural critic, "Communications," *The Listener*, 9 July 1970.

The costs of Quebec remaining within Confederation may be as high as those of separating. We shall all pay heavily, whatever the outcome.

Abraham Rotstein, political economist, *Postcript to Power Corrupted: The October Crisis and the Repression of Quebec* (1971) edited by Abraham Rotstein.

The Quebec writer has invented a country. It is now up to the country to tell us if the writing is a lie or the hall that leads to History.

Jacques Godbout, author and filmmaker, "Notre Libération" (1972), *Le réformiste: textes tranquilles* (1975).

It could have a highly "distinctive flag" too: two jackasses eating the leaves off one maple tree.

Eugene Forsey, historian, commenting on a "national" flag for Quebec, *Freedom and Order* (1974).

I will fight separatism to the end of my career. We would lose 200,000 people, more. Today we have to go on our knees to Wall Street because we need the money. Separate, we would be flat on our face to Wall Street.

Robert Bourassa, Quebec Premier, quoted by Richard Gwyn in *The Toronto Star*, 29 April 1975.

Like an adolescent, it wants to be independent. But, my God, it also wants to be paid an allowance by its father.

Pierre Elliott Trudeau, Prime Minister, interview in *Le Monde*, 13 May 1977, translated and published by John Honderich in *The Toronto Star*, 13 May 1977.

Something can be said for kissing Quebec goodbye. I've always said one of the greatest advances in the 20th century was the peaceful separation of Norway from Sweden in 1905.

Kenneth Boulding, British-born American economist, address, Conference on Social and Economic Change in Canada, Couchiching Conference, 2 Aug. 1977, quoted by Daniel Stoffman in *The Globe and Mail* the following day.

They set tables in New York to listen to Lévesque who claimed he was George Washington. Then Trudeau went to the States and claimed he was Abraham Lincoln. The Americans were confused.

Lines from the narration of the NFB-CBC documentary about René Lévesque and Pierre Elliott Trudeau, *The Champions* (1978) written and directed by **Donald Brittain**.

The same Canadians who can argue eloquently that justice and good sense, both, are on the side of Estonia, Latvia, Lithuania, Basque, Croatian, Walloon, Kurdish or Palestinian separatists can maintain that Quebec separatists must be out of their minds to want something unnecessary and impractical.

Jane Jacobs, urban commentator, *The Question of Separatism: Quebec and the Struggle over Sovereignty* (1980).

If the arm wants to cut itself off, the head should decide whether it will.

Pierre Elliott Trudeau, Prime Minister, opposing the Quebec referendum of 1980, quoted by Thelma McCormack in "The Problem with Polls," *The Canadian Forum*, July–Aug. 1992.

In every part of Canada there are strong separatist feelings, and separatism can lead only to increased American penetration, especially economic and ideological. This is not to say that such penetration must be sinister, merely that it is the opposite of what separatism aims at.

Northrop Frye, cultural critic, "Levels of Cultural Identity" (1989), *The Eternal Act of Creation: Essays, 1979–1990* (1993) edited by Robert D. Denham.

Let's get the scorpions out of the bottle. They may even learn to live side by side in harmony.

Jacques Parizeau, leader of the Parti Québécois, employing Sir Winston Churchill's image, addressing a joint meeting of the Empire Club and the Canadian Club, Toronto, 11 Dec. 1990, quoted by Konrad Yakabuski in *The Toronto Star* the following day.

"This Land is My Land" is one thing, "This is my land" is another.

Louis Dudek, poet and aphorist, "The Separatists," *Small Perfect Things* (1991).

Quebec is part of Canada as much as a cat in the mouth of a crocodile is part of the crocodile.

Yves Beauchemin, playwright, quoted by David Olive in "Notre Pays," *The Globe and Mail's Report on Business Magazine*, Aug. 1991.

If Canada is unacceptable, it's unacceptable completely. You can't be a part-time Canadian.

Brian Mulroney, Prime Minister, press conference, Baie-Comeau, Que., 14 Nov. 1991, quoted by Alan Freeman in *The Globe and Mail* the following day. Mulroney was responding to the assurances of Parti Québécois leader Jacques Parizeau that citizens of an independent Quebec would retain Canadian citizenship and currency.

Ladies and gentlemen, if you are not moved to preserve Canada for reasons of the soul, you should, at least, preserve it for reasons of the pocket.

Matthew Barrett, chairman, Bank of Montreal, address to the Canadian Club, quoted by Canadian Press, *The Globe and Mail*, 19 Nov. 1991.

It's come to the point that we're talking about humiliation on every street corner.

Jean Chrétien, Leader of the Opposition, quoted by Ingrid Peritz in *The Montreal Gazette*, 28 Dec. 1991.

When I looked at Canada, I never thought of a piece of the entity being separate. It was borderless, a continuum from sea to sea. There were no lines on the map or street signs up. I saw it as a united part, and I felt proud.

Roberta Bondar, astronaut aboard the *Discovery*, 22–30 Jan. 1992, *Maclean's*, 24 Feb. 1992.

So please don't fall apart—don't let us down. My country, Russia, is watching Canada much more attentively than you can imagine.

Arkadi Tcherkassov, Russian geographer "Our Man in Moscow," *Grainews*, July 1992.

My separatist friends show a fascination for small countries—Sweden, Lithuania, Holland, Costa Rica. Deep in their hearts, I'm sure they share with me the special relationship that other Canadians entertain with vastness. This giant country might be too big for small minds.

Roch Carrier, author, "Canada Is a Grand Dream," *Canadian Living*, September 1992.

In Quebec, humiliation is decidedly selective.

Pierre Elliott Trudeau, former Prime Minister, referring to the provincial premier's tactics in negotiating "profitable federalism" with the rest of Canada, "Trudeau Speaks Out," *Maclean's*, 28 Sept. 1992.

If all the provinces were separated by water, tensions would dissolve.

Leonard Cohen, poet and songwriter, quoted by Brian D. Johnson in "Life of a Lady's Man," *Maclean's*, 7 Dec. 1992.

Separatism, n. The longest-running dramatic entertainment on the continent, even surpassing the Broadway run of Agatha Christie's equally tiresome *The Mousetrap*.

David Olive, editor, *Canadian Political Babble* (1993).

Canada was not conceived in an act of passion, nor has it been maintained at a pitch of patriotic fervour. It would be a mistake to end it that way—with fiery speeches and hot blood flowing.

Gordon Gibson, B.C. Liberal leader, *Plan B: The Future of the Rest of Canada* (1994) issued by the Fraser Institute.

Since Confederation seven generations of Canadians—French-speaking, English-speaking, and immigrants from around the world—have flourished, economically and culturally, under a regime of peace, order, and occasional good government. To throw this lightly away is a folly almost beyond belief.

Michael Bliss, historian and columnist, *The Toronto Star*, 20 May 1994.

We can separate as long as we all stick together.

Malapropism attributed to Bloc Québécois leader **Lucien Bouchard**, 21 June 1994.

Quebeckers will reflect on whether it would be "normal" to follow the lead of those who wish to separate from Canada.... It is not often that I agree with them. But this time I do. Canada is not a normal country. Canada is an extraordinary country.

Jean Chrétien, Prime Minister, address, Canadian Chamber of Commerce, Quebec City, 18 Sept. 1994, quoted by Susan Delacourt and Rhéal Séguin in *The Globe and Mail* the following day. In the 1970s and 1980s, René Lévesque used the adjective normal to modify the noun country, the notion being that Quebec's provincial status was abnormal, whereas any future sovereign status would be normal. In the 1990s, Jacques Parizeau extolled "un peuple normal," and Lucien Bouchard rhapsodized about "un pays normal."

When you have seventy per cent of your French population that feel in their hearts that they are Quebecers first, and when they want all decisions taken in Quebec City, only two things can happen. Either they leave and give themselves a real country, or they stay and they provide you with a never-ending visit to the dentist.

Jacques Parizeau, Quebec Premier, address, Canadian Club of Toronto, 22 Nov. 1994, published in *The Toronto Star* the following day.

Separating because of our complaints about federalism would be like amputating a leg to cure a sprain.

Daniel Johnson, Liberal leader, address, National Assembly, 30 Nov. 1994, quoted by Robert McKenzie in *The Toronto Star*, 1 Dec. 1994. Johnson's comparison between separation and amputation was made and reported prior to knowledge that Lucien Bouchard's leg would need to be amputated.

The sovereigntist project must quickly take a turn which will bring it closer to Quebeckers.

Lucien Bouchard, Bloc Québécois leader, party convention, Montreal, 9 April 1995, as quoted by Rhéal Séguin and Tu Thanh Ha in *The Globe and Mail* the following day. Bouchard used the French word *virage*, meaning "road turn," to indicate a "turning away" from participating in a referendum on Quebec independence, as advocated by

Quebec Premier Jacques Parizeau, to one on provisional sovereignty-association. Later, in Quebec City, Parizeau noted, "It should be well understood that a Yes vote in the referendum on sovereignty in 1995 will lead to Quebec sovereignty."

Quebec, incidentally, will not leave Canada during the next millennium, realizing that to settle its claims of nationhood would be far too risky and expensive an undertaking, but that negotiating them is perpetually profitable.

Peter C. Newman, journalist, "The Dawn of a New Millennium," *Maclean's*, 30 Dec. 1996.

But Canada is about to become a major news story, for it is closer to dissolution than many realize. O Canada might well become No Canada. America could end up with a bunch of weak, quarrelsome, and suspicious neighbours on its northern border.

Mortimer B. Zuckerman, Montreal-born publisher and editor-in-chief, *U.S. News & World Report*, 14 July 1997.

If they have the thrill of smoke, darkness and ancient yearnings, our side will have to have daylight, reason and hope. The politics of civility has to fight hard against the politics of desire.

Vivian Rakoff, psychiatrist, psychological profile of Lucien Bouchard and the Quebec psyche, "Just What Was Written," *The Globe and Mail*, 26 Aug. 1997.

It's for Quebec to decide.

Slogan of the **Parti Québécois** used at rallies to mark the federal government's decision to request the Supreme Court to consider the legality of a unilateral declaration of independence, as noted by Rhéal Séguin in *The Globe and Mail*, 21 Feb. 1998.

The Quebec issue, as it is called, is an indispensable topic for Canadian conversation. If all else fails, it can be taken up with the comforting knowledge that nothing new will be said.

John Kenneth Galbraith, economist and essayist, *Name-Dropping: From FDR On* (1999).

Quebeckers don't really want to separate. They just want to keep getting pregnant so they'll receive a bigger welfare cheque from the rest of Canada.

Jan Wong, columnist, "Why Should I? This Is My Home," *The Globe and Mail*, 26 Nov. 1999.

We are winning the battle against our enemies. It is time for someone who can win over our friends.

William Johnson, retiring President of Alliance Quebec, "Why I'm Leaving," *The Globe and Mail*, 2 Feb. 2000.

SERVICE

What a fellow does for others is far more fun than what he does for himself. I suppose they call me a manufacturer, a maker that is. Perhaps I am—but there's more satisfaction in making people useful and happy than in all other kinds of manufacturing in all the world.

R.S. McLaughlin, automotive manufacturer and philanthropist, interviewed by R.E. Knowles in *The Toronto Star*, 28 July 1928.

Service is the rent we pay for the privilege of living on this earth.

N. Eldon Tanner, former oil executive and Mormon elder, quoted by Stephen R. Covey in *The Seven Habits of Highly Effective People: Restoring the Character Ethic* (1989).

The Rotarians own the town, the Kiwanians run it, and the Lions do all the work—and have all the fun.

Proverbial lore of service clubs recalled "several years ago" by Kiwanis Club member Milt Hamilton, Toronto, 4 Nov. 1991.

Throughout my life, but especially in my retirement, the incidents that gave me the deepest sense of satisfaction were those connected with service to others.

*

To sum up: One felt that the things that differentiated a true person as a human being was the reliability of their dedication to serving others.

Robert McClure, medical missionary, interviewed by Mike McManus, TVO, reproduced in *The Toronto Star*, 14 Nov. 1991.

SETTLEMENT

Besides, it has been found that colonization is at all times unfavourable to the fur trade.

Lord Selkirk, colonist, *Statement Respecting The*

Earl of Selkirk's Settlement upon the Red River in North America (1817).

The aloofness of Canada, not less inhabited perhaps, but so far less humanized than Asia, struck me with awe, and an immense admiration for the courage that had tackled it.

Freya Stark, British traveller, *Beyond Euphrates* (1951).

No country is ever settled just once. Each new generation must settle it again in their imaginations.

John Bemrose, writer, "Adventures in History," *Maclean's*, 14 Dec. 1992.

SEWAGE

Canada's urban sewage-treatment systems are a disgrace from sea to stinking sea.

Adapted from the report of the Vancouver-based **Sierra Legal Defence Fund**, executive director Greg McDade, as reported by Dan Westell in *The Globe and Mail*, 15 June 1994. Westell observed, "If the annual volume of untreated sewage were piled on the 7,800-kilometre Trans-Canada Highway, the report says, it would cover the road to a depth of nine metres."

SEX

See also DESIRE, HOMOSEXUALITY, LOVE, MEN & WOMEN, PORNOGRAPHY, PROSTITUTION, SEXUAL OFFENCES

Free love

The words *free love*, long identified with licentiousness and bohemianism, may well have been introduced by **John Humphrey Noyes**, founder of the community at Oneida, N.Y., 1847. With his followers he settled in Ontario in 1878. He died at Niagara Falls, Ont., in 1886.

Carol was as hot as a Quebec heater.

Description of an adolescent girl's sexuality in **Robertson Davies**' novel *The Manticore* (1972).

Balls have their place, a yard away from the brain.

George Woodcock, author, referring to descriptions of sexual practices in literature, "Fragments from a Tenth-hour Journal," *Northern Journey*, Fall 1974.

Sex Is the Invention of a Very Clever Venereal Disease

Sign on a wall in the horror movie about a rampant infection called *They Came from Within* (1975) directed by David Cronenberg.

It has been observed that every function of which the human body is capable—every one—has been performed, at one time or another, in the back seat of a taxi.

John Johnson, cabbie and writer, *Taxi! True Stories from Behind the Wheel* (1978).

Sex occupies the thoughts of most human beings more of the time, and far more urgently, than any other single interest.

J.F.M. Hunter, philosopher, *Thinking about Sex and Love* (1980).

In an ultimate sense, the function of human sexuality is to maintain the bonds of mutual affection and nurturance. This is essential to the peaceful survival of our race. Instead of causing shame, caring and sensual tenderness must be accepted as vital forces in our lives. Sensuality is, in fact, the most effective remedy for the violence within ourselves and within the family.

Cyril Greenland, psychiatric social worker, "Violence and the Family," *Canadian Journal of Public Health*, Feb. 1980.

One of the reasons sex is so popular is that it's centrally located.

Frank Zingrone, communications theorist, address, Ontario Conference of Teachers of English, Oct. 1982.

Sex is the beginning of our identity, out of which most of us don't ever grow, even in the androgynous face of great age.

Jane Rule, writer, "Morality in Literature," *A Hot-Eyed Moderate* (1986).

We read sex manuals that said a man should learn to play a woman like a violin. Nobody said a word about a woman learning to play a man like a flute.

Margaret Atwood, author, "If You Can't Say Something Nice, Don't Say Anything at All," *Language in Her Eye: Views on Writing and Gender by Canadian Women Writing in English* (1990) edited by Libby Scheier, Sarah Sheard, and Eleanor Wachtel.

Her vowels were full of sex, her consonants of money.

Line from **Edward Phillips**' novel *Sunday Best* (1990).

There are other things too... it's just a kind of spasm... rather like a cough.

Robertson Davies, novelist, referring to the contemporary preoccupation with the orgasm, interviewed by Harry Rasky on *The Magic Season of Robertson Davies*, CBC-TV, 27 Dec. 1990.

More dreams are destroyed in bed than are ever found there.

Robin Skelton, poet and aphorist, *A Devious Dictionary* (1991).

We have what I called an omni-sexuality. Which does not recognize the sorts of normal barriers and liaisons and taboos. And to the extent that I'm interested in exploring stuff that's beyond taboo, I would explore not just bisexuality but any kind of sexuality. Dog sexuality. Animal sexuality. Insect sexuality. Whatever.

David Cronenberg, film director, interview, *Rolling Stone*, 6 Feb. 1992.

In the era of AIDS, CyberSex may be the ultimate in safe sex.

Frank Ogden, futurologist. referring to artificial electronic stimuli, 14 Nov. 1992.

I don't think a man ever gets over that first sight of the naked woman. I think that's Eve standing over him, that's the morning and the dew on the skin. And I think that's the major content of every man's imagination. All the sad adventures in pornography and love and song are just steps on the path towards that holy vision.

Leonard Cohen, poet and songwriter, quoted by Brian D. Johnson in "Life of a Lady's Man," *Maclean's*, 7 Dec. 1992.

To be old is to be sexually oppressed; first the old values inhabit, then the younger generation disapproves and finally society sets up formal barriers to accessibility of sexual partners.

Benjamin Schlesinger, sociologist, "The Sexless Years or Sex Rediscovered," *Seniors and Sexuality: Experiencing Intimacy in Later Life* (1995) edited by Robynne Neugebauer-Visano.

In the Buddha's gesture of touching, the earth bears witness. In sex, perhaps the earth of our flesh bears witness to the reality behind our illusions.

Tim Ward, traveller, *Arousing the Goddess* (1996).

Most teenage girls do not have a clue of what it means to own sex.

Kate Fillion, journalist, *Lip Service: The Truth about Women's Darker Side in Love, Sex, and Friendship* (1996).

The central dogma of the baby boomers: the belief that sex, so long as it's consensual, ought never to be subject to moral scrutiny at all.

David Frum, neo-conservative commentator, arguing that only sex within marriage is sacrosanct, quoted by Andrew Sullivan, "Going Down Screaming," *The New York Times Magazine*, 11 Oct. 1998.

If a man doesn't get an erection when he sees a heron, then he's not functioning. Flesh and spirit are one.

Attributed to writer **Scott Symons** as adapted by Sarah Hampson in an interview, "CanLit's Bad Boy Is Back," *The Globe and Mail*, 8 June 2000.

SEXUAL OFFENCES See also CRIME, SEX

In my rape fantasy, the man overwhelms me—not because I'm worthless and need to be subjugated but because I am so sexy I have made him lose control.

Susan Swan, author, "Desire and the Mythology of Feminity," *Language in Her Eye: Views on Writing and Gender by Canadian Women Writing in English* (1990) edited by Libby Scheier, Sarah Sheard, and Eleanor Wachtel."

I think that sexism is racism in disguise.

Shirley Solomon, host of CTV's *The Shirley Show*, quoted by Paula Todd in *Homemaker's*, Sept. 1992.

Apparently just about everybody who quits their job is being sexually harassed. We must have one hell of a lot of attractive people. I have to admit to you that I have never been sexually harassed myself. If I were I would certainly want to make it known that I had been so favoured.

John Crosbie, Minister of Fisheries and Oceans, speech, Lewisporte, Nfld., 11 Feb. 1993, quoted by Tim Harper in *The Toronto Star* two days later. He had in mind women workers who quit their jobs because of sexual harassment and then claimed Unemployment Insurance benefits.

Harrassment... falls short of assault, or any other criminal act, much less a violent criminal act. It is not the crime of the century, though sex panic more and more stigmatizes it as though it were.

John Fekete, philosopher, *Moral Panic: Biopolitics Rising* (2nd ed., 1995).

Ladies, as distinct from women, are rarely raped.

Attributed to columnist **McKenzie Porter** in an article in *The Toronto Telegram* in 1975 by Peter Worthington, "Irrepressible Ken Porter," *The Toronto Sun*, 11 April 1999.

SHARING

Give a man a fish and he will have food for a day. Teach a man to fish and he will have food for a lifetime.

Attributed to **M.M. Coady**, adult educator and co-founder of the self-help Antigonish Movement in Antigonish, N.S., in 1929.

Sharing: that's what a confederation is about. We are still in the process of inventing our country. Canada is able to become the country the whole planet will look up to when it is time to move away from tribalism and embrace the 21st century.

Roch Carrier, author, "Canada Is a Grand Dream," *Canadian Living*, September 1992.

Sharing is one of the most basic words in Inuktitut. We like to use that word, but it seems to me that we rarely practice it to the extent that Inuit do.

James Houston, author and artist, *Confessions of an Igloo Dweller* (1995).

SHIPS & SAILING See also SPORTS, TRAVEL

And even after I was big / And had to go to school, / My mind was often far away / Aboard the Ships of Yule.

Last verse of **Bliss Carman**'s poem "The Ships of Yule" (1912), *Bliss Carman's Poems* (1929).

We spoke of the racing tides off Vancouver, and the lonely pine-clad ridges gunning up to the snow-peaks of the Selkirks, to which we had travelled once upon a time in search of sport.

Description of the adventures of two British sportsmen in **John Buchan**'s story "The Kings of Orion," *The Moon Endureth: Tales and Fancies* (1912).

Never again will I ever sail / With a drunken captain and a heavy gale.

Final couplet of the folksong "Canso Strait," *Songs and Ballads from Nova Scotia* (1932) edited by Helen Creighton.

I never wanted to be better than any other man. I always wanted to be just as good.

Angus Walters, captain of the schooner *Bluenose*, quoted by Feenie Ziner in *Bluenose: Queen of the Grand Banks* (1970).

Perhaps the implacable ice holds them still. Perhaps in one or another of those endless, gigantic ice pressure ridges shifting, sinking, reshaping themselves forever in the ice streams that flow between the islands of the Canadian archipelago, *Erebus* and *Terror* are still carried, hidden and secret.

Rudy Wiebe, novelist, referring to the lost vessels of Sir John Franklin's Arctic expedition, *Playing Dead: A Contemplation Concerning the Arctic* (1989).

Shipwrecks are like dreams, lying beyond the observable everyday world. They draw us into places we do not belong, confirming that there are times when reason and fact are no match for enduring mysteries.

Joseph MacInnis, undersea explorer, *Fitzgerald's Gorm: The Wreck of the Edmund Fitzgerald* (1997).

SHOES

Indeed, in some tribal languages the word for *shoe* is *bata* because, for a long time, that was the only kind of footwear local people had ever known.

Thomas J. Bata, world head of the Bata Shoe Company, referring to sales in African countries, *Bata: Shoemaker to the World* (1990) written with Sonja Sinclair.

According to an anecdote that has become part of Bata folklore, two salesmen were sent overseas to explore the possibility of selling shoes in Africa. One of them cabled home: "Nobody wearing shoes. No market possibilities. Returning home soonest possible." The other one, a true Bata disciple, had a completely different reaction. "Everybody barefoot," he informed head office. "Tremendous sales opportunities."

Thomas J. Bata, world head of the Bata Shoe Company, discussing postwar sales, *Bata: Shoemaker to the World* (1990) written with Sonja Sinclair.

SHOPPING

You can buy better things for half the money in Canada.

C.L. Norton and **John Habberton**, travellers and satirists, crossing from the United States into Canada, *Canoeing in Kanuckia or Haps and Mishaps* (1878).

Americans have their Benedict Arnolds, Norway gave the world Vidkun Quisling and Canadians have cross-border shoppers. They all have something in common: they're traitors.

Arthur Milnes, journalist, "Betrayal at the Border, *The Globe and Mail*, 9 Dec. 1991.

Canadians seek bargains south of the border with gusto. As the saying goes, "The heart may be worn on the left but the wallet is usually worn on the right." It is becoming rarer to see consumers buy products of their own nation on nationalistic grounds alone.

Kimon Valaskakis, economist, University of Montreal, "A Prescription for Canada Inc.," *The Globe and Mail*, 31 Oct. 1992.

Shopping is the 20th-century version of hunting. Equipped with plastic cards rather than blowpipes, shoppers are driven by an atavistic bloodlust to stalk the dense retail jungles in search of that wary and succulent prey, the bargain.

Attributed to **Steven Levy**, sociologist and producer of Toronto's One of a Kind craft show, by John Barber in *The Globe and Mail*, 26 Nov. 1992.

SHOW BUSINESS See also CELEBRITIES, HOLLYWOOD

I was a German comedian, but like I told you, I lost my accent one day when they sank the Lusitania. That night I just took off the chin piece I used to wear, and I became a Jew comedian. It was at the Chase Theatre in Toronto.

Groucho Marx, comedian, reminiscing how his career took an important turn in Toronto in 1915, quoted by Charlotte Chandler in *Hello, I Must Be Going* (1978). She quoted the most famous of the Marx brothers as saying, "When we got to Toronto, it was ten below, and the audience was forty below."

As far back as I can remember, I wanted to be slightly grand, and Dovercourt Road wasn't quite the place for that.

Beatrice Lillie, entertainer, referring to her humble birth and upbringing in a red-brick house at No. 68 Dovercourt Road, Toronto, *Every Other Inch a Lady* (1972) written with John Philip and James Brough.

I'm not really part of show business . . . I live in Toronto.

Anne Murray, singer, appearing on TV's *The Merv Griffin Show*, quoted by Dennis Braithwaite in *The Toronto Star*, 12 Feb. 1975.

My first act got started in Toronto. I was at Shea's for a whole year, then I was in Montreal for a year. . . . When I went back to the States, they advertised me as a Canadian comedian.

Red Skelton, U.S. comedian, reminiscing about his early years in vaudeville, quoted by H.J. Kirchhoff in *The Globe and Mail*, 17 March 1989.

It's called show business, because it's half-business. Both words matter.

Sandra Shamas, comic, quoted by Liam Lacey in *The Globe and Mail*, 4 Jan. 1992.

I'm there to ask questions on the audience's behalf. If you put your own agenda ahead of the audience's, become too impressed with your own ideas at the expense of the people watching, then you betray a trust.

Bill Cameron, broadcaster and journalist, quoted by Roderick Jamer in *TV Guide*, 22 Aug. 1992.

We're the only festival in town where you have access to superstars.

Greg Gatenby, literary organizer, Harbourfront's International Festival of Authors, quoted by *eye*, 15 Oct. 1992.

I wasn't born in Canada, but if I have a choice, I will be next time.

Red Skelton, comedian, quoted in an open Letter to the Editor written by Tom Kalyn, promoter, *The Red Skelton Show*, published as an advertisement headed "Red Skelton" in *The Globe and Mail*, 25 Oct. 1997.

Lorne Michaels, who has had more influence on American television comedy than anyone in the last quarter-century, suavely summed up the northern condition. "In a country where civility and moderation are celebrated," he said, "show business seemed like showing off." He asserted, for example, that a Canadian would never have made a film called *It's a Wonderful Life* because "that would be bragging." He envisioned the Canadian version would have been titled *It's an All Right Life*.

Sarah Vowell, columnist, reporting on a panel on Canadian comedy at New York's 92nd Street YMCA, "American Squirm: Canuck Yuks," "Salon," Internet, 27 Jan. 1999. She concluded, "Short makes self-loathing enchanting."

SIGNS

Sometimes I misread a sign—though recently I saw one in Mexico that said, "*No Maltrate las Señales*" (Do not maltreat the signs), and I try not to.

Kildare Dobbs, essayist, Introduction, *Reading the Time* (1968).

The statement that "no one ever died from getting lost" is untrue, irrelevant, and wholly unworthy of us.

Paul Arthur and **Romedi Passini**, designers, *Wayfinding: People, Signs, and Architecture* (1992).

SIKH PEOPLE

Vancouver was another fertile field for Sikh militants. The talk over there was of power only growing from the barrel of a gun, of suicide missions. These organizations, however they might differ ideologically, all had one strain in common: They were devoted to the cult of violence.

Shiva Naipaul, essayist, "The Death of Indira Gandhi" (1984), *An Unfinished Journey* (1986).

I wore my best turban.

Harbhajan Minhas, Sikh veteran of World War II, who wore his turban and uniform to meet with Queen Elizabeth II, Victoria, B.C., quoted by Michael Smyth in the *Winnipeg Free Press*, 21 Aug. 1994.

This is an ambitious people. You're going to see a Sikh premier, why not a Sikh prime minister?

Adds Jas Mohal, reporter for BCTV, anticipating the B.C. premiership of Punjabi-born lawyer Ujjal Dosanjh, "first premier of colour," quoted by Jennifer Hunter and Chris Wood, "Sikh Power," *Maclean's*, 21 Feb. 2000.

SILENCE See also SOUND

Have little care that Life is brief, / And less that art is long. / Success is in the silences, / Though fame is in the song.

Lines from **Bliss Carman**'s poem "Envoi," *Bliss Carman's Poems* (1929).

The silence of our Western forests was so profound that our ears could scarcely comprehend it. If you spoke your voice came back to you as your face is thrown back to you in a mirror. It seemed as if the forest were so full of silence that there was no room for sounds.

Emily Carr, artist, "Silence and Pioneers," *The Book of Small* (1942).

Silence is a pocket of possibility. Anything can happen to break it.

R. Murray Schafer, composer and theorist, *Ear Cleaning: Notes for an Experimental Music Course* (1967).

There is really no such thing as silence. When there is no external racket to drown it out, we are left with the insistent, inescapable sound of our own thoughts, and there are many people to whom thinking, even on the most humble, day-dreaming level, is torture.

Robertson Davies, man-of-letters, commencement address, Toronto French School, 18 June 1982, FTS's *Bi-Line* (1982).

If men are silent, books will find a voice.

Line from a poem in **Steve McCaffery**'s *Panopticon* (1984).

In all-important human affairs, silence is the ultimate contempt.

Nancy Logan, writer, "Bosom Buddies, *Toronto Life Fashion*, Sept. 1992.

SIN

I have no doubt at all the Devil grins, / As seas of ink I spatter. / Ye gods, forgive my "literary" sins— / The other kind don't matter.

Lines from **Robert W. Service**'s verse "Proem," *The Spell of the Yukon and Other Verses* (1907).

Live in the large! Dare greatly, and if you must sin—sin nobly!

W.L. Grant, Principal of Upper Canada College in the 1920s, characteristic exhortation to students, paraphrasing one of Luther's letters to Melancthon, recalled by one-time student Robertson Davies, as noted by Judith Skelton Grant in *Robertson Davies: Man of Myth* (1994).

Oh, the greatest sin—I'm convinced of this—is cruelty. In either man or woman. I can forgive, or try to forgive anything else. And the queen virtue, by the same token, is kindness.

Nellie L. McClung, pioneer writer, quoted by R.E. Knowles in *The Toronto Star,* 18 Nov. 1937.

Betting, Beer, Bingo

The three "terrible sins" according to **James Muchmore**, Moderator of the General Council of the United Church of Canada, 1962–64.

Original sin means that there is no way of separating means from ends, good from bad, vision from history, without God.

Northrop Frye, cultural critic, Entry 731, Notebook 1997, *Northrop Frye Newsletter,* Summer 1997.

SINCERITY

To convince others, you must first convince yourself. Sheer sincerity can carry an audience.

J.R. (Joey) Smallwood, Premier of Newfoundland, quoted by Richard Gwyn in *Smallwood: The Unlikely Revolutionary* (1968).

SINGAPORE

This Singapore—is it in the Commonwealth?

Attributed to B.C. Premier **William Vander Zalm**, preparing to meet a dignitary from Singapore, a long-time member of the Commonwealth, as quoted by David Olive in *Canadian Political Babble* (1993).

SKATING See also SPORTS

I skate the way I think Isadora Duncan danced. I'm trying to explore every facet of my personality. I'm criticized as flamboyant, arrogant, and melodramatic. I'm black and white. I'm yes and no. I try to live my life touching extremes.

Toller Cranston, champion skater, quoted in *Canada Today/D'Aujourd'hui,* Oct. 1977.

Sportsmanship is, above all, the most important thing. What happens today is not the most important thing in the world. Respect for your competitors is one of the most important things.

Elvis Stojko, figure-skating personality, quoted in the *Winnipeg Free Press,* 27 March 1994.

Then there's the incredible feeling of skating itself, of getting on this shiny, slippery surface and moving faster than your feet would otherwise move, of feeling the breeze that you've created yourself in the act of skating.

Ken Dryden, former hockey personality, speaking about the resolve of architect Frank Gehry in his sixty-fifth year to learn to skate, testimonial dinner tendered the Toronto-born architect by the University of Toronto, "Hockey Lessons," *The Globe and Mail,* 28 Nov. 1998.

SKIING See also SPORTS

Whoever seeth this image shall not faint or fall today. *Regardes à St. Christophe et t'en va rassureé.*

Consolation from a wayside shrine for skiers, **Saint-Sauveur**, Laurentian Mountains, 1931, as noted by Robert Ayre in "The Laurentians Remembered," *The Laurentians: Painters in a Landscape* (1978) edited by Mela Constantinidi.

There was no point in trying to ski well and finish fifth or tenth. I wanted to ski awesome and finish first. This was my last chance to come home with a medal.

Kerrin Lee-Gartner, champion skier, winning the Gold Medal for downhill skiing at the 1992 Winter Olympics at Albertville, France, 15 Feb. 1992, quoted by Dave Perkins in *The Toronto Star* the following day.

SKY

Nowhere else will you find such wide skies, so much air or freedom, except when snow dwarfs and suffocates every prospect. But there, too, there can be a white and scintillating splendour not to be found elsewhere.

Sir Osbert Sitwell, English traveller and writer, *The Four Continents: Being More Discursions on Travel, Art and Life* (1954).

The sequestered brilliance of Canadian skies.

Image from a poem attributed to the American poet **Marianne Moore** but not located in *The Complete Prose of Marianne Moore* (1986) edited by Patricia C. Willis.

SLAVERY See also BLACKS

It was the 18th of October, 1830, in the morning, when my feet first touched the Canadian shore. I threw myself on the ground, rolled in the sand, seized handfuls of it and kissed them, and danced around, till, in the eyes of several who were present, I passed for a madman.

Josiah Henson, most famous of the fugitive slaves and the model for the fictional Uncle Tom in Harriet Beecher Stowe's novel *Uncle Tom's Cabin; or, Life Among the Lowly* (1852), thus described in *An Autobiography* (1881) his joy and relief upon reaching freedom from slavery in Upper Canada (present-day Ontario). His tulipwood cabin stands at Dresden, north of Chatham, Ont.

Farewell, old Master, / That is enough for me, / I'm going straight to Canada / Where coloured men are free!

Song sung to the tune of "Oh Susanna" by former black slaves who had "crossed the line" from the United States into the Canadian provinces, reproduced by Lena Newman in *The John A. Macdonald Album* (1974).

SLEEP

I do not believe in the despair of people who are able to sleep. When the mind can still resort to this, the body is not really ill. And with time the body can always cure the mind.

André Laurendeau, editor, *Une vie d'enfer* (1965).

The reason people sleep is that those who walked about in the dark didn't survive.

Louis Dudek, poet and aphorist, "Epigrams," *Small Perfect Things* (1991).

Sometimes I want to go to sleep and merge with the foggy world of dreams and not return to this, our real world.

Thoughts of the narrator of **Douglas Coupland**'s novel *Life after God* (1994).

SMILES

That's how I went "cold pan"—or frozen faced, if that conveys more to you. I took my woes on to the stage with me, and people laughed. There is a psychological reason why they should laugh at a melancholy person, but I'm not going into that now.

Ned Sparks, character actor in the movies who popularized the "dead-pan" expression, quoted in *Film Week*, 11 Jan. 1936.

SMOKING See also TOBACCO

Far away in St. Malo a statue is being raised to Jacques Cartier, to the first white man to smoke a pipe, to the first modern man.

Endre Ady, Hungarian poet and essayist, "The First Pipe-Smoker" (23 July 1905), *The Explosive Country: A Selection of Articles and Studies 1898–1916* (1977) translated by G.F. Cushing, edited by Erzsébet Vezér.

I decided it would be easier / to give up smoking / than girl watching.

Lyrics of **Terry Rowe**'s song "An Addiction" from *You and I, and Love* (1975).

Cigarette smokers are not interested in tobacco.

Marshall McLuhan, communications pioneer, quoted by Hugh Kenner in "Marshall McLuhan, R.I.P." (1981), *Mazes: Essays by Hugh Kenner* (1989).

Having smoking sections in restaurants is like having urinating and non-urinating sections in swimming pools.

Garfield Mahood, executive director of the Non-Smokers' Rights Association, quoted by Konrad Yakabuski in *The Toronto Star*, 19 March 1994.

Women have begun to smoke for the same reason that men are stopping. Each is meeting the other halfway: Men are increasing their sensitivity by letting their bodies talk to them, while women are decreasing their sensitivity by reducing the volume of information their bodies naturally give them.

Derrick de Kerckhove, communications specialist, quoted by Philip Marchand, "Wired Would Apply to Author in Many Senses," *The Toronto Star*, 12 July 1995.

Why is it that the chief executives of the companies that produce Player's, Matinee, Export,

Winston and Camel aren't called "drug lords"? Why is it that cigarettes are "sold," but illegal drugs are "trafficked"? Why is it the value of shares in the global traffic in killer tobacco are reported in the business pages, and nobody wonders about the morality of it? Why isn't the "international tobacco industry" known as the "world narcotic syndicate"?

Bob Hunter, columnist, "Enviro," *eye*, 6 Jan. 1996.

The parents are responsible and do not smoke in front of the children. The children are wily and do not smoke in front of the parents.

Richard Needham, columnist, quoted by Michael Kesterton in *The Globe and Mail*, 20 July 1996.

SNOBBERY

Ontario snobbery is timidity, another form of the reticence which underlies so much of what is wrong with us. Our Leading Citizens are not really sure of themselves; they don't quite know what has made them leading citizens, or what will keep them leading citizens.... In their insecurity they crowd together. So do sheep.

E.K. Brown, critic, "Now, Take Ontario" (1947), *Responses and Evaluations: Essays on Canada* (1977) edited by David Staines.

SNOW See also WINTER

There was life in all things. Snow shovels could go about by themselves, could move from one place to another without having to be carried. That is why we now, when in solitary places, never dare to stick a snow shovel into the snow. We are afraid lest it should come alive and go off on its own. So we always lay snow shovels down in the snow, so that they do not stand up. Thus all things were alive in the olden days.

Eskimo legend "In the Olden Days" recalled by **Aqikhivik** and quoted by Knud Rasmussen in *Intellectual Culture of the Caribou Eskimos: Iglulik and Caribou Eskimo Texts: Report of the Fifth Thule Expedition, 1921–24* (1930).

Howsoever it be, the Snow is very profitable for the fruits of the earth, to preserve them against the frost, and to serve them as a furgowne.

Marc Lescarbot, French lawyer and sometime colonist, "The Voyage of Monsieur de Monts into New France, written by Marke Lescarbot" (1606), *Hakluytus Posthumus, or Purchas His Pilgrimes: Contayning a History of the World in Sea Voyages and Lande Travells by Englishmen and Others* (1625) by Samuel Purchas, reproduced in 1905.

An Arctic traveller, by burying himself in snow, will sleep more warmly than in any other wrap, and even a slight fall of snow over his blanket serves as a warm coverlet.

William Carpenter Bompas, Bishop, *Northern Lights on the Bible: Drawn from a Bishop's Experience during Twenty-five Years in the Great North-West* (1893).

... my sunny nature didn't recover its equilibrium till I got away from everybody into the white world here—it started snowing yesterday afternoon and hasn't ceased yet, so Canada is looking as it should.

Mrs. Patrick Campbell, touring British actress, writing in her diary, Hamilton, Ont., 11 Dec. 1907, quoted by Alan Dent in Mrs. Patrick Campbell (1961). She toured Canada eight times between 1907 and 1916.

You people, with your snow, don't need any irrigation, the snow breaks up the soil, saturates it, starts the idea of harvest in its heart. Congratulate Canada, for me, on her copious snow.

Jan Christian Smuts, Prime Minister, Union of South Africa, interviewed in Toronto by R. E. Knowles, *The Toronto Star*, 3 Jan. 1930.

A heavy snowfall in December meant that winter had come,—the deepest reality of Canadian life.

Line descriptive of the season in **Willa Cather**'s historical novel *Shadows on the Rock* (1946).

... for an instant the flakes stopped falling, the light of the sky came through so that the city of Ottawa was revealed, as though it were the Heavenly City itself, glittering in its heights and depths of snow, a collection of too-heavy, dark stone buildings, the weight of them and their high, enormous roofs eased for the instant by the snow, the public monuments, models of commonsense, converted temporarily into snowmen that would melt away at the sun's caress.

Sir Osbert Sitwell, English traveller and writer,

The Four Continents: Being More Discursions on Travel, Art and Life (1954).

Mons pays ce n'est pas un pays c'est l'hiver / Mon jardin ce n'est pas un jardin c'est la plaine / Mon chemin ce n'est pas un chemin c'est la neige / Mon pays ce n'est pas un pays c'est l'hiver

Verse from poet and chansonnier **Gilles Vigneault**'s poem "Mon Pays" (My Country), *Avec les vieux mots* (1965). He set the lyrics to music and "Mon Pays" was accepted as the unofficial anthem of Quebec. English translation: "My country is not a country it's the winter / My garden is not a garden it's the plain / My road is not a road it's the snow / My country is not a country it's the winter."

Acadian driftwood / gypsy tailwinds / They call my home / the land of snow.

Verse from **Robbie Robertson**'s "Acadian Driftwood" from the album *Northern Lights—Southern Cross* (1975), quoted by Douglas Fetherling in *Some Day Soon: Essays on Canadian Songwriters* (1991).

Until I came to Canada I never knew that "snow" was a four-letter word.

Attributed to Buenos Aires–born author and anthologist **Alberto Manguel**, April 1988.

You wonder why there isn't as much snow as before? We aren't worthy of walking in it.

Stuart McLean, broadcaster, "What's the Matter with Rubber Boots?" *The Morningside World of Stuart McLean* (1989).

In winter, / snow falls / without permission. // But I let it fall anyway.

Lines from **Ariel Grue Lee**'s poem "Snow," *Many-Mouthed Birds: Contemporary Writing by Chinese Canadians* (1991) edited by Bennett Lee and Jim Wong-Chu.

There's a blizzard any time you want to do something in Saskatchewan.

Maggie Siggins, investigative journalist, resident of Regina, quoted by Henry Mietkiewicz in *The Toronto Star*, 23 Nov. 1991.

Preparations are well under way at our house for canning a family-sized supply of this year's snow. Let's hope they are at yours, too. Time is running out.

Joey Slinger, humorist, "The Snow of Yesteryear," *If It's a Jungle Out There, Why Do I Have to Mow the Lawn* (1992).

When it snows on the West Coast, ignore it. Maybe it will go away. No matter how many years in a row it snows, no matter how deep the snow is, remember: *It does not snow on the West Coast.*

Miro Cernetig, columnist, quoting from *The Lampoon*, "Vancouver," *The Globe and Mail*, 25 Jan. 1996.

SOCCER See also SPORTS

The reason soccer is the globe's most popular sport is simple. You don't need skates. You don't need bats. You don't need shoulder pads, kidney pads, cleats, knee pads and helmets. All you have to do is run. All day. Nonstop.

Allan Fotheringham, columnist, "The Gentlemen of Summer," *Maclean's*, 20 June 1994.

SOCIAL CREDIT See also POLITICAL PARTIES

Social Credit is the world's new road to prosperity and contentment. It bears the marks of strength, stability and scientific accuracy.

William Aberhart, Alberta Premier, interviewed by R.E. Knowles in *The Toronto Star*, 13 Sept. 1935.

Well, take Alberta as a sample. We hold that the province itself is the source of wealth. That province, like any other corporate entity, should, and does, declare dividends. Our citizens are the shareholders.

William Aberhart, Alberta Premier, explaining the basis of his Social Credit theory, interviewed by R.E. Knowles in *The Toronto Star*, 13 Sept. 1935.

Social Credit means just one thing, "That which is physically possible, desirable and morally right, must be made financially possible."

W.A.C. Bennett, Premier of British Columbia, quoted by Roger Keene in *Conversations with W.A.C. Bennett* (1980).

SOCIALISM See also IDEOLOGIES, NEW DEMOCRATIC PARTY, WELFARE STATE

The cause of socialism is the cause of love and hope and humanity: the cause of competition is the cause of anarchy, pessimism, and a disbelief in a possible Manhood for human nature just emeging from its barbarous infancy.

Archibald Lampman, poet, "Untitled Essay on Socialism" (1886), *Archibald Lampman: Selected Prose* (1975) edited by Barrie Davies.

I am convinced that we may develop in Canada a distinctive type of socialism. I refuse to follow slavishly the British model or the American model or the Russian model. We in Canada will solve our problems along our own lines.

J.S. Woodsworth, social reformer, president's address at the founding of the Co-operative Commonwealth Confederation (CCF), 1 Aug. 1933, quoted by Michiel Horn in *The League for Social Reconstruction: Intellectual Origins of the Democratic Left in Canada, 1930–1942* (1980).

The trouble with socialists is that they let their bleeding hearts go to their bloody heads.

T.C. (Tommy) Douglas, CCF-NDP leader, quoted in *Maclean's*, 12 July 1993.

I've fathered two parties now, and lost my political fertility. This isn't my swan song. It's my stork song.

F.R. Scott, National Chairman of the CCF, drafter of the preamble of the NDP constitution, bowing out at the NDP founding convention in 1961, quoted in *Time*, 1 May 1964.

So socialism in Canada, when it comes, will be stamped as strongly by Canadian tradition as the Cuban revolution was by Cuban tradition. It will be as Canadian as blueberry pie.

Leslie Morris, Communist, "Socialism Crosses the Atlantic," *The Canadian Tribune*, 19 June 1961, *Selected Writings of Leslie Morris: 1923–1964* (1970).

A socialist society must be one in which there is democratic control of all institutions which have a major effect on men's lives and where there is equal opportunity for creative non-exploitative self-development. It is now time to go beyond the welfare state.

"The Waffle Manifesto: For an Independent Socialist Canada" (1969) reprinted in *The Canadian Forum*, Dec. 1989.

True Christianity is the path to socialism and socialism is Christianity in action.

Tim Buck, leader of the Communist Party of Canada, quoted by Oscar Ryan in *Tim Buck: A Conscience for Canada* (1975).

Socialism goes into the gut, it has echoes of the class struggle, it has an international bond, and with all its sometimes messianic imperfection, it strives for a new society and dreams of utopia.

Stephen Lewis, former leader of the Ontario NDP, quoted in *The Toronto Star*, 8 Nov. 1978.

Socialism and pleasure are not necessarily a contradiction in terms.

Ed Broadbent, NDP leader, quoted in *Today*, 20 June 1981.

The working class and the employing class have nothing in common. There can be no peace as long as hunger and want are found among millions of working people and the few, who make up the employing class, have all the good things of life.

Preamble of the "Industrial Workers of the World," *The Canadian Wobbly Songbook* (1990) compiled by Jerzy (George) Dymny.

Canada's two enemies—separatists and socialists—have contributed mightily toward the deindustrialization and economic malaise in this country. Both are more similar than most realize: they attack wealthy creators and replace them with public-sector enterprises, an oxymoron in most cases.

Diane Francis, columnist, *The Financial Post*, 17 Dec. 1991.

The only serious functioning Marxists left in the West are the senior management of large, usually transnational corporations. The only serious Marxist thinkers are neo-conservative.

John Ralston Saul, author, *The Doubter's Companion: A Dictionary of Aggressive Common Sense* (1994).

The Western world, especially Canada, is far more socialistic than China has ever been, with its free public education, universal medicare, unemployment insurance, old-age pensions and government funding for television.

Jan Wong, correspondent, *Red China Blues: My Long March from Mao to Now* (1996).

The choice isn't between capitalism and socialism. The question is what kind of capitalism do we want to have.

Bob Rae, first socialist Premier of Ontario, remark made on 14 Dec. 1994, as quoted by James Laxer in *In Search of a New Left* (1996).

SOCIAL PROGRAMS See also MEDICARE, PENSIONS

A great city is not to be judged only by its beautiful buildings, its clean streets, its subway system or its harbourfront. The true measure of civilization rests upon how it cares for its vulnerable members.

Reva Gerstein, sociologist, quoted by André Picard in *The Globe and Mail*, 26 April 1991.

When I'm giving a speech, I often tell my audiences this: "We cannot do well by those truly in need if we insist on doing the same thing for everyone."

John Crispo, economist, *Making Canada Work: Competing in the Global Economy* (1992).

Every country has its national monuments—focal points that come to attain enormous emotional importance as unifying symbols of pride in its history and its special attributes. The United States, for instance, has its Statue of Liberty, its Grand Canyon, its Jefferson and Lincoln memorials, and so on. Canada is perhaps unique, however, in that our real national "monuments" are neither statues nor places. Our monuments are our social programs, our railways, our CBC.

Brian Mulroney, Prime Minister, quoted by George Radwanski and Julia Luttrell in *The Will of a Nation* (1992).

You can't be both gatekeeper and purse-snatcher at the same time.

Gary Filmon, Manitoba Premier, conference of provincial premiers and territorial leaders, St. John's, Nfld., 25 Aug. 1995, quoted by Edward Greenspon and Richard Mackie in *The Globe and Mail* the following day. Filmon was objecting to the attempt of Ottawa to reduce fiscal transfers for social programs and yet impose national standards and dictate social policy.

I'm an optimist in the long run, but what I didn't know—and I don't think politicians know—is how we are going to make it through the night, with the rich getting richer and the poor poorer.

Matthew Barrett, CEO, Bank of Montreal, as quoted by Ron Graham in *All the King's Horses* (1995).

No matter how deep the social program cuts of the federal Liberals and provincial Conservatives may become, there exists a basic sense among Canadians—which must ultimately be reflected by our politicians—that the uneducated, the sick, the poor and the elderly should not be allowed to fend for themselves.

Peter C. Newman, columnist, "The Nation's Business," *Maclean's*, 5 Feb. 1996.

A nationality cannot define itself by its social programmes. And a distinctive foreign policy doesn't emerge from a bland altruism punctuated by irritating the generally benign neighbouring presence which is the chief fact of Canada's political life.

Conrad Black, publisher, "Taking Canada Seriously," *International Journal*, Winter 1997–98.

Canada's social safety net became a hammock.

Conrad Black, publisher, commenting on changes since the 1960s led by the Trudeau administrations, "Out of Uncle Sam's Shadow," *National Post*, 11 Jan. 2000.

SOCIAL SCIENCE

As the late Harold Innis observed, the risk of being a social scientist in Canada is that one may die laughing.

Dave Godfrey and **Mel Watkins**, editor and political scientist, *Gordon to Watkins to You—Documentary: The Battle for Control of Our Economy* (1970).

SOCIAL UNION

The Government will not use its spending power to create new shared-cost programs in areas of exclusive provincial jurisdiction without the consent of a majority of the provinces. Any new program will be designed so that non-participating provinces will be compensated, provided they establish equivalent or comparable initiatives.

*

The Government will work with the provinces and Canadians to develop agreed-upon values and principles to underlie the social union and to explore new approaches to decision making in social policy.

Roméo LeBlanc, Governor General, Speech from the Throne, House of Commons, 27 Feb. 1996. This constitutes an early reference to the concept of a "social union" (coupled with the notion of a limitation on new shared-cost programs), a subject discussed by the provincial premiers, Saskatoon, 10 Aug. 1998.

SOCIAL WORK

For me, politics is a vehicle to achieve things—not a power trip, not a game of charades that you play with the vested interests, but a natural extension of social work, a way to alleviate misery.

Dave Barrett, B.C. Premier and former social worker, quoted by Christina Newman in *The Globe and Mail*, 1 March 1975.

SOCIETY See also CLASS, SOCIAL; ESTABLISHMENT

A lady will be a lady, even in the plainest dress; a vulgar minded woman will never be a lady, in the most costly garments.

Catharine Parr Traill, pioneer writer, *The Canadian Settler's Guide* (1855).

There may be little courtesy in the manners of the people, but there is plenty of generosity; no French politesse, but a ready hand; no good breeding, but a willing heart. Society is in a rough rude state out here, but there is something about it which I like, for all that; nothing like pride, nothing artificial, as among our poor upper classes at home, no gulf separating rich from poor.

G.T. Borrett, traveller, *Letters from Canada and the United States* (1865).

In Canada, you can be outside society and still feel a sense of security.

David Steinberg, Winnipeg-born comedian, quoted by Peter Goddard in *Maclean's*, March 1971.

A very grim future awaits the elaborate urban civilization which has grown up in Canada during the past thirty years. Life will be much less easy and comfortable, and decidedly more costly; nothing can long delay the inevitable approach of the change.

Donald G. Creighton, historian, "Surviving in the Post-Keynesian Era" (1975), *The Passionate Observer: Selected Writings* (1980).

Kick below, suck above.

Maxim not quite attributed to socialite **Sondra Gotlieb** by Allan Fotheringham, *Maclean's*, 21 Nov. 1983.

We do not need a society that permits, but one that accepts.

Robin Skelton, poet and aphorist, *A Devious Dictionary* (1991).

The pillars of society have hearts of stone.

John Hofsess, founder of Right to Die, characteristic remark, April 1992.

There's nothing wrong with overdogs.

E. Graydon Carter, Canadian-born editor of *Vanity Fair*, quoted by Liam Lacey in *The Globe and Mail*, 1 Jan. 1994.

Society was once a canvas to be described and altered by newspapers with a clear sense of mission—material, moral or political. Society is now more a mystery to be explored and unravelled by them.

William Thorsell, editor-in-chief, "Opening Bravo," *The Globe and Mail*, 5 March 1994.

Once the great dialectic was capital versus labour. Now it's the conflict between the comfortable and the deprived. And the comfortable see government as the threat because it is the only hope for the deprived.

John Kenneth Galbraith, economist and author, quoted by John B. Judis in *Mother Jones*, April 1994.

I believe that our ability to reassert the citizen-based society is dependent upon our rediscovery of the simple concepts of disinterest and participation.

John Ralston Saul, author, *The Unconscious Civilization* (1995).

Of this we can be certain: A society is mad when it cannot accept the diversity of its own identity, when it denies itself freedom of choice, when it sets one of its people against the other, as we are so clearly warned in Mark 3:25.

Alberto Manguel, man-of-letters, "Kidnap Tale Echoes Grimly," *The Globe and Mail*, 5 July 1997. "And if a house be divided against itelf, that kingdom cannot stand" (Mark 3:25).

SOLITUDE

In Canada, Walden Pond is a glacier.

B.W. Powe, commentator, *The Solitary Outlaw* (1987).

There aren't two solitudes in this country; there are 26 million.

Peter C. Newman, author and columnist, *Maclean's*, 10 Feb. 1992. (Approximately 30 million in 2000.)

That's what I would miss most if I went away—the isolation. I like to be alone a lot. Canada is a good place to feel alone.

Robert Davidson, Haida artist, extolling the merits of the West Coast, "My Canada Includes...," *Maclean's*, 3 Jan. 1994.

SOMALIA AFFAIR

Canada, Canada, Canada.

Dying screams of **Shidane Arone**, Somali teenager who was caught intruding on the Canadian Forces base near Belet Huen, Somalia, and was tortured and beaten to death by commandos from a subunit of the Canadian Airborne Regiment, 16 March 1994, quoted by Brian Bergman and Luke Fisher in *Maclean's*, 28 March 1994.

It never dawned on me that I needed to have an agenda or that I needed to have minutes.

General John Boyle, Chief of Defence Staff, testifying before the Somalia Inquiry, stating that no records were kept of meetings of two working groups on the Somalia affair during 1993–94, Ottawa, 12 Aug. 1996, quoted by Paul Korning, "Boyle Breaks Somalia Silence," *The Globe and Mail*, 13 Aug. 1996.

Somalia will never die.

Peter Desbarats, Commissioner, reacting on 12 March 1997 to the federal government's arbitrary decision to end the deliberations of the Commission of Inquiry, *Somalia Cover-up* (1997). Desbarats concluded, "My hunch is that most of the Somalia story will be known within the next five to ten years. It's even possible that further revelations could result in the appointment of another inquiry to complete our work."

SONGS See also MUSIC

All songs are born in man out in the great wilderness. Without ourselves knowing how it happens, they come with the breath, words and tones that are not daily speech.

Kilimé, Eskimo shaman, referring to poetry and song, quoted by Peter Freuchen in *The Book of the Eskimos* (1961) edited by Dagmar Freuchen.

I'll keep rolling along, / Deep in my heart is a song, / Here on the range I belong, / Drifting along with the tumbling tumbleweeds.

Last verse of the song "Tumbling Tumbleweeds" (1934), words and music by the cowboy singer **Bob Nowlan**, New Brunswick-born leader of the Sons of the Pioneers.

It would be wonderful if I could live to see Canada made a singing nation.

Attributed to **Edward Johnson**, Ontario-born operatic tenor, General Manager of the Metropolitan Opera in New York City from 1935 to 1950.

Land of the silver birch, / Home of the beaver, / Where still the mighty moose / Wanders at will! / Blue lake and rocky shore, / I will return once more. / Boom did-dy boom boom, boom did-dy boom boom, boom did-dy boom boom, boom.

First of four verses and refrain of "Land of the Silver Birch" arranged for the Girl Guides of Canada as a camp song by **John Arthur Cozens** of Toronto, as noted by Mark Gollam in his obituary in the *National Post*, 19 May 1999. This is part of the official text, as arranged by Cozens for the Vaughan District (Toronto) Girl Guide Choir (conducted by his wife) in January 1951.

I tell myself it's not the singing, it's the interpreting. Unless you interpret, you're just making noises.

Alan Mills, folksinger noted for his husky voice and gruff manner, quoted by Mavis Gallant in *The Montreal Standard*, 10 Feb. 1951.

Evangelist songs stir people to good, but trade union songs stir people to hate and to seek their own advancement.

Helen Creighton, folklorist, letter to Carmen Roy, 17 March 1960, quoted by Ian McKay in "Helen Creighton and the Politics of Antimodernism," *Myth and Milieu: Atlantic Literature and Culture 1918–1939* (1993) edited by Gwendolyn Davies.

What can I say about songwriting? I don't know anything about it. To ask me about songwriting is like asking a patient to talk about a disease he was born with. Above all, you have to leave room in life to dream.

Buffy Sainte-Marie, singer-composer, *The Buffy Sainte-Marie Songbook* (1971).

We have stopped singing. And singing is primal, the elemental expression.

R. Murray Schafer, composer and theorist, quoted in *Time*, 4 Sept. 1972.

I try to put into my songs all that I feel. And I feel a lot of things—like a woman, like a Québécoise, like a citizen of the world.

Pauline Julien, singer, comment during a concert, Guelph, Ont., quoted by Ray Conlogue in *The Globe and Mail*, 17 May 1977.

Songs, stories are beyond value; they are the memory and wisdom of a people, the particular individual rivers of the sea of life which constitutes us all.

Rudy Wiebe, novelist and essayist, *Playing Dead: A Contemplation Concerning the Arctic* (1989).

He didn't invent me. I was a person—and an artist—long before I met Leonard Cohen.

Suzanne Verdal, Quebec dancer and performer, referring to herself as the inspiration in 1977 for Leonard Cohen's song "Suzanne," quoted in *The Globe and Mail*, 25 May 1992.

If I knew where songs came from I would go there more often.

Leonard Cohen, poet and songwriter, interviewed by Karen Schoemer in *The New York Times*, 29 Nov. 1992.

Simply put, men tend to sing outside the home and women sing within it.

Edith Fowke, folklorist, Introduction, *A Family Heritage: The Story and Songs of LaRena Clark* (1994) by Edith Fowke with Jay Rahn.

SOUND See also MUSIC, NOISE, SILENCE

The limits of the powers of the human voice from time immemorial had been set by the size of an audience physically present. These were now simply removed. A single voice addressing a single audience on a single occasion could at least theoretically address the entire population of the earth.

Eric A. Havelock, Toronto-educated classicist at Yale University, (1967), *The Muse Learns to Write: Reflections on Orality and Literacy from Antiquity to the Present* (1986).

Today all sounds belong to a continuous field of possibilities lying *within the comprehensive dominion of music.*

R. Murray Schafer, composer and theorist, *The New Soundscape: A Handbook for the Modern Music Teacher* (1969).

Any environment has sounds that a composer learns to be sensitive to. I have been interested in sounds of the past in southern Ontario for some time. It gives you a certain identification with where you are, if you know what was there before you came.

John Beckwith, composer and musicologist, quoted by Susan Carson in *Weekend Magazine*, 11 March 1972.

Today we accept recorded and broadcast sound as perfectly normal, even though it has differentiated us from all listeners before us on this earth.

R. Murray Schafer, composer and theorist, "Dub," *The Canadian Forum*, Nov. 1994.

Above us another music, the planets and stars and their radiophonic hum.

B.W. Powe, cultural commentator, coining a new word "Electroscape," *Outage: A Journey into Electric City* (1995).

SOUTH AFRICA

I should like to travel up and down this enormous country which I am persuaded and most firmly believe is going to be one of the great countries of the world.

General Jan Christian Smuts, South African leader, "Freemasonry of Empire," 3 Jan. 1930, *Addresses Delivered before The Canadian Club of Toronto: Season of 1929–30* (1930).

My hope is that they will return to the Commonwealth in due course. There will always be a light in the Commonwealth window.

John G. Diefenbaker, Prime Minister, address in Ottawa following the 1961 Commonwealth Prime Ministers' Conference in London, England, at which Diefenbaker insisted that the Commonwealth declare the principle of racial equality, which meant that South Africa would withdraw its application for continued membership as a republic. Quoted by Peter C. Newman in *Renegade in Power: The Diefenbaker Years* (1963).

I try to occupy the high moral ground so that the future leaders of South Africa will know where Canada stood.

Brian Mulroney, Prime Minister, explaining the government's opposition to South Africa's apartheid policy, Commonwealth Conference, Kuala Lumpur, 24 Oct. 1989.

You have made me feel like a young man again, with my batteries recharged.

Nelson Mandela, President of the Republic of South Africa, addressing 40,000 school-age children, SkyDome, Toronto, 25 Sept. 1998, quoted by Marcus Gee and Virginia Galt in *The Globe and Mail* the following day.

SOUTH AMERICA

In short, the degree of Canadian ignorance about Latin America resembles the ignorance the United States is said to harbour about matters Canadian. Indeed, one cannot escape the conclusion that Canadian ignorance of Latin America is rather more profound than American ignorance of Canada.

Robin W. Winks, historian, "Canada and the Three Americas: Her Hemispheric Role," *Friends So Different: Essays on Canada and the United States in the 1980s* (1989) edited by Lansing Lamont and J. Duncan Edmonds.

SOUTHEAST ASIA

The economic boom, so familiar to Europeans and North Americans, even up to four years ago, has now moved to the Near West, once known as the Far East. Today the Orient is just like anywhere else, only a non-stop flight away.

Frank Ogden, futurologist, remark, 10 Feb. 1993.

SOVEREIGNTY

See also PARTITION, QUEBEC, REFERENDA, SECESSION, SEPARATISM, SOVEREIGNTY-ASSOCIATION

Pretty soon we'll read in one-inch headlines, "Sovereignty makes you bald."

Jacques Parizeau, Parti Québécois leader, ridiculing hypothetical objections to Quebec separatism, quoted by Peter C. Newman in *Maclean's*, 16 Sept. 1991.

Sovereignty makes you bald. I was wrong. It appears that sovereignty makes you impotent.

Jacques Parizeau, leader, Parti Québécois, ridiculing the scare tactics of opponents of Quebec separatism, quoted by Robert McKenzie in *The Toronto Star*, 15 Dec. 1991.

The central dilemma in Canada today, the great festering contradiction that has been with us for 125 years, comes down to this: French Canadians aspire to nationhood while English Canadians fear the loss of it.

John Fraser, columnist, "The Last Laugh," *Saturday Night*, March 1992.

Quebec has been encouraged to believe it can have the painless assumption of the benefits of sovereignty without forfeiting the comforts of Confederation.

Conrad Black, publisher, address, Canadian Club of Toronto, 26 Oct. 1992, quoted by Bob Papoe in *The Toronto Star* the next day.

It is so well kept, maybe the best kept nation in the world, and these golden chains make its liberation difficult to achieve.

Maurice Séguin, historian, quoted by Robert Comeau in an interview with Gilles Gougeon in *A History of Quebec Nationalism* (1994) translated by Louisa Blair, Robert Chodos, and Jane Ubertino.

Sovereignty is not worth a single life.

Daniel Latouche, political scientist, quoted by André Picard, "Québécois Voices," *The Globe and Mail*, 30 June 1994.

Quebec has the choice of being equal to British Columbia in a much decentralized Canada, or equal to Angola in the United Nations.

Gordon Gibson, former Member of Parliament, *Thirty Million Musketeers* (1995).

Une caisse de douze.

Daniel Paillé, Quebec Minister of Industry and Commerce, responding at a public meeting to the question about the "cost" of Quebec's independence, quoted by columnist Lysiane Gagnon, as quoted by André Picard in "Québécois Voices,"

The Globe and Mail, 16 Feb. 1995. It translates "a twelve-pack," i.e., a case of twelve beers. Picard observed, "The mathematics of his quip is that transfer payments from Ottawa to Quebec work out to about $600 a person, or $12 a week, the cost of a 12-pack of beer in a Montreal corner store."

What I'd like is a sovereign Quebec in a strong Canada.

Monologue called "The Pride of Being a Quebecker" written and delivered by Quebec comic **Yvon Deschamps**, as quoted by Lysiane Gagnon, "Inside Quebec," *The Globe and Mail,* 11 March 1995.

Péquistan, Québecistan

Derisive names for an independent Quebec, derived from Péquiste (a member of the Parti Québécois) and the Islamic Republic of Pakistan, Sept. 1995.

We, the people of Quebec, declare that we are free to choose our future. / We, the people of Quebec, through the voice of our National Assembly, proclaim: Quebec is a sovereign country.

Text of the Preamble to the Declaration of Sovereignty Bill, written by a committee consisting of singer **Gilles Vigneault**, playwright **Marie Laberge**, sociologist **Fernand Dumont**, and constitutional-law specialists **Andrée Lajoie** and **Henri Brun**. The document was released at the Grand Theatre, Quebec City, 6 Sept. 1995. The text was tabled in the National Assembly, 7 Sept. 1995, and published in *The Toronto Star* that day.

I know many Haitians who are sovereigntists... but I have never met a Jamaican who was a sovereigntist.

Jacques Parizeau, former Quebec Premier, address, Upper Canada College, Toronto, 18 Feb. 1997, suggesting it was not "money and the ethnic vote" that defeated the 2nd Quebec Referendum on Sovereignty but "language," "Parizeau Comments Attacked," *The Globe and Mail,* 20 Feb. 1997.

I'm convinced that this will happen by the end of my mandate.

Lucien Bouchard, Quebec Premier, expressing his belief that Quebec will be a sovereign country within four years (presumably by the year 2003), television interview, Quebec City, 18 Nov. 1999, quoted by Robert McKenzie in *The Toronto Star* the following day.

SOVEREIGNTY-ASSOCIATION See also PARTITION, QUEBEC, REFERENDA, SOVEREIGNTY

These people are, to adapt a delightful phrase of the late M. Duplessis, "separatists without knowing it." They do not want separation, but they do want things which can be got only by separation. They are asking for dry water, boiling ice, sour sugar, stationary motion.

Eugene Forsey, constitutional authority, on special constitutional status for Quebec, "Concepts of Federalism: Some Canadian Aspects," *Concepts of Federalism* (1965) edited by Gordon Hawkins.

What we intend to bring about, if people agree in a referendum and give us the bargaining power for it, is independence and association.

René Lévesque, Quebec Premier, quoted by Richard Simon in his introduction to *Must Canada Fail?* (1977).

The Péquistes have started a ping-pong game with two words: Sovereignty-association. In combination, the two words have no meaning, but they preoccupy editorial writers and baffle everyone, even Anglo-Saxons, while the government prepares to get re-elected.

Roger Lemelin, writer and publisher, address, Canadian Press, annual dinner, 2 May 1979, quoted in *The Toronto Star,* 4 May 1979.

The phrase sovereignty-association has two elements meaning "independent" and "connected," and thus it is a thumbnail description of the human condition itself.

Jane Jacobs, urban commentator, *The Question of Separatism: Quebec and the Struggle over Sovereignty* (1980).

The chances are that Quebec would be worse off, economically and in other ways, if it were to become an independent country; and the chances are that most Quebeckers sense it. That is why so many separatists, who tend to be an intellectual elite, like to talk of "sovereignty-association," a weasel expression designed to persuade Quebeckers that they can have their gâteau and eat it.

Editorial feature, "Survey on Canada," *The Economist,* 19 June 1991, reprinted in *The Globe and Mail,* 19 July 1991.

Abjuring sovereignty or sovereignty-association (the latter an oxymoron if there ever was one), they will probably settle for something called renewed federalism, whereby Ottawa will surrender still more of its powers to Quebec.

Mordecai Richler, journalist and author, "A Reporter at Large: Inside/Outside," *The New Yorker,* 23 Sept. 1991.

Le Quebec, ma patrie. Le Canada, mon pays. "Quebec is my homeland. Canada is my country."

Paradoxical statement of the Quebec dilemma, according to **Lysiane Gagnon** in *The Globe and Mail,* 4 April 1992.

SOVIET UNION See also COMMUNISM, RUSSIAN PEOPLE

Certainly, over the portals of Russia should be inscribed "Abandon Old Conceptions All Ye Who Enter Here."

Norman Bethune, physician, surgeon, and revolutionary, "Reflections on Return from 'Through the Looking Glass,'" Montreal address, 20 Dec. 1935, quoted by Roderick Stewart in *The Mind of Norman Bethune* (1977).

The great power of the future promises to be not the United States or Great Britain, but Russia; and the problem of the future is how to live with her on the best terms.

A.L. Burt, historian, letter dated 27 April 1944, quoted by Lewis H. Thomas in *The Renaissance of Canadian History: A Biography of A.L. Burt* (1975).

I am Mr. Brown to everybody, including my children.

Igor Gouzenko, Soviet defector in Ottawa in 1945, explaining his assumed name and identity, noted by Frank R. Joubin in *Not for Gold Alone: The Memoirs of a Prospector* (1986) written with D. McCormack Smyth.

This must be credited as a merit of the Soviet regime: its police character has been brought to a height of perfection.

Ironic observation made in **Igor Gouzenko**'s novel *The Fall of a Titan* (1954) translated from the Russian by Mervyn Black.

Just because Joe Stalin says that two and two are four, I am not going to stop saying the same thing.

James G. Endicott, peace activist, quoted in *The Prince Albert News Herald,* 2 March 1949, as noted by Stephen Endicott in *James G. Endicott: Rebel Out of China* (1980).

You know, it's an awesome responsibility to have to ask yourself each day, "What will Khruschev do?"

John G. Diefenbaker, Prime Minister, speech, St. John's, Nfld., 16 March 1963.

It is our belief that our two countries, as neighbours who often come up against similar problems, could do much in the present conditions to improve the international climate. The joint struggle waged by our peoples in the years of the Second World War against the common enemy—Hitler's Germany—is vivid proof that we have good reason for feeling this way.

Andrei Gromyko, Soviet Minister of Foreign Affairs, address, Ottawa, Oct. 1969, quoted by V. Makhotin in *USSR-Canada: Good-Neighbourly Co-operation* (1974), a booklet issued by the Novosti Press Agency Publishing House, Moscow.

Do you realize that you live in *paradise?* No country in the world has the luck and the opportunities that you have here.

Mrs. Andrei Gromyko, wife of the Soviet Minister of Foreign Affairs, addressing Margaret Trudeau on a visit to 24 Sussex Drive, quoted by Trudeau in *Beyond Reason* (1979).

The price of a can of Coca-Cola at the Mirabel airport vending machine equals one-tenth of our regular monthly salary—yes, sir!

Arkadi Tcherkassov, Russian geographer, "Our Man in Moscow," *Grainews,* June 1992.

We will be your students.

Boris Yeltsin, Russian leader, referring to democracy and prosperity in Canada with respect to their absence in the former Soviet Union, address, joint sitting of the Senate and the House of Commons, Ottawa, 19 June 1992, quoted by Warren Caragata in *The Toronto Star* the following day.

SPACE See also ASTRONOMY, UNIVERSE

You must understand that we're here / to emulsify the stars / and level the protons out through space / Do you think we're not also on Mars?

Lines from **Earle Birney**'s poem "Remarks Decoded from Outer Space" (1945), *The Collected Poems of Earle Birney* (1975).

Air Canada says it has accepted 2,300 reservations for flights to the Moon in the past five days. It might be noted that more than one hundred have been made by men for their mothers-in-law.

News briefing from **NASA's Mission Control Centre** at Houston, Texas, to the Apollo 11 mission to the Moon, shortly before splashdown, 24 July 1969, quoted by Gene Farmer and Dora Jane Hamblin in *First on the Moon* (1970).

Our ultimate destiny—or at least a very attractive ultimate destiny—is for humanity to solve all its own problems, and become an island of highly developed and sophisticated matter that contacts other such islands.

Jon Lomberg, space artist, quoted by Robin Snelson in *Future Life*, Feb. 1980.

We are the first generation to have seen our planet under the gaze of eternity, not from this mountain top or that city tower, but from an astronaut's window, revolving mist-wrapped in the cobalt darkness of space. We are the first generation to have lived under the shared threat of ecological and nuclear catastrophe. Progress, the passage from savagery to civilization, now conveys us towards apocalypse, the end of time.

Michael Ignatieff, essayist, *The Needs of Strangers* (1985).

Dear God, we have infected the very stars with our fears and hatreds.

Rudy Wiebe, novelist, referring specifically to missiles and satellites illuminated in the night sky of the North, *Playing Dead: A Contemplation Concerning the Arctic* (1989).

The world is united under the gaze of the satellite, much as it was under the scare of the bomb.

Derrick de Kerckhove, communications theorist, "From Bureaucracy to Telecracy," *McLuhan Studies*, Volume I, 1992.

Winter or no winter... it's absolutely beautiful and spectacular. There is absolutely nothing boring. There is no boring place anywhere on the planet.

Roberta Bondar, astronaut, describing the appearance of "the blue planet" from Space Shuttle *Discovery*, orbiting the Earth, conversation with Prime Minister Mulroney, 28 Jan. 1992, quoted by Stephen Strauss in *The Globe and Mail* the following day. The *Discovery* was in Earth orbit from 22–30 Jan. 1999.

As we orbited over Canada, my crewmates joked, "We're going over Canada—boring. It's snowbound and inhospitable." But the snow brought out the beauty. It gave it different dimensions. The rivers were clear because of the ice. The first time we passed over, I was playing a tape of *O Canada* sung by a policeman in the Soo.

Roberta Bondar, astronaut aboard the Space Shuttle *Discovery*, 22–30 Jan. 1992, *Maclean's*, 24 Feb. 1992.

There is a place in space for Canada.

Stephen MacLean, astronaut aboard the Space Shuttle *Discovery*, interviewed in Houston, Texas, by Michael Smith in *The Toronto Star*, 30 Oct. 1992.

It may be that humans of the future will have a choice between living with gravity or living without it.

Lydia Dotto, science writer, *The Astronauts: Canada's Voyageurs in Space* (1993).

Who can say whether, in the planetary entourage of the Star Bêta Pictoris, hominoids may not be the guinea pigs of guinea pigs? Perhaps, in the neighbourhood of Capella, rats show them off in their traveling circuses.

Hubert Reeves, astrophysicist, *Malicorne: Earthly Reflections of an Astrophysicist* (1993) translated from the French edition of 1990 by Donald Winkler.

I'm really looking forward to trying to get a good photograph of the arm with Canada written there on it in big print with some recognizable part of the country down underneath.

Chris Hadfield, astronaut, scheduled to operate the Remote Manipulator Arm (Canadarm) aboard the Space Shuttle *Atlantis*, quoted by

Joseph Hall, "Canadian in Space Gets Window Seat," *The Toronto Star*, 5 Nov. 1995.

There are more ants / than people / on this planet— // it's the anthill of the Milky Way

Lines from **Nelson Ball**'s poem "Anthill," *The Concrete Air* (1996).

The reason we are going into outer space is to explore inner space.

*

Why not be part of something magnificent?

David Williams, physician and astronaut, anticipating the first space flight to the planet Mars, CBC-TV's *The National*, 15 April 1998.

Twenty-four hours before launch date and here stood the very orbiter I will ride to space or to oblivion. But ride the mighty rocket, ride I will.

Julie Payette, Canadian-born astronaut, text of an e-mail message sent to her sister Maude Payette the day before her scheduled flight into space aboard the Space Shuttle *Discovery*, launched 27 May 1999, quoted in *Maclean's*, 17 May 1999.

Ad finem ultimum

Motto of the **Canadian Space Agency / Agence Spatiale**, based in Montreal, from its coat of arms, as noted by Jennifer Hunter, *Maclean's*, 24 Jan. 2000. The Latin inscription translates "Towards the final frontier," a possible allusion to the motto of the starship *Enterprise* on TV's *Star Trek*.

SPANISH CIVIL WAR See also SPANISH PEOPLE, WAR

It ought to be plain to democratic countries what we're up against now, for the conflict is a straight fight between fascism and democracy.

Norman Bethune, physician and revolutionary, interviewed in Toronto in June 1937, reprinted in *The Toronto Star*, 13 Sept. 1992.

To that pale disc we raise our clenched fists, / And to those nameless dead our vows renew, / "Comrades, who fought for freedom and the future world, / Who died for us, we will remember you."

Last of three verses of **Norman Bethune**'s poem "Red Moon," *The Canadian Forum*, July 1937.

SPANISH PEOPLE See also SPANISH CIVIL WAR

It was dawn for Britain but twilight for Spain.

Wording on an official plaque, Spanish Banks, Vancouver. On 22 June 1792, Captain George Vancouver parlayed with Captains Galiano and Valdez and accepted Spain's surrender of the Northwest Coast.

By the start of the third millennium, Spanish, not French, will be the second language in Canada.

Frank Ogden, futurologist, characteristic remark, made in 1985.

SPEECH & SPEECHES See also LANGUAGE

If you have anything to tell me of importance, for God's sake begin at the end.

Line from **Sara Jeannette Duncan**'s novel *The Imperialist* (1904).

No hoock, no spooch.

Stephen Leacock, humorist, message telegraphed to organizers of a speech in Buffalo, N.Y., when Leacock was stopped at the border by a customs officer who relieved him of his flask, recalled by Allan Anderson in *Remembering Leacock* (1983).

Talking is an art—or perhaps I should say, good talking is an art.

Neil M. Morrison, supervisor of talks on CBC Radio from 1943 to 1954, *CBC News*, 6 Feb. 1949.

Before I speak, I want to say something.

Attributed to Créditiste leader **Réal Caouette**, prefacing a political speech, Magog, Que., in the 1960s.

It's no good looking like an Eskimo if you can't speak like one.

Abraham Okpik, Inuit elder, "What Does It Mean to Be an Eskimo?" *North*, March–April 1963.

The length of a speech does not matter. A ten-minute speech can be too long, and a week-long speech can be short.

Stanley Knowles, Member of Parliament, commenting on the NDP filibuster, House of Commons, 9 Feb. 1977.

There is nothing more exterior than writing. The moment it is done it is forever outside.

There is nothing more interior than speech, than the body's saying.

George Bowering, poet and author, Introduction, *Fred Wah's Selected Poems: Loki Is Buried at Smoky Creek* (1980).

He had that flat Canadian accent, like a file on soft metal.

Description of the speech of an Indian from Campbell River, B.C., adrift in Seattle, Wash., in **A.E. Maxwell**'s detective novel *The King of Nothing* (1992).

Today's speeches are written for the fifteen-second clip. The rest is fill.

Bill Neville, political adviser, quoted by Charlotte Gray in *Saturday Night*, March 1992.

Canadians are noticeably inclined to turn a statement into a question by means of a rising intonation: this expresses hope that there are no objections, and simultaneously requests a sign from the listener that the statement has been understood.

Margaret Visser, social commentator, "'I Mean, You Know, Like . . . '," *The Way We Are* (1994).

Good English is that spoken by the reasonably educated people in one's specific geographical location.

W.H. Brodie, supervisor of Broadcast Language, CBC from 1940s to 1960s, as recalled by broadcaster Max Ferguson, correspondence, 3 April 1996.

If you accept the accent, you accept the person.

Jehane Benoît, cooking authority, quoted by Bee McGuire in *Today*, 12 April 1980.

Strange as it may seem, what human beings fear more than death is public speaking!

Peter Urs Bender, motivational speaker, *Secrets of Power Presentations* (6th edition, 1991).

The Canadian voice strikes the untuned English ear as so distinctively "American" that the British take little care to distinguish their Commonwealth fellow citizens from those of the Great Republic to the south.

John Keegan, British historian, *Travels of a Military Historian in North America* (1995).

The best way to save face is to keep the bottom part of it shut.

Jeffrey Simpson, columnist, quoting an adage, "Verbatim," *The Globe and Mail*, 18 April 1996.

I have now been waiting two hours to give my address to you. . . . It is Box 519, High River, Alberta, and I am going there right now.

W.O. Mitchell, raconteur, after waiting to address an audience on the Prairies, *An Evening with W.O. Mitchell: A Collection of the Author's Best Loved Performance Pieces* (1997) edited by Barbara and Armond Mitchell.

SPEED

If you are moving at the speed of light, you are already there.

Marshall McLuhan, communications pioneer, Montreal International Book Fair, quoted by Christie McCormick in *The Montreal Gazette*, 16 May 1975.

SPIRIT See also SPIRIT, NATIONAL

Our world needs a soul, it needs a spirit. . . . Our world has an urgent need for a *spiritual élite*.

Georges P. Vanier, future Governor General, address to the Institut Catholique, Paris, 26 Nov. 1952, quoted by Jean Vanier in his book *In Weakness, Strength* (1971).

The world has always had its doom criers, calamity howlers and pedlars of pessimism and now they are in full cry. But the human race is invincible and always has been. Deep down in the human spirit there is something eternal and you and I are part of it.

Gordon Sinclair, broadcaster and author, *Will Gordon Sinclair Please Sit Down* (1975).

SPIRIT, NATIONAL See also SPIRIT

A wise nation preserves its records, gathers up its muniments, decorates the tombs of its illustrious dead, repairs its great public structures, and fosters national pride and love of country, by perpetual references to the sacrifices and glories of the past.

Joseph Howe, publisher and statesman, address, Framingham, Mass., Aug. 31, *Poems and Essays* (1874).

The immense size and progress of this country impresses itself upon one more every day.

The Canadian National Spirit and personality is becoming so powerful and self-contained that I do not think we need fear the future.

Winston Churchill, English statesman, address, Ottawa, August 1929, quoted by Alexander Rose, "Winston's Great Canadian Love Affair," *National Post*, 1 May 1999.

No Canadian has ever been known to sell his mother but we provide collective testimony to the existence of a country ever ready to peddle the dreams of its forefathers.

John Meisel, political scientist, address, Unity Conference, Ottawa, *The Toronto Star*, 15 Oct. 1977.

It may be that out of the loneliness of a vast land can come a strengthening of a man's spirit, making him feel he is really something in himself.

Morley Callaghan, novelist, "Canada," *The Toronto Star*, 1 July 1978.

Surely no other country on earth has so much variety. Surely no other land can be so beautiful and yet, at times, so cantankerous. So generous to the human spirit and yet, without warning, so cruel.

Barry Broadfoot, oral historian, Foreword, *The Beauty of Canada* (1978), a collection of photographs by Lorne Edmond Green.

SPIRITS See also ANGELS, BELIEF, SPIRITUALISM

Brownies, like fairies and goblins, are imaginary little sprites, who are supposed to delight in harmless pranks and helpful deeds. They work and sport while weary households sleep, and never allow themselves to be seen by mortal eyes.

Palmer Cox, artist, Editorial Note, *The Brownies: Their Book* (1887). This was the first of thirteen volumes of early comic art involving the elf-like Brownies drawn by Palmer Cox who lived in Granby, Que.

It seems to me that with fuller knowledge and with fresh means of vision these people are destined to become just as solid and real as the Eskimos.

Sir Arthur Conan Doyle, novelist and spiritualist, writing about "little people" in photographs known as the Cottingley Fairies, *The Coming of the Fairies* (1922).

Spirits can assist the shaman not only in foretelling but in changing the future.

David E. Young, **Grant C. Ingram**, and **Lise Swartz**, anthropologists, referring to the belief and practice of Cree healer Russell Willier, *Cry of the Eagle: Encounters with a Cree Healer* (1989).

Humanity has always been attended by invisible beings.

Joe Fisher, journalist and psychic, *Hungry Ghosts* (1990).

SPIRITUALISM See also BELIEF, SPIRITS

Here, Mr. Split-foot, do as I do.

Maggie Fox, pioneer medium, snapping her fingers two or three times and being answered by the same number of raps, Hydesville, New York, 31 March 1848, quoted by R.G. Pressing in *Rappings that Startled the World* (Lily Dale, 1940s). These "spirit-rappings" at the hands of Maggie and Katie Fox, born at Consecon, Canada East (Ontario), launched the movement of Modern Spiritualism.

If spiritualism were true, what a fate to look forward to, every dunce and adventurer having a right to put questions to you, for which in other days you would have knocked him down!

George Brown, editor and publisher, referring to the practices of mediums and the vogue for "table-rapping," "Spiritualism," *The Daily Globe* (Toronto), 28 Nov. 1873.

The credit on the playscript reads: "By Patricia Joudry. Transmitted by the spirits of Willa Cather and George Bernard Shaw." Willa had had a finger in it, and my messages from Shaw stated that he wanted billing for her.

Patricia Joudry, playwright and medium, *Spirit River to Angels' Roost: Religions I Have Loved and Left* (1977). The credit line appeared on an unproduced and unpublished dramatic play titled *Years of Your Father,* which was "dictated to" Joudry in England in the 1960s.

SPIRITUALITY See also BELIEF

Cutting through Spiritual Materialism

Title of a widely read book published in 1973 by **Chogyam Trungpa Rinpoche**, Tibetan Buddhist missionary in the West, who established his international headquarters in Halifax prior to his death there on 4 April 1987.

If a visitor to Canada were to ask me where the holiest of holy places of this country were to be found, I would be quick to respond that there are but three. One is the line of silent stone figures marching along the ridges that mark ancient shorelines of Pleistocene seas at Eskimo Point in the Northwest Territories. A second is the sculpture in glowing yellow cedar of "The Raven and the First Men," by Bill Reid, the Haida master carver, at the Museum of Anthropology at U.B.C. Last, but most impressive of all, is the village of Ninstints at daybreak when the raven's cry once more brings the world into being.

George F. MacDonald, archaeologist, Preface, *Ninstints: Haida World Heritage Site* (1983).

The people with the fewest material goods are often those with the richest spiritual values... People with the least wealth are often the most generous and hospitable.

Peter Worthington, correspondent, *Looking for Trouble: A Journalist's Life... and Then Some* (1984).

Secularism today simply implies a generalized silence in culture about the whole category of man's spiritual needs.

Michael Ignatieff, essayist, *The Needs of Strangers* (1985).

Geographically, Canada is a very vast country, and spiritually, she can become extremely fertile.

Sri Chinmoy, Hindu spiritual leader who lectured at sixteen Canadian universities, *My Maple Tree: An Indian Spiritual Master Shares His Light with the Awakened Soul of Canada* (1977).

And there, at Huronia, occurred perhaps the most interesting encounter: Christian liturgy of the Word intertwined with the rituals of the original religion of the Canadian Indians. It was a pilgrimage to the beginnings: Christianity in Canada was planted in soil already prepared by the traditional religiosity of the Huron and other Indian and Inuit tribes.

John Paul II, Pontiff, sermon, Midland, Ont., quoted by George Radwanski in *The Toronto Star*, 20 Oct. 1984.

All I have learned is that enlightenment won't do me any good. The perceiving ego won't feel any of it.

Tim Ward, journalist, student of Buddhism in a monastery in Northern Thailand, *What the Buddha Never Taught* (1990).

I do not know what "enlightenment" is. I still get tired, catch colds and argue with my children about cleaning their room and eating their dinner. But my life has changed and I wake up most mornings eager to see how the adventure will unfold, knowing I have the energy, strength and humour to meet it with enthusiasm.

Oriah Mountain Dreamer, Native teacher, *Confessions of a Spiritual Thrillseeker: Medicine Teachings from the Grandmothers* (1991).

Most Canadian executives' idea of spirituality these days is to pray every night that they'll have a job the next morning.

Peter C. Newman, columnist, "Business Watch," *Maclean's*, 12 April 1993.

My spiritual and physical life are completely entwined with the garden. It's a nourishing wellspring of energy and strength. It impels me on into the future. It is here I do my worshipping.

Marjorie Harris, writer and gardener, *The Healing Garden* (1996).

SPORTS

See also ATHLETES, AUTOMOBILE RACING, BASEBALL, BASKETBALL, BOXING, CURLING, CYCLING, FISH & FISHING, FOOTBALL, GOLF, HOCKEY, HORSES & HORSE RACING, LACROSSE, OLYMPIC GAMES, RUNNING, SHIPS & SAILING, SKATING, SKIING, SOCCER, SWIMMING, TENNIS, TOBOGANNING, WALKING, WEIGHTLIFTING, WRESTLING

Eleven men can put on white flannel trousers and call themselves a cricket team, on which an entirely new set of obligations, almost a new set of personalities, are wrapped about them. Women could never be a team of anything.

Stephen Leacock, humorist, "The Woman Question," *Essays and Literary Studies* (1916).

My definition of a pro is a guy who plays even when he's hurting.

Attributed to football player **Angelo Mosca** who retired from the Hamilton Tiger Cats in 1972.

Fables endure in sport as though carved in marble. Like heirlooms they come down through generations, with old men deceiving themselves with falsehoods of their own creation, which are repeated by kids.

Dick Beddoes, sports columnist, *The Globe and Mail*, April 1973.

Whatever you do, whatever you endeavour, have fun.

Michael Francis (King) Clancy, hockey personality, advice at a dinner in his honour, Royal York Hotel, Toronto, quoted by Dick Beddoes in *The Globe and Mail*, 18 March 1975.

The trouble with many sports figures is that anything less than a puff is a knife.

Trent Frayne, sports columnist, referring to reporting and profiling, *The Canadian*, 29 Jan. 1977.

Little leagues too often make little men out of little boys.

Dick Beddoes, sports personality, addressing the overemphasis on winning in children's sports, TVO's *Speaking Out*, 1978.

When that one great scorekeeper comes to write your name, it's not whether you won or lost, but how many paid to get into the game.

Attributed to sports personality **Herb Capozzi** according to Vancouver promoter Thomas Butler as quoted in *The Globe and Mail*, 4 Aug. 1979.

It doesn't matter who wins. If the game is good, we all win.

Characteristic remark of the sports personality **Dick Beddoes**, recalled at his memorial service, Toronto, 24 Aug. 1991.

Sport is a great way to build confidence and it's made me realize that when you work hard at something, anything can happen.

Silken Laumann, champion rower, quoted by Scott Taylor in the *Winnipeg Free Press*, 9 Aug. 1992.

A nation of young people is a society of hockey and tennis players. A nation of older people is a society of gardeners and walkers.

David K. Foot and **Daniel Stoffman**, demographer and journalist, *Boom, Bust & Echo: How to Profit from the Coming Demographic Shift* (1996).

Rowing is so dumb that it's won by the team that can go *backwards* the fastest. It's the only racing sport in which the winner can see the losers.

Sam Orbaum, Montreal-raised Israeli columnist, "But Seriously," *The Jerusalem Post Magazine*, 26 July 1996.

I have decided I am finally growing up. I am losing interest in sport. This must be a sign of maturity.

Allan Fotheringham, columnist, *Maclean's*, 27 Oct. 1997.

SPRING See also SEASONS

The Canadian springtime is the most invigorating and powerful in the world / Beneath the thick blanket of snow and ice / Suddenly / Generous nature

Lines from French traveller and writer **Blaise Cendrars**' poem "The North" (1924), *Blaise Cendrars: Complete Poems* (1992) translated by Ron Padgett.

A great many people are wholly unaware that the soft, sweet musical thrill they can hear among the other night sounds of early spring is the love song of the warty toad.

Greg Clark, newspaperman, quoted by Barry Conn Hughes in *The City*, 18 March 1979.

SRI LANKA

Saviour of Ceylon

Sobriquet of **Leonard Birchall**, Canadian airman aboard a Catalina flying boat, making its first reconnaissance flight out of Ceylon (as Sri Lanka was then called), 4 April 1942, who radioed information about a Japanese fleet streaming toward the South Asian island for a surprise attack, as noted by Peter Goodspeed in *The Toronto Star*, 13 Aug. 1994.

You must be surrounded by Sri Lankans—I call Don Mills "Sri Lanka West."

Arthur C. Clarke, scientist and science-fiction author, long-time resident of Colombo, Sri Lanka, letter to John Robert Colombo, resident of Toronto, 21 April 1997.

STANDARDS

The nice thing about standards is there are so many to choose from.

Attributed to **Matthew Fox**, member of the construction industry, by editor Roger Burford Mason, Jan. 1998.

STATESMANSHIP

A statesman has been defined as "a politician held upright by equal pressures from all sides."

Ed Finn, commentator, *The Toronto Star*, 1 Sept. 1975.

A statesman is a man who can solve great problems which wouldn't exist if there were no statesmen.

John G. Diefenbaker, former Prime Minister, lines written in the scrapbook of Gary Lautens, quoted in Diefenbaker's obituary, *The Toronto Star*, 17 Aug. 1979.

No comments on politics. I'm a statesman now.

Attributed to former Prime Minister **Brian Mulroney** when asked for his reactions to the federal leadership debate, "Briefly Noted," *The Globe and Mail*, 15 May 1997.

STATISTICS

Statistical tables are like skeletons. Perhaps that is the reason so many people view them with awe.

John Porter, sociologist, *Canadian Social Structure: A Statistical Profile* (1967).

Just as the journalist has ousted the serious writer of poetry and fiction, the statistician is replacing the statesman.

Irving Layton, poet and aphorist, *The Whole Bloody Bird (obs, aphs & Pomes)* (1969).

Some people use statistics as a drunk uses a lamp post—for support rather than illumination.

Marshall McLuhan, communications pioneer, quoted by Richard J. Schoeck in *Who Was Marshall McLuhan?* (1994) edited by Barrington Nevitt and Maurice McLuhan.

STOCK MARKET See also FINANCE, MONEY

There will be 100 pages dealing with the social structure of the city of Toronto, which is in fact a vast mining camp.... When the mines are booming, the Ontario stock-exchange is a bull market, it blooms and flourishes, and Montreal declines. It is vice-versa, too, of course.

Wyndham Lewis, British artist, "Hill 100: Outline for an Unwritten Novel" (1942), *Wyndham Lewis in Canada* (1971) edited by George Woodcock.

Scam Capital of the World

Title of an article critical of the Vancouver Stock Exchange written by journalist **Joe Queenan** and published in *Forbes*, 29 May 1989. The feisty author wrote, "The VSE, founded in 1907, is the longest-standing joke in North America, the Cubs included." He concluded: "There isn't much gold in Vancouver, but there's still plenty of brass."

Stock market, n. A den of equities, where the person who manages to look smart for more than ten minutes probably deserves his reputation for sagacity.

David Olive, business commentator, *White Knights and Poison Pills: A Cynic's Dictionary of Business Jargon* (1990).

A further rule is that when a mood of excitement pervades a market or surrounds an investment prospect, when there is a claim of unique opportunity based on special foresight, all sensible people should circle the wagons; it is the time for caution.

John Kenneth Galbraith, economist and essayist, *A Short History of Financial Euphoria* (1990, 1993).

You have to know what you *don't* know when you play the stock market.

Alexander Tadich, stock trader and writer, *Rampaging Bulls: Outfox Promoters at Their Own Game on Any Penny Stock Market* (1992).

In the end, we are all speculators. You can quote me.

Alexander Tadich, stock trader and writer, *Rampaging Bulls: Outfox Promoters at Their Own Game on Any Penny Stock Market* (1992).

Insider trading would stop cold if we hanged a half-dozen culprits at the corner of King and Bay. (Well, maybe two dozen in Vancouver.)

H.S. Bhabra, novelist, "Progressive Culling," *The Globe and Mail*, 20 Sept., 1994.

STORIES See also FICTION, LEGENDS, LITERATURE

Nothing is more essential to our lives than stories—the only things of equal importance are food, shelter, human love and some kind of religious activity.

Hugh Hood, novelist, quoted by John Metcalf in *Sixteen by Twelve* (1970).

One may read a book alone (in fact most of us prefer that) but one cannot tell a story alone, which is why any language changes so drastically when it moves from oral to written form.

Rudy Wiebe, novelist, *Playing Dead: A Contemplation Concerning the Arctic* (1989).

I suppose history has taught me this: every person has an individual story. The stories have similar patterns, but each is unique and particular.... One of the beautiful things about telling stories is that you never tell them completely.

Rudy Wiebe, novelist, interviewed by Linda Hutcheon in *Other Solitudes: Canadian Multicultural Fictions* (1990) edited by Linda Hutcheon and Marion Richmond.

Stories are memories / that must be shared with the Universe;, / because if they aren't / the Universe becomes a much smaller place.

Drew Hayden Taylor, dramatist, epigram, *Toronto at Dreamer's Rock* (1990).

In our community everybody is a storyteller, but not everybody would choose that as an occupation.

*

I don't believe that those stories should be recorded by anybody except us. I don't think that you have any right to come into my community and tell my stories for me. I can speak for myself. I share them with you, and you can read them. And if you come into my circle, and I tell you the stories, then you should respect that you're invited into the circle.

Maria Campbell, Métis storyteller and writer, interviewed by Hartmut Lutz in *Contemporary Challenges: Conversations with Canadian Native Authors* (1991).

The people who have control of your stories, control of your voice, also have control of your destiny, your culture.

Lenore Keeshig-Tobias, Ojibway storyteller and writer, interviewed by Hartmut Lutz in *Contemporary Challenges: Conversations with Canadian Native Authors* (1991).

An ancient metaphor: thought is a thread, and the raconteur is a spinner of yarns—but the true storyteller, the poet, is a weaver.

Robert Bringhurst, author and typographer, *The Elements of Typographic Style* (1992, 2nd ed., 1996).

It is as if the opening words of both St. John and Genesis were/are: "In the beginning was the story."

James Reaney, poet, "'Cutting Up Didoes,'" *University of Toronto Quarterly*, Spring 1992.

A tale told in Avenue Road entered western memory.

Edmund Carpenter, anthropologist, "Remembering Explorations," *Canadian Notes & Queries*, Spring 1992. Walking on Toronto's Avenue Road in the 1950s, Carpenter learned the story of the Elephant Man from the scientist Ashley Montague; fifteen years later, Carpenter told the story to an editor in New York who drew it to the attention of the playwright Bernard Pomerance who wrote the stage play *The Elephant Man* on which was based the film.

Five hundred and fifty generations have lived here. Only the stories we tell each other will create us as a true Canadian people.

Rudy Wiebe, novelist, acceptance speech, Governor General's Awards, Montreal, 15 Nov. 1994, quoted by Ray Conlogue in *The Globe and Mail* the following day.

We generate stories for you because you don't save the ones that are yours.

Observation from **Douglas Coupland**'s novel *Microserfs* (1995).

I know of no culture which does not tell stories, and the core stories of every culture partake of the sacred. We cannot speak our most profound thoughts, but through stories we can show them in action and when we do, they move hearts and consciences as well as minds.

Silver Donald Cameron, columnist, *The Halifax Herald*, 17 May 1998.

Stories are central to the life of every people. On the other hand, no people or community or nation, and especially no political authority, can have exclusive rights to interpret its own history. We know too well what happens when they try.

Robert Bringhurst, poet and translator of Haida stories, "Since When Has Culture Been about Genetics," *The Globe and Mail*, 22 Nov. 1999.

STRATEGY

Well, my strategy has always been to stay on course unless a change of course, is announced. And if it is, of course, we will announce it.

Attributed to Prime Minister **John Turner** by Diane Francis, "The Insiders," *The Toronto Star*, July 1984.

STRATFORD FESTIVAL See also PLACES: COMMUNITIES; THEATRE

I am intensely interested to produce Shakespeare on a stage which might produce the actor-audience relation for which he wrote—viz., the audience closely racked ROUND the actors.... I assume that at Stratford, Ont., the stage and the audience are still to be made, and if I could influence their design I would be very happy to do so.

Tyrone Guthrie, British theatre director, letter to Dora Mavor Moore, 11 May 1952, accepting an invitation to visit Stratford, Ont., to explore the possibility of establishing a Shakespearian stage there, a concept he entertained in the 1940s, published in *The Toronto Star*, 17 May 1971.

The Presbyterians aren't speaking to the Anglicans and the Anglicans were snubbing the Catholics. By the time the festival opened, the Baptists were offering flowers to the Anglicans and the Presbyterians were buying bottles of Scotch for the [Tyrone] Guthries... but it wasn't bought locally. The Presbyterians went to Hamilton.

Sir Alec Guinness, British actor, recalling his experiences in the Ontario city that sponsored the Stratford Shakespearian Festival in 1953, quoted by Herbert Whittaker in *The Globe and Mail*, 10 May 1977.

The only thing that can seriously and permanently weaken the Festival is a failure of the courageous and high-minded impulse which originally set it going. That would be failure indeed, and the whole marrow of the organization would be diseased by it.

Robertson Davies, man-of-letters, Introduction, *The Fourth Annual Festival of Drama* (Festival Program, 1956).

For Canada itself, the Charlottetown Festival is already of greater value than the one in Stratford.

Nathan Cohen, critic, quoted by Mavor Moore in *Maclean's*, 4 June 1966. The Stratford Shakespearian Festival opened in Stratford in 1953; the Charlottetown Festival was founded in Charlottetown in 1965.

Blow winds and crack your cheeks... Canada: 6, Russia: 5!

William Hutt, actor, introducing the score during the final game in the 1972 Canada-U.S.S.R. hockey series during the heath scene of a production of *King Lear* for students at the Stratford Festival, as noted by Keith Garebian in *William Hutt: A Theatre Portrait* (1989). "Realizing what the Lear had just announced, the students released a thunderous ovation. They cheered and screamed, and stamped their feet.... Finally realizing that the play was continuing, the audience settled down and was remarkably alert for the remainder of the show."

He inspired—and demanded—absolute loyalty. "Robin is a genius" became the opening remark of Festival people to visitors from the outside world, and this became a standing joke among sceptical non-members of the faith.

Martin Knelman, journalist, referring to the Stratford Festival's brilliant artistic director Robin Philips, *A Stratford Tempest* (1982).

Each year the miracle renews: we band of artists are released into the adventure again; to renew the act of faith in the recreation of the spirit of imagination. For it is that unique gift that is ours (our joy and our sorrow too): to delve into the stuff of our lives, and dig up with absolute fidelity and accuracy our happiness, our ecstasy, our pain, our misery, our laughter, our ironies, our intimacies passionate and unidentifiable—hot or icy cold; all unguarded and uncensored, free and truthful—and through the medium of the text, allow the audience to receive the substantiation of our truth into their truth, their reality.

"A Letter to the Company on the First Day of Rehearsals, February 20, 1995," composed by actor **Nicholas Pennell** on his death bed, read to the assembled members of the Stratford Festival, printed in the memorial brochure "A Celebration of the Life of Nicholas Pennell," Festival Theatre, Stratford, Ont., 26 Feb. 1995.

STREET PEOPLE See also POVERTY

Though the boulevards of Paris are the living rooms of the people, the streets of Toronto are the bedrooms of the people.

Pat Capponi, social activist, quoted by Cary Fagan in *City Hall and Mrs. God* (1990).

I hope to see a time of much greater concern for the welfare of others—a time when no one ignores the man or woman sleeping on the sidewalk.

June Callwood, humanitarian, "My Hope for the Future," advertisement for The Tomorrow Fund, *Toronto Life*, Sept. 1996.

STRESS See also RELAXATION

Stress is the state manifested by a specific syndrome which consists of all the nonspecifically induced changes within a biologic system.

Hans Selye, specialist in stress, *The Stress of Life* (1956). A simpler definition also appears in the book: "Stress is essentially the rate of all the wear and tear caused by life." Selye distinguished between good stress, which he termed eustress, and distress, or bad stress.

I wish you love at home, happiness in your work, and success with your stress.

Peter G. Hanson, physician and stress specialist, *Stress for Success: Thriving on Stress at Work* (1989).

STRIKES See also UNIONS

If I have to shed my blood, I would prefer to do it here, where I know it would be for freedom.

Fred J. Dixon, labour representative, anti-conscription rally in 1917, quoted by John Herd Thompson in *The Harvests of War: The Prairie West, 1914–1918* (1978).

You can not salt the eagle's tail, / Nor limit thought's dominion. / You can not put ideas in jail, / You can't deport opinion.

First (and also final) verse of **Edmund Vance Cooke**'s seventeen-verse poem "Sedition" concerning the charges of seditious conspiracy that were brought against leaders of the Winnipeg General Strike, *The Industrial Banner*, 20 March 1920. Reproduced by N. Brian Davis in *The Poetry of the Canadian People, 1720–1920* (1976).

SUBSIDIES

When governments enter the picture, subsidies cannot be far behind.

Charles Lynch, newspaperman, quoted by Hal Herbert in the House of Commons, Ottawa, 8 May 1975.

You can't run a train across the country until the tracks are laid. You can't broadcast a program nationally without a distributing microwave network linking transmission outlets. In publishing you can't sell books until you have the means of distributing them nationally. There seems to be a rule in Canada. Subsidize, but for God's sake don't merchandise.

Harry Boyle, broadcaster and author, address, Books of Our Own Conference, Toronto, 14–15 Oct. 1976, quoted in *Books of Our Own*, Nov. 1976.

Subsidies are the accepted way of redistributing the wealth to those with the most political clout.

James H. Boren, neologist, *Fuzzify! Borenwords and Strategies for Bureaucratic Success* (1982).

SUBURBS

Multiplication by subdivision.

Fred Gardiner, Chairman of Metropolitan Toronto, reference to the growth of subdivisions such as Toronto's Don Mills in the 1950s, noted by Christopher Hume, "Don of an Old Dream," *The Toronto Star*, 5 Dec. 1999.

SUCCESS See also ACHIEVEMENTS, WINNING

Knowles: "Are you satisfied, on the whole, with the life you've had, Miss Arden?"

Arden: "Yes, I am, I believe, honestly, that mine has been a useful life—and that's the real measure of success after all."

Interview with Canadian-born beautician **Elizabeth Arden** conducted in Toronto by **R.E. Knowles**, *The Toronto Star*, 19 Nov. 1938.

My experience has always been that it is the simple things that are usually most successful.

Ed Mirvish, merchandiser and showman, "Foster the Inherent Human Quality," *Probings: A Collection of Essays Contributed to the Canadian Mental Health Association for Its Golden Jubilee 1918–1968* (1968).

Success requires a special quality of mind, not the highest.

Edgar Z. Friedenberg, social scientist, "Class Conflict and Moral Indignation," *The Disposal of Liberty and Other Industrial Wastes* (1975).

The trouble with success is that it is a poor preparation for failure.

Attributed to humorist **Eric Nicol**, Dec. 1976.

Success in this country is like a train; the train comes, it leaves, the sound leaves with it. Suddenly there's silence. Waiting for the next train. Those gaps we create very well in this country. We've got to close the gaps.

Gordon Pinsent, actor and writer, interviewed by Marcia Douglas in *Maclean's*, 15 May 1978.

I'm not mediocre enough to be successful.

Mendelson Joe, artist-composer-performer, born Joe Mendelson, characteristic remark, Dec. 1978.

Where I come from there's a name for people who quit: We call them quitters.

Charlie McKenzie, concierge, Rhinoceros Party of Canada, quoted by Stewart MacLeod in *Maclean's*, 30 March 1992.

Start at the top; ask nothing of others you will not ask of yourself. Go fast; you can't leap a canyon in two jumps. There are no sacred cows. Be honest; don't sugarcoat it. Keep it simple. Communicate from the top. Be prepared to take the heat.

Ralph Klein, Alberta Premier, seven secrets of success, according to Robert Mason Lee, "The West," *The Globe and Mail*, 10 Dec. 1994.

It is easier to fail than succeed because when you fail nobody expects you to succeed.

Larry Solway, veteran broadcaster, maxim, 21 Oct. 1996.

SUFFERING See PAIN & SUFFERING

SUICIDE See also DEATH, EUTHANASIA

One suddenly starts thinking about suicide as the last stage of his or her own inner revolt. Suddenly it seems more dignified to die than to live.

Lines from **Marie-Claire Blais**' novel *Vivre! Vivre!* (1969) as quoted by Claude Janelle in *Citations québécoises modernes* (1976).

Death and taxes—the only inevitabilities. Even taxes may change, but we all face dying at some point. Yet acceptance of one's personal death is mitigated by the experience of continuity with both past and future. Species annihilation, on the other hand, means a relatively swift (on the scale of civilization), deliberately induced end to history, culture, science, biological reproduction, and memory. It is the ultimate human rejection of the gift of life, an act that requires a new word to describe it: *omnicide*. It is difficult to comprehend omnicide, but it may be possible to discern the preparations for it, and prevent its happening.

Rosalie Bertell, nuclear regulatory consultant, "Radioactivity: No Immediate Danger?" *Ms.*, Sept.–Oct. 1991.

It's probably the only way we can give our death a meaning.

Because otherwise it's completely arbitrary.

David Cronenberg, film director, referring to suicide, interview, *Rolling Stone*, 6 Feb. 1992.

The suicide rate in Canada is twice the murder rate.

John Hofsess, founder of Right to Die, Victoria, observation, April 1992.

Who owns my life?

Question associated with **Sue Rodriguez**, Lou Gehrig's disease sufferer, quoted by Deborah Wilson in *The Globe and Mail*, 20 May 1993. Rodriguez appealed to the Supreme Court of Canada to create a constitutional exemption to the provision of the Criminal Code that requires the criminal prosecution of anyone, physician or otherwise, who might assist her in her death. Her appeal was denied.

Please, my near and dear ones, forgive me and understand. I hope this potion works. My spirit is already in another country and my body has been a damn nuisance. I have been so fortunate.

Margaret Laurence, novelist, suicide note to family and friends upon taking an overdose, Peterborough, Ont., 5 Jan. 1987, quoted by CP, *The Hamilton Spectator*, 28 July 1997.

I want to say it out loud and clearly: Don't let yourself mistake suicide—or suicidal thinking—for some kind of summary of a life. It's not. It's a lonely, private, furious moment that sometimes gets acted upon. But it's a moment of illness; it really isn't a report card.

David Gilmour, writer and broadcaster, address, University of Toronto, 13 Oct. 1999, printed as "The Moment I Understood the Logic of Suicide," *National Post*, 26 Oct. 1999.

SUMMER See also SEASONS

It is a transitory joy, this Canadian summer, one so fleeting that even its difficulties are treasured for the simple reason that a cut lawn holds the smell of fresh-mown grass, a troublesome tent the promise of a light rain drumming through the night.

Roy MacGregor, columnist, *Ottawa Citizen*, 16 May 1987.

Ah, but Canada *does* have a summer. It's the time that separates one hockey season from another.

Sam Orbaum, Montreal-raised Israeli columnist, "But Seriously," *The Jerusalem Post Magazine*, 19 April 1996.

SUN

Those sundowns!—even his pen could not do them full justice. Down the length of College Street, right out into the west, a path of brittle pink as the sun declined, and a sky ranging from blue to hyacinth, mauve, lime green, until the final blaze of ruddy gold spread over everything, even the squat little trams, like bed-bugs, which clang along this busy highway.

Sarah Coulton Campion, biographer and daughter of the British historian G.G. Coulton, *Father: A Portrait* (1948). The biographer and the historian and his wife spent the years 1943–44 in Toronto where Coulton, then in his eighties, taught history at the University of Toronto. The daughter is describing sunset over College Street in downtown Toronto.

The sun never sets / it is we who rise / & think / to shine.

Lines from **Earle Birney**'s poem "Copernican Fix" (1983), *Last Makings* (1991).

SUPERNATURAL See also BELIEF

Communication with the dead, prophecy and telepathy were topics I had discussed at adolescent pajama parties, then abandoned as a sign of maturity. However, I was unwilling to discard a compelling experience just because it was at odds with a preconception.

Sylvia Fraser, novelist and journalist, *The Book of Strange: A Journey* (1992).

SUPERSTITION See also BELIEF

We have no understanding of truth when hotels refuse to number a floor "13" because people think that number is unlucky.

Brock Chisholm, first Director-General of the World Health Organization, speech, 4 Nov. 1945, Ottawa, quoted by Allan Irving in *Brock Chisholm: Doctor to the World* (1998).

SUPREME COURT See COURTS

SURVIVAL

The long-term solution, our hope for life and survival, can only derive from personal development.

Hubert Reeves, astrophysicist, *Malicorne: Earthly Reflections of an Astrophysicist* (1993) translated from the French edition of 1990 by Donald Winkler.

Survival, as I keep trying to say in my various ways, is all.

Margaret Laurence, novelist, "The City," *The Toronto Star*, 15 April 1970, reprinted 26 April 1992.

Survival now would seem to depend upon the extension of consciousness itself as environment. This extension has already begun with the computer and has been anticipated in our obsession with ESP and occult awareness.

Marshall McLuhan, communications pioneer, observation made in 1972, "A McLuhan Sourcebook," *The Essential McLuhan* (1995) edited by Eric McLuhan and Frank Zingrone.

It is clear that in order to survive... we will thus have not only to tolerate one another, but to love one another in a way which will require of us an unprecedented desire to change ourselves.

Pierre Elliott Trudeau, Prime Minister, opening address, United Nations Conference on the Habitat, Vancouver, quoted by Michael Benedict in *The Toronto Star*, 31 May 1976.

The fear of "disappearing" is deeply ingrained in the French-Canadian psyche, and no word sums up more accurately the history of Quebec than the word *survival*.

Lysiane Gagnon, columnist, *The Globe and Mail*, 22 Aug. 1992.

Have we survived?
Yes. But only in Quebec.

Margaret Atwood, author, rephrasing the argument of her study *Survival* (1972), "Survival, Then and Now," *Maclean's*, 1 July 1999.

SWEARING

The young have their four-letter words and I have my own which I'd suggest to them if they want to get ahead in this world—work, duty, risk, guts, zest.

Richard Needham, columnist, quoted by Michael Kesterton in *The Globe and Mail*, 20 July 1996.

SWIMMING See also SPORTS

I really did it for Canada.

Cindy Nicholas, champion swimmer, reception committee, Toronto, 6 Aug. 1975, following her successful crossing (in record time for a woman) of the English Channel, reported by E. Kaye Fulton in *The Toronto Star*, 7 Aug. 1975.

SWISS PEOPLE

The English-speaking Canadians would do well to take their cue from the German-speaking Swiss, who make a point of knowing French and speaking it to their Francophone Swiss compatriots. Mutual linguistic courtesy is one of the social bonds that hold the Swiss people together.

Arnold J. Toynbee, historian, "Canada's Identity and Bilingualism," *The Globe and Mail*, 30 March 1961.

For decades, Canada ranked with Switzerland as one of the Western world's dullest countries. Nothing ever happened there. The part-time correspondents who served the foreign media were hard put to find anything newsworthy to report; the few bureau chiefs of those foreign journals that maintained offices in Ottawa, either for reasons of prestige or because of traditional links, were often reduced to reporting the mysterious movements of caribou herds in the Arctic.

F.S. Manor, journalist, "Canada's Crisis: The Causes," *Foreign Policy*, Winter 1977–78.

SYMBOLS See also EMBLEMS, NATIONAL

The national symbol in Canada is not the cowboy or the covered wagon—those self-reliant symbols of rough justice individually dispensed—but the opposite, the "Mountie," the long representative and guarantor of central authority in barely policed areas who "always gets his man."

Abraham Rotstein, economist, "Canada: The New Nationalism," *Foreign Affairs*, Oct. 1976, included by Grant S. McClellan in *Canada in Transition* (1977).

On the left and right sides of the maple leaf on the Canadian flag you'll see the faces of two men (liberal and conservative?) arguing with each other. A few decades ago the Canadian dollar bill had to be re-engraved because the face of a demon accidentally turned up in the Queen's hair just behind her left ear.

Martin Gardner, polymath, "The Great Stone Face," *The New Age: Notes of a Fringe Watcher* (1988).

T

TALENT

There is nothing so much of a curse—in the pursuit of artistic triumph—as a half a talent. If that's all a beginner has, better to leave the whole business alone.

Walter Huston, Toronto-born actor, interviewed by R.E. Knowles in *The Toronto Star,* 18 April 1935.

I've always said that talent of any kind comes in a variety of packages—black, white, brown, yellow, tall, short, fat, thin, monsterlike or gentle.

Oscar Peterson, jazz pianist, quoted by Richard Palmer in *Oscar Peterson* (1984).

I believe that Canadians, especially English-Canadians, must rid themselves of this disease, which is unique to Canada among developed nations, that talent is spread equally across the country like skin over a body. It is not.

Greg Gatenby, artistic director, Harbourfront Reading Series, panel on culture in the Greater Toronto Area, *The Toronto Star,* 8 July 1995.

Talent is not enough—just ask Céline Dion.

Peter Urs Bender, motivational speaker, characteristic remark, 11 May 2000.

TASTE

Good taste is a sin of omission. It leaves out direct awareness of forms and situations.

Marshall McLuhan, communications pioneer, *Through the Vanishing Point: Space in Poetry and Painting* (1968) with Harley Parker.

Good taste can be defined as making war while refusing to say shit.

Robert Fulford, columnist and author, "Perfect Bad Taste" (1970), *Crisis at the Victory Burlesk: Culture, Politics and Other Diversions* (1968).

It is breath wasted to argue articles of faith (religion, politics, economics, golf) or matters of taste (wine, women, theatre, Toronto).

Eric Nicol, humorist, *Letters to My Son* (1974).

A man can tell me all about his tastes in food, clothes & women & tell me nothing. One remark about, say, Beethoven and I've got him....

Northrop Frye, cultural critic, diary entry, 20 Aug. 1942, *Northrop Frye Newsletter,* Fall 1996.

TAXES See also FINANCE, GOODS & SERVICES TAX

The force of folly can no further go, / Than taxing men that they may richer grow.

Sir Richard John Cartwright, recalling a couplet against taxation, address, House of Commons, 3 March 1885.

Nothing will be gained by the crude methods of socialism, by taxing the middle class, the intelligent, hard-working, thoughtful, industrious people—the real strength of the nation—out of existence, and replacing them by parasites who expect everything to be done for them and do nothing for themselves or for their children.

Helen MacMurchy, physician and author, *Infant Mortality: Special Report* (1910).

The promises of yesterday are the taxes of today.

W.L. Mackenzie King, Leader of the Opposition, statement made in 1931, quoted by David Olive in *Canadian Political Babble* (1993).

Taxes should be on people, not business, as they prosper so all prosper. Only a nut would tax the goose that lays the golden egg. You feed it without restrictions and tax the guy that gets the egg.

John Bulloch, President, Canadian Federation of Independent Businesses, advertisement, *The Globe and Mail,* 4 Oct. 1974.

A woman of the street, since she charges for her affection, contributes to Gross National Product, at least in principle. A lovely and loving mistress does not.

John Kenneth Galbraith, economist and author, *Almost Everyone's Guide to Economics* (1978) written with Nicole Salinger.

Smile and the world smiles with you; tax and you tax alone.

Attributed to former Metro Chairman **F.G. Gardiner**, noted in his obituary, *The Globe and Mail,* 23 Aug. 1983.

Scientific Research Tax Credit (SRTC)

"[Marshall] (Mickey) Cohen [Deputy Minister of Finance] played a key role in shaping the SRTC into its final, unfortunate form," explained Linda McQuaig in *Behind Closed Doors* (1987) in a reference to the system of transferable credits—"tax breaks"—to corporations, which drained the Treasury and resulted in no discernible scientific research.

First there is plunder, then tribute, and finally tax. The first goes with slavery, the second with tenantry, the third with wages.

Louis Dudek, poet and aphorist, entry for 1984, *Notebooks 1960–1994* (1994).

In many of the companies that are corporate welfare bums, receptionists pay more in income tax than the companies do.

Cameron Smith, author, *Love & Solidarity: A Pictorial History of the NDP* (1992). The phrase "corporate welfare bums" goes back to 1972 and is associated with NDP leader David Lewis.

The Hudson Bay Company has decided it no longer will be involved in fur trading. That leaves all the trapping and skinning to the federal government.

Dave Broadfoot, comedian, quoted by Sid Adilman in *The Toronto Star*, 4 Jan. 1992.

In short, tax evasion is a response to tax invasion.

Pierre Lemieux, economist, "A Few Words in Support of Tax Evasion," *The Globe and Mail*, 31 Jan. 1994.

It's a blessing to pay tax.

Irving Feldman, accountant, characteristic remark heard in his Toronto office at "income-tax time," 30 April 1993.

The time has come to call for taxation of all the churches and religious institutions. People who wish to practise their religion or philosophy should obviously be allowed to do so as their democratic right, but without being subsidized by the state (by people who do not share their dogmas or beliefs).

Henry Morgentaler, physician, Honourary President of the Humanist Association of Canada, "Humanism Today," *Humanist in Canada*, Winter 1995/96.

Few exercises in social argument are made so obviously in defence of financial self-interest as those brought forward by the rich against their taxes. It always boils down to the slightly improbable case that the rich are not working because they have too little income, the poor because they have too much. Or, calling on my rural Ontario origins in Elgin County, to what may be called the horse-and-sparrow theory—this holds that if you feed the horse enough oats, some will pass through to the road for the sparrows. Perhaps, who knows?

John Kenneth Galbraith, economist and essayist, *The Socially Concerned Today* (1998).

We want American-style taxes and European-style services. The result has been Canadian-style deficits, from which we are finally weaning ourselves.

Bob Rae, columnist, "The Provinces," *The Globe and Mail*, 23 Dec. 1998.

50c (+ taxes); higher outside Greater Toronto

Per-copy price notice, masthead of the *National Post*, 20 May 1999.

Taxes are the arterial sclerosis of the economy. They gum up the veins of business.

Robert Mundell, Ontario-born economist, professor at New York's Columbia University, 1999 Nobel laureate in Economics, quoted by Peter Shawn Taylor, "Nobel Prize a Triumph for a Low-Key Economic Maverick," *National Post*, 14 Oct. 1999.

TEACHERS & TEACHING

See also EDUCATION

Only by pursuing knowledge, that is, by constantly enlarging his own intellectual horizons, can the teacher retain his original freshness and enthusiasm.

Irving Layton, poet, noted in 1955, *Taking Sides: The Collected Social and Political Writings* (1977) edited by Howard Aster.

For a teacher, patience has to be a substitute for heroism.

Northrop Frye, cultural critic, quoted in *Maclean's*, 5 April 1982.

You cannot teach a bird to fly, only how to let go its branch and begin to fall.

Tim Ward, traveller, *What the Buddha Never Taught* (1990).

A university professor's job has two parts, advancing some branch of learning and teaching it to others, and the publication that issues from this employment hardly counts as writing and seldom merits reading.

Francis Sparshott, philosopher, entry, *Contemporary Authors Autobiography Series* (1992), Volume 15.

The only authority in the classroom is the authority of the subject taught, not the teacher.

Northrop Frye, cultural critic, interviewed by David Cayley in *Northrop Frye in Conversation* (1992).

Teaching is a passing on, *an act of future*. The expert may expand the range of what is possible, but the teacher expands the range of who can do the possible.

Ken Dryden, goalkeeper and student of education, "Verbatim," *The Globe and Mail*, 22 July 1996.

TEARS

One of the mysteries that man has so far failed to solve is the reason why a woman cries when she is glad.

Bob Edwards, publisher, *The Eye Opener*, Summer Annual, 1921, *The Wit and Wisdom of Bob Edwards* (1976) edited by Hugh Dempsey.

At my lowest moments, I cry for the sadness of the world.

William Shatner, television personality, quoted in the TV documentary *William Shatner: At Home in the Universe*, CBC-TV, 2 Nov. 1999.

TECHNOLOGY See also EDUCATION, SCIENCE & SCIENTISTS

Technology was a basic resource that improved, or self-multiplied, with each repeated opportunity of its application.

Buckminster Fuller, inventor and designer, recalling the insight he gained from his apprenticeship in 1913–14 as a machine fitter at a new cotton mill in Sherbrooke, Que., *Ideas and Integrities: A Spontaneous Autobiographical Disclosure* (1968) edited by Robert W. Marks.

Technology is the metaphysics of our age, you know, it is the way being appears to us, and certainly we're rushing into the future with no categories by which we can judge it.

George P. Grant, philosopher, interviewed by Gad Horowitz, *Journal of Canadian Studies*, Aug. 1969.

The most human thing about people is technology.

Marshall McLuhan, communications pioneer, quoted by John Robert Colombo in *Colombo's Canadian References* (1976).

I regard all machines as malignant demons: The best thing they can do is come apart in my hands.

Northrop Frye, cultural critic, quoted by Gillian Cosgrove in *The Toronto Star*, 7 Aug. 1980.

Cyberpunk

The word cyberpunk and the concept of virtual reality (computer stimulation of sensory experience) were introduced and popularized by the Vancouver-based, science-fiction writer **William Gibson** in the title story of his collection *Burning Chrome* (1980) and amplified in his novel *Neuromancer* (1984). Tom Shippey, "Inside the Screen," *The Times Literary Supplement*, 30 April 1993.

The revolutionary element is built into contemporary society everywhere. A technological revolution makes the world more uniform: one cannot take off in a jet plane and expect a radically different way of life in the place where the plane lands.

Northrop Frye, cultural critic, "The Meeting of Past and Future in William Morris" (1982), *Myth and Metaphor: Selected Essays, 1974–1988* (1990), edited by Robert D. Denham.

A technological society, after all, is one in which everyone has access to technology. It is the most universal availability of technology, not just its presence, that distinguishes the rich countries from the poor.

Witold Rybczynski, essayist, *Taming the Tiger: The Struggle to Control Technology* (1983).

Canadians live under the remarkable illusion that we are a technologically advanced people. Everything around us denies that assumption. We are, in many ways, a Third World country, selling our natural resources in exchange for the high technology of the industrialized world.

David Suzuki, scientist and broadcaster, "A Planet for the Taking," *The Canadian Forum*, Feb. 1985.

Canada's prosperity essentially rests on its ability to export modern technology, expertise and information.

Frank Feather, futurologist, *G-Forces: Reinventing the World—The 35 Global Forces Restructuring Our World* (1989).

I believe that, in the end, technology is going to do more to destroy capitalism than all the revolutions in history.

Gerald Bull, arms engineer, assassinated in Brussels, 22 March 1990, quoted by Dale Grand in *Wilderness of Mirrors: The Life of Gerald Bull* (1991).

But the essence of the new technological society is that it's not an infrastructure outside our lives. Increasingly, it's the infrastructure within which we live.

Heather Menzies, writer, "Hyping the Highway," *The Canadian Forum*, June 1994.

Technology's not something you can put back in the black box and return to Radio Shack. It's the vaccinations you've had and all that metal in your teeth. It's everything, the whole thing that makes us what we are. There is absolutely no option. Whatever it is, we're going there. We can't say, "Oh no, back to nature! because nature no longer exists. We messed with it too much."

William Gibson, novelist, quoted by Mark Shainblum and Mathew Friedman, "Post Modern Sublime," *SOL Rising*, Jan. 1997.

By 2050, most people will have implants in their heads, bringing them any information they want, whenever they want it, just by thinking about it.

Robert J. Sawyer, science-fiction writer, "The Next Century," *The Globe and Mail*, 1 Jan. 2000.

TELECOMMUNICATIONS See also COMMUNICATIONS

Canadian stories have a place on the information highway.

Ted Rogers, President, Rogers Communications Inc., statement made in Toronto, 19 Dec. 1994, following regulatory commission approval of the $3.1 billion takeover of Maclean Hunter Ltd., quoted by Harvey Enchin in *The Globe and Mail* the following day.

TELEPHONE See also COMMUNICATIONS

The telephone was conceived in Brantford in 1874, and born in Boston in 1875.

Alexander Graham Bell, inventor of the telephone, address, "The Substance of My Latest Research" (1917), *Empire Club of Canada: Addresses Delivered to the Members* (1919). The date of its invention was 10 March 1876.

Yes, Aleck, it is I, your father, speaking.

Alexander Melville Bell, language instructor for the deaf, thus identified himself on the world's first long-distance telephone call, heard by his son, Alexander Graham Bell, inventor of the telephone, 10 Aug. 1876. The father, speaking into a primitive transmitter in Brantford, was heard by the son in a shoe store in Paris, Ont., thirteen kilometres away. The son replied by telegraph in Morse code and later called it "the first transmission of speech to a distance."

Trying to guess who it is when the telephone rings provides the average woman with lots of excitement.

Bob Edwards, publisher, *The Eye Opener*, 9 March 1918, *The Wit and Wisdom of Bob Edwards* (1976) edited by Hugh Dempsey.

The telephone is a most useful invention. We can discuss important matters, spread peace and love by persuading others as we talk. It was invented in Canada by Alexander Bell.

Mohandas K. Gandhi, Indian pundit, addressing a group of school children in Wardha, Central India, July 1935.

"Yes" and "Oui" are the two rudest words in their respective dictionaries when used to answer the phone.

Tim Burke, columnist, *The Montreal Gazette*, 12 Jan. 1983.

The Long Distance Feeling

Television advertising campaign to promote long-distance sponsored by **Bell Canada** and created by **McKim Advertising**, noted by Jerry Goodis in *Goodis: Shaking the Canadian Advertising Tree* (1991).

TELEVISION See also ACTORS & ACTING, BROADCASTING, CULTURE, NEWS

Cue the elephant! Cue the goddamn elephant!

Sydney Newman, TV producer, issuing commands to floor director Harry Rasky, during the experimental broadcast of a live show from Toronto's CNE, late summer 1952, quoted by Knowlton Nash in *Cue the Elephant! Backstage Tales at the CBC* (1996). "The elephant, slated to perform in the opening scene, was being uncooperative," noted Nash, who added, "The elephant was a harbinger of live television's capricious nature."

A TV licence is a licence to print money.

Roy Thomson, publishing and television executive, boast made to fellow businessmen after his company, Scottish Television Limited, based in Edinburgh, Scotland, was awarded the licence to operate a national television service, 19 June 1957. (Even more profitable was North Sea Oil.) As Thomson noted in his memoirs, *After I Was Sixty* (1975), "Perhaps this remark was injudicious but it was certainly right." When he visited China, he met Chou En-lai who inquired, "Is it not true, then, that you had a licence to print money?"

Broadcasting has been called the fifth estate. I believe cable will become the sixth estate.

Jack Kent Cooke, financier with extensive cable interests, quoted in the 1960s by Adrian Havill in *The Last Mogul* (1992).

Since the point of focus for a TV set is the viewer, television is Orientalizing us by causing us all to begin to look within ourselves.

Marshall McLuhan, communications pioneer, commenting on his own observations, "Playboy Interview" (1969) conducted by Eric Norden, *The Essential McLuhan* (1995) edited by Eric McLuhan and Frank Zingrone.

Television is a vicarious projection of the self into experience, tending, in the distant future, toward the actual projection of self into experience.

Elwy Yost, TV host, "You Are the Broadcast," *A Media Mosaic: Canadian Communications through a Critical Eye* (1971) edited by Walt McDayter.

It has often been said that Britain has the best television in the world. Milton Shulman... believes that this assessment is smug and inaccurate. The most he will concede is that Britain's television is the "least worst" in the world.

Wording of the jacket copy and central theme of *The Least Worst Television in the World* (1973) by **Milton Shulman**, Toronto-born, London-based journalist, drama critic, and TV producer. Shulman noted, "No other media or art form in mankind's history has been absorbed in such massive doses by so many people."

Television's influence is much too subtle to be detected by its victims.

Milton Shulman, TV personality, *The Ravenous Eye: The Impact of the Fifth Factor* (1973).

In the movie, you go outside into the world. In television you go inside yourself.

Marshall McLuhan, communications pioneer, observation made in 1967, "A McLuhan Sourcebook," *The Essential McLuhan* (1995) edited by Eric McLuhan and Frank Zingrone.

All TV networks should end with the letters BS.

Louis Dudek, man-of-letters, *Epigrams* (1975).

Let us make a profit so that we can make Canadian programs.

Allan Slaught, President, Global Television Network, statement, CRTC hearing in Ottawa, 5 Nov. 1975, to justify the Ontario mini-network's policy of importing American shows rather than mounting Canadian shows, quoted by Blaik Kirby in *The Globe and Mail* the following day.

The human head is almost the only thing that appears on television close to life size. The TV screen is perfectly adapted to carrying the talking head.

Robert MacNeil, broadcaster and memoirist, *The Right Place at the Right Time* (1982).

I remember the Golden Age of Television very well. It was black and white, and you could usually see the stagehands.

Johnny Wayne, comedian and partner of Frank Shuster, quoted by Clyde Gilmour in *The Toronto Star*, 17 April 1982.

Videographer

Videocam operator **Danny Petkovsek** became

the world's first "videographer" when Toronto's CITY-TV commissioned and televised his documentary *Raymond: No Fixed Address.* As noted by Liam Lacey in *The Globe and Mail,* 22 June 1993, a videographer is a one-person videocam crew who photographs live action, dispensing with writer, producer, narrator, etc.

Why is public television so important? Because, unlike commercial television, it is committed to the idea of broadcasting as a public good. It does not exist to serve commerce or political manipulation, but the needs of citizens for knowledge and ideas and cultural development.

Bernard Ostry, Chairman, TVO, quoted in *The New York Times,* 31 Dec. 1989.

We have handed over this most powerful medium to a foreign country. Nowhere else in the world has one country imported the total television output of another country.

Denis Harvey, CBC-TV executive, address, conference on global television, Toronto, 31 Nov. 1990, quoted by Christopher Harris in *The Globe and Mail* the following day.

Maybe there are only two kinds of people in this world: those who watch TV because they are bored, and those who are bored because they watch TV.

Don Gillmor, columnist, *The Globe and Mail,* 27 May 1992.

American civilization has to *de-theatricalize* itself, I think, from the prison of television.

Northrop Frye, cultural critic, "Notebook 1993," edited by Robert D. Denham, *Northrop Frye Newsletter,* Summer 1993.

When Americans watch TV, they're watching TV, but when Canadians watch TV, they're watching *American* TV.

Martin Short, comic, remark, quoted by Rick Marin in "The Most Entertaining Americans? Canadians," *The New York Times,* 27 June 1993.

The biggest difference is that 90 per cent of all French TV programs are produced here in Quebec, so Quebecers have a real sense of who they are. In English Canada it's the reverse and so they have less of a sense of identity.

Jean Morin, advertising executive, quoted by Brian Dunn, "Why Quebec Advertising Is Different: Advertising Supplement," *Advertising Age,* 22 Nov. 1993.

The producing of television shows today is a lot like what Henry Ford did in 1908. Having spent some years trying to make a great car, he came to the conclusion that he would never succeed. So he said, "To hell with it," and he went on to make a *lot* of cars.

Alex Barris, TV writer, characteristic remark, Dec. 1993.

One of the joys of working on television is that you feel as if you've got friends everywhere.

Pamela Wallin, TV personality, quoted by Joyce Singer in *Today's Seniors,* Aug. 1994.

You know, to work in television is to be relentlessly besieged by criticisms of television's distortion, violence and banality, mostly by people who earn a living with the competition—print.

Moses Znaimer, television executive, interviewed by Antonia Zerbisias in *The Toronto Star,* 8 April 1995.

Television is the triumph of the image over the printed word. / The true nature of television is flow, not show; process, not conclusion. / As worldwide television expands, the demand for local programming increases. / The best TV tells me what happened to me, today. / TV is as much about the people bringing you the story as the story itself. / In the past, TV's chief operating skill was political. In the future it will be, it will have to be, mastery of the craft itself. / Print created illiteracy. TV is democratic. Everybody gets it. / TV creates immediate consensus, subject to immediate change. / There never was a mass audience, except by compulsion. / Television is not a problem to be managed, but an instrument to be played.

Moses Znaimer, television executive, "The Ten Commandments of Television," promotion for CBC-TV's special *Introducing TVTV: The Television Revolution,* advertisement, *The Globe and Mail,* 8 April 1995.

I was born in 1948. I can't recall a world before television, but I know I must have experienced one.

William Gibson, author, "The Net Is a Waste of Time," *The New York Times Magazine*, 14 July 1996.

The object of much commercial television is to numb viewers into a state of mind that welcomes advertising intrusions instead of rejecting them.

Patrick Watson, TV personality, "A Project for Canada," *Maclean's*, 5 April 1999.

I didn't know it then, but one of the secrets of success on television is, if you can't be beautiful, be memorable.

Brian Linehan, showbusiness interviewer, quoted by Peter Urs Bender and George Torok in *Secrets of Power Marketing* (1999).

Canada is the most wire-cabled country in the world because the entire population would suffer glottal stops, if not mass palpitations and hyperventilation, without U.S. television.

Conrad Black, publisher, "Out of Uncle Sam's Shadow," *National Post*, 11 Jan. 2000.

TEMPERATURE See also WEATHER

There are always vanities, follies, hypocrisies in any country, even on the frontier, but they don't really thrive at forty below. At that temperature the chief concern is to keep warm.

Paul Hiebert, humorist, "The Comic Spirit at Forty Below Zero," *Manitoba in Literature* (1970) edited by R.G. Collins and Kenneth McRobbie.

TENNIS See also SPORTS

A middle-class version of professional wrestling.

John Ralston Saul, author, *The Doubter's Companion: A Dictionary of Aggressive Common Sense* (1994).

TERRITORIES See NORTHWEST TERRITORIES, THE NORTH, NUNAVUT, YUKON TERRITORY

TERRORISM See also OCTOBER CRISIS

The movement for independence was our first and last chance to live differently from American suburbanites. And we blew it.

Pierre Vallières, one-time revolutionary, Front de Libération du Québec (FLQ) sympathizer, *Impossible Quebec* (1980).

If you can toss a bomb into a pub in Ireland it won't be long before you can toss a nuclear bomb into London.

Bob Hunter, activist and columnist, remark made in 1972, recalled in his column in *eye*, 25 March 1992.

Once, returning from a brief journey, I found the secretary had been replaced, which was no great surprise in itself, except that the new girl, a colossus of over six foot, could neither type nor take shorthand. Running into a journalist friend in the street, I discovered rather late that le *tout-Paris* evidently knew already, that my new secretary was a French-Canadian activist who had been apprehended while trying to blow up the Statue of Liberty. It would, of course, be unreasonable to expect such a person to be able to type.

I put my foot down on this occasion, since I didn't think that anyone with an idea as monstrously silly as blowing up a statue would be capable of understanding any thought expressed more quietly. Overnight I became a reactionary and a capitalist hyena, I must say, with some relief.

Peter Ustinov, British actor married to Québécoise actress Suzanne Plechette, responsible for hiring nannies and secretaries, describing their life together in France, *Dear Me* (1977).

It makes one conscious of the small things in life that really count—friendship, family... and clean water.

André Deschenes, consultant held hostage for five days by Peru's Tupac Amaru rebels in Lima, remarks upon release, quoted by Linda Diebel in *The Toronto Star*, 24 Dec. 1996.

THANKSGIVING See HOLIDAYS

THEATRE See also ACTORS & ACTING, CULTURE, LITERATURE, STRATFORD FESTIVAL

Ladies and gentlemen... thank you with all my heart for myself and comrades, and more especially for my co-worker, Miss Terry, for the right-royal Canadian, I will say British, welcome you have given us.

Henry Irving, English actor, after-curtain address, Opera House, Toronto, quoted by Joseph Hatton in *Henry Irving's Impressions of America: Narrated in a Series of Sketches, Chronicles, and Conversations* (1884).

One day the famous French actress Sarah Bernhardt came to Montreal to play the role of Hamlet. In the British sector there was much advertising of this unique opportunity, but in the French-Catholic areas warnings were posted to keep the population from the theatre in which an actress performed wearing trousers.

Otto Hahn, German-born atomic scientist, describing his visit to Montreal, 1905–06, *Otto Hahn: A Scientific Autobiography* (1966) edited by Willy Ley.

The Canadian Players in "Saint Joan" by Bernard Shaw. Curtain Time 8:00 p.m. or One Hour After the Train Arrives

Notice on the poster announcing the appearance of the **Canadian Players** troop at Moosonee, arriving on the Ontario Northland Railroad, 1950s, as noted in *Also in the Cast: Memoirs of Tony van Bridge* (1995).

Canadian theatre? what is it? If only playwrights, actors and producers north of Niagara would turn their eyes from Broadway and look around them at a place called Canada!

John Coulter, playwright, speech in 1947, quoted by Betty Lee in *Love and Whisky: The Story of the Dominion Drama Festival* (1973).

Melodrama has never seemed to me to be an outworn mode of theatre; I see melodrama all around me in daily life, and whenever I pick up a newspaper I find melodramatic plots on every page.

Robertson Davies, man-of-letters, quoted by Geraldine Anthony in *Stage Voices: Twelve Canadian Playwrights Talk about Their Lives and Work* (1978).

Canadian theatre's most valuable contribution may well turn out to be its *dis*similarity from American theatre, its offering to the world of not only an alternative North American theatre but a model for greater diversity in general.

Mavor Moore, man-of-the-theatre, "Northern Renaissance: The Saga of Canada's Theatre," *Friends So Different: Essays on Canada and the United States in the 1980s* (1989) edited by Lansing Lamont and J. Duncan Edmonds.

Going to the theatre is a small indulgence for most people. And they need it.

Garth Drabinsky, theatre impresario, "Big Ideas," quoted by Ken Mark in *The Village Post*, April 1995.

People go to the theatre not to feel good. They go there to feel.

Robert Lepage, director, "Words to Remember," *The Globe and Mail*, 28 Dec. 1996.

Theatre is about putting a strong visual image together with honest talk.

Christopher Newton, theatre director, quoted by Robert Cushman, "Mr. Newton's Profession," *National Post*, 15 May 1999.

THERAPY

The time is coming when the basic therapeutic insights must become part of the human environment in which we live: the family, the school, the office, every institution and association of men must become, or at least attempt to be, a therapeutic community.

Gregory Baum, theologian, "The Human Community," *Probings: A Collection of Essays Contributed to the Canadian Mental Health Association for its Golden Jubilee 1918–1968* (1968).

Roses have more problems than cabbages.

David Lewis, psychiatrist, referring to Margaret Trudeau's hospitalization, quoted by Marilyn Dunlop in *The Toronto Star*, 20 Sept. 1974.

Therapy is *not* the real world. It is intimacy without friendship. Its goal is to provide you with the tools to succeed on the outside, and the caring, reassurance and support to fail on the inside. You rehearse your life in therapy; you live it in the world.

Jack Muskat, psychologist, "Fifth Column," *The Globe and Mail*, 28 Nov. 1994.

THIRD WORLD See also HUNGER, POVERTY

Canada is the only Third World country with snow.

Tim Burke, columnist, *The Montreal Gazette*, 12 Jan. 1983.

Canada is, basically, one step away from being a Third World country. We have a different view of world affairs, a different colour of information about the world. We have to pay a lot more attention to what's going on around us than most Americans feel they have to, because we don't feel like we control it.

Bruce Cockburn, folk-rock singer, comparing Canada and the United States, quoted by Brad Coswald in the *Winnipeg Free Press*, 20 May 1992.

When you come back from the Third World, in this case Morocco, you realize that Canada, despite all its bitching, moaning, whining, complaining, is a *very* rich country. Even in a tiny town it shows.

Scott Symons, author, "Deliquescence in Canada," *The Idler*, July–Aug. 1992.

In fact, nothing has done more to undermine the ability of Third World populations to feed and support themselves than the billions spent on megaproject development.

Patricia Adams, Executive Director, *Probe International*, mailing, Jan. 1995.

THOUGHTS See also INTELLIGENCE

I wonder if, to those living thousands of years in the future, our current thinking will also seem naïve and no more profound than the picture-writing of the cave men.

Peter M. Millman, astronomer, *This Universe of Space* (1961).

Think until it hurts.

Roy Thomson, newspaper publisher, maxim, interviewed by the host of TVO's *The Education of Mike McManus*, 15 Sept. 1975.

Possession of the capacity for thought makes us a thought-dominated species.

Donald Hebb, psychologist, "A World of Thought," *Essay on Mind* (1980).

Research is hard, writing harder, but thinking hardest of all.

Robert Fulford, columnist, address, Editors' Association of Canada, Toronto, 22 Jan. 1996, quoted in *Edition*, March 1996.

TIBET

The last stronghold of the wicked one.

Description of the religion of Bon and Buddhism found in Tibet, associated with **Susie Carson Rijnhart**, Christian missionary, born in Strathroy, Ont., *With the Tibetans in Tent and Temple: Narrative of Four Years' Residence on the Tibetan Border, and of a Journey into the Far Interior* (1901). She entered Tibet but failed to reach Lhasa; after four years of intensive missionary activity, she found no converts. She returned to Canada and lies buried in Chatham, Ont.

It looks as if communism will soon include the strange, praying Buddhists on the roof of the world.

Matthew Halton, correspondent and newspaperman, "Communism Comes to Shangri-la," *The Toronto Star*, 8 April 1950.

Deeper into the mystery of Tibet which keeps turning out, on closer inspection, to be no mystery at all, but the most ordinary of ordinaries.

Observation made by a character in **Mark Frutkin's** novel *Invading Tibet* (1991).

TIME See also FUTURE, PAST, PRESENT, TODAY

The man who made time made lots of it. If you rush too fast, you'll shorten your days.

Traditional wisdom of a Dene Elder at Fort Simpson, N.W.T., quoted in *Canada's Northwest Territories: 1992 Explorers' Guide* (1991).

Cosmopolitan Time

Original name for what came to be called Standard Time proposed by **Sir Sandford Fleming**, the engineer who introduced the concept of global time-reckoning, Washington Meridian Conference, Oct. 1884; "Time-Reckoning" (1879), *Proceedings of the Canadian Institute*, Toronto (1884).

A man can always find time to do a thing if he has the inclination.

Bob Edwards, publisher, *The Eye Opener*, Summer Annual, 1920.

Time is the small change of eternity.

Irving Layton, poet and aphorist, *The Whole Bloody Bird (obs, aphs & Pomes)* (1969).

The world will end at midnight tonight; 11:30 in Newfoundland.

CBC Radio listeners are reminded whenever they hear a program announcement of the fact that Newfoundland's time is thirty minutes "ahead" of mainland time regardless of time zone. The catch-phrase is attributed to **Tom Cahill**, CBC producer in St. John's, Nfld., and was discussed in Peter Gzowski's book about *This Country in the Morning* (1974).

The search for perfection is not an end in itself. The demands of other branches of science, including space research, are pushing hard on the heels of the timekeeper. Even so, among the units of science, no other unit is known with greater precision than the unit of time.

Malcolm M. Thomson, scientist, *The Beginning of the Long Dash: A History of Timekeeping in Canada* (1978). The National Research Council Time Signal, heard over CBC Radio each day at 1:00 p.m. EST, may be the world's longest-running if shortest radio program. Its duration is as short as fifteen seconds. It runs: "The beginning of the long dash, followed by ten seconds of silence, indicates exactly one o'clock. . . . "

In everyone's life, time moves slowly for a while, like a snowball on a mountainside, but then it tumbles faster and faster and, in a speeding avalanche, thunders to its end.

Harry Bruce, essayist, "Yesterday's Children: It's Cruel of Them to Grow so Fast," *Today Magazine*, 18 Oct. 1980.

My work naturally makes me a slave of the clock. Refusing to wear a watch is my little gesture of personal liberation.

Barbara Frum, TV personality, quoted by Clyde Gilmour in *The Toronto Star*, 12 Dec. 1981.

There is nothing like anticipation for slowing time (and fulfillment for spending it).

Ronald Wright, author, *Time Among the Maya: Travels in Belize, Guatemala, and Mexico* (1989).

Our perception that we have "no time" is one of the distinctive marks of modern Western culture.

Margaret Visser, author, *The Rituals of Dinner: The Origins, Evolution, Eccentricities, and Pleasures of Table Manners* (1991).

TITLES See also AWARDS & HONOURS

In London I'm Lord Thomson, in Toronto I'm Ken. I have two sets of Christmas cards and two sets of stationery. You might say I'm having my cake and eating it too. I'm honouring a promise to my father by being Lord Thomson, and at the same time I can just be Ken.

Ken Thomson, CEO of the Thomson Corporation, son of its founder Roy Thomson, first Lord Thomson of Fleet, known as "Old Roy," quoted by David MacFarlane in *Saturday Night*, Oct. 1980. The full title of "Young Ken" is Lord Thomson of Fleet and of Northbridge in the City of Edinburgh.

TOAST

May you live as long as you want to, and may you want to as long as you live.

Sir Edwin Leather, Canadian-born former Governor of Bermuda, reciting his favourite toast, Toronto, 14 Nov. 1980.

TOBACCO See also SMOKING

Smoking can kill you / Smoking during pregnancy can harm your baby / Cigarettes can cause fatal lung cancer / Cigarettes are addictive / Tobacco smoke can harm your children

Warnings required by law to occupy one-quarter of the front of cigarette packages, announced by **Benoît Bouchard**, Minister of Health, 19 March 1993, quoted by Geoffrey York in *The Globe and Mail* the following day.

Smoking is to heart specialists as skiing is to chiropractors.

Maurus E. Mallon, aphorist, 26 March 1993.

If the tobacco farmer can get subsidies, why not his victims?

Bob Hunter, columnist, "Enviro," *eye*, 6 Jan. 1996.

TOBOGGANING See also SPORTS

Oh, it was awful—wonderful—magnificent! . . . I have never experienced anything so surprising,—it is like flying; for a moment you cannot breathe!

Ellen Terry, English actress, tobogganing with Henry Irving's stage manager Bram Stoker, Toronto, quoted by Joseph Hatton in Henry Irving's *Impressions of America: Narrated in a Series of Sketches, Chronicles, and Conversations* (1884).

Sleighing; down the goat hill, absurdly unable to get rid of the fear of a fall. I can make myself run the risk of it, but cannot avoid the instinctive stiffening against it, which shows that one should never let oneself get out of the practice of these moral tests, any more than of the physical.

Freya Stark, traveller and writer, observation recorded in a notebook, entry for 16 Jan. 1929, Creston, B.C., *Beyond Euphrates* (1951).

TODAY See also TIME

Today is the tomorrow you worried about yesterday.

Well-known saying attributed to ornithologist **Jack Miner** who operated his migratory bird sanctuary (1904–44) at Kingsville, Ont.

TOLERANCE

The tolerance of differences is the measure of civilization.

Vincent Massey, Governor General (1952–59), quoted by U.S. President Richard Nixon, address, joint sitting of the Senate and the House of Commons, 14 April 1972.

Solving your problems throughout your recent history, you Canadians have shown to the world that there is something you have per capita more than any other nation, and that is tolerance.

Arkadi Tcherkassov, geographer, "Our Man in Moscow," *Grainews*, July 1992.

We have matured from a nation of two solitudes to a nation of about forty-three solitudes.

Rick Green, comedian and host of TVO's *Prisoners of Gravity*, "My Canada Includes...," *Maclean's*, 3 Jan. 1994.

TOONIE See LOONIE

TORONTO See also ONTARIO

Now, for this night, let's harbour here in York.

Line from the Third Part of *King Henry VI* (1590–92), Act IV, Scene VII, by **William Shakespeare**. It is traditionally maintained that this line was spoken by Lieutenant-Governor John Graves Simcoe as he stepped ashore at the bay, named York, later Toronto, 13 May 1793; it remains the motto of the city's York Club.

The trade of York is very trifling; and it owes its present population and magnitude entirely to its being the seat of government, for it is destitute of every natural advantage except that of a good harbour.

John Howison, traveller, describing early Toronto, *Sketches of Upper Canada: Domestic, Local, and Characteristic* (1821).

I, however, didn't care much about Toronto; there was too much assumption of exclusiveness, without just grounds *to go upon*, and I left the place then, as I do now, without any intention of returning to it.

Horton Rhys, British actor, *A Theatrical Trip for a Wager! Through Canada and the United States* (1861).

Toronto as a city is not generally attractive to a traveller. The country around it is flat; and, though it stands on a lake, that lake has no attributes of beauty.

Anthony Trollope, English novelist and traveller, *North America* (1862).

Toronto is 12 miles long, one way, within the city limits; the poor live at one end and work at the other—and not a car on Sunday. These families are as exiled as if the Atlantic flowed between them, but as long as God and the clergy are gratified what of it?

Mark Twain, humorist, entry written in *Mark Twain's Notebook* (1935), edited by Albert Bigelow Paine, after being interviewed, 27 July 1895, by Marie Joussaye, a reporter with the *Toronto Globe*, who had agitated in vain against religious groups for Sunday streetcar service, as noted by Taylor Roberts, "Mark Twain and Sunday Streetcars: An Interview in Winnipeg," *Mark Twain Journal*, Fall 1990.

I went to Toronto last Sunday. It was closed.

Remark made in reference to the city's pre-1960 restrictive Blue Laws, attributed to any number of comedians, notably **W.C. Fields** in the 1920s.

"And how do you like Toronto?" was my first question of the far-travelled Emma.

"Much—in the summer," was the reply; "just now, however, I'd sooner be in the Riviera."

Emma Goldman, anarchist, sometime resident of Toronto, interviewed by R.E. Knowles in *The Toronto Star*, 24 Jan. 1934.

I love all of you, my fellow Torontonians.... I am prouder of Canada than Canada can possibly be of me.

Mary Pickford, silent-film star, paying a return visit on May 1934 to Toronto where she was born, in *The Toronto Star's Centennial Magazine: The Hundred*, Nov. 1992.

Mary and I frequently meet each other—and, I need hardly add, Toronto and Torontonians are our principal line of chatter.

Walter Huston, actor, father of director John Huston and grandfather of actress Anjelica Huston, referring to the silent film star Mary Pickford, another former Torontonian in Hollywood, interviewed by R.E. Knowles in *The Toronto Star*, 18 April 1935.

There is no church in Heaven, whereas Toronto can boast four hundred—and frequently does.

Gilbert Norwood, British writer, "Is This Paradise?" *Spoken in Jest* (1938).

And there live girls who've never gone / To Havergal or Bishop Strachan.

Couplet referring to two exclusive girls' schools, from **Earle Birney**'s poem "Eagle Island" (1938), *The Collected Poems of Earle Birney* (1975).

My taxi approached a towering Gothic pile. There were never any Goths in Canada, but there are a goodly number of Gothic buildings.

Wyndham Lewis, British artist and author, referring to the student union Hart House on the campus of the University of Toronto, *America, I Presume* (1940).

She had good luck. She married a Canadian. She has a Ford automobile. She lives in Toronto.

Speech of Christine, destitute cabaret singer in postwar Germany, played by Marlene Dietrich, referring to her sister who married a Canadian and moved to Toronto, in the movie *Witness for the Prosecution* (1957) written by **Michael Wilding**.

One sensed a fear of becoming an appendage of the giant neighbour across the great lake ... the process of osmosis with the United States contributed materially to the progress of the province. But it also aroused ... a great deal of melancholy.

Charles de Gaulle, President of France, writing about Toronto on his third and penultimate trip to Canada in 1960, *Memoirs of Hope: Renewal, 1958–62: Endeavour 1962–* (1970) translated by Terence Kilmartin.

... Toronto, a city of penetrating gloom in which Scottish dourness is pierced, from time to time, by unexpected flashes of gaiety.

Alan Pryce-Jones, critic for the *Sunday Telegraph*, reviewing Edmund Wilson's study *O Canada* (1967).

It's better to run to Trana / Than to stay in a place you don't wanta.

Couplet from a musical routine written and performed by **Groucho Marx**, part of his record album *An Evening with Groucho* (1967).

As a relatively recent transplant from New York, I am frequently asked whether I find Toronto sufficiently exciting. I find it almost too exciting. The suspense is scary. Here is the most hopeful and healthy city in North America, still unmangled, still with options. Few of us profit from the mistakes of others, and perhaps Toronto will prove to share this disability. If so, I am grateful at least to have enjoyed this great city before its destruction.

Jane Jacobs, urban commentator, "A City Getting Hooked on the Expressway Drug," *The Globe and Mail*, 1 Nov. 1969.

This is a city of skyscrapers, tall black towers standing back on tiptoe, cheating about which is the taller. It is a lonely city, a drugstore city, where the cheap counter food is munched by sad, lonely women already preparing at six in the evening for bed and television.

Robert Morley, British actor, referring to Toronto's New City Hall, *The London Observer*, 4 Dec. 1972.

I have two brothers. One is alive, the other lives in Toronto.

Eric Nicol, humorist, *Letters to My Son* (1974).

But how shall we define Toronto now?

A forest of neighbourhoods—situated between the world's widest expressway and the world's tallest tower—all dedicated to keeping cars out and buildings low.

A vista of suburbs—split-levels and apartment towers stretching to the horizon—crisscrossed by lovely ravines and garish festivals of free enterprise.

William Kilbourn, historian, Introduction, *The Toronto Book* (1976).

What I like best about Toronto is that life there still moves at a leisurely and civilized pace. In the Maritimes we have to run just to keep from being thrown off the treadmill and onto the welfare rolls.

Alden Nowlan, poet and columnist, *The City*, 1 Jan. 1977.

The longest designated street in the world is Yonge Street, which runs north and west from Toronto, Canada. The first stretch, completed on February 16, 1796, ran 34 1/2 miles. Its official length, now extended to Rainy River at the Manitoba–Minnesota border, is 1,171.1 miles.

Norris and **Ross McWhirter**, editors, *Guinness Book of World Records* (1978).

I'm impressed by the gratifying amount of light here. Light is a blessing, representing what is more desirable in life, including love, compassion and decency.

John Cheever, American novelist, visiting Toronto during Indian summer, quoted by Ken Adachi in *The Toronto Star*, 11 Nov. 1978.

In Toronto, the place where I was born and still live, one old city seems to have been piled on another, and now there's another, and it is a strange new crazy quilt on the lake.

Morley Callaghan, novelist, "Canada," *The Toronto Star*, 1 July 1978.

Hasn't Toronto changed? We used to be forced to go to Loblaws to buy ice cream—just for excitement.

Judith Krantz, New York–based popular novelist, recalling the early 1960s when she lived in Toronto, quoted by Ken Adachi in *The Toronto Star*, 15 March 1981.

Canadians are often scolded for their diffidence and lack of sense of identity, but the positive side of that is, I think, shown by the ability of Toronto to absorb this tremendous and cosmopolitan influx with what seems to me a minimum of tension.

Northrop Frye, cultural critic, "The View from Here" (1983), *Myth and Metaphor: Selected Essays, 1974–1988* (1990) edited by Robert D. Denham.

Toronto (n.) Generic term for anything which comes out in a gush despite all your careful efforts to let it out gently, e.g., flour into a white sauce, tomato ketchup on to fried fish, sperm into a human being, etc.

Douglas Adams and **John Lloyd**, English humorists, *The Meaning of Liff* (1983).

Canada is a little more European than the United States.... It's so clean—it reminds me of Switzerland.

Hans Küng, Swiss-born theologian, teaching at the University of Toronto, quoted by Kelley Teahen, "Visiting Theologian," *The Globe and Mail*, 18 Sept. 1985.

Toronto is a kind of New York operated by the Swiss.

Peter Ustinov, theatre personality, appreciative comment, interviewed by John Bentley Mays in *The Globe and Mail*, 1 Aug. 1987. When reminded of the insight at a reception on 20 June 1992, quoted in the same newspaper the following day, Ustinov replied, "I've been here so many times, I've learned it's really run by the Canadians."

There are more Italians in Toronto than in Milan; the Canadian city also has the second-largest Chinese population on the continent and more West Indians than anywhere else outside those sunny islands.

Steve Veale, travel writer, "Toronto," *The Penguin Guide to Canada* (1989, 1991) edited by Alan Tucker.

To me Toronto is the city in which to walk.

Umberto Eco, Italian scholar, frequent visitor, letter of 13 Jan. 1989 to Greg Gatenby who quoted it in *The Wild Is Always There: Canada through the Eyes of Foreign Writers* (1993) and noted, "Apart from his hometown of Bologna, he has lived in Toronto longer than he has lived in any other city."

Canada's very receptive to experimental fiction. Toronto is a very articulate and literary town.

Jerzy Kosinski, Polish-born American fiction-writer, interviewed in New York City, quoted by Pearl Sheffy Gefen in *The Globe and Mail*, 18 May 1991.

It's a very easy place to shoot movies, and the people here are nice, but you never find yourself seriously compelled by the city. I never thought like: "It's too bad I'm shooting today because I could be at the top of the CN Tower."

Nora Ephron, American writer and director, on location, quoted by John Fitzgerald in *The Globe and Mail*, 14 June 1991.

What Mecca is to Islam, what Rome is to the Pope, Toronto is to me.

Timothy Leary, author, referring to his indebtedness to the late Marshall McLuhan during the course of a talk in Toronto, quoted by Susan Kastner in *The Toronto Star*, 30 June 1991. "McLuhan said I needed something snappy to sell me. Something like 'The Pepsi Generation.' It came to me afterwards in the shower: Tune in, turn on, drop out. So to a great extent, Marshall McLuhan is responsible for me."

I can't think of anything sweeter in the world than Toronto in the summer time.

Barbara Amiel, columnist based in London, England, interviewed by Peter Gzowski on CBC Radio's *Morningside*, 14 April 1992.

Whatever buildings I saw in Toronto remained in my mind and came out in the form of Metropolis.

Joe Shuster, comic-book artist and creator (with writer Jerry Siegel) of "Superman," recalling his youthful years in Toronto in the early 1930s as a *Star* paperboy, interviewed in Los Angeles by journalist Henry Mietkiewicz, *The Toronto Star*, 26 April 1992. Clark Kent was a reporter for "the Daily Star," then "the Daily Planet," finally a TV station.

Toronto is a progressive, avant-garde city. It's so far advanced over anything I've seen in the States.

Philip Johnson, U.S. architect, assessing Toronto's new highrise complexes, quoted by David Lasker in *The Globe and Mail*, 3 Sept. 1992.

Toronto is where if you ask a waiter, "What is the *soupe du jour?*" he will reply, "It's the soup of the day, sir."

Mordecai Richler, author and host of the BBC-TV special *Oh, Canada! Oh, Quebec!*, telecast in the United Kingdom on 29 Sept. 1992, as noted by David Israelson in *The Toronto Star* the following day.

The only reason Toronto is no longer the dullest city on earth is that it is no longer full of anglo-Canadians.

Joel Garreau, journalist and author, quoted by Lawrence Martin in *Pledge of Allegiance* (1993).

One day, perhaps, the presence of the ravines will force us to redraw our mental picture of the urban region we inhabit. We may even decide that Toronto, properly understood, is not a big city that contains some parks but a big park that contains a city.

Robert Fulford, journalist, "Sunken Treasures," *Toronto Life*, Aug. 1993.

But he had married her, taken her for four years to Toronto, and when that self-imposed banishment grew irksome they had returned to London, now with two babies.

Reference to the background of a murder victim and his wife in **P.D. James**' mystery novel *Original Sin* (1994).

London is romantic and historically splendid; Paris is infinitely beautiful and has an air of louche aristocracy; Vienna has an ambiguity of spirit—a bittersweet savour—which enchants me. But Toronto—flat-footed, hard-breathing, hard-aspiring Toronto—has a very special place in my heart, like a love one is somewhat ashamed of but cannot banish.

Thoughts of the narrator of **Robertson Davies**' novel *The Cunning Man* (1994).

Toronto the Good Enough

George Yabu, interior designer, quoted by John Barber, "Toronto," *The Globe and Mail*, 10 Aug. 1994.

It's a nice place, it's easy going and nobody bugs you. It's a nice place in the summer. I wouldn't want to come here in the wintertime.

Mick Jagger, leader of the Rolling Stones rock group, explaining why he selected Toronto to prepare for his 1994 Voodoo Lounge world tour, and later his 1997 Bridges to Babylon world tour, quoted by Betsy Powell in *The Toronto Star*, 20 Aug. 1994.

Torontonians are the only people on Earth who believe that sin is a failure of education, that sex is a branch of public health, and that beauty is the outward manifestation of virtue. We disapprove of litter. We won't tolerate slums.

Joe Berridge, urban planner, "Is Toronto Different from U.S. Cities? Was It Planned that Way?" *The Globe and Mail*, 10 April 1995.

Toronto was a young city, it had no old age, no middle ages. It had made its own contracts. How fortunate to start so late in history, without the baggage of Britain.

Thoughts of a character in **Margaret Drabble**'s novel *The Witch of Exmoor* (1996).

In short, Greater Toronto will be the place where people and businesses that can choose to be anywhere, choose to be.

Report of the **Greater Toronto Area Task Force**, chaired by Anne Golden, released 17 Jan. 1996, advance text published as "A Vision for Greater Toronto," *The Globe and Mail*, 15 Jan. 1996. With this report Metropolitan (Metro) Toronto came to be known as the Greater Toronto Area (GTA).

Toronto... got all excited, a decade ago, of advertising itself as a "world-class city." Cities that are world-class—minor burgs such as Rome or Paris—don't boast about being world-class. They know it and never think about it.

Allan Fotheringham, columnist, "The Decline of Tranta the Good," *Maclean's*, 5 Feb. 1996.

The real miracle of Toronto might be that the "most hopeful and healthy city in North America" emerged almost by inadvertence, while people were looking elsewhere.

Richard Conniff, U.S. journalist, "Toronto," *National Geographic*, June 1996. The quoted words are those of urban writer and resident Jane Jacobs.

If Toronto had been in the Soviet Union, what would it have been called? Retrograd.

Nick Auf der Maur, "Page Two Column," *The Montreal Gazette*, 18 Sept. 1996.

How can you fault the safest city in North America?

Sue Zesiger, writer, "Best Cities," *Fortune*, 11 Nov. 1996. This is the article that found Toronto to be the world's leading city for "workability and livability," followed by London, Singapore, Paris, and Hong Kong."

Toronto is a big city that dreams of being little. It adores smallness. It's a metropolis with the mind of a village.

Robert Fulford, cultural commentator, "City of Imagination," *Maclean's*, 17 March 1997.

I don't know what my map of Toronto consists of, but it includes Connecticut, New York, and Pennsylvania.

Attributed to theatre impresario **Garth Drabinsky** during a discussion about mental maps of home cities by David Crombie, speech, University of Toronto, 7 Nov. 1997.

Toronto is such a problem to those of us from God's Country. It's clean. Everything works. Crime is discouraged, the subway routes are comprehensible. It's impossible not to wonder: Where did we go wrong?

Robert Stone, U.S. novelist, following a visit to the Harbourfront International Authors Festival, "American Apostle," *The New York Review of Books*, 26 March 1998.

In London, people ask you what school you went to. In New York, they ask you who you work for. In Toronto, they ask you what street you live on and how much you paid for your house—if they don't know already.

*

When someone tells me they don't like Toronto, I always ask, "What part?" It is a city of *quartiers*, a city that is unplanned, a city that completely changes character from neighbourhood to neighbourhood.

Allan Gotlieb, Chairman, Ontario Heritage Foundation, address, 7 April 1999, forum on Toronto's city plan, "What Makes a Great City?" *The Globe and Mail*, 12 April 1999.

McLuhan said the world would shrink to a global village. He never mentioned that Bloor and Yonge might be one of its major intersections.

Mitch Potter, reporter, "Bright Lights, Big City," *The Toronto Star*, 6 June 1999.

When the world dreams of America, it is dreaming of Toronto....

*

I would tell Torontonians how liberating I found their town—not stuck in its old image, as England or America might be, and yet not too precipitously clinging to a new one—they would look bewildered, express their pride with an apology or a shrug, define their city by telling me everything it wasn't. One curiosity of being a foreigner everywhere is that one finds oneself discerning Edens where the locals see only Purgatories.

*

I found myself telling Torontonians that their city had all Manhattan's software without, so to speak, its hard drive.

Pico Iyer, traveller, *The Global Soul: Jet Lag, Shopping Malls and the Search for Home* (2000).

TOTEM POLES See also NATIVE ART

I suggested . . . that the Department of Justice would like us to change the captions under the picture of the totem poles of Ninstints to read that those poles were carved by extraterrestrials.

Elizabeth E. May, social activist, referring to the fact that a reference in a booklet to the ancestral rights of the Haida people of the Queen Charlotte Islands, B.C., troubled the federal government, *Paradise Won: The Struggle for South Moresby* (1991).

TOURISM See also TRAVEL

Hospitalité Spoken Here

Slogan using French and English words authorized for use by the tourism department of the **Province of Quebec** during the administration of Jean Lesage (1960–66).

Canada. The World Next Door

Theme for an advertising campaign created for Tourism Canada by John McIntyre of **Camp Associates Advertising** for use in the United States, launched 5 March 1986; *Changing Opinions: The Marketing of Canada. The World Next Door* (Tourism Canada, 1986). It consisted of three, sixty-second television commercials: Wild World, Old World, New World.

There is nothing wrong with being a tourist, nothing uncomfortable about it if you are insensitive to how funny you look to the natives and simply enjoy how funny they look to you.

Jane Rule, writer, "Funny People," *A Hot-Eyed Moderate* (1986).

More money, time, and equipment are involved in tourism than an any other single business.

Frank Ogden, futurologist, *Ogdenisms: The Frank Ogden Quote Book* (1994).

The world needs more CANADA

Motto of the advertising supplement for **Eastern Canada** in *The New York Times*, 12 May 1996.

This year, about 16 million Americans are expected to make overnight stays in your country. Allowing for some duplication, that means that 5 per cent of the U.S. population will visit Canada this year.

James Brooke, Canadian bureau chief, *The New York Times*, "Why *The New York Times*'s Canada Bureau Isn't in Canada," *The Globe and Mail*, 4 Oct. 1999.

TOYS

Little boys never grow up. Their toys just get more expensive.

Don Harron, humorist, speaking in the guise of the comic character Valerie Rosedale, quoted by Martha Harron in *A Parent Contradiction* (1988).

TRADE & COMMERCE See also FOREIGN AFFAIRS, FREE TRADE

Sir John Macdonald and the Canadian Parliament have decreed that the people of Manitoba shall sell their wheat in Montreal and Toronto, and trade with Ontario and Quebec. God and Nature have decreed that they shall sell their wheat in and trade with St. Paul, Minneapolis, and other contiguous western cities.

J.W. Longley, Attorney General of Nova Scotia and professed annexationist, "Current Objections to Commercial Union Considered," *Handbook of Commercial Union: A Collection of Papers Read before the Commercial Union Club, Toronto* (1888) edited by Graeme Mercer Adams.

Canadians don't export. We allow others to import from us.

Jean-Luc Pepin, Minister of Trade and Commerce (1965–72), characteristic remark.

The dilemma is that it is always easy to be a "Boy Scout" in areas that are of little direct concern to Canada's own economic interests. The foreign service always has more latitude to talk about bananas than to talk about wheat.

Pamela A. McDougall, commissioner, *Report of the Royal Commission on Conditions of Foreign*

Service, 1981, as quoted by Michael Valpy, "Bananas and Wheat," *The Globe and Mail*, 14 Jan. 1982.

America's biggest trading partner is Canada. Its trade with Ontario alone exceeds its trade with Japan. The nations have been moving toward an open market since the 1800s. Four-fifths of trade was free already.

Priit J. Vesilind, writer, "Common Ground, Different Dreams," *National Geographic*, March 1990.

There is not another mechanism devised by man that will have a more civilizing influence on the lives of nations than trade. Fair and freer trade.

Brian Mulroney, Prime Minister, quoted in *Maclean's*, 25 June 1990.

There are more medieval trade barriers between Victoria and St. John's than from Great Britain to Greece.

Heading on an advertisement placed by the **Certified General Accountants of Canada** in *The Globe and Mail's Report on Business*, 21 August 1992.

Every day people, ideas and goods stream across our border. Bilateral trade now is more than a billion Canadian dollars every day—I learned to say that—and about $270 billion United States dollars last year. It is by far the world's largest bilateral relationship. Our trade with each other has become an essential pillar in the architecture of both our economies.

Bill Clinton, U.S. President, address, joint meeting of the House of Commons and the Senate of Canada, Ottawa, Senate Debates, 23 Feb. 1995.

The U.S. trades more with Ontario than with Japan, and conducts more trade with Canada in one week than with Africa in a year.

James Brooke, Canadian bureau chief, *The New York Times*, "Why *The New York Times*'s Canada Bureau Isn't in Canada," *The Globe and Mail*, 4 Oct. 1999.

TRADITION See also ANCESTRY, HERITAGE, PAST

I have traversed five or six hundred leagues in Canada without finding a single memorial of bygone times; no one there knows anything of the doings of his great-grandfather. May we not see in that the primitive condition of mankind?

Complaint of "the Child of Nature," an unnamed Huron Indian, abducted from the Old World and taken to France where he was Christianized and imprisoned, in the French author **Voltaire**'s work of satire "The Child of Nature" (1767) included in *Zadig and Other Tales* (1923) translated by R. Bruce Boswell.

I heard a friend exclaim, when speaking of the want of interest this country possessed, "It is the most unpoetical of all lands; there is no scope for imagination; here all is new—the very soil seems newly formed; there is no hoary ancient grandeur in these woods; no recollections of former deeds connected with the country.

Catharine Parr Traill, pioneer writer, letter of 9 May 1833, *The Backwoods of Canada: Being Letters from the Wife of an Emigrant Officer* (1836).

Let us make haste to write down the stories and traditions of the people, before they are forgotten.

English translation of the motto of *Soirées canadiennes*, the literary monthly published in Quebec City from 1861 to 1865; the motto was devised by folklorist **Joseph-Charles Taché**.

If all of us / Who need roots / Start digging / At the same time / There just aren't / Going to be enough spades / To go around.

Lines from **Raymond Souster**'s poem "The Need for Roots," quoted by Milton Wilson, "Recent Canadian Verse," *Contexts of Canadian Criticism* (1971) edited by Eli Mandel.

TRAINS See RAILWAYS

TRANS-CANADA HIGHWAY

Nine-tenths of Canada's people live near the slender belt of the Trans-Canada Highway.

Wes Rataushk, writer, *Silver Highway: A Celebration of the Trans-Canada Highway* (1988).

TRANSLATION

Translation is a strange, self-effacing craft in which perfection is unattainable and the ultimate sign of success is not to be noticed.

Paul Wilson, translator, "Keepers of the Looking-Glass," *The Brick Reader* (1991) edited by Linda Spalding and Michael Ondaatje.

Translation is the art of re-imagining, in other languages and through other eyes, that which a certain text appears to be saying.

Alberto Manguel, essayist, "The Right Word Is Often a Stranger," *The Globe and Mail*, 18 April 1992.

The poet moves from life to language, the translator moves from language to life; both, like the immigrant, try to identify the invisible, what's between the lines, the mysterious implications.

Line from **Anne Michaels**' novel *Fugitive Pieces* (1996).

TRAVEL See also AUTOMOBILES, AVIATION, RAILWAYS, SHIPS & SAILING, TOURISM

We arrived finally at the (so-called) "best hotel in town." May a kind fortune preserve us from the worst!

Henry Van Dyke, essayist, visiting Winnipeg, "The Red River of the North," *Harper's New Monthly Magazine*, May 1880.

The more you travel in Canada west of the Lakehead the more you think of the country as an act of will. Its central reality—more real and more central even than the grain elevator—is the telephone book.

Michael Macklem, publisher, "A Book a Mile," *The Tamarack Review*, No. 55, 1970.

Nobody foresaw that cars would "make" the motor roads and create suburbia. Nor did anyone anticipate that roads would put a "concrete kimono" on the community and destroy cities.

Marshall McLuhan, communications pioneer, *Take Today: The Executive as Dropout* (1972) with Barrington Nevitt.

There are four classes of travel—first, second, third, and with children.

Richard Needham, newspaper columnist, *The Wit and Wisdom of Richard Needham* (1977).

It's like our visit to the moon / or to that other star: / I guess you go for nothing / if you really want to go that far.

Last line of **Leonard Cohen**'s song "Death of a Lady's Man" from the album *Death of a Lady's Man* (1978).

Canadians go south to the Caribbean to avoid the winter cold, south to New York City to flee provincialism, and south over the border to avoid exorbitant liquor taxes and Sunday store closures. In Canada, south is the direction of escape....

Witold Rybczynski, architect and essayist, *The Most Beautiful House in the World* (1989).

I always feared there would come a time in my travels when suddenly it would all be futile, when I'd understand there was no purpose to the journey. Then I'd just go home.

Tim Ward, traveller, *What the Buddha Never Taught* (1990).

Canadian history began 20,000 years ago when primitive people came across the land bridge from Asia to watch the quarter-finals of the national Hockey League playoffs, which are still going on.

Dave Barry, U.S. travel guide writer, *Dave Barry's Only Travel Guide You'll Ever Need* (1991).

Canada the Good is a slogan that Canadian publicists, it seems, are not brave enough to adopt; they go on and on about those Rockies, those tiresome Mounties, kilted guards of honour and corners of olde France, but they are too timid to offer the grandest of all tourist inducements: that by coming to Canada you are very likely visiting the freest, fairest and kindest society that mankind has yet evolved.

Jan Morris, Anglo-Welsh traveller, "In Praise of Canada," *The Toronto Star*, 15 June 1992.

I have no desire to be elsewhere. I have no need for elsewhere. *Elsewhere* is in the mind.

Timothy Findley, novelist, "When You Write about This Country," *The Canadian Forum*, Sept. 1992.

There are two stoplights in the 2,000-kilometre stretch of the Trans-Canada highway between Sydney, Cape Breton, and Windsor, Ontario. I could see them both from my office in the high rise.

Philip Milner, author and academic, *The Yankee Professor's Guide to Life in Nova Scotia* (1993).

Writing about travel, whether imaginary or the narrative of actual events, is, I suggest, one of the great arteries of world literature, into which flow vast tributaries of experience, and which feed as abundantly as the past floods of the Nile our imaginative conceptions of the world of life.

George Woodcock, author and traveller, "Travel and the Exorcism of Boredom," *Queen's Quarterly*, Summer 1994.

The road ran along the river, into the northern spruce, to Quebec. Because it went to Canada, the road had a blue mood of lonely distances and night travel.

Lines about Labrador from **E. Annie Proulx**'s story "A Country Killing," *Atlantic Monthly*, Nov. 1994.

TREES See also FORESTS

Many a terrible secret is hid by those silent woods....

From the last sentence of **Sir Arthur Conan Doyle**'s historical novel *The Refugees: A Tale of Two Continents* (1893) set in the days of New France.

In the deepest part of the forest beats the heart of a country / A people without a forest is a people in decline.

Lines attributed to Prime Minister **Sir Wilfrid Laurier**, inspired by a visit to Lac Témiscouata and adjoining regions on Quebec's South Shore, noted in *Bas-Saint-Laurent: Tourist Guide* (7th ed., 1991).

They are dying because they cannot stand the city. And the city comes nearer and nearer all the time.

Ernest Hemingway, reporter, "Cars Slaying Toronto's Splendid Old Oak Trees" (1923), republished in *The Toronto Star*, 1 March 1992.

Martin lived in British Columbia... and when Martin spoke of those mighty forests, his voice changed, it became almost reverential; for this young man loved trees with a primitive instinct, with a strange and inexplicable devotion.

Description of the character Martin Hallam in **Radcliffe Hall**'s once-controversial novel *The Well of Loneliness* (1928)

I rarely feel so free in social intercourse with humans as I always feel with trees.

Lionel LeMoine FitzGerald, artist, letter to Bertram Brooker, 19 Feb. 1937, quoted by Paul Duval in *Four Decades: The Canadian Group of Painters and Their Contemporaries—1930–1970* (1972).

The Douglas fir, also known as the Douglas spruce, is neither a fir nor a spruce—but a pine tree.

Robert L. Ripley, cartoonist and columnist, *Ripley's Mammoth Believe It or Not!* (1955).

Did you know that trees talk? Well they do. They talk to each other, and they'll talk to you if you listen. Trouble is, white people don't listen.... I have learned a lot from trees: sometimes about the weather, sometimes about animals, sometimes about the great Spirit.

Tatanga Mani, Stoney Indian also known as Walking Buffalo, *Tatanga Mani: Walking Buffalo of the Stonies* (1969) edited by Grant MacEwan.

Pine's the Canadian tree / and not the maple, / pines reflected in cold rivers.

Lines from **John Ferns**' title poem in *Pine's the Canadian Tree: An Anthology* (1975) edited by Dorothy S. Murphy.

TROUBLE

A man who goes out to meet trouble will have a short walk.

Bob Edwards, publisher, *The Eye Opener*, Summer Annual, 1920.

Do not face trouble; outface it.

Robin Skelton, poet and aphorist, *A Devious Dictionary* (1991).

I guess the good Lord knew / I was born with a thorn in my shoe.

Lines from **Gene MacLellan**'s song "Thorn in My Shoe" (1970), quoted in his obituary by Barbara MacAndrew in *The Globe and Mail*, 28 Jan. 1995.

"Sorry for your trouble."

It's one of the great Nova Scotian phrases, precise, economical, eloquent. When someone has died, it's what you say to the family. It's exactly what you mean, and it says everything.

Silver Donald Cameron, columnist, *The Halifax Herald*, 23 June 1998.

TRUDEAU, PIERRE ELLIOTT See also POLITICIANS

If all politicians were like Mr. Trudeau, there would be world peace.

John Lennon, formerly of the Beatles, press conference following a meeting that he and his wife Yoko Ono had with Prime Minister Trudeau, Parliament Hill, Ottawa, 22 Nov. 1969; quoted by Trudeau in his *Memoirs* (1993).

In Pierre Elliott Trudeau, Canada has at last produced a political leader worthy of assassination.

Irving Layton, poet and aphorist, *The Whole Bloody Bird (obs, aphs & Pomes)* (1969).

Trudeau is able to wear this corporate image which is not private or personal. He gets it, as far as I know, from his Indian heritage. He must be forty percent Indian, like many French Canadians, and I think this corporate tribal mask is his greatest asset. Nobody can penetrate it. He has no personal point of view on anything.

Marshall McLuhan, communications pioneer, quoted by Peter C. Newman in "The Table Talk of Marshall McLuhan," *Maclean's*, June 1971.

Trudeaucrats

Term first used with reference to Prime Minister Trudeau's entourage in Ottawa by sports columnist **Dick Beddoes** in *The Globe and Mail*, 2 Aug. 1976.

My judgement, as of now, is that I am the best.

Pierre Elliott Trudeau, Prime Minister, press conference following the defeat of his government, 22 May 1979, quoted by Andrew Szende and David Blaikie in *The Toronto Star*, 20 July 1979. When the reporters sniggered, Trudeau looked surprised and asked, "What's so funny about that?"

When I shine, he shines.

Margaret Trudeau, wife of Prime Minister Trudeau, open-line radio program, CKOY Ottawa, as noted in *The Toronto Star*, 6 Feb. 1976.

More importantly, he chose to marry into a younger generation which, despite its present flat tummies, high, firm breasts and wholesome expressions, has fewer inner resources and whose particular ethos puts no premium on duty, loyalty or sacrifice at the expense of self-fulfilment.

Auberon Waugh, columnist, "Found under a Stone," *The Spectator*, 19 March 1977.

I'm the woman who gave freedom a bad name.

Line from the one-woman revue *Maggie and Pierre* (1980) written and performed by **Linda Griffiths**, who impersonated both the Prime Minister and his estranged wife Margaret Sinclair.

Thank you for being the first Canadian Prime Minister who's never been dull.

F.R. Scott, poet and professor of law, addressing guest speaker Pierre Elliott Trudeau, Scott's 70th birthday celebration, Montreal, *Brick: A Journal of Reviews*, No. 30, Summer 1987.

Whether you like him or not, he gave Canada its present international image.

Arkadi Tcherkassov, Russian geographer, "Our Man in Moscow," *Grainews*, July 1992.

Almost everything he did over the next four years was decisive, dramatic and disastrous. Almost everything he bequeathed has been repealed, denied or destructive.

William Thorsell, columnist, referring to the legacy of the Trudeau years in office, "Pierre Trudeau and the Dance of the Acolytes," *The Globe and Mail*, 24 Jan. 1998.

He seems impatient at being a Canadian.

Observation about Trudeau made by an unnamed European journalist covering the G-7 Summit in Venice in 1978, as noted by Richard Gwyn, "Opinion," *The Toronto Star*, 5 April 1998.

Don't bury me yet.

Pierre Elliott Trudeau, former Prime Minister, subject of a three-day academic conference at York University, telegram sent from Europe, quoted by Hugh Winsor, "The Power Game," *The Globe and Mail*, 26 Oct. 1998.

He haunts us all.

Stephen Clarkson, academic and author, referring to Pierre Elliott Trudeau, *Trudeau and Our Times: Magnificent Obsession / Heroic Delusion* (1990).

English Canada needs a strong central government; I recognize that. If I were an anglophone, I would think exactly like Trudeau.

Lucien Bouchard, Conservative Cabinet Minister who formed the separatist Bloc Québécois, quoted by Graham Fraser in *The Globe and Mail*, 3 Nov. 1990.

I suppose if you're Mr. Trudeau, it's kind of difficult when you get up in the morning and you look in the mirror and you know you've seen perfection for the last time all day.

Brian Mulroney, Prime Minister, ad hominem attack on Trudeau's constitutional concerns during public debate on the Charlottetown Accord, press conference, Ottawa, quoted by Carl Goar in *The Toronto Star*, 26 Sept. 1992.

In international affairs he stood head and shoulders above statesmen of other NATO countries who are blinded by their hostility to socialism and either cannot or will not recognize the situation as it is.

Andrei Gromyko, Soviet foreign minister, writing in his memoirs, as quoted by Trudeau in his *Memoirs* (1993).

As long as there are fascinating new places to explore, new pathways to discover through the forests, new stars to notice in the wilderness, new experiences to share and books to read, I will remain—God willing—a happy man.

Pierre Elliott Trudeau, former Prime Minister, *Memoirs* (1993).

The frustration Mr. Trudeau brought about in English Canada is one of the most disastrous factors in our recent history.

Lucien Bouchard, open letter, published in *The Montreal Gazette*, 10 Feb. 1996.

A man who believed in Canada and tried to give it his best.

Pierre Elliott Trudeau, former Prime Minister, upon being asked how he would like to be remembered, interviewed by Peter Gzowski on CBC Radio's *Morningside*, 22 Oct. 1996.

TRUST

I haven't become cynical, but the scales have fallen from my eyes. At one time, you believed that if you worked hard, you made a living. Life made sense, institutions were there to support you, government to represent you, and you could trust other people. Now nobody believes in anybody anymore.

Wendy Mesley, TV commentator, quoted by Matt Cohen in "Wild about Wendy," *Toronto Life*, June 1997.

TRUTH

Truth is mighty—mighty scarce.

Bob Edwards, publisher, *The Eye Opener*, 31 May 1919, *The Wit and Wisdom of Bob Edwards* (1976) edited by Hugh Dempsey.

I do not want to pull through life like a thread that has no knot. I want to leave something behind when I go; some small legacy of truth, some word that will shine in a dark place.

Nellie L. McClung, suffragette, *Our Nell: A Scrapbook Biography of Nellie L. McClung* (1979).

Truth should be the predominating thing. I know Truth is one of the first victims of war.

J.S. Woodsworth, M.P., House of Commons, 8 Sept. 1939.

In seeking absolute truth we aim at the unattainable, and must be content with broken portions.

Sir William Osler, physician and professor, quoted by William Bennett Bean in *Sir William Osler: Aphorisms from His Bedside Teachings and Writings* (1950).

Telling the truth is really the most powerful thing you can do.

Alice Munro, author, quoted by Val Cleary in *Quill & Quire*, March 1974.

Being truthful is more important than being a leader.

Robert L. Stanfield, former Conservative leader, "Sayings of the Week," *The London Observer*, 2 June 1974.

People feel uncomfortable at some of the things that are said at these hearings. Native people speak their minds quite openly and some people don't like what they say. White people speak their minds quite openly and others don't like what they say. But my only client is truth.

Thomas R. Berger, Justice and Royal Commissioner, quoted by Martin O'Malley in *The Past and Future Land: An Account of the Berger Inquiry into the Mackenzie Valley Pipeline* (1976).

What is true must be repeated. The inevitable may be more tolerable if confessed.

John Kenneth Galbraith, economist and essayist, *Almost Everyone's Guide to Economics* (1978) written with Nicole Salinger.

Why this should be, I cannot say, but there's always mystery in truth, perhaps most of all when life and art fuse imperceptibly.

Edmund Carpenter, anthropologist, Introduction to Stephen Guin Williams' photographs *In the Middle: The Inuit Today* (1983).

There is a story, among the Dene people of northern Canada, of a young Cree boy who was called to be a witness at a trial held by whites. He was asked by the judge to swear "to tell the truth, the whole truth, and nothing but the truth."

"Oh, no!" he replied. "I can't do that. I can only tell you what I know."

Dennis Murphy, communications theorist, "Taking Media on Their Own Terms: The Integration of the Human and the Technological" (1988), *Who Was Marshall McLuhan?* (1994) edited by Barrington Nevitt and Maurice McLuhan.

Truth is not necessarily stranger than fiction, but coincidence can sometimes be.

Line from **Edward Phillips**' novel *Sunday Best* (1990).

The truth that matters to people is not factual truth but moral truth; not a narrative that tells *what* happened but a narrative that explains *why* it happened and who is responsible.

Michael Ignatieff, author, "Articles of Faith," *Index on Censorship*, Sept.–Oct. 1996, as reprinted in "Readings," *Harper's*, March 1997.

There's a precise moment when we reject contradiction. This moment of choice is the lie we will live by. What is dearest to us is often dearer to us than truth.

Thoughts of a character in **Anne Michaels**' novel *Fugitive Pieces* (1996).

TURKEY

I was expecting many things in Canada to be better than they had been in Turkey, but in some respects I felt a certain shallowness in the Canadian attitude towards life and greater depth in the Turkish.

Murat Yagan, teacher of traditions from the Caucasus Mountains who arrived in Vancouver in the mid-1960s, *I Come from Behind Kaf Mountain: The Spiritual Autobiography of Murat Yagan* (1984) edited by Patricia Johnston and Joan McIntyre.

TURTLE ISLAND

Turtle Island encompasses the whole North American continent, Ellesmere Island in the north representing the head, Labrador representing one of the flippers, Florida another flipper, Mexico the tail, California another flipper, Alaska another flipper, and then the shell is divided into thirteen areas. There is a custodian in each area—and we belong to one of them. In our language we use the word Spoo-pii to describe the Turtle, which means an area which is high.

Stan Knowlton, Sik-ooh-Kotoki Friendship Society, Lethbridge, Alta., 25 May 1993, quoted in *Perspectives and Realities: Volume 4: Report of the Royal Commission on Aboriginal Peoples* (1996), co-chaired by René Dussault and Georges Erasmus.

TWENTIETH CENTURY See also

TWENTY-FIRST CENTURY

The twentieth century belongs to Canada.

Sir Wilfrid Laurier, Prime Minister, address, Canadian Club of Ottawa, 18 Jan. 1904. This is the most celebrated of Canadian quotations. What Laurier actually said on that occasion was "The nineteenth century was the century of the United States. I think we can claim that it is Canada that shall fill the twentieth century." Soon thereafter the words took on a life of their own and assumed the shape of the familiar aphorism "The twentieth century belongs to Canada." Since then the remark has been accepted as an index of national aspiration as measured against national achievement. In the 1900s it was regarded as prophetic; in the 2000s, as ironic.

The aphorism has caused parody and commentary. Over two dozen variations on the words and theme appear in *Colombo's Canadian Quotations* (1974), four more in *Colombo's New Canadian Quotations* (1987), four additions in *The Dictionary of Canadian Quotations* (1991), and ten in all in *Colombo's All-Time Great Canadian Quotations* (1994). Ten additional variations on the theme appear here.

It has been observed on the floor of this House, as well as outside of this House, that as the nineteenth century had been the century of the United States, so the twentieth century would be the century of Canada. This option has not been deemed extravagant. On this continent and across the waters, it has been accepted as the statement of a truth, beyond controversy.

Sir Wilfrid Laurier, Prime Minister, House of Commons, 21 Feb. 1905.

Our day is tomorrow.

Stephen Leacock, humorist, concluding sentence of *Canada: The Foundations of Its Future* (1941).

The twentieth century is the bathroom's century. True, the bathroom shares that century with the Dominion of Canada.... Let us say, then, that the twentieth century is the century of Canada and of the bathroom.

B.K. Sandwell, editor and essayist, "I Sing the Bathroom," *The Diversions of Duchesstown and Other Essays* (1955).

Adolescent dreams of glory haunt the Canadian consciousness (and unconsciousness), some naive and some sophisticated. In the naive area are the predictions that the twentieth century belongs to Canada, that our cities will become much bigger than they ought to be, or like Edmonton and Vancouver, "gateways" to somewhere else, reconstructed Northwest Passages. The more sophisticated usually take the form of a Messianic complex about Canadian culture, for Canadian culture, no less than Alberta, has always been "next year country."

Northrop Frye, cultural critic, "Conclusion to a Literary History of Canada" (1965), *The Bush Garden: Essays on the Canadian Imagination* (1971).

Colonial-minded until the 1960s, Canadians were never in a position to belong to the twentieth century, let alone to pretend that it belonged to us. But we are a society now just beginning to live in the post-modern world of Expo '67.

William Kilbourn, historian, "Some Feelings about the United States," *The New Romans: Candid Canadian Opinions in the U.S.* (1968) edited by Al Purdy.

The Twentieth Century may belong to Canada, but Canada belongs to the Chase Manhattan Bank.

Richard Needham, newspaper columnist, *The Globe and Mail*, 6 Dec. 1976.

Canada's Good Destiny myth—framed in the country's most celebrated aphorism: Laurier's misquoted prophecy that the 20th century belongs to Canada—is running on empty with just seven years of the century left. Canadians do not have good feelings about themselves or their country.

Michael Valpy, columnist, *The Globe and Mail*, 4 June 1993.

Canada might not even belong to the 21st century.

David O'Brien, Chairman of Canadian Pacific Ltd., Calgary, 19 May 1999, quoted by Claudia Cattaneo in the *National Post* the following day.

The 21st century will belong to China.

Allan Fotheringham, columnist, millennial prediction, *Maclean's*, 1 Jan. 2000.

Okay, okay, Wilfrid Laurier got it wrong. The 20th century didn't belong to Canada. Instead, this country belongs to the 21st century, belongs to it more completely than just about any other of the 188 member-states of the United Nations.

Richard Gwyn, columnist, "Home and Away," *The Toronto Star*, 1 Jan. 2000.

TWENTY-FIRST CENTURY See also

TWENTIETH CENTURY

As was the case with reciprocity, Laurier was wrong. Let's ensure that it will be the *twenty-first century* that belongs to Canada!

Mel Hurtig, publisher and nationalist, speech made in 1990, *At Twilight in the Country: Memoirs of a Canadian Nationalist* (1996).

The twentieth century belonged to the United States. So would the twenty-first—and Canada had to be in position to tag along.

Lawrence Martin, journalist and author, *Pledge of Allegiance: The Americanization of Canada in the Mulroney Years* (1993).

Canada does work a lot better than most people think, and, unless we screw it up more by surrendering to the decentralizers and the racialist impulse underlying separation, it certainly will inherit the 21st century.

Michael Bliss, historian, "Opinion," *The Toronto Star*, 28 June 1996.

The next millennium will not belong to Canada—or to anyone else, east of Hawaii. This will be the age of the Asian Tigers and Dragons, the ripening of China as the world's dominant power.

Peter C. Newman, journalist, "The Dawn of a New Millennium," *Maclean's*, 30 Dec. 1996.

I believe the twenty-first century will be the Pacific century.

Jean Chrétien, Prime Minister, address, National Press Club, Washington, D.C., 9 April 1997, quoted by Graham Fraser, "Chrétien Adjusts Warmth Dial," *The Globe and Mail*, the following day.

I will give all my energy to see that the 21st century will be a great century for the Canada again.

Jean Chrétien, Prime Minister, expressing in unidiomatic English gratitude for his government's majority and hopes for the country's well-being in the future, election night coverage, CBC-TV, 2 June 1997.

In the twenty-first century, this country will be united on the basis of equality of citizens and provinces or it is unlikely to be united at all.

Preston Manning, Reform leader, interviewed by Dale Eisler in *Maclean's*, 16 June 1997.

Perhaps Ontario's new motto could be: "The 21st century belongs to Ontario."

William Christian, political scientist, "Independence," *The Globe and Mail*, 2 Oct. 1997.

TWO NATIONS See also DISTINCT SOCIETY

Resolution: That Canada is and should be a federal state. That Canada is composed of two founding peoples (*deux nations*) with historic rights who have been joined by people from many lands. That the constitution should be such as to permit and encourage their full and harmonious growth and development in equality throughout Canada.

Resolution of the Montmorency Conference on National Unity, Montmorency, Que., 7–10 Aug. 1967.

You may not agree with me, but the theory that Canada is two nations can only lead to division and dissension and finally to de-confederation.

John G. Diefenbaker, former Prime Minister, address, Conservative convention, Toronto, 7 Sept. 1967, quoted by Robert C. Coates in *The Night of the Knives* (1969). Diefenbaker dismissed the Two Nations theory as "a ferry boat to disaster."

TWOONIE See LOONIE

TYPOGRAPHY See also DESIGN

Typographic design starts in a composing stick.

Carl Dair, typographer, originally a compositor and printer, statement reproduced in the privately printed volume "Carl Dair in Quotes" (*Wrongfount 6*, 1968).

Typography is the craft of endowing human language with a durable visual form, and thus with an independent existence. Its heartwood is calligraphy—the dance, on a tiny stage, of the living, speaking hand—and its roots reach into living soil, though its branches may be hung each year with new machines. So long as the root lives, typography remains a source of true delight, true knowledge, true surprise.

Robert Bringhurst, author and typographer, *The Elements of Typographic Style* (1992, 2nd ed., 1996).

U

UFOs See UNIDENTIFIED FLYING OBJECTS

UGLINESS

I think that the general insensitivity of the eye is a very real problem in our society. We tolerate ugliness all around us—in our houses, our furnishings, our cars, our outdoor signs and billboards. Ugliness is the norm; that which is beautiful is conspicuous, and being conspicuous, people are not too sure that they want it.

Carl Dair, typographer, address, opening of *Typography 62 Exhibition*, Education Centre, Toronto, 8 Jan. 1963.

UKRAINIAN PEOPLE

Flee, flee, for here you have no hand, and there you will have plenty of land. Here you are drudges; there you will be masters.

Ivan Pylypiw, advocate of Ukrainian immigration to Canada, encouraging fellow villagers of Nebyliw, Western Ukraine, to settle the Canadian Northwest, 1892–93; he and fellow villager Wasyl Eleniak became the first Ukrainian immigrants, 7 Sept. 1891.

The Ukrainian prairies gave us our souls, but the Canadian prairies have stirred us up to sing.

Ivan Danylchuk, Ukraine-born, Saskatoon-based poet, Preface, *Day Dawns* (1929) as translated by Watson Kirkconnell in *Canadian Overtones* (1935).

I said to Mr. Khruschev, "Give the Ukrainians the vote!" Then he got mad and that's when he took off one of his shoes, you remember, and hammered the table with it.

John G. Diefenbaker, Prime Minister, address, Ukrainian Centre, Montreal, election campaign of 1962, quoted by Peter Dempson in *Assignment Ottawa: Seventeen Years in the Press Gallery* (1968). He boasted that his remark had brought about the Soviet Premier's shoe-banging episode at the United Nations. Although Diefenbaker did address the UN General Assembly on the subject of free elections in the Soviet sphere of influence in 1960, Nikita Khruschev was not then present. Some sixteen days later he banged the table with his shoe during an address made by a delegate from the Philippines.

When I was travelling through the Ukraine I felt at home because it was like Manitoba with the poplar trees, the land, and the crops. Those people brought all the right tools, and they brought seed. They got here and within no time at all they had built log cabins and tilled the land.

W.D. Valgardson, author, interviewed by Judith Miller in *Other Solitudes: Canadian Multicultural Fictions* (1990) edited by Linda Hutcheon and Marion Richmond.

If you ask an average Russian what he knows of Canada, he would start with ice hockey, then mumble something about Indian trappers and French-Canadian voyageurs and loggers, and then add firmly: It's the country where *our* Ukrainians grow wheat!"

Arkadi Tcherkassov, geographer, "A Homesick Russian's Thoughts about the Ukraine—in the Heart of Labrador!" *Grainews*, June 1994.

UNDERSTANDING

Understanding is neither a point of view nor a value judgment. To understand something is to grasp its multiple facets simultaneously in their constantly changing relationships to each other, and to environments, both visible and invisible.

Barrington Nevitt, communications consultant, *The Communication Ecology: Re-presentation versus Replica* (1982).

That takes understanding, and most of us don't have much these days. We're just name-calling and "them and us-ing," as human beings have always done. But we don't have to do that. We can do better.

Buffy Sainte-Marie, singer and war protester, quoted by Daryl Jung in *Now*, 14 April 1988.

UNEMPLOYMENT See also LABOUR

Quebec youth are having rather a hard time. Especially the student class. You see, so many are workless, on their graduation. And that, as you will see, contributes to the upbuilding of the Quebec "nationalism" of which we have spoken already. They see, and believe, that the choice jobs fall into more or less alien hands. And that, of course, brings its own reaction.

C.G. (Chubby) Power, Liberal Cabinet Minister, interviewed by R.E. Knowles in *The Toronto Star*, 3 March 1937.

All other problems and all other desires tend to disappear when one is out of work. An economic recession is a national problem; unemployment is a personal problem.

Pierre Elliott Trudeau, Prime Minister, address, Saskatchewan Liberals, Regina, 13 Feb. 1971.

Canadians don't hate unemployment but they hate the unemployed.

Reuben Baetz, executive director, Canadian Council on Social Development, quoted in *The Vancouver Sun*, 28 Feb. 1972.

Would that wars rather than men went unwaged.

Maurus E. Mallon, aphorist, June 1993.

A more interesting way of stating this problem of definition is that 30 per cent (some 820 million people) of the world's labour force is either unemployed or not earning a subsistence wage.

John Ralston Saul, author, *The Doubter's Companion: A Dictionary of Aggressive Common Sense* (1994).

UNGAVA See also QUEBEC

In trying to decide to which situation the government has shown the least sensitivity, one has a rich field of choice; but the heartless imposition of low-flying NATO planes over Innu lands in the Ungava peninsula is probably the winner. One could not find a better example anywhere of a government failing to represent the interests of its people.

Boyce Richardson, journalist, "Concealed Contempt," *The Canadian Forum*, Dec. 1989.

All of northern Quebec, Ungava, was incorporated in the province in 1912. Ungava was, and arguably still is, the land of the Crees, whose protection was a federal responsibility devolved as an administrative convenience, but not irrevocably, to Quebec. If Quebec should one day declare itself independent, it should expect to lose more than half its territory the following day when the Crees likewise declare themselves independent—by taking much of the mighty James Bay project with them.

John Grimond, editor, "Survey on Canada," *The Economist*, 19 June 1991, reprinted in *The Globe and Mail* the same day.

UNIDENTIFIED FLYING OBJECTS See also EXTRATERRESTRIAL LIFE

Some considerations affecting the interpretations of reports of unidentified flying objects.

First recorded use of the words unidentified flying objects to describe anomalous aerial craft, presumably extraterrestrial in origin, formerly called flying saucers, may well be in the Canadian government document titled "Report on Visit to USAF Headquarters / Directorate of Intelligence / May 15–19" dated 23 May 1950, part of "Project Second Story" and presumably written by **Wilbert Smith**, a flying-saucer enthusiast with the Department of Transport.

CANADA: A HAVEN FOR UFOS?

Heading on a magazine article that Roy Neary (actor Richard Dreyfuss) rips from the wall of his room, briefly visible in Steven Spielberg's movie *Close Encounters of the Third Kind* (1977).

I don't know why, but there are more UFO sightings in Canada than anywhere else in the world.

J. Alen Hynek, director, Centre for UFO Studies, quoted by Sidney Katz, "UFO Researcher Sure He'll Meet Spacemen from Distant Stars," *The Toronto Star*, 19 March 1977.

Some people believe I am crazy. I don't care.

Claude Vorilhon, French journalist known as the cult leader Rael, founder of the Raelian movement, now based in Quebec, author of the book *The Message Given to Me by Extra-terrestrials: They Took Me to Their Planet* (1978).

The evidence is overwhelming that Planet Earth is being visited by extraterrestrial spacecraft, that the subject of UFOs represents a kind of Cosmic Watergate, and that none of the arguments made by the small group of "noisy negativists" stand up under careful scrutiny.

Stanton T. Friedman, flying-saucer enthusiast, resident of New Brunswick, characteristic observations, 15 Jan. 1991.

One woman wrote to me that I was right about the abduction phenomenon, but that I left out the most important thing, that during the night aliens were going to downtown Toronto and rearranging the buildings.

Budd Hopkins, investigator of alien abductions, commentary, *Alien Discussions: Proceedings of the Abduction Study Conference held at MIT, Cambridge, MA* (1994) edited by David E. Pritchard and John E. Mack.

No one can think about the subject and be relaxed.

Dwight Whalen, researcher, referring to UFOS, Niagara Falls, Ont., 19 July 1996.

UNION OF SOVIET SOCIALIST REPUBLICS See SOVIET UNION

UNIONS See also CAPITALISM, LABOUR, STRIKES

Grass will grow, the river will reach the sea, the boy will become a man, and labour will come into its own.

Fred J. Dixon, leader of the Winnipeg General Strike, defence speech, rebutting the charge of seditious conspiracy and defending the cause of labour, Winnipeg, 13–14 Feb. 1920.

You know my origins; I have always been with, and one of, the workers, and I have neither the desire nor the ability to swing at this late date to the other side. In my official capacity I have travelled the middle of the road, but now that you have put the extreme alternative to me, my place is marching with the workers rather than riding with General Motors. At this late date I cannot oppose unionism and the workers and labour as a whole.

David A. Croll, Ontario Minister of Public Welfare, Labour, and Municipal Affairs, letter of resignation over a matter of principle to Ontario Premier Mitchell Hepburn, 14 April 1937, published in *The Toronto Star* the following day.

Wherever we look around the world, we find that the happiest and most progressive democracies are also the ones where unions flourish.

F.R. Scott, constitutional law authority, "The Relationship of the White Collar Worker and Unions" (1942), *A New Endeavour: Selected Political Essays, Letters, and Addresses* (1986) edited by Michiel Horn.

A central objective of Canadian socialists must be to further the democratization process in industry. The Canadian trade union movement throughout its history has waged a democratic battle against the so-called rights or prerogatives of ownership and management.

"The Waffle Manifesto: For an Independent Socialist Canada" (1969) reprinted in *The Canadian Forum*, Dec. 1989.

If the public can't see the justice of our cause, then to hell with the public!

Joe Davidson, President, Canadian Union of Postal Workers, referring to the inconvenience that a national postal strike would cause the public, Aug. 1975, quoted by Walter Stewart in *The Canadian*, 8 Oct. 1977.

Unions will survive in our society because, though they are heir to all the faults of humanity, they are the creation of humanity's highest virtues.

Desmond Morton, historian, *Working People* (1980) written by Terry Copp.

Unions: the people who brought you paid vacations

Slogan, advertisement sponsored by the **United Steelworkers**, *The Canadian Forum*, June 1998.

Canadian economic life should be legislatively insulated from the lobotomized, Luddite dishonesty of many of our labour leaders. The right to strike against the public interest should be abolished and the right to strike generally curtailed, while fair employment practices are rigorously enforced.

Conrad Black, publisher, "Out of Uncle Sam's Shadow," *National Post*, 11 Jan. 2000.

UNITED EMPIRE LOYALISTS

They Sacrified Everything Save Honour.

Inscription on the cairn dedicated to the memory of the United Empire Loyalists, Tusket, N.S. The historian **Robert B. Blauveldt** chose the words for the monument, which was unveiled in 1964. The designations "United Empire Loyalist" and "U.E." for "Unity of Empire" were chosen by Lord Dorchester, Governor-in-Chief of British North America, 9 Nov. 1789, as "a Marke of Honour" for families of immigrants who fled the Thirteen Colonies between 1776 and 1783 to settle in British North America.

One Flag, One Throne, One Empire.

Motto of the **Imperial Order, Daughters of the Empire** (IODE), a women's patriotic and philanthropic organization. Its first provincial chapter was formed by Margaret Murray in Fredericton, N.B., 13 Feb. 1900. Some ninety years later the IODE boasts ten thousand members in chapters from coast to coast.

And how are the Daughters today?

Elizabeth II, Queen of Canada, addressing members of the Imperial Order, Daughters of the Empire, Chatham, N.B., 16 July 1976, quoted by Gerald Utting in *The Toronto Star* the following day.

UNITED KINGDOM See also BRITISH EMPIRE & COMMONWEALTH, ENGLISH PEOPLE, IRISH PEOPLE, SCOTTISH PEOPLE, WELSH PEOPLE

We must seriously consider our Canadian position, which is most illegitimate. An Army maintained in a country which does not even permit us to govern it! What an anomaly!. . . . What is the use of these colonial dead weights which we do not govern?

Benjamin Disraeli, British Chancellor of the Exchequer, letter to Lord Derby, 1866, quoted by Gwynne Dyer and Tina Viljoen, commentator and TV producer, *The Defence of Canada: In the Arms of the Empire* (1990).

I had grown up only half Canadian, because I felt more than half British.

Robert MacNeil, broadcaster and memoirist, discussing his Scottish-English ancestry and his birth in Halifax, *The Right Place at the Right Time* (1982).

We have just passed an Immigration Bill to keep out the West Indians. My God, I would pass an Immigration Bill to keep out the Canadians. They have done nothing but damage to this country.

Robert Boothby, English observer, quoted by Robert Fulford in *The Globe and Mail*, 2 Oct. 1996.

UNITED NATIONS See also PEACEKEEPING & PEACEMAKING

I've seen more common sense expressed around the table in a farm house than I have around the table in the United Nations committee room.

Lester B. Pearson, former President of the UN's Security Council, CBC-TV's *First Person Singular*, 19 Aug. 1974.

Mankind urgently needs a system of enforceable international law and an agency that commands universal respect and trust to arbitrate differences, or humanity is doomed.

Frank R. Joubin, prospector, *Not for Gold Alone: The Memoirs of a Prospector* (1986) written with D. McCormack Smyth.

The United Nations will soon have 250 members. What makes you think 20th-century Canada will still be one of them?

Frank Ogden, futurologist, "Constructive Destruction Will Let in the Future," "As Prime Minister, I Would..." *Canada's Brightest Offer Innovative Solutions for a More Prosperous and United Country: Volume Two* (1996) with a foreword by Frank Stronach.

We'll throw a party if we win the gold medal in hockey, but not, apparently, if we win the gold medal for having the best society.

John Godfrey and **Rob McLean**, commentators, referring to the United Nations Human Development Index which in the 1990s regularly rated Canada as the best country in which to live, *The Canada We Want: Competing Visions for the New Millennium* (1999).

UNITED STATES OF AMERICA See also ALASKA; AMERICA; BORDER, CANADIAN-AMERICAN; CALIFORNIA; CANADA & THE UNITED STATES; FLORIDA

Come then, ye generous citizens, range yourselves under the standard of general liberty, against which all the force and artifices of tyranny will never be able to prevail.

George Washington, future U.S. President, proclamation, "The Inhabitants of Canada" (1774), quoted by Gilbert Parker and Claude G. Bryan in *Old Quebec: The Fortress of New France* (1903).

The American experience is too precious to be entrusted to present-day American patriots only.

William Kilbourn, historian, "Some Feelings about the United States," *The New Romans: Candid Canadian Opinions in the U.S.* (1968) edited by Al Purdy.

If Canadians cease to exist it is more likely to be death by hypnosis than by foreign investment. The vitality of the American media, from the NBC to *Penthouse*, is such that Canadians are losing consciousness of themselves.

John W. Holmes, political commentator, *Saturday Night*, July 1974.

In fact, the key to our own future security may lie in both Mexico and Canada becoming stronger countries than they are today.

Ronald Reagan, former film actor and Governor of California, announcing his candidacy for the U.S. presidency, address, New York City, 13 Nov. 1979.

One of the blessings of Canadian life is there is no "Canadian way of life," but a unity under allegiance to the Crown, admitting of a thousand diversities.

George Ignatieff, Russian-born former diplomat, *Cultures and Writers: A Cultural Dialogue of Ethnic Writers* (1983) edited by Yvonne Grabowski.

Americans believe not only "My country, right or wrong" but also "My country, right or wrong, is right."

Attributed to the columnist **Stuart Trueman** in *Add Ten Years to Your Life* (1989).

Americans are easy targets for derision because they take themselves so seriously. Indeed, I have noticed that all countries that own atom bombs take themselves seriously.

Sam Orbaum, Montreal-raised Israeli columnist, "Friday Feuilleton," *The Jerusalem Post*, 28 Jan. 1991.

I love the country but I can't stand the scene.

Line from **Leonard Cohen**'s song "Democracy" on the album *The Future* (1992).

There is nothing wrong with Americans dreaming of a republic which, by the year 2000, encompasses the Maritime and Western provinces of Canada, the Yukon and Northwest Territories all the way to the Pole.

Pat Buchanan, U.S. conservative commentator and perennial presidental candidate, quoted by Lawrence Martin in *Pledge of Allegiance* (1993).

In 1966 I thought that Americans were the salt of the earth: and so wherever they walked, nothing would ever grow again.

Douglas Fetherling, author, former draft-resister, *Travels by Night* (1994).

UNITY, NATIONAL

You, the League of Five Nations Chiefs, be firm so that if a tree should fall upon your joined hands, it shall not separate you or weaken your hold. So, shall the strength of union be preserved.

Article of the "Great Law of Peace" of the **Iroquois Confederacy**, reproduced by Craig MacLaine and Michael S. Baxendale in *This Land Is Our Land: The Mohawk Revolt at Oka* (1991).

Canada has achieved internal unity and material strength, and has grown in stature in the world community, by solving problems that might have hopelessly divided and weakened a less gifted people.

Harry S. Truman, U.S. President, address, joint sitting of the Senate and the House of Commons, 11 June 1947.

Identity is local and regional, rooted in the imagination and in works of culture; unity is national in reference, international in perspective, and rooted in political feeling.

Northrop Frye, cultural critic, *The Bush Garden: Essays on the Canadian Imagination* (1971).

The only real miracle of Canada's togetherness is that we have not yet torn each other limb from limb, and I am beginning to believe the size of the country is responsible, rather than its sweetness. There has always been plenty of room to dodge.

Walter Stewart, author, *But Not in Canada!* (1976).

Malevolence has not imprisoned us in two worlds. A sense of justice and fair play has.

Barbara Frum, interviewer and broadcaster, describing how the Canadian Broadcasting Corporation / Société Radio-Canada has acted to divide rather than unite Canada by maintaining two separate services in English and French, address, Destiny Canada Conference, York University, Toronto, 28 June 1977, quoted by Ron Lowman in *The Toronto Star* the following day.

Whatever the outcome of the present challenge to national unity, the important thing is how, as Canadians, we respond to the pressures generated by the challenge. The more our individual reactions are altruistic and based on what is good for the country rather than ourselves, the more positive the karma we shall inherit as citizens of a New Canada.

Ted G. Davy, editor, "Canada's Karma," *The Canadian Theosophist*, July–Aug. 1977.

I tell you, there can be no long-term prosperity or guarantee of freedom in Canada without unity. Unity is the keystone. Unity is fundamental.

Roger Lemelin, writer and publisher, address, Canadian Press, annual dinner, 2 May 1979, quoted in *The Toronto Star*, 4 May 1979.

So what holds us together? The Bay? Bell? Canadian Tire? Big Macs? Labatts? Molson's? Gretzky? The CN Tower, Expo 86, the Calgary Winter Olympics? Love/hate of the Yanks? None of the above? Great! Funny country, eh?

Charles Lynch, newspaperman, *A Funny Way to Run a Country: Further Memoirs of a Political Voyeur* (1986).

I keep telling people across this country, when I talk to aboriginal people and to non-aboriginals, that when you talk about unity, that it's going to be the aboriginal people that will keep this country together.

Elijah Harper, former Chief of the Red Sucker Lake Reserve, Manitoba M.L.A., addressing a Native conference at McMaster University, Hamilton, 18 May 1991, quoted by Barbara Brown in *The Hamilton Spectator*, 21 May 1991.

Canada was safely and solidly together *until* communications began to spot regional disparities. *Lack of communication* held the country together. With TV, Louis Riel would have succeeded.

Frank Zingrone, communications specialist, *The Toronto Star*, 3 Aug. 1993.

UNIVERSE See also SPACE

When daylight gives place to starlight we are transported from the earth to the universe, and to the thoughts which the contemplation of the universe begets.

Goldwin Smith, essayist, *Guesses at the Riddle of Existence and Other Essays on Kindred Subjects* (1897).

Our universe is vastly more mysterious than science has grasped. There are no accidents in the universe. I believe there is a cosmic plan for us and this belief is based on facts not on faith.

Allen Spraggett, author, quoted by Nancy Reynolds in *The Niagara Falls Review*, 24 Aug. 1976.

In the time it takes to read this sentence, the universe will increase in volume by 100 trillion cubic light-years.... The creatures who inhabit one planet of one star of one galaxy among billions now know the extent, if not the ultimate meaning, of the visible universe.

Terence Dickinson, astronomer, referring to man's understanding of the cosmos, *NightWatch: An Equinox Guide to Viewing the Universe* (1983, 1989).

For the Greeks, the word "cosmos" meant the universe, order, and beauty in the universe. Our word "cosmetic" derives from this.

Hubert Reeves, astrophysicist, *Malicorne: Earthly Reflections of an Astrophysicist* (1993) translated from the French by Donald Winkler.

Lovers who praise perfection's form / In one who keeps their ardour warm / Opine the universe to be / An accidental oddity.

Lines from **Robert Finch**'s poem "Oxymoron," *Miracle at the Jetty* (1991).

UNIVERSITIES See COLLEGES & UNIVERSITIES

U.S.S.R. See SOVIET UNION

UTOPIA

Political utopias are a form of nostalgia for an imagined past projected on to the future as a wish.

Michael Ignatieff, essayist, *The Needs of Strangers* (1985).

We are living in truly terrifying times, where utopias become literally inconceivable and the visibility ahead is closing down to zero.

Judith Merril, science-fiction personality, Afterword, *Ark of Ice: Canadian Futurefiction* (1992) edited by Lesley Choyce.

The one place I've never lived in is a perfect world.

John Sewell, urban critic, address, Hart House, University of Toronto, 14 Oct. 1997.

V

VALUE & VALUES

But it is from the deep sense of humane values commonly shared, which underlies them, that we draw our truest strength.

Sir Campbell Stuart, Montreal-born chief of propaganda in London in World War II, referring to Canada's relationship with Britain and the States, *Opportunity Knocks Once* (1952).

I learned... not to trust value judgments too much, even when they come from the pit of the stomach, which is where the sixteenth-century alchemist Helmont located the soul.

Northrop Frye, cultural critic, "The World as Music and Idea in Wagner's Parsifal" (1982), *Myth and Metaphor: Selected Essays, 1974–1988* (1990), edited by Robert D. Denham.

The calculation of costs has replaced the estimation of values.

Robin Skelton, man-of-letters, aphorism, May 1990.

Whatever our origin, we have enough in common to bind us far more strongly than now.

What are these values and ideas?

Freedom and dignity in diversity, with openness to all cultures and races; a sensitive democracy; social solidarity; an orderly, safe society; a clean environment; the often outspoken idea of North; a peace-supporting, more independent role in an increasingly interdependent world; a yearning to love this country in any way each individual chooses, with no apology—the right to be a Canadian in different ways, times and places, or not very much at all.

Keith Spicer, Commissioner, *Citizens' Forum on Canada's Future: Report to the People and Government of Canada*, published as a special feature of *The Toronto Star, The Globe and Mail,* and other newspapers, 29 June 1991.

The values of Canada are those of both a caring and a competitive society, but the country is under pressure in this Global Village.

Geraldine Kenney-Wallace, scientist and university president, *Finding Common Ground* (1992) edited by Jean Chrétien.

If everything is for sale, nothing has any value.

Walter Stewart, journalist, *Too Big to Fail: Olympia & York: The Story Behind the Headlines* (1993).

As I see it, the new mental picture of Canadians has been shaped by three major quests: for personal autonomy, for pleasure, and for spiritual fulfilment. In all three pursuits, the accent is on "personal."

Michael Adams, pollster, *Sex in the Snow: Canadian Social Values at the End of the Millennium* (1997).

Deliver value and make clients and prospects aware of all that you give. Emphasizing your perceived value is an effective marketing tool, Remember, Total Value = Real Value + Perceived Value.

George Torok, motivational speaker, "Presentation Matters," *Contact: Canada's Sales and Marketing Magazine*, Jan. 2000.

Everything of value today is invisible. If you can see it and touch it, forget it.

Frank Ogden, futurologist, aphorism, 7 March 2000.

VANCOUVER See also BRITISH COLUMBIA

To describe the beauties of this region will, on some future occasion, be a very grateful task to the pen of a skilled panegyrist.

Captain George Vancouver, English navigator, describing the site of the future city of Vancouver, Spring 1792, *A Voyage of Discovery to the North Pacific Ocean and Round the World* (1798).

I knew the Vancouver audience would be English, and therefore no trouble to talk to; otherwise it would have been insane for me to try to succeed with such a dilapidated voice.

Mark Twain, humorist and recitalist, writing to H.H. Rogers, 17 Aug. 1895, concerning his throat problems and his speaking engagement in Vancouver, quoted by Philip V. Allingham in "Mark Twain in Vancouver, British Columbia: August, 1895," *Mark Twain Journal*, Fall 1990.

Tyre and Sidon,—where are they? / Where is the trade of Carthage now? / Here is Vancouver on English Bay, / With tomorrow's light on her brow!

Last of seven stanzas of **Bliss Carman**'s poem "Vancouver" (1922), *Bliss Carman's Poems.*

Vancouver is lovely. There is no other word for it.

Sir Arthur Conan Doyle, author and traveller, *Our Second American Adventure* (1923).

Vancouver rain, Vancouver rain, / Again I hear its soft refrain / Tap-tapping on the window pane.

Verse quoted by **Robert W. Service** in *Harper of Heaven: A Further Adventure into Memory* (1948).

Oriental Vancouver.

Allen Ginsberg, poet, characterizing the city in 1956, *Allen Ginsberg Journals: Mid-Fifties (1954–1958)* (1995) edited by Gordon Ball.

Canadian cities like Vancouver are really still on the edge of wild country, where life can be rough indeed. A man can take part in a television programme and then return to something like a log cabin.

J.B. Priestley, English bookman and broadcaster, impressions of a five-city tour, "Canadian Notes and Impressions," BBC's *The Listener,* 31 May 1956.

Vancouver: A terrible hole.

Brendan Behan, Irish playwright, *The Wit of Brendan Behan* (1968) compiled by Sean McCann.

Nowhere else have I encountered this strange marriage of sea and forest.

Description of Vancouver's Stanley Park from French author and traveller **Michel Tournier**'s novel *Gemini* (1975).

Tawdry and romantic, bourgeois and raunchy at once, Vancouver is where the small ambitions flourish and the large dreams move furtively.

Silver Donald Cameron, journalist, *Weekend Magazine,* 19 April 1975.

Vancouver *is* the edge of the frontier and it attracts (it would be strange if it did not) a certain type of people.

Allan Fotheringham, columnist, Epilogue, *The Vancouver Book* (1976) by Chuck Davis. "Narcissus-on-the-Pacific" is one of Fotheringham's epithets for Vancouver.

The idea that Vancouver people really put quality of life as they see it—comfort, beaches, recreation areas and green spaces—far above economic growth amazes me.... If I moved here I would be, without question, anti-growth.... That makes Vancouver, outside of Marin County, the most limits-to-growth place I know.

Herman Kahn, director, Hudson Institute, referring to Los Angeles' Marin County, remark, 12 Nov. 1978.

In the '70s, I became fifty years old. I moved to Vancouver. Oddly enough I discovered that there were other joyful matters besides constitutional reform, the Quebec Referendum, and the latest Canadian political polls—*me.*

Laurier LaPierre, Quebec-born, Vancouver-based historian, quoted by Anna Porter and Marjorie Harris in *Farewell to the 70s: A Canadian Salute to a Confusing Decade* (1979).

Vancouver (n.) The technical name for one of those huge trucks with whirling brushes on the bottom used to clean streets.

Douglas Adams and **John Lloyd**, humorists, *The Meaning of Liff* (1983).

Nor does the proximity of mountains make the city itself any lovelier. You can see the Alps from Milan, but that doesn't do much for Milan itself. No, Vancouver is beautiful from *outside* Vancouver.

Stephen Brook, English travel writer, *Maple Leaf Rag: Travels across Canada* (1987).

If I dare make a prophecy, as a matter of fact, I would myself hazard an unpopular guess that in fifty years' time Vancouver will be much as it is today, only less so.

Jan Morris, Anglo-Welsh travel writer, "Too Nice for Words," *Saturday Night,* Feb. 1988.

This expansion has transformed Vancouver into the second busiest port in North America, surpassed only by New York. Vancouver now handles more cargo than Toronto, Halifax, Quebec, and Montreal combined.

Alan F.J. Artibise, planning consultant, "Canada as an Urban Nation," *Daedalus: Journal of the*

American Academy of Arts and Sciences, "In Search of Canada," Fall 1988.

Besides being home to the VSE, this city of 1.5 million people is the hallucinogen capital of North America.... A huge proportion of Canadian drug traffic flows through British Columbia, which also happens to be the magic mushroom capital of the world.

Joe Queenan, journalist, referring to the Vancouver Stock Exchange as well as to mind-altering drugs, "Scam Capital of the World," *Forbes,* 29 May 1989.

The paradox of Vancouver—so many inward-looking social groups in a beautiful outdoor setting—is the root of the city's strengths and weaknesses.

Liam Lacey, correspondent, "The Paradox in Paradise," *The Globe and Mail,* 29 June 1991.

Hongcouver, as it is now known, is evolving faster than any other Canadian city, as Montreal fades in bilingual boredom and Toronto hungers for being an American clone.

Allan Fotheringham, columnist, *Maclean's,* 24 Aug. 1992.

Unless we move more swiftly than during the past decade of economic decline, especially in Canada and the U.S., that funny Vancouver joke may not go over so well in Kansas City. "Why did the Asian cross the road?" "To buy the other side, silly."

Frank Ogden, futurologist, characteristic observation, March 1993.

The beauty of Vancouver has inspired our work here.

Bill Clinton, U.S. President, press conference, conclusion of the summit meeting with Russian President Boris Yeltsin, Vancouver, quoted by Deborah Wilson in *The Globe and Mail,* 6 April 1993.

It's a nice city. But it's as good a place for horror to happen as any.

Wes Craven, director of horror movies, on location in Vancouver for *A Nightmare on Elm Street,* quoted by Andrew Ryan in *TV Guide,* 18 June 1994.

Vancouver. Spectacular by Nature. / You can ski and sail in the same day. / Vancouver has the highest ratio of foreign-born population of any city in the world, according to a local survey of published statistics. / Paris has fashion. Venice has canals. New Orleans jazz. And Vancouver has ... wait for it ... literature.

Information package, **Tourism Vancouver**, 1 Oct. 1995.

You've probably heard that we can ski within sight of downtown Vancouver and be on the water catching a spring salmon, all in the space of thirty minutes. It's true—as long as your skis have quick-release bindings. Otherwise, it might take up to forty-five minutes.

Denny Boyd, columnist, quoted in the information package, Tourism Vancouver, 1 Oct. 1995.

We have a lot more in common with Hong Kong and Singapore than we have with Ontario and Quebec.

Attributed to B.C. Premier **Mike Harcourt**, referring to Vancouver, by David Beers in "Vancouver Arts," *The Globe and Mail,* 2 Nov. 1995.

Vancouver has taught Central Canadians to worry about vaudeville.

William Thorsell, editor-in-chief, referring to the urban political scene, quoted in "Vancouver Arts," *The Globe and Mail,* 2 Nov. 1995.

I just wish it was like the old days, easy parking everywhere.

Douglas Coupland, novelist, referring to changes taking place in Vancouver, quoted by David Beers in "Vancouver Arts," *The Globe and Mail,* 2 Nov. 1995.

Perched on the edge of a continent, Vancouverites have learned to make a living on the margins.

Christopher Dafoe, arts critic, "Vancouver Arts," *The Globe and Mail,* 2 Nov. 1995.

People still come here for essentially the same two reasons—exploitative or utopian—and neither one of those two streams leads naturally to expressions of collective identity.

Robert Mason Lee, arts columnist, quoted in "Vancouver Arts," *The Globe and Mail,* 2 Nov. 1995.

My new home in the West End is, near as I can tell, the only high-rise society in North

America where I can walk without fear at midnight, where I can imagine safely raising a child.

David Beers, journalist, referring to the lifestyle of Vancouver, "Sustainable Fantasy," "Vancouver Arts," *The Globe and Mail*, 2 Nov. 1995.

No longer road's end, Vancouver suddenly lies at the centre of a new geography of power, a confluence not of rivers or railroads but of time zones. Here is that rare spot where you can talk to Europe in the morning and Asia the same afternoon, making Vancouver ideal for trans-shipping digitized wealth.

David Beers, journalist, referring to the lifestyle of Vancouver, "Sustainable Fantasy," "Vancouver Arts," *The Globe and Mail*, 2 Nov. 1995.

I see this association of the city and mental and physical freedom as an important and valuable tradition not to be lost. I see myself as the symbolic descendant of that fleeing serf, and that is why I feel such pleasure at becoming a Freeman of my own city.

George Woodcock, man-of-letters, accepting the Freedom of the City Award, Vancouver, 1995, quoted by Alan Twigg, "Larger Lives," *The Globe and Mail*, 23 Dec. 1995.

Part of growing up in West Vancouver was to feel as if you were growing up in the middle of nowhere: a zero-history, zero-ideology bond-issuing construct teetering on the edge of the continent....

Douglas Coupland, author, *Polaroids from the Dead* (1996).

I like this new Vancouver... it's a city unlike any other city on Earth. It's clean and smart and beautiful and tolerant and getting wiser every day. We're pretty much the world's youngest city. This is our strength. We have the time and the free will to create our vision and it seems we're doing a good job of it.

Douglas Coupland, author, "Coupland's Vancouver," *Vancouver*, Oct. 1997.

Vancouver is a very nice place if you like 400 inches of rainfall a day. It is kind of like a tropical rain forest without the tropics.

David Duchovny, co-star of the *X-Files* television series filmed in Vancouver, comment made on the talk-show *Late Night with Conan O'Brien*, quoted by Christopher Dafoe in *The Globe and Mail*, 25 October 1997.

Vancouver is very clean and very lovely. But you have to use Canadian money there. It's very strange.

Charlize Theron, movie actor, "People," *National Post*, 24 Jan. 2000.

VANCOUVER ISLAND See also BRITISH COLUMBIA

Vancouver Island is weighing anchor, heading for the South Pacific.

Phyllis Webb, poet, "And Things Get Stranger Every Day," "Bank of Montreal: A Portrait of Canada," *Saturday Night*, May 1992.

VANDER ZALM, WILLIAM See also POLITICIANS, PREMIERS

There's nothing much more to find out about Bill Vander Zalm that isn't already known.

William Vander Zalm, future B.C. Premier, commenting on himself, 19 July 1982, quoted by Stephen Osborne and Mary Schendlinger in *Quotations from Chairman Zalm* (1988).

What is the sound of one hand clapping? The sound of Zalm Thought!

Stephen Osborne and **Mary Schendlinger**, compilers, *Quotations from Chairman Zalm* (1988). According to columnist Orland French, B.C. Premier William Vander Zalm is the originator of the peculiar kind of malapropism called "Zalm Thought"; he likened Vander Zalm to "a gardener who reaps his words before he sows his thoughts."

I only wish I knew him before his lobotomy.

Kim Campbell, Socred M.L.A., March 1988, quoted by Tim Harper in *The Toronto Star*, 27 March 1993.

In the last two weeks it seems to have gone from Vandermania to Zalmnesia.

Pun attributed to B.C. Opposition leader **Mike Harcourt** with reference to the resignation of B.C. Premier William Vander Zalm, CBC Radio, 17 April 1991.

VANITY

It is a fine thing to be a trifle vain. Too much modesty does not pay in this world.

Kit Coleman, columnist in the 1880s and 1890s,

quoted by Ted Ferguson in *Kit Coleman: Queen of Hearts* (1978).

VEGETARIANISM See also FOOD & DRINK

In the best Anglo-Saxon tradition, I'm almost totally indifferent to the process of eating and, quite frankly, can just barely manage to open cans. Furthermore, my basic attitude toward food is that it's a time-consuming nuisance—I have, by the way, become virtually a vegetarian in the past decade—and I would be only too delighted if one could effectively sustain oneself with all necessary nutritional elements by the simple intake of X capsules per day.

Glenn Gould, pianist, letter of 20 Jan. 1973, *Glenn Gould: Selected Letters* (1992) edited by John P.L. Roberts and Ghyslaine Guertin.

Wagner thought everyone should become vegetarian.... The lakes of the north of Canada, he wrote, are chock-full of vegetarian panthers and tigers. (This may have been true in Wagner's day. But there weren't any left last time I looked.)

David W. Barber, opera commentator, obscure reference to German composer Richard Wagner, *When the Fat Lady Sings: Opera History as It Ought To Be Taught* (1990).

If you are an "average meateater," its literature finger-wags, you'll consume precisely 12 cows, 29 hogs, 2 sheep, 37 turkeys, 984 chickens, and 408 kilograms of fish (and a partridge in a pear tree) in your lifetime.

Jeremy Ferguson, journalist, referring to information from the Toronto Vegetarian Association, "Consuming Passions," *The Globe and Mail*, 22 Jan. 1992.

VICE

Variety is the spice of vice.

Kent L. Bowman, aphorist, "A Is for Aphorisms," *The House Poets: Eight Toronto Poets* (1974) edited by Hans Jewinski.

Seek the balance between pleasure and honour; all else is vice.

L.S. Cattarini, aphorist, "Confessions of a New-Victorian," *Generation of Swine* (1995).

VICTIMS

You just can't win.

"Canadian slang expression" according to British lexicographer **Eric Partridge** in *Partridge's Dictionary of Slang* (1974).

Everyone must vacillate between a vision of himself as plaintiff and as defendant, as Abel and as Cain. And the world must always seem to be either the Garden of Eden, from which he is about to be expelled, or a circle of hell, into which he has wandered like Dante or Orpheus only to find that he can't get out. How guilty the innocent always feel, how innocent the guilty.

Thoughts of a character in **Jane Rule**'s novel *The Desert of the Heart* (1964).

This above all, to refuse to be a victim. Unless I can do that I am nothing.

Thoughts of the narrator of **Margaret Atwood**'s novel *Surfacing* (1972)

I refuse to be victimized and I refuse to *not document* how people are victimized.

Brian McKenna, TV personality, co-producer with Terry McKenna of CBC-TV's *The Valour and the Horror*, quoted by Anne Collins, "The Battle over 'The Valour and the Horror'" *Saturday Night*, May 1993.

In Canada, government-designated victims outnumber the entire population because of the possibility of accumulating conditions of victimization like food stamps....

Conrad Black, capitalist, "Après-Referendum Scenarios," *The Globe and Mail*, 21 Feb. 1995.

The identification of victimizer is difficult to accept. So we all cry out that we are victims, as only victims can claim purity. We can effect change only when we don the cloak of victimizer.

Joy Kogawa, author, interviewed by Lisa Hobbs Birnie in *Western Lights: Fourteen Distinctive British Columbians* (1996).

Victimology proved unable to generate objects of commodity value.

Douglas Coupland, novelist, "Agree/Disagree: 55 Statements about the Culture," *The New Republic*, 2 Aug. 1995.

All of us, it can't be denied, are victimized from time to time. But this is quite different from believing ourselves to be victims all the time.

That is a state of mind, more often than not in large part unconscious. It is buried in our mythology. Or rather, this is deformed mythology—mythology become mystification.

John Ralston Saul, author, *Reflections of a Siamese Twin: Canada at the End of the Twentieth Century* (1997).

VICTORIA See also BRITISH COLUMBIA

All that is required to render the place enjoyable is *society,* and it certainly does want a dozen good familes to settle there before it is endurable as a residence for a Governor's wife and daughters. The people are *entirely respectable,* but decidedly *plebian* and *narrow minded*.... They are modest respectable people—but very underbred, and of course the men are not improved by such associations.

Charles Kean, actor, letter, 22 June 1865, *Letters of Mr. and Mrs. Charles Kean Relating to Their American Tours* (1945) edited by William G.B. Carson. Keane and his theatrical troupe toured North America in 1831–33, 1845–47, 1864, and 1865.

I suggest that it is not a good climate where bananas and yams flourish if men decay. Canada, excepting Victoria, B.C., has a working rather than a loafing climate.

Vilhjalmur Stefansson, Arctic explorer, address, "Abolishing the Arctic," Empire Club of Canada, Toronto, 25 Oct. 1928.

So stands tranquil Victoria in her Island setting—Western as West can be before earth's gentle rounding pulls West east again.

Emily Carr, artist, "Grown Up," *The Book of Small* (1942).

In Eastern Canada they persist in regarding Vancouver and Victoria as one entity: The Coast. They little realize the impenetrability of the Tweed Curtain that separates Victoria from the rest of Canada.

Tony Emery, art curator, talk, CBC Radio, 4 Oct. 1955.

Both the city and metropolitan area had the highest proportion of population 65 and over among their Canadian counterparts, 21.4% and 18.1%, respectively, in 1996.

John Newcomb, "Victoria, B.C.," *The Canadian Encyclopedia: Year 2000 Edition* (1999).

VICTORIA DAY See HOLIDAYS

VICTORY

It is a delusion of the victor that history has come to an end. The certainty that it hasn't is the comfort of the defeated.

Vivian Rakoff, psychiatrist, insight from a dream, Montreal, Oct. 1967.

Never say that this is the final journey; the hour of fulfillment still will be ours.

Inscription on the headstone of NDP leader **David Lewis**, who died in Ottawa, 23 May 1981, a quotation from the marching song of Jewish partisans during World War II, noted by Cameron Smith in *Unfinished Journey: The Lewis Family* (1989).

VIDEO

This "vigilante video" force will change the way laws are enforced.

*

Within ten years, a good portion of the video you watch will be shot by you and your friends. A new world of images is evolving.

Frank Ogden, futurologist and coiner of the term "vigilante video" with respect to readily available camcorders, *Sunday Magazine,* 7 April 1991.

VIETNAM WAR See also WAR, WAR RESISTERS

I feel reasonably certain that were I a Vietnamese today I would enlist with my people against any government imposed on us by foreigners.

Brock Chisholm, first Director-General of the World Health Organization, speech, 1965, quoted by Allan Irving in *Brock Chisholm: Doctor to the World* (1998).

There is no ideology at the rice-roots level, only the sense that the mills of the gods grind slowly, and they grind woe.

Line of narration of CBC-TV's *Mills of the Gods* (1965), a documentary about the Vietnamese peasants trapped in a lifetime of war, written and spoken by documentary filmmaker **Beryl Fox** and broadcast to much controversy.

Bombing Pause, a temporary cessation of bombing to determine whether the opponent wishes to negotiate; a concession to create an atmosphere of negotiation.

The phrase was probably introduced into debate about the war in Vietnam by Canadian Prime Minister Lester Pearson, in a speech in Philadelphia on April 2, 1965. Pearson, who as Canada's Minister of External Affairs had won a Nobel Peace Prize, suggested that President Johnson ought to order a "pause" in bombing North Vietnam, which might bring about peace talks.

William Safire, columnist, *Safire's Political Dictionary: An Enlarged, Up-to-Date Edition of the New Language of Politics* (1968). Indeed, the first such "bombing pause" was commenced 13 May 1965 and lasted six days.

In the barbarous war in Vietnam, Canada has supported the United States through its membership on the International Control Commission and through sales of arms and strategic resources to the American military-industrial complex.

"The Waffle Manifesto: For an Independent Socialist Canada" (1969) reprinted in *The Canadian Forum*, Dec. 1989.

My son would have voted for the President / this year his first time, being twenty-one, / if he were not in jail or a refugee / in Canada, and if he were not dead / like the Republic....

Lines from **Paul Goodman**'s poem "Chicago" (1968), *Homespun of Oatmeal Gray* (1969).

Too hot! Too hot!

Kim Phuc, nine-year-old Vietnamese girl, running naked along a road in Vietnam, aflame with napalm, accompanied by her two brothers, photographed momentously by Associated Press photographer Nick Ut, June 1972; Kim Phuc, with her husband and family, became Toronto residents, as noted by Peter Cheney in *The Toronto Star*, 6 Feb. 1997.

They knew the score, and they expected nothing better from anybody than what generally happened. They were infallibly correct, infallibly polite, infallibly professional. There was a quiet confidence about them.... And if the Canadians were ironic and wryly humorous about it, they were also hardheaded as hell.

James Jones, novelist and correspondent, describing individual Canadians who participated in the Vietnam War, *Viet Journal* (1974).

Television brought the brutality of war into the comfort of the living room. Vietnam was lost in the living rooms of America—not on the battlefields of Vietnam.

Marshall McLuhan, communications pioneer, address, Montreal International Book Fair, quoted by Christie McCormick in *The Montreal Gazette*, 16 May 1975.

I have always regarded sneaking off to Canada to avoid the draft as an act of craven puppyhood. It seems to me that if you're going to resist, the only proper thing to do is *resist*, by either going the conscientious objector route or going to jail. Admittedly this is a lot less fun than cavorting with the baby seals north of the 49th parallel, but that's the breaks.

Cecil Adams, U.S. columnist, discussing American war resisters, *The Straight Dope: A Compendium of Human Knowledge* (1984).

If it had been a different war, I might have enlisted, but I believed that doing so for this war would have made me no different than the "good Germans" who fought for Hitler.

Stephen Eaton Hume, American-born writer living in Vancouver, grandson of Pugwash founder Cyrus Eaton, quoted by Alan Haig-Brown in *Hell No, We Won't Go: Vietnam Draft Resisters in Canada* (1996).

VIOLENCE See also HOCKEY VIOLENCE

I suggest, therefore, if you want to save a fantastic blood bath on this planet which would be dramatic, cathartic and tragic in the Greek sense, we turn off TV totally, for good.

Marshall McLuhan, communications pioneer, panel discussion, St. Michael's College, Toronto, Dec. 1970, quoted by Robert O'Driscoll in *The Canadian Forum*, May 1981.

Those who complain that our history is dull may be failing to recognize its greatest blessing—an extraordinary lack of violence.

Bernard Ostry, Secretary General, National Museums of Canada, quoted by Helen Worthington in *The Toronto Star*, 5 Nov. 1977.

I'm not going to be shy about using the sword if something illegal is attempted in the Province of Quebec.

Pierre Elliott Trudeau, Prime Minister, interviewed by Bruce Phillips, taped 20 Dec. 1977, telecast on the CTV Network on 1 Jan. 1978 and published in *The Globe and Mail* the next day.

If we were born to violence, we'd have fangs. If we let ourselves hate too much, we get ulcers. So I put what's wrong down to the system, not to human nature. And the system can be changed.

David Fennario, playwright, quoted by Ray Conlogue in *The Globe and Mail*, 4 Oct. 1980.

You're a soldier? Me too.

René Jalbert, former career soldier, sergeant-at-arms and head of security at Quebec's National Assembly, Quebec City, addressing Corporal Dennis Lortie of the Canadian Armed Forces, 8 May 1984. From the Speaker's Chair, Lortie shot and killed three people and injured thirteen others. After five hours of conversation, Jalbert persuaded Lortie to surrender. Quoted by CP in Jalbert's obituary, *The Toronto Star*, 22 Jan. 1996.

Violence is never the answer, unless, of course, *you're* winning.

Maurus E. Mallon, aphorist, observation made in July 1992.

Violence has been allowed to contaminate sex, and then sex is blamed as the cause of violence. Not only are we dealing with panic about violence, but also a sex panic fed by a born-again puritanism masked as biofeminist concern for women's safety.

John Fekete, philosopher, *Moral Panic: Biopolitics Rising* (2nd ed., 1995).

If you're a stranger in this strange land and a Canadian says, "Freeze," he's only talking about the weather. You don't have to fear for your life. Not right away, anyway.

Arthur Black, broadcaster and humorist, referring to differences between the United States and Canada, *Black in the Saddle Again* (1996).

There's nobody more dangerous to a woman than a weak and vengeful man with a fist, or a club, or a gun.

Margaret Wente, columnist, "Counterpoint," *The Globe and Mail*, 22 June 2000.

VIRTUAL REALITY

The whole question of virtual reality will be meaningless in that scenario. We'll be inside the computer, and we won't even realize it.

*

In a science fiction story, you need a rocket or a time machine. What they're mainly for is to move the characters and further the plot. I chose cyberspace.

William Gibson, science-fiction novelist, referring to his conception of cyberspace or virtual reality, quoted by Ric Dolphin in *Maclean's*, 14 Dec. 1992.

VIRTUES

Talking about virtue is a luxury that should be indulged in only after you have practised it for a lifetime.

Louis Dudek, poet and aphorist, "Epigrams," *Small Perfect Things* (1991).

Eventually virtue can come to anyone, just by the elimination of alternatives.

Thought of a character in **Joan Barfoot**'s novel *Keeping in Touch* (1994).

There are Canadian virtues—grit, tolerance, opportunity, civility, compassions, and equality—and they should be part of any definition of national character.

J.L. Granatstein, historian, *Yankee Go Home: Canadians and Anti-Americanism* (1996).

VISION

Who sees a vision bright and bold / Hath found a treasure of pure gold....

Lines from **Isabella Valancy Crawford**'s poem "Who Sees a Vision" (1884), *The Collected Poems of Isabella Valancy Crawford* (1905) edited by J.W. Garvin.

We have wanted to discover and create a new heaven and new earth here in Canada, and to make others see it.

Raymond Knister, author, "Canadian Literati" (1920s), *Poems, Stories and Essays* (1975) edited by David Arnason.

Never cheat on your own vision.

Ludmilla Chiriaeff, founder and artistic directory of Les Grands Ballets Canadiens (1958–74), characteristic remark, quoted by Linda Howe-Beck in her obituary, "Lives Lived," *The Globe and Mail*, 9 Oct. 1996.

My children, I desire you to pray for unity of all children, from the Land of the Rising Sun,

Japan, to the Land of the Maple Leaf, Canada, and I desire unity among all children.

Message attributed to the **Virgin Mary**, delivered in English on 13 Sept. 1992 by Marie Danielle, Sister of the Immaculate Heart, L'Avenir, near Drummondville, Que., as quoted by Mike King in *The Montreal Gazette*, 25 Sept. 1992.

Seeing is no longer believing. We may soon have to revert to secrecy, like cultural militias, in order to regain the sacred iconic power of ancient archetypes, which we had almost lost....

Frank Zingrone, academic, "A Psychic Visitation by the White Goddess," *Gazette* (York University), 8 Oct. 1997.

VOCATION

I felt no special sense of vocation. If God had created me to become a chemist, he had neglected to inform me of the fact.

John C. Polanyi, scientist and Nobel laureate, "No Genuine Ivory Tower Is Ever Irrelevant," *The Vancouver Sun*, 9 Sept. 1989.

VOTES See also ELECTIONS

Some days we count the votes around this table and other days we weigh them. Today we'll weigh them.

Arthur Vining Davis, Chairman, Aluminum Company of America, alluding to his practice when faced with resistance of assessing the stock value of each of his directors, quoted by Peter C. Newman in *The Canadian Establishment: Volume One* (1975).

Why do people vote Liberal or Conservative, even after they have indicated dissatisfaction with their traditional party?

I think the reason is that when they are in the polling booth and as they hold the pencil, poised to bring it down onto the ballot, the ghost of their Liberal or Conservative grandfather appears, grabs the pencil, and makes the X for them.

David Lewis, NDP leader (1971–75), characteristic remark, heard in Oct. 1974.

WAGES

But Schreyer was unwilling to rest on his laurels: He created quite a stir in Winnipeg when he announced that as a long-term project he favoured an incomes' policy under which the highest salaries in Manitoba should not be more than two and a half times greater than the lowest wages.

Ivan Avakumovic, historian, referring to the NDP Premier Ed Schreyer of Manitoba, later Governor General, quoted in *The Commonwealth*, Vancouver, 19 May 1976, *Socialism in Canada: A Study of the CCF-NDP in Federal and Provincial Politics* (1978).

WALES See WELSH PEOPLE

WALKING See also SPORTS

Walking on two legs is an extremely complicated way of getting around, and even though we adopted this method millions of years ago, we're still feeling the effects of having done it.

Jay Ingram, science writer and broadcaster, "The Science of Walking," *The Science of Everyday Life* (1991).

Always, everywhere, people have walked, veining the earth with paths, visible and invisible, symmetrical or meandering.

*

Walking is a mobile form of waiting.

Thomas A. Clark, poet, "In Praise of Walking," *Wild Culture: Specimens from The Journal of Wild Culture* (1992) edited by Whitney Smith and Christopher Lowry.

Walking. Trans-Canada. Clyde McRae walked 3,764 miles from Halifax to Vancouver in 96 days, from May 1 to August 4, 1973.

Peter Matthews, editor, *The Guinness Book of Records* (1996).

WAR See also CANADIAN ARMED FORCES, COLD WAR, DEFENCE, GULF CRISIS, KOREAN WAR, REBELLIONS, SPANISH CIVIL WAR, VIETNAM WAR, WAR CRIMES, WAR DEAD, WAR OF 1812, WAR RESISTERS, WORLD WAR I, WORLD WAR II, WORLD WAR III

Canada is only an eternal topic for unhappy wars, and I am fed up and fuming.

Voltaire, French author, letter of 21 Nov. 1759, quoted by Greg Gatenby in *The Wild Is Always There: Canada through the Eyes of Foreign Writers* (1993).

War is everywhere. When Britain is at war, Canada is at war; there is no distinction. If Great Britain, to which we are subject, is at war with any nation Canada becomes liable to invasion, and so Canada is at war.

Sir Wilfrid Laurier, Prime Minister, House of Commons, 17 Jan. 1910.

It would be seen by the world that Canada, a daughter of Old England, intends to stand by her in this great conflict. When the call comes our answer goes at once, and it goes in the classical language of the British answer to the call of duty: "Ready, aye, ready."

Sir Wilfrid Laurier, Leader of the Opposition, during the special war session at the time of the Chanak Affair, House of Commons, 19 Aug. 1922. "Ready, aye, ready" is the traditional British response to the call to arms. It is also the motto of the Marlboroughs. The war-cry was sounded in English Canada from the Crimean War to the Suez Crisis. With respect to Canada's readiness to stand by Britain in times of need, the battle-cry was invoked by George Monro Grant, Sir Wilfrid Laurier, and Arthur Meighen.

We live in a fire-proof house, far from inflammable materials.

Raoul Dandurand, delegate, speech, classic expression of Canadian isolationism, League of Nations Assembly, The Hague, 2 Oct. 1924, *Documents on Canadian Foreign Policy: 1917–1939* (1962), edited by Walter A. Riddell.

Whatever our ideals may be there is no hope for peace until people realize that the causes of war are economic. Under the present rule of hopeless economic chaos I don't see any chance of eliminating war. It's a matter of international justice much more than one of policemen.

Norman Bethune, physician and revolutionary, interviewed in Toronto in June 1937 by William Strange and reprinted in *The Toronto Star*, 13 Sept. 1992.

I envy the department of war the huge sums that are available when war is on. Why are not these sums available in peace time?

J.S. Woodsworth, M.P., House of Commons, 8 Sept. 1939.

The two world wars and ever-recurring economic crises are the modern equivalents of the Black Death.

John A. Irving, philosopher, *Science and Values: Explorations in Philosophy and the Social Sciences* (1952).

And human history lies so close to the history of men's wars that the angels themselves would be hard put to imagine a history free of carnage.

André Laurendeau, editor, "Jesus, Mahomet, and Marx Reconciled in Chaos" (1963), *André Laurendeau: Witness for Quebec* (1973) translated by Philip Stratford.

The war has dirtied the snow.

Last line of **Roch Carrier**'s novel *La Guerre, Yes Sir!* (1968) translated in 1970 by Sheila Fischman.

War lasts as long as businessmen find it profitable.

Lines from **Jacques Lamarche**'s novel *La dynastie des Lanthier* (1973).

Things done in wartime by men and women should not be marked down in a big book for posterity. Wartime is when no rules apply.

Barry Broadfoot, oral historian, *Six War Years 1939–1945: Memories of Canadians at Home and Abroad* (1974).

An elderly man in the audience asked General Macnamara, "Would you please identify for us Canada's enemy?" The general replied, "Canada's enemy today is the potential for a nuclear war."

Mel Hurtig, nationalist and publisher, referring to Brigadier-General Don Macnamara, Introduction, *The True North Strong & Free? Proceedings of a Public Inquiry into Canadian Defence Policy and Nuclear Arms* (1987).

There may be just wars, but no holy wars, because the "good" side is never holy and the "bad" side is still human.

Northrop Frye, cultural critic, *The Double Vision: Language and Meaning in Religion* (1991).

War has always had a high price, in money, in misery and in lives, but we shouldn't fool ourselves. We've gone on fighting wars all down our history because we were willing to pay the price; but in more and more of the world, as time goes on, we simply cannot afford to pay the price of war at all any more. There's nothing in the world that's worth blowing the whole world up for.

Gwynne Dyer, military affairs analyst, speech, University of Winnipeg, *Winnipeg Free Press*, 28 Feb. 1991.

There exist cultures with no history of all-out war and no word for enemy.

Rosalie Bertell, anti-nuclear activist, *No Immediate Danger? Prognosis for a Radioactive Earth* (1985).

It is odd, too, that it is not the excitement and horror of wars that remain foremost in his mind, but the masses of ordinary people struggling, often unsuccessfully, just to arrive.

Jack Cahill, war correspondent, *Words of War* (1987).

In the period 1945–89, 127 wars were fought. All but two of them have been in, or between, developing countries. Virtually every one of them has had the potential of escalating into a much broader conflict.

Ivan Head, president, International Development Research Centre, quoted by Gerald Utting in *The Toronto Star*, 20 July 1991.

The Canadians in the First World War and the Second World War were phenomenally warlike. They were a striking force on the Western Front in 1918. They were a huge force in Bomber Command, bombing the hell out of Germany. And now suddenly Canada's into peacekeeping, with the greatest peacekeeping tradition in the world.

John Keegan, British military historian, interviewed in Toronto by Marcus Gee in *The Globe and Mail*, 11 Nov. 1994.

I keep having a vision of a guide or preacher or some professional haranguer standing in front of a war cemetery in Flanders with a million crosses behind him and explaining how human aggressiveness has such essential survival value.

Northrop Frye, cultural critic, Entry 49, Notebook 1991, *Northrop Frye Newsletter*, Summer 1997.

WAR CRIMES See also WAR

I am disappointed about the Canadians. I expected better.

Simon Wiesenthal, director, Jewish Documentation Centre, Vienna, long critical of Canada's willingness to harbour known war criminals and its unwillingness to act against them, notably against former Ukrainian Nazis, including Albert Helmut Rauca, the first suspect (in 1982) to be extradited for war crimes, quoted by Ann Walmsley in *Maclean's*, 9 Dec. 1985.

Justice is justice, and within the strict limits of what is possible, it should be done. Justice will also serve the interests of truth. But the truth will not necessarily be believed, and it is putting too much faith in truth to believe that it can heal. All one can say is that leaving war crimes unpunished is worse: it permits societies to indulge, unopposed, their fantasies of denial.

Michael Ignatieff, author, "Articles of Faith," *Index on Censorship*, Sept.–Oct. 1996, as reprinted in "Readings," *Harper's*, March 1997.

WAR DEAD See also EPITAPHS, MEMORIALS, WAR

MORTEM VIRTUS COMMUNEM / FAMAM HISTORIA / MONUMENTUM POSTERITAS DEDIT

Inscription in Latin, Wolfe and Montcalm Monument, Governor's Garden, Chateau Frontenac, Quebec City, commemorating the deaths of James Wolfe and the Marquis de Montcalm, Battle of the Plains of Abraham in 1759. The unadorned inscription, submitted in competition by lawyer and versifier **John Charlton Fisher**, dates from 1828. The official English translation reads "Valour Gave Them a Common Death / History a Common Fame / Posterity a Common Monument."

Aux Braves / To the Brave

Inscription on the fluted iron column that honours the fallen forces, both French and British, 28 April 1760, **National Historic Site**, Sainte-Foy, Que.

In Flanders fields the poppies blow / Between the crosses, row on row, / That mark our place; and in the sky / The larks, still bravely singing, fly / Scarce heard amid the guns below. // We are the Dead. Short days ago / We lived, felt dawn, saw sunset glow. / Loved, and were loved, and now we lie / In Flanders fields. // Take up our quarrel with the foe: / To you from failing hands we throw / The torch; be yours to hold it high. / If ye break faith with us who die / We shall not sleep, though poppies grow / In Flanders fields.

The text of **Major John McCrae**'s sonnet "In Flanders Fields" (1915), the most familiar poem occasioned by the Great War. It was written on 3 May 1915, during the Second Battle of Ypres, Belgium, by McCrae, who was First Brigade surgeon in the Canadian Field Artillery. It appeared anonymously in *Punch*, 8 Dec. 1915. McCrae died in France on 28 Jan. 1918, and is buried at the Wimereux Cemetery, Boulogne, France, never knowing the fame of his poem. Since that year, "In Flanders Fields" has been recited as part of the official Armistice Day program on 11 Nov. and has become an integral part of all Remembrance Day ceremonies in Canada. *In Flanders Fields and Other Poems* (1919) edited by Sir Andrew Macphail.

Yes, it is a wonderful thing to think of all those men that have gone, and to think of those cemeteries out there, as well as the men who have come back, more or less maimed, and to think of the wonderful sacrifice which has won us this peace.

Canon F.G. Scott, Chaplain, Canadian Army in the Great War, "Personal Reminiscences of the War," 27 Oct. 1919, *The Canadian Club Year Book: 1919–20* (1920).

Read how free men throughout this land kept faith in the hour of trial, and in the day of battle, remembering the traditions they had been taught, counting life nothing without liberty.

Inscription on the wall of the **Memorial Chamber**, Peace Tower, Centre Block, Parliament Buildings, Ottawa, "the holiest spot on Canadian soil," prepared in 1919, dedicated 1 July 1927. Reproduced by Wilfrid Eggleston in *The Queen's Choice: A Story of Canada's Capital* (1961).

A soldier of the Great War / Known to God

Inscription on innumerable headstones, cemetery,

Faubourg-d'Amiens, Arras, France, Aug. 1936. As Sir Robert Borden wrote in *Letters to Limbo* (1971) edited by Henry Borden, "No words can adequately describe the wonderful simplicity and beauty of these homes of the dead. Nowhere did I see the words 'Unknown Soldier'; where identification had failed, the inscription read: 'A soldier of the Great War,' and then, at the bottom of the stone were the words, 'Known to God.'"

They gave me a name. They called me the Unknown Soldier. Kings and statesmen came and bowed before me; archbishops prayed; soldiers stood at stiff attention...I longed to speak, but words would not come.

Lines from the prose poem "Resurrection" written by **Horace Brown**, writer and later Toronto alderman, broadcast on CBC Radio, 11 Nov. 1935, as recited by Leslie Chance. Two years later Boris Karloff recited it on NBC's *The Rudy Vallee Hour* and elicited thousands of requests for reprints. The text appears in Brown's collection *Encore* (1977).

It marks the scene of feats of arms which history will long remember and Canada can never forget.

Edward VIII, King of England and Canada, address, dedication, Vimy Ridge Memorial, France, 26 July 1936. The Battle of Vimy Ridge, 9–12 April 1917, claimed 3,598 Canadians lives.

They will never know the beauty of this place, see the seasons change, enjoy nature's chorus. All we enjoy we owe to them, men and women who lie buried in the earth of foreign lands and in the seven seas. Dedicated to the memory of the Canadians who died overseas in the service of their country and so preserved our heritage.

Inscription on a monument to commemorate the war dead, Cabot Trail, Cape Breton Island, N.S. It was transcribed by Jeff Walker and published in *The Toronto Star*, 10 Nov. 1992. The moving inscription in French and English was composed by writer **Michael Cobb** of the Department of Veterans' Affairs. To mark the centennial of the National Parks Commission in 1985, one such monument was erected in each province and territory.

Canada and Canadians have had freedom and the fruits of victory since 1945...and had we not fought, freedom would have been lost. Was it worth it? Was it worth the death, the maiming, the unending pain? That is a terrible question if posed by someone who lost a son, a husband, or a brother at Ortona, or H.M.C.S. *St. Croix*, or in a Lancaster over the Ruhr. Even so, there can only be one answer. Was it worth it? Oh, yes.

J.L. Granatstein and **Desmond Morton**, historians, *A Nation Forged in Fire: Canadians and the Second World War, 1939–1945* (1989).

Thank you forever.

Message written in English in the *Book of Remembrance* by a local Dutch visitor to the Canadian War Cemetery, Bergen-op-Zoom, Holland, noted by Douglas MacArthur in *The Globe and Mail*, 11 Nov. 1989.

From today, London will have a distinguished memorial which will bear witness to those brave Canadians who fought and died in two world wars.

Elizabeth II, Queen of Canada, dedication, Canada Memorial, Green Park, London, England, 3 June 1994. Prime Minister Jean Chrétien described the monument, sculpted by Pierre Granche from granite from the Canadian Shield decorated with 1,000 bronze maple leaves, as "a small piece of Canada in the heart of London." Nearly 110,000 Canadians died in foreign combat. The unveiling commemorated the 50th anniversary of the D-Day landing, the Allied invasion of Occupied France.

WAR MEASURES ACT See also OCTOBER CRISIS

What French Canada as a whole thought of the War Measures Act was dramatically shown by the Gallup Poll of December 5th: 86% approved. English-speaking Canada approved 89%. I have never known such unanimity between French and English on any matter so easily capable of dividing them—especially when there are so many politicos and journalists desperately trying to divide them.

F.R. Scott, constitutional law specialist, "The War Measures Act in Retrospect" (1971), *A New Endeavour: Selected Political Essays, Letters, and Addresses* (1986) edited by Michiel Horn.

WAR OF 1812 See also WAR

Push on, brave York Volunteers!

Sir Isaac Brock, Commander of the British and

militia forces, last command, issued to the militia brought to the Niagara Peninsula from York, Upper Canada (later, Toronto, Ont.), and pressed into the Battle of Queenston Heights, 13 Oct. 1812. Upon issuing the command, Brock fell to an American sniper's bullet. Quoted by military historian C.P. Stacey, "Brock's Muniments," *Books in Canada*, Aug.–Sept. 1980.

It was at Queenston I gained the secret plan laid to capture Captain Fitzgibbon and his party. I was determined if possible to save them. I had much difficulty in getting through the American guards. They were ten miles out in the country.... The scene by moonlight to some might have been grand, but to a weak woman certainly terrifying. With difficulty I got one of the chiefs to go with me to their commander. With the intelligence I gave him he formed his plans and saved the country.

Laura Secord, heroine of the War of 1812, describing her valorous trek through the Niagara woods to alert the English to a planned American attack, 22 June 1813, quoted by J.M. Harper in *The Annals of the War: Illustrated by a Selection of Historical Ballads* (1915).

Our lives are in the hands of the Great Spirit. We are determined to defend our lands, and if it is his will, we wish to leave our bones upon them.

Tecumseh, Shawnee war chief, final oration, Fort Malden, U.C., Oct. 1813, translated by Major John Richardson, quoted by Don Gutteridge in *Tecumseh* (1976).

But let the rash intruder dare / To touch our darling strand, / The martial fires / That thrilled our sires / Would light him from the land.

Refrain of **Charles Sangster**'s martial poem "Song for Canada," *Songs of the Great Dominion* (1889), edited by W.D. Lighthall.

As Canadians look down "the corridors of Time," they will always see those flashes from the musketry at Lundy's Lane, and hear the bugles which drove the invaders of their country from the woods of Chateauguay.

Sir John Bourinot, historian, "The Makers of the Dominion of Canada: VIII, The Canadian Heroes of the War of 1812–15," *The Canadian Magazine*, June 1898.

Have we not stood stood together in the van: / Whether at Queenston Heights, or Lundy's Lane?

Couplet from the verse "Canada to Britain" in *The Land of Napioa and Other Essays in Prose and Verse* (1896) composed by **Bertram Tennyson**, Canadian-based nephew of the poet laureate.

Every nation may, without offence to its neighbours, commemorate its heroes, their deeds of arms, and their noble deaths. This is no taunting boast of victory, no revival of long-passed animosities, but a noble tribute....

Edward VII, Prince of Wales, address on the laying of the cornerstone of Brock's Monument, Queenston Heights, 18 Sept. 1860, reproduced by Henry James Morgan in *Tour of H.R.H. the Prince of Wales through British America and the United States* (1860).

WAR RESISTERS See also VIETNAM WAR

I think those kids who have lived in Sweden or Canada... have been punished long enough.

Jimmy Carter, U.S. presidential candidate, referring to his promise to extend pardons to all U.S. war resisters, election campaign, quoted in *Maclean's*, 31 May 1976.

Now, getting down to your question: there is no treaty between the U.S. and Canada that permits U.S. authorities to haul your ass, or any other portion of your anatomy, back down here for draft evasion. The existing treaties, which antedate the Vietnam era by a considerable stretch, permit extradition only for offences that are *recognized as crimes in Canada.* Since Canada has no draft, it has no such thing as draft evasion. On the other hand, you can be extradited for desertion once you've actually been inducted into the military.

Cecil Adams, U.S. columnist, discussing U.S. war resisters, *The Straight Dope: A Compendium of Human Knowledge* (1984).

WEAPONRY See also FIREARMS, WAR

She is a pretty good gun, I think.

John C. Garand, toolmaker and inventor, born near Quebec, based in Springfield, Mass., referring to his invention in 1933 of the semi-automatic rifle, originally called the Garand, now known as M1 for Model No. 1, "You Asked Us," *The Toronto Star*, 21 Nov. 1991.

With the advent of nuclear weaponry, another phrase is often used in place of balance of power—"balance of terror," coined by Canadian Prime Minister Lester Pearson in 1955.

William Safire, columnist, *Safire's Political Dictionary: An Enlarged, Up-to-Date Edition of the New Language of Politics* (1968).

Remember the old TV western *Have Gun Will Travel?* Did you know that the name for that program came from a Canadian? Yeah. CBC-TV producer by the name of Fletcher Markle, as a matter of fact. I only bring it up because it represents possibly the last time Canadians were on the leading edge of handgun sensibility.

Arthur Black, broadcaster and humorist, "Is That a Six-shooter That I See Before Me?" *That Old Black Magic* (1989).

We are living in the midst of a permanent wartime economy. The most important capital good produced in the West today is weaponry. The most important sector in international trade is not oil or automobiles or airplanes. It is armaments.

John Ralston Saul, author, *Voltaire's Bastards: The Dictatorship of Reason in the West* (1992).

One thing you can say— / if you don't mind puns— / re the U.S.A. / it sticks to its guns."

Barry Brent, poetaster, No. 600, *The Amusings of Jeremy Fine* (1994).

WASTE MANAGEMENT

There may be life in the fermentation of a dunghill. But who can imagine himself blest in the prospect of sharing it?

Goldwin Smith, essayist, "Is There Another Life?" *Guesses at the Riddle of Existence and Other Essays on Kindred Subjects* (1987).

In Greek mythology, Hercules cleansed the Stables of Augeas during his Twelve Labours by diverting the river Alpheus to flow through them. The Ontario Waste Management Corporation failed to emulate the Herculean feat in 16 years, even after diverting rivers of red ink into waste management problems.

Tom Davey, editor and publisher, "Editorial Comment," *Environment Science & Engineering*, Jan. 1995.

Not long ago an activist in Ontario was demanding zero discharges from all industrial operations. It was pointed out to him that absolute zero could not be achieved because of the laws of organic chemistry. Unabashed—and in all seriousness—the activist then said that the laws of organic chemistry must be repealed.

Tom Davey, editor and publisher, "Canada's Water Quality Record," *Environmental Science & Engineering*, March 1995.

WATER See also JAMES BAY PROJECT

I don't want to be a dog in the manger about this. But if people are not going to use it, can't we sell it for good hard cash?

Pierre Elliott Trudeau, Prime Minister, on the export of surplus water to the United States, CBC-TV's *Under Attack*, Feb. 1970.

His dream has always been to flood Quebec from one border to another. He's happy to live in a lake as long as he can get electricity out of it.

Georges Erasmus, National Chief, Assembly of First Nations, on Quebec Premier Robert Bourassa's proposed James Bay 2 Project, quoted by Tim Tiner in *Now*, 17 March 1988.

Though we ordinarily think that rivers run from the heights of land and mountains to eventually vanish in the sea, when you approach a river from the ocean it becomes much more enlightening to recognize that rivers are the gnarled fresh fingers of the sea reaching for the mountain.

Rudy Wiebe, novelist, *Playing Dead: A Contemplation Concerning the Arctic* (1989).

Just as air links all forms of life in interdependence, so, too, does water. The water that we drink in Canada was once transpired from the canopy of the Amazon rain forest or evaporated from the steppes of the Soviet Union.

Anita Gordon and **David Suzuki**, science broadcasters, *It's a Matter of Survival* (1990).

For a nation upstream to divert water, robbing those downstream... increasingly will be regarded as equivalent to armed invasion. And yet considering the flow of people, raw materials, foodstuffs, airborne waste and water across international borders, it is evident that we are all of us upstream of someone and correspondingly likely to be involved in conflict.

John C. Polanyi, scientist, *Ecodecision Magazine*, Sept. 1991.

The sight of millions of Westerners drinking bottled water is a reminder of our disconnection from reality.

John Ralston Saul, author, *The Doubter's Companion: A Dictionary of Aggressive Common Sense* (1994).

The actual basic water needs of humans are quite small—a mere two litres of drinking water per day. The cost of supplying treated potable water to consumers varies, but is in the range of 40 to 60 cents a cubic metre of 1,000 litres. So it actually costs consumers less than one cent per day for this life-sustaining fluid. Soft drinks can cost $1,000 a cubic metre while Scotch whisky can often be over $20,000 a cubic metre.

Tom Davey, editor and publisher, "Canada's Water Quality Record," *Environmental Science & Engineering*, March 1995.

The motor of economic growth was once fuelled by oil; in the next millennium, the precious fuel will be water.

Peter C. Newman, journalist, "The Dawn of a New Millennium," *Maclean's*, 30 Dec. 1996.

There's nothing wrong with the water in the Miramichi.... I've been walking on it for years.

Frank McKenna, Premier of New Brunswick, responding in the Legislature, 12 Feb. 1997, to criticisms about the quality of the water in the province's central Miramichi region, noted by *The Globe and Mail* the following day.

It is also a cliché to say that the world is not short of water, but rapidly running short of usable water.

Marq de Villiers, commentator, *Water* (1999).

WEALTH See also MONEY

Lives of millionaires remind us / How to get dishonest spoil, / And departing leave behind us / Millions wrung from sons of toil.

First of seven verses of "The Mammon Worshippers," *The Labour Union*, Feb. 1883, reproduced by N. Brian Davis in *The Poetry of the Canadian People, 1720–1920* (1976).

What purports to be compassion for the poor is generally hatred and envy of the rich.

Richard Needham, newspaper columnist, *The Wit and Wisdom of Richard Needham* (1977).

I've never known anyone to make a million doing something he hated.

Jean-Marc Chaput, business consultant, quoted by James Quig in *The Canadian*, 11 March 1978.

Alberta tends to create wealth; Toronto tends to reshuffle it.

Alexander Ross, editor, quoted by Allan Fotheringham in *Maclean's*, 2 Feb. 1981.

I once heard Dr. Morton Shulman make a comment that really hits home. The purpose of acquiring wealth, he said, was to enjoy life more.

Gordon Pape, financial writer, *Building Wealth: Achieving Your Financial Goals* (1988).

The success of the wealthy is important for the maintenance of the unfortunate.

Michael Walker, head, Fraser Institute, quoted by Eric Kierans and Walter Stewart in *Wrong End of the Rainbow* (1988).

For real wealth and real power in Canada, inherit it, marry it or forget it.

Walter Stewart, journalist, quoted by Stephen McHale in *The Globe and Mail*, 23 Jan. 1991.

The prize is *wealth creation*—a bigger pie can offer everyone a larger slice.

Nuala Beck, financial writer, *EXCELerate: Growing in the New Economy* (1995).

Abundance renders all issues personal and apolitical.

Douglas Coupland, novelist, "Agree/Disagree: 55 Statements about the Culture," *The New Republic*, 2 Aug. 1995.

I never met a millionaire who was rich enough.

Jean Chrétien, Prime Minister, address, Economic Club of New York, March 1998, as quoted by John R. MacArthur, *The Globe and Mail*, 20 March 1998. As MacArthur, publisher of *Harper's Magazine* and member of the audience, observed, "A few people chuckled at this clumsily delivered jibe, but given the large number of millionaires in attendance I suspect what I heard beneath the laughter was the simultaneous grinding of a thousand sets of privately insured teeth. We don't make fun of the rich down here nowadays; it simply isn't done."

WEATHER See also CLIMATE, SEASONS, TEMPERATURE

The weather broke at last. One might say it smashed itself over their heads.

Seasonal change in Labrador described in **H.G. Wells**' novel *Marriage* (1912).

They have it 60° below zero in Calgary—an uncivilized climate. I notice people do not seem to get more hardened to the cold. The only way to be hardened to uncomfortable conditions is not to know of a comfortable one.

Freya Stark, traveller and writer, observation recorded in notebook, entry for 31 Jan. 1929, Creston, B.C., *Beyond Euphrates* (1951).

When I first came down here, the people used to ask me, "How do you like the weather out here?" My answer was, "I like it because I have been freezing all last winter," but lately after being here three and a half months in this terrible heat, I am beginning to change my tune.

Abraham Okpik, Eskimo elder, "Life in the South," *Northern Affairs Bulletin*, Sept.–Oct. 1959.

Canadians love to sit in the dark trembling with fear at weather forecasts.

Robert Morley, British actor, CBC-TV interview in 1972, quoted by Lorraine Monk in *Between Friends/Entre Amis* (1976).

We are the northern edge of the New World. We are the weather of ourselves. The search for the Northwest Passage is always part of our dream, and of our nightmare too. We look for a route through the weather. It reveals itself in our architecture. In our clothing. In our sports. "My country is this fire burning under the snow."

Robert Kroetsch, author and poet, "Canada Is a Poem," *Divided We Stand* (1977) edited by Gary Geddes.

This is the situation: An Arctic low seeps down from Ungava. A howling blizzard roars in from the Great Lakes. A savage gale tears up from the south. Freezing drizzle slashes in from the North Atlantic. They all meet, shake hands, rejoice and do their things over the Atlantic provinces.

Ray Guy, humorist, "January's Awful; But, Thank God, At Least We're Safe from Killer Crocodiles," *Ray Guy's Best* (1987).

The weather was next. I could see it was still raining. What did British Columbia mean to me? It was still *snowing* in other parts of Canada.

Susan Musgrave, columnist, "Other Parts of Canada," *Great Musgrave* (1989).

If we are boring, there's certainly nothing boring about our meteorology.

David Phillips, climatologist, Environment Canada, *The Day Niagara Falls Ran Dry!: Canadian Weather Facts and Trivia* (1993).

Sunshine always seems brighter after rain. As if each puddle has captured a sunbeam. A glow in the heart of the water. The eyes of the earth.

Lines from **Dany Laferrière**'s novel *An Aroma of Coffee* (1994) translated by David Homel.

In Newfoundland they say, if you don't like the weather outside your front window, look out your back window.

David Phillips, climatologist, Environment Canada, recalling a folk saying, CBC Radio, 7 Dec. 1994.

I guess now that we're no longer Number 1, some people will be disappointed.

David Phillips, climatologist, Environment Canada, "Quotables," *The Hamilton Spectator*, 25 Feb. 1995. In the words of the *Spectator*, "Canada is no longer the coldest country on Earth. Russia is now in top spot with an average yearly temperature of −5.3°C. Canada came in at −4.4, and Outer Mongolia a distant third at −0.7."

People such as Margaret Atwood and Lucien Bouchard, who wonder whether there really is a Canada, should spend a winter in Snag. Maybe longer.

William Thorsell, columnist, "Where the Sun Stays up until All Hours," *The Globe and Mail*, 21 June 1997. He is referring to the fact that the coldest temperature ever recorded in Canada was −63°C. at Snag, Y.T., 3 Feb. 1947.

If we could predict the weather perfectly, it would take all the fun out of being Canadian.

David Phillips, climatologist, interviewed on CBC Radio, 8 Oct. 1997.

Right now the climate changes about four times a year.

Michael Enright, host of CBC Radio's *This Morning*, commenting on climate change and global warming, 6 April 1998.

WEIGHT See also DIET

Fat men are good-natured because good-natured men are usually fat.

Bob Edwards, publisher, *The Eye Opener*, 22 May 1915, *The Wit and Wisdom of Bob Edwards* (1976) edited by Hugh Dempsey.

There's a truth at the bottom of it—every woman should be fat enough to stand the strain of life.

Elizabeth Arden, cosmetics manufacturer, interviewed by R.E. Knowles in *The Toronto Star*, 16 April 1936.

History seems to be destitute of fat lovers.

Raymond Canale, Italian-born, Toronto-based aphorist, 1975.

It is easiest to fast / just after eating.

Robert Priest, aphorist, *Time Release Poems* (1997).

WEIGHTLIFTING See also SPORTS

Be that as it may, Louis Cyr, the boy of Saint-Cyprien, descendant of modest Canadian peasants, brought honour to his country and his feats in fact made his name as famous in the annals of human strength as those legendary heroes, Hercules, Milo of Croton, and Samson.

Ben Weider, writer, conclusion of *The Strongest Man in History: Louis Cyr, Amazing Canadian* (1976). Cyr worked as a Montreal policeman; a statue was erected in his memory in Montreal. He was modest and is believed to have stated, "My father was the strongest man who ever lived—bar none."

WELFARE See also WELFARE STATE

People who are picked up every time they fall down develop this peculiar habit of falling down.

Richard Needham, newspaper columnist, *The Wit and Wisdom of Richard Needham* (1977).

Farewell fathers make for welfare mothers.

Maurus E. Mallon, aphorist, *Compendulum* (1995).

The weather is nicer in B.C.

David Tsubouchi, Ontario's Minister of Social Services, reply made on 25 July 1995 to a Toronto reporter's query about the effect of planned reductions in provincial welfare benefits, which would leave them lower than those in British Columbia, quoted by Craig McInnes in *The Globe and Mail*, 27 July 1995.

Should the Welfare State for Corporations Be Rolled Back?

Abraham Rotstein, political scientist, suggesting that the title of "Should the Welfare State Be Rolled Back?" be changed to the one above, CBC Radio's *Ideas*, 2 April 1996.

WELFARE STATE See also SOCIALISM, WELFARE

Any man or woman intent on leading Canada into the twenty-first century will have to champion something more inspiring than the attainment of a basic living standard for his people. He will have to concern himself much more with the *quality* of the lives Canadians lead. His appeal will have to move beyond the welfare state (which offers only palliatives for existing inequalities) and concentrate on the environmental barriers to social progress. His government will have to concern itself primarily with Canadian society's capacity for self-fulfilment.

Peter C. Newman, author, contributor to *If I Were Prime Minister* (1987) edited by Mel Hurtig.

There is a spectre haunting the leading industrial nations and that spectre is the death of the welfare state.

Sylvia Ostry, economist, address, conference on "The Public Good: Lessons for the Third Millennium," St. Francis Xavier University, Antigonish, N.S., quoted by Hugh Winsor in *The Globe and Mail*, 8 July 1996. The line echoes the opening of Marx's *Communist Manifesto* (1848), which states that the spectre of communism is haunting Europe.

WELSH PEOPLE See also BRITISH EMPIRE & COMMONWEALTH, UNITED KINGDOM

There is, indeed, a mythical tribe of Welsh Indians identified by some with the Tuscarora, a tribe affiliated with the Iroquois, speaking Welsh and supposed to be descendants of the followers of a Prince Madoc who landed in America in the year 1170. Following the American War of Independence, some of the Tuscarora Indians joined the Grand River Reservation in Ontario.

John Murray Gibbon, nationalist and publicist, discussing fanciful origins of some Native North American groups, *Canadian Mosaic: The Making of a Northern Nation* (1938).

I am a Welsh separatist myself, dedicated to the independence of Wales from England, and the issues that have animated Montreal during the past thirty years are very familiar to me. We also have a language and a culture to defend against great odds, we think of continental Europe as Montrealers think of the U.S., and we too fluctuate, decade by decade, in conviction, apathy, or despair.

Jan Morris, Anglo-Welsh travel writer, "The Battle for Montreal," *Saturday Night*, July 1988.

To the Celts, speech, not silence, was golden.

Observation made in **Robertson Davies**' novel *Murther & Walking Spirits* (1991).

WESTERN PROVINCES See also ALBERTA, BRITISH COLUMBIA, MANITOBA, PRAIRIE PROVINCES, SASKATCHEWAN

There is something bigger than fact: the underlying spirit, all it stands for, the mood, the vastness, the wildness, the Western breath of go-to-the-devil-if-you-don't-like-it, the eternal big spaceness of it. Oh the West! I'm of it and I love it.

Emily Carr, artist, *Hundreds and Thousands* (1966).

It was the fate of the West to become the colony of a colony which brought to its new imperial role neither imagination, liberality, nor magnanimity.

W.L. Morton, historian, "Cleo in Canada: The Interpretation of Canadian History," *The University of Toronto Quarterly*, April 1946.

The history of the West is a chronicle of voyages, a ceaseless ebb and flow from east to west and west to east of human beings in search of fur, buffalo, land, wealth, salvation. The quest never ends. Waves of people wash across the prairies and disappear, cast up on the island promontories of the island cities or wrecked at last on the beaches of Vancouver where they spend the last days of their lives gazing wistfully out to sea.

Heather Robertson, memoirist, *Grass Roots* (1973).

There are more left-handed Mormon streakers in the West than there are Western separatists.

Adapted from a remark attributed to nationalist **Mel Hurtig** by Dick Beddoes in *The Globe and Mail*, 17 Dec. 1976.

I just think you Westerners should take over this country.... if you are so smart.

Pierre Elliott Trudeau, Prime Minister, campaign speech, Edmonton, 9 March 1978, quoted by Andrew Szende in *The Toronto Star* the next day.

Like many of you, my grandfather came west from Ontario not to leave Canada but to build it, and now for Western Canadians that's possible as never before.

Joe Clark, Prime Minister, address, Calgary, 13 Nov. 1979, quoted by Terrance Wills in *The Toronto Star*, 17 Nov. 1979.

Anyone who talks about western alienation is a fruit-cake, a nut-ball, a tinkertoy, a jerk, you name it. Alienation is a typical media fascination.... Sure B.C. is different. Every part of the country is different.

Dave Barrett, B.C. Leader of the Opposition, quoted by Stanley Meisler in *The Los Angeles Times* and reprinted in *Canada Today/D'Aujourd'hui*, Oct. 1980.

We are the orphans of Confederation and we resent it.

I.H. (Izzy) Asper, owner of the Global Television Network, expressing Western grievances against Central Canada, quoted in *The Globe and Mail*, 16 Dec. 1989.

As a British Columbian, I prefer to call British Columbia the True West. Alberta,

Saskatchewan, and Manitoba are the Near East; Ontario and Quebec the Middle East; and the Atlantic provinces the Far East.

Gordon Campbell, Vancouver Mayor, quoted by Peter C. Newman, "Essay," *Maclean's*, 24 Aug. 1992.

WHALES & WHALING See also ANIMALS

Ned Land, a Canadian by birth, knew no equal in his dangerous occupation. Skill, coolness, audacity, and cunning: he possessed them all in a superior degree, and it must be an astute whale to escape the stroke of his harpoon.

Description of the Quebec-born whaler Ned Land, "the prince of harpooners," in French author **Jules Verne**'s fantastic-adventure novel *20,000 Leagues Under the Sea* (1991).

WHEAT See also AGRICULTURE

It is a matter of pride with our orators that in the North-West wheat can be successfully grown some eight hundred miles north of the International boundary, and that the Territories can support a population of fifty millions.

A.T. Hunter, Captain, "The Fatuous Insolence of Canadians," Address to the Empire Club of Canada, Toronto, 4 Feb. 1904.

All the rocking wheat of Canada, ripening now, / has not so much of strength as the body of one woman / sweet in ear, nor so much to give / though it feed nations.

Lines from **D.H. Lawrence**'s poem "Manifesto," *Look! We Have Come Through* (1917).

There is no more exhilarating sight in the west than the prospect of the binders at work on the sea-wide, sky-skirted prairie, with the golden grain gleaming under the August sun and above and about all the cloudless blue dome of heaven.

Reginald A.H. Buller, biologist, "Wheat in the West" (1924), *Canada: A Portrait: The Official Handbook of Present Conditions and Recent Progress* (54th edition, 1992).

Help Win the War by Growing Less Wheat

Wording on posters on Prairie grain elevators during World War II, recalled by T.D. Douglas and quoted by Peter Stursberg in *Diefenbaker: Leadership Gained, 1956–62* (1975).

WHITE ANGLO-SAXON PROTESTANT

I'm always very proud of the fact that I was brought up as a WASP. It means that I belong to the only group in society that it is entirely safe to ridicule.

Northrop Frye, cultural critic, "The Critic and the Writer," address, Learned Societies, McGill University, Montreal, May 1972, *Northrop Frye Newsletter*, Winter 1991–92.

I'm white, I'm straight, I'm sorry / What's worse I'm WASP and male / I'm so middle-class that / I make Wonderbread seem stale.

Opening lines of the comic song "I'm White, I'm Straight, I'm Sorry" (1992) composed by **Mark Leiren-Young** and **Kevin Crofton** for their show and album *Local Anxiety: Forgive Us We're Canadian* (1994).

WHITEHORSE See also YUKON TERRITORY

The city hosts the territory's only hospital, the main campus of Yukon College, and offices of four levels of government.

Paul M. Koroscil and **Steven Smyth**, contributors, "Whitehorse, Y.T.," *The Canadian Encyclopedia: Year 2000 Edition* (1999).

WILDERNESS See also ECOLOGY, NATURE, THE NORTH, WILDLIFE

We were Caesars, being nobody to contradict us.

Pierre-Esprit Radisson, coureur de bois, "Lake Superior Voyage" (1661), *The Explorations of Pierre-Esprit Radisson* (1961) edited by Arthur T. Adams. Radisson is referring to social conditions and lack of restraints in the area of Lake Superior in the 17th century. Peter C. Newman titled the second volume of his history of the Hudson's Bay Company *Caesars of the Wilderness* (1987).

Everyone should take two trips into the wilderness each year, each of six months duration.

Ernest Thompson Seton, naturalist, quoted by Andrew Nikiforuk, "Fifth Column," *The Globe and Mail*, 12 Aug. 1994.

The history of Canada for about three hundred years was a struggle to escape from the wilderness, and for the last half century has been a desperate attempt to escape into it.

Bruce Hutchison, author and publisher, remark

made in 1953, quoted by Reginald Eyre Watters in *British Columbia: A Centennial Anthology* (1958).

A friend defines wilderness as a place where you could be eaten.

Anne Edwards, **Patrick Morrow**, and **Arthur Twomey**, adventurers, *Exploring the Purcell Wilderness* (1978).

Nearly every Canadian feels, as a special part of his national identity, a closeness to the wilderness; and many a Canadian's personal identity is bound up with the pleasure he takes in wilderness activities.

Hugh Brody, author, *Maps and Dreams: Indians and the British Columbia Frontier* (1981).

This is something that all Canadians know, the feel of the wild even in the heart of the city.

Wade Davis, ethnobotanist and essayist, *Shadows in the Sun* (1992).

As long as there is a wilderness, I know there is a larger part of myself that I can always visit, vast tracts of territory lying dormant, craving exploration and providing sanctity.

Thoughts of the narrator of **Douglas Coupland**'s novel *Life after God* (1994).

... before we enter the hinterlands, before the air becomes too brittle and too cold to breathe, before we enter that place where life becomes harsh, where we must become animals in order to survive.

Douglas Coupland, author, *Polaroids from the Dead* (1996).

Heart of the Canadian Wilderness

Civic motto of Thompson, Man., according to Anita Lienert, "A Tale of Three Cities," *Management Review*, July–Aug. 1997.

WILDLIFE See ANIMALS, ECOLOGY, NATURE, WILDERNESS

Only once in these long Canadian wanderings was the deep peace of the wilderness savagely broken. It happened in the maple woods about midnight when I was cold and my fire was low.

John Muir, botanist, future founder of the Sierra Club, who spent two years (1864–66) on a farm at Meaford, Canada West (Ont.), exploring the region south of Georgian Bay, letter, *The Life and Letters of John Muir* (1924) edited by William Frederic Badé. He described (at some length) the threat of wolves in the Georgian Bay area.

"I often say," he mused, as if to himself, "when I'm asked, or when I ask myself, where I get the courage to face my great and cultured audiences—I say, to them or to myself—'behind it all is the wilderness, and the strange, spectral, wonderful life there.' It never lies to me. It sticks to me till the end."

Grey Owl, author and naturalist, referring to the lectures he delivered at the invitation of England's aristocracy, interviewed by R.E. Knowles in *The Toronto Star*, 2 March 1936.

WILL POWER

Where there is a will there is a delay.

Albert W.J. Harper, Ottawa aphorist, *Thoughts and Afterthoughts* (1984).

Any mountain is movable.

Silken Laumann, Olympic rower, overcoming a leg injury to compete and place in the 1992 Summer Olympics at Barcelona, quoted by Emily Mitchell in *Time*, 27 July 1992.

WINE See also ALCOHOL, DRINKING, FOOD & DRINK

I find that the public generally prefer native wines after they have begun to use them.

William Haskins, Hamilton winemaker, report to the Ontario Agricultural Committee, 1880, quoted by Tony Aspler in *Vintage Canada* (1984).

God has His own sense of humour. He gave grapes for making wine not to Quebec, but to Ontario.

Richard J. Needham, newspaper columnist, *A Friend in Needham* (1969).

If wine is unfaithful to a great tradition, it is not merely scolded, it is scorned. Hence the terms "cloudy," "dead," "sour," "corky," "vinegary," "sulfurous," "bitter," "neurotic." (And "foxy," which should appear only in a Canadian dictionary because it is the only distinctive adjective widely used to describe the taste of certain Canadian-made wines.)

Percy Rowe, oenologist, *Red, White and Rosé: Enjoying Wines in Canada* (1978).

We boast the largest per capita consumption of wine in any city in North America.

Information package, **Tourism Vancouver**, Oct. 1995.

White wine is fine, but it's mere gastronomic foreplay.

Tony Aspler, wine specialist, "Vintage Point," *The Toronto Star*, 4 Oct. 1995.

There are two stages in an oenophile's life. The first is the discovery of wine; the second, the revelation of *fine wine*.

Tony Aspler, wine specialist, *Travels with My Corkscrew: Memoirs of a Wine Lover* (1997).

WINNING See also SUCCESS

When you're ahead and winning, don't "frig" with the sails.

Attributed to **Angus Walters**, captain of the schooner *Bluenose*, during the International Fishermen's Trophy Races (1921–38).

I've gone through this life, met a lot of people, had a lot of dealings, been fortunate, worked hard, seen things as bad as the worst fightin' and killin' in the wars, seen plenty of nice things too, and I've come out of it all believin' absolutely in this: "The good guys win out in the end."

Conn Smythe, hockey personality, quoted by Jack Batten in *The Canadian*, 8 Oct. 1977.

Winning brings with it such an immense momentum. Everything fits, everything works. Every new thing is made to fit and work. Everything just *is*.

Ken Dryden, hockey star and writer, *The Game: A Thoughtful and Provocative Look at a Life in Hockey* (1983).

A winner is a person who can lose... but doesn't make a habit of it.

Peter Urs Bender, business motivator, characteristic remark, 20 May 2000.

WINNIPEG See also MANITOBA

The most interesting object in Winnipeg—perhaps we may say the only thing which has anything of the picturesque about it—is Fort Garry, the head-quarters of "the Governor and company of adventurers of England trading into Hudson's Bay."

Henry Van Dyke, essayist, visiting Winnipeg, "The Red River of the North," *Harper's New Monthly Magazine*, May 1880.

The city seems lying in a dream, content for the moment with having shown her magnificent possibilities; yet there is a certainty in her very repose that some day, and sooner perhaps than even the optimists think, she will arise and fulfill them.

Sara Jeannette Duncan, novelist and essayist, writing about Winnipeg in 1888, *Sara Jeannette Duncan: Selected Journalism* (1978) edited by Thomas E. Tausky.

I have never seen real mud since I left the Missouri till to-day. Then when I looked out and saw the mud in the side streets I said, "Here I am at home again." In the east either the poverty of the soil or the extent of the pavements precludes the possibility of real mud, and I am rather glad to see it again.

Mark Twain, humorist, interviewed prior to a lecture in Winnipeg, *The Winnipeg Daily Tribune*, 26 July 1895; quoted by Norton D. Kinghorn in "Mark Twain in the Red River Valley of the North," *Minnesota History*, Winter 1977.

This provincial cut-off town boasts a good symphony, a fine ballet company, and one of the three best repertory theatres on the North American continent. No middle-western city in the United States, with the exception of Chicago, had until ten years ago comparable cultural organizations.

Agnes de Mille, U.S. ballet director, visit in 1963, quoted in *Canada Today/D'Aujourd'hui*, June 1982.

A trip to Winnipeg, as flat and on the whole as small-minded as ever.

André Laurendeau, Quebec nationalist, diary entry for 1965, "A Québécois Journal," translated by Pat Smart, *The Canadian Forum*, Nov. 1990.

I needed a place where I could move mountains or carry larger stones than Sisyphus, and here was the place for it. I realized that the very lack of drums and trumpets, the non-existence of slogans and parades, with nobody telling me what I'm supposed to believe as a Canadian, the very lack of being pasted all over with slogans, gave me a kind of freedom for my mind and for my spirit and my creative energies that I had never experienced before in my life.

John Hirsch, Hungarian-born theatre director, "On Becoming Canadian" (1965), *Concepts of Federalism* (1965) edited by Gordon Hawkins.

...know that Winnipeg / (200 miles south and not big enough / for a place on the map of the world / in the post office), that Winnipeg / is where the world begins.

Lines from a poem by **Dale Zieroth**, quoted by George Woodcock in *The Meeting of Time and Space* (1981).

Some Torontonians think of Winnipeg, when they think of it at all, much as they would a bruised lip. They believe both locations are best covered with ice.

James H. Gray, Winnipeg-based historian, *The Toronto Star*, 20 Sept. 1981.

A common negative image conveyed through the national media is that Portage and Main is the coldest spot in Canada.

Price Waterhouse study of Winnipeg's image and assets, quoted by Geoffrey York in *The Globe and Mail*, 24 Feb. 1990. York noted the popular quip about Winnipegers enjoying (or enduring) "ten months of snow and two months of winter."

For example, had there been a Free Trade Agreement in place a couple of generations ago, where would Winnipeg be today? Where would Calgary be? W.H. Loewen, chairman of Comcheq Services Ltd., puts it well: "Instead of being midway between Toronto and Vancouver, Winnipeg would be north of Bismarck."

Mel Hurtig, nationalist, *The Betrayal of Canada* (1991).

Recently, when somebody suggested that "the new Canada"—if it even comes into being—might be wise to select Winnipeg as its seat of government, a great hoot of laughter was heard across the nation. Winnipeg! The very idea had them rolling in the aisles. It was similar to the laughter that was heard in the mid-nineteenth century when word reached Kingston, Montreal, and Toronto that Queen Victoria felt that Ottawa would do nicely.

Christopher Dafoe, columnist, *Winnipeg Free Press*, 2 Feb. 1992. On CBC Radio's *Morningside*, commentator Eric Kierans had suggested, somewhat tongue-in-cheek, that the national capital of TROC (The Rest of Canada) might be moved from Ottawa to a more central location, Winnipeg.

Winnipeg, at one time, was known as "The Gateway to the West." When you arrived in Winnipeg on the CPR you were entering the West. By the same token, I suppose, it could be regarded as the "Gateway to the East" if you happened to be heading for Toronto or Montreal on the Grand Trunk.

Christopher Dafoe, columnist, *Winnipeg Free Press*, 6 Nov. 1993.

Geographical location in the centre of Canada provides those of us resident in Winnipeg the advantage and the opportunity to look out at both the east and west with a clear unobstructed view of this great country of ours. We are not, as some might believe, in the middle of nowhere. We are in the middle of a country that is the envy of every other country that I have had the opportunity to visit during my travels.

Hartley T. Richardson, James Richardson & Sons, Limited, remark, *National and Global Perspectives* (Business Council on National Issues), Autumn 1995.

Winnipeg is the optimum size for a city. Some days I feel like I know everyone I meet downtown.

Carol Shields, novelist, interviewed in *Snapshots: Canada, The World Next Door*, Jan. 1996.

We have long boasted in this city that we have more beautiful women per capita than any other city in the world.

Tom Oleson, columnist, noting the presence in the city of a talent scout for *Playboy*, *Winnipeg Free Press*, 18 Aug. 1996.

This handsome agglomeration of skyscrapers lies in the middle of relative emptiness, and it shows what can be done when people are sensible and imaginative.

*

In Winnipeg there is negligible discord. Yes, Winnipeg is an eye-opener. Its faults are shared by all humanity; its virtues are its own.

Peter Ustinov, theatre personality, quoted in *The*

European, as noted by Michael Kesterton in "Social Studies," *The Globe and Mail*, 15 Oct. 1996.

WINTER See also SEASONS, SNOW

It is in Ottawa that you get the essence of the Canadian winter. Winnipeg is too miserably cold; Toronto too damp; Montreal too given to thaws; but Ottawa is the typical Canadian winter city one used to read about long ago.

Kit Coleman, columnist in the 1880s and 1890s, quoted by Ted Ferguson in *Kit Coleman: Queen of Hearts* (1978).

I took part in the life of the Canadian winter, and liked the kind, courageous people, more heroic than they knew. I learned to skate, went sleighing with my father, or watched the wood-cutters sawing up our trees on the "mountain."

Freya Stark, English traveller and author, *Beyond Euphrates: Autobiography, 1928–1933* (1951). She is describing wintering in 1928–29 in B.C.'s Kootenay Valley.

A heavy snowfall in December meant that winter had come,—the deepest reality of Canadian life.

Description from **Willa Cather**'s novel *Shadows on the Rock* (1931).

For it's forty below in the winter, / And it's twenty below in the fall. / It just rises to zero in summer, / And we don't have a springtime at all.

Refrain of the song "Forty Below," a parody of the folk song "Red River Valley." Once believed to be traditional, the lyrics were written by the journalist **Christopher Dafoe** and published in his column "Coffee Break by Wink," *Winnipeg Free Press*, 29 May 1959.

Yes, this is a cold country. Cold with the snow and frost that have entered into the bloodstream and packed ice around the heart; cold with fear, ignorance, repression, denial. Only alcohol consumed in great quantities can temporarily dissolve this hard pack of ice.

Irving Layton, poet, Introduction, *Love Where the Nights Are Long* (1962).

In Europe, winter is just one of the four seasons. In Canada it's a deluge of snow, a desert of cold. It gives the country a fifth dimension.

Jacques Ferron, author, quoted by Norman Sheffe, editor of *Many Cultures, Many Heritages* (1975).

All our Canadian winters! The necessity to adapt to extreme change is at least part of the stimulus of the northness of Canada; it may have something to do with that resourcefulness for which I believe Canadians have some reputation.

Kathleen Coburn, scholar, *In Pursuit of Coleridge* (1977).

The winter is very hard in Canada.... The thermometer is much more sensitive than the human being.

Jorge Luis Borges, man-of-letters, interviewed by Raul Galvez in Buenos Aires, Argentina, June 1985, *From the Ashen Land of the Virgins* (1988).

Oh Canadian love, Canadian love / It's either forty below or it's ninety above. / And though it's hard to be yearning / When you're freezing or burning / Like the dollar we keep falling in Canadian love.

Verse from singer-performer **Marie-Lynn Hammond**'s "Canadian Love," quoted by Ellen Schwartz in *Born a Woman: Seven Canadian Women Singer-Songwriters* (1988).

We have hot summers and resplendent autumns, but it is winter that establishes the character of our country and our psychology. The Canadian mood.

Thoughts of the narrator of **Robertson Davies**' novel *Murther & Walking Spirits* (1991).

The winters are cold, so we have to warm each other with our feelings.

Mitsou, pop singer, "My Canada Includes...," *Maclean's*, 3 Jan. 1994.

In Canada, the colder the winter is, the warmer the people are.

Jean Charest, Prime Minister, *My Road to Québec* (1998).

WISDOM See also INTELLIGENCE

All true wisdom is only to be learned far from the dwellings of men, in the great solitudes; and it can only be attained through suffering. Suffering and privation are the only things that can open the mind of man to that which is hidden from his fellows.

Igjugarjuk, Caribou Eskimo shaman, quoted by Knud Rasmussen in *Across Arctic America: Narrative of the Fifth Thule Expedition* (1927).

Humanity has to travel a hard road to wisdom, and it has to travel it with bleeding feet.

Nellie L. McClung, suffragette, *In Times Like These* (1915).

Wisdom may be rented, so to speak, on the experience of other people, but we buy it at an inordinate price before we make it our own forever.

Thoughts of a character in **Robertson Davies**' novel *Leaven of Malice* (1954).

It is cruel for the old to inflict their disillusioned wisdom on the young. Fortunately, it is also impossible.

Irving Layton, poet, Foreword, *The Covenant* (1977).

The function of the wise isn't to run the show, but to clean up the messes made by the fools who do.

Richard Needham, columnist, "A Writer's World," *The Globe and Mail*, 16 May 1980.

In this world the follies of the rich pass for wise sayings.

John Kenneth Galbraith, economist and essayist, *The Culture of Contentment* (1992).

WISHES

I would like world peace and my own apartment.

Reply to the question of what she wants, offered an unnamed Miss Canada contestant in the 1970s, as noted by Trina McQueen, "Reporting on Women," *The Globe and Mail*, 5 March 1994.

The WOW Project is the Golden Rule in action. / WOW is Wishing Only Well for yourself and for your world. / We Wish Only Well, and we want to brighten the world! WOW invites you to look at life with the wonder of a child, and see all the different reasons to say WOW! / Reach out... and WOW the world!

"The WOW Project," initiated by the activist **Carmen Colombo** in Montreal in 1996. The explanations come from the project's homepage on the Internet, March 1997.

WIT See also HUMOUR & HUMORISTS

Nothing is as fleeting as a moment of wit on television.

David Steinberg, Winnipeg-born comedian, quoted in *The New York Times Magazine*, 25 April 1971.

The pun is the highest form of wit. Wit is the subtlest form of knowledge.

Eric McLuhan, communications theorist, quoted by Olivia Ward in *The Toronto Star*, 30 March 1980.

The wit of a graduate student is like champagne—Canadian champagne.

Line from **Robertson Davies**' story "The Ghost Who Vanished by Degrees," *High Spirits* (1982).

WOLVES See also ANIMALS

The wolf will not attack a man. I risked $100 cash money, to be paid to anyone who could prove the contrary. I still have that $100 in the safe and sacred depository of my jeans-pocket. And no fewer than 42 claimants tried to have it transferred, but in vain. A wolf will not attack a man.... And any who claims he ever was is a liar.

J.W. Curran, publisher of *The Sault Star*, interviewed by R.E. Knowles in *The Toronto Star*, 27 Nov. 1933.

In the end, there were no simple answers. No heroes... no villains... only silence.

Last words of the movie *Never Cry Wolf* (1983) narrated by the scientist named Tyler (played by actor Charles Martin Smith), based on **Farley Mowat**'s 1963 book of the same name, photographed in northern British Columbia, the Yukon, and Alaska.

WOMEN See also FEMINISM, MANKIND, MEN & WOMEN, MONTREAL MASSACRE, WOMEN'S RIGHTS, YVETTES

The lineal descent of the people of the Five Nations shall run in the female line. Women shall be considered the Progenitors of the Nation. They shall own the land and the soil. Men and women shall follow the status of their mothers.

Article of the "Great Law of Peace" of the **Iroquois Confederacy**, reproduced by Craig MacLaine and Michael S. Baxendale in *This Land Is Our Land: The Mohawk Revolt at Oka* (1991).

There are some differences between the ladies of *Quebec,* and those of *Montreal;* those of the last place seemed to be generally handsomer than those of the former. Their behaviour likewise seemed to me to be somewhat too free at *Quebec,* and of a more becoming modesty at *Montreal.*

Peter Kalm, Swedish naturalist and traveller in 1748, *Travels into North America* (1772), translated from the Swedish by J.R. Foster.

A woman of taste is always an engaging object.

Thomas McCulloch, satirist, *Letters of Mephibosheth Stepsure* (1821), a work of humour edited by Douglas Lochhead as *The Stepsure Letters* (1960).

Girls should be educated to fit them for the sphere of life for which they are destined—that of the homemaker.

Adelaide Hoodless, founder of the Women's Institute in 1897, quoted by Ruth Howes in *Adelaide Hoodless: Woman with a Vision* (1965).

A woman is more influenced by what she suspects than by what she is told.

Bob Edwards, publisher, *The Eye Opener,* 3 Nov. 1917, *The Wit and Wisdom of Bob Edwards* (1976) edited by Hugh Dempsey.

A girl of sixteen pretends to know a lot more than a woman of thirty will admit she knows.

Bob Edwards, publisher, *The Eye Opener,* Summer Annual, 1924, *The Best of Bob Edwards* (1975) edited by Hugh Dempsey.

Few women are enrolled among the makers of Canada. Yet in all save the earliest years they have formed nearly half the population and have done almost half the work. But historians and businessmen tell us little of the part they have played. The woman's stage was set not in the limelight but in the firelight.

Isabel Skelton, traveller, *The Backwoodswoman* (1924).

When I hear men talk about women being the angel of the home I always, mentally at least, shrug my shoulders in doubt. I do not want to be the angel of any home; I want for myself what I want for other women, absolute equality. After that is secured then men and women can take turns at being angels.

Agnes Macphail, first female Member of Parliament, House of Commons, 26 Feb. 1925.

Our discontents are passing. We may yet live to see the day when women will be no longer news! And it cannot come too soon. I want to be a peaceful, happy human, pursuing my unimpeded way through life, never having to explain, defend or apologize for my sex.

Nellie L. McClung, suffragette, "A Retrospect" (1929), quoted by Linda Rasmussen et al., in *A Harvest Yet to Reap: A History of Prairie Women* (1976).

As Goethe said, it is the Eternal Feminine that beckons us ever onward: he did not mention the Eternal Old Woman who holds us back.

Observation attributed to the fictional character Samuel Marchbanks in **Robertson Davies**' collection *Samuel Marchbanks' Almanack* (1967).

But the women we really love are the women who complete us, who have the qualities we can borrow and so become something nearer to whole men.

Thoughts of a character in **Robertson Davies**' novel *The Manticore* (1972).

If women were running the show, there wouldn't be any wars, but there would be some savage duels.

Richard Needham, newspaper columnist, *The Wit and Wisdom of Richard Needham* (1977).

Economists could get a very sudden increase in the GNP by discovering and including the unpaid labour of women.

John Kenneth Galbraith, economist and essayist, *Almost Everyone's Guide to Economics* (1978) written with Nicole Salinger.

An abandoned woman was like a dog you kicked when the real object of your wrath wasn't available.

Thoughts of a character in **Jane Rule**'s novel *After the Fire* (1989).

One of my favourite pleasures is to say "menopause" out loud in a fancy restaurant and see all the heads turn.

Janine O'Leary Cobb, publisher of a newsletter

A Friend Indeed, quoted by Rod Mickleburgh in *The Globe and Mail*, 30 May 1991.

I guess I'll never understand women—not even the six-year-olds.

Gary Lautens, humorist, "Leaving Home—Sort Of," *The Best of Gary Lautens* (1995).

Women have climbed higher on the scale of virtue, higher than man, I have always believed that. But people say, and I believe it, that when they fall, women reach a level of baseness that the most vile men could not reach.

Jean Bienvenue, Justice of the Quebec Superior Court, controversial opinion expressed from the bench while sentencing a woman convicted of the murder of her husband, Trois-Rivières, Que., 6 Dec. 1995, quoted by André Picard in *The Globe and Mail*, 9 Dec. 1995. The remarks were examined by a disciplinary proceeding which ended in a recommendation that Judge Bienvenue be removed from office.

Being a woman in politics is something like being Ginger Rogers. You have to dance as well as Fred Astaire—backwards in heels!

Audrey McLaughlin, former NDP leader, quoted in "The Agnes Macphail Fund" letter, June 1996.

Forgive me for saying this, but what would happen if we were all PMSed the same week? Can you imagine what the Parliament of Canada would be like?

Deborah Grey, M.P., addressing a political fund-raising dinner, Edmonton, 20 March 1997, quoted by David Vienneau in *The Toronto Star*, 22 March 1997. The Reform Member of Parliament thus referred to Pre-Menstrual Syndrome (PMS) in an attempt to ridicule the Liberal election strategy to recruit more women candidates. The plan backfired.

The Women of Influence lunches I spoke at in Canada featured cold noodle salad and polystyrene chicken thighs, suggesting more plainly than words could that Canadian businesswomen have at their command small influence and less money.

Germaine Greer, Australian-born author, describing a book-promotion and lecture tour, "Letter from New York," *The Times Literary Supplement*, 7 Aug. 1999.

WOMEN'S RIGHTS See also RIGHTS, WOMEN

The Rights of Women are now beginning to be better understood, and to bring to light her long-buried capabilities. It has lately been discovered that woman is the equal of man; equal in counsel, equal in debate, equal in judgment, equal in eloquence, equal in courage, equal in every quality but that of brute force—a poor superiority, enjoyed by him in common with the beasts of burden.

Dramatic speech in the play *The Female Consistory of Brockville* (1856) written by "**Caroli Candidus**," as quoted by Beth Kaplan in *Communiqué*, May 1975.

No woman capable of doing higher work should consent to become a man's drudge, at any man's bidding. I am not a stickler for women's rights but I am for women's pluck and independence.

Kit Coleman, columnist in the 1880s and 1890s, quoted by Ted Ferguson in *Kit Coleman: Queen of Hearts* (1978).

We'll have true equality when we have as many incompetent women in senior positions as incompetent men.

Sheelagh Whittaker, businesswoman, address, Montreal, 12 Dec. 1991.

We church-going Roman Catholics participate in a pattern of discrimination against women that is illegal everywhere except in the church. The federal and provincial governments—which rightly insist other Canadian institutions address gender issues in hiring, promotion, and pay equity—say nothing to the Church, whose discrimination is the most blatant.

Philip Milner, author and academic, *The Yankee Professor's Guide to Life in Nova Scotia* (1993).

WORDS

Too many words are fatal to religious devotion. The heart and the mouth do not open simultaneously.

Marie de l'Incarnation, missionary, quoted by Agnes Repplier in *Mère Marie of the Ursulines: A Study in Adventure* (1931).

I have made all my journeys by means of words. We send our words out to reconnoitre, and they bring back reports on the countries they have seen. We see from these reports whether the countries are real, fairly real, or surreal.

Hector de Saint-Denys-Garneau, poet, *The Journal of Saint-Denys-Garneau* (1962) translated by John Glassco.

In those parts of the world where the older civilizations are seated . . . the map is more ancient than the alphabet.

Leslie H. Neatby, historian, *In Quest of the North West Passage* (1958).

A French Canadian once remarked to me with perplexity, "Our national differences are shown by the fact that all English swear words are about sex and all of ours are about the church." Who is oppressed by what?

James C. Paupst and **Toni Robinson**, physician and writer, *Breakdown or Break-through: Self-Discovery through Change* (1980).

You can find many excuses for a poem but only one reason for a word.

Line from a poem in **Steve McCaffery**'s *Knowledge Never Knew* (1983).

Like sketching, like metaphor, illustrative language testifies to the freedom of every human being.

Graeme Nicholson, philosopher, *Seeing and Reading* (1984).

We need words to keep us human.

Michael Ignatieff, essayist, *The Needs of Strangers* (1985).

Is that the flesh made word / or is that the flesh-made word?

Line from a poem in **Fred Wah**'s *Music at the Heart of Thinking* (1987).

If all the words of all the Harlequin books sold last year were laid end to end, they would stretch 1,000 times around the earth or 93 times to the moon. That's a distance of one-quarter of the way to the sun.

Publicists, **Harlequin Enterprises Limited**, *The Harlequin Story: Harlequin Fun Facts* (1988).

All words are part of the Word.

Northrop Frye, cultural critic, interviewed by Harry Rasky on *The Great Teacher: Northrop Frye*, CBC-TV, 25 Dec. 1989.

It used to be the most important person in the community was the blacksmith. Now it's the wordsmith.

Morris C. Shumiatcher, advocate, obiter dictum, 1 Dec. 1993.

Lathomenon. It's derived from Greek, as all good words are. It's a beautiful opposite of phenomenon because it takes existence for granted. When something exists and is apparent, it is a phenomenon. When it exists but isn't apparent, it is a lathomenon.

Endel Tulving, psychologist concerned with memory, University of Toronto, quoted by Karina Dahlin and Alfred Holden, "Simply the Best," *University of Toronto Magazine*, Summer 1994.

WORK See also CAREERS, EMPLOYMENT, LABOUR

We are made to work—and as long as the Lord gives me a continuation of health and energy—I am determined to work and work with a will.

Timothy Eaton, merchant, letter, 28 April 1870, quoted by Joy L. Santink in *Timothy Eaton and the Rise of His Department Store* (1990).

Don't work all your life to make a living,—but work to live all your life.

Jack Miner, conservationist, advice written in the autograph album kept by J. Alex Edmison of Ottawa, signed: "'Uncle' Jack Miner / August 3rd—1924—Camp Ahmek, Algonquin Park," Ont.

A man feels impelled to do something to keep awake.

Sir William Mulock, financier and philanthropist, interviewed by R.E. Knowles in *The Toronto Star*, 30 Nov. 1928.

At play, man uses all his faculties; at work, he specializes.

Marshall McLuhan, communications pioneer, "The Art of Wychwood Park," *Toronto Life*, April 1970, as quoted in *Who Was Marshall McLuhan?* (1994) edited by Barrington Nevitt and Maurice McLuhan.

You cannot take your *work* too seriously—only yourself. Let other people give you the attention you deserve, and concentrate on deserving it.

Eric Nicol, humorist, *One Man's Media—and How to Write for Them* (1973).

One secret of happiness in life is always to have some work left over at the end of the day.

Richard Needham, newspaper columnist, *The Wit and Wisdom of Richard Needham* (1977).

Employment Equity

The words "employment equity," which refer to the equality of men and women in the workplace, were coined and the concept was defined by **Rosalie Abella**, jurist and chairperson of the Royal Commission on Employment Equity, the report of which was released in 1984.

It doesn't matter what my qualifications are, all some people will see are my pierced ears.

Roberta Bondar, physician and astronaut, commenting on how men view women who work in high technology, quoted by Trish Crawford in *The Toronto Star*, 2 Aug. 1987.

I used to have a motto back in my concert days and it served me in good stead for a number of years... some inner voice said to me, "Who ever said it's supposed to be fun?" That became my motto.

Glenn Gould, pianist, interviewed by Ulla Colgrass in *For the Love of Music* (1988).

McJob.

Neologism devised to refer to a low-skill, low-pay work in the service industry, first used by **Doug Coupland** in his novel *Generation X: Tales from an Accelerated Culture* (1991).

Dad always told us if you work hard you can't go wrong. You may not get what you want, but you will get something.

Jean Charest, Minister of the Environment and Conservative leadership candidate, referring to his father's advice, interviewed by Patrick Doyle, "The Charest Factor," *The Toronto Star*, 15 May 1993.

I get jolly well tired of managing a multinational public company by day and doing the ironing when I get home at night.

Lynne Stethem, founder of Angoss Software Corp., Toronto, quoted by Ellen Roseman, "The Glare of Going Public," *The Globe and Mail*, 29 Nov. 1993.

Think like a man, act like a lady, work like a dog.

Hazel McCallion, long-time Mayor of Mississauga, Ont., business conference, Toronto, 19 Jan. 1999.

WORLD

See also CANADA & THE WORLD

The most obvious thing about our world is that it is incomprehensible.

Alberto Manguel, editor, Introduction, *Canadian Mystery Stories* (1991).

The world, in brief, needs Canada.

Charles, Prince of Wales, address, Queen's University, Kingston, Ont., 28 Oct. 1991, quoted in *The Globe and Mail* the following day.

Canada sits near the top of the world with a better view of what goes on to the south.

Lesley Choyce, editor, Introduction, *Ark of Ice: Canadian Futurefiction* (1992).

The world is constantly renewed, out of its own nature, in space and time, and we ourselves are one extraordinary example of its creative power. The complete structure, its immense order and possibility, cannot be entirely imagined or understood, yet we are present before it, in its totality and in its detail, from day to day. To that extent it is an open secret, forever revealing itself.

Louis Dudek, poet and aphorist, Preface, *The Birth of Reason* (1994).

WORLD CLASS

A phrase used by provincial cities and second-rate entertainment and sports events, as well as a wide variety of insecure individuals, to assert that they are not provincial or second-rate, thereby confirming that they are.

John Ralston Saul, author, *The Doubter's Companion: A Dictionary of Aggressive Common Sense* (1994).

WORLD WAR I

See also WAR, WORLD WAR II, WORLD WAR III

In the name of religion, of freedom, of loyalty to the British flag, the French Canadians are being called upon to go and fight the Prussians of Europe. Are we to allow the Prussians of Ontario to impose as masters their dominion in the very heart of the Canadian Confederation, under the shelter of the British flag and British institutions . . . ?

Henri Bourassa, publisher and nationalist, editorial, *Le Devoir*, 21 Dec. 1914.

The Canadians played a part of such distinction that thenceforward they were marked out as storm troops; for the remainder of the war they were brought along to head the assault in one great battle after another. Whenever the Germans found the Canadian Corps coming into the line they prepared for the worst.

David Lloyd George, British Prime Minister, following the Battles of the Somme in 1916, quoted by F.G.C. Stanley in *Canada's Soldiers: The Military History of an Unmilitary People* (3rd ed., 1974).

If anyone can do it, it will be the Canadians.

Sir Julian Byng, British commander, on being informed in Jan. 1917 that he was leading the Canadian Corps in the assault on Vimy Ridge, France; quoted by Vince Leah in the *Winnipeg Free Press*, 9 April 1992.

Canada has profited the most and suffered the least from this war of any of the nations of the empire.

N.W. Rowell, politician, diary entry, 8 July 1919, quoted by Margaret Prang in *N.W. Rowell: Ontario Nationalist* (1975).

"We are here! We are here! / Soldiers all! / Good cheer! We are near! / Ontario! Ontario! / Toronto! Montreal!"

Lines from the martial poem "The Bugles of Canada," *The Poems of Arthur Conan Doyle* (1922), composed by **Sir Arthur Conan Doyle**, British novelist and sometime versifier, who explained, "In war time a Canadian Division was encamped near my house. I used to fashion their bugle calls into the names of their distant land. Hence these verses."

Canadian soldiers had a distinguished record in World War I, but they had to fight for recognition.

Eric Nicol, humorist, "The War Years" (1967), *Still a Nicol: The Best of Eric Nicol* (1972) edited by Alan Walker.

Son, millions of men have just stood up in their graves and saluted you.

Timothy Findley, novelist, recalling the reaction of his father, a war veteran, after reading his novel *The Wars* (1977), quoted by Roy MacGregor in *The Canadian*, 17 Dec. 1977.

Tread softly at Passchendaele, because you tread upon a dream of what we might have become.

Last line of **Sandra Gwyn**'s *Tapestry of War: A Private View of Canadians in the Great War* (1992). In this line there is a memorable echo of W.B. Yeats. Many Canadians and other Allies died in the vicinity of Passchendaele Ridge northeast of Ypres in southwest Belgium. Gwyn wrote, "It was at Passchendaele that the Great War reached its nadir of horror."

WORLD WAR II

See also WAR, WORLD WAR I, WORLD WAR III

While we are urged to fight for freedom and democracy, it should be remembered that war is the very negation of both. The victor may win; but if he does, it is by adopting the selfsame tactics which he condemns in his enemy.

J.S. Woodsworth, M.P., declining to make unanimous the motion that a state of war exists with Germany through the invocation of the War Measures Act, House of Commons, 8 Sept. 1939.

Come . . . if you dare!

Last words of the NFB film *Churchill's Island* (1939–41) exclaimed by narrator **Lorne Greene**. The words anticipate the Battle of Britain. They are heard over the arresting shot of a cannon overlooking the English Channel trained on Northern Europe. The documentary was directed by Stuart Legg, as noted by D.B. Jones in *The Best Butler in the Business: Tom Daly of the National Film Board of Canada* (1996).

Give us your aluminum and we will turn your pots and pans into Spitfires and Hurricanes, Blenheims and Wellingtons.

Patriotic appeal to the homefront for pots and pans and other material useful in the war effort issued in July 1940 by **Lord Beaverbrook**, who served in Britain's War Cabinet and was in charge of aircraft production, quoted in *Chronicle of the Second World War* (1990) edited by Derrick Mercer.

We shall fight on the beaches, we shall fight on the landing grounds, we shall fight in the fields and in the streets, we shall fight in the hills; we shall never surrender. And even if, which I do not for a moment believe, this island or a large part of it, were subjugated and starving, then our Empire beyond the seas, armed and guarded by the British Fleet, would carry on the struggle, until, in God's good time, the New World, with all its power and might, steps forth to the rescue and the liberation of the Old.

Winston Churchill, British wartime leader, address, British House of Commons, London, England, 4 June 1940; there is a veiled allusion to Canada in the words "our Empire beyond the seas" and to the United States in the words "the New World."

Major-General J. Hamilton Roberts... had told his men that Dieppe would be a piece of cake; each year on the anniversary of the debacle a small parcel would arrive in his mail bearing a stale piece of cake to remind him of his words.

David J. Bercuson, historian, referring to the Canadian general who led the ill-fated Dieppe Raid, 19 Aug. 1942, *Maple Leaf against the Axis: Canada's Second World War* (1994).

When I warned them that Britain would fight on alone, whatever they did, their generals told their Prime Minister and his divided cabinet, "In three weeks England will have her neck wrung like a chicken." Some chicken! Some neck!

Sir Winston Churchill, British Prime Minister, address, joint meeting of the Senate and the House of Commons, Ottawa, 30 Dec. 1941. Churchill was referring to the cowardly generals of France in the most inspired, widely reported, and fondly remembered address ever delivered on Canadian soil. Afterwards Churchill repaired to the Speaker's Chamber, where he sat for Yousuf Karsh's camera. Karsh's portrait, which caught Churchill's famous "bulldog" expression, is the most celebrated photograph ever taken on Canadian soil.

My fadder fight against you last time. We give you one good lickin' den we do it again.

Defiance expressed with exuberance by Johnny the Trapper (played by **Laurence Olivier**), the simple French Canadian who falls into the hands of cold-blooded Nazi spies who are making their way from Hudson Bay to the still-neutral United States in the movie *The 49th Parallel* (1942).

Perhaps, dramatic as it is, the current landing of numerous French Canadians on the Normandy coast will help reestablish a vital link, missing for almost two centuries.

André Breton, French surrealist and traveller, *Arcanum 17* (1944) translated from the French in 1994 by Zack Rogow.

For instance, the Van Doos, as English Canada pronounced *le royal 22e régiment* (*vingt-deuxième*), had a distinguished record in both wars, never losing a battle. In World War II, during the invasion scare in Britain, it was the Van Doos who mounted guard at Buckingham Palace in in London.

F.S. Manor, journalist, "Canada's Crisis: The Causes," *Foreign Policy*, Winter 1977–78.

Paris is free. Paris is happy again.

Matthew Halton, war correspondent, covering the liberation of Paris, broadcast, CBC Radio, 26 Aug. 1944.

You're going to die, and I would too, rather than go back to Canada.

Nancy Astor, socialite-turned-nurse when Cliveden, her English estate, was converted into a hospital for Canadian soldiers, addressing patients who had lost their will to live, quoted by John Halpern in *Eminent Georgians* (1995).

He's a Canadian. Doesn't he realize he's in this too?

Protest of the Englishman (played by actor **Robert Morley**) about the ignorance of international affairs shown by the Canadian captain Charlie Allnut (Humphrey Bogart) in the movie *The African Queen* (1951).

The Germans stole our food, the Canadians our heart!

Message on a postcard printed in Holland depicting the Dutch peoples' affection for their Canadian liberators in World War II. Quoted by David Kaufman and Michiel Horn in *A Liberation Album: Canadians in the Netherlands: 1944–45* (1980).

Words like "freedom" and "democracy" tend to make Canadians blush and scrape their toes in the dirt of embarrassment. But the war against fascism was about freedom and democracy. There is too much naïveté afoot these days, a feeling that no war can be a just war, that no cause can be worth dying for. The horrors of the Vietnam War and the ominous shadow of the nuclear arms race have made most Canadians unable to realize that once it was different.

J.L. Granatstein and **Desmond Morton**, historians, *A Nation Forged in Fire: Canadians and the Second World War 1939–1945* (1989).

A missing million.

Phrase employed by researcher **James Bacque** to refer to the number of German prisoners-of-war said to be unaccountably dead or missing at the end of World War II in his article "The Last Dirty Secret of World War Two," *Saturday Night*, Sept. 1989, and thereafter in his book *Other Losses: An Investigation into the Mass Deaths of German Prisoners at the Hands of the French and Americans after World War II* (1989). The words "Other Losses" come from an Allied report dated 2 June 1945. Bacque's conclusions were dismissed by historian Günter Bischof and biographer Stephen E. Ambrose in *Eisenhower and the German POWs: Facts against Falsehood* (1992). Defence expert John Keegan dismissed the notion as "Bacque's canard" in "James Bacque and the 'Missing Million,'" *The Times Literary Supplement*, 23 July 1993.

We feel very contrite about the unbearable sufferings and hardships brought upon the peoples of the Asia Pacific by the actions of the Japanese state. I expressed this formally to Prime Minister Mulroney. By saying that, I expressed my apology for the unbearable suffering and pain that was caused by the Japanese state against the Canadian people who experienced such sufferings.

Toshiki Kaifu, Japan's Prime Minister, admitting guilt concerning treatment of Allied prisoners of war during World War II, press conference following a private meeting with Prime Minister Mulroney, Tokyo, 28 May 1991, quoted by Edith Terry and Rudy Platiel in *The Globe and Mail* the following day.

The Talmud declares: "He who saves one life saves the whole world." Between 1939 and 1945, Canada's soldiers, sailors, and airmen willingly went into harm's way to fight the Axis, until it was shattered. In doing so, they helped save the world many times over.

David J. Bercuson, historian, *Maple Leaf against the Axis: Canada's Second World War* (1994).

On the beach behind us, Canadians gave their lives so the world would be a better place. In death they were not anglophones or francophones, not from the West or the East, not Christians or Jews, not aboriginal people or immigrants. They were Canadians.

Jean Chrétien, Prime Minister, address to commemorate the 50th anniversary of the D-Day Invasion, delivered at Juno Beach, France, 6 June 1994, as quoted by Allan Thompson in *The Toronto Star* the next day. On the very first day of the D-Day invasion, 6 June 1944, 359 Canadians died.

WORLD WAR III

See also WAR, WORLD WAR I, WORLD WAR II

There will be no second prizes in the next world war.

John G. Diefenbaker, former Prime Minister, speech, House of Commons, 23 May 1967.

Two Canadians, quite convinced of the imminence and inevitability of a Third World War which Canada could not escape, decided to emigrate to a place that would be safe because it was isolated, poor, virtually unpopulated and had an uninviting climate. They researched various possibilities before discovering their haven of peace far from all artillery and bombs. The couple then duly departed—to the Falklands.

Jean-Charles de Fontbrune, French scholar, *Nostradamus 2: Into the Twenty-first Century* (1984) translated by Alexis Lykiard.

By the decade 2020–30, a major war between the Great Powers was as unthinkable as one between Canada and the United States had been the century before.

Line from **Arthur C. Clarke**'s futuristic novel *2061: Odyssey Three* (1987).

I have three young children at home and I want to leave for them a world free of nuclear war. This would be the greatest gift all politicians could give to the children of the world.

Brian Mulroney, Prime Minister, quoted by William Walker in *The Toronto Star*, 17 Sept. 1988.

WORRY

Yesterday's neglect causes two-thirds of today's worries.

Bob Edwards, publisher, *The Eye Opener*, 12 May 1919, *The Wit and Wisdom of Bob Edwards* (1976) edited by Hugh Dempsey.

WORSHIP

Reverence all life. Emulate my patience. Unfold the mysteries of God and even of pebbles. Do it as a learner of life, a revealer. Let your dominion be over yourself, and let your expanding consciousness see God's life in all things.... Praise God forever, and praise Him in the vastness of all life.

Sentiments attributed to the "Cosmic Angel of Stone," a deva or spirit entity which speaks through medium **Dorothy Maclean**, author of *To Hear the Angels Sing* (1980).

WRESTLING See also SPORTS

When I was down, all of Canada bent down to pick me up.

Maurice "Mad Dog" Vachon, former professional wrestler, who when disabled in an accident in 1987 sought a seat in Parliament, quoted by Donald McKenzie in the *Winnipeg Free Press*, 27 July 1992.

WRITERS & WRITING See also BOOKS; LITERATURE; MAGAZINES; POETS & POETRY; WRITERS & WRITING, CANADIAN

Your Highness, I have had other compliments paid me, but none equal to this one. I have never before had a salute fired in my honour.

Mark Twain, humorist, addressing Governor General Lord Lorne, whose guest he was at the opening of Parliament, Ottawa, May 1883, quoted by Stephen Leacock in "Mark Twain in Canada," *Queen's Quarterly*, Spring, 1935.

I write for life's sake, and have no time for art for art's sake. Oscar Wilde believed in art for art's sake, and see what he has become, but art for life's sake becomes a Browning. Humanity is the thing. Too many write about flowers when there is suffering in the world.

Wilson MacDonald, poet, quoted in *The Calgary Herald*, 20 Nov. 1923, reproduced by Stan Dragland in *Wilson MacDonald's Western Tour, 1923–24: A Collage of Letters* (1975).

I believe in drawing up my chair to my desk and going to it. I rise early—and begin. Always morning work. Give me till 11:00 a.m., and the rest of the day can belong to anyone who wants it.

Stephen Leacock, humorist, interviewed by R.E. Knowles in *The Toronto Star*, 16 Feb. 1933.

Don't go to New York or Toronto or Montreal, stay at home. Go to the blacksmith's shop, the barber shop, the back stoop of a farmhouse.

W.O. Mitchell, author, dispensing advice to would-be writers, at a meeting of the Canadian Authors' Association, Vancouver, noted in "Successful Author Finds Fan Mail Bit Embarrassing," *The Vancouver Sun*, 11 Jan. 1947.

Always write short stories seventeen pages long.

Arthur Mayse, Canadian contributor of short stories to *Saturday Evening Post*, advice given in 1949 to Hugh Garner, who called it "the best advice I ever got about writing short stories" in *One Damn Thing after Another* (1973).

Write! Write! Get up every morning at five and write before the day begins!

F.R. Scott, poet and constitutional law professor, advice in the 1950s to McGill student Ruth R. Wisse, recalled in "My Life without Leonard Cohen," *Commentary*, Oct. 1995.

There's no distinction in not being ready and not being appreciated. In the long run the honest writer with the authentic talent always triumphs. He stands up. The world's best sellers oddly enough, over a period say of fifty years, turn out to be written by the world's best writers.

Morley Callaghan, author, "Novelist," *Canada: Proceedings of the Canadian Writers' Conference* (1956) edited by George Whalley.

In a biography, keep the poor man alive.

William Kilbourn, historian and biographer, address, Winnipeg CAA Convention in 1957, quoted by Stan Obodiac in *My Experiences at a Canadian Authors' Convention* (1957).

There are two kinds of writers: the one who tries to see the world out of his own eyes, and the other one, the commercial writer, who tries to see the world out of the eyes of others.

Nathan Cohen, critic, "Heroes of the Richler View," *The Tamarack Review*, Winter 1958.

Writers *may* think, but they *must* feel.

Robertson Davies, man-of-letters, address, 1970, *Robertson Davies: The Well-Tempered Critic: One Man's View of Theatre and Letters in Canada* (1981) edited by Judith Skelton Grant.

He was an egocentric monster, but he was also the most completely free spirit I ever met.

Gerald Robitaille, Montreal-born writer who served as the personal secretary of Henry Miller—in Paris from 1953 and in California from 1967—until the publication of *Le Père Miller* (1971), his book of candid memoirs, quoted by Don Bell in *The Toronto Star*, 22 June 1980.

Take similes, for example. Why does the outlook have to be bleak? Why can't it be as bleak as the view from the Ford Hotel? And why must a person be as dull as can be? Why can't he be as dull as Sunday noon in Moncton? With metaphors, hyperbole and so on it is the same. An enterprising person could pass a short lifetime Canadianizing them all.

Doug Fetherling, writer, "Even When We Swear We're All Colonials," *Saturday Night*, May 1971.

It's easy to produce writers, but a public is much harder to come by.

Marshall McLuhan, communications pioneer, interviewed by Linda Sandler in *Miss Chatelaine*, 3 Sept. 1974.

Writers are eye-witnesses, I-witnesses.

Margaret Atwood, author, "Paradoxes and Dilemmas: The Woman as Writer," *Women in the Canadian Mosaic* (1976) edited by Gwen Matheson.

Once I've thought of it, it just spills out. Writing is like controlled dreaming.

John Gray, playwright, quoted by Stephen Godfrey in *The Globe and Mail*, 7 Sept. 1985.

I can no longer keep a journal. My life erases / everything I write.

Lines from a poem in **Robert Kroetsch**'s *Seed Catalogue* (1986).

Clear prose indicates the absence of thought.

Attributed to communications pioneer **Marshall McLuhan** by Marsh Jeanneret in *God and Mammon* (1989).

A scholar dedicates a lifetime to one field; a writer can flit about and sample many.

Ronald Wright, author, *Time among the Maya: Travels in Belize, Guatemala, and Mexico* (1989).

EXCREMENT $8.00 / SLIMY REGENERATE LITERATURE / WORST SELLING AUTHOR

Wording on signs sported by maverick and sometimes self-published fiction writer **Crad Kilodney**, who hawked his books at Toronto's street corners, noted by Stuart McLean on CBC Radio's *Morningside*, 9 Jan. 1989.

Generally speaking, the most respected fiction writers in Canada are Margaret Atwood and Robertson Davies, but no one churns out a body of fiction of as consistently high a quality as the companies listed on the VSE.

Joe Queenan, U.S. journalist, referring to the Vancouver Stock Exchange, "Scam Capital of the World," *Forbes*, 29 May 1989.

Speak the flesh. Kiss and *tell* with anger, grace, humour and sometimes, love.

Lorna Crozier, poet, "Speaking the Flesh," *Language in Her Eye: Views on Writing and Gender by Canadian Women Writing in English* (1990) edited by Libby Scheier, Sarah Sheard, and Eleanor Wachtel.

Like the evening television news, this is a work of fiction. All resemblances to real persons and things, living or dead, is purely intentional—unless they find it objectionable, of course.

Brian Fawcett, novelist, *Acknowledgements, Public Eye: An Investigation into the Disappearance of the World* (1990).

I guess I write to trick reality into revealing itself.

George Bowering, author, "Selected Errata," *The Brick Reader* (1991) edited by Linda Spalding and Michael Ondaatje.

Writers are at their best as terrorists—sometimes social terrorists, sometimes political, sometimes terrorists of the heart. If a writer is good, he will be all three at once.

John Ralston Saul, author, *Voltaire's Bastards: The Dictatorship of Reason in the West* (1992).

Authors' conventions point up the difference between writing and writering. Writering consists of loud, self-promoting bombast on every topic under the sun. Mental mediocrity guised as omniscience.

Maurus E. Mallon, aphorist, 29 July 1992.

Writers are only different from other people in that they have a specific ability to tell stories.

Josef Skvorecky, author, quoted by Billy Markus in *eye*, 15 Oct. 1992.

I write to complete the world, to add an eighth day to creation.

Antonine Maillet, Acadian writer, quoted by Hubert Reeves in *Malicorne: Earthly Reflections of an Astrophysicist* (1993) translated from the French edition of 1990 by Donald Winkler.

So the short answer to "Why do you write" is—I suppose I write for some of the same reasons I read: to live a double life; to go places I haven't been; to examine life on Earth; to come to know people in ways, and at depths, that are otherwise impossible to be surmised. Whatever their other reasons, I think all writers write as part of this sort of continuum: to give back something of what they themselves have received.

Margaret Atwood, author, "Why I Write," *The Toronto Star*, 5 June 1993.

Style may attract; only substance holds.

Neil Bissoondath, author, "A Day in the Life of *The Globe and Mail*," *The Globe and Mail*, 5 March 1994.

As a rule, authors are soft-shelled. Most of their writing time is spent alone, wrestling with the angel, and talking to themselves, and bumping into the furniture.

Margaret Atwood, author, remarks, Harbourfront, Toronto, 11 June 1994.

The mind cannot absorb what the ass cannot endure.

Greg Gatenby, literary director, giving advice to authors before their twenty-minute public readings, Harbourfront's International Festival of Authors, quoted by Stephen Smith in *Toronto Life*, Oct. 1994.

I still do not know what impels anyone of sound mind to leave dry land and spend a lifetime describing people who do not exist.... Perhaps a writer is, in fact, a child in disguise, with a child's lucid view of grown-ups, accurate as to atmosphere, improvising when it tries to make sense of adult behaviour.

Mavis Gallant, author, Introduction, *Selected Stories* (1996).

A diary tells you what a writer did and thought about himself, a journal what he thought about the world.

Louis Dudek, poet and aphorist, "Bitter Pills," *Reality Games* (1998).

WRITERS & WRITING, CANADIAN

See also ATWOOD, MARGARET; BERTON, PIERRE; CALLAGHAN, MORLEY; COHEN, LEONARD; COHEN, NATHAN; DAVIES, ROBERTSON; FRYE, NORTHROP; LEACOCK, STEPHEN; LITERATURE; MCLUHAN, MARSHALL; MOWAT, FARLEY; RICHLER, MORDECAI; WRITERS & WRITING

Let me see, there was the Canadian author of *Maria Chapdelaine*, was there not?

Hugh Walpole, English novelist, interviewed in Toronto by R.E. Knowles, *The Toronto Star*, 27 Jan. 1930. Knowles had mischievously asked his interviewee for the names of Canadian novelists. Walpole came up with Mazo de la Roche, Ralph Connor, Raymond Knister, and Frederick Niven. Knowles admitted his unfamiliarity with the last two names.

And anybody sailing up the St. Lawrence will see where the *legend* of Canada begins, which is behind all literature.

G.K. Chesterton, English writer, address at a luncheon held in honour of Rudyard Kipling sponsored by the Canadian Literary Society and recorded by the BBC, London, England, 1933; "Visiting Canada," *The Chesterton Review*, Nov. 1996.

A poet or a novelist of great talent born in Upper Canada would not be much better off than an Eskimo, nor would the cultural gift he had to bestow stand a better chance of enriching the life of his people.

Wyndham Lewis, British artist, "Nature's Place in Canadian Culture" (1940–44), *Wyndham Lewis in Canada* (1971) edited by George Woodcock.

Rex Mottram exerted himself to make a good impression. He was a handsome fellow with dark hair growing low on his forehead and heavy black eyebrows. He spoke with an engaging Canadian accent. One quickly learned all that he wished one to know about him....

Description of the Montreal-born, London-based financier (and bigamist) in **Evelyn Waugh**'s novel *Brideshead Revisited* (1945). Waugh modelled the character of Mottram on the English politician Brendan Bracken.

A society of some thousands of the greatest Canadian writers.

F.R. Scott, poet, referring to the membership of the Canadian Authors' Association, quoted by Ken Lefolii in *Maclean's*, 11 April 1959.

Boy Meets Girl in Winnipeg and Who Cares?

Hugh MacLennan, novelist and essayist, title of an essay included in *Scotchman's Return and Other Essays* (1960). MacLennan argued that Canadian editors, publishers, and readers prefer their romances and dramas set in foreign locales rather than in presumably non-romantic and non-dramatic places such as Winnipeg.

Take my advice, desert John, and fly to Italy with me! There, on the sunny hills, we shall write such poems, such novels, such plays, as shall make the soul of Lily Brook, Nellie McClung, and Laura Salverson shrivel with envy!

Mazo de la Roche, novelist, undated early letter to fellow writer Katherine Hale, quoted by Ronald Hambleton in *Mazo de la Roche of Jalna* (1966).

Human experience deeply felt in Moose Jaw and brought successfully to paper can be read in Ghana with a sense of recognition. Our best writers know this instinctively.

Walter O'Hearn, newspaperman, *Lady Chatterley, Latterly* (1963).

Naive Canadian writers tried to prove there was something uniquely interesting in Canada. Sophisticated ones confessed, with a defeated smile, that there was nothing interesting about Canada at all.

Ronald Bryden, critic, "Live on the Margin" (1965), *Canada: A Guide to the Peaceable Kingdom* (1970) edited by William Kilbourn.

The job of the writer in Canada is not only to tell the housewife in Saskatoon that Citadel Hill is in Halifax, but to tell her why and in what ways she is different from a housewife in Denver. And why it is worth staying different.

Ray Smith, author, quoted in *Maclean's*, May 1972.

Here we should also note Gustave's apocryphal ancestry: he liked to claim that he had Red Indian blood in his veins. This seems to have been not quite the case; though one of his ancestors did emigrate to Canada in the seventeenth century and become a beaver-trapper.

Julian Barnes, English author, referring to the French novelist Gustave Flaubert, *Flaubert's Parrot* (1984).

The success of a Canadian author is measured in airplane miles and Gzowski minutes.

Attributed to writer **Ray Smith** by CBC Radio producer Peter Kavanagh in 1986 in Sydney, N.S. Smith had in mind authors' national book promotion tours culminating in exposure on CBC Radio's *Morningside* hosted by Peter Gzowski.

America will swallow you up, Canada is best.

V.S. Naipaul, Trinidadian author based in London, advising his nephew Neil Bissoondath to leave Trinidad and settle in Canada rather than England or the United States. Quoted by Ken Adachi in *The Toronto Star*, 27 Aug. 1988.

Maybe one of the problems with literature in Canada is that writers are known for their roles rather than their books.

Matt Cohen, novelist, interviewed by Mervin Butovsky, in *Other Solitudes: Canadian Multicultural Fictions* (1990) edited by Linda Hutcheon and Marion Richmond.

Canada wouldn't know it had great writers if it had them.

Louis Dudek, poet and aphorist, "Epigrams," *Small Perfect Things* (1991).

If you can set a book in Alpha Centauri, you sure as shit can set it in Toronto.

Tanya Huff, author of urban gothic fantasy novels set in Toronto, quoted by Shlomo Schwartzberg in *Now*, 26 March 1992.

The English Patient is the book most frequently begun by readers and not finished since Stephen Hawkings' *A Brief History of Time*. The readers who love it, however, really love it.

Philip Marchand, book columnist, referring to Michael Ondaatje's much-praised and filmed novel, "What I Really Think," *Saturday Night*, Oct. 1997.

And my best wish of all, may you be read forever.

Adrienne Clarkson, Governor General, dispensing the Governor General's Literary Awards, Rideau Hall, Ottawa, 16 Nov. 1999, published in "Canada Must Make Her Own Music," *The Globe and Mail* the following day.

Once upon a time, Canadian writers went to America or Europe to find themselves or develop their voices; now, it seems, more and more writers from elsewhere are coming to Canada to join in the action of a new kind of self-definition.

Pico Iyer, American travel writer, "Exile Fiction," *Saturday Night*, Dec. 1999–Jan. 2000.

X

X has been a linguistically challenged letter. Its sound, *ks*, is a tongue-twister to the English speaker when it occurs initially in a word. From *Xanadu* to *xylophone*, it ends up as *z*. It comes from the Greek *khi* (*k* aspirate), the twenty-second letter of the Greek alphabet. A Canadian scholar who is engaged in undercover activities and wishes to disguise his country of origin could write that he comes from *Xanada*, though not say it. The *x* spelling would keep him hidden in the alphabetical order. It would also be linguistically correct because the *C* of *Canada*, being in a stressed open syllable, is actually *k* aspirate, as in words of Greek origin, like character.

Thomas M. Paikeday, Canadian lexicographer and compiler of *The User's Webster Dictionary* (2000), personal communication, 29 Feb. 2000.

Y

YELLOWKNIFE See also NORTHWEST TERRITORIES

Where am I? I will give you some clues. The fish is arctic char, the meat is musk ox, the minister's cultural territories embrace a third of all Canada, the chat-show hostess is a Dene, and the birds are those irrepressible rascals of northern legend, those first cousins of the monkey-gods, the ravens.

I am in Yellowknife, "YK," capital city of the Northwest Territories.

Jan Morris, Anglo-Welsh travel writer, "Wild Blue-Yonder City," *Saturday Night*, Nov. 1989.

YVETTES See also WOMEN

Yvette... A woman who limits her activities to household duties and outings with her husband, as opposed to a "liberated" woman.

Léandre Bergeron, lexicographer, *The Québécois Dictionary* (1982).

You would be a bunch of Yvettes.

Lise Payette, Quebec Cabinet Minister, women's gathering, Quebec City, 30 March 1980. First she dismissed as les Yvettes (Plain Janes) those women who planned to vote No in the first Quebec referendum; then she referred to Liberal leader Claude Ryan's wife Madeleine as "an Yvette," to widespread outrage.

YOUTH See also AGE

Most people who are old enough to know better often wish they were young enough not to.

Bob Edwards, publisher, *The Eye Opener*, 20 April 1912.

One of the really notable achievements of twentieth century Canada has been to make the young old before their time.

Thoughts of a character in **Robertson Davies**' novel *Tempest-Tost* (1951).

Grown-ups get old and forget how to play. / They keep their appointments / And lose each day. / They work too hard and wash their ears, / They smile too little / And hold back tears. / They forget about magic, they forget how to sing. / I wouldn't be grown-up for anything.

Rhyme recited by a youngster in **Betty Jane Wylie**'s play *Kingsayer* (1978).

The adolescent or teenager is a twentieth-century invention, and a most ill-advised one.

Northrop Frye, cultural critic, "Literature as a Critique of Pure Reason" (1983), *Myth and Metaphor: Selected Essays, 1974–1988* (1990) edited by Robert D. Denham.

My message is very simple. Work hard, have confidence in yourself, realize that life is not fair, but if you stay in school and be prepared, it gets fairer. Last, but not least, is to stay away from alcohol and drugs.

Lincoln Alexander, Lieutenant-Governor of Ontario, advice to youth, quoted by Barbara Turnbull in *The Toronto Star*, 29 Oct. 1989.

There is very little people in their early twenties can tell me that I don't already know, except about computers.

Thought of a character in **Edward Phillips**' novel *Sunday Best* (1990).

It's the three I's—they think they're immortal, immune and infertile. I see it as a massive power trip. By breaking the rules, they're testing their own power.

Mary Sue McCarthy, educationalist, discussing the attitude of today's youth, quoted by Janice Dineen in *The Toronto Star*, 18 May 1991.

One generation is IBM. The next is Macintosh. They can communicate, but they're different.

Douglas Coupland, social satirist, interviewed on CBC *Prime Time News*, 4 November 1992.

When I was young, I swore that when I was old enough I'd never forget what it was like to be young.

Sam Orbaum, Montreal-raised Israeli columnist, "But Seriously," *The Jerusalem Post Magazine*, 15 Dec. 1995.

YUGOSLAVIA

Dubrovnik? They bombed *our* city.

Roger Burford Mason, Toronto-based author and editor, recalling a visit with his wife, Aileen, to the most scenic city in Yugoslavia, the scene of fighting during the country's civil war, *The Toronto Star,* 4 Nov. 1991.

We all loved Yugoslavia. Why didn't the Yugoslavs?

Myrna Kostash, author, interviewed by Mark Abley in "The Culture of Nationalism," *The Canadian Forum,* Sept. 1994.

YUKON TERRITORY

See also GOLD, KLONDIKE, THE NORTH, NUNAVUT, WHITEHORSE

A bunch of the boys were whooping it up in the Malamute saloon; / The kid that handles the music-box was hitting a rag-time tune; / Back of the bar, in a solo game, sat Dangerous Dan McGrew, / And watching his luck was his light-o-love, the lady that's known as Lou.

*

There are strange things done in the midnight sun / By the men who moil for gold; / The Arctic trails have their secret tales / That would make your blood run cold; / The Northern Lights have seen queer sights, / But the queerest they ever did see / Was that night on the marge of Lake Lebarge / I cremated Sam McGee.

Opening verses of two of **Robert W. Service**'s most popular ballads, "The Shooting of Dan McGrew" and "The Cremation of Sam McGee," *Songs of a Sourdough* (1907).

Out of the Yukon / Came a broad-shouldered man; / A man without pity, / A man without land.

Lines from **Magnus Bourque**'s song "The Ballad of Albert J." (1966), a song composed about Albert Johnson, the Mad Trapper, as quoted by Rudy Wiebe in "Notes on a Possible Legend," *Figures in a Ground: Canadian Essays in Modern Literature Collected in Honour of Sheila Watson* (1978) edited by Diane Bessai and David Jackel.

We, the Indians of the Yukon, object to... being treated like squatters in our own country. We accepted the white man in this country, fed him, looked after him when he was sick, showed him the way of the North, helped him to find the gold; helped him build and respected him in his own rights. For this we have received very little in return. We feel the people of the North owe us a great deal and we would like the Government of Canada to see that we get a fair settlement for the use of the land.

Elijah Smith, Whitehorse chief, addressing Jean Chrétien, Minister of Indian Affairs, 1968, quoted in *Perspectives and Realities: Volume 4: Report of the Royal Commission on Aboriginal Peoples* (1996), co-chaired by René Dussault and Georges Erasmus.

Guns and blood are *not* the North. I'm more scared in Toronto traffic than in Ross River.

Max Fraser, northern journalist, quoted by Val Ross in *The Globe and Mail,* 28 Sept. 1991.

The laughter reaches even into the chilly Alaskan Yukon when Bob Hope and Bing Crosby get together for *Road to Utopia,* the hilarious fourth entry in the classic "Road" series.

Promotional copy (creating a new political entity "Alaskan Yukon") that appeared on the carton of the 1980s video-cassette of the comedy movie *Road to Utopia* (1945).

Yukoners call areas beyond the territory "outside." My newspaper even capitalizes the word. But only in winter does a more profound meaning of that term come to mind. The real outside, the world beyond the gentle border of the sky, reasserts its power. We go inside, into our homes and offices and cozy corner tables in restaurants, to contemplate the outside—the edge of our world and the fringes of our imagination.

John Dunn, journalist with the *Whitehorse Star,* "Contrasts," *The Globe and Mail,* 18 Dec. 1990.

My suggestion was to consider selling the Yukon to a country like Taiwan, which with $88 billion in foreign reserves is the cash-richest country on the planet. Maybe, for $200/250 billion, they might be interested. Say $50 billion down and $10 billion a year for 15–20 years. If present residents of the Yukon were offered $100,000 to move, they might consider this a form of "early retirement." Native people should get $100,000 each and have the choice of staying or moving. Quite possibly their new owners might treat them better than the previous ones.

Frank Ogden, futurologist, *Ogdenisms: The Frank Ogden Quote Book* (1994).

Z

ZEN

Zen is something no one undertands but all applaud with at least one hand.

Irena F. Karafilly, novelist and aphorist, "Thoughts for the Millennium from A to Z," *The Montreal Gazette*, 30 Dec. 1999.

ZOOS See also ANIMALS

The future of zoos is not in elephants and tigers. The future of zoos depends upon the interpretation to the public of the inter-relationship of living things.

Tommy Thompson, parks commissioner, characteristic observation, made upon assuming the directorship of the Metropolitan Toronto Zoo, 15 June 1978.

I think zoos are an abomination. And the rationales we use: zoos educate the public. Educate them to what? We educate them to think about putting animals—and we are one—in cages. The other rationale is preserving endangered species. That's bullshit.

Farley Mowat, naturalist and author, interviewed by Alan Twigg in *Strong Voices: Conversations with Fifty Canadian Authors* (1988).

The fact that my grandchildren will grow up in a world in which tigers exist only in zoos, books, and videos pains my soul.

David Suzuki, environmentalist, "The Case of Keeping Wild Tigers," *Earth Time: Essays* (1998).

ZZZZ

Can you hear that *zzzz*? That's the sound of people asleep, snoring, while the future with all its opportunities roars by them.

Frank Ogden, futurologist, interviewed by Lisa Hobbs Birnie in *Western Lights: Fourteen Distinctive British Columbians* (1996).

INDEX

The letter *a* or *b* after the page number indicates the left-hand or right-hand column of the page on which the quotation will be found. Unattributed quotations appear under Anonymous.